COMPUTER ARCHITECTURE AND ORGANISATION

(A Practical Approach)

- **Concepts**
- **Principles**
- **Case Studies**
- **Experiments**

Er. RAJIV CHOPRA

Asst. Prof. (CSE/IT)
Deportment of CSE/IT
GTBIT, GGSIPU, Delhi
BE(CSE); M.I.T; M.Tech (IT)
(USIT, GGSIPU, Delhi)
CCEH—Certified

S.CHAND
PUBLISHING

S Chand And Company Limited
(ISO 9001 Certified Company)

S Chand And Company Limited

(ISO 9001 Certified Company)

Head Office: D-92, Sector–2, Noida – 201301, U.P. (India), Ph. 91-120-4682700

Registered Office: A-27, 2nd Floor, Mohan Co-operative Industrial Estate, New Delhi – 110 044, Phone: 011-49731800

S. CHAND PUBLISHING

www.**schandpublishing.com**; e-mail: **info@schandpublishing.com**

Marketing Offices:

Chennai	:	Ph: 23632120; chennai@schandpublishing.com
Guwahati	:	Ph: 2738811, 2735640; guwahati@schandpublishing.com
Hyderabad	:	Ph: 40186018; hyderabad@schandpublishing.com
Jalandhar	:	Ph: 4645630; jalandhar@schandpublishing.com
Kolkata	:	Ph: 23357458, 23353914; kolkata@schandpublishing.com
Lucknow	:	Ph: 4003633; lucknow@schandpublishing.com
Mumbai	:	Ph: 25000297; mumbai@schandpublishing.com
Patna	:	Ph: 2260011; patna@schandpublishing.com

First Edition 2014

Reprint 2025

ISBN: 978-81-219-4224-9 **Product Code:** H3ACA50INFT10ENAA14O

PRINTED IN INDIA

By Vikas Publishing House Private Limited, Plot 20/4, Site-IV, Industrial Area Sahibabad, Ghaziabad – 201 010 and Published by S Chand And Company Limited, A-27, 2nd Floor, Mohan Co-operative Industrial Estate, New Delhi – 110 044.

PREFACE

Many books on Computer System Architecture and Organization are available in the market but they are not complete, are very formal and dry. My attempt is to make CSA and CO very simple so that a student feels as if the teacher is sitting behind him and guiding him. This text is bolstered with many examples and CASE STUDIES. Also included in this text are the experiments to be performed in CSA and CO lab. Every effort has been made to alleviate the treatment of the book for easy flow of understanding of the students as well as the professors alike.

Any suggestions to further enhance the quality of the book will be highly acknowledged.

Er. RAJIV CHOPRA

ACKNOWLEDGEMENT

Writing a good book not only requires sincere efforts and hard work but also the blessings of the omnipresent GOD. I thank the support given by S. Bhatnagar, Mr. Madan, his colleagues and the entire team of S. Chand for publishing this book in a nice format. I also acknowledge the support given by my parents-DR. J. R. CHOPRA (Ex-Professor of Physics) and Mrs. Sushma Chopra (Ex-Principal) during the writing of this book. Lastly, I acknowledge my twin babies-Arjeesh (son) and Arshitha (daughter) and my wife Shakti Chopra for their patience and motivations.

CONTENTS

CHAPTER 1 BOOLEAN ALGEBRA AND BASIC BUILDING BLOCKS

1.0 INTRODUCTION

Shannon (1938) developed the **switching algebra** for designing telephone switching systems. It is actually a subset of a more general algebra known as **Boolean algebra** that was developed by Boole in 1815-64. **Boolean algebra is a branch of abstract algebra closely related to other branches such as group theory and linear algebra.**

As we know that group theory deals with groups, linear algebra with vector spaces, similarly Boolean algebra treat Boolean algebras as the models of the equational theory of two values. So, Boolean algebra is algebra of logic.

Switching circuits are also called as **logic circuits, gate circuits and digital circuits.**

NOTE: Switching algebra is also called as Boolean algebra.

The terms Switching expression and Boolean expressions are used inter changeably. Boolean algebra is a system of mathematical logic. It is an algebraic system consisting of the set of element (0, 1), **two binary operators** (OR and AND) and one unary operator called NOT. It is the basic mathematical tool in the analysis and synthesis of switching circuits. **Please understand that any complex logic statement can be expressed by a Boolean function.** The Boolean algebra is governed by certain well-developed rules and laws. Any single variable or a function of the variables can have a value of either a 0 or a 1. The binary digits 0 and 1 are used to represent the two voltage levels that occur within the digital logic circuit. The usual **convention** is to follow positive logic i.e., binary 1 represents the higher of the two voltage levels (+5V) and binary 0 represents the lower of the two Voltage levels (0V). **Please note that no other voltages ever occur at the inputs or outputs. Also note that any voltage above some level (like 2V or 2V etc.) is treated as logic 1 and any voltage below some level (0.8V, say) is treated as logic 0, logic 1 means TRUE, ON, HIGH and Logic 0 means FALSE, OFF, LOW.**

But Boolean algebra is different from ordinary algebra and the binary number system.

In Boolean Algebra

(*a*) $A + A = A$

(*b*) $A - A = A$

This is so because the variable A has only a logical value. It doesn't have any numerical significance.

In Ordinary Algebra

(*a*) $A + A = 2A$

(*b*) $A - A = A^2$.

This is so because the variable A has a numerical value here.

In Boolean algebra, 1 + 1 = 1, whereas in the binary number system, 1 + 1 = 10 and in ordinary algebra, 1 + 1 = 2. There is nothing like subtraction or division in Boolean algebra. **Also note that the there are no negative or fractional numbers in Boolean algebra.** In Boolean algebra, the multiplication and addition of the variables and functions are also only logical. They represent logic operations. Logical multiplication is the same as AND operation and logical addition is the same as the OR operation. There are only two constants 0 and 1 within the Boolean system. Whereas in ordinary algebra, you can have any number of constants, A variable or function of variables in Boolean algebra can assume only two values, either a 0 or a 1, whereas the variables or functions in ordinary algebra can assume an infinite number of values.

> **NOTE:** (1) In Boolean algebra,
> (*a*) If A = 1, then A ≠ 0
> (*b*) If A = 0, then A ≠ 1.
> (2) Any functional relation in Boolean algebra can be proved by the method of perfect induction. It is a method of proof whereby a functional relation is verified for every possible combination of values that the variables may assume. We form a truth-table here. It shows how a logic circuit responds to various combinations of logic levels at its inputs.

1.1 BOOLEAN ALGEBRA VERSUS SWITCHING ALGEBRA

The switching algebra is a two-valued Boolean algebra defined on a set of operators OR (+) and AND (–) defined by the truth table below:

OR:

X	*Y*	*X* + *Y*
0	0	0
0	1	1
1	0	1
1	1	1

AND:

X	*Y*	*X.Y*
0	0	0
0	1	0
1	0	0
1	1	1

Please note that in the above definition, the set B is now completely defined. This is also true for the operators (+) and (–). Because 1 is used to represent *True* and 0 is used to represent *False*.

In Switching algebra, the value of a logic variable and be either 1 or 0. The information represented by such a logic variable is a bit.

1.2 TRUTH TABLES

A table which lists all possible combinations of input variables and the corresponding outputs is called as a truth-table. It shows how the logic circuit's output responds to various combinations of logic levels at the input. A truth table having 2 inputs will have 2^2 possible combinations. Similarly, a truth table with 3-inputs will have 2^3 (= 8) possible combinations. **In general, for n independent variables, there are a total of 2^n combinations.**

They are used for simplification of the Boolean function. They are used to derive equivalent Boolean functions to get logic diagrams using different logic gates.

1.3 DUALITY PRINCIPLE

In a positive logic system, the more positive of the two voltage levels is represented by a 1 and the more negative by a 0.

In a negative logic system, the more positive of the two voltage levels is represented by a 0 and the more negative by a 1. **Please understand that this distinction between positive and negative logic systems is very important because an OR gate in the positive logic system becomes an AND gate in the negative logic system and vice-versa.** So, positive and negative logics give rise to a *basic duality* in all Boolean identities. When changing from one logic system to another, 0 becomes 1 and 1 becomes 0. ***Also, understand that an AND gate becomes on OR gate and an OR gate becomes an AND gate.***

Rule: "Given a Boolean identity, we can produce a dual identity by changing all '+' signs to '.' signs, all '.' signs to '+' signs and complementing all 0s and 1s. The variables are not complemented in this process."

The advantage of the duality concept is that once a theorem or statement is proved, the dual also this stands proved. **This is called as the principle of duality.**

An examination of **Huntington's postulates** reveals a certain symmetry i.e., the postulates come in pairs. One of the postulates in each pair can be obtained from the other one by two ways –

(*a*) By interchanging the two binary operators

(*b*) By interchanging the two identity elements when they appear explicitly.

So, one of the commutative laws can be obtained from the other by interchanging the operators (+) and (.). The same is true of the two distribution laws.

> **NOTE:** Whenever some result (theorem) is deduced from the postulates, the duality principle can be invoked as proof of the dual theorem.

Some dual entities are given in table 1.

Given Expression	It's Dual
$\overline{0} = 1$	$\overline{1} = 0$
$0.1 = 0$	$1 + 0 = 1$
$0.0 = 0$	$1 + 1 = 1$
$1.1 = 1$	$1 + 1 = 1$
$A.0 = 0$	$A + 1 = 1$
$A.1 = A$	$A + 0 = A$
$A.A = A$	$A + A = A$

Given Expression	It's Dual
$A.\bar{A}=0$	$A+\bar{A}=1$
$A.B=B.A$	$A+B=B+A$ (Commutation)
$A.(B.C)=(A.B).C$	$A+(B+C)=(A+B)+C$ (Association)
$A.(B+C)=A$	$A+AB=A$ (Duality Theorem)
$A.(A+B)=AB+AC$	$A+BC=(A+B)(A+C)$ (Distribution)
$A(A+B)=A$	$A+AB=A$ (Duality Theorem)
$A.(A.B)=A.B$	$A+A+B=A+B$
$\overline{AB}=\bar{A}+\bar{B}$	$\overline{A+B}=\overline{AB}$ (De-Morgan's Theorem)
$(A+B)(\bar{A}+C)(B+C)=(A+B)(\bar{A}+C)$	$AB+\bar{A}C+BCC=AB+\bar{A}C$
$(A+C)(\bar{A}+B)=AB+\bar{A}C$	$AC+\bar{A}B=(ACB)(\bar{A}+C)$
$A+\bar{B}C=(A+\bar{B})(A+C)$	$A(\bar{B}+C)=(A\bar{B}+AC)$
$(A+B)(C+D)=AC+AD+BC+BD$	$(AB+CD)=(A+C)(A+D)(B+C)(B+D)$
$A+B=AB+AB+A\bar{B}$	$AB=(A+B)(\bar{A}+B)(A+\bar{B})$
$A+B(\overline{C+\overline{DE}})=A+B\bar{C}DE$	$A[B(\overline{C+\overline{D+E}})]=A(B+\bar{C}+D+E)$
$\overline{\overline{AB}+\bar{A}+AB}=0$	$\overline{\overline{AB}.\bar{A}.(A+B)}=1$
$AB+\overline{AC}+A\bar{B}C(AB+C)=1$	$(A+B)(\overline{A+C}).[(A+\bar{B}+C)+(A+B)C]=0$
$ABD+ABCD+ABD$	$(A+B+D)(A+B+C+D)=(A+B+D)$
$\overline{A\bar{B}+ABC}+A(B+A\bar{B})=0$	$\overline{(A+\bar{B}).(A+B+C)}.(A+[B(A+\bar{B})])=1$
$A+\bar{B}C(A+\bar{B}C)=A+\bar{B}C$	$A.[(\bar{B}+C)+A.(\bar{B}+C)]=A.(\bar{B}+C)$

1.4 DUALITY THEOREM

We can derive one Boolean function from another by the following rules–

1. Changing each OR sign to an AND sign.
2. Changing each AND sign to an OR sign.
3. Complementing any 0 or 1 appearing in the expression.

We are in a position to solve some examples now.

EXAMPLE 1: Given $AB' + A'B = C$. Show that $AC' + A'C = B$.

SOLUTION: *Given:* $AB' + A'B = C$ ...(1)

To prove: $AC' + A'C = B$ ...(2)

Proof: Substitute the value of C (from 1) in equation-2 we get :

$$A[AB' + A'B']' + A'[AB'+A'B]$$

$$= A[(AB')' (A'B')'] + A'AB' + A'A'B$$

$$= A[(A' + B)(A + B')] + O.B' + A'B$$

$$= A[A'B' + AB] + O + A'B$$

$$= AA'B' + AAB + A'B$$

$$= O + AB + A'B \quad [\because A + A' = 1]$$
$$= B$$

Hence proved.

EXAMPLE 2: Show that the dual of the Boolean function

$$\boldsymbol{F = A'B + AB'} \text{ is equal to its complement.}$$

SOLUTION: $E = A'B + AB'$

$\therefore$ $F' = (A'B + AB')'$ [Complementing both sides]

$= (A'B)' - (AB')'$ [De Morgan's law]

$= [(CA')' + B'] - [A' + (B')']$

$= [A + B'].[A' + B]$

$= AB + A'B'$

From Duality principle, the dual of

$$F = (A' + B).\ (A + B')$$
$$= A'B' + AB$$
$$= F'(A, B)$$

EXAMPLE 3: What are the differences between Boolean postulates and Boolean Theorems? Give some examples.

SOLUTION: Fundamental conditions or self-evident propositions are called as ***postulates.*** The postulates for Boolean Algebra originate from the three basic logic operations – AND, OR and NOT. These postulates define the operation of AND, OR and NOT. So, these are the results of these basic operations.

For example: Boolean postulates are –

1. $0.0 = 0$
2. $0 - 1 = 0$ — Are derived from AND operation
3. $1.0 = 0$
4. $1.1 = 1$
5. $0 + 0 = 0$
6. $0 + 1 = 1$ — Are derived from OR operation
7. $1 + 0 = 1$
8. $1 + 1 = 1$
9. $\overline{0} = 1$ — Are derived from NOT operation.
10. $\overline{1} = 0$

With the help of Boolean postulates many useful theorems (called as Boolean theorems) have been derived.

For example: Boolean theorems are :

1. $0.X = 0$
2. $X.0 = 0$
3. $A.X = X$
4. $X.1 = X$

5. $X+0=X$
6. $0+X=X$
7. $X+1=1$
8. $1+X=1$
9. $X.X=X$
10. $X.\overline{X}=0$
11. $X+X=X$
12. $X+\overline{X}=1$
13. $\overline{\overline{X}}=X$
14. $X+Y=Y+X$
15. $X.Y=Y.X$
16. $X(YZ)=(XY).Z=XYZ$
17. $(X+Y)+Z=X+(Y+Z)=X+Y+Z$
18. $X.(Y+Z)=XY+XZ$
19. $X+YZ=(X+Y).(X+Z)$
20. $X+XY=X$
21. $X(X+Y)=X$
22. $XY+X\overline{Y}=X$
23. $(X+Y)(X+\overline{Y})=X$
24. $\overline{X.Y.Z...}=\overline{X}+\overline{Y}+\overline{Z}+....$
25. $\overline{X+Y+Z+...}=\overline{X}.\overline{Y}.\overline{Z}.....$

EXAMPLE 4: Simplify the following:

$$F = \overline{(x+y)}.\overline{(\overline{x}+\overline{y})}.$$

SOLUTION: Using De-Morgan's theorem-

$$= \overline{x}.\overline{y}.(\overline{\overline{x}}).(\overline{\overline{y}})$$

$$= \; = \overline{x}.\overline{y}..x.y$$

$$= \; = x\overline{x}.y\overline{y}$$

$$= 0 \qquad [\because x\overline{x}=0 \text{ and } y\overline{y}=0]$$

EXAMPLE 5: Find the dual of the equation

$$X+XY = X.$$

SOLUTION: It's dual is $X.(X+Y)=X$

NOTE: In this process of dual finding, literals are not complemented.

1.5 DIFFERENT FORMS OF BOOLEAN FUNCTIONS

Basically, there are 6 types of forms of Boolean functions. They are as follows:

(*a*) **Monomial: Any Boolean function which does not include the operation '+' and or '.' is called a Monomial. For eg., xy, xy', y etc.**

(*b*) **Polynomial: Boolean functions having '+' and '.' are called as polynomials. It implies that the sum of monomial functions is a polynomial. i.e.,**

$$\text{Polynomial} = f(\text{Monomial})$$

For eg. $y + xz, x + y + z$ etc.

(*c*) **Minimal Boolean Function (MBF): If there are *n*-variables, then the product of all the *n*-variables taken together is called as a Boolean function of *n*-variables.**

For eg.,

$xy, x'y, y'x$ etc. are minimal Boolean functions for two-variables.

$xyz, x'yz, x'y'z, x'y'z'$ etc. are minimal Boolean functions for three-variables.

Tip: The number of minimal Boolean functions in n-variables will be 2^n.

(*d*) **Normal Boolean Function (NBF): If a Boolean function of *n*-variables involves all the *n*-variables in it, then it is called as a Normal Boolean Function.** The variable x can be selected in two ways – x or x'.

For eg. $x + y, x' + y$ etc. are NBF of 2-variables, x and y.

(*e*) **Canonical Form:** A Boolean function, $F(x_1, x_2, ..., x_n)$ of n-variables, when expressed as a polynomial in the form of sum of products (SOP) or product of sum (POS) in such a way that each term involves all the n-variables, either complemented or uncomplemented, then it is known as **Canonical form** (or expanded form) *of the given Boolean function.*

For e.g.

$$F(x, y) = (x + y) + xy$$
$$F(x, y, z) = x'y'z' + xyz$$

NOTE: Canonical forms of Boolean function are basic form that we obtain from reading a function from the truth-table.

(*f*) **Standard Form:** Here, the number of variables in each term may be one, two or any number of variables.

$$F(x, y, z) = y + xyz + yz$$
$$F(x, y, z) = (x + y')(x' + y)$$

1.6 K-MAPS AND SOLVED EXAMPLES

Simplifying Boolean expressions is not easy. Till now, we have simplified Boolean functions algebraically only. But it is not an efficient method. So, we use another method called as **a Karnaugh map method or K-map in short. K-map is defined as a chart or a graph tool that is composed of an arrangement of adjacent cells each representing a particular combination of variables in sum or product form.** It provides an area to represent every row of a truth-table. Like a truth-table, it is a means of showing the relationship between logic inputs and the desired output. K-maps can be used for problems with any number of variables but when number of variables becomes five or more than K-map becomes very complex. So, it is usually limited to six variables. **In general, an n-variable function can have 2^n possible combinations.** So, a two-variable K-map will have 2^2 =

4 cells or square.

A three variable map will have 2^3 = 8 cells or squares and a four variable map will have 2^4 = 16 cells and so on. Each square represents one minterm or maxterm. Each of the product terms in standard SOP form is called a s a **minterm** and each of the sum terms in the standard POS form is called a **maxterm. Please understand that the minterms and maxterms are usually represented as binary words in terms of 0s and 1s, instead of actual variables.**

> NOTE: A standard SOP form can always be converted to a standard POS form by treating the missing minterms of the SOP form as the maxterms of the POS form and vice versa.

K-maps can be of 2, 3, 4, 5, and 6 variables. Let us study these now.

Two-Variable K-map

A two variable K-map has 2^2 = 4 squares. Each such square is called a **cell.** It is shown in Fig. 1.

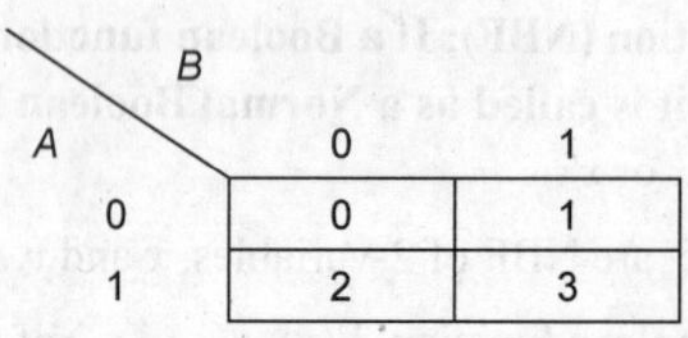

Row No.	A	B	Minterm	Maxterm
0	0	0	$\bar{A}\bar{B}$	$A + B$
1	0	1	$\bar{A}B$	$A + \bar{B}$
2	1	0	$A\bar{B}$	$\bar{A} + B$
3	1	1	AB	$\bar{A} + \bar{B}$

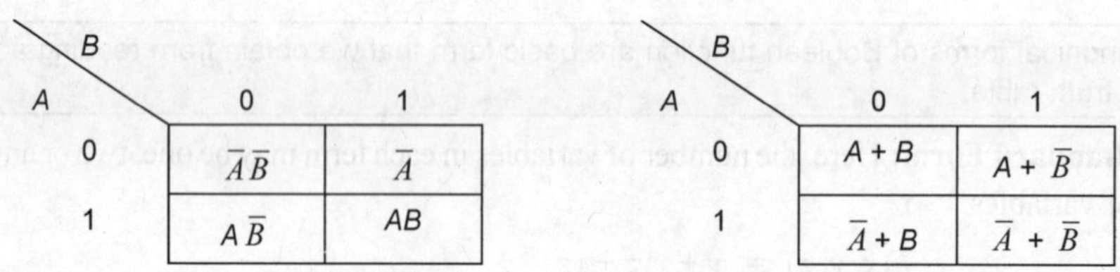

Fig. 1.1. 2-Variable K-map

There are four minterms or maxterms for two variable. So, the map consists of four squares one for each minterm or maxterm as shown in Fig. 1.1. **Please note that for each row of the truth table, for each maxterm or for each maxterm there is one specific square in the K-map.** For e.g. first row and 2nd column corresponds to *AB* (minterm) or *A* + *A* + *B* (maxterm). They give the binary number (01), whose decimal equivalent is 1.

Three Variables K-map

A three-variable K-map is shown in Fig. 1.2

A \ BC	00	01	11	10
0	0	1	3	2
1	4	5	7	6

A \ BC	00	01	11	10
0	$\bar{A}\bar{B}\bar{C}$	$\bar{A}\bar{B}C$	$\bar{A}BC$	$\bar{A}B\bar{C}$
1	$A\bar{B}\bar{C}$	$A\bar{B}C$	ABC	$AB\bar{C}$

A \ BC	00	01	11	10
0	$A+B+C$	$A+B+\bar{C}$	$A+\bar{B}+\bar{C}$	$A+\bar{B}+C$
1	$\bar{A}+B+C$	$\bar{A}+B+\bar{C}$	$\bar{A}+\bar{B}+\bar{C}$	$\bar{A}+\bar{B}+C$

Fig. 1.2. 3-Variable K-map

Because there are three binary variables, so the number of squares are 8 (=2^3) squares (or cells), one for each minterm or maxterm. **Please note that the minterms or maxterms are not arranged in a binary sequence. Also note that each square differs from its preceding or succeeding square by one bit only just like our reflected or Gray Codes. Each square corresponds to one of the combination of three variables.**

For eg. the square 2 (from fig. 1.2) corresponds to first row and fourth column, that gives $\bar{A}B\bar{C}$ minterm or $A+\bar{B}+C$ maxterm which corresponds to binary number 010 whose decimal equivalent is 2.

Four Variable K-maps

A K-map for four variables is shown in Fig. 1.3

AB \ CD	00	01	11	10
00	0	1	3	2
01	4	5	7	6
11	12	13	15	14
10	8	9	11	10

AB \ CD	00	01	11	10
00	$\bar{A}\bar{B}\bar{C}\bar{D}$	$\bar{A}\bar{B}\bar{C}D$	$\bar{A}\bar{B}CD$	$\bar{A}\bar{B}C\bar{D}$
10	$\bar{A}B\bar{C}\bar{D}$	$\bar{A}B\bar{C}D$	$\bar{A}BCD$	$\bar{A}BC\bar{D}$
11	$AB\bar{C}\bar{D}$	$AB\bar{C}D$	$ABCD$	$ABC\bar{D}$
10	$A\bar{B}\bar{C}\bar{D}$	$A\bar{B}\bar{C}D$	$A\bar{B}CD$	$A\bar{B}C\bar{D}$

AB \ CD	00	01	11	10
00	$A+B+C+D$	$A+B+C+\bar{D}$	$A+B+\bar{C}+\bar{D}$	$A+B+\bar{C}+D$
01	$A+\bar{B}+C+D$	$A+\bar{B}+C+\bar{D}$	$A+\bar{B}+\bar{C}+\bar{D}$	$A+\bar{B}+\bar{C}+D$
11	$\bar{A}+\bar{B}+C+D$	$\bar{A}+\bar{B}+C+\bar{D}$	$\bar{A}+\bar{B}+\bar{C}+\bar{D}$	$\bar{A}+\bar{B}+\bar{C}+D$
10	$\bar{A}+B+C+D$	$\bar{A}+B+C+\bar{D}$	$\bar{A}+B+\bar{C}+\bar{D}$	$\bar{A}+B+\bar{C}+D$

Fig. 1.3. 4-Variable K-map

Please note that there are 16 minterms or 16 maxterms. These are shown in Fig. 1.3. **Also note that any two adjacent. Squares in the K-map differ by one variable which is primed in one square and unprimed in the other.**

Five and Six Variable K-maps

A five – variable expression has $2^5 = 32$ possible combinations of input variables. A five variable map looks like –

$A = 0$

BC \ DE	00	01	11	10
00	0	1	3	2
01	4	5	7	6
11	12	13	15	14
10	8	9	11	10

$A = 1$

BC \ DE	00	01	11	10
00	16	17	19	18
01	20	21	23	22
11	28	29	31	30
10	24	25	27	26

Fig. 1.4(a). 5-Variable K-map

$D = 0$

BC \ EF	00	01	11	10
00	0	1	3	2
01	8	9	11	10
11	24	25	27	26
10	16	17	19	18

$D = 1$

BC	10	11	01	00
00	6	7	5	4
01	14	15	16	12
11	30	31	29	28
10	22	23	21	20

BC \ EF	00	01	11	10
10	48	49	51	50
11	56	57	59	58
01	40	41	43	42
00	32	33	35	34

BC \ BE	10	11	01	00
10	54	55	53	52
11	62	63	61	60
01	46	47	45	44
00	38	39	37	36

Fig. 1.4 (b). 6-Variable K-map

In Fig. 1.4(a), 32 squares of the K-map are divided into 2 blocks of 16 squares each. The **left block** represents minterms from m_0 to m_{15} in which $A = 0$ and the **right block** represents minterms from m_{16} to m_{31} in which $A = 1$. **Please understand that a 5-variable K-map may contain 2-squares, 4-squares, 8-squares, 16 = squares or 32-squares involving these two blocks. Also understand that the squares in these blocks are said to be adjacent if on superimposing one block on top of another, the squares coincide with one another.** The squares are read by dropping out the variables that change.

Similarly, a six-variable K-map can have $2^6 = 64$ possible combinations. These 64 squares of the K-map are divided into four blocks on the map represents a minterm or a maxterm. The values of A and D remain constant for all minterms (maxterms) in each block. The **top left block** represents minterms (m_0 to m_{27}) in which $A = 0$ and $D = 0$. The **top right block** represents minterms (m_4 to m_{31}) in which $A = 0$ and $D = 1$.

The *bottom* **left block** represents minterms (m_{32} to m_{43}) in which $A = 1$ and $D = 0$.

Also, the **bottom right** *block* represent minterms (m_{44} to m_{63}) in which $A = 1$ and $D = 1$.

Please understand that 6-variables K-map may contain 2-squares, 4-squares, 8-squares, 16-squares, 32-squares or 64-squares involving these four blocks. Also understand that the squares are said to be adjacent in two blocks, if upon superimposing one-block on top of another block, the squares coincides with one another.

> **NOTE:** Diagonal cells like (m_{18}, m_{45}) are NOT adjacent to each other.

Limitations of 5 and 6 Variable K-map

Although these maps preserve all features of the previous maps yet it is observed that the number of squares become very large and hence a reasonable selection of adjacent squares becomes more difficult.

K-map Reduction

For economical gate implementation it is essential to express logic function in its simple algebraic form. The **main intention** in the design of a digital circuit is **that its cost should be as low as possible.** To design a circuit with the least cost, the expression used to realize that circuit must be minimal. **Please note that because the cost is roughly proportional to the number of gate inputs in the circuit, an expression is considered minimal only if it corresponds to the least possible number of gate inputs. Also note that there is no guarantee that the minimal expression obtained from the K-map in the SOP form is the real minimal.** To get a real minimal expression, we obtain the minimal expressions for any problem in both SOP and POS forms by using the K-maps and then takes the minimal of these two minimals. We follow certain rules for K-map reduction. These rules are as follows:

Rule 1: Plot the K-map and enter 1's in those cells corresponding to the combinations for which function value is 1, then enter 0's in the other cells. In general, place 1s (0s) corresponding to the minterm (maxterms) of the SOP (POS) expression.

Rule 2: Examine the map for 1's that cannot be combined with any other 1 cell and form groups with such single 1. That is, check the K-map for 1s (0s) which are not adjacent to any other 1(0). They are isolated minterms (maxterms).

Rule 3: Check for those 1s (0s) which are adjacent to only one other 1(0) and make them pairs (2 squares). That is, identify the 1s that can be combined with a single other 1s in only one way. A group of 2 cells is called as a **pair.**

Rule 4: Group the 1s which results in groups of 4-cells but are not part of an 8-cells group. A group of 4 cells is called as **quad.** They must geometrically form a square or a rectangle.

Rule 5: Group the 1s that can be combined with seven others to make a group of eight-adjacent ones in only one way. A group of 8 cells is called as an **octet.**

Rule 6: Check for any 1s (0s) that have not been combined yet and combine them into bigger squares if possible. That is, form more pairs, quads and octets to include those 1s that have not yet been grouped. **Please understand that the grouping may not be unique but it should be in an optimum manner. Also note that there can be overlapping of groups if they include common 1's.**

Rule 7: Ignore any superfluous (or redundant) group.

Rule 8: Finally, read the map. When one or more than one variable appear in other complemented and uncomplemented form within a group than that variable (s) is eliminated $(a+\bar{a}=1)$ from the term corresponding to that group. Variables that are same for all the cells of the group must appear in the term corresponding to that group.

> **NOTE: A two cells (pair) will eliminate one-variable, a group of four cells (quad) eliminate two variables, and an eight cell eliminates three variables. Similarly, a group of 2^n cell eliminates *n*-variables.**

We are in a position to solve some examples on K-maps now.

EXAMPLE 1: Simplify the function, $F = AB\bar{C} + ABC$ by K-map method.

SOLUTION: We draw a K-map for three variables (i.e., *A*, *B* & *C*) firstly –

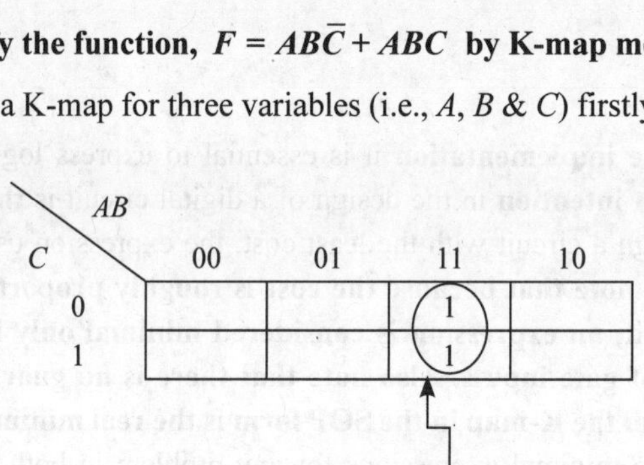

$\therefore F = AB$ is its simplified form. This is so because we find here that the squares containing 1s are adjacent squares. So, they can be groped together. The variables *AB* are common to both squares, so they are selected. There is no other variable common to both the squares. So, common variables, C and $\bar{C}$ are discarded.

EXAMPLE 2. Simplify the Boolean function:

$$F = \bar{x}yx + \bar{x}y\bar{z} + x\bar{y}z + x\bar{y}\bar{z}$$

SOLUTION:

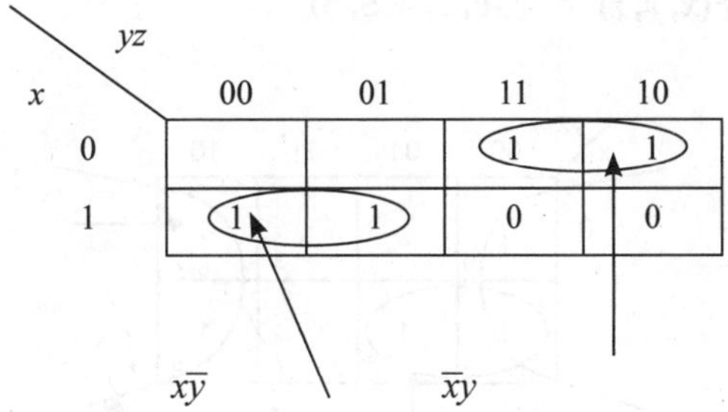

$\therefore \qquad F = \bar{x}y + x\bar{y}$

EXAMPLE 3: Simplify $F = \bar{A}.\bar{B}.C + \bar{A}.B.C$ using K-maps.

SOLUTION: A 3-variable K-map is as follows:

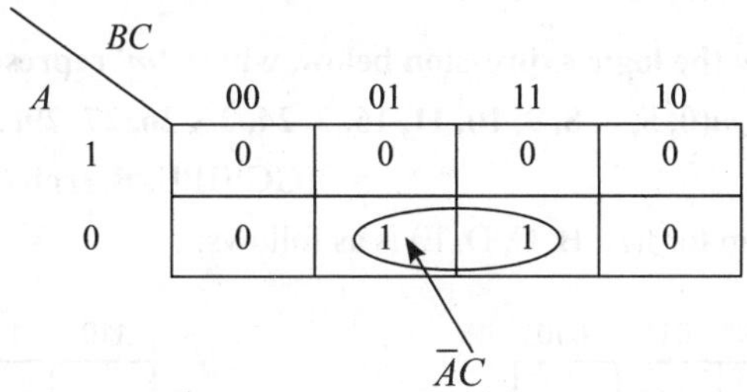

$\therefore \qquad F = \bar{A}C$

EXAMPLE 4: Simplify the Boolean function

$$F = \bar{x}yz + x\bar{y}\bar{z} + xyz + xy\bar{z}.$$

SOLUTION:

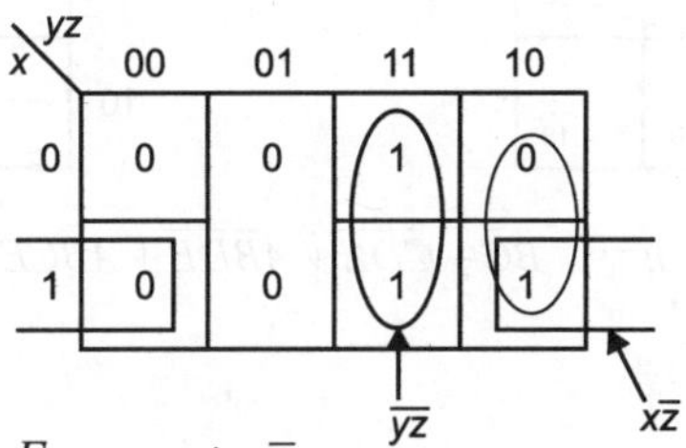

$\therefore \qquad F = yz + x\bar{z}$

EXAMPLE 5: Simplify the Boolean function

$$F = \bar{A}C + \bar{A}B + A\bar{B}C + BC$$

SOLUTION:

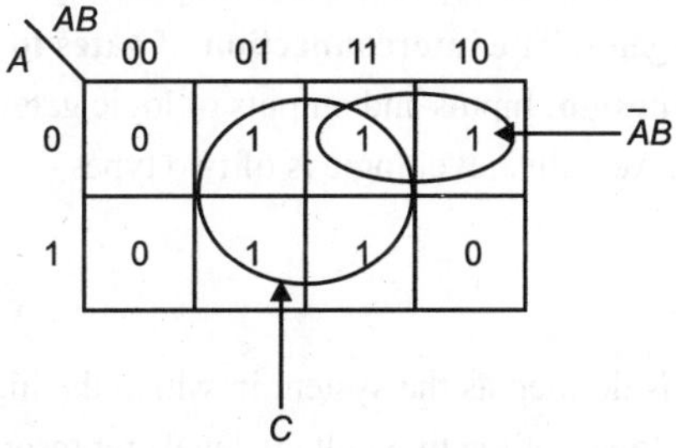

$\therefore \qquad F = C + \bar{A}B$

EXAMPLE 6: Simplify:

$$F(x, y, z) = \Sigma(0, 2, 4, 5, 6)$$

SOLUTION:

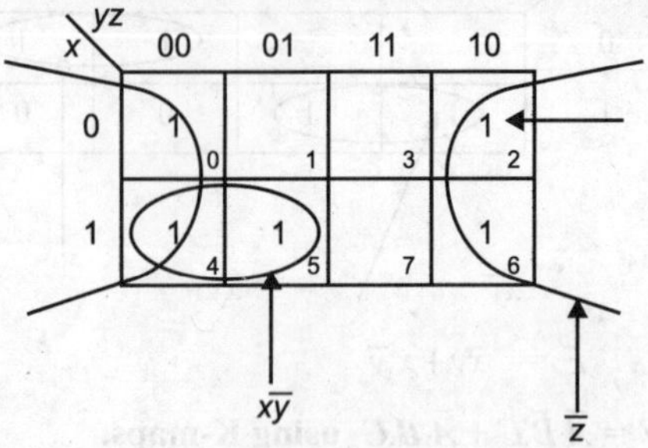

$\therefore$ $$F(x, y, z) = \overline{Z} + x\overline{y}$$

EXAMPLE 7: Simplify the logic expression below, where '*m*' represents maxterms –
***f*(*A*, *B*, *C*, *D*, *E*) = Σ*m*(0, 5, 6, 8, 9, 10, 11, 16, 2, 24, 25, 26, 27, 29, 31)**

[GGSIPU, B.Tech (ECE/EEE) – May 2005]

SOLUTION: The K-map for f(A, B, C, D, E) is as follows:

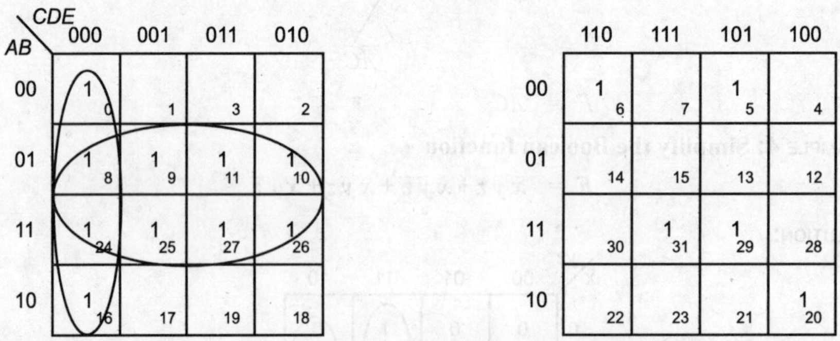

$\therefore$ $$F = B\overline{C} + \overline{C}\overline{D}\overline{E} + A\overline{B}\overline{D}\overline{E} + ABCE + \overline{A}\overline{B}CDE + \overline{A}\overline{B}C\overline{D}E$$

1.7 LOGIC GATES

An electronic circuit which performs a logic operation is called as a logic gate. They are the fundamental building blocks of digital systems. In Boolean Algebra, there are only three basic operations: AND, OR and NOT. These three basic operations are also called as **logic operations** that are implemented with the help of logic gates. Complex logic operations are performed by interconnecting these logical gates. **The interconnection of gates to perform a variety of logical operations is called as logic design.** Inputs and outputs of logic gates can occur only in two levels. These are logic 1 and logic 0. Actually, level logic is of two types –

(*a*) Positive logic

(*b*) Negative logic.

A **positive logic system** is defined as the system in which the higher of the two voltage levels represents the logic 1 and the lower of the two voltage levels represent logic – 0.

A **negative logic system** is defined as the system in which the lower of the two voltage levels represents logic-1 and the higher of the two voltage levels represents the logic-0.

Let us study these basic gates now.

AND Gate

An AND gate has two or more inputs but only one output. It's logic symbol is –

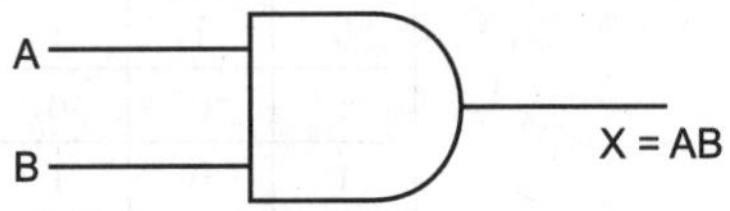

Fig. 1.5(a). Logic Symbol

Inputs		Output
A	*B*	*X*
0	0	0
0	1	0
1	0	0
1	1	1

Fig. (1.5(b). Truth Table

Only when A = B = 1, the output X = 1, else it is all zero. That is why an AND gate is also called as ***all or nothing gate.***

We can extend our AND gate for three input also –

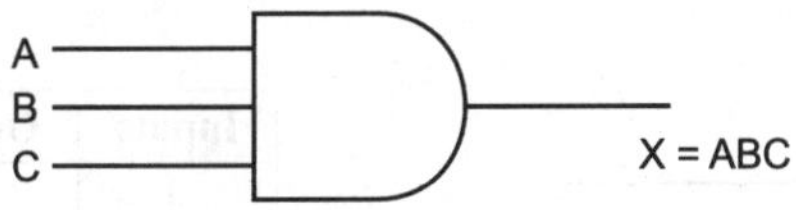

Fig. 1.5(c)

Inputs			Output
A	*B*	*C*	*X*
0	0	0	0
0	0	1	0
0	1	0	0
0	1	1	0
1	0	0	0
1	0	1	0
1	1	0	0
1	1	1	1

NOTE: An AND gate with inputs as *A, B, C, D, ...* will have the Boolean output expression as *F = A. B. C. D.....* or *F = ABCD.*

OR Gate: An OR gate has two or more inputs and only one output. It is a device whose output is 1, even if one of its inputs is 1. That is why an OR gate is also called as an any or all gate. **Please note that it can also be called as an inclusive OR gate because it includes the condition both the inputs can be presented.**

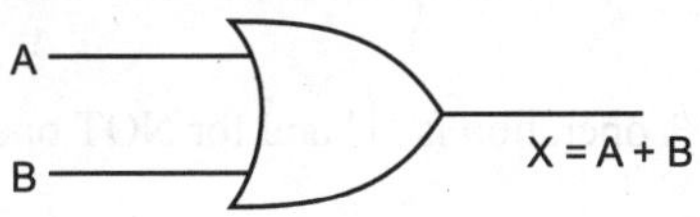

Fig. 1.6(a). Logic symbol

Inputs		Output
A	*B*	*X*
0	0	0
0	1	1
1	0	1
1	1	1

Fig. 1.6(b). Truth Table

We can extend our OR gate for three inputs also –

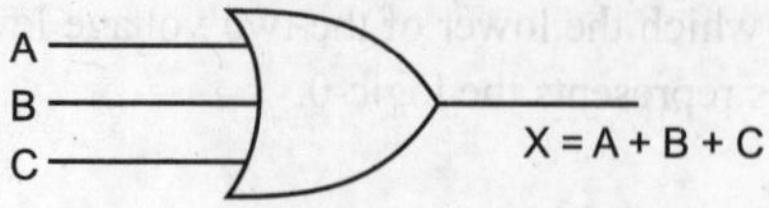

Fig. 1.6(c)

Inputs			Output
A	*B*	*C*	*X*
0	0	0	0
0	0	1	1
0	1	0	1
0	1	1	1
1	0	0	1
1	0	1	1
1	1	0	1
1	1	1	1

Fig. 1.6 (d)

NOTE: An OR gate symbol is '+'. An OR gate with inputs as *A*, *B*, *C*, *D*, ... will have the Boolean output expression as $F = A + B + C + D + ...$ or $F = A$ or B or C or D or ....

NOT gate / Inverter / Inhibitor / Complement

A NOT gate or inverter or inhibitor has only one input and one output. It is a device whose output is always the complement of its input.

Its logic symbol is

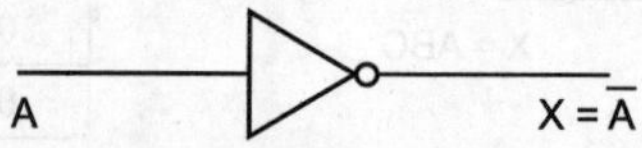

Fig. 1.7(a) Logic Symbol

Inputs	Output
A	*X*
0	1
1	0

The output expression is $X = \overline{A}$.

Before we discuss other types of gates, please remember the following points –

1. These gates are fabricated on an IC chip.

   For eg. IC 7408 contains four 2 – inputs AND gates.

   IC 7432 contains four 2 – input OR gates.

   IC 7404 contains 6 inverters.

2. Logic circuits of any complexity can be realized using AND, OR and NOT gates. Such logic circuits which uses three gates only are called as AND/OR Invert or **AOI logic circuits.**
3. Logic circuits which use AND gates and OR gates only are called as AND/OR i.e., AO logic circuits.
4. The symbol for AND operation is '.' (dot), for OR operation is '+' and for NOT operation is '–' (bar).
5. Logical operation is also called as a **switching operation.**
6. Input and outputs of logic gates can occur in two levels only. These two levels are 0 and 1 or LOW and HIGH or OFF and ON or FALSE and TRUE respectively.

1.8 DERIVED GATES

Although any Boolean expression can be realized by using the AND, OR and NOT gates yet there are two more gates that have been derived from these gates. The two gates are very popular and are named as **the NAND gate and the NOR gates.** Only one, type of gate i.e., either NAND or NOR is sufficient for the realization of any logical expression. **Therefore, these two gates are also known as Universal gates or Universal building blocks. Please note that both NAND and NOR gates can perform all the three basic logic functions (AND, OR and NOT). So, AOI logic can be converted to NAND logic or NOR logic.**

NAND Gates

The NOT-AND operation is also known as NAND operation i.e., AND gate followed by a NOT gate. NAND means NOT the AND i.e. the AND output is NOTed. It is two or more inputs and only one output. So, we can draw now –

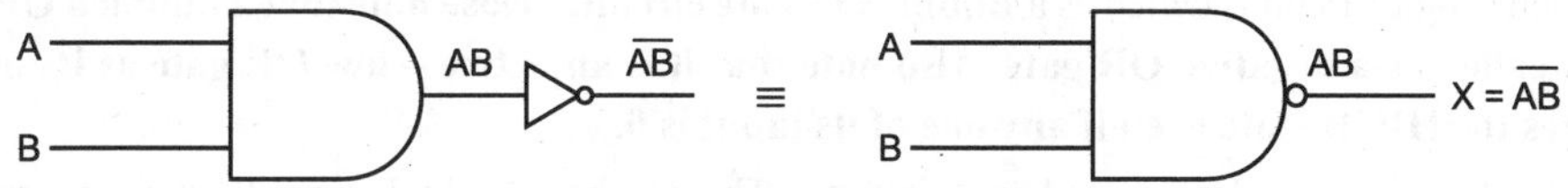

Fig. 1.8(a). Logic Symbol

Inputs		Output
A	*B*	*X*
0	0	1
0	1	1
1	0	1
1	1	0

Fig. 1.8(b). NAND Truth Table

Its truth table is shown in Fig. 1.8(b).

Similarly, a three-input NAND gate has the following logic symbol and truth table

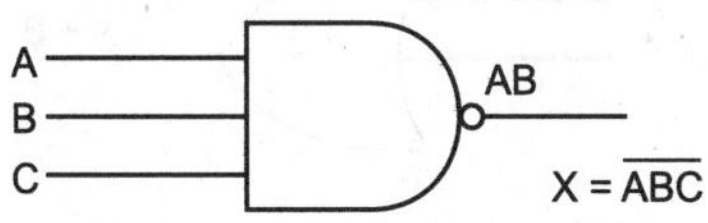

Fig. 1.8(c). Input NAND Gate

Inputs			Output
A	*B*	*C*	*X*
0	0	0	1
0	0	1	1
0	1	0	1
0	1	1	1
1	0	0	1
1	0	1	1
1	1	0	1
1	1	1	0

Fig. 1.8 (d). Truth Table (3-input)

From the figure 1.8(b), we observe that when either $A = 0$ or $B = 0$ or when both $A = B = 0$, the output $(X) = 1$. That is, if either $\overline{A} = 1$ or $\overline{B} = 1$ or both $\overline{A}$ and $\overline{B}$ are equal to 1. **Therefore, the NAND gate can perform the OR function.** This means that –

$$X = \overline{A} + \overline{B} = \overline{AB}$$

Hence, a NAND gate can be realized by the above equation also i.e., two NOT gates and one OR gate are needed. Diagrammatically,

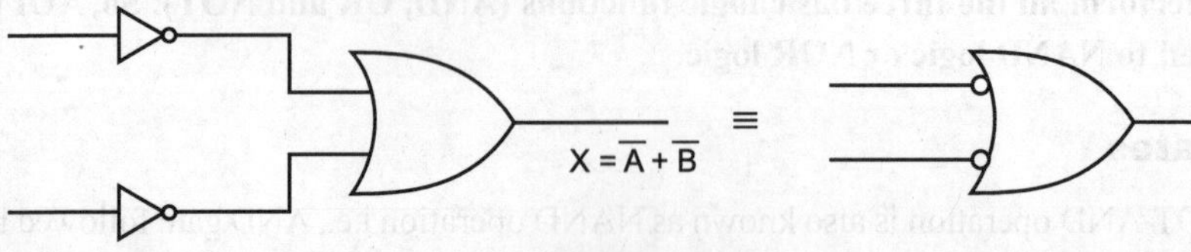

Fig. 1.9. Bubbled OR Gate

Such a logic circuit is called as a **Bubble OR gate circuit. Please note that a bubbled OR gate is also called as a negative OR gate. Also note that it is an active – low OR gate as its output assumes the HIGH state even if any one of its input is 0.**

A NAND gate can also be used as an inverter. This can be done by laying all its input terminals together and applying the signal to be inverted to the common terminal. This is shown in Fig. 1.10.

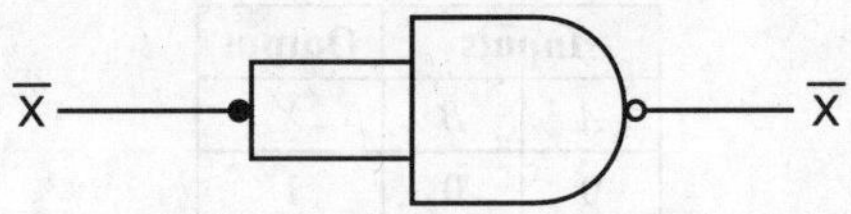

Fig. 1.10 (a). NAND as an inverter

Another way is to connect all its input terminals except one, to logic 1 and applying the signal to be inverted to the remaining terminal as shown in Fig. 1.10(b).

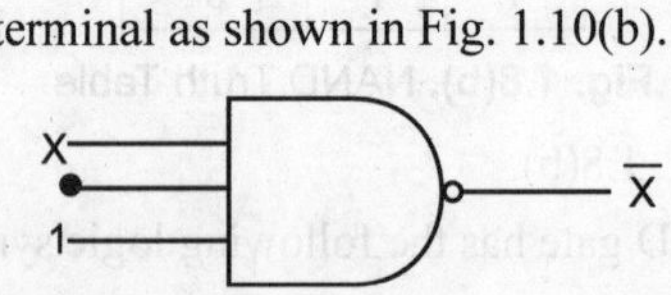

Fig. 1.10(b). NAND gate as a controlled inverter

The following gate is bubbled NAND gate.

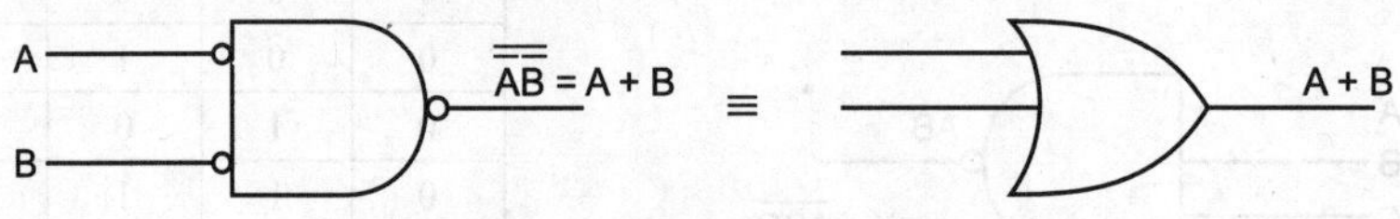

Fig. 1.11. Bubbled NAND gate

> **NOTE:** IC 7400 has four 2-input NAND gates
> IC 7410 has three 3-input NAND gates
> IC 7480 has two 4-input NAND gates
> IC 7430 has one 8-input NAND gates

Many other logic operations can be realized using NAND gates:

(*a*) This is an AND gate using NAND gates only.

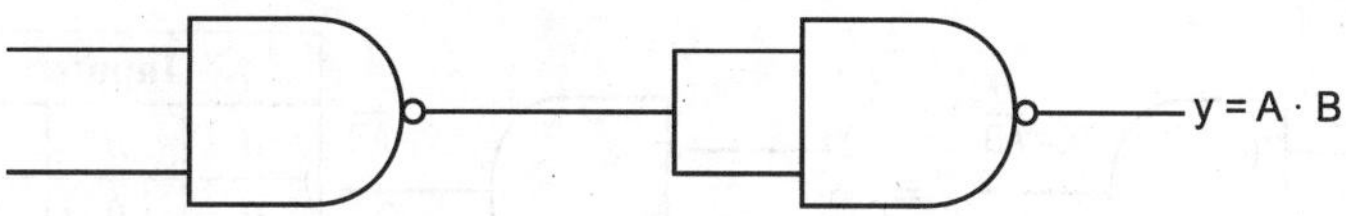

(*b*) This essentially is an OR gate using NAND gates only.

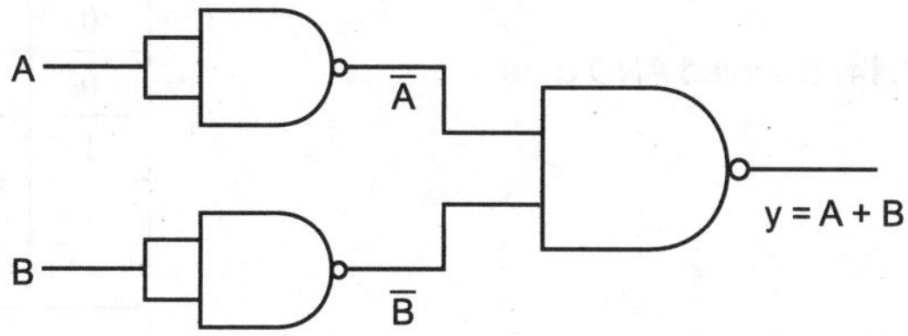

(*c*) This is an EX OR gate using NAND gates only.

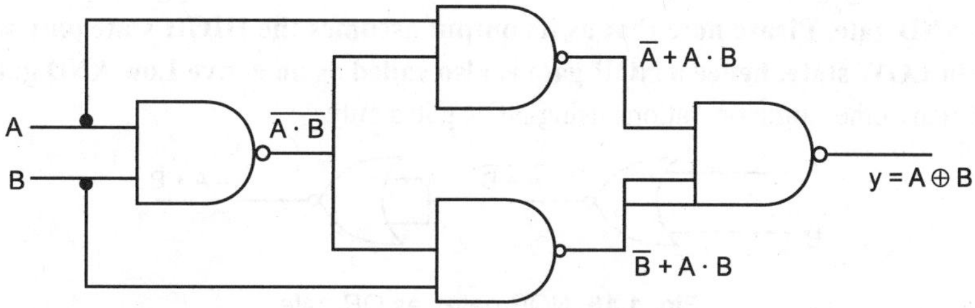

NOR Gates

The NOR gate operates like an OR gate followed by an Inverter (NOT gate). NOR means NOT or i.e., the OR output is NOTed. So, a NOR gate is a combination of an OR gate and a NOT gate i.e.

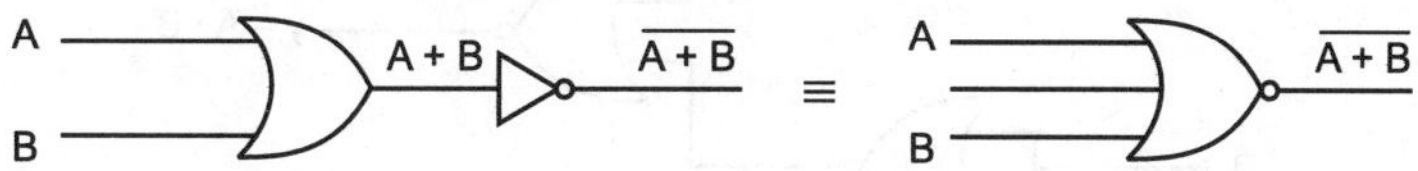

Fig. 1.12. Formation of a two input NOR gate.

Its truth table is –

Inputs		Output
A	*B*	*X*
0	0	1
0	1	0
1	0	0
1	1	0

Similarly, a three-input NAND gate is shown in Fig. 1.13.

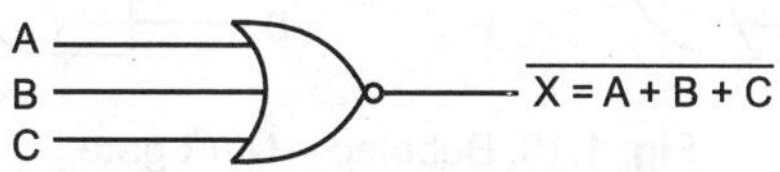

Fig. 1.13. Three Input NOR gate

Its truth table is also shown

The following is a Bubbled AND gate:

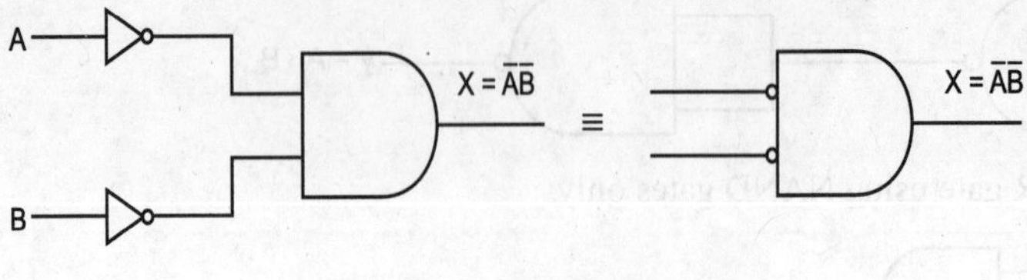

Fig. 1.14. Bubbled AND gate

Inputs			Output
A	*B*	*C*	*X*
0	0	0	1
0	0	1	0
0	1	0	0
0	1	1	0
1	0	0	0
1	0	1	0
1	1	0	0
1	1	1	0

Thus, an AND gate with inverted inputs is called as **a bubbled AND gate. It is also called as a negative AND gate. Please note that as its output assumes the HIGH state only when all its inputs are in LOW state, hence a NOR gate is also called as an active Low AND gate.** Also we can realize many other logic operations using NOR gates only –

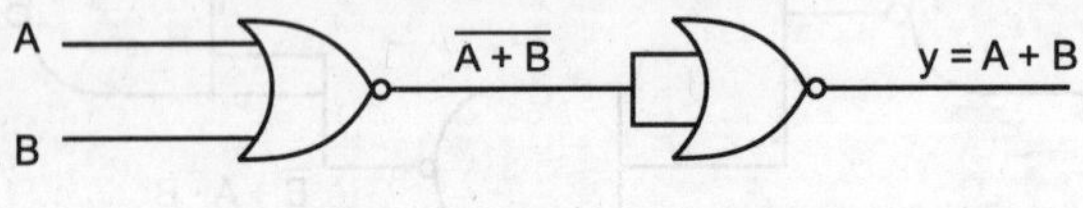

Fig. 1.15. NOR gates as OR gate.

Similarly, an AND operation can be realized using NOR gates only –

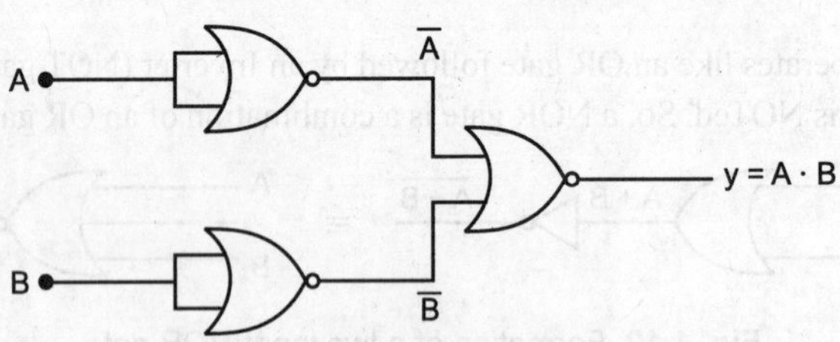

Fig. 1.16. NOR gates as AND gate.

Just like a NAND gate, a NOR gate can also be used as an inverter i.e.

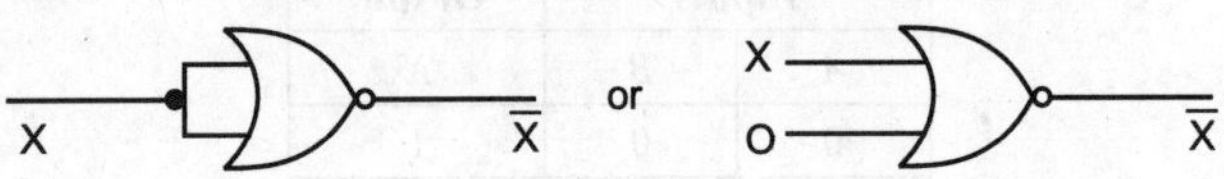

Fig. 1.17. NOR gate as an inverter

The following gate is bubbled – NOR gate

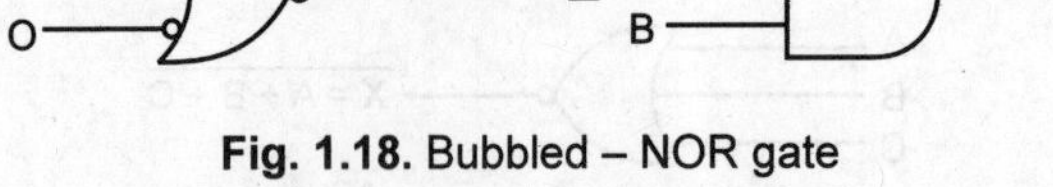

Fig. 1.18. Bubbled – NOR gate

> **NOTE:** IC 7402 has four 2-input NOR gates
> IC 7427 has three 3-input NOR gates
> IC 7425 has two 4-input NOR gates

The cost of a large digital system (like a computer) will be less if the variety of logic gates is reduced. **Please understand that the cost of a digital system depends on the variety and not so much on the multiplicity of component. Also understand that most of the digital systems use only one type of gate – NAND or NOR to produce any Boolean function.** This has an economic advantage.

Exclusive – OR (X – OR) gate

The X-OR gate has a high output only when an odd number of inputs is high. Its logic symbol and truth table are shown in Fig. 1.19.

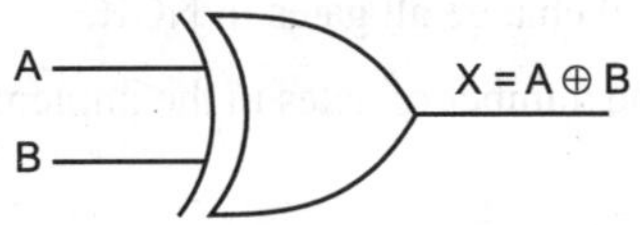

Fig. 1.19(*a*). Logic Symbol

Inputs		Output
A	*B*	*X*
0	0	0
0	1	1
1	0	1
1	1	0

Fig. 1.19(b). Truth Table

From Fig. 1.19(a), it is clear that an XOR gate produces an output of 1 only when the inputs are not equal. **That is why it is called as an anti-coincidence gate or inequality detector. Please note the following points –**

1. The output of an X-OR gate is the module sum of its two inputs.
2. Three or more variable XOR gates do not exist.
3. When more than two variables are to be used or XORed than a number of two-input XOR gates will be used.
4. The output of an EX-OR gate is

$$f = AB' + A'B$$

If $\quad B = 1, \quad f = A.0 + A'.1 = O + A' = A'$

If $\quad B = 0, \quad f = A.1 + A'.0 = A + O = A$

$\therefore \quad 1 \oplus A = A' \quad \text{and} \quad O \oplus A = A$

Thus, EXOR gate can be used as a controlled inverter with one input as A, the other (control) input is B. An EXOR gate is a *true / complement unit*. It is shown in Fig. 1.20.

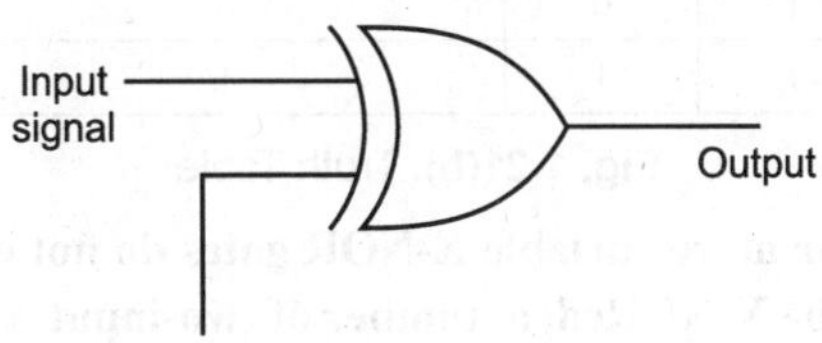

Fig. 1.20. A controlled Inverter

Its truth table is

Input Signal	Controlled Signal	Output $y = A \oplus B$
0	0	$0 = A$
0	1	$1 = \overline{A}$
1	0	$1 = A$
1	1	$0 = \overline{A}$

5. To design *NAND only* circuits, convert the desired logic expression to SOP form, then draw the corresponding two levels AND OR circuit and change all gates to NAND.
6. To design *NOR only* circuit, convert the desired logic expression to POS form, then draw the corresponding two level OR – AND circuit and change all gates to NOR.
7. Always simplify the function in order to reduce the number of gates in the implementation.
8. TL-IC 7486 contains four X-OR gates.

   CMOS IC 74C86 contains four XOR gates.

   HCMOS IC 74 HC 86 contains for XOR gates.

Exclusive NOR (X-NOR) Gate

An X-NOR gate gives high output for both inputs low and both inputs high. **It is also called a coincidence gate because its output is 1 only when its inputs coincide. It can be used an equality detector because it output 1 only when its inputs are equal.** Its logic symbol and truth table is given in Fig. 1.21.

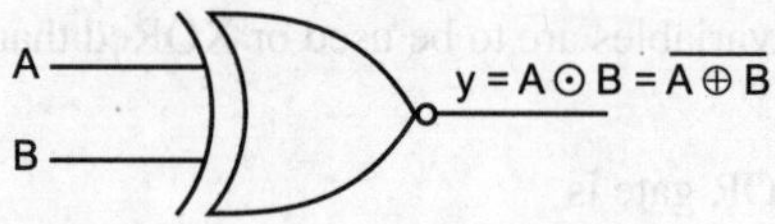

Fig. 1.21(a). Logic Symbol

Inputs		Output
A	B	$y = A \odot B = \overline{A \oplus B}$
0	0	1
0	1	0
1	0	0
1	1	1

Fig. 1.21(b). Truth Table

Please note that three or more variable X-NOR gates do not exist. Also note that when a number of variables are to be X-NORed, a number of two-input X-NOR gates can be used.

An X-NOR gate can be used as an inverter by connecting one of the two input terminate to logic 0 and feeding the input sequence to be inverted to the other terminal. It is shown in Fig. 1.22.

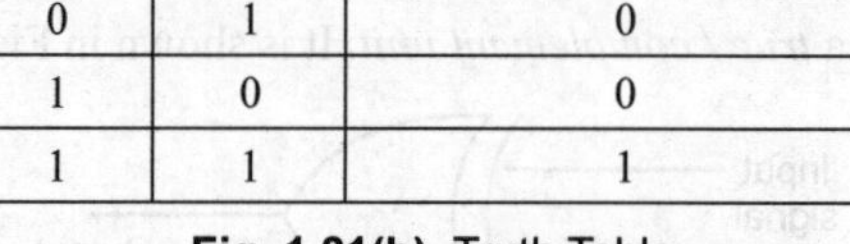

Fig. 1.22. X-NOR gate as an inverter

If input = 0, output, X = 1

If input = 1, output $X = 1 \odot 0 = 0$

So, we can say that an X-NOR can be used as **a controlled inverter** i.e., one of its inputs can be used to decide whether the signal at the other input will be inverted or not. **Before we go further, please remember the following points-**

1. Although $A \odot B = \overline{A \oplus B}$ but $A \odot B \odot C \neq \overline{A \oplus B \oplus C}$.
2. X-NOR gate can be used as a comparator too.
3. TTL IC 7415266, CMOS IC 74C 266 and HCMOS IC 74HC 266, all contain for X-NOR gates.

We are in a position to solve some examples now.

EXAMPLE 1: (*a*) Simplify the following Boolean function

$$Z = [(A + B)' + B']'$$

(*b*) Show the logic diagram of the Boolean function using NAND gates.

SOLUTION: (*a*)

$$Z = [A + B)' + B']'$$

$$= [A'B' + B'] \quad \text{[Using De-Morgan's Law]}$$

$$= (B')' \quad \text{[Using Absorption law]}$$

$$= B \quad \text{[Using Involution law]}$$

(*b*) $Z = B$

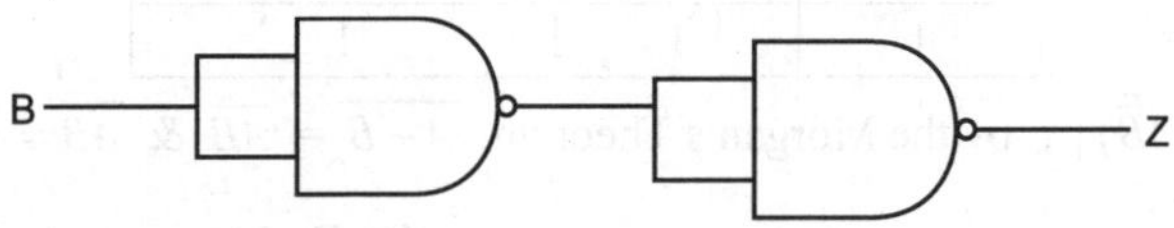

EXAMPLE 2: ***Show that***

$(A + B)\overline{AB}$ is equivalent to $A \oplus B$. Also, construct the corresponding logic diagrams.

SOLUTION: Considering L.H.S. firstly,

A	B	$A + B$	AB	$\overline{AB}$	$(A + B)(\overline{AB})$
0	0	0	0	1	0
0	1	1	0	1	1
1	0	1	0	1	1
1	1	1	1	0	0

Now, consider R.H.S. i.e. $A \oplus B$

A	B	$A \oplus B$
0	0	0
0	1	1
1	0	1
1	1	0

From these two truth-tables we observe that last two columns are same.

Hence, $A \oplus B = (A + B) AB.$

Now, we construct its logic diagrams –

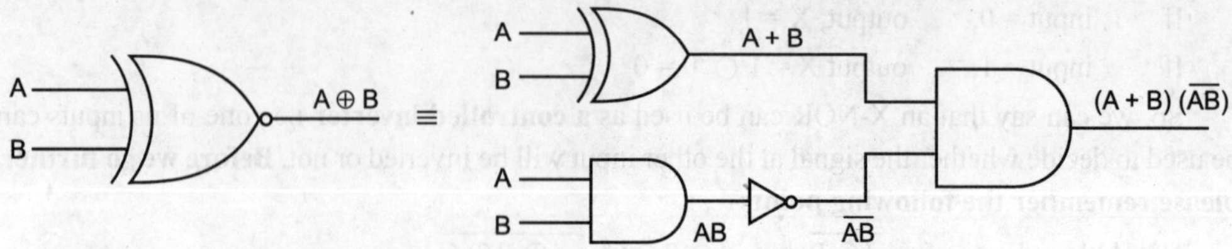

EXAMPLE 3: How an EX-NOR can be obtained using NAND gate only? Sketch the circuit diagram.

SOLUTION: The EX-NOR gate is

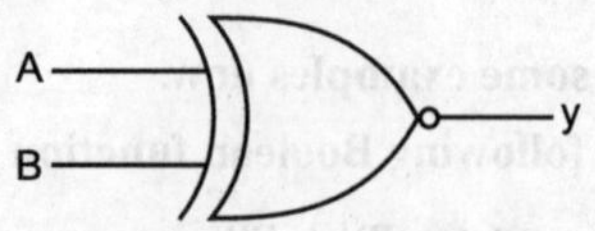

$$y = \overline{A \oplus B}$$
$$= AB + \bar{A}.\bar{B}$$

A	*B*	$y = AB + \bar{A}.\bar{B}$
0	0	1
0	1	0
1	0	0
1	1	1

Let $y = \overline{(\overline{AB})}.\overline{(\overline{A}\overline{B})}$ [$\because$ by the Morgan's Theorem, $\overline{A+B} = \bar{A}\bar{B}$ & $\overline{AB} = \bar{A}+\bar{B}$]

$= \overline{\overline{AB}} + \overline{\overline{\bar{A}\bar{B}}}$ [By De Morgan's theorem, $\overline{A+B} = \bar{A}\bar{B}$]

$= AB + \bar{A}\bar{B}$

$\boxed{y = A \odot B}$.

Its circuit diagram is –

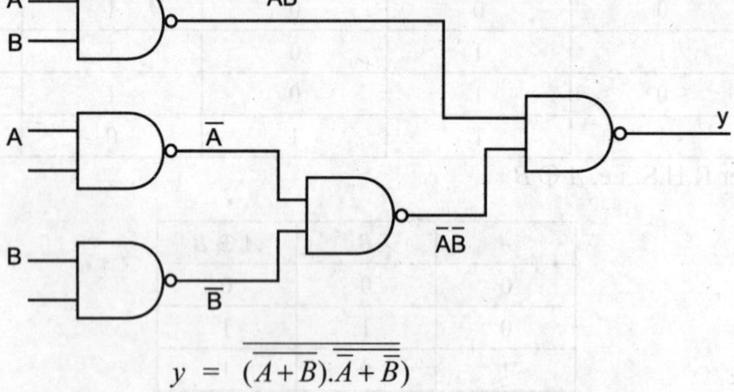

i.e. $y = \overline{(\overline{A+B}).\overline{\bar{A}+\bar{B}}}$

EXAMPLE 4: Draw the diagram of digital circuit for

$$F = AB + BC + CD \text{ using NAND to NAND logic.}$$

SOLUTION:

$$F = AB + BC + CD$$

$= (A \text{ NAND } B) \text{ NAND } (B \text{ NAND } C) \text{ NAND } (C \text{ NAND } D)$

∴ Logic circuit is –

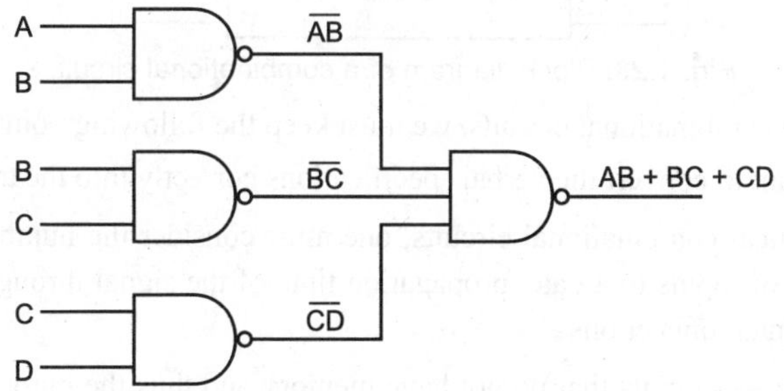

$$\therefore \quad F = y = \overline{\overline{AB}.\overline{BC}.\overline{CD}} \qquad \text{(From Fig.)}$$

$$= \overline{\overline{AB}} + \overline{\overline{BC}} + \overline{\overline{CD}}$$

$$= AB + BC + CD$$

EXAMPLE 5: Make a 4-input NAND gate using 2-input NAND gates.

SOLUTION: Let the four inputs be A, B, C, and D and the output be y.

$$\therefore \quad y = \overline{A.B.C.D}$$

$$\text{or} \quad \overline{\overline{y}} = \overline{\overline{A.B.C.D}}$$

$$= (A.B).(C.D.)$$

$$= (\overline{\overline{A.B}}).(\overline{\overline{C.D}})$$

$$\text{or} \quad \overline{\overline{y}} = \overline{y_1}\,\overline{y_2}$$

$$\therefore \quad y = \overline{\overline{y_1}\,\overline{y_2}}$$

$$y_1 = \overline{A.B} \qquad and \qquad y_2 = \overline{C.D}$$

Its circuit diagram is –

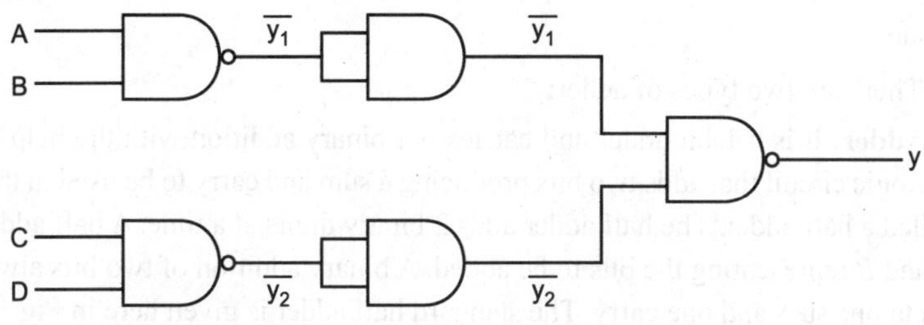

1.9 COMBINATIONAL CIRCUITS

–HA, FA, MUX, DEMUX

A combinational circuit consists of logic gates whose outputs at any time are determined from the present combination of inputs only. A combinational circuit consists of input variables, logic gates and output variables. These combinational circuits that are used to perform some function are known as **combinational logic.** In general, a combinational circuit has n-inputs and *m*-outputs i.e.

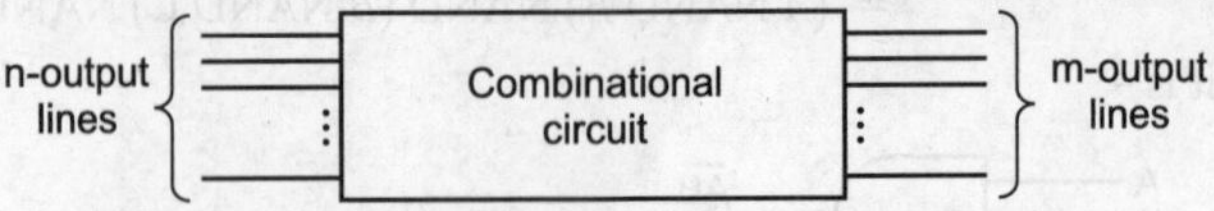

Fig. 1.23. Block diagram of a combinational circuit.

While designing combinational circuits, we must keep the following points in mind:

1. It is important to convert the verbal specifications correctly into the truth table.
2. For economical combinational circuits, one must consider the number of gates required, the number of inputs to a gate, propagation time of the signal through the circuit and the number of interconnections.
3. These are those circuits that do not have memory and thus the outputs are obtained from the inputs only.
4. They are faster as the delay between the input and the output is due to the propagation delay of gates only.
5. They are easy to design.

The design procedure involves the following steps:

Step 1: The problem is stated.

Step 2: The number of available input variables and required output variables is determined.

Step 3: The input and output variables are assigned letter symbols.

Step 4: The truth table that defines the required relationship between inputs and outputs is derived.

Step 5: The simplified Boolean function for each output is obtained.

Step 6: The logic diagram is drawn

The design and maintenance of digital computers are greatly facilitated by the Boolean algebra and logic circuits. Logic gates have several applications to the computers. Given below are some useful applications.

1. Adders (Half Adder, Full Adder)
2. Encoder

Adders: There are two types of adder:

***(a)* Half Adder**: It is a 1-bit adder and carries out binary addition with the help of X-OR and AND gates. A logic circuit that adds two bits producing a sum and carry to be used in the next higher position is called a half adder. The half adder adds 2 binary digits at a time. A half adder consists of two inputs *A* and *B* representing the bits to be added. A binary addition of two bits always produces 2 bit output data one sum and one carry. The standard half adder is given here in Fig. 1.24.

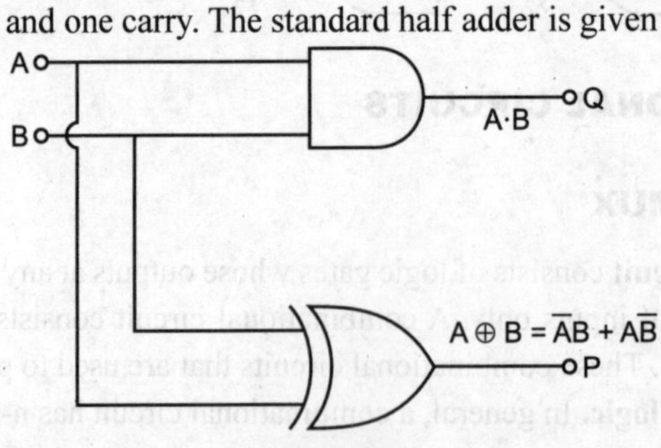

Fig. 1.24

The output of the exclusive OR gate is called the SUM, while the output of the AND gate is the CARRY.

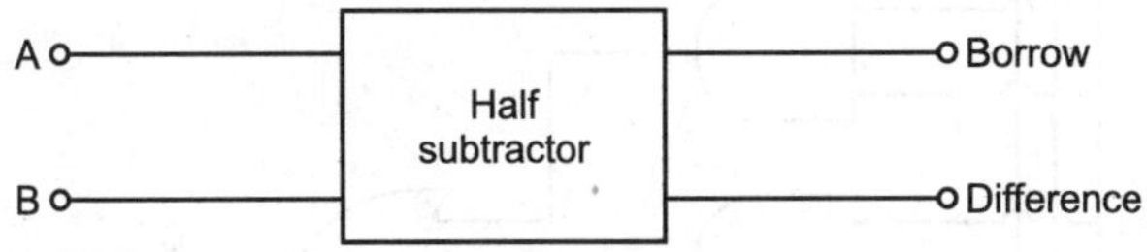

Fig. 1.25

The symbol of half adder is shown in Fig. 1.25. The truth table of half adder is given below:

Input		Output	
A	***B***	**Sum (S)**	**Carry (C)**
0	0	0	0
0	1	1	0
1	0	1	0
1	1	0	1

The AND gate produces a high output only when both inputs are high while exclusive of produces a high output if either inputs, but not both, is high. From the truth tale it is clear

(*i*) If input $A = 0, B = 0$, then human response will be 0 plus 0 is equal to 0 with carry but half adder response: SUM = 0 and CARRY = 0.

(*ii*) If input $A = 0, B = 1$, then human response will be 0 plus 1 is 1 with a carry of half-adder response: SUM = 1 and CARRY = 0.

(*iii*) If input $A = 1, B = 0$, then human response will be 1 plus 0 is 1 with a carry of half adder response: SUM = 1 and CARRY = 0.

(*iv*) If input $A = 1$ and $B = 1$, then human response will be 1 plus 1 is 0 with a carry of half adder response: SUM = 0 and CARRY = 1.

(*b*) Full Adder: It is logic circuit that can add three bits. It produces two outputs: SUM and CARRY. For the higher order columns, we have to use a full adder, a logic circuit third add 3 bits at a time. The third bit is the carry from lower column. This implies that they are logic circuit with three inputs and two inputs. The Boolean equations for SUM and CARRY.

$$\text{SUM} = X \oplus Y \oplus Z$$

$$\text{CARRY} = XY + YZ + ZX$$

i.e. SUM equals *X XOR Y XOR Z*

CARRY equals *XY OR YZ OR ZX*

With three inputs and two outputs full adder is shown in Fig. 1.26.

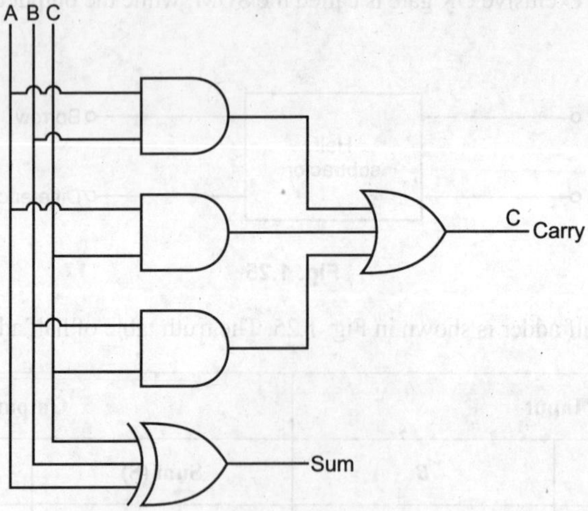

Fig. 1.26

The symbol of full adder is shown in Fig. 1.27. It three inputs usually called the CARRY IN between it comes from lower-order column. There are outputs, SUM and CARRY. The output C ARRY IS the CARRY OUT because it goes to the next or order.

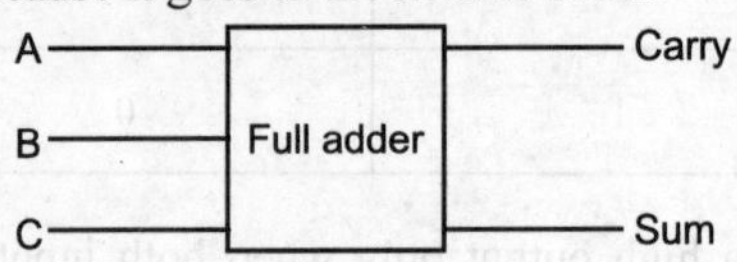

Fig. 1.27

The truth table of full-adder is given below:

A	*B*	*C*	CARRY	SUM
0	0	0	0	0
0	0	1	0	1
0	1	0	0	1
0	1	1	1	0
1	0	0	0	1
1	0	1	1	0
1	1	0	1	0
1	1	1	1	1

From the truth table we can conclude:

(*i*) When $A = 0$, $B = 0$ and $C = 0$, then human response will be 0 plus 0 plus 0 is 0 with a carry of 0 but full adder response : SUM = 0 and CARRY = 0.

(*ii*) When $A = 0$, $B = 0$, $C = 1$, the human response will be 0 plus 0 plus 1 is 1 with a carry of 0 but the full adder response : SUM = 1, CARRY = 0.

(*iii*) Now we are taking fourth entry when $A = 0$, $B = 1$, $C = 1$, then the human response will be 0 plus 1 is 0 with a carry of 1 but full adder response : SUM = 0 and CARRY = 1.

(*iv*) Last entry, input $A = 1$, $B = 1$, $C = 1$ then the human response will be with a carry of 1 but full adder response: SUM = 1 and CARRY = 1.

So we cay say that, the full adder captures in electronic circuitry, the methods we use when we add 3 bits at a time. The full-adder can do more than a millions second. Besides that, it never gets tired or bored, or asks for a raise.

***(c)* Half Subtractor:** A half subtractor is a combinational logic circuit that subtracts two bits and produces their difference. Half subtractor consists of one XOR and with two inputs *A* and *B* representing the bits to be subtracted and two outputs *P* and the output of XOR gate and this output generate the difference and *R* represents Borrow. This output generates the borrow shown in Fig. 1.28

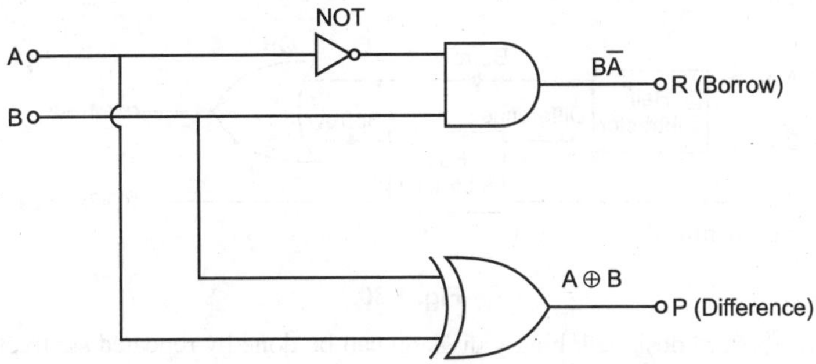

Fig. 1.28

The standard block diagram of half subtractor is shown in Fig. 1.29

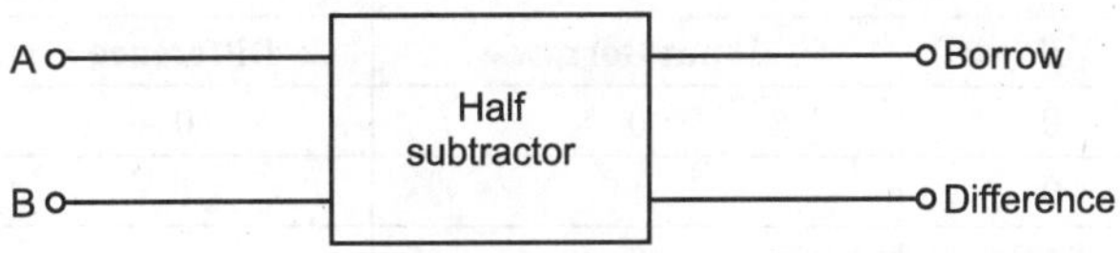

Fig. 1.29

The truth table of half subtractor is given below:

Input		Output	
A	***B***	$P = A \oplus B$	$R = B\overline{A}$
0	0	0	0
0	1	1	1
1	0	1	0
1	1	0	0

With two inputs *A* and *B* there are four distinct cases :

(*i*) When $A = 0, B = 0$

Borrow $R = B\overline{A} = 0.\ 1 = 0$ and difference

$P = A \oplus B + A\overline{B} + \overline{A}B = 0.1 + 1.0 = 0 + 0 = 0$

(ii) When $A = 0, B = 1$

Borrow $R = B\overline{A} = 1.1 = 1$. and difference

$P = A \oplus B = A\overline{B} + \overline{A}B = 0.0 + 1.1 = 0 + 1 = 1$

(*iii*) When $A = 1, B = 0$

Borrow $R = R = B\overline{A} = 0.0 = 0$ and difference

$$P = A \oplus B + A\overline{B} + \overline{A}B = 1.1 + 0.0 = 1 + 0 = 0$$

(*iv*) When $A = 1, B = 1$

Borrow $R = B\overline{A} = 1.0 = 0$ and difference

$$P = A \oplus B + A\overline{B} + \overline{A}B = 1.0 + 0.1 = 0 + 0 = 0$$

(*d*) Full Subtractor: A full subtractor is analogous to full-adder and can be used to handle binary numbers at a time. A full subtractor can be designed by using two half subtractor OR gate as shown in Fig. 1.30.

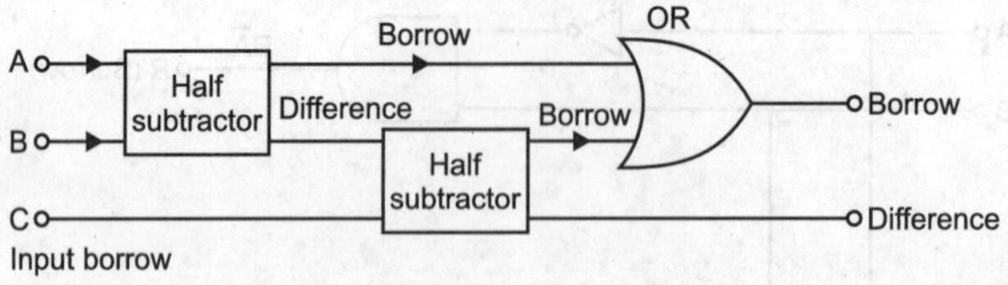

Fig. 1.30

Then subtractors are designed, binary division can be done by repeated subtractions and need some sequential circuit. In full subtractor, there are three inputs, namely A (minuend), and borrow C. The borrow digit C is subtracted from input A. The truth table for subtractor is given below:

Input			Output	
A	***B***	**Input Borrow**	**Difference**	**Borrow**
0	0	0	0	0
0	0	1	1	1
0	1	0	1	1
0	1	1	0	1
1	0	0	1	0
1	0	1	0	0
1	1	0	0	0
1	1	1	1	1

Multiplexers: In modern days it is important to transfer data or information from one place to another place. This data is transmitted directly through wires. In digital system, these data are transferred in form the form of bits. For a long distance these wire send data through telephone lines or cables. To send more data at a time we need a number of cable lines, hence the cost and size of these would be too expensive and large. To avoid these use a single wire and the data is sent over a single wire in serial form. Thus the device for this purpose is called ***multiplexers***. It is also called ***data selector***. Hence a multiplexer with number of inputs but a single output is shown in Figure 1.31.

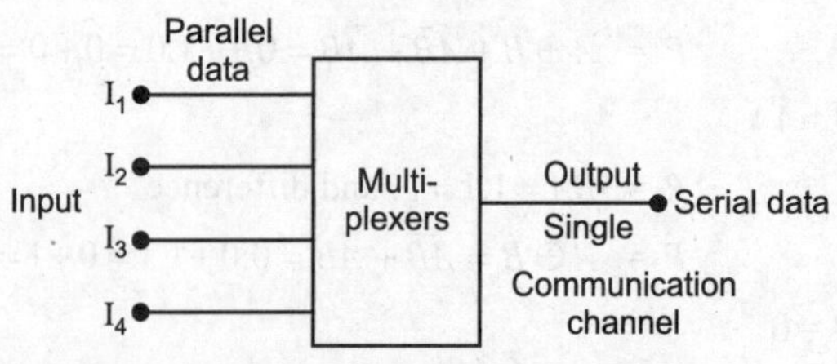

Fig. 1.31

Similarly, we have demultiplexers which have a single input bit a number of outputs (opposite that of a multiplexer). Thus for transmission of data or information we need a multiplexer and recollect the data in the serial form we need a demultiplexer (as shown).

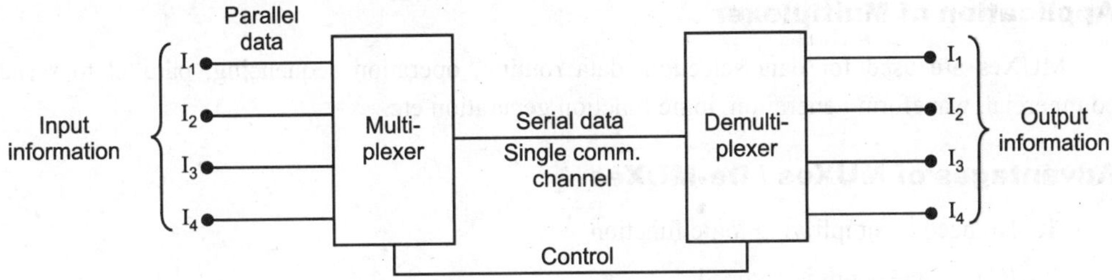

Fig. 1.32

The selection of the input lines is controlled by selection lines, for this first we input lines in the form of 2^n e.g., if there is 4 input line we have 2^2 input lines. Now we have n selection line for example for 2^3 i.e. 8 input lines, we have 3 (as $n = 3$). Suppose we have 6 input lines then we need at least 2^3 input lines out of which is working chance number of selection lines is 3. Consider a multiplexer having 4 input and output terminals, here number of selection line, $n = 2$ we have

$$4 = 2^2 \text{ compare with } 2^n$$

We get $n = 2$, number of selection line = 2 (S_0, S_1)

Let the four input lines be I_0, I_1, I_2, I_3

We have

O/P	S_1	S_0
I_0	0	0
I_1	0	1
I_2	1	0
I_3	1	1

Hence the circuit for 4 input terminals multiplexer is:

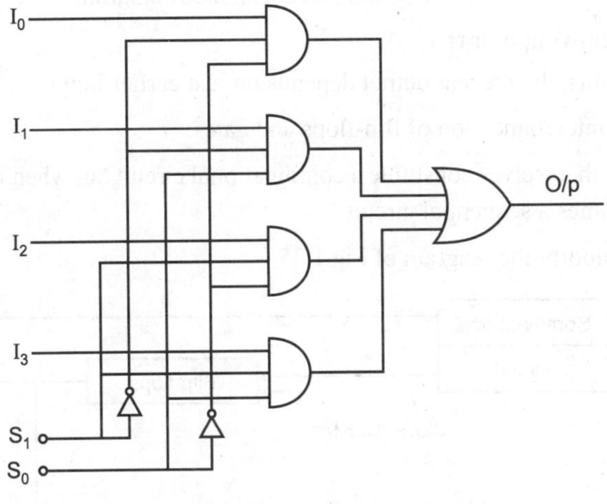

Fig. 1.33

We get O/P as I_0 if $S_1 = 0, S_0 = 0$
Same method for I_1, I_2 and I_3 may be used.

Application of Multiplexer

MUXes are used for data selection, data routing, operation sequencing, parallel to serial commercial, waveform generation, logic function generation etc.

Advantages of MUXes / De-MUXes

1. No need of simplifying logic function
2. IC package count is reduced.
3. Better reliability as now we have external wired connections.
4. Easy to charge the logic function that has been implemented.

1.10 SEQUENTIAL CIRCUITS

It is defined as a combination of a combinational circuit and memory elements connected in the feedback path. The memory elements are devices capable of storing binary information. Please understand that it is this binary information, stored at any given time that defines the state of the sequential circuit. Also note that the sequential circuit receives binary information from external inputs. The conclusion is that a sequential circuit is specified by a time sequence of inputs, outputs and internal states. It's block diagram is shown in Fig. 1.34.

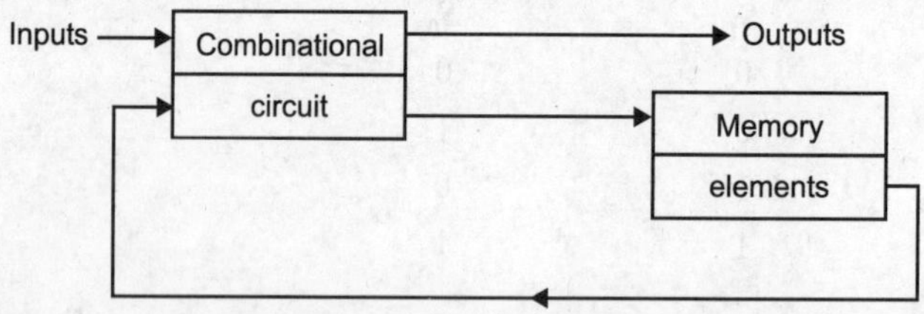

Fig. 1.34. Sequential circuit block diagram

Keep in mind the following points

1. In these circuits, the present output depends on just earlier input.
2. They are an interconnection of flip-flops and gates.
3. The gates by themselves constitute a combinational circuit but when included with the flip-flops, it becomes a sequential circuit.
4. So, we can modify the diagram of Fig 1.35.

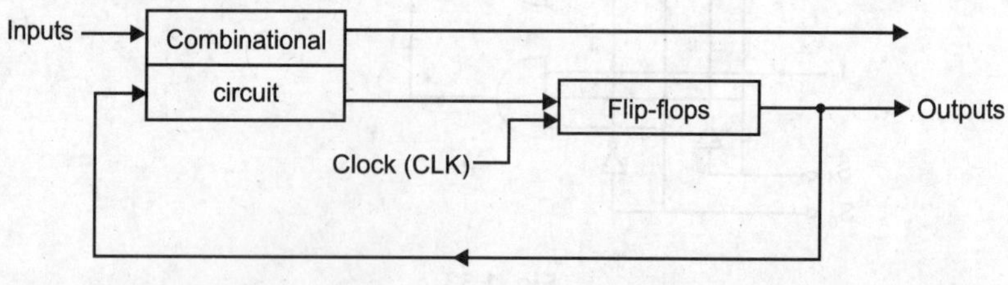

Fig. 1.35. Modified block diagram of sequential circuits.

5. Sequential circuits examples are – counters, shift registers, serial adders, sequence generators etc.

Before we go further, let us tabulate the differences between the two, in the next section.

1.11 COMPARISON OF COMBINATIONAL AND SEQUENTIAL CIRCUITS

Combinational Circuits	Sequential circuits
1. Are those circuits whose output variables at any instant of time are determined solely by the present values of its inputs.	1. Are those circuits whose present values of outputs are determined by the present values of its inputs and its present state.
2. No need of memory elements.	2. Memory elements are needed to store the past history of the input variables.
3. Its behavior is described by the set of output functions.	3. Its behavior is described by the set of next-state functions and the set of output functions.
4. More hardware is required to realize these circuits.	4. Lesser hardware is required to realize these circuits.
5. Are faster in speed as the delay between input and output is due to propagation delay of gates only.	5. Are slower in speed.
6. More expensive circuits.	6. Cheaper circuits.
7. Easier to design	7. Harder to design.
Example : Parallel adders, subtractor, encoders, decoders, MUXes, DeMUXes etc.	**Example:** Counters, shift registers, serial Adders, sequence generators etc.

Sequential circuits are of two types:

(*a*) Asynchronous sequential circuit.

(*b*) Synchronous sequential circuit.

Asynchronous Sequential Circuits

A sequential circuit whose output depends on the sequence in which the input changes is known as an asynchronous sequential circuit. These circuits are ***not*** controlled by clock i.e., those circuits in which averts occur whenever the inputs are applied are called as asynchronous sequential circuits.

Synchronous Sequential Circuits

A sequential circuit whose output behavior depends on the input at discrete time is called as a synchronous sequential circuit. These circuits are controlled by the clock. **A clock is a periodically generated pulse by a pulse generator. That is why they are also called as clocked sequential circuits.**

Let us compare the two in a tabular form now.

Synchronous Sequential Circuits	Asynchronous sequential circuits
1. Here, the memory elements are clocked FFs.	1. Here, the memory elements are either unclocked FFs or time delay elements.
2. Any change in input can affect memory elements when OK is activated.	2. Change in input can affect memory elements at any instant of time.

Synchronous Sequential Circuits	Asynchronous sequential circuits
3. They depend on the speed of clock	3. They are faster circuits.
4. They are easier to design.	4. They are difficult to design.

1.12 DON'T CARE CONDITIONS

Usually in truth tables or in some Boolean functions, all minterms have specific value of 0 or 1. But a situation may arise where the minterms don't have specific values. Such minterms are called as **unspecified or incomplete variables. These minterms are denoted by ϕ or d and are called as don't care entries.** These entries are entered in the K-map along with the minterm and can be combined with 1's or 0's depending upon which combination will eliminate maximum number of literals.

1.13 PARALLEL BINARY ADDERS (4-BIT)

Single bit full or Half Adders do not perform any useful function. To add two 4-bit numbers a 4-bit adder is required. Four single bit Full-Adders are connected together to form a 4-bit Parallel Adder capable of adding two 4-bit binary numbers.

The two 4-bit numbers *A* and *B* are applied at the circuit inputs $A_{0.3}$ and $B_{0.3}$ respectively. The 4-bit Sum output of the Parallel Adder is available at outputs $S_{0.3}$. The Carry In to the circuit is set to 0 (C_{in} = 0). The Carry is available at C_{001}.

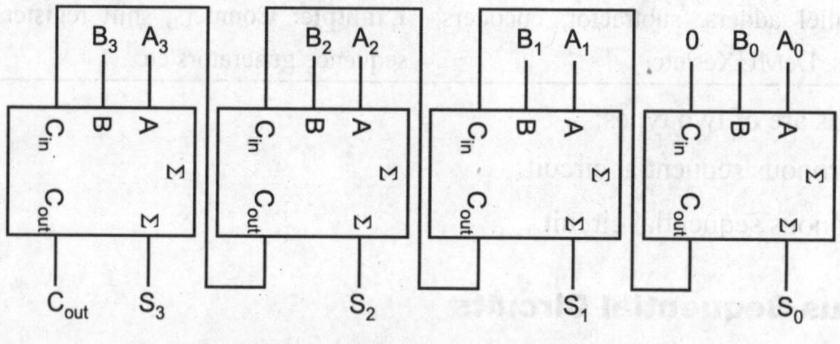

Fig. 1.36. 4-bit parallel Binary Adder

1.14 ENCODERS AND DECODERS

Encoder is a combinational circuit that has 2^n input or less input lines and n output lines. It is shown in Fig. 1.37.

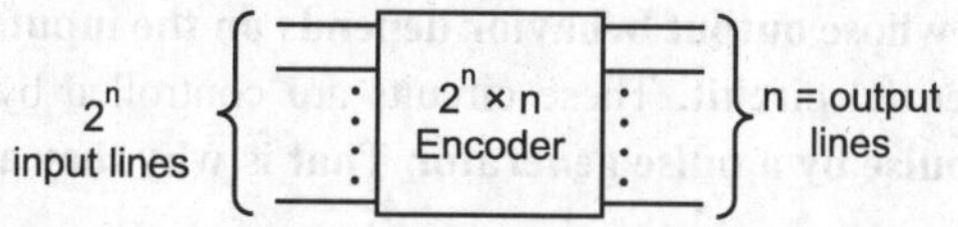

Fig. 1.37. Encoder (e.g. octal to binary encoder)

Each input is associated with an *n*-bit binary code and one input is supposed to be active (to be '1') at a time. **Please note that the *n*-outputs of the encoder supply the binary code associated with the active input. Also note that an encoder performs the reverse operation of a decoder.** Let us now see what a decoder is?

Decoder is a combinational circuit that has *n*-inputs and 2^n outputs. They assign an *n*-bit binary code to each output. So, it receives an *n*-bit input code and activates a single output. It may also have an enable input that enables or disables the decoder. For e.g. (3 × 8) decoder **Priority encoders** are more sophisticated types of encoders that assign priorities to the inputs. They allow more than one input to be active at a time. The output binary code corresponds to the active input with the highest priority. **Please understand that here each priority is expressed as a number that equals the number of the input assigned to.** This means that input-5 has a higher priority than input-4; input-4 has a higher priority than input-3 and so on.

To meet the larger input need, several similar chips need to be connected in such a way that we get a desired. IC. This is done by using enable input terminals. **The expansion process of decoders involves the following steps:**

Step 1: Calculate the number of available decoder needed to design desired decoder.

Step 2: Connect input lines.

Step 3: Connect output lines of each chip in parallel.

Step 4: Output lines of any level are connected with enable inputs of next succeeding level.

We are in a position to solve some problems now.

EXAMPLE 1: A (4 × 16) decoder is needed. How many (2 × 4) decoders are required?

SOLUTION: At level – 1 (m_1), we need $= \frac{16}{4} = 4$ decoders

At level-2 ($\underline{m}_2$), we need $= \frac{4}{4} = 1$ decoders.

EXAMPLE 2: Construct a (4 × 16) decoder using two (3 × 8) decoders with enable input.

SOLUTION:

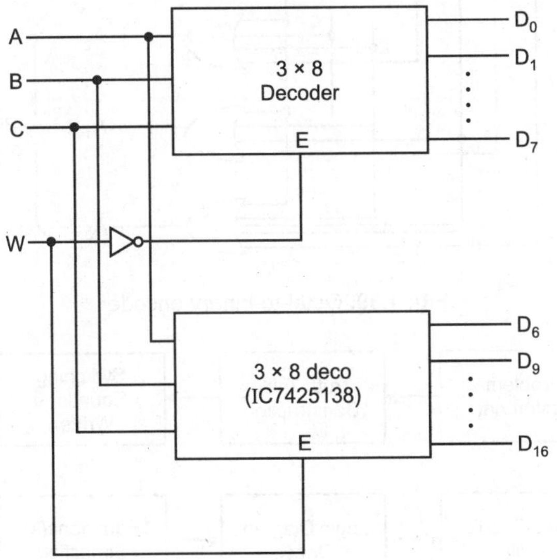

Fig. 1.38

EXAMPLE 3: Design an octal-to-binary encoder.

SOLUTION: An octal to binary encoder means it is an 8-input to 3-output encoder. Its truth table is

Octal	Binary		
	A_2	A_1	A_0
0 (D_0)	0	0	0
1 (D_1)	0	0	1
2 (D_2)	0	1	0
3 (D_3)	0	1	1
4 (D_4)	1	0	0
5 (D_5)	1	0	1
6 (D_6)	1	1	0
7 (D_7)	1	1	1

We observe here that $A_2 = 1$ if any of the digits D_4 or D_5 or D_6 or D_7 is a 1.

$$\therefore \quad A_2 = D_4 + D_5 + D_6 + D_7$$

Similarly,

$$A_1 = D_2 + D_3 + D_6 + D_7$$

and

$$A_0 = D_1 + D_3 + D_5 + D_7$$

Please note that D_0 is NOT present in any of the expressions above, so D_0 is a don't care.

Hence, we now draw its logic circuit –

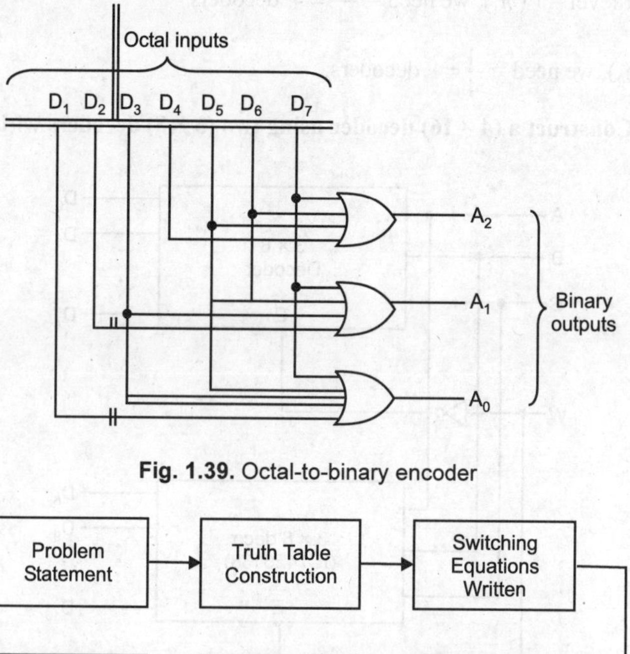

Fig. 1.39. Octal-to-binary encoder

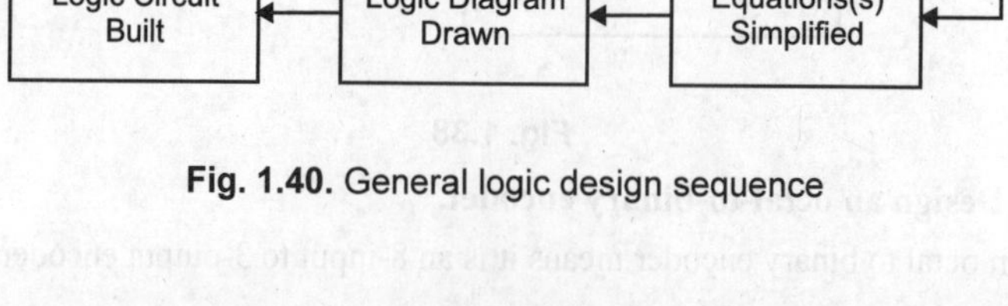

Fig. 1.40. General logic design sequence

1.15 PROLEM STATEMENTS TO TRUTH TABLES

Before any combinational logic system can be designed it must be defined. Proper statement of a problem is the most important part of any digital design task. Once correctly and clearly stated, any problem can be converted to the necessary logic for implementation. Figure 1.40 illustrates the sequence of design tasks in a general way.

Notice that the first task is to define the problem to be solved. Nothing can occur until that is correctly accomplished. The problem is then "rewritten" in the form of a truth table. From the truth table, the switching equations can be written and simplified and the logic diagram drawn. The logic diagram can be realized using any one of the three main digital integrated circuit families: transistor-transistor logic (TTL), emitter-coupled logic (ECL), or complementary metal-oxide silicon (CMOS). Practical applications rarely come in a prepackaged "truth table." ready for logic design. Truth tables must be constructed from verbal problem descriptions. Examples are given here to develop a sense of constructing truth tables from verbal problem statements.

EXAMPLE 1: A NASA system consists of three computers, two of which are on-line (connected to the system) at any given time. The system uses three computers to ensure safety in spacecraft operation through redundancy. If one computer experiences a problem it is taken off-line and another computer is brought on-line. Sele-checking diagnostics determines one computer fails it must be switched off-line. No more than two computers are to be on-line at any given time. Design the control logic to connect or disconnect the computers. In the event that two computers are unavailable, generate a warning and allow the third computer to come on-line. If all three computers are unavailable generate a second warning signal that invokes emergency procedures.

SOLUTION: Determine input and output variables and assign names.

Let variables represent the operation status of the three computers. C_1 is computer 1, C_2 is computer 2, and C_3 is computer 3. When $C_1 = 1$, for example, then that computer has failed. Let O_1, O_2 and O_3 be the computer disconnect control signal outputs. If $O_x = 1$, for example, then that computer is connected. Let W_1 and W_2 be the two warning output signals. If $W_x = 1$, then the warning is activated.

Construct a truth table that generates the proper output responses based on input variable values. Because three input variables exist an eight row truth table is needed (one row for each input combination. Each connect/disconnect control signal is generated based on the values of the computer operation status signals and the requirement for two computers to be available. For instance, if $C_1 = C_2 = C_3 = 0$, then all three computers are operational; which two are brought on-line is the designer's choice. In this example computers 2 and 3 are connected. The second case, when $C_1 = C_2 = 0$ and $C_3 = 1$, computer 3 has failed, so computers 1 and 2 are switched on-line. The truth table (Table 3.2) illustrates all of the output values for each of the input combinations. A separate equation must be written for each output variable.

Table 1.1: Truth Table for Example 1

C_1	C_2	C_3	O_1	O_2	O_3	W_1	W_2
0	0	0	0	1	1	0	0
0	0	1	1	1	0	0	0
0	1	0	1	0	1	0	0
0	1	1	1	0	0	1	0

C_1	C_2	C_3	O_1	O_2	O_3	W_1	W_2
1	0	0	0	1	1	0	0
1	0	1	0	1	0	1	0
1	1	0	0	0	1	1	0
1	1	1	0	0	0	0	1

EXAMPLE 2: Design a combinational logic truth table so that an output is generated indicating when a majority of four inputs is true.

SOLUTION: The circuit has four inputs and a single output. Let I_1, I_2, I_3, and I_4 represent the input variables, and O_1 be the output variable.

A majority occurs any time three or more of the input variables are true. The truth table (see Table 3.3) must contain 16 rows, 1 for each input permutation.

Table 1.2: Truth Table for Example 2

I_4	I_3	I_2	I_1	O_1
0	0	0	0	0
0	0	0	1	0
0	0	1	0	0
0	0	1	1	0
0	1	0	0	0
0	1	0	1	0
0	1	1	0	0
0	1	1	1	1
1	0	0	0	0
1	0	0	1	0
1	0	1	0	0
1	0	1	1	1
1	1	0	0-	0
1	1	0	1	1
1	1	1	0	1
1	1	1	1	1

EXAMPLE 3: A conveyor system brings raw material in from three different sources. The three sources converge into a single output conveyor. Sensors mounted adjacent to each source conveyor indicate the presence of raw material. All four conveyors have separate motors so they can be individually controlled. Each source conveyor can have a different speed. The output product flow rate is fixed; it can be turned only on or off. The output product rate must match the source flow rates. To accomplish these following conditions must be met. If source 1 has product, then sources 2 and 3 must be turned off; if source 1 is empty, then either 2 or 3 or both can be turned on. In the event that no product is available from the three sources, the output conveyor must be turned off. If no product is available, the respective source conveyor must be turned off.

SOLUTION: A diagram illustrating the conveyor system with the product switches and motors helps us to visualize the problem and define the variables. This diagram is shown in Figure. Table 3 is a truth table for this example.

Table 1.3: Truth Table for example 3

S3	*S2*	*S1*	M_4	M_3	M_2	M_1
0	0	0	0	0	0	0
0	0	1	1	0	0	1
0	1	0	1	0	1	0
0	1	1	1	0	0	1
1	0	0	1	1	0	0
1	0	1	1	0	0	1
1	1	0	1	1	1	0
1	1	1	1	0	0	1

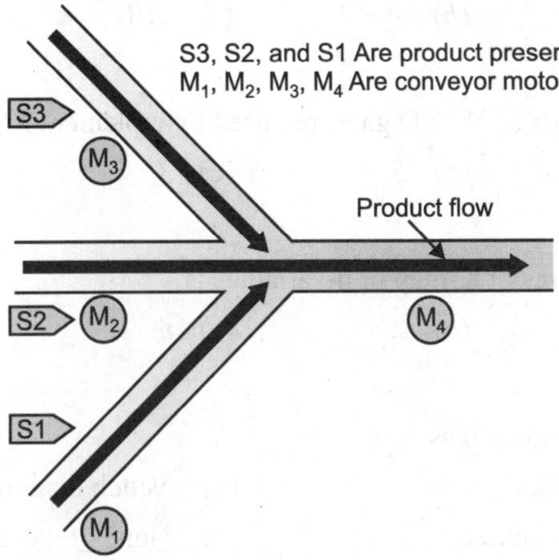

Once the truth table is complete, "think" your way through it by careful comparison with the original problem description. In many real world applications, the original problem statement may be incompletely defined. When that occurs, additional discussions or investigation into the objectives is necessary. In some cases several "passes" or trials may be necessary to accurately define the problem.

In summary, the process of converting a verbal problem statement into a truth table involves the following steps:

1. Determine the input variables and output variables that are involved.
2. Assign mnemonic or letter or number symbols to each variable.
3. Determine the size of the truth table; how many input combinations exist: $2^x = y$ where x = number of input variables and y = number of combinations.
4. Construct a truth table containing all of the input variable combinations.
5. By careful reading of the problem statement determine the combinations of inputs that cause a given output to be true.

SUMMARY

In this chapter we have studied Boolean algebra. The basic building blocks of a digital system are also studied. Various methods to reduce Boolean expression to its SOP or POS form using K-maps have been dealt in these chapters. Also many examples based on Word problems have been solved.

MULTIPLE CHOICE QUESTIONS [MCQs]

Q. 1. A NOT gate can have

(*a*) 1 input (*b*) 2 inputs (*c*) 3 inputs (*d*) any number

Ans. (*a*)

Q. 2. The operation that is commutative but not associative is

(*a*) AND (*b*) OR (*c*) EX-OR (*d*) NAND

Ans. (*d*)

Q. 3. A bulb is controlled by two switches A and B. The bulb glows only when both switches A and B are ON. It's Boolean expression is

(*a*) AB (*b*) $A + B$ (*c*) $\overline{AB}$ (*d*) $\overline{A+B}$

Ans. (*a*)

Q. 4. Minimum number of NAND gates required to implement XOR gate is

(*a*) 4 (*b*) 5 (*c*) 3 (*d*) 2

Ans. (*a*)

Q. 5. Number of squares in K-map of n-variables is -

(*a*) $2n$ (*b*) 2^n (*c*) n (*d*) 2^{n-1}

Ans. (*c*)

Q. 6. K-maps are also known as

(*a*) Venn diagrams (*b*) Veitch diagrams

(*c*) Sequence diagram (*d*) None of the above

Ans. (*b*)

Q. 7. A NOT gate is also called as a

(*a*) Inhibitor (*b*) Exhibitor

(*c*) Multivibrator (*d*) None of the above

Ans. (*a*)

Q. 8. Universal gates are

(*a*) AND-OR (*b*) OR-NOR (*c*) NAND-NOR (*d*) OR-EXOR

Ans. (*c*)

Q. 9. A MUX is also called as a

(*a*) Data Rejector (*b*) Data Selector

(*c*) Date Manipulator (*d*) None of the above

Ans. (*b*)

Q. 10. Memory element are NOT required in

(*a*) Combination circuits (*b*) Sequential circuits

(*c*) Linear circuits (*d*) Electronic circuits

Ans. (*a*)

Q. 11. A decoder is a combinational circuit that has

(*a*) *N*-inputs, n-output. (*b*) *n*-input, n^2-outputs

(*c*) *n*-inputs, 2^n-outpus. (*d*) 2^n-inputs, *n*-outputs

Ans. (*c*)

Q. 12. An encoder performs the reverse operation of a

(*a*) Decoder (*b*) MUX (*c*) De-MUX (*d*) Adders

Ans. (*a*)

Q. 13. When we move from one square to an adjacent square in a K-map, the number of variables that change are

(*a*) one (*b*) two (*c*) three (*d*) four

Ans. (*a*)

Q. 14. For the definition of K-map cells, which code has been used

(*a*) BCD code (*b*) Binary code (*c*) Gray code (*d*) None of the above

Ans. (*c*)

Q. 15. *n*-bit parallel adder has

(*a*) $(n+1)$FAs (*b*) $(n-1)$ FAs (c) *n* FAs (*d*) 2*n* FAs

Ans. (*c*)

Q. 16. The number of selector lines needed in a single input n-output De-MUX is

(*a*) 2 (*b*) *n* (*c*) 2^n (*d*) $\log_2 n$

Ans. (*d*)

Q. 17. The process of keeping the binary number designations of the rows and columns in Gray code is called as

(*a*) Logical ordering (*b*) Serial ordering

(*c*) Serial ordering (*d*) Adjacency ordering

Ans. (*c*)

Q. 18. The main criterion in the design of digitial circuits is

(*a*) Cost (*b*) Time (*c*) Manpower (*d*) None of the above

Ans. (*a*)

Q. 19. A 8-square cell is

(*a*) Pair (*b*) Quad (*c*) Octet (*d*) None of the above

Ans. (*c*)

Q. 20. A demultiplexer is also called as a

(*a*) Selector (*b*) Distributor (*c*) Actor (*d*) None of the above

Ans. (*b*)

Q. 21. The minimum number of selection lines required for selecting one out of *n*-input lines is

(*a*) $m = \log n * \log 2$ (*b*) $m = \log n/\log 2$

(*c*) $m = \log n + \log 2$ (*d*) None of the above

Ans. (*b*)

Q. 22. For applications like data selection, data routing, operation sequencing, parallel to serial conversion, wave form generations etc. we can use

(*a*) MUXes (*b*) De-MUXes (*c*) Encoders *d*) Decoders

Ans. (*a*)

Q. 23. To store n-bits of information, the number of Flip-Flops required are

(*a*) n (*b*) n^2 (*c*) $n*n$ (*d*) n^3

Ans. (*a*)

Q. 24. A transient caused by hazardous behavior of a logic circuit is known as

(*a*) Switch (*b*) Glitch (*c*) Pitch (*d*) None of the above

Ans. (*b*)

Q. 25. It is possible to implement any Boolean function of *n*-variables with

(*a*) 2^n (*b*) 2^{n-1} MUXes (*c*) $2n$ MUXes (*d*) None of the above

Ans. (*b*)

CONCEPTUAL SHORT QUESTIONS WITH ANSWERS

QUESTION 1: Determine by means of truth table, the validity of De-Morgan's theorem for three variables:

$$(ABC)' = A' + B' + C'.$$

SOLUTION 1:

A	*B*	*C*	*ABC*	*(ABC)'*
0	0	0	0	1
0	0	1	0	1
0	1	0	0	1
0	1	1	0	1
1	0	0	0	1
1	0	1	0	1
1	1	0	0	1
1	1	1	1	0

Now,

A'	*B'*	*C'*	*A' + B' + C'*
1	1	1	1
1	1	0	1
1	0	1	1
1	0	0	1
0	1	1	1
0	1	0	1
0	0	1	1
0	0	0	0

$$\therefore \quad (ABC)' = A' + B' + C'$$

QUESTION 2: List the truth-table for a three variable EX-OR (odd) function.

SOLUTION 2:

A	B	C	$A \oplus B$	$A \oplus B \oplus C$
0	0	0	0	0
0	0	1	0	1
0	1	0	1	1
0	1	1	1	0
1	0	0	1	1
1	0	1	1	0
1	1	0	0	0
1	1	1	0	1

QUESTION 3: Simplify the following expression using Boolean Algebra

(*a*) $A + AB$ (*b*) $AB + AB'$

(*c*) $A'BC + AC$ (*d*) $A'B + ABC' + ABC$

SOLUTION 3: (*a*) $A + AB$

$$= A(1 + B)$$
$$= A \quad \because [(1 + B) = 1]$$

(*b*) $AB + AB'$

$$= A(B + B') \quad [\because B + B' = 1]$$
$$= A$$

(*c*) $A'BC + AC$

$$= C(A'B + A)$$
$$= C(A' + A)(B + A) \quad [\because A + A' = 1]$$
$$= (A + B)C$$

(*d*) $A'B + ABC' + ABC$

$$= A'B + AB(C' + C)$$
$$= A'B + AB$$
$$= B(A' + A)$$
$$= B$$

QUESTION 4: Simplify the following expression using Boolean algebra:

(*a*) $AB + A(CD + DC')$ (*b*) $(BC' + A'D)(AB' + CD')$

SOLUTION 4: (*a*) $AB + A(CD + CD')$

$$= AB + AC(D + D')$$
$$= A(B + C)$$

(*b*) $(BC' + AD)(AB' + CD')$

$$= ABB'C' + A'AB'D + BCC'D' + A'CD'D$$
$$= 0 \text{ (Since } AA' = 0)$$

QUESTION 5: Using De-Morgan's theorem, show that:

(*a*) $(A + B)'(A' + B')' = 0$ (*b*) $A + A'B + A'B' = 1$

SOLUTION 5: (*a*) $(A + B)(A' + B') = (A'B')(AB)$

(*b*) $A + A'B + A'B' = A + A'(B + B')$

$$= A + A' \qquad [\because B + B' = 1]$$

$$= 1$$

QUESTION 6: Given the Boolean expression

$$FF = x'y + xyz'$$

(*a*) Derive an algebraic, expression for the complement F'

(*b*) Show that F.F′ = 0

(*c*) Show that $F + F' = 1$

SOLUTION 6: $F = x'y + xyz'$

(*a*)

$$F' = (x + y').(x' + y' + z)$$
$$= xx' + x'y' + xy' + y' + xz + yz'$$
$$= y'(1 + x' + x + z) + xz$$
$$= y' + xz.$$

(*b*)

$$\text{F.F}' = (x'y + xyz')(y' + xz)$$
$$= x'yy + xyz'y' + x'yxz + xyz'xz$$
$$= 0$$

(*c*)

$$F + F' = x'y + xyz' + y' + xz(y + y')$$
$$= x'y + xy(z' + z) + y'(1 + xz)$$
$$= x'y + xy + y'$$
$$= y(x' + x) + y'$$
$$= y + y' = 1$$

QUESTION 7: Given the Boolean function

$$F = xy'z + x'y'z + xyz$$

(*a*) List the truth table of the function.

(*b*) Draw the logic diagram using the original Boolean expression.

(*c*) Simplify the algebraic expression using Boolean algebra.

SOLUTION 7:

x	y	z	F
0	0	0	0
0	0	1	1
0	1	0	0
0	1	1	0
1	0	0	0
1	0	1	1
1	1	0	0
1	1	1	1

(*b*) Its logic diagram is

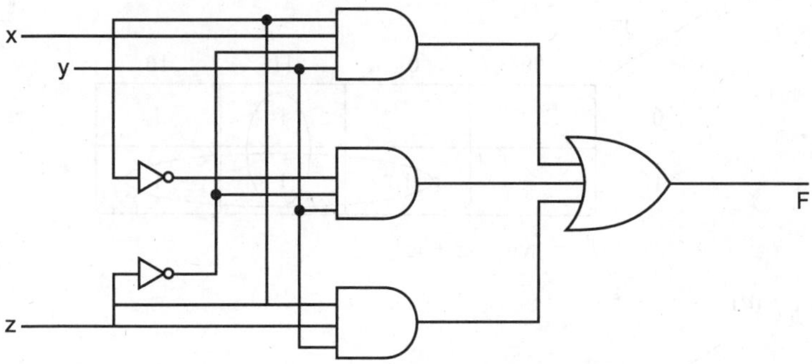

(*c*) $$F = xy'z + x'y'z + xyz$$
$$= y'z(x + x') + xz(y + y)$$
$$= y'z + xz$$

Its logic diagram is –

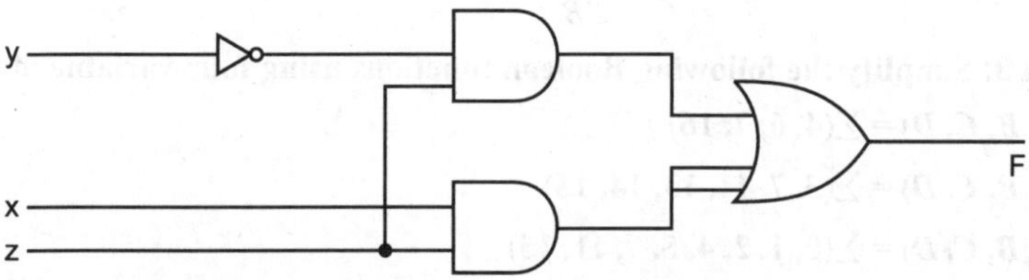

QUESTION 8: Simplify the following Boolean functions using three variable maps:

(*a*) $F(x, y, z) = \Sigma(0, 1, 5, 7)$ **(*b*) $F(x, y, z) = \Sigma(1, 2, 3, 6, 7)$**

(*c*) $F(x, y, z) = \Sigma(3, 5, 6, 7)$ **(*d*) $F(A, B, C) = \Sigma(0, 2, 3, 4,6)$**

SOLUTION 8: (*a*)

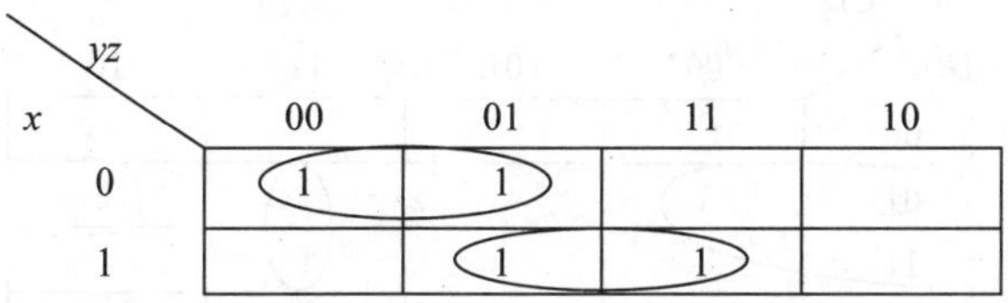

$\therefore$ $$F = x'y' + yz$$

(*b*)

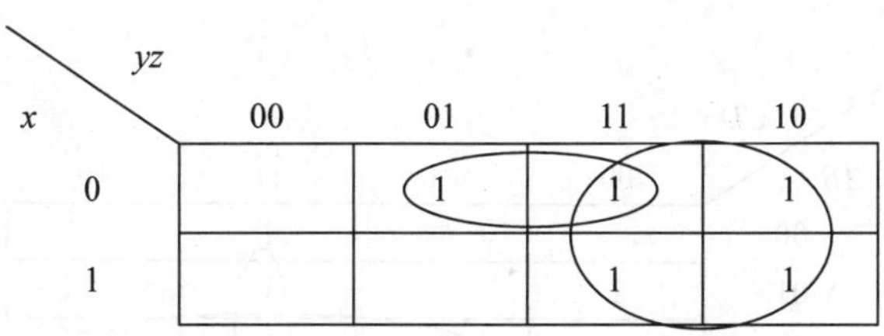

$\therefore$ $$F = y + x'z$$

(*c*)

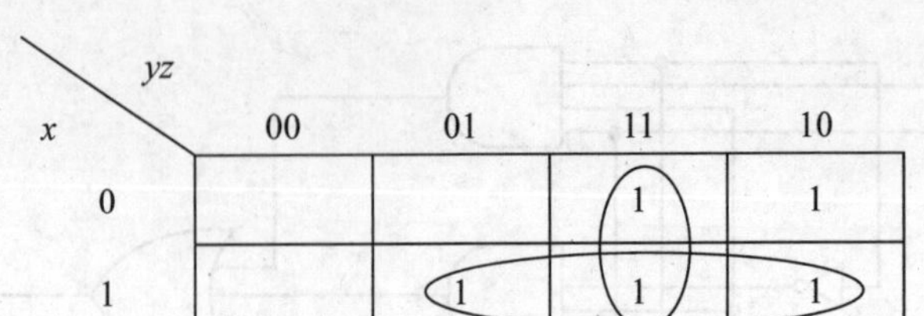

$\therefore \quad F = xy + xz + yz$

(*d*)

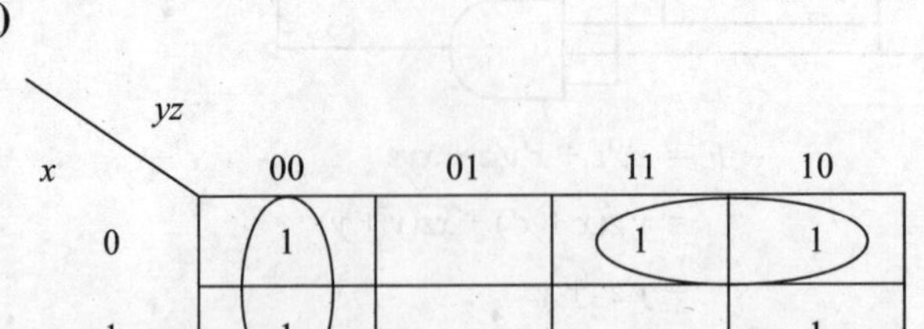

$\therefore \quad F = C + A'B$

QUESTION 9: Simplify the following Boolean functions using four-variable maps

(*a*) $F(A, B, C, D) = \sum(4, 6, 7, 16)$

(*b*) $F(A, B, C, D) = \sum(3, 7, 11, 13, 14, 15)$

(*c*) $F(A, B, C, D) = \sum(0, 1, 2, 4, 5, 7, 11, 15)$

(d) $F(A, B, C, D) = \sum(0, 2, 4, 5, 6, 7, 8, 11, 13, 15)$

SOLUTION 9:

(*a*)

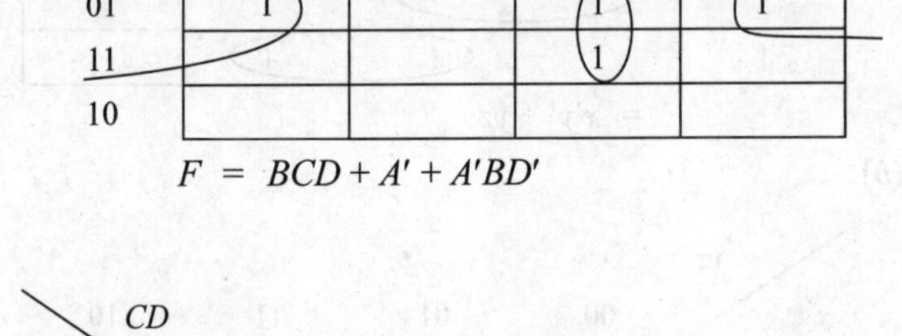

$\therefore \quad F = BCD + A' + A'BD'$

(*b*)

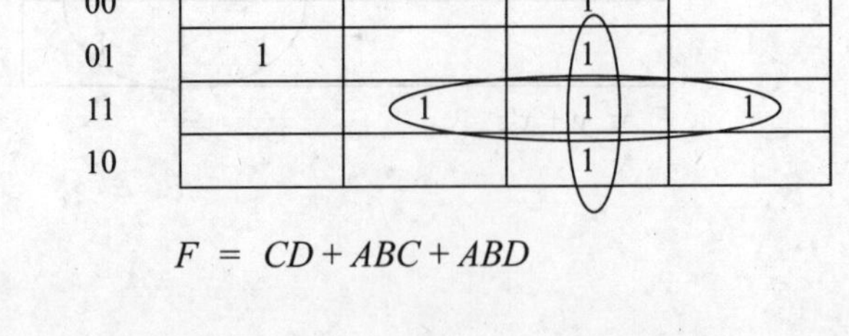

$\therefore \quad F = CD + ABC + ABD$

(*c*)

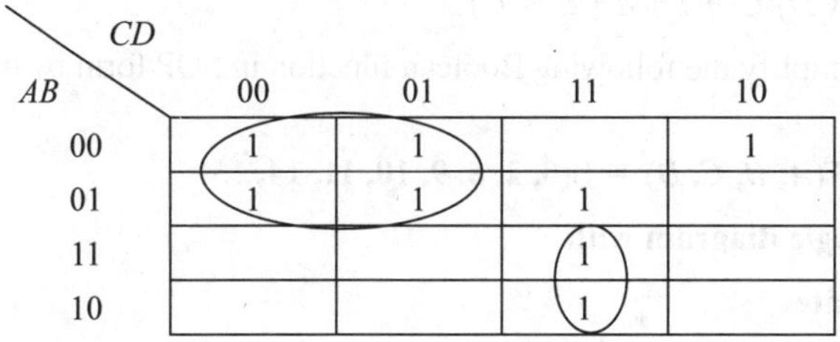

$\therefore \qquad F = A'C' + A'B'D' + ACD + A'BD$

(*d*) The k-map is shown below–

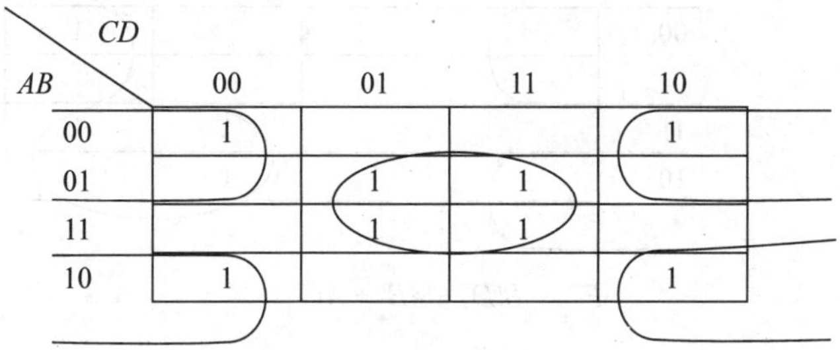

$\therefore \qquad F = BD + B'D' + A'B$

QUESTION 10: Simplify the following expression in

(*a*) SOP form **(*b*) POS form**

1. $x'y' \; y'z' + zy' + xy$ **2.** $AC' + B'D + A'CD + ABCD$

[MDU – BE(CSE) – 4th Sem, May 2008]

SOLUTION 10: (*a*)

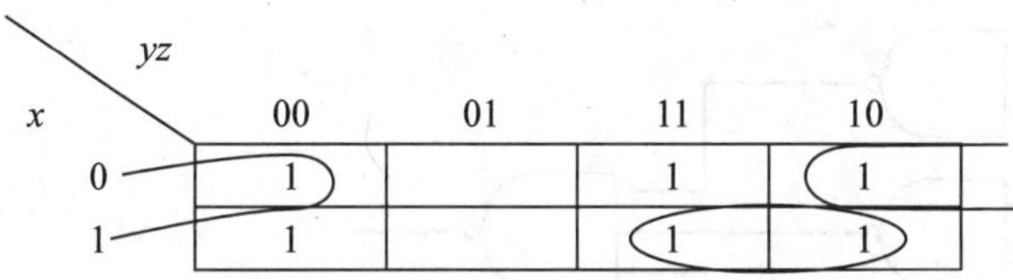

(*i*) $F = xy + z'$

$F = x'z + y'z$

(*ii*) $F = (x + z')(y + z')$

(*b*)

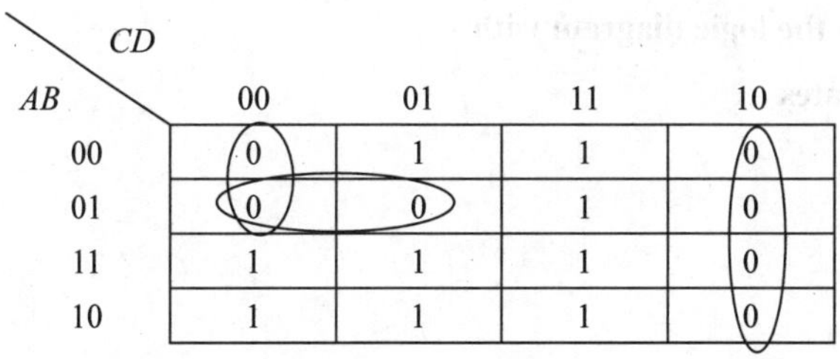

(*i*) $F = AC' + CD + B'D$

(*ii*) $F = (A + D)(C' + D)(A + B' + C)$

Question 11: Simplify the following Boolean function in SOP form by means of four variable map-

$$\mathbf{F(A, B, C, D) = S(0, 2, 8, 9, 10, 11, 14, 15)}$$

Draw the logic diagram with

(*a*) AND-OR gates

(*b*) NAND gates.

Solution 11:

AB \ CD	00	01	11	10
00	1			1
01				
11			1	1
10	1	1	1	1

$\therefore \quad F = B'D' + AB' + AC$

(*a*)

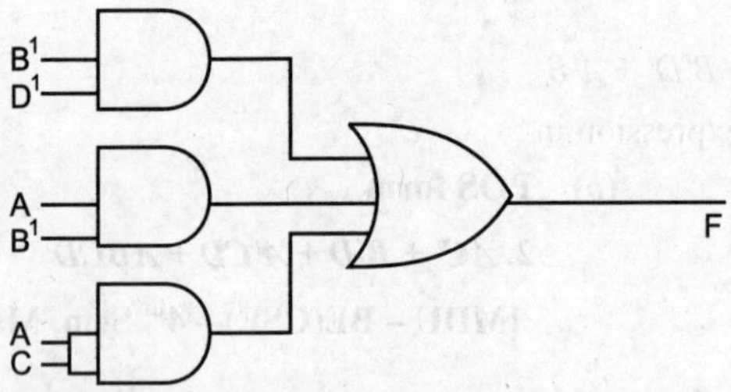

(*b*)

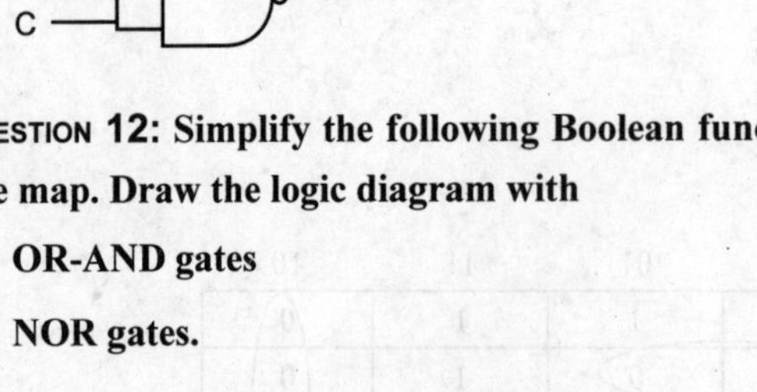

Question 12: Simplify the following Boolean function in POS form by means of a four-variable map. Draw the logic diagram with

(*a*) OR-AND gates

(*b*) NOR gates.

SOLUTION 12:

wx \ yz	00	01	11	10
00	0	0	1	1
01	1	1	1	1
11	0	0	1	1
10	0	0	1	1

$\therefore$

$$F = wy' + x'y + wx'z'$$

$$F = (w' + y)(x + y)(w' + x + z')$$

(*a*)

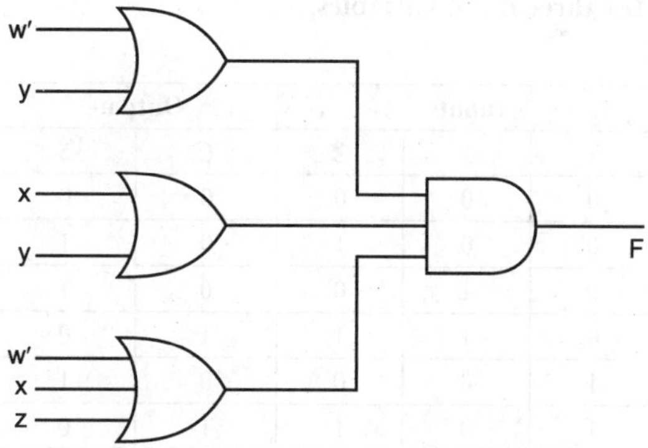

(*b*)

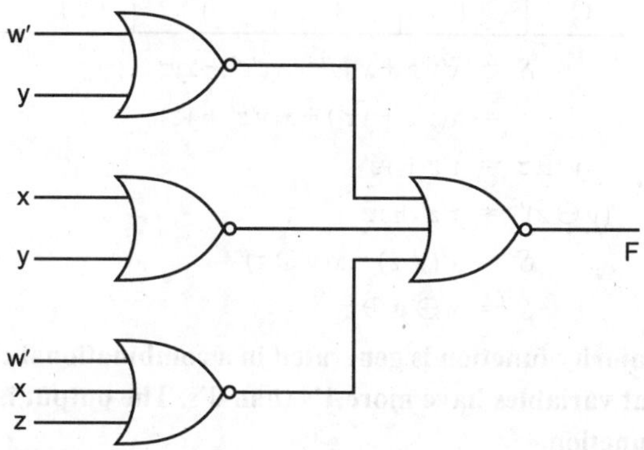

for the expression derived above.

QUESTION 13: Simplify the Boolean function *F* together with the don't care conditions, *d*, in

(*a*) SOP form **(b) POS form**

$$F(w, x, y, z) = \Sigma(0, 1, 2, 3, 7, 8, 10)$$

$$d(w, x, y, z) = (\Sigma(5, 6, 11, 15)$$

SOLUTION 13: We draw its K-map first –

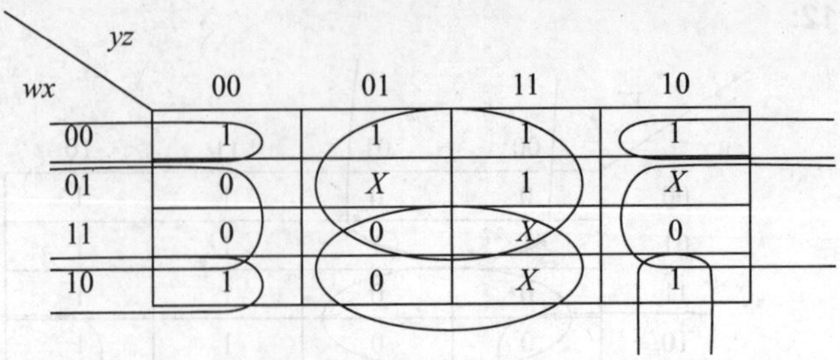

$\therefore$ $$F = x'z' = w'z$$

(*ii*) $$F = (x' + z)\,(w' + z')$$

QUESTION 14: Using table given below, derive the Boolean expression for the S(sum) output of the full-adder in SOP form. Then by algebraic manipulation show that *S* can be expressed as the exclusive OR of the three input variables.

SOLUTION 14:

Inputs			Outputs	
X	*Y*	*Z*	*C*	*S*
0	0	0	0	0
0	0	1	0	1
0	1	0	0	1
0	1	1	1	0
1	0	0	0	1
1	0	1	1	0
1	1	0	1	0
1	1	1	1	1

$\therefore$ $$S = x'y'z + x'yz' + xy'z' + xyz$$

$$= x(y'z + yz') + x(y'z' + yz)$$

But $$y \oplus z = y'z + yz'$$

and $$(y \oplus z)' = y'z' + yz$$

$\therefore$ $$S = x'(y\ z) = x(y \oplus z)'$$

or $$S = x \oplus y \oplus z$$

QUESTION 15: A majority function is generated in a combinational circuit when the output is equal to 1 if the input variables have more 1's than 0's. The output is 0 otherwise. Design a three input majority function.

SOLUTION 15:

x	*y*	*Z*	*F*
0	0	0	0
0	0	1	0
0	1	0	0
0	1	1	1
1	0	0	0
1	0	1	1

x	*y*	*Z*	*F*
1	1	0	1
1	1	1	1

x \ *yz*	00	01	11	10
0	0	0	1	0
1	0	1	1	1

$\therefore \quad F = xy + xz + yz$

QUESTION 16: Design a full adder circuit using only NAND gates.

(VNS Gujrat University, Dec. 2007, JNTU, AP, March 2009)

SOLUTION 16: The Boolean expression for the full adder sum and carry can be written as

$$S = A'B'C + AB'C' + A'BC' + ABC$$

$$C = AB + BC + CA = [(AB)')(BC)'(CA)']'$$

The NAND gate realization of sum and carry are shown in Fig 1.41.

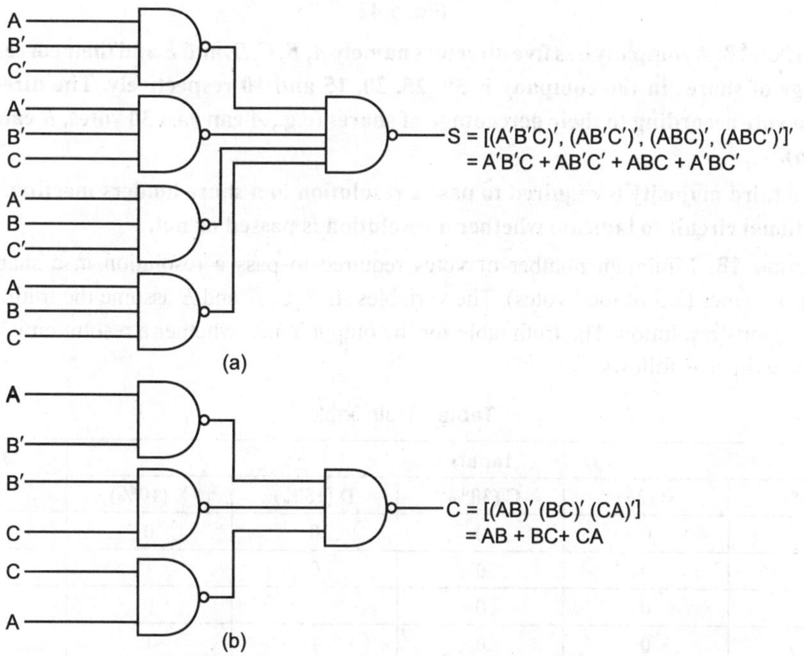

Fig. 1.41. Implementing full adder sum and carry with NAND gate.

QUESTION 17: Obtain NAND logic diagram of a full adder from the Boolean function

$$C = xy + yz + xz$$

$$S = \bar{C}\,(x + y + z) + xyz$$

(RGPV – June 2003)

SOLUTION 17:

$$C = xy + yz + xz$$

$$= [(xy)'\,(yz)'\,(xz)']$$

$$S = \bar{C}\,(x + y + z) + xyz$$

$$= \{[x'y'z')' \ \overline{C}\ ]'. (xyz)\}'$$

The NAND gate realization of sum *S* and carry *C* are shown in Fig. 1.42.

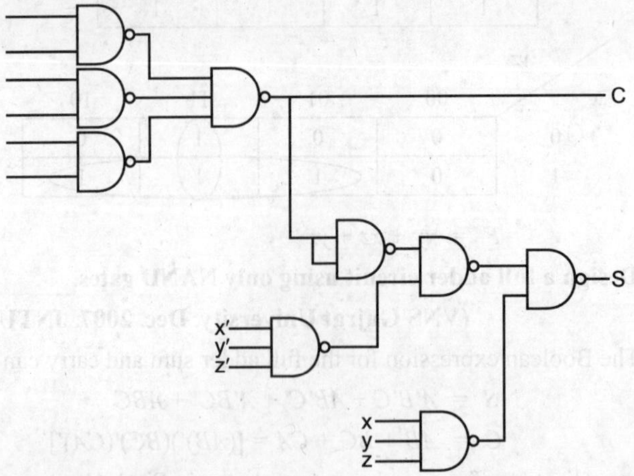

Fig. 1.42

QUESTION 18: A company has five directors namely *A*, *B*, *C*, *D*, and *E* and their corresponding percentage of shares in the company is 30, 25, 20, 15 and 10 respectively. The directors are eligible to vote according to their percentage of shares (e.g., *A* can cast 30 votes, *B* can 25 votes and so on).

A two third majority is required to pass a resolution in a share holders meeting. Design a combinational circuit to indicate whether a resolution is passed or not.

SOLUTION 18: Minimum number of votes required to pass a resolution in a share-holders meeting is 67 votes (2/3 of total votes). The variables *A*, *B*, *C*, *D* and *E* assume the truth value 1 if director supports resolution. The truth table for the output Y i.e., whether a resolution is passed or not, can be written as follows.

Table : Truth Table

Inputs					Output
A (30%)	B (25)	C (20%)	D (15%)	E (10%)	*Y*
0	0	0	0	0	0
0	0	0	0	1	0
0	0	0	1	0	0
0	0	0	1	1	0
0	0	1	0	0	0
0	0	1	0	1	0
0	0	1	1	0	0
0	0	1	1	1	0
0	1	0	0	0	0
0	1	0	0	1	0
0	1	0	1	0	0
0	1	0	1	1	0

Inputs					Output
A (30%)	B (25)	C (20%)	D (15%)	E (10%)	Y
0	1	1	0	0	0
0	1	1	0	1	0
0	1	1	1	0	0
0	1	1	1	1	1
1	0	0	0	0	0
1	0	0	0	1	0
1	0	0	1	0	0
1	0	0	1	1	0
1	0	1	0	0	0
1	0	1	0	1	0
1	0	1	1	0	0
1	0	1	1	1	1
1	1	0	0	0	0
1	1	0	0	1	0
1	1	0	1	0	1
1	1	0	1	1	1
1	1	1	0	0	1
1	1	1	0	1	1
1	1	1	1	0	1
1	1	1	1	1	1

From the above table, the expression for Y can be written as –

$$Y = \Sigma m(15, 23, 26, 27, 28, 29, 30, 31)$$

DE \ ABC	000	001	011	010	110	111	101	100
00	0 0	4 0	12 0	8 0	24 0	28 1	20 0	16 0
01	1 0	5 0	13 0	9 0	25 0	29 1	21 0	17 0
11	3 0	7 0	15 1	11 0	27 1	31 1	23 1	19 0
10	2 0	6 0	14 0	10 0	26 1	30 1	22 0	18 0

Fig. 1.43.(a)

In the 5 variable K-map shown in fig 1.42(a) there are two quads and two pairs. The simplified expression is given by

$$Y = ABC + ABD + ACDE + BCDE$$

Now the above expression can be implemented as shown in Fig. 1.43(b)

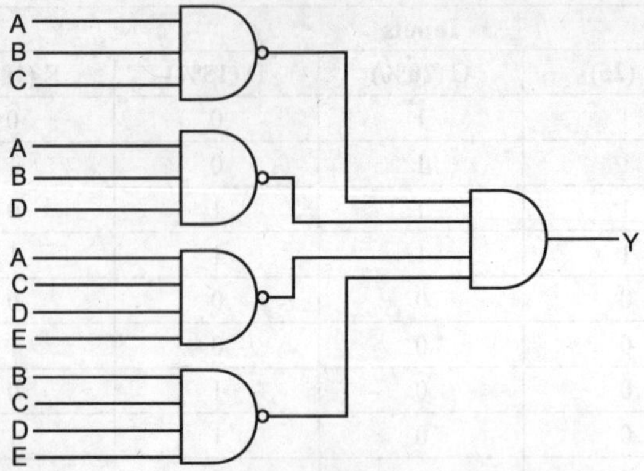

Fig. 1.43(b)

QUESTION 19: Four persons, members of a TVB panel game, each have an ON/OFF button that is used to record their opinion of a certain pop record. Instead of recording individual scores, some data processing is required such that the score board shows a HIT when the majority vote is in favor of and a MISS if it is against. Provision must also be made for TIE. From this verbal statement

(*a*) Derive the truth tables separately for HIT, MISS and TIE

(*b*) Extract SOP and POS for each of the three outputs

(*c*) Simplify the equation in SOP form

SOLUTION 19: From the word description of the problem, the truth table for the output HIT pairs and TIE can be written as follows:

Table

Inputs				Output		
A	*B*	*C*	*D*	HIT	MISS	TIE
0	0	0	0	0	1	0
0	0	0	1	0	1	0
0	0	1	0	0	1	0
0	0	1	1	0	0	1
0	1	0	0	0	1	0
0	1	0	1	0	0	1
0	1	1	0	0	0	1
0	1	1	1	1	0	0
1	0	0	0	0	1	0
1	0	0	1	0	0	1
1	0	1	0	0	0	1
1	0	1	1	1	0	0
1	1	0	0	0	0	1
1	1	0	1	1	0	0
1	1	1	0	1	0	0
1	1	1	1	1	0	0

(*b*) The sum of product form of HIT, MIS and TIE are given by

$$HIT = A'BCD + AB'CD + ABC'D + ABCD' + ABCD$$

$$MISS = A'B'C'D' + A'B'C'D' + A'B'C'D' + A'B'C'D' + A'B'C'D'$$

$$TIE = A'B'CD + A'BC'D + A'BCD' + AB'C'D + A'BC'D + ABC'D'$$

The product of a sum form of HIT, MISS and TIE are given by

$$HIT = (A + B' + C' + D')(A' + B + C'\ D')(A' + B' + C + D').(A' + B' + C + D)\ (A' + B' + C' + D')$$

$$MISS = (A + B + C + D)(A + B + C + D')(A + B + C' + D).\ (A + B' + C + D)(A' + B + C + D)$$

$$TIE = (A + B + C' + D')(A + B' + C + D')(A + B' + C' + D)(A' + B + C + D')\ (A + B' + C + D')(A' + B' + C + D)$$

AB \ CD	00	01	11	10
::	0	0	0	0
::	0	0	1	0
::	0	1	1	1
::	0	0	1	0

Fig. 1.44(a). K-map for HIT

AB \ CD	00	01	11	10
00	1	1	0	1
01	1	0	0	0
11	0	0	0	0
10	1	0	0	0

Fig. 1.44(b). k-map for MISS

AB \ CD	00	01	11	10
00	0	0	1	0
01	0	1	0	1
11	1	0	0	0
10	0	1	0	1

Fig. 1.44c. K-map for TIE

Now, the simplified expressions are –

$$HIT = ACD + BCD + ABC + ABD$$

$$MISS = A'B'C' + A'C'D' + B'C'D' + A'B'D$$

$$TIE = A'B'CD + A'BC'D + A'BCD' + ABC'D' + AB'C'D + AB'CD'$$

QUESTION 20: Design a combinational circuit with three inputs x, y, z and three outputs *A*, *B* and *C*. When the binary input is 0, 1, 2, or 3, the binary output is one greater than the input. When the binary input is 4, 5, 6, or 7, the binary output is one less than the input.

[MDU, BE(CSE) – 4th Sem, May 2007)]

SOLUTION 20: We draw its truth table first –

x	*y*	*z*	*A*	*B*	*C*
0	0	0	0	0	1
0	0	1	0	1	0
0	1	0	0	1	1
0	1	1	1	0	0

x	*y*	*z*	*A*	*B*	*C*
1	0	0	0	1	1
1	0	1	1	0	0
1	1	0	1	0	1
1	1	1	1	1	0

x \ *yz*	00	01	11	10
0	0	0	1	0
1	0	1	1	1

x \ *yz*	00	01	11	10
0	0	1	0	1
1	1	0	*1*	0

$$A = xy + xz\ yz \qquad B = x \oplus y \oplus z$$

From truth-table, we find that

$$C = Z'$$

∴ Required combinational circuit is –

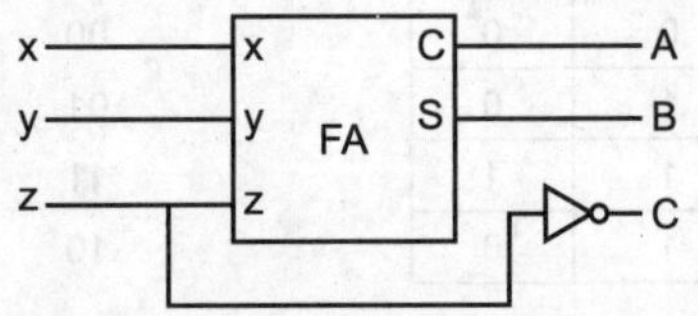

QUESTION 21: Design the following circuits

(*a*) Multiplier using shift method

(*b*) Parallel multiplier

(*c*) Binary Divider

SOLUTION 21: (*a*) Multiplier using Shift Method

To understand the multiplication process using shift method, consider the multiplication of two 4-bit binary numbers 1010 and 1011, as an example.

```
      1 0 1 0          → Multiplicand
    × 1 0 1 1          → Multiplier
  -----------
      1 0 1 0          → Partial product 1
    1 0 1 0            → Partial product 2
  0 0 0 0              → Partial product 3
1 0 1 0                → Partial product 4
1 1 0 1 1 1 0
-------------
```

From the above multiplication process, one can easily understand that if the multiplier is 1, then the multiplicand is simply copied as a partial product; if the multiplier bit is 0, then the partial product is 0. Whenever a partial product is obtained, it is shifted one bit to the left of the previous partial product. This process is continued until all the multiplier bits are checked, and then the partial products are added. This multiplication process, i.e. multiplication by a partial product addition and shifting, can be implemented using the block diagram shown in Fig. 1.45.

In the diagram shown in Fig. 1.45, the 4-bit multiplier is stored in a register $Y(Y_3Y_2Y_1Y_0)$, the 4-bit multiplicand is stored in register $M(M_3M_2M_1M_0)$ and the X register $(X_4X_3X_2X_1X_0)$ is initially cleared to 00000. Here, to perform multiplication, the least significant bit of the multiplier bit (Y_0) is checked whether it is 0 or 1. If $Y_0 = 1$, the number in the multiplicand register (M) is added with the least significant 4-bits of X-register ($X_3X_2X_1X_0$; X_4 is to store carry in addition process) and the combined X and Y register is shifted to the right by 1 bit. If performing any addition, this process has to be repeated four times to perform 4-bit multiplication. Now, the multiplication result $(R_7R_6R_5R_4R_3R_2R_1R_0)$ will be available in X and Y registers $(X_3X_2X_1X_0\ Y_3Y_2Y_1Y_0)$.

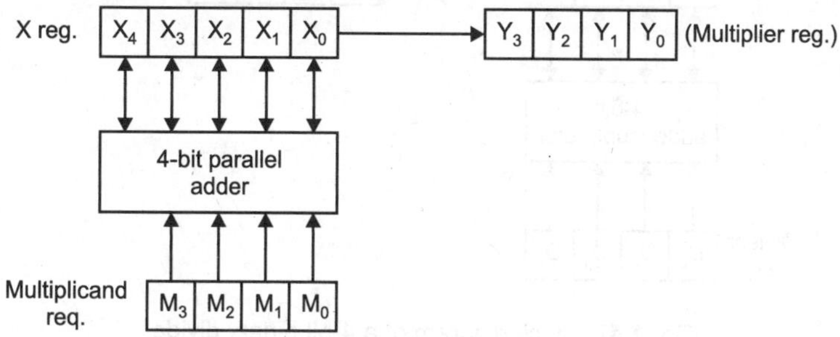

Fig. 1.45. 4-bit binary multiplier using shift method

(*a*) Parallel Multiplier

The 4-bit multiplier using shift method requires 4 cycles of addition and shifting operations, but it requires only a single 4-bit parallel adder.

It requires three 4-bit parallel binary adders and 16 numbers of 2-input AND gates. Here, each group of 4 AND gates is used to obtain partial products while 4-bit parallel adders are used to add the partial products. Since the generation of partial products and their additions are performed in parallel in the group of AND gates and 4-bit adders respectively, the multiplication result $(P_7P_6P_5P_4P_3P_2P_1P_0)$ will be available at the output immediately after the propagation delay in the multiplier circuit.

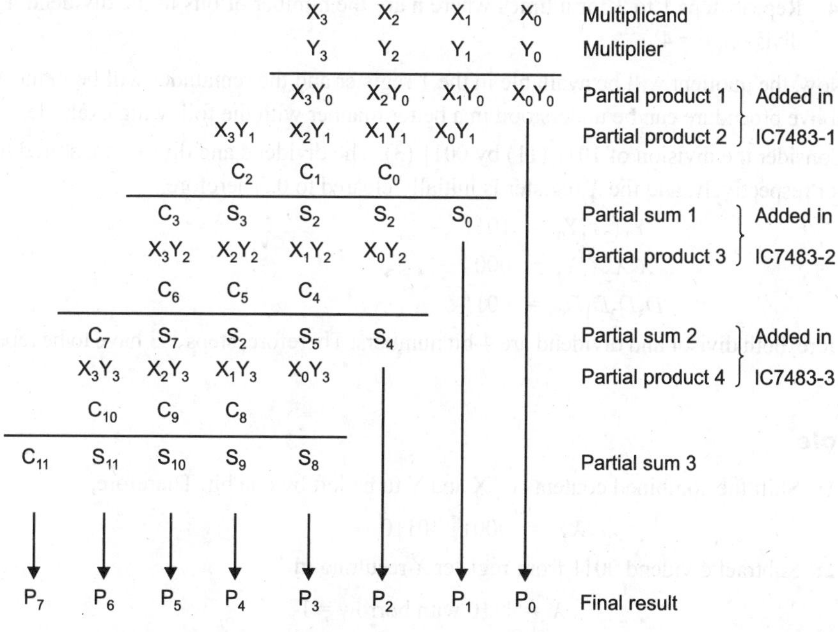

Fig. 1.46. Symbolic form of binary multiplication process

The operation of the parallel multiplier can be understood in a better manner from the symbolic form of binary multiplication process shown in Fig. 1.46.

(b) Binary Divider

Division is the most difficult and time consuming operation for a general purpose computer. A block diagram of a binary divider unit using restoring technique for division is shown in Fig. 1.47.

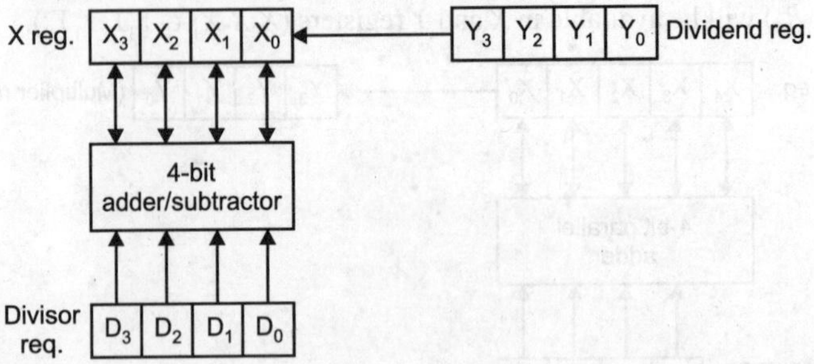

Fig. 1.47. Block diagram of a 4-bit binary divider

Here, the dividend is stored in the dividend register $Y(Y_3Y_2Y_1Y_0)$, the divisor is stored in the divisor register $D(D_3D_2D_1D_0)$ and initially the X register $(X_3X_2X_1X_0)$ is cleared.

The procedure for division operation using the circuit shown in Fig. 1.47 is explained as follows:

1. Shift the combined content of X and Y registers to the left by one bit.
2. Perform trial subtraction by subtracting the content D register from the content of X register.
3. If there is no borrow in the previous subtraction, put 1 in the LSB of Y register, else restore the original content of X register by adding the contents of D register with the contents of X register.
4. Repeat steps 1 to 3 for n times where n are the number of bits in the dividend. For a 4-bit division, $n = 4$.

Now, the quotient will be available in the Y register and the remainder will be in the X register. The above procedure can be understood in a better manner with the following example.

Consider the division of 1011 (11) by 0011 (3). The dividend and divisor are stored in Y and D register respectively, and the X register is initially cleared to 0. Therefore,

$$Y_3Y_2Y_1Y_0 = 1011$$
$$X_3X_2X_1X_0 = 000$$
$$D_3D_2D_1D_0 = 0011$$

Here, both divisor and dividend are 4-bit numbers. Therefore, steps 1-3 have to be repeated four times.

I Cycle

Step 1: Shift the combined contents of X and Y to be left by one bit. Therefore,

$$XY = 0001 \quad 0110$$

Step 2: Subtract dividend 0011 from register X resulting in

$$X = 1110 \text{ with borrow} = 1$$

Step 3: Since borrow = 1, restore the original content in *X* register by adding dividend 0011 with the content of x register 1110. Now,

$$XY = 0001 \quad 0110$$

II Cycle

Step 1: Shift the combined contents of *X* and *Y* to be left by one bit. Therefore,

$$XY = 0010 \quad 1100$$

Step 2: Subtract dividend 0011 from *X* register resulting in

$$X = 111 \text{ with borrow} = 1$$

Step 3: Since borrow = 1, restore the original content in *X* register by adding dividend 0011 with the content of *X* register 1111. Now,

$$XY = 0010 \quad 1100$$

III Cycle

Step 1: Shift the combined contents of X and Y to the left by one bit. Therefore,

$$XY = 101 \quad 1000$$

Step 2: Subtract dividend 0011 from register X which results in

$$X = 0010 \text{ with borrow} = 0$$

Step 3: Since borrow = 0, put 1 in the LSB of *Y* register (Y_0). Therefore,

$$XY = 0010\,1001$$

IV Cycle

Step 1: Shift the combined contents of X and Y to the left by one bit. Therefore,

$$XY = 0101 \quad 0010$$

Step 2: Since borrow = 0, put 1 in the LSB of Y register (Y_0). Therefore,

$$XY = 0010 \quad 0011$$

Now, the quotient 0011 (3) is available in the *Y* register and the remainder 0010 (2) is available

QUESTION 22: Define what is a K-map? How do you map? How do we reduce Boolean expression in SOP form using K-maps? Discuss various methods what is map rolling? Also give the method to derive POS Boolean expression using K-map? Give sufficient examples and explain.

SOLUTION 22: Truth table provides a nice and natural way to list all the values of a function. There are ways to represent functional values. One of them is Karnaugh Map named after its origi-Maurice Karnaugh. These maps also called Veitch diagrams. Karnaugh map is a graphical display of the fundamental products in a truth table. Karnaugh map is nothing but a rectangle made of certain number of squares, . ach square representing a Maxterm or Minterm.

Sum of Products, Reduction using K-map: In S-O-P reduction each square of K-map represents a minterm of the given function. If there are n variables, then there would be a map of 2^n square, each representing a minterm.

2-variable K-map for S-O-P reduction and representing minterms are given in Fig.

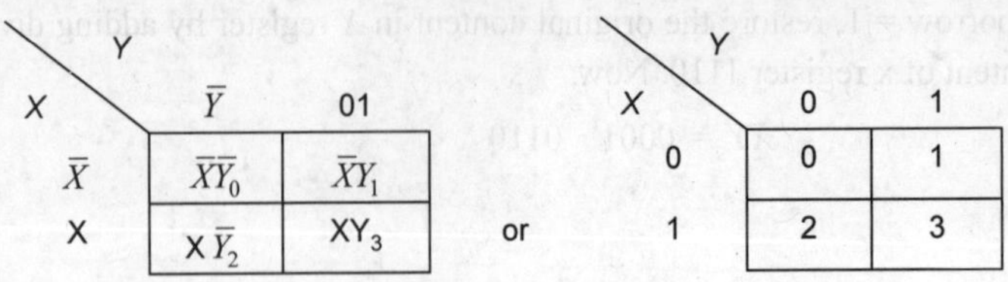

Fig. 1.48

3-variable K-map for S-O-P reduction and representing minterms are given in Fig.

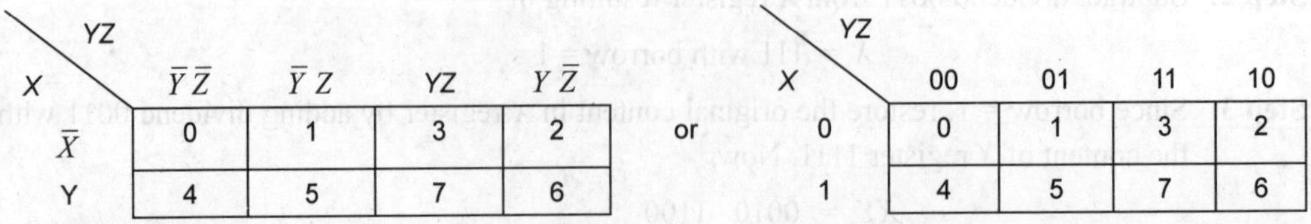

4-variable K-maps for S-O-P reduction and representing minterms are given in Fig. 1.49. Note in every square a number is written. These subscripted numbers denote that this square corresponds to that number's minterm. For example in three variable maps $X\bar{Y}\bar{Z}$ box has been given number 4 which means this square corresponds to m_2. Similarly box number 6 means it corresponds to m_6 and so on. Notice the numbering scheme here, it is 0, 1, 3, 2, then 4, 5, 7, 6 and so on. Always squares are marked using this scheme while making a K-map. Observe carefully above given K-map. See the binary number at the top of K-map. These do not follow binary progression; instead they differ by one place when moving from left to right (00, 01, 11, 10). It is done so that only one variable changes from complemented to uncomplemented form or vice-versa i.e., $\overline{A}\overline{B}$, AB, AB, $A\overline{B}$. The binary code 00, 01, 11, 10 is called Gray code and is a binary code in which each successive number differs only in one place.

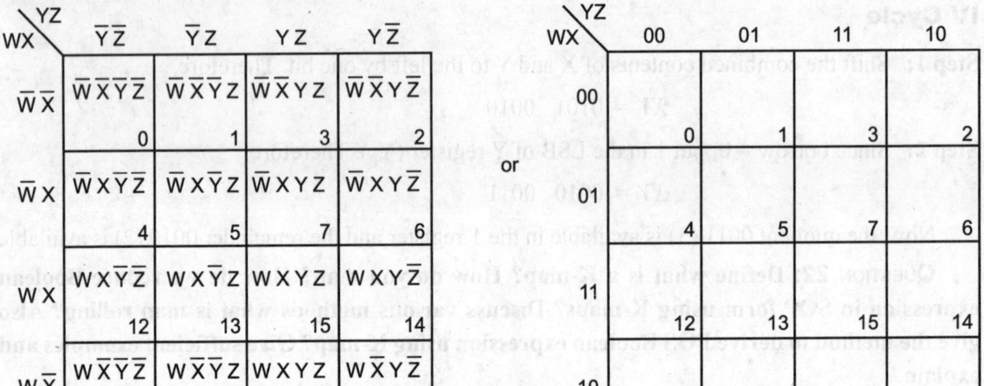

Fig. 1.49

How to Map in K-maps? We will take an example of 2- variable map to illustrate. Suppose we have to make a K-map of given truth table.

A	*B*	*F*
0	0	0
0	1	0

A	*B*	*F*
1	0	1
1	1	1

The canonical S-O-P expression for this table is $F = A\overline{B} + AB$ or $F = \Sigma(2, 3)$. Now output is noted in the given truth table. Here, in minterms m_2 and m_3 the output is 1. Thus we consider m_2 and m_3 and enter 0's in all blank squares. Similarly for 3-variable and 4-variable enter 1's for all outputs and then enter 0's in the rest of squares.

How to reduce Boolean expression in S-O-P form using K-map? For reducing the Boolean expression, we have to mark pairs, quads and octets.

Method 1

Reduction of a pair: Consider the following K-map

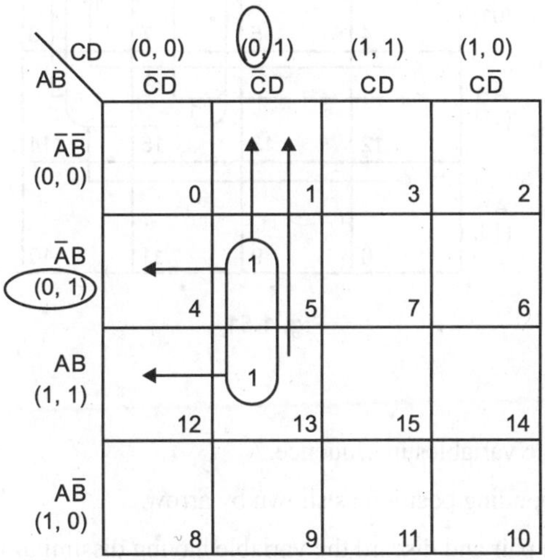

Fig. 1.50

Consider the pair (m_5, m_{13}) we have to firstly write down the variable used sequentially and then write down the corresponding number of both the entries (as shown by arrow for, m_5 that the value of *A*, *B* is (0, 1) and the value of *C*, *D* is (0, 1) same for m_{13}.

	A	*B*	*C*	*D*
For $m_5 \rightarrow$	0	1	0	1
For $m_{13} \rightarrow$	1	1	0	1

After this choose the same pair e.g., B, C, D, leave the dissimilar pair e.g., A we get by F_i ( )

B	*C*	*D*
1	0	1
1	0	1
B	$\overline{C}$	D

Now write down the same variable for the pair of one's for example B and D place a bar (–) for the variable having a pair of zeros for example C in Fig. 1.51.

The Boolean expression for the given pair (m_5, m_{13}) we have

$$f(A, B, C, D) = B\bar{C}D$$

Please note that the same method is used for the reduction of quad, octet also.

Reduction of a quad: Consider the quad (m_6, m_7, m_{14}) in the following K-map.

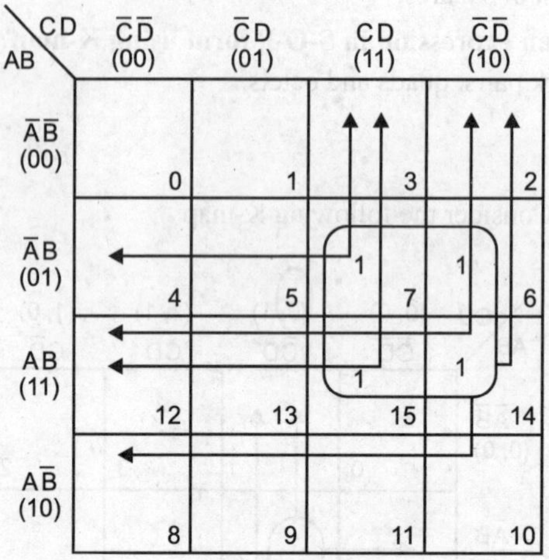

Fig. 1.51

Methods

1. Write down all the variables in sequence.
2. Enter the corresponding position as shown by arrow.
3. Choose the same pair and discard the variable having dissimilar pair.
4. Write down the variables as such for the pair of one's and take complement (or place a bar) of the variable having a pair of zeros.

We get:

	A	*B*	*C*	*D*
For m_7 →	0	1	1	1
For m_6 →	0	1	1	0
For m_{15} →	1	1	1	1
For m_{14} →	1	1	1	0

[Discard A and D because they contain dissimilar pair]

Hence, Boolean expression for the quad is given by

$$f(A, B, C, D) = BC$$

Reduction of an octet: Same methods as of pair and quad. Consider the following octet.

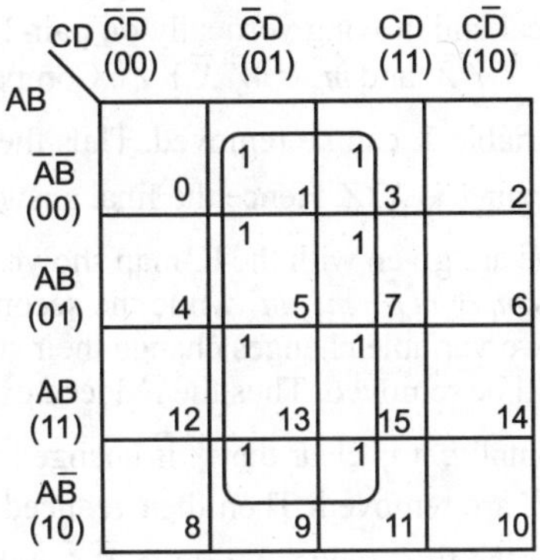

Fig. 1.52

We have

	A	B	C	D
For $m_1 \rightarrow$	0	0	0	1
For $m_3 \rightarrow$	0	0	1	1
For $m_5 \rightarrow$	0	1	0	1
For $m_7 \rightarrow$	0	1	1	1
For $m_{13} \rightarrow$	1	1	0	1
For $m_{15} \rightarrow$	1	1	1	1
For $m_9 \rightarrow$	1	0	0	1
For $m_{11} \rightarrow$	1	0	1	1

Since, A, B, C have dissimilar terms hence are discarded but D has similar group of one's hence is written as such. So we get the Boolean expression for the octet as—

$$f(A, B, C, D) = D$$

Same method can apply for P.O.S. K-map but in this case for the group of 1's we write $\overline{A}$ and for group of 0's we write A.

Method II

Reduction of a Pair: To reduce the Boolean expression, adjacent 1's are encircled. If 2-adjacent 1's are encircled, it makes a pair, if 4 adjacent 1's are encircled, it makes a quad, if 8-adjacent 1's are encircled, and it makes an octet.

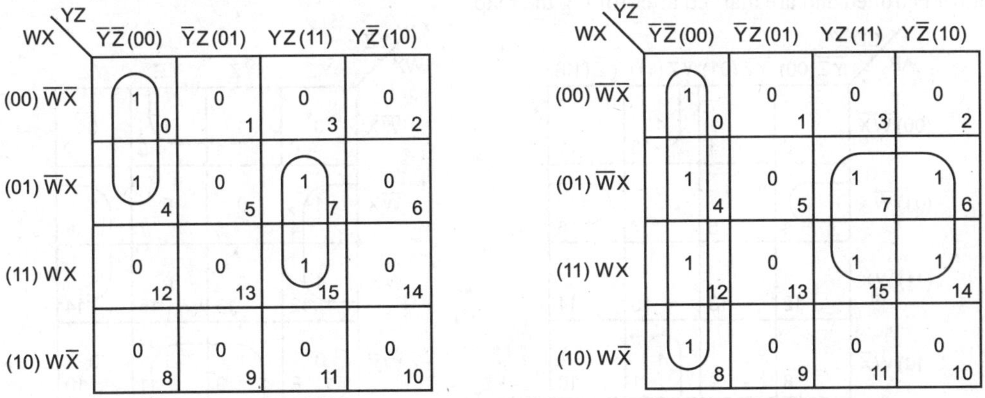

Fig. 1.53

Observe that pair-1 is vertical and moving vertically on pair-1, see one variable *X* is changing its state from $\bar{X}$ to X as m_0 is $\bar{W}\bar{X}\bar{Y}\bar{Z}$ and m_4 is $\bar{W}X\bar{Y}\bar{Z}$. Compare the two and we see $\bar{W}\bar{X}\bar{Y}\bar{Z}$ changes to $\bar{W}X\bar{Y}\bar{Z}$. So the variable X can be removed. Thus the answer of pair 1 is $\bar{W}\bar{Y}\bar{Z}$ and similarly the answer of another pair 1 is *XYZ*. Hence the final answer will be $\bar{W}\bar{Y}\bar{Z} + XYZ$.

Reduction of a Quad: If we are given with the K-map shown in Fig. 1.54 in which two quads have been marked. First quad is $m_0 + m_4 + m_{12}\ m_8$ while the second quad is $m_7 + m_6 + m_{15} + m_{14}$, when we move across quad-1, two variable changes change their states i.e. *W* and *X* changing their states. So these two variables will be removed. Thus the reduced expression will be $\bar{Y}\bar{Z}$. Similarly for second quad, moving horizontally, it is clear that *Z* is changed by $\bar{Z}$ and on moving vertically $\bar{W}$ is changed by *W* so *Z* and *W* are removed. Then their reduced form will be *XY*. Therefore the reduced form of both the quad or the final reduced form is $\bar{Y}\bar{Z} + YZ$.

Reduction of an Octet: Let us consider a K-map with octet shown in Fig. 1.54.

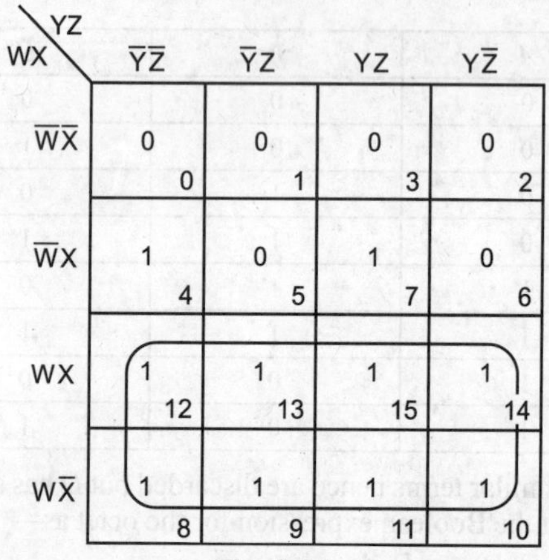

Fig. 1.54

Moving vertically one variable *X* is removed and moving horizontally two variables *Y* and *Z* are removed. Thus the eliminating *X*, *Y* and *Z*, the reduced expression will be only *W*.

Map Rolling: Now we shall try to understand the map rolling i.e. roll the map. For this we consider a map as if its left edges are touching the right edges and top edges are touching bottom edges. Then its opposite edges squares and corner squares are considered contiguous. As even in opposite edge squares and is corner squares only one variable changes its state from complemented to uncomplemented state or vice-versa. Therefore, while marking the pairs, quads and octets, map must be rolled and are marked after rolling the map.

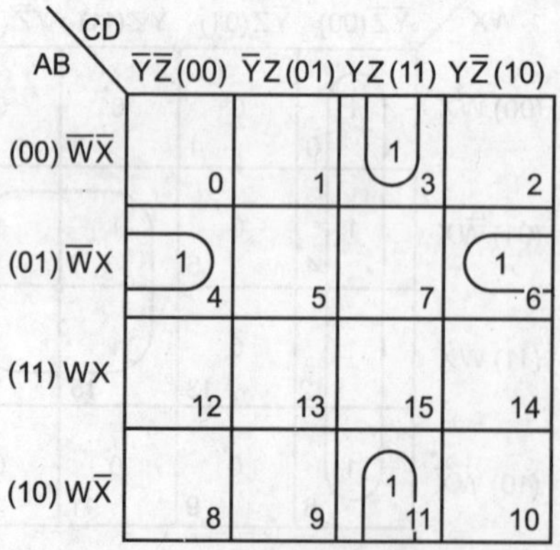

Fig. 1.55

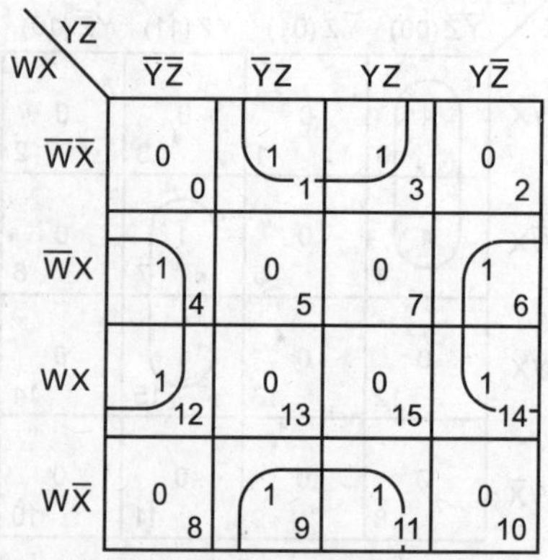

Fig. 1.56(a)

In the above K-map there are two groups marked i.e., one pair is $m_3 + m_{11}$ and other pair is $m_4 + m_6$. The reduced expression for fist pair is $\bar{X} Y Z$ and the reduced expression for second pair is $\bar{W} X \bar{Z}$. Hence the final expression is $\bar{X} Y Z + \bar{W} X \bar{Z}$.

In the above K-map two quads have been marked. One quad is $m_1 + m_3 + m_9 + m_{11}$ and second quad is $m_4 + m_6 + m_{12} + m_{14}$. The reduced expression for first quad is $X\bar{Z}$.

Thus the final expression is $\bar{X} Z + X\bar{Z}$. We can take another K-map of quad for more convenience. In Fig. 1.56(b) there are one quad only and the reduced expression for this will be $\bar{X} \bar{Z}$.

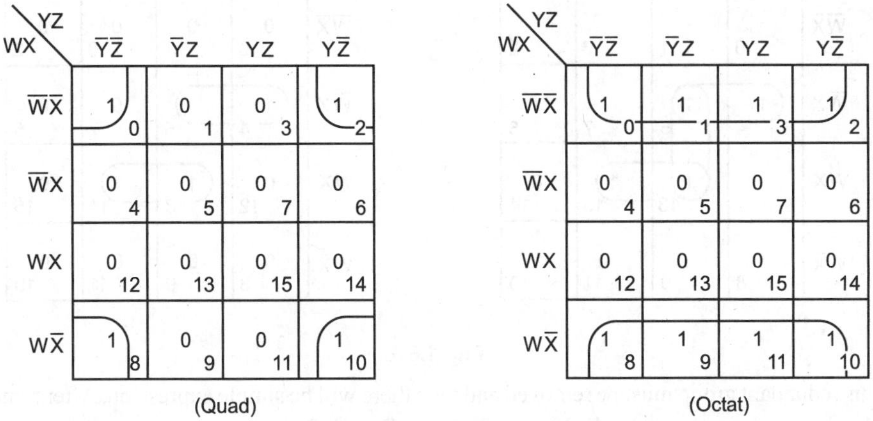

Fig. 1.56(c)

In fig. there are one octat only therefore the reduced expression for octat will be $\bar{X}$ only.

Overlapping Groups: Here overlapping means the same 1 can be encircled more than once. For example, if the following K-map is given.

From this K-map we observe that 1 for m_1 and m_{14} has been encircled twice. Once for pair $(m_5 + m_7)$ and again for quad $(m_7 + m_6 + m_{15} + m_{14})$ and similarly m_{14} for the quad and for pair $(m_{14} + m_{10})$. Overlapping always leads to simpler expressions.

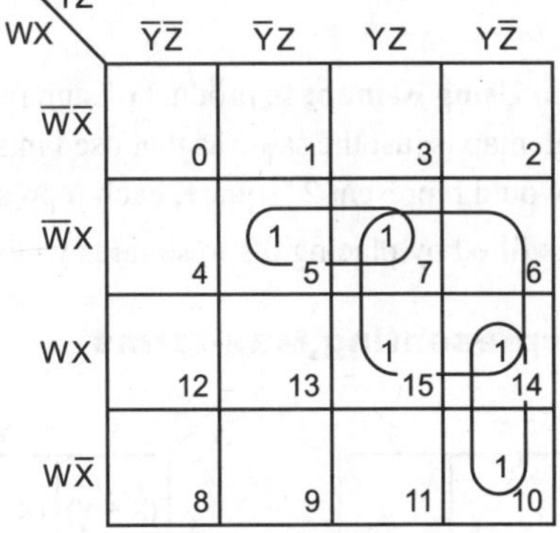

For first $(m_5 + m_7)$ expression, the reduced form is $\bar{W} X Z$ and for second expression is XY while for third expression is $W X \bar{Z}$. Therefore the final reduced expression for this K-map is

$\bar{W} X Z + X Y + W X \bar{Z}$.

Redundant Group: Redundant group is a group whose all 1's are overlapped by other groups (i.e. pairs, quads, octats). The example is given below.

Fig. 1.57 has a redundant group. In this there are three pairs, first pair is $(m_4 + m_5)$, second is $(m_5 + m_{13})$ and third is $(m_{13} + m_{15})$. Here, the second pair is redundant group as its all 1's are attached to other groups. The reduced expression is

$$\overline{W}\,X\,\overline{Y} + X\,\overline{Y}\,Z + W\,X\,Z$$

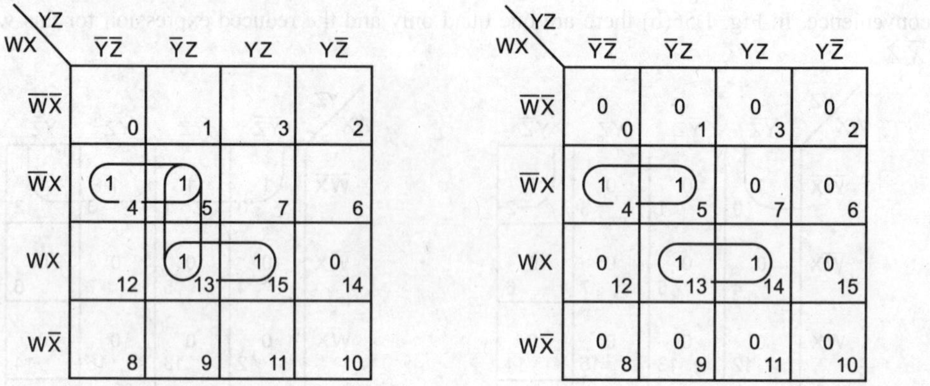

Fig. 1.57

This redundant group must be removed and then there will be simple expression. After removing the redundant group, we can get th eK-map shown in Fig. 1.58.

The reduced expression for K-map in Fig. 1.58(b) will be

$$\overline{W}\,X\,\overline{Y} + W\,X\,Z$$

Don't care condition: Normally in the truth table or in some boolean functions all minterm have specific value 0 or 1 but situation may arise where the minterms does not have specific values. Such minterm are called **unspecified or incomplete variables.** These minterms are denoted by ϕ or *d* and are called **don't care entries**. These entries are entered in the K-map along with the minterm and can be combined with 1's or 0's depending upon which combination will eliminate maximum number of literals. These don't cares are like wild in poker because you can let them stand for whatever you like.

Product of Sum Reduction Using K-map: In product of sum reduction, each square of K-map represents a Maxterm. Karnaugh map is just the same as that used in sum of product production. For a function of n variables, map would represent 2^n square, each representing a Maxterm.

For P-O-S reduction map is filled by placing 0's in squares whose Maxterms lead to output 0.

Two Variable K-map Representing Max-terms

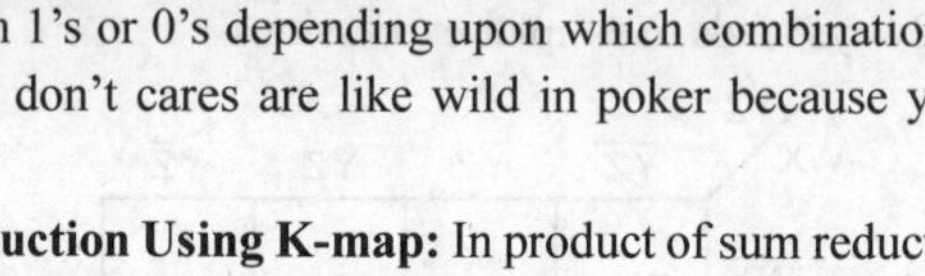

Fig. 1.58

Three Variable K-map Representing Max-terms

X \ YZ	00	01	11	10
0	0	1	3	2
1	4	5	7	6

or

X \ YZ	YZ	$Y\overline{Z}$	$\overline{Y}\overline{Z}$	$\overline{Y}Z$
X	$X + Y + Z$ 0	$X + Y + \overline{Z}$ 1	$X + \overline{Y} + \overline{Z}$ 3	$X + \overline{Y} + Z$ 2
$\overline{X}$	$\overline{X} + Y + Z$ 4	$\overline{X} + Y + \overline{Z}$ 5	$\overline{X} + \overline{Y} + \overline{Z}$ 7	$\overline{X} + \overline{Y} + Z$ 6

Fig. 1.59

Four Variable K-map Representing Min-terms

The major difference between S-O-P K-map and P-O-S K-map is that, P-O-S map complemented letters represent 1's and uncomplemented letters represent 0's whereas it is just opposite in S-O-P K-map. In Figs. 1.57, 1.57, 1.58 for 0's uncomplemented letters appear and for 1's complemented letters appear.

WX \ YZ	00	01	11	10
00	0	1	3	2
01	4	5	7	6
11	12	13	15	14
10	8	9	11	10

or

WX \ YZ	YZ	$Y\overline{Z}$	$\overline{Y}\overline{Z}$	$\overline{Y}Z$
WX	$W+X+Y+Z$ 0	$W+X+Y+Z$ 1	$W+X+\overline{Y}+\overline{Z}$ 3	$W+X+\overline{Y}+Z$ 2
$W\overline{X}$	$W+\overline{X}+Y+Z$ 4	$W+\overline{X}+Y+\overline{Z}$ 5	$W+\overline{X}+\overline{Y}+\overline{Z}$ 7	$W+\overline{X}+\overline{Y}+Z$ 6
$\overline{W}\overline{X}$	$W+\overline{X}+Y+Z$ 12	$\overline{W}+\overline{X}+Y+\overline{Z}$ 13	$\overline{W}+\overline{X}+\overline{Y}+\overline{Z}$ 15	$\overline{W}+\overline{X}+\overline{Y}+Z$ 14
$\overline{W}X$	$\overline{W}+X+Y+Z$ 8	$\overline{W}+X+Y+Z$ 9	$\overline{W}+X+\overline{Y}+\overline{Z}$ 11	$\overline{W}+X+\overline{Y}+Z$ 10

Fig. 1.60

Method To Derive P-O-S Boolean Expression Using K-Map

The rules of S-O-P expression and P-O-S expression are same except for one thing i.e. for P-O-S expression adjacent 0's are encircled in the form of pairs, quads and octats. The rules for deriving P-O-S boolean expression can be understood as:

1. First of all we prepare a truth table of given function.
2. Draw an empty K-map for given function i.e. for two variable, three variable K-map and so on.
3. Map the given function by entering 0's for the outputs as 0 in the corresponding squares i.e. if M_6 M_8 are 0's then squares no. 6 and 13 will be having 0's.
4. Enter 1's in all left squares.

5. Encircle adjacent 0's in the form of pairs, quads and octats and do not forget to roll the map and overlap.
6. Write the reduced expression for all the groups and AND (.) them.

QUESTION 23: Differentiate between a Latch and a Flip-Flop.

SOLUTION 23:

Latch	Flip Flop
1. They are level sensitive	1. They are edge sensitive.
2. Latch is faster.	2. They are slower.
3. They do not have a clock signal.	3. They depend on clock signals.
4. They take lesser number of gates and lesser power to work.	4. They take more number of gates and more power to work.
5. Latch is sensitive to glitches on enable pair.	5. Flip flop is immune to glitches.

EXERCISE QUESTIONS

Q. 1. (*a*) Explain with a logic diagram, the working of a full-adder.

(*b*) Explain the action of multiplexer with suitable diagrams.

[PTU, MCA – 3rd Sem., 2009]

Q. 2. What do you mean by a multiplexer? Design a (4 ×1) MUX using AND, OR and NOT gate.

[MDU, BE (CSE) – 4th Sem., May 2007]

Q. 3. Explain Full adder. **[MDU, BE(CSE), 4th Sem., May 2008]**

Q. 4. Design basic gates with the help of universal gats only

[MDU, BE (CSE) – 4th Sem., Dec. 2008]

Q. 5. Compare and contrast encoder with a multiplexer?

[MDU, BE (CSE) – 4th Sem., Dec., 2008]

Q. 6. Differentiate between demultiplexer and decoder

[MDU, BE (CSE) - 4th Sem., May 2009 & Dec. 2009]

Q. 7. Draw and explain circuit diagram for the implementation of given function using NAND gates only.

$$y = A\bar{B}C + \overline{A\bar{B}C} + \bar{A}D$$

[MDU, BE (CSE) – 4th Sem., Dec. 2009]

CHAPTER 2

COMPUTER ORGANIZATION (CO) VERSUS COMPUTER ARCHITECTURE (CA)

2.0 INTRODUCTION

Computer organization deals with the study of the behavior and structure of different building blocks of a computer system. **Computer design refers to the transformation of the behavior to the corresponding structure. And the detailed study of the art / science of dividing the system functions in software and hardware modules and establishing the interface among them is known as a computer architecture.**

Merging of computer and the communication technologies has already ushered in a significant technological revolution. This in turn will lead to the merging of electronics with computer. New and innovative designs to suit the specific requirements of the changing scenario are expected to further evolve in the near future. Hence, computer organization study is a must.

2.1 TABULAR COMPARISON OF CO AND CA

Computer architecture is a science for designing a computer system. Just as a building architect prepares a design for a building, in a similar fashion a **computer architect** designs a high performance-system at a reasonable cost, fulfilling all other requirements. Computer architecture provides various attributes to the computer system which are needed by a machine language programmer or a system software designer to develop a program. It is a conceptual model.

Computer Organization gives an in-depth picture of its functional structure and logical interconnections between different functional blocks. Actually, it includes the computer hardware. **Please understand that two computers with same architecture can have different organization. And two computers having same organization differ in their architecture. Also note that for designing a computer, its architecture is fixed first and then its organization is decided.**

Tip: Architecture indicates its hardware whereas the organization reveals its performance

Let us tabulate the differences between CO and CA now.

Computer Organization	Computer Architecture
1. It deals more with the interface between software and hardware.	1. It deals more with the lower level details.
2. It deals with Hardware System Architecture (HSA).	2. It deals with Instruction Set Architecture (ISA).

Computer Organization	Computer Architecture
3. The task is to find out and investigate the organizational structure for its proper operation.	3. It investigates instruction formats, instruction set and addressing technology. It also includes the specifications of various functional modules like CPU and memories.
4. While designing, it is not fixed first.	4. Firstly, computer's architecture is fixed and then its organization is decided.
5. It reveals computer's performance	5. It reveals computer's hardware.

2.2 HIERARCHY OF STRUCTURE OF COMPUTER SYSTEM

The structure of a computer system is the arrangement of its components and their relationships. The physical implementation of the computer design depends on its technology. **Please note that two computers of same organization designed at a course of period would have different component technology due to which their hardware circuit is different. Also note that the architecture of these may or may not be the same.** Its structure can be defined using three basic building blocks –

Computer design.

Computer organization

Computer architecture.

That is –

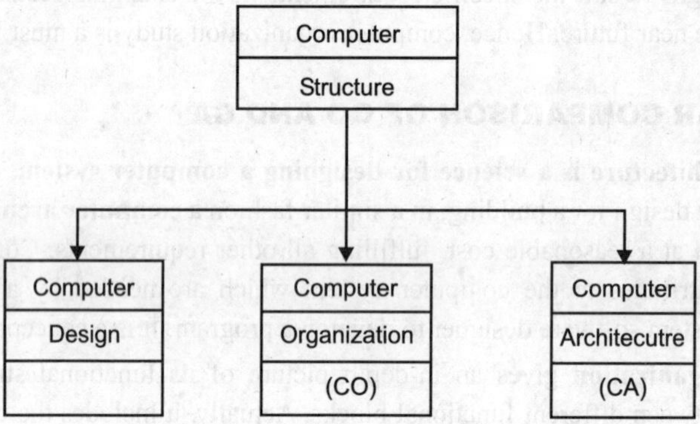

Fig. 2.1. Structural Hierarchy of a Computer System

We have already defined these terms in previous section.

2.3 ISA VS HSA

ISA or Instruction-set architecture determines the computational characteristics of a computer. ISA is an **abstraction** on the interface between the hardware on the interface between the hardware and the low-level software. It is an abstract image of a system as seen by the programmer. This is shown in Fig. 2.2

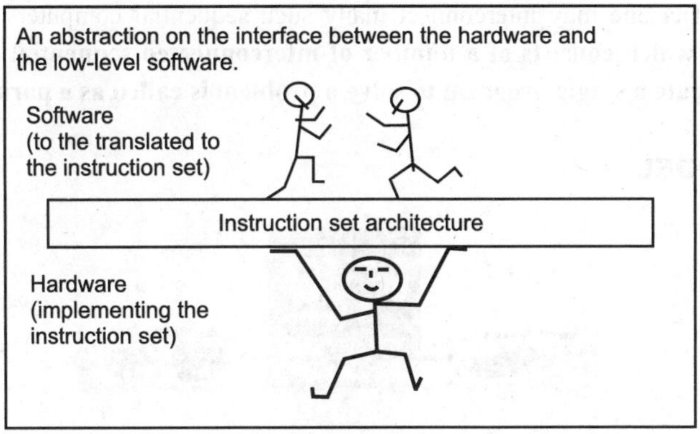

Fig. 2.2. ISA

HSA or Hardware System Architecture is a low level, more detailed and concrete description of a system that involves how the different parts of the system are interconnected and how they interoperate in order to implement the ISA.

Programmers write programs in different languages, programs are compiled, executables are generated. All this is a part of ISA. **Please note that this ISA has nothing to do with the description of the implementation of the computer, which is HSA. Also note that ISA is a kind of focal point.**

2.4 BASIC NEUMANN'S ARCHITECTURE

As we know that a single computer consists of an input unit, a program memory, ALU and an output unit. The arithmetic and logic unit (ALU) and the control unit (CU) together form a CPU. A CPU is also named as **processing element or PE or a microprocessor** (MP). In 1940, John Von Neumann proposed a stored-program concept based computer which is also known as a sequential computer or a uniprocessor or Von-Neumann's machine or the conventional computer. It is shown below in Fig. 2.3

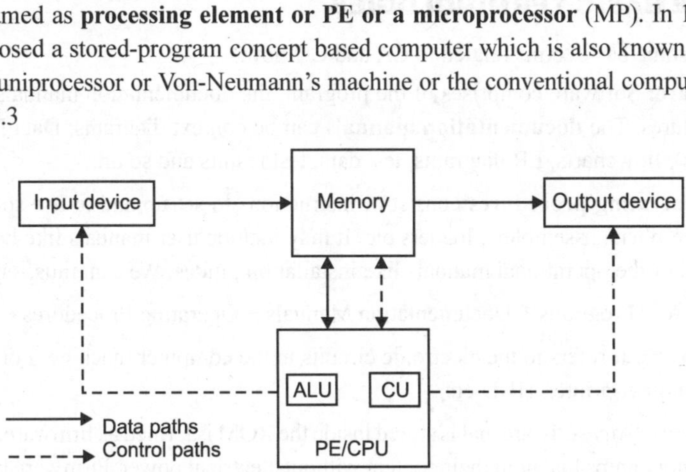

Fig. 2.3. Von Neumann's conventional computer

Working: The PE retrieves one instruction of the program at a time, interprets it and executes it. The operation of this computer is thus sequential. At a time, PE can execute only one instruction. The speed of this sequential computer is thus limited by the speed at which a PE can retrieve instructions and data from memory and the speed at which it can process retrieved data. To increase the speed of processing of data one may interconnect many such sequential computers to work together. **Such a computer which consists of a number of interconnected sequential computers which cooperatively execute a single program to solve a problem is called as a parallel computer.**

2.5 IPO MODEL

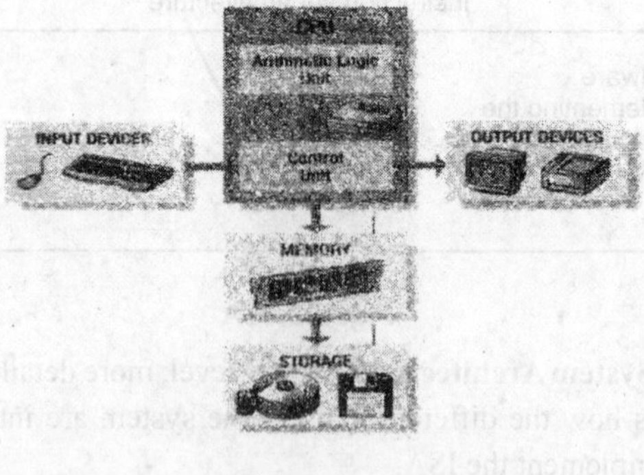

Fig. 2.4. IPO Model of a computer

Inputs (I): Those devices that convert human written programs into computer understandable form. That is, input data is converted to binary form.

Process (P): It executes a program. It is also called as a CPU or Processing Element. It consists of control Unit (CU), ALU and memory.

Output (O): Those devices that convert binary data to human understandable form. This forms an IPO model.

2.6 SOME BASIC TERMINOLOGIES

We define some basic terms related to CA and CO now.

1. **Software:** Software comprises of the program, the documentation manuals and operating procedures. The **documentation manuals** can be context diagrams, Data Flow Diagrams (DFDs), flowcharts, ER diagrams, test data, test results and so on.

   The **Operating procedures** consist of instructions to set up and to use software systems like compliers, assemblers, loaders etc. It may include user manuals like beginners guide, tutorial or the operational manuals like installation guides. We can, thus, say that –

   Software = Programs + Documentation Manuals + Operating Procedures

2. **Hardware:** It refers to the electronic circuits in the computer machine. For e.g. keyboard, CPU, mouse, printer, HDD etc.

3. **Firmware:** Any software that is stored inside the ROM is termed as firmware. It is a category of memory chips that hold their content without electrical power. Firmware becomes "hard-software" when holding program code.

4. **Shareware:** Software distributed through information services that are free of charge on trial basic. If you use it, you pay for it, for which you receive additional documentation, support or possibly the next upgrade at no cost.

5. **Vaporware:** Many systems are so complex that even during their development phase they are never finished. These systems are called as vaporware.

6. **System Software:** Programs used to control the computer and run application programs. For. e.g, OS, DBMS etc.
7. **Application Software:** The software used in PCs fall under this category. For. e.g, MS-WORD, MS-EXCEL, MS-POWERPOINT, Spreadsheets, small DBMS etc.
8. **Analog Computers:** These devices that process infinitely varying signals like voltage or frequencies are called as analog computers. For e.g.: thermometer, voltmeter etc.
9. **Digital Computers:** Computer that accepts and processes data that has been converted into binary numbers. For e.g., All common computers are digital.
10. **Hybrid Computers:** A digital computer that processes analog signals which have been converted into digital form. For eg.: It is used in process control and robotics.
11. **Middle ware:** It is software that operates at the level between an application program and a network.
12. **Freeware:** Some software are available free of cost. They can be downloaded from Internet. Such software's are called as freeware.

2.7 COMPUTER EVOLUTION AND GENERATIONS

We are now in a position to review some historical milestones in the computer development to assess the state-of-the art computing.

Milestones of Computer development are as follows-

There are two major stages in the development of computers:

1. Mechanical / Electromechanical
2. Electronic

Till 1945, computers were built with mechanical or electromechanical parts.

Abacus was the earliest mechanical computer used in China in 500 B.C. It is manually operated and used to perform decimal arithmetic with carry propagation digit by digit.

After the Abacus, the following are the major milestones in the history of computing as follows:

1. In 1962, Blaise Pascal built a mechanical adder / subtractor in France.
2. In 1827, Charles Babbage designed a difference engine in England for polynomial evaluation.
3. In 1941, Konrad Luse built first binary mechanical computer, in Germany. This computer was designed for general purpose computations.
4. In 1944, Howard Aiken proposed very first electromechanical decimal computer, for general purpose computations. IBM also built Harvard Mark I.

Please note that the speed and the reliability of these computers were greatly limited due to use of moving mechanical parts. With the introduction of electronics, the moving parts in mechanical computers were replaced by high mobility electrons and computers became electronic computers. Now, electric signals were used for information transmission. The speed of electric signal was almost equal to the speed of light. (Remember: $c = 3 \times 10^8$ m/s).

Computer Generations

The state of improvement in the development of a product is known as generation. Different technologies have been used for manufacturing the computer hardware. Various computer generations are tabulated next:

Generations	Technology & Architecture	Software and Applications	Popular Examples
First (1945-54)	Vacuum tubes and relay memories, CPU driven by PC and Accumulator, fixed-point arithmetic.	Machine / Assembly languages, single user, no subroutine linkage, programmed I/O using CPU.	ENIAC, Princeton IAS, Mark-I, EDVAC, IBM 650/701.
Second (1955-64)	Transistor, core memories, I/O processor, floating-point calculations.	High-level language (HLL) used with compilers, subroutine libraries, batch processing monitor.	ATLAS, B-5000, PDP-1, IBM0-7090, CDC-1604.
Third (1965-74)	Integrated circuits (SSI/ MSI), Microprogramming, pipelining, cache and lookahead processors.	Multiprogramming and time-sharing OS, multiuser applications.	IBM 360/370, CDC 6600, TI-ASC, HP-2100, PDP-8
Fourth (1975-90)	LSI/VLSI and Semiconductor memory, multiprocessors, vector supercomputers, multicomputers	Multiprocessor OS, languages, compilers and environments for parallel processing.	XAV 9000, Intel 8080, Cray XMP, IBM 3090.
Fifth (1991-Present)	ULSI/VHSIC processors, memory and switches, high density packaging, scalable architectures.	Massively parallel processing, grand challenge applications, heterogeneous processing.	IBM RS-16000, Fujitsu VPP 500, Intel Paragon.

Please note that here with each new generation; the circuitry becomes smaller and more advanced. The speed, power and memory of computers is proportionately increased due to miniaturization. That is, due to reduction in sizes of circuitry and hardware devices. Each generation is characterized by a major technological development. **Also note that the latest generation computers inherited all good features and eliminated bad features in previous generations.**

We shall now explain each of these generations in detail.

1. **First Generation (1945-1954):** This generation used vacuum tubes and relay memories interconnected by insulated wires. The first generation computers have a single CPU (uniprocessor) that perform serial fixed point arithmetic using program counter (PC), branch predictions and an accumulator. The CPU was involved in l memory access and Input/output operations. Machine and assembly languages were used.

EXAMPLES:

(*a*) **ENIAC.** Electronic Numerical Integrator and Calculator. Built at Moore School of University of Pennsylvania in 1950.

(*b*) **IBM 70.** The first electronic stored program commercial computer built by IBM in 1953.

2. **Second Generations (1955-1964):** This generation used the discrete transistors, diodes and magnetic ferrite cores interconnected by printed circuits. Index registers, floating point arithmetic, multiplexed memory and I/O processor were introduced. High level languages (HLL) like FORTRAN, ALGOL and COBOL were introduced with compilers, subroutine libraries and batch processing monitors. In 1957, Irving Reed developed Register Transfer Language (RTL) for the systematic design for digital computers.

   EXAMPLE:

   (*a*) IBM 7090: The stretch computer built in 1962: Composed of instruction look ahead and error correcting memories.

   (*b*) Univac LARC: Livermore Atomic Research Computer.

3. **Third Generations (1965-74):** This generation used integrated circuits (ICs) both in logic and memory in SSI and MSI.

   Multilayered printed circuits were used. Micro- programmed control became popular to close up the speed gap between CPU and main memory. Pipelining and cache memory were introduced. Multiprogramming and time sharing were implemented.

   EXAMPLES:

   1. IBM 360/370 Series.
   2. CDC 6600 / 7600 Series.
   3. Texas Instruments ASC.
   4. PDP-8 Series.

4. **Fourth Generation (1975-1990):** It is uses LSI and VLSI. Core memory was replaced by semiconductors memory. Parallel computers appeared in various architectures. Shared or distributed memory or optional vector hardware were used. Multiprocessing operating system, special languages and compliers were developed.

   EXAMPLES:

   1. VAX 9000
   2. Cray XMP
   3. IBM-3090

5. **Fifth Generation (1991-Present):** This generation is marked by the use of high density and high speed processor and memory chips. VLSI technology is now more improved. **For example,** 64-bit 150 MHz microprocessors are now available on a single chip with over one million transistors.

   These machines emphasize massively parallel processing (MPP). Scalable and latency tolerant architectures are being adopted using VLSI, Silicon, Gas technologies, high density packaging and optical technologies.

   The performance of Fifth generations computers will be crossing even Tera Flops (10^{12}) range i.e., 10^{12} floating point operations per second. By using heterogeneous processing and thus a network of heterogeneous computers along with the shared memory can solve large scale problems now.

EXAMPLES:

1. MPP – Cray Research
2. CMS – Thinking machines Corporation
3. Paragon – Intel Super Computer

2.8 BASIC COMPUTER ORGANISATION – MULTILEVEL VIEWPOINT OF A MACHINE

Computers are organized as different levels; with each level built on its predecessor. Each level here represents a different level of abstraction. By designing and analyzing computers in this way, reduces design complexity as we are doing abstraction.

Today machines of upto 6 levels do exist. These levels are shown in Fig. 2.5

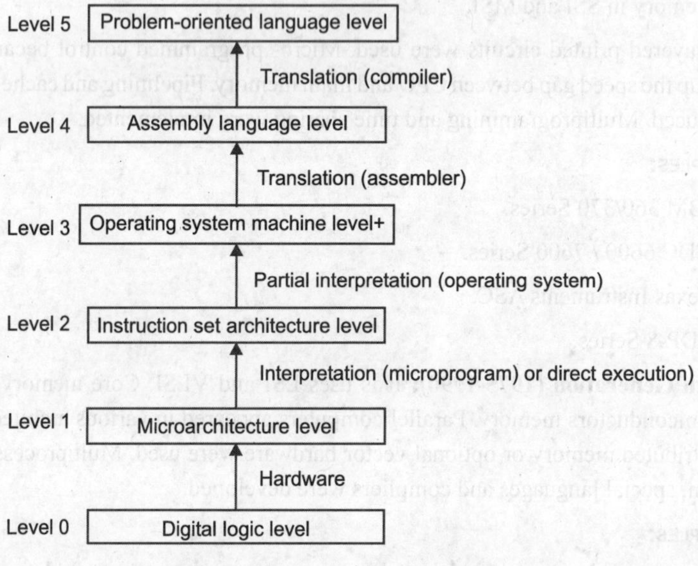

Fig. 2.5. A Six-level Computer

Level 0, the digital logic level, is the machine's true hardware. Its circuits carry out the machine language programs of level 1. For the sake of completeness, we should mention the existence of yet another level below our level 0. This level, which is not shown in figure 25 and falls within the realm of electrical engineering, is called the ***device level.*** At this level, the designer sees individual transistors, which are the lowest-level primitives for computer designers.

The next level up is the micro architecture level. At this level we see a collection of (typically) 8 to 32 registers that form a local memory and a circuit called an **ALU** (Arithmetic Logic Unit) that is capable of performing simple arithmetic operations. The registers are connected to the ALU to form a data path, over which the data flow. The basic operation of the data path consists of selecting one or two registers having the ALU operate on them, for example, adding them together, with the result being stored back in some register.

On some machines the operation of the data path is controlled by a program called a microprogram. On other machines the data path is controlled directly by hardware.

On machines with software control of the data path, the microprogram is an interpreter for the instructions at level 2. It fetches, examines, and executes instructions one by one, using the data path to do so. For example, for an ADD instruction, the instruction would be fetched, its operands located and brought into registers, the sum computed by the ALU, and finally the result routed back to the place it belongs. On a machine with hardwired control of the data path, similar steps would take place, but without an explicit stored program to control the interpretation of the level 2 instructions.

At level 2 we have a level that we will call the instruction Set Architecture level or (ISA level). Every computer manufacturer publishes a manual for each of the computers it sells, entitled **Machine Language Reference Manual** or something similar. These manuals are really about the ISA level not the underlying levels. When they describe the machine's instruction set, they are in fact describing the instructions carried out interpretively by the microprogram or hardware execution circuits. If a computer manufacturer provides two interpreters for one of its machines, interpreting two different ISA levels, it would need to provide two "machine language" reference manuals, one for each interpreter.

The next level, the operating system machine level, is usually a hybrid level. Most of the instructions in its language are also in the ISA level. In addition, there is a set of new instructions, a different memory organization, the ability to run two or more programs concurrently, and various other features. More variation exists between level 3 designs than between those at either level 1 or level 2.

The new facilities added at level 3 are carried out by an interpreter running at level 2, which, historically, has been called an operating system. Those level 3 instructions identical to level 2's are carried out directly by the microprogram (or hardwired control) not by the operating system. In other words, some of the level 3 instructions are interpreted by the operating system and some of the level 3 instructions are interpreted directly by the microprogram.

There is a fundamental break between levels 3 and 4. The lowest three levels are not designed for use by the average garden-variety programmer. Instead they are intended primarily for running the interpreters and translators needed to support the higher levels. **These interpreters and translators are written by people called as systems programmers who specialize in designing and implementing new virtual machines.** Levels 4 and above are intended for the applications programmer with a problem to solve.

Another change occurring at level 4 is the method by which the higher levels are supported. Levels 2 and 3 are always interpreted. Levels 4, 5 and above are usually, although not always, supported by translation.

Yet another difference between levels 1, 2 and 3 on the one hand, and levels 4, 5, and higher, on the other, is the nature of the language provided. The machine languages of levels 1, 2 and 3 are numeric. Programs in them consist of long series of numbers, which are fine for machines but bad for people. Starting at level4, the languages contain words and abbreviations meaningful to people. Level 4, the assembly language level, is really a symbolic form for one of the underlying languages. This level provides a method for people to write programs for levels 1, 2 and 3 in a form that is not as unpleasant as the virtual machine languages themselves. Programs in assembly language are first translated to level 1, 2 or 3 language and then interpreted by the appropriate virtual or actual machine. The program that performs the translation is called an **assembler.**

Level 5 consists of languages designed to be used by application progammers. *For eg.* HLL like C/C++, IAVA2 LISP and T-PROLOG.

These programs are generally translated to level 3 or level 4 by special translators like **compilers.**

2.9 MOORE'S LAW

46 years ago, Intel cofounder Gordon Moore published his observation that the number of translators that could be put on a silicon chip doubled about every two years. It means that the computer capacity would also increase geometrically.

At the time, Moore believed that this growth might continue for "perhaps 10 years". In fact, he was off by three decades and counting. Overtime, advances in chip technology have proceeded almost like clockwork, with capacity sometimes doubling even faster. This spring, Intel announced yet another new chip that keeps Moore's law right on track.

Intel says a vertical ridge on its new 22 nm. Ivy Bridge 3D Tri-Gate Chip creates much more real estate for transistors. "Just as skycrapers set urban planners optimize available.

Space by building upward, Intel's 3D tri-gate transistor structure provides a way to manage density, "according to May 2011 announcement. But how long can this doubling go on?

At one extreme pessimists argue that it can't continue for two much longer- that circuits are becoming so tiny now that physics will prevent it. Already, the scale is difficult to comprehend – Intel's May release noted that "More than 6 million 22 nm Tri-Gate transistors could fit in the period at the end of this sentence." The pessimists say that the shock of running into a wall will be a terrible blow to the high-tech sector, which has worked in an environment of exponential growth for years.

At the other extreme, some futurists contend that Moore's law will hold for many more decades. Indeed, they say, we stand at the cusp of a "singularity", another point like the invention of agriculture or the industrial revolution when suddenly everything changes.

2.10 LIMITATIONS OF COMPUTER TECHNOLOGY

Many limiting factors guide the growth and the performance of computer technology. Some of the factors are –

(*a*) Speed of light ($c = 3 \times 10^8$ m/s).

(*b*) Speed of operation.

(*c*) Amount of data to be handled.

(*d*) Device reliability (i.e., failure free operation).

(*e*) Networking and communication facilities.

(*f*) Cost of computer usage.

SUMMARY

In this chapter, we have learnt the differences between computer architecture and computer organization. The basic computer architecture and basic computer organization have been discussed. We focus on computer evolution and its generation too. Inspite of this there are some limiting factors and laws that govern this computer industry. They have been explained.

MULTIPLE CHOICE QUESTIONS [MCQs]

Q. 1. The science of designing a computer system is called as

(*a*) Computer architecture (*b*) Computer design

(*c*) Computer organization (*d*) None of the above

Ans. (*a*)

Q. 2. For designing a computer –

(*a*) Architecture is fixed first (*b*) Organisation is fixed first.

(*c*) Both are fixed first (*d*) None of the above.

Ans. (*a*)

Q. 3. Architecture indicates its hardware, whereas organization reveals its

(*a*) Design (*b*) Speed (*c*) Performance (*d*) None of the above

Ans. (*c*)

Q. 4. ISA means –

(*a*) IS-A relationship (*b*) Instruction Set Architecture

(*c*) Intra Set Architecture (*d*) None of the above

Ans. (*b*)

Q. 5. HAS means –

(*a*) HAS-A relationship (*b*) Hardware System Architecture

(*c*) High Speed Access (*d*) None of the above

Ans. (*b*)

Q. 6. The stored program concept was given by

(*a*) Berry Boehm (*b*) John Von Neumann

(*c*) Charles Babbage (*d*) Jacobson

Ans. (*b*)

Q. 7. A software is

(*a*) Programs only

(*b*) Programs + Compilers

(*c*) Programs + documentation manuals operating procedures

(*d*) None of the above.

Ans. (*c*)

Q. 8. A thermometer will be a

(*a*) Analog computer (*b*) Digital computer

(*c*) Super computer (*d*) Hybrid computer

Ans. (*a*)

Q. 9. PDP-8 is put under

(*a*) First Generation (*b*) Second Generation

(*c*) Third Generation (*d*) None of the above

Ans. (*c*)

Q. 10. On some machines, the operation of the data path is controlled by a program called as -

(*a*) Microprograms (*b*) Macroprogram

(*c*) Firmware (*d*) None of the above

Ans. (*a*)

CONCEPTUAL SHORT QUESTIONS WITH ANSWERS

QUESTION 1: What are the functional requirements in a computer system?

SOLUTION 1: The functional requirements in a computer system are as shown in Fig.-

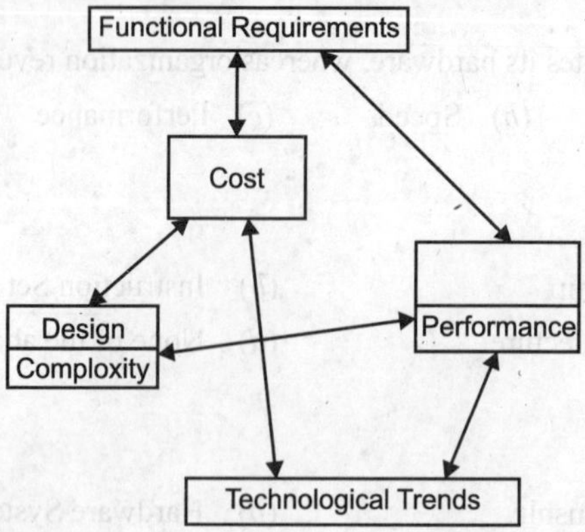

QUESTION 2: Comparison between Livewares and Firmwares

SOLUTION 2: Livewares: All persons connected with computers form a **Liveware.**

Firmwares: Any software that is stored inside the ROM is a firmware.

QUESTION 3: Compare SRAM and DRAM. [MDU,BE(CSE)– 4th Sem, 2006]

SOLUTION 3: We tabulate the difference between the two.

sRAM	dRAM
1. Each sRAM cell is a Flip Flop.	1. Each dRAM unit consist of one MOSFET and capacitor.
2. More number of components per cell.	2. Lesser number of components per cell.
3. No refreshing is required.	3. Refreshing is required.
4. More cost.	4. Lesser cost.
5. Are faster memories	5. Are slower memories.
6. Loses it's contents as power is switched off.	6. Loses it's content but slowly as the capacitor discharges
7. More access time	7. Lesser access times.

QUESTION 4: What is a semantic gap?

SOLUTION 4: It is defined as a measure of difference between the concepts in HLL and the concepts in the computer architecture.

QUESTION 5: What parameters are considered for computer performance?

SOLUTION 5: Some of the factors are as follows –

(*a*) MIPS rate.

(*b*) What kind of instruction?

(*c*) CPU size – 16 or 32 or 64 bit.

(*d*) Effectiveness of an instruction.

(*e*) FLOPS, MFLOPS, GFLOPS and TFLOPS range.

EXERCISE QUESTIONS

Q. 1. Briefly explain stored program organization.

[GGSIPU, B.Tech. (CSE) – 5th Sem., Dec. 2008] & MDU, BE (CSE) – 4th Sem., 2006].

Q. 2. Explain architecture of computer system. **[GGSIPU, B. Tech. (CSE) – Dec. 2009].**

Q. 3. Define the term computer architecture. **[GGSIPU, B.Tech. (CSE) –Dec. 2010]**

Q. 4. What do you mean by structured organization? Briefly discuss multilevel view point of a machine. **[MDU, BE (CSE) – 4th Sem., 2005 and 2007].**

Q. 5. (*a*) Mention four components of computer system.

(*b*) List any four external memory storages. **[B.Sc. (CS) - Madras Univ., April 2011]**

Q. 6. Explain the significance of a layered architecture. **[PTU, B.Tech. (CSE) – 3rd Sem., 2009]**

Q. 7. Write short notes on ISA. **[DTU (DCE) – ME (CS) – 2004-05].**

CHAPTER 3

REGISTER TRANSFER LANGUAGE (RTL)

3.0 INTRODUCTION

According to Wilkes (1951), an orderly method of designing the control unit of a conventional computer is called as **microprogramming.** It is based on the analogy between sequence of transfer required to execute a machine instruction and the sequence of individual instructions in conventional user program. Each step is called as a **microinstruction** and the complete set of steps required to process a machine instruction is called as a **microprogram.**

A group of flip-flops is called as a **register** and we need to understand what operations are performed on the data in the register. RTL or Register Transfer Language is a symbolic language used to:

(*a*) describe internal organization of digital computers

(*b*) facilitate the design process of digital systems.

3.1 MICROOPERATION DEFINITION AND CHARACTERISTICS

Arithmetic and logic unit performs various operations on the data stored in the registers. **The operations executed on data stored in register are called as microoperations. Please note that a microoperation is an elementary operation performed on the information stored in one or more registers. Also note that the result of the microoperation may be stored in source register or it may be stored in another register. For e.g.,** Load, store, clear, shift, count etc. are microoperations. A sequence of microoperations is performed to complete one operation. A microoperation requires only one clock pulse for execution if the operation is done in parallel.

For e.g a bidirectional shift register is able to perform right shift and left shift microoperations.

4-types of microoperations are encountered here –

(*a*) Register Transfer

Microoperations: They transfer binary information from one register to another.

(*b*) Arithmetic microoperations:

It performs arithmetic operations on numeric data stored in registers.

(*c*) Logic microoperations

They perform bit manipulation operations on non-numeric data stored in registers.

(*d*) Shift microoperations

They perform shift operations on the data stored in registers.

3.2 RTL DEFINITION

RTL or Register Transfer language is a symbolic language for digital system design. It is a HDL or hardware description language for digital system design. We can specify **data transfers and data manipulations** that can take place in a digital system. One can also specify the **conditions** under which these transfers take place. And each such conditional data transfer pair is called as a **microoperation. Please understand that by specifying the microoperations properly, we can specify the entire digital system.**

RTL was developed by Chris Fraser and J. Davidson of University of Arizona (in 1980s). It is used by GNU C Compiler, gcc and other compilers. It is a language used to describe the operations of instructions within a processor. It describes the requirements of data and control units in terms of digital logic. **Also understand that each instruction from the architecture's instruction set is defined in RTL.** So, RTL acts as an intermediate code for a machine with an infinite number of registers for machine-independent optimization.

3.3 BASIC SYMBOLS USED FOR REGISTER TRANSFERS

Say, we want to multiply two numbers. Then, the microoperations to be performed are as follows:

1. Load first number in register 1.
2. Load second number in register 2.
3. Perform multiply microoperation.
4. Store the result in the destination register.

Here, all microoperations have been given in words but it is a lengthy descriptive explanation. Hence, it is preferred to use symbolic notations ot describe the microoperations. The following table describes the basic symbols for register transfer.

Symbol	Description	Examples
1. Letters	Denotes a register	MAR, *IR*, *R*2
2. Numerals Parenthesis ( )	Denotes a part of a register	R_1(7–0) is, bits 7–0 of register , *R*1
3. Arrow ←	Denotes transfer of information	$R_2 \leftarrow R_1$
4. Comma ,	Separates two microoperations that are performed simultaneously	$R_2 \leftarrow R_1$, $R_1 \leftarrow R_2$
5. Colon :	Separates control function from microoperations.	$T : R2 \leftarrow R1$

The symbolic notation used to describe the microoperation belongs to transfer among registers that forms a syntax or statement of a RTL.

For eg. The statement denotes a transfer of the content of register R_1 into register R_2. After transfer, the contents of register R_2 are replaced by the content of register R_1. **But please note that the contents of register R_1 remain unchanged.** The term register transfer implies the availability of hardware logic circuit that can perform a stated microoperation and transfer the result of operation to the same or another register. **Also note that as we have various higher-level programming languages, similarly we have RTL to specify microoperation.** Each statement is RTL specifies a unique microoperation.

The individual flip flops in an *n*-bit register are numbered in sequence from 0 to $n - 1$, from right (number – 0) towards left. When we say register transfer, it implies that –

(*a*) Circuits are available from the outputs of the source register to the inputs of the destination register.

(*b*) The destination register has a parallel load capability.

A register is represented by a rectangular box with the name of the register inside.

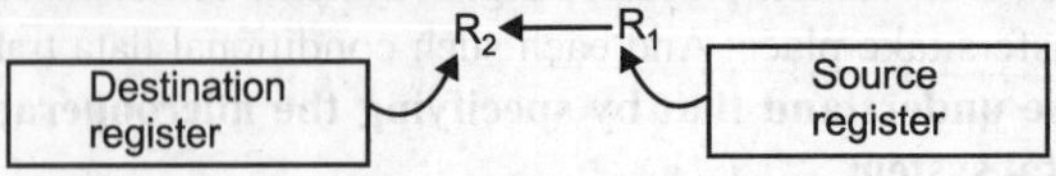

RTL also allows specifying control conditions in the statement. It uses control variable along with a colon at LHS of the statement. Such a function is called as a **control function** that is a Boolean variable used to initiate a sequence of operations. When it is in one binary state, it **initiates** an operation else in other state it **inhibits** the operation.

For e.g. $T : R_2 \leftarrow R_1$.

Here, T is a control variable having value equal to 1 or 0. This statement indicates that the content of R_1 are transferred to R_2 only when $T = 1$ else the transfer operation is not performed. This is similar to if-then-else statement in HLLS. It means that if $T = 1$ then $R_2 \leftarrow R_1$. Note that in this statement, control condition is terminated with a colon.

Before we discuss further, let us solve an example now.

EXAMPLE 1: Consider two 3-bit registers. It is desired to transfer the contents of one register to another. Write RTL statements to accomplish the same Draw its block diagram and its timing diagram.

SOLUTION 3:

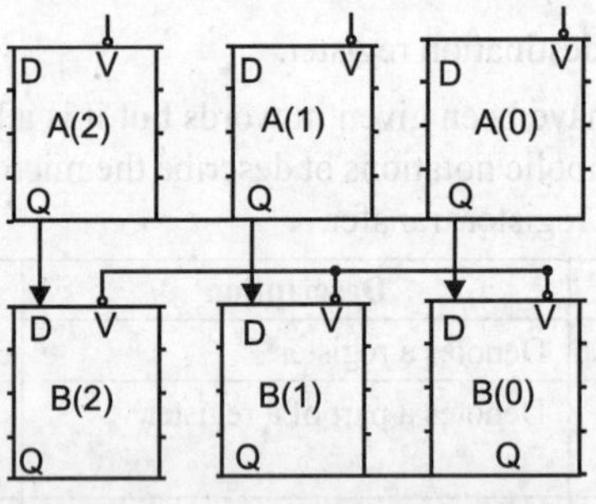

Fig. 3.1. Implementing a register transfer

Microoperations are synchronized with the help of clock signal. The microoperation is initiated either at the rising edge or at the falling edge of the clock signal depending on the circuit. Fig. 3.1 shows two 3-bit registers A and B. **Please note that each bit storage in the register is implemented by one flip flop.** Bit-2 in register A is indicated by $A(2)$, bit-1 by $A(1)$ and bit-0 by $A(0)$. Similarly, we proceed for register-B. **Also note that the rightmost bit is always bit-0, with the bit numbers increasing from right to left.** In general, if a register contains n-bits then the left most bit is numbered n–1.

$$\therefore \quad \text{Reg} - A = A(2), A(1), A(0)$$

$$\text{Reg} - B = B(2), B(1), B(0)$$

Working: When a CLK (clock) pulse is applied to all the three flip-flops of register-B then the contents flip-flops of register-A will be transferred / copied to the corresponding flip-flops of register-B.

$\therefore$ We now write its RTL statements

$B(2) \leftarrow A(2); \quad B(1) \leftarrow A(1); \quad B(0) \leftarrow A(0)$

or simplify, $B \leftarrow A$.

Next, we draw its block diagram.

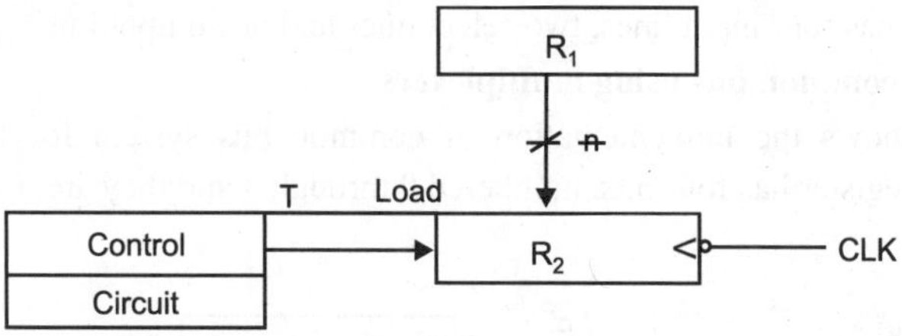

Fig. 3.2. Block diagram for microoperation given.

Here 'n' is the number of bits in the registers. Register (R_2) has a load input that is activated by the control variable, T. It is synchronized with the clock signal.

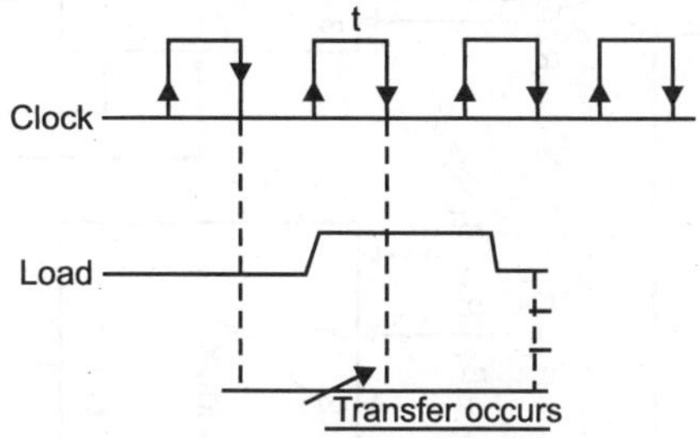

Fig. 3.3. Timing diagram

Please note here that the block is not included as a variable in the register transfer statements. It is assumed that all transfers occur during a clock edge transfers occur during a clock edge transition – either +ve or –ve. **If hardware permits both, then two microoperations can be executed at the same time.** Both these microoperation will be separated by a comma in a statement.

3.4 BUS AND MEMORY TRANSFERS

A bus is a group of wires. It consists of a set of common lines one for each bit of a register to carry binary information. **Control signals** determine which register is selected by the bus. **A common bus scheme** is used to minimize the number of wires within a system. **By a common bus scheme we mean a set of common lines, one for each bit of a register through which binary information is transferred once at a time.** Control signals determine which is the source register and which is a destination register for that particular transfer.

3.5 IMPLEMENTING COMMON BUS USING - MUX AND TRI-STATE BUFFERS

The common bus scheme is implemented in two ways –

(*a*) Using multiplexers (MUX)

(*b*) Using tri-state bus buffers.

Method-1: Constructing common bus system using multiplexers (MUXes)

The number of MUXes needed to construct the bus is equal to 'n', where 'n' is the number of bits in each register. The size of each MUX is ($K \times 1$) where 'K' is the number of registers in the digital system.

We consider the implementation of common bus system for four registers using MUXes. Each register has four bits (numbered from 0 through 3) and they are routed through MUXes to the common bus. Here, **four MUXes are used to select four bits of the source register.** As shown in Fig. 3.4, each MUX has four input lines, two select lines and one output line.

Implementation of common bus using multiplexers

The Fig. 3.4 shows the implementation of common bus system for four registers using multiplexers. Each register has four bits, numbered 0 through 3 and they are

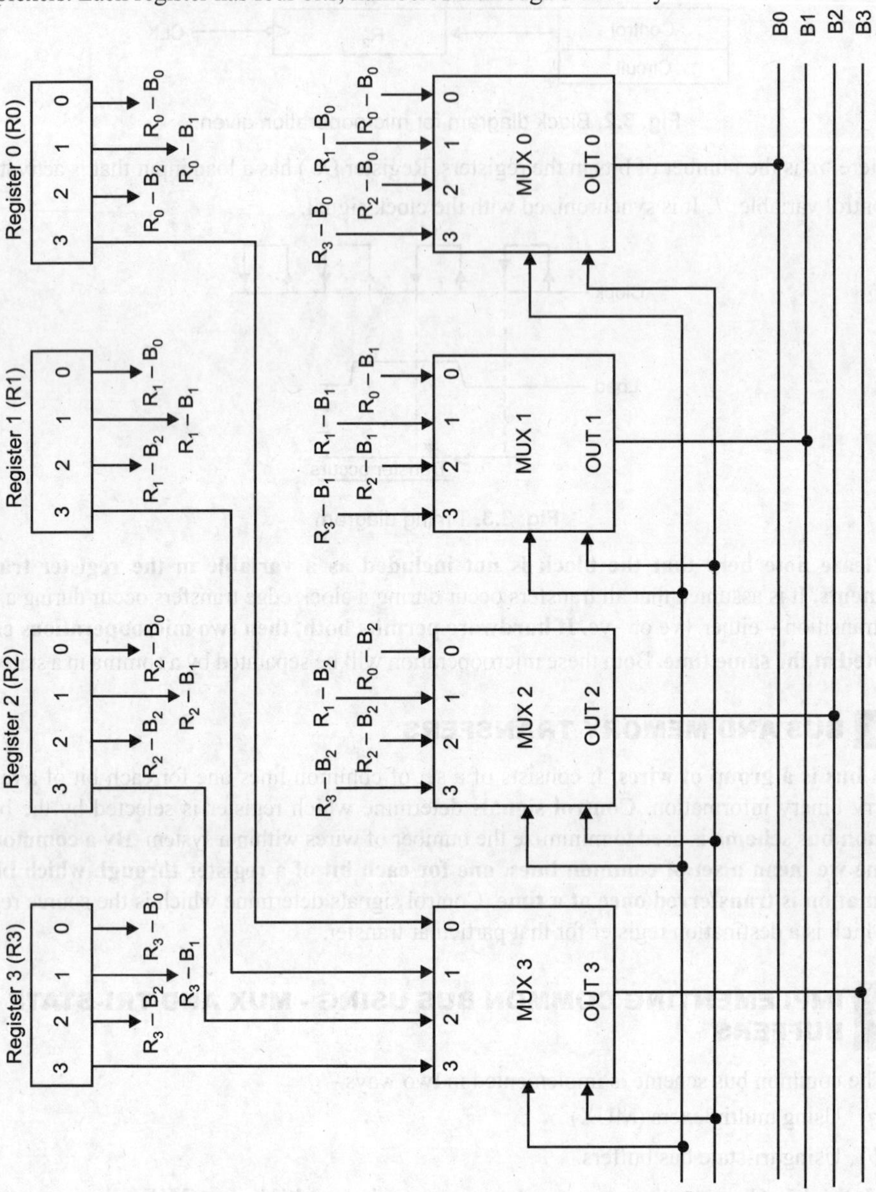

Fig. 3.4. Common bus system using MUXes.

The four input lines of multiplexer-0 (MUX 0) are connected to the bit-0 outputs of four registers such that bit-0 of register is connected to input-0, bit-0 of register 1 is connected to input-1, bit-0 of register-2 is connected to input-2 and bit-0 of register-3 is connected to input-3. Similarly, inputs for MUX-1 are connected to bit-1 outputs, inputs for MUX-2 are connected to bit-2 and inputs for MUX-3 are connected to bit-3 outputs of registers 0 through 3. In Fig. 3.1, for simplicity, only input connections for MUX-3 are physically shown. To show other connections, labels are used. **Two same labels have connection between them.** For instance, bit-2 ($B_0 - B_2$)) output of register is connected to the input 0 for MUX 2.,

The two selection lines S_1 and S_0 are connected to the selection inputs of all four MUXes. These lines chose the four bits of one register and transfer them into the four-line common bus through OUT lines.

When $S_1S_0 = 00$, the input 0 of all four MUXes are selected applied to the outputs to transfer them on the common bus. As a result, a common bus receives the contents of register-0 as the outputs of register -0 are connected to the input-0 of the MUXes. Similarly, the content of register-1 are transferred on the common bus when $S_1S_0 = 01$. The selection line truth table is shown below:

S_1	S_0	Selected Register
0	0	Reg–0
0	1	Reg–1
1	0	Reg–2
1	1	Reg–3

Please note that in general, a common bus system will have *n*-multiplexers and *n*-line common bus where *n* represents the number of bits in each register and *K* number of inputs to each multiplexers where *K* represents the total number of register. Also note that the size of each MUX will be $K \times 1$. For example, A common bus for 8-registers of 6-bits each requires 16-MUXes. Each MUX must have 8 data input lines and 3 selection lines to multiplex one significant bit in the eight registers.

The data transfers from a bus to any destination register can be accomplished by connecting the bus lines to the inputs of all destination registers and activating the load control input of the particular (selected) destination register.

In RTL notation form, we can specify the transfer of data between two registers considering a bus as follows:

$BUS \leftarrow R_1, \quad R_2 \leftarrow BUS$

Here, the content of register, $R1$ is placed on the bus and then the content of the bus is loaded into the register $R2$ by activating its load control input. Since buses always exist in the system, so most of the times we prefer direct method of representing data transfer between register.

∴ Above data transfer is specified as $R2 \leftarrow R1$.

Method II : Constructing common bus system using tri-state buffer

A tri-state gate is a digital circuit that has three states – HIGH (logic-1), LOW (logic-0) and a **high impedance state. High impedance state behaves like an open circuit which means that out put is disconnected.** It does not have any logical significance. As we know that a bus is a common connection between number of registers and other units. Hence, the data transfer through tri-states gates may require larger sinking and sourcing of current. **The tri-state gate which provides more sinking and sourcing capacities is called as a tri-state buffer.** Its logic symbol is –

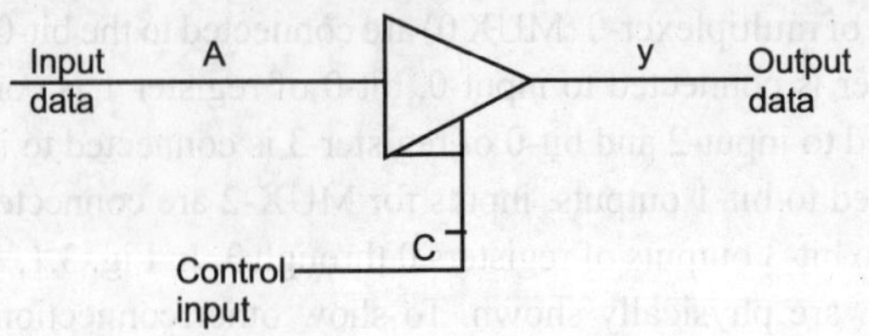

Fig. 3.5. Tri-state buffer symbol

NOTE: When $C = 1$, $y = A$
When $C = 0$, y = High impedance.

As shown in Fig. 3.6, the control input (C) decides the state of the output. When control input (C) = 1, the data available at the output i.e., $y = A$. Whereas when control input (C) = 0, the output goes to a high-impedance state. **Before we discuss further, please remember the following points:**

1. The outputs of the three state buffers connected together to form a single bus line.
2. The **Control inputs** to the buffers determine which of the normal inputs will communicate with the bus line.
3. The **Connected buffers** must be **controlled.** Only one tri-state buffer can be active at a time keeping all other in a high impedance state.
4. **Use decoders** so that only one control input is active at a time.
5. **When the enable input (E) of the decoder is 0,** all of its four outputs are 0 and the bus line is in a HIGH-impedance state because all four buffers are disabled.
6. **When the enable input (E) is active,** one of the three-state buffers will be active, depending on the binary value ion the selected inputs of the decoder.

All this is shown in Fig. 3.7.

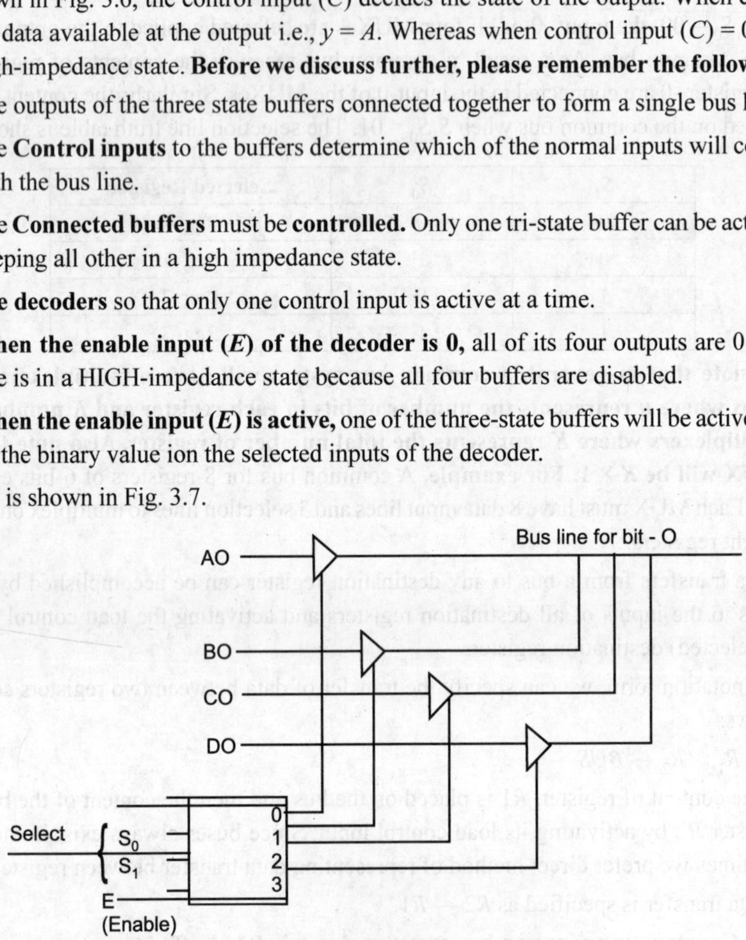

Fig. 3.6. Bus line with 3-state buffers

3.6 MEMORY TRANSFER

A memory is a collection of flip-flops or storage cells. Each cell stores 1-bit of information. The memory stores binary information in groups of bits called as **Words.** Each word has an address that is called as a **memory address.** So, any word can be accessed from main memory by specifying corresponding address. **The process transfer of information from a memory word to the outside environment is called as a read operation and the transfer of new information to be stored into the memory is called as a write operation.**

Please note that it is the number of words in the memory that decides the size of the memory and the number of address bits.

For eg. : 8-bit address can access upto $2^8 = 256$ different words.

Also understand that the number of bits that can be read or written at a time is decided by the word length, i.e., number of bits in one word, of the memory.

For eg. Consider a memory unit that receives the address from a register called as the address register (*AR*). The data are transferred to another register called as the data register (*DR*). Then the read operation can be stated as –

Read : $DR \leftarrow M[AR]$

In read operation, the address of the memory word is specific by address register, *AR*. The data word read from the memory is loaded into the data register, *DR*. The letter, *M* shows memory word whose address is specified by address register, *AR*. **The control signal, Read**, indicates that the operation is performed only when Read signal is active. Once the data is available in the *DR* register it can be transferred to any other register within the CPU.

For eg. it can be transferred to register, *R*2, as follows –

$$R2 \leftarrow DR$$

Please note that for above operation the activation of Read signal is not necessary as it is needed only when the data is read from a memory unit.

The write operation can be stated as –

Write : $M[AR] \leftarrow DR$.

The write operation, transfers the contents of a data register to a memory word (*M*) selected by the address in the address register, *AR*.

The control signal, Write, shows that the operation is performed only when **Write** signal is active. When it is necessary to transfer data from any other CPU register to the memory, we have to transfer the data from that register to the data register *DR* before write operation.

For eg. if we want to transfer data from register *R*1 to the memory whose address is in AR then this operation can be shown as –

$$DR \leftarrow R1$$

Write: $M[AR] \leftarrow DR$

3.7 ARITHEMATIC, TRANSFER LOGICAL AND SHIFT MICROOPERATIONS

As already explained, Microoperations are the elementary operations performed on data stored in registers or in me ıory microoperations are of our types –

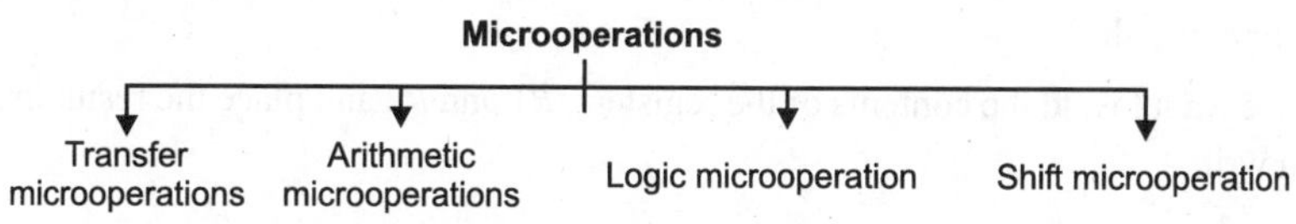

Fig. 3.7. Types of Microoperations

Transfer Microoperations

The microoperations that transfer information from one register to another are known as transfer microoperations. Data may be transferred from a register to memory or vice versa.

Arithmetic Microoperations

The microoperations that perform arithmetic operations on data stored in registers.

Logic Microoperations

This operation performs bit manipulation on data in one or two registers.

Shift Microoperations

This operation shifts data in a register.

Let us study these in detail now.

Transfer Microoperations

We have discussed about transfer microoperations earlier too. **But the following points must be kept in mind –**

1. Depending on how the registers are attached to each other it is possible to do more than one register transfers by comma but keep them on the same line.

   For e.g. $R2 \leftarrow R1, R1 \leftarrow R3$

It means that the contents of register -1 are transferred to register-2 and **at the same time** the contents of register-3 are transferred to register-1.

e.g. 2: If $C = 1$, then $R2 \leftarrow R5$ can be written in RTL as –

$$C : R2 \leftarrow R5$$

But if we want $R2 \leftarrow R5$ operation when $C = 0$, then we may write as –

$$\overline{C} : R2 \leftarrow R5.$$

Please understand that these microoperations do the transfer of information from one register to another but do not change the content at the time of transfer. But other microoperations discussed next do change the information contents.

II. Arithmetic Microoperations

The basic arithmetic operations are –

(*a*) Add.

(*b*) Subtract.

(*c*) Increment.

(*d*) Decrement.

(*e*) Arithmetic shift.

Say, if we want to add the contents of the registers, $R1$ and $R2$ and place the result in $R0$ register then we can write –

$$R0 \leftarrow R1 + R2$$

Please note that the symbol '+' here refers to the actual binary addition and this could be done using a binary ripple carry adder / subtract. Also note that there is no multiplication or division here. The table below shows various arithmetic micro operations -

Table 3.1. Arithmetic Microoperation

Operations	Symbolic Representation	Description
1. Add	$R3 \leftarrow R1 + R2$	Contents of $R1$ and $R2$ are added and result is transferred to $R3$.
2. Subtract	$R3 \leftarrow R1 - R2$	Contents of $R2$ are subtracted from contents of $R1$ and the result is stored in $R3$.
3. 1s complement	$\overline{R3}$	Complement the contents of $R3$.
4. 2s complement	$\overline{R3} + 1$	Complement the contents of $R3$ and ad 1 to it.
5. 2s complement subtraction	$R3 \leftarrow R1 + \overline{R2} + 1$	Add $R1$ and the 2s complement $R2$.
6. Increment	$R2 \leftarrow R2 + 1$	Increment contents of $R2$ one.
7. Decrement	$R1 \leftarrow R1 - 1$	Decrement the contents of $R1$ by one.

NOTE: In statement,

$$K1 + K2 : R0 \leftarrow R1 + R2$$

'+' in ($K1 + K2$) represents 'OR' whereas in $R2 + R3$, '+' representing binary addition.

We discuss a **Binary Adder** now.

A binary adder is a digital circuit that adds two binary numbers of any lengths. A binary adder is instructed with full-adder circuits connected in cascade.

DO YOU KNOW?

An n-bit binary adder requires n full adders.

The logic circuit that performs the addition of two binary digits and produce a sum and carry output is called as a **half adder.** However, a circuit that adds two bits and a previous carry is called as a **Full adder** i.e.

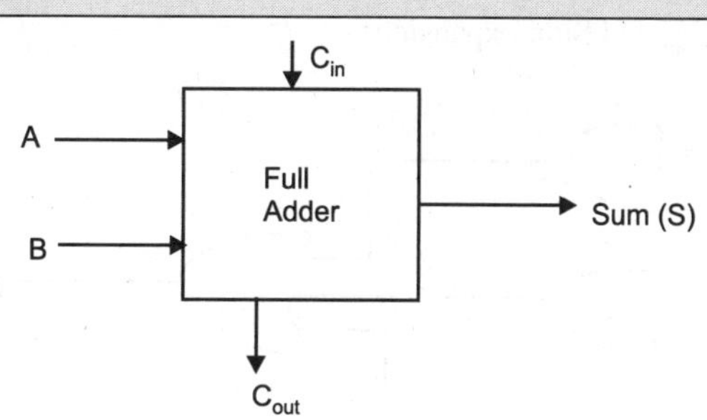

Fig. 3.8(a). FA block diagram

Inputs			Outputs	
A	***B***	***C***	**Carry**	**Sum**
0	0	0	0	0
0	0	1	0	1
0	1	0	0	1
0	1	1	1	0
1	0	0	0	1
1	0	1	1	0
1	1	0	1	0
1	1	0	1	1

Fig. 3.8(b). Truth table of FA

Simplification using K-maps

(*a*) For carry (C_{out})

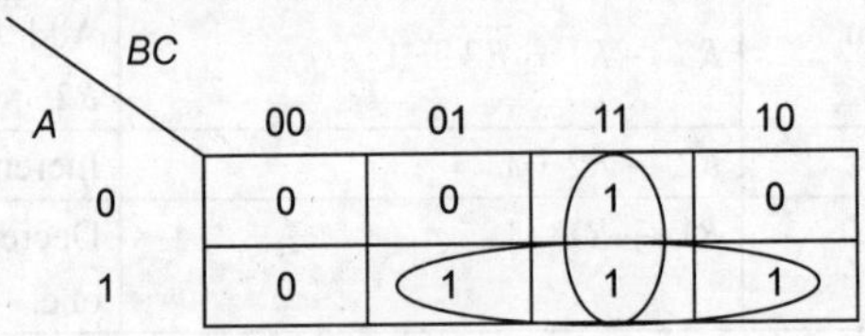

$$\therefore \quad C_{out} = AB + AC_{in} + BC_{in}$$

(*b*) For sum (*S*) –

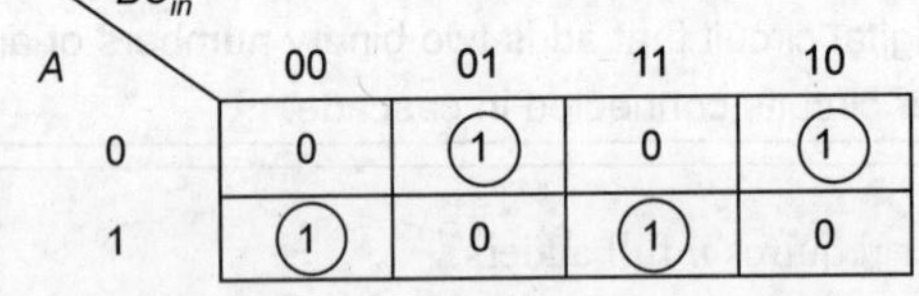

$$\therefore \quad \text{Sum} = \bar{A}\bar{B}C_{in} + \bar{A}B\bar{C}_{in} + A\bar{B}\bar{C}_{in} + ABC_{in}$$

$$\therefore \quad \text{Sum} = A \oplus B \oplus C_{in}.$$

Logic diagrams for C_{out} and Sum expansions

(*a*) C_{out} –

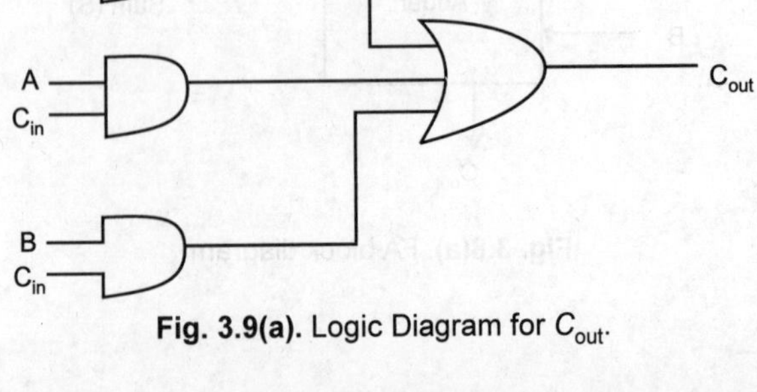

Fig. 3.9(a). Logic Diagram for C_{out}.

(*b*) For Sum

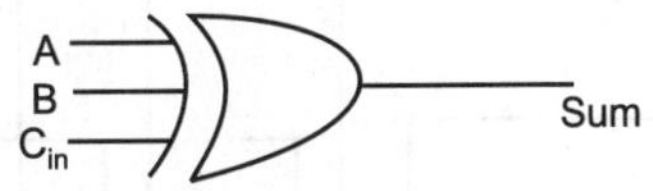

Fig. 3.10(b). Logic diagram for sum

Parallel Adder

A single FA is capable of adding two one-bit numbers and an input carry. But to add binary numbers with more than one bit, additional FAs must be employed. **An '*n*-bit' parallel adder can be constructed using '*n*' number of FAs circuits in cascades.**

It means that the carry output of each adder is connected to the carry input of the next higher order adder. It is shown in Fig. 3.11.

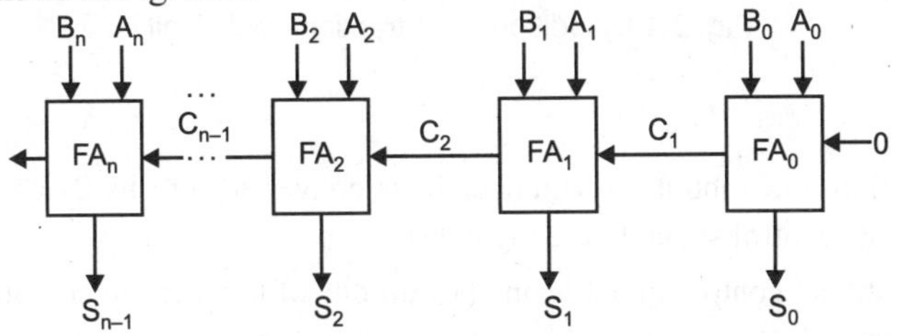

Fig. 3.11. An *n*-bit parallel adder

Please note that either a *HA* can be used for the least significant position or the carry input of a *FA* is made 0 because there is no carry in the least significant bit position.

Parallel Subtractor

As we know that, the subtraction $(A - B)$ using 2s complement method is –

$$(A - B) = [\text{A} + \text{2s complement of B}]$$

And 2s complement of B = 1s complement of $B + 1$.

Now, the 1s complement can be implemented with inverters and a one can be added to the sum through the input carry. Its logic diagram is shown in Fig. 3.12.

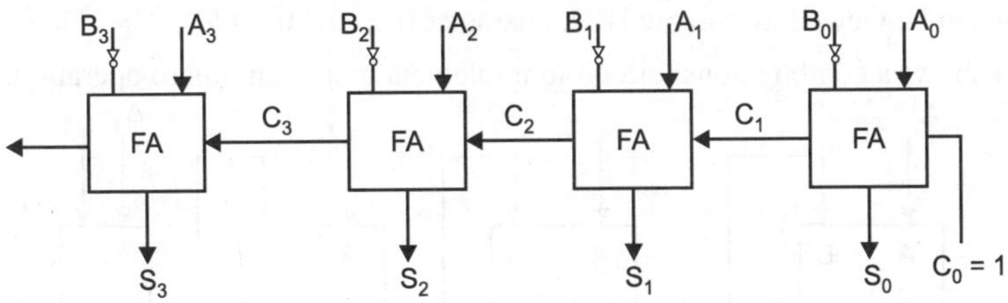

Fig. 3.12. 4-bit parallel subtractor

Addition / Subtraction Logic Unit

Number a and number b are the two inputs for n-bit adder. It consists of n-bit adder, 2s complement circuit and an overflow detector logic circuit. It is shown in Fig. 3.13.

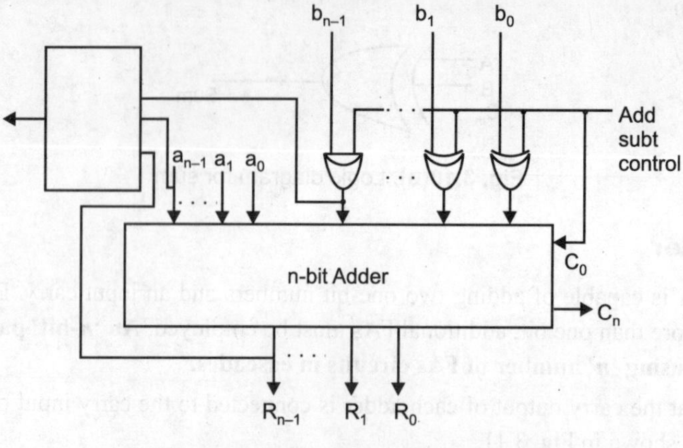

Fig. 3.13. Addition / Subtraction Logic Unit.

Working

To do subtraction, the subtrahend (number b) is converted into its 2s complement form by making Add/ Subtract control signal to the logic one

When Add / subtract control signal is one (1), all bits of number are complemented and carry zero (C_0) is set to one.

$\therefore$ n-bit adder give the result as $R = a + \overline{b} + 1$.

Where $\overline{b} + 1$ represents 2s complement of number, b.

Binary Incrementer

A binary counter is one in which every time the count enable is active, the clock pulse transition increments the count. A counter is a sequential circuit. A 4-bit incrementer has 4-input lines and one increment flag (IF).

If IF = 1 (Set), the output is (input + 1).

As if IF = 0 (reset), the output is the input itself.

The output is just 4-output lines and a carry line. So, we need 4- HAs to achieve this, A 4-bit binary output can be viewed as a single HEX character (i.e., 0100 = 4h).

Fig. 3.14 shows a combinational circuit to implement increment micro operation.

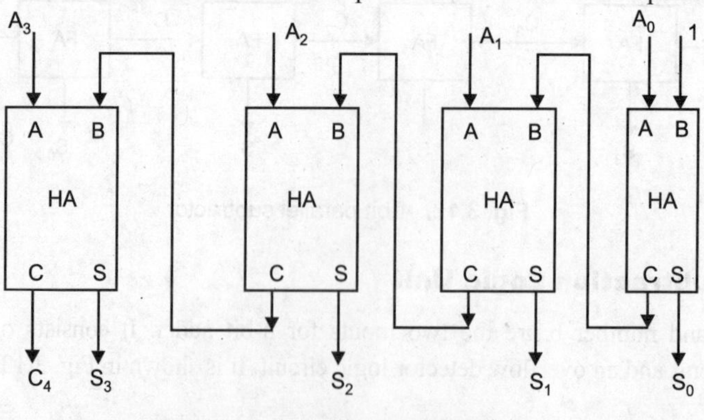

Fig. 3.14. 4-bit Binary Incrementer.

Working

One of the inputs to the best significant HA is connected to logic-1 and the other input is connected to the least significant bit (LSB) of the number to be incremented. The output carry from the lower order HA is connected to one of the inputs of the next higher order HA. This circuit gets the four bit number from bits A_0 through A_3, adds one to it and generates the incremented output in S_0 through S_3. If number to be incremented is 111 the output carry C_4 is generated and we get 0000 at S_0 through S_3.

The arithmetic microoperation can be implemented in one composite arithmetic circuit. **Please understand that the basic component of an arithmetic circuit is the parallel adder. Also understand that by controlling the data inputs to the adder, it is possible to obtain different types of arithmetic operations.** Let us tabulate these operations now.

Table 3.2. Implementation of basic arithmetic operations

Function	Implementation
1. $Y \leftarrow A$	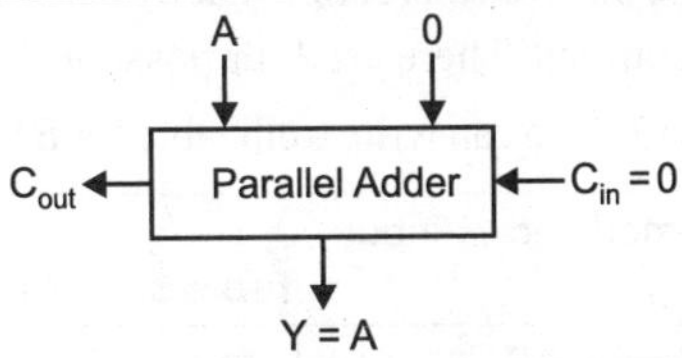
2. $Y \leftarrow A + 1$	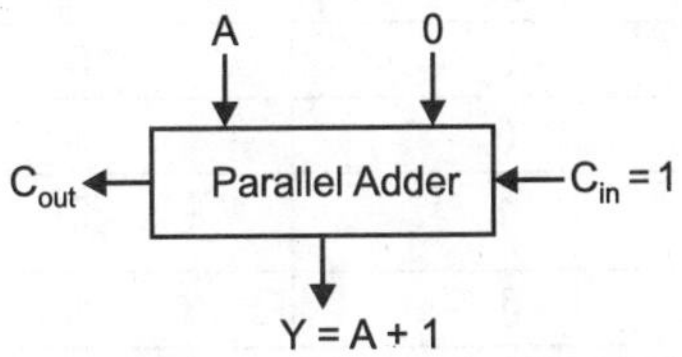
3. $Y \leftarrow A + B$	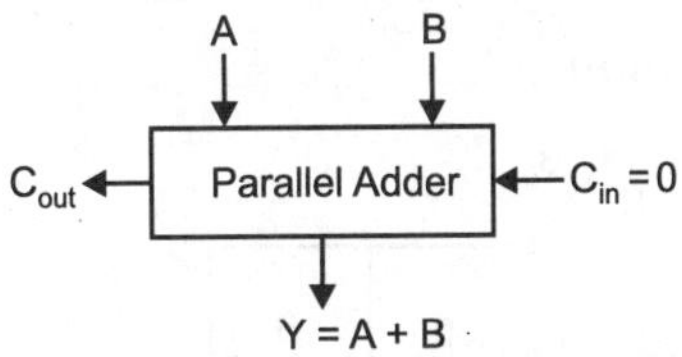
4. $Y \leftarrow A + B + 1$	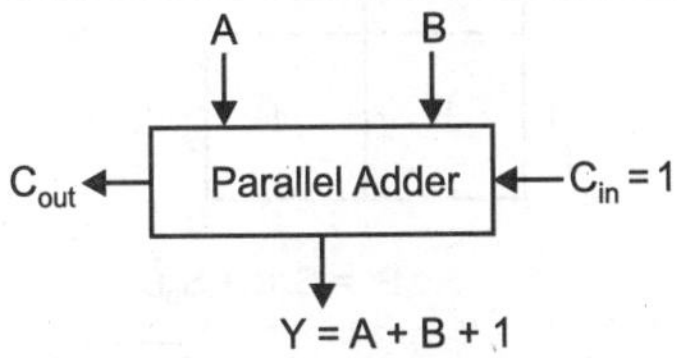
5. $Y \leftarrow A + \overline{B}$	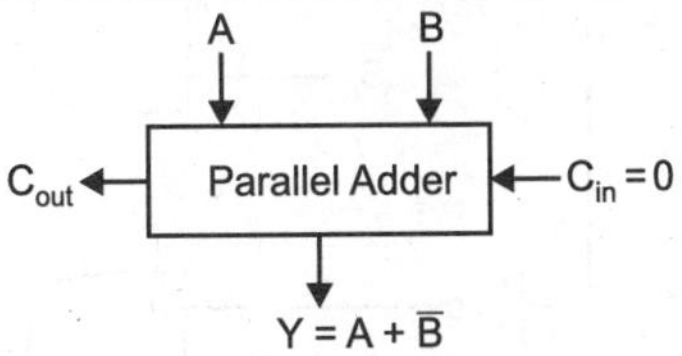
6. $Y = A + \overline{B} + 1$	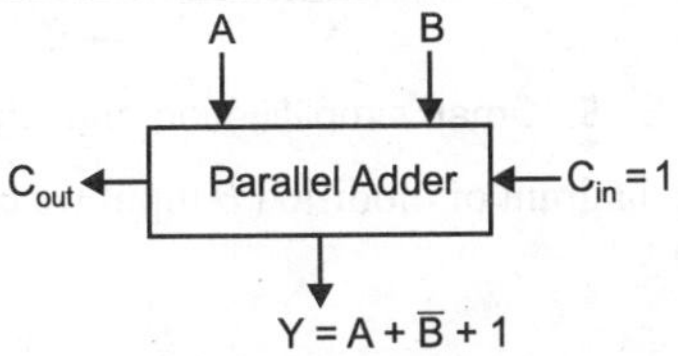

Function	Implementation
7. $Y = A - 1$	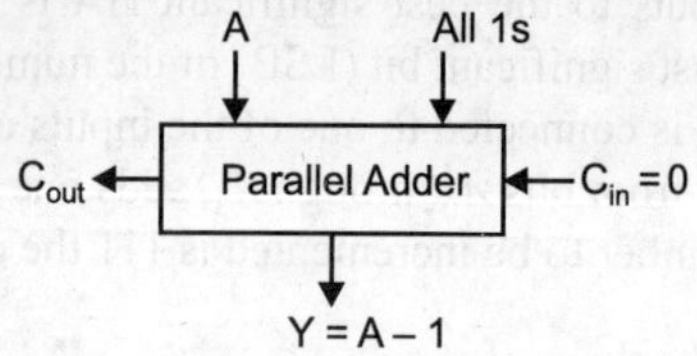
8. $Y = A$	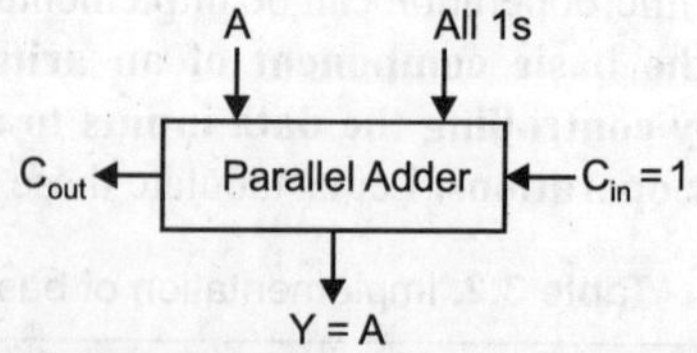

Looking at Table 3.3 we can realize that by selecting proper B and C_{in} inputs we can implement basic arithmetic operations. There are four possible B inputs 0 and 1.

Refereeing Table 3.3 we can write truth table for B input with respect to S_0 and S_1 signals as follows:

NOTE: *B* indicates modified *B* input.

Table 3.3. Truth table

S_1	S_0	B'
0	0	0
0	1	B
1	0	$\overline{B}$
1	1	1

K-map Simplification

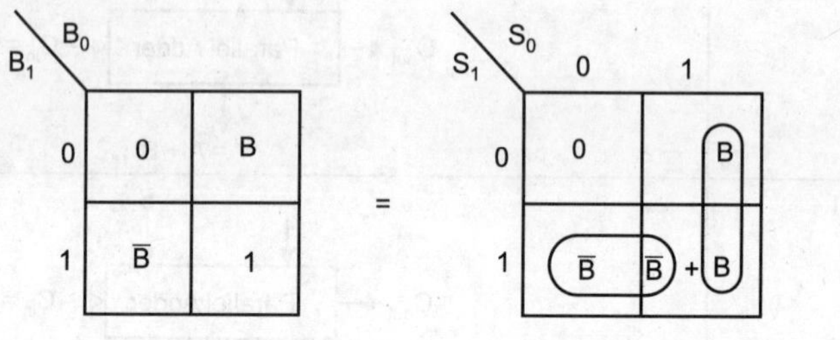

$$\therefore B' = S_1\overline{B} + S_0B$$

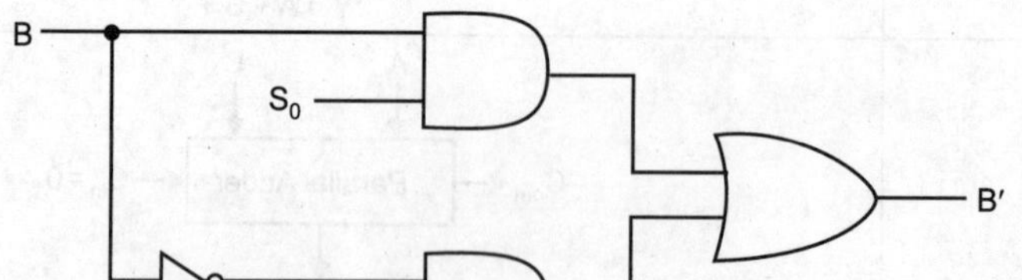

Fig. 3.15. K-map simplification and logic diagram of modified *B* input

Using the logic diagram of modified *B* input we can draw the logic diagram of aithmetic circuit as shown in Fig. 3.16

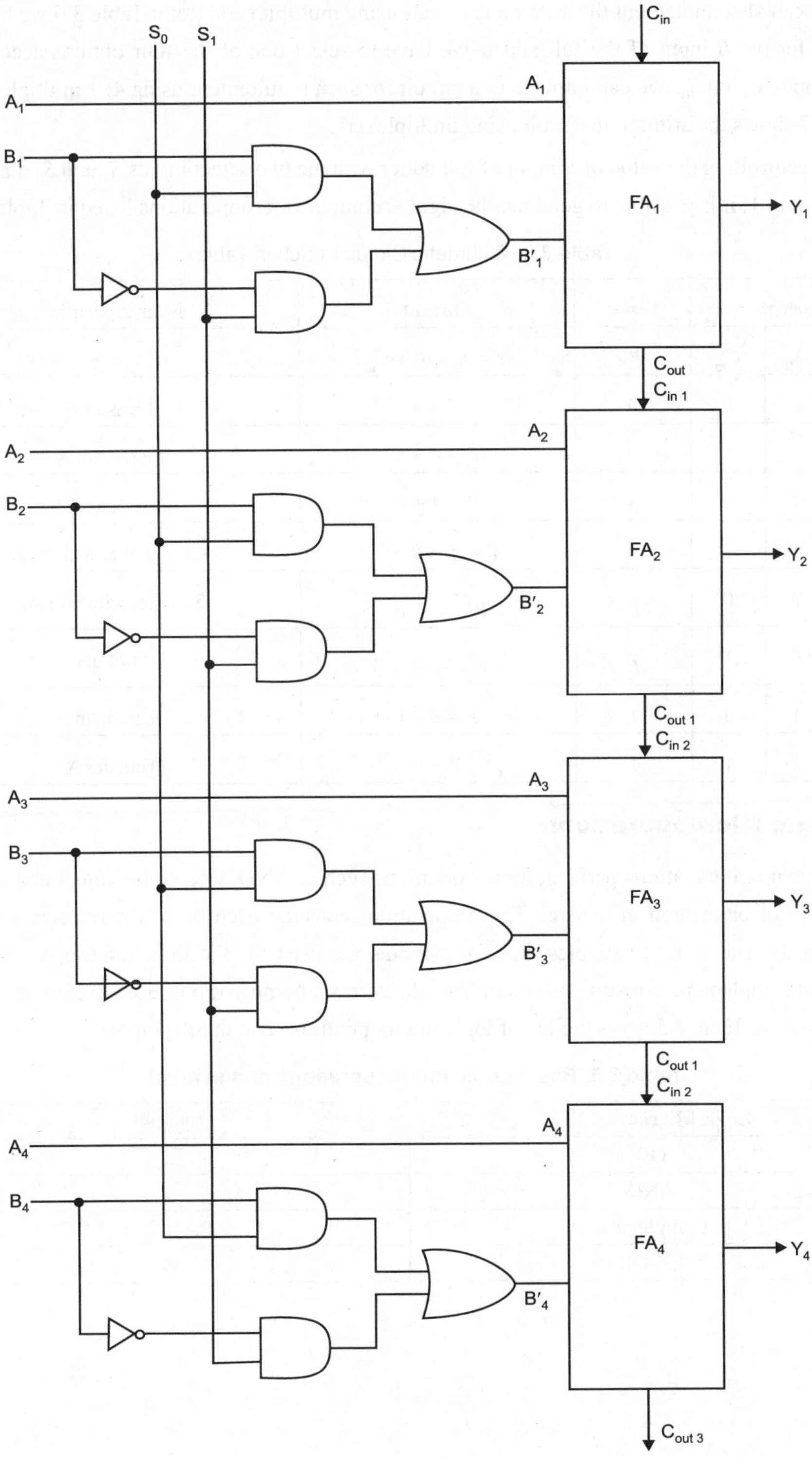

Fig. 3.16. Logic diagram of arithmetic circuit

We can also implement the arithmetic circuit using multiplexers. Refer Table 3.6 we have four options for the B input of the full adder. We have to select one of the four options according to select input S_1 and S_0. We can implement a circuit for such requirement using 4: 1 multiplexer. The Fig. 3.17 shows the arithmetic circuit using multiplexers.

By controlling the value of B input of full adder with the two select inputs S_1 and S_0 making C_{in} equal to 0 to 1, it is possible to generate the eight arithmetic microoperations listed in Table 3.4.

Table 3.4. Arithmetic Circuit Function Table

Select			Input	Output	Microoperation
S_1	S_0	C_{in}	B'	$Y = A + B' + C_{in}$	
0	0	0	0	$Y = A$	Transfer A
0	0	1	0	$Y = A + 1$	Increment A
0	1	0	B	$Y = A + B$	Add A and B
0	1	1	B	$Y = A + B + 1$	Add A and B with carry
1	0	0	$\overline{B}$	$Y = A + \overline{B}$	Subtract with borrow
1	0	1	$\overline{B}$	$Y = A + \overline{B} + 1$	Subtract
1	1	0	1	$Y = A - 1$	Decrement A
1	1	1	1	$Y = A$	Transfer A

III. Logic Microoperations

Logic microoperations perform logic operations such as AND, OR, complement and XOR on the strings of bits stored in register. These operations consider each bit of the register separately and treat them as binary variables. Special symbols are used for the logic microoperations OR, AND and complement to distinguish them from the corresponding symbols used to express Boolean functions. The Table 3.5 gives the list of logic microoperations and their symbols.

Table 3.5. Basic Logic microoperations and symbols

Logic Microoperation	Symbol
OR	$\vee$
AND	$\wedge$
Complement	Bar ($\overline{}$)
EX-OR	$\oplus$

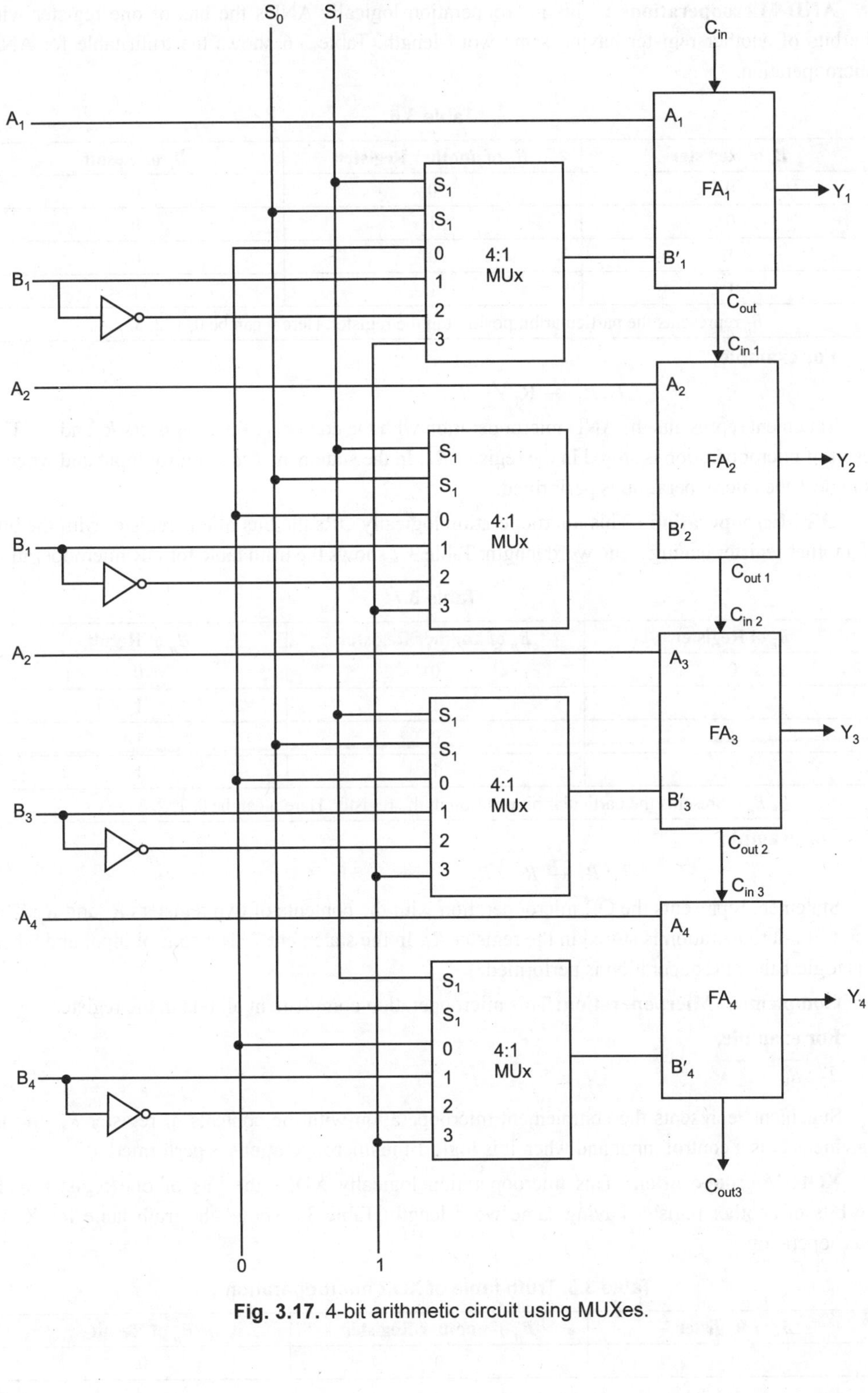

Fig. 3.17. 4-bit arithmetic circuit using MUXes.

AND Microoperations : This microoperation logically ANDs the bits of one register with the bits of another register having same word length. Table 3.6 shows the truth table for AND microoperation.

Table 3.6

B_n of Register	B_n of another Register	B_n of Result
0	0	0
0	1	0
1	0	0
1	1	1
B_n represents the particular bit position in the register. Here n can be 0, 1, 2, 3, ...		

For example,

$$T : R_1 \leftarrow \mathrm{R}_1 \wedge R_2.$$

Statement represents the AND microoperation with the contents of two registers R_1 and R_2. The result of microoperation is stored in the register $R1$. In the statement T is a control input and when it is logic 1 the microoperation is performed.

OR Microoperation : This microoperation logically ORs the bits of one register with the bits of another register having same word length. Table 3.7 shows the truth table for OR microoperation

Table 3.7

B_n of Register	B_n of another Register	B_n of Result
0	0	0
0	1	1
1	0	1
1	1	1
B_n represents the particular bit position in the register. Here n can be 0, 1, 2, 3, ...		

For example

$$T_1 : R_1 \leftarrow R_1 \vee R_2$$

Statement represents the OR microoperation with the contents of two registers R_1 and R_2. The result of microoperation is stored in the register R_1. In the statement T_1 is a control input and when it is logic 1 the microoperation is performed.

Complement Microoperation: This microoperation complement all bits in the register.

For example,

$T_2 : \overline{R_1}$

Statement represents the complement microoperation with the contents of register R_1. In the statement T_2 is a control input and when it is logic 1 the microoperations is performed.

XOR Microoperation: This microoperation logically XORs the bits of one register with the bits of another register having same word length. Table 3.8 shows the truth table for XOR microoperation.

Table 3.8. Truth table of XOR microoperation

B_n of Register	B_n of another Register	B_n of Result
0	0	0

B_n of Register	B_n of another Register	B_n of Result
0	1	1
1	0	1
1	1	0
B_n represents the particular bit position in the register. Here n can be 0, 1, 2, 3, ...		

For example,

$$T: R_1 \leftarrow R_1 \oplus R_2$$

Statement represents the XOR microoperation with the contents of two registers R_1 and R_2. The result of microoperation is stored in the register R_1. In the statement T is a control input and when it is logic 1 the microoperation is performed.

Symbols

It is important to note that the symbols used to represent operation between two binary variables of a control function are different from the symbols used to represent operations between two registers. For example, in the statement

$$T + S: R_1 \neg R_2 + R_3, R_4 \neg R_5 \vee R_6$$

The sign between T and S is an OR operation between two binary variables of a control function. The + between R_2 and R_3 specifies an add microoperation. The OR microoperation is represented by the symbol $\vee$ between registers R_5 and R_6.

The table 3.9 shows the operation symbol used for two binary variables of a control function and symbols used to specify the operation between two registers.

Table 3.9 Symbols

Operation	Symbols used in control function	Symbol used in register operations
AND		$\wedge$
OR	+	$\vee$
XOR	$\oplus$	$\oplus$

With two binary variables and four logic microoperations we can perform six logic microoperations. These are listed in Table 3.10.

Table 1.10. List of Logic Microoperations

Boolean function	Microoperation	Name of Operation
$F_0 = 0$	$F \leftarrow 0$	Clear
$F_1 = AB$	$F \leftarrow A \wedge B$	AND
$F_2 = A\overline{B}$	$F \leftarrow A \wedge \overline{B}$	AND with second operand complemented
$F_3 = A$	$F \leftarrow A$	Transfer A
$F_4 = \overline{A}B$	$F \leftarrow \overline{A} \wedge B$	AND with first operand complemented
$F_5 = B$	$F \leftarrow B$	Transfer B
$F_6 = A \oplus B$	$F \leftarrow A \oplus B$	Exclusive OR
$F_7 = A + B$	$F \leftarrow A \vee B$	OR
$F_8 = \overline{(A + B)}$	$F \leftarrow \overline{A \vee B}$	NOR

Boolean function	Microoperation	Name of Operation
$F_9 = \overline{A \oplus B}$	$F \leftarrow \overline{A \oplus B}$	Exclusive NOR
$F_{10} = \overline{B}$	$F \leftarrow \overline{B}$	Complement B
$F_{11} = A + \overline{B}$	$F \leftarrow A \vee \overline{B}$	OR with second operand complemented
$F_{12} = \overline{A}$	$F \leftarrow \overline{A}$	Complement A
$F_{13} = \overline{A} + B$	$F \leftarrow \overline{A} \vee B$	OR with first operand complemented
$F_{14} = \overline{AB}$	$F \leftarrow \overline{A \wedge B}$	NAND
$F_{15} = 1$	$F \leftarrow$ all 1's	Set to all 1's

Hardware Implementation

The design of logic circuit is comparatively simple than the design of arithmetic circuit. Fig. 3.18 shows the function table and the logic diagram for logic circuit.

S_1	S_2	Output	Function
0	0	$Z = A \vee B$	OR
0	1	$Z = A \oplus B$	XOR
1	01	$Z = A \wedge B$	AND
1	1	$Z = \overline{A}$	NOT

(*a*) Function table

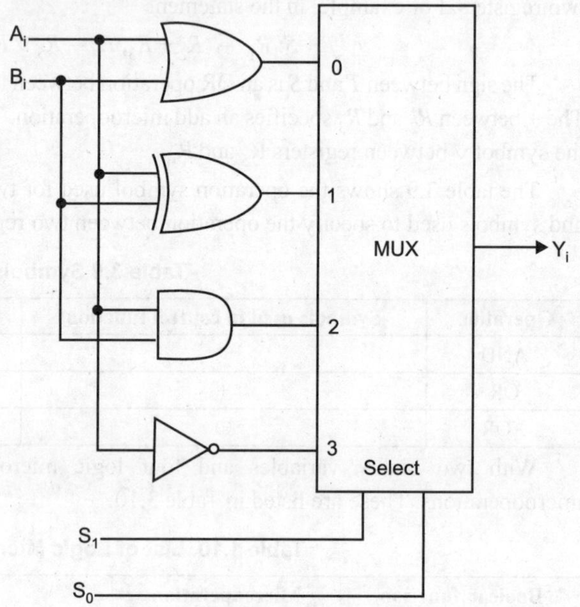

Fig. 3.18. Logic Circuit

NOTE: The logic diagram shown in Fig. 3.18(b) is repeated in times for *n*-bit logic circuit. Therefore, inputs *A* and *B*, and output *Y* are shown with subscript *i* where *i* = 1, 2, ... *n*.

Applications

Logic microoperations are used to manipulate individual bits or a portion of a word stored in a register. They are used to change bit values, delete a group of bits, or insert new bit values into a register. Let us see some examples of manipulation of individual bits or portion of a word. In these examples, bits of one register (designated by *A*) are manipulated by logic microoperations as a function of the bits of another register (designated by *B*).

EXAMPLE 1: Selective Set

This operation sets to 1 the bits in register A where there are corresponding 1s in register B. It does not affect bit positions that have 0's in B. We know that in OR operation result is logic 1 when one of the inputs are both logic 1. Therefore, the OR microoperation can be used to selectively set the bits of a register.

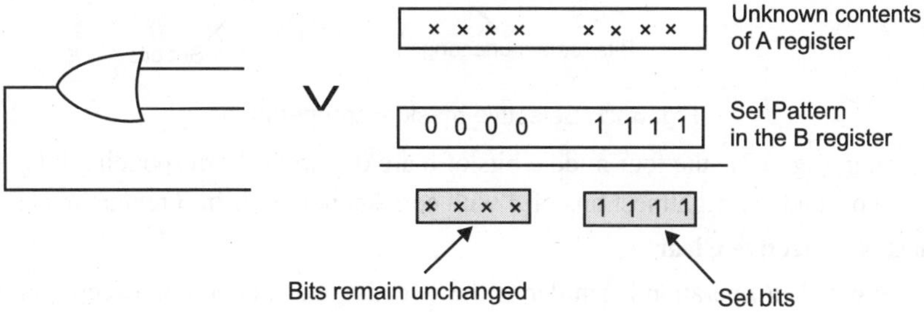

Fig. 3.19: Selective set microoperation

As shown in the Fig. 3.19, the rightmost four bits of *B* are 1's, so the corresponding bits of *A* are set. It is important to note that X indicates unknown bits it can be either 0 or 1. The left most four bits of A with corresponding 0's in *B* remain unchanged.

EXAMPLE 2: Selective – Complement

This operation complements bit in A where there are corresponding 1's in *B*. Does not affect bit positions that have 0's in *B*. Referring the truth table of EX-OR microoperation we can realize that when one of the input is logic 1, the output complement of the other input. Therefore, the EX-OR microoperation can be used to selectively complement the bits of a register.

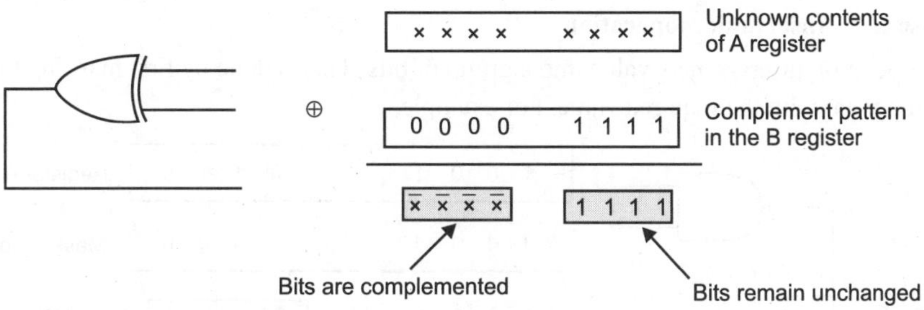

Fig. 3.20. Selective complement microoperation

As shown in the Fig. 1.36, the leftmost four bits of B are 1's, so the corresponding bits of A are complemented. The right most four bits of corresponding 0's in B remain unchanged.

EXAMPLE 3: Selective Mask

This operation clears to 0 the bits in A only where there are corresponding 0's in B. We know that in AND operation result is logic 0 when one of the inputs is both logic 0. Therefore, the AND microoperation can be used to selectively mask the bits of register.

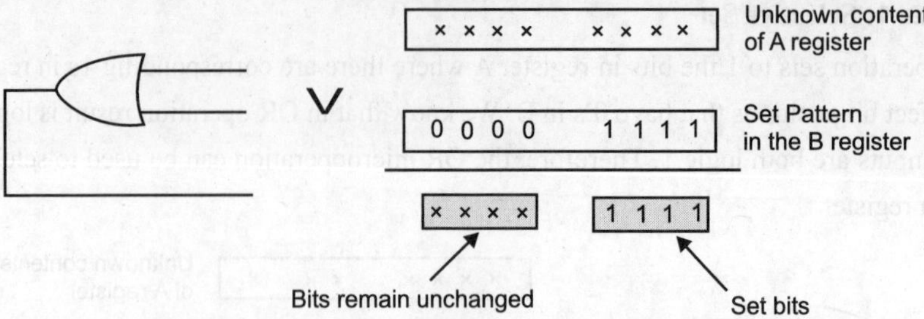

Fig. 3.21. Selective mask microoperation

As shown in Fig. 3.21, the four middle bits of b are 0's, so the corresponding bits are cleared. The two left most and two rightmost bits of *A* with corresponding 1's in *B* remain unchanged.

Example 4: Selective Clear

The selective clear operation is similar to the selective mask operation except that the bits of *A* are cleared only when there are corresponding 1's in *B*. This operation can be performed using AND operation with complemented *B* input.

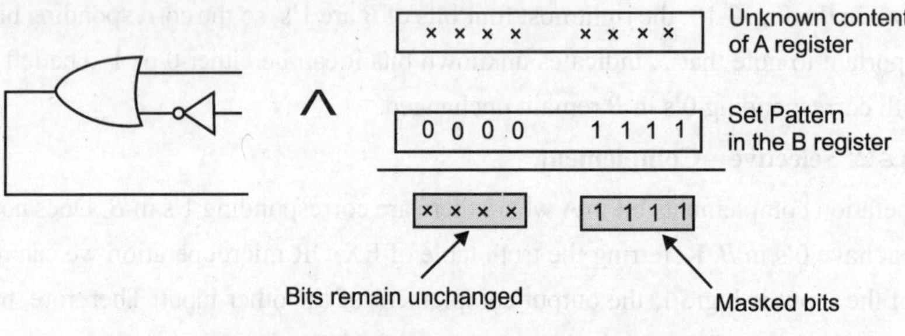

Fig. 3.22. Selective clear microoperation

Example 5: Insert microoperation

The operation inserts a new value into a group of bits. This is done by first masking to bits and then ORing them with the required value. For example,

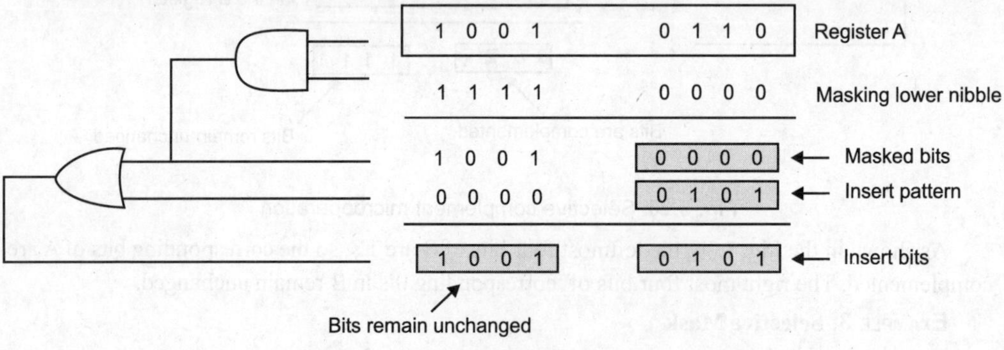

Fig. 3.23

IV Shift Microoperations

Shift microoperations are used to shift the contents of a register to the left or the right. This functionality of shift microoperation is useful for serial transfer of data. When the bits are shifted, first flip-flop in the register receives its binary information from the serial input and the last flip flop of register gives the information to the serial output. During, a shift left operation the serial input transfers a bit into the rightmost position. During a shift-right operation the serial input transfers a bit into the leftmost position. There are three types of shift operations.

3.8 ARITHMETIC LOGIC SHIFT UNITS

We have seen that individual registers perform microoperations directly without using any ALU. This is the design of arithmetic and logic circuits for a simple ALU. Instead of having individual registers performing the microoperations directly, computers can use a number of storage registers that are then connected to common operational unit i.e., ALU. Thus, by combining both the circuits with the help of a MUX, we get an arithmetic and logic circuit as shown in Fig. 3.24.

Fig. 3.24 shows one stage of an arithmetic logic shift unit,. The subscript '*i*' designates a typical stage. Inputs – A_i and B_i are applied to both the arithmetic and logic units. Inputs S_1 and S_0 are used to select a particular microoperation. At the output, a (4 × 1) MUX is used to choose between an arithmetic output in y_i and a logic output in Z_i. The data in the MUX are selected with inputs S_3 and S_2. The other two data inputs to the MUX receive inputs A_{i-1} for shift left operation and A_{i+1} for shift left operation and A_{i+1} for shift right operation. **Please note that the diagram of Fig. 3.24 shows just one typical stage. Also note that this circuit must be reported n-times for an *n*-bit ALU.** For a multistage ALU, the output carry C_{i+1} of a previous arithmetic stage must be connected to the input carry C_i of the next stage in sequence.

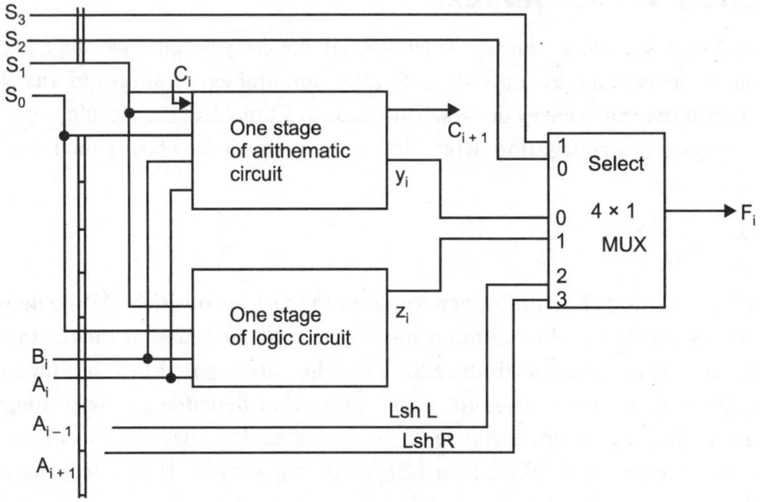

Fig. 3.24. One stage of arithmetic logic shift circuit

The table below gives a list of operations that can be performed using circuit of Fig. 3.24. This table shows 14 operations of ALU.

Select Inputs

Table 3.11. Function table for arithmetic logic shift circuit

S	S_0	S_1	S_0	C_{in}	Operation	Function
0	0	0	0	0	$F = A$	Transfer A

S	S_0	S_1	S_0	C_{in}	Operation	Function
0	0	0	0	1	$F = A + 1$	Increment A
0	0	0	1	0	$F = A + B$	Addition of A and B
0	0	0	1	1	$F = A + B + 1$	Add with carry
0	0	1	0	0	$F = A + B'$	Subtract with borrow
0	0	1	0	1	$F = A + B' + 1$	Subtraction
0	0	1	1	0	$F = A\ 1$	Decrement A
0	0	1	1	1	$F = 1$	Transfer A
0	1	0	0	X	$F = A \wedge B$	AND
0	1	0	1	X	$F = A \vee B$	OR
0	1	1	0	X	$F = A \oplus B$	XOR
0	1	1	1	X	$F = A'$	Complement a
1	0	X	X	X	$F = \text{shr } A$	Shift right A into F
1	1	X	X	X	$F = \text{shl } A$	Shift left A into F

Herein, the **first eight operations are arithmetic operations** and are selected when $S_3\ S_2 = 00$. The **next four are logic operations** and are selected when $S_3S_2 = 01$. **The last two operations are shift operations** and are selected when $S_3S_2 = 10$ and $S_3S_2 = 11$. The carry input has no effect during logic and shift operations and hence marked as don't care.

3.9 DESIGN OF FAST ADDERS

We have already studied a n-bit full adder wherein the carry output each stage is connected to the carry input of the next higher-order stage. **So, the sum and carry output of any stage cannot be produced until the input carry occurs.** This leads to a time delay in the addition process. This delay is known as **carry propagation delay**. Say, we want to add two binary numbers.

```
  0 1 1 0     (6)
+ 0 0 1 1     (3)
  1 0 1 0     (9)
```

Please note here that the sum bit generated in the last bit position (MSB) depends on the carry that was generated by the addition in the previous positions. It means that the adder will not produce correct result until the LSB carry has propagated through the intermediate full-adders. Also note that it represents a time delay that depends on the propagation delay produced in each full-adder. For instance, if we say that each *FA* has a delay of 20ns then S_3 will not reach its correct value, until 50 ns, after LSB carry is generated. Hence, total time required to perform addition is = 60 + 20 = 80 ns.

DO YOU KNOW?

Extending this adder circuit to add a grater number of bits will make situation more worse.

In general, carry propagation delay and sum propagation delay are measured in terms of gate delays.

Observe figures 3.5 and 3.6, we find that for a full adder,

C_{out} needs two gate delays and sum needs one gate delay.

But when we connect such FA circuits in cascade to generate *n*-bit ripple adder as shown in Fig. 3.25,

C_{n-1} is available after $2(n-1)$ gate delays

S_{n-1} is one XOR gate delay later

andfinal carryout, C_n, is available after $2n$ gate delays.

$\therefore$ For a 4-bit ripple adder,

C_4 is available after $8(2 \times 4)$ gate delay

C_3 is available after $6[2(4-1)]$ gate delays

and S_3 is available in 7 gate delays.

Now, we need to eliminate this inter-stage carry delay. **This process of eliminating inter stage carry delay is called as look-ahead-carry-addition.** In this method, we use logic gates to look at the low-order bits of the ***Augend*** *and* ***addend*** to check if a higher-order carry is to be generated. Two functions – carry generate and carry propagate are used.

Consider a *FA* circuit as below:

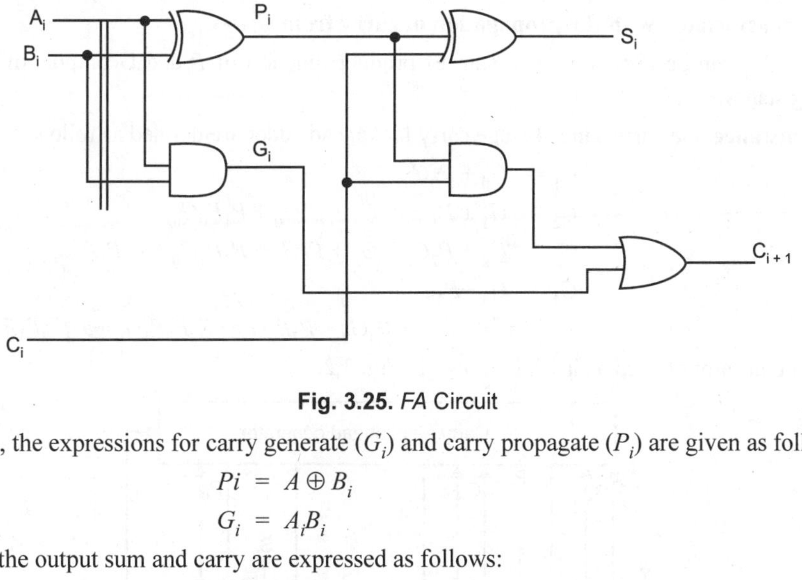

Fig. 3.25. *FA* Circuit

Then, the expressions for carry generate (G_i) and carry propagate (P_i) are given as follows.

$$Pi = A \oplus B_i \quad \ldots(1)$$

and

$$G_i = A_iB_i \quad \ldots(2)$$

And the output sum and carry are expressed as follows:

$$S_i = P_i \oplus C_i \quad \ldots(3)$$

$$C_{i+1} = G_i + P_iC_i \quad \ldots(4)$$

How? Let us prove it now.

Given:

$$\begin{aligned} C_{i+1} &= G_i + P_iC_i \quad \ldots(4) \\ &= A_iB_i + (A_i \oplus B_i)C_i \qquad [\because P_i = A_i + B_i \text{ and } G_i = A_iB_i] \\ &= A_iB_i + (\overline{A}_iB_i + A_i\overline{B}_i)C_i \\ &= A_iB_i(C_i + 1) + \overline{A}_iB_iC_i + A_i\overline{B}_iC_i \\ &= A_iB_iC_i + A_iB_i + \overline{A}_iB_iC_i + A_i\overline{B}_iC_i \end{aligned}$$

$$= A_iB_i + A_iC_i(B_i + \overline{B}_i) + \overline{A}_iB_iC_i$$
$$= A_iB_i + A_iC_i + \overline{A}_iB_iC_i$$
$$= A_iB_i(C_i + 1) + A_iC_i + \overline{A}_iB_iC_i$$
$$= A_iB_iC_i + A_iB_i + A_iC_i + \overline{A}_iB_iC_i$$
$$= B_iC_i(A_i + \overline{A}_i) + A_iB_i + A_iC_i$$
$$= B_iC_i + A_iB_i + A_iC_i$$
$$= A_iB_i + (A_i + B_i)C_i \quad \ldots(5)$$

Comparing equation-4 and equation-5 i.e.,

$$C_{i+1} = G_i + P_iC_i$$

and $$C_{i+1} = A_iB_i + (A_i + B_i)C_i$$

we find that –

$$G_i = A_iB_i$$

and $$P_i = A_i + B_i.$$ Hence proved.

Please note that G_i is called as a carry generate and it produces a carry when both A_i and B_i are 1, regardless of the input carry. Also note that P_i is called as a carry propagate because it is a term associated with the propagation of carry from C_i to C_{i+1}.

Also, C_{i+1} can be expressed as a sum of product function of P and G outputs of all of the preceding stages.

For instance, the carries in a 4-stage carry lookahead adder are defined as follows:

$$C_1 = G_0 + P_0C_{in}$$
$$C_2 = G_1 + P_1C_1 = G_1 + P_1G_0 + P_1P_0C_{in}$$
$$C_3 = G_2 + P_2C_2 = G_2 + P_2G_1 + P_2P_1G_0 + P_2P_1P_0C_{in}$$
$$C_4 = G_3 + P_3C_3$$
$$= G_3 + P_3G_2 + P_3P_2G_1 + P_3P_2P_1G_0 + P_3P_2P_1P_0C_{in}$$

A general form of such a circuit is shown in Fig. 3.26

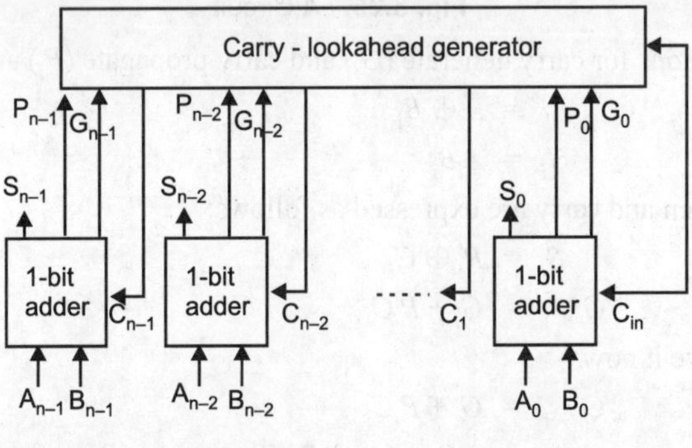

Fig. 3.26. Generalized Carry Lookahead adder circuit

The sum equation of stage-i, S_i is given by

$$S_i = A_i \oplus B_i \oplus C_i$$

As $$S_i = P_i \oplus G_i \oplus C_i$$

How? Let us prove this now.

We conversely assume that

$$S_i = P_i \oplus G_i \oplus C_i$$

where $P_i = A_i + B_i$ (proved earlier)

and $G_i = A_i B_i$

$$\therefore \quad S_i = (A_i + B_i) \oplus (A_i B_i) \oplus C_i$$

$$= [\overline{(A_i + B_i)}(A_i B_i) + (A_i + B_i)\overline{(A_i + B_i)}] \oplus C_i$$

$$= [(\overline{A}_i + \overline{B}_i)(A_i B_i) + (A_i + B_i)(\overline{A}_i + \overline{B}_i)] \oplus C_i$$

$$= [O + A_i\overline{A}_i + A_i\overline{B}_i + \overline{A}_i B_i + B_i\overline{B}_i] \oplus C_i$$

$$= (A_i\overline{B}_i + \overline{A}_i B_i) \oplus C_i$$

$$= A_i \oplus B_i \oplus C_i$$

But from Fig. 3.27, we find that

$$S_i = P_i \oplus C_i$$

or $S_i = A_i \oplus B_i \oplus C_i$

Hence, $S_i = P_i \oplus G_i \oplus C_i$ Proved.

After combining all these equations and the modified sum equations, we draw a 4-bit carry lookahead adder as shown in Fig. 3.27.

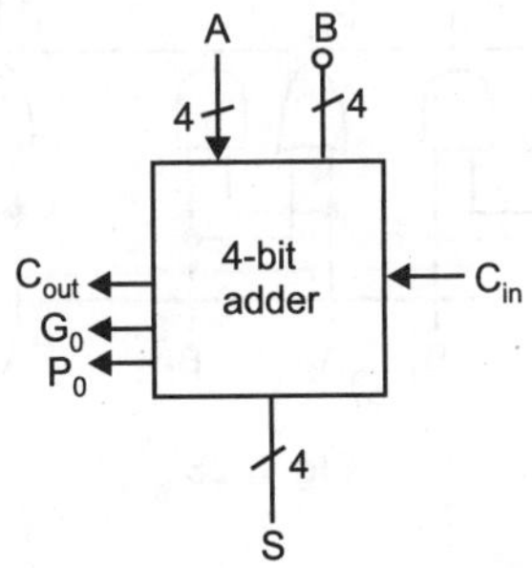

Fig. 3.27. 4-bit carry lookahead adder.

Please note (from figure 3.27) that one gate delay is needed to develop all P_i and G_i signals. It is followed by two gate delays in the AND OR circuit for C_{i+1}. After a further XOR gate delay, all sum bits are available. So, independent of *n*, the *n*-bit addition process requires only 4-gate delays and all carries can be obtained within 3 gate delays after the signals *A*, *B* and C_{in} are applied. **Also note that a 4-bit ripple carry adder (in comparison) requires 7 gate delays for S_3 and 8 gate delays for c_4.** We can cascade such 4-bit carry lookahead adders to form a 16-bit or 32-bit adder. We require four -4bit carry lookahead adders to form 16-bit carry look ahead adder and eight 4-bit carry lookahead adders to form 32-bit adder, the carry out (C_4) forms the low-order 4-bit adder. It is available 3 gate delays after the input operands *A*, *B* and C_0 are applied to the 32-bit adder. Then, C_3 is available at the output of the second adder after a further 2 gate-delays. C_{12} is available after a further 2 gate delays and soon.

Finally, C_{28}, the carry-in to the high-order 4-bit adder, is available after a total of $(6 \times 2) + 3 = 15$ gate delays. C_{32} is available after 2-gate delays i.e., after 17 gate delays and S_{31} is available after 3 gate delays i.e. 18 gate used then these gate delays are very less compared to total delays of 63 and 64 for S_{31} and C_{32}.

What about multilevel generate and propagate functions.

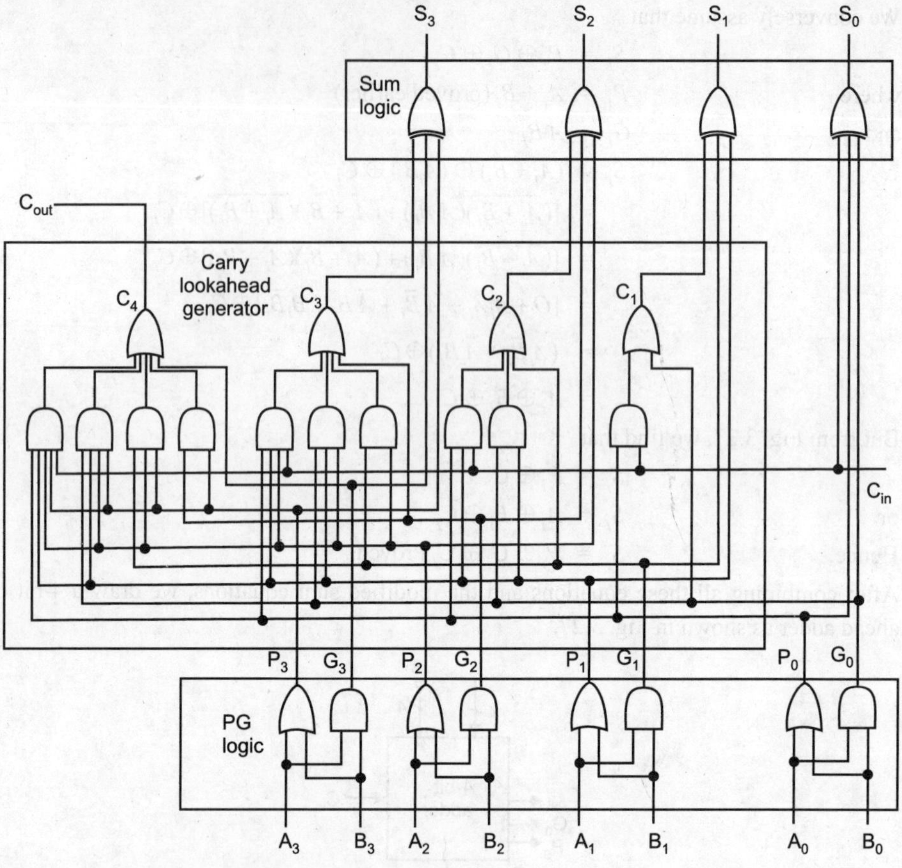

Fig. 3.28

Multilevel Generate and Propagate Functions

In the 32-bit adder just discussed the carries C_4, C_8, C_{12}, ... ripple through 4-bit adder blocks with two gate delays per clock. This is analogous to the way individual carries ripple through each bit stage in a ripple-carry adder. By use of multi-level block generate and propagate functions, it is possible to use the lookahead approach to develop the carries C_4, C_8, C_{12}, ... in parallel in a multi-level carry-lookahead circuit. The FIg. 3.28 shows a 16-bit adder implemented using in 4-bit adder blocks. Here, blocks provide new output functions defined as G_k^i and the where $K = 0$ for the first 4-bit block, K – 1 for the second 4-bit block and so on. In the first block,

$$P_0^1 = P_3P_2P_1P_0$$

$$G_{10} = G_3 + P_2G_2 + P_3P_2G_1 + P_3P_2P_1G_0$$

Therefore, we can use first-level G_i and P_i function to determine whether bit stage generator or propagates a carry, and we can use the second level G_K^1 and P_K^1 functions to determine whether block K generates or propagates a carry. With these new functions available, it is not necessary to wait for carries to ripple through the 4-bit blocks. Looking at Fig. 3.29, we can determine C_{16} as

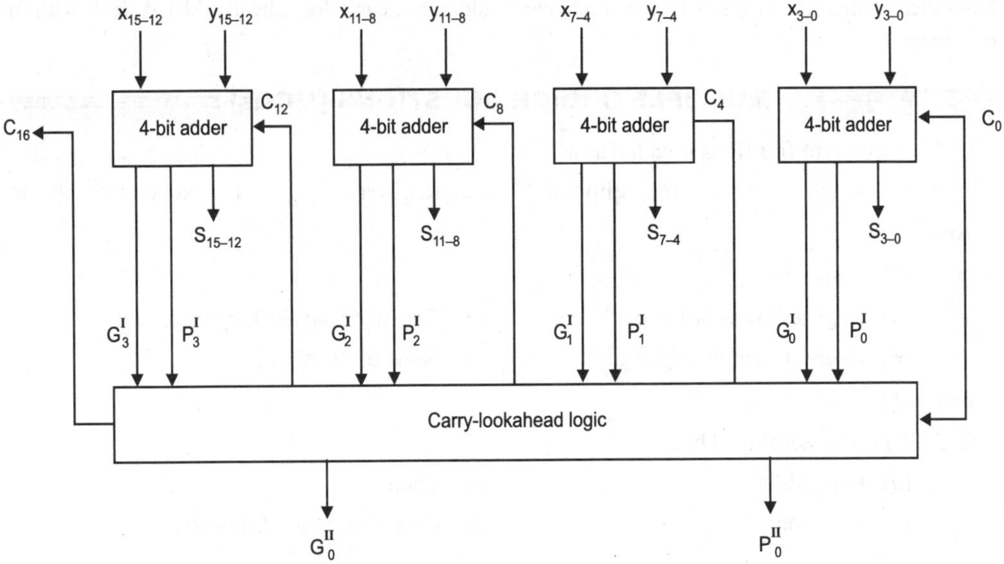

Fig. 3.29. 16-bit carry-lookahead adder built from 4 –bit adders

$$C_6^1 = G_3^1 + P_3^1 G_2^1 + P_3^1 P_2^1 G_1^1 + P_3^1 P_2^1 G_0^1 + P_3^1 P_2^1 P_0^1 C_0$$

The above expression is identical in form to the expression for C_4; only variable names are different. Therefore, the structure of the carry-lookahead circuit in Fig. 3.29 is identical to the carry-lookahead circuit shown in the Fig. 3.28. However, **please note that the carries C_4, C_8, C_{12} and C_{16} generated internally by 4-bit adder blocks are not needed in the Fig. 1.49 because they are generated by the multi-level carry lookahead circuits.**

Let us see the delay in producing outputs from the 16-bit carry-ahead adder. The delay in developing the carries produced by the carry-lookahead circuits is two gate delays more than the delay needed to develop the G_K^1 and P_K^1 functions. The G_K^1 and P_K^1 functions require two gate delays and one gate delay, respectively, after the generation of G_i and P_i. Therefore, all carries produced by the carry-lookahead circuits are available 5 gate delays after A, B and C_0 are applied as inputs. The carry C_{15} is generated inside the higher-order 4-bit block in the Fig. 3.29 in two gate delays after C_{12} followed by S_{15} in one further gate delays. Therefore, S_{15} is available after 8 gate delays. These delays, 5 gate delays for C_{16} and 8 gate delays for S_{15} are less as compared to 9 and 10 gate delays for C_{16} and S_{15} in cascaded 4-bit carry-lookahead adder blocks, respectively.

We can cascade two 16-bit adders to implement 32-bit adder. Here, only two more gate delays are required to get C_{32} and S_{31} and C_{16} and S_{15} respectively. Therefore, C_{32} is available after 7 gate delays and S_{31} is available after 10 gate delays. These delays are less compared to 18 and 17 gate delays for the same outputs if the 32-bit adders of built from a cascade of eight 4-bit adders.

If we go for the third level then we can build 64-bit using four 16-bit adders. Delays through this adder will be 12 gate delays for S_{63} and 7 gate delays for C_{64}.

SUMMARY

RTL has been dealt in detail in this chapter. Basically, there are two types of parallel adders – ripple carry adder and carry look ahead adder. They differ in the way the carry bits are generated. A ripple carry adder becomes slow once the number of bits is increased. The time taken by the LSB carry to propagate to MSB stage is more. This is known as a **ripple carry problem.** So, we use a carry look-ahead adder that is faster than a ripple carry adder. So, carry lookahead adder is dealt with in this chapter.

MULTIPLE CHOICE QUESTIONS [MCQs]

Q. 1. A group of flip-flops is called as a

(*a*) Latch (*b*) Flip flop (*c*) Register (*d*) None of the above

Ans. (*c*)

Q. 2. RTL stands for

(*a*) Register Transfer logic (*b*) Register Transfer Language

(*c*) Register Temporary Logic (*d*) None of the above

Ans. (*b*)

Q. 3. RTL was developed by

(*a*) Barry Boehm (*b*) Chen

(*c*) Jacobson (*d*) Chris Fraser and Davidson

Ans. (*d*)

Q. 4. To specify microoperations we have

(*a*) TTL (*b*) RTL (*c*) STL (*d*) None of the above

Ans. (*b*)

Q. 5. 1 Flip-flop means

(*a*) 1-bit (*b*) 2-bit (*c*) 3-bit (*d*) 4-bit

Ans. (*a*)

Q. 6. To minimize the number of wires in a system, we use

(*a*) Common bus scheme (*b*) Common bus arbitration

(*c*) Common bus Transfer (*d*) None of the above

Ans. (*a*)

Q. 7. The tri-state gate which provides more sinking and sourcing capacities is called as a -

(*a*) Bi-state buffer (*b*) Buffer

(*c*) Tri-state buffer (*d*) None of the above

Ans (*c*)

Q. 8. A memory is a collection of

(*a*) Registers (*b*) Flip Flops (*c*) RAM (*d*) ROM

Ans. (*b*)

Q. 9. Using 2s complement method, $(A - B)$ is given by

(*a*) A-2s complement of B (*b*) B – 2s complement of A.

(*c*) A + 2s complement of B (*d*) None of the above

Ans. (*c*)

Q. 10. For a look-ahead carry adder, the expression for sum and carry are –

(*a*) $S_i = P_i \oplus G_i$
$C_{i+1} = G_i + P_i C_i$

(*b*) $S_i = P_i + G_i$
$C_{i+1} = G_i \oplus P_i C_i$

(*c*) $S_i = P_i \oplus C_i$
$C_{i+1} = G_i + P_i C_i$

(*d*) None of the above

Ans. (*c*)

CONCEPTUAL SHORT QUESTIONS WITH ANSWERS

Q. 1. Show that block diagram of the hardware that implements the following register transfer statement

$$yT_2 : R_2 \leftarrow R_1, \quad R_1 \leftarrow R_2$$

Ans.

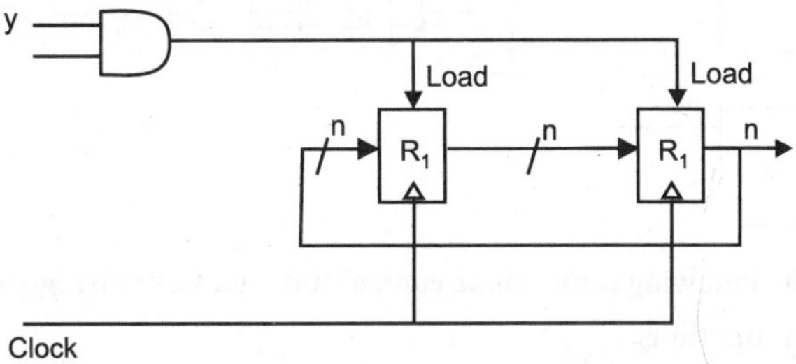

Q. 2. The outputs of four registers R_0, R_1, R_2 and R_3 are connected through 4 to 1-line multiplexers to the inputs of a fifth register, R_5. Each register is eight bits long. The required transfers are dictated by four timing variables to through T_3 as follows:

$$T_0 : R_5 \leftarrow R_0$$
$$T_1 : R_5 \leftarrow R_1$$
$$T_2 : R_5 \leftarrow R_2$$
$$T_3 : R_5 \leftarrow R_3$$

The timing variables are mutually exclusive, which means that only one variable is equal to 1 at any given time while the other three are equal to 0. Draw a block diagram showing the hardware implementation of the register transfers. Include the connections necessary from the four timing variables to the selection inputs of the multiplexers and to load input of register R_5

Ans.

T_0	T_1	T_2	T_3	S_1	S_0	R_3
0	0	0	0	X	X	0
1	0	0	0	0	0	1
0	1	0	0	0	1	1
0	0	1	0	1	0	1
0	0	0	1	1	1	1

$\therefore$

$$S_1 = T_2 + T_3$$
$$S_0 = T_1 + T_3$$

and $\qquad$ Load $= T_0 + T_1 + T_2 + T_3$

So, we draw now.

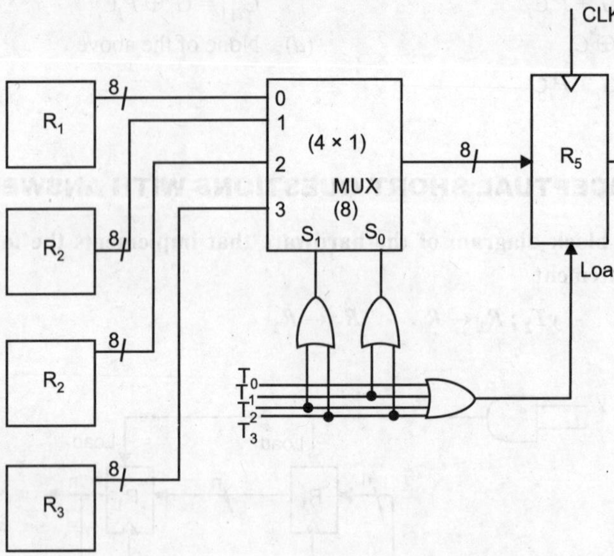

Q. 3. Represent the following conditional, control statement by two register transfer statement with control functions.

If ($P = 1$) then

($R_1 \leftarrow R_2$)

Else if ($Q = 1$) then

($R_1 \leftarrow R_3$) [GGSIPU, B.Tech (CSE) – 5th Sem., Dec. 2005]

Ans. $3 : P : R_1 \leftarrow R_2$

$P'Q : R_1 \leftarrow R_3$

Q. 4. What has to be done to the bus system of figure given below to be able to transfer information from any register to any other register, specifically, show the connections that must be included to provide a path from the outputs of register C to the inputs of register A.

Ans. Connect the 4-line common bus to the four inputs of each register. Provide a "Load" control input in each register. Provide a clock input for each register.

To transfer from register C to register A :

Apply $S_1S_0 = 10$ (to select C for the enable the load input of A and apply a clock pulse).

Q. 5. Draw a diagram of a bus system similar to the one-shown in figure below but use three-state buffers and a decoder instead of the multiplexers.

Ans.

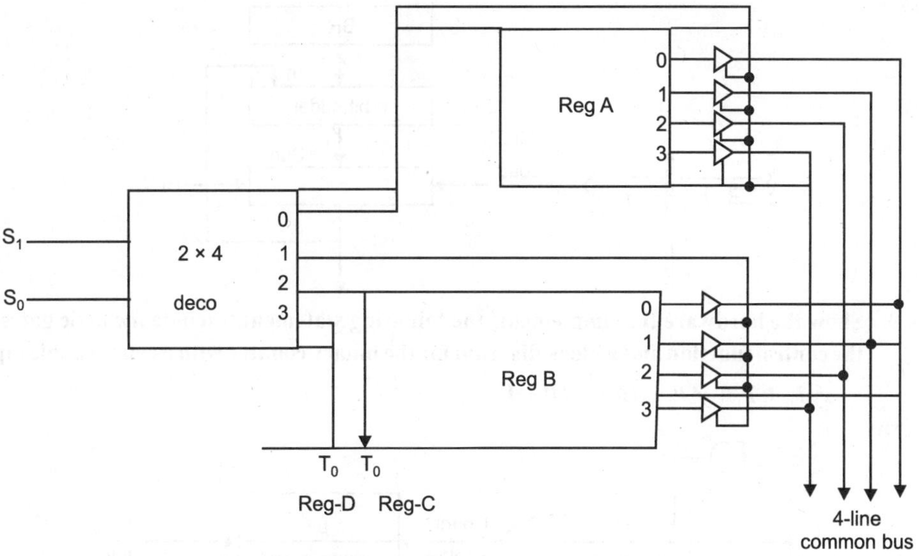

Q. 6. A digital computer has a common bus system for 16-registers of 32-bits each. The bus is constructed with multiplexers.

(*a*) How many selection inputs are there in each multiplexer?

(*b*) What size of MUXes are needed?

(*c*) How many mulitplexers are there in the bus?

Ans. (*a*) 4 selection lines are needed to select one of 16 registers.

(*b*) (16 * 1) MUXes are needed.

(*c*) 32 MUXes, one for each of the registers.

Q. 7. The following transfer statements specify a memory. Explain the memory operation in each case

(a) $R_2 \leftarrow M[AR]$ (*b*) $M[AR] \leftarrow R_3$ (*c*) $R_5 \leftarrow M[R_5]$

Ans. (*a*) Read memory word specified by the address in *AR* into register R_2.

(*b*) Write content of register R_3 into the memory word specified by the address in *AR*.

(*c*) Read memory word specified by the address in R_5 and transfer content to R_5 (destroys previous value).

Q. 8. Draw the block diagram for the hardware that implements the following statements:

$$x + yz: AR \leftarrow AR + BR$$

where AR and BR are two *n*-bit registers and *x*, *y* and *z* are control variables. Include the logic gates for the control function. (Remember that the symbol + designates an OR operation in a control or Boolean function but that it represents an arithmetic plus in a microoperation) [GGSIPU, B.Tech. (CSE)-5th Sem., Dec. 2005]

Ans.

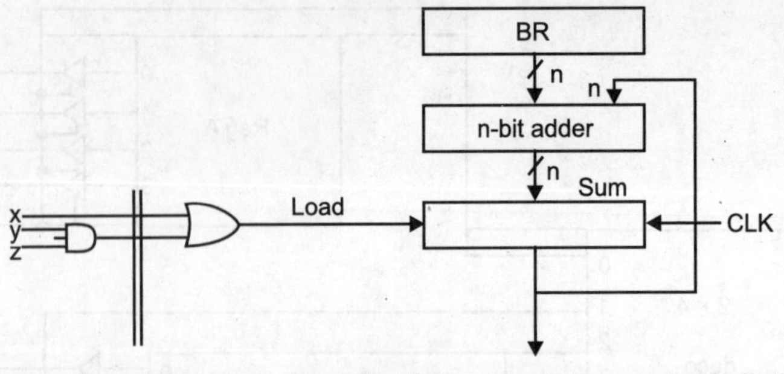

Q. 9. Show the hardware that implements the following statement. Include the logic gates for the control function and a block diagram for the binary counter with a count enable input.

$$xyT_0 + T_1 + y'T_2 : AR \leftarrow AR + 1$$

Ans.

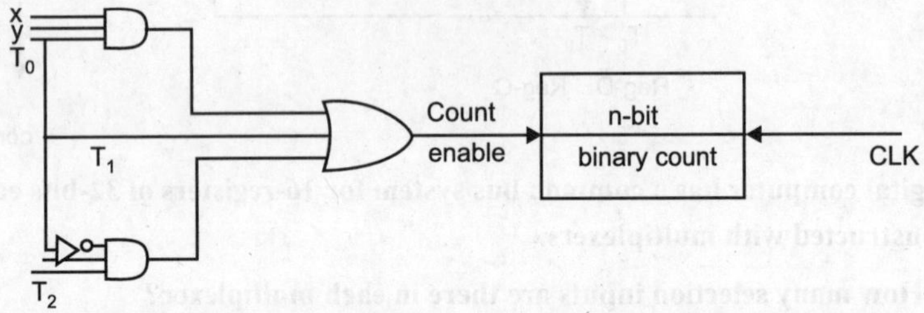

Q. 10. Consider the following register transfer statements for two 4-bit registers R_1 and R_2.

$$xT : R_1 \leftarrow R_1 + R_2$$
$$x'T : R_1 \leftarrow R_2$$

Every time that variable $T = 1$, either the content of R_2 is added to the content of R_1 if $x = 1$ or the content of R_2 is transferred to R_1 if $x = 0$. Draw a diagram showing the hardware implementation of the two statements. Use block diagrams for the two 4-bit registers, 4-bit adder and a quadruple 2-to-1-lien MUX that selects the inputs to R_1. In the diagram, show now the control variables x and T select the inputs of the MUXes and the load input of register R_1.

Ans.

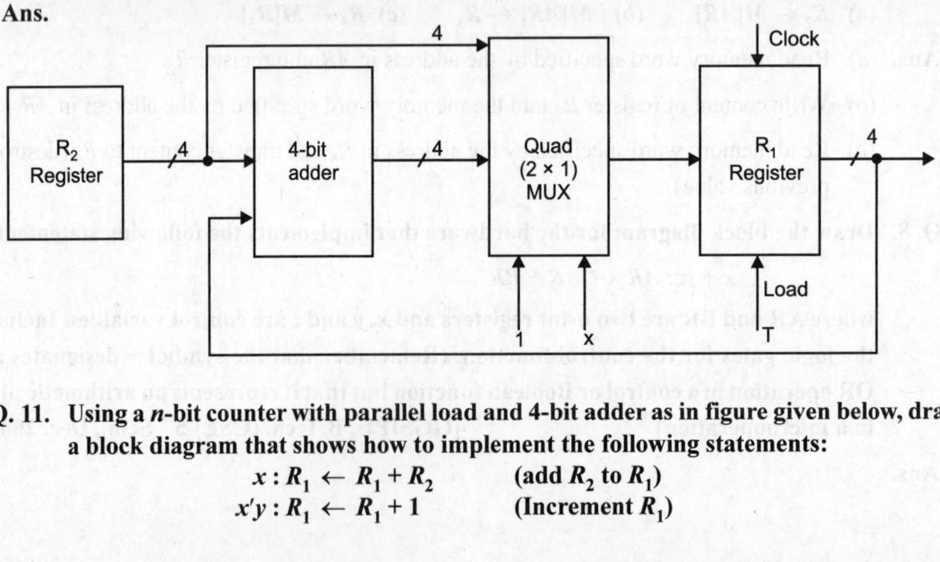

Q. 11. Using a n-bit counter with parallel load and 4-bit adder as in figure given below, draw a block diagram that shows how to implement the following statements:

$$x : R_1 \leftarrow R_1 + R_2 \qquad \textbf{(add } R_2 \textbf{ to } R_1\textbf{)}$$
$$x'y : R_1 \leftarrow R_1 + 1 \qquad \textbf{(Increment } R_1\textbf{)}$$

Where R_1 is a counter with parallel load and R_2 is a 4-bit register.

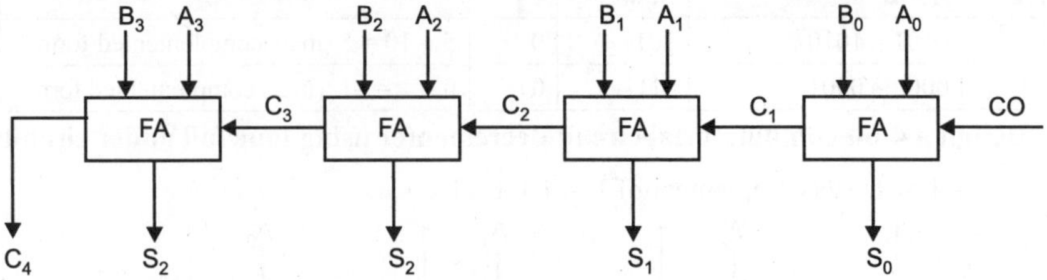

Fig. 3.30 4-bit binary adder

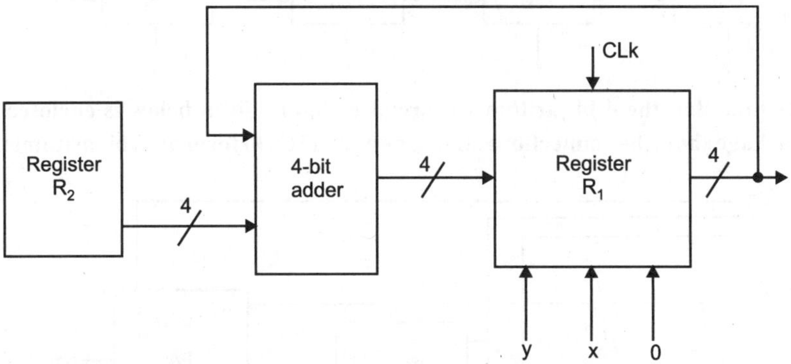

Q. 12. The adder subtractor circuit of figure given below has the following values for input mode *M* and date inputs *A* and *B*. In each case, determine the values of the outputs : S_3, S_2, S_1, S_0 and C_4.

	M	*A*	*B*
(*a*)	0	0111	0110
(*b*)	0	1000	1001
(*c*)	1	1100	1000
(*d*)	1	0101	1010
(*e*)	1	0000	0001

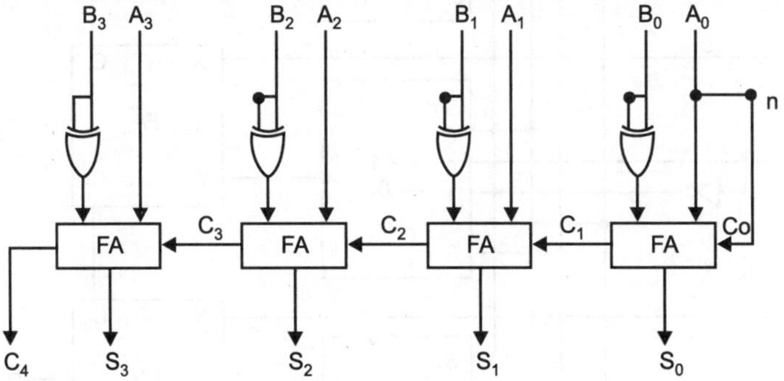

Fig. 3.31. 4-bit adder-subtractor

M	*A* + *B*	Sum	C_4	
0	0111 + 0110	1101	0	7 + 6 = 13
0	1000 + 1001	0001	1	8 + 9 = 16 + 1
1	1100 – 1000	0100	1	12 – 8 = 4

M	*A* + *B*	Sum	C_4	
1	0101 – 1010	1011	0	5 – 10 = 5 (in 2s complemented form)
1	0000 – 0001	1111	0	0 – 1 = –1 (in 2s complemented form)

Q. 13. Design a 4-bit combinatorial circuit decrementer using four full adder circuits.

Ans. $\because A - 1 = A + \text{2s complement of } 1 = A + 1111$

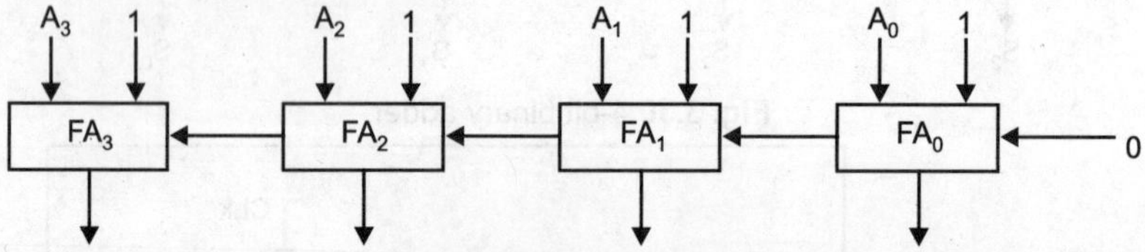

Q. 14. Assume that the 4-bit arithmetic circuit of figure given below is enclosed in one IC package show the connections among two such ICs to form an 8-bit arithmetic circuits.

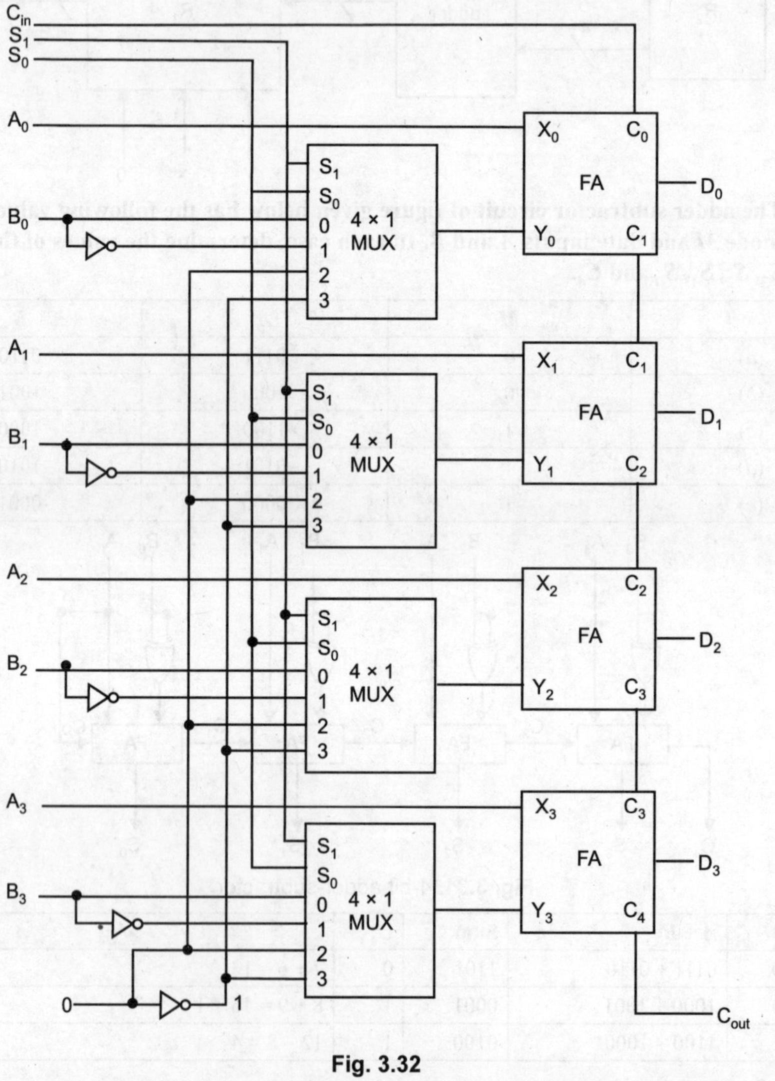

Fig. 3.32

Ans.

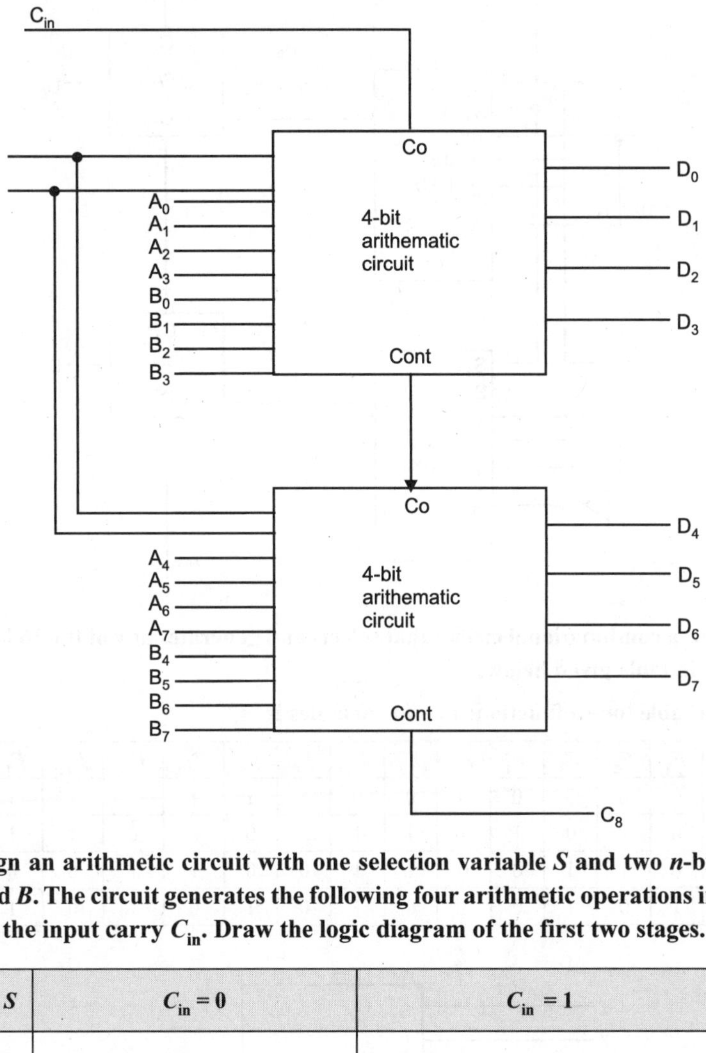

Q. 15. Design an arithmetic circuit with one selection variable S and two n-bit data inputs A and B. The circuit generates the following four arithmetic operations in conjunction with the input carry C_{in}. Draw the logic diagram of the first two stages.

S	$C_{in} = 0$	$C_{in} = 1$
0	$D = A + B$ (add)	$D = A + 1$ (increment)
1	$D = A - 1$ (decrement)	$D = A + \overline{B} + 1$ (Subtract)

Ans.

S	C_{in}	X	Y	
0	0	A	B	$(A + B)$
0	1	A	0	$(A + 1)$
1	0	A	1	$(A - 1)$
1	1	A	$\overline{B}$	$(A - B)$

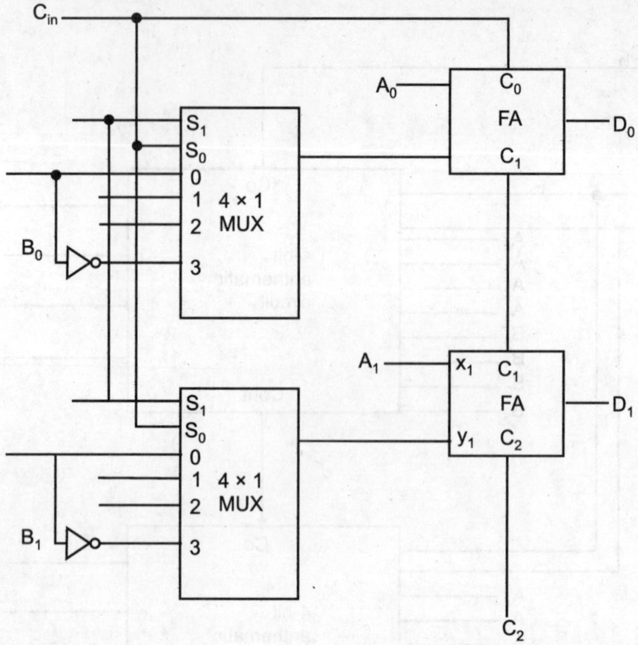

Q. 16. Derive a combinational circuit that selects and generates any of the 16 logic functions listed in table given below:

Truth table for 16 functions of two variables is

x	y	F_0	F_1	F_2	F_3	F_4	F_5	F_6	F_7	F_8	F_9	F_{10}	F_{11}	F_{12}	F_{13}	F_{14}	F_{15}
0	0	0	0	0	0	0	0	0	0	1	1	1	1	1	1	1	1
0	1	0	0	0	0	1	1	1	1	0	0	0	0	1	1	1	1
1	0	0	0	1	1	0	0	1	1	0	0	1	1	0	0	1	1
1	1	0	1	0	1	0	1	0	1	0	1	0	1	0	1	0	1

Ans.

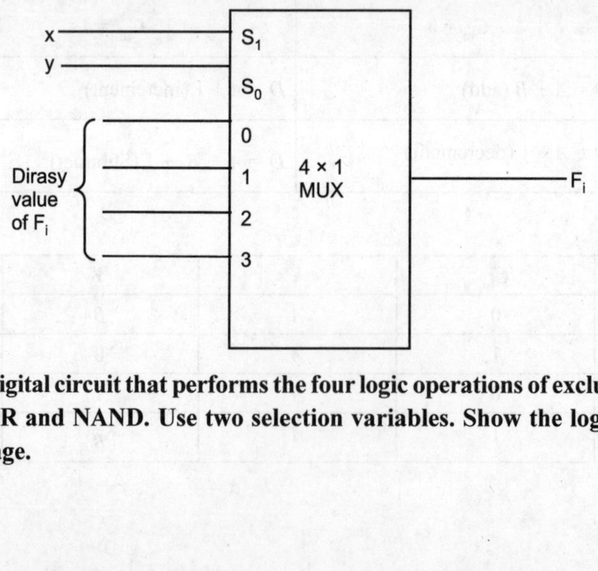

Q. 17. Design a digital circuit that performs the four logic operations of exclusive OR, exclusive NOR, NOR and NAND. Use two selection variables. Show the logic diagram of one typical stage.

Ans.

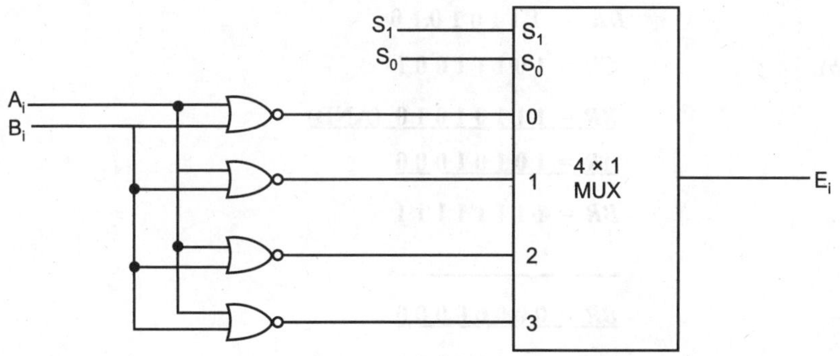

Q. 18. Register *A* holds the 8-bit binary 11011001. Determine the *B* operand and the logic microoperation to be performed ion order to change the value in A to :

(*a*) 01101101 (*b*) 11111101 [GGSIPU, B.Tech.(CSE) – 5th Sem., 2005)

Ans. (*a*) $A = 1\,1\,0\,1\,1\,0\,0\,1$

$\underline{B = 1\,0\,1\,1\,0\,1\,0\,0\ +}$

$A \leftarrow A \oplus B$ $\quad 0\,1\,1\,0\,1\,1\,0\,1$

(*b*) $A = 1\,1\,0\,1\,1\,0\,0\,1$ **(OR)**

$\underline{B = 1\,1\,1\,1\,1\,1\,0\,1}$

$A \leftarrow A \vee B$ $\quad 1\,1\,1\,1\,1\,1\,0\,1$

Q. 21. The 8-bit registers. *AR*, *BR*, *CR* and *DR* initially have the following values:

$AR = 111110010$

$BR = 111111111$

$CR = 10111001$

$DR = 11101010$

Determine the 8-bit values in each register after the execution of the following sequence of microoperations.

$AR \leftarrow AR + BR$ **Add *BR* to *AR***

$CR \leftarrow CR \wedge DR,\ BR \leftarrow BR + 1$ **AND *DR* TO *CR*, increment *BR***

$AR \leftarrow AR - CR$ **Subtract *CR* from *AR***

[GGSIPU, B.Tech. (CSE) – 5th Sem., Dec. 2004]

Ans. (*a*) $AR = 1\,1\,1\,1\,0\,0\,1\,0$

$\underline{BR = 1\,1\,1\,1\,1\,1\,1\,1\ (+)}$

$\underline{AR = 1\,1\,1\,1\,0\,0\,0\,1}$

$\therefore$ $BR = 1\,1\,1\,1\,1\,1\,1\,1$

CR = 1 0 1 1 1 0 0 1

DR = 1 1 1 0 1 0 1 0

(*b*) CR = 1 0 1 1 1 0 0 1

BR = 1 1 1 0 1 0 1 0 (AND)

AR = 1 0 1 0 1 0 0 0

∴ BR = 1 1 1 1 1 1 1 1

+1

BR = 0 0 0 0 0 0 0 0

AR = 1 1 1 1 0 0 0 1

DR = 1 1 1 0 1 0 1 0

(*c*) AR = 1 1 1 1 0 0 0 1

CR = 1 0 1 0 1 0 0 0 (–)

AR = 0 1 0 0 1 0 0 1

∴ BR = 0 0 0 0 0 0 0 0

CR = 1 0 1 0 1 0 0 0

DR = 1 1 1 0 1 0 1 0

Q. 20. An 8-bit register contains the binary value 10011100. What is the register value after arithmetic shift right? Starting from the initial number 10011100, determine the register value after an arithmetic shift left and state whether there is an overflow.

Ans. R = 100 111 00

Arithmetic right shift = 11001110

Arithmetic left shift = 00111000

An overflow occurs because a negative number is changed to positive.

Q. 21. Starting from an initial value of R = 11011101, determine the sequence of binary values in R after a logical shift-left, followed by a circular shift-right, followed by a logical shift-right and a circular shift-left.

Ans. R = 11011101

Logical shift left = 10111010

Circular shift right = 01011101

Logical shift right = 00101110

Circular shift left = 01011100

Q. 22. What is the value of output *h* in figure given below if input a is 1001, $S = 1$, $I_R = 1$ and $F_L = 0$?

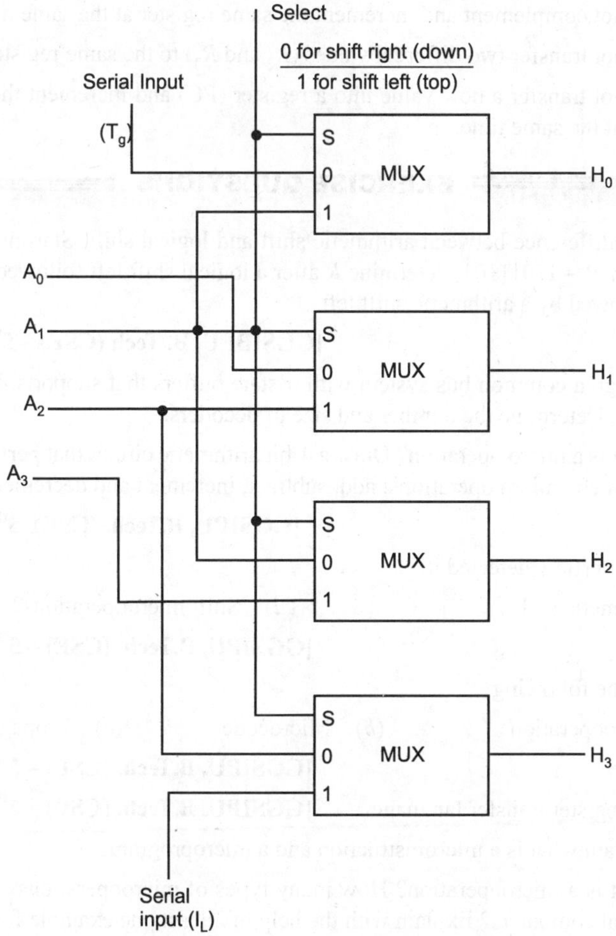

Fig. 1.33. 4-bit combinational circuit shifter

Function Table

Select	*Output*			
S	H_0	H_1	H_2	H_3
0	I_R	A_0	A_1	A_2
1	A_1	A_2	A_3	T_L

Ans. $S = 1$, Shift left

	A_0	A_1	A_2	A_3	I_L
	1	0	0	1	0
H =	0	0	1	0	Shift left

Q. 23. What is wrong with the following register transfer statements

(*a*) $xT : AR \leftarrow AR,\ AR \leftarrow 0$

(*b*) $yT : R_1 \leftarrow R_2,\ R_1 \leftarrow R_3$

(*c*) $zT : PC \leftarrow AR,\ PC \leftarrow PC + 1$?

Ans. (*a*) Cannot complement and increment the same register at the same time.

(*b*) Cannot transfer two different values (R_2 and R_3) to the same register

(*c*) Cannot transfer a new value into a register (PC) and increment the original value by one at the same time.

EXERCISE QUESTIONS

Q. 1. State the difference between arithmetic shift and logical shift. Starting from initial value of register R = 11011101, determine R after a logical shift left followed by a circular shift right followed by a arithmetic shift left.

[GGSIBPU, B. Tech (CSE) – 5th Sem. Dec. 2004]

Q. 2. (*a*) Design a common bus system with tristate buffers that supports 8-registers of 8-bits each. Determine the number and size of decoders.

(*b*) What is a micro operation? Draw a 4-bit arithmetic circuit that performs the following arithmetic micro operations: add, subtract, increment and decrement.

[GGSIPU, B.Tech. (CSE) 5th Sem., Dec. 2005]

Q. 3. How is overflow detected in

(*i*) arithmetic and (*ii*) Shift microoperations?

[GGSIPU, B.Tech. (CSE) – 5th Sem., Dec. 2005]

Q. 4. Explain the following:

(*a*) Microoperation (*b*) Microcode (*c*) Propagation delay

[GGSIPU, B.Tech. (CSE) – 5th Sem., Dec. 2008]

Q. 5. Explain register transfer language. **[GGSIPU, B.Tech. (CSE) – 5th Sem., Dec. 2009]**

Q. 6. (*a*) Explain what is a microinstruction and a microprogram.

(*b*) What is a microoperation? How many types of microoperations are mostly found in digital computers? Explain with the help of atleast one example for each category.

[GGSIPU, B.Tech. (CSE) – 5th Sem., Dec. 2010]

Q. 7. (*a*) Show the hardware to implement the following RTL code:

(*i*) $\alpha : X \leftarrow X + Y$

(*ii*) $\beta : X \leftarrow X + Y' + 1$

(*iii*) $\gamma : X \leftarrow X \oplus Y$

Also show the hardware to implement all three of the RTL statements in one combined system. Control hardware ensures that no more than one of the control signals α, β, and γ is active at any time.

(*b*) Define the following

(*a*) Micro-operation

(*b*) Micro-instruction

(c) Micro-program

(*d*) Micro-code

(*e*) Instruction. **[DTU (DCE) – ME (CS) – 3rd Sem., 2004-05]**

Q. 8. Write short notes on – Fast carry adder **[PTU, B.Tech. (CSE) – 3rd Sem., 2009]**

CHAPTER 4

BUS AND MEMORY

4.0 INTRODUCTION

In mainframe computers, there is a **separate path** from each source register to each destination register for connecting them. Every source point was directly connected to every destination point. This results in a very **high hardware cost** as a large number of wires are desired now. So, in mini and micro computers, bus concept is used. A bus is a group of wires that are used to sent data and information. This bus is a **shared common path** for several resources. A single wire carries a signal to multiple units. But at any instant only two units are logically linked. The main benefit of bus method is to reduce cost of connecting wires and associated driver/receiver circuits. But it has some disadvantages also like low speed due to sharing.

4.1 BUS AND SYSTEM BUS

A bus is defined as a group of wires that serves a single purpose. The major parts of the microcomputer are connected to each other by three sets of parallel lines called as **system buses**. Some pass data; some pass address and others acts as **control lines.** These lines are **daisy chained** from one device to the next.

4.2 TYPES OF SYSTEM BUS

Buses are of three types –

(*a*) Address bus

(*b*) Data bus

(*c*) Control Bus

Let us define them now.

Address Bus: The bus over which the CPU sends out the address of the memory location is called as the address bus. The address bus carries the address of the memory location to write to or read from. The address bus may consist of 16, 20, 24 or 32 parallel signal lines. **If there are *N* address lines then it can directly address 2^N memory locations. For eg.,** If the number of address lines N = 16 then it can address.

$$2^{16} = 65,536 \text{ or } 64\text{K memory locations.}$$

Figure. 4.1 shows the address bus, control and data bus. The address bus is unidirectional as shown by an arrow.

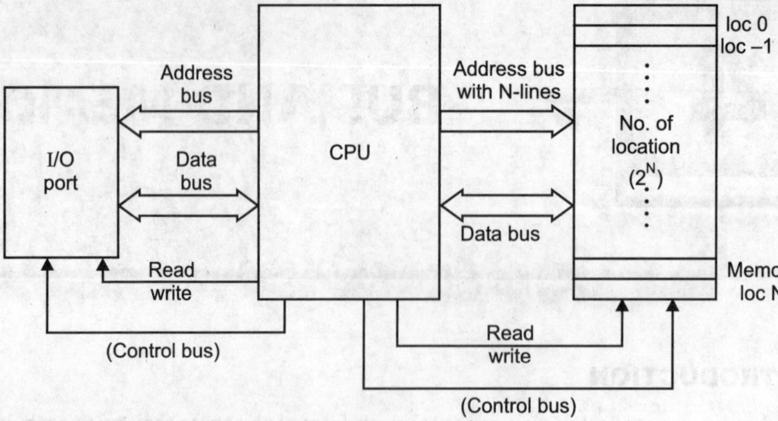

Fig. 4.1. Three types of buses

The address bus is also used to send the port address on the address bus when the CPU reads data from or writes data to a port.

Data Bus: The data bus consists of 8, 16, or 32 parallel lines. It is a **bidirectional bus.** It means the data can get transferred from CPU to memory and vice versa. Data bus connects the I/O ports and CPU.

Hence, CPU can write data to or read it from the memory or I/O ports. **Please understand that the number of data lines used in the data bus is equal to the size of data word being written or read. Also note that many devices in the system will connect their outputs to the some data bus but only one device will have its output enabled at a time so that there is no collision of data.** To avoid multiple devices to put their outputs simultaneously on the data bus, all devices getting connected to the data bus should have three state outputs. This helps in disabling the outputs of the devices which should be stopped from connecting their outputs to the data bus.

Control Bus: The control bus is used for sending control signals to the memory and I/O devices. The control bus consists of 4 to 10 parallel signals lines. The CPU sends signals on the control bus to enable the outputs of addressed memory devices or I/O port devices.

For e.g, Memory read, memory write, I/O read and I/O write.

We are in a position to solve some examples now.

EXAMPLE 1: If 1,048,576 memory locations each capable of storing an 8-bit data are to be addressed by a CPU, then calculate the number of address and data lines required.

SOLUTION: As we know that, Number of locations to be addressed, $M = 2^N$

Where N is no. of address lines.

Given: 1,048,576 = M

That is, 1,048,576 = 2^N

∴ Log_a 1,048,576 = N

or N = 20.

∵ No. of data lines is always equal to the number of data bits.

∵ No. of data lines is 8.

EXAMPLE 2: What will be the total capacity of 20-bit address lines CPU?

SOLUTION: 20-Bit address lines show the total capacity of the memory.

∴ Main memory has a capacity of = 2^{20}.

EXAMPLE 3: What is a bus? Draw the logic diagram of a 4-bit bus involving two input and output registers using multiplexers.

SOLUTION: A **bus** is a set of connections between two or more components which are designed to transfer several bits of a word from a specific source to destination. It is a **shared media** of information transfer.

The logic diagram of a 4-bit bus is shown in Fig.

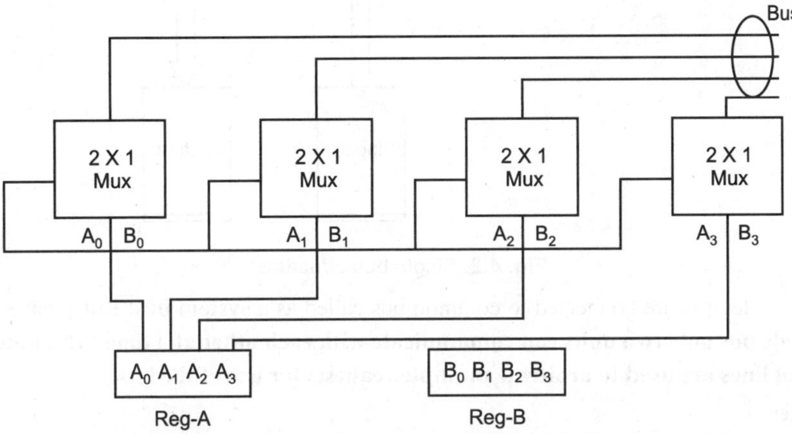

EXAMPLE 4: A digital computer system has a common bus system for 16-bit registers. The size of each register is 32-bits each. The bus is constructed using multiplexers.

(a) How many selection inputs are needed for each multiplexer?

(b) What is the size of multiplexer needed?

(c) How many multiplexes are needed?

[GSSIPU, B.Tech. (CSE/ IT/ ECE) 5th sem., 2011]

SOLUTION: Given:

Size of register = 32 bits

Size of register = 16

(a) Size of MUX = No. of registers

∴ Size of MUX = 16 × 1

(b) No. of selection bits (n) –

As 2^n = size of MUX = 16

or $2^n = 2^4$

∴ $n = 4$

∴ No. of selection bits = 4.

(c) No. of MUXes = Size of register = 32 (given)

4.3 SINGLE (UNI) BUS STRUCTURE

When address, data and control bus are shown by single bus then it is called as a system bus. Such an interconnection bus structure is called as a **single bus structure**. It is shown in Fig. 4.2.

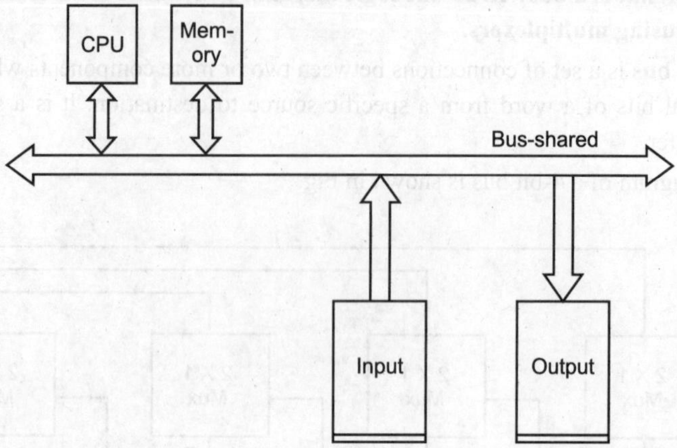

Fig. 4.2. Single bus structure.

Here, all devices are connected to common bus called as a **system bus. But please note that with a single bus only two units can communicate with each other at a time. Also note that the bus control lines are used to arbitrate multiple requests for use of the bus.**

Advantages

1. Its cost is low.
2. It is a flexible structure.

The complexity of the bus control logic depends on the amount of translation needed between the system bus and CPU, the timing requirements, whether or not interrupt management is included and the size of the overall system. **If system is small** then, control signals of the CPU could be used directly to reduce handshaking logic. Even drivers and receivers are not needed now for data and address lines. On the other hand, **larger system** with several interfaces need both bus driver and receiver circuits connected to the bus so as to maintain sufficient signal quality.

Many CPUs use time-multiplexed address and data buses to reduce the number of pins. Actually, during the first part of the bus cycle, address is present on this bus. Later on the same bus is used for data transfer purpose. Hence, initially latches are required to hold the address sent by the CPU. Even interrupt priority management is optional in a system. It is not needed in the systems that use software priority management. The complex system includes hardware for managing the I/O interrupts to increase the efficiency of a system. Many devices like PIC or priority interrupts controllers does the same.

4.4 TYPES OF BUSES

1.4.1 Synchronous and Asynchronous Buses

When several devices like CPU, memory and I/O devices are connected it acts as a **bus-master** and the other unit acts as a **bus-slave**. A master supervises a slave. Usually, CPU is a bus master and memory and I/O devices are slaves. **But please remember that I/O controllers also serve as bus-masters.** Only bus masters can initiate data transfers even if slaves make a request for data transfers.

Also note that once the data transfer is initiated, both master and slave participate equally in the data transfer process. This data transfer can be done by two methods –

(*a*) Synchronous data transfer.

(*b*) Asynchronous data transfer.

Let us study them one by one now.

(*a*) Synchronous data transfer

In this method, all devices will derive the timing information from a common clock. Signal. Next, we draw a timing diagram for synchronous I/O transfer as in Fig. 4.3.

(1) At time, t_0, CPU places the device address on the address lines of system bus and sets the control lines to perform the input operation.

(2) During time, $t_0 - t_1$, the addressed device gets the address and it recognizes that an input operation is requested.

(3) At time, t_1, address device places its data on the data bus.

(4) At time, t_2, CPU reads the data lines and loads the data from data bus into its input buffer.

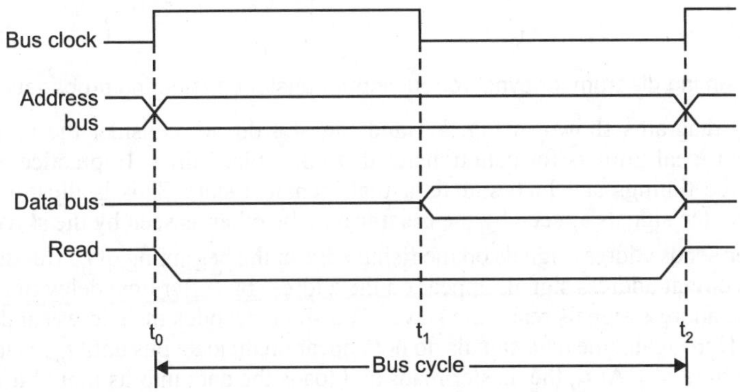

Fig. 4.3. Timing diagram for synchronous input transfers

Similarly, the timing diagram for an output operation is shown in Fig. 4.4. Herein, CPU places output data on the data lines when it transmits the address and control line information.

1. At time, t_1 the addressed device reads the data lines and loads the data into its data buffer.
2. CPU assumes that at t_2, the output data have been received by the I/O device and the cycle ends.

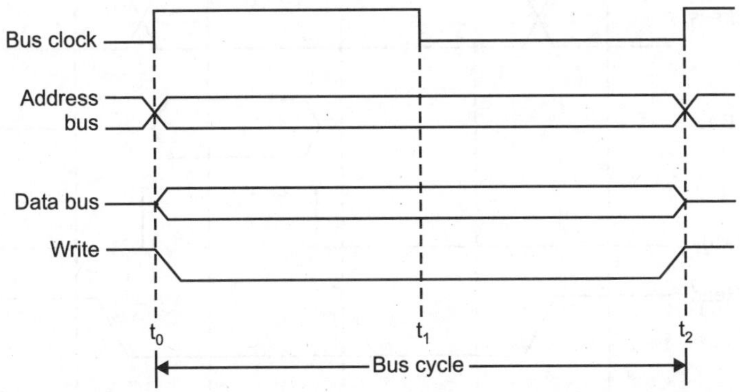

Fig. 4.4. Timing diagram for synchronous output transfer

In synchronous system, the clock pulse width should be chosen such that it is greater than the maximum propagation delay between the processor and any of the devices connected to the bus. **During read operation,** the clock pulse width must be large enough to allow all devices to decode the address and control signals so that the addressed device can be ready to respond at time t_1.

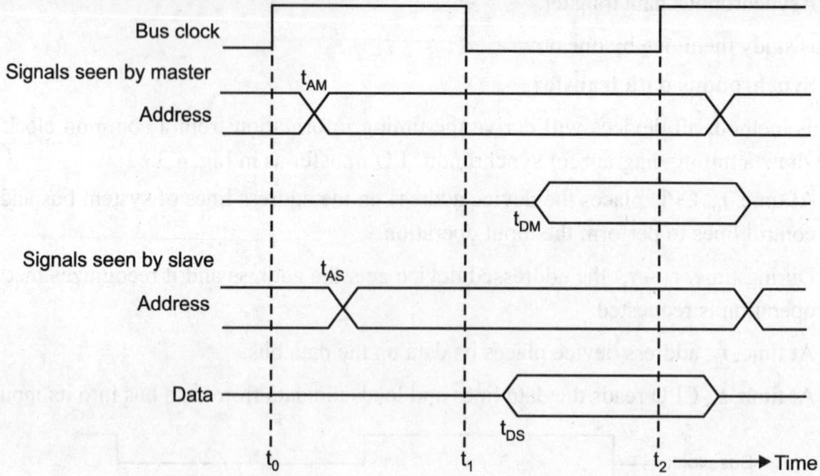

Fig. 4.5. Timing diagram for synchronous input transfer considering propagation delays

The timing diagrams shown in Fig. 4.3 and Fig. 4.4 do not consider the propagation delay so they represent ideal timings for data transfer that takes place lines. In practice the propagation delays, delays the timings at which signals actually change state. This is illustrated in Fig. 4.5. Figure 4.5 shows the signals as seen by the **master** and the other as seen by the **slave.**

The master sends address signals on the rising edge at the beginning of t_0. But due to the delays in the bus drive circuit address signals appear on the address bus after time delay of t_{AM}. After some delay, at t_{AS}, the address signals reach the slave. **The slave** decodes the address and at t_1 sends the requested data. Here again, the data signals do not appear on the data bus until t_{ps}. Data signals reach to the master at time t_{DM}. At t_2, the master reads and loads the data into its input buffer. The time $t_2 - t_{DM}$ is known as data setup time for master's input buffer. The data must continue to be valid after t_2 for a period equal to the hold time of the master's input buffer.

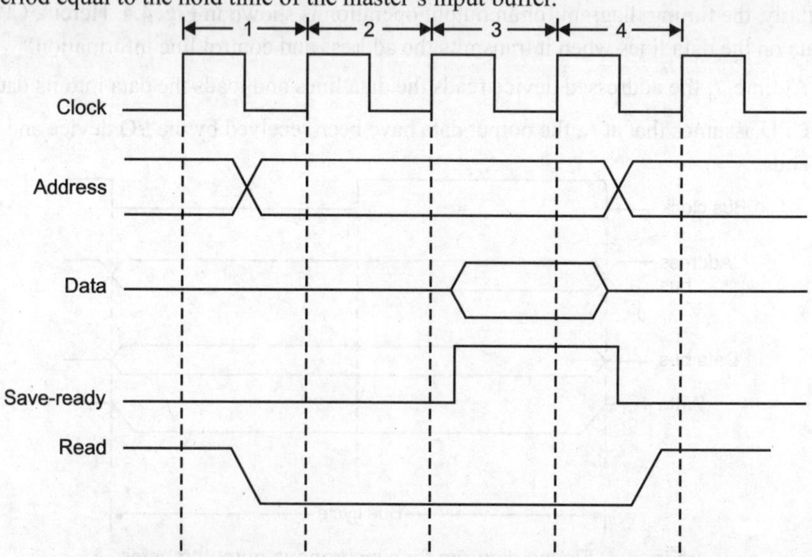

Fig. 4.6. Modified synchronous input data transfer with multiple clock cycles

Disadvantages

1. Because a transfer has to be completed within one clock cycle, the clock period, $t_2 - t_0$, must be selected to accommodate the longest delays on the bus and the slowest device interface. This forces all devices to operate at the speed of the slowest device.
2. There is no way determining whether the slave is responding to data transfer or not.

To overcome above mentioned limitations most of the buses includes control signals that represent a response from the device and use high frequency clock signals such that a complete data transfer cycle would span several clock cycles. Then, the number of clock cycles involved can vary from one device to another and operating speed is not decided by the slowest device. The Fig. 4.6 shows the timing diagram for modified synchronous input data transfer with multiple clock cycles.

(*b*) Asynchronous data transfer

In asynchronous bus, the common clock is eliminated and data transfer on the system bus is achieved by the use of a hand shake between the processor and the device being addressed. Here, the clock line is replaced by two control signals Ready and Accept.

(*a*) **For input operation,** processor places the address and sets the control lines to perform the input operation at t_0. It then indicates at t_1 to the addressed device that it is ready to accept data by activating the Ready line. *W* hen the addressed device receives, the Ready signals, it places the data on the data bus at t_2 and then informs the accept line. Upon activation of Accept line processor reads data from the data bus and loads it into the input buffer. The timing diagram for input operation is as shown in Fig. 4.7. At t_4 processor removes the address and controls information from bus.

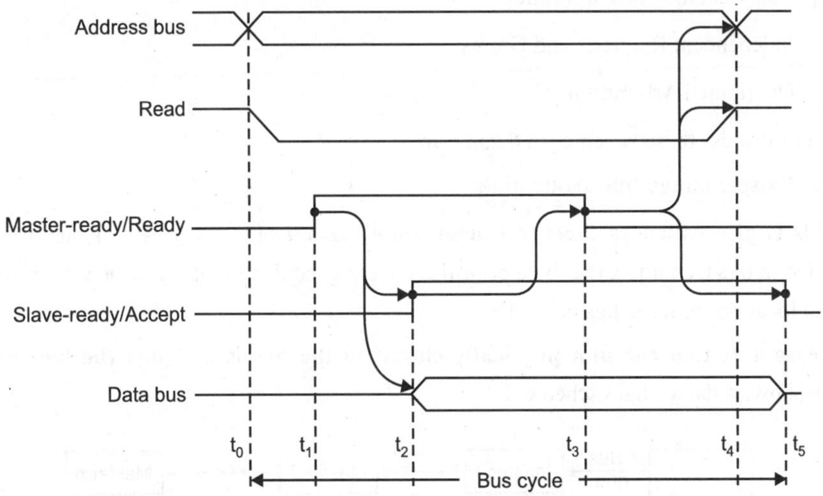

Fig. 4.7. Timing diagram for asynchronous input transfer

When the device interface receives the 1 to 0 transition of master ready signal, it removes the data and slave-ready signal from the bus. This completes the input data transfer.

(*b*) **For output operation,** processor places the address, data and sets the control lines to perform the output operation. It then indicates to the addressed device that it has send data by activating Ready signal. The addressed device reads the data into its input buffer when it receives Ready signal. It then indicates that it has done so by activating the Accept signal.

The timing diagram for **output operation** is as shown ion Fig. 4.8.

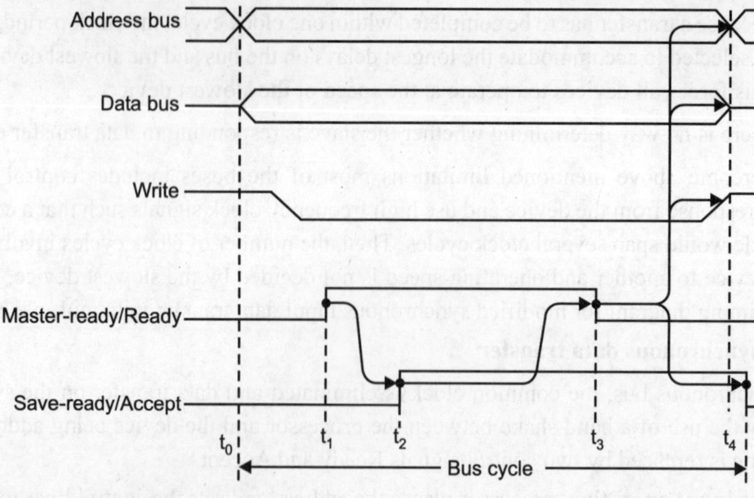

Fig. 4.8. Timing diagram for asynchronous output transfer

4.4.2 BUS ARBITRATIONS

The process of selecting the next bus master is known as arbitration. The duration of a master's control of the bus is called bus tenure. The different bus arbitration schemes are:

(*a*) Daisy-chained bus arbitration.

(*b*) Independent Requests and Grants.

(*c*) Distributed Arbitration.

Let us discuss these schemes in detail now.

1. Daisy-chained bus arbitration

This is also called as a central arbitration scheme. It uses a central bus arbiter or bus controller. In this technique, the fixed priorities are assigned to all units or devices according to their physical location from the bus controller.

Please note that the unit physically closest to the bus is assigned the highest priority. Fig. 4.9 shows a daisy chain scheme.

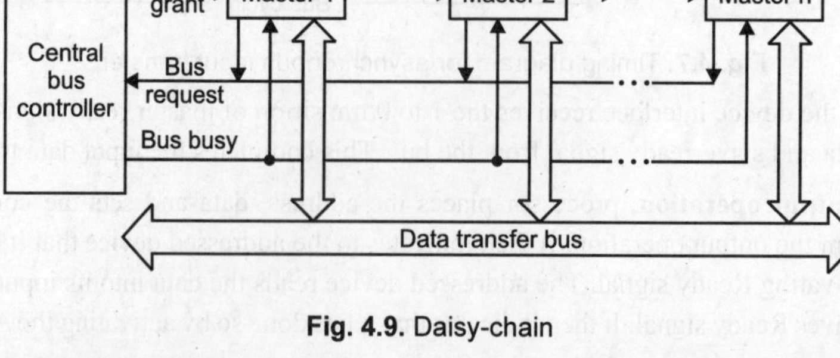

Fig. 4.9. Daisy-chain

Observe that the potential masters are **daisy-chained in a cascade.** A fixed priority is set in a daisy-chain **from left to right. Whenever a higher-priority device fails, all the lower priority devices on the right of the daisy-chain cannot use the bus. Please note that we need to bypass a failing device** or **remove the device from the daisy-chain itself.**

The bus transaction timing is shown in Fig. 4.10 below:

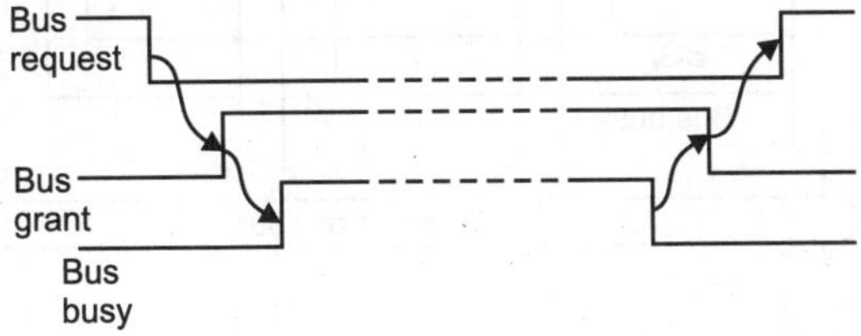

Fig. 4.10. Daisy-chain bus timing

Each master can send a bus request. However, all requests share the same bus-request line. A shown in Fig. 4.10, the bus is busy only when the Grant of Bus is given and grant is given if a bus is requested. The reverse process occurs when the bus is released.

Advantages of Daisy-chaining

1. Simplicity
2. Low cost.
3. It requires the minimum number of control lines irrespectively of the expansion of the system or number of master units.

Drawbacks of Daisy-chaining

1. The priorities of the units are dependent on their physical location.
2. The bus arbitration is slow because of the propagation delay of bus grant signal.
3. When the system is expanded, the propagation delay goes on increasing for the newly added units.
4. The failure of one unit breaks down the system ahead from failed unit.

II. Independent Requests and Grants

It is also possible to have a independent multiple bus-request and bus-grant signal lines for each potential master.

In this scheme, no daisy-chaining is used. Still we have a common central arbiter. Fig. 4.11 shows independent requests with a central arbiter.

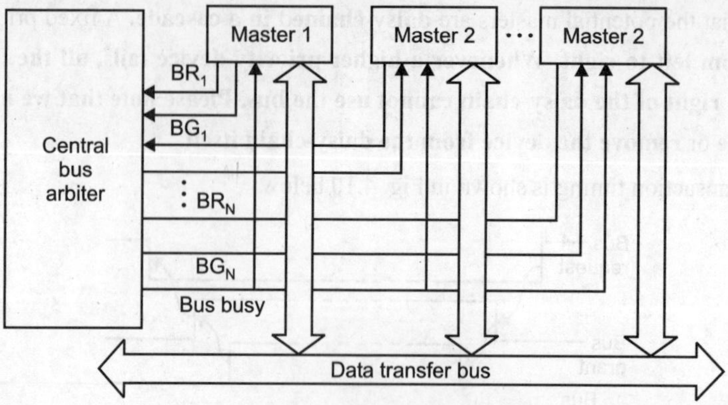

Fig. 4.11. Independent requests method.

Advantages of this scheme are as follows:

1. More flexibility is provided by bus lines.
2. Faster arbitration as compared to daisy-chaining.

Disadvantages of this scheme –

Large number of arbitration lines are required.

III. Distributed Arbitration

In this scheme, each Master has its own arbiter. Each of these arbiters is given a unique arbitration number (id). This id is used to resolve arbitrations. When two or more devices complete for the bus, the winner is the one whose arbitration number is largest.

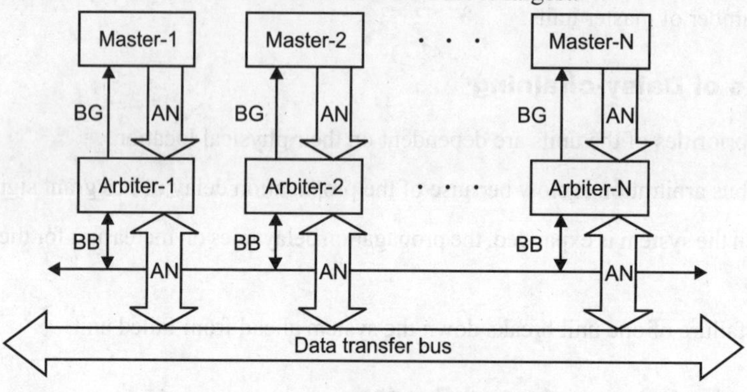

Fig. 4.12. Distributed arbiter scheme.

As distributed arbiter scheme is shown Fig. 4.12

BG – Bus Grant.

BB – Bus Busy

AN – Arbitration Number.

All masters (1 to N) send their arbitration numbers to the shared bus request grant (SBRG) lines on the arbitration bus via their own arbiters.

Each arbiter compares the resulting number on the SBRG lines with its own arbitration number. If the SBRG number is grater, the requester is dismissed. At the end, the winner's arbitration number remains on the arbitration bus after the current bus takes the control of the bus. **Please note that this policy is also priority based. For example,** Multibus II and Future bus use such a scheme.

4.5 TYPES OF BUSES

4.5.1 ISA Bus

ISA stands for **Industry Standard Architecture** in context of **buses** but it stands for **instruction Set Architecture** in terms of **machine levels.** It does not take full advantage of 32-bit address bus and 32-bit data bus of a 32-bit microprocessor. It reduces the data transfer rate of the system. This problem can be solved to some extent using a 32-bit bus between the CPU and memory and employing a cache on the motherboard of the computer.

Its **advantage** is its low cost and availability of many peripheral boards for it.

Its **disadvantage** is that it is not suitable for a multi-user and multitasking system because of its low data transfer rate.

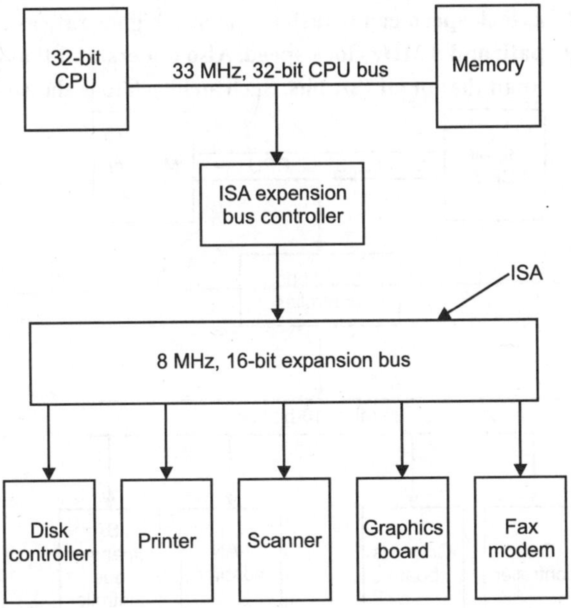

Fig. 4.13. Typical ISA bus architecture for 32-bit CPU

4.5.2 EISA Bus

EISA stands for **Extended Industry Standard Architecture**. It is used in 32-bit address bus and 32-bit data bus to fulfill the needs of a 32-bit microprocessor. **Please note that the data transfer rate of EISA is twice that of ISA.** For a multiuser / multitasking system ISA bus is not suitable because it has low data transfer rate and there is no mechanisms. **Also note that EISA bus architectures are suitable for multiuser system.** The EISA bus system is 100% compatible with ISA 8-bit and 16-bit expansion boards and software.

EISA connector contains two layers of contacts. The **top layer contacts** are the contacts for ISA signals and the **bottom layer** contacts are the contacts for additional EISA signals.

Do You Know?

The physical size of ISA bus connector and EISA bus are same. So, either ISA or EISA cards can be inserted in the EISA connector slot.

4.5.3 MCA Bus

MCA stands for **Micro Channel Architecture.** MCA bus has been developed by IBM. MCA contains the same types of signals and performs the same function as an EISA bus but same function as an EISA but the MCA and EISA bus architecture are completely incompatible. Both MCA and EISA are intelligent buses with high band width

4.5.4 Local BUS

ISA, EISA and MCA buses are not able to fulfill the data transfer rate required by 32-bit and 64-bit microprocessor available today. **Please understand that a local bus system with its 32-bit data path and 33 MHz clock speed can transfer data at a higher rate as compared to ISA bus which has 16-bit data path and 8 MHz clock speed. Also understand that its data transfer rate is about 6 times faster than that of an ISA bus.** Such architecture is shown in Fig. 4.14

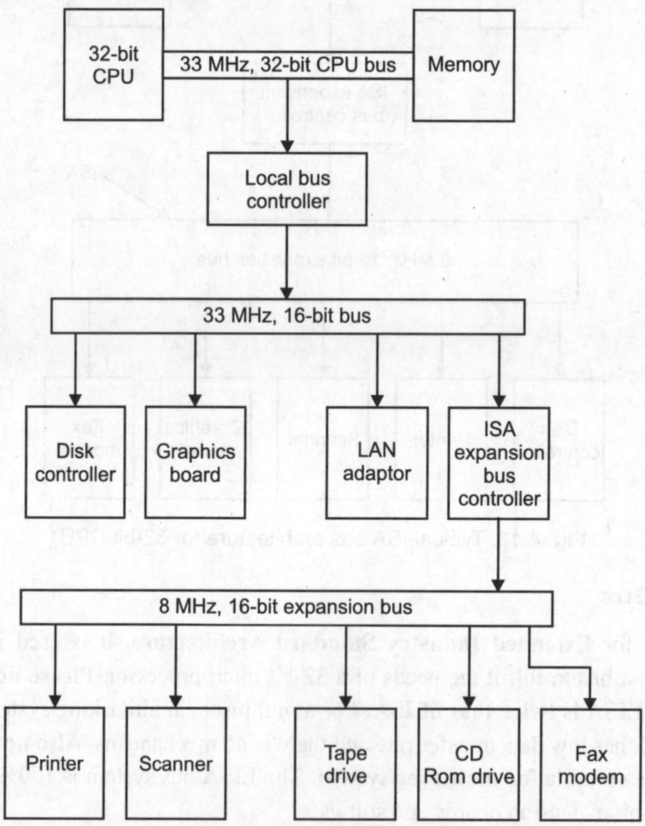

Fig. 4.14. Local Bus Architecture

There are two local bus standards –

(*i*) Video Electronics Standards Association (VESA) VL.

(*ii*) Peripheral Component Interconnected (PCI).

Let us explain these now.

VL bus is VESA local bus developed in 1992. It is suitable for graphics applications but it cannot be used to improve the speed of other compatible peripherals. The VL architecture incorporates a bus controller to CPU. The VL bus recently uses a 64-bit expansion capability and a physical slot. It includes only one hardware interrupt control line which is used to look into an ISA, EISA or MCA bus.

In 1992, VL BUS 20 ver. was released with the release of Intel's 64-bit Pentium microprocessor and it provides a 64-bit interface.

PCI (or Peripheral component Interconnect) was developed by Intel. It is a 32-bit local bus which extends the processor's own local bus. It can be expanded to 64-bit, if required. It is a costly system. **Please remember that the PCI bus system is able to support ten devices because PCI**

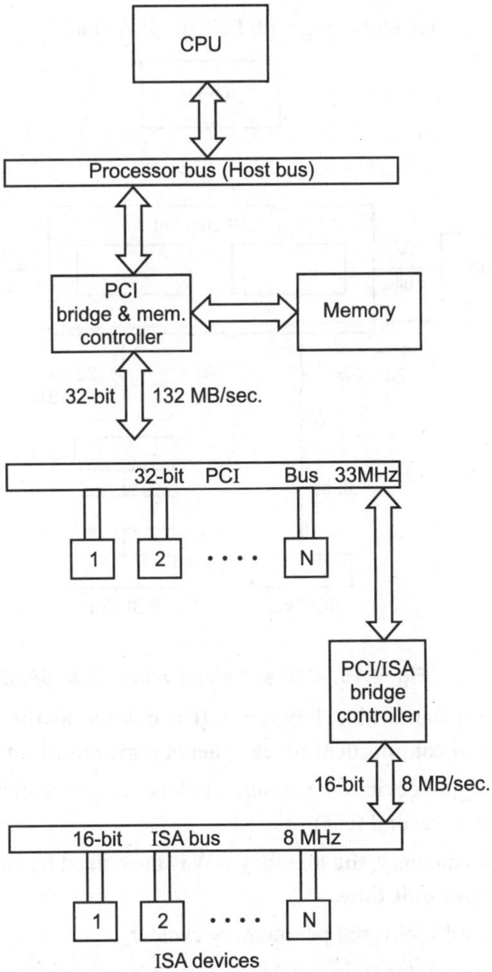

Fig. 4.15. PCI bus and ISA bus shown together

devices do not electrically load down the CPU bus. On the other hand, VL bus supports only three local bus peripherals. The PCI bus system can transfer data at a rate of 130 MB per second at 33 MHz. It is a high performance connection between the motherboard components and expansion boards of a system. The PCI bus employs connector (188 pins for a 64-bit system). PCI specifies for two types of connection-5V system and 3.3 V on power system. Its design has ability to support future generations of peripherals. PCI bus architecture is shown in Fig. 4.15.

4.5.5 AGP

It stands for **Accelerated Graphics Port.** It is a 32-bit expansion slot or bus. It is specifically designed for video card. It is an improvement over PCI bus. **AGP generates and processes pixels.** It receives commands from the CPU and then converts the graphics command into a data stream and keeps analog to digital converter (ADC) that receives information from the local memory and controls the intensity of RGB (Read, Blue and Green) electron beam. It's data transfer rate is 528 MB/Sec or more. It operates at the processor bus speed. It handles data transfer to PCI bus simultaneously.

Fig. 4.16 shows an AGP slot along with PCI and ISA slots.

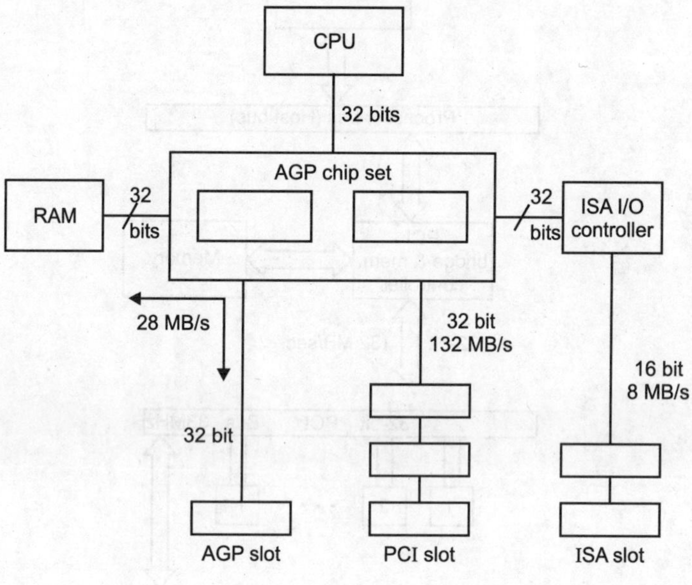

Fig. 4.16. AGP slot along with PCI & ISA slots

We define the term Bandwidth (BW) here. **It is defined as the amount of data that can be transmitted via a given communication channel in a given unit of time.**

For e.g. BW of digital devices is measured in bits per second (bps) and that of analog devices is measured in cycles per second (cps).

In the case of main memory, **the memory BW is measured by the number of memory words that can be accessed per unit time.**

So, W = No. of words delivered per memory cycle, t_m.

∴ Maximum Memory Bandwidth (BM) is given by –

$$B_m = \frac{W}{b_m} \text{ (words/s or bytes/s)}$$

The concept of BW becomes very important when we talk of memory and I/O devices as these devices are sequential, like disks and tapes. Depending upon the latencies and rotational delays, there may be variations in the data transfer rates. Hence, **we define the Bandwidth of a disk as the average data transfer rate.**

For a CPU, the B.W. is measured as the maximum CPU computation rate, B_p. Let t_p be the time taken for processor cycle, t_m be the cycle time for main memory, t_d be the cycle time for I/O devices. As per relationship,

$$t_d > t_m > t_p$$

Before we go further, let us solve an example now.

EXAMPLE 1: A 32-bit PCI system operates at 33 MHz. Calculate the bandwidth.

SOLUTION: Given:

$$\text{Clock frequency } (f) = 33 \text{ MHz}$$

$$\therefore \quad \text{Period} = \frac{1}{f} = \frac{1}{(33 \times 10^6)}$$

One bus cycle transfer 4-bytes in one clock cycle.

$$\therefore \quad \text{B.W.} = 4 \times 33 \times 10^6 \text{ bytes}$$

$$= 133 \text{ MB/sec.}$$

4.5.6 USB-Universal Serial Bus

USB excels the RS 232C serial port in several aspects –

(*a*) Easy installation.

(*b*) Faster transfer rate.

(*c*) Simple cabling.

(*d*) Multiple device connections.

The **main features of USB** are as follows:

1. 127 different devices can be connected on a single USB bus.
2. Initial USB standard supported 12 Mbps transfer rate while USB 2.0 supports **higher rates.**
3. It can support **wide range of low B.W. devices** also like keyboard, mouse, joystick, FDD, printer, scanner etc.
4. Each device is connected to an USB hub. The USB hub is an intelligent unit interacting with the PC on one side and the peripheral devices on other sides. It looks like a multi-tiered star topology. So, a single USB hub **establishes presence of multiple USB devices up to 127.**
5. A USBA device can be connected without powering off a PC. The **plug and play** feature in the BIOS and the USB devices take care of detection, device recognition and handling. The user is totally relieved of configuration procedure.
6. USB controller in PC detects the **presence or absence** of the USB devices.
7. USBs assign an **appropriate level of electrical power.**
8. USBs are **easy to install** as they need only one cable.
9. CPU or software initiates every transaction on the USB bus. So, the overhead on the software increases when large number of peripherals is connected. **Hence, USBs are said to be host centric.**
10. **Wireless USB** called as WUSB has also been developed.

4.5.7 IEEE 1394, 1284 and 488 bus

IEE 1394 (Firewire)

Firewire was initially introduced by Apple-PC and later on standardized by IEEE 1394. It is a **standard** for high-speed serial data transfer. Firewire's connector connects a number of serial devices in a daisy chain fashion. Even multimedia devices can be connected. Some of the main features of **Firewire** are as follows:

1. It is limited to shorter distances than USB bus.
2. Both (USB + Firewire) can be used so that a device serves as a link to another device.
3. It is faster than USB bus – 400 Mbps (30 times higher B.W. than USB).
4. Multiple devices, up to 63, can be connected.
5. Each device on a firewire bus forms a node unlike USB.
6. Firewire supports **isochronous data transfers** that are suitable for digital video and other time critical media. **Please understand that the isochronous data transfer guarantees timely delivery of data between the nodes.** This is so because once a device is connected to the firewire bus, it consumes on allocated portion of the bandwidth so as to assure the **timely delivery of data.** Automatically, the bus allocates 10 MB/sec for serial command overhead and the rest for the devices. **Also understand that once the firewire bus bandwidth is exhausted, it does not recognize the remaining devices.**
7. It supports DMA transfers also unlike USB.
8. This cable can be **easily extended** also. Actually, it is possible to plug in a device to a PC and then plug other device into the device which has already been connected.
9. IEEE 1394 (or firewire) has four wires – two for power supply and two for sending data and commands.

IEEE 1284

Its main features are –

1. It is a standard to interface peripheral device to the parallel port of a computer.
2. Devices like printer, CD-ROM, HDD etc. can be easily connected to a parallel port.
3. It has five modes of operation.
   ***(a)* Centronics mode / compatibility mode.** It is used for printer connection.
   ***(b)* EPP (Enhance Parallel Port) and ECP (Extended Capability Port). EPP** is a super parallel port design for bidirectional data flow. Its data transfer rate is up to 2 MBPs. It was developed by Intel, Xirecon and Zenith. **ECP** (by HP) provides channels to transfer data simultaneously. **For eg.** In a print-fax-scan machine, it is possible to print and receive fax simultaneously.

IEEE 488

1. To connect various devices, HP, developed HP Interface bus (HPTB). IEEE later on accepted it as a standard called as IEEE 488.
2. It is also known as a General Purpose Interface BUS (GPIB).
3. It uses 24-wire cable.
4. 8-10 devices can be connected in a daisy-chain fashion.

5. The bus includes 8 **bidirectional data lines, five bus management lines and three handshake lines.** Here, the bidirectional lines are used to transfer data, addresses, commands and status bytes. The **handshake signals** coordinate the transfer of data bytes on the data lines. Whereas the bus management lines send signals for resort, interrupt etc. to indicate for instance, end of data block transfer.

4.6 TIMING AND CONTROL

In a computer, the timing for all registers is controlled by a master clock generator. The clock pulses do not change the state of a register unless the register is enabled by a control signal. The control signals are generated in the control unit and provide control inputs for the multiplexer's in the common bus, control inputs in a processor registers and micro operations for the accumulator.

There are two types of control organizations –

(*a*) Hardwired control.

(*b*) Microprogrammed control.

Let us define and compare them in a tabular form.

Features	Hardwired Control	Microprogrammed control
1. Speed	Fast	Slow
2. Control functions	Implemented in hardware	Implement in software
3. Flexibility	Not flexible to accommodate new system specifications or new instructions.	More flexible to accommodate new system specification or new instructions redesign is required easier.
4. Ability to handle large instruction sets.	Somewhat difficult	Easier.
5. Ability to support OS	Very difficult	Easy
6. Design process	Somewhat complicated	Orderly and syst4matic
7. Applications	Mostly RISC microprocessors	Mainframes and some microprocessor
8. Instruction set size	Under 100 instructions	Over 100 instructions
9. ROM Size	–	2K to 10 K by 20-400 bit microinstructions.
10. Chip area efficiency	Uses least area	Uses more area.

4.7 INSTRUCTION CYCLE, MACHINE CYCLE AQND *T*-STATES

The CPU fetches one instruction from the memory at a time and executes it. **The sequence of steps required by the CPU to fetch and execute on instruction is called as an instruction cycle (IC).** An IC consists of a fetch cycle and an execute cycle i.e.

Total time required to execute an instruction $(IC) = FC + EC$

Where FC = Time required for fetch cycle.

EC = Time required for execution cycle.

Please understand that the fetch and execute cycles are carried out in synchronization with the clock. Also, understand that in the fetch cycle, CPU fetches the opcode of the instruction from the memory. And the steps required to acquire the data from the memory and complete the operation that is specified in the instruction is the job of the **Execute Cycle (EC).**

Actually, an **instruction fetch operation** causes an instruction byte that consists of opcode, to be fetched from the memory. The fetch operation involves three steps –

Step 1: Send the address of the next instruction to the memory.

Step 2: Get the instruction code from the memory.

Step 3: Update the program counter (PC).

To start with, the CPU sends the address of the memory location from where the opcode is to be fetched. Then, the CPU reads that instruction byte in the instruction decoder. The instruction is then decoded in the instruction decoder where the type of instruction, its size and the task to be completed is specified. The CPU transfers the opcode, data and address depending on the **entire process called as decoding**. So, we can show these fetch – execute cycle as follows:

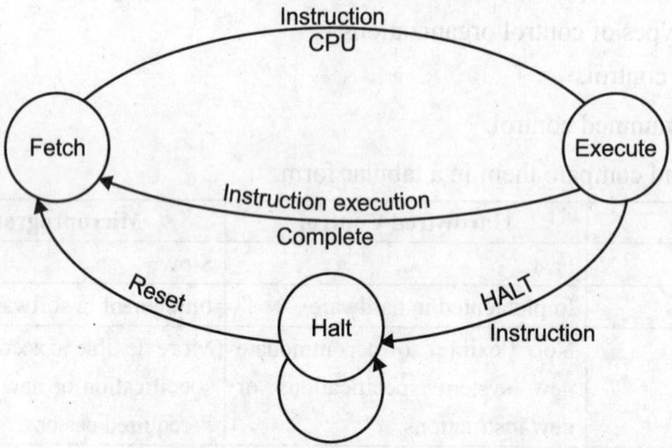

Fig. 4.17. STD for fetch – execute cycle

From Fig. 4.17, it is crystal clear that the fetch and execute cycles of instruction will toggle among, from one to the other. Firstly, the fetch operation is completed and thus now the instruction code is available. The CPU then executes this instruction and will go for fetch operation of the next instruction. **Please note that the switching shown in the state transition diagram (STD) of figure 4.17, is applicable for all instructions except HALT (HLT) instruction. Also note that when the HALT instruction is executed, CPU enters the HALT Loop.** So, it will not go for fetch operation. CPU will remain in the HALT loop and will poll (check) for the reset signal. When a reset is applied, it will return back to fetch operation. **Let us tabulate the differences between the fetch cycle (FC) and execution cycle (EC) in a tabular form now.**

Fetch Cycle	Execution Cycle
1. The CPU performs fetch cycle to access instruction codes from program memory.	1. The CPU performs execution cycles to access data memory, stack memory and I/O devices.
2. During a fetch cycle, the CPU performs only **read operation**.	2. During an execution cycle, the CPU performs **either read or write operation.**
3. The number of fetch cycles present in an instruction cycle depends upon the length of instruction like, for a 2-byte instruction,	3. The number of execution cycles present in an instruction cyclic depends upon the type of instruction, addressing mode and the length of the operand.

Fetch Cycle	Execution Cycle
4. Here, the contents of PC are placed on the address bus.	4. The contents of stack printer (SP), GPRs (General Purpose Registers), temporary registers are placed on the address bus.
5. PC is incremented by 1.	5. PC is NOT incremented.

On the other hand, **the time required by the CPU or microprocessor to complete the operation of accessing memory or I/O device is called as a machine cycle.** So, operations like opcode fetch, memory read, memory write, I/O read, I/O write are all performed in a machine cycle. Thus, an instruction cycle (IC) consists of several machine cycles. Actually, CPU performs an operation in a specific time period i.e. specific clock cycles. **Each clock cycle is called as a T-state. And the number of T-states required to perform an operation is called as a machine cycle.** This relationship is shown in Fig. 4.18.

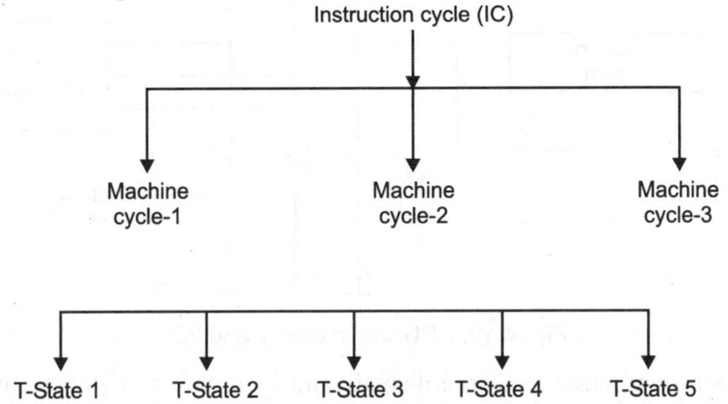

Fig. 4.18. Relationship between IC, MC and T-states

Each machine cycle consists of 3 to 6 clock periods/cycles which are known as T-states. **Please note here that one IC consists of 1 to 5 machine cycles and 1 machine cycle consists of 3 to 6 *T*-states.**

For eg. There are seven different types of machine cycles in 8085 microprocessor. There are three status signals – IO/M, *S*1 and *S*0. **Please note that these status signals identity each type of machine cycle. Also note that these signals are generated at the beginning of each machine cycle and they remain valid for the entire duration of the cycle.**

4.8 CPU WITH MEMORY AND I/O

As we know that the CPU acts as the brain of our computer system. It is the **heart** of any system but CPU has a limited storage capacity. So, it depends on memory to hold data and programs and to save results. We have a simple equation for CPU now.

CPU = Control Unit + ALU + Registers

A **Control unit** monitors the sequences of instructions, **ALU or Arithmetic and Logic Unit**, performs a simple arithmetic and logical operations. **But please understand that every different processor type has its own design of different instruction-set, register, buses, microoperations, machine instructions, addressing modes and so on. Also understand that it is our CPU that fetches, decodes and executes program instructions.**

A CPU with memory and I/O are shown in Fig. 4.19. From figure we find that CPU has two main parts – Data Path and Control path.

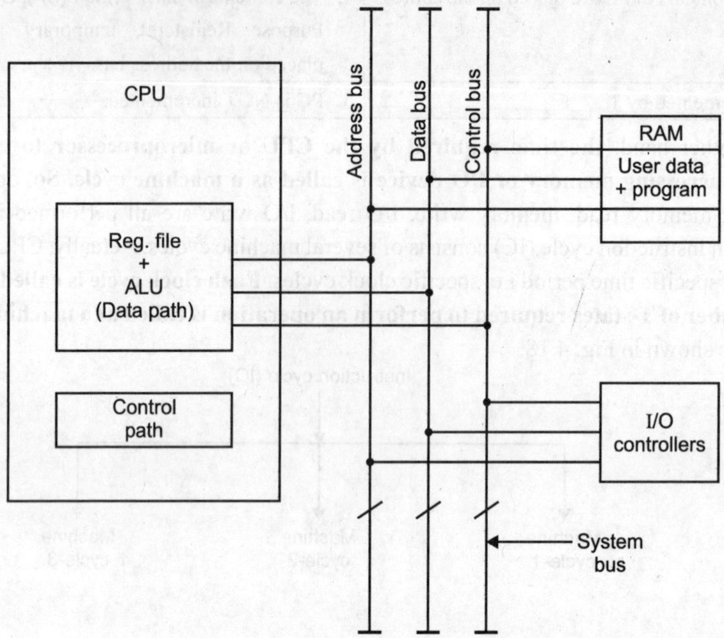

Fig. 4.19. CPU with memory and I/O

The **data path** unit consists of an arithmetic and logic unit and storage registers that are interconnected by a data bus-which itself is connected to the main memory.

The **Register File / Array** is a storage location within the CPU. **Please note that registers hold data that can be readily accessed by CPU as registers are faster than memories. Also note that registers can be implemented using D flip-flops.**

ALU is a complex unit that needs to be designed. It performs all arithmetic (like addition subtraction, left and right shifts, multiply and divide unit etc) and logical operations (like AND, OR, NOT, NAND, NOR etc.).

The **Control Path** (see Fig. 4.19) decodes and monitors the execution of instructions and coordinates the operations. It is the system clock that synchronizes the activities of the CPU (measured in clock cycles (GHz)). Various CPU components perform operations as per the signals generated by the control unit. We shall study this a bit later. ALU works as directed by the control unit. **Please understand that it is this control unit that determines which actions to carry out according to the values in the PC (Program counter) register and a status register.** To synchronize these activities, a fixed number of **clock cycles** are required. It is this clock frequency (in MHz or GHz) that determines the speed with which all operations are carried out.

4.9 SIMPLE CPU FUNCTIONS

A CPU fetches instruction (i.e. binary executable like .EXE files) from the main memory. Each instruction (e.g. add, load, store etc.) must be decoded in the CPU. Once the instruction is decoded in the CPU, it can be executed by issuing commands to ALU and manipulating operands in the

CPU registers. After one instruction is completed, the next one can be fetched from the memory for execution. So, a CPU execution cycle is shown in Fig. 4.20. It shows four steps –

1. **Fetch:** To fetch next instruction using PC from Main Memory Instruction Register (IR).
2. **Decode:** To understand or interpret the instruction.
3. **Operand fetch:** To get data from main memory or I/O.
4. **Execute:** To run the instruction and send back the result of computation to memory or I/O device.

Hence, we can say that a CPU performs an instruction cycle (IC). IC is defined as a procedure the CPU goes through to process an instruction again and again to complete a program.

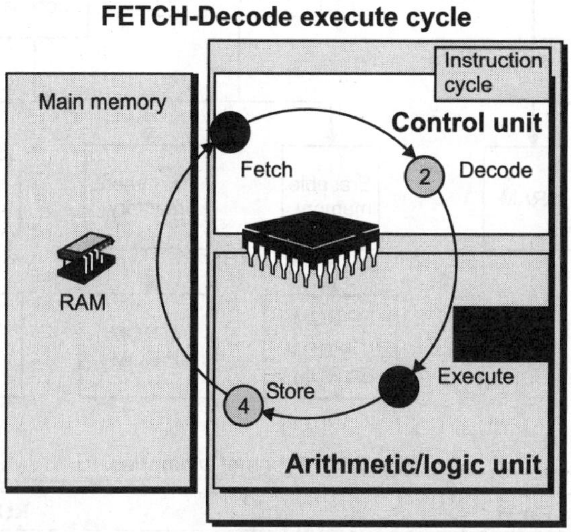

Fig. 4.20. CPU in a loop

4.10 MEMORY AND ITS TYPES

Memory is needed to store data (called as data memory) and programs (called as a program memory). Memory is viewed as a set of contiguous bytes. Each byte has an address. **The total number of bits, a memory can store is called as its capacity.** A byte is comprised of 8-bits where each of these bits is a **flip flop or a cell.** Memories are classified as follows –

Basically, memory is of two types –

(*a*) Prime or Main Memory (MM).

(*b*) Secondary or AUX Memory.

Prime memory (or primary) is of two types –

(*a*) RAM – Random Access Memory.

(*b*) ROM – Read Only Memory.

Let us compare RAM and ROM in a tabular form now.

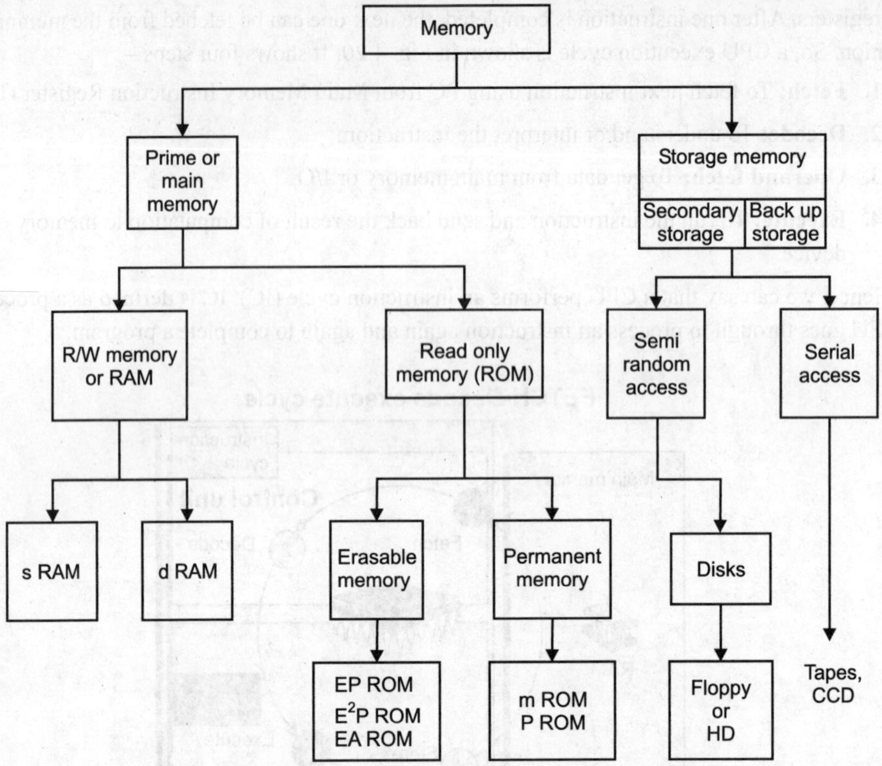

Fig. 4.21. Types of Memories

RAM	ROM
1. Only reading and writing can be done.	1. Only reading can be done.
2. It is a sort of temporary storage.	2. It is a sort of permanent storage.
3. It is of two types – sRAM and dRAM	3. It is of three types – PROM, EPROM / E^{2}PROM and EAROM.
4. It is used in calculators, computers etc.	4. It can be used in computers, embedded storages etc.
5. It is volatile memory i.e. contents are erased when electrical power is switched off.	5. It is non-volatile as contents are not lost.

RAM is of two types –

(*a*) sRAM or static RAM.

(*b*) dRAM or dynamic RAM.

Let us compare the two in a tabular form.

sRAM	dRAM
1. Each sRAM cell is a flip-flop	1. Each DRAM cell consists of one MOSFET and a capacitor.
2. It has more number of components per cell.	2. It has only 20 components as above.
3. Refreshing is not required.	3. Refreshing is periodically done.

sRAM	dRAM
(4) They are faster memories.	(4) They are slower memories.
(5) It is costlier.	(5) It is cheaper
(6) They are not used as a system's main RAM because of its high cost and lower memory density.	(6) They have high density and low cost/bit that makes them suitable for system's main RAM.

RAM is also of various types –

(*a*) PROM : Programmable ROM

A user can program these ROMs using a PROM programmer. It is programmed only after its fabrication i.e., the contents are permanently fixed.

(*b*) EPROM : Erasable Programmable ROM

We can erase and re-program ROMs either by using UV light (EPROMs) or using electricity (EAROM). EPROM has a quartz window installed on the chip to erase its contents by exposing it to UV light. This exposure is done for 10-15 minutes.

NOTE:	1. UV rays will erase cells at a time.
	2. All erased locations will store a 1.

Also note that selective erasing is not possible here as all locations get erased at a time.

E^2PROM or EE-PROM stores data in form of charges. It uses low voltages (20-26 V) for erasing or programming. We can even erase a particular memory location. This is called as **selective erasing.** It uses MOS circuitry.

4.11 SRAM VERSUS DRAM

Let us comprise sRAM and dRAM now (i.e., static and dynamic RAMs).

sRAM	dRAM
1. Each sRAM cell is a flip-flop.	1. Each DRAM unit consists of one MOSFET and a capacitor.
2. It has more number of components per cell.	2. It has lesser number of components per cell (only two).
3. It has lesser memory cells per unit area.	3. It has more memory cells per unit area.
4. Refreshing is not required as there are no capacitors.	4. Refreshing is required periodically as it uses capacitor and capacitors store charge
5. They are more costly.	5. They are less costly.
6. They are faster memories as their access times are less.	6. They are slower memories as their access times are more.
7. They consume less power.	7. They consume more power.

For example, a ($2^{20} \times 16$) sRAM contains 2^{20} = 4 M words each 16 bytes long. The RAM would need 20 address lines. The total storage capacity is $2^{20} \times 16 = 2^{24}$ bits.

Static RAM

Static RAM is a type of RAM that holds its data without external refresh, for as long as power is supplied the circuit. This is contrasted to dynamic RAM (DRAM), which must be refreshed many times per second in order to hold its data contents. SRAMs are used for specific applications within the PC, where the strengths outweigh their weaknesses compared to DRAM:

- **Simplicity:** SRAMs don't require external refresh circuitry or other work in order for them to keep their data intact.
- **Speed:** SRAM is faster than DRAM.

In contrast, SRAMs have the following weaknesses, compared to DRAMs:

- **Cost:** SRAM is, byte for byte, several times more expensive than DRAM.
- **Size:** SRAMs taken up much more space than DRAMs (which is part of why the cost if higher).

These advantages and disadvantages taken together obviously show that performance-wise, **SRAM is superior to DRAM**, and we would use it exclusively if only we could do so economically. Unfortunately, 32 MB of SRAM would be prohibitively large and costly, which is why DRAM is used for system memory. SRAMs are used instead for level 1 cache and level 2 cache memory, for which it is perfectly suited; cache memory needs to be very fast, and not very large.

SRAM is manufactured in a way similar to how processors are: Highly-integrated transistor patterns photo-etched into silicon. Each SRAM bit is comprised of between four and six transistors, so SRAM takes up much more space compared to DRAM, which uses only one (plus a capacitor). Because an SRAM chip is comprised of thousands or millions of identical cells, it is much easier to make than a CPU, which is a large die with a non-repetitive structure. This is one reason why RAM chips cost much less than processors do.

Dynamic RAM

Dynamic RAM is a type of RAM that only holds its data if it is continuously accessed by special logic called a **refresh circuit.** Many hundreds of times each second, this circuitry reads the contents of each memory cell, whether the memory cell is being used at that time by the computer or not. Due to the way in which the cells are constructed the reading action itself refreshes the contents of the memory. If this is not done regularly, then the DRAM will lose its contents, even if it continues to have power supplied to it. **This refreshing action is the reason as why the memory is called dynamic.**

All PCs use DRAM for their main system memory, instead of SRAM; even though DRAMs are slower than SRAMs and require the overhead of the refresh circuitry. It may seem wired to want to make the computer's memory out of something that can only hold a value of a fraction of a second. In fact, DRAMs are both more complicated and slower than SRAMs.

The reason that DRAMs are used is simple: They are much cheaper and take up much less space, typically 1/4 of the silicon area of SRAMs or less. To build a 64 MB core memory from SRAMs would be very expensive. The overhead of the refresh circuit is tolerated in order to allow the use of large amounts of inexpensive, compact memory. The refresh circuitry itself is almost never a problem; many years of using DRAM has caused the design of these circuits to be all but perfected.

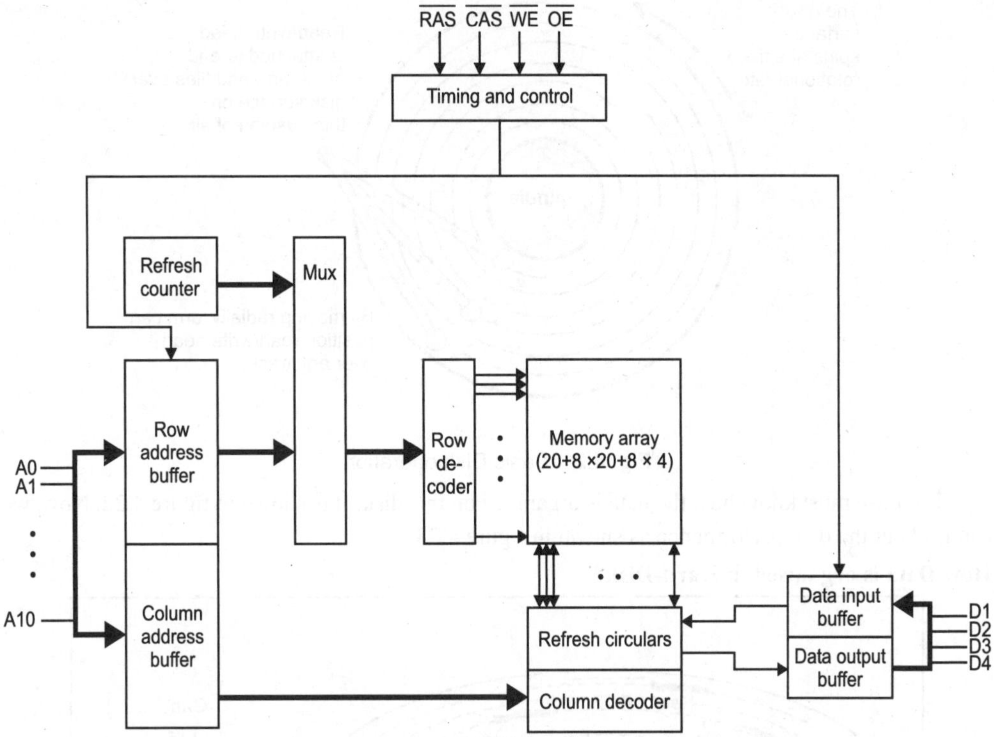

DRAMs are smaller and less expensive than SRAMs because SRAMs are made from four to six transistors (or more) per bit, DRAMs use only one, plus a capacitor. The capacitor, when energized, holds an electrical charge if the bit contains a "1" or no change if it contains a "0". The transistor is used to read the contents of the capacitor. The problem with capacitors is that they only hold a charge for a short period of time, and then it fades away. These capacitors are tiny, so their charges fade particularly quickly. This is why the refresh circuitry is needed: to read the contents of every cell and refresh them with a fresh "charge" before the contents fade away and are lost. Refreshing is done by reading every "row" in the memory chip one row at a time; the process of reading the contents of each capacitor re-establishes the charge. DRAM is manufactured using a similar process to how processors are : a silicon substrate is etched with a patterns that make the transistors and capacitors (and support structures) that comprise each bit. DRAM costs much less than a processor because it is a series of simple, repeated structures, so there isn't the complexity of making a single chip with several million individually-located transistors. There are many different kinds of specific DRAM technologies and speeds that they are available in.

4.12 DISK CAPACITY

First of all let us see, the disk operation.

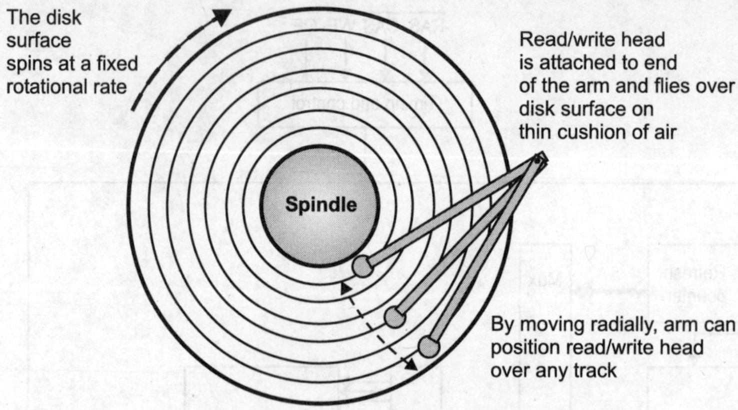

Fig. 4.21. Basic Disk operation

Then, we must know how the data is organized on this disk. It is shown in figure 4.22. Now, we can find out the disk performance as shown in figure 4.23.

How Data is organised in Hard-Disk?

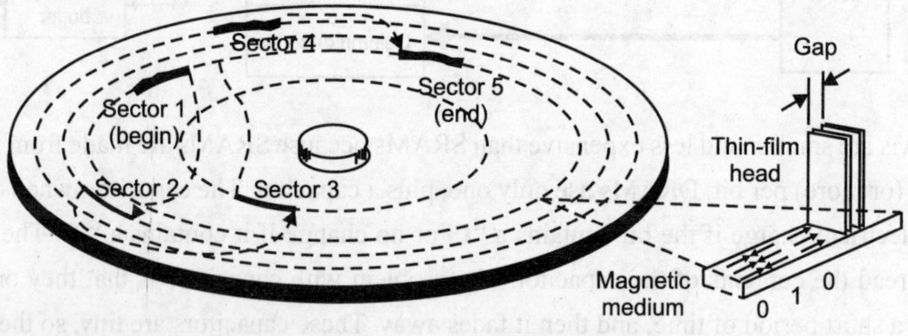

Magnetic recording along the tracks and the red/write head.

0	16	32	48	1	17	33	49	2	
30	46	62	15	31	47	0	16	32	
60	13	29	45	61	14	30	46	62	
27	43	59	12	28	44	60	13	29	

Logical numbering of sectors on several adjacent tracks.

Fig. 4.22. Data Organisation on Disk

Disk Speed

1. **Seek time:** The time in moving head to correct track.
2. **Rotational Latency:** It is the waiting time for data to rotate under head.

$$\textbf{Access Time} = \left(\frac{\textbf{Seek}}{\textbf{time}}\right) + \left(\frac{\textbf{Latency}}{\textbf{time}}\right)$$

Disk performance

Seek time = a + b(c – 1) + b(c – 1)$^{1/2}$

Average rotational latency = (30/rpm) s = (30 000/rpm) ms

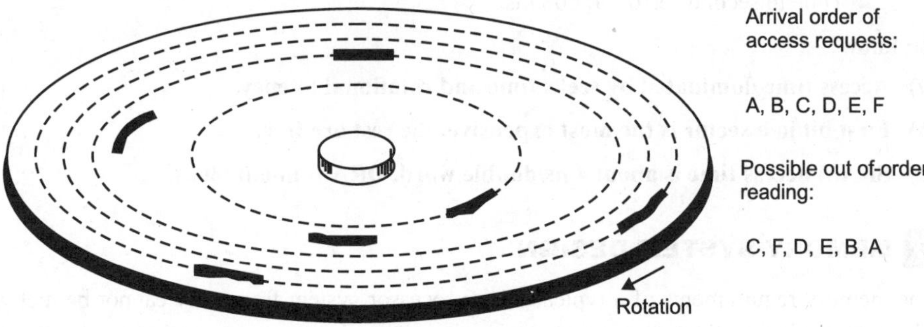

Reducing average seek time and rotational latency by performing dis accesses out of order.

Fig. 4.23. Disk performance

Disk Access Time

Average time to access a specific sector approximated by:

$$T_{access} = T_{avg}\ \textbf{seek} + T_{avg}\ \textbf{rotation} + T_{avg}\ \textbf{transfer-seek-time}\ (T_{avg}\ \textbf{seek})$$

- Time to position heads over cylinder containing target sector.
- Typical T_{avg} seek = 3-5 ms

Rotational Latency (T_{avg} Rotation)

- Time waiting for first bit of largest sector to pass under R/W head.
- T_{avg} rotation = 1/2 × 1/RPMs × 60 sec/1 min. For example, 3 ms for 10,00 rpm disk.

Transfer Time (T_{avg} Transfer)

- Time to read the bits in the target sector.

  T_{avg} transfer = 1/RPM × 1/(avg # sectors/ track) × 6 secs/1 min

  For example, 0.006 ms for 10,000 rpm disk with 1,000 sectors/track Given: 512-byte sectors, 86 MB/s data transfer rate.

Disk Access Time: Example

Given

- Rotational rate = 7,200 rpm
- Average seek time = 5 ms
- Avg # sectors / track = 1000

Derived Average Time to Access Random Sector

- T_{avg} rotation = 1/2 × (60 secs/7200 RPM) × 1000 ms/sec = 4 ms.
- T_{avg} transfer =- 60/7200 RPM × 1/400 secs/track × 1000 ms/sec = 0.008 ms.
  - T_{access} = 5 ms + 4 ms + 0.008 ms = 9.008 ms.
  - Time to second sector : 0.008 ms

Do you know?

(*a*) **Access time dominated by seeks time and rotational latency.**

(*b*) **First bit in a sector is the most expensive, the rest are free.**

(*c*) **SRAM access time is about 4 ns/double word, DRAM about 60 ns.**

4.13 MEMORY SYSTEM DESIGN

The memory requirements of a typical microprocessor system frequently cannot be met with a single memory device. Several memory devices must then be interconnected to form a memory system. In a memory system, capacity is expanded **by increasing the number of words and/or by increasing the word length** above that attainable from a single memory device. Word length is increased by placing the outputs of two or more memory devices in parallel. For example, m, 16 K × 1-bit memories can be arranged in parallel to make a 16 K × m-bit memory system.

The number of words in a memory system is increased by multiplexing outputs from two or more memory devices. Memory devices have features that facilitate this. For example, chip select or chip enable inputs are provided on individual memory devices for this purpose.

A memory system with an increased number of words requires a provision for address expansion. **Expanding the number of memory address bits to which the memory system responds.** The number of address bits that a microprocessor provides dictates its **memory address space** or the range of memory locations it can be directly address. A memory system can be designed to fill the entire memory address space of microprocessor with which it is used, although most applications do not require that much memory.

Depending on the size of the memory system, external address decoding logic, in addition to the memory's chip select inputs, may also be required for address expansion. This external logic decodes the additional address it's required to select a memory device. MSI decoders, which decode two, three, or four inputs, are often used for this purpose.

The additional address lines required for memory expansion are connected to the decoder's inputs, and the decoder's outputs provide the signals for the chip select inputs of the memory devices. Decoders, themselves, may also have one or more enable inputs for the purpose of interconnecting decoders to create a larger decoder.

When memory devices are combined to form a memory system, with an expanded number of words, the corresponding data outputs of the memory devices must be multiplexed to form a single set of data outputs for the entire memory system. The output buffers on each memory devices are three-state to allow the multiplexing of output data from several memory devices. Address decoding logic decodes the higher order address bits and enables the three-state outputs of only one memory device.

Memory systems are designed to provide the required amount of ROM and RWM needed for a particular application. **The design steps may be described as follows:**

1. Estimate the amount of ROM and RWM required for the application.
2. Determine the address boundaries for each type of memory. Draw an initial memory map.
3. Select the memory devices to be used.
4. Determine the arrangement of memory devices necessary to provide the required word length and number of words. Draw the detailed memory map.
5. Design the address decoding logic.
6. Determine the buffering required, if any.
7. Determine the required speed of the memory devices.

SUMMARY

In this chapter, we have studied about bus and memory. We have seen how an instruction is executed by the CPU. Various bus standards have been dealt with. We have also seen the internal disk organization and computed its capacity. Finally, we have listed the steps needed for a good memory design.

MULTIPLE CHOICE QUESTIONS [MCQs]

Q. 1. A group of wires performing a single function is known as a

(*a*) Cable (*b*) UTP
(*c*) Bus (*d*) None of the above

Ans. (*c*)

Q. 2. The bus over which the CPU send out the address of the memory location is called as a –

(*a*) Address Bus (*b*) Data bus
(*c*) Control Bus (*d*) Common bus

Ans. (*a*)

Q. 3. If there are N address lines then it can directly address

(*a*) 2^N memory locations (*b*) 2N memory locations
(*c*) $2 + N$ memory locations (*d*) N^2 memory locations

Ans. (*a*)

Q. 4. Which of the following must be a bidirectional bus

(*a*) Address bus (*b*) Data bus
(*c*) Control bus (*d*) Common bus

Ans. (*b*)

Q. 5. A daisy chained bus arbitration scheme is also called as

(*a*) Control arbitration (*b*) Main arbitration
(*c*) Distributed arbitration (*d*) None of the above

Ans. (*a*)

Q. 6. In context of users, IS a stand for

(*a*) Instruction set (*b*) Industry set architecture
(*c*) Industry Standard Architecture (*d*) None of the above

Ans. (*c*)

Q. 7. AGP stands for

(*a*) Accelerated Graphics Port (*b*) Accumulated General Port

(*c*) A greedy protocol (*d*) None of the above

Ans. (*a*)

Q. 8. On a single USB bus, how many devices can be connected

(*a*) 125 (*b*) 126 (*c*) 127 (*d*) 128

Ans. (*c*)

Q. 9. Firewire refers to

(*a*) IEEE 1394 (*b*) IEEE 8023 (*c*) IEEE 1284 (*d*) IEEE 488

Ans. (*a*)

Q. 10. Which of the following is true for an instruction cycle (IC) –

(*a*) $IC = FC$ (*b*) $IC = FC - EC$

(*c*) $IC = FC * EC$ (*d*) $IC = FC + EC$

Ans. (*d*)

CONCEPTUAL SHORT QUESTIONS WITH ANSWERS

QUESTION 1: Distinguish between a bus structure and a non-bus structure.

SOLUTION: Let us tabulate the differences between the two –

BUS Structure	Non-BUS structure
1. Many units share a common set of lines. So, a cheaper structure.	1. More number of wires is used. Hence, a costlier structure.
2. Clashes may occur. **For eg.** When CPU is reading an instruction from memory, data must enter into CPU only and not to other units.	2. Clashes are not possible.
3. Additional control circuitry is needed to avoid clashes.	3. No additional control circuitry is needed as no clashes occur here.
4. Simultaneous communication is not possible.	4. Simultaneous communication is possible.
5. Lesser transfer speed	5. More transfer speed.

QUESTION 2: A bus has a width of 16 bits and a frequency of 133 MHz. Find the transfer speed in bits/s, bytes/s, KB/s and MB/s.

SOLUTION: Transfer speed of bus $= 16 \times 133 \times 10^6$

$$= 2128 \times 10^6 \text{ bits/s}$$

$$= 2128 \times \frac{10^6}{8} = 266\times10^6 \text{ bytes/s}$$

$$= \frac{266\times10^6}{1000} = 266\times10^3 \text{ KB/s}$$

$$= \frac{266\times10^3}{1000} = 266 \text{ MB/s}$$

QUESTION 3: Generally there are two buses within a computer. What are they? Explain.

SOLUTION: There are two types of buses in a computer –

(*a*) **Internal bus /Front side Bus (FSB).**

(*b*) **Expansion bus / input-output bus.**

The **internal bus or FSB** allows the processor to communicate with one another. It is mainly used to add new devices using **expansion slots** connected to the I/O bus.

QUESTION 4: What are the various parameters that can be used to evaluate the performance of a memory unit? **[MDU, BE (CSE) – 4th Sem, May 2007]**

SOLUTION: Various parameters are as follows:

1. **Speed:** It is defined as the number of bits processed per second.
2. **Cost:** Cost of device increases as the size increase.
3. **Size:** Size can be measured in bytes, MB, GB, TB, PB etc.
4. **Efficiency:** Minimal memory is being used or not, also becomes an important parameter.

QUESTION 5: Explain the organization of main memory.

[MDU, BE (CSE) – 4th sem., Dec. 2008]

SOLUTION: Main memory organization: RAM and ROM Chips

Typical RAM chip

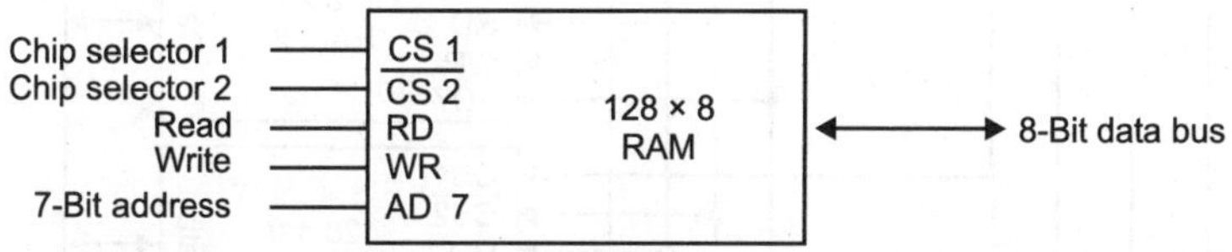

CSI	$\overline{CS2}$	*RD*	*WR*	**Memory function**	**State of data bus**
00	×	×	Inhibit	High-impedance	
1	1	×	×	Inhibit	High-impedance
1	0	0	0	Inhibit	High-impedance
1	0	0	1	Write	Input data to RAM
1	0	1	×	Read	Output data
1	1	×	×	Inhibit	High-impedance

Typical ROM chip:

Memory Address map.

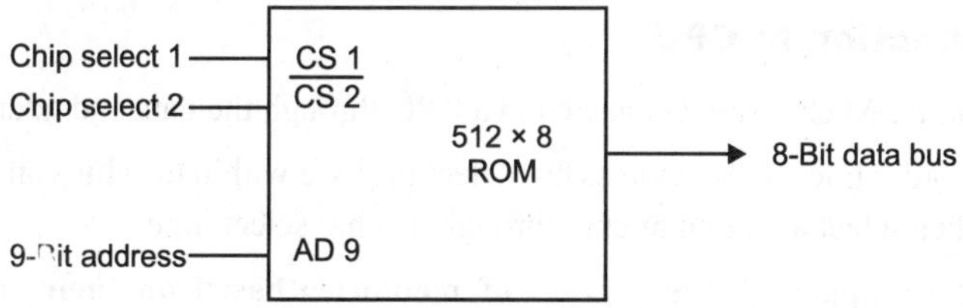

Address space assignment to each memory chip

Example: 512 bytes RAM and 512 bytes ROM.

Component	Hex addresses	Address bus 10	9	8	7	6	5	4	3	2	1
RAM1	000-007F	0	0	0	×	×	×	×	×	×	×
RAM 2	0080-00FF	0	0	1	×	×	×	×	×	×	×
RAM 3	0100-017F	0	1	0	×	×	×	×	×	×	×
RAM 4	0180-01FF	0	1	1	×	×	×	×	×	×	×
ROM	0200-03FF	1	×	×	×	×	×	×	×	×	×

Connection of memory to CPU

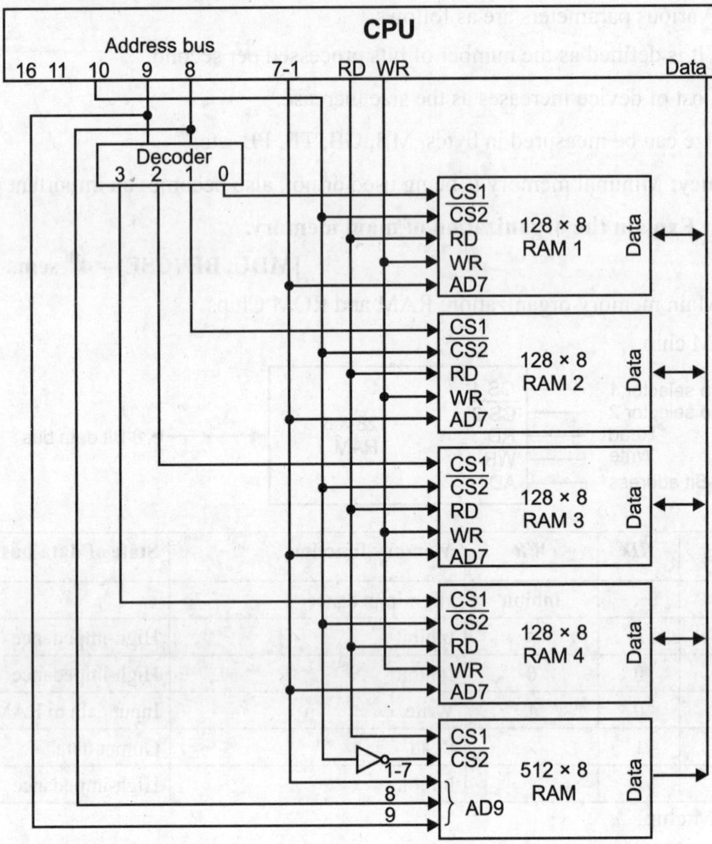

Memory Connection to CPU

- RAM and ROM chips are connected to a CPU through the data and address buses.
- The low-order lines in the address bus select the byte within the chips and other lines in the address bus select a particular chip through its chip select inputs.

QUESTION 6: Compare different types of memories based on their category, Erasure mechanism, write mechanisms and volatility

SOLUTION:

Memory	Category	Erasure	Write Mechanism	Volatility
1. RAM	Read-write memory	Electrically byte level	Electrically	Volatile
2. ROM	Read-only Memory	Not possible	Mask	
PROM				Non-volatile
3. EPROM 4. E^{2}PROM	Read only memory	UV light, chip level Electrically, byte level	Electrically	
5. Flash Memory		Electrically block level		

QUESTION 7: Discuss the key characteristics of memory systems.

[MDU, BE (CSE) - 4th Sem., 2007]

SOLUTION: The key characteristics of computer memory systems are shown in table below:

Location	Performance
Processor: Main Memory secondary Memory	**Access time:** Cycle time Transfer rate
Capacity: Word size Number of words	**Physical type**: Semiconductor, Magnetic Optical Magnetic-Optical
Unit of transfer : Word Block	**Physical Characteristics:** Volatile/Non-volatile Erasable/Non- erasable organization.
Access Method: Sequential random associative.	

QUESTION 8: Compare and contrast the access times on magnetic disks to that of magnetic tapes.

SOLUTION: Let us tabulate the comparisons:

Access time on disk	Access time on tape
1. Access time is a sum of seek time and latency time.	1. Access time is a sequential
2. No rewinding.	2. If head is on nth record, the traverse (n–1) previous record, it has to start again.
3. Random and direct access.	3. Sequential access.
4. Range is approx. 10^{-7}	4. Range is approx. 10^{-1}.

EXERCISE QUESTIONS

Q. 1. Differentiate between hardwired control and microprogrammed control.

[GGSIPU, B.Tech. (CSE)-5th Sem., Dec. 2004 & Dec. 2006].

Q. 2. How EISA differs from ISA. **[GGSIPU, B.Tech. (CSE)-5th Sem., Dec. 2004]**

Q. 3. Write short notes on – General purpose instrumentation bus IEEE 498

[GGSIPU, B.Tech. (CSE)-5th Sem., Dec. 2005].

Q. 4. (*a*) Explain the timing sequence of instruction cycle.

(*b*) Explain the architecture of computer system.

[GGSIPU, B.Tech. (CSE)-5th Sem., Dec. 2005]

Q. 5. Why microprogrammed control unit so called?

[GGSIPU, B.Tech. (CSE)-5th Sem., Dec. 2010]

Q. 6. Explain the difference between Hardware control memory and micro programmed control memory. **[GGSIPU, B.Tech. (CSE)-4th Sem., 2000, 2004]**

Q. 7. Write note on magnetic tapes and magnetic drums [MDU, BE (CSE)-4th Sem., 2001]

Q. 8. Draw a flowchart for computer cycle control and explain it.

[MDU, BE (CSE)-4th Sem., 2002]

Q. 9. Draw and explain the detailed data path of a typical register based CPU.

[MDU, BE (CSE)-4th Sem., 2005]

Q. 10. Briefly discuss about sRAM and dRAM and its organization

[MDU, BE (CSE)-4th Sem., 2005, 2006]

Q. 11. How a computer instruction is executed? Draw the instruction cycle

[MDU, BE (CSE)-4th Sem., 2006]

Q. 12. (*a*) Define the term instruction cycle.

(*b*) What the functions of control unit.

(*c*) Compare sRAM and dRAM.

(*d*) Explain the structure and functions of magnetic disk storage.

(*e*) Explain the hardwired implementation of control unit.

[B.Sc. (CS); Madras Univ., April 2011]

Q. 13. (*a*) Discuss the data transfer mechanism of the PCI bus.

(*b*) What are various types of ROM? Discuss the methods of programming ROMs.

(*c*) What is an instruction execution cycle?

(*d*) What is the function performed by timing and control unit in a microprocessor?

[PTU, MCA – 3rd Sem., 2009]

Q. 14. What are the various types of performance metrics? **[PTU, B.Tech. (CSE) – 3rd Sem., 2009]**

Q. 15. Differentiate between hardwired control and microprogammed control. Is it possible that a hardwired control be associated with a control memory?

[DTU (DCE) – ME (CS), 2004-05]

CHAPTER 5

INSTRUCTION SET ARCHITECTURE (ISA), CPU ARCHITECTURE & CONTROL DESIGN

5.0 INTRODUCTION

Processor designing is not an easy task. A processor or CPU or processing element or microprocessor has many roles at various levels. These roles are as follows:

(*a*) **At system level,** CPU has 2 main functions i.e., program execution and interfacing with other subsystems like memory.

(*b*) **At architectural level,** CPU consists of PC, Accumulator, Stack, Flags, interrupt vectors and so on. Each instruction specifies a major role known as a **macro-operation.** The exact macro-operation for an instruction is indicated in the opcode part of that instruction.

(*c*) **At Register transfer level,** CPU has a set of digital modules like registers, adders, counters, MUXes, decoders, flip-flips etc.

(*d*) **At gate level,** CPU consists of the hardware circuitry which perform microoperations.

> **DO YOU KNOW?**
>
> *Practically speaking, there is an overlap between register-transfer level and gate-level due to usage of LSIs and VLSIs.*

So, a processor design involves the following steps –

Step 1: Understand each instruction clearly. Define the macro-operation in terms of the given computer architecture.

Step 2: Identify the hardware resources needed to implement the macro-operation in terms of programmer visible hardware like flags, registers, stack, flip-flops etc.

Step 3: Translate each macro-operation as one or more register transfer operations.

Step 4: Design the datapath i.e., a collection of functional units, required for performing the register transfer operations and identify the control points. These datapath circuits are analyzed so that they can be reduced by containing the designs for various instructions and eliminating the redundant circuits.

Step 5: List the timing sequence of control signals required to activate the control points.

5.1 ISA DEFINITION AND CPU INTERNAL STORAGE

ISA or instruction set architecture is the part of computer architecture that is concerned with programming. It includes a specification of the set of all binary codes (Opcode). ISA is an **abstraction** on the interface between the hardware and the low-level software. **The set of opcodes for a particular ISA is also known as the machine language for ISA.** ISA comprises of the following:

(*a*) Instruction Formats.

(*b*) Addressing Modes.

(*c*) Operations inside instruction set.

(*d*) Encoding of instructions.

(*e*) Data Storage.

Actually, ISA is distinguished from the micro architecture which is the set of processor design techniques used to implement the instruction set. **Please remember that when engineers design micro-architectures, they use Register Transfer Language (RTL) to define the operation of each instruction of an ISA. Also remember that ISA can be emulated in software by an interpreter but this emulation will be slow as compared to running the programs on the hardware implementing that ISA.**

> **DO YOU KNOW?**
>
> *It is a common practice for vendors of new ISA or micro-architecture to make software emulators available to software developers before the hardware implementation is ready.*

CPU (or simply a processor) performs some basic functions as shown in figure 5.1.

To perform these functions of figure 5.1, CPU is divided into different, specific functional units. From Fig. 5.2, we observe that these are three main parts of a CPU –

(*a*) ALU

(*b*) Registers

(*c*) Control Unit.

Also, there is an internal data bus used to transmit data between these parts. Let us explain them one by one now.

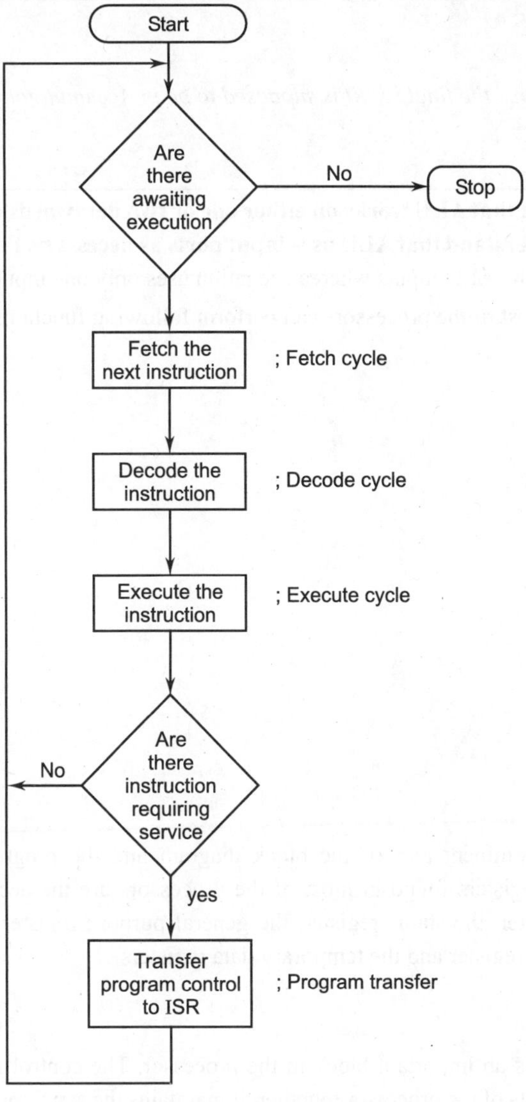

Fig. 5.1. Flowchart showing CPU functions

ALU

Arithmetic and logic unit contains the processors data processing logic. It has two inputs and an output. The internal data bus of CU is connected to the two inputs of ALU through the temporary register and the accumulator. The ALU's single output is connected to the internal data bus. It allows sending the output of ALU over the bus to any device connected to the bus. Within CPU, it is register-A (also called as an Accumulator) that gives data to ALU and after performing the operation, the resulting data word is sent to the register A and stored there.

DO YOU KNOW?

After all operations, the final result is supposed to be in Accumulator, by default.

Please understand that ALU works on either one or two datawords depending on the kind of operation. Also understand that ALU uses input ports as necessary. For instance, the multiply operation uses both of the ALU inputs whereas negation uses only one input.

The ALU of the most of the processors can perform following functions:

1. Addition
2. Subtraction
3. AND
4. OR
5. Exclusive OR
6. Complement
7. Shift right
8. Shift left
9. Increment
10. Decrement

Registers

Registers are a prominent part of the block diagram and the programming model of any processor. The basic registers found in most of the processors are the accumulator, the program counter, the stack pointer, the status register, the general purpose registers, the memory address register, the instruction register and the temporary data registers.

Control Logic

The control logic is an important block in the processor. The control logic is responsible for working of all other parts of the processor together. It maintains the synchronization in operation, of different parts in the processor. The synchronization is achieved with the help of one of the control logic's major external inputs, processor's clock. The clock is a signal which is the basis of all the timings inside the processor.

Usually processor's control logic is microprogrammed. This means that the organisation of the control logic itself is much like the organisation of a very special purpose processor.

The control logic receives the signal from instruction decoder which decodes the instruction stored in the instruction register. The control logic then generates the control signals necessary to carry out this instruction. The control logic does a few other special functions. It looks after the processor power-up sequence. It also processes interrupts. An interrupt is like a request to the processor from other external devices such as the memory and I/O. The interrupt asks the processor to execute a special program. We shall study this a bit later in this chapter.

Internal Data Bus

The internal data bus connects the different parts of processor together and it enables the communication between these parts. The data transfer through this internal data bus is controlled by control logic.

Processor's internal data bus is usually connected to an external data bus. Due to this processor can communicate with external memory or I/O devices. Usually the internal data bus is connected to the external data bus by logic called a **bi-directional bus (transreceiver)**.

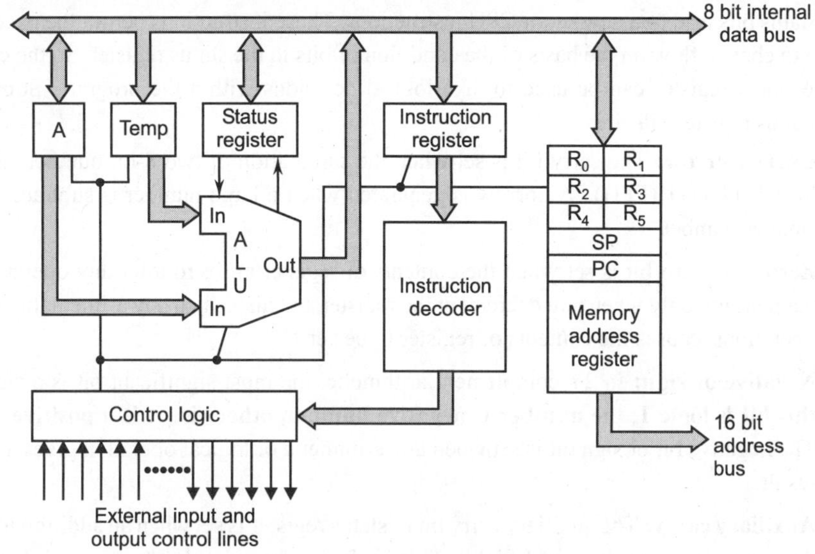

Fig. 5.2. General Processor Organisation

We have seen that processor consists of various registers. These registers are used for different purposes. Let us study the functioning of these registers one by one.

The Accumulator

The accumulator is the major working register of CPU. Most of the time it is used to hold the data for manipulation. Whenever the operation processes two words whether arithmetically or logically, the accumulator contains one of the words. The other word may be present in another register or in a memory location. Most of the times the result of an arithmetic or logical operation is placed in the accumulator. In such cases, after execution of instruction original contents of accumulator are lost because they are overwritten.

The accumulator is also used for data transfer between an I/O port and a memory location or between one memory location and another.

The Program Counter(PC)

The program counter is one of the most important registers in the CPU. As mentioned earlier, a program is a series of instruction stored in the memory. These instructions tell the CPU exactly how to solve problem. **It is important that these instructions must be executed in a proper order to get the correct result.** This sequence of instruction execution is monitored by the program counter. It keeps track of which instruction is being used and what the next instruction will be.

The program counter gives the address of memory location from where the next instruction is to be fetched. Due to this, the length of the program counter decides the maximum program length in bytes. **For example,** CPU that has 16 bit program counter can address 2^{16} bytes (64 KB of memory).

The Status Register

The status register is used to store the results of certain condition when certain operations are performed during execution of the program. **The status register is also referred to as flag register.** ALU operations and certain register operations may set or reset one or more bits in the status register. Status bits lead to a new set of CPU instructions. These instructions permit the execution of a program to change flow on the basis of the condition of bits in the status register. So the condition bits in the status register can be used to take logical decisions within the program. Some of the common status register bits are:

1. **Carry/Borrow:** The carry bit is set when the summation of two 8-bit numbers is greater than 1111 1111 (FFH). A borrow is generated when a large number is subtracted from a smaller number.
2. **Zero:** The zero bit is set when the contents of register are zero after any operation. This happens not only when you decrement the register, but also when any arithematic or logical operations, causes the contents of register to be zero.
3. **Negative or sign:** In 2's complement arithmetic, the most significant bit is a sign bit. **If this bit is logic 1, the number is negative number, otherwise it is a positive number.** The negative bit or sign bit is set when any arithmetic or logical operation gives a negative result.
4. **Auxiliary carry:** The auxiliary carry bit of status register is set when an addition in the first 4 bits causes a carry into the fifth bit. **This is often referred as half carry or intermediate carry.** This is used in the BCD arithmetic.
5. **Overflow Flag:** In 2's complement arithmetic, most significant bit is used to represent sign and remaining bits are used to represent magnitude of a number (see Fig 5.3). This flag is set if the result of a signed operation is too large to fit in the number of bits available (7-bits for 8-bit numbers it represents).

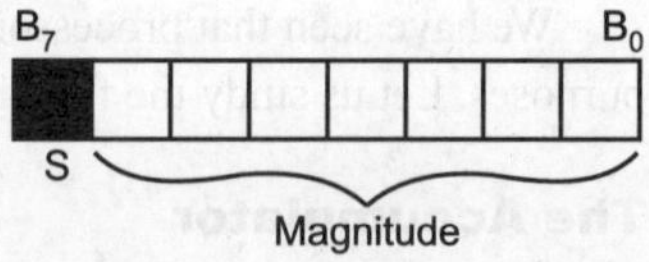

Fig. 5.3

   For example, if you add the 8-bit sign number 01110110 (+118 decimal) and the 8 bit sign signed number 00110110 (+54 decimal). The result will be 10101100 (+172 decimal), which is the correct binary result, but in this case it is too large to fit in the 7-bits allowed for the magnitude in an 8-bit signed number. The overflow flag will be set after this operation to indicate that the result of the addition has overflowed into the sign bit.

6. **Parity:** When the result of an operation leaves the indicated register with an even number of 1s, parity bit is set.

The Stack Pointer

The stack is special reserved area in the computer memory used to store the contents of the registers and return address of the PC in case of subroutine programs.

The memory address of the stack area is given by a special register called the **stack pointer**. Like the Program Counter, the Stack Pointer automatically points to the next available location in the memory (Fig. 5.4).

Please note that as you go on storing (pushing) data on the stack, the stack pointer always points the last data placed on the stack and when you try to remove (pop) data you always get the last data placed on the stack. This kind of stack operation is called LIFO (last-in first-out) operation.

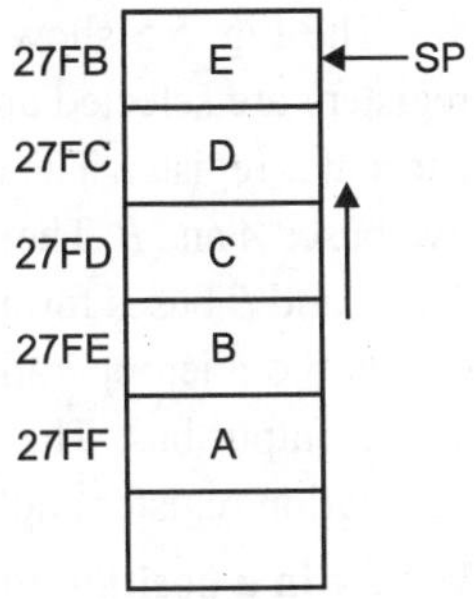

Fig. 5.4

General Purpose Registers

In addition to the special purpose register discussed above, most CPUs have other registers called general purpose registers. The general purpose register are used as simple storage area, mainly these are used to store intermediate results of the operation. Getting the operand from the general purpose registers is faster than from memory, so it is better to have sufficient number of general purpose registers.

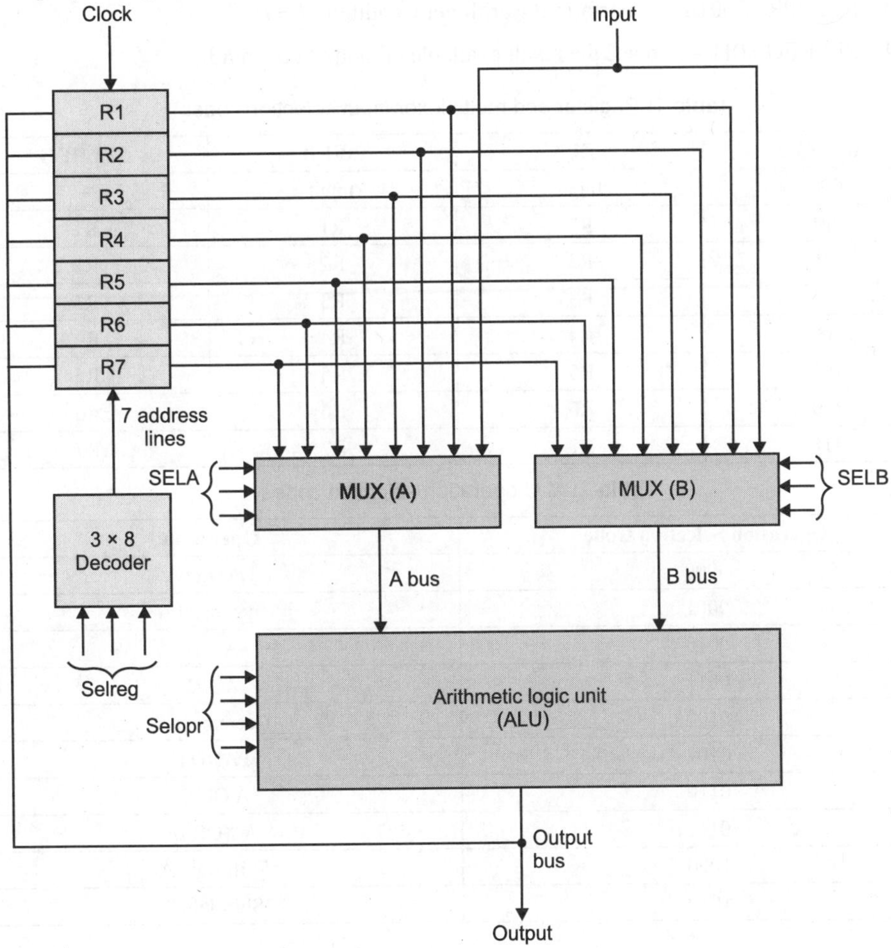

Fig. 5.5. General bus organization for CPU registers

The Fig. 5.5 shows the general bus organization for seven CPU registers. It shows that how registers are selected and how data flows between register and ALU. A decoder is used to select a particular register. The output of each register is connected to two multiplexers (MUX) to form the two buses *A* and *B*. The selection lines in each multiplexer select the input data for the particular bus. The *A* and *B* buses form the two inputs of an arithmetic logic unit (ALU). The operation select lines decide the microoperation to be performed by ALU. The result of the microoperation is available at the output bus. The output bus is connected to the inputs of all registers, thereby selecting a destination register and it is possible to store the result in it.

We are in a position to solve an example now

EXAMPLE 1: It is desired to perform the operation, $R3 \leftarrow R1 + R2$. What binary selection variables are needed to the select inputs. Refer to figure 5.5

SOLUTION: To perform the operation $R3 \leftarrow R1 + R2$ we have to provide following binary selection variables to the select inputs (Refer Tables 1 and 2).

1. SELA : 001 – to place the contents of R1 into bus A.
2. SELB : 010 – to place the contents of R2 into bus B.
3. SELOPR : 10010 – to perform the arithmetic addition $A + B$.
4. SELREG : 011 – to place the result available on output bus in *R*3.

Table 1: Register and multiplexer input selection codes

Binary Code	SELA	SELB	SELREG
000	Input	Input	–
001	R1	R1	R1
010	R2	R2	R2
011	R3	R3	R3
100	R4	R4	R4
101	R5	R5	R5
110	R6	R6	R6
111	R7	R7	R7

Table 2: ALU operation selection codes

Operation Selection Code	Operation
0000	Transfer A
0001	Increment A
0010	A + B
0011	A – B
0100	Decrement A
0101	A AND B
0110	A OR B
0111	A XOR B
1000	Shift right A
1010	Shift left A

5.2 LEVELS OF ISA

ISA-1

As already mentioned, ISA or Instruction set Architecture is an abstraction on the interface between the hardware and the low-level software.

ISA-2

ISA includes everything that the programmers need to know to make the machine code work correctly. Designers can now talk about functions independently from the hardware that performs these functions. **Please understand that this abstraction allows many implementations of varying cost and performance to run identical software.**

ISA-3

ISA is determined by the following:

(*a*) Data types, data structures.

(*b*) Encoding and representations

(*c*) Instruction formats

(*d*) Instruction set.

(*e*) Addressing modes

ISA-4

(*a*) Instruction format or encoding.

(*b*) Location of operands and results.

(*c*) Data type and size.

(*d*) Operations supported.

(*e*) Jumps and branches.

ISA-5

(*a*) Language of machine (Instruction set).

(*b*) More primitive than HLL.

(*c*) More restrictive instructions.

ISA-6

(*a*) Assembly or machine language.

(*b*) Assembly language provides convenient symbolic representation, machine language is the underlying reality.

(*c*) Assembly can provide **pseudo-instructions.** For eg., "move $a0, $a1" exist only in assembly, the actual instruction is "Add $a0, $a1, $Zen."

(*d*) When considering performance, you should count real instructions.

ISA-7

That is, represented instructions in computer –

(a) Assembly Language

ADD $R0, R1, R2$; $(R0) \leftarrow (R1) + (R2)$

(b) Machine Language

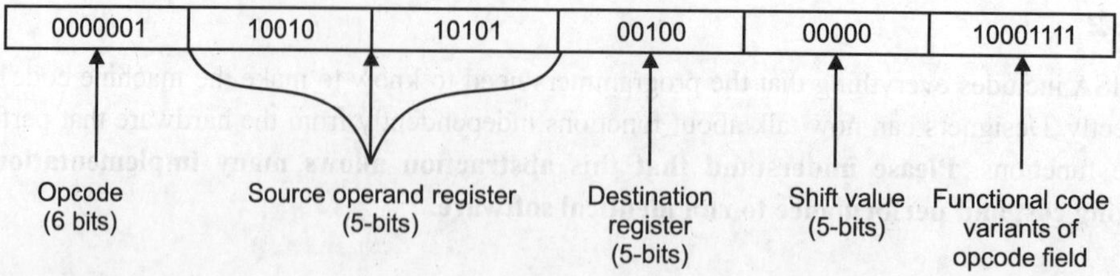

Note: These ISA's are carried out at microlevel in micro-coded CPU.

5.3 INSTRUTION FORMATS

An instruction is a command given to a computer to perform a specified operation on some given data and the format is which the instruction is specified is known as an instruction format. An instruction format defines the layout of the bits of an instruction. It must include opcode, zero or more operands and the addressing mode for each operand.

For eg. In instruction, ADD $R1, R0$.

(*a*) ADD is the opcode.

(*b*) $R1$ and $R0$ are the address fields.

The number of address fields in the instruction format depends on the internal organization of the CPU. Operations specified by the computer instructions are executed on some data stored in memory or some registers.

Please note that the operands residing on memory are specified by memory address and operands residing on processor registers are specified by register address. Also note that a register address is a binary number of K-bits that defines one of the 2^k registers in the CPU. So, if a CPU has register from $R0$ to $R15$, then address of each registers will be of four bits.

The instruction length is usually kept on multiple of the character length or memory transfer length which is usually 8-bits. With this length we will always get an integral number of instructions during a fetch cycle. Once the instruction length is fixed, it is necessary to allocate the number of bits for opcode, operand(s) and addressing modes. **For an instruction format of a given length, if more number of bits is allocated to opcode field, then lesser number of bits is available for addressing.** The bits allocation for addressing can be determined by the factors given below:

(*a*) Number of addressing modes.

(*b*) Number of operands.

(*c*) Number of CPU registers.

(*d*) Number of register sets.

(*e*) Number of address lines.

(*f*) Address granularity (i.e., address can refer to a byte, word or a double word).

These factors simplify the task of allocating in the instruction.

DO YOU KNOW?	The instruction format of a processor also changes according to the address references in the instruction.

Let us now study various instruction types according to the address references.

5.3.1 Zero-address Instruction

Zero-address Instructions can be defined as the computational instructions in which the address field is not present. Generally, stack organized computers (to be discussed shortly) use this type of addressing field. Mostly, they use **PUSH** and **POP** instructions. Actually, the given notation of the operation is converted into Reverse Polish Notation (discussed in Section 5.12 of this chapter). In order to evaluate arithmetic expression in a stack computer, it is to be entered in reverse polish notation form.

In these instructions, the locations of all operands are defined **implicitly**. Such instructions are found in machines that store operands in a structure called as a **pushdown stack.** Stack-oriented machines do not contain any accumulator or general purpose registers (GPRs).

Examples: Burrough's B5000 (main frame), HP 3000 (mini computers) are stack-oriented machines.

5.3.2 One-address Instructions

One address instructions use an implied accumulator (AC) register for all data manipulation, i.e. they contain only one address field.

For e.g,

ADD B

This instruction adds the contents of variable A into the processor register called as an **accumulator (AC)** and stores the sum back into the accumulator destroying the previous contents of the accumulator. In this instruction, the second operand is assumed implicitly, in a unique location accumulator. **For. eg.** STORE B

This instruction copies the contents of accumulator into memory location B.

Please note from these examples that the operand specified in the instruction can be either source operand or destination operand depending on the instruction. Also note that, in one address instructions the implied operand (accumulator) can be either source or destination depending on the instruction.

For eg. In instruction, LOAD A, the operand-specified is a **source operand** as it copies the contents of memory location A into the accumulator. On the other hand, the operand specified in the STORE B instruction is a **destination operand.**

For multiplication and division, a temporary register is used. The address of the second register is assumed to be accumulator.

Example: DDP-8, HP 2116, MC6800, Intel 8085 etc.

5.3.3 Two-address Instructions

In this format, each address field specify either a processor register or a memory word i.e., they contain two address fields.

For eg., ADD *A*, *B*

It adds the contents of register (variables) *A* and *B* and stores the sum in register *A*, destroying its previous contents. So, here operand *A* is a source operand and operand *B* serves as both source and destination operand.

Please understand that to represent this instruction, lesser number of bits is required as compared to three-address instructions (to be discussed next). Also note that the number of bits required to represent two address instructions includes:

1. **Bits required specifying the two memory addresses of the two operands i.e,** 2n bits.
2. **Bits required to specify the operation.**
3. **Examples:** IBM 360/370, PDP-11, Intel 8086.

5.3.4 Three-address Instructions

A three-address instruction represented as follows-

ADD *A*, *B*, *C*

where *A*, *B*, *C* are the variables.

These variable names are assigned to different memory locations. In this instruction, operands A and B are called as **source operands** and operand C is called as **destination operand.** And ADD is the operation to be performed on the operands. **The number of bits required to represent such instructions includes –**

1. **Bits required specifying the three memory addresses of the three operands. If n-bits are required to specify one memory address, 3n bits are required to specify three memory addresses.**
2. **Bits required to specify the operation**

The **main advantage** of this three-address format is that it results in shorter programs when evaluating arithmetic expression but require **larger space** to specify three addresses, (many bits are needed now).

Example: Cyber-170, CD-6600 etc.

Summary / Conclusions

We conclude from the above discussion that the instruction with only one address will require lesser number of bits to represent it and an instruction with three addresses will require more number of bits to represent it. **Please understand that it means that to access entire instruction from the memory, the instruction with three addresses requires more memory accesses while the instruction with one address requires lesser memory access.** The speed of the instruction execution is mainly dependent on how much memory accesses it requires for the execution. **Also note that if memory accesses are more, more time is required to execute the instruction**. It means that the execution time for three address instruction is more than the execution time for one address instructions. Thus, to have a less execution time, we have to use instructions with minimum memory accessed. To achieve this, instead of referring the operands from memory it is advised to refer operands from processor registers. When machine level language programs are generated by compiles from high level languages, the **intelligent compiler** sees that the maximum references to the operands lie in the processor registers.

Before we discuss further, let us solve some problems now.

EXAMPLE 1. **Evaluate the following arithmetic expression using 3-address, 2-address, 1-address and 0-address instructions to show the effect on computer program.**

$$X = (A + B)*(C - D)$$

SOLUTION: In the above arithmetic expression, variables A, B, C and D are given. We will assume that the operands are stored at memory addresses, A, B, C and D. The result will be stored above memory address X. In the program, ADD SUB and MUL are used for arithmetic operations. MOV is used for the transfer operations. LOAD and STORE are used for transfer to and from memory and AC register. $R1$, $R2$ are general purpose registers and T is the address of temporary memory location to store intermediate result.

Three-Address Instructions

ADD $R1, A, B$	$R1 \leftarrow M[A] + M[B]$
SUB $R2, C, D$	$R2 \leftarrow M[C] - M[D]$
MUL $X, R1, R2$	$M[X] \leftarrow R1 * R2$

Two-Address Instruction

MOV $R1, A$	$R1 \leftarrow M[A]$
ABD $R1, B$	$R1 \leftarrow R1 + M[B]$
MOV $R2, C$	$R2 \leftarrow M[C]$
SUB $R2, D$	$R2 \leftarrow R2 - M[D]$
MUL $R1, R2$	$R1 \leftarrow R1 * R2$
MOV $X, R1$	$M[X] \leftarrow R1$

One Address Instruction

LOAD A	$AC \leftarrow M[A]$
AND B	$AC \leftarrow AC + M[B]$
STORE T	$M[T] \leftarrow AC$
LOAD C	$AC \leftarrow M[C]$
SUB D	$AC \leftarrow AC - M[D]$
NUL T	$AC \leftarrow AC * M[T]$
STORE X	$M[X] \leftarrow AC$

Zero Address Instruction

Given expression is

$$X = (A + B)*(C - D)$$

Reverse Polish notation of the given expression is evaluated as-

$$X = AB + *CD-$$
$$= AB + CD - *$$

PUSH A	TOS ← A
PUSH B	TOS ← B
ADD	TOS ← $(A+B)$
PUSH C	TOS ← C
PUSH D	TOS ← D
SUB	TOS ← $(C-D)$
MUL	TOS ← $(A+B)*(C-D)$
POP X	M[X] ← TOS

EXAMPLE 2: Evaluate the following arithmetic expressions using 3-address, 2-address, 1-address and 0-address instructions to show the effect on the computer program

$$X = (A+B)*(C+D).$$

SOLUTION: ADD, SUB, DIV and MUL are used for arithmetic operations, MOV for the transfer operation. LOAD and STORE for transfer to and from memory and *AC* register. We will assume that the operands are in memory addresses *A*, *B*, *C* and *D* and the result must be stored in memory address *X*. *R*1, *R*2 are the registers and T is the address of temporary memory location used to store intermediate result.

Three-Address Instruction

ADD $R1, A, B$	$R1 \leftarrow M[A] + M[B]$
ADD $R2, C, D$	$R2 \leftarrow M[C] + M[D]$
MUL $X, R1, R2$	$X \leftarrow R1 * R2$

The symbol $M[A]$ denotes the operand at memory address symbolized by *A*.

The advantage of the three-address format is that it results in shorter programs when evaluating arithmetic expressions.

Two-Address Instruction

MOV $R1, A$	$R1 \leftarrow M[A]$
ADD $R1, B$	$R1 \leftarrow R1 + M[B]$
MOV $R2, C$	$R2 \leftarrow M[C]$
ADD $R2, D$	$R2 \leftarrow R2\ M[D]$
MUL $R1, R2$	$R1 \leftarrow R1 * R2$
MOV $X, R1$	$M[X] \leftarrow R1$

One-Address Instructions

One address instruction uses an accumulator (AC) register for all data manipulations.

LOAD A	$AC \leftarrow M[A]$
ADD B	$AC \leftarrow AC + M[B]$
STORE T	$M[T] \leftarrow AC$
LOAD C	$AC \leftarrow M[C]$
ADD D	$AC \leftarrow AC + M[D]$
MUL T	$AC \neg AC * M[T]$
STORE X	$M[X] \neg AC$

All operations are done between the *AC* register and a memory operand. *T* is the address of a temporary memory location required for storing intermediate result.

Zero-Address Instruction

To evaluate arithmetic expression for zero-address machine, the expression must be in reverse polish notation. Also, the instructions like ADD, MUL do not require an operand field. It simply pops up the two top most operands from the stack, performs the operation and places the result on top of the stack. However, PUSH and POP instructions requires an address field to specify the operand that communicates with the stack. TOS stands for top of stack.

The reverse polish notation of expression is as follows:

$$X = (A+B) * (C+D) \text{ is evaluated as}$$
$$= (AB+) * (CD+)$$
$$= AB + CD+ *$$

PUSH A	TOS $\leftarrow A$
PUSH B	TOS $\leftarrow B$
ADD	TOS $\leftarrow A+B$
PUSH C	TOS $\leftarrow C$
PUSH D	TOS $\leftarrow D$
ADD	TOS $\leftarrow C+D$
MUL	TOS $\leftarrow (A+B) * (C+D)$
POP X	$M[X] \leftarrow$ TOS

5.4 ADDRESSING MODES

Each instruction needs data on which it has to perform the specified operation. The operand (data) may be in the accumulator, general purpose register or in the some specified memory location. Hence, there are various ways of specifying data. **The techniques of specifying the address of the data are known as a addressing modes, And the address of an operand is known as effective address.**

Addressing modes are used to –

(*a*) Give programming versatility to the user.

(*b*) Reduce the number of bits in the address field of the instruction.

(*c*) Provide flexibility for writing programs.

The effective address (or *EA*) of an operand is the address of (pointer to) the main memory or reference location in which the operand is contained i.e.,

$$\text{Operand} = [EA]$$

Before we categorize the addressing modes, the following points must be kept in mind-

1. Different operands will use different addressing modes.
2. One or more bits in the instruction format can be used as a **mode field.** The value of the mode field determines which addressing mode is to be used.
3. The **effective address (*EA*)** will be either main memory or the register's address.

Actually, there are 12 types of addressing modes. Out of these 12, 8085 uses first five modes only. These addressing modes are follows:

1. Direct (or absolute) addressing.
2. Register addressing.
3. Register indirect addressing.
4. Immediate addressing.
5. Implicit addressing.
6. Indexed addressing.
7. Based addressing
8. Based indexed addressing.
9. Relative addressing.
10. Relative indexed addressing
11. Page addressing.
12. Stack addressing.

Let us study these one by one now.

1. Direct (or absolute) addressing

In direct addressing the address of the data (operand) is specified within the instruction. Examples of direct addressing are:

(a) **STA 2500 H:** Store the contents of the accumulator in the memory location 2500 H.

(b) **LDA 2500 H**: Load accumulator with the contents of the memory location 2500 H.

In example (*a*) above, 2500 H is the memory address where data are to be stored. The memory address 2500H is given in the instruction itself. In this case it is understood that the source of data is accumulator.

(c) **IN 01**: Read data from an input device whose address is 01.

In this instruction 01 is the address of an input device from where data is to be read, in instruction, it is implied that the data will be transferred from the input device to the accumulator.

2. Register addressing

In the register addressing the operands are located in general-purpose registers. In other words the contents of a register are the operand. Therefore, only the names of the registers are to be specified in the instruction. **Examples of register addressing are:**

(a) **MOV *A, B*:** Transfer the contents of register B to register A.

The opcode of this instruction is 78H. In addition to the operation to be performed, the opcode also specifies the addresses of the registers mentioned in the instruction. The opcode 78H binary from is 01111000. The first two bits 01 denote MOV operation, the next three bits are the binary code of register A and the last three bits 000 are the binary code of register B of 8085.

(b) **ADD B:** Add the contents of the register B to the contents of the accumulator. The opcode of this instruction is 80H. In the binary form the code is 10000000. The first five bits 10000 specify the operation to be performed, i.e., ADD. The last three bits 000 are the binary code of register B.

3. **Register indirect addressing**

In the register indirect addressing, the address of the operand is given indirectly. The contents of a register or a register-pair are the address of the operand. Compare this with the register addressing where the content of the register is the operand. **Examples are:**

(*i*) **LXI H, 2400H**	:	Load H-L pair with 2400H.
MOV A, M	:	Move the content of the memory location, whose address is in H-L pair (i.e., 2400 H), to the accumulator.

In this example MOV A, M is an example of register indirect addressing. For MOV A, M instruction the operand is in a memory location whose address is not directly given in this instruction. The address of the memory location is stored in H-L pair, which has been specified by the earlier instruction in the program i.e., LXI H, 2400H.

(*ii*) **LXI H, 2200 H**	:	Load H-L pair with 2200 H
ADD M	:	Add the contents of the memory location, whose address H-L pair, to the contents of the accumulator

In this example the instruction ADD M is an example of register indirect addressing.

4. **Immediate addressing**

In immediate addressing the operand is given in the instruction itself. The examples of immediate addressing are:

(*i*) **MV1 A, 06**	:	Move 06 to the accumulator.
(*ii*) **ADI 05**	:	Add 05 to the content of the accumulator.
(*iii*) **LXI H, 2500H**	:	Load H-L pair with 2500H.

5. **Implicit addressing**

This mode of addressing is also called **implied addressing or inherent addressing.** These instructions operate on only one operand, which is in the accumulator. So address need not be specified. Such addressing is known as **implicit addressing. Examples are:**

(*i*) RAL	:	Rotate the contents of the accumulator left through carry
(*ii*) RLC	:	Rotate the contents of the accumulator left.
(*iii*) CMA	:	Take complement of the contents of the accumulator.

Many instructions use two operands. For one of the operands they use implicit addressing while for the other operand they employ any one of the other addressing modes.

Before, we discuss further, we must define certain terms related to these addressing modes.

(*a*) Effective Address (EA)

A large memory is divided into **segments.** The memory address of an operand consists of two components:

(*a*) Starting address of the segment.

(*b*) An offset.

The **starting address** of the segment is supplied by the processor. The operand is placed at an **offset** within the segment with a reference to the starting address of the segment. The **offset** is three offset address elements – displacement, base and index. **The combination depends on the addressing mode of an instruction to be executed. This offset is also called as an effective address. Please understand that the memory address of an operand is given by-**

$$\begin{pmatrix}\text{Memory address}\\ \text{of an operand}\end{pmatrix} = \begin{pmatrix}\text{Starting address of}\\ \text{memory segment}\end{pmatrix} + (\text{offset})$$

(*b*) Displacement: It is an 8-bit or 16-bit immediate value given in the instruction.

(*c*) Base: It is the content of the base register.

(*d*) Index: It is the content of the index register.

Some more addressing modes are discussed now.

6. Indexed addressing

The operand's offset is determined by adding an 8-bit or 16-bit displacement given in the content of the index register.

7. Based addressing

This mode of addressing the operand's offset is the sum of the content of the base register and the 8-bit or 16-bit displacement given in the instruction.

8. Based indexed addressing.

In this mode of addressing, the operand's offset and the sum of the content of the register are added together to form the effective address. The base register contains base address and the index register contains an index.

9. Relative addressing

In relative addressing, signed displacement is added to the current value of the program counter to form the effective address. This mode of the addressing is commonly used in branch or group instructions. The displacement is a signed quantity so as to allow either a forward or backward jump from the location pointed out by the program counter. **This mode is also known as *PC relative addressing*.** The effective address specifies that the memory location is in relation to the current value of the program counter.

10. Relative indexed addressing

It is mode of addressing in which the contents of the program counter and the contents of the register are added together to form the effective address.

11. Page addressing

In page mode of addressing the memory is divided into a number of equal length pages. The page size is 256 bytes for 8-bit microprocessors and 4 KB for 16-bit microprocessors. The address contains a page register to hold page number. The instruction contains an offset that indicates the address within the page with reference to the starting address. The numbering of pages is done in such a way that in case of 16-bit memory, the 8-bit page number contained in the page register indicates 8 MSBs of the operand. The advantage of this mode of addressing is that a fewer bits in the instruction indicate the memory address. This result in shorter instruction and faster microprocessors provide paged addressing. In such a case the paged addressing is restricted only to the first 256 memory to 8 MSBs of the address of these 256 memory locations are zero **and this page is called 0-page (or base page).** Such mode of addressing is called 0-page addressing.

12. Stack addressing

In this mode of addressing, the address of the operand is specified by the stack pointer (SP). Instruction is shortest because it does not include any address of the memory **location or mention any register** (just like implied mode of addressing). The contents of SP are automatically incremented or decremented after each stack operation. PUSH instruction is used to save the contents of a register pair into the stack. The POP instruction is used to transfer the contents from the stack to the register-pair. SP contains the address of the memory location of the stack from (or to) which data is to be transferred.

The stack addressing is employed in the following cases:

(*i*) When PUSH and POP instructions are used in a program by the programme.

(*ii*) When CALL instruction is used to call a subroutine. Before a program jumps in the main program to a sub-routine the contents of the PC are save when program goes back from the subroutine to the main program the contents of PC are restored. For this RET instruction is used at the end of a subroutine. This uses stack addresses.

(*iii*) When interrupt occurs the contents of important registers are saved onto the stack. For this stack addressing is used.

5.5 CISC VS RISC VS/ MISC

Powerful General purpose microprocessors may be divided into two groups *i.e.,*

(*i*) Pure complex instruction set computer (CISC) processors.

(*ii*) Pure reduced instruction set computer (RISC) processors.

Examples of CISC processors are **the** 8086, 80186, 80286 and 80386 belonging to INTEL family and 68000 and 68040 from MOTOROLA family.

Please note that 80386 is the last pure CISC model of the Intel family because 80486 **has the facility of RISC technology partially.**

The CISC microprocessors have :

- **Complex** machine instructions.
- **Micro-encoding** of machine instructions.
- Best addressing capability.
- Smaller number of useful registers.

Reduced Instruction Set Computer (RISC) have faster clock rates, ranging from 20 to 120 MHz. For example: Intel i860, SPARC, IBM RS/6000 etc. are some of the RISC processors.

5.6 ADVANCED PROCESSOR TECHNOLOGY

By the year 2010 (the year of common wealth games!!!), a single VLSI chip will have more than 1 billion transistors.

Pipelining has been used in RISC machines. RISC processors have been succeeded by super scalar processors that execute multiple instructions in one clock cycle. Very Large Instruction word (VLIW) processors are those in which one instruction word encodes more than one operation. As per the **Moore's Law -"The number of transistors which can be integrated in a chip has been doubling every 18 months".** To enhance the speed of PEs, we now make use of multithreading,

VLIW and vector processors. What we actually observe is that as technology evolves rapidly, the clock rates of PEs also slowly move from lower to higher speeds. We shall also study about the super pipelined processors. These computers use multiphase clocks with clock rate ranging from 100 to 500 MHz. Vector computers (to be discussed) use this approach. We should also understand that a scalar processor is different from a vector processor. This is shown in Fig. 5.6. Also shown in Fig. 5.7 is the working of a vector processor. What we observe from Fig. 5.6 and Fig. 5.7 is that in case of a scalar processor - one-result/many clock cycles is produced while in case of vector processors one result/clock is produced.

SCALAR VS VECTOR PROCESSING

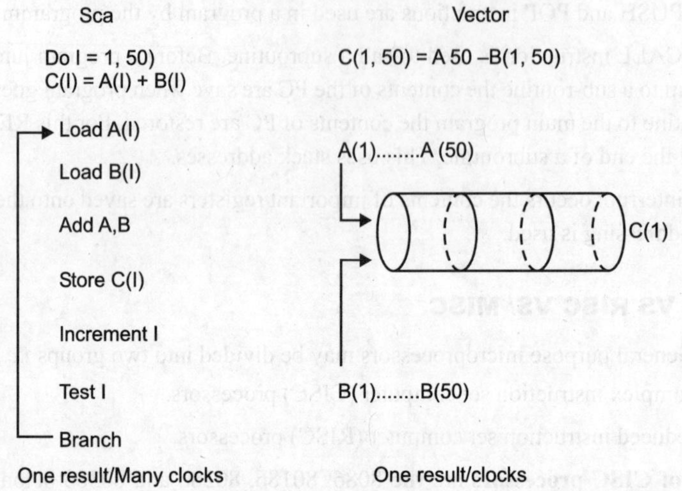

Fig. 5.6. Scalar V/s Vector Processing

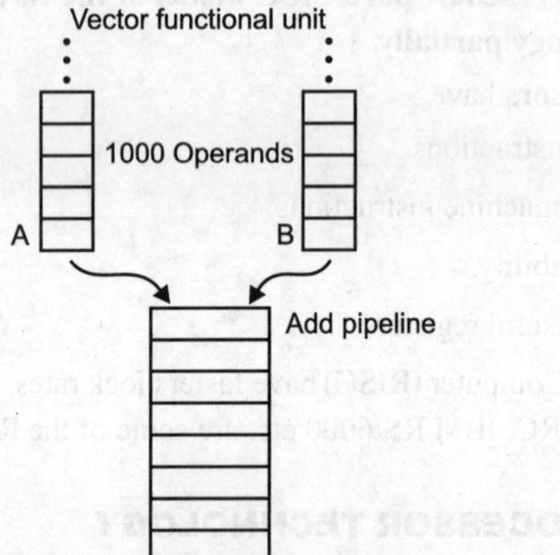

Fig. 5.7. Vector Processing

Please note that a base scalar processor is defined as a system in which one instruction is issued per cycle. There is one-cycle latency (delay) for a simple operation and a one-cycle latency (delay) between the instruction issues.

As we already know that the execution of any instruction requires four phases:

Fetch---------> Decode --------- > Execute ---------> Write-back (results)
(F) (D) (E) (W)

Further assuming that we have an instruction pipeline (like an assembly line production) which receives successive instructions from it's input side and it executes them in an overlapped fashion. Then, we can have three different cases.

Case 1 : Execution in a base scalar processor

Herein, if I draw a graph showing its execution of instruction then we get the following

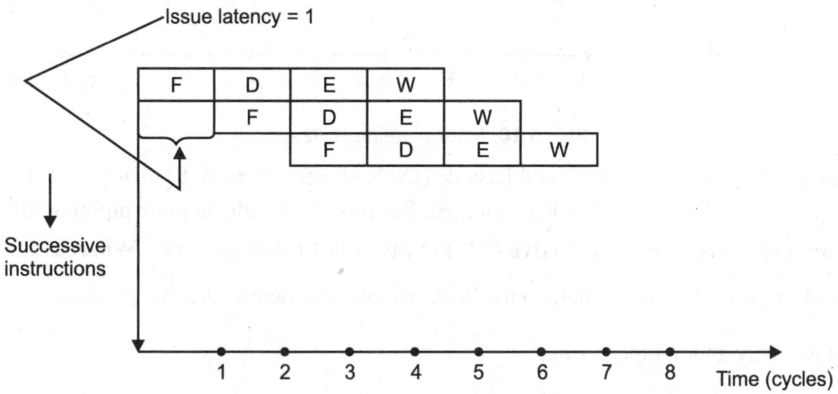

Fig. 5.8. A base scalar processor showing pipelining.

So, here in Fig. 5.8 we find that the pipeline utilization can be improved if successive instructions can execute at the rate of one per cycle.

Case 2 : Pipeline underutilization

Can't we have an issue-latency of more than one? Yes, why not. Say, the issue latency is 2 now. So, we draw Fig. 5.9.

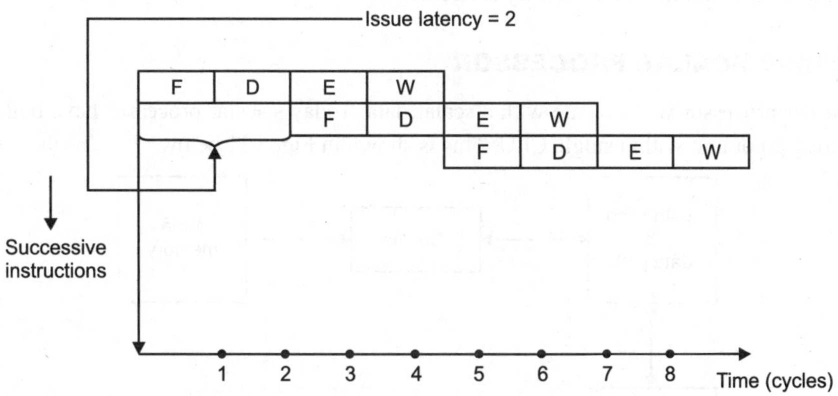

Fig. 5.9. Pipeline underutilization with 2 issue latency

It is observed from Fig. 5.9 that if the issue-latency between two instructions is increased (from 1 to 2) then the pipeline can be **underutilized.**

Case 3 : Poor pipeline utilization

It is also possible to combine two pipeline stages into one stage. So, we draw another Fig. 5.10.

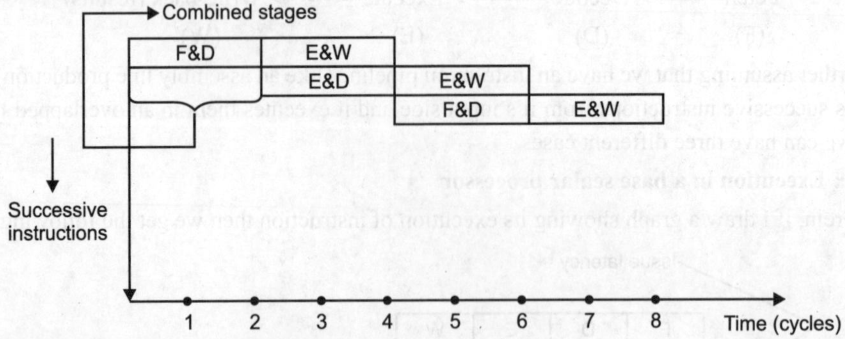

Fig. 5.10. Poor pipeline utilization.

Herein, 2 phases i.e. Fetch (*F*) and Decode (*D*0 have been merged. Similarly, Execute (*E*) and write-back results (*W*) phases have been merged. But this also results in **poor pipeline utilization.**

Please note here that the effective CPI for case I is 1 (ideal pipeline). **Whereas for case II, it is 2 and in case** III, it is $\frac{1}{2}$ (half) only. What we observe here is that the pipeline utilization is falling down only and not increasing.

5.7 INSTRUCTION-SET ARCHITECTURES

One of the important aspects of Computer architecture is the design – set for a processor. It is the instruction set chosen for a particular computer that determines the way in which machine language programs are constructed. A computer **with a large number of instructions is called as a complex instruction set computer** (CISC). Computer that uses a few instructions with simple constructs are called as **reduced instruction set computer (RISC).** These instructions can be executed at a faster -within the CPU with minimum memory references

5.8 CISC SCALAR PROCESSOR

A scalar processor will execute with a scalar data. Today's scalar processor have both integer and floating point unit within single CPU. This is shown in Fig. 5.11 below.

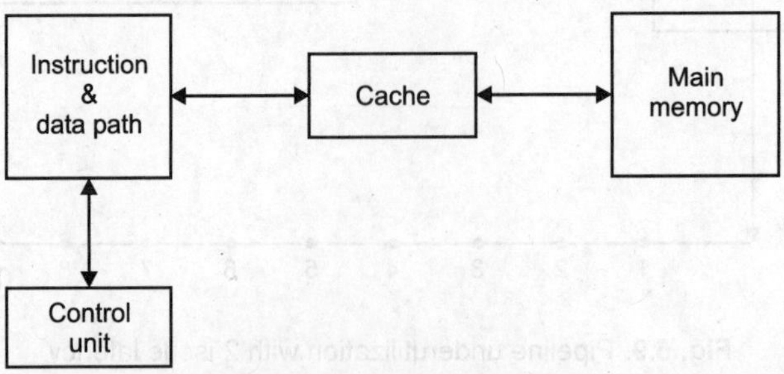

Fig. 5.11. CISC architecture.

We can use a single chip or many chips to construct a CISC scalar processor. **Please note that ideally, a CISC scalar processor should have a performance equal to that of a base scalar processor** (discussed earlier). However, in CISC machines under pipelining may occur due to data dependence, resource conflicts, branches, jumps and other reasons.

For example: *VAX* 8600, i486, M68040 are CISC processors. Others include 8086, 80186/286/386, M68000 etc.

By convention — CISC architecture (Fig. 5.11) uses a unified cache. **A unified cache** holds both instructions and data. So, same bus is used.

5.9 RISC SCALAR PROCESSORS

These processors issue one instructions per cycle. Some of the features of RISC are-

(*a*) Reduced instruction set.

(*b*) Simpler instructions.

(*c*) Hardwired control unit.

(*d*) Few addressing modes.

(*e*) Instruction pipelining.

For Example: Intel i860, M88100, and 29000 are some RISC processors. A RISC architecture is shown in Fig. 5.12.

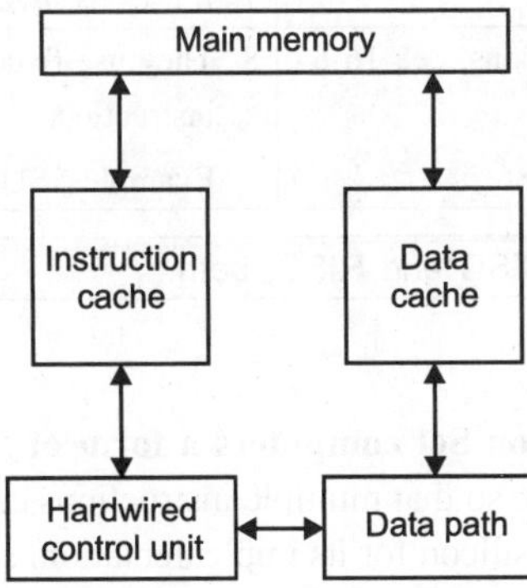

Fig. 5.12. A RISC Architecture.

In RISC machines, we have separate instruction (I) and data (D), caches. Say, we want to multiply 2 numbers being stored in a 2D- memory

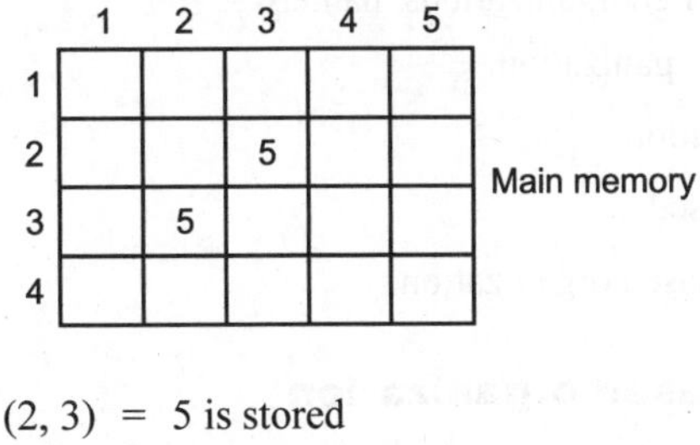

At memory location (2, 3) = 5 is stored

At memory location (3, 2) = 5 is stored.

Then, CISC machine will multiply them in one instruction as follows:

MULT : 2: 3, 3 : 2

Whereas RISC machine will use many instructions as follows:

Load *A*, 2 : 3 : Get First Number

Load *b*, 3 : 2 : Get Second number

Prod *A*, *B* : Multiply them i.e., $A \leftarrow A * B$

Store 2 : 3, *A* : Move results from *A* to ; Mem. Loc. 2 : 3

In CISC approach, very little RAM is required to store instruction. The emphasis is on building complex instructions directly into the hardware. But in RISC approach, more RAM is required.

Comparison of Cisc and Risc in Tabular Form

CISC	RISC
1. These computers use large set of instructions.	1. These computers use small set of instructions.
2. They support 12-24 addressing modes.	2. They support only 3-5 addressing modes.
3. They use 8-24 general purpose register (GPRS).	3. They use 32-192 GPRs.
4. They mostly have a unified cache.	4. They use separate (split) data and instruction cache.
5. Clock rates are between 33-50 MHz.	5. Clock rates are between 50-150 MHz.
6. CPI is between 2 and 15.	6. Average CPI is less than 1.5
7. It uses micro coded control logic.	7. It uses hardwired control logic.
8. They use variable format instructions, i.e., 16-64 bits per instruction. Examples: 8086, 186, 286, 386, 486.	8. They use fixed instruction format i.e. 32 bits per instruction. Examples: SUN SPARC, i860 etc.

Note: Pentium has features of CISC and RISC, both.

MISC

MISC or Minimal Instruction Set computers a form of stack machine where there are few separate instructions (16-64), so that multiple instructions can be fitted into a single machine word. They need small amount of silicon for its implementation, so they can be easily realized in a multi-core form. MISC's code density is similar to RISC.

5.10 DIFFERENT TYPES OF CPU ORGANIZATIONS

There are four types of CPU organizations, namely –

(*a*) Accumulator based organization.

(*b*) Stack based organization.

(*c*) General Register Based.

(*d*) Memory / Register based organization.

5.10.1 Accumulator based organization

Here, the operations can take place between accumulator and the operand (in instruction) only.

For eg. EDSAC uses this organization.

These types of computers use one address operands.

E.g. $A = B + C$

Pseudo op	Process
LOAD B	$AC \leftarrow M[B]$
ADD C	$AC \leftarrow AC + M[C]$
STORE A	$M[A] \leftarrow AC$

5.10.2 Stack based organization

Data operated on by program can be stored in the CPU register and in the computer memory. It can be organised properly for easy access. **For example,** the data stress of similar data type can be organised in the form of arrays and can be accessed using array pointers. Like array data structure, most of the computers supports an important data structure known as a stack.

A stack is a list of data elements, usually words or bytes, with the accessing restriction that the elements can be added or removed\ at one end of the list only. This end is called the **top** of the stack, and the other end is called the **bottom of the stack.** As only one end is used for adding and removing data elements, the element stored last is the first element retrieved. Thus stack structure is also known as **Last IN First-out (LIFO) list.** The terms **Push** and **Top** are used to describe placing a row data element on the stack and removing the top data element from the stack, respectively.

The stack in the digital computer is a part of register unit or memory unit with a registrar that holds the address for the stack. **The part of register array or memory used for stack is called stack area and the register used to hold the address of stack is called stack pointer. The value of the stack pointer** always point at the **top data element on the stack.**

Two Types of Stacks are there

I. Register Stack

As mentioned earlier, a stack can be placed in a portion of a memory unit or it can be organized as a collection of a finite number of CU registers. The Fig. 5.13 shows the organization of a 32-word register stack. The stack pointer holds the address of the register that is currently the top of stack. As shown in the Fig. 5.13 four data elements 10, 20, 30 and 40 are placed in the stack. The data element 40 is on the top of stack, therefore, the content of SP is now 4.

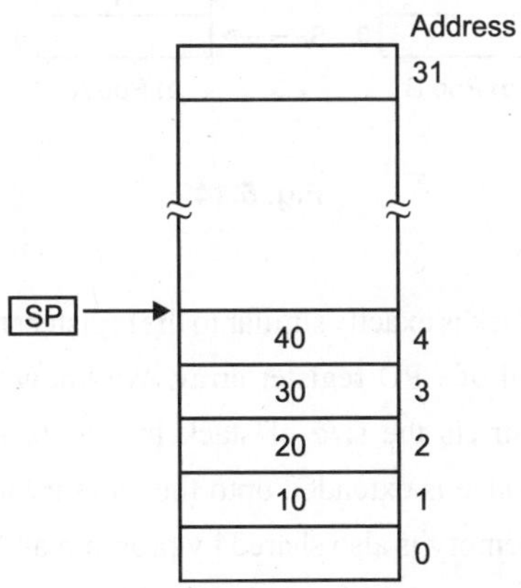

Fig. 5.13. Block diagram of a 32-word register stack

To remove the top data element, the stack is popped by reading the register at address 4 and decrementing the content of SP. The data element 30 is now on top of the stack since SP holds address 3. To insert a new data element, stack is pushed by incrementing SP and writing a data element on the incremented location in the stack.

In 32 word stack, the stack pointer is a 5-bit register, because $2^5 = 32$. Initially, it is clear to 0 and stack is said to be empty. When data element is pushed on the stack, the stack pointer is incremented so that it points to the address of the next higher register and then the data element is written in the register pointed by stack pointer. If SP reaches 31 and one more data element is pushed then SP is incremented to 0 and data element is stored in the register 0. Now there is no more empty register in the stack and stack is said to be FULL. The Fig. 5.14 shows the operation of stack when specified sequence of instructions are executed.

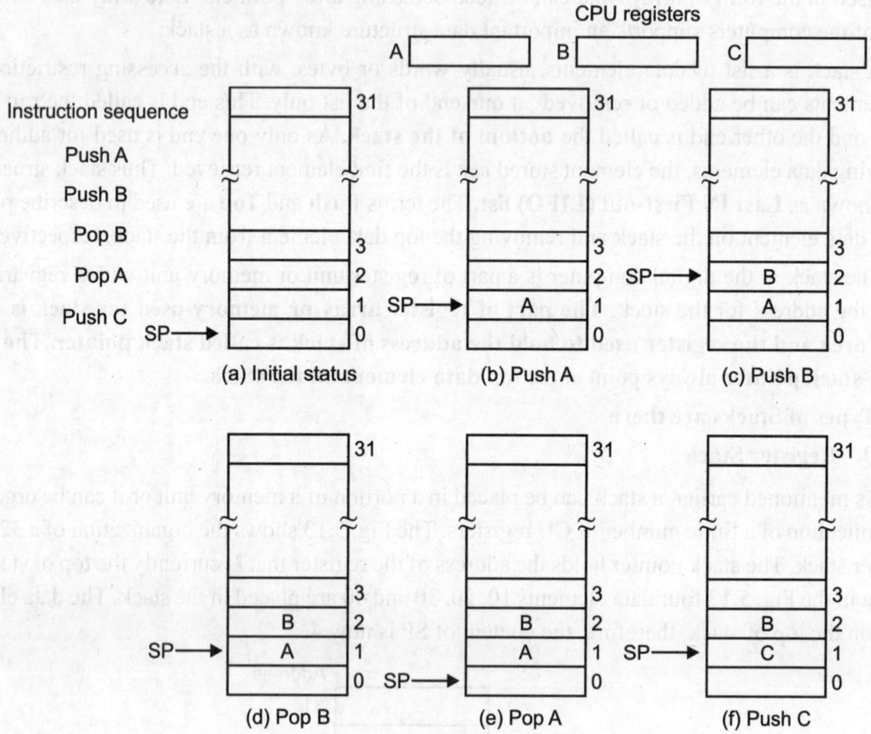

Fig. 5.14

II. Memory Stack

The operation of memory stack is exactly similar to the register stack. However, it is implemented using computer memory instead of CPU register array. We know that, the number of registers in the CPU are limited and it restricts the size of stack in the stack computer. But when stack is implemented using memory its size is extended upto the memory addressing capacity of the CPU. But truly speaking, computer memory is also shared by program and data, as shown in the Fig. 5.15. Hence a part of computer memory is used for the stack. **The memory stack has an advantage of large size but the operation on it is slower than that of register stack. This is because register stack is internal to the CPU and does not need any memory access.**

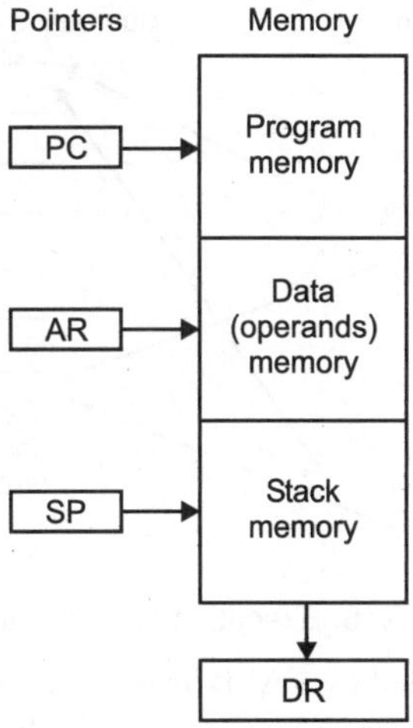

Fig. 5.15. Sharing of Computer memory by program, data and stack areas

In the stack organized computers instruction's operands are stored at the top of the stack, so data processing instructions do not need to contain addresses as they do in a conventional, Von Neumann computer. The add operation $A + B$ is specified for a stack computer by the following sequence of three instructions:

PUSH A

PUSH B

ADD

The first PUSH instruction loads A into top of stack (TOS). Execution of PUSH $-B$ causes A's location to become TOS + 1 and places B in the new TOS immediately above A. To execute ADD, the top two words of the stack are popped into the ALU where they are added, and the sum is pushed back into the stack. As shown by program sequence, in the stack computer, operator is specified after the operands i.e., $A\ B\ +$ Instead of $A + B$. **This method of representing arithmetic expression is known as Reverse Polish Notation,** named after the Polish logician Jan Siewicz Lucka. Therefore we can say the stack computer evaluates arithmetic and other expressions using a reverse polish notation format.

In most conventional computers, stack is used to implement subroutine call and return instructions. In some situations, it is better to execute part of a program that is not in sequence (don't confuse with logical sequence) with the main program. **For example,** there may be a part of program that must be repeated many times during the execution of the entire program. Rather than writing repeated part of the program again and again, the programmer can write that part only once. This part is written separately. **The part of the program which is written separately is called subroutine**. The Fig. 5.16 shows how the main and subroutine program are executed.

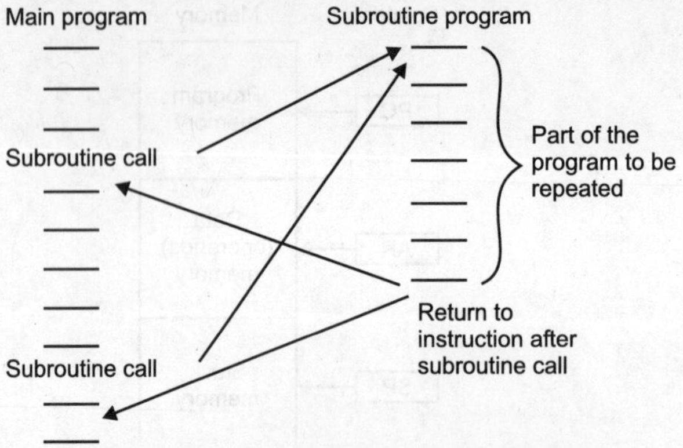

Fig. 5.16. Execution of subroutine programs

When the subroutine is called by CALL instruction the current of PC are pushed on the stack and after execution of subroutine program the content of PC as we popped back in the PC to execute the next instruction after the CALL.

5.10.3 General Register Based Organization

It has already been discussed in figure 5.5 and Section 5.1.

5.10.4 Memory / Register Based Organization

Most computers do not provide hardware to check **stack overflow** (i.e., full stack) or **stack underflow** (i.e., employ stack). This must be done by our software. This organization is shown in Fig. 5.17.

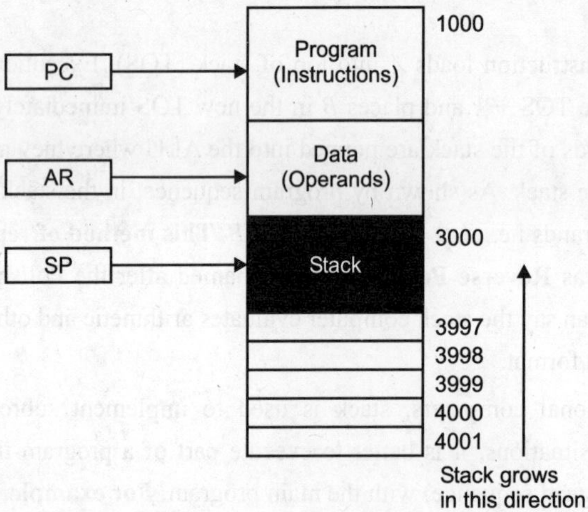

Fig. 5.17. Memory / Register based CPU organization.

5.11 DIFFERENT INTERNAL BUS STRUCTURES IN CPU

We know that bus is a group of community action lines or data paths, which connects different functional units and the different types of arrangement of buses is called **bus structure.** There are essentially three bus structures.

1. **Common-bus structure or single-bus organization** (Fig. 5.18).

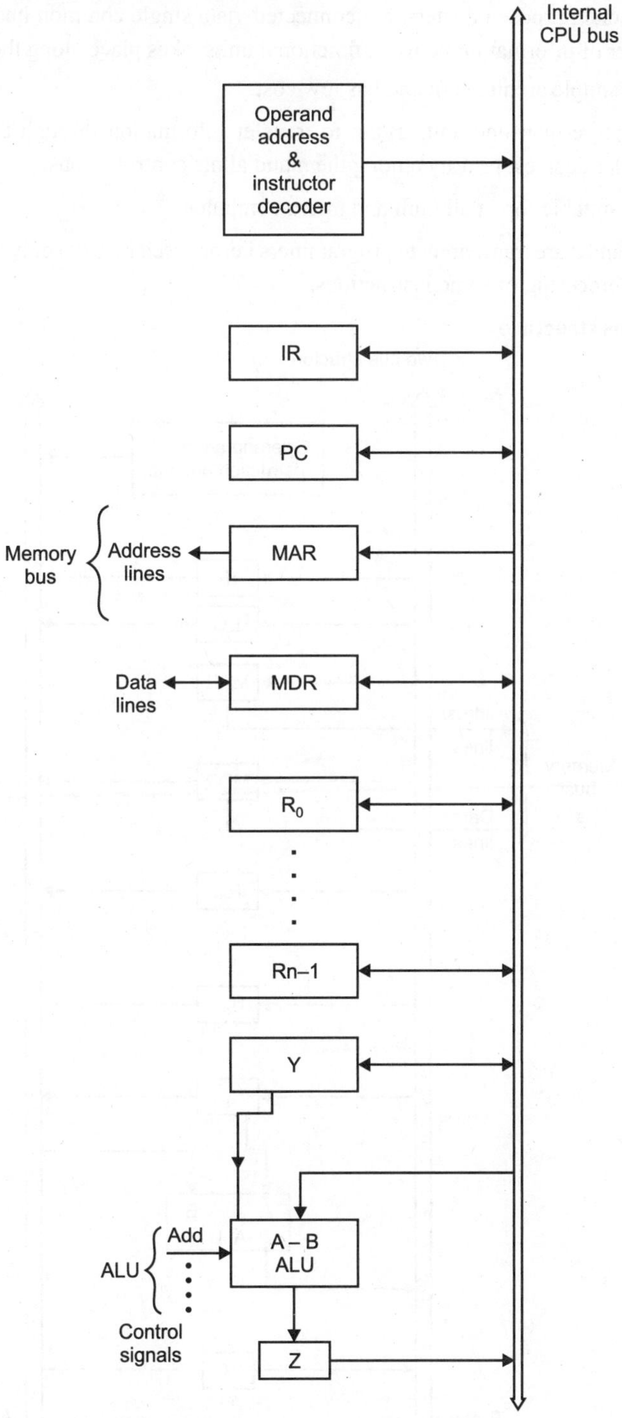

Fig. 5.18. Single bus organisation

2. **Two bus structure** (Fig. 5.19).
3. **Three bus structure** (Fig. 5.20).

In a **common bus structure**, the functional units like arithmetic logic unit, CPU-general purpose and special purpose registers, are connected via a single common bus which is internal to CPU. All transfer of information between functional units takes place along the common bus.

- This is simple architecture and has low cost.
- When more than one unit, trying to transfer information through the bus, then the bus controller decides, priority among them and allots control of bus.
- This is suitable for small mini and micro computer.
- Reg. *Y* and *Z* are transparent to programmers i.e. are used by CPU only for temporary storage during procesing of some instructions.

(ii) Two bus structure

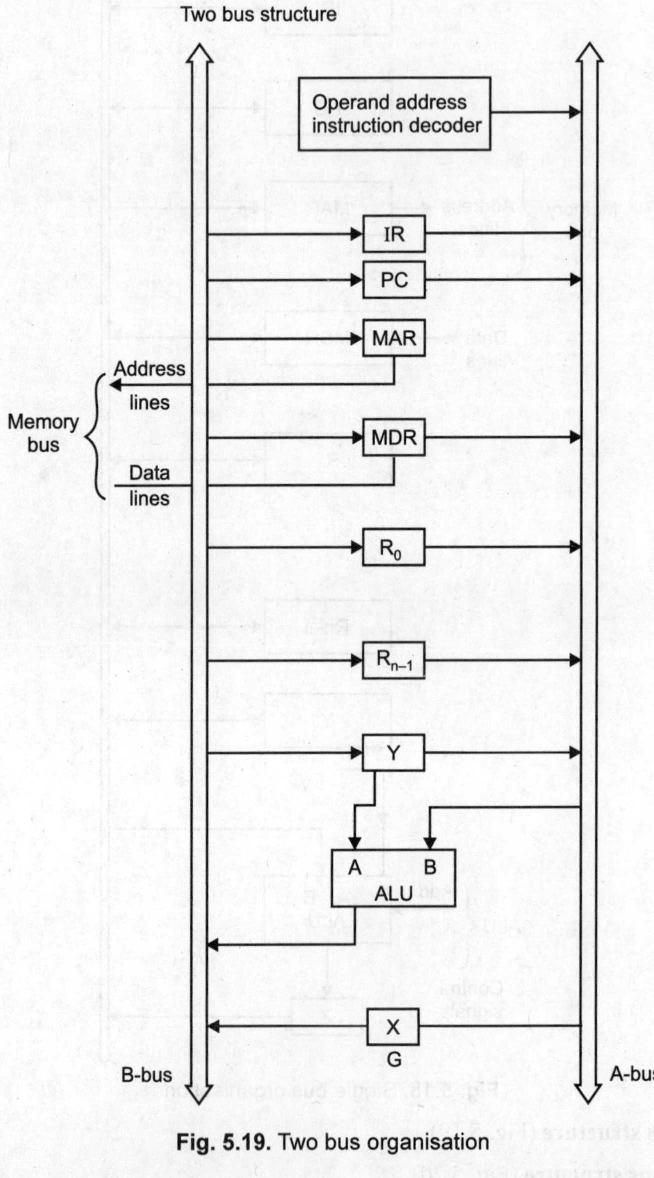

Fig. 5.19. Two bus organisation

- This arrangement consists of two bus — *A* and *B* so that all register inputs are connected to *B* bus and all register outputs are connected to *A* Bus, and both buses are connected to each other through a bustie (*G*) or busenable.
- The purpose of bustie is to isolate the buses when disabled and transfer the data on bus *A* to bus *B* when enabled.
- Since there are two buses, it is possible to have parallelism in operation to some extent.
- As more than one outputs are connected to bus, so control is complex.

(iii) Three Bus structure

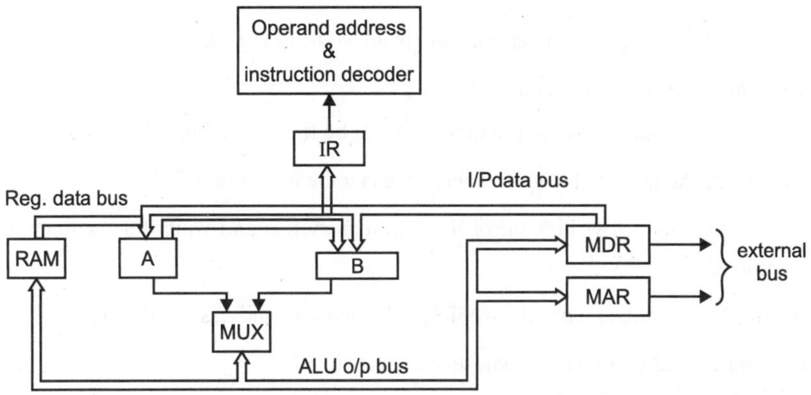

Fig. 5.20. Three bus organisation

- This arrangement consists of three buses output data, bus, register data bus and all output bus with each bus is connected to only one output at a time and a number of inputs.
- As only one O/P is connected to bus so but transfers are fast and simpler control.
- However, its needs multiplexers to select buses.
- *A* & *B* are work-registers.
- A these are 3 buses, so 30-transfers can take place simultaneously.

Thus we find that by providing more data paths, it is possible to reduce the number of clock cycles needed to execute an instruction.

5.12 FETCHING AND STORING DATA WORDS

How do you fetch a data word, from external memory?

The data, stored in a memory location, is identified by a unique address e.g. 20A0, 20A1 etc.,

- This memory address, is transferred to the memory address register (MAR), by CPU (memory fetch).
- Then CPU connects the read control line of memory bus and words until the read function is completed.
- When read function is completed (i.e. contents of addressed memory location are available on data bus), it is indicated by control signal called memory function completed (MFC)

and when MFC is enabled (1) the contents of data bus are loaded into memory data register (MDR).

E.g. transfer data QRS register R2 from location specified in register R1.

Step 1: MAR ← [*R*1] ; Obtain address of location where data stored is in R1 register into MAR.

Step 2: Read ; Enable read control signal on memory bus.

Step 3: Wait ; Wait until MFC = 1 so that contents of location on data bus and inturn into MDR.

Step 4: *R*2 ← [MDR] ; Transfer contents from MDR to reg. R2.

How do you store data word into memory?

- The data word to be loaded into memory is to be first loaded into MDR.
- Obtains the address of location where data is to be loaded into MR.
- Then, CPU enables write control line in memory bus and waits for memory function to complete.
- When MFC = 1, data word from MDR is loaded into addressed location.

  Load data word in a location whose address is in *R*1.

  The data word is in *R*2.

  We have to store data word into address of memory specified in *R*1.

Step 1 : MAR ← [*R*1]: ; Obtain address of location where data stored into MAR.

Step 2: MDR ← [*R*2] ; Obtain data into MDR.

Step 3 : Write ; Enable write control signal to place contents of MDR in data bus.

Step 4 : Wait ; Wait until MFC to get enabled so that data on bus is loaded into location in *R*1.

5.13 REGISTER TRANSGFER WITH I/O GATING

Register Transfer

There are two types of transfers of information from source register to destination register.

In a **parallel transfer** all bits from source register are transferred simultaneously to destination register, during one clock pulse.

In a **serial transfer**, information is transferred one bit at a time by shifting each bit from source register to destination register which is achieved by shift registers.

- Transfer of information from source register to common bus – parallel transfer.
- Four register *A*, *B*, *C* and *D* are connected to common bus lines.

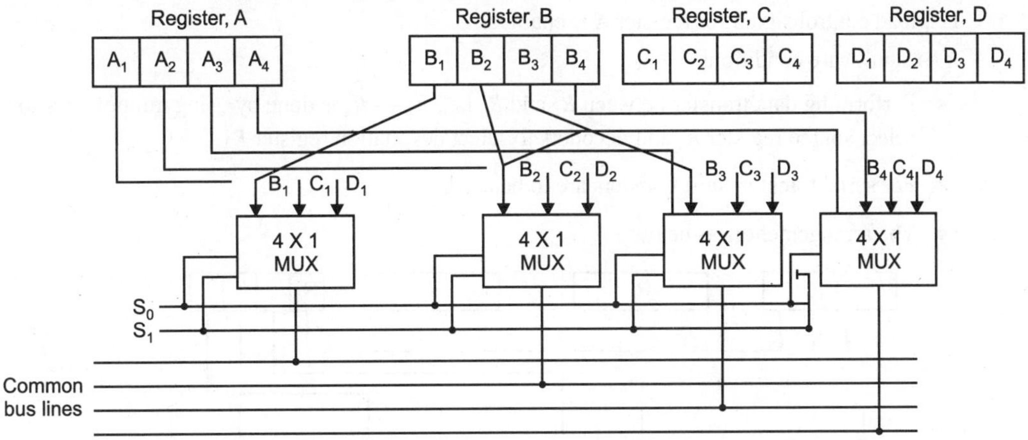

- At a time one register contents are available on common bus, by using multiplexers as below.
- The select signals are as below:

S_0	S_1	Register selected
0	0	*A*
0	1	*B*
1	0	*C*
1	1	*D*

When S_0, S_1 are 0, 0 then Register A contents, A_1, A_2, A_3, A_4 are available on common bus.

- **Transferring information from Common bus to selected register.**

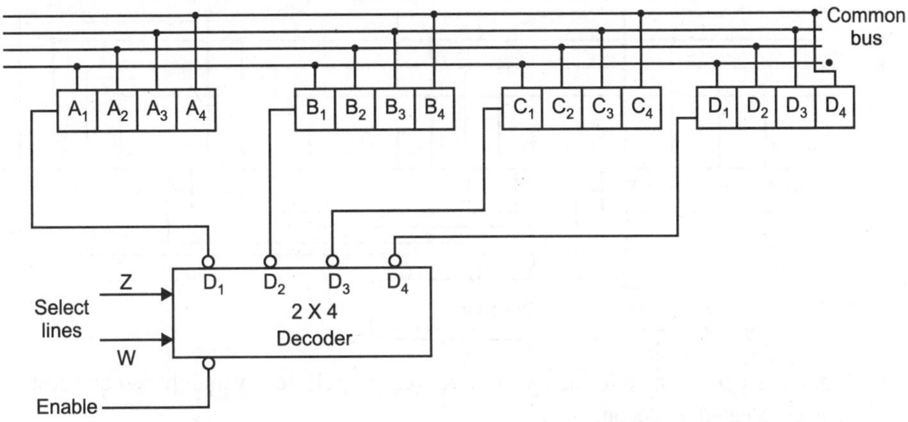

Enable	*Z*	*W*	Selected destination register
0	0	0	Register *A*
0	0	1	*B*
0	1	0	*C*
0	1	1	*D*
1	*X*	*X*	No register selected

i.e., load control signal for register A is enabled.

$X \rightarrow$ don't care conditions

- Performing data transfer between R_1 and R_4 i.e., $R_1 \leftarrow R_4$ is done by using multiplexers to select source register R_4 and decoders to select destination register $R1$.
- For serial transfer, shift registers are to be used.
- The arrangement is as below.

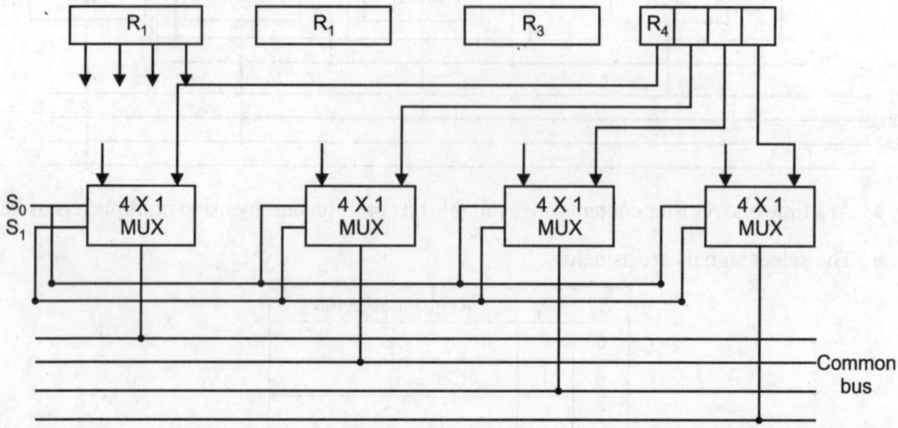

Step 1: Control signals $S_0 = 1$, $S_1 = 1$ to select R_4. So that contents of R_4 are placed on data bus

Step 2: Select destination reg. with control signals enable = 0, $z = 0$, $w = 0$ so that contents on data bus are placed into R_1.

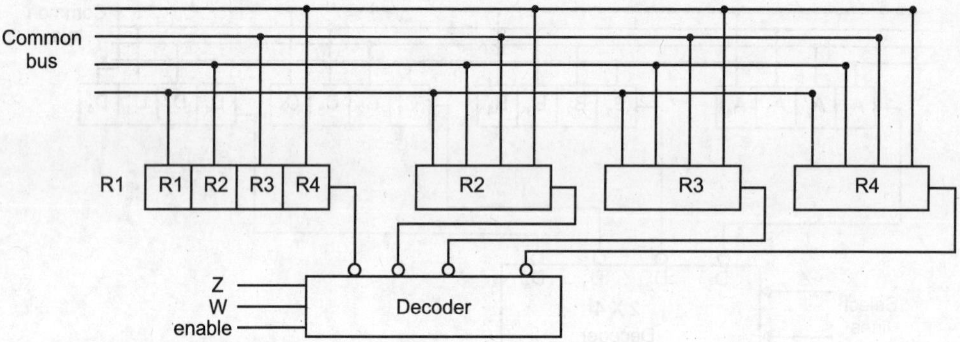

- Arithmetic operation performed with source register selected by multiplexer and destination register selected by decoders.

Control Signals

1. MUX A select signals enabled to place $R2$ on A bus.
2. MUX B select signal enabled to place $R3$ on B bus.
3. In ALU function selector, add signals are enabled to perform $R2 + R3$.

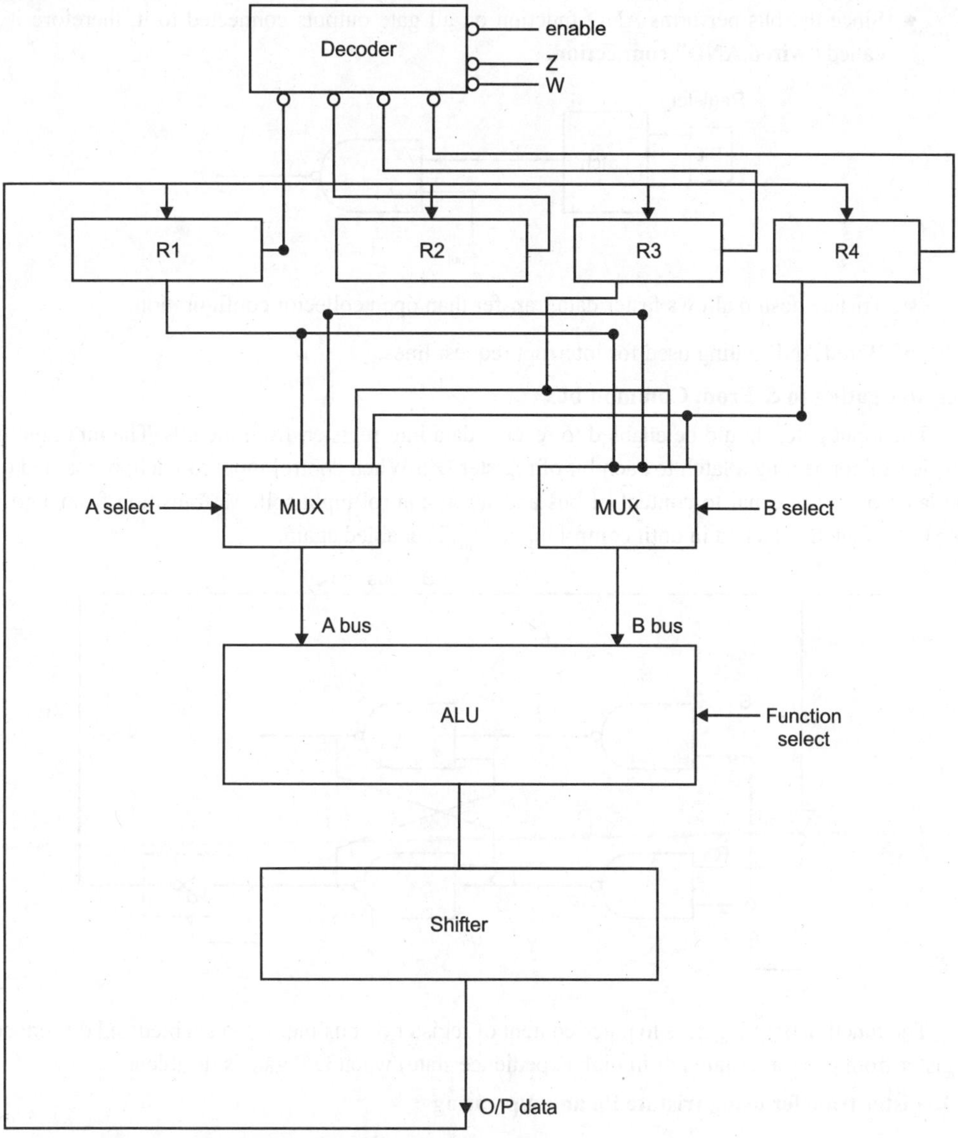

4. Shift select enable to place ALU on output bus.
5. Decoder select to replace result into R_1 ($z = 0, w = 0$).

This is achieved by gate with tristate O/O as shown in Fig. When control input (Z_{out}) is enabled, contents of register bit is placed on bus line and when Z_{out} is disabled register is isolated from bus.

- I/O gating can also achieved by means of open collector (for bipolar) or opendrain (for MOS) gates.
- Therefore an open collector NAND gate is used.
  - When Z_{out} is high, bit stored in the latch (from register bit) is loaded on bus line.
  - When Z_{out} is low bus is in idle (1) state. Thus allows data to the bus is transferred from other register.

- Since the bus performs AND function on all gate outputs connected to it, therefore it is called **"wired AND" connection.**

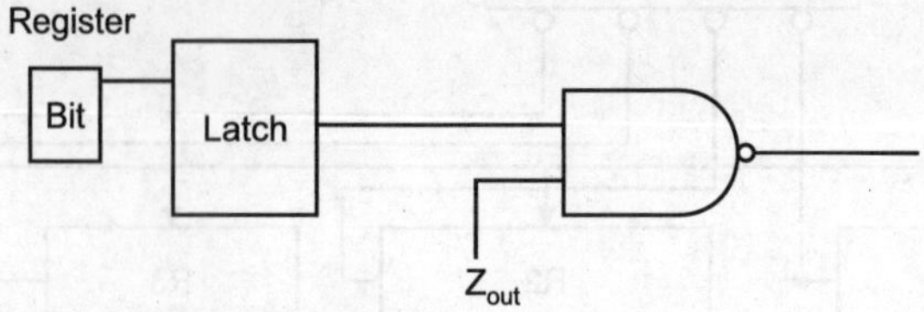

- Tristate design allows faster data transfer than open collector configuration.
- Wired AND gating used for interrupt request lines.

Register gating to & From Common bus

The input gate, should be enabled to receive data into register, from the bus. The input gating consists of connecting a latch to each bit of register (Z). When control input to latch, is enabled (1) the latch output is equal to content of bus and when control input follows transition from 1 to 0. The O/P of latch is locked in until control input (Z_{in}) is enabled again.

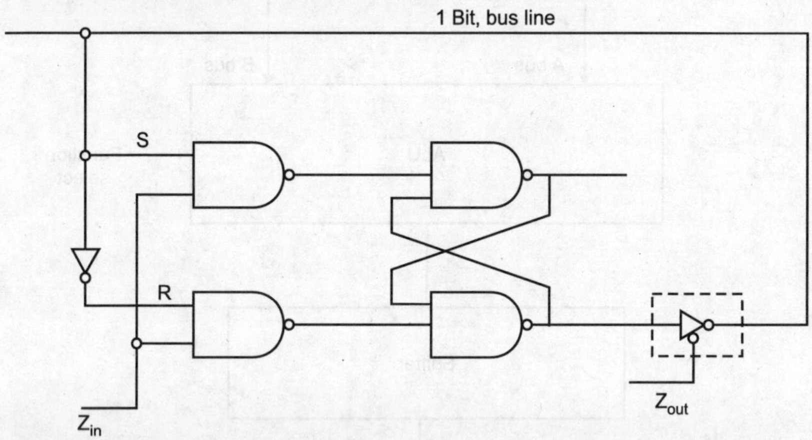

The function of O/P gate is to place content of register on busline, when enabled and disconnect register from bus (or tristated or in high expedience state) when O/P gate is disabled.

A Register transfer using tristate i/p and o/p gating

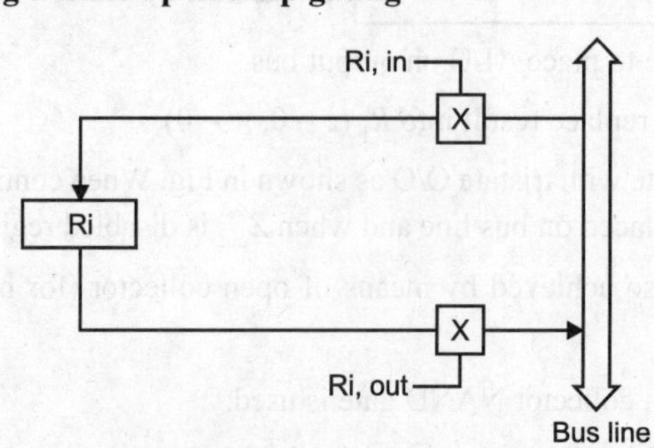

- To enable data transfer between register and bus lines, input and output gatings are provided.
- The register R_i is connected to bus via input gate and output gate.

- The input gate is controlled by R_i in control signal and O/p gate by R_i out signal.
- To place register content on bus, the control line of output gate R_i out is enabled and to place bus line content on register bit the O/p gate control line R_{in} is enabled e.g. obtain register transfer in common bus for following case $R_1 \leftarrow R_4$.

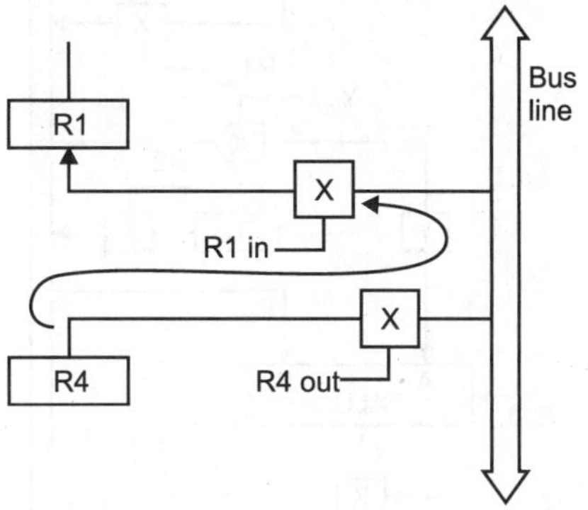

Step 1: Enable control line of output gate of R_4 to place its content onbus.

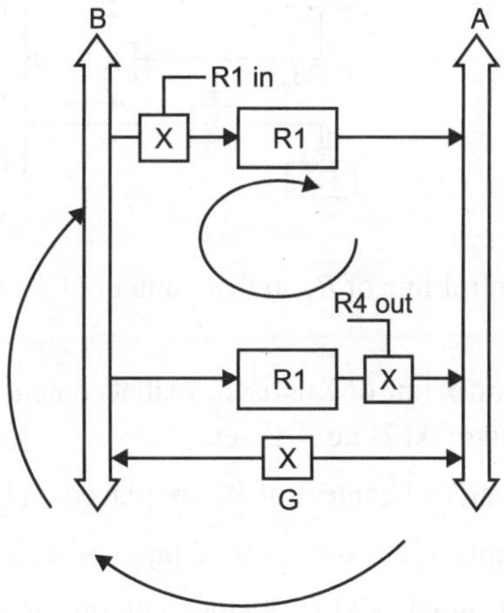

Step 2: Enable control line of input gate of R_1 to place content of bus input R_1.

In two bus structure, $R_1 \leftarrow R_4$ performed is as below:

Step 1: Enable output gate control line $R_{4\,out}$ to place content of R_4 on A bus.

Step 2: Enable busline, so that data on A bus are transferred to B bus.

Step 3: Enable input gate control line of R_1 so that content on B bus are loaded into R_1 register

- **Performing arithmetic operation: Using Input/output gating**

$$R3 \leftarrow [R1] + [R2]$$

- We know that ALU is complemented with combinational circuits and therefore has no internal storage (flip-flops). Thus, one of operand is placed into temporary register (r) and the second operand is directly gated from bus. So that both operands are available simultaneously, at the inputs of ALU.

- The steps to perform $R_5 \leftarrow [R1] + [R2]$ are as below:

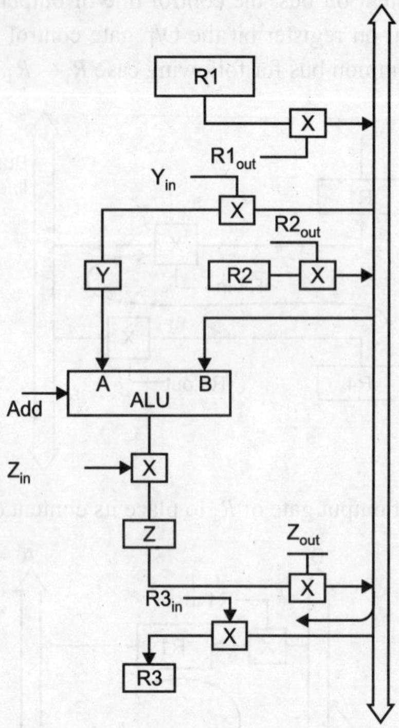

Step 1: Enable output gate control line of R_1 so that content of R_1 are loaded onto common bus to $\boldsymbol{R_{1out}}$ **is set.**

Step 2: Enabled input (gate control line of Y register, so that content of bus are loaded into Y register and available at A input of ALU i.e. Y is set.

Step 3: Enable O/p gate of $R2$ so that content of $R2$ are placed on bus i.e. R_2out set.

Step 4: Directly gate the contents of bus onto second input of ALU.

Step 5: Enable the add control signal in ALU. So that both operands available at A & B in input of ALU are added.

Step 6: Enable input control line Z_{in} of Z reg so that result is placed into Z register i.e. Z_{in} set.

Step 7: Enable output control line Z_{out} of Z reg so that result in Z are loaded into bus Z_{out} set.

Step 8: Enable input control line R_{3in} of R_3 reg so that contents of bus are loaded onto R_3 reg i.e., R_3 in set.

These above 8 microoperations may be grouped. So that they can be done in 3 micro operations as below [1], R_{1out}, Y in (2) R_{2out}, Add, Z_{in} (3) Z_{out}, R_{3in}

Arithmetic Operations in Two Bus Structure

E.g. $R_3 \leftarrow [R1] + [R2]$

1. R_{1out}, G_{enable}, Y_{in}

- Place contents of R_1 on B bus by R_{1out} set.
- The enable G so that content on B bus red transfer to A bus.

- Enable Y_{in} so that content on *A* bus loaded line *Y* and available at *A* input of ALU.
- Directly gate second operand from *R*2 and available at *B* input of ALU.
- Enable add control lien of ALU & result in ALU directly gated to *B* bus and enable R_3 in to place result in R_3.

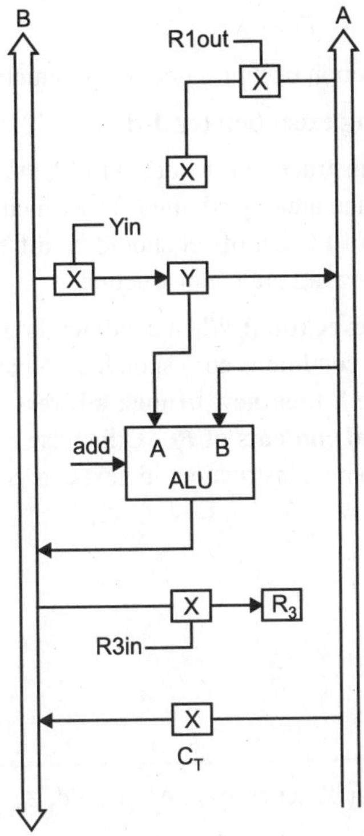

5.14 EXECUTION OF ONE COMPLETE INSTRUCTION

This essentially consist of two cycles called fetch cycle and execution cycle together called instruction cycle

- The **fetch cycle**, consist of fetching the instruction (opcode) from external memory location where address is specified in program counter, and loading it into instruction register (IR), Within the CPU.
- Before memory read function is completed, (i.e. placing opcode into database and intune into IR) the program counter contents get updated so that it contains address of next instruction, to be fetched from memory.

  $$PC \leftarrow PC + K$$

  Where *K* is word length of memory. $K = 1$, when instruction occupies one word in memory.
- The above steps are repeated until complete instruction is loaded into *IR*, when instruction occupies more than one word in memories.

  $(IC = FC + EC)$
- The execution phase begins as soon as fetch phase is completed (i.e. instruction is loaded into *IR*).

- The instruction decoding circuit, enables the appropriate control signals and perform the operation, as indicated in *I.R*.
- Straight-line-execution. In this, while waiting for instruction to be placed into *IR* (i.e. memory read) the *PC* is updated so that it points to next consecutive location, which contains the next instruction code.

$$PC \leftarrow PC + K$$

where $K = 1$ when instruction occupies one word in memory.

- **Unconditional branching execution (eg JMP)**

  In this as soon as branch instruction is loaded into *IR*, the *PC* is loaded with branch address. The branch address is calculated by adding offset which is specified, in instruction, to the current updated content of PC i.e. offset should be different between branch address and address immediately following branch instruction.

- **Conditional branching execution:** When condition branch instruction like *jnz*, *jc*, jnc etc. is stored in *IR*, the status conditions corresponding to conditions in instruction is checked. **If conditions are satisfied, then new branch address is loaded into *PC* by adding the offset to current updated contents of *PC*.** Otherwise normal execution is done since *PC* now updated to point it to next instruction, in next consecutive location E.g. Add NUM, *R*1

Step 1: Fetch instruction.

Step 2: Fetch first operand.

Step 3: Perform addition.

Step 4: Load result into *R*1.

Control Sequence

1. PC_{out}, MAR_{in}, Read, Clear *Y*, set carry in ALU, Add, Z_{in}.
2. Z_{out}, PC_{in}, wait for MFC.
3. MD R_{out}, IR_{in}.
4. Add field of IR_{out}, MAR_{in}, Read.
5. $R1_{out}$ Y_{in}, Wait for MFC.
6. MDR_{out}, Add, Z_{in}
7. Z_{out}, R_{in}
8. end

Unconditional Branching

1. PC_{out}, MAR_{in}, Read, Clear *Y*, set any in ALU, Add, Z_{in}.
2. Z_{out}, PC_{in}, Wait for MFC.
3. MDR_{out}, IR_{in}
4. PC_{out}, Y_{in}
5. Add Field of IR_{out}, Add, Z_{in}
6. Z_{out}, PC_{in}
7. end

Conditional Branching

- If branch instruction is jump if negative, then CPU checks negative flag which if set i.e. condition satisfied then control transfers to end and next instruction cycle, begins.
- If condition is not satisfied, then new value of branch address is calculated by adding offset, X, specified in instruction address field with current updated contents of PC and loaded into PC so that control transfers to new branch address.

5.15 GENERATING COINTROL SIGNALS BY TWO METHODS

There are **two methods of control** used (i) Hardwired control (2) Microprogrammed control

- **Hardwired Controller**

1. We know that, a counter driven by an external clock is required to know, how many steps are needed to execute an instruction in IR. As each state of counter corresponds to each step.
2. The instruction decoder, interprets content of instruction register and depending upon the outer protection, control signals are generated.
3. We are also required to know the condition code and status flags, (when IR is a conditional branch instruction) to generate appropriate control signals.

The above 3 information is necessary to generate appropriate control signals which is achieved as below:

> **NOTE:** Using hard wired logic in camps is an old method and now-a-days μpc- method of generation of control signals is used.

The arrangement, based on above, **three facts**, (i.e., number of steps indicated by counter contents of *IR* for which decoder / encoder and status conditional codes checked), consists of counter driven by clock, a decoder/ encoder block and status flags with conditional codes block as shown.

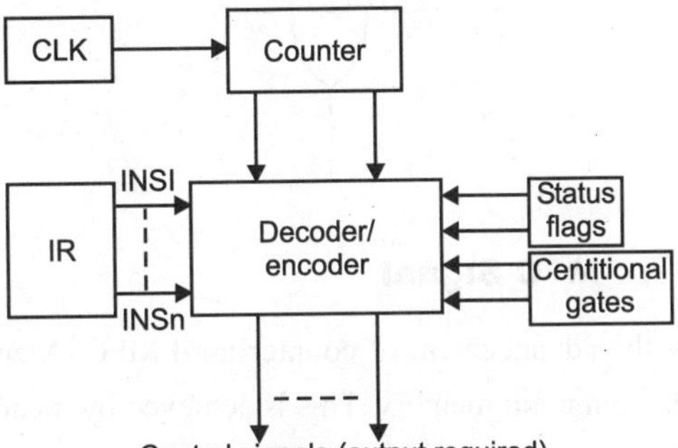

- The counter provided with step decoder provides signal to each step in execution of instruction
- Detailed block diagram is given on next page.
- Instruction decoder consists of signals INS1 to INSn for instructions.
- When an instruction is loaded into *IR* then corresponding INS signal enabled and all other lines are disabled.

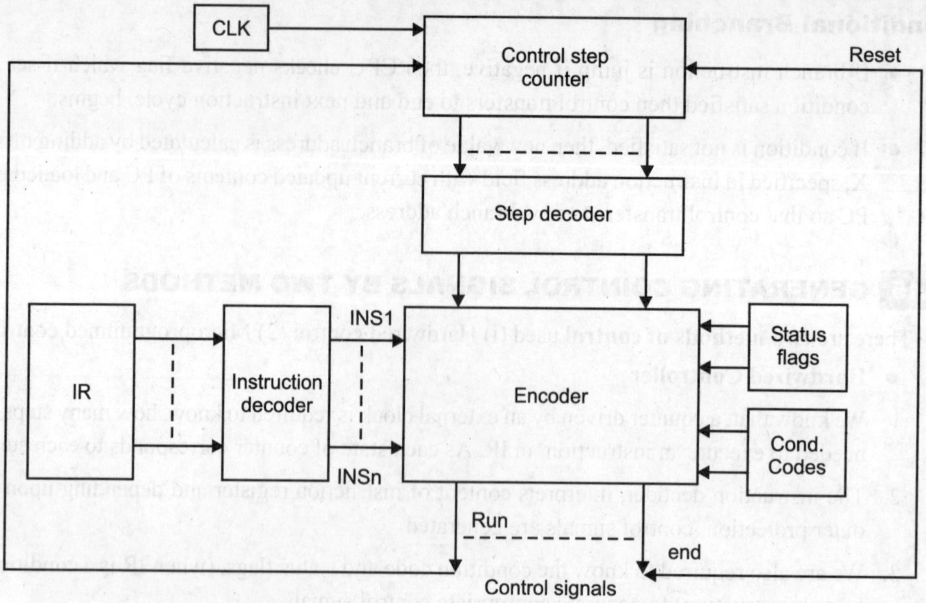

Generation of Control Signs: e.g. Z_{in} control signal enabled during time slot T_1, during T_6 for ADD instruction, during T_5 for branch instruction etc.

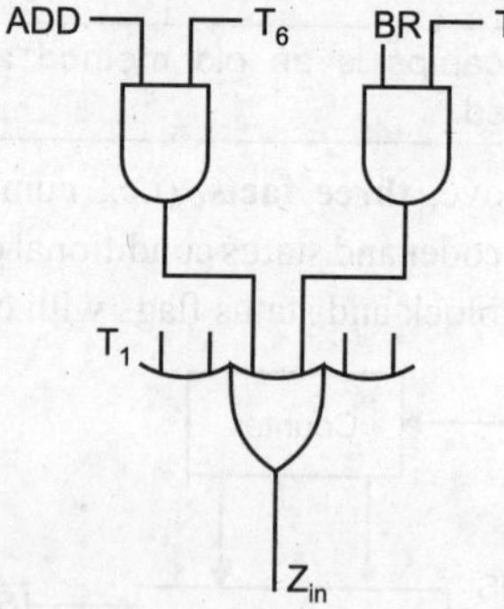

Generation of Wait for MFC Signal

- We need to delay the advancement of counter until MFC (Memory Function Complete) signal is received, from main memory. This is achieved by means of RUN signal wherein wherever run is active, counter is advanced. When WMFC signals generated, RUN becomes 0 and counting is inhibited and CPU remains in wait state until MFC is received.
- Also, as MFC is generated from memory which is not synchronous in with CPU clock and therefore to synchronise MFC with CPU clock, a flip flop is used.
- Both required, for generation of RUN signal and modified circuit to synchronize MFC with CPU clock, as shown below.

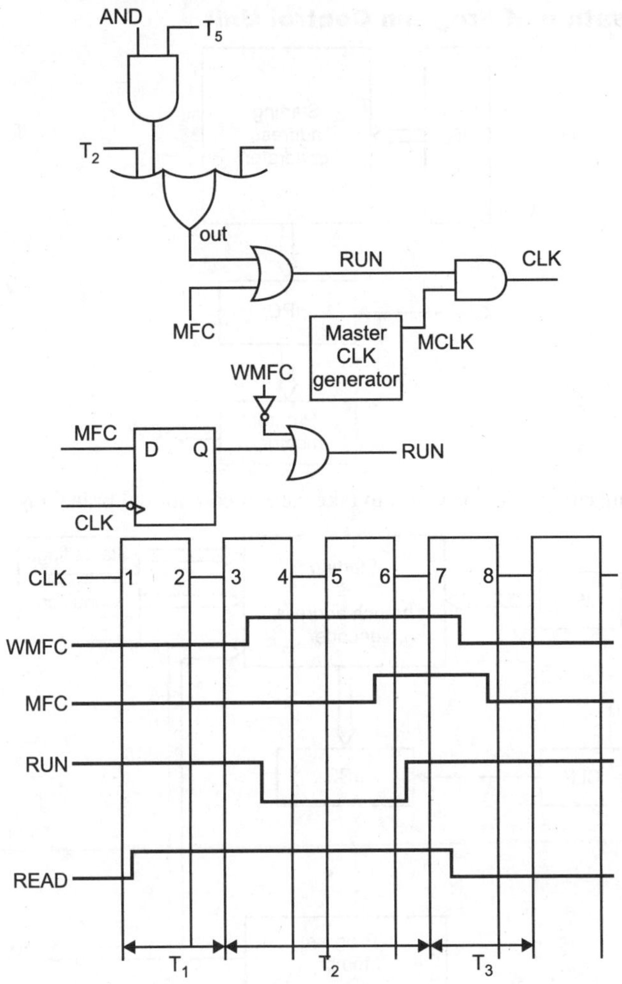

Construed individual boils of this indicate different control signals.

- In a microprogram each control lood is called as micro **instruction.**
- Microprogram is stored in special memory within CPU called **microprogram memory.**
- **To read control words sequentially, microprogram control (μpc) used.**
- Whenever a new instruction is loaded into i.e., μpc is incrementally, loaded with starting address of corresponding the program.
- μpc **is incriminated automatically** to Read successive control words in a μ-program.
- To take care of branching chinch micro instructions are included.
- To take care of conditional branching micro instructions specify cohich of instruction register should be checked as a condition for branching to take place.
- μpc is loaded with **first in** μ-program when **"end"** instruction encountered.
- μpc loaded with **starting address** when new instruction is loaded into IR.
- When branch μ-instruction encountered and if branch condition satisfied then μpc loaded with branch address.

Basic Organisation of Program Control Unit

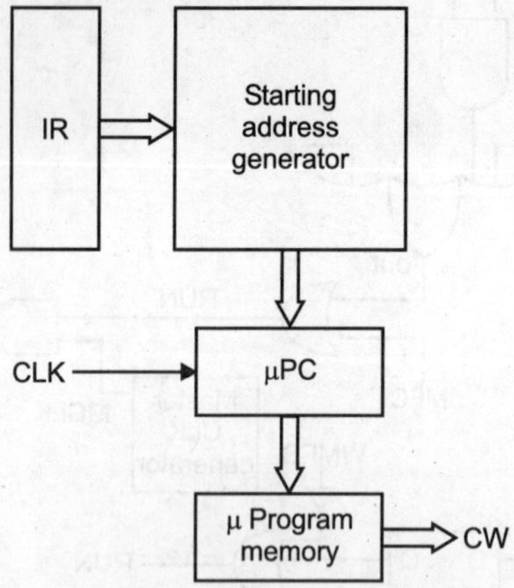

Modified organisation of control unit to take care of conditional branching.

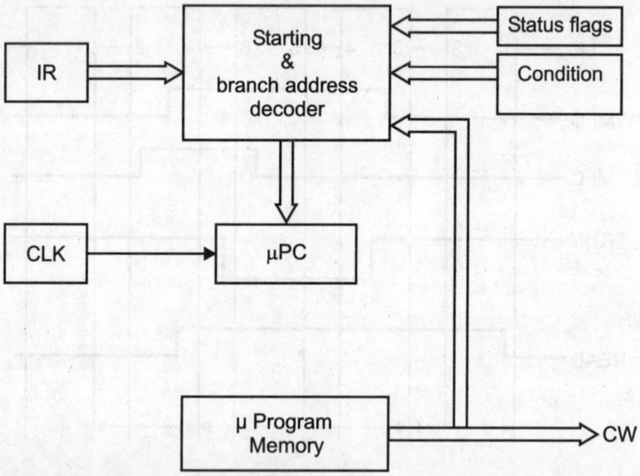

Advantages of μ Programmed Control

- As instruction corresponds to μ program, so set of μ programs define set of instruction. We can change instruction set by changing μ programs. This flexibility is not possible in hardware controllers.
- Execution of an instruction depends upon fetch time of corresponding μ program. So, speed of microprogram, memory should be fast.
- ROM is used for μ program storage, as contents of μ program memory are not changed frequently.
- It also facilitates the addition of new instructions to existing machines.. μ_p control is more efficient and orderly as we don't need 1 clock after every one instruction is executed.

Disadvantages of Microprogammed Control

1. A μP control unit is slower than hardwired CU. This is so because time required to access the microinstructions from (control Memory (CM) is more).

2. The flexibility is achieved at some extra hardware cost due to control memory (CM) and its access circuiting.

Before we discuss further let us solve some examples based on control designs now.

EXAMPLE 1: Write a combined micro routine that can implement that BGT (Branch if > 0), BPL (Branch if plus) and *BR* (Branch unconditionally) instructions. The branch conditions for the BGT and BPL instructions are–

$$Z + (N \text{ XOR } V) = 0$$

and $N = 0$ **respectively.**

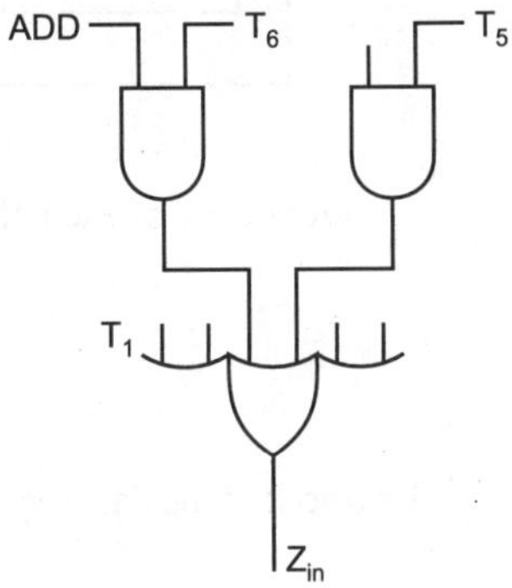

Find the following now

(*a*) Total number of microinstructions required.

(*b*) Total number of microinstructions required if a separate microroutine is used for each machine instruction.

SOLUTION: For bus organization, we write the microroutines for all three branches given in the question –

(*a*) Combined Microroutine –

Address	Microinstruction
0	PC_{out}, MAR_{in}, Read, Y_{in}, Select C, Add, Z_{in}
1	Z_{out}, PC_{in}, WMFC
2	MDR_{out}, IR_{in}

According to the opcode in instruction register (IR), branching is made to the starting address of appropriate microroutine.

(*b*) Unconditional Branch

15	Offset-field-of-IR_{out},
	Select Y, Add, Z_{in}
16	Z_{out}, PC_{in}, End

(*c*) Branch if plus

25	If N = 1 then branch to microinstruction
26	Offset-field-of, IR_{out}, Select
27	Z_{out}, PC_{in}, End.

(*d*) Branch if > 0

35	If $Z + (N \text{ XOR } V) = 1$ then branch
16	Offset-field-of, IR_{out}, Select
2	Z_{out} , PC_{in}, End.

Please note here that the first three microinstructions in the combined microroutine are used to fetch the opcode. The total number of microinstruction required are 11. Also note that if a separate microroutine is used for each machine instruction then 17 microinstructions are required in all.

EXAMPLE 2: The microprogrammed control organization in figure below has the following propagation delay times— 40ns to generate the next address, 10ns to transfer the address into the control address register, 40ns to cross the control memory ROM, 10ns to transfer the microinstruction into the control data register and 40ns to perform the required

microoperations specified by the control word. What is the maximum clock frequency that the control can use? What would the clock frequency be if the control data register is not used? Given

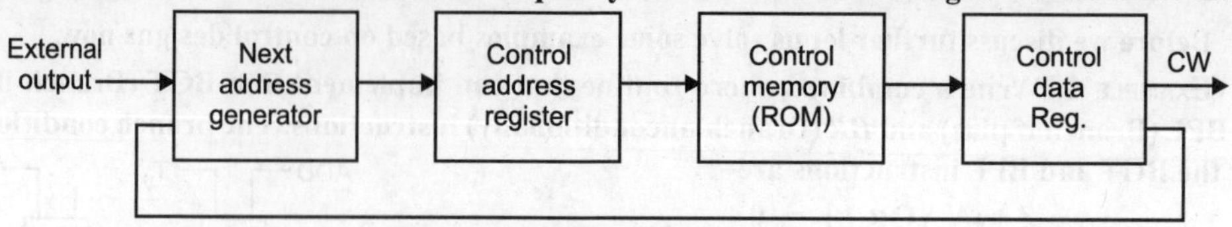

Fig. 5.21. μP control organization

$$\text{Frequency of each clock} = \frac{1}{100\times10^{-9}}$$

$$= \frac{100}{100}\times10^{6}$$

$$= 10 \text{ MHz}$$

SOLUTION: If the data register is removed, we can use a single phase clock with a frequency of –

$$= \frac{1}{90\times10^{-9}}$$

$$= 11.1 \text{ MHz}$$

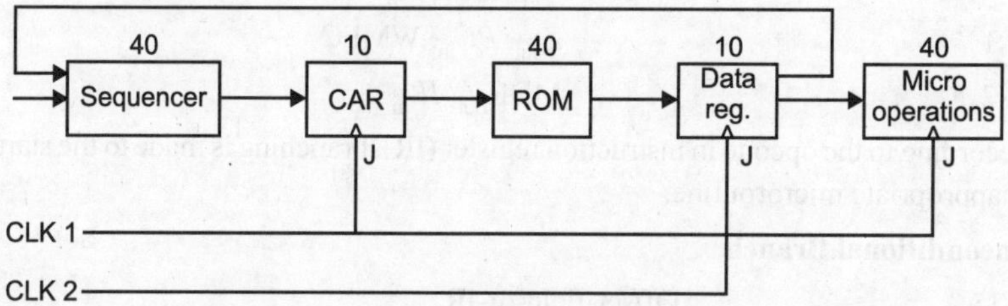

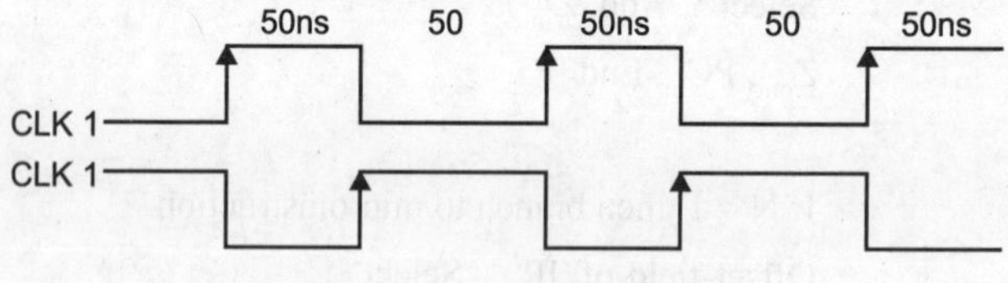

5.16 REVERSE POLISH NOTATION (RPN)

In late 1950s, Australian philosopher and computer Scientists Charles L. Hamblin suggested to place the operator after the operands. Such a notation, he called as a **Reverse Polish Notation (RPN) or postfix expression. For eg.,** The following RPN expression will multiply 3 and 3 to give 9.

3 3 *

E.g. 2 : (3 + 4)*5 can be expressed in RPN as

3 4+ 5 *

E.g. 3$A + B$ is expressed as $AB +$ in RPN.

Properties of RPN

1. Brackets are not required to represent the order of evaluation or grouping of terms.
2. RPN expressions are simply evaluated from left to right. This simplifies the computation of the expression within computer programs.

3. Stack organization used RPNs to evaluate arithmetic expressions.
4. Reading the expression from left to right, the following operations are performed-
   (*a*) If a value appears next in the expression, push this value on to the stack.
   (*b*) If an operator appears next, pop two items from the top of the stack and push the result of the operation on to the stack.
5. Basically, there are three methods of representing arithmetic expressions –
   (*a*) $A + B$ = Infix form.
   (*b*) $+ AB$ = Prefix (or polish) form.
   (*c*) $AB +$ = Postfix (or RPN) form.
   But our **stack uses RPN form.**
6. A standard infix form expression can be converted to an RPN expression using a parsing algorithm as recursive descent parse.

RPN Algorithm

A stack based algorithm for evaluation of postfix (or RPN) expressions is –

*S*1 : Get a token (operator or operand) from the input text.

*S*2 : **If the token is an operand,** push it onto the top of the stack.

*S*3 : **If the token is an operator,** pop the two operands from the stack, perform the operation and push the result onto the top of the stack.

*S*4 : Repeat step-1 to steps-3, until there are no more tokens.

The result is the value at the top of the stack. **We are in a position to solve some examples now.**

EXAMPLE 1: Convert the following infix expression into its RPN form-
$(x + y)*[z*(w + v) + s]$

SOLUTION: The two-sub expression $(x + y)$ and $(w + v)$ will be solved first. Thus, the postfix expression for these are –

$xy +$

and $wv +$ respectively.

Now, in square brackets, z will be multiplied by $(w + v)$.

∴ It's postfix form is $zwv + *$,

This is then added to s i.e.,

$zwv + *s +$.

Finally, $xy +$ and $zwv + *s +$

will be multiplied together to get

$xy + zwv + *s + *$

EXAMPLE 2: How stack is used to compute this RPN
2 3 4 * + . ?

SOLUTION: We draw a table here –

Token	Action	Stack contents
2	Push 2	{2}
3	Push 3	{2, 3}
4	Push 4	{2, 3, 4}
*	Pop 4, pop3 MUL, Push 12	{2, 12}
+	Pop 12, pop 2, add, Push 14	{14}

Below we show the stack contents –

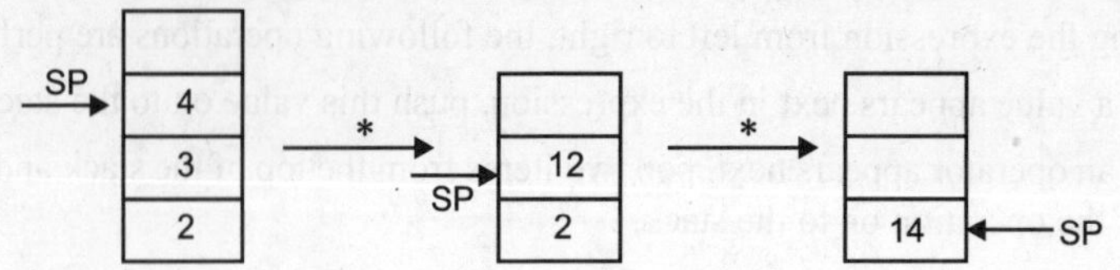

∴ Final result of 2 3 4 * +

RPN is 14.

EXAMPLE 3: Show the stack states during the execution of –

$$Z = W + (3 * (x - y)) + 2(v + u)$$

[UPTU, BE(CSE) -4th Sem., May 2003]

SOLUTION: In RPN, the given expression is expressed as –

$xy - 3 * vu * 2 * w + +$

Say, $x = 5$

$y = 2$

$v = 3$

$u = 4$

and $w = 6$

Then the stack contents are –

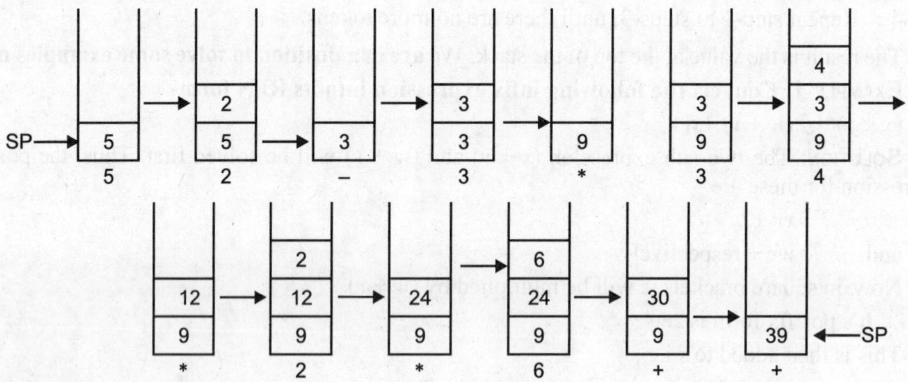

∴ Final result is 39 inside stack. The stack pointer position is also shown in the above simulation.

5.17 A CASE STUDY ON RISC, CISC AND ITS APPLICATIONS

We have already discussed about RISC and CISC. But here we would like to highlight that RISC architecture was designed to satisfy the following properties –

1. **Register-to-Register Operations**

   SPARC (Scalable Processor Architecture) is a RISC microprocessor architecture given in 1985 by Sun Microsystems. SPARC is scalable across a wide range of semiconductor technologies, chip implementations and system configurations. SPARC is flexible. It is a flexible integration of cache, memory management and floating point units. So, processors are produced at a price that is suitable for systems ranging from leap-tops to super computers. Solaris runs on SPARC-based systems.

SPARC architecture includes register **window.** SPARC has 32 GPRS, **8 global registers** and 24 registers are in **register window.** A window consists of **three groups** of 8 registers – the **out, local** and in **registers.** They are as follows:

Register Group	Register Address	Use
1. Global	*r*[0] – *r*[7]	Contains values that vary little between execution.
2. Out	*r*[8] – *r*[15]	Contain outgoing parameters.
3. Local	*r*[16] – *r*[23]	Contain scratch registers.
4. In	*r*[24] – *r*[31]	Contain incoming parameters

SPARC can have 2 to 32 windows. Most implementations have 7 to 8 windows. At any given time, **only one window is visible that is determined by the current window pointer (CWP).** This is a five-bit value that can be decremented or incremented by **SAVE** and **RESTORE** instructions respectively. These instructions are generally executed on the **procedure call and return** respectively. The **register window overlap partially**. So the output register become the **in registers** of the called procedure. Thus, the memory traffic is reduced when going up and down the procedure call. Since this is a frequency operation, so performance is improved.

The overlapping is shown below in Fig. 5.22

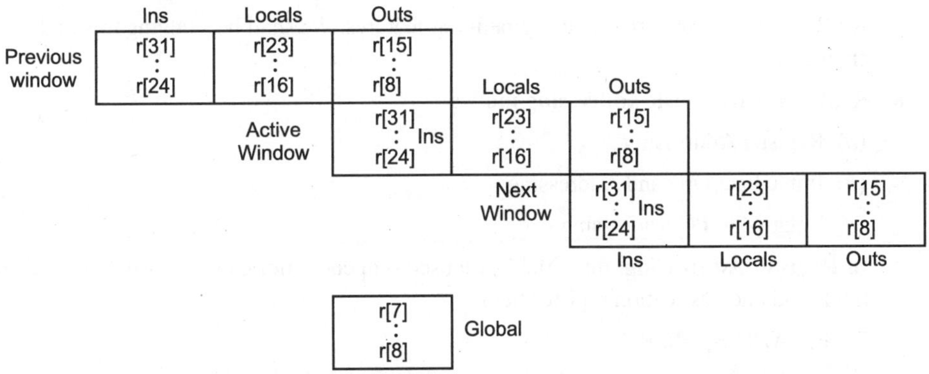

Fig. 5.22. Three overlapping register windows and global registers.

When a function is called, the **in register** may contain arguments that can be used. The *local registers* be used for anything while the function executes. The **out registers** are used to pass arguments to functions that it calls.

Register windows are also used to save the processor contexts when traps or interrupts occur. The SPARC OS always ensure that there is a register window not being used below the current one. If a trap occurs then the current workspace pointer (CWP) is decremented and the new window saves the processor context.

2. **One Instruction per cycle**

In RISC processors (like SPARC, MIPS R3000, IBM, RS/6000 etc.) there is one instruction per machine cycle. We define a machine cycle as the time it takes to fetch two operands from registers, perform an ALU operation and store the result in a register. That is the reason as to why RISC machine instructions are not complicated and can execute about as fast as microinstructions on CISC machines (like Pentium).

3. **Hardwired Instructions**

With simple, one cycle instruction, there is no need for microinstruction. The machine instructions can be hardwired. **Please understand that these instructions are executed**

faster than the instructions implemented with the microinstructions as it is not mandatory to access a microprogram control memory (CM) during instruction execution.

4. **Reduced number of instructions**

   RISC processors provide **limited** number of instructions only. This simplifies the control unit design.

5. **Simple Addressing Modes**

   All RISC instructions use simple register addressing modes. Several other addressing modes are also used like displacement mode and PC relative mode. **Please note that it does not support complex addressing modes. Also note that the complex addressing modes are synthesized in software itself from the simple modes available in RISC.**

6. **Simple Instruction Format**

   RISC processors use simple instruction formats with fixed length of instruction. The instruction length is aligned on word boundaries. Opcodes are fixed. So, with fixed fields, **opcode decoding and register operand addressing can occur simultaneously.** It simplifies the design. Even instruction fetching is optimized as the word lengths are fetched.

7. **Pipelining**

   All RISC processors provide this pipelining features. We shall be studying this in detail in chapter 8.

8. **RISC has three basic addressing modes –**

   (*a*) Register Addressing

   (*b*) Immediate Operand Addressing

   (*c*) Relative to PC Addressing.

   In Register Addressing, three fields are used – opcode, field, one or two source register fields and one destination register field.

   For eg., ADD R_1, R_2, R_3

   For eg., 2 LD (R_1), R_2

   For eg., $R_3 \leftarrow M[R_1 + R_2]$

   In immediate operand addressing, the second source is an immediate operand.

   For eg., ADD R_1, # 850, R_2

   i.e., $R_2 \leftarrow R_1 + 850$

   In relative to PC Addressing, the instruction consists of three fields – opcode field, condition field and address field. **Opcode field** specifies the operation, **condition field** specifies one of the many possible branch conditions and **address field** specifies the signed offset which is to be added to the contents of PC to compute new address when branch condition is satisfied. For e.g., JMP COND, R_1 (R_2)

   i.e., $PC \leftarrow R_1 + R_2$ if the condition is satisfied.

9. The control unit (CU) for RISC machines require lesser chip area (about 10% of total chip area). On the other hand, in CISC machines over 50% of area is taken by CU only. Thus, on a RISC VLSI chip, more space is free for other features like cache, floating point unit, I/O etc. Thus, now RISC designers can provide a large number of CPU registers on the chip. So, throughput is also increased. As a result, we can increase the **regularization factor** of the chip. It is given by a formula –

$$\textbf{Regularization Factor } (RF) = \frac{\textbf{Total no. of devices on chip}}{\textbf{No. of drawn devices}}$$

Here, the numerator term excludes ROMs. And drawn devices (in denominator) includes registers, ALUs, contents etc. **Please note that as this regularization factor increases, the VLSI design cost decreases.**

10. Because of the uniformity of the instruction size and the duration of execution, the wait cycle period in the pipeline is also reduced to a minimum.
11. RISC machines are faster as the CU is smaller, so fewer gates are used and hence shorter propagation delays are observed.
12. Faster decoding as the decoding system is small and simple
13. As a large number of CPU registers are used, thus their is reduction in number of memory accesses.
14. More reliability (failure free operation) as design errors will be less.
15. Even virtual memory management (discussed in chapter 6) becomes easier here.
16. RISC compilers are simple and small as the number of instructions in RISC machines are also less. Thus, lesser compiler development costs.
17. Availability of large number of CPU register permits a more efficient code optimization in a compiler by maximizing the number of faster register to register operations and minimizing the number of slower memory accesses.
18. Register windows in RISC allow fast parameter passing between procedures. This constitute a direct support of HLL handling of subroutines and procedures.
19. A RISC program is a about 30% longer than a CISC program. Actually, a number of functions performed on CISC machine by a single instruction will require 2, 3 or more instructions on a RISC machine. Thus, RISC code becomes longer and needs more memory.
20. RISC machines have a large **on-chip register file i.e., a CPU register file.** RISC keeps the operands or intermediate results or even data in this file, which is needed later. So, the overall traffic of data between the memory and the CPU is reduced. This increases RISC speed. Also, a large register set allows efficient parameter passing between procedures. Because otherwise if small register set is there, then most of the parameters will be stored in memory which tends to be slow.

A large CPU register file can allow to implement data structures like stack and queue on the CPU-chip itself. **Also note that a large number of identical registers on the CPU chip increases its regularization factor (RF). Thus, it reduces the cost of VLSI design.**

On the other hand, on-chip CPU Register file has some drawbacks also. It has more sophisticated decoding system which increases the access time to any of its registers. It takes more chip space.

An **alternative approach** could be to use a **cache memory**. As already explained, a cache is a small, additional, supportive memory that supports CPU. It consists of sRAM.

Compassion of large on-chip CPU register file and cache memory approaches.

Let us see the effect of cache and on-chip register file on RISC performance in form of a graph-

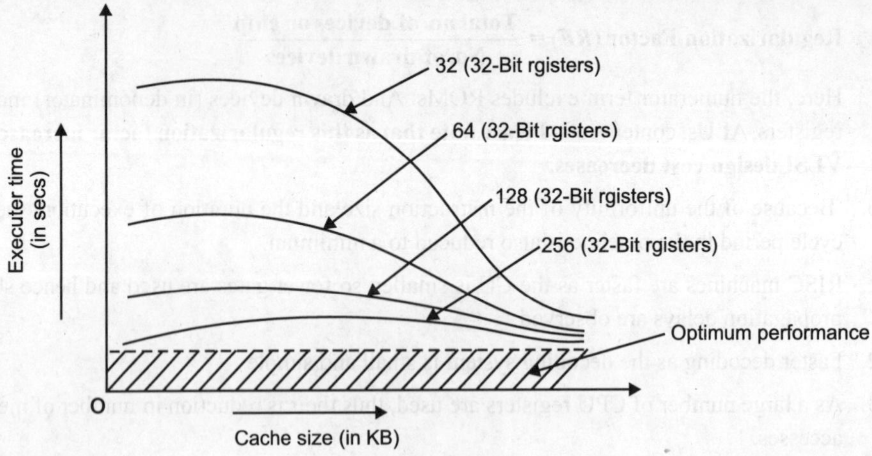

Fig. 5.23

In graph of Fig. 5.23, the four curves represent four different sizes of register file (i.e., 32, 64, 128 and 256 registers). Also, it is observed from the graph that as the register numbers are doubled (say, from 32 to 64), the performance also improves considerably.

Applications of CISC & RISC Machines

CISC (like Pentiums) are not a substitute for CISC but RISC is now taking an increased share of the micro industry today. RISCs are being used in various fields like WLANs, NICs, Mobile systems, security controller applications, intelligent traffic systems, Internet devices and so on.

SUMMARY

In this chapter, we have studied about the CPU and control design. We have classified computers RISC, CISC and MISC. A case study on RISC is also given.

MULTIPLE CHOICE QUESTIONS [MCQs]

Q. 1. At gate level CPU performs –

(*a*) Macro-operations (*b*) Pseudo-operations.

(*c*) Micro-operations (*d*) None of the above

Ans. (*b*)

Q. 2. After all operations are over, the final result (by default) is stored in

(*a*) Accumulator (*b*) B-register

(*c*) *PC* (*d*) *SP*

Ans. (*a*)

Q. 3. A command given to a computer to perform a specified operation on some given data and format is known as –

(*a*) Instruction Format (*b*) IEEE Format

(*c*) IETE Format (*d*) ISTE Format

Ans. (*a*)

Q. 4. An example of one address instruction machine is

(*a*) PDP-8 (*b*) Intel i5

(*c*) AMD (*d*) Cray XMP

Ans. (*a*)

Q. 5. The memory address of an operand is given by

(*a*) Base address + Memory Size of Segment

(*b*) Base Address + Memory Size

(*c*) Starting address + offset of memory

(*d*) None of the above

Ans. (*c*)

Q. 6. A form of stack based machines is

(*a*) CISC (*b*) RISC

(*c*) MISC (*d*) None of the above

Ans. (*c*)

Q. 7. MAR stands for

(*a*) Memory Address Register (*b*) Memory After Register

(*c*) Memory Arithmetic Register (*d*) None of the above

Ans. (*a*)

Q. **8. Stack organization uses**

(*a*) Infix forms (*b*) Postfix forms

(*c*) Prefix forms (*d*) Prenex forms

Ans. (*b*)

Q. 9. SPARC can have

(*a*) 2 to 4 windows (*b*) 2 to 32 windows

(*c*) 2 to 42 windows (*d*) 2 to 82 windows

Ans. (*b*)

Q. 10. As RF increases, VLSI design cost-

(*a*) Increases (*b*) Decreases

(*c*) Remains Stable (*d*) None of the above

Ans. (*b*)

Q. 11. Aging registers are

(*a*) Counters to show how long ago their associated pages have been referenced.

(*b*) Register to keep track of when the program was last accessed.

(*c*) Counters to keep track of last accessed instruction.

(*d*) None of the above

Ans. (*a*)

Q. 12. Stack overflow causes

(*a*) Hardware Interrupt (*b*) External Interrupt

(*c*) Internal Interrupt (*d*) Software Interrupt

Ans. (*c*)

Q. 13. After fetching the instruction from the memory, the binary code of the instruction goes to

(a) *IR* (*b*) *PC* (*c*) Accumulator (*d*) *IP*

Ans. (*a*)

Q. 14. Zero address instructions are applied in a special memory organization called

(*a*) *PC* (*b*) Instruction decoder

(*c*) Stack (*d*) None of the above

Ans. (*c*)

CONCEPTUAL SHORT QUESTIONS WITH ANSWERS

Q. 1. Compare one-address and three-address instruction machines in a tabular form

[GGSIPU, B.Tech. (CSE) - 5th Sem., Dec. 2004]

Ans.

One-address instruction machine	Three-address instruction machines
1. These machines are also known as **accumulator machines.**	1. These machines are also known as **general purpose machines.**
2. All instructions have a maximum of one operand	2. All instructions have a maximum of 2-3 operands.
3. Are more fast machines	3. Are slower machines.
4. Simple formats	4. Complex formats.
5. Large programs For. e.g., ADD 05	5. Small programs. For eg. ADD *R*1, *R*2

Q. 2. An instruction set of a machine has the following characteristics –

- The instruction consists of
  - **(*a*) An opcode**
  - **(*b*) 3-operand addresses.**
  - **(*c*) First operand is a register operand.**
  - **(*d*) Remaining two operands can be immediate, memory or register operands.**
- **The addressing modes used in this machine are –**
  - **(*a*) Immediate addressing**
  - **(*b*) Register addressing**
  - **(*c*) Direct Indirect addressing**
  - **(*d*) Indirect addressing.**
- **The machine has 16 GPRs and 16 address registers.**
- **The machine has 2 MB RAM.**
- **The machine contains 200 operations.**

The operations can be performed either on byte data or on word data as specified by instruction. Design suitable instruction formats for this machine. You may assume variable length instructions. State the assumptions if any. What will be the maximum value for an undersigned integer to be used as immediate operand for this machine?

Ans. 2 **GIVEN:** 2MB RAM

$$\text{i.e., } 2\text{ MB} = 2 \times 10^6$$
$$= 2 \times 10^3 \times 10^3$$
$$= 2 \times 2^{10} \times 2^{10}$$
$$= 2^{21}$$

$\therefore$ Address Bus = (21 bits) – (Memory address)

Formats available –

RRR RSS RII

RRS RRI

RSI

$\because$ 6 instruction formats are used for 200 operations.

$\Rightarrow$ $200 = 2^8$

$\therefore$ 8 bits for opcode.

Assumptions

Immediate address = 1 or 2 byte (8 bits) depending on one byte or word.

Opcode = 1 byte (8 bits long).

$\therefore$ 4 bits for selecting 16 GPRs.

4 bits for selecting address register.

Let Address Register size = 16 bits

$\therefore$ Maximum size of one signed unit is $2^{16} - 1 = 65{,}533$

For 32 bits, $2^{32} - 1$

$$= 4294967296 - 1$$
$$= 4294967295$$

Q. 3. How many memory references will be needed to fetch and execute –

1. **A single operand (memory or register) instruction having indirect addressing mode.**
2. **A branch instruction using indirect addressing mode . Please mention the assumption (if any)**

Ans.

1. Two (2) Memory references for fetching operand,
   One (1) memory reference for fetching instruction
   $\therefore$ 2 + 1 = 3 Memory references are required for fetch and execute.
2. Two (2) memory references for fetching branch address, one memory reference for instruction fetching..
   $\therefore$ 3 memory references in all.

Q. 4. What is the maximum address space that a processor can access directly if it is connected to a –

(*a*) 16 bit memory. **(*b*) 8 bit memory.**

Ans. (*a*) ∵ Memory address space that a CPU can access = $2^{\text{no. of bits of memory}}$.

$= 2^{16} = 65,536$ address space (can be accessed by CPU directly).

(*b*) Similarly, for 8-bit memory -

$= 2^{8} = 256$ address space (can be accessed by processor directly).

Q. 5. How many memory references will be needed to fetch and execute the following instruction

(Assume 1 memory word = 16 bits, size of instruction = 16 or 32 bits)

1. **A MOV instruction using register indirect addressing scheme for both the operands.**
2. **An ADD instruction with one register, one memory (direct) and one 16-bit immediate operands.**
3. **A subroutine call instruction using relative addressing.**
4. **A shift instruction to a memory (direct) perand.**
5. **Incrementing a counter using auto-incrementing addressing mode**

Ans. 1. **5 Memory references** are needed

– Two each for fetching 2 operands

– One for instruction fetching of 16 bits.

2. **3 Memory references** are needed.

– One for direct mode fetching.

– Two for instruction

3. **2 memory references** needed.

– One for incrementing PC

– One for loading subroutine instruction address.

4. **2 Memory references** needed.

– One for direct operand fetching

– One for instruction fetching.

5. **1 memory reference** instruction.

Q. 6. Assume that:

Contents of Register BX = 687DL. Contents of Register SI = 213Bh. Offset / Displacement in the instruction = B234 h

Find the effective address using the above registers and offset (wherever applicable) if the following addressing modes are used –

1. **Register addressing (using BX).**
2. **Register indirect addressing (Using BX).**
3. **Based Index**
4. **Based Index Relative.**

Ans. (*i*) No of effective address as operand is directly ion register

(*ii*) $EA =$ 687 Dh.

(*iii*) $EA =$ 687 Dh
+213 Bh
89B8h

(*iv*) EA = 687 Dh
213 Bh
+B234 h
13BECh

Q. 7. Write short notes on –

(*a*) Machine start up and reset vector.

(*b*) Wilkes control.

(*c*) Dual use of microinstruction bits.

Ans. (*a*) Machine start up and reset vector

The control unit (CU) is also responsible for initializing various registers during the start-ups of the machine. The control unit loads a hardware generated address in the PC and starts execution of the instruction stored in that location. This hardware generated address may be the address of the first instruction to be executed. **The address of the first instruction is known as the reset vector.** In the first, case, the CU starts its normal operation immediately after loading the reset vector address machines, the CU must first fetch the reset vector into the program counter (PC) before beginning its normal operation. **Please note that the reset vector address machines allow generality of design to the machine architects.** It means that the machine architects will not have to assign the starting address of the startup program to be executed in the memory. They just need to assign the address of the reset vector in the memory. **Also note that different reset vector values can be chosen on the same machine allowing more flexibility.**

For eg. If we have two different start up routines for two different OS, then by changing the reset vector value in the memory, we can change the loading of the OS. However, both OS can reside on the main memory at the same time.

(*b*) Wilkes Control

Microprogramming requires the execution of microinstruction. A microinstruction has two parts –

1. A set of **control fields** that specify the control signals to be activated.
2. An **address field** that contains the address in control memory of the next microinstruction to be executed.

Maurice *V*, Wilkes, the inventor of microprogramming, each bit K_i of control field corresponds to a distinct control line, C_i.

where $K_i = 1$ in current microinstruction $\rightarrow$ C_i is activated.

Else C_i remains inactive.

Every program CU should be able to respond to external signals or conditions. We can satisfy this requirement by introducing some form of switch (S) controlled by an external condition that allows the current microinstruction to select one of the two possible address fields. The third microinstruction may be followed by the microinstruction with address 100 or 101, as determined by the external condition. This feature makes conditional branches within a microprogram possible.

(*c*) Dual use of microinstruction bits

One bit is needed in the microinstruction to indicate whether this is a control microinstruction or a branching microinstruction. In case, the microinstruction contains control signals, then the next microinstruction address is calculated either by using the opcode of IR or it is the address of the next microinstruction in sequence. In this technique, an extra cycle is needed for branch microinstructions which is not desired.

Q. 8. The memory unit of a computer has 256 K words of 32 bits each. The computer has an instruction format with four fields: an operation code field, a mode field to specify one of the seven addressing modes, a register address field to specify one of 60 processor registers and a memory address. Specify the instruction format and the number of bits in each field if the instruction is in one word memory

[MDU, BE (CSE) – 4th Sem., 2000]

Ans. Memory unit = 256 K words = 2^{18} words.

$\therefore$ 18 bits memory address is required.

Given : 60 CPU registers

We know that, $2^5 < 60 < 2^6$.

$\therefore$ 6 bits are required for register address. Also, note that there are 7 addressing modes and $2^2 < 7 < 2^3$.

$\therefore$ We need 3 bits to specify 7 addressing modes.

Total number of bits in instruction format is 32.

$\therefore$ No. of bits in opcode field

$$= 32 - (18 + 6 + 3)$$
$$= 32 - 27$$
$$= 5 \text{ bits}$$

The instruction format is –

32 bits

Opcode	Mode	Reg. addr.	Mam. addr.
5 bits	3 bits	6 bits	18 bits

Q. 9. Write a program to evaluate arithmetic expression

$$X = (A - B) * (((C - D*)E/F)/G)$$

(*a*) Using a general register computer with three address instructions.

(*b*) Using a general register computer with two address instructions.

(*c*) Using an accumulator type computer with one address instructions.

(*d*) Using stack organized computer with zero address instructions.

Ans. $X = (A - B) * (((C - D * E)/F)/G)$

Three Address instructions:

SUB $R1, A, B$	$R1 \leftarrow M[A] - M[B]$
MUL $R2, D, E$	$R2 \leftarrow M[D] - M[E]$
SUB $R2, C, R2$	$R2 \leftarrow M[C] - R2$
DIV $R2, R2, F$	$R2 \leftarrow R2/M[F]$
DIV $R2, R2, G$	$R2 \leftarrow R2/M[G]$
MUL $X, R1, R2$	$M[X] \leftarrow R1 * R2$

(b) Two Address Instructions

MOV $R1, A$	$R1 \leftarrow M[A]$
SUB $R1, B$	$R1 \leftarrow R1 - M[B]$
MOV $R2, D$	$R2 \leftarrow M[D]$
MUL $R2, E$	$R2 \leftarrow R2 * M[E]$
MOV $X, R2$	$M[X] \leftarrow R2$
MOV $R2, C$	$R2 \leftarrow M[C]$
SUB $R2, X$	$R2 \leftarrow R2 - M[X]$
DIV $R2, F$	$R2 \leftarrow R2/M[F]$
DIV $R2, G$	$R2 \leftarrow R2/M[G]$
MUL $R1, R2$	$R1 \leftarrow R1 * R2$
MOV $X, R1$	$M[X] \leftarrow R1$

(c) One Address Instructions

LOAD A	$AC \leftarrow M[A]$
SUB B	$AC \leftarrow AC - M[B]$
STORE T	$M[T] \leftarrow AC$
LOAD D	$AC \leftarrow M[D]$
MUL E	$AC \leftarrow AC * E$
STORE X	$M[X] \leftarrow M[C]$
LOAD C	$AC \leftarrow M[C]$
SUB X	$AC \leftarrow AC - M[X]$
DIV F	$AC \leftarrow AC / M[P]$
DIV G	$AC \leftarrow AC / M[G]$
MUL T	$AC \leftarrow AC * M[T]$
STORE	$M[X] \leftarrow AC$

(d) For stack rganized computer, the expression must be in reverse polish notation

$$X = (A - B) * (((C - D * E) / F) / G)$$
$$= AB - *(((C - DE*)/F/G)$$
$$= AB - *(((CDE*-)/F)/G)$$
$$= AB -* (CDE* - F)/)/G)$$

$= AB -* CDE* - F/G/$

$= AB - CDE* - F/G/*$

Thus, the RPN of given arithmetic expression is $AB -* CDE* - F/G/*$

Zero Address Instruction:

PUSH *A*	TOS ← *A*
PUSH *B*	TOS ← *B*
SUB	TOS ← *A* – *B*
PUSH *C*	TOS ← *C*
PUSH *D*	TOS ← *D*
PUSH *E*	TOS ← *E*
MUL	TOS ← *D* * *E*
SUB	TOS ← *C* – *D* * *E*
PUSH *F*	TOS ← *F*
DIV	TOS ← (*C* – *D* * *E*)/*F*
PUSH *G*	TOS ← *G*
DIV	TOS ← ((*C* – *D* * *E*)/*F*)/*G*
MUL	TOS ← (*A* – *B*) * (((*C* – *D* * *E*)/*F*)/*G*)
POP *X*	*M*[*X*] ← TOS

Q. 10. Write a program to evaluate arithmetic expression

$$X = \frac{(A-B)+C*(D*E-F)}{G+H*K}$$

(*a*) Using a general register compute with three address instructions.

(*b*) Using a general register computer with two address instructions.

(*c*) Using an accumulator type compute with one address instructions.

(*d*) Using stack organized computer with zero address instructions.

Ans. (*a*) Three address instruction:

SUB *R*1, *A*, *B*	*R*1 ← *M*[*A*] – *M*[*B*]
MUL *R*2, *D*, *E*	*R*2 ← *M*[*D*] * *M*[*E*]
MUL *R*2, *R*2, *C*	*R*2 ← *R*2* *M*[*C*]
ADD *R*1, *R*1, *R*2	*R*1 ← *R*1 + *R*2
MUL *R*2, *H*, *K*	*R*2 ← *M*[*H*] * *M*[*K*]
ADD *R*2, *G*, *R*2	*R*2 ← *M*[*G*] + *R*2
DIV *X*, *R*, *R*1	*M*[*X*] ← *R*1/*R*2

(*b*) Two Address instruction:

MOV *R*1, *A*	*R*1 ← *M*[*A*]
SUB *R*1, *B*	*R*1 ← *R*1 – *M*[*B*]

MOV $R2, D$	$R2 \leftarrow M[D]$
MUL $R2, E$	$R2 \leftarrow R2 * M[E]$
SUB $R2, F$	$R2 \leftarrow R2 - M[F]$
MUL $R2, C$	$R2 \leftarrow R2 * M[C]$
ADD $R1, R2$	$R1 \leftarrow R1 + R2$
MOV $R2, H$	$R2 \leftarrow M[H]$
MUL $R2, K$	$R2 \leftarrow R2 * M[K]$
ADD $R1, G$	$R2 \leftarrow R2 + M[G]$
DIV $R1, R2$	$R1 \leftarrow R1/R2$
MOV $X, R1$	$M[X] \leftarrow R1$

(*c*) One Address Instruction

LOAD D	$AC \leftarrow M[D]$
MUL E	$AC \leftarrow AC * M[E]$
SUB F	$AC \leftarrow AC - M[F]$
MUL C	$AC \leftarrow AC * M[C]$
STORE T	$M[T] \leftarrow AC$
LOAD A	$AC \leftarrow M[A]$
SUB B	$AC \leftarrow AC - M[B]$
ADD T	$AC \leftarrow AC + M[T]$
STORE T	$M[T] \leftarrow AC$
LOAD H	$AC \leftarrow M[H]$
MUL K	$AC \leftarrow AC * M[K]$
ADD G	$AC \leftarrow AC + M[G]$
STORE X	$M[X] \leftarrow AC$
LOAD T	$AC \leftarrow M[T]$
DIV X	$AC \leftarrow AC/M[X]$
STORE X	$M[X] \leftarrow AC$

(*d*) For stack organized computer, the expression must be in reveres polish notations

$$X = \frac{(A-B)+C*(D*E-F)}{G+H*K}$$

$$= \frac{AB-*C*(DE*-F)}{G+HK*}$$

$$= \frac{AB-+C*DE*F-}{G+HK*}$$

$$= \frac{AB-+CDE*F-*}{GHK*+}$$

$$= \frac{AB-CDE*F-*+}{GHK*+}$$

$$= AB - CDE * F - * + GHK * + /$$

Thus, the reverse polish notation of given arithmetic expression is

$AB - CDE * F - * + GHK * + /$

Zero Address Instruction:

PUSH A	TOS $\leftarrow A$
PUSH B	TOS $\leftarrow B$
SUB	TOS $\leftarrow A - B$
PUSH C	TOS $\leftarrow C$
PUSH D	TOS $\leftarrow D$
PUSH E	TOS $\leftarrow E$
MUL	TOS $\leftarrow D * E$
PUSH F	TOS $\leftarrow F$
SUB	TOS $\leftarrow D * E - F$
MUL	TOS $\leftarrow C * (D * E - F)$
ADD	TOS $\leftarrow A - B + C * (D * E - F)$
PUSH G	TOS $\leftarrow G$
PUSH H	TOS $\leftarrow H$
PUSH K	TOS $\leftarrow K$
MUL	TOS $\leftarrow H * K$
ADD	TOS $\leftarrow G + H * K$
DIV	TOS $\leftarrow \dfrac{A - B + C*(D*E - F)}{G + H*K}$
POP X	$M[X] \leftarrow$ TOS

Q. 11. What are the techniques for modification or generation of branch address?

Ans. There are three techniques which are discussed below:

I. Bit-ORing: In this technique, the branch address is determined by ORing particular bit or bits with the current address of the microinstruction. **For example,** if the current address is 170 and the branch address is 172 then the branch address can be generated by ORing 02(bit 1), with the current address.

II. Using Condition Variables: In this technique the condition variables are used to modify the contents of the cm address register directly, thus eliminating whole or in part the need for branch addresses in microinstructions. **For example,** let the condition variable CY indicates occurrence of CY = 1, and no carry when CY = 0. Suppose that we want to execute a SKIP_ON_CARRY microinstruction. This can be done by logically connectivity CY to the count enable input of μpc at an appropriate point in the microinstruction cycle. This allows the overflow condition to increment μpc an extra time, thus performing the desired skip operation.

III. Wide-Branch Addressing: Generating branch addresses becomes more difficult as the numer of branch increases. In such situations Programmable Logic Array can be used to generate the required branch addresses. This simple and inexpensive way of generating branch addresses is known as **wide-branch addressing.** Here, the opcode of a machine instruction is translated into the starting address of the corresponding micro-routine. This is achieved by connecting the opcode bits of the instruction register as inputs to the PLA, which acts as a decoder. The output of the PLA is the address of the desired microroutine.

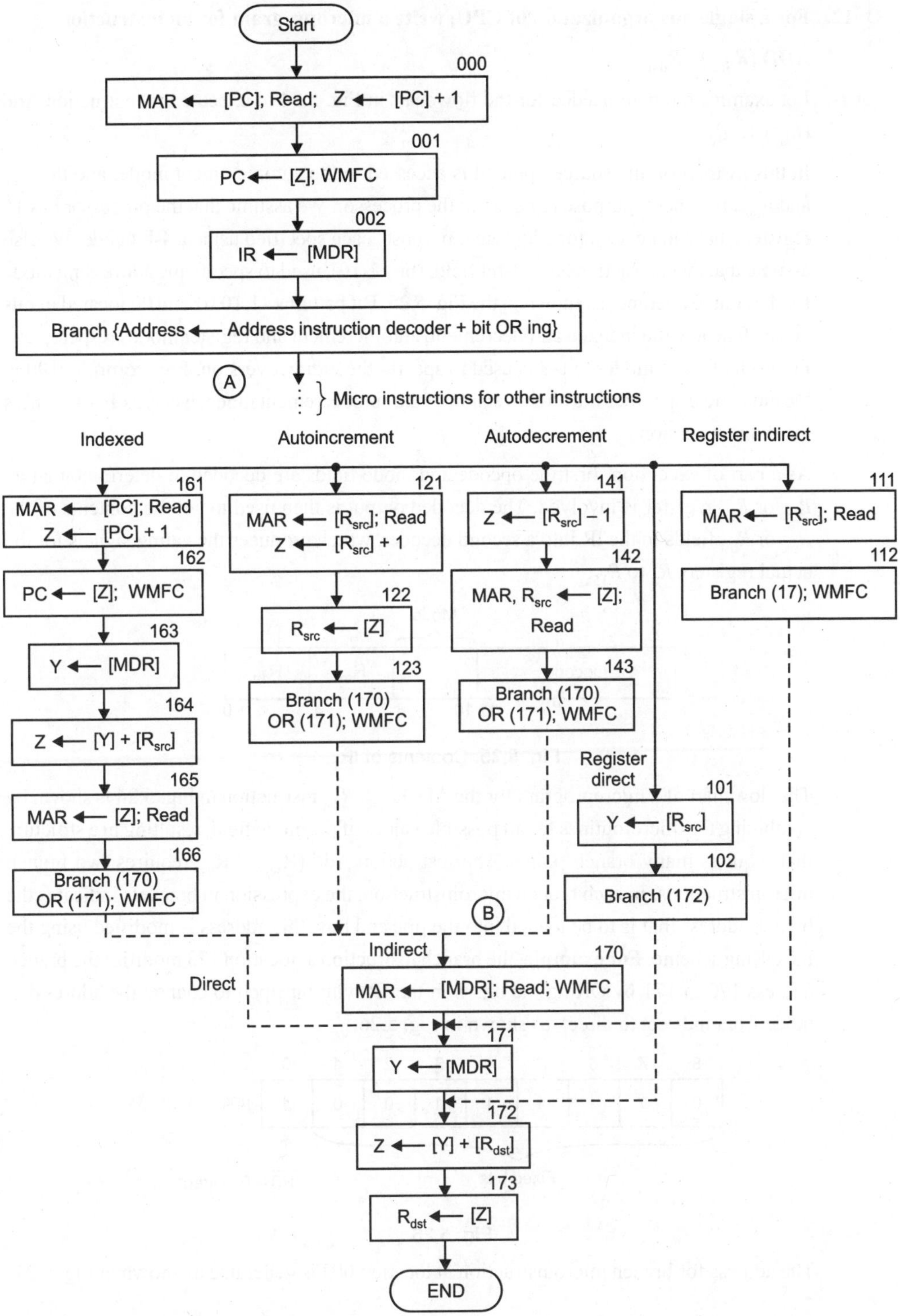

Fig. 5.24. Flowchart of a microprogram for the ADDsrc, R_{dst} instruction

Q. 12. For a single bus organization of CPU, write a microprogram for an instruction ADD (R_{Src}), R_{dst}

Ans. Let examine the path needed for the flowchart in Fig. 5.24 to execute the instruction Add (R_{src}) +, R_{dst}.

In this instruction the source operand is accessed in the autoincrement mode, and the R_{src} and R_{dst} are general purpose registers in the processor. We assume that the processor has 16 registers that can be used for addressing purpose, each specified using a 4-bit code. We also assume that the instruction has a 3-bit field, (bits 8-10), used to specify the addressing mode for the source operand, as shown in the Fig. 5.25. Bit patterns 11,10,01 and 00 located in bits 10 and 9 denote the indexed autodecrement, autoincrement and register modes respectively. For each of these modes, bit–8 is used to specify the indirect version. **For example,** 100 in the mode field specifies the direct version of the autodecrement mode, whereas 101 specifies the indirect version.

As a part of execution, first the opcode and mode fields are decoded to determine that an R_{src} or R_{dst} register is involved. The decoded output is then used to get the contents of the R_{src} or R_{dst} fields in the IR into a second decoder, which produces the gating signals for the actual registers R_0 to R_{15}.

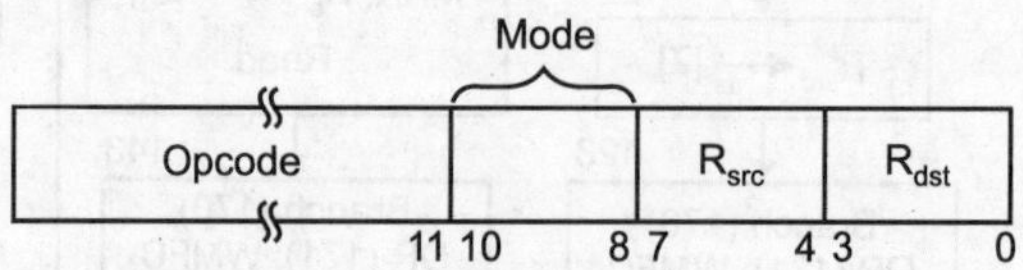

Fig. 5.25. Contents of IR

The flowchart of a microprogram for the ADD R_{src}, R_{dst} instruction in Fig. 5.24 is shown by combining the microroutines for all possible values of the mode field, resulting in a structure that requires many branch points. The instruction Add (R_{scr})+, R_{dst} requires two branch microinstructions. In each branch microinstruction, the expression in brackets indicates the branch address that is to be loaded into the μpc and how this address is modified using the bit-ORing scheme. **For example**, the branch instruction at location 123 modifies the branch address 170 to 171 by ORing the bits-8 in the IR with bit μpc0 to change the addressing mode from indirect to direct, as shown in Fig. 5.26.

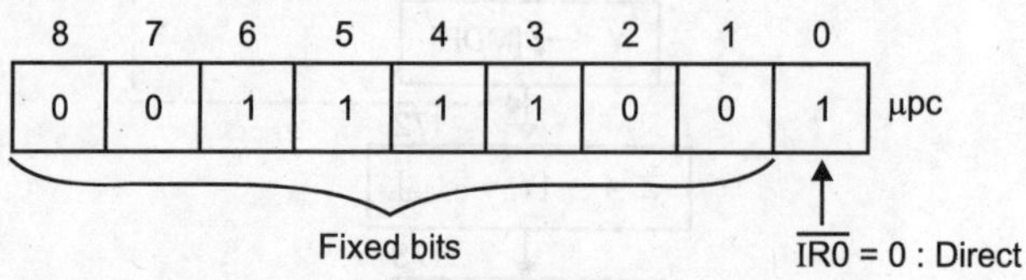

Fig. 5.26

The address for branch microinstruction at location 003 is generated as shown in Fig. 5.27.

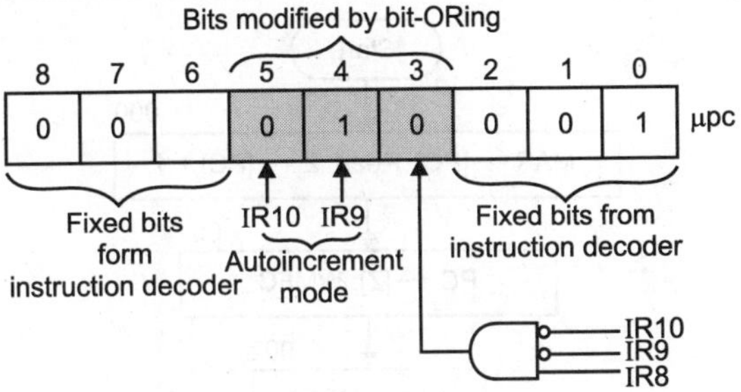

Fig. 5.27. Bit ORing for branch microinstruction at location 003

The table gives the microinstruction sequence for the execution of Add (R_{src}), R_{dst} instruction

Table 5.1: Microinstruction for Add (R_{src})+, R_{dst}

Address (Octal)	Microinstruction
000	PC_{out}, MAR_{in}, Y_{in}, Select C, Add, Z_{in}
001	Z_{out}, PC_{in}, MWFC
002	MDR_{out}, IR_{in}
003	μBranch $\left\{\begin{matrix} \mu pc \leftarrow (101)_8 \text{ from instruction decoder} \\ \mu pc_{5,4} \leftarrow [IR_{10,9}], \mu pc_3 \leftarrow [\overline{IR}_{10}].[\overline{IR}_9].[IR_8] \end{matrix}\right\}$ i.e. $\mu pc_{5,4,3} \leftarrow (010)_2$
⋮	
121	R_{srcout}, MAR_{in}, Read, Select C, Add, Z_{in}
122	Z_{out}, R_{srcin}
123	μBranch {$\mu pc \leftarrow (170)_8$ from instruction decoder $\mu pc_0 \leftarrow \overline{IR_8}$} , WMFC
⋮	
171	MDR_{out}, Y_{in}
172	R_{dstout}, Select Y, Add, Z_{in}
173	Z_{out}, R_{dstout}, End

Q. 13. For a single bus organization of CPU, draw a flowchart of a microprogram for instruction

ADD(R_{src})+, R_{dst}

Ans. The flow-chart is –

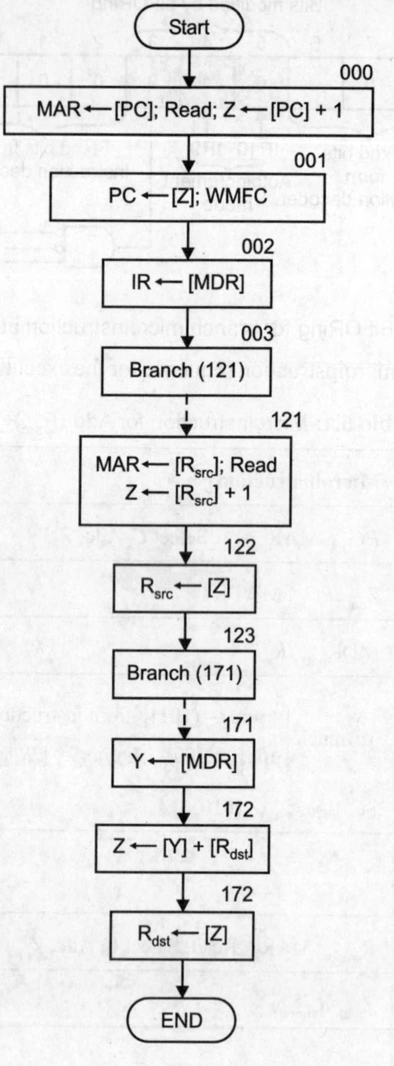

Q. 14. For a single bus organization of data paths inside the CPU, write μp of microinstruction and draw flowchart of microprogram for the following instruction –

MOV $(R_{src})+$, R_{dst}.

[Note: R_{dst} uses direct and R_{src} uses autoincrement addressing].

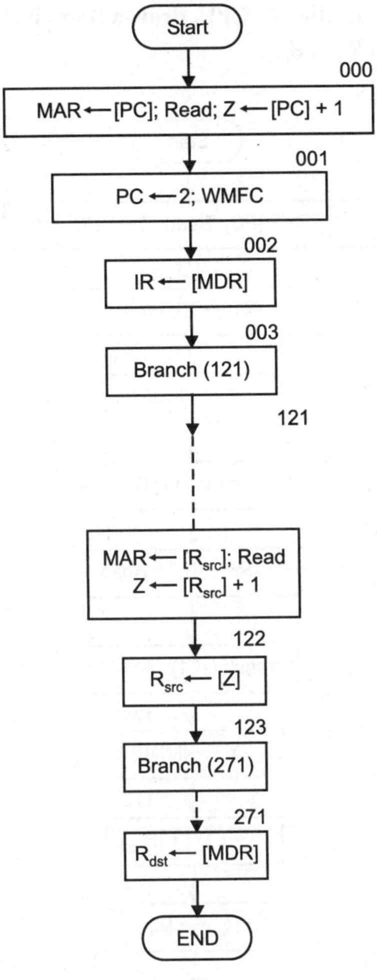

Fig. 5.28

Address (Octal)	Microinstruction
000	PC_{out}, MAR_{in}, Read, Y_{in}, Select C, Add, Z_{in}
001	Z_{out}, PC_{in}, MWFC
002	MDR_{out}, IR_{in}
003	
⋮	$\mu\text{Branch}\left\{\begin{array}{l}\mu\text{pc} \leftarrow (101)_8 \text{ from instruction decoder} \\ \mu\text{pc}_{5,4} \leftarrow [IR_{10,9}],\ \mu pc_3 \leftarrow [\overline{IR}_{10}].[\overline{IR}_9].[IR_8]\end{array}\right\}$
121	R_{srcout}, MAR_{in}, Read, Select C, Add, Z_{in}
122	Z_{out}, R_{srcin}
123	$\mu\text{Branch}\{\mu pc \leftarrow (270)_8 \text{ from instruction decoder } \ \mu pc_0 \leftarrow \overline{IR}_8\}$, WMFC
271	MDR_{out}, R_{dstin}, End

15. For a single bus organisation of CPU, draw a flow chart and write microinstructions for instruction ADD (R_{src}), R_{dst}.

Ans. Flow chart is as follows –

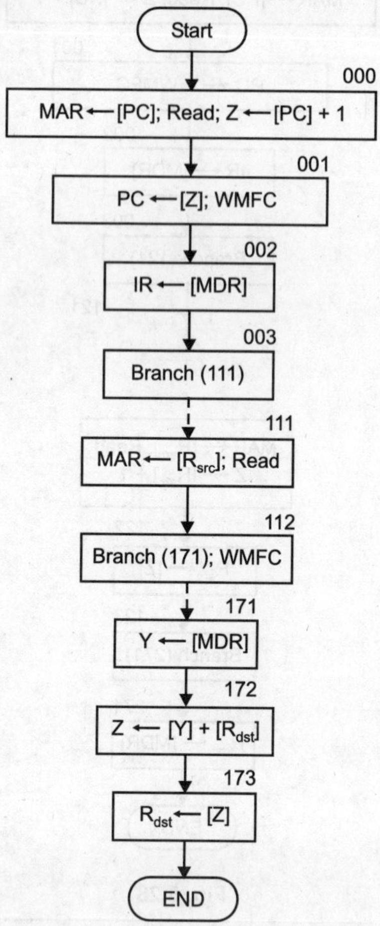

Microinstructions

Table 5.2: Microinstruction for Add (R_{src}), R_{dst}

Address (Octal)	Microinstruction
000	PC_{out}, MAR_{in}, Read, Y_{in}, Select C, Add, Z_{in}
001	Z_{out}, PC_{in}, MWFC
002	MDR_{out}, IR_{in}
003	$\mu\text{Branch}\left\{\begin{array}{l}\mu pc \leftarrow (101)_8 \text{ from instruction decoder} \\ \mu pc_{5,4} \leftarrow [IR_{10,9}],\ \mu pc_3 \leftarrow [\overline{IR}_{10}].[\overline{IR}_9].[IR_8]\end{array}\right\}$
111	R_{srcout}, MAR_{in}, Read μBranch{$\mu pc \leftarrow (170)_8$ from instruction decoder $\mu\ pc_0 \leftarrow \overline{IR_8}$ }, WMFC
112	μBranch {$\mu pc \leftarrow (170)_8$ from instruction decoder $\mu pc_0 \leftarrow \overline{IR_8}$), WMFC

Address (Octal)	Microinstruction
⋮	
171	MDR_{out}, Y_{in}
172	R_{srcout}, Select Y, Add, Z_{in}
173	Z_{out}, R_{dstout}, End

Q. 16. For a single bus organization of CPU draw a flowchart and write microinstructions for instruction ADD-(R_{src}), R_{dst}.

Ans. Flowchart and microinstructions are –

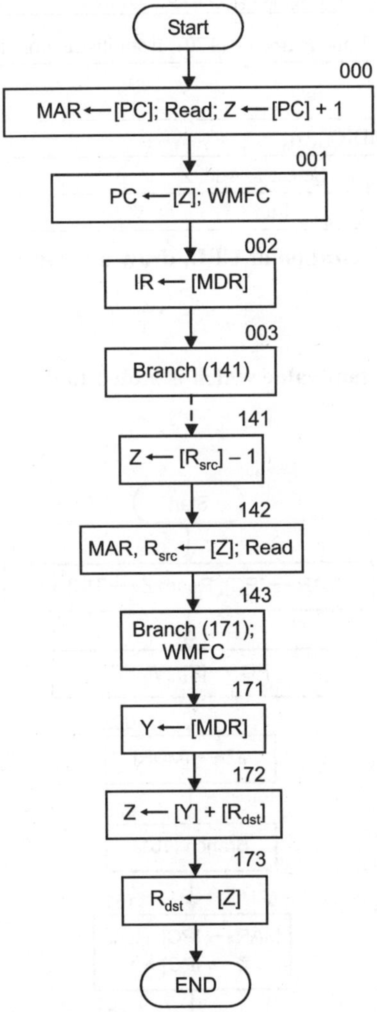

Table 5.3: Microinstruction for Add-(R_{src}), R_{dst}

Address (Octal)	Microinstruction
000	PC_{out}, MAR_{in}, Read, Y_{in}, Select C, Add, Z_{in}
001	Z_{out}, PC_{in}, MWFC

Address (Octal)	Microinstruction
002	MDR_{out}, IR_{in}
003	μBranch $\left\{ \begin{array}{l} \mu pc \leftarrow (101)_8 \text{ from instruction decoder} \\ \mu pc_{5,4} \leftarrow [IR_{10.9}], \mu pc_3 \leftarrow [\overline{IR_{10}}].[\overline{IR_9}].[IR_8] \end{array} \right\}$ i.e. $\mu pc_{5,4.3} \leftarrow (010)_2$
141	R_{srcout}, Select C, Sub, Z_{in} μBranch{$\mu pc \leftarrow (170)_8$ from instruction decoder $\mu pc_0 \leftarrow \overline{IR_8}$ }, WMFC
142	MAR_{in}, R_{srcin}, Z_{out}, Read
143	μBranch {$\mu pc \leftarrow (170)_8$ from instruction decoder $\mu pc_0 \leftarrow \overline{IR_8}$}, WMFC
⋮	
171	MDR_{out}, Y_{in}
172	R_{srcout}, Select Y, Add, Z_{in}
173	Z_{out}, R_{dstin}, End

Q. 17. For a single bus organization of CPU, draw a flowchart and write microinstruction for instruction –

Add $_{const}(R_{src}), R_{dst}$

where const is a constant value which is added to the contents of R_{src} to generate the EA.

Ans. It's flowchart is –

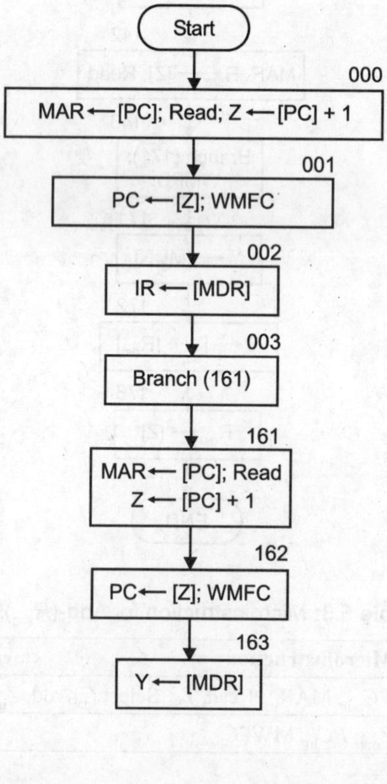

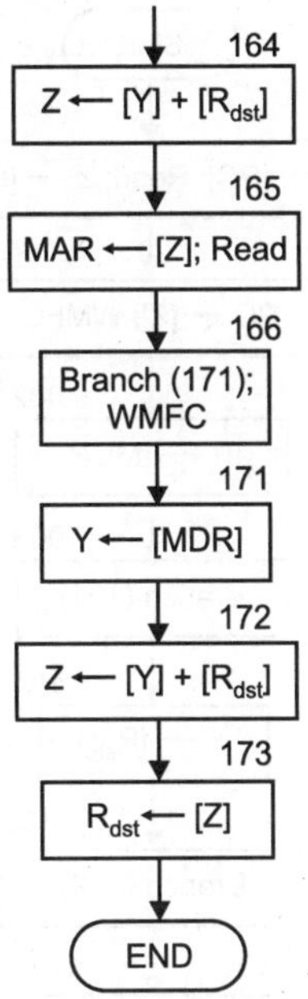

Table 5.4: Microinstruction for Add const (R_{src}), R_{dst}

Address (Octal)	Microinstruction
000	PC_{out}, MAR_{in}, Read, Y_{in}, Select C, Add, Z_{in}
001	Z_{out}, PC_{in}, MWFC
002	MDR_{out}, IR_{in}
003	$\mu\text{Branch}\begin{cases}\mu pc \leftarrow (101)_B \text{ from instruction decoder} \\ \mu pc_{5,4} \leftarrow [IR_{10,9}],\ \mu pc_3 \leftarrow [\overline{IR_{10}}].[\overline{IR_9}].[\overline{IR_8}]\end{cases}$
161	PC_{out}, MAR_{in}, Read, Y_{in}, Select C, Add, Z_{in}
162	Z_{out}, PC_{in}, MWFC
163	MDR_{out}, Y_{in}
164	R_{srcout}, Select Y, Add, Z_{in}
165	Z_{out}, MAR_{in}, Read
166	$\mu\text{Branch}\{\mu pc \leftarrow (170)_8$ from instruction decoder $\mu pc_0 \leftarrow \overline{IR_8}\}$, WMFC
⋮	
171	MDR_{out}, Y_{in}
172	R_{srcout}, Select Y, Add, Z_{in}
173	Z_{out}, R_{dstin}, End

Q. 18. For a single bus organization of CPU, draw a flowchart and write microinstructions for instruction ADD R_{src}, R_{dst}.

Ans. It's flowchart is –

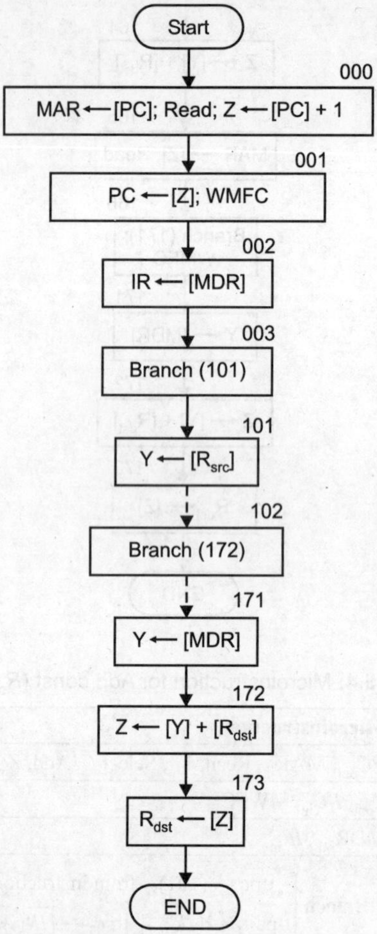

Microinstructions are as follows

Table 5.5: Microinstruction for Add (R_{src}), R_{dst}

Address (Octal)	Microinstruction
000	PC_{out}, MAR_{in}, Read, Y_{in}, Select C, Add, Z_{in}
001	Z_{out}, PC_{in}, MWFC
002	MDR_{out}, IR_{in}
003	$\mu\text{Branch}\left\{\begin{array}{l}\mu pc \leftarrow (101)_8 \text{ from instruction decoder} \\ \mu pc_{5,4} \leftarrow [IR_{10,9}], \mu pc_3 \leftarrow [\overline{IR}_{10}].[\overline{IR}_9].[IR_8]\end{array}\right\}$ i.e., $MPC_{5,4,3} \leftarrow (000)_2$
101	R_{srcout}, Y_{in}
102	μBranch $\{\mu pc \leftarrow (170)_8$ from instruction decoder, $\mu pc_0 \leftarrow \overline{IR_8}$), WMFC
171	MDR_{out}, Y_{in}
172	R_{dstout}, Select Y, Add, Z_{in}
173	Z_{out}, R_{dstin}, End

Q. 19. Evaluate the expression 5 6 2 + * 1 2 4 / –. Show the stack contents

Ans. Given : 5 6 2 + * 1 2 4 / –

Steps	Input Symbol	Stack	Intermediate Calculations
1	5; Push it	5	
2	6; Push it	5, 6	
3.	2; Push it.	5, 6, 2	
4	+; pop 2 elements & evaluate them	5	6+2 = 8
5.	Push this result = 8	5, 8	
6.	* ; pop 2 elements & evaluate them	Empty	5*8 = 40
7.	Push this result = 40	40	
8.	12; Push it	40, 12	
9.	4; Push it	40, 12, 4	
10.	/ ; pop 2 elements and evaluate them	40	12 / 4 = 3
11.	Push this result = 3	40, 3	
12.	– ; pop 2 elements & evaluate them.	Empty	40 – 3 = 37
13.	Push this result = 37	37	
14.	No more input symbols / elements		∴ 37 is the result

Q. 20. The content of PC in the basic computer is 3AF (all nos. are in HEX). The content of AC is 7EC3. The content of memory at address 3AF is 932 E. The content of memory at address 32E is 09AC. The content of memory at address 9AC is 8B9F.

(*a*) What is the instruction that will be fetched and executed next?

(*b*) Show the binary operation that will be performed in the AC when the instruction is executed.

(*c*) Give the contents of registers *PC*, *AR*, *DR*, *AC* and *IR* in HEX and the values of *E*, *I* and the sequence counter SC in binary at the end of the instruction cycle

[GGSIPU, B.Tech (CSE)- 5th Sem., Dec. 2006 and Dec. 2008]

Ans. (*a*)

$$9 = (1001)_2$$

$$I = \frac{1001}{1ADD}$$

∴ ADD I 32 E.

(*b*)

$$AC = \text{7EC3 (ADD)}$$

$$DR = \frac{8B9F}{0A62}$$

Memory

3AF	932E
32E	09AC
9AC	8B9F
	AC = 7EC3

(*c*) $PC = 3AF + 1$

$= 3B0$ $IR = 932E$

$AR = 9AC$ $E = 1$

$DR = 8B9F$ $I = 1$

$AC = 0A62$ $SC = 0000.$

Q. 21. A computer uses a memory unit with 256 K words of 32-bits each. A binary instruction code is stored in one word of memory. The instruction has four parts : an indirect bit, and operation code, a register code part to specify and one of 64 registers and an address part.

(*a*) How many bits are there in the operation code, the register code part and the address part?

(*b*) Draw the instruction word format and indicate the number of bits in each part.

(*c*) How many bits are there in the data and address inputs of the memory?

[GGSIPU, B. Tech. (CSE) – 5th Sem., Dec. 2004]

Ans. $\because$ $256 = 2^8 \times 2^{10} = 2^{18}$ and $64 = 2^6$

(*a*) Address : 18 bits

Register Code : 6 bits

Indirect bit $= \frac{1}{25}$ bits

$32 - 25 = 7$ bits for opcode = 32 bits.

(*b*)

1	7	6	18
I	Opcode	Register	Address

= 32 bits

(*c*) Date : 32 bits;

Address : 18 bits.

Q. 22. What is the difference between a direct and indirect address instruction? How many references to memory are needed for each type of instruction to bring an operand into a processor register? [GGSIPU, B. Tech. (CSE) – 5th Sem., Dec. 2004]

Ans. A direct address instruction needs two memory references –

1. Read instruction.
2. Read operand.

On the other hand, an indirect address instruction needs three memory references—

1. Read instruction.
2. Read EA (Effective Address).
3. Read operand.

23. What are the two instructions needed in the basic computer in order to set the *E* flip-flop to 1?

And. CLE; Clear *E*

CME ; Complement *E*

Q. 24. Make the following changes to the basic computer.

(*a*) Add a register to the bus system CTR (count register) to be selected with

$$S_2S_1S_0 = 000$$

(*b*) Replace the ISZ instruction with an instruction that loads a number into CTR.

LDC Address CTR ← M[Address]

(*c*) Add a register reference instruction, ICSZ: Increment CTR and skip next instruction if zero. Discuss the advantage of this change.

Ans. Convert the ISZ instruction from a memory reference instruction to a register-reference instruction. The new instruction ICSZ can be executed at time T_3 instead of time T_6, a savings of **3 clock cycles.**

25. Define the following:

(*a*) Microprocessors.

(*b*) Microoperation.

(*c*) Microinstruction.

(*d*) Microprogram.

(*e*) Microcode. **[GGSIPU, B.Tech. (CSE/IT/ECE) – 5th Sem., 2011]**

Ans. (*a*) Microprocessor

It is a small size CPU which acts as a heart of a microcomputer. **For. eg:** Intel 8085, 8086/8086/88; Pentiums, i10.

(*b*) Microoperation

It is an elementary digital computer operation.

(*c*) Micro-instruction

It is an instruction stored in control memory

(*d*) Microprogram

It is an sequence of microninstructions.

(*e*) Microcode

It is same as micro-program.

26. A control memory has 4096 words of 24 bits each.

(*a*) How many bits are there in the control address register?

(*b*) How many bits are there in each of the inputs going into MUX?

(*c*) What are the number of inputs in each MUX and how many MUXes are needed?

Ans. $CM = 2^{12} \times 24$

(*a*) 12 bits

(*b*) 12 bits.

(*c*) 12 MUXes, each of size (4 × 1).

Q. 27. Using the mapping procedure described in figure given below, give the first micro-instruction address for the following opcodes—

(*a*) **0010** (*b*) **1011** (*c*) **1111**

Computer Instruction		1	0	1	1		
Mapping bits:	0	X	X	X	X	0	0
Microinstruction address	0	1	0	1	1	0	0

Fig. 5.29. Mapping from instruction code to microinstruction address.

Ans. (*a*) 0 0 0 1 0 0 0 = 8

(*b*) 0 1 0 1 1 0 0 = 44

(*c*) 0 1 1 1 1 0 0 = 60

Q. 28. Formulate a mapping procedure that provides eight consecutive microinstructions for each routine. The operation code has six bits and the control memory has 2048 words.

Ans. Given: Opcode = 6 bits

Control memory address = 11 bits.

$$00\left|\begin{matrix} X\ X\ X\ X\ X\ X \\ X\ X\ X\ X\ X\ X \end{matrix}\right|000$$

Q. 29. Give the 9-bit microoperation field for the following micro-operations

(*a*) $AC \leftarrow AC + 1, DR \leftarrow DR + 1$

(*b*) $PC \leftarrow PC + 1, DR \leftarrow M[AR]$

(*c*) $DR \leftarrow AC, AC \leftarrow DR$

Ans.

	*F*1	*F*2	*F*3
(*a*)	011	110	000
(*b*)	000	100	101
(*c*)	100	101	000

Q. 30. Let *SP* = 000000 in the stack of figure given below. How many items are there in the stack if :

(*a*) FULL = 1 and EMPTY = 0?

(*b*) FULL = 0 and EMPTY = 1?

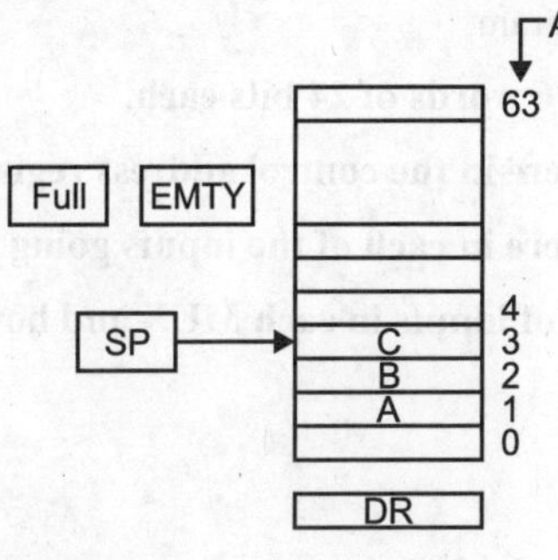

Ans. (*a*) Stack full with 64 items.

(*b*) Stack empty.

Q. 31. A stack is organized such that *SP* always points at the next empty location on the stack. This means that *SP* can be initialized to 4000 in figure given below and the first item in the stack is stored in location 4000. List the microoperations for the push and pop operations

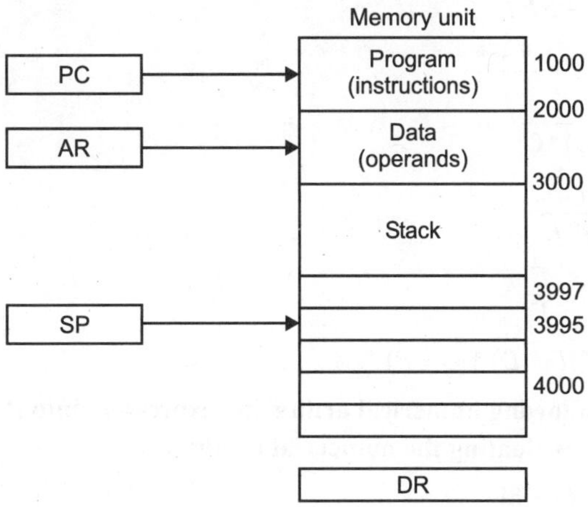

Fig. 5.30. Memory with program, data and stack segments

Ans. PUSH : $M[SP] \leftarrow DR$

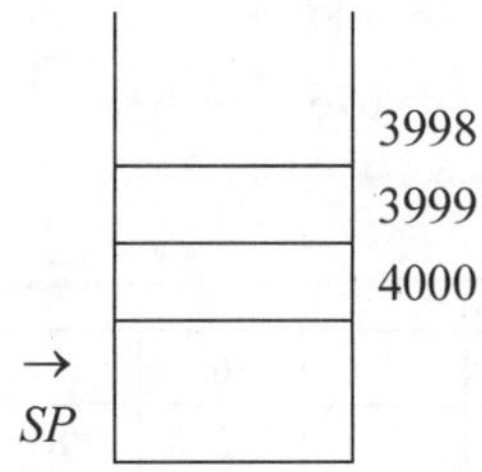

$SP \leftarrow SP - 1$

POP : $SP \leftarrow SP + 1$

$DR \leftarrow M[SP]$

Q. 32. Convert the following arithmetic expressions from infix to RPN –

(*a*) $A*B + C*D + E*F$.

(*b*) $A*B + A*(B*D + C*E)$

(*c*) $A + B*[C*D + E*(F + G)]$

(*d*) $A*[B + C*(D + E)]\ F * (G + H)$.

[GGSIPU, B. Tech (CSE)- 5th Sem., Dec. 2008 & Dec. 2011]

Ans. (*a*) $AB * CD * E * ++$.

(*b*) $AB * ABD * CE * + * +$

(*c*) $FG + E * CD * + B * A +$

(*d*) ABCDE + * + * FGH + * /.

Q. 33. Convert the following RPNs to infix notations –

(*a*) ABCDE + * – /

(*b*) ABCDE * / – +

(c) *ABC * /D – EF / +*

(*d*) ABCDEFG + * + * + *.

Ans. (*a*) $\frac{A}{B-(D+E)*C}$

(*b*) $A+B-\frac{C}{D*E}$

(*c*) $\frac{A}{B*C}-D+\frac{E}{F}$

(*d*) $(((F+G)*E+D)*C+B)*A$

Q. 34. Convert the following numerical arithmetic expression into RPN and show the stack operations for evaluating the numerical result

(3 + 4) [10(2 + 6) + 8]

Ans. Now, (3 + 4) [10(2 + 6) + 8]

= 7 [80 + 8]

= 7.88

= 616

RPN is : 34 + 26 + 10 * 8 + *

and stack contents are –

				6		10		8		
	4		2	2	8	8	80	80	88	
3	3	7	7	7	7	7	7	7	7	616
3	4	+	2	6	+	10	*	8	+	+

Q. 35. A FIFO memory organization stores information in such a manner that the item that is stored is the first item that is retrieved. Show how a FIFO memory operates with three counters. A write counter WC holds the address for writing into memory. A real counter RC holds the address for reading from memory. An available storage counter ASC indicates the number of words stored in FIFO. ASC is incremented for every word stored and decremented for every item that is retrieved.

Ans. **WRITE** (if not full):

$M[WC] \leftarrow DR$

$WC \leftarrow WC+1$

$ASC \leftarrow ASC+1$

READ (if not empty):

$DR \leftarrow M[RC]$

$RC \leftarrow RC+1$

$ASC \leftarrow ASC-1$

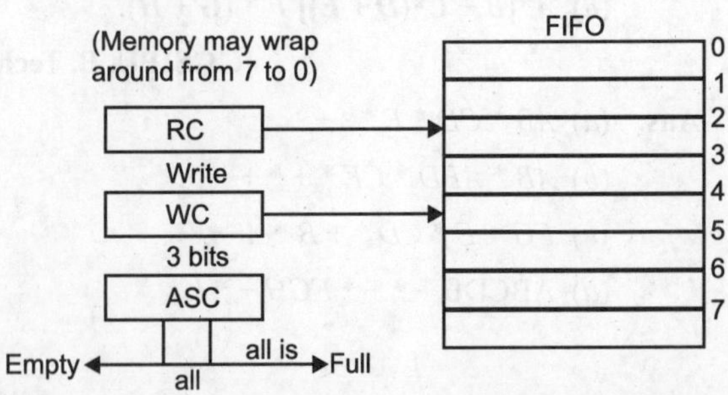

Q. 36. A computer has 32 bit instruction and 12-bit addresses. If there are 250 two-address instructions, how many one-address instructions can be formulated?

[GGSIPU, B. Tech. (CSE) 5th Sem., Dec. 2005]

Ans.

8	12	12	= 32 bits
Opcode	Address	Address	

(Two-address instructions)

$2^8 = 256$ combinations

$256 - 250 = 6$ combinations can be used for one address.

Opcode	Address

6×2^{12} (one-address instructions)

∴ Maximum number of one address instruction

$$= 6 \times 2^{12}$$
$$= 24{,}576$$

Q. 37. The memory unit of an computer has 256 K words of 32 bits each. The computer has an instruction format with four fields: an operation code field, code field, a mode field to specify one of the seven addressing modes, a register address field to specify one of 60 processor registers and a memory address. Specify the instruction format and the number of bits in each field if the instruction is in one memory word.

Ans. ∵ $256\text{ K} = 2^8 \times 2^{10} = 2^{18}$

∴ Address = 18 bits long

Mode = 3 bits long

Register = 6 bits long

27 bits

Opcode = + 5

32 bits

∴ Instruction format is as follows –

Opcode	Mode	Register	Address	
5	3	6	18	= (32 bits)

Q. 38. A two-word instruction is stored in memory at an address designated by the symbol, *W*. The address field of the instruction (stored at *W* + 1) is designated by the symbol *Y*. The operand used during the execution of instruction is stored at an address symbolized by *Z*. An index register contains the value of *X*. State how *Z* is calculated from the other addresses if the addressing mode of the instruction is –

(*a*) Direct **(*b*) Indirect**

(*c*) Relative **(*d*) Indexed**

[GGSIPU, B.Tech. (CSE) – 5th Sem., Dec. 2005; DTU(DCE) – ME(CS) – 2005]

Ans.

Register	Address	Memory
PC	W	Opcode Mode
	$W+1$	Y
$XR = X$	$W+2$	Next instruction
	Z	Operand

Now, let Z = Effective address

(*a*) Direct : $Z = Y$

(*b*) Indirect : $Z = M[Y]$

(*c*) Relative : $Z = Y + W + 2$

(*d*) Indexed : $Z = Y + X$

Q. 39. A relative mode branch type of instruction stored in memory at an address equivalent to decimal 750. The branch is made to an address equivalent to decimal 500.

(*a*) What should be the value of the relative address field of the instruction (in decimal)?

(*b*) Determine the relative address value in binary using 12-bits (Why must the number be in 2s complement?)

(*c*) Determine the binary value in PC after the fetch phase and calculate the binary-value of 500. Then show that the binary value in PC plus the relative address calculated in part b is equal to the binary value of 500.

Ans. (*a*) Relative address = 500 – 751 = –251

(*b*) 251 = 000011111011

–251 = 111100000101

(*c*) PC = 751 = 001011101111

RA = –251 = 111100000101

EA = 500 = 000111110100

Q. 40. How many times does the control unit refer to memory when it fetches and executes an indirect addressing modes instruction, if the instruction is –

(*a*) A computational type requiring an operand from memory

(*b*) A branch type.

Ans. Let us assume one word per instruction or operand.

(*a*) Computational type:

Fetch instruction

Fetch Effective Address

Fetch operand

$\therefore$ 3 memory references

(*b*) Branch type:

Fetch instruction

Fetch effective address and transfer to PC

$\therefore$ 2 Memory references

Q. 41. What must the address field of an indexed addressing mode instruction be to make it the same as a register indirect mode instruction?

Ans. The address part of the indexed mode instruction must be set to **zero**.

Q. 42. An instruction is stored at location 300 with its address field at location 301. The address field has the value 400. A processor register *R*1 contains the number 200. Evaluate the effective address if the addressing mode of the instruction is–

(*a*) direct.

(*b*) immediate.

(*c*) relative.

(*d*) register indirect.

(*e*) index with R1 as the index register.

[GGSIPU, B. Tech. (CSE) – 5th Sem., Dec. 2004]

Ans. Let us draw the memory view firstly.

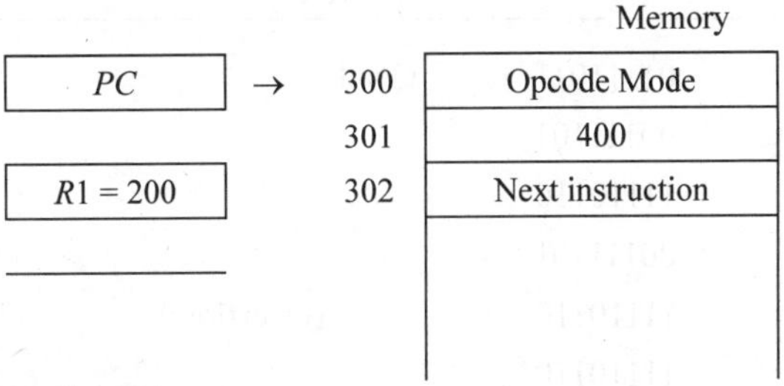

∴ The corresponding EAs are –

(*a*) Direct: 400

(*b*) Immediate: 301

(*c*) Relative: 302 + 400 = 702

(*d*) Register indirect: 200

(*e*) Indexed: 200 + 400 = 600

Q. 43. Assuming an 8-bit computer, show the multiple precision addition of the two 32-bit unsigned numbers listed below using the add with carry instruction. Each byte is expressed as a two-digit hexadecimal number. (6E, C3567A) + (13556B8F)

Ans.

1 = *C*	*O* = *C*	1 = *C*	0 = Reset initial carry	
6E	C3	56	7A	
13	55	6B	8F	
82	18	C2	09	Add with carry

Q. 44. Given the 16-bit value 1001101011001101, what operation must be performed in order to –

(*a*) Clear to 0, the first 8 bits.

(*b*) Set to 1, the last 8 bits.

(*c*) Complement the middle 8 bits? [GGSIP, B.Tech. (CSE) – 5th Sem., Dec. 2005]

Ans. (*a*) AND with : 0000000011111111

(*b*) OR with : 0000000011111111

(*c*) XOR with : 0000111111110000

Q. 45. An 8-bit shift register contains the value 01111011 and the carry bit is equal to 1. Perform the eight shift operations given by the instructions listed in Table given below. Each time, start from the initial value given above.

Table 5.6: Typical shift instructions

Name	**Mnemonic**
Logical shift right	SHR
Logical shift left	SHL
Arithmetic shift right	SHRA
Arithmetic shift left	SHLA
Rotate right	ROR
Rotate left	ROL
Rotate right through carry	RORC
Rotate left through carry	ROL C

Ans. Initial : 01111011 C = 1

SHR : 00111101

SHL : 11110110

SHRA : 00111101

SHLA : 11110110 (Overflow)

ROL : 11110110

RORC : 10111101

ROLC : 11110111

Q. 46. Show that the circuit labelled as 'check for zero output' in figure given below is an 8-bit NOR gate –

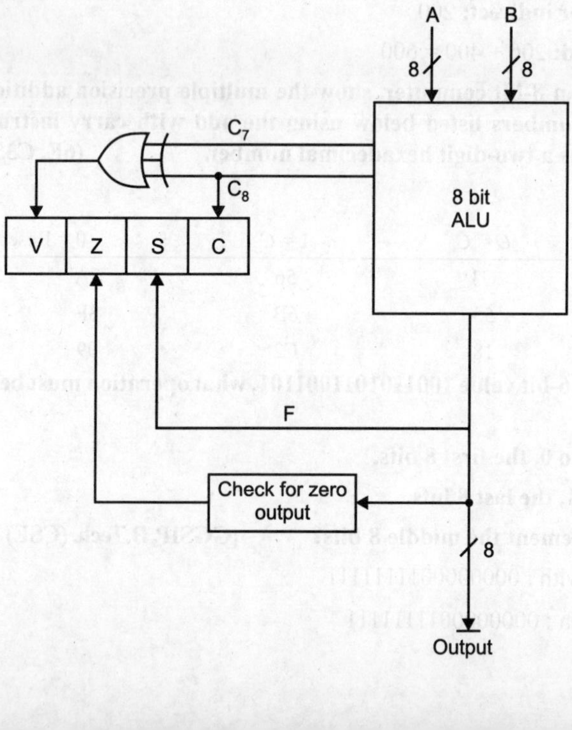

Ans. $Z = F_0' F_1' F_2' F_3' F_4' F_5' F_6' F_7'$

$= (F_0 + F_1 + F_2 + F_3 + F_4 + F_5 + F_6 + F_7)'$

Q. 47. A computer responds to an interrupt request signal by pushing onto the stack the contents of PC and the current PSW. It reads a new PSW from memory from a location given by an interrupt address symbolized by IAD. The first address of the service program is taken from memory at location IAD + 1.

(a) List the sequence of microoperations for the interrupt cycle.

(b) List the sequence of microoperations for the return from interrupt instruction.

Ans. (*a*) $SP \leftarrow SP - 1$

$M[SP] \leftarrow PSW$

$SP \leftarrow SP - 1$

$M[SP] \leftarrow PC$

$TR \leftarrow IAD$; *TR* is temporary register

$PSW \leftarrow M[TR]$

$TR \leftarrow TR + 1$

$PC \leftarrow M[TR]$

Go to the fetch phase.

(*b*) $PC \leftarrow M[SP]$

$SP \leftarrow SP + 1$

$PSW \leftarrow M[SP]$

$SP \leftarrow SP + 1$

Q. 48. Three computers use register windows with the following characteristics. Determine the window size and the total number of registers in each computer.

	Computer 1	Computer 2	Computer 3
Global Registers	10	8	16
Local registers	10	8	16
Common registers	6	8	16
Number of windows	8	4	16

[GGSIPU, B.Tech. (CSE) – 5th Sem., Dec. 2005]

Ans. $\therefore$ Window size $= L + 2C + G$

$\therefore$ Computer 1 : 10 + 12 + 10 = 32

Computer 2 : 8 + 16 + 8 = 32

Computer 3 : 16 + 32 + 16 = 64.

$\because$ Register file $= (L + C)W + G$

Computer 1 : (10 + 6)8 + 10

= 16*8 + 10

= 138

Computer 2 : $(8 + 8)4 + 8$

$= 16*4 + 8$

$= 72$

Computer 3 : $(16 + 16)16 + 16$

$= 32*16 + 16$

$= 528$

Q. 49. Given an example of a RISC-I instruction that will perform the following operations –

(*a*) Decrement a register.

(*b*) Complement a register.

(*c*) Negate a register.

(*d*) Clear a register to O.

(*e*) Divide a signed number by 4.

(*f*) No operation.

Ans. (*a*) SUB *R*22, # 1, *R*22; (*R*22 ← *R*22 – 1 i.e., subtract 1).

(*b*) XOR *R*22, # – 1, *R*22; *R*22 ← *R*22 ⊕ all 1s ($X \oplus 1 = X'$).

(*c*) SUB *R*0, *R*22, *R*22; *R*22 ← 0 – *R*22

(*d*) ADD *R*0, *R*0, *R*22; *R*22 ← 0 + 0

(*e*) SRA *R*22, $2, *R*22; Arithmetic shift right twice

(*f*) OR *R*1, *R*1, *R*1; *R*1 ← *R*1 *VR*1

or ADD *R*1, *R*0, *R*1; *R*1 ← *R*1 + 0

or SLL *R*1, # 0, *R*1; Shift left 0 times

Q. 50. Write the RISC-I instructions in assembly language that will cause a jump to address 3200 if the Z(zero) status bit is equal to 1.

(*a*) Using immediate mode.

(*b*) Using a relative address mode (assume that PC = 3400)

Ans. (*a*) JMP Z, # 3200, (R0); PC ← 0 + 3200

(*b*) JMPR Z, –200; PC ← 3400 + (–200)

51. What are the various techniques of grouping of control signals? Compare them. Also give their advantages and disadvantages. [MDU, BE (CSE) – 4th Sem., 2002]

Ans. The grouping of control signals can be done either by using techniques called as **vertical organisation** or by using technique called **horizontal organisation**. The encoded scheme that use compact codes to specify only a small number of controls functions in each microinstruction are referred to as a **vertical organization.** On other hand, the minimally encoded scheme, in which resources can be controlled with a single instruction, is called a **horizontal organization.**

The Table shows the comparison between horizontal and vertical organisation.

Table 5.7: Differences

S.No.	Horizontal	Vertical
1.	Long formats	Short formats
2.	Ability to express a high degree of parallelism	Limited ability to express parallel microoperations
3.	Little encoding of the control information	Considerable encoding of the control information
4.	Useful when higher operating speed is desired.	Slower operating speeds.

The advantages and disadvantages of horizontal and vertical organisations are summarized as follows:

1. The horizontal organisation approach is suitable when operating speed of computer is a critical factor and where the machine structure allows parallel usage of number of resources.
2. Vertical approach results in slower operations speed but less bits are required in the microinstruction.
3. In vertical approach, the significant factor is the reduced requirement for the parallel hardware required to handle the execution of microinstructions.

52. Compare hardwired and μPC in tabular form

[GGSIPU, B.Tech. (CSE) – 5th Sem., Dec. 2004] & [MDU, BE (CSE) – 4th Sem., 2004]

Attribute	Hardwired Control	Microprogrammed Control
Speed	Fast	Slow
Control functions	Implemented in hardware	Implemented in software
Flexibility	Not flexible, to accommodate new system specifications or new instructions	More flexible, to accommodate new system specification or new instructions redesign is required
Ability to handle large complex instruction sets	Some what difficult	Easier
Ability to support operating systems and diagnostic features	Very difficult (unless anticipated during design)	Easy
Design process	Somewhat complicated	Orderly and systematic
Applications	Mostly RISC microprocessors	Mainframes, some microprocessors
Instruction set Size	Usually under 100 instructions	Usually over 100 instructions
ROM size	–	2K to 10K by 20-400 bit microinstructions
Chip area efficiency	Uses least area	Uses more area.

EXERCISE QUESTIONS

Q. 1. (*a*) State the difference between arithmetic shift and logical shift. Start from initial value of register $R = 11011101$. Determine R after a logical shift left followed by a circular shift right followed by a arithmetic shift left.

(*b*) What is Reverse Polish Notation. Convert the following expressions to RPN –

(*i*) $W + X * [Y * Z + P*Q*(R - S)]$

(*ii*) $W - X * W + [P*(R+S) - Q]$

(*c*) Evaluate the following arithmetic expressions using stack operation by first converting it to RPN –

(4*5) + (7*4) – (3*6). **[GGSIPU, B.Tech. (CSE) – 5th Sem., Dec. 2004]**

2. (*a*) What are addressing modes. Give two advantages of using them. How many references to memory are needed by direct and indirect address instruction to bring the operand into a CPU register.

(*b*) An instruction is stored at location 8000 with its address field at location 8001. The address field has the value 4000. A processor register, R contains the numeral 20. Find the effective address if the addressing mode is –

(*i*) direct.

(*ii*) Immediate

(*iii*) Relative

(*iv*) Register indirect

[GGSIPU, B.Tech. (CSE) – 5th Sem., Dec. 2004; 2008; 2009 & 2010]

Q. 3. Which of the following pairs of reverse polish formulae are mathematically equivalent?

(*i*) $AB + C +$ and $ABC + +$

(*ii*) $AB * C +$ and $ABC + *$. **[GGSPU, B.Tech. (CSE) – 5th Sem., Dec. 2005]**

Q. 4. (*a*) Explain in brief with example all the different types of addressing modes.

(*b*) Explain the basic features of RISC and CISC computers.

[GGSIPU, B.Tech. (CSE) – 5th Sem., Dec. 2005, 2006, 2007, 2009]

Q. 5. (*a*) Explain Polish Notation. Give one example each to illustrate polish notation and RPN.

(*b*) Express (3*4) + (5*6) to RPN **[GGSIPU, B.Tech. (CSE) – 5th Sem., Dec. 2008]**

Q. 6. What are addressing modes? Explain the following with the help of suitable examples :

(*i*) Implied mode
(*ii*) Register mode
(*iii*) Direct address mode
(*iv*) Relative address mode
(*v*) Immediate mode
(*vi*) Register indirect
(*vii*) Indirect address
(*viii*) Base Register addressing mode

[GGSIPU, B.Tech. (CSE) – 5th Sem., Dec. 2010] & [MDU, BE (CSE) – 4th Sem., 2000, 2001, 2004, 2005, 2006]

Q. 7. Write a program to evaluate the arithmetic statement. With suitable comments, using –

$$X = (A + B*C) / CD - E*F + G*H)$$

(*a*) Three address machine.

(*b*) Two address machine.

(*c*) One address machine.

(*d*) Zero address machine. **[MDU, BE. (CSE) – 4th Sem., 2002]**

Q. 8. Write a program to evaluate the following arithmetic statements using–

(*i*) 3-address instructions.

(*ii*) 2-address instructions.

(*iii*) 1-address instructions.

$$X = \frac{\left[A * \frac{B}{C} + D\right].E}{\frac{D}{E} * F + \frac{C}{A} + B}$$

[MDU, BE (CSE) 4th Sem. 2004]

Q. 9. (*a*) What do you mean by ISA? How it affects the design of a computer system?

(*b*) Briefly discuss stored program concept. **[MDU, BE (CSE) – 4th Sem., 2006]**

Q. 10. Compare RISC and CISC processors.

[Madras Univ., B.Sc. (CS); April 2011] & [PTU, MCA – 3rd Sem., 2009] & [PTU, B.Tech. (CSE) - 3rd Sem. 2009]

Q. 11. Differentiate between hardwired control and μPC. Is it possible a hardwired control associated with a control memory. **[DTU (DCE) – ME(CS) – 2004-05]**

Q. 12. Explain in detail the RISC pipeline why is the cache miss penalty, greater in deeply pipelined processor?

[GGSIPU, B.Tech. (CSE)- 5th Sem., Second Term. Exam., Nov. 2011]

[Hint : Students are advised to refer to Chapter 8 of this book]

Q. 13. A computer has 16 registers, an ALU with 32 operations and a shifter with eight operations. All connected to a common bus system.

(*a*) Formulate a control word for a microoperation.

(*b*) Specify the number of bits in each field on the control word and give a general encoding scheme. **[GGSIPU, B.Tech. (CSE/IT/ECE) – 5th Sem., 2011]**

Q. 14. What is the difference between a direct and indirect address instruction? How many references to memory are needed for each type of instruction to bring an operand into a processor register? **[GGSIPU, B.Tech. (CSE)/IT/ECE) – 5th Sem., 2011]**

CHAPTER 6

MEMORY, ITS HIERARCHY AND ITS TYPES

6.0 INTRODUCTION

Memory refers to a sequence of bytes of storage that has different vital functions. The memory of a microcomputer (or PC) is the space where both program and data are stored before execution, during execution and after execution. The storage that is controlled by the CPU is known as an **online storage**. For eg. a magnetic disk directly connected with CPU is an online disk file. A storage device not under the control of CPU is the **offline storage.** Most modern computers today are based on the stored program concept given by John Von Neumann in 1970s. **Please note that the user programs and user data are initially stored on auxiliary or secondary memory devices from where they are brought to the main memory by the operating system. Also note that memory is logically organized as a linear array of locations or addresses with addresses ranging from 0 to maximum memory size that the processor can address.**

> Do you know? Memory addresses are assigned either by the programmer or by the system software in octal or in hexadecimal forms.

To choose computer's memory, four parameters are considered :

(*a*) Capacity

(*b*) Speed

(*c*) Latency

(*d*) Bandwidth.

Let us define these one by one now.

Capacity: A memory that has m-addresses and a word length n-bits, has a capacity of (m*n) bits.

Speed: It is measured by two parameters –

(*a*) Access time (t_A).

(*b*) Cycle time (t_c).

The access time (t_A) is defined as the time taken by the memory to complete a read operation from the instant of receiving the read control signal.

> Tip : Generally, the access time for read and write is equal.

The cycle time (t_c) is defined as the minimum time interval necessary from the initiation of one memory operation to the initiation of next memory operation. It comes into picture where two successive memory read operations have to be performed. **During first read operation, the second read cannot be initiated.** This is so because after first read, the data that is read (and is available after its t_A) **can be used immediately by the CPU but the memory is still busy with some internal operations, for some more time called as the recovery time (t_R).** It is only after this t_R that the next operation can be started. Thus, we can write that –

$$\boxed{t_c = t_A + t_R}$$

Latency: It is defined as the access time for the first access in a series of accesses.

Bandwidth: It is defined as the data transfer rate by the memory. It is given by number of bytes per second.

Memories are classified as follows:

1. **On the basis of role**
   (*a*) Main memory.
   (*b*) Secondary memory.
   (*c*) Cache memory.
   (*d*) Virtual memory.
2. **On the basis of access**
   (*a*) RAM.
   (*b*) Sequential access memory.
3. **On the basis of capacity**
   (*a*) R/W memory.
   (*b*) ROM.
4. **On the basis of technology**
   (*a*) Core memory.
   (*b*) Semiconductor memory.

We have already studied these in previous chapters.

6.1 MEMORY HIERARCHY

Practically there is a very large speed gap between CPU and memory. **Memory is about 1000 times slower than CPU**. To close up this speed gap, a hierarchical memory system is used. The memory hierarchy system consists of all storage devices employed in a system from slow but high capacity auxilllary memory to a relatively faster main memory, to as even smaller and faster cache memory accessible to the high speed logic. Each memory is involved with different levels in the memory hierarchy system. The reason for having two or three levels of memory hierarchy is economics. The memory hierarchy is shown in Fig. 6.1 below.

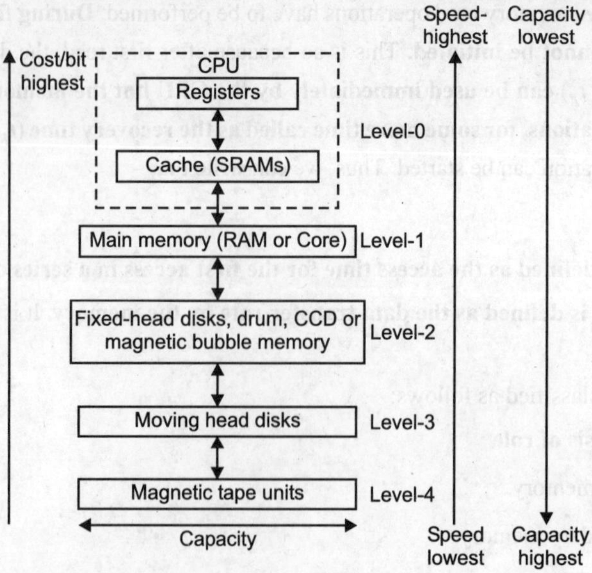

Fig. 6.1. Memory hierarchy

Please note that to make an efficient computer system, it is not possible to rely only on a single memory component but in a multilevel memory hierarchy. As shown in Fig. 6.1. Register file is the innermost level of memory. It is directly addressable by ALU. Next layer is cache memory. Cache memory acts on buffer between CPU and the main memory (MM). Main memory can be accessed in blocks by using multiway interleaving across parallel memory modules. At the outer levels of hierarchy, disks and tape units are used to establish the virtual memory space. This hierarchy of Fig. 6.1 is used to **broaden the memory bandwidth so that it will match with the bandwidth of the CPU.**

Five parameters characterize this memory technology :

(*a*) Access time (t_i) : It is defined as the round-trip time from the CPU to the ith level memory. It can range from a few nanoseconds (*ns*) *t* microseconds (μ*S*).

(*b*) Memory size : It is defined as the number of bytes or words in level i.

(c) Cost: The cost of the *i*th level memory is estimated by the formula:

$$\boxed{C_i * S_i}$$

Where C_i cost / byte

S_i – No. of bytes / words in level *i*.

(*d*) Bandwidth (b_i) : It is defined as the rate at which information is transferred between adjacent levels.

(*e*) Unit of transfer (x_i) : It is defined as the grain size for data transfers between the levels *i* and *i* + 1.

Please note that the memory devices at a lower level are faster to access, smaller in size, more expensive per byte, having a higher bandwidth and using a smaller unit to transfer as compared with those at a higher level. Also note here that:

$$\boxed{\begin{array}{l} t_{i-1} < t_i \\ S_{i-1} < S_i \\ C_{i-1} > C_i \\ b_{i-1} > b_i \\ x_{i-1} < x_i \end{array}}$$

Where $i \leftarrow 0$ to 4

For e.g., $i = 0$ means CPU register level.

$i = 1$ means main memory.

⋮

$i = 4$ means tape units.

6.2 CHARACTERISTICS OF MEMORY HIERARCHY

(a) Inclusion

As shown in Fig. 6.2, M_1 corresponds to cache, M_2 corresponds to main memory, M_3 corresponds disk storage. The inclusion property states that :

$$\boxed{M_1 \subset M_2 \subset M_3 \subset ... \subset M_n}$$

It means that all information is originally stored in the outermost level, M_n. During the processing, subsets of M_n are copied into M_{n-1}. Similarly, subsets of M_{n-1} are copied into M_{n-2} and so on.

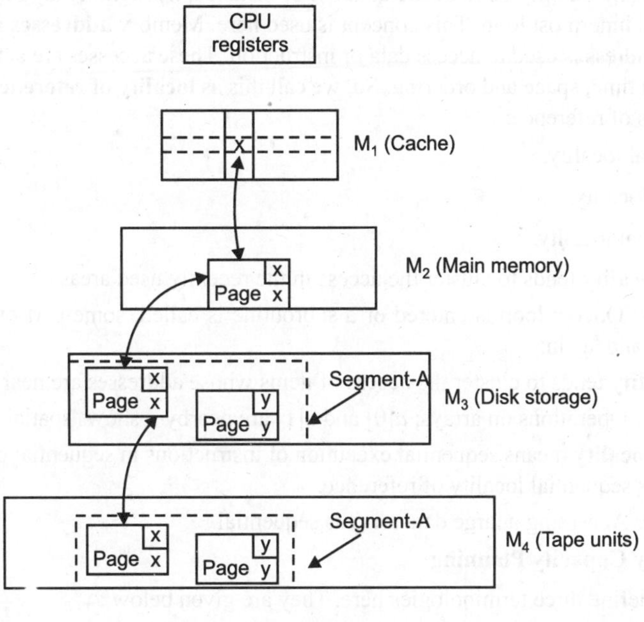

Fig. 6.2. Inclusion property

If an information is found in M_i then copies of the same word (8, 16 and 32 bits) will also be found in upper levels M_{i+1}, M_{i+2}, ..., M_n (for $i \leftarrow 1$ to 4 above).

Please note that a word stored in M_{i+1} may not be found in M_i. So, if a word is missing at level M_i then it implies that it is also missing from all the lower levels, i.e., M_{i+1}, M_{i+2}, ..., M_1. As shown in Fig. 6.2, the highest level is the backup storage where everything can be found.

Note that the information transfer between the CPU and cache is in terms of **words** i.e. 4 or 8 bytes each depending on the **word length of a machine.**

(*b*) Coherence

The coherence property means that the copies of the same information item at the successive memory levels must be consistent. This simply means that if a word is changed in the cache (M_1-level) then copies of that word must be updated immediately at the higher levels. But the memory hierarchy is to be maintained.

> **Tip** : Store frequently used information at the lower levels (say, M_1) so that access time of memory is minimal.

How this is done?

In general there are two techniques for maintaining the coherence in this memory hierarchy:

(*a*) **Write-Though (WT):** It means an immediate update in M_{i+1} if a word is modified in M_i ($i \leftarrow 1, 2, ..., n-1$).

(*b*) **Write-Back (WB):** It means delaying the update in M_{i+1} until the word being modified in M_i is replaced or removed from M_i.

(*c*) Locality of Reference

According to Hennessy and Patterson's (1990) 90-10 rule – **A typical program may spend 90% of its execution time on only 10% of the code."** For instance, a program may be spending most of its time on nested innermost loop. This concept is used here. Memory **addresses are generated by the CPU.** This address is used to access data or instruction. These accesses are actually clustered in certain regions in time, space and ordering. So, we call this as **locality of reference**. There are three types of localities of reference:

1. Temporal locality.
2. Spatial locality.
3. Sequential locality.

Temporal locality tends to cluster the access in the recently used areas.

For example: Once a loop is entered or a subroutine is called, some part of program will be referenced again and again.

Spatial locality tends to cluster the access of items whose addresses are near to one another.

For example: Operations on arrays; *a*[0] and *a*[1] are nearby – shows spatial locality.

Sequential locality means sequential execution of instructions in sequential order or accessing of an array shows sequential locality of reference.

For example: Accessing a large data array is sequential.

(*d*) Memory Capacity Planning

We need to define three terminologies here. They are given below :

1. **Hit Ratio (h_i):** Referring back to our Fig. 6.1 of memory hierarchy, we say that when an information item is found at M_i, it is a **hit** else it is a **miss** so, we define the **hit-ratio (h_i) at M_i as the probability that an information item will be found in M_i. So, miss-ratio** at M_i is defined as $(1 - h_i)$.

Please note here that the hit-ratios are independent random variables with their values between 0 and 1.

The access frequency to M_i is given by

$$f_i = (1-h_i)(1-h_2)\ldots(1-h_{i-1})h_i$$

Also $$\sum_{i=1}^{n} f_i = 1$$

Actually, $$f_1 >> f_2 >> f_3 >> \ldots >> f_n.$$

This implies that the inner levels of the memory are accessed more often than the outer levels of the memory.

2. **Effective Access Time (T_{eff}) :** T_{eff} of a memory hierarchy is defined as follows:

$$T_{eff} = \sum_{i=1}^{n} f_i . t_i$$

$$= h_1 t_1 + (1-h_1)h_2 t_2 + (1-h_1)(1-h_2)h_2 t_3 + \ldots + (1-h_1)(1-h_2)\ldots(1-h_{n-1})t_n.$$

T_{eff} depends on the program's behaviour and the memory design choices.

3. **Total cost of memory hierarchy (C_{total}) :** It is given by the formula:

$$C_{total} = \sum_{i=1}^{n} C_i . S_i$$

It means that the cost is distributed over n levels. Because $C_1 > C_2 > C_3 > \ldots C_n$ so we have to choose $S_1 < S_2 < S_3 < \ldots S_n$.

An **ideal design** of memory hierarchy should have following parameters:

(*a*) $T_{eff} \approx t_1$ (of M_1).

(*b*) $C_{total} \approx C_n$ (of M_n).

Practically, this is not possible due to the tradeoffs among n-levels.

Our problem now is to minimize

$$T_{eff} = \sum_{i=1}^{n} f_i . t_i$$

and the constraints are :

So, $$C_{total} = \sum_{i=1}^{n} C_i . S_i < C_0$$

We need to manage the tradeoffs among t_i, C_i, S_i and f_i (or h_i) at all levels ($i \leftarrow 1$ to n).

We are in a position to solve a problem now.

EXAMPLE 1: Cc nsider a three level memory hierarchy ($M_1 - M_3$) as shown below:

Memory level	Access time	Capacity	Cost/KB
M_1 (cache)	$t_1 = 25$ ns	$S_1 = 512$ KB	$C_1 = \$1.25$
M_2 (MM)	$t_2 = ?$	$S_2 = 32$ MB	$C_2 = \$0.2$
M_3 (Disk)	$t_3 = 4$ ns	$S_3 = ?$	$C_3 = \$0.0002$

It is desired that :

$$T_{eff} = 10.04\ \mu s$$
$$h_1 = 0.98 \text{ (for } M_1)$$
$$h_2 = 0.9 \text{ (for } M_2).$$

But $$C_{total} \leq \$15000.$$

Find S_3, t_2 (marked as ? in table)?

SOLUTION: We know that the cost of memory hierarchy is given by the formula:

$$C = C_1S_1 + C_2S_2 + C_3S_3 \leq 15000$$

or 1.25 (512) + 0.2 (32) + 0.0002(S_3) = 15000

or $$S_3 = \textbf{39.8 Gbytes}$$

Now

$$T_{eff} = h_1t_1 + (1 - h_1)h_2t_2 + (1 - h_1)(1 - h_2)h_3t_3 \leq 10.04$$

or $$10.04 \times 10^{-6} = 0.98 \times 25 \times 10^{-9} + 0.02 \times 0.9 \times t_2 + 0.02 \times 0.1 \times 1 \times 4 \times 10^{-3}$$

or $$t_2 = \textbf{903 ns.}$$

Now, if someone wants to double the main-memory (M_2) from 32 MB to 64 MB such a case, cache hit ratio is unaffected but the hit ratio of main memory (M_2) may increase. T_{eff} will also increase accordingly.

6.3 CACHE MEMORY

The transfer of information from main memory (MM) to cache memory is conducted in units of cache blocks (or cache lines)

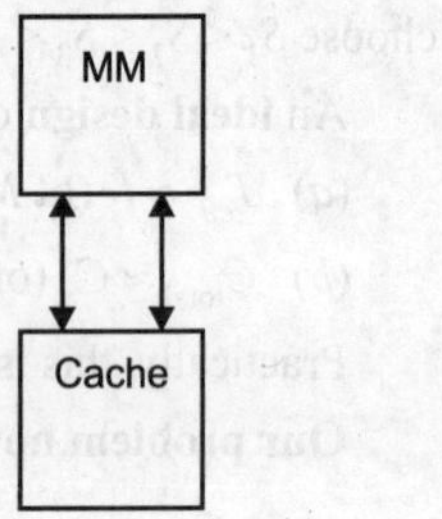

Fig. 6.3. MM and Cache memory

4 block placement schemes are as follows:

(*a*) Direct mapping cache.

(*b*) Fully Associative cache.

(*c*) Set-Associative cache.

(*d*) Sector mapping cache.

Block in caches are called as **'block frames'** in order to distinguish them from **'blocks'** of MM.

Block-frames (of cache) are denoted as $\overline{B}_i$ for $i \leftarrow 0$ to m.

and Blocks (of MM) are denoted as B_j for $j \leftarrow 0$ to n.

Now, various mappings can be defined from the set $| B_j |$ to $| \overline{B}_i |$

Also, we assume that $n >> m$ where $n = 2^s$ ad $m = 2^r$

Each block (of MM) or block frame (of cache) is assume to have b-words where $b = 2^w$.

$$\text{Cache has} = m.b \text{ .words}$$
$$= 2^r . 2^2 \text{ words}$$
$$= 2^{r+w} \text{ words}$$

and $$\text{M.M. has} = n.b \text{ words}$$
$$= 2^s . 2^w \text{ words}$$
$$= 2^{s+w} \text{ words}$$

where these words have $(s + w)$ bits, when the block frames are divided into $v = 2^t$ sets, then

$$\frac{m}{v} = \frac{2^r}{2^t} = 2^{r-t} = K \text{ blocks are in each set.}$$

I. Direct-Mapping Cache

- It is based on direct mapping of $\frac{n}{m} = \frac{2^s}{2^r} = 2^{s-r}$ memory blocks to one block frame in cache.
- Block B_j of MM is mapped to block-frame, $\overline{B}_i$ of cache, if $i = j$ and 4, i.e., $B_j \rightarrow \overline{B}_i$ if $i = j \bmod 4$.

There is a unique block frame $\overline{B}_i$ that each B_j can load into. There is no way to implement block replacement policy.

This direct mapping is very rigid but is the simplest cache organization to implement. Direct mapping is shown next:

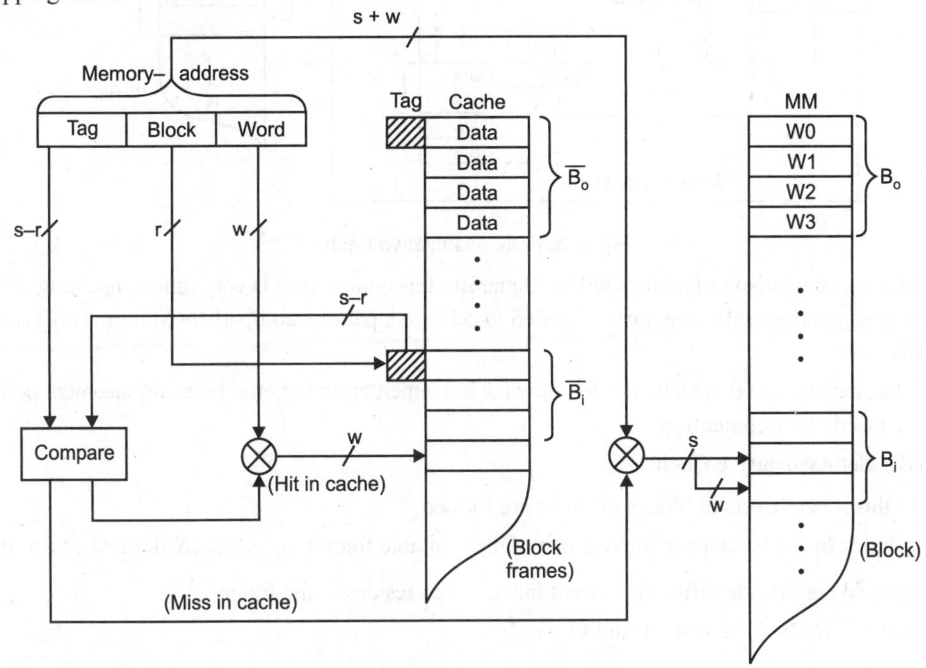

Fig. 6.4. Cache /Memory addressing

Working: We assume a case where each block contains four words (i.e. w = 2 bits).

Now, the memory address is divided into three fields:

w bits $\rightarrow$ word offset within each block

s bits $\rightarrow$ specify address in M.M.

$(s - r)$ bits (leftmost) $\rightarrow$ The tag to be matched.

Once the block $\overline{B}_i$ is uniquely identified by this field, the tag associated with the addressed block is compared with the tag in the memory address.

A cache hit occurs when the two tags match. Otherwise a cache miss occurs. In case of a cache hit, the word offset is used to identify the desired data word within the addressed block.

When a miss occurs, the entire memory address (s + w bits) is used to access the MM. The first 5 bits locate the addressed block and the lower w bits locate the word within the block.

II. Fully associative Cache

In this method, the tags are compared with all blocks tags in the cache.

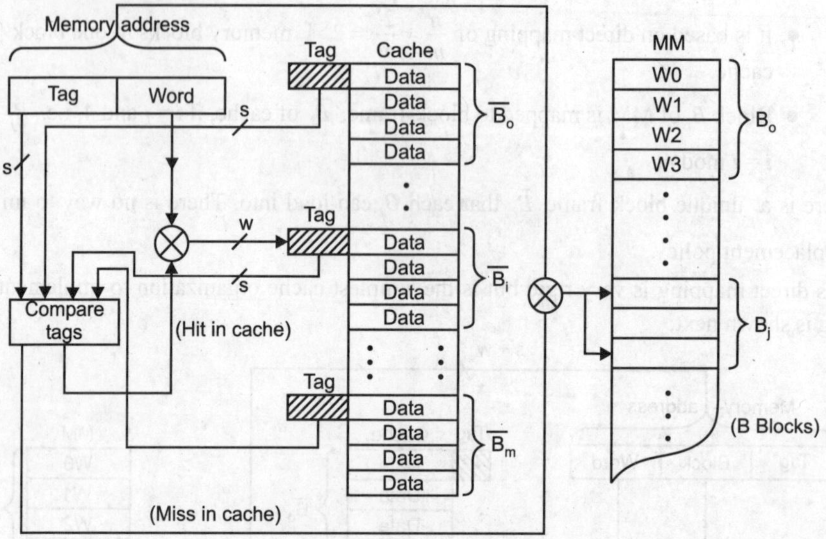

Fig. 6.5. Fully associative cache.

Herein, comparison of all tags will be done. But this comparison is very time consuming. Thus CAM-content addressable memory is needed to achieve a parallel comparison of tags. This is a bit costlier.

The advantage of this method is to allow the implementation of better block replacement policy with reduced block contention.

III. Set Associative Cache

In this scheme, sets of blocks of cache are formed.

A block B_j can be mapped into anyone of the available frames $\overline{B}_i$ in a set S_i defined below. It is the matched tag that identifies the current block which resides in the frame.

So, $B_j \to \overline{B}_i \in S_i$ if $j \pmod{v} = i$

If k represents set size,

m represents cache block frames

Then No. of sets of blocks, $\boxed{v = \dfrac{m}{k}}$

where k may be 2, 4, 8, 16 or 64 (depending on need).

For e.g.,

If $k = 2$ (i.e., 2 blocks in each set)

$m = 7$ (i.e. total no. fo blocks-frame in cache)

Then $v = \dfrac{7}{2} = 4$

i.e., there will be 4 sets of 2 blocks (as $k = 2$)

Also, $\quad 2^d = v(d - \text{bit set number is used to identify each set})$

or $\quad 2^d = 4$ (as above)

$$= 2^2$$

$\therefore \quad d = 2$ for our e.g..

$\therefore$ 2 bit tag is required.

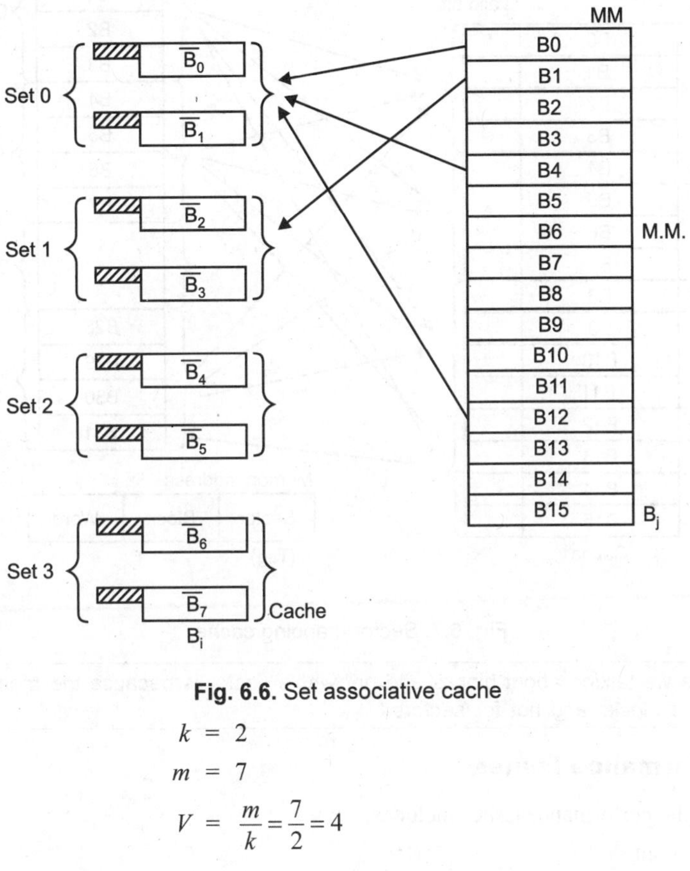

Fig. 6.6. Set associative cache

Here $\quad k = 2$

$\quad m = 7$

$\therefore \quad V = \dfrac{m}{k} = \dfrac{7}{2} = 4$

If $\quad j = 0$

then (0 mod v) = (0 mod 4) = 0; So, B_0 goes into S_0.

IV. Sector Mapping Cache

In this scheme, we partition both the cache and main memory (MM) into fixed-sized sectors.

- Each sector of MM can be placed in any of the available sector-frames.
- If a matched sector-frame is found (a cache hit), the block field is used to locate the desired block within the sector frame.
- If a cache miss occurs, only the missing block is fetched from the MM and brought into a similar block frame in an available sector.

So, i^{th} block in a sector $\rightarrow$ is placed into i^{th} block frame in a destined sector frame.

Also a valid bit is attached to each block frame to indicate whether the block is valid or invalid. When the contents of a block frame are replaced, the remaining block frame in the same sector are marked invalid. Only the **most recently replaced block frame in a sector** is marked valid for reference.

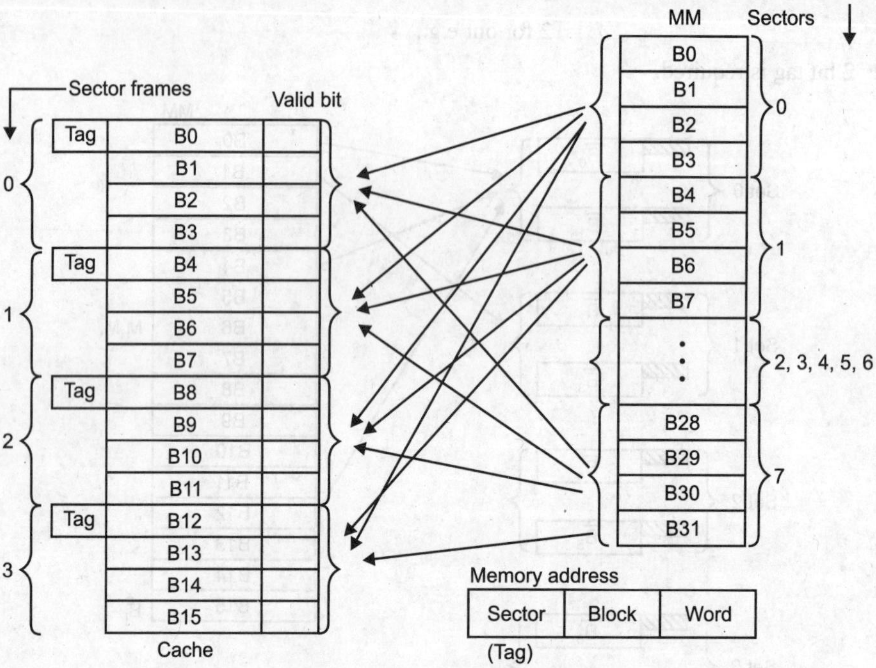

Fig. 6.7. Sector mapping cache.

> **NOTE:** Why are we talking about blocks and not whole sector is because the memory requests are destined for blocks and not for sectors.

Cache Performance Issues

Various cache performance issues includes:

(*a*) Cycle count.

(*b*) Hit ratio.

(*c*) Effect of block size.

(*d*) Effect of set number.

Tradeoffs exist between these issues.

1. Cycle counts

The cache speed depends on:

(*a*) Underlying static or dynamic RAM technology

(*b*) Cache organization and

(*c*) Cache hit ratios.

As shown in Fig. 6.8 below, the graph is between cycle count (y-axis) and cache size, set number and block size (on x-axis).

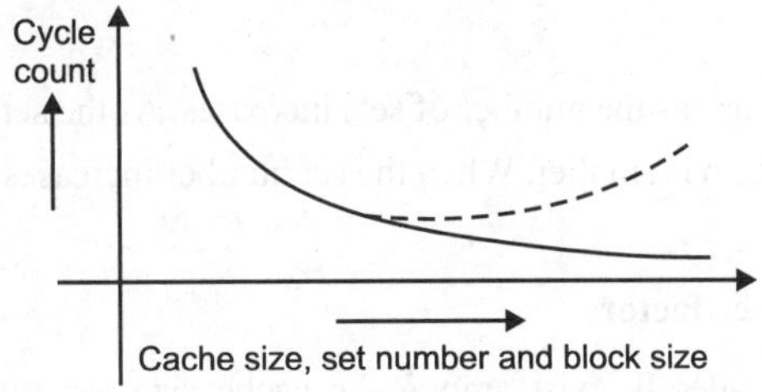

Fig. 6.8. Cycle count versus cache size and other parameter.

The cycle count decreases almost linearly with the increasing value of the above cache parameters. **Please note here that the decreasing trend becomes flat and after a certain point turns into an increasing trend as shown by the dashed line.**

2. Hit Ratios

As shown in Fig. 6.9 **hit ratio increases with respect to increasing cache size.**

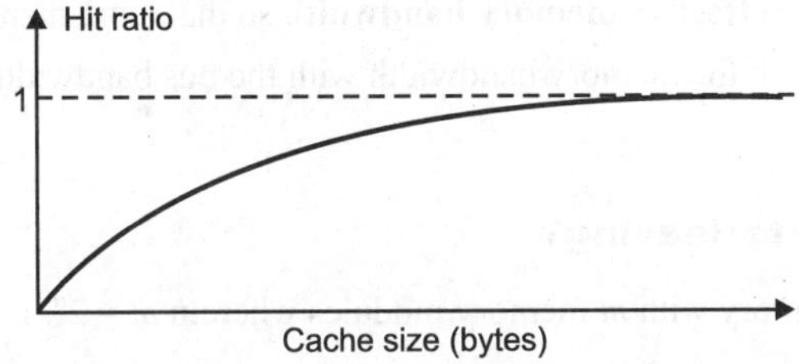

Fig. 6.9. Hit ratio v/s cache size

Please note that when the cache size approaches infinitely, a 100% hit ratio is expected. However, this never happens. It is because the cache size is always bounded by a limited budget. Graph of above Fig. 6.9 can be given by equation $1\text{-}C^{-0.5}$, where C is the total cache size.

3. Block Sizes

Let us now draw a graph between Hit ratio (y-axis) and block size (bytes) on x-axis. This is shown below in Fig. 6.10.

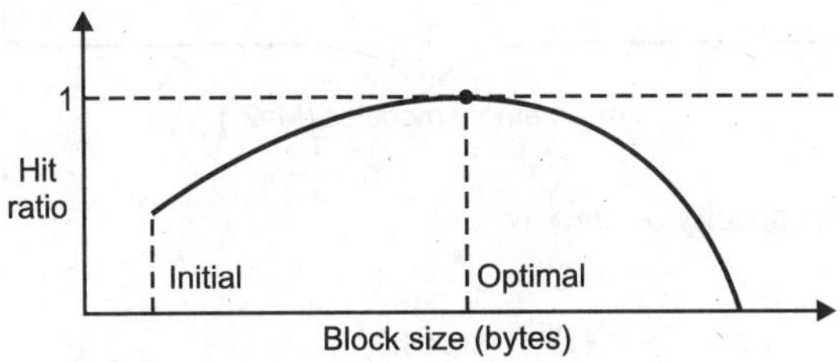

Fig. 6.10. Hit ratio v/s block size.

As the block size increases, initially, the hit ratio also increases. This is because of spatial locality in referencing larger instruction/data blocks. Hit ratio then reaches its peak value at a certain block size. After this point as shown in Fig. 6.10, the hit ratio decreases with further increase in the block size. This is because of the mismatch between program behaviour and block size.

Please note that the hit ratio become zero (0) when the block size equal the entire cache size.

4. Set numbers

The hit ratio may decrease as the number of sets increases. As the set number increases from 32 to 256, the decrease in hit ratio is smaller. When the set number increases to 512 and beyond, the hit ratio decreases faster.

5. Other Performance factors

Now, we know that tradeoffs exist among the cache size, set number, block size and the memory speed. Multilevel cache also offer options for expanding the cache effects. An optimal cache hierarchy design is a must.

Interleaved Memory Organization

In this technique, the system memory is divided into a number of memory modules and arranges addressing so that successive words in the address space are placed in different modules. Our objective is to broaden the **effective memory bandwidth** so that more memory can be accessed per unit time. We need to match the memory bandwidth with the bus bandwidth and with the processor bandwidth.

What is Memory Interleaving?

Consider a main memory with m memory modules wherein $m = 2^a$. Each has $W = 2^b$ words of memory cells. That is,

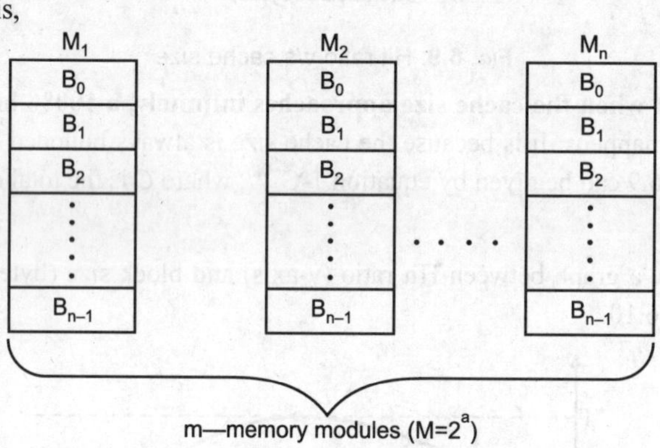

$$\therefore \quad \text{Total memory capacity} = m \times w$$
$$= 2^a \times 2^b$$
$$= 2^{a+b} \text{ words.}$$

These memory words are assigned linear addresses.

There are two address formats for memory interleaving:

1. Low-order interleaving.
2. High-order interleaving.

Let us discuss these formats one by one.

1. **Low-order interleaving** spreads the contiguous memory locations across the m modules horizontally. This is shown in Fig. 6.11 below:

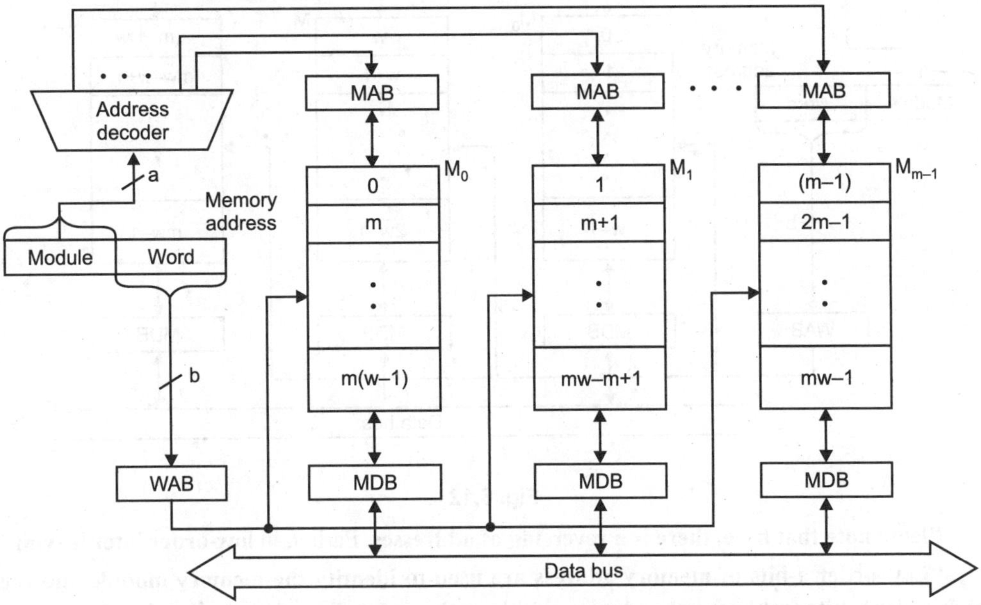

Fig. 6.11. Low order m-way interleaving

MAB : Module Address Buffer.

MDB : Memory Data Buffer.

WAB : Word Address Buffer.

The **low-order** a – bits of the memory address are used to identify the memory module. The high-order b-bits are the word addresses within each module. **Please note that the same word address is applied to all memory modules simultaneously**. An address decoder is used to distribute module addresses.

2. **High-order interleaving:** It uses **high-order** a-bits as the module address and the **low-order** *b*-bits as the word address within each module. Contiguous memory locations are thus assigned to the same memory module. In each memory cycle, only one word is accessed from each module. So, this type of interleaving cannot support block access of contiguous locations. It is shown in Fig. 6.12. below:

MAB : Module Address Buffer.

MDB : Memory Data Buffer.

WAB : Word Address Buffer.

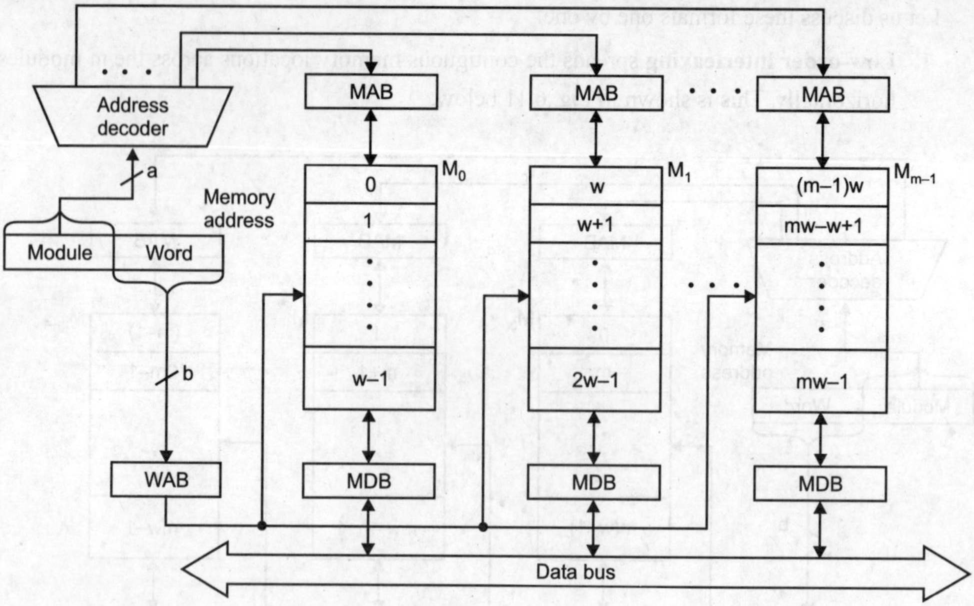

Fig. 6.12

Please note that here, there is a reversing of addresses. Earlier, in **low-order inter leaving.**

"Low-order a-bits of memory address are used to identify the memory module and the high-order b-bits are the word addresses within each module." On the other hand, in **high order interleaving.**

"High-order a-bits are used as the module address and the low-order b-bits as the word address within each module."

Note that a single memory module is assumed to deliver one word per memory cycle and thus has a bandwidth of 1.

What is memory bandwidth?

The memory bandwidth (B) of an m-way interleaved memory is upper-bounded by m and lower bounded by:

1. According to Hellerman, for uniprocessor,

$$B = m^{0.56} = \sqrt{m}$$

where m is the number of interleaved memory modules.

If $m = 16$ then $B = \sqrt{16} = 4$

This means that if 16 memory modules are used, then the effective memory bandwidth is four times that of a single module.

What is fault tolerance?

It is easier to locate faulty memory modules in a memory bank of *m*-memory modules due to memory interleaving. However, this fault isolation cannot be carried out in low-order interleaved memory in which a module failure may affect the entire memory bank. Thus, **low-order interleaving memory is not fault-tolerant.**

Comparisons of these 4-techniques

In general, direct mapping caches have larger miss ratios than set-associative caches. However, simulation results on some data has shown **that the gap diminishes as the size of caches gets larger. For e.g,** can 8 KB two-way set associative cache with set size of 32 bytes has a **miss ratio difference** off 0.013 in comparison with a direct mapping cache of the same size. However, for the caches with 32 KB, the difference is 0.005. **This phenomenon is seen because the miss ratio of all kinds of caches decreases as the cache size increases.**

Direct mapping caches have smaller average access times for sufficiently large cache sizes. The reason is that a set-associative cache requires extra gates and hence has a longer hit access time (t_c) than a direct-mapping cache. Another reason is that the gap between the direct-mapping cache's miss-ratio and set-associative cache's miss ratio diminishes as the caches get larger. Hence, set associative organisation is preferred for small caches while direct-mapping organization is preferred for larger caches.

6.4 VIRTUAL MEMORY TECHNOLOGY

The main memory is also known as a physical memory but this memory is limited in size. To solve this problem auxiliary memory is also used. A memory hierarchy consisting of **main memory and auxiliary memory is known as virtual memory.**

Auxiliary or back up memory can be like disk arrays. Only active programs or some portions of them are stored in physical memory at one time. All programs are loaded in and out of the physical memory dynamically under the control of O.S. Without virtual memory, it is impossible to implement multiprogramming or time sharing features. Each word in the physical memory is given a **physical address**. This forms a **physical address space. Virtual address are generated by CU at compile time**. This is shown below in Fig. 6.13.

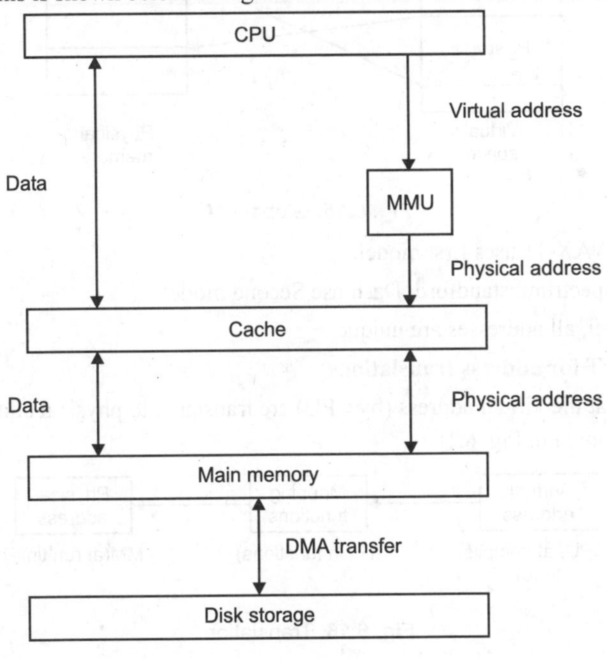

Fig. 6.13. Virtual memory organization.

As shown in Fig. 6.13 above, that the **CPU generates virtual addresses that are to be translated to physical addresses and that too at run time.** This is done by a special hardware called as **Memory Management Unit or MMU.**

There are 2 ways of having virtual memories:

(*a*) Private virtual memory.

(*b*) Global virtual memory

In private virtual memory space model, each processor has its own private virtual adress space. These virtual addresses are mapped to the same physical memory that is shared by all the processors. This is shown in Fig. 6.14.

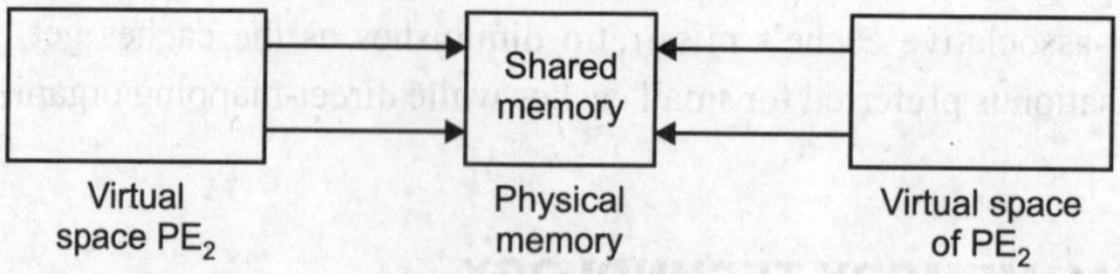

Fig. 6.14. Private VM.

In global virtual memory space model, a single global virtual space is formed. We don't have different spaces for PEs now. This is shown in Fig. 6.15.

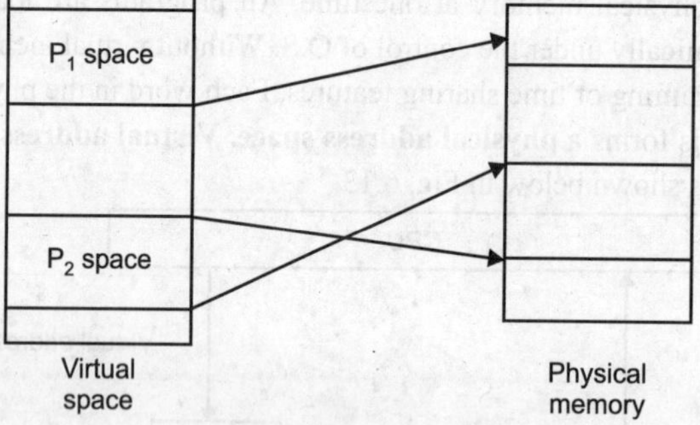

Fig. 6.15. Global VM.

Applications: VAX-11 uses first model.

IBM-801, HP spectrum, standford, Dash use Second model.

In Second model, all addresses are unique.

Role of TLB and PT for address translations

As we know that the virtual address (by CPU) are translated to physical address at run time by MMU. That is, as shown in Fig. 6.16.

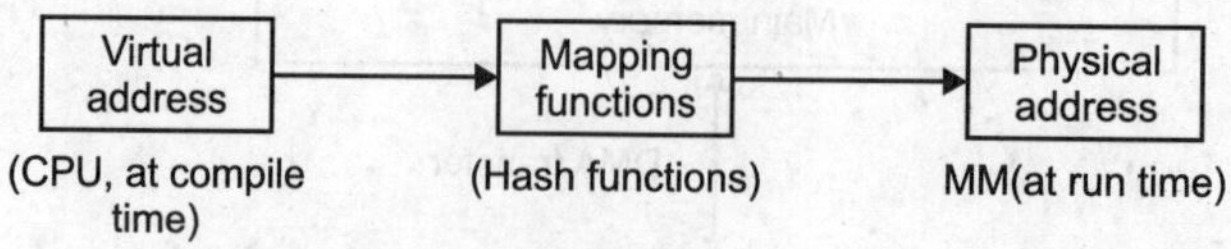

Fig. 6.16. Translation

Basically, we have translation maps that are in form of:

(*a*) Translation Lookaside Buffer (TLB)

(*b*) Page Tables (PTs).

On the basis of **locality of reference,** a particular **working set of pages** is referenced within a given context or time window. The use of TLB and PT is shown below in Fig. 6.17.

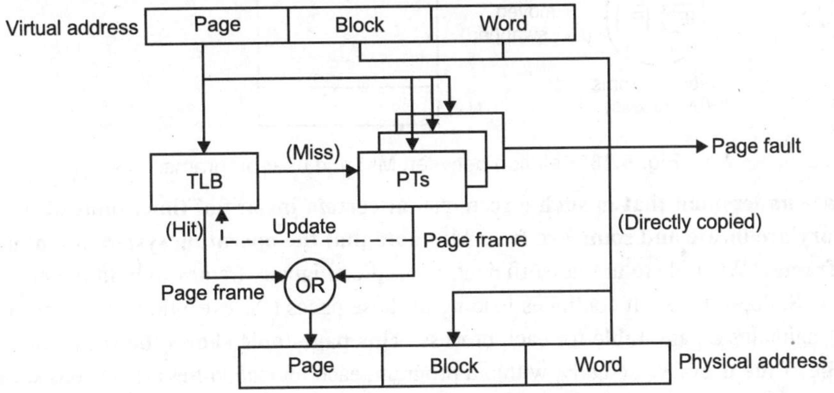

Fig. 6.17. Role of TLB and PT during address translations

We observe that each virtual address is divided into three fields – virtual **page** number, cache **block** number and **word** address within the block. Our objective is to produce the physical address (at bottom of Fig. 6.17) having page frame number, block number and the word address.

How it works? There are some steps:

Step 1: The virtual page number (leftmost field) is used to search through the TLB for a match. This TLB can be an associative memory or content addressable memory (CAM) or part of cache memory. TLB is a high-speed look up table. It stores recently referenced page entries.

> **NOTE:** Page entry = Virtual page number + page frame number

The pages belonging to the same working set will be directly translated using the TLB entries.

Step 2: **If there is a match (or hit) in the TLB**, the page frame number is retrieved from the matched page entry. However, the cache block (middle field) and the word address are copied directly.

Step 3: **If there is no match (or miss) in the TLB,** a hashed pointer is used to identify one of the page tables where the desired page frame number can be retrieved.

6.5 PAGING

Assume that the **user program** (or process) is divided into small fixed sized chunks of the same size and the memory is divided into chunks of same size. We call these chunks of a process as **pages** and those of memory as **frames** (or page frames). Then, the chunks of a process could be assigned to available chunks of memory.

That is,

User program (or Process) → Pages

Memory (Main) → Frames.

It means that

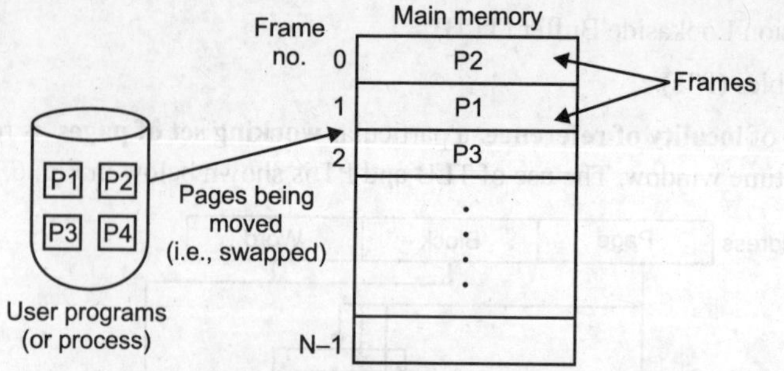

Fig. 6.18. Relation between MM and user programs.

Please understand that in such a scenario, at certain instant of time, some of the frames in memory are in use and some are free. Also note that the operating system maintains a list of free frames. When there are no sufficient, unused contiguous frames to hold the process then also our O.S. doesn't stop. It continues loading of those pages (for execution). In order to achieve this, OS maintains a **page-table** for each process. **This page-table shows the frame location for each page of the process.** Actually, within a program, each logical address (LA) consist of a page number and an offset within the page. In paging technique, the logical-to-physical (i.e., program to memory) address translation is still done by the processor hardware. This means that the processor must know how to access the page table of the current process. With the input of LA (page number, offset), the processor uses the page table to produce a physical address (frame number, offset). This entire technique is shown in Fig. 6.19.

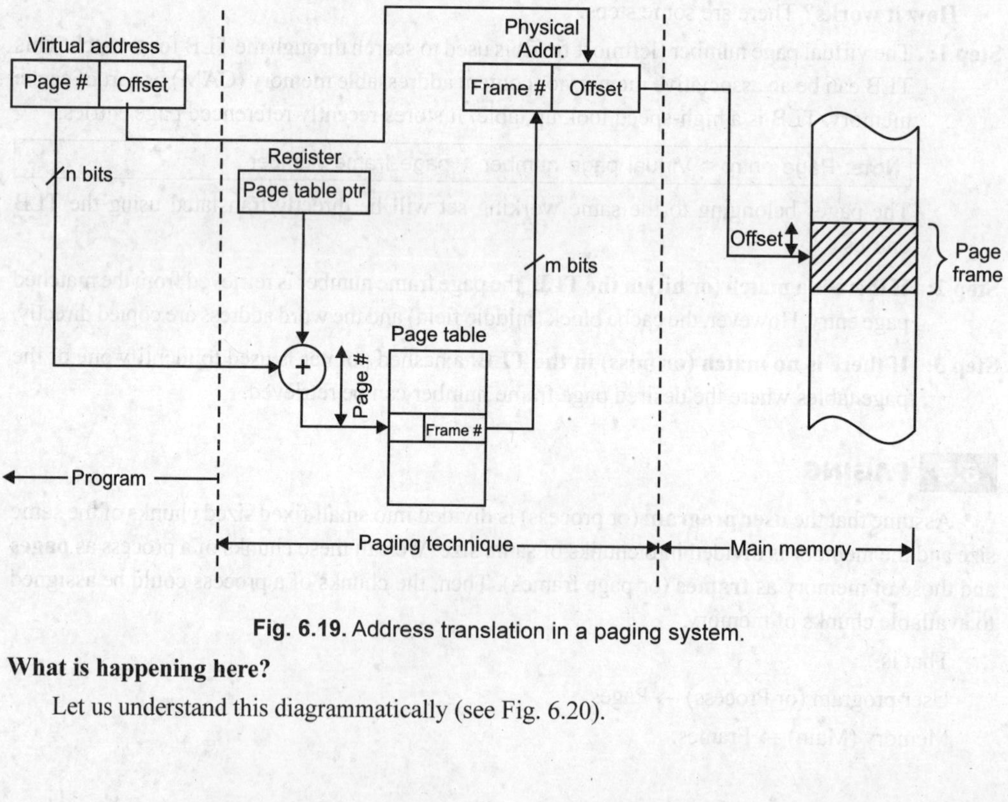

Fig. 6.19. Address translation in a paging system.

What is happening here?

Let us understand this diagrammatically (see Fig. 6.20).

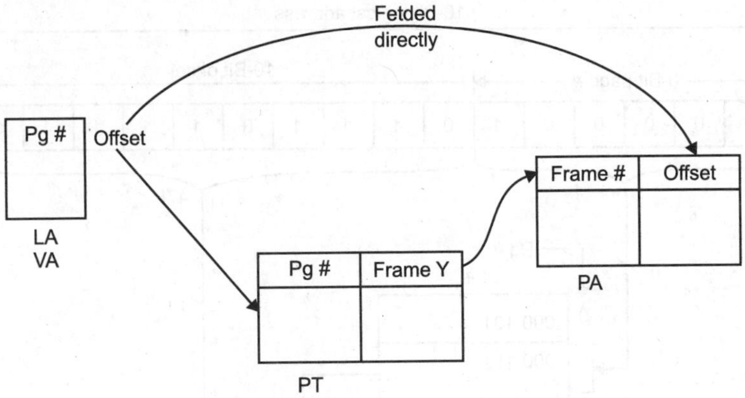

Fig. 6.20. Simplified diagram of Fig. 6.19.

What is available to us is logical or virtual address. Thus, LA comprises of –

LA (Pg #, Offset)

Using it's Pg #, and the frame # a page table, is created. To generate required physical address (PA) to map to main memory, the OS adds frame # of page table and the offset of logical address to form physical address of MM. This is how mapping and address translation is done.

Let us consider an example to understand this.

Say, logical address = 1502 (LA)

Page size = 1K

and address bus is 16 bits wide.

$$\therefore \quad \frac{LA}{page\ size} = \frac{1502}{1K} = \frac{1502}{1024}$$

$\therefore$ quotient = 6

remainder = 10.

With a page-size of 1K, an offset field of 10 bits is needed, leaving 6-bits for the page number. So, a program can consist of a maximum of $2^6 = 64$ pages of 1KB each.

Also, since $\frac{1K}{64} = \frac{2^{10}}{2^6} = 2^4$ = Entries in Page Table (PT).

Let us see this diagrammatically now.

$\because \quad (1502)_{10} = (0000010111011110)_2$

i.e., 16 bit logical address

6 bit (pg #) 10-bit (offset)

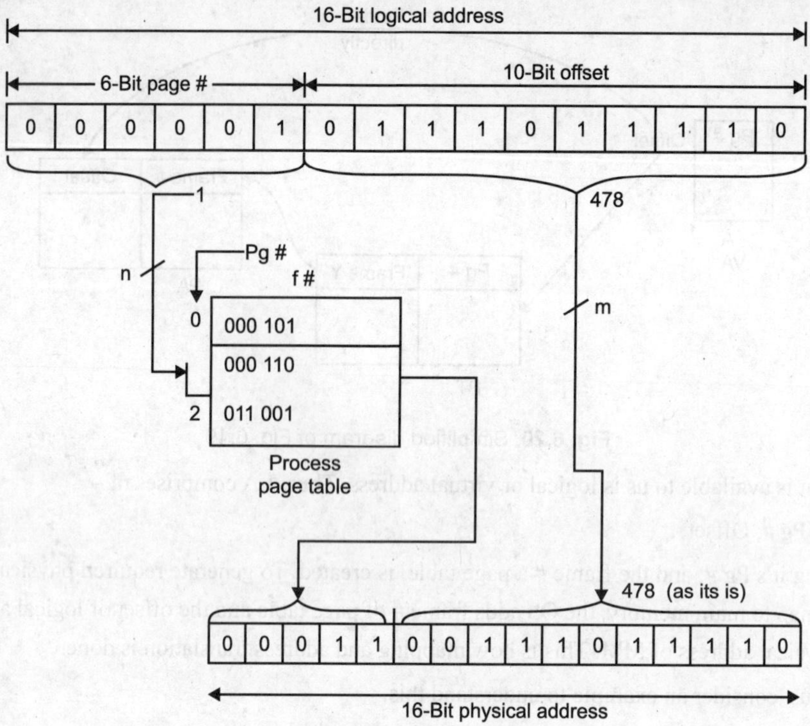

Fig. 6.21. A paging example

$\therefore$ $LA = 1502 = (0000010111011110)_2$ is page number 1, offset 478.

Say, that this page is residing in main memory frame $6 = (00110)_2$.

Then PA is frame no. 6, Offset 478.

$$\therefore \qquad PA = (0001100111011110)_2.$$

6.6 SEGMENTATION

It is also possible to divide a user program into a number of segments. Here, all segment need not necessarily of same length. But segments do have a maximum segment limit. In segmentation, the logical address comprises of a segment number and an offset. **Paging is invisible to the programmer whereas segmentation is visible and it is the programmer to the compiler that will assign programs and data may be further broken down into multiple segments.** This technique uses a segment table for each process and a list of free blocks of main memory. **Please understand that when a process enters the running state, the address of its segment table is loaded into a special register used by the memory management hardware.**

The address translation in segmentation scheme is used as follows –

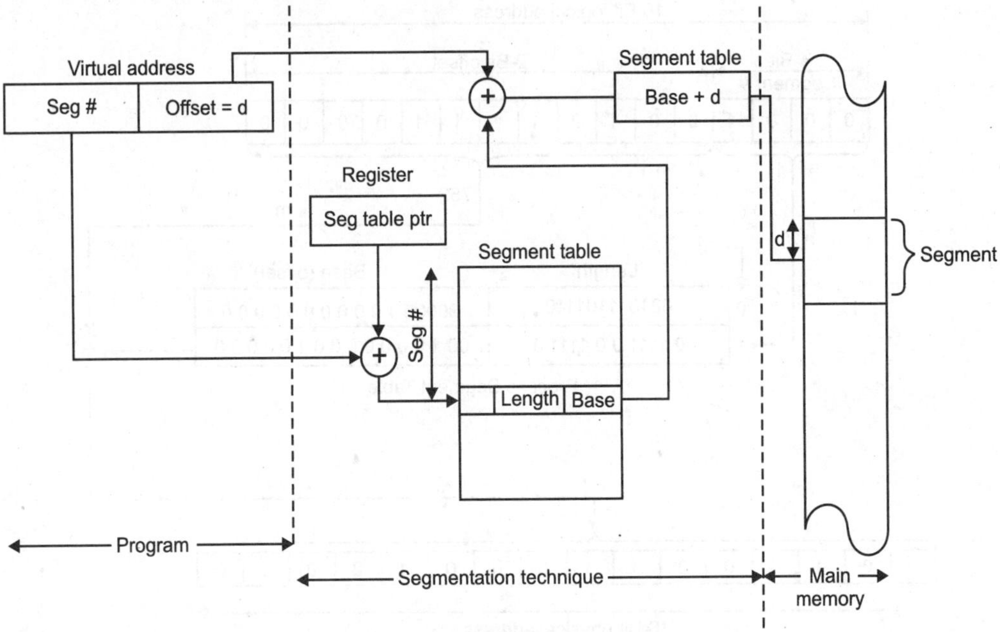

Fig. 6.22. Address Translation in a Segmentation System

Please note that each process has its own segment table and when all of its segments are loaded into the main memory, the segment table for a process is created and loaded into main memory. Also note that each segment table entry contains the starting address of the corresponding segment in main memory as well as the length of the segment. The basic mechanisms is still the same i.e., to read a word from memory involves the translation of a virtual or logical address (consisting of segment number and offset) into a physical address using a segment table. **The segment table is of variable length depending on the size of the process. So, we cannot hold it in registers. Instead, it must be in main memory to be accessed.** This is shown in Fig. 6.22. When a particular process is running, a register holds the starting address of the segment table for that process. Let us take an example to understand this.

Say, we have the **logical address** (LA) as –

$(0001001011110000)_2$

Now, this is segment number 1, offset 752. The aim is to convert this LA (or virtual address) into actual or physical address (PA). This is done as follows and is shown in Fig. 6.23.

Suppose that this segment is residing in main memory starting at Physical Address (PA) –

$(0010000000100000)_2$.

Then, the Physical Address (PA) is –

$$\begin{array}{r} 0010000000100000 \\ +\quad 001011110000 \\ \hline 0010001100010000 \\ \hline \end{array}$$

This entire procedure is shown in Fig. 6.23 on the next page .

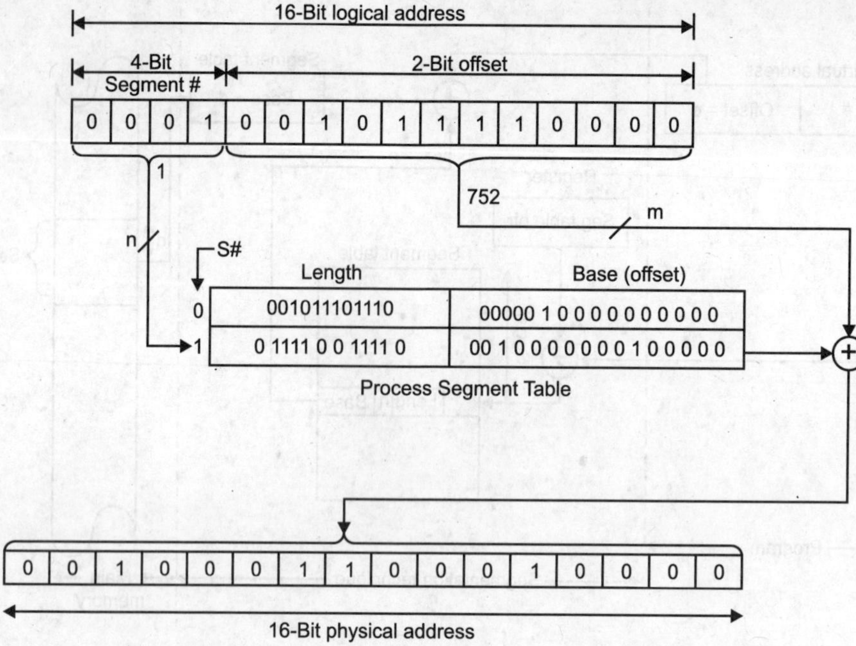

Fig. 6.23. A Segmentation Example

So, we conclude that a process is divided into a number of segments that need not be of equal size. When a process is brought in all of its segments are loaded into available regions of memory and a segment table is set up.

6.7 COMPARISON OF PAGING, SEGMENTATION AND VIRTUAL MEMORY TECHNIQUES

Initially, our system used to work using overlays. From overlay structures we shifted to paging schema, from paging we shifted to segmentation schema and finally now we use virtual memory schema. Let us first of all tabulate the differences between paging and segmentation.

Paging	Segmentation
1. In paging scheme, the main memory is partitioned into frames (or blocks).	1. The segmentation scheme, the main memory is partitioned into segments.
2. The logical address space is divided into pages by the compiler or Memory Management Unit (MMU).	2. The logical address space is divided into segments as specified by the programmers.
3. This scheme suffers form internal fragmentation or page breaks.	3. This scheme suffered from external fragmentation.
4. The OS maintains a free frames list; there is no need to search for free.	4. The OS maintains the particulars of available memory
5. The OS maintains a page table for mapping between frames and pages.	5. The OS maintains a segment maps table for mapping purpose.
6. This scheme does not support the user's view of memory.	6. This scheme supports user's view of memory.

Paging	Segmentation
7. Processor uses the page number and displacement to calculate absolute address (p, d)	7. Processor uses the segment number and displacement to calculate the absolute address (*s*, *d*).

Paging may be of two types –

(*a*) Simple paging (or discussed above).

(*b*) Virtual Memory Paging.

Similarly, segmentation may be of two types –

(*a*) Simple segmentation (as discussed),

(*b*) Virtual Memory segmentation.

Let us compare them in a tabular form –

Simple Paging	Virtual Memory Paging
1. All the **pages** of a process must be in main memory for a process to run.	Not all pages of a process need be in main memory frames for a process to run.
2. Pages are read together (for a process).	Pages may be read in, as needed.
3. Lesser number of processes can be maintained.	More number of processes can be maintained.
4. Page table entries are less complex.	Page table entries become more complex.
5. Page tables are stored in real memory.	Page tables are stored in virtual memory (i.e., on disk).

Similarly, we compare simple segmentation and virtual memory segmentation in a tabular form –

Simple Segmentation	Virtual Memory Segmentation
1. All the **segments** of a process must be in the main memory for a process to run.	1. Not all segments of a process need to be in main memory frames for the process to run.
2. Segments are read together.	2. Segments may be read in as needed.
3. Lesser number of processes can be maintained.	3. More number of processes can be maintain3d.
4. Segment table entries are less complex	4. Segment table entries are more complex.
5. Segment tables are stored in real memory.	5. Segment tables are stored in virtual memory (i.e., on disk).

6.8 DEMAND PAGING

It is a scheme in which a page is not loaded into a main memory from the secondary memory, until it is needed. So, in demand paging, pages are loaded only on demand and not in advance. The advantage here is that now lesser I/O is needed, less memory is needed, factor response and more users serviced now. **Please note that in this scheme, rather than swapping the entire program in memory, only those pages are swapped which are required currently by the system.**

Implementation of demand paging

To implement demand paging, it is necessary for the O.S. to keep track of which pages are currently in use. The page map table (PMT) contains an entry bit for each virtual page of the related process. **For each page actually swapped in memory, page map table points to the actual location that contains the corresponding page frame and entry bit is set and marked as YES**

if it is in memory. If a particular page is not in memory then the entry bit is reset and marked as 'NO'. If a program during execution never accesses those pages which are marked as 'NO' there will be no problem and the execution proceeds normally. This is shown in Fig. 6.24 below:

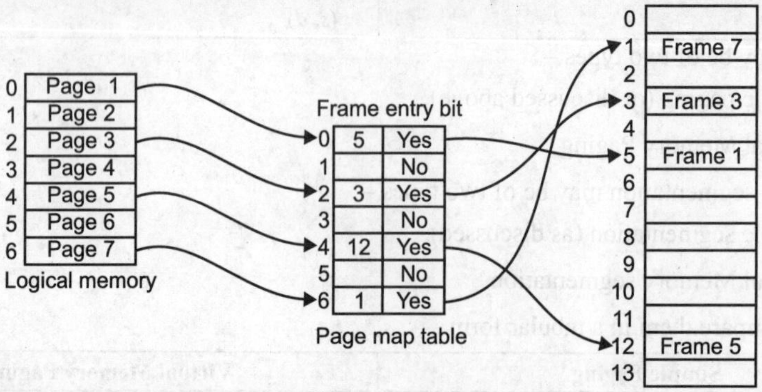

Fig. 6.24. Implementation of demand paging scheme

If a program tries to access a page that was not swapped in memory then page fault occurs. **Please note that a page fault trap is the result of the OS failure to bring a valid part of the program into memory in an attempt to minimize swapping overhead and physical memory requirement.** When the running program experiences a page fault, it must be suspended until the missing page is swapped in main memory. **Also note that since the disk access time is usually several orders of magnitude longer than the main memory cycle time, so the O.S. can schedule another process during this period.**

Hardware requirements to support demand paging–

The hardware requirement to support demand paging is the same as the hardware for paging, that is –

(*a*) A page map table (PMT) with the ability to mark YES and NO for page entry.

(*b*) A hard disk to hold those pages that are not in memory.

Performance of Demand Paging

1. Page fault rate, p, is given as –

   $0 \leq p \leq 1.0$

   i.e. if $p = 0$ then no page faults

   if $p = 1$ then every reference is a fault.

2. Effective Access Time (EAT) is given as follows-

   EAT = $(1 - p)$ * Memory access + p (page fault overhead) + (swap page out) + (swap page in) + (Restart overhead).

6.8.1 Pure Demand Paging

Pure demand paging is the form of demand paging in which not even a single page is loaded into memory initially. Therefore, the very first instruction causes a page fault in this case. This kind of demand paging may significantly decrease the performance of a computer system by generally increasing the effective access time of memory. If 'm_t' represents the memory access time and 'p' is the probability of occurrence of a page fault then the effective access time (EAT) is given by the formula-

$$\text{EAT} = (1-p) * m_t + p * \text{page-fault time}$$

We are in a position to solve some problems now.

EXAMPLE 1: Suppose we have a demand-paged memory. The page table is held in registers. It takes 8 milliseconds to service a page fault if an empty page is available or the replaced page is not modified and 20 milliseconds if the page replaced is modified. Memory access time is 100 nanoseconds.

Assume that the page to be replaced is modified 70 percent of the time. What is the maximum acceptable page-fault rate for an effective access time of an more than 200 nanoseconds?

SOLUTION: From the given conditions, we get

$$0.2\ \mu s = (1-P) * 0.1\ \mu s + (0.3\,P) * 8 \text{ millisec.} + (0.7P) * 20 \text{ millisec.}$$

or $$1 = -P + 2400\,P + 14000\,P$$

$$[\because 100 \text{ ns } 0.1\ \mu s \text{ sec } \& \ 200 \text{ ns} = 0.2\mu \text{ sec}]$$

or $$1 = 16399\,P$$

or $$\boldsymbol{P = 0.00006}$$

EXAMPLE 2: Consider a demand-paging system with a paging disk that has an average access and transfer time of 20 milliseconds.

Addresses are translated through a page table in main memory with an access time of 1 microsecond per memory access. Thus, each memory reference through the page table takes two accesses. To improve this time, we have added an associative memory that reduces access time to one memory reference, if the page-table entry is in the associative memory.

Assume that 80 percent of the accesses are in the associative memory and that, of the remaining 10 percent (or 2 percent of the total) causes page faults. What is the effective memory access time?

SOLUTION: Effective Access Time (EAT) = (0.8)(1 sec) + (0.1)(2 sec) + (0.1) (5002 sec)

$$= 501.2 \text{ secs}$$

$$= 0.5 \text{ millisec.}$$

6.9 ASSOCIATIVE MEMORIES

An associate memory is made up of an array of similar cells. One of those cells is shown in Fig. 6.25.

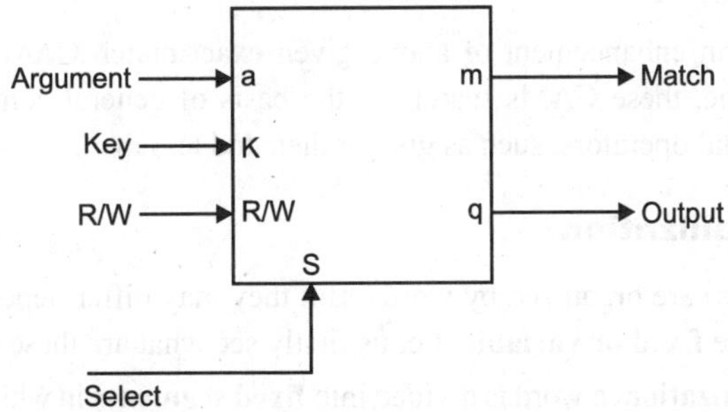

Fig. 6.25. Associative Memory Cell-block diagram

It has four inputs –

(*a*) **Argument bit** (a),

(*b*) Corresponding **key bit (K),**

(*c*) **R/W line** to specify the operation to be performed.

(*d*) **Select line 5**, to select the particular cell for read or write.

It (cell) has **two outputs** –

(*a*) **Match bit (m)** – It shows if the data stored in the cell match with the argument bit a

(*b*) **Data output (q)**

The match bit is set to 1 if the key bit K is 0.

Comparisons of RAM and CAM

1. In case of RAMs, the stored data is identified by means of a unique address given to each data item. On the other hand, the data stored in an associative memory is accessed by the content of data itself. That is why associative memories CAMs or content addressable memories (CAM) are named as CAM or AM.
2. In general, a search time for a particular piece of data in a RAM having n- words will take t*f(n) time.

   where '*t*' is the time taken to fetch and compare one word of memory.

   and '*f*' is an increasing function of n.

Also note that *f* is an increasing function of *n* if and only if $f(n_1) < f(n_2)$ for all $n_1 < n_2$. **So, when *n* increases, the search time also increases.** On the other hand, in case of a CAM having *n*-words, the search time is almost independent of *n* because all the words may be searched in parallel. **Please note that only one cycle time is required to determine if the desired word is in memory. Also note that if the desired word is in memory then one more cycle time is required to retrieve it.**

Types of CAMs

CAMs are put under two categories :

(*a*) **Exact Match CAM**

These CAMs address data based on equality with certain key data.

(*b*) **Comparison CAM**

These CAMs are an enhancement of above given exact match CAMs. Rather than doing a search on equality alone, these CAMs search on the basis of general comparison. These CAMs support various relational operators, such as greater than and less than.

CAM (or AM) Organization

All CAMs (or AMs) are organized by words. But they may differ depending on whether their logical organizations are **fixed or variable.** Let us firstly see what are these?

(*a*) **In fixed organization,** a word is divided into **fixed segments** in which any segment may be used for interrogation. Depending on the application, a segment of a word may be further defined as the **key segment and each bit of this segment must be used for interrogation purpose.**

(*b*) **In variable organization**, the word may be divided into **fixed segments** but any part of a segment may be used for the purpose of interrogation.

NOTE: In its most general form, the CAM will be fully interrogable i.e., it will allow any combination of bits in the word to be searched for

We shall be, however, concerned with fully interrogatable CAMs with exact match capacity. We now draw a block diagram of an associative memory having *m*-words and *n*-bits per word. It is shown in Fig. 6.26.

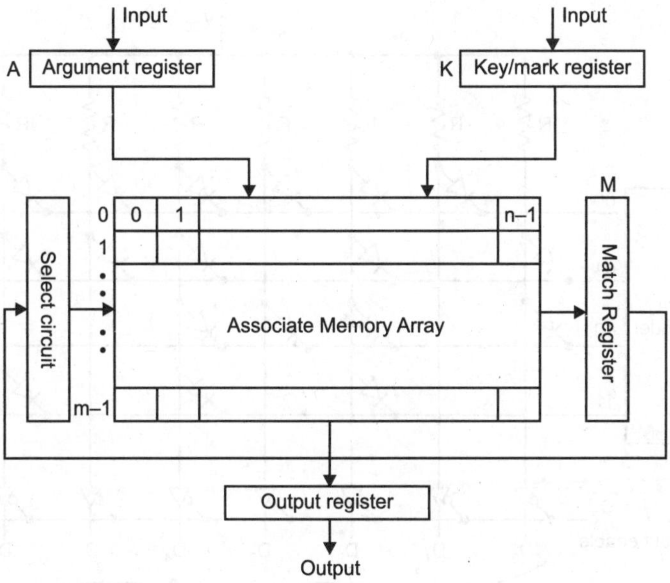

Fig. 6.26. Block diagram of an Associative Memory

Working: The argument register (A) and the key register (K) are both n-bits long, one for each bit of a word. Before the search process starts, the word to be searched is loaded into the argument register, A. The segment of interest to the word is specified by the bit positions having 1's in the key register, K. Once the argument and key registers are set, each word in memory is compared in parallel with the content of A. **If a word matches the argument**, the corresponding bit in the match register M, is set. Thus, M has m-bits, one for each word in memory. If more than one bit is set to 1 in M, the select circuit determines which word is to be read. For instance, all matching entries may be read out in some predetermined order.

Applications of CAM

1. To do a parallel search (by data association), each word needs to have a dedicated circuit for itself. This adds to additional hardware costs as with each word, the cost of AMs also increases. So, CAM is used in applications where search time is significant to the proper implementation of the task under execution.

2. CAMs may be used as the highest level of memory of real-time systems in military applications that require a large number of memory accesses.
3. CAMs may be used for pattern recognitions too.

6.10 MEMORY ORGANIZATION

Let us now study ROM and RAM organizations.

6.10.1 ROM and Its Organization

First, we will see the simple ROM. Fig. 6.27 shows a very simple four byte diode ROM.

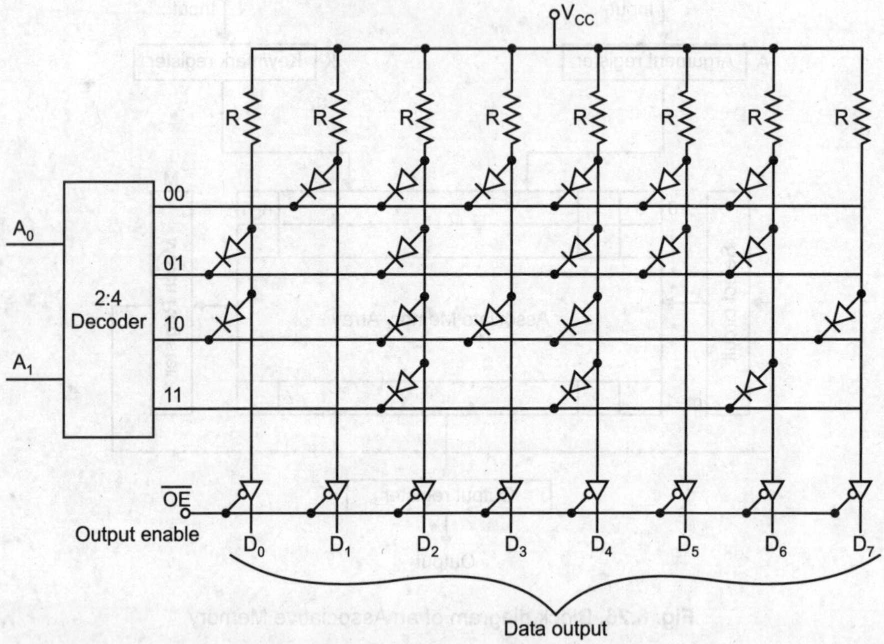

Fig. 6.27. Simple four byte diode ROM

Diode ROM consists of only diodes and a decoder. As shown in the Fig. 6.27 address lines A_0 and A_1 are decoded by 2 : 4 decoder and used to select one of the four rows. As decoder output is active low, it places a logic 0 on the selected row. Each output data line goes to logic 0 if a diode connects the otuput data column to the selected row. Data is available on the output data lines only when output enable (OE) signal is low. Table shows the contents of ROM at four locations.

Table 6.1: Contents of ROM

Address in binary	Binary Data								Data in Hex
	D_0	D_1	D_2	D_3	D_4	D_5	D_6	D_7	
00	1	0	1	0	0	1	0	1	A5
01	0	1	0	1	0	0	0	1	51
10	0	1	0	0	0	1	1	0	46
11	1	1	0	1	0	1	0	1	D5

Now-a-days ROMs use MOS technology instead of diode. Fig. 6.28 shows for nibble (half-byte) ROM using MOS transistors. Here, diodes and pull up resistors are replaced by MOS transistors. The address on the address lines (A_0 and A_1) is decoded by 2 : 4 decoder. Decoder selects one of the four rows making it logic 0. The inverter connected at the output of decoder inverts the state of selected row (i.er. logic 1). Therefore, each output data line goes to logic 0 if a gate of MOS transistor is connected to row select lines. When gate of the MOS transistor is connected to the selected row, MOS transistor is turned on. This pulls the corresponding column data line to logic 0.

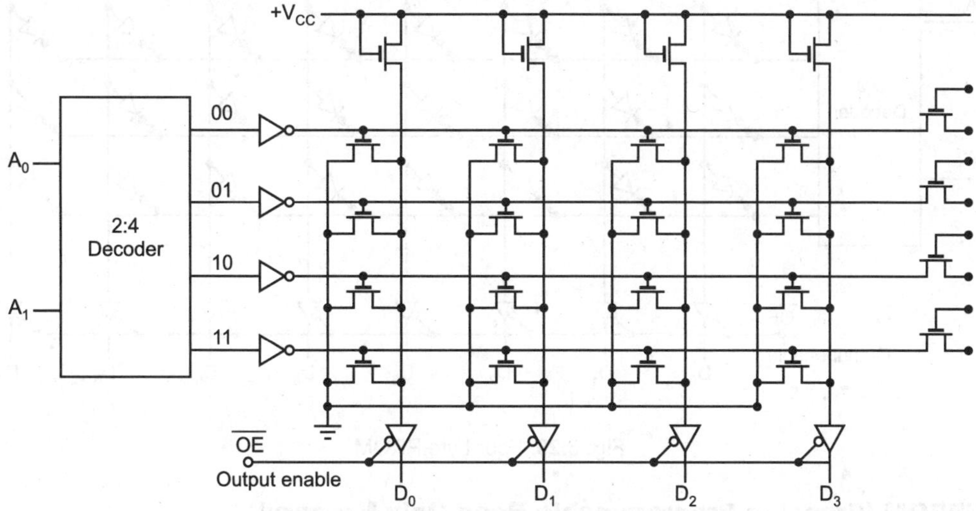

Fig. 6.28. Simple four half-byte ROM

In integrated circuits, a thin metalized layer connects the gates of some transistors to the row select lines. The gate connections of the MOS transistors depend on the date to be stored in the ROM. Therefore, according to the user truth table manufacturer can deposit thin layer of metal to connect gates of the transistors. Once the pattern/mask is decided, it is possible to make thousands of such ROMs. These ROMs are called **Mask-programmed ROMs.** Masked ROMs are used in microprocessor based toys, TV games, home computers and other such high volume consumer products.

PROM (Programmable Read Only Memory)

In Fig. 6.29, a four byte PROM as shown. It has diodes in every bit position, therefore, the output is initially all 0s. Each diode, however has a feasible link in series with it. By addressing bit and applying proper current pulse at the corresponding output, we can blow out the fuse, storing logic 1 a that bit position. The fuse uses material like michrome and polycrystalline. For blowing the fuse it is necessary to pass around 20 to 50 mA of current for period 5 to 20 μs. **The blowing of fuses according to the truth table is called programming of ROM.** The user can program PROMs with special PROM programmer. The PROM programmer selectively burns the fuses according to the bit pattern to be stored. This process is also known as **burning of PROM.** The PROMs are one time programmable. Once programmed, the information stored is permanent.

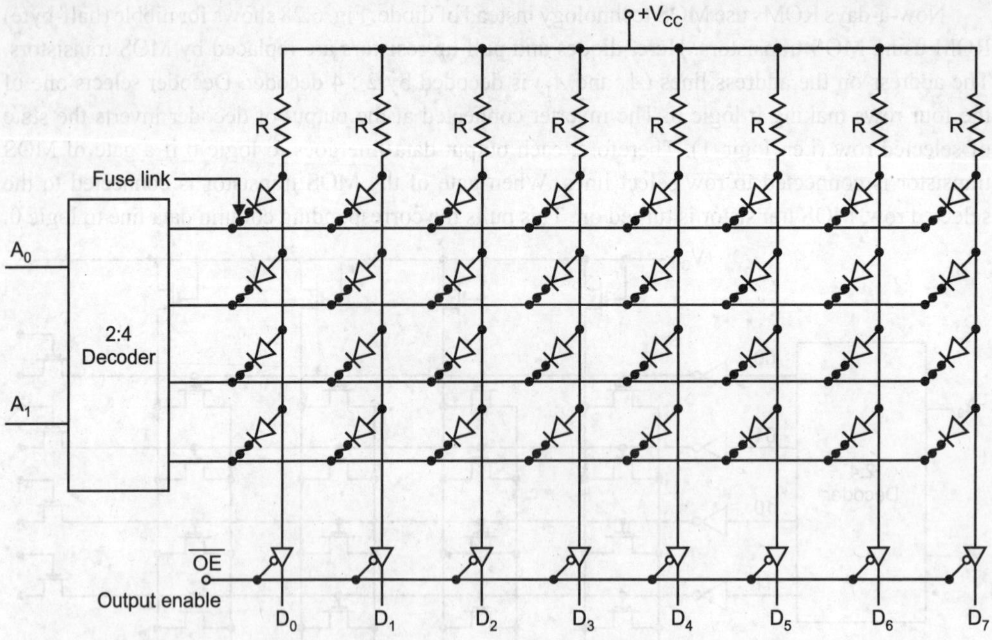

Fig. 6.29. Four byte PROM

EPROM (Erasable Programmable Read Only Memory)

Erasable programmable ROMs use MOS circuitry. They store 1s and 0s as a packet of charge in a buried layer of the IC chip. EPROMs can be programmed b the user with a special EPROM programmer. **Please note that we can erase the stored data in the EPROMs by exposing the chip to ultraviolet light through its quartz window for 15 to 20 minutes, as shown in the Fig. 6.30**

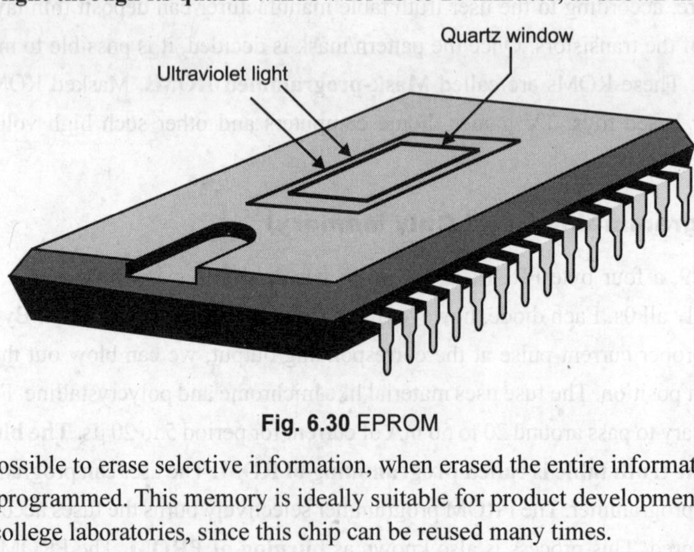

Fig. 6.30 EPROM

It is not possible to erase selective information, when erased the entire information is lost. The chip can be reprogrammed. This memory is ideally suitable for product development, experimental projects, and college laboratories, since this chip can be reused many times.

EPROM Programming

When erased each cell in the EPROM contains 1. Data is introduced by selectively programming 0s into the desired bit locations. Although only 0s will be programmed both 1s and 0s can be presented in the data.

During programming address and data are applied to address and data pins of the EPROM. When the address and data are stable, programe pulse is applied to the program input of the EPROM. The program pulse duration is around 50 ms and its amplitude depends on EPROM 1C. It is typically 5.5 V to 25 V. In EPROM it is possible to program any location at any time-either individually, sequentially, or at random.

EEPROM (Electrical Erasable Programmable Read Only Memory)

Electrically erasable programmable ROMs also use MOS circuitry very similar to that of EPROM. Data is stored as charge or no charge on an insulated layer or a insulated floating gate in the device. The insulating layer is made very thin (< 200i). Therefore, a volatage as low as 20 to 25 V can be used to move charges across the thin barrier in either direction for programming or erasing. EEPROM allows selecting erasing at the register level rather than erasing all the information since the information can be changed by using electrical signals. The EEPROM memory also has a speical chip erase mode by which entire chip can be erased in 10 ms. This time is quite small as compared to time required to erase EPROM, and it can be erased and reprogrammed with device in the circuit. However, EEPROMS are most expensive and least dense ROMs.

Let us now discuss RAM organization.

RAM Organization

RAMs are distinguished by the fact that each storage location can be accessed independently. The access time (t_A) and cycle time (t_M) for every location are constant and independent of its position.

10.0.1.ID RAM Organization

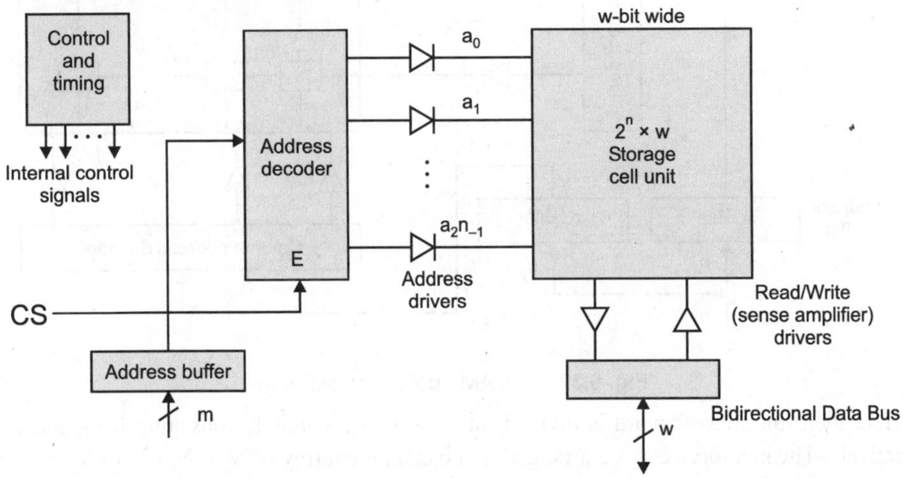

Fig. 6.31. ID-RAM Organization

A storage unit is composed of a large number of (2^n) addressable locations. Each of which is a 2-bit wide word. Individual bits are not directly addressable. We address a word at a time (unless w=1). This type of RAM is referred as $2^n \times w$ bit memory as shown in Figure 6.31

Working of RAM

First the address of the location to be accessed is transferred to the RAM address buffer via address lines. The address decoder, selects the location in the memory cell unit. A control line indicates the type of access to be performed. **In a read operation**, the requested locations contents are transferred from the memory unit to the data buffer and from there to the bus. **For a write operation**, the word to be stored is transferred from the data be to the selected location in the memory unit. Since we never simultaneously the a read and write operation, so the data bus is a bi-directional data bus.

The memory unit is made up of many identical 1-bit memory cells and the interconnections. The actual number of lines connected to the cell and the functions depend on the memory technology used and the addressing schemes . In general each cell is connected to a set of data, address, and control signals.

A RAM's storage cells are physically arranged into regular arrays to reduce the cost of the connections between the cells and the access circuitry. The memory address ids partitioned into d components so that address A_i of cell becomes a d dimensional vector ($A_{i,1}$ $A_{i,2}$ ... $A_{i,d}$) = A_i. Each of the d parts of the address word goes to a separate address decoder and a separate set of address drivers. A cell is selected by simultaneously activating all d of a address lines. A memory unit with this kind of addressing is said to be **dimensional.**

The most common RAM organization is the 2D RAM organization also called row-column scheme as shown in figure 6.32. The data and control circuity is omitted for simplicity.

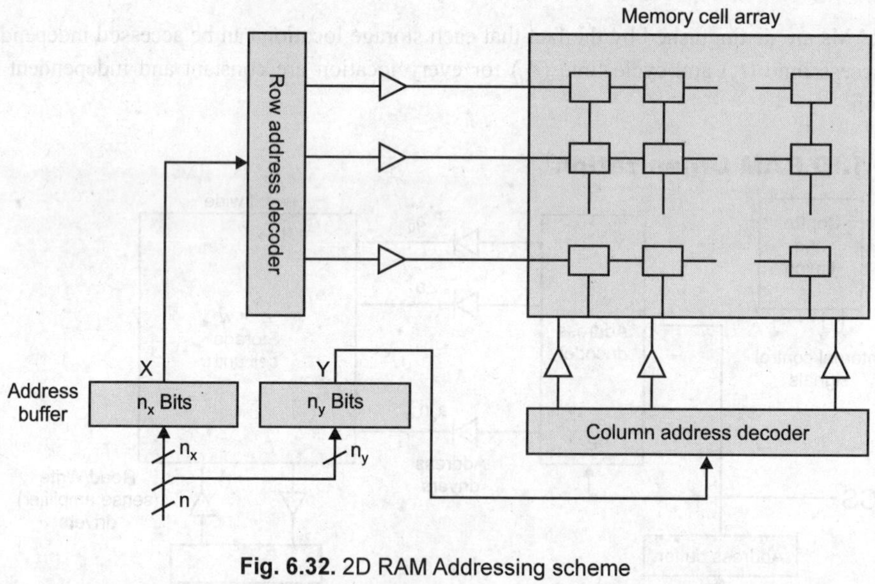

Fig. 6.32. 2D RAM Addressing scheme

Here the n-bit address word is divided into two parts. X and Y, consisting of n_x and n_y bits respectively. The memory cells are arranged in a rectangular array of $N_x \times N_y$ where $N_x = 2^{nx}$ rows and $N_y = 2^{ny}$ columns. The total number of cells in memory is $N = N_xN_y$. A cell is selected by the coincidence of signals applied to its X and Y address lines.

Advantages of 2D Organization

The 2D organization requires much less access circuitry compared to a 1D organization of the same storage capacity. If $N_x = N_y = \sqrt{N}$, the number of address drivers needed is instead, N in case of 1D organization. **For example** if $N = 16$ then $N_x = N_y = \sqrt{16} = 4$. We need two 1 out of 4 address decoders instead of a single 1-out of -16 address decoder which is more complex. In addition, the 2D organization is a good match for the inherently two dimensional layout structures allowed by VISI technology.

RAM Design

A RAM chip contains all required access circuitry, including address decoders, drivers, and control circuits. Figure 6.33 shows a general $2^n \times w$ –bit RAM IC.

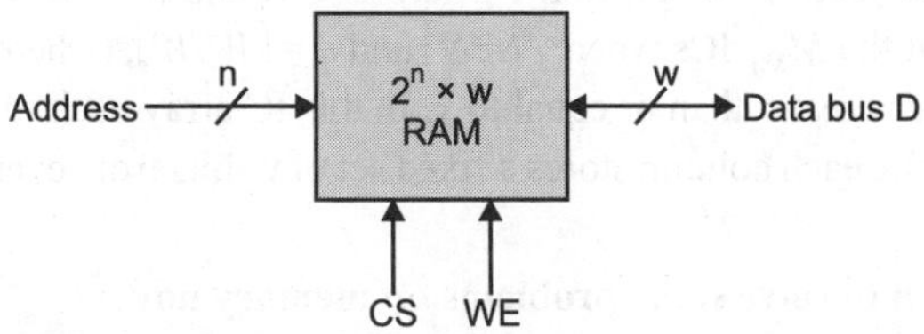

Fig. 6.33. A RAM Chip Showing its Major Control Signals

There are 2^n words so we require n address lines. The words are *w*-bit wide hence data bus has w lines. WE is the write enable line, for memory, write operation WE = 1 and for memory read operation WE = 0. The chip select (CS) initiates a memory operation. A memory is accessed for Read and Write operations only when CS = 1. The RAM of figure 6.34 has a bidrectional data bus *D*. This is directly wired to all addressable storage locations. For a write operations, WE = 1, allowing *D* to act as an input bus to all storage locations. Only the address locations, (value specified by address bus) actually stores the word received on *D*. For a read operation, WE = 0. So, only the addressed memory location transfers its data to *D*.

Memory cells are usually organized in the form of an array, in which each cell is capable of storing one bit of information. One such organization is shown in Fig. 6.34. Each row of the cells constitutes a memory word, and all cells of a row are connected to a common line referred to as word line, which is driven by the address decoder on the chip. Fig. 6.34(a) shows a memory chip consistency of 16 words of 8-bits each, which is usually referred to as a 16 × 8 organization. To address 16 words we need 4 address lines as $2^4 = 16$. For this we need a (4 × 16) decoder.

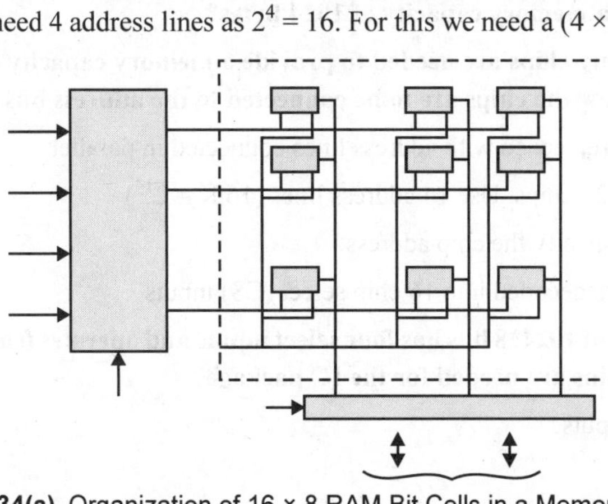

Fig. 6.34(a). Organization of 16 × 8 RAM Bit Cells in a Memory Chip

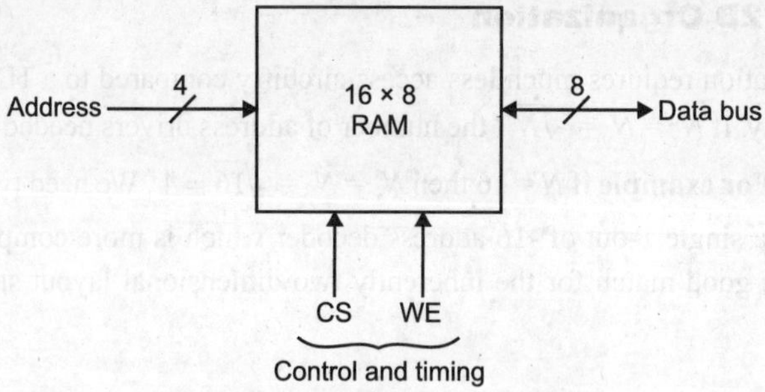

Fig. 6.34(b). Block Diagram of 16 × 8 RAM Memory Chip

Let us now examine how to design a RAM chip. Given that $N \times W$-bit RAM ICs denoted as $M_{N \times W}$. How do we design a $N' \times W'$ bit RAM where $N' \geq N$ and $W' \geq W$. A general approach is to construct a $p \times q$ array of the M_{NW} ICs where $\lceil N'/N \rceil$ and $q = \lceil W'/W \rceil$, (where $\lceil x \rceil$ denotes the ceiling on x), the smallest integer greater than or equal to x. In this IC array each row stores N word except possibly the last row, while each column stores a fixed set of w-bits from every word except possibly the last column.

We are in a position to solve some problems on memory now.

Q. 1. (*a*) How many 128 × 8 RAM chips are needed to provide a memory capacity of 2048 bytes?

(*b*) How many lines of the address bus must be used to access 2048 bytes of memory? How many of these lines will be common to all chips?

(*c*) How many lines must be decoded for chip and select? Specify the size of the decoders

Ans. (*a*) $\dfrac{2048}{138} = 16$ chips

(*b*) $2048 = 2^{11}$; 11 lines to address 2048 bytes

$128 = 2^7$; 7 lines to address each chip and 4 lines to decoder for selecting 16 chips

(*c*) (4*16) decoder.

Q. 2. A computer uses RAM chips of (1024*1) capacity.

(*a*) How many chips are needed and how should their address lines be connected to provide a memory capacity of 1024 bytes?

(*b*) How many chips are needed to provide a memory capacity of 16 KB? Explain in words how the chips are to be connected to the address bus.

Ans. (*a*) 8 chips are needed with address lines connected in parallel.

(*b*) 16*8 = 128 chips. Use 14 address lines ($16\text{ K} = 2^{14}$)

10 lines specify the chip address.

4 lines are decoded into 16 chip select (CS) inputs

Q. 3. A ROM chip of 1024*8 bits has four select inputs and operates from a 5V power supply. How many pins are needed for the IC package?

Ans. 10 pins for inputs,

4 for chip select,

8 for outputs and 2 for power.

∴ 24 pins are needed in all.

Q. 4. You are given a (16*8) bit RAM chip. Construct a (16*16) bit RAM organization

Given : $N = N' = 16$

$W = 8$

$W' = 16$

Ans. Now, $p = \frac{16}{16} = 1, \qquad q = \frac{16}{8} = 2.$

∴ We need $(p*q) = (1*2)$ array of bisc (16*8) RAM chip. This is shown in Fig. 6.35

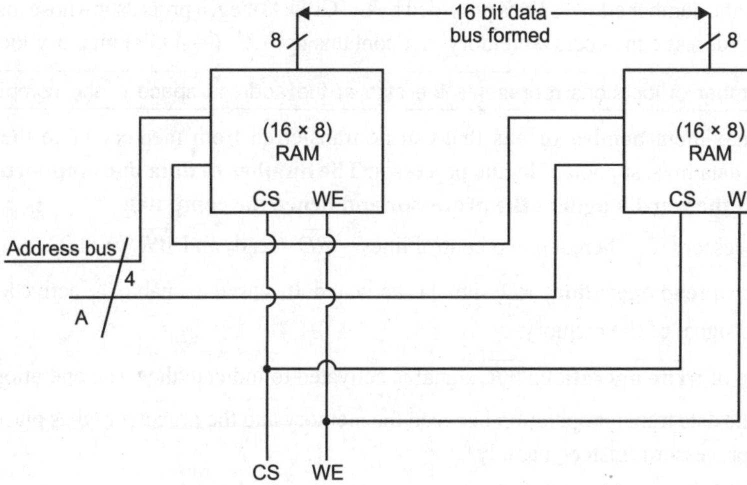

Fig. 6.35. A(16*16) RAM using (16´8) Chip

Please note two things here:

1. All address and control lines are connected in the same way to each IC.
2. Their 8-bit data buses are concentrated to form a single 16-bit wide bus.

Q. 5. A computer employs RAM chips of (256 × 8) and ROM chips of (10^{24} × 8). The computer system needs 2KB of RAM, 4 KB of ROM and four interface units, each with four registers. A memory mapped I/O configuration is used. The two highest order bits of the address bus are assigned 00 for RAM, 01 for ROM and 10 for interface registers.

(*a*) How many RAM and ROM chips are needed.

(*b*) How a memory address maps for the system?

(*c*) Give t'ıe address range in HEX for RAM, ROM and interface.

Ans. RAM chips needed $= \frac{2048}{256} = 8$ chips

[$\because 2048 = 2^{11}, 256 = 2^8$]

ROM chips needed $= \frac{4096}{1024} = 4$ chips

[$\because$ 4096 = 2^{12}, 1024 = 2^{10}]

Interface, 4*4 = 16 registers [16 = 2^4]

$\therefore$ Let us draw the address map now.

Component	Address	16 15 14 13	12 11 10 9	8 7 6 5
RAM	0000-07FF	0 0 0 0	0 3 X 8	X X X X
ROM	4000-4FFF	0 0 0 1	2 X 4 X X	X X X X
Interface	8000-800F	1 0 0 0	0 0 0 0	0 0 0 0

6.11 INTERFACING MEMORY TO CPU

As already mentioned, the maximum size of memory that can be used in any computer is calculated form the number address lines provided by the CPU. For eg. a processor whose instructions generate 32-bit address can access a memory that contains upto 2^{32} (= 4 GB) memory locations.

NOTE: The number of locations represents the size of the address space of the computer.

Also the maximum number of bits that can be transferred from memory or to the memory depends on the data lines supported by the processor. **The number of data lines supported by the processor gives the word length of the processor and hence the computer.**

On the processor (*IC*), there are two control lines – $\overline{RD}$ (read) and $\overline{WR}$ (write).

(*a*) In case of **read operation,** $\overline{RD}$ signal is activated. It is used to enable the active low output enable signal of the memory.

(*b*) In case of **write operation**, $\overline{WR}$ signal is activated to indicate the write operation.

Actually, the data transfer operation between the memory and the processor takes place through the use of two processor registers, namely-

(*a*) MAR (Memory Address Register).

(*b*) MDR (Memory Data Register).

This is shown in Fig. 6.36.

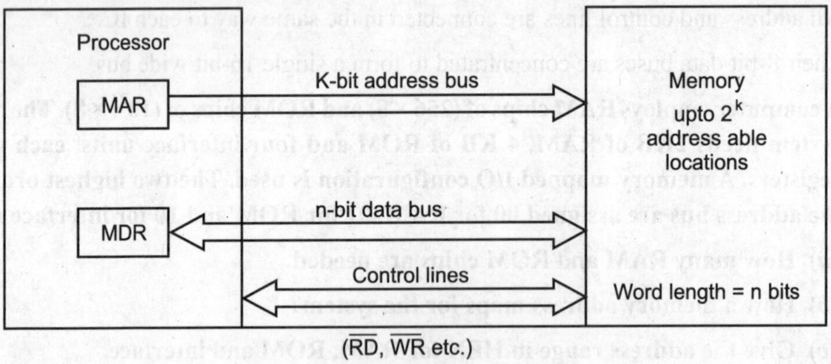

Fig. 6.36. Memory-to-CPU Interfacing (connections)

Herein, if MAR is K-bit long and MDR is *n*-bit long then it is possible to access 2^k memory locations. During one memory cycle, it is possible to transfer *n*-bit data.

6.12 PAGE REPLACEMENT ALGORITHMS

When the processor need to execute a particular page, that page is not available in main memory, this situation is said to be a **page fault**. When the page fault occurs, this page replacement will be needed. The word **page replacement means select a victim page in the main memory, replace that page with the required page from the backing store (Disk).** The students may have a doubt, how to select a victim page. **The answer is simple page replacement algorithms**. The page replacement algorithms select the victim pages.

Now a days the number of page replacement algorithms are available. Each operating system has its own page replacement policy. Now we consider some of the popular page replacement algorithms.

I. FIFO Algorithm : (First in First Out Algorithms)

FIFO is the simplest page replacement algorithm, the idea behind this is **Replace a page that page is the oldest page of all the pages of main memory or replace the page that has been in memory longest**. FIFO focuses on the length of time the page has been in memory rather than how much the page is being used. To illustrate the page replacement algorithm, we shall use the reference string.

0 1 2 3 0 1 2 3 0 1 2 3 4 5 6 7

for memory with 3 frames. This example incurs 16 page faults under FIFO, as show in the table.

Table FIFO Behaviour

Frame	0	1	2	3	0	1	2	3	0	1	2	3	4	5	6	7
0	0*	0	0	3*	3	3	2*	2	2	1*	1	1	4*	4	4	7*
1		1*	1	1	0*	0	0	3*	3	3	2*	2	2	5*	5	5
2			2*	2	2	1*	1	1	0*	0	0	3*	3	3	6*	6
	✓	✓	✓	✓	✓	✓	✓	✓	✓	✓	✓	✓	✓	✓	✓	✓

This example incurs 16 pages faults. The symbol "*" indicates the new page in the memory. The symbol "✓" indicates page fault. The performance of the page replacement algorithm is measured through the page fault rate.

∴ Page fault rate = Number of page faults / Number of bits in the reference string

$$= 16/16 = 100\%$$

If an algorithm having the least page fault rate, we can say that the algorithm is the best one.

If the required page is in the main memory, then page replacement is not required, in that situation we use the 'x', symbol Consider the next example,

The reference string is 0, 1, 2, 3, 2, 5, 6, 3, 4, 6, 3, 7, 3, 1, 5, 3, 6, 4, 3, 4, 2, 3, 4, 5, 1. For a memory with 4 frames. This example incurs 12 page faults. See the table below.

Table FIFO behaviour

Frame	1	2	3	2	5	6	3	4	6	3	7	3	1
0	1*	1	1	1	1	6*	6	6	6*	6	6	6	1*
1	–	2*	2	2*	2	2	2	4*	4	4	4	4	4
2	–	–	3*	3	3	3	3*	3	3	3*	7*	7	7
3	–	–	–	–	5*	5	5	5	5	5	5	3*	3
	✓	✓	✓	X	✓	✓		✓	✓	X	X	✓	✓

Frame	5	3	6	3	4	2	4	3	4	5	1
0	1	1	1	1	1	2*	2	2	2	2	2
1	5*	5	5	5	5	5	5	3*	3	3	3
2	7	7	6*	6	6	6	6	6	6	5*	5
3	3	3*	3	3*	4*	4	4*	4	4	4	1*
	✓	X	✓	X	✓	✓	X	✓	X	✓	✓

Page fault rate – 16/24 = 75%

II. Optimal Page Replacement Algorithm

The optimal page replacement algorithm has the lowest page fault rate of all algorithms. The criteria of this algorithm is **Replace a page that will not be used for the longest period of time.** To illustrate this algorithm, consider the reference stirring 1, 2, 3, 2, 5, 6, 3, 4, 6, 3, 4, 6, 3, 7, 3, 1, 5, 3, 6, 3, 4, 2, 4, 3, 4, 5, 1. Assume that the memory size is four frames. Consider the table to calculate the page fault rate.

Table Optimal Behaviour

Frame	1	2	3	2	5	6	3	4	6	3	7	3	1
0	1*	1	1	1	1	6*	1	1	1	1	1	1	1*
1		2*	2	2*	2	6*	6	6	6*	6	6	6	6
2			3*	3	3	3	3*	3	3	3*	3	3*	3
3					5*	5	5	4*	4	4	7*	7	7
	✓	✓	✓	X	✓	✓	X	✓	X	X	✓	X	✓

Frame	5	3	6	3	4	2	4	3	4	5	1
0	1	1	1	1	1	2*	2	2	2	2	1*
1	6	6	6*	6	4*	4	4*	4	4*	4	4
2	3	3*	3	3*	3	3	3	3*	3	3	3
3	5*	5	5	5	5	5	5	5	5	5*	5
	✓	X	X	X	✓	✓	X	X	X	X	✓

∴ Page fault = 11/24

The optimal page replacement algorithm is difficult to implement, because it requires future knowledge of reference string, so this algorithm is used mainly for comparison studies.

III. LRU (Least Recently Used Algorithm)

The criteria of this algorithm is **Replace page that has not been used for the longest period of time**. This strategy is the **page replacement algorithm looking backward in time, rather than forward**. To illustrate the algorithm consider the reference the string.

0, 1, 2, 3, 0, 1, 2, 3, 0, 1, 2, 3, 4, 5, 6, 7 with 3 main frames.

Frame	0	1	2	3	0	1	2	3	0	1	2	3	4	5	6	7
0	0*	0	0	3*	3	3	2*	2	2	1	1*	1	4*	4	4	7*
1		1*	1	1	0*	0	0	3*	3	3	2	2*	2	5*	5	5
2			2*	2	2	1*	1	1	0*	0	0	3	3	3	6*	6
	✓	✓	✓	✓	✓	✓	✓	✓	✓	✓	✓	✓	✓	✓	✓	✓

∴ Page fault rate = 16/16 = 100%.

IV. Least Frequently Used Algorithm (LFU)

The least frequently used algorithm **selects a page for replacement, if the page has not been used often in the past (or) replace page that page has smallest count.** For this algorithm each page maintains a counter, whose counter value shows the least count, replace that page. The reason for this selection is that an actively used page should have a large reference count, so don't replace the actively used page. The frequency counter is reset each time a page is loaded. To illustrate this algorithm consider below reference string.

0 1 2 3 0 1 2 3 0 1 2 3 4 5 6 7 with 3 memory frames

Table LFU Algorithm

Frame	0	1	2	3	0	1	2	3	0	1	2	3	4	5	6	7
0	0*	0	0	0	0+	0	0	0	0+	01	0	3*	3	3	3	3
1		1*	1	1	1	1+	1	3*	3	1*	1	1	1	1	1	1
2			2	3*	3	3	2*	2	2	2	2+	2	4	5*	6*	7*
	✓	✓	✓	✓	X	X	✓	✓	X	✓	X	✓	✓	✓	✓	✓

∴ Page fault = 12/16.

V. Most Frequently used Algorithm (MFU)

The criteria of this algorithm is replace a page that has the maximum frequency count of all pages. The implementation of this algorithm is fairly expensive.

VI. Belady's Anomaly

The general principle is if the number of frames is increased, the page fault rate will be decreased. For example consider the following reference string.

7 0 1 2 0 3 0 4 2 3 0 3 2 1 2 0 1 7 0 1

If we apply the FIFO algorithm with 3 frames, there are 15 page faults, if we increase to 4 frames, there are 12 page faults. But consider the reference string, given below:

1, 2, 3, 4, 1, 2, 5, 1, 2, 3, 4, 5

The number of page faults for 4 frames (10) is greater than the number of faults for 3 frames (9). This result is most unexpected and is known as **Belady's Anomaly.**

Table 4 Frames

Frame	1	2	3	4	1	2	5	1	2	3	4	5
0	1	1	1	1	1+	1	5*	5	5	5	4	4
1		2	2	2	2	2+	2	1*	1	1	1	5
2			3	3	3	3	3	3	2*	2	2	2
3					4	4	4	4	4	3	3	3
	✓	✓	✓	✓	X	X	✓	✓	✓	✓	✓	✓

∴ Page fault for 4 frames = 10/12

With 3 Frames

Frame	1	2	3	4	1	2	5	1	2	3	4	5
0	1*	1	1	4	4	4	5*	5	5	5	5	5+
1		2*	2	2*	1	1	1	1	1	3	3	3

2			3*	3	3*	2	2	2	2	2	4	4
	✓	✓	✓	✓	✓	✓	✓	✓	✓	✓	✓	✓

∴ Page fault for 3 frames = 9/12

Belady's Anomaly was not always true, it is applicable only to FIFO algorithm.

SUMMARY

In this chapter, we have studied a very vital part of our computer i.e., Memory. We have also studied the roles of cache and virtual memories. Various OS policies like paging and segmentation have been explained. Interfacing of memory to CPU has been dealt with. Different page replacement algorithms have been discussed.

MULTIPLE CHOICE QUESTIONS [MCQs]

Q. 1. A sequence of consecutive bytes is known as –

(*a*) Memory (*b*) CPU

(*c*) Printer (*d*) None of the above

Ans. (*a*)

Q. 2. Generally, the access time for read and write is

(*a*) Different (*b*) Same

(*c*) One less than the other (*d*) None of the above

Ans. (*b*)

Q. 3. The access time (t_A) cycle time (t_c) and recovery time (t_R) are related by the equation:

a) $t_A = t_C + t_R$ (*b*) $t_A = t_C * t_R$

(*c*) $t_c = t_A / t_R$ (*d*) $t_c = t_A + t_R$

Ans. (*d*)

Q. 4. The fastest memory is

(*a*) RAM (*b*) ROM

(*c*) Register (*d*) None of the above

Ans. (*c*)

Q. 5. As we come down the memory hierarchy, cost / bit

(*a*) Increases (*b*) Decreases

(*c*) Remains same (*d*) None of the above

Ans. (*b*)

Q. 6. MMU stands for

(*a*) Main Memory Unit (*b*) Memory Management Unit

(*c*) Mass Memory Unit (*d*) None of the above

Ans. (*a*)

Q. 7. Main memory is divided into

(*a*) Pages (*b*) Frames (*c*) Blocks (*d*) Caches

Ans. (*b*)

Q. 8. User programs (or Processes) are divided into

(*a*) Pages (*b*) Frames (*c*) Blocks (*d*) Caches

Ans. (*a*)

Q. 9. A form of demand paging in which not even a single page is loaded into memory initially

(*a*) Impure demand paging (*b*) Pure demand paging

(*c*) Non-demand paging (*d*) None of the above

Ans. (*b*)

Q. 10. CAMs are

(*a*) Caches only (*b*) RAMs

(*c*) ROMs (*d*) Associative Memories

Ans. (*d*)

Q. 11. The blowing of fuses according to the truth table is known as

(*a*) Programming of ROM (*b*) Refreshing of ROM

(*c*) Clearing of ROM (*d*) None of the above

Ans. (*a*)

Q. 12. EPROMs use

(*a*) MOS circuitry (*b*) FET circuitry

(*c*) BJT circuitry (*d*) PNP circuitry

Ans. (*a*)

Q. 13. EPROMs erasure involves

(*a*) 5 mins (*b*) 30 mins (*c*) 15-20 mins (*d*) 1 hour

Ans. (*c*)

Q. 14. MDR stands for

(*a*) Memory Accumulator Advanced (*b*) Memory Data Register

(*c*) Memory Default Register d) Nene of the above

Ans. (*b*)

Q. 15. The lowest page fault rate is seen in

(*a*) Optimal algorithm (*b*) FIFO algorithm

(*c*) LRU algorithm (*d*) None of the above

Ans. (*a*)

CONCEPTUAL SHORT QUESTIONS WITH ANSWERS

Q. 1. Give a comparison of sRAM and dRAM taking their advantages and disadvantages, manufacturing technology and densities.

Ans. Taking the advantages and disadvantages of RAM together we can summarize that performance wise SRAM is superior to DRAM, and we would use it exclusively, if only we could do so economically. Unfortunately 512 MB of SRAM would be prohibitively large and costly, therefore DRAM is used for system memory. SRAMs are used instead for level

1 cache and level 2 cache memory for which it is perfectly suited, (cache memory needs to be very fast and not very large).

SRAM and DRAMs are manufactured in similar way i.e. highly integrated transistor patterns are photo-etched into silicon. Each SRAM bit is comprised of between 4 to 6 transistors, therefore SRAM takes up much more space compared to DRAM, which uses only one transistor (plus a capacitor).

Bipolar memories are generally used only when very fast operation is the primary requirement. High power dissipation in bipolar circuits makes it difficult to achieve high density. Hence, a memory implemented with bipolar memory chips requires a relatively large number of chips.

Dynamic MOS memory is the predominant technology used in computer main memories. The high densities achievable in this technology make the implementation of large memories economically attractive.

Static MOS memory chips have higher densities and slightly longer access times than bipolar chips. They have lower densities than dynamic memories, but are easier to use because they do not require refreshing.

Q. 2. A memory has 12 address lines and 8 data lines. Find –

(*a*) Number of Register. **(*b*) Word length**

If memory has 8192 memory locations then how many address lines are there? Can you summarize the memory capacities and their corresponding address lines required for memory interfacing?

Ans Given:

Address lines = 12

Data lines = 8

$\therefore$ No. of registers (memory locations) = $2^N = 2^{12} = 4096$

Word length = M bit = 8 bit

If memory has 8192 locations then it has 13 address lines.

Let us put it in a tabular form for various memory capacities —

Memory Capacity	Address Lines required
1 K (1024) locations	10
2 K (2048)	5
4 K (4096)	12
8 K (8192)	13
16 K (16384)	14
32 K (32,768)	16
64 K (65, 536)	16

Q. 3. Compare:

(*a*) Direct Mapping.

(*b*) Associative Mapping

(*c*) Set Associative Mapping

Ans.

Direct Mapping	Associative Mapping	Set Associative Mapping
1. A block of data from the main memory has only **one possible location** in the cache.	1. A block of data from main memory can be placed into **any cache block position.**	1. A block of data from main memory can map into a **particular block location** of any direct mapped cache.
2. It requires only one comparison	2. It requires comparison with all tag bits.	2. The number of comparisons required are equal to the number of blocks per set.
3. Lesser searching time is needed	3. More searching time is needed.	3. Searching time increases with number of blocks per set.
4. Main memory address is divided into three fields – TAG, block and WORD.	4. Main memory address is divided into **two field** only – TAG and WORD.	4. Main Mamory address is divided into three field - TAG, SET and WORD.
5. **Cahce Hit-Ratio (CHR) decreases** if processor needs to accessame memory location form two different pages of the main memory frequently.	5. **Cache-Hit-Ratio (CHR) has no effect** if processor needs to access same memory location from two different pages of the main memory (MM) frequently.	5. The effect of reduction in **Cache-Hit-Ratio (CHR)** in case of frequency access to the two different pages of the main memory is reduced.

Q. 4. Draw a 4-by-2 associative memory array. Explain its construction and working with a neat sketch. Derive a Boolean expression for each bit of the match-register.

Ans. We draw the (4 × 2) associative memory array, first of all

1. **When the read operation is selected**, the argument is matched with the words whose select lines are set to 1. The match output of each cell is then ANDed together to generate the match bit for that particular word.
2. **When the write operation is selected,** the argument bits are stored in the selected word.

   Let us now derive the Boolean expression for each bit M_i of the match register.

Derivation

Say, W_{ij} denote the jth bit of the ith word in the memory.

A_j and K_j denote the jth bit of A and K respectively,

M_i denote the ith bit of M.

Further, suppose that –

$$x_j = A_j W_{ij} + \overline{A}_j \overline{W}_{ij} \qquad (\text{for } j \leftarrow 0, 1, 2, \ldots n-1)$$

That is,

$$\begin{bmatrix} x_j = 1, & \text{if } W_{ij} \text{ matches } A_j \\ x_j = 0, & \text{otherwise} \end{bmatrix}$$

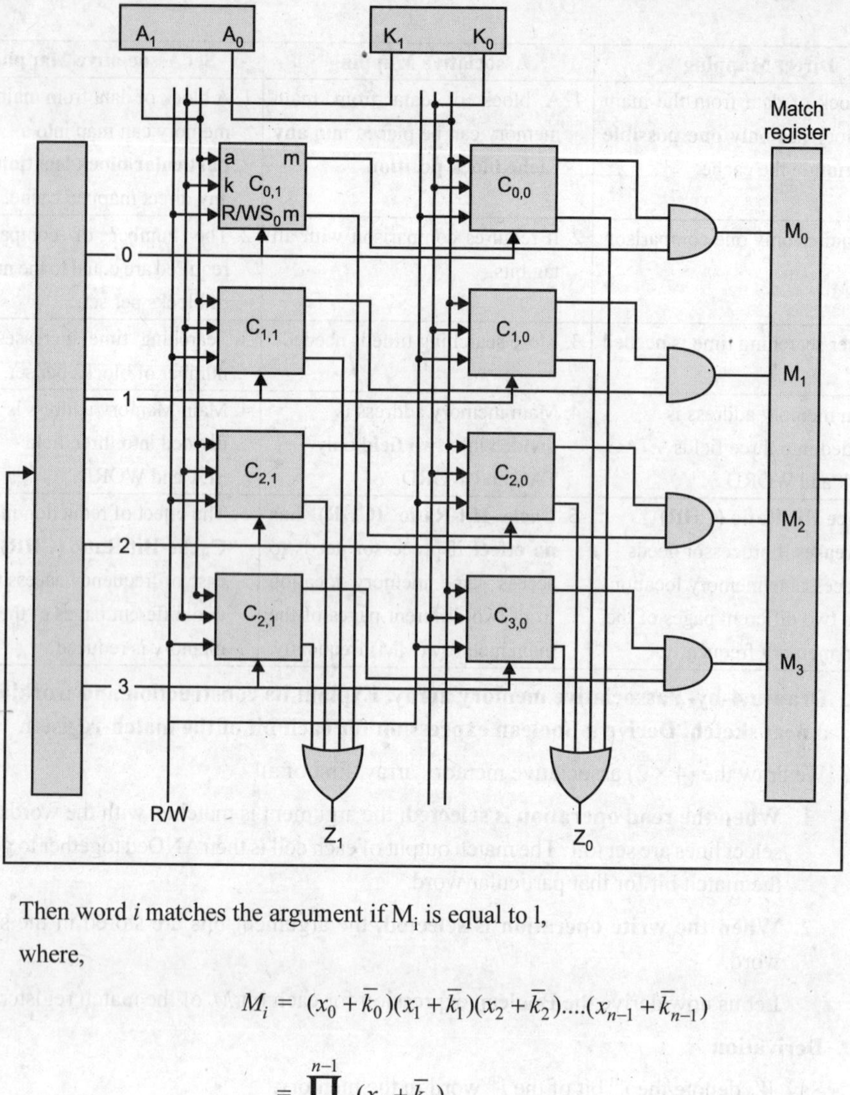

Then word *i* matches the argument if M_i is equal to 1,

where,

$$M_i = (x_0 + \bar{k}_0)(x_1 + \bar{k}_1)(x_2 + \bar{k}_2)....(x_{n-1} + \bar{k}_{n-1})$$

$$= \prod_{j=0}^{n-1} (x_j + \bar{k}_j)$$

$$\therefore \qquad M_i = \prod_{j=0}^{n-1} (A_j W_{ij} + \bar{A}_j \bar{W}_{ij} + \bar{k}_j)$$

Hence, derived.

Working:

Let us show its working for one word of associative memory,

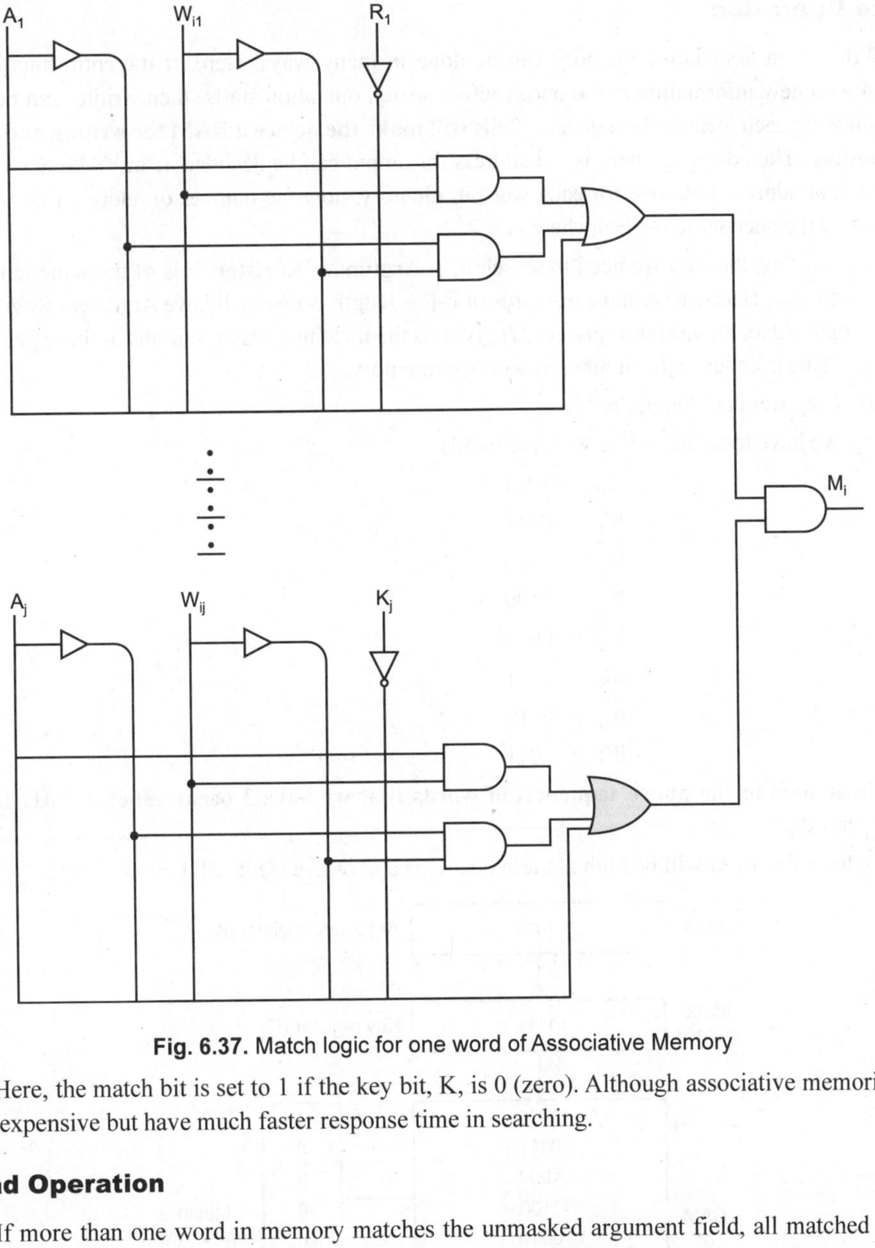

Fig. 6.37. Match logic for one word of Associative Memory

Here, the match bit is set to 1 if the key bit, K, is 0 (zero). Although associative memories are very expensive but have much faster response time in searching.

Read Operation

If more than one word in memory matches the unmasked argument field, all matched words will have 1s in the corresponding bit position of the match register. So, it is necessary to scan the bits of the match register one at a time. **Please understand that the matched words are read in sequence by applying a read signal to each word line whose corresponding M_i bit is at 1.** Actually, in most of the applications, the associative memory storesd a table with no two identical items under a given key. In this scenario, only one word may match the unmasked argument field. **Also understand that by connecting the output, M_i, directly to the read line in the same word position, the content of the matched word will appear at the output.** Also if we exclude words having a zero content, an all-zero output will indicate that no match occurred and that the searched item is not available in the memory.

Write Operation

Write to an associative memory can be done in many ways. Here, if the entire memory is loaded with new information at the once (before search operation starts) then writing can be done by addressing each location in sequence. **This will make the device a RAM for writing and CAM for reading.** The advantage here is the address for output can be decoded as in RAM. So, instead of having *m* address line, one for each word in memory, now the number of address lines can be reduced by the decoder to *d*-lines where $m = 2^d$.

For eg., Say, the data we need to search is in **Argument Register**. It is of the same length as of the word size. Because we have m-words of n-bits length, so we will have Argument Register of n-bits length. Also, the **match register (*M*)** gives us the matching result in terms of those particular bits high. This is equal to the number of words in memory.

So *M*-register is of length, *m*-bits.

Say, we have to search 1011. We have words

$$W_0 = 1011$$
$$W_1 = 0111$$
$$W_2 = 1000$$
$$W_3 = 1100$$
$$W_4 = 0010$$
$$W_5 = 1011$$
$$W_6 = 0111$$
$$W_7 = 1011$$

Please note in the above sequence, of words that we have 3 occurresnce of 1011 i.e., at W_0, W_5 and W_7.

So, the value of *M* will be high at these positions and otherwise it will be low. That is,

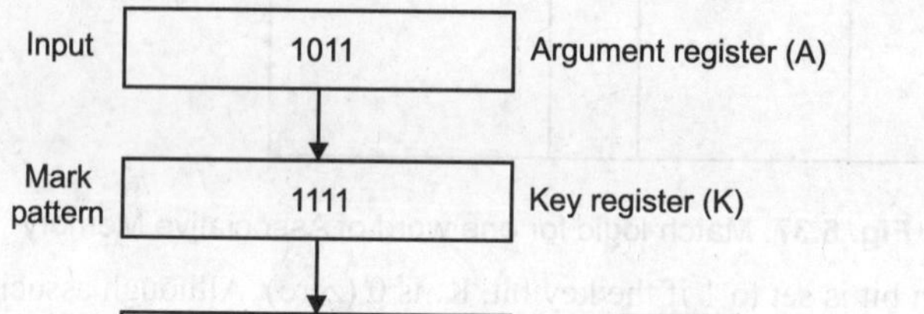

∴ Key Register = 1111.

It represents that it is matching all bits of argument register (*A*) to every word of CAM (or AM). Say, we need to choose only some bits for checking as we want all words ending with one. Then the value of key register (*k*) will be 0001; (as we are just matching only the last bit).

∴ Match Register (M)(has = [11000111].

Q. 5. From (16*8) bit RAM, how will you construct a (64*8) bit RAM. Increase the number of stored words by a factor of 4. [UPTU, B. Tech. (CSE), 4th Sem., 2002]

Ans. We follow a general approach as explained earlier.

$$p = \frac{64}{16} = 4 \text{ and } q = \frac{8}{8} = 1$$

∴ $A(p \times q)$ i.e., (4*1) array of (16*8) RAM chips is-

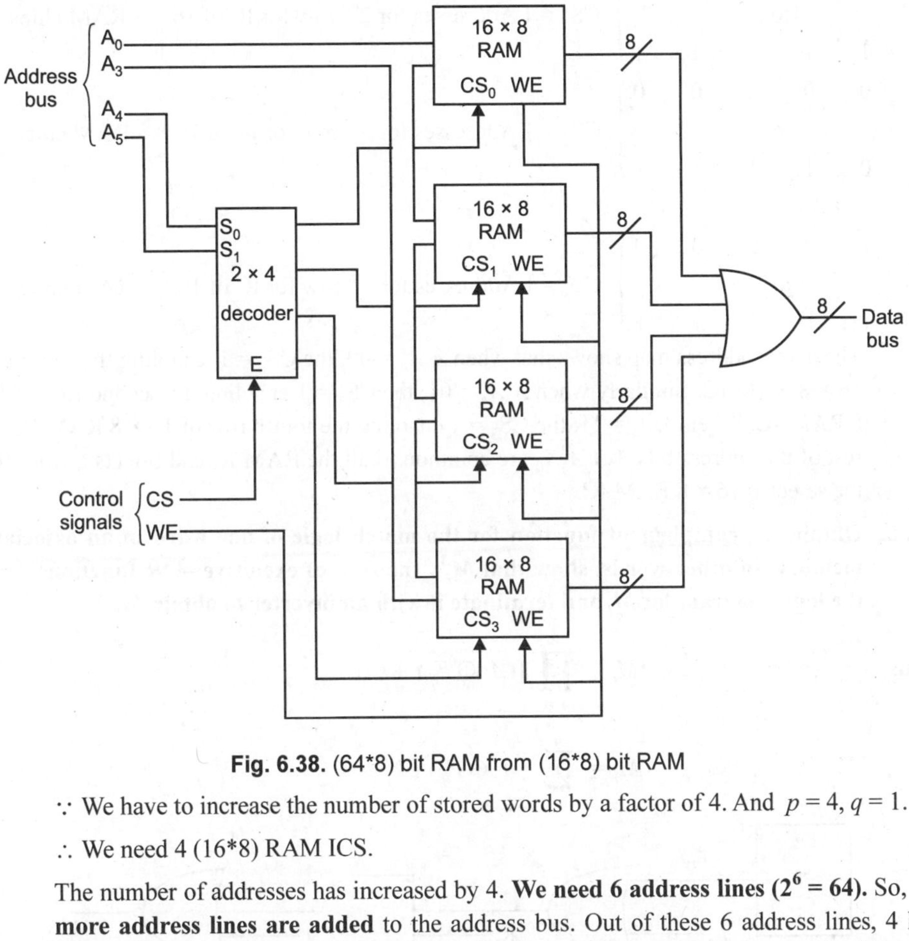

Fig. 6.38. (64*8) bit RAM from (16*8) bit RAM

∵ We have to increase the number of stored words by a factor of 4. And $p = 4, q = 1$.

∴ We need 4 (16*8) RAM ICS.

The number of addresses has increased by 4. **We need 6 address lines (2^6 = 64).** So, **two more address lines are added** to the address bus. Out of these 6 address lines, 4 least significant address lines are required to select 16 words from each 16*8 RAM chip and 2 most significant address lines are required to select one of the 4 RAM ICs. Furthermore a 2 × 4 decoder is needed to decode the two MSB address bits A_4 and A_5. The original 4 address lines are connected to the 4-bit address bus of each RAM ICs. The 2-additional address lines act as selection inputs to the decoder. Each decoder output line is connected to the CS inputs of the RAMs in the same row, ensuring that the row has a unique address. The output buses of all RAM IC's can be wired together without additional logic. The remaining control line WE is attached to every RAM IC as before. The external CS line is connected to the chip enable input E of the decoder. Making this line $E = 0$ disables the decoder forcing all CS lines to the individual RAM ICs to 0 so that they are all deactivated.

The address map of this RAM organization is shown below:

A_5	A_4	A_3	A_2	A_1	A_0	
0	0	0	0	0	0	
		to				$CS_0 = 1$ Addresses for Ist row for IC of 16 × 8 RAM chips
0	0	1	1	1	1	
0	1	0	0	0	0	
		to				$CS_1 = 1$ Addresses for 2nd row for IC of 16 × 8 RAM chips
0	1	1	1	1	1	
1	0	0	0	0	0	
		to				$CS_2 = 1$ Addresses for 3rd row for IC of 16 × 8 RAM chips
1	0	1	1	1	1	
1	1	0	0	0	0	
		to				$CS_3 = 1$ Addresses for 4th row for IC of 16 × 8 RAM chips
1	1	1	1	1	1	

The above address map shows that when $A_5A_4 = 00$, the $CS_0 = 1$, enabling the first row of 16 × 8 RAM IC. Similarly when $A_5A_4 = 01$, the $CS_1 = 1$ enabling the second row of 16 × 8 RAM IC. When $A_5A_4 = 11$, the $CS_3 = 1$ enabling the fourth row of 16 × 8 RAM IC. The rest of the address bits $A_3A_2A_1A_0$ are common to all the RAM IC and selects a word from the selected 16 × 8 RAM IC.

Q. 6. Obtain the complement function for the match logic of one word in an associative memory. In other words, show that M_i^1s the sum of exclusive –OR functions. Draw the logic diagram for M_i and terminate it with an inverter to obtain M.

Ans.

$$M_i = \prod_{j=1}^{n} [(A_j \oplus F_{ij})' + k_j']$$

$$M_i' = \sum_{j=1}^{n} (A_j \oplus F_{ij}) + k_j$$

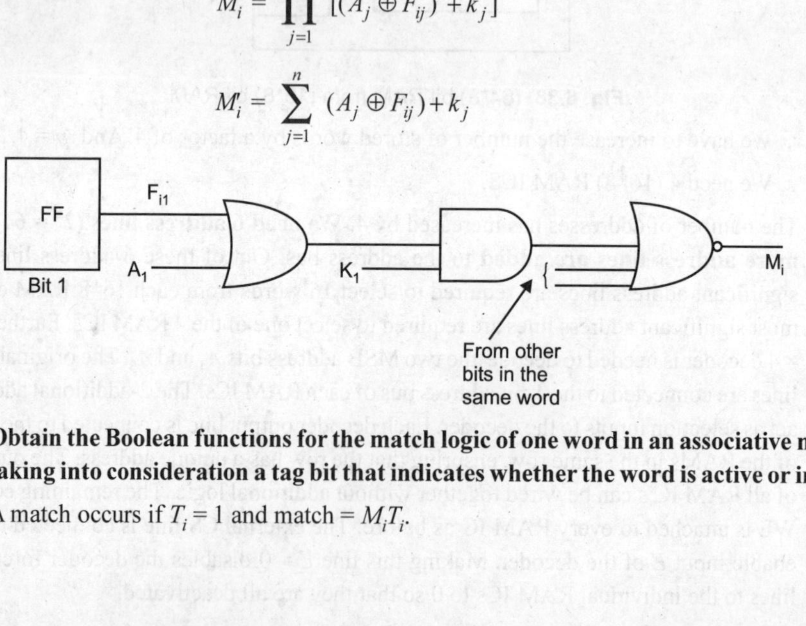

Q. 7. Obtain the Boolean functions for the match logic of one word in an associative memory taking into consideration a tag bit that indicates whether the word is active or inactive.

Ans. A match occurs if $T_i = 1$ and match $= M_iT_i$.

Q. 8. What additional logic is required to give a no-match result for a word in an associative memory when all key bits are zeros?

Ans. $M_i = \left[\prod_{j=1}^{n} A_j F_{ij} + A'_j F'_{ij} + k'_j\right] (k_1 + k_2 + k_3 + ... + k_n)$

Q. 9. Describe in words and by means of a block diagram how multiple matched words can be read out from an associative memory.

Ans. A d-bit counter drives a d-to-m decoder where $2^d = m$, (where m = no. of words in memory). For each count, the M_i bit is checked and if 1, the corresponding read signal for word – i is activated.

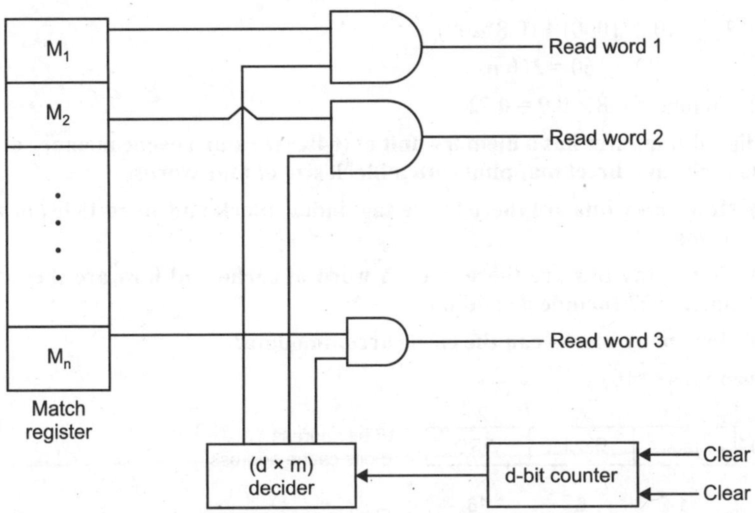

Q. 10. A two way set associative cache memory uses blocks of four words. The cache can accommodate a total of 2048 words from main memory. The main memory size is (128 K * 32).

(*a*) Formulate all pertinent information required to construct the cache memory

(*b*) What is the size of the cache memory?

Ans. Given : 128 K = 2^{17}.

For a set size of 2, index address has 10 bits to accommodate, 2048/2 = 1024 words of cache.

(*a*)

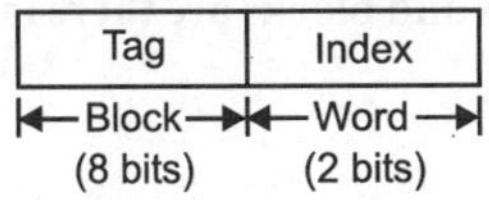

(*b*)

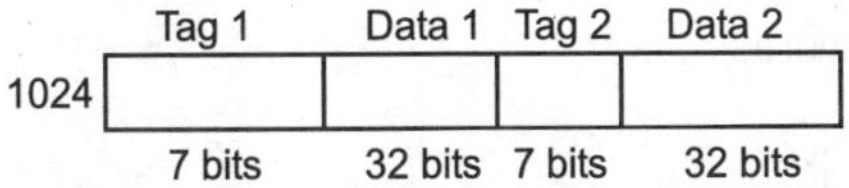

$\therefore$ Size of cache memory = 1024*2 (7 + 32)

= 1024 * 78

Q. 11. The access of a cache memory is 100 ns and that of main memory is 1000 ns. It is estimated that 80% of the memory request are for read and the remaining 20% for write. The hit-ratio for read access only is 0.9. A write-through procedure is used.

(*a*) What is the average access time of the system considering only memory read cycles?

(*b*) What is the average access time of the system for both read and write requests?

(*c*) What is the hit ratio taking into consideration the write cycles?

Ans. (*a*) $T_{avg} = \underbrace{(0.9 \times 100)}_{\text{cache-access}} + \underbrace{(0.1*1100)}_{\text{memory access}}$

$= 90 + 110$

$= \mathbf{200\ ns}$

(*b*) $T_{avg} = (0.2*1000) + (0.8*200)$

$= 200 + 160 = \mathbf{360\ ns}$

(*c*) Hit ratio $= 0.8 \times 0.9 = \mathbf{0.72.}$

Q. 12. A digital computer has a memory unit of (64K*16) and a cache memory of 1 K words. The cache uss direct mapping with a block size of four words.

(*a*) How many bits are there in the tag, index, block and word fields of the address format?

(*b*) How many bits are there in each word of cache and how are they divided into functions? Include a valid bit.

(*c*) How many blocks can the cache accommodate?

Ans. Given : (64K*16)

(*a*)

6	8	2
Tag	Block	WRD

= 16 bit address
=10 bits cache address

(*b*)

1	6	16
V	Tag	Data

= 23 bit in each word of cache

∴ 16-bit address

and 16-bit data.

(*c*) $2^8 = 256$ blocks of 4 words each.

Q. 13. An address space is specified by 24-bits and the corresponding memory space by 16-bits.

(*a*) How many words are there in the address space?

(*b*) How many words are there in the memory space?

(*c*) If a page consists of 2K words, how many pages and blocks are there in the system?

Ans. (*a*) Address space = 24 bits

$2^{24} = 16$ M words

(*b*) Memory space = 16 bits

$2^{16} = 64$K words.

(*c*) $\frac{16M}{2K} = 8$ K pages

and $\frac{16M}{2K} = = 32$ blocks.

Q. 14. A virtual memory has a page size of 1K words. There are eight pages and four blocks. The associative memory page table contains the following entries:

Page	**Block**
0	**3**
1	**1**
4	**2**
6	**0**

Making a list of all virtual addresses (in decimal) that will cause a page fault if used by the CPU.

Ans. The pages which are not in the main memory are :

Page A	Address	Address that will cause fault
2	2K	2048-3071
3	3K	3072-4095
5	5K	5120-6143
7	7K	7168-8191

Q. 15. A virtual memory system has an address space of 8K words, a memory space of 4K words and page block sizes of 1K words (shown in figure). The following page reference changes occur during a given time interval. (Only page changes as listed. If the same page is reference again, it is not listed twice).

4 2 0 1 2 6 1 4 0 1 0 2 3 5 7

Determine the four pages that are resident in main memory after each page reference change if the replacement algorithm used is –

(*a*) FIFO **(*b*) LRU**

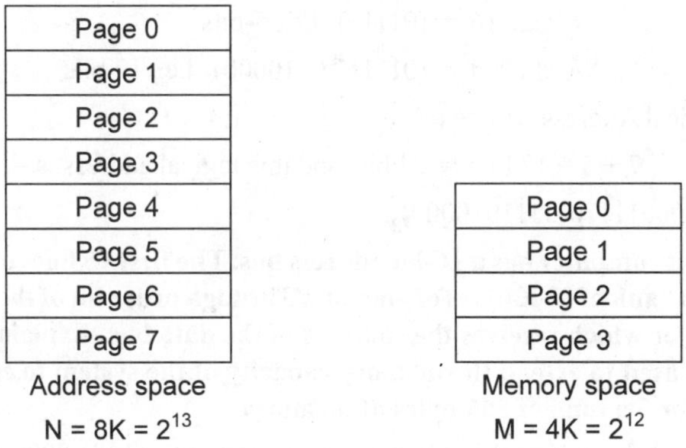

Fig. 6.39. Address space and memory space split into groups of 1k words

Ans. Given reference string is–

4, 0, 0, 1, 2, 6, 1, 4, 0, 1, 0, 2, 3, 5, 7

We draw a table to show how FIFO and LIFO words.

Page Reference	Pages in Main Memory	Contents of FIFO	Pages in Memory	LRU Most record
Initial	0124	4201	0124	4201
2	0124	4201	0124	4012
6	0126	2016	0126	0126
1	0126	2016	0126	0261
4	0146	0164	1246	2614
0	0146	0164	0146	6140
1	0146	0164	0146	6401
0	0146	0164	0146	6410
2	0146	1642	0124	4102
3	2346	6423	0123	1023
5	2345	4235	0235	0235
7	2357	2357	2357	2357

Q. 16. The logical address space in a computer system consists of 128 Segments. Each segment can have upto 32 pages of 4K words in each. Physical memory consist of 4K blocks of 4K words in each. Formulate the logical and physical address formats.

Ans. Logical Address

7 bits	5 bits	12 bits
Segment	Page	Word

= 24 bits

Physical Address

12 bits	12 bits
Block	Word

Q. 17. Give the binary number of the logical address formulated in question No. 16 above for segment 36 and word number 2000 in page 15.

Ans. Given

$$\text{Segment } 36 = (0100100)_2 \text{ i.e., 7-bits}$$

$$\text{Page } 16 = (01111)_2 \text{ i.e., 5-bits}$$

$$\text{Word } 2000 = (011111\ 0910000)_2 \text{ i.e., 12 bits}$$

$\therefore$ Logical Address will be of

$$7 + 5 + 12 \text{ bits} = 24 \text{ bits and this logical address is –}$$

$(010010001111011111010000)_2$.

Q. 18. An 8-bit computer has a 16-bit address bus. The first 15 lines of the address are used to select a bank of 32 K bytes of memory. The high order bit of the address is used to select a register which receives the contents of the data bus. Explain how this configuration can be used to extend the memory capacity of the system to eight banks of 32K bytes each, for 5 a total of 256 bytes of memory.

Ans. The processor selects the external register with an address 8000 Hex. Each bank of 32 kB are selected by address 0000-7FFF. The processor loads an 8-bit number into the register with a single 1 and seven 0s. Each output of the register selects one of the 8 banks of 32 bytes through 2 chip select (CS) inputs. A memory bank can be changed by changing the number in the register.

Q. 19. A magnetic disk system has the following parameters:

T_S : average time to position the magnetic head over a track.

R : Rotation speed of disk in revolutions per second.

N_t : No. of bits per trace.

N_{S+} : No. of bits per sector.

Calculate the average time, T_a, that it will take to read one sector.

Ans. Average time, T_a is given by = $T_a = T_s$ + (time for half revolution) + (time to read a sector)

$$T_a = T_s + \frac{1}{2R} + \frac{N_S}{N_t} \times \frac{1}{R}$$

Q. 20. What is the transfer rate of an eight track magnetic tape whose speed is 120 inches per second and whose density is 1600 bits per inch?

Ans. An eight-track tape reads 8-bits (one character) at the same time.

Transfer rate = 1600* 1230

= 192,000 character / sec.

Q. 21. Construct a 128 MB RAM from 2M × 4 bit RAM IC. Also 1 out of 2^k decoder ICs are available for $k \times 3$, as wellas ICs containing standard logic gates. Out goal is to minimize the total numbers of ICs used. Solve this using two approaches:

(*i*) Each RAM chip has single chp select line CS

(*ii*) Each RAM chip has two chip select lines CS_1 and CS_2.

Ans.

Approach I

Assuming each RAM chip has a single chip select line CS. To construct 128 MB RAM from 2M × 4 bit RAM. We are given N' = 128MB, N = 2M × 4, W' = 8 bit and W = 4 bit.

$$\therefore \qquad p = \lceil 128/2 \rceil = 64$$

$$\text{and} \qquad q = \lceil 8/4 \rceil = 2$$

We can organize 128 MB RAM as a 64 × 2 array of 2M × 4 RAM ICs. To address 128 MB locations we need 27 address line says 2^{27} = 128 MB.

Out of these 27 address lines, given each IC has 2M locations, we need 21 address lines to select 2M locations as 2^{21} = 2M. Therefore, address $A_{20} \ldots A_0$ will go in each IC. There are 64 rows of 2M ICs, so we needs 6-bits to select one of these 64 ICs.

But we are provided with 1-out-of-2^k decoder ICs where $K \leq 3$. Taking $K = 3$ we are provided with 3 × 8 decoder IC. With the single 3 × 8 decoder we can select only 8 ICs. To select 64 ICs we need 8 such decoder. Now to distinguish which of these 8 decoder selects one of the 64 ICs we need another 3 × 8 decoder. These makes a two level decoder tree as shown in figure. The first level has one 3 × 8 decoder which select one of the eight 3 × 8 decoders from the second level of decoders, which in turn selects one of the 64 IC's.

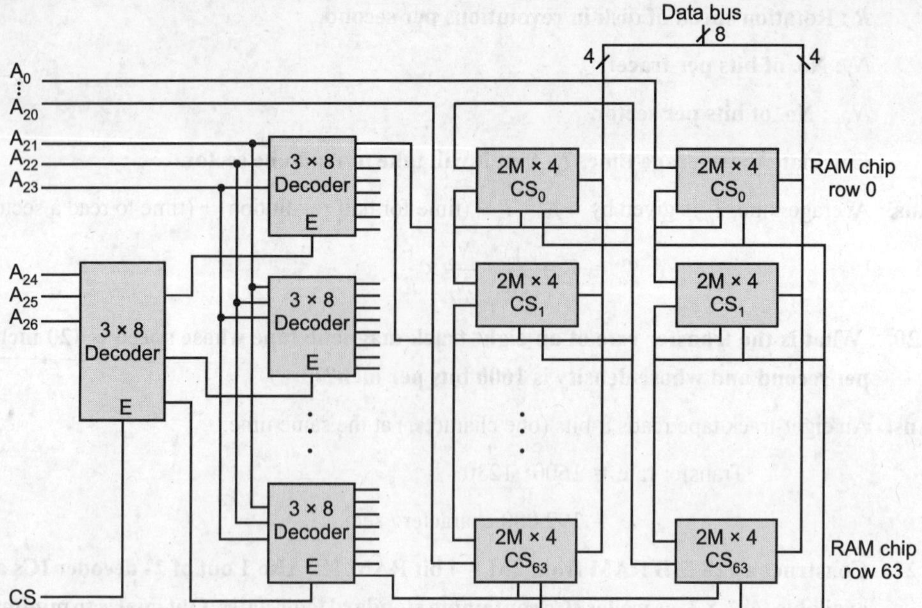

Fig. 6.40. Constructing 128 MB RAM from 2M × 4 bit RAM ICs and 12-out-of-2^3 Decoder ICs

We use two level decoder tree of 3 × 8 decoders. Address lines A_{26} A_{25} A_{24} selects the first level decoder output, address lines A_{23} A_{22} A_{21} selects the second level decoder output. In total 6-bits of address lines A_{26} ...A_{21} selects one of the 64 chips rows. Address lines A_{20} ... A_0 selects a word in the above selected RAM chip.

Approach II

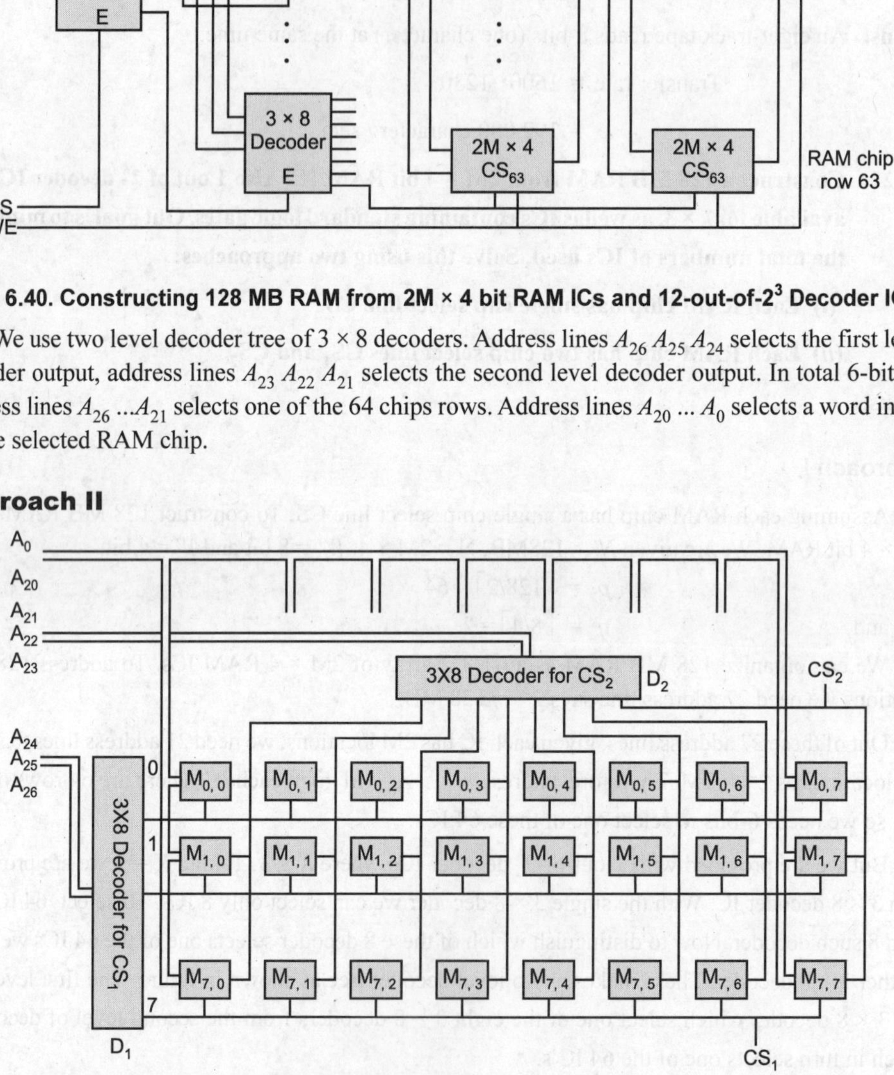

Fig. 6.41. 2-D Array Organization for RAMs with two chip select lines CS_1 and CS_2

Assuming each RAM IC has two chips select lines CS_1 and CS_2 and is enabled if and only if $CS_1 = CS_2 = 1$. A less costly solution is possible when each RAM IC is having two chip enable lines CS_1 and CS_2 such that both enable lines must be active to enable the IC. Then the 64 rows of ICs, which form a 1-D memory array in figure I can be reorganized into the 2-D8×8 structure of ICs as shown in figure II.

Now only two 3 × 8 decoders are needed. Decoder D_1 to address the 8 rows of RAM ICs and decoder D_2 to address the 8 columns of RAM ICs. Each output of D_1 is connected to the CS_1 to all RAM ICs' in a distinct column. Thus address bits A_{26} .. A_{21} select a unique IC in the 2-D array (address bits A_{26} ... A_{24} selects a row of ICs and address bits A_{23} ... A_{21} selects a column of ICs), and address bit A_{20} ... A_0 selects one of the address from the selected IC. Also since the word size is 1 byte, there is a pair $M_{i,j}$ of RAM ICs at every row column but for simplicity sake it is not shown in the figure.

22. What is cache flushing?

Ans. The on-chip cache can be flushed by external hardware of software. **The process of clearing of all valid bits of all lines in the cache is known as cache flushing.**

External hardware activates the FLUSH pin for flushing the cache. While our **software** may use INVD or WBINVD instructions to flush the cache.

23. A computer has 16 MB main memory and 64 KB cache. The block size is 16 bytes.

(*i*) How many cache lines does the computer have?

(*ii*) How many blocks does the main memory have?

(*iii*) Give the starting address of memory blocks which are directly mapped to cache lines.

(*iv*) Explain how a given address is retrieved from the memory system.

Ans. (*i*) Cache size is 64KB (given) = $2^6 \times 2^{10}$ bytes.

Block size is 16 KB.

$$\therefore \text{ No. of cache lines} = \frac{2^{16}}{2^4} = 2^{12} = 4\text{K}.$$

(*ii*) $$\text{No. of blocks is main memory} = \frac{2^{24}}{2^4} = 2^{20}.$$

(*iii*) As there are 4K cache lines and 1 M blocks.

$$\therefore \text{ No. of blocks mapped into each cache line} = \frac{2^{20}}{2^{12}} = 2^8 = 256.$$

Please remember that at any time only one of these blocks will occupy a cache line.

The mapping is given below. **Also note that the addresses are in HEX.**

	Cache line Address	Block No.s (Depth = 16 bytes)			
	000	00000	01000		FF000
	001	00001	01001		FF001
	002	00002	01002		FF002
4K	003	-	01003		FF003
cache	⋮	⋮	⋮	…	
lines	00f	0000f	0100f		FF00F
	⋮				
	FFF	00FFF	01FFF		FFFFF
	Tags	00	01	…	FF

Totally 256 Blocks exist.

∴ In Cache line address $(000)_H$ one of the 256 blocks can be mapped as shown in table.

(*iv*) The main memory (MM) address is divided into three parts

Memory address bits = 24

Tag	Cache line no	Byte address
8-bits (2 HEX)	12-bits (3 HEX)	4-bits (1 HEX)

So, given the address, the 12 bits cache line number is used to locate the cache line where the memory block is mapped.

Then, the 8-bit tag is matched with the starting address in the block stored in cache line. If it matches it is in the cache and is retrieved, otherwise it has to be retrieved from the main memory (MM).

Q. 24. Derive the logic of one cell and of an entire word for an associative memory that has an output indicator when the unmasked argument is greater than (but not equal to) the word in the associative memory.

Ans. Say,

$$x_j = A_jF_{ij} + A'_jF'_{ij}$$

[Argument bit = memory word bit]

Output indicator, $G_i = 1$ if :

$A_jF'_{ij} = 1$ *and* $K = 1$ [First bit is $A = 1$ while $F_{i1} = 0$]

or if $x_1A_2F'_{i2} = 1$ and $K_2 = 1$ [First pair of bits are equal and second bit is $A = 1$ while $f_{i2} = 0$]

$$G_i = (A_1F'_{i1} + K'_1)(x_1A_2F'_{i2} + k'_2)(x_1x_2A_3F'_{i3} + k'_3) \dots (x_1x_2 \dots x_{n-1}A_nF'_{in} + k'_n)$$

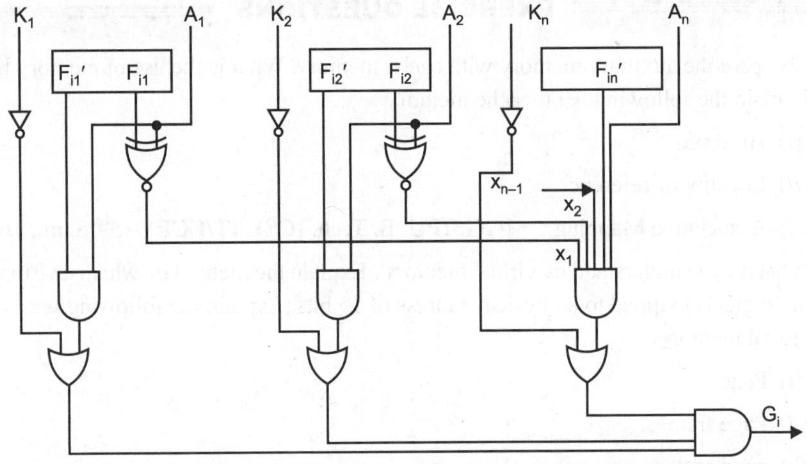

Q. 25. A four-way set associative cache memory has four words in each set. A replacement procedure based on the least recently used (LRU) algorithm is implemented by means of 2-bit counters associated with each word in the set. A value in the range 0 to 3 9n thus recorded for each work. When a hit occurs, the counter associated with the referenced world is set to 0, those counters with values originally lower than the referenced one are incriminated by 1, and all other remain unchanged. If a miss occurs, the word with counter is set to 0. The other three counters are incriminated by1. Show that this procedure works for the following sequence of word reference:

***A, B, C, D, B, E, D, A, C, E, C, E,* (Start with *A, B, C, D,* as the initial four words, with word A being the least recently used).**

Ans. Sequence : *A B C D E B E D A C E C E*

LRU

↓

Counter value =	3 2 1 0
Initial words =	A B C D
B is a hit	A C D B
E is a miss	C D B E
D is a hit	C B E D
A is a miss	B E D A
C is a miss	E D A C
E is a hit	D A C E
C is a hit	D A E C
E is a hit	D A C E

EXERCISE QUESTIONS

Q. 1. Compare the auxiliary memory with cache memory. What is the use of memory hierarchy. Explain the following w.r.t. cache memory

(*i*) Hit Ratio

(*ii*) Locality of reference

(*iii*) Associative Mapping **[GGSIPU, B. Tech. (CSE/IT/ECE) – 5th Sem., Dec. 2004]**

Q. 2. What do you understand by virtual memory? Explain the method by which a virtual address of 20 bits is mapped to a physical address of 15 bits. Explain the following with respect to virtual memory

(*i*) Page

(*ii*) Page frames.

(*iii*) page replacement

(*iv*) Page fault **[GGSIPU, B. Tech (CSE/IT/ECE) – 5th Sem., Dec. 2004]**

Q. 3. (*a*) A machine has a 32 bit byte addressable virtual address space. The page size is 8 KB. How many pages of virtual address space exist?

(*b*) A computer has pages of virtual address space but only has 4 page frames. Initially memory is empty. A program references the virtual pages in the order 0, 7, 2, 5, 8, 9, 2, 4. Which reference causes a page fault with LRU and FIFO?

[GGSIPU, B.Tech. (CSE/IT/ECE) – 5th Sem., Dec. 2005]

Q. 4. (*a*) Explain how cache memory may be organized using associative mapping.

(*b*) (*i*) How many 128 × 8 RAM chips are needed to provide a memory capacity of 2048 bytes.

(*ii*) How many lines of the address busd must be used to access 2048 by lets of memory? How many of these lines will be common to all chips?

(*iii*) How many lines must be decoded for chip select? Specify the size of the decoders?

(*c*) Explain why can't we have a single large main memory instead of a hierarchy of memory.

[GGSIPU, B.Tech. (CSE/IT/ECE) – 5th Sem., 2006]

Q. 5. "The cache memory is employed in computer systems to compensate for the speed differential between main memory access time and speed of processor logic." Discuss and justify the above statement. **[GGSIPU, B. Tech. (CSE/IT/ECE) – 5th Sem., Dec. 2008]**

Q. 6. (*a*) Discuss memory hierarchy

(*b*) Explain CAM **[GGSIPU, B. Tech. (CSE/IT/ECE) – 5th Sem., Dec. 2009]**

Q. 7. Write short notes on the following:

(*a*) Memory hierarchy in a computer system.

(*b*) Memory address map.

(*c*) Associative memory.

(*d*) Set-associative mapping

[GGSIPU, B. Tech. (CSE/IT/ECE) – 5th Sem., Dec. 2010]

Q. 8. (*a*) Explain memory hierarchy in a computer system.

(*b*) A computer uses RAM chips of (1024*1) capacity –

(*i*) How many chips are needed and how should their address lines be connected to provide a memory capacity of 1024 bytes?

(*ii*) How many chips are needed to provide a memory capacity of 16 KB? Explain in words, how the chips are to be connected to the address bus.

(*c*) Explain cache coherence.

[GGSIPU, B. Tech. (CSE/IT/ECE) – 5th Sem., Dec. 2010]

Q. 9. What is cache memory? Explain different mapping procedures. Also mention their advantages and disadvantages. **[MDU, BE (CSE) – 4th Sem. 2000]**

Q. 10. (*a*) What is cache memory? Explain the write-through and write-back method to write in cache.

(*b*) What do you understand by mapping? Explain direct mapping cache organization.

(*c*) How interleaved memory is useful in multiprocessor system?

[MDU, BE (CSE) – 4th Sem. 2002]

Q. 11. Obtain the Boolean function for match logic of on-word in an associative memory taking into consideration a tag bit that indicates whether word is active or inactive.

[MDU, BE (CSE) – 4th Sem. 2002]

Q. 12. (*a*) Discuss the advantages of interleaved memory.

(*b*) How do we read from associative memory? **[MDU, BE (CSE) – 4th Sem. 2004]**

Q. 13. (*a*) Which is the fastest memory in the memory hierarchy? Why memory hierarchy is needed?

(*b*) Briefly discuss the following –

(*i*) Static and dynamic RAM and its organization

(*ii*) Total Memory hierarchy. **[MDU, BE (CSE) – 4th Sem. 2005]**

Q. 14. (*a*) Compare characteristics of sRAM and dRAM.

(*b*) What is the design principle for cache memory? Discuss the following cache mapping scheme.

(*i*) Direct cache mapping.

(*ii*) Associative cache mapping. **[MDU, BE (CSE) – 4th Sem. 2006]**

Q. 15. (*a*) What do you mean by cache memory? Draw and explain the block diagram of cache memory.

(*b*) What are the various parameters that can be used to evaluate the performance of a memory unit? **[MDU, BE (CSE) – 4th Sem. 2007]**

Q. 16. Explain the principles of cache design. **[Madras University, B.Sc. (CS) – April 2011]**

Q. 17. (*a*) What are the various types of ROM? Discuss the methods of programming ROMs.

(*b*) Discuss the various mapping schemes used in cache design, compare the scheme in terms of cost and performance. **[MCA–3rd Sem. PTU 2009]**

Q. 18. (*a*) Give the function of memory address and MBR.

(*b*) Give the features of a RAM cell. **[MCA– 3rd Sem. 2009]**

Q. 19. (*a*) What is a memory hierarchy? Explain with the help of diagram.

(*b*) Explain the importance of interleaved memory.

(*c*) What is the need of virtual memory? **[B.Tech. (CSE) – 3rd Sem., PTU 2009]**

Q. 20. Show the layout of a cache for a CPU that can address (1M × 16) of memory: the cache holds (8K × 16) of data and has the following mapping strategies. Give the number of bits per location and the total number of locations –

(*i*) Fully Associative.

(*ii*) Direct Mapped.

(*iii*) Two-Way set Associative.

(*iv*) Four-way set Associative. **[DTU (DCE) – ME (CS) 2004-05]**

CHAPTER 7

INPUT AND OUTPUT PROCESSING (IOP)

7.0 INTRODUCTION

Computer is required to communicate with external environment though Input / Output or I/O subsystem. The essential features of communications are:

(a) **CPU** which receives information (data and program) is faster processing device.

(b) **Peripherals** are slower devices (like keyboard, printer etc.) or faster storage devices (like magnetic disks).

(c) Manner of operation of CPU is different from peripherals (or I/O devices).

The requirements of CPU are that –

1. It should be able to identify (or select) I/O device, for a transfer (read / write) operation.
2. It should be able to send and receive data.
3. It should coordinate CPU operations with that of I/O operations.

Few examples of input and output devices are given below:

Input Devices

Keyboards
Light pen
Mouse
Card punch
Digitizer
Optical scanner
Joy sticks
Touch panels
Data gloves
Track balls.

Output Devices

Video Display Terminal (VDU)
Graphics terminal

Card Reader

Plotter

Printers

Disk (I/O)

Tapes (I/O)

7.1 INPUT / OUTPUT INTERFACE

The interface is a circuit, between peripheral and processor, which provides a method to transfer data between internal memory, CPU registers and external Input / output devices. Types of I/O are shown in Fig. 7.0.

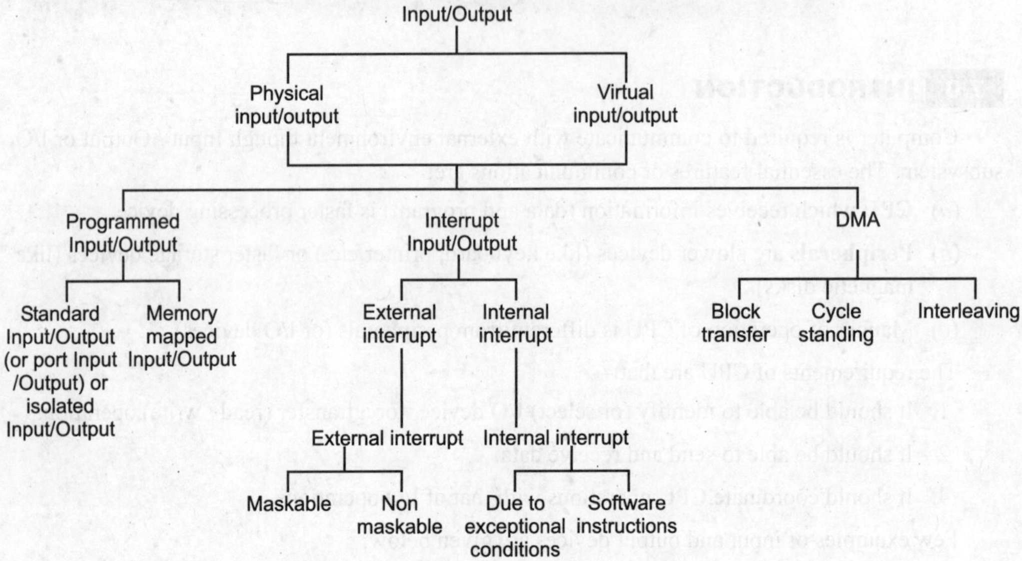

Fig. 7.0. Types of I10

The purposes of interfaces are to resolve the following differences:

(*i*) **Mode of operation**

The I/O devices are electro mechanical and electromagnetic and CPU is electronic device and thus mode of operation of CPU and I/O devices differs.

(*ii*) **Rate of Transfer**

The data transfer rate of peripherals is either very slow or faster compared to CPU transfer rate.

(*iii*) **Change of format**

The data format of I/O devices is different from word format of processor.

(*iv*) **Synchronisation**

The operation of CPU must be synchronized with I/O devices.

(*v*) **Isolation**

The operation of each peripheral should not disturb other peripherals and CPU.

Also interface should have a decoder to decode the address meaning it should be able to identify device to be serviced.

Interface should have the circuitry to **test device readiness** by checking status flag of device, and when ready, should be able to enable interrupt to CPU.

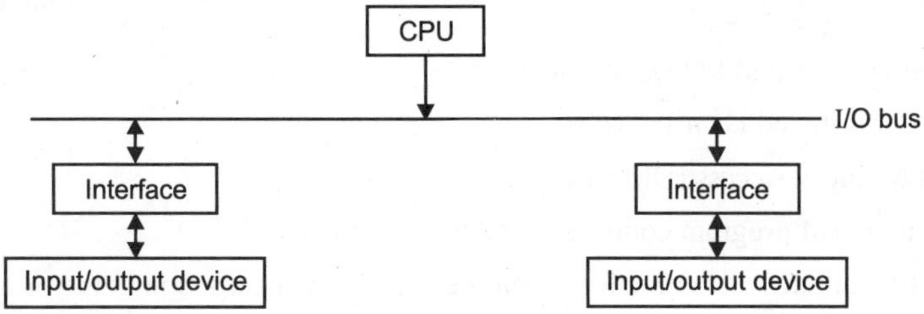

Interface module is shown in Fig. 7.1

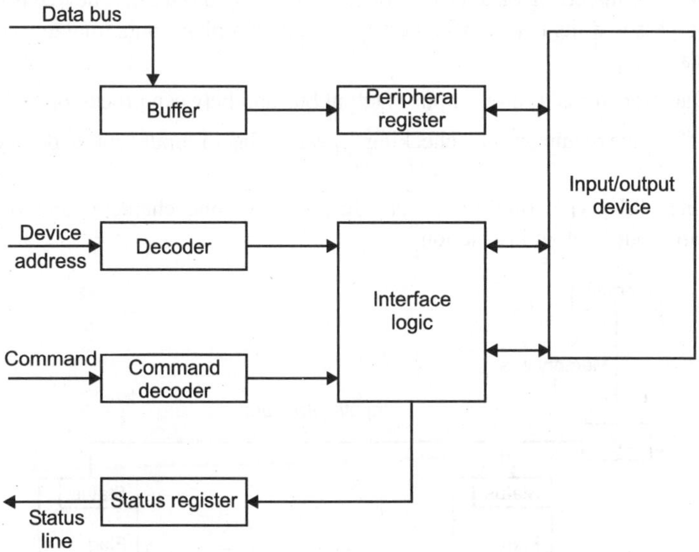

Fig. 7.2. Connection of I/O Bus to interface to I/O

The interface module consists of interface logic with address decoder and command decoder and buffer and status registers.

Each I/O device has its own interface and I/O bus is connected to all interfaces.

Address decoder in interface, monitors address lines, when its I/O address is detected on address lines it decodes and activate path between I/O bus and peripheral.

At the same time I/O command is placed on data lines and command decoder decodes and is applied to interface control to activate specified command.

Interface has buffer register for holding data being transferred through I/O bus.

Peripheral Registers hold data in turn for I/O device.

Status register: Stores status of device and interface status such as buffer full, ready to rescue data etc. to indicate to CPU.

Also interface **synchronises data flow** between **CPU and peripheral.** As for input synchronisation, interface accepts data from peripheral at **peripheral transmission rate** and for output synchronisation it sends data at a rate peripheral can accept.

7.2 Modes of Transfer

There are three possible modes of data transfer between CPU and I/O devices. They are as follows:

(*i*) Program Controlled I/O Data Transfer.

(*ii*) Interrupt Initiated Data Transfer.

(*iii*) Direct Memory Access (DMA) Transfer

I. The features of program controlled I/O are as below:

- CPU initiates, data transfer, when it executes I/O instruction in the program.
- **Execution of one I/O instruction causes one word of data to be transferred.**
- While transferring data, processor stays in a loop program, if device is not ready. Thus processor waits until device gets ready and completes data transfer when devices are ready.
- Data transfer is through Input / Output bus and between processor and peripheral.

Checking of device readiness is by checking the status flag of Input / output device, continuously by the CPU.

For example, Tele typewriter which can handle only one character and one character is transferred by an Input / output instruction.

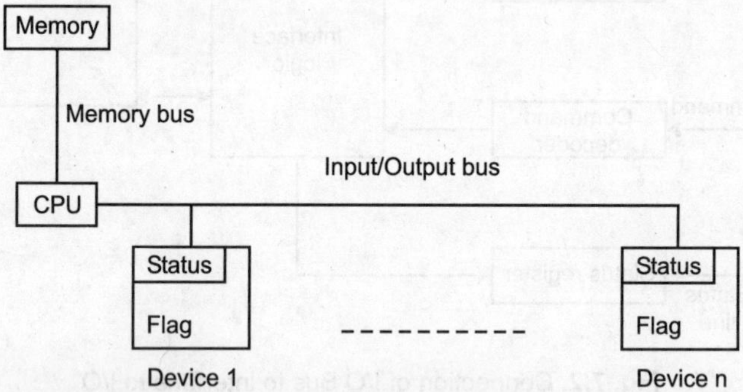

Fig. 7.3. Program Controlled Input / Output

This technique is used for low speed devices only.

II. Interrupt Initiated I/O transfer

The features of this method are as follows:

- CPU initiates data transfer by issuing **special command** to interface to send interrupt when device is ready.
- Interface keeps monitoring the device continuously and CPU executes other programs other than I/O operations.
- When I/O device, is ready, to receive or send data, interface generates interrupt request to CPU.
- When CPU receives interrupt, it completes the current instruction execution and branches to interrupt service routine, to perform data transfer, and then returns back to, from where it has branched.
- CPU time is saved as "interface", monitors device-status-flag, for its readiness.

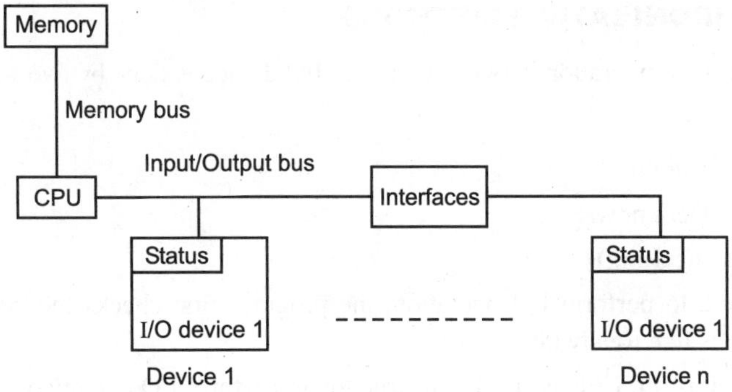

Fig. 7.4. Interrupt Initiated I/O transfer

III. DMA Transfer

- CPU initiates data transfer by supplying to interface with starting memory address (from and to data transferred) and number of words of data and mode of transfer (i.e. Read / Write).
- DMA interface transfers data to and from memory through memory bus.
- When CPU initiates data transfer by supplying more information and issues special GO command,
- When GO command is received by DMA controller, it requests memory cycle through memory bus (steal memory cycle from CPU) and performs data transfer in blocks independently and directly to and from memory and I/O (i.e. CPU relinquishes the control of buses).
- CPU performs other functions when data transfer is not performed.

Fig. 7.5. DMA Transfers

This is useful when large blocks of data are to be transferred, at high speed, without interference of CPU, directly between I/O device and memory.

Application of DMA Transfers

1. It is useful for updating the display in an interactive terminal. Typically, an image of screen display of terminal is kept in memory which can be updated under program control. **Please understand that the contents of memory are transferred to screen periodically by means of these DMA transfers only.**
2. Faster transfer of information.

7.3 SYNCHRONISATION METHODS

Synchronisation of operation between CPU and I/O device is done by two ways:

(*a*) Polling.

(*b*) Interrupt Method.

Let us discuss them now.

Polling (or status checking)

In this method, to perform I/O operation, the program first checks the device readiness by testing its status bits like Ready bit.

When ready bit is set, CPU issues I/O instruction to perform I/O operation.

Thus before issuing I/O instruction, CPU polls all devices for their readiness.

In 8085 ready bit is connected to control line ready which is active when device is ready to receive data and CPU senses control line until it is active. Until device is not ready CPU is in wait loop.

II. Interrupt

In this method, CPU does not check the device readiness.

However, device when ready to interrupts CPU and CPU completes its current instruction and branches its control to interrupt service routine to service I/O device.

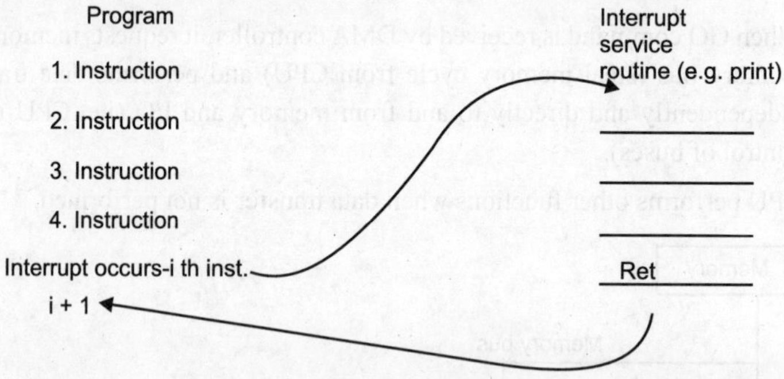

While interrupt occurs when CPU executing instruction, i, it completes it, then branches to service routine. When routine is executed, the control returns back to $(i+1)^{th}$ instruction.

Interrupt Handling

1. When device is ready to send / receive data, device activates interrupt request.
2. CPU interrupts program being executed, when CPU receives interrupt request.
3. Interrupts disabled
4. CPU acknowledges to device that it has received interrupt request signal.
5. CPU performs the operation needed for I/O device which interrupted CPU.
6. Enables interrupts.
7. CPU resumes execution of interrupted program.
8. The effect of interrupt request from device cause CPU to suspend its current program to be executed. However, arrival of interrupts should be controlled as they can arrive at any time.

i.e. CPU should ignore interrupt requests in certain situations, while program it is executing should not be interrupted until end instruction.

9. When interrupt occurs interrupt line is active, it should be deactivated as soon as CPU accepts request. Otherwise this single interrupt request is treated as erroneous multiple interrupt request and causes system to go into infinite loop. These problems, we can enable and disable interrupts as follows:

To overcome these problems, we can enable and disable interrupts as follows:

1. The first instruction is, disable interrupt in interrupt service routine and last would be enable interrupts. Thus, it ensures that CPU is not interrupted until it completes the service routine execution.
2. Before executing interrupt service routine, disable automatically all the interrupts. This is done by CPU, by setting the interrupt bit in program status (PS) register to disable interrupts and resets this bit to enable interrupts.

Interrupt request signal is accepted by CPU only when it raises from 0 to 1- level i.e. CPU responds to interrupt request only to leading edge of this signal.

Thus, single interrupt request signal cannot be treated as erroneous multiple requests.

7.4 DMA

DMA stands for Direct Memory Access. When the processor wishes to read or write a block of data, it issues a command to the DMA module. The following information is sent to the DMA module:

(*a*) Whether a read or write is requested.

(*b*) The address of the I/O device involved.

(*c*) Starting location in memory (to read from or write into).

(*d*) The number of words to be read or written.

The processor relinquishes (frees) the control of all three types of buses. It does some other work. So, now CPU has delegated the work of I/O to the DMA module. The DMA module transfers the entire block of data, one word at a time, directly to or from memory without going through the processor. When the transfer is complete, the DMA module sends an interrupt signal to the processor. **Please note here that the processor is involved only at the beginning and at the end of the transfer.** DMA module needs to take control of the bus to transfer data to and from memory. The processor pauses for one bus cycle i.e., the time it takes to transfer one word across the bus. **Also understand that the overall effect is to cause the processor to execute more slowly during a DMA transfer wl en processor access to the bus is required. DMA is (efficient) better for a multiple –word I/O transfer than interrupt-driven or programmed I/O.**

DMA module controls the exchange of data between the main memory and an I/O module over the system bus. It is shown in Fig. 7.6.

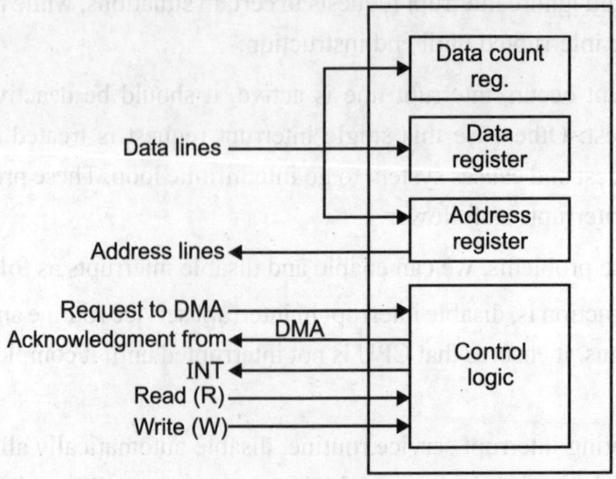

Fig. 7.6. Basic DMA Block Diagram

WORKING: When the processor wishes to read or write a block of data, it issues a command to the DMA module. The following information is sent to the DMA module:-

(*a*) Whether Read/Write is requested on R or W lines respectively (between processor and DMA module).

(*b*) Data lines (see figure 7.6) communicate the address of the I/O device involved.

(*c*) Starting address of memory location (from where read/write is to be done) is also communicated on the data lines and is stored in the Address register by the DMA module.

(*d*) Number of words to be read or written are again communicated via data lines only but stored in data count register.

The Processor now continues with other work. (Note that CPU should not be idle). When the transfer is complete, the DMA module sends an interrupt signal to the processor.

Applications of DMA

Figure 7.7 shows the role of DMA in a computer system.

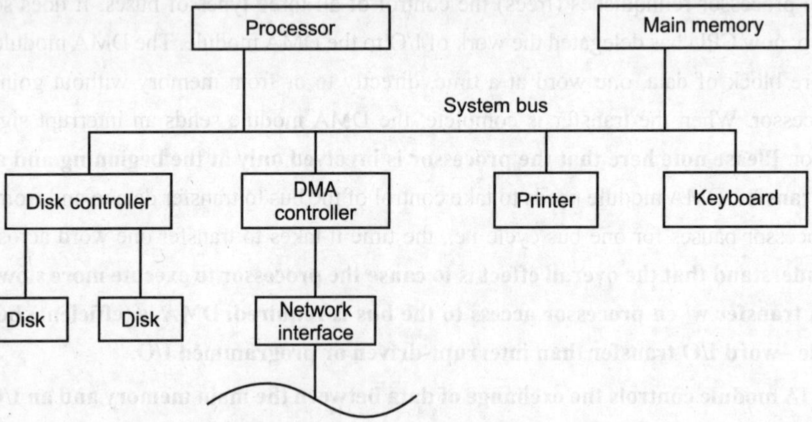

Fig. 7.7. Use of DMA controller

DMA is used to connect a high speed network to the system bus. DMA controller handles the data transfer between high speed network and the computer system. It is also used to transfer data between processor and floppy disk with the help of floppy disk controller (FDC).

Let us now see the working of DMA controller to transfer data between I/O device (like floppy, CDs etc) and the processor.

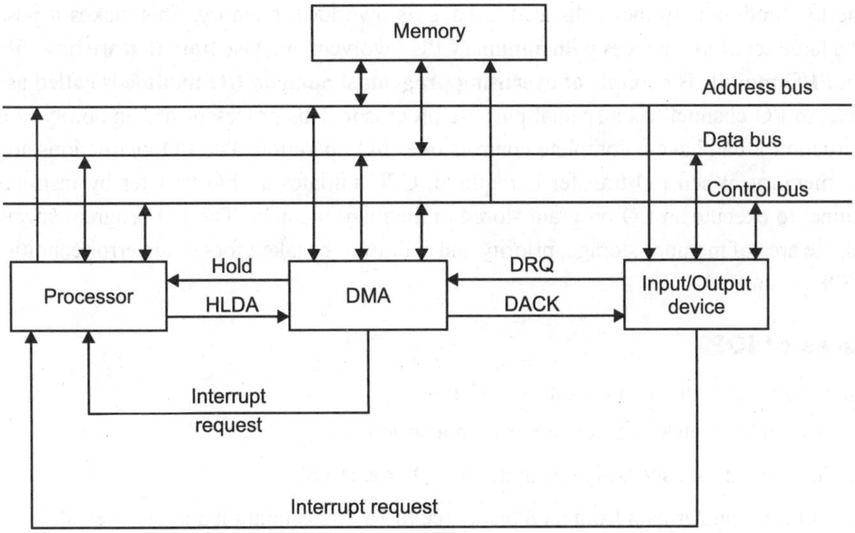

Fig. 7.8. Data transfer between I/O device and processor

When processor needs some data from the disk, it sends a series of command words to registers inside I/O device (like FDC of floppy disks or CDs etc). While the I/O device is busy, in the mean time, the processor loads the DMA data counter and address register.

Please remember that –

(*a*) The **data counter register** is loaded with count equal to the number of bytes to be transferred to or from the memory.

(*b*) The **address register** is loaded with the starting address of the memory.

When the controller reads the first byte of data from a sector, it sends DMA request (DRQ) signal to the DMA controller. DMA request sends a hold request signal to the HOLD input of the processor. The processor then floats (frees) its buses and sends a HOLD-acknowledgement signal to the DMA controller. The DMA controller then sends and the first transfer address on the bus and asserts the DACK′ input of the I/O device (say, FDC for example) to tell it that the DMA transfer is under way. When the number of bytes specified in the DMA controller initialization has been transferred, the DMA controller asserts the EOP′ (End-of-Process) signal which is connected to the TC (Terminal Count) input of the I/O device. This causes the I/O device to generate interrupt signal to tell the processor that the requested block of data has been read from disk to buffer in memory. In a similar fashion, d: a can be written into the disk.

7.5 I/O PROCESSOR (IOP) AND I/O CHANNELS

Usually, a peripheral device is controlled directly by the CPU. Then, a controller is added to CPU to control peripheral devices with some programming facility. Interrupts may be used here.

This saves CPU time that was required for polling of I/O device. DMA controller is introduced to give direct access to memory for I/O module. The I/O module is then enhanced to become a processor with a specialized instruction set tailored for I/O. **Please understand that an IOP is capable of executing an I/O program in memory as per the directions given by CPU. It can execute I/O program without CPU intervention**

The I/O module is further enhanced to have its own local memory. This makes it possible to control a large set of I/O devices with minimal CPU involvement. **Also note that we have observed here that I/O module is capable of executing programs. Such an I/O module is called as an I/O channel.** An I/O channel has a special purpose processor. This processor has an ability to execute I/O instruction it can have a complete controls over I/O operation. The I/O instructions are stored in main memory. When I/O transfer is required, CPU initiates an I/O transfer by instructing the I/O channel to execute an I/O program stored in the main memory. The I/O program specifies the devices, the area of memory storage, priority and actions to be taken for certain error conditions. For eg. IC 8089 is an IOP.

Features of IOP

The following are the main features of IOP –

1. An IOP can fetch and execute its own instructions.
2. Instructions are specially designed for I/O processing.
3. I/O can transfer data from an 8 bit source to 16 bit destination and vice versa.
4. IOP does all work involved in an I/O transfer like device setup, programmed I/O and DMA operation.
5. Communication between IOP and CPU is through, **memory based control blocks. CPU defines tasks in the control blocks to locate a program sequence called as a channel program.**
6. IOP supports **multiprocessing environments** also. Both CPU and IOP can do processing simultaneously.

7.6 SERIAL AND PARALLEL COMMUNICATION

Both serial and parallel means of data transfers are used by microprocessors.

But most microprocessors are designed for parallel communication. **In parallel communication, please remember the following points:-**

1. Number of lines required to transfer data depends on the number of bits to be transferred.
2. **All bits** are transferred at a time.
3. It is useful whenever data is to be transferred between nearby devices like **CPU and printer.**
4. The transfer process is very fast.

   For instance, to transfer 8 bits, 8 lines are required and all 8 bits will be transferred simultaneously.
5. It is more useful for small distances only.

In serial communication please remember the following points:

1. Data is transferred serially on a single line.

2. Same hardware configuration that was used for parallel transfer can be used for serial data transfers too.
3. **One bit** is transferred at a time over a single line.
4. The transfer process is slow.
5. Data transmission over a long distance is impractical and costlier as the increase in cabling increases its cost too.

For eg. Parallel communication is not useful for devices like tapes or a CRT terminal. For these devices serial communication is used.

Let us tabulate the differences between the two now.

Serial data transfer	Parallel data transfer
1. Only one bit of data is transferred at a time.	1. All bits (usually, 8 bits) are transferred at a time.
2. Only two lines are needed to connect.	2. 8 lines are required for 8 bit data.
3. Data transfer is slow.	3. Data transfer is fast.
4. It is useful for longer distances.	4. It is useful for shorter distances.
For e. g. Tapes and CRT terminal use serial communication.	For e.g. CPU and printer use parallel communication for data transfers.

Serial data communication may be in

(*a*) Simplex mode.

(*b*) Half duplex mode.

(*c*) Full duplex mode.

Simplex: Data transfer is in one direction

For e.g. Transmission from a computer to the printer.

Half Duplex: It allows data transfer in both the direction but not simultaneously.

For e.g. A walkie – talkie.

Full Duplex: It allows data transfer in both the directions simultaneously.

For e.g. Transmission through telephone lines.

Data transfer scheme may be –

(*a*) Asynchronous.

(*b*) Synchronous.

Let us summarize the differences between the two in a tabular form.

Asynchronous data transfer	Synchronous data transfer
1. It transfers only one character at a time.	1. It transfers a block of characters at a time
2. Start and stop bits are used for each character.	2. No start and stop bits are used.
3. Lesser speeds as more overheads are involved here	3. Higher speeds as overheads are spread over a frame (or packets of data bytes).
4. Two separate clock inputs are used for transmitter and receiver.	4. Only one clock is used for both transmitter and receiver.
5. It is used for data transfer rates $<= 20\ K$ bits per second.	5. It is used for data transfer rates $>=20\ K$ bits per second.

7.7 I/O AND MEMORY BUSES

CPU issues I/O command simultaneously, with address of device to which it is meant. The command decoder in interface module decodes and specified command is activated in interface logic. The I/O instruction format is as follows:

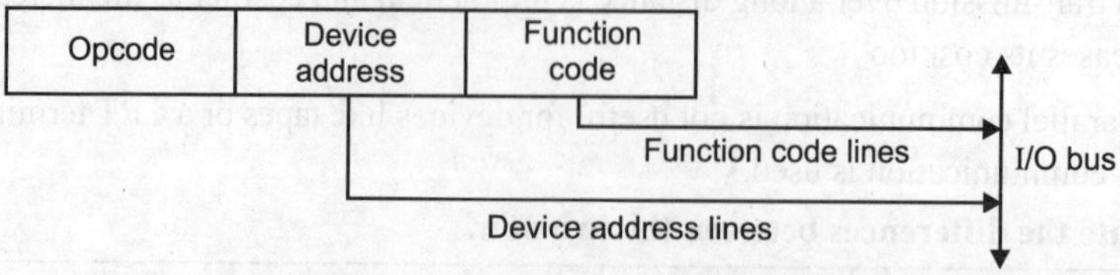

It consists of **opcode** which specifies that instruction an I/O instruction device address, which specify to which device, command is meant for and **function code** specifying command for I/O interface.

Types of I/O commands:

There are 4 types of I/O commands that an interface may receive when addressed by CPU. They are as follows:

1. **Control Command**

   This command issued to activate peripherals.

   E.g. Rewind tape for tape drives.

2. **Test Command**

   This is issued to interface by CPU to test the conditions of I/O device and conditions in interface, such as buffer full, device not ready etc.

3. **Data Output Command**

   (*a*) Issued by CPU to interface when it outputs data to peripheral.

   (*b*) Interface accepts data from I/O bus and stores in buffer register for peripheral.

4. **Data Input Command**

   (*a*) Issued by CPU when it wants to input data from peripheral.

   (*b*) Interface receives data from peripheral and stores in buffer register for CPU.

7.8 I/O INTERFACING TECHNIQUES

Many processors (microprocessors) isolate memory and I/O system. It partitions memory from I/O using software's. This software has instructions that specifically address memory and other instruction that specifically access I/O. **Please understand that when these instructions are decoded by the processor, an appropriate control signal is generated to activate either memory or I/O operation.** So I/O devices can be interfaced to a computer system's I/O in two ways-

(*a*) Memory mapped I/O.

(*b*) I/O mapped I/O.

In 8085, for instance, this is done by the M/IO signal pin on its IC.

Note: In 8085,

(*a*) M/IO′ = 1 means processor is communicating with memory.

(*b*) M/IO′ = 0 means processor is communicating with I/O.

Let us study these two techniques now.

I. Memory – mapped I/O

A method in which the total memory address space is partitioned is shown in Fig. 7.9

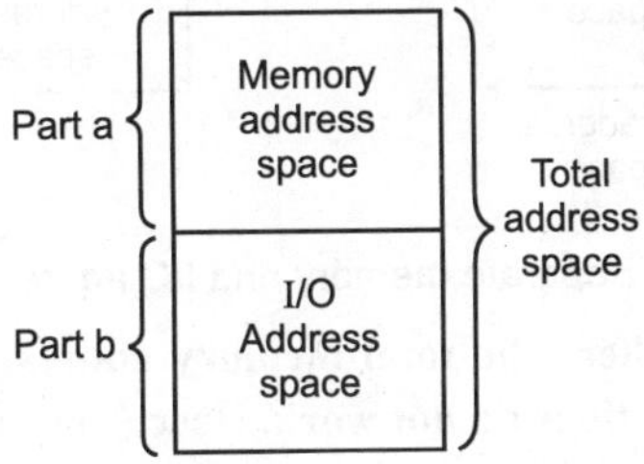

Fig. 7.9. Division of total address space

In this technique, a memory reference instruction that causes data to be fetched from or stored at the address specified, automatically becomes an I/O instruction if that address is made an address of an I/O port. The usual memory related instructions are used for I/O related operations. The special I/O instructions are not required. **Please remember the following points regarding memory mapped I/O:-**

1. I/O devices, here, are treated as memory locations.
2. There will be no separation like memory or I/O.
3. Each I/O device will have 16 bit address.
4. The control signals used will be the same as memory (MEMR' and MEMW').
5. Interfacing between the I/O and processor will be same as single memory location.
6. The number of device I/O will be 64 K, (shared by I/O and memory).

We now draw, Fig. 7.10 that show programmed I/O with memory mapped I/O.

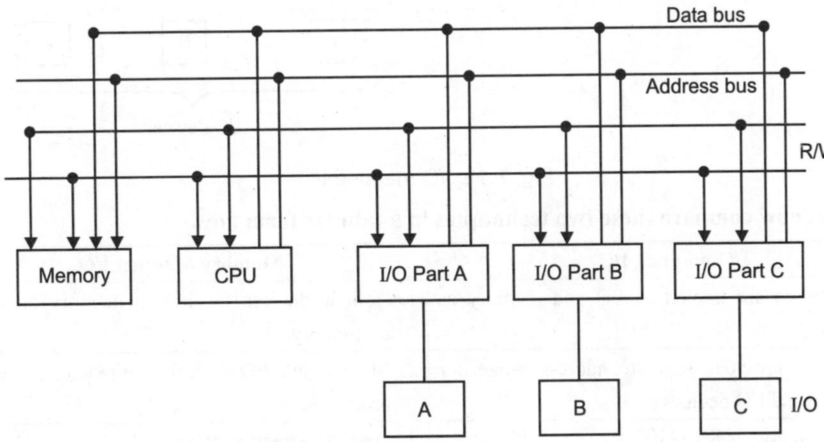

Fig 7.10

II. I/O Mapped I/O

When we divide the total address space as in method-I we are actually reducing memory address space. To avoid this reduction, we allocate a different I/O address space. This is shown in Fig 7.11.

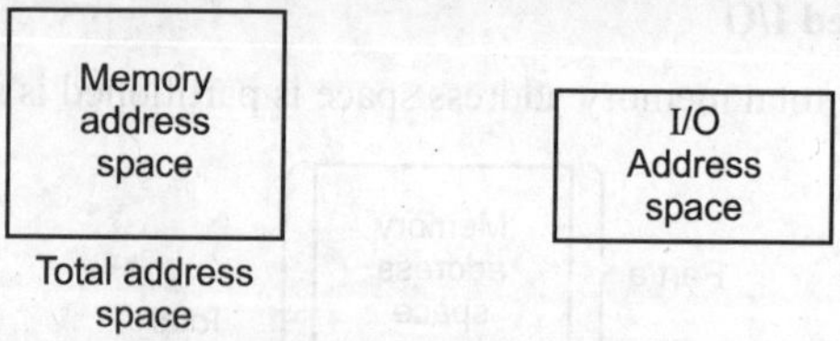

Fig 7.11. Separate memory and I/O address space

Please note that although here the total memory address space has not been used but now the memory related instructions do not work. Hence, the processor can only use this mode. Hence, the processor can only use this mode if it has special instructions for I/O related operation (like I/O read, I/O write etc). **Also note the following points regarding I/O Mapped I/O:-**

1. Here, the I/O device is treated as I/O device only.
2. Each I/O device uses 8 bits of address lines.
   Hence, $2^8 = 256$ I/O devices can be connected to the system.
3. 256 input and 256 output devices can be connected. We now draw Fig. 7.12 that shows programmed I/O with I/O mapped I/O.

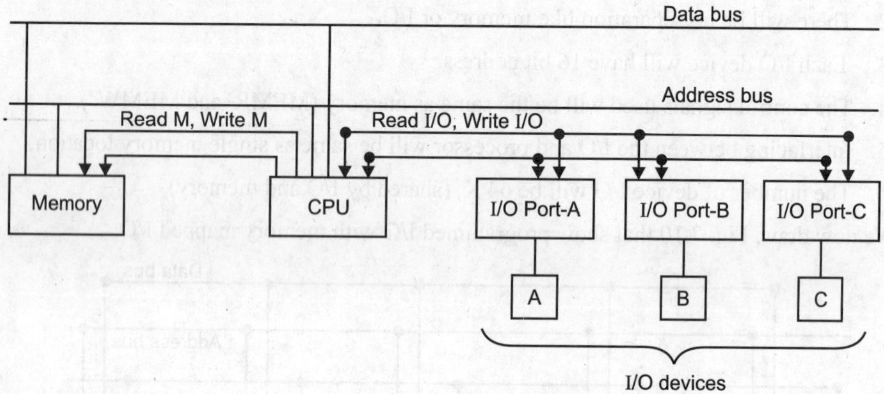

Fig. 7.12. I/O mapped I/O

Let us now compare these two techniques in a tabular form now.

I/O mapped I/O	Memory Mapped I/O
1. I/O devices are treated as I/O and memory as memory.	1. Both the devices (i.e., I/O and memory) are treated as memory.
2. Processor provides separate address range for memory and I/O devices.	2. Memory and I/O share the entire address range of processor.
3. Device address is 8/16 bits.	3. Device address is 20 bits.
4. Processor provides less address lines for accessing I/O hence, less decoding is required.	4. Processor provides more address lines for accessing memory. So, more decoding is required.

I/O mapped I/O	Memory Mapped I/O
5. Control signals used for I/O are IOR′ and IOW′.	5. Control signals used for I/O are MEMR′ and MEMW′.
6. Special instructions like IN and OUT are used.	6. All memory related instruction can be used to communicate with I/O.
7. Data transfers between accumulator and I/O devices is allowed.	7. Data transfer is possible between any register and I/O.
8. Lesser hardware is required as only 8/16 bits of address decoding is required.	8. More hardware is required as 20 bits address decoding is needed.
9. Arithmetic and logical operations are not possible with direct data from I/O devices.	9. Arithmetic and logical operations can be performed on direct data from I/O device.
10. Total number of devices that can be connected are – 1 MB memory. 65,535 (max) input devices. 65,535 (max) output devices.	10. Total number of devices that can be connected will be only 1 MB as it is shared between memory and I/O.

III. Interrupt – Driven I/O

In this method, the processor initiates the I/O device to get ready. Then it executes its main program instead of remaining in a program loop to check the status of the I/O device. **Please understand that whenever an I/O device is ready for the data transfer, an interrupt signal is sent to the processor.** When the processor is interrupted, it stops the execution of the program and transfers control to the **ISR (Interrupt Service Routine)**. ISR performs the data transfer. **Also understand that after the data transfer is over, the control is returned to the point where it was interrupted. ISR is different from a normal subroutine** because the address of ISR is predefined or it is available in **Interrupt Vector Table (IVT),** whereas a subroutine address is to be given in subroutine's CALL instruction. **Please note that IRET instruction is used to return from the ISR whereas RET instruction is used to return from subroutine. Also note that IRET instruction restores flag contents along with CS and IP, whereas RET instruction restores only CS and IP Contents.**

DO YOU KNOW?

A normal program can be interrupted by three (3) methods –

- By external signal.
- By a special program's instruction.
- By the occurrence of some condition.

SUMMARY

The messiest aspect of computer architecture design is the design of I/O. This is because of the availability of wide variety of I/O devices. I/O interface is a hardware component. Asynchronous data transfers include two methods- strobe control and handshaking. We have also studied about the three ways of data transfers between I/O and memory. We found that the process where a memory cycle is taken by DMA from CPU is known as **cycle stealing.** We also learnt that if a system consists of both CPU and IOP, then CPU acts as a master processor and IOP is a slave processor.

MULTIPLE CHOICE QUESTIONS [MCQs]

Q. 1. A circuit between peripheral and processor used to transfer data is known as –

(*a*) Interface (*b*) Poll (*c*) IOP (*d*) None of the above

Ans. (*a*)

Q. 2. During DMA transfer, which of the following techniques is used –?

(*a*) Memory stealing. (*b*) Memory leakage.

(*c*) Cycle stealing. (*d*) None of the above

Ans. (*c*)

Q. 3. Cycle stealing transfers –

(*a*) Half data word. (*b*) One block of data.

(*c*) One byte of data at a time. (*d*) None of the above.

Ans . (*c*)

Q. 4. During DMA transfers, CPU relinquishes the control of –

(*a*) IOP (*b*) Printers

(*c*) Data and address bus. (*d*) None of the above

Ans. (*c*)

Q. 5. An interrupt in which the branch address is assigned to a fixed location in memory is known as –

(*a*) Non- vectored interrupt (*b*) Vectored interrupt.

(*c*) Maskable interrupt (*d*) None of the above

Ans. (*a*)

Q. 6. The interrupt that can be masked is called as-

(*a*) NMI (*b*) Maskable Interrupt

(*c*) Software Interrupt (*d*) None of the above.

Ans. (*b*)

Q. 7. An interrupt to read input from the keyboard is an example of a-

(*a*) Software Interrupt (*b*) Hardware Interrupt

(*c*) NMI (*d*) None of the above

Ans. (*a*)

Q. 8 Transmission through telephone lines is an example of –

(*a*) Simplex mode (*b*) Half duplex mode

(*c*) Full duplex mode (*d*) None of the above

Ans. (*c*)

Q. 9. In I/O Mapped I/O, device address is-

(*a*) 16/32 bits. (*b*) 8/16 bits.

(*c*) 20 bits. (*d*) 40 bits.

Ans. (*b*)

Q. 10. In memory mapped I/O, device address is-

(*a*) 20 bits (*b*) 40 bits (*c*) 80 bits (*d*) 120 bits

Ans. (*a*)

Q. 11. To return from ISR, we use –

(*a*) RET instruction (*b*) CALL instruction

(*c*) IRET instruction. (*d*) JMP instruction.

Ans. (*c*)

Q. 12. An example of Intel's IOP is –

(*a*) 8085 (*b*) 8086 (*c*) 8087 (*d*) 8089

Ans. (*d*)

CONCEPTUAL SHORT QUESTIONS WITH ANSWERS

Q. 1 Compare the three data transfer techniques in a tabular form.

Ans.

Programmed Mode	Interrupt Mode	DMA Mode
1. To check device ready status, the I/O routine software will loop on.	Here, the device controller hardware raises interrupt.	Here, the device controller hardware raises DMA request.
2. To read from or write to the device controller, it used INPUT or OUTPUT instructions in the I/O routine.	It also uses INPUT or OUTPUT instruction in the I/O routine.	It uses DMA ACK Signal from DMA controller along with IOR/ IOW.
3. To read from or write data to memory Move (or Load) instruction is used in the I/O routine.	To read from or write data to memory, move instruction is used in the I/O routine.	Here, memory write or read operation is done by DMA.
4. I/O routine generates addresses of memory locations.	I/O routine generates addresses of memory locations.	DMA controller generates address of memory locations
5. I/O routine indicates end of data transfer.	I/O routine shows end of data transfer.	DMA controller shows end of data transfer.

Q. 2. Distinguish between data channel and DMA controller.

Ans. Let us tabulate the differences.

Data Channel	DMA Controller
1. It fetches the command parameters from the main memory.	1. The software issues these parameters to the different registers of DMA controller.
2. It accepts data from memory/ I/O controller and then issues it to the I/O controller/memory.	2. It coordinates the data transfer between the memory and the I/O controller.
3. It provides a buffer of one word.	3. Data does not pass through the DMA controller.
4. It performs error checking.	4. It doesn't perform any error checking.
5. It is a costlier device.	5. It is a low cost, LSI chip.

Q. 3. DMA uses three different data transfer schemes. What are they? Discuss each scheme. [UPTU, BE (CSE) – 4th Sem. 2001, 2002, 2003, 2004, 2005, 2006, 2007, 2008, 2009, 2010, 2011]

Ans. DMA uses three different data transfer schemes –

(*a*) Burst mode DMA transfer.

(*b*) Cycle stealing.

(*c*) Transparent (or hidden) DMA.

Let us explain these one by one now.

I. Burst- mode/ Block- mode transfer DMA

In this technique, two or more data bytes are transferred continuously. The processor is disconnected from the system bus during DMA transfer. **Plea0se note that it means that the MicroProcessor cannot execute its own program during this transfer. Also note that n- number of DMA cycles is added into the machine cycles of the microprocessor where 'n' denotes the number of bytes to be transferred.** The algorithm is very simple:

1 The DMA controller sends HOLD signal to the process and waits for HLDA (Hold-acknowledge) signal.

2 After receiving HLDA signal, the DMA controller gains control of the system bus and executes a DMA cycle to transfer one byte.

3 After the transfer of one byte, it increments the memory address and decrements counter and transfers next byte.

4 Repeat steps 1 to 3, till all data bytes are transferred between memory and I/O devices.

5 After all bytes of data have been transferred, the DMA controller disables HOLD signal and enters into slave mode. It is the fastest DMA mode.

II. Cycle stealing/Single-byte transfer mode

The process of taking (or stealing) memory cycle from CPU by DMA is known as cycle stealing.

Basic principle

"The DMA controller transfers one data word at a time returns the control of buses to CPU. The CPU merely delays its operation for one memory cycle to allow the direct memory I/O transfer to steal one memory cycle".

Only one byte is transferred at a time. **It is slower than the burst mode of transfer because only one DMA cycle is added between two machine cycles of the processor.** The algorithm is very simple:-

1. The DMA controller sends HOLD signal to the processor and waits for HLDA signal.
2. After receiving HLDA signal, the DMA controller gains control of the system bus and execute only one DMA cycle.
3. After the transfer of one byte. It disable HOLD signal and enters into slave mode.
4. The CPU now gains the control of the system bus and executes next machine cycle. If the count is not zero and next data is available then DMA controller sends HOLD signal to the processor and transfer next byte of data block.

III. Hidden/Transparent Mode

In this mode, CPU executes some states during which it floats the address and data buses. During these states, CPU is isolated from the system bus. The DMA controller transfers data between memory and I/O devices during these states and this operation is transparent to the processor. **This is the slowest DMA transfer mode because it requires some logic to detect the states when the processor is floating the buses.**

NOTE: In this mode, the instruction execution speed of processor is not reduced.

Q. 4. Distinguish between external and internal interrupts.

Ans. The differences are tabulated below:

External Interrupts	Internal Interrupts
1. The interrupts generated by the hardware circuits outside the CPU are known as **external interrupts.**	1. The interrupts generated within the CPU are known as **internal interrupts.**
2. These are basically hardware interrupts.	2. These may be hardware or software interrupts.
3. The hardware interrupts are generated by the circuits	3. The software interrupts generated by an instruction in the program.
Example are – A power sensing circuit may generate an external interrupts. Console switch may generate an external interrupt Timer counter generates timer interrupt when its count reaches zero.	**Examples are –** Divide-by-Zero. Stack overflow. Protection violation All these will generate internal interrupts.

Q. 5. Compare hardware interrupt and software interrupt in a tabular form.

Ans. The differences are as follows:

Software Interrupt	Hardware Interrupt
1. It is a synchronous event.	1. It is an asynchronous event.
2. An interrupt that is requested by executing an instruction (software)	2. An interrupt that is requested by external device.
3. Here, program counter PC is incremented.	3. Here, PC is not incremented.
4. It cannot be ignored or masked.	4. It can be masked.
5. It is used in program debugging and does not improve system throughput.	5. It is used to interface peripheral in interrupt driven I/O and improves through put of the system.

Q. 6. Compare Non -Maskable (NMI) and maskable interrupts (MI).

Ans. The differences are as follows:

NMI	MI
1. It cannot be ignored or masked.	1. It can be ignored or masked.
2. It has a higher priority.	2. It has a lower priority.
3. Its response time is low.	3. Its response time is high.
4. During power failures, smoke detection etc, it is used.	4. It is used to interface peripherals.

Q. 7. How many character per second can be transmitted over a 1200 band line in each of the following modes (Assume a character code of eight bits):

(*a*) Synchronous Serial Transmission.

(*b*) Asynchronous Serial Transmission with two stop bits.

(*c*) Asynchronous serial transmission with one stop bit?

[GGSIPU, B. Tech (CS E) – 5th sem., Dec. 2008]

Ans. (*a*) 1200/8 = 150 Characters/second (cps).

(*b*) 1200/ (8+1(start-bit) + 2(stop-bits) = 1200/11 = 109 cps.

(*c*) 1200/ (8+1(start-bit) + 1(stop-bit) = 1200/10 = 120 cps.

Q. 8. Give peripheral devices that produce an acceptable output for a person to understand.

Ans. The list is as follows-

1. Printers (all types).
2. Digital plotter.
3. Graphics display.
4. Voice output.
5. DAC – Digital- to- Analog converter.

Q. 9. Indicate whether the following constitute a control, status or data transfer commands –

(*a*) skip next instruction if flag is set.

(*b*) seek a given record on a magnetic disk.

(*c*) check if I/O device is ready.

(*d*) move printer paper to beginning of next page.

(*e*) read interface status register.

Ans.

(*a*) **Status command.** It checks the status of flag bit.

(*b*) **Control command.** It moves magnetic head in disk.

(*c*) **Status command.** It checks if device power is ON.

(*d*) **Control command.** It moves the paper position.

(*e*) **Data input command.** It reads a value of a register.

Q. 10. Give six status conditions for the setting of individual bits in the status register of an asynchronous communication interface.

Ans. The six (6) status conditions are as follows –

1. Output flag to indicate when transmission register is empty.
2. Input flag to indicate when receiver register is full.
3. Enable interrupt if any flag is set.
4. Parity error.
5. Framing error.
6. Overrun error.

Q. 11. Information is inserted into a FIFO buffer at a rate of *m*- bytes per second. The information is deleted at a rate of n byte per second. The maximum capacity of the buffer is k- bytes.

(*a*) How long does it take for an empty buffer to fill up when $m>n$?

(*b*) How long does it take for a full buffer to empty when $m<n$?

(*c*) Is the FIFO buffer needed if $m = n$?

Ans. (*a*) $\frac{k \text{ bytes}}{(m-n) \text{ bytes/sec}} = \frac{k}{m-n \text{ sec.}} = k/_{m-n}$ secs.

(*b*) $m/m-n$ sec.

(*c*) No need for FIFO.

Q. 12. In most computers an interrupt is recognized only after the execution of the instruction. Consider the possibility of acknowledging the interrupt of any time during the execution of an instruction. Discuss the difficulty that may arise.

Ans. If an interrupt is recognized in the middle of an instruction execution, it is necessary to save all of the information from control register in addition to the processor register. The state of the CPU to be saved is more complex.

Q. 13. Consider a computer without a priority interrupt hardware. Any one of many sources can interrupt the computer and any interrupt request results in storing the return address and branching to a common interrupt routine. Explain how a priority can be established in ISR.

Ans. The service routine checks the flags in sequence to determine which one is set. The first flag that is checked has the highest priority level. The priority level of the other sources corresponds to the order is which the flags are checked.

Q. 14. What programming steps are required to check when a source interrupts the computer while it is still being serviced by a pervious interrupt request from the same source?

Ans. We set the MASK bit belonging to the interrupt source. So, it can interrupt again. At the beginning of the service routine check the value of the return address within the source service program, then the same source has interrupted again while being serviced.

Q. 15. Why are read and write control lines in a DMA controller bidirectional? Under what conditions and for what purpose are they used as outputs?

Ans. During CPU and DMA controller's communication, the read and write lines are used as inputs from the CPU to the DMA controller. But when the DMA controller communicates with memory then the read and writes lines are used as outputs from DMA to memory.

Q. 16. A DMA controller transfers 16 bit words to memory using cycle stealing. The words are assembled from a device that transmits characters at a rate of 2400 cps. The CPU is fetching and executing instruction at an average rate of 1 million instructions per second. By how much will the CPU be slowed down because of the DMA transfer?

Ans. Now, CPU refers to memory (on average once or more) every 1 μsec ($1/10^6$)

Characters arrive one every 1/2400 = **416.6 μsec**

Two characters of 8 bits each are packed into a 16 bit word every 2x416.6 = **833.3 μsec.**

So, CPU is slowed down by –

$= 1/833.3 \times 100\%$

$= 0.12\%$ (Ans)

Q. 17. Why does DMA have priority over the CPU when both request a memory transfer?

Ans. The CPU can wait to fetch instructions and data from memory without any damage occurring except loss of time. DMA usually transfer data from a device that cannot be stopped since information continues to flow so loss of data may occur.

Q. 18. The address of terminal connected to a data communication processor consists of two letters of the alphabet or a letter followed by one of the 10 numerals. How many different addresses can be formulated.

Ans. There are 26 letters and 10 numerals.

Address that can be formed = (26*26) + (26*10)

= (676 + 260)

= 936 addresses.

Q. 19. List a possible line procedure and the character sequence for the communication between a data communication processor and a remote terminal. The processor inquires if the terminal is operative. The terminal responds with yes or no. If the response is yes, the processor sends a block of text.

Ans. The processor transmits the address of the terminal followed by ENQ (enquiry) code – 00000101. The terminal responds with either ACK (acknowledge) or NAK (Negative acknowledge) or the terminal does not responds during a timeout period. If the processor receives an ACK, it sends a block of text.

Q. 20. A data communication link employs the character controlled protocol with data transparency using the DLE character. The text message that the transmitter sends between STX and ETX is as follows:

DLE STX DLE DLE ETX DLE DLE ETX DLE ETX

What is the binary value of the transparent text data?

Ans. DLE STX DLE DLE ETX DLE DLE ETX DLE ETX i.e.,

Delete STX delete DLE ETX delete DLE ETX delete ETX

So, 32-bit text is as follows:

$(0001\ 0000\ 1000\ 0011\ 0001\ 0000\ 1000\ 0011)_2$

Q. 21. What is the minimum number of bits that a frame must have in the bit oriented protocol?

Ans. 32 bits between two flags and 48 bits including the flags.

Q. 22. Show how the zero insertion word in the bit- oriented protocol, when a zero followed by the 10 bits, that represents the binary equivalent of 1023 are transmitted.

Ans. Information to be sent (1023) is

$(01111111111)_2$

After zero insertion, information transmitted is – $(011111011111 0)_2$

And, information received after detection is – $(01111111111)_2$

Q. 23. The addresses assigned to the four registers of the I/O interface of figure given below are equal to the binary equivalent of 12, 13, 14 and 15. Show the external circuit that must be connected between an 8-bit I/O address from the CPU and the CS, RS1 and RS0 inputs of the interface.

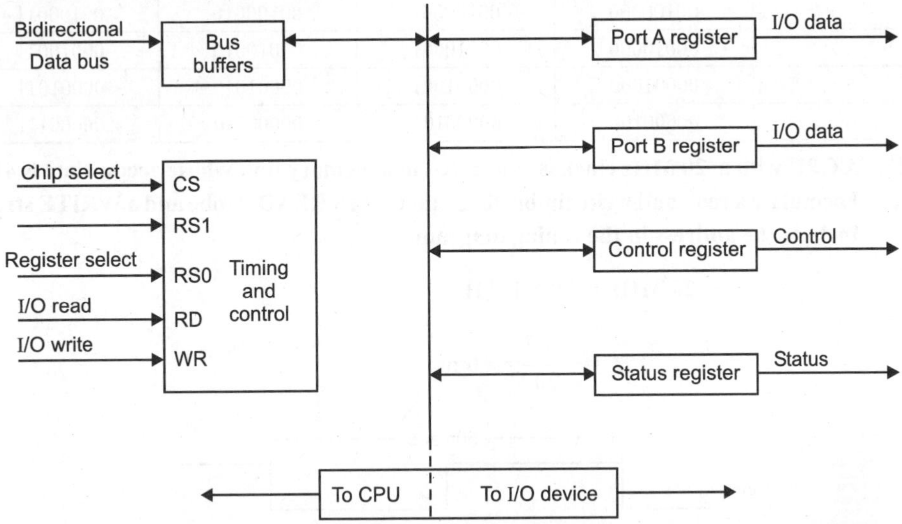

CS	RS1	RS0	Register Selected
0	X	X	None: data bus in high impedance
1	0	0	Port A register
1	0	1	Port B register
1	1	0	Control Register
1	1	1	Status register

$A_7 \; - A_2 \, A_1 \, A_0$

12 = 0 0 0 0 1 1 0 0 $\quad$ $CS = A_2 \, A_3 \, A'_4 \, A'_5 A'_6 A'_7$

13 = 0 0 0 0 1 1 0 1 $\quad$ $RS1 = A_1$

14 = 0 0 0 0 1 1 1 0 $\quad$ $RS0 = A_0$

15 = 0 0 0 0 1 1 1 1

To CS $\quad$ RS1 RS0

Q. 24. Six interface units of the type shown in figure given in Q 23 are connected to CPU that uses an I/O address of eight bits. Each one of the six chip select (CS) inputs is connected to i different address lines. Thus the high order address line is connected to the CS input of the first interface unit and the sixth address line is connected to the CS input of the sixth interface unit. The two low order address lines are connected to the RS1 and RS0 of all six interface units. Determine the 8 Bit address of each register in each interface.

Ans.

Interface	Part A	Part B	Control Reg.	Status Reg.
1	10000000	10000001	10000010	10000011
2	01000000	01000001	01000010	01000011
3	00100000	00100001	00100010	00100011
4	00010000	00010001	00010010	00010011
5	00001000	00001001	00001010	00001011
6	00000100	00000101	00000110	00000111

Q. 25. A CPU with a 20 MHz clock is connected to a memory unit whose access time is 40ns. Formulate a read and write timing diagram using a READ strobe and a WRITE strobe. Include the address in the timing diagram.

$$20 \text{ MHz} = 20 \times 10^6 \text{ Hz}$$

$$T = \frac{10^{-6}}{20} = 50 \text{ ns}$$

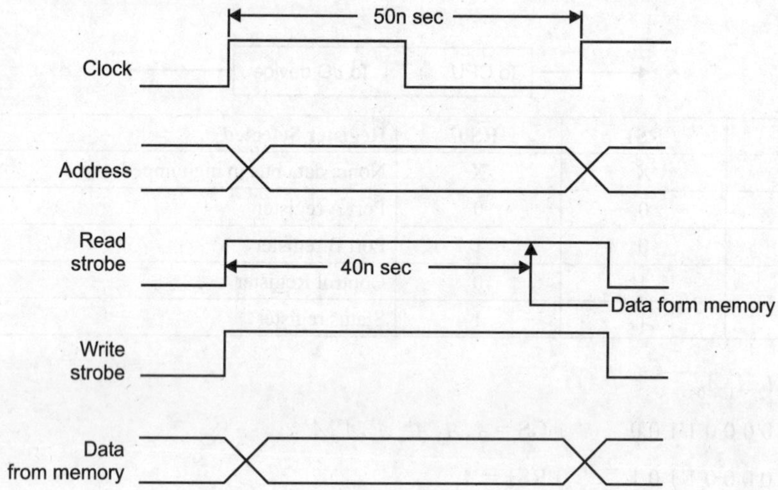

Q. 26. The asynchronous communication interface shown in the figure given below is connected between a CPU and a printer. Draw a flowchart that describes the sequence of operations in the transmitter portion of the interface when the CPU sends characters to be printed.

CS	RS	Operation	Register Selected
0	X	x	None: data bus in high impedance
1	0	WR	Transmitter register
1	1	WR	Control Register
1	0	RD	Receiver Register
1	1	RD	Status Register

Block diagram of a typical asynchronous communication interface is on next page.

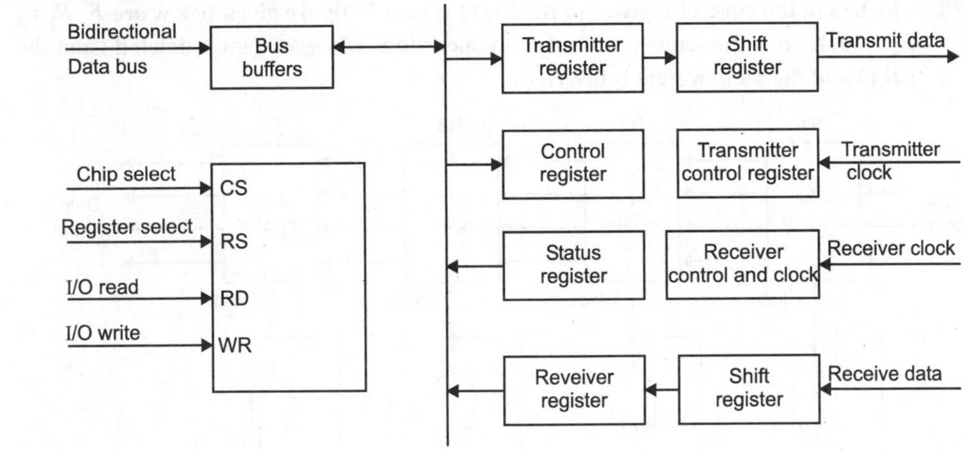

Ans. Output flag is a bit in status register.

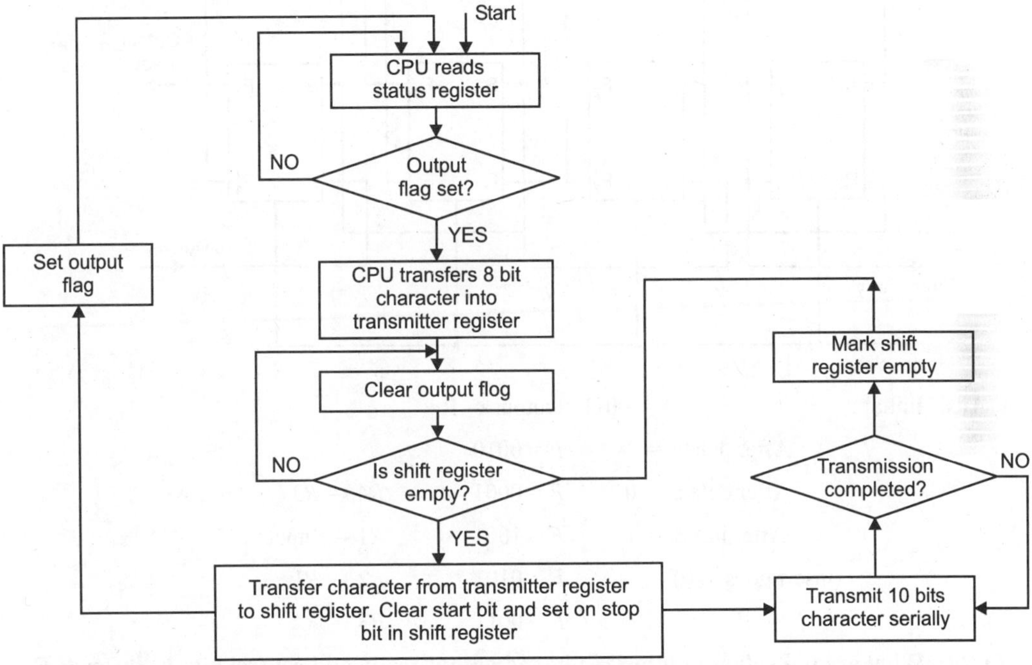

Q. 27. How many bits are there in the transmitter shift register of figure given in Q. 26 when the interface is attached to terminal that needs one stop bit? List the bits in the shift register when the letter *W* is transmitted using ASCII with even parity.

Ans. 10 Bits : Start bit + 7 ASCII + parity + stop bit.

From table in Q 26 ASCII $W = 1010111$

With even parity = 11010111

With start and stop bits = 1110101110

Q. 28. The bits in the control register of the FIFO shown in figure given below are F_1 F_2 F_3 F_4 = 0011. Give the sequence of internal operations when an item is deleted from the FIFO and then a new item is inserted.

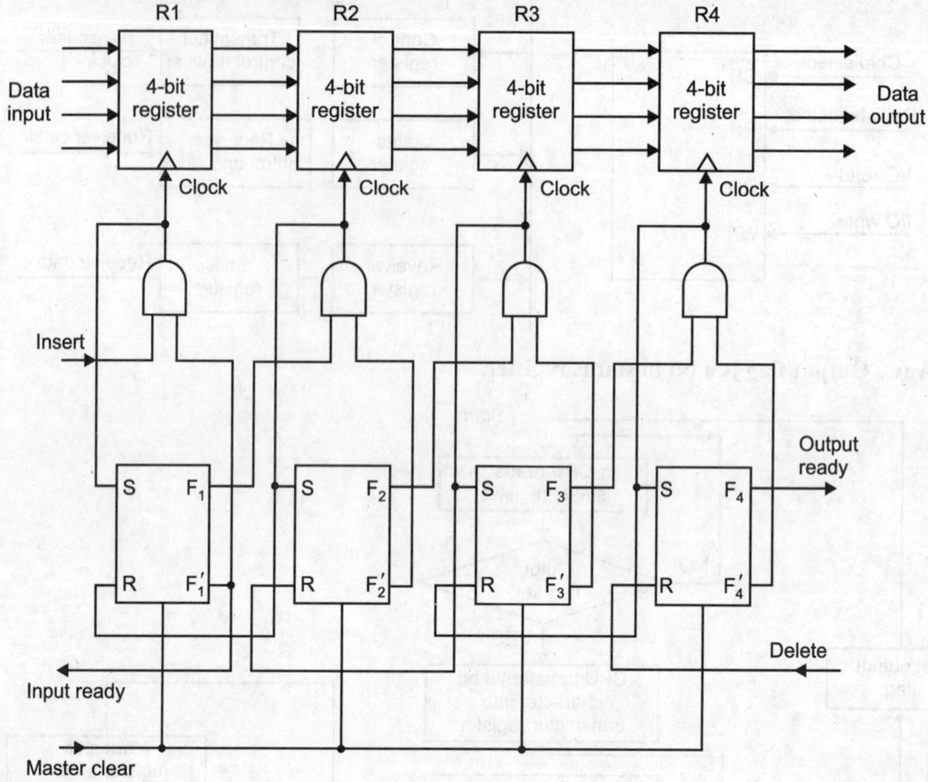

Ans. Initial F = 0011 Output ← R4

After delete = 1	$F = 0010$	
After delete = 0	$F = 0001$	$R4 \leftarrow R3$
After insert = 1	$F = 1001$	$R1 \leftarrow$ Input
(insert goes to 0)	$F = 0101$	$R2 \leftarrow R1$
	$F = 0011$	$R3 \leftarrow R2$

Q. 29. What are the values of input ready and output ready and control bits F_1 through F_4 in figure given in Q. 29 when

(*a*) The buffer is empty?

(*b*) The buffer is full?

(*c*) The buffer contains two data items?

Ans.

	Input ready	Output ready	$F_1 - F_4$
(*a*) Empty buffer	1	0	0000
(*b*) Full buffer	0	1	1111
(*c*) Two items	1	1	0011

Q. 30. Show a block diagram similar to figure given below for the data transfer from a CPU to an interface and then to an I/O device. Determine a procedure for setting and cleaning the flag bit.

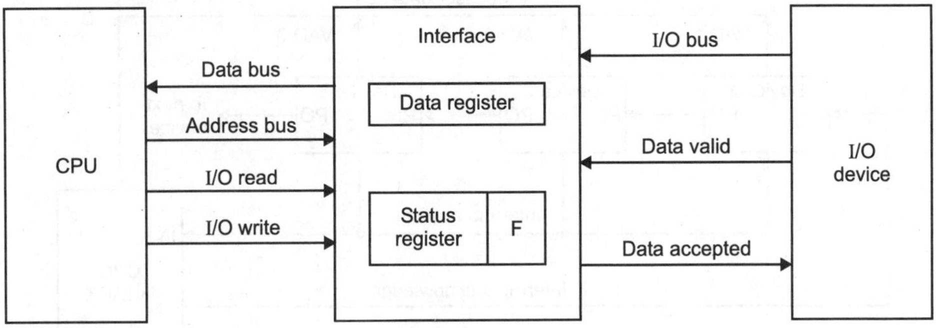

Fig. 7.13. Data transfer from I/o device to CPU

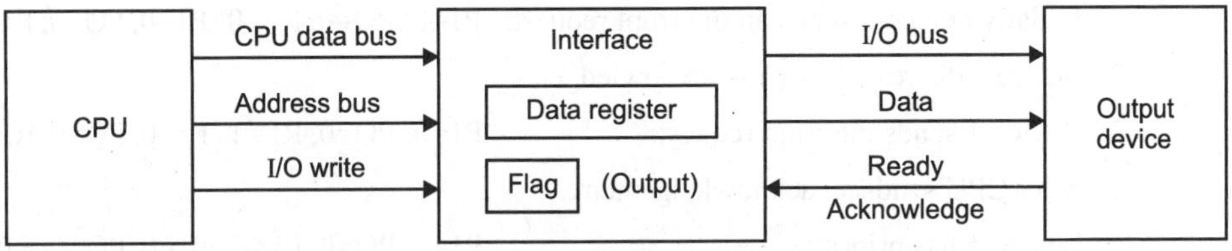

Ans. Flag = 0 if data registered full (After CPU writes data)

Flag = 1 if data register empty (After the transfer to device)

When flag goes to 0, enable "Data ready" and place data on I/O bus. When "Acknowledge" is enabled, set the flag to 1 and disable "ready" handshake line.

Q. 31. Using the configuration established in Prob. 30, obtain a flowchart for the CPU program to output data.

CPU program flow chart:

Ans.

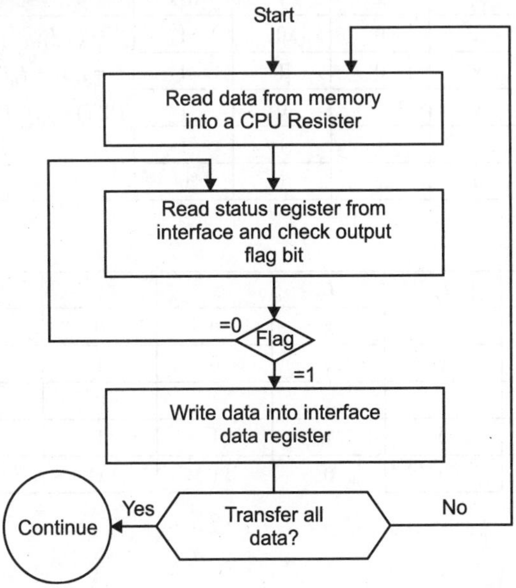

Q. 32. What happen in the daisy chain priority interrupt shown in figure given below when device 1 requests an interrupt after device 2 has sent an interrupt request to the CPU but before the CPU responds with the Interrupt Acknowledge?

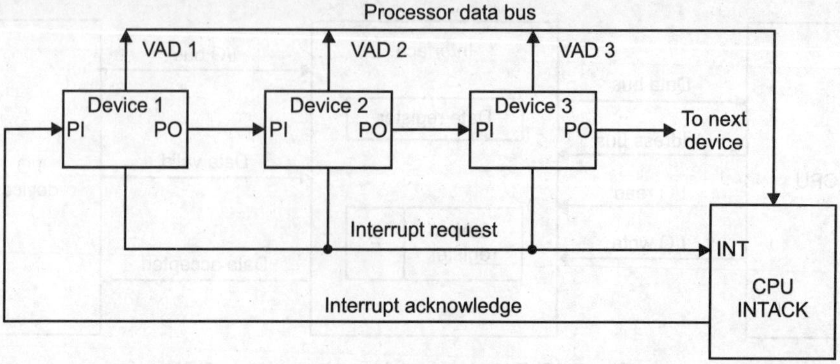

Ans.

	Device 1	Device 2
1. Initially device-2 sends an interrupt request:	P1=0, PO=0, RF=0	P1=0, PO=0, RF=1
2. Before CPU responds with acknowledge, Device-1 sends interrupt request:	P1=0, PO=0, RF=1	P1=0, PO=0, RF=1
4. After CPU sends an acknowledgement, Device-1 has priority:	P1=1, PO=0, RF=1	P1=0, PO=0, RF=1
	VAD enable =1	VAD enable =0

Q. 33. Using combinational circuit design techniques derive the Boolean expressions in table given below for the priority encoder. Draw the logic diagram of the circuit.

Table priority encoder truth table

Inputs				Outputs			Boolean functions
I_o	I_1	I_2	I_3	x	y	IST	
1	x	x	x	0	0	1	$X = I'_0 I'_1$
0	1	x	x	0	1	1	$Y = I'_0 I_1 + I'_0 I'_2$
0	0	1	x	1	0	1	$(\text{IST}) = I_0 + I_1 + I_2 + I_3$
0	0	0	1	1	1	1	
0	0	0	0	x	x	0	

Ans.

I_o	I_1	I_2	I_3	x	y	IST
1	x	x	x	0	0	1
0	1	x	x	0	1	1
0	0	1	x	1	0	1
0	0	0	1	1	1	1
0	0	0	0	x	x	0

Hence, map simplification is as follows:

$x = I'_0 I'_1$ $\qquad$ $y = I'_0 I_1 + I'_0 I'_2$

Q. 34. Design parallel priority interrupt hardware for system with 8 interrupt sources.

Ans. It is given in the figure below, needs 8 AND gates and an 8 × 3 decoder.

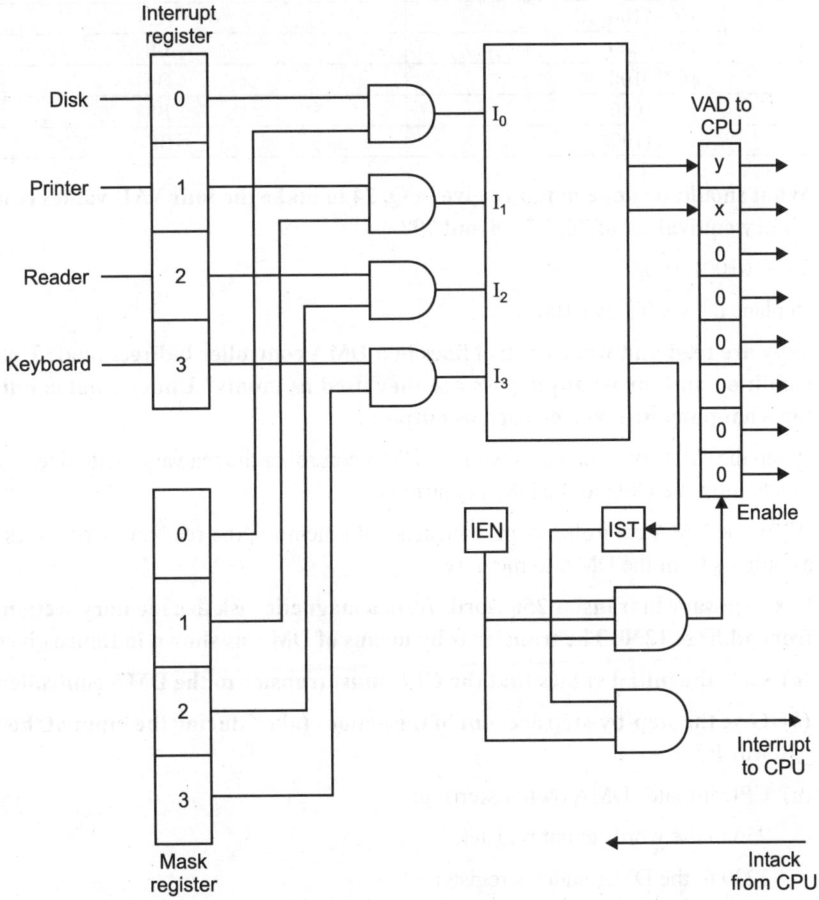

Q. 35. Obtain the truth table of an 8x3 priority encoder. Assume that the three outputs *xyz* from the priority encoder are used to provide a vector address of the form 101*xyz*00. List the eight vector addresses starting from the one with the highest priority.

Ans. (*a*)

I_0	I_1	I_2	I_3	I_4	I_5	I_6	I_7	*xyz*	IST
1	*x*	*x*	*x*	*x*	*x*	*x*	*x*	000	1
0	1	*x*	*x*	*x*	*x*	*x*	*x*	001	1
0	0	1	*x*	*x*	*x*	*x*	*x*	010	1
0	0	0	1	*x*	*x*	*x*	*x*	011	1
0	0	0	0	1	*x*	*x*	*x*	100	1
0	0	0	0	0	1	x	x	101	1
0	0	0	0	0	0	0	1	111	1
0	0	0	0	0	0	0	0	*xxx*	0

(*b*)

Binary	Hexadecimal
10100000	A0
10100100	A4
10101000	A2
10101100	AC
10110000	B0
10110100	B4
10111000	B8
10111100	BC

Q. 36. What should be done in figure give in Q. 34 to make the four VAD values equal to the binary equivalent of 76, 77, 78 and 79?

Ans. 76 = $(01001100)_2$

Replace the six 0's by 010011xy

Q. 37. Why are read and write control lines in a DMA controller bidirectional? Under what condition and for what purpose are they used as inputs? Under what condition and for what purpose are they used as outputs?

Ans. When the CPU communicates with the DMA controller the read and write lines are used as inputs form the CPU to the DMA controller.

When the DMA controller communicates with memory, the read and write lines are used as outputs from the DMA to memory.

Q. 38. It is necessary to transfer 256 words from a magnetic disk to a memory section starting from address 1230. The transfer is by means of DMA as shown in figure given below:

(*a*) Give the initial values that the CPU must transfer to the DMA controller.

(*b*) Give the step-by-step account of the actions taken during the input of the first two words.

Ans. (*a*) CPU initiates DMA by transferring:

256 to the words count register.

1230 to the DMA address register.

Bits to the control register to specify write operations.

(*b*) (*i*) I/O device sends a DMA request.

(*ii*) DMA sends BR (bus request) to CPU.

(*iii*) CPU responds with a BG (bus grant).

(*iv*) Contents of DMA address register are placed in address bus.

(*v*) DMA sends "DMA acknowledge" to I/O device and enables the write control line to memory.

(*vi*) Data word is placed on data bus by I/O device.

(*vii*) Increment DMA address register by 1 and decrement DMA word count register by 1.

(*viii*) Repeat steps 4-7 for each data word transferred.

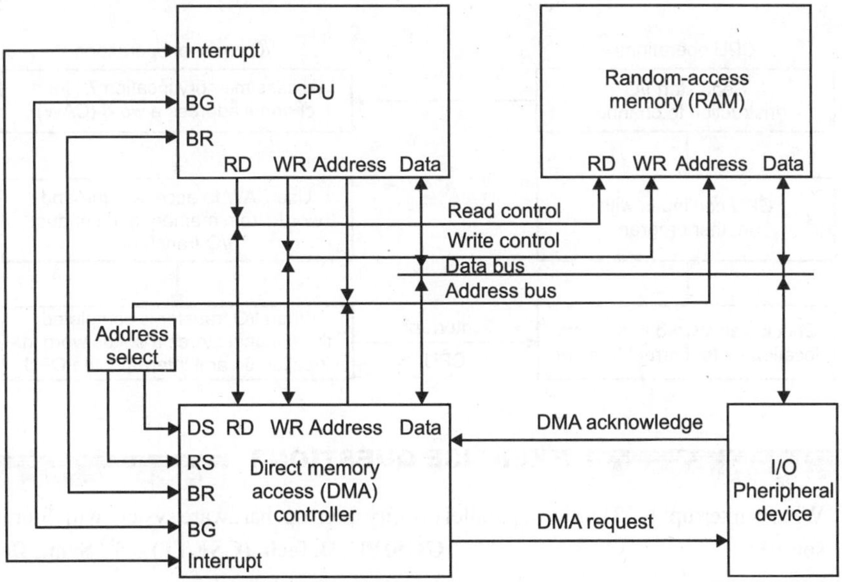

Fig. 7.13. DMA transfer in a computer system

Q. 39. Draw a flowchart similar to the one is figure given below that describes the CPU-I/O channel communication in the IBM 370.

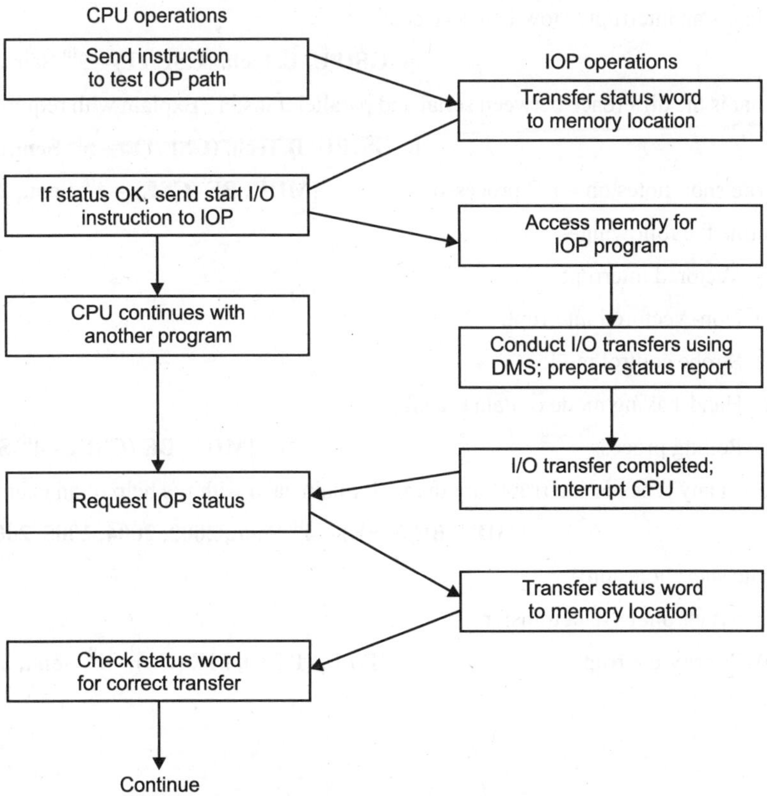

Fig. 7.14. CPU-IOP Communication

Ans.

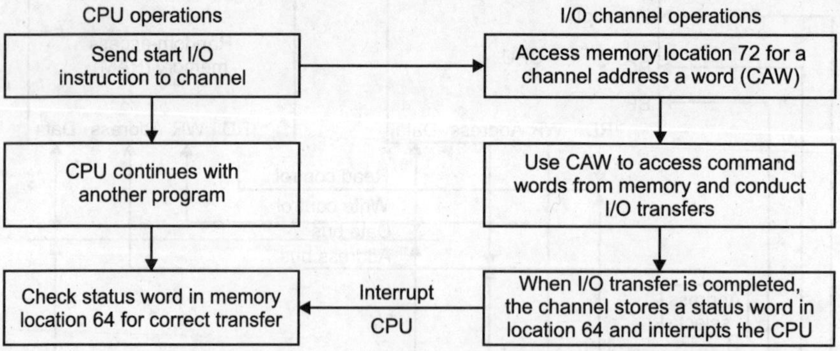

EXERCISE QUESTIONS

Q. 1. What is interrupt I/O? Design a parallel priority interrupt hardware system with four interrupt source. **[GGSIPU, B.Tech. (CSE/IT) – 5th Sem., Dec 2006]**

Q. 2. Explain IPC and synchronization. Give suitable example. **[GGSIPU, B.Tech. (CSE/IT) – 5th Sem, Dec. 2006]**

Q. 3. Explain priority interrupt. **[GGSIPU, B.Tech. (CSE/IT) – 5th Sem., Dec. 2009]**

Q. 4. What is an interrupt? How is it serviced? **[GGSIPU, B.Tech. (CSE/IT) – 5th Sem., Dec 2010]**

Q. 5. What is the difference between serial and parallel transfer? Explain with required example. **[GGSIPU, B.Tech. (CSE/IT) – 5th Sem., Dec. 2011]**

Q. 6. Write short notes on – I/O processor. **[MDU, BE (CSE) – 4th Sem., 2000- 2001]**

Q. 7. Define the following –

(*a*) Vectored interrupt.

(*b*) Non- vectored interrupt.

(*c*) Strobe control mode.

(*d*) Handshaking mode of data transfer.

(*e*) Polling process. **[MDU, BE (CSE) – 4th Sem., 2001]**

Q. 8. How many types of interrupts are there? Explain each with the help of an example. **[MDU, BE (CSE) – 4th Sem., 2002, 2004, 2005, 2006 & 2007]**

Q. 9. Write short notes on –

(*a*) Synchronous data transfer.

(*b*) Priority interrupt. **[DTU, (DCE), ME (CS) – 4th Sem., 2004- 2005]**

CHAPTER

8 PARALLEL PROCESSING

8.0 INTRODUCTION TO PARALLEL COMPUTING

Maximization of CPU performance has always been the lust for any computer architect. But certainly this is not an easy task. This is due to several reasons. One of the reasons is the simultaneous operation of complex multiple data paths. We remember Sidney Fembach's statement: **"Today's large computers (mainframes) would have been considered 'Supercomputer', 10 to 20 years ago. Similarly, today's supercomputers will be considered 'State-of-the art' standard equipment 10 to 20 years from now."**

There are two approaches for improving the performance of a computer:-

1.. By improving the performance of a single computer.

2. By Parallel Processing.

Basically, we can achieve parallelism within the CPU and with many CPUs. Within the CPU, we have just one CPU, so parallelism can be achieved by multitasking, pipelining and so on. **Such architecture is called as a uniprocessor system.** Also, it is known as **Von Neumann's architecture** (that is, conventional system or a sequential machine). In such a system, we can increase the speed by many methods like increasing the clock rate (from MHz to GHz) or by using faster memories and caches, pipelining at instruction level etc. But this approach has already reached its maximum limit. So, we go for the second approach. In second approach, we use many CPUs (also called as processing elements) to solve a given problem. The architecture used to solve these problems are known as **advanced computer architectures** and the algorithms are known as **Parallel Algorithms.** Programming of these computers is known as **Parallel Programming.** In fact, advanced computer architectures are centred on the concept of parallel processing.

8.1 NEED FOR PARALLELCOMPUTING

There are several reasons as to why we need parallel computing. Some of the reasons are given below:

1. To refine physical models such as those of complex molecules and crystals, to verify new theories and to solve newer problems of science we need computers which can perform several billions of arithmetic calculations per second. This requires parallel computers (or Supercomputers).

2. To model global weather forecasts, we need large sets of non-linear partial differential equations. Hundreds of mega-flops' speed and large memory size have been found essential to solve such real-time weather forecast equations.

3. To model interaction between atoms and understand micro behaviour of materials, quantum and structural chemists need high speed computing.

4. Molecular biologists require modelling very complex genetic structures and needing interactive three dimensional graphics facilities to aid their understanding.

5. To create realistic graphic images to display results of simulation of aircraft landing and spacecraft docking requires very high speed computation.

6. To save time and cost - Time is saved as parallel computing is very fast. Cost is saved as multiple cheap computing resources can also be used.

7. To provide concurrency; i.e., parallel execution of tasks.

NOTE: 1. **Mega Flops-** A machine which is capable of performing one floating-point operation every 10 n sec has a speed of $\left(\frac{1}{10^{-8}}\right) = 100$ Mega flops i.e., 100 million (mega) floating-point operations per second.

2. **Concurrency-** To do multiple things at the same time.

8.2 CONSTRAINTS OF CONVENTIONAL ARCHITECTURE

8.2.1 Von Neumann's Architecture

As we know that a single computer consists of an input unit, a program memory, ALU and an output unit. The arithmetic and logic unit (ALU) and the control unit (CU) together forms a CPU. A CPU is also named as a **processing element or PE or a** microprocessor (μP). **In 1940, John Von Neumann proposed a stored-program concept based computer which is also known as a sequential computer or a uniprocessor or Von-Neumann's machine or the conventional computer. It is shown below in Fig 8.1.**

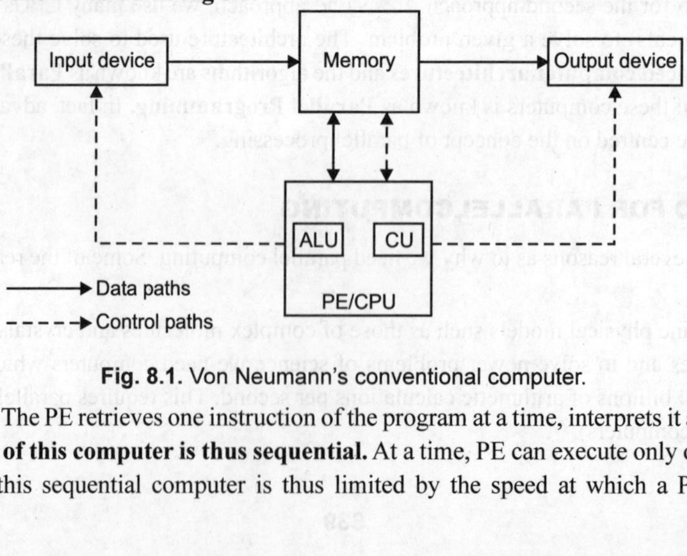

Fig. 8.1. Von Neumann's conventional computer.

Working: The PE retrieves one instruction of the program at a time, interprets it and executes it. The **operation of this computer is thus sequential.** At a time, PE can execute only one instruction. The speed of this sequential computer is thus limited by the speed at which a PE can retrieve instructions and data from memory and the speed at which it can process retrieved data. To increase the speed of processing of data one may interconnect many such sequential computers to work together. **Such a computer which consists of a number of interconnected sequential computers which cooperatively execute a single program to solve a problem is called as a parallel computer.**

Let us now tabulate some differences between sequential (or Von Neumann or conventional) computers versus Parallel computer (or Supercomputers). They are as follows:-

Table 8.1: Differences between Sequential and Parallel computers

Sequential or Von Neumann Computers	Parallel or Supercomputers
1. Are uniprocessor systems i.e., they have only 1 CPU (or PE).	1. Are multiprocessor systems i.e., they have many CPU (or PEs).
2. They can execute only I instruction at a time	2. They can execute several instructions at a time.
3. There speed is limited as we know that the speed of light ($c = 3 \times 10^8$m/s) is also limited.	3. There is no limitation of speeds. We now have supercomputers working at Mega Flops (MFLOPS) and Tera Flops (TFLOPS) range.
4. It is quite expensive to make single CPU faster.	4. It is less expensive if we use larger number of fast commodity processors to achieve the better performance.
5. These computers are found in Laboratories of colleges, industries. For eg: Pentium mP	5. They are not commonly found. Some centres like CDAC in NOIDA and Pune have PARAM Supercomputers which has been developed in INDIA. CRAY-l, CRAY-YMP, CRAY-XMP are some other examples of Supercomputers that have been developed by USA, JUGENE by Europe.

8.2.2 Limitations of Sequential Machines

1. Only single instructions execution at a time makes these computers slower.
2. The speed of electronic devices used in PE has already reached to a saturation level. The limiting factor being the speed of the light.
3. It is very expensive to make a single processor of a sequential machine faster.
4. Its speed is directly proportional to the speed at which the data can move through hardware.
5. The speed of this computer is also limited by the speed at which PE can retrieve data and instructions from memory.

8.3 COMPUTER GENERATIONS

The state of improvement in the development of a product is known as generation. Different technologies have been used for manufacturing the computer hardware. Various Computer generations are tabulated next

Generations	Technology & Architecture	Software and Applications	Popular Examples
First (1945-54)	Vacuum tubes & relay memories, CPU driven by PC and Accumulator, fixed-point arithmetic.	Machine/Assembly languages, single user, no subroutine linkage, programmed I/O using CPU.	ENIAC, Princeton IAS, Mark-I, EDVAC, IBM 650/701.
Second (1955-64)	Transistors, core memories, I/O processor, floating-point calculations.	High-level language (HLL) used with compilers, subroutine libraries, batch processing monitor.	ATLAS, B-5000, PDP-1, IBM-7090, CDC-1604
Third (1965-74)	Integrated circuits (SSI/ MSI), microprogramming, pipelining, cache and lookahead processors.	Multiprogramming and time-sharing OS, multiuser applications.	IBM 360/370, CDC 6600, T-ASC, HP-2100, PDP-8.
Fourth (1975-90)	LSI/ VLSI and Semiconductor memory, multiprocessors, vector supercomputers, multi computers.	Multiprocessor OS, languages, compilers and environments for parallel processing.	VAX 9000, Intel 8080, Cray XMP, IBM 3090.
Fifth (1991-Present)	ULSI/VHSIC processors, memory and switches, high density packaging, scalable architectures.	Massively parallel processing, grand challenge applications, heterogeneous processing.	IBM RS — 16000, Fujitsu VPP 500, Intel Paragon.

Please note that here with each new generation; the circuitry becomes smaller and more advanced. The speed, power and memory of computers is proportionately increased due to **miniaturization.** That is, due to reduction in sizes of circuitry and hardware devices. Each generation is characterized by a major technological development. **Also note that the latest generation computers inherited all good features and eliminated bad features in previous generations.**

We shall now explain each of these generations in detail.

1. **First Generation (1945—1954):** This generation used vacuum tubes and relay memories interconnected by insulated wires. The first generation computers had a single CPU (uniprocessor) that was performing serial fixed point arithmetic using program counter (PC), branch predictions and an accumulator. The CPU was involved in all memory access and Input/output operations. Machine and assembly languages were used.

   EXAMPLES:

   (*a*) **ENIAC:** Electronic Numerical Integrator and Calculator. Built at Moore School of University of Pennsylvania in 1950.

   (*b*) **IBM 70:** The first electronic stored program commercial computer built by IBM in 1953.

2. **Second Generations (1955-1964):** This generation used the discrete transistors, diodes and magnetic ferrite cores interconnected by printed circuits. Index registers, floating point

arithmetic, multiplexed memory and I/O processor were introduced. High level languages (HLL) like FORTRAN, ALGOL and COBOL were introduced with compilers, subroutine libraries and batch processing monitors. In 1957, Irving Reed developed Register Transfer Language (RU) for the systematic design of digital computers.

EXAMPLES:

(*a*) **IBM 7090:** The stretch computer, built in 1962 : Composed of instruction look ahead and error correcting memories.

(*b*) **Univac LARC:** Livermore Atomic Research Computer.

3. **Third Generations (1965-74):** This generation used integrated circuits (ICs) both in logic and memory in SSI and MSI.

   Multilayered printed circuits were used. Micro-programmed control became popular to close up the speed gap between CPU and main memory. Pipelining and cache memory were introduced. Multiprogramming and time sharing were implemented.

   EXAMPLES:

   1. IBM 360/370 Series.
   2. CDC 6600/7600 Series.
   3. Texas Instruments ASC.
   4. PDP-8 Series.

4. **Fourth Generation (1975-1990):** It used LSI and VLSI. Core memory was replaced by semiconductors memory. Parallel computers appeared in various architectures. Shared or distributed memory or optional vector hardware were used. Multiprocessing operating system, special languages and compilers were developed.

   EXAMPLES:

   1. VAX 9000
   2. Cray XMP
   3. IBM-3090

5. **Fifth Generation (1991-Present):** This generation is marked by the use of high density and high speed processor and memory chips. VLSI technology is now more improved. For example, 64-bit 150 MHz microprocessors are now available on a single chip with over one million transistors.

These machines emphasize **M**assively **P**arallel **P**rocessing (MPP). Scalable and latency tolerant architectures are being adopted using VLSI, Silicon, Gas technologies, high density packaging and optical technologies.

The performance of fifth generation computers will be crossing even Tera Flops (10^{12}) range i.e., 10^{12} floating point operations per second. By using heterogeneous processing and thus a network of heterogeneous computers along with the shared memory can solve large scale problems now.

EXAMPLES:

1. MPP — Cray Research
2. CMS — Thinking Machines Corporation
3. Paragon — Intel Super Computer V.
4. PARAM--- India's Super Computer.

8.4 THE STATE OF COMPUTING

There are some grand challenge problems in the field of super computers. Some of them are as follows

- Global weather forecasting.
- Environmental modelling.
- Cosmology.
- Astrophysics.
- Aerodynamics.
- Artificial Intelligence.
- Superconductor modelling.
- Computer vision.
- Quantum mechanics.

And so on. All these applications are computationally intensive. So, we now need very fast computers. These are, naturally, the Supercomputers.

As per the special issue of IEEE on Heterogeneous computing — June 1993, the editor Cherry Pancake described the requirements of **Quantum Chromo-Dynamics.** It is the study of subatomic structure. The experiment involved in **this study demands a CRAY Supercomputer to run for 24 hours/day for 1500 years to get the required atomic details.**

8.5 EVOLUTION OF PARALLEL PROCESSORS

8.5.1 Parallel Processing Basic Terminologies

1. **Parallel processing:** It is defined as the process of information processing that emphasizes the concurrent manipulation of data elements belonging to one or more processes solving a single problem.
2. **Parallel Computer:** It is defined as a multiple processor computer capable of parallel processing.
3. **Supercomputer:** It is defined as a general purpose computer'capable of solving individual problems at extremely high computational speeds, compared with other computers built during the same time.
4. **Throughput:** The throughput of a device is the number of results it produces per unit time: There are many ways to improve the throughput of a device. The speed at which the devices operate can be increased or the concurrency can be increased. **Please note that by 'Concurrency', we mean the number of operations that are being performed at any one time.**
5. **Pipelining:** A pipelined computation is divided into a number of steps called segments/ stages. The output of one segment is input of the next segment. This forms a pipe. **Please note here that the work rate of the pipeline is equal to the sum of work rates of each of the segment. Also note that, it is possible to achieve pipelining with and within CPU.**

6. **Data Parallelism:** It is the use of multiple functional units to apply the same operation simultaneously to the elements of a data set. **Please note that in this type of parallelism, the data set is broken up but not the algorithms.** For instance, Engineering and scientific programs use this -type of parallelism.
7. **Speed Up:** It is defined as the **ratio between the time needed for the most efficient sequential algorithm to perform a computation (t_s) and that of the time needed to perform the same computation on a machine incorporating pipelining and / or parallelism (t_p). Mathematically,** $S(n) = t_s / t_p$
8. **Degree of Parallelism: It is defined as the total number of processors required to execute a program in each such time period.** An efficient parallel program has a high degree of parallelism.

   Parallelism is of two types:

   (*a*) **Hardware Parallelism** — It is built into the machine's architecture.

   (*b*) **Software Parallelism** — It is exploited by the concurrent execution of machine language instructions in a program.

8.5.2 Features of parallel processors

There are some interesting features of Parallel Processing/Computers. They are discussed next:

1. **Better Quality Solutions**: When arithmetic operations are distributed to many computers, each one does a smaller number of arithmetic operations. Thus, the rounding-off errors are lower when parallel computers are used.
2. **Better Algorithms:** The availability of many computers which can work simultaneously leads to different algorithms which are not relevant for purely sequential computers. It is possible to explore different facets of a solution simultaneously using several processors and these give better insight to solutions of several physical problems. -
3. **Better Storage Distribution:** Certain types of parallel computing systems provide much larger storage which is distributed. Access to the storage is faster in each computer. This feature is of special interest in many applications such as information retrieval and computer aided design.
4. **Greater Reliability:** In-principle, a parallel Computer will work even if a processor fails. We can build a parallel computer's hardware and software for better fault tolerance.

8.5.3 Evolution

We are now in a position to review some historical milestones in the computer development to assess the state-of-the-art computing.

Milestones of Computer development are as follows — there are two major stages in the development of computers:

1. Mechanical/Electromechanical.
2. Electronic.

Till 1945, computers were built with mechanical or electromechanical parts.

Abacus was the earliest mechanical computer used in China in 500 B.C. It is manually operated and used to perform decimal arithmetic with carry propagation digit by digit.

After the Abacus, the following are the major milestones in the history of computing as follows:

1. In 1940, Blaise Pascal built a mechanical adder/subtaractor in France.
2. In 1827, Charles Babbage designed a difference engine in England for polynomial evaluation
3. In 1941, Konrad Luse built first binary mechanical computer, in Germany. This computer was designed for general purpose computations.
4. In 1944, Howard Aiken proposed very first electromechanical decimal computer, for general purpose computations. IBM also built Harvard Mark I.

Please note that the speed and the reliability of these computers was greatly limited due to use of moving mechanical parts. With the introduction of electronics, the moving parts in mechanical computers were replaced by high mobility electrons and computers became electronic computers. Now, electric signals were used for information transmission. The speed of electric signal is almost equal to the speed of light. (Remember: $c = 3 \times 10^8$m/s).

8.5.4 Future Trends

During the past 10 years, the trends indicated by ever faster networks, distributed systems and multiprocessor computer architectures suggest that parallelism is the future of computing.

From the application point of view, the mainstream usage of computers is experiencing a trend of four ascending levels of sophistication —

- Data Processing.
- Information Processing.
- Knowledge Processing.
- Intelligence Processing.

The relationship between these four levels is demonstrated by a Venn-diagram as shown below in Fig. 8.2.

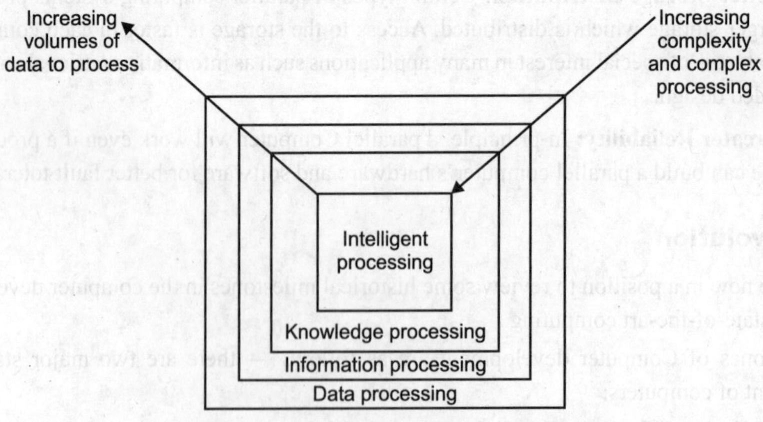

Fig. 8.2. Space diagram for 4-levels of sophistication.

From the Fig. 8.2, it is clear that the space for data processing is largest. Herein, you have increased volume of data to process. At the same time, there is less complexity at this level. However, at the next level i.e., Information processing level, more degree of parallelism has been found which is higher than that at data processing level. Similarly, knowledge processing has more complexity than Information processing. And finally, intelligent processing has maximum complexity. It is because intelligent processing involves the use of Artificial intelligence (Al) languages. AT is the branch of computer science that deals with non-algorithmic approach of problem solving. So, these tasks are quite complex. Hottest area of Al is Neural Networks. It is successful in number of disciplines like voice recognition and natural language processing. Quantum computations, molecular and nanotechnology will drastically change the trends of future computing.

8.6 PARALLELISM IN UNIPROCESSOR SYSTEM

8.6.1 Uniprocessor Architecture

The system with a single central processor or PE is called as a Uniprocessor System. A typical uniprocessor computer has 3 main parts-

(*a*) The Main Memory (MM),

(*b*) he Central Processing Unit (CPU),

(*c*) The Input-Output (I/O) Subsystem.

Example Systems:

1. Mainframe Computer IBM system 370/Model 168 uniprocessor.
2. Super minicomputer VAX-11/780 by DEC.

However, we will study the system architecture of mainframe IBM system 370/Model 168 uniprocessor. Its architecture is shown below

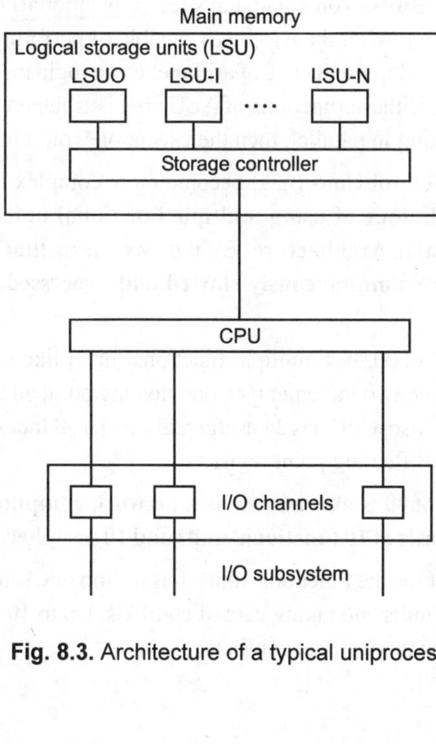

Fig. 8.3. Architecture of a typical uniprocessor

As it is clear from the above Fig. 8.3 that IBM-370 mainframe uniprocessor has three main parts:

1. **Main Memory (MM):** This uniprocessor has four units called as **Logical Storage Units (LSUs).** So, N = 4 for IBM-370 machine. These four LSUs are four way interleaving. We shall be explaining interleaving in subsequent chapters. The storage controller provides the multiport connections between the CPU and the four LSUs.
2. **CPU:** The CPU contains the instruction decoding and execution units as well as a cache.
3. **I/O Subsystem:** The peripherals are connected to the system via high speed I/O channels which operate asynchronously with the CPU.

8.6.2 Parallel Processing Mechanisms for Uniprocessors

To achieve parallelism in uniprocessor systems a number of parallel processing mechanisms have been developed. They are as follows:

(*a*) Multiple functional units.

(*b*) Parallelism and pipelining within the CPU.

(*c*) Overlapped CPU and I/O operations.

(*d*) Use of hierarchical memory system.

(*e*) Balancing of subsystem bandwidths.

(*f*) Multiprogramming and time sharing.

Now, we shall explain each of these techniques of introducing parallelism in uniprocessor systems one by one.

1. **Multiple functional Units:** Von Neumann's (or conventional) computers consist of only one ALU (within CPU). Also, the ALU was capable of performing only one function at a time. So, execution of a long sequence of arithmetic and logic instructions would have been very slow. Therefore, if these functions of ALU are distributed to multiple and specialized functional units working in parallel, then the execution would be faster.

   In such a case, the Control Units (CU) become more complex but a higher throughput is achievable. **This technique of using multiple functional units in a single processor is called as a Superscalar Architecture.** By this, **we mean that multiple instructions of a single program are simultaneously started and processed, in parallel, in different functional units.**

   For example : CDC 6600, has multiple functional units like one fixed point adder, two multipliers, one divider, two incrementers, one floating point adder, one shifter, one logical unit, one branch unit. Also, CPU has 24 useful registers i.e., 8 Index Registers (IR), 8 operand address registers and 8 floating point registers.

   Note that the CDC-6600 is also known as a network computer. This is because it has one CPU which consists of 10 functional units and 10 peripherals and control processor.

   The program does not see the functional units. It is the job of CU to take care of instruction's routing to functional units and taking care of conflicts. Up to 10 instructions can be issued in the CPU, as long as there are no conflicts.

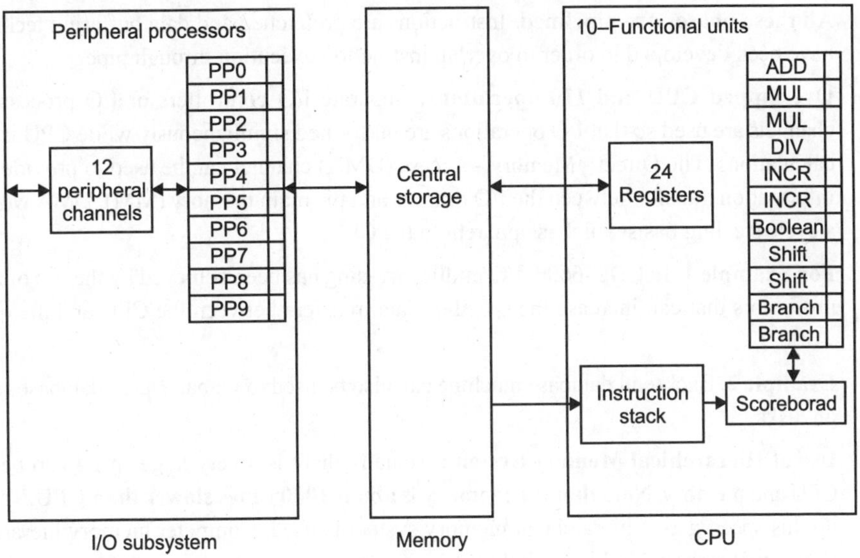

Fig 8.4. CDC-5500 uniprocessor with 10—functional units.

CDC-6600 was designed in year 1964. Its 10 functional units can operate in parallel.

There is a Scoreboard used to check the availability of functional units and registers required.

The central processor consists up of an instruction stack that can store eight words of 60 bits. The instructions are 16-bit and 30-bit long.

How concurrency is achieved in CDC-6600 uniprocessor?

- CDC-6600 has an instruction prefetch facility. So, 8 words of 60 bits each can be prefetched.
- CDC-6600 has 10 functional units with a Scoreboard that provides a queue and a reservation scheme.
- 32-way memory interleaving.
- 10 peripheral processors with own memory for I/O programs.

2. **Parallelism and Pipelining within the CPU:** We must understand that the use of multiple functional units is a form of parallelism within the CPU. In first generation, old machines we used to have bit serial address. But now, almost all CPUs make use of parallel adders - like carry-look ahead adder and carry-save adders.

   High speed multiplier recoding and convergence division are the techniques for exploring parallelism and the sharing of hardware resources for the functions of multiply and divide.

   Instruction execution is performed in a cycle of events as shown below:

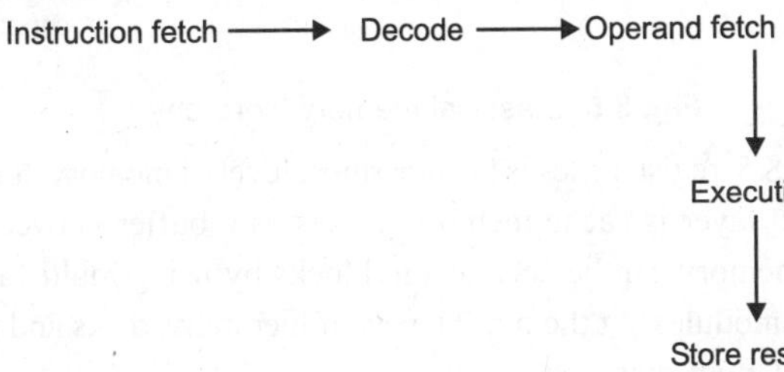

All these phases are pipelined. Instructions are prefetched and data buffering techniques have been developed in order to overlap instruction execution through pipe.

3. **Overlapped CPU and 110 operations:** Separate I/O controllers or I/O processors or channels are used so that I/O operations are performed simultaneously while CPU is doing calculations. The Direct - Memory - Access (DMA) channel can be used to provide direct information transfer between the I/O devices and the main memory (MM). DMA works on a cycle stealing basis which is apparent to the CPU.

   For Example 1. In CDC-6600, I/O multiprocessing has been achieved by the use of 10 I/O processors that can increase the speed of data transfers between the CPU and the outside world.

   Example 2. Back-end database machine can also be used to manage large databases stored on disks.

4. **Use of Hierarchical Memory System:** Actually there is a very large speed gap between CPU and memory. **Note that the memory is about 1000 times slower than CPU.** To close up this speed gap, a hierarchical memory system is used. Computer memory hierarchy is conceptually shown in Fig 8.5 below.

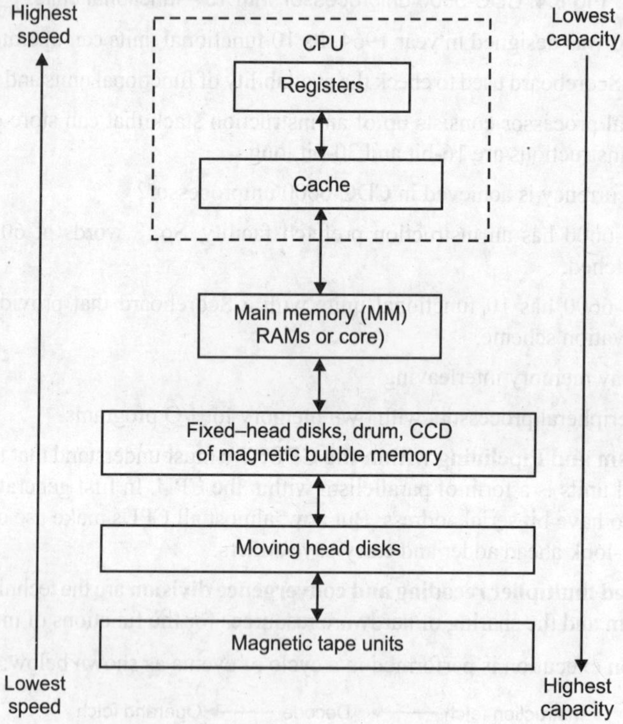

Fig. 8.5. Classical memory hierarchy

As shown in Fig. 8.5, register files is the innermost level of memory. It is directly addressable by he ALU. Next layer is cache memory. It acts as a buffer between CPU and the main memory. Main memory can be accessed in blocks by using multiway interleaving across parallel memory modules. At the outer levels of hierarchy, disks and tape units are used to establish a virtual memory space.

Please note that the hierarchy illustrated above is used to broaden the memory bandwidth so that it matches the bandwidth of CPU.

5. **Balancing of Subsystem Bandwidths:** As discussed earlier also, that as per Von- Neumann's architecture, a computer has three parts, namely:

   (*a*) CPU

   (*b*) Main Memory (MM) and

   (*c*) I/O devices.

Also, we know that

ALU + CU = CPU (or PE or MPU)

However, out of these three subsystems, **CPU is the fastest unit and I/O devices are the slowest devices.** The main memory is between the two devices, i.e., CPU and I/O. The performance of these subsystems is measured in terms of their bandwidths. We shall now define the term 'bandwidth'. It is defined below:

"Bandwidth is defined as the number of operations performed per unit time."

or

"Bandwidth is defined as the maximum rate in millions of bits per second (MBPS) at which information can be transferred to or from a memory unit".

Bandwidths may be related to the main memories, processrs I/O or even the utilization Bandwidths. We shall now define these one by one.

(***a***) **Main Memory bandwidth (B_m):** It is defined as the number of memory words that can be accessed (either fetch or store) per unit time. To avoid bottleneck between the subsystem, their processing bandwidths should be matched. Let W be number of words delivered per memory cycle and *tm* be memory cycle time in seconds, then memory bandwidth B_m is equal to.

$$B_m = \frac{W}{t_m} = \text{(words/second or bytes/second).}$$

(***b***) **Bandwidth of processor (B_p): It is the maximum CPU computation rate.** For e.g. Cray — 1 processor bandwidth (B_p) = 160 megaflops (MFLOPS).

IBM 370/168 processor bandwidth = 12.5 (million instructions per second) MIPS.

(B_P – Denotes processor bandwidth).

(**c**) **I/O Bandwidth (B_d): It is defined as average data transfer rate.** For e.g. Modern disc drive has B_d = 1 megabyte/second.

(***d***) **Utilization Bandwidths:** In practice, utilization bandwidths of these subsytems are lower than actual bandwidths.

1. Utilization bandwidth of memory B_m^u.

   Rough measure of B_m^u is defined as follows.

$$B_m^u = \frac{B_m}{\sqrt{M}}$$

   M is the number of interleaved memory modules in the memory system. e.g. for IBM 3033 uniprocessor; M = 8

$$B_m^u = \frac{B_m}{\sqrt{8}}$$

It can read eight double words (8 byte each) from an eight way interleaved memory system per each memory cycle tm = 456ns.

$$B = \frac{8*8bytes}{456ns}$$

$$B = 140 \text{ megabytes/sec.}$$

$$B_m^u = \frac{140}{\sqrt{8}}$$

$$= 49.5 \text{ megabytes/sec.}$$

(e) Utilization Bandwidth of CPU B_p^u: It is decided by measuring number of output results (in words) per second.

Let R_ω be number of words results and T be the total CPU time required to generate R_ω results, then

$$B_p^u = \frac{R_\omega}{T_p} \text{ (words/sec.)}$$

(f) Utilization Bandwidth of I/O devices (B_d^u): It is lower than their actual Bandwidth, B_d. In practice, relationship between the bandwidths of major subsytems in a high performance uniprocessor is observed as follows:

$$B_m \geq B_m^u \geq B_p \geq B_p^u \geq B_d$$

Hence it is clear that main memory has highest bandwidth.

Also if t_p, is processor cycle time, t_m is memory cycle time and t_d is average access time of I/O devices then relation between t_p, t_m and t_d is observed as follows

$$t_d > t_m > t_p$$

The above relationship implies that there is unbalance in the speeds of major subsystems and the processing power of these subsystems is required to be matched to obtain better performance.

The two major techniques used for balancing subsystem bandwidths are as follows:

1. **Bandwidth Balancing between CPU and Memory:** The difference in the speed of CPU and the main memory can be covered up by using fast cache memory between them as shown in Fig. 8.6.

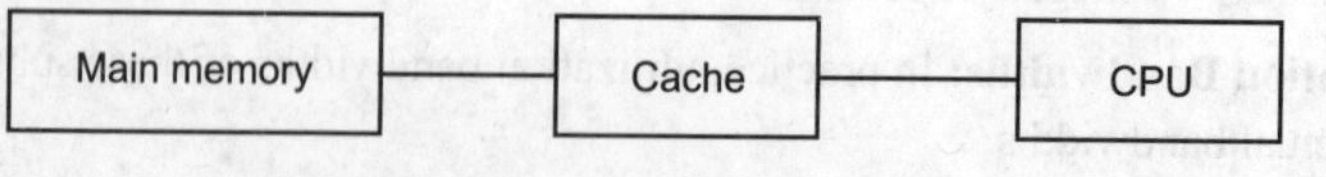

Fig 8.6. Cache Memory for Balancing Bandwidth of CPU and Memory

Access time of cache (t_c) should be equal to speed of CPU i.e. $t_c = t_p$.

The part of memory words are first loaded into cache memory. Hence immediate instructions and data will be available from the cache to the CPU. Cache acts as a data/ instruction buffer. However cache memories are costly and hence it is not economical to use them in bulk.

2. **Bandwidth Balancing between Memory and I/O (Input-Output) devices:** To balance the speed of I/O devices and memory, input-output channels with different speeds are used

between the slow I/O devices and the main memory. The function of these I/O channels is to act as a buffer and also provide multiplexing transfer the data from multiple I/O devices into main memory by stealing CPU cycles. In addition to this, the filtering of the irrelevant data before transferring to main memory can provide a faster and more effective data transfer rate.

Ideally for a totally balanced system, entire memory bandwidth should be watched with the bandwidth sum of the processor and I/O devices.

i.e., $B_p^u + B_d = B_m^u$

where $B_p^u = B_m$

and $B_m^u = B_m$

Tremendous hardware and software support is required to achieve this total balance.

8.6.3 Multiprogramming and Time Sharing

In addition to above hardware approaches for increasing speed of uniprocessor system, following software approaches are also used to achieve concurrency.

1. Multiprogramming and
2. Time sharing

1. **Multiprogramming :** It is possible to achieve a high degree of resource sharing among many user programs even in presence of single CPU.

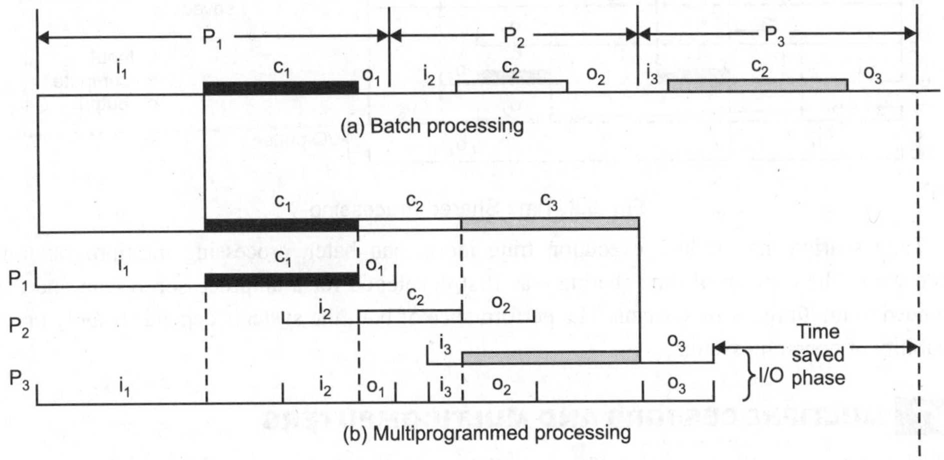

Fig. 8.7

In Fig 8.7 (a) conventional batch processing is illustrated by sequential execution. Following notations are used for operations

i → input

C → compute

O → output

There may be more than one process active in a computer in the same time interval. Some of these processes might be competing for memory, some will be I/O processors and others might demanding CPU. Some computer programs are CPU - bound (Computation intensive) and some are I/O bound (input output intensive). Execution of various types of such programs can be mixed to balance the bandwidths among various functional units. There will be better resource utilization by means of program interleaving through overlapping I/O and CPU operations. **This interleaving of CPU and I/O operations among several programs is called multiprogramming.** Refer Fig. 8.7 (b).

Whenever I/O operations in processors P_1 is going on, system scheduler can switch CPU to process P_2. So P_1 and P_2 (more than one) processes will be executing simultaneously in the system. When P_2 is over, the CPU can be switched to P_3. It can be noted that there is overlapped CPU and I/O operation and CPU wait time is greatly reduced. The programs can be mixed across the boundary of user's tasks and systems processes. Multiprogramming reduces the total execution time. The process P_1, P_2 and so on, may belong to the same or different programs.

2. **Time sharing:** In multiprogramming, CPU is shared by many programs. Sometimes, certain program occupies CPU for very long time and hence other programs have to wait. This problem can be solved by using a time sharing operating system. **The basic concept is to allot fixed or variable time slices to multiple programs.** Hence time sharing O.S. gives equal opportunities to all programs demanding CPU time.

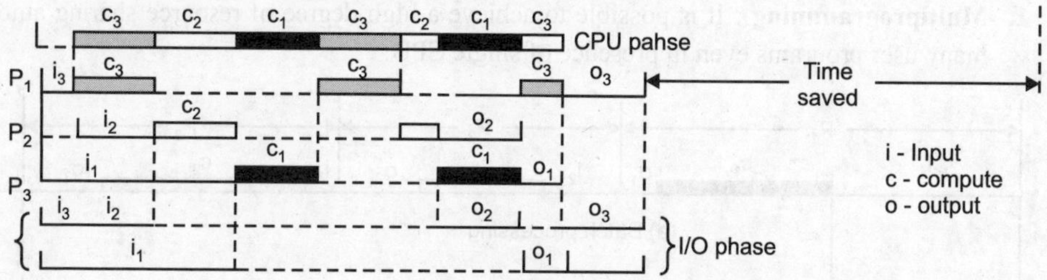

Fig. 8.8. Time Shared Processing

Time sharing may reduce execution time more than batch processing multiprogramming approaches. The concept of time sharing was first developed for a uniprocessor system and then extended to multiprocessor systems. The performance of both the systems depends heavily on the capability of operating system.

8.7 MULTIPROCESSORS AND MULTICOMPUTERS

There are two main categories of the parallel computers. Before categorizing them let us see their definitions. **A multiprocessor is a single computer in which multiple processors exist. The complete system comprises of many (multiple) processors.** The processors are interconnected through an **Interconnection Network. They share common resources** like memory and I/O devices. They have **just one** O.S. Even though many computers exist, **it behaves as a single computer only. Whereas in a multicomputer system, multiple autonomous computers are interconnected by the network.** Also, the communication among them is not mandatory. **So, we can say that the distributed memory MIMD (Multiple Instruction Multiple Data) architectures are called as multicomputers. While Shared memory MIMD architectures are called as multiprocessors.**

We are now in a position to tabulate the differences between the two. They are given below:

Multiprocessors	Multicomputer
1. It is a **single computer** in which multiple processors exist.	1. It has **multiple** (many) autonomons computers.
2. Although many PEs are used but these PEs do not have their own individual memories. In fact, **sharing of memory and I/O resources** is done. So, they are also known as shared memory	2. Here also many PEs (or CPUs) exist but each FE has its own memory arid I/o resources. **No sharing** occurs in this case. So, they are also known as **Distributed memory multicomputers.**
3. The communication among PEs is must.	3. The communication among PEs is not mandatory.
4. They use **dynamic networks** wherein the communication links can be reconfigured by setting the active switching unit of the system.	4. They use **static network** wherein the connection of switching units is fixed and is typically, realized as direct or point to-point connections. These networks are also known as direct networks.
5. They are also called as **tightly-coupled** systems due to the high degree of resource sharing. E.g. The Sequent symmetry S-81	5. They are also called as **loosely-coupled** as there is no resource sharing. E.g. Message Passing Multicomputer.

Next we shall describe the two main categories of parallel computers.

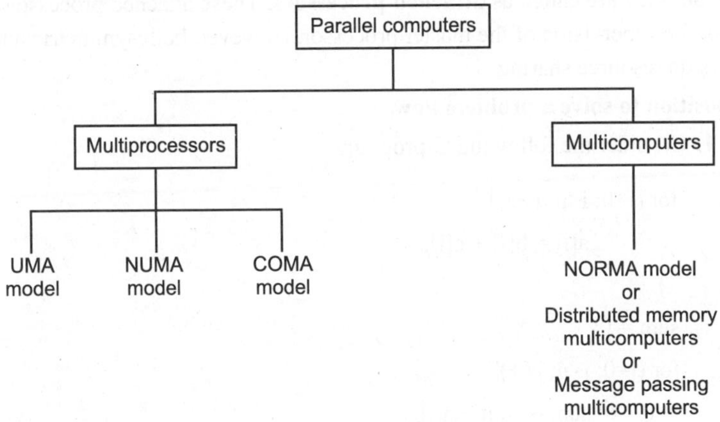

Fig. 8.9. Categories of Parallel computers multiprocessors and multi computers.

I. The UMA Model

As shown in Fig. 8.10, in this model, the physical memory is uniformly shared by all the processors. All processors (PE_1......PE_n) have equal access time to all memory words. **This is the reason as to why they are called as uniform memory access computers. Please note that in this architecture, each processor (CPU/PE) may have its own private cache memory. The peripherals (I/O) devices are also shared. Since there is a high degree of resource (memory and I/O) sharing, so these systems are also known as tightly coupled systems.** At the centre of Fig 8.10, we can also see a System Interconnection Network which can be common bus architecture, a crossbar switch or a multistage network.

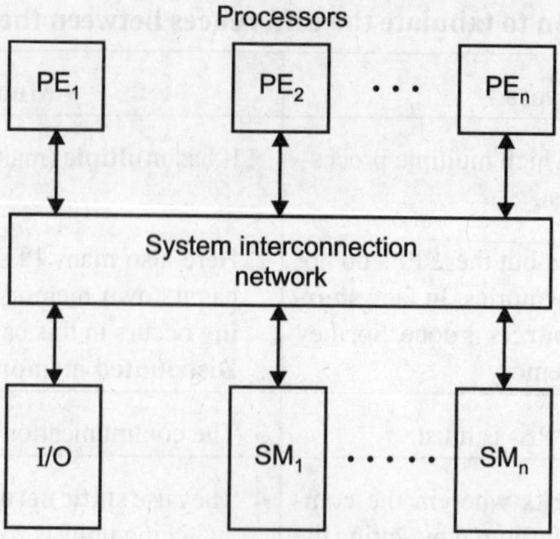

Fig. 8.10. UMA Model

When all processors (or PEs) have equal access to all peripheral devices then the system is called as a **symmetric multiprocessor**. So, now all the processors are equally capable of running the executive programs like OS Kernel or I/O service routines. **Whereas in an asymmetric multiprocessor**, only one or a subset of processors are executive-capable. It is the job of master processor (or an executive) to execute the 0.S. and the handle I/O. The remaining processors have no I/O capability. So, they are called as **attached processors.** These attached processors execute user programs under the supervision of the master processor. However, both symmetric and asymmetric multiprocessors do resource sharing.

We are in a position to solve a problem now.

EXAMPLE 1: Consider the following C-program-

```
for (i=0; i<n; i++){
        a[i] = b[i] + c[i];
}
sum = 0;
for (j=0; j<n; j++)|
        sum = sum + a[j];
}
```

This program is to execute firstly on a uniprocessor or sequential (or conventional or Von Neumann) machine. How many machine cycles are required? Now, if this program is run on a M-processor system, how many cycles are required? Compare your results. Assume that:

$N = 2^{20}$ ***elements in the array***

Average no. of cycles required = 200 cycles

$M = 256$ ***(PEs CPU Processors)***

How much is the efficiency?

SOLUTION: Let us first of all number the lines of the code in given program

```
For (i=0; i<n; i++){            L1
        a [i] = b[i]+ c[i];     L2
```

```
    }                                   L3
          sum =0;                       L4
    for (i=0; j<n; j++){                L5
          sum = sum + a[j];             L6
    }                                   L7
```

Suppose now that line no. 2, 4 and 6 take 1 machine cycle to execute. For simplicity, let us ignore line no. 1, 3, 5 and 7. Further assume that k-cycles are needed for each interprocessor communication using a shared memory. We also assume that the arrays are already loaded in the main memory. We ignore bus contentions also.

Now, we have 2 cases:

Case 1: If the program is executed on the conventional or sequential machine then we finds that the i-for loop requires N cycles and also j-loop requires N cycles (Note loop contains N-recursive iterations). So, sequential execution of above program requires 2 N cycles (totally).

Case 2: If the program is executed on a multiprocessor with M-processors then the total numbers of cycles required is

$$2\,N/M + (K+1)\log_2 M \text{ cycles}$$

Why? This is because addition of each pair of partial sums requires K-cycles through shared memory. To merge all partial sums, an *l*-level binary adder is required, where = $\log_2$ M. This adder tree takes *l*(K + 1) cycles to merge the M partial sums sequentially from the leaves to the root of the tree. Hence, the result.

Now, we are given that:

$$N = 2^{20}, M=256=2^8, K = 200$$

∴ **Sequential execution takes** = 2N (cycles)

$$= 2^1 \text{ x } 2^{20} \text{ cycles}$$

$$= 2^{21} \text{ machine cycles.}$$

And Parallel execution takes = $\dfrac{2N}{M} + (K+1)\log_2 M\,(\text{cycles})$

$$= 2 \times \frac{2^{20}}{256} + (200+1)_{\log_2} 256$$

$$= 2^1 \times \frac{2^{20}}{2^8} + (200+1)_{\log_2} 256$$

$$= 2^{21-8} + 201 \log_2 2^8$$

$$= 2^{12} + 201 \times 8 \log_2 2$$

$$= 2^{12} + 1608 \times 1$$

$$= 212 + 1608 = \textbf{9800 cycles.}$$

Whereas actual speed-up obtained is 214 only. So,

Efficiency (η) = (214/256) * 100% = **83.6%**

∴ **Efficiency of 83.6% is achieved by parallel processing.**

Applications of UMA Model:

1. It is suitable for general purpose and time-sharing applications by multiple users.

2. It can be used to speed up the execution of a single large program in time-critical applications.

II. The NUMA Model

It is a sort of shared memory multiprocessor only. In these computers the access time varies with the location of the memory word. There are two possibilities of NUM.A model. One is to have the shared memory that is physically distributed to all PEs. This memory is called as local memory (LM). This is shown in Fig 8.11 below:

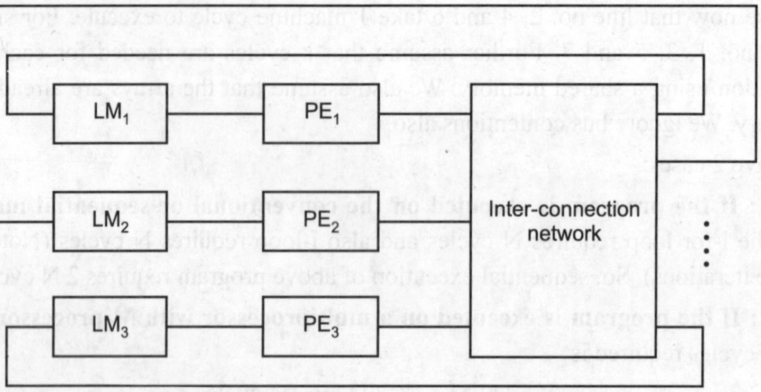

Fig. 8.11. Shared Memory NUMA Model.

Please note that here the collection of all 1ocal memories forms a global address space (GAS) that is accessible by all processors. The BBN Butterfly system is its example.

Another model is known as a hierarchical cluster model. **In this model, instead of distributed memories, a global shared memory is added to a multiprocessor system.**

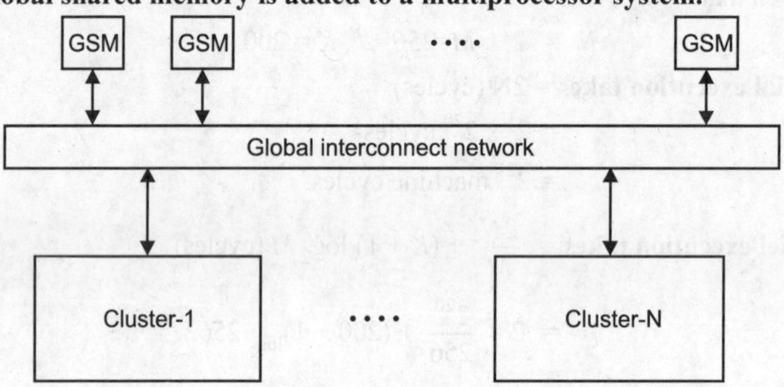

Fig 8.12. Globally shared memory multiprocessor.

A **Cluster** comprises of many PEs, shared memory of each PE and a cluster interconnection network. So, we have three types of memory accesses. They are as follows:

(*a*) Local memory access (within cluster)

(*b*) Global memory access (GSM)

(*c*) Remote memory access.

Please note that the local memory access is fastest. Then comes the global memory access. Then, finally, we have the slowest one, that is, the remote memory access. Also note that, each cluster is itself an UMA or NUMA multiprocessor. The clusters are connected to GSM. This entire system is collectively known as a NUMA multiprocessor. There are two important points to be kept in mind. They are:

(*a*) All processors belonging to the same cluster are allowed to unformly access the cluster shared-memory.

(*b*) All clusters have equal access to global memory.

NOTE :	Speed of local Speed memory (LM)	>	Shared of cluster memory	>	Speed of GSM

Example System: The Cedar Multiprocessor by University of Illinois.

III. The COMA Model

We can easily understand this model if we understand this equation

Multiprocessor + Cache memory = COMA Model

Examples of COMA machines:

- Data Diffusion Machine (DDM) by Swedish Institute of Computer Science.
- KSR-1 machine by Kendall Square Research.

A COMA model is shown below in Fig. 8.13.

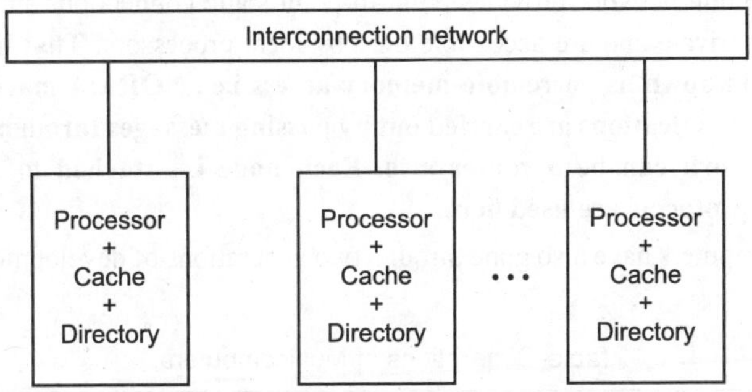

Fig. 8.13 COMA Model

So, now **distributed memories have been converted to caches**. There is no memory hierarchy now. All these cache form a global address space. If cache access is remote (far-off) then distributed cache Directories help.

Other variants of COMA also exist. **For instance,** cache coherent non-uniform memory access (CC-NUMA) model. For e.g. Stanford Dash is a CC-NUMA model. Also note that machines like SS-S81 is known as a **minisupercomputer.** IBM-390 model are also known as **high-end mainframes or near-supercomputers.**

Applications: General purpose multi-user applications need multiprocessors.

We shall describe multi-computers now (Category-II).

I NORMA machines /Message passing multi-computer/ Distributed memory multicomputers.

These machines consist up of multiple computers. These multiple computers are known as **nodes. A node is an autonomous computer consisting of a processor, local memory, attached disks or I/O Peripherals.** These nodes are also interconnected by a **message passing network.** This network of CEs may be in Mesh, Ring, Torus, Hypercube etc. forms. Such a computer is shown below in Fig. 8.14.

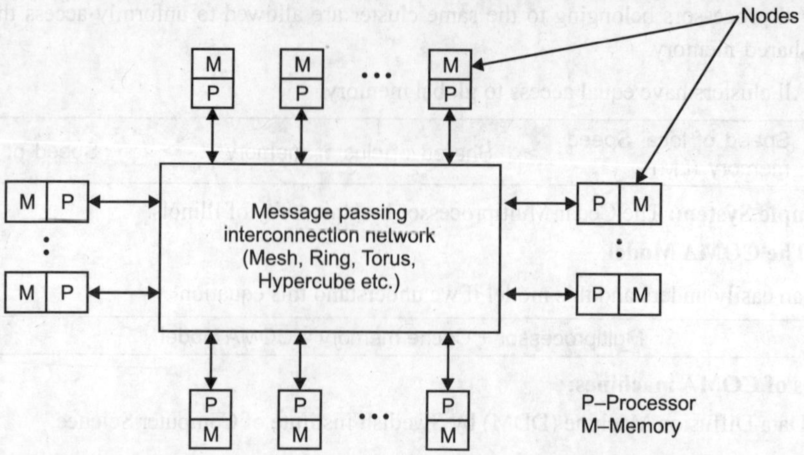

Fig 8.14. NORMA machine/ message passing multicomputer / Distributed memory MultiComputer

The interconnection network provides point-to-point static connections among the nodes. All local memories are private and are accessible only by local processors. **That is why these multi computers are also known as no-remote-memory-access i.e., NORMA machines. Please note that inter node communications are carried out by passing messages through static connection network. This network can be a router also. Each node is attached to a router. Certain message—passing protocols are used here.**

These multi computers have also gone through two generations of development. They are given below in the table

Table-Generations of Multicomputers.

Generation	Technology and Architecture	Example Systems
First (1983-87)	• Processor board technology • Hypercube architecture	• Intel iPSC / 1 • Caltech cosmic
Second (1988-1992)	• Hardware message routing • Mesh architecture	• Paragon by Intel. • Parsys Super Node 1000
Third (1993-1997)	• VLSI • Fine-grain multicomputers	• MIT j-machine • Caltech Mosaic

8.8 INTRODUCTION TO PARALLEL COMPUTING

Now, we discuss about vector supercomputers first.

It is a register-to-register architecture. The scalar processor has scalar functional pipelines while the vector processor has vector functional pipelines. The vector processor has vector registers which are programmable. The working is very complex. If the decoded instruction is a **scalar operation** then it is directly executed by scalar processor using scalar functional pipelines. Else, if the instruction is decoded as a **vector operation**, it is sent to vector control unit. It supervises flow of vector data between MM and vector functional pipes. As shown in Fig. 8.15, the program and data from the host computer are loaded into the Main Memory (MM). Both are decoded by the scalar unit first.

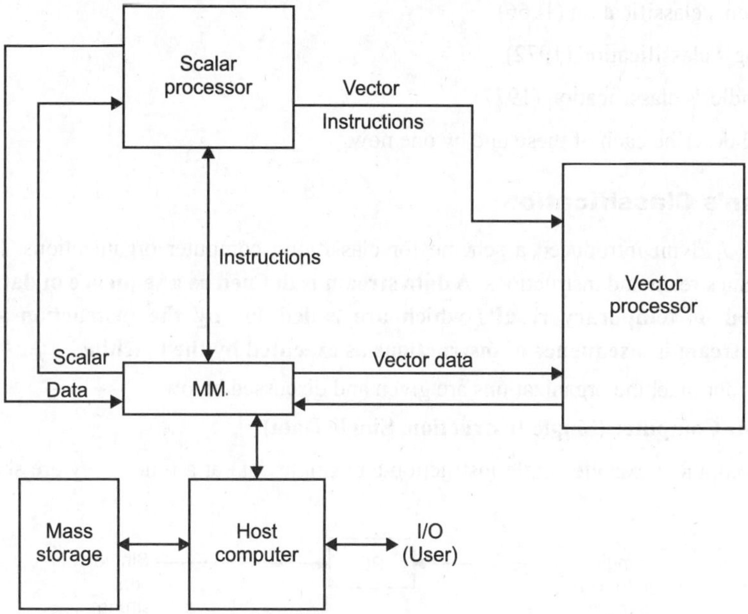

Fig. 8.15. A vector supercomputer

Another **variant** of vector supercomputers is based on memory-to-memory. It uses a vector stream unit to replace vector registers. Retrieval of operands (vector) and results is done directly from the main memory in superwords (like 512 bits).

Example system: Cyber—205, Cray—YMP

NOTE: Number of vector registers and functional pipelines in a vector processor are fixed.

Next, we discuss about SIMD computers in short. They will be discussed in detail in subsequent chapters.

SIMD Model: A single Instruction Multiple Data (SIMD) can be specified by 5-parameters:-

$$\text{SIMD}(M) = (N, C, I, M, R) \text{ Where}$$

'*N*'- represents the number of PEs in the machine

'*C*'- represents a set of instructions.

'*I*'- represents a set of instructions that are broadcast by the CU to all PEs.

'*M*'- represents a set of masking schemes for masking or demasking certain PEs.

'*R*'- represents a set of data-routing functions.

For example: Master Computer (MP—1 family) which has processors (or PEs) ranging from 1024 to 16,384 PEs with 1.3 GFlops rate. Each of this PE has 16 kB local memory. It supports Fortran-77, UNIX OS, debuggers and so on.

We shall be describing SIMD computers in detail again in subsequent chapters.

8.9 PARALLEL ARCHITECTURAL CLASSIFICATION SCHEMES

There are three computer architectural classifications based on the multiplicity of instruction and data stream. They are given below:

1. Flynn's classification (1966)
2. Feng's classification (1972)
3. Handler's classification (1977)

We shall describe each of these one by one now.

8.9.1 Flynn's Classification

Michael *J* Flynn introduced a scheme for classifying computer organizations. He uses the concept of data stream and instructions. **A data stream is defined as a sequence of data including input, partial or temporary results which are called for by the instruction stream. An instruction stream is a sequence of instructions as executed by the machine.**

Flynn's four machine organizations are given and discussed below:

1. **SISD Computer (Single Instruction, Single Data)**

These computers execute single instruction and single data at a time. They are shown in Fig. 8.16. below:

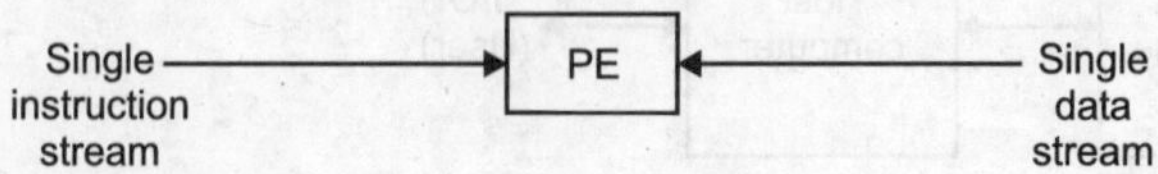

Fig 8.16. SISD Computer

For example: Von Neumann's sequential computer (or uniprocessors) falls under this category, IBM 701, VAXI1, CDC6600.

2. **SIMD Computer (Single instruction, Multiple Data)**

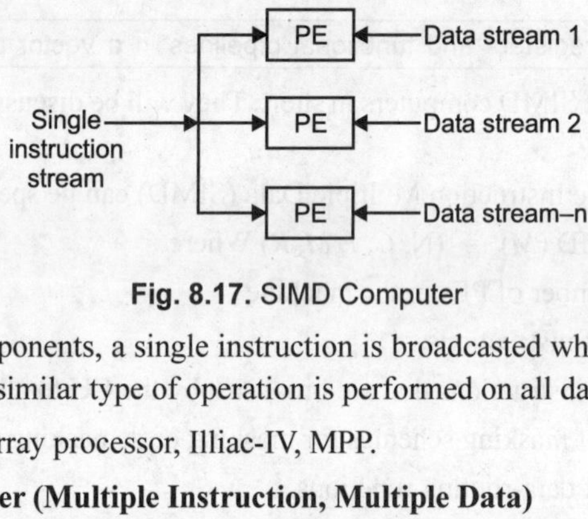

Fig. 8.17. SIMD Computer

So, in these components, a single instruction is broadcasted which operates on many data streams. Hence, similar type of operation is performed on all data streams.

For example: Array processor, Illiac-IV, MPP.

3. **MIMD Computer (Multiple Instruction, Multiple Data)**

In these computers, individual PEs operates on programs having their own instructions and data. So, we have many (multiple) instructions working or operating on many data streams.

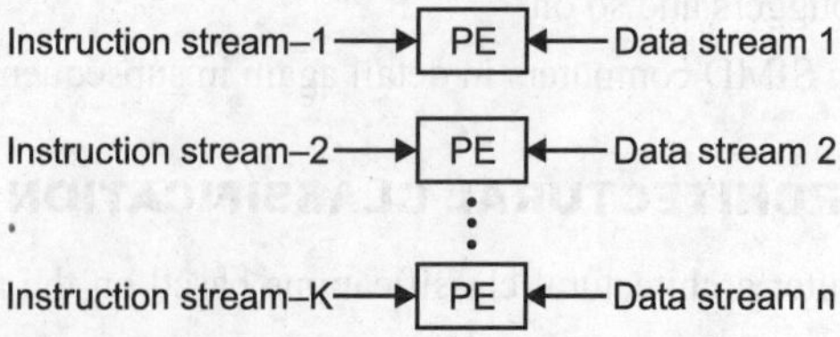

Fig 8.18. MIMD Computer

For example: Multiprocessors are put under this category, IBM 370, Cray—2, UNIVAC 1100/80.

4. **MISD Computer (Multiple Instruction and Single Data)**

   In this category, multiple instructions operate on a single data stream. That is,

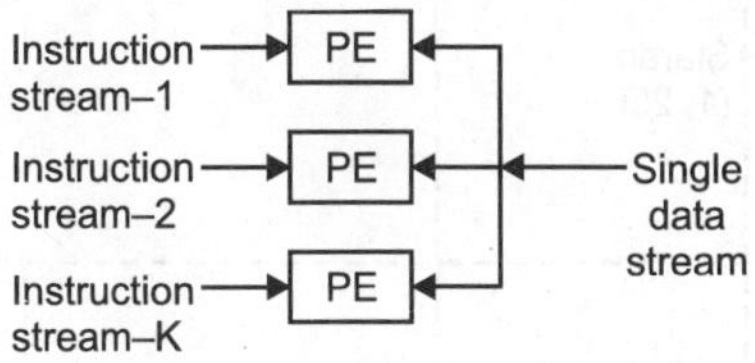

Fig 8.19. MISD Computers

For eg.: Systolic Array

8.9.2 Feng's Classification

Tse-Yun Feng has suggested the use of the degree of Parallelism to classify various computer architectures. First of all we must define what is meant by maximum degree of Parallelism. **It is defined as the maximum number of bits that can be processed within a unit time by a computer system. It is represented by P.**

Let P_i be the number of bits that can be processed within the ith processor cycle (or i^{th} clock period). Consider T processor cycles indexed by $i = 1, 2, ..., T$. Then, the average parallelism degree P_a is defined by :

$$P_a = \frac{\Sigma_{i=1}^{T} P_i}{T}$$

Generally, $P_i < P$.

∴ We define the utilization rate (μ) of a computer system within T cycles by:

$$\mu = \frac{P_a}{P} = \frac{\Sigma_{i=1}^{T} P_i}{T.P}$$

If the computing power of the processor is fully utilized i.e., the parallelism is fully exploited, then we have $P_, = P$ for all I and $\mu = 1$ for 100% utilization. The utilization rate depends on the applications program being executed.

Thus, computer can be classified based on their maximum parallelism degree. Fig. 1.20 demonstrates this classification.

As shown in Fig. 8.20, **the horizontal axis shows the word length, n.** The **vertical axis corresponds to the bit slice length, m. Please note here that both length measures are in terms of the number of bits contained in a word or in a bit slice. A bit slice is a string of bits, one from each of the words at the same vertical bit position.**

Now, the maximum parallelism degree, $P(c)$ of a given computer system C is represented by the product of the word length, W, and the bit slice length, m, that is

$$P(c) = n.\,m$$

Here, the pair (n, m) corresponds to a point in a computer space corresponding to a particular computer, shown by the coordinate system in the graph of Fig. 8.20. **Please note that $P(c)$ is equal to the area of the rectangle defined by the integer's n and m.** There are four types of processing methods that can be seen from Fig. 8.20

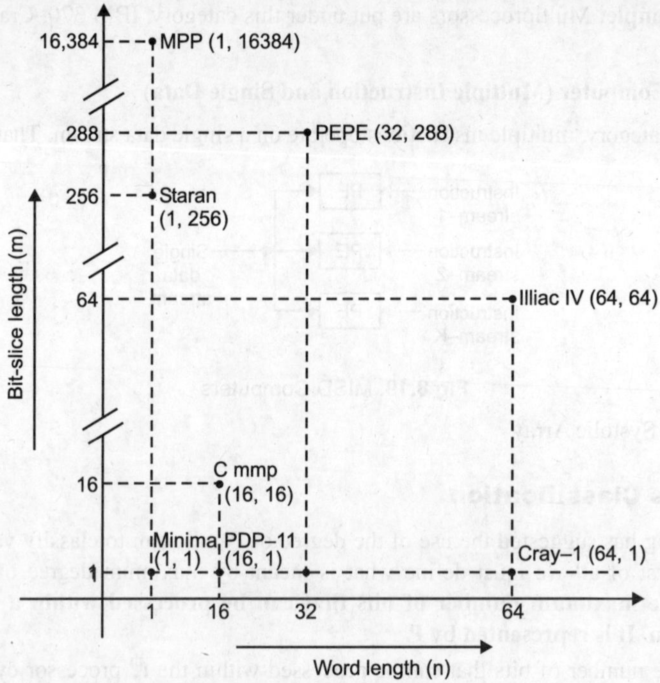

Fig 8.20. Feng's classification

1. Word-serial and bit-serial (WSBS).
2. Word-parallel and bit-serial (WPBS).
3. Word-serial and bit-parallel (WSBP).
4. Word-parallel and bit-parallel (WPBP).

Fig 8.21 below shows the word slice and bit slice.

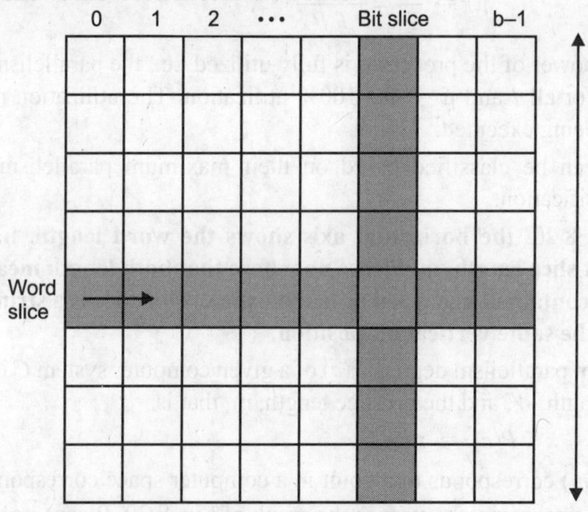

Fig 8.21. Word slice and bit slice.

Let us explain these four types of processing methods with respect to Fig. 8.21.

Method-I: WSBS processing method (where $n = m = 1$)

It is also known as bit serial processing because one bit is processed at a time. This method was only used in first generation computers.

For example: The "MINIMA."

Method-II: WPBS processing method (where $n = 1$, $m > 1$)

It is also known as **bit-slice or bis-processing.** In this method, an m-bit-slice is processed at a time.

For example: STARAN and MPP (by Goodyear Aerospace).

Method-III: WSBP processing method (where $n > 1$ and $m = 1$)

It is also known as **word-slice processing** as it processes one word on n—bits at a time. It is found in most existing computers.

For example: IBM-370, CDC 6600.

Method IV: WPBP processing method (where $n > 1$ and $m > 1$)

This is known as **fully parallel processing or simply parallel processing**. Here an array of (n x m) bits is processed simultaneously.

Please note that this is the fastest processing mode out of the four models.

For example: ILLIAC IV and PEPE.

We summarize Feng's classification in a tabular form now. It is given below:

MODE	COMPUTER MODEL (manufacturer)	Degree of Parallelism (n, m)
1. WSPS ($n = m = 1$)	• The 'MINIMA' (unknown)	(1, 1)
2. WPBS ($n = 1$, $m > 1$) (bit-slice processing)	• STARAN (Goodyear Aerospace) • MPP (Goodyear Aerospace) • DAP (ICL, England)	(1, 256) (1,16,384) (1,4096)
3. WSBP ($n > 1$, $m = 1$) (Word slice processing)	• IBM 370 • CDC 6600 • Burrough 770 • VAX 11 (DEC)	(64,1) (60,1) (48,1) (16,1)
4. WPBP ($n > 1$, $m > 1$)(fully parallel processing)	• Illiac - IV (Burroughs) • TI-ASC(T1) • C.mmp (CMU) • S-I (LCNL)	(64,64) (64,32) (16,16) (36,16)

8.9.3 Handlers Classification

Handler's classification is based on the degree of parallelism versus degree of pipelining that is built into the hardware structures of a computer system. Here, the parallel- pipeline processing is considered at three subsystem levels-

1. **Processor Control Unit (PCU)** i.e., CPU.
2. **Arithmetic Logic Unit (ALU)** i.e., PE.

3. **Bit Level Circuit (BLC)** i.e., combinational logic circuitry needed to perform 1-bit operations in the ALU.

A computer system X, can be characterized by a triplet containing six independent entities as follows:

$$T(X) = < K X K', D X D', W X W' >$$

Where

K = the number of processors (PCUs) within the computer.

D = the number of ALUs or PEs under the control of one PCU.

W = the word length of an ALU or of a PE.

W' = the number of pipeline stages in all ALUs or in a PE

D' = the number of ALUs that can be pipelined.

K = the number of PCUs that can be pipelined.

For example:

Texas Instrument's Advanced Scientific Computer (TI— ASC) has following specifications:

$$T(\text{ASC}) = <1 \times 1, 4 \times 1, 64 \times 8>$$

$$= <1, 4, 64 \times 8>$$

It has one controller controlling four arithmetic pipelines and each has 64—bit word length and eight stages.

Please note that whenever the second entity i.e., *K'*, *D'* or *W'* equals to 1, we drop it, since pipelining of one stage or of one unit is meaningless.

Also note that, in many computers, the number of stages in different functional units is variable. In such cases, the range of pipeline stages is indicated within parenthesis. For example, Cray-1 Supercomputer contains a variable number of pipeline stages in all ALUs. So, a variable range of I to 14 is used. That is,

$$T(\text{Cray-1}) = <1, 12 \times 8, 64 \times (1 \sim 14)>$$

For Cray-1, the pipeline chaining degree is a variable with a maximum value equal to 8.

Let us consider another example. CDC 6600, has a CPU with an ALU that has 10 specialized hardware functions, each of word length of 60-bits. Furthermore, CDC-6600 has 10 peripheral I/O processor which can operate in parallel. Each I/O processor has one ALU with a word length of 12-bits. So, we say that:

$$T(\text{CDC}) = T(\text{CPU}) * T(\text{I/O Processor})$$

$$= <1, 1 * 10, 60> * <10, 1, 12>$$

Yet, in another example of Illiac-IV, we state its system specification as follows

T(Illiac-IV) $=< 1, 64, 64 >$

Note here that K′, D′ and W′ are being omitted as they are all 1.

8.9.4 Classification based on Coupling between Processing Elements (PEs)

Coupling refers to the way in which PEs cooperate with one another. A system may be:

1. **Loosely Coupled: The degree of coupling between the PEs is less.**

   Example: A parallel computer consisting of workstations connected together by **LAN (like Ethernet) is loosely coupled.** In this case, each one of the workstations works independently. If they want to cooperate, they will exchange messages. Thus, logically they are autonomous and physically they do not share any memory and communicate via I/O channels.

2. **Tightly coupled: The degree of coupling between the PEs is more.** A tightly coupled parallel computer shares a common main memory (MM). So, the communication among PEs is very fast. The cooperation may be at the level of instructions also. It is carried out by each PE as they share a common memory.

   We have already tabulated the differences in the beginning of this chapter.

8.9.5 Classification based on Modes of Access Memory

This has already been discussed in this chapter.

8.9.6 Classification based on Grain Size

We shall now describe this type of classification. What is a grain size? We define it as follows

"The quantum of work done by a PE before it communicates with another processor is called as the grain size."

It determines the frequency of communication between PEs during the solution of a problem. This will correspond to the number of instructions carried out by PE before it sends the results to a cooperating PE. The grain sizes are classified as

(*a*) Very fine grain.

(*b*) Fine grain.

(*c*) Medium grain.

(*d*) Coarse grain.

We shall explain each one by one.

Very fine grain parallelism: Instruction level parallelism is exploited by having multiple functional units and overlapping steps during instruction execution. Thus, ILP exploits very fine grain parallelism and VLIW processor uses it effectively..

Fine grain parallelism: It will correspond to a thread. A thread may be the instructions belonging to one iteration of a loop, typically 100 machine instructions. Tightly coupled parallel computers can exploit fine grain parallelism effectively as the processors cooperate via a shared memory and time to access a shared memory is small (a few machine cycles).

Medium grain parallelism: It will correspond to a procedure (or subroutine). This grain is formed of 100 machine instructions.

Coarse grain parallelism: It will correspond to a complete program.

Please note that loosely coupled parallel computers can exploit only medium or coarse grain parallelism as the time to communicate results using a communication network will be a few 100 clock cycles and the quantum of work done by processors must be larger than this.

8.10 INSTRUCTION LEVEL PARALLELISM AND THREAD LEVEL PARALLELISM

Pipelining can overlap the execution of instructions when they are independent of one another. **This potential overlap among instructions is called as instruction level parallelism (ILP).** It is so called since then the instructions can be evaluated in parallel.

The amount of parallelism available within a basic block (a straight line code sequence with no branches) is quite small. For a typical MIPS program1 the average dynamic branch frequency is between 15% and 25%. It means that between four and seven instructions execute a pair of branches. Since, these instructions are likely to depend upon one another; the amount of overlap we can exploit within a basic block is likely to be much less than the average basic blocks size. To obtain substantial performance-enhancement, we must exploit ILP across multiple basic blocks.

Actually, processing of instructions in parallel requires three major tasks. They are-

Task 1: Checking dependencies between instructions to determine which instructions can be grouped together for parallel execution. Parallelism among instructions must be exploited by finding sequences of unrelated instructions that can be overlapped in the pipeline. This increases pipeline utilization (i.e., it is now full).

Task 2: Dynamic scheduling is used where the hardware rearranges instruction execution to reduce the hazards.

Task 3: Score boarding is the process of allowing instructions to execute out of order when there are sufficient resources and no data dependencies.

Thread Level parallelism (TLP) means use of multiple threads of execution that are inherently parallel. A thread is a separate process with its own instructions and data. A thread may be a process that is part of a parallel program or it may represent an independent program on its own. A thread has all states for it to execute.

TLP is an important alternative to ILP because it could be more cost-effective to exploit than ILP.

8.11 PERFORMANCE OF PARALLEL PROCESSORS — METRICS & MEASURES

The program behaviour and the machine capability need to be matched for an ideal. performance from a machine. It is not easy to achieve this perfect match. Better hardware technology, innovative architectural features and better resource management can enhance machine capability. However, it is difficult to predict program behaviour. This is because it depends totally on the application and run-time conditions. Other factors like algorithm design, data structures, language efficiency, programmer skill and technology, also affect the program behaviour.

Also note that the machine performance may change from program to program. So, it is difficult to achieve peak performance in real—life applications.

Next, we shall discuss the fundamental factors that affect the performance of a computer. They are as follows—

1. **Parallel Run Time, ($T(n)$): It is defined as the time required to run a program on an n—processor computer**

   If $n = 1$, $T(1)$ denotes the run time of a program on a single processor (Sequential). .

2. **Speed-up, ($S(n)$):** It is defined as the ratio of the time taken to run a program on a single processor ($T(1)$) to the time taken to run if on a parallel computer with identical processors ($T(n)$).

$$\therefore \qquad S(n) = \frac{T(1)}{T(n)}$$

Speed-up metric is a quantitative measure of performance. It denotes the relative benefit of running a program in parallel.

3. **Parallelism Profile in Programs: Degree of parallelism is the measure of the extent to which software Parallelism and hardware parallelism match.** There are 2 things that we usually talk about —

1. Degree of Parallelism (DOP) 2. Average Parallelism.

The execution of a program on a parallel computer may use different number of processors at different time periods during the execution cycle. For each time period, **the number of processors used to execute a program is defined as the degree of parallelism (DOP). Please note that DOP is a discrete time function, assuming only non-negative i.e., positive integer values. The plot of DOP as a function of time is called as the parallelism profile of a given program.**

Average Parallelism is, however, different. Consider a parallel computer consisting of n-**homogeneous processors.** The maximum parallelism in a profile is m'. In ideal case n >> m. The computing capacity (Δ) of a single processor is approximated by the execution rate, such as MIPS or MFLOPS, without considering the penalties from memory access, communication latency or system overhead. When *'i'* processors are busy during an observation period, we have DOP = *i*.

So, the total amount of work 'W' (instructions or computations) performed is proportional to the area under the profile curve.

$$W = \Delta \int_{t_1}^{t_z} DOP(t)dt$$

$$= \Delta \sum_{i=1}^{m} i \cdot t_1$$

Where

$$t_i = \text{total amount of time that DOP} = i \text{ and}$$

$$\sum_{i=1}^{m} t_i = (t_2 - t_1) \text{ is the total elapsed time.}$$

Then, the average parallelism is given by

$$A = \frac{1}{t_2 - t_1} \int_{t_1}^{t_2} DOP(t)dt$$

For example: Consider the Fig. 8.22 below:

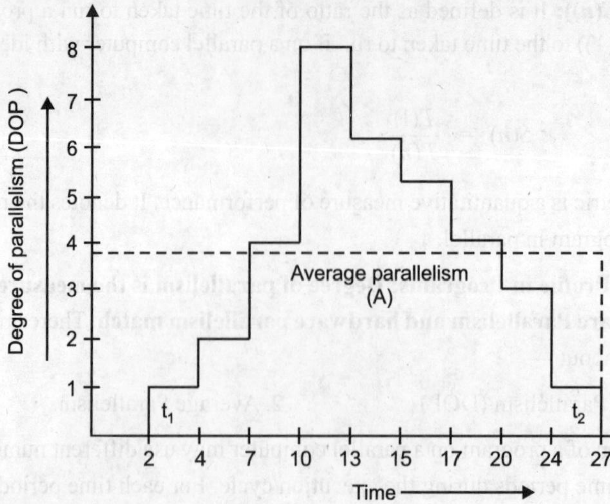

Fig 8.22. Parallelism profile at an algorithm

It is crystal clear from Fig. 8.22 that the parallelism profile '*m*' increases from 1 to 8 and then decreases to 0 during the time period (t_1, t_2). So, the average parallelism A is computed.

4. **Clock rate and CPI:** It is the clock that drives the CPU. It has a constant cycle time, τ, τ is measured in nanoseconds. Clock rate is defined as the inverse of cycle time.

$$f = \frac{1}{\tau}$$

Where '*f*' is the frequency (or clock rate).

The program size is decided by its **instruction count** (I_c) i.e., **the number of machine instructions to be executed in the program.** Different machine instructions require different number of clock cycles to execute. Therefore, cycles per instruction (CPI) becomes an important parameter to measure the time taken to execute each instruction.

$$\text{CPI} = \frac{\text{CPU clock cycles for a program}}{\textit{Instruction Count}}$$

But CPU Time = (CPU clock cycles for a program) × (clock cycle time) ...(1)

But $\tau = \dfrac{1}{f}$ ...(2)

Where

$$\text{CPU Time} = \frac{\text{CPU clock cycles for a program}}{\textit{Clock rate}}$$

But CPU Time = Instruction Count * CPI

(from equation - 1)

$$\therefore \quad = \frac{\textit{Instruction count. Clock cycle time}}{\textit{Clock Rate}}$$

$$\therefore \quad \text{CPU Time } (T) = I_c \times \text{CPI} \times \tau$$

or $$T = \frac{Seconds}{Program} = \frac{Instructions}{Program} \times \frac{Cycles}{Instruction} \times \frac{Seconds}{Cycle}$$

Where I_c = instruction count in a program

and τ = clock period.

5. **MIPS Rate and MFLOPS:** Let C be the total number of clock cycles required execute a given program. Then, the CPU time (T) is given by:

$$T = C \times \tau = \frac{C}{f}$$

$\therefore$ $$\text{CPI} = \frac{C}{I_C}$$

and $$T = I_c \times \text{CPI} \times \tau$$

$$= I_c \times \frac{\text{CPI}}{f}$$

The speed of the processor is usually measured in terms of **million instructions per second** (MIPS).

$$\text{MIPS rate} = \frac{I_C}{T \times 10^6} = \frac{f}{\text{CPI} \times 10^6}$$

$$\text{MIPS} = \frac{f \times I_C}{C \times 10^6}$$

MIPS rate varies with the clock rate (0. instruction count (4) and CPI of a given machine.

MFLOPS — Million Floating Point Operations per Second is emerging as a performance measure. MIPS and MFLOPS ratings are not convertible because they measure different ranges of operations. Both are used to describe instruction execution rate and floating point capability of a parallel computer.

6. **Efficiency ($E(n)$ or η): Efficiency of a program, on n processors is defined as the ratio of speed—up achieved and the number of processors used to achieve it.**

$\therefore$ $$\eta = E(n) = \frac{s(n)}{n} = \frac{Actual\ speed - up}{Ideal\ Speed - up}$$

$$= \frac{T(1)}{n[T(n)]}$$

Where $T(1)$ = Time taken to execute a program on sequential or uniprocessor system.

$T(n)$ = Time taken to execute same program with n number of processors by parallel system.

Please note that E(n) or η is the measure of the fraction of time for which a processor, is usefully employed.

$\therefore$ $$1 \le S(n) \le n$$

and $$\frac{1}{n} \le n \le 1$$

Also note that the maximum efficiency of 1 is never achieved due to parallel overheads.

Consider Fig. 8.23 below. It shows three different curves:

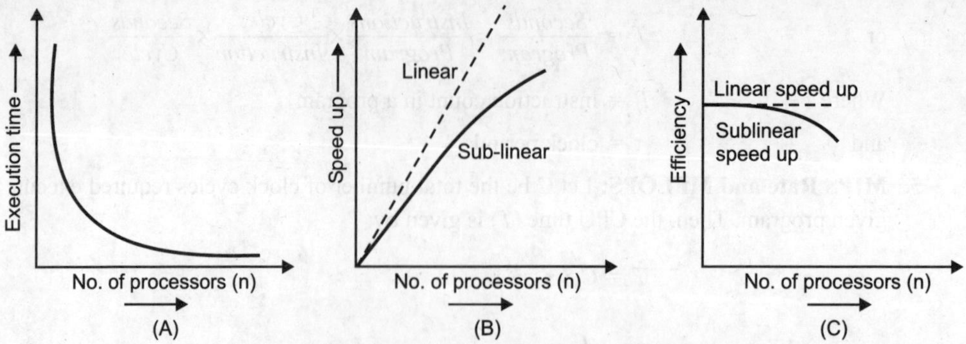

Fig. 8.23

Ideally, the speed-up should be linear. But generally it decreases due to parallel overhead. Parallel computers do not achieve linear speed-up or an efficiency of one because of parallel overheads due to Inter process communications, load imbalance, intertask synchronization etc. All the above sources are application or problem dependent. Efficiency indicates the actual speed-up achieved as compared with maximum value. Efficiency is lowest when the entire program is executed sequentially on a single processor and it is maximum when all n processors are fully utilized during complete execution period.

7. **Redundancy, *R*(*n*):** If $O(n)$ represents the total number of unit operations performed by a n-processor system then Redundancy in a parallel computation is defined as-

$$R(n) = \frac{O(n)}{O(1)}$$

It indicates the extent of matching between software parallelism and the hardware parallelism. It is obvious that $1 <= R(n) <= n$.

8. **Utilization, *U*(*n*) :** System utilization signifies the percentage of resources like processors, memories etc. that are busy during the execution of parallel program. It is defined as:

$$U(n) = R(n).\,E(n) = \frac{O(n)}{nT(n)}$$

9. **Quality of Parallelism, *Q*(*n*): *Q*(*n*) is directly proportional to speed-up , *S*(*n*), and efficiency, *E*(*n*) and inversely related to redundancy, *R*(n). It is given by the formula:-**

$$\mathbf{Q(n) = S(n).\,E(n) / R(n)}$$

$Q(n)$ is always upper-bounded by speed-up, $S(n)$ as $E(n) < 1$ and $R(n) < n$.

10. **Throughput Rate, W_s: A system throughput is defined as the number of programs executed per unit time on the system. Mathematically,**

$$W_S = \frac{Program}{Second} \quad \text{(system throughput)}$$

11. **CPU Throughput, *Wp*: It is given by the number of instructions executed per second. Mathematically,**

$$W_p = \frac{f}{I_C \times CPI}$$

Where f = clock rate

I_c = Instruction Count

CPI = Cycle/instructions.

$$W_p = \frac{MIPS \times 10^6}{I_C} \text{ (from equation 9)}$$

But $W_s < W_p$, due to additional overheads of the system because of I/O, compiler and OS, when multiple programs are interleaved for CPU execution by multiprogramming or time sharing operations.

Scalability Metrics

The following metrics affect the scalability of a system—

1. **Machine size (*n*):** The number of processors employed in a parallel computer system. A large machine size means more resources and more computing power.
2. **Clock rate (*f*):** It determines the basic machine cycle. We try to build a machine with components like CPUs, Memory, bus, network etc. driven by a clock which can scale up with better technology.
3. **Problem size (*s*):** The amount of computational workload or the number of data points used to solve a given problem. The problem size(s) is directly proportional to the sequential execution time $T(s, 1)$ for a uniprocessor system because each data point may demand one or more operations.
4. **CPU time (*T*):** The actual CPU time (in secs) elapsed in executing a given progranl on a parallel machine with n processors collectively. This is parallel execution time) denoted as $T(s, n)$ and is a function of both s and n.
5. **I/O demand (*d*):** The I/O demand in moving the program, data and results associated with a given application run. The I/O operations may overlap 'with the CPU, operations in a multiprogrammed environment.
6. **Memory Capacity (*m*):** The amount of main memory (in bytes or words) used in a program execution. **Please note that the problem size, the program size, the algorithms affect the memory demand and the data structures used. Also note that the memory demand varies dynamically during program execution.** Here, we refer to the maximum number of memory words demanded virtual memory is almost unlimited with a 64 bit address space. It is the physical memory, which is limited in capacity.
7. **Communication overhead (*h*):** The amount of time spent for interprocessor communication, synchronization, remote memory access etc. This overhead includes all non-computing operations, which do not involve the CPUs or I/O devices. This overhead $h(s, n)$ is a function of s and n and is not the part of $T(s, n)$. For a uniprocessor system, the overhead $h(s, 1) = 0$.
8. **Computer Cost (*c*):** The total cost of hardware and software resources required to carry out the execution of a program.
9. **Programming overhead (*p*):** The development overhead associated with an application program. Programming overhead (p) may slow down software productivity and thus requires a high cost. Unless stated, both computer cost and programming cost are ignored in our scalability analysis.

NOTE: Depending on the computational objectives and resource constraints imposed, one can fix some of the above parameters and optimize the remaining ones to achieve the highest performance with the lowest cost.

Hence, we say,

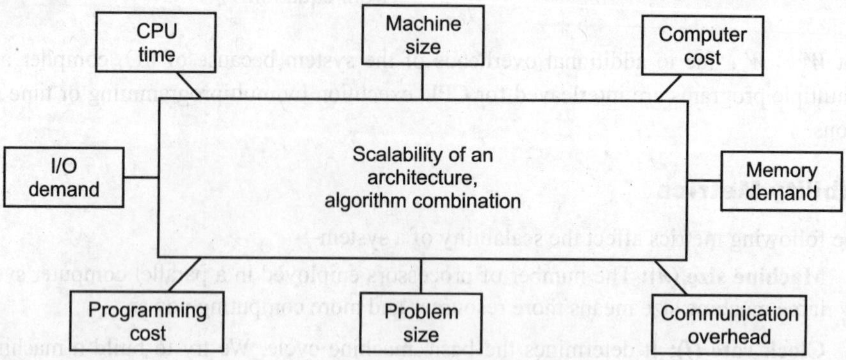

Fig. 8.24

We can compare programmability with scalability

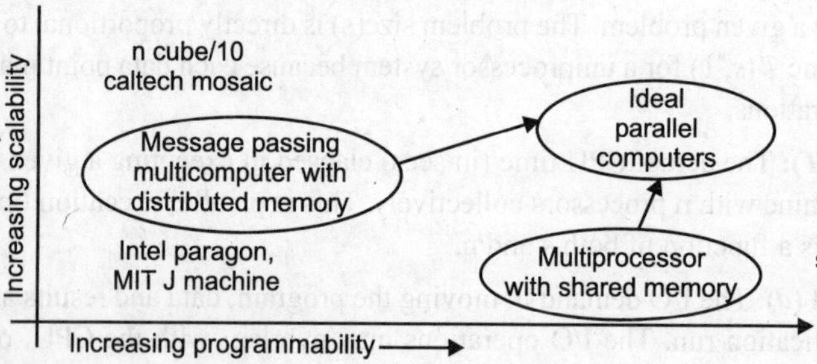

8.12 SPEED UP PERFORMANCE LAWS

Now, we are in a position to discuss some laws related to the speed—up of supercomputer or parallel computers.

8.12.1 Amdahl's Law - for fixed workload

Assuming there will be some parts that are only executed on one processor, the deal situation would be for all available processors to operate simultaneously for the other times. If the fraction of computation that cannot be divided into concurrent tasks is, *f* and n]o overhead incurs when the computation is divided into concurrent parts, the time to perform the computation with n processors is given by.

$$ft_s + (1-f)\, t_s/n$$

So, we draw now.

Illustrated is the case with a single serial part at the beginning of computation, but the serial part could be distributed throughout the computation. Hence the speed up factor is given by:

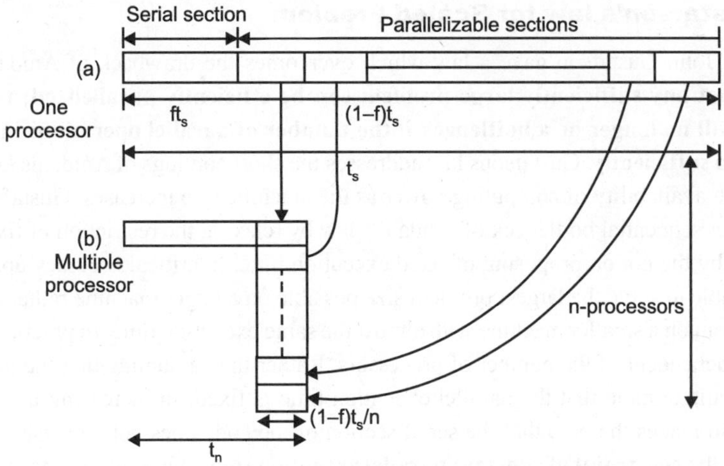

Fig. 8.25. Amdahl's law

$$S(n) = \frac{t_s}{ft_s + \frac{(1-f)t_s}{n}} = \frac{n}{1+(n-1)f}$$

This equation is known as Amdahl's law.

If we plot $S(n)$ versus, n, no. of processors, we get:

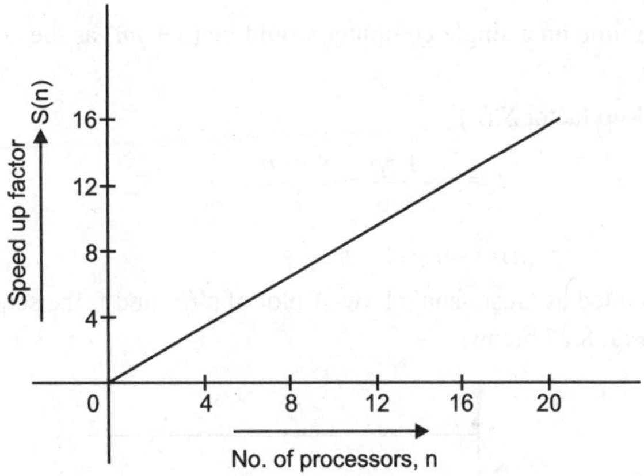

Fig 8.26. Speed-up versus n

We see that indeed a speed improvement is indicated. Even with an infinite number of processors, the minimum speed up is limited of 1/f, i.e.

$$\underset{n \to \infty}{S(n)} = \frac{1}{f}$$

Shortcomings of Amdahl's Law:

1. The work load cannot scale to match the available computing power as the machine size increases. Hence, the fixed load prevents scalability in performance.
2. The sequential bottleneck is a serious problem.

8.12.2 Gustafson's law for Scaled Problem

In 1988, John Gustafson gave a law which overcomes the drawback of Amdahls law. **This law states that any sufficiently large problem can be efficiently parallelized; the sequential operations will no longer be a bottleneck if the number of parallel operations in the problem is scaled—up sufficiently.** Gustafsons law addresses the short comings of Amdahls law that cannot scale to match availability of computing power as the machine size increases. Gustafson suggested a solution over sequential bottleneck of Amdahl's law by relaxing the restriction of fixed size of the problem and by the notion proposing of fixed execution time. In critical accuracy application, it is always desirable to solve the largest problem size possible on a larger machine rather than solving a smaller problem on a smaller machine with almost the same execution time. In practice, the problem size is not independent of the number of processors. Rather than assuming that the problem size is fixed, we should assume that the parallel execution time is fixed. In increasing the problem size, Gustafson also makes the case that the serial section of the code does not increase as the problem size. So, with the **constraint of constant parallel execution time,** the resulting speed-up factor will be numerically different from Amdahl's speed-up factor and is called as scaled sped-up factor.

In Amdahl's law, we fix the total execution time on a single processor as a constant. But, in Gustafson's law, the parallel execution time is constant rather than the serial execution time. Let us now derive the Gustafson's equation.

Let the execution time of the parallel computer be a serial part and a parallel part, $S + p$. For convenience, let

$$S + p = 1 \text{ (say)}$$

So, the execution time on a single computer would be $(S + pn)$ as the n parallel parts must be executed sequentially.

$\therefore$ Scaled speed-up factor $S'(n)$

$$= \frac{S+np}{S+p} = \frac{S+np}{1} \qquad \text{(from (1))}$$

$$S'(n) = n + (1 - n)s$$

This equation is called as Gustafson's Law. A plot of s'(n) and f, the sequential fraction of the program is shown in Fig. 8.27 below.

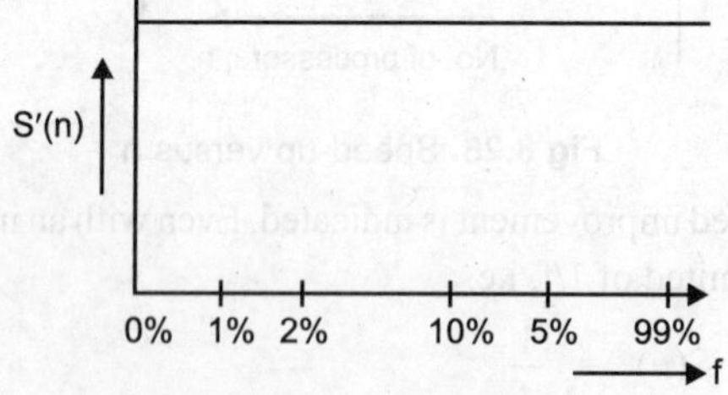

Fig. 8.27. Effect of Gustafson's law

Please note that the slope of the curve of Fig. 8.27 is much more flatter than in case of S(n) in Amdahl's law.

Suppose that we had a serial section of 5% and 20 PEs, then as per the definitions of Gustafsons law, the scaled speed up factor is

$$S'(n) = 0.05 + 0.95(20)$$
$$= 19.05$$

Whereas it is only 10.26 according to the Amdahl's law. Speed-ups of 1021, 1020 and 1016 have been achieved in practice with 1024 PEs. Thus, we can conclude that there will not be a problem of sequential bottleneck when the problem can scale to match the available computing power.

8.12.3 Memory bounded Speed-up Model — Sun and Ni's Law

In 1993, Xian-He Sun and Lionel Ni proposed this law. They developed a memory-bounded speed-up model. The idea was to solve the largest possible problem, limited only by the available memory capacity. This may result in some increase in execution time to achieve scalable performance. This law is a generalisation of Amdahfs law and Gustafson's law. The model maximizes the use of both CPU and memory capacity.

Let us derive its equation now.

Say, M = represents the memory requirement of a given problem.

and W = represent the computational workload.

Now, M and W are related to each other depending on the address space and the architectural constraints.

let $W = g(M)$

or $M = g^{-1}(W)$

In a multicomputer, the total memory capacity increases linearly with the number of nodes available. The execution time, T, will be a function of number of a processors, n and the workload, W and will also be related to memory requirement, M.

$\therefore$ $T = f(M)$

or $M = f^{-1}(T)$

The enhanced memory can be related to the execution time of the scaled workload as follows

$$T^* = f^*(nM)$$

Where nM is the increased memory capacity of n processor machine.

Now, $f^*.(nM) = F(n).F(M)$

$= F(n).T(n,W)$

where $T(n, W) = F(M)$

and f^* is a homogeneous function.

$F(n)$ reflects the increase in the execution time as memory increase n-times.

So, a fixed memory speed - up is given by :

$$S^*(n) = \frac{T_s + F(n)T_p(n, W)}{T_s + \dfrac{F(n)(T_p(n, w)}{n}}$$

$$= \frac{\alpha + F(n)(1-\alpha)}{\alpha + \dfrac{F(n)(1-\alpha)}{n}}$$

Where

$$T = T_s + T_p$$

T = Total execution time

T_s = Execution time for sequential load

T_p = Execution time for parallel load

α = Sequential fraction of a program

This equation of $S^*(n)$ for fixed-memory speed-up has been derived above on the basis of two assumptions

1. All the individual memory spaces forms a global address space. It means that there is a distributed shared memory space.
2. Full memory capacity is used up for solving scaled problem.

Now, three special cases arise.

Case 1: When $F(n) = 1$

This is when the problem size is fixed. In this case, the fixed memory speedup becomes equivalent to Amdahl's law, when fixed workload is given.

Case 2: When $F(n) = n$

This is when workload increases n-times, when memory is increased n-times.

So, the fixed memory speed up becomes equivalent to Gustsfson's law, when execution time is fixed.

Case 3: When $F(n) \geq n$

This is the case in which the computational workload increases faster than the memory requirement. Thus, memory bound or fixed memory model may give a higher speed up than the fixed execution time (Gustafsons) model. **So, we conclude that:-**

1. **Amdahl's law and Gustafson's law are special cases of Sun and Ni's law.**
2. **When computation grows faster than the memory requirement, the memory bound model may yield a higher speed up and better resource utilization.**

$$S_n^* \geq S_n' \geq S$$

8.13 CASE STUDY OF INTEL ITANIUM PROCESSOR

The first implementation. of IA-64 architecture is Itanium processor. It was jointly developed by HP and Intel. It has a blend of superscalar features.

The block diagram of Itanium processor is shown in Fig. 8.28. From the Fig. 8.28 it is clear that Itanium architecture includes

(*a*) Upto 6 instructions of 64—bit per clock cycle can be executed.

(*b*) It has 128 General Purpose Registers (GPRs)

(*c*) It has 3 level cache.

(*d*) It has large address space : 50 bit physical/64—bit virtual.

(*e*) Very few transistors in each core.

(*J*) It has nine functional units. All of them are pipelined.

(*g*) Instructions are fetched from LI cache.

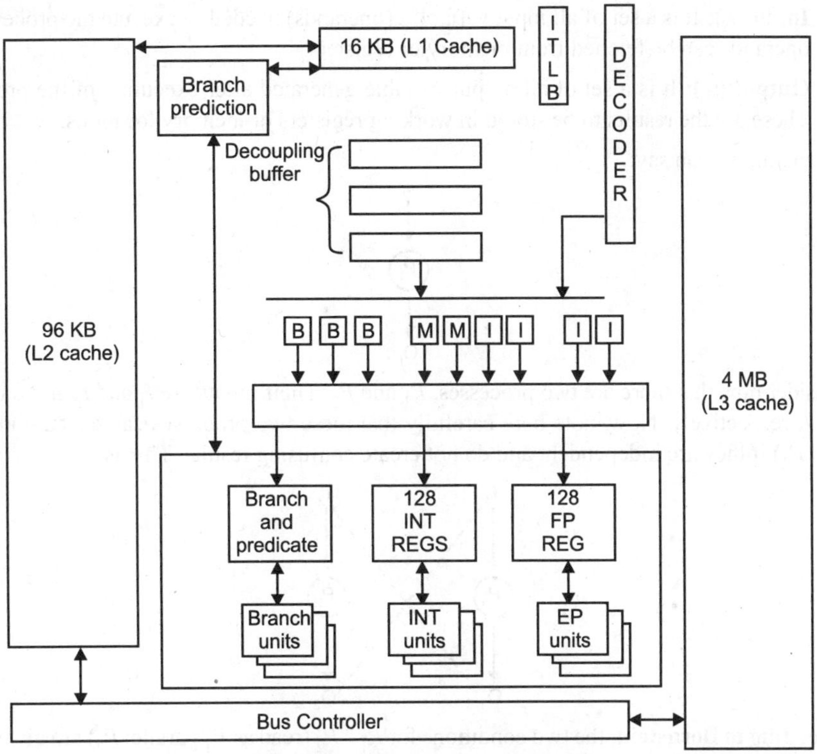

Fig. 8.28. Block diagram of Itanium CPU.

(*h*) **Decoupling** buffer is used to hold upto 8 bundles of instructions. It is fed by $L1$ instruction cache.

The organization of Itanium CPU is simpler than a conventional superscalar organization. No reservation stations (to study later on), no reorder buffers and no memory ordering buffers are observed. There is no register dependency—detection logic. It is replaced by explicit parallelism.

There are three levels of cache $L1$, $L2$ and $L3$. $L1$ cache is divided into a 16 KB instruction cache and a 16 KB data cache.

Each of these is a 4 way set associative with 32 byte line size. $L2$ cache is of 96 KB and is 6-way set associative with 64 byte line size. $L1$ and $L2$ caches are on chip with CPU. $L3$ cache is off-chip but on the same package as the processor.

8.14 CONDITIONS OF PARALLELISM (BERNSTEIN'S CONDITIONS)

The aim of a parallel programmer is to exploit parallelism in a given problem. And the ability to execute several program segments in parallel requires each segment to be independent of the other segments. This independence may be data independence, control independence and resource independence. But it is important to understand that all modules/programs need not be independent, i.e., they are depend nt. We need to identify such critical statements and to parallelize them.

Bernstein (in 1966), gave a set of conditions on the basis of which two (2) processes can execute in Parallel.

According to Bernstein—

(*a*) **Process (P_i):** It is a software entity.

(*b*) **Input (I_i):** It is a set of all input variables (operands) needed to execute the process. These operands can be fetched from memory or registers.

(*c*) **Output (0_i):** It is a set of all output variable generated after execution of the process, P_i. These are the results to be stored in working registers or memory locations.

In general, we can say:

Consider now that there are two processes, P_1 and P_2. Their inputs are I_1 and I_2 and outputs are O_1 and O_2 respectively. Now, note here carefully that these two processes can execute in parallel (i.e., $P_1 \parallel P_2$) if they are independent and do not create confusing results. That is,

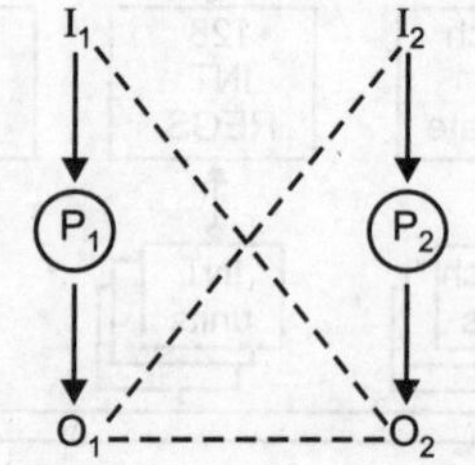

According to Bernstein, the two conditions for $P_1 \parallel P_2$ (read as P_1 parallel P_2) are given below:

Condition I: $I_1 \cap O_2 = \phi$ (these three conditions are known as

Condition II : $I_2 \cap O_1 = \phi$ Bernstein conditions).

Condition III : $O_1 \cap O_2 = \phi$

In general, a set of processes, $P_1, P_2, \ldots P_k$ can execute in parallel if Bernstein's conditions are satisfied on a pair wise basis. This means that:-

$P_1 \parallel P_2 \parallel P_3 \parallel \ldots\ldots\ldots P_k$ if and only if $P_i \parallel P_j$ for all $i \neq j$.

NOTE: This is true if the output of one process will not be used as input to the other process.

Properties of Parallelism Relation (||)

The following are the properties of parallelism relation in general:

1. **Commutativity:** The parallelism relation (||) is commutative, i.e. $P_i \parallel P_j$ implies $P_j \parallel P_i$.
2. **Non-transitivity:** The parallelism relation (II) is not transitive i.e., if $P_i \parallel P_j$ and $P_j \parallel P_k$, then $P_i \neq P_k$ (i.e., $P1$ does not parallelize with P_k)
3. **Associativity:** The parallelism relation is associative. That is, $(P_i \parallel P_j) \parallel P_k = P_i \parallel (P_j \parallel P_k)$

Please note that the condition $I_i \cap I_j \neq \phi$ does not prevent parallelism between two processes. However, violation of any of the three Bernstein's conditions prohibits parallelism between two processes. There are many program constructs that may prohibit parallelism.

Any statements or processes which depend on run-time conditions are not transformed to parallel form. **For example,** If statements or conditional branches. Recursions also prohibit parallelism.

In general, data dependence, control dependence and resource dependence all will prevent parallelism from being exploited.

Our aim is to identify these dependencies so that parallelization of such segments can be done.

Before discussing these dependencies, we must solve a problem now.

EXAMPLE 8.1: Consider the following five instructions P_1 to P_5 for some program where each instruction represents one process. Assume that each statement requires one step to execute. There is no pipelining. Show how sequential execution and parallel executions can be done.

P_1 : $C = D \times E$

P_2 : $M = G + C$

P_3 : $A = B + C$

P_4 : $C = L + M$

P_5 : $F = G \div E$

SOLUTION: If these five processes, $P_1 - P_5$ are executed **sequentially** then we find that 5 steps are needed. That is,

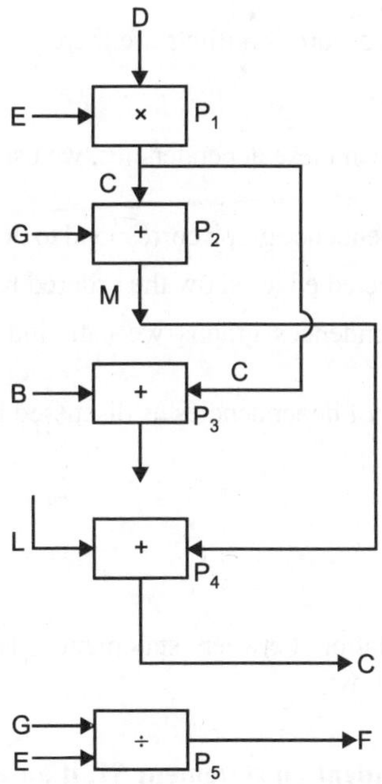

Fig. 8.28. Sequential Executive of P1 - P5

∴ Sequential execution requires 5-steps as shown in Fig. 8.28.

Now consider the parallel execution case. If two adders are available simultaneously, the parallel execution requires only three steps. That is,

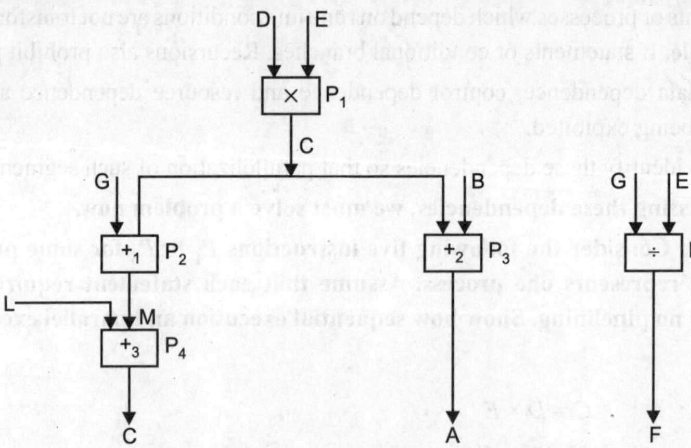

Fig. 8.29 Parallel execution of $P_1 - P_5$

∴ Parallel Execution requires **3 steps only.** From Fig. 8.29, it is clear that:

$$\left.\begin{array}{l} P_1 \parallel P_5 \\ P_2 \parallel P_3 \\ P_2 \parallel P_{5e} \\ P_5 \parallel P_3 \\ P_4 \parallel P_5 \end{array}\right\} \quad \text{i.e. } P_2 \parallel P_3 \parallel P_5 \text{ is thus possible.}$$

and this is possible only if no resource conflicts are there.

Types of Dependencies

To describe the relations between these dependencies, we usually draw dependence graphs. We use the following terms here:

1. **Nodes:** The nodes of a dependence graph correspond to the program statements/ instructions.
2. **Directed Edges:** The directed edges show the ordered relations among the statements.

When we analyze these dependences graphs we can find out the areas where chances of parallelization exist.

There are three (3) main types of dependencies as discussed below:

1. **Data Dependence.**
2. **Control Dependence.**
3. **Resource Dependence.**

I. Data Dependence

It represents an ordering relation between statements. There are five (5) types of data dependencies. They are defined below:

(*a*) Flow dependence:

A statement *S*2 is flow-dependent on statement *S*1, if an execution path exists from *S*1 to *S*2. It is denoted as follows:

$$S1 \longrightarrow S2$$

Here, there should be atleast one output of *S*1 that feeds *S*2 as an input.

(*b*) Antidependence:

A statement *S*2 is antidependent on statement *S*1, if ***S*2 follows *S*1 in program order and if the output of *S*2 overlaps the input to *S*1.** It is denoted as follows:

$$S1 \;\longrightarrow\!\!\!\!\!\!\!\!+\;\; S2 \text{ (with a crossed bar)}$$

(c) Output dependence:

Two statements are **output dependent if they produce** (or write) **the same output variable**. It is denoted by:

$$S1 \longrightarrow S2$$

(d) I/O dependence:

It occurs because the same file is referenced by both I/O statements. It is not because the same variable is involved. **Note that read and write are I/O statements.**

(e) Unknown dependence:

There are some critical situations wherein dependencies cannot be determined. This is known as **unknown dependency.**

For examples:

1. Subscript of a variable is itself subscribed e.g. a [*i*[*j*]].
2. Subscript does not contain the loop index variable. e.g. a [ ].
3. A variable appears twice with subscripts having different coefficients of the loop variable.
4. Subscript is nonlinear in the loop index variable.

When any of these situations exists, we say unknown dependencies exist. **We are in a position to solve some problems now.**

EXAMPLE 8.2: Given the following four statements *S*1 - *S*4. Find out the data dependencies by drawing its data dependence graph:

***S*1**	:	**Load *R*1, *A***
***S*2**	:	**Add *R*2, *R*1**
***S*3**	:	**Move *R*1, *R*3**
***S*4**	:	**Store *B*, *R*1**

SOLUTION: We find that:

(*a*) *S*2 is **flow dependent** on *S*1 because the variable A is passed via register, *R*1. So,

$$S1 \longrightarrow S2$$

(*b*) *S*3 is **anti dependent** on *S*2 because of the conflicts in register contents of *R*1. So,

$$S2 \longrightarrow\!\!\!\!\!\!\!+\;\; S3$$

(*c*) *S*3 is **output dependent** on *S*1 because they both modify the same register, *R*1. So, we draw its dependence graph:

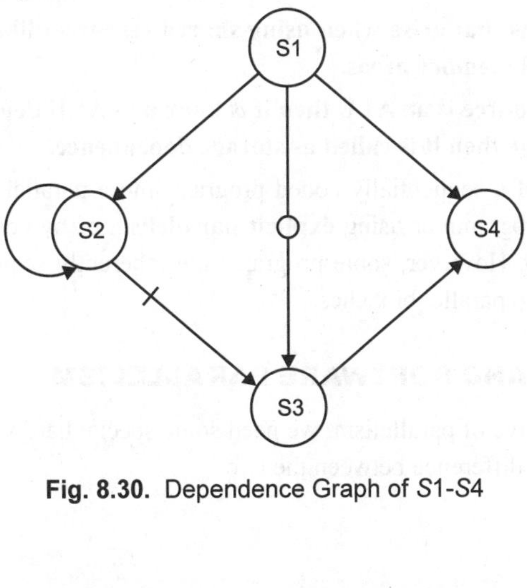

Fig. 8.30. Dependence Graph of *S*1-*S*4

NOTE: that it is not necessary that statements will always be related. For example, *S*2 and *S*4 in above graph of Fig. 8.30 are totally independent.

EXAMPLE 8.3: Consider another code snippet with some I/O operations

*S*1	:	Read (4), *A*(*I*)
*S*2	:	Rewind (4)
*S*3	:	Write (4), *B*(*I*)
*S*4	:	Rewind (4).

Find dependencies and draw its dependence graph?

SOLUTION: We find that

(*a*) *S*1 and *S*3 (read and write statements) are I/O dependent on each other because they both access the same file from the tape unit 4.

(*b*) No other dependency is found here. So, we draw its dependency graph now:

Fig. 8.31. Shows I/O dependence

II. Control Dependence

A situation where the order of execution of statements cannot be determined before run-time. For e.g., the *IF* statement of FORTRAN will not be resolved until run-time. Different branches of *IF*, may introduce or eliminate data dependencies among instructions.

Consider 2 Situations now.

Situation 1: Control independent loops	Situation 2: Control dependent loops
Do 10 *I* = 1, *N* *A*(*I*) = *C*(*I*) If (*A* (*I*). LT. 0) *A*(*I*) = 1 10 CONTINUE	Do 20 *I* = 1, *N* If (*A* (*I*-1). *EQ*. 0) *A* (*I*) = 0 20 CONTINUE

What I want to show from these two scenarios is that in situation II, Wherein control dependency exists; parallelism is not exploited. Better compilers are now needed to exploit more parallelism.

III. Resource Dependence

It means the conflicts that arise when using shared resources like integer units, floating-point units, registers and memory areas.

If the conflicting resource is an ALU then it is known as ALU dependence. If the conflicts involve workplace storage then it is called as storage dependence.

The transformation of a sequentially coded program into a parallel executable form is done either manually by the programmer using **explicit parallelism** or by compiler detecting **implicit parallelism** automatically. However, some programs are inherently sequential in nature. So they cannot be decomposed into parallel branches.

8.15 HARDWARE AND SOFTWARE PARALLELISM

To achieve our objective of parallelism, we need some special hardware and software support. We shall now tabulate the difference between the two.

Hardware Parallelism	Software Parallelism
1. It is build into the machines architecture and hardware multiplicity. It is also known as machine parallelism.	1. It is exploited by the concurrent execution of machine language instructions in a program as coded by a programmer or as generated by a high-level language compiler.
2. It is a function of cost and performance trade offs.	2. It is a function of algorithm, programming style and compiler optimization.
3. It displays what is the resource utilization.	3. It displays patterns of simultaneously executable operations.

8.16 PROGRAM PARTITIONING AND SCHEDULING

We need to understand the terminologies first. They are discussed below:

(*a*) **Grain size or granularity: It is a measure of the amount of computation involved in a Software Process.**

(*b*) **Grain: It is a program segment that is chosen for parallel processing.**

(*c*) **Latency: It is a time measure of the communication overhead incurred between machine subsystems.**

For example: The time required by a PE to access the memory is known as the memory latency. Now we shall discuss about the levels of parallelism.

8.16.1 Levels of parallelism

Parallelism has been explored at five levels of processing. This is shown below in Figure 8.28.

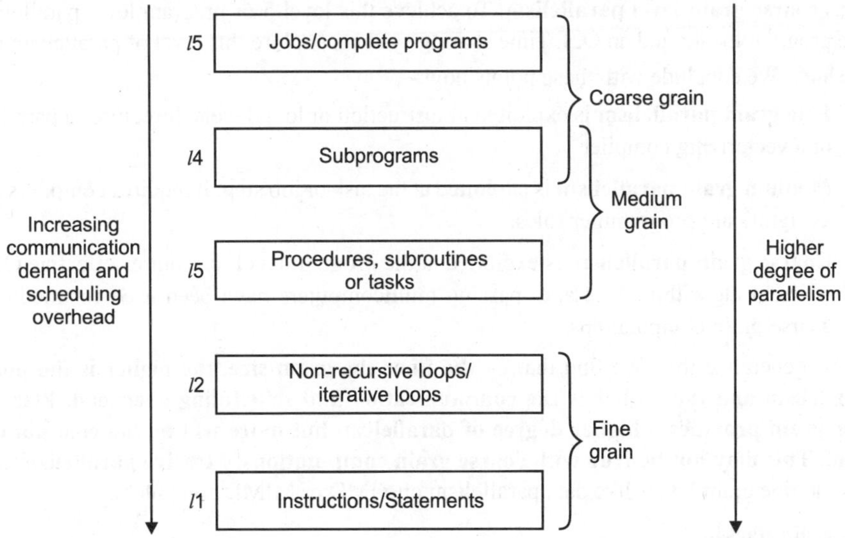

Level- 1 Instruction Level/Statement level parallelism

At this level of parallelism, a typical grain (or programs segment) consists of **less than 20 instructions. So, it is called as fine grain parallelism. Please note that the lower the level (in Fig. 8.28), the finer will be the granularity of the software processes.**

The advantage of this type of parallelism is the fact that at this level there will be huge amount of parallelism available. For doing so, we also need an optimizing compiler. It is a compiler which automatically detects parallelism. It converts the source code to a parallel form which can be understood by the run-time system. **Also note that detecting instruction level parallelism by an ordinary programmer in a source code is difficult.**

Level-2: Loop level parallelism

At the loop level, a grain size will have less than 500 instructions. (whereas in level 1 above we had just 20). What we can do is that if some loop operations are non-recursive and independent in successive iterations then we can vectorize them for pipelined execution. **Note that it is difficult to parallelize recursive loops.** This level of parallelism is better and finer as compared to level-3 and level-5. This type of grain is very suitable for a parallel computer.

Level-3 Procedure level parallelism

At this level, a typical graph corresponds to medium size at the task, procedural, subroutine or functional levels. The grain size is usually less than 2000 instructions. **Please note that the detection of parallelism at this level is much more difficult than at the fine-grain levels.** The programmers, however, need to work hard. They must restructure a program at this level. They need compilers also.

Level-4: Subprogram level parallelism

At this level, a typical grain corresponds to subprograms or job steps. The grain size is **thousands of instructions.** Earlier, the parallelism at this level has been exploited by algorithm designers or programmers and not by the compilers.

Level-5 Job/Program level parallelism

At this level, the grain corresponds to the independent jobs or programs for parallel execution. The grain size can be from **tens of thousands of instruction in a single program.** So, it is also known as **coarse grain level parallelism**. To achieve this level-5 or program level parallelism we need the program loader and an O.S. Time sharing systems explore this level of parallelism only.

Conclusions: We conclude with these points now:-

1. **Fine grain parallelism** is exploited at instruction or loop levels. It requires a parallelizing or a vectorizing compiler.
2. **Medium grain parallelism** is exploited at the task or job step. It requires compilers as well as significant programmer roles.
3. **Coarse grain parallelism** is exploited at the program level. It requires effective O.S. and efficient algorithm. Message- passing multicomputers have been used for medium and coarse-grain computations.

Let us generalize this. We find that — **the finer the grain size, the higher is the potential for parallelism and the higher is the communication and scheduling overhead. Please note that fine grain provides a higher degree of parallelism but more will be the communication overhead. This may not be true with coarse grain computations. Massive parallelism** is often found at the fine grain levels like data parallelism on SIMD or MIMD computers.

What is grain packing?

This approach was introduced by Lewis in 1988 for parallel programming. The **idea of grain packing** is to apply fine grain first in order to achieve a higher degree of parallelism. Then we combine (pack) multiple fine-grain nodes into a coarse-grain node if it can eliminate unnecessary communication delays or reduce scheduling overhead. Usually, all fine-grain operations within a single coarse-grain node are assigned to the same CPU for execution. Fine-grain partition of a program demands more inter processor communication than that required in a coarse-grain partition. Thus, grain packing offers a trade off between parallelism and communication overhead. Grain packing removes communication delays. **Also note that the internal delays among fine grain operations within the same coarse-grain node are negligible.** This is due to the fact that communication delay is contributed mainly by inter-PE delays and not by the delays within the same processor. Hence, the choice of optimal grain size is must. It is only then we can achieve the shortest schedule for the nodes on a parallel computer. **We are in a position to solve some problems now.**

EXAMPLE 1: Consider the following program —

Begin

1. a:=1
2. b:=2
3. c:=3
4. d:=4
5. e:=5
6. f:=6
7. g:=a*b
8. h:=c*d
9. i:=d*e
10. j:=e*f
11. k:=d*f
12. 1:=j*k
13. m: = 4*1
14. n:= 3*m
15. o : = n*i
16. p: = o*h
17. q : = p*q

Show fine grain program graph before packing. Convert it to a coarse grain program graph after packing. [GGSIPU, M-Tech (IT) 6th sem., May 2003]

SOLUTION. We draw the program graph. It shows the structure of a program. Each node in this graph corresponds to a computational unit in the program. The grain size is measured by the number of basic machine cycles - both processor and measured cycles that are needed to execute all the operations within the node. How a node is represented?

It is shown below

(n, s) denotes (node-number, grain-size)

(x, i) denotes (input, delay)

(z, k) denotes (output, delay)

(y, j) and (g, h) are other inputs and outputs respectively.

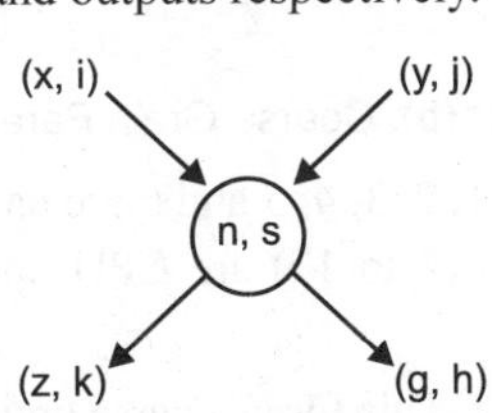

So, the grain size reflects the number of computations involve in a program segment. Fine-grain nodes have a smaller grain size and coarse-grain nodes have a larger grain size.

So, we draw its fine grain program graph first.

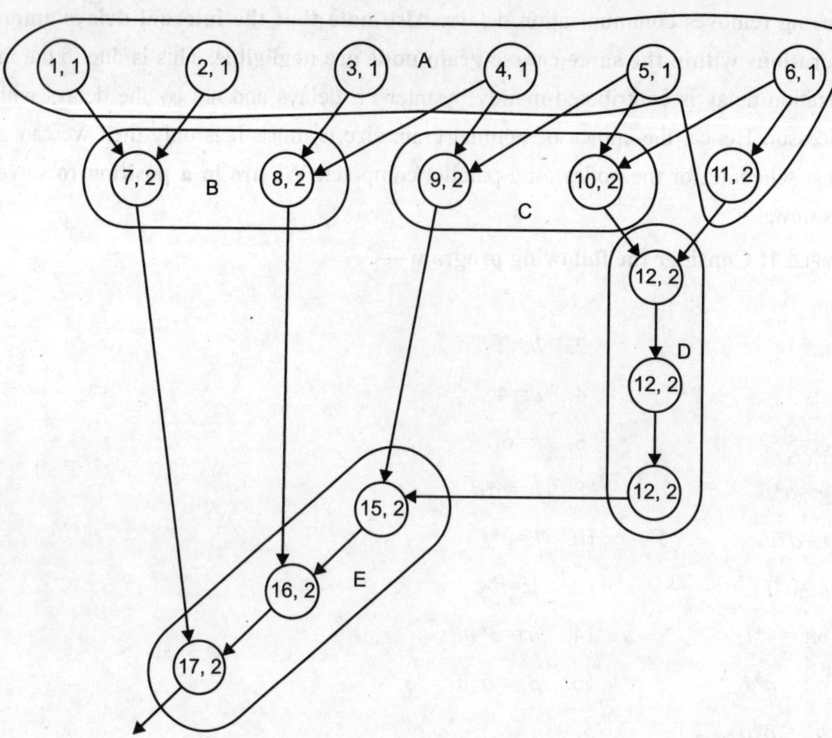

Fig. 8.31(a). Fine grain parallelism

So, we convert it to a coarse grain program graph now.

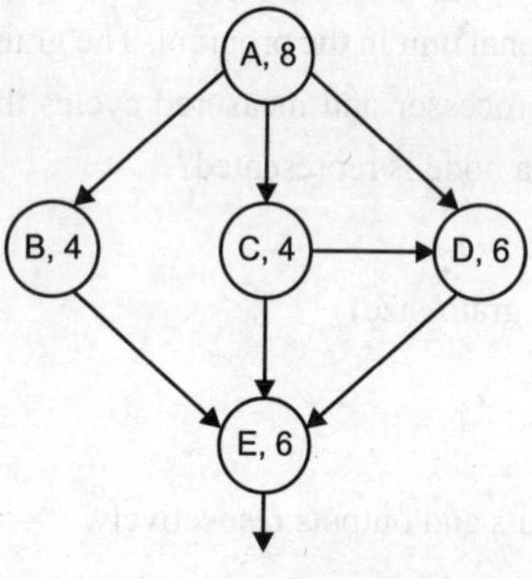

Fig. 8.31(b). Coarse Grain Parallelism

In **Figure** - ***a***, we find that nodes 1, 2, 3, 4, 5 and 6 are data fetch operations from / to memory that takes one cycle. All other nodes (7 to 17) are CPU operations, each requiring 2 cycles to complete.

In **Figure** - ***b***, we do grain packing. This forms coarse grain nodes with larger grain sizes (from 4 to 8 as shown in Fig. b). **Please note that the node (A, 8) in Fig. b, is obtained by combining the nodes (1, 1), (2, 1), (3, 1), (4, 1), (5, 1), (6, 1) and (11, 2) of Fig. a.** And the grain size of node - A is the summation of all grain sizes of all these nodes i.e., (1 + 1 + 1 + 1 + 1 + 1 + 2 = 8). So, we get (A, 8). Similarly, other packings are done.

EXAMPLE 8.2: Draw dependence graphs for the following programs:

(*a*) *S*1: *A*=*B*+*D*	(*b*) *S*1: *X*—SIN(*Y*)
*S*2: *C*=*A**3	*S*2: *Z*=*X*+*W*
*S*3: *A*=*A*+*C*	*S*3: *Y*= – 2.5**W*
*S*4: *E*=*A*/2	*S*4: *X*= cos (*Z*)

SOLUTION:

(*a*) 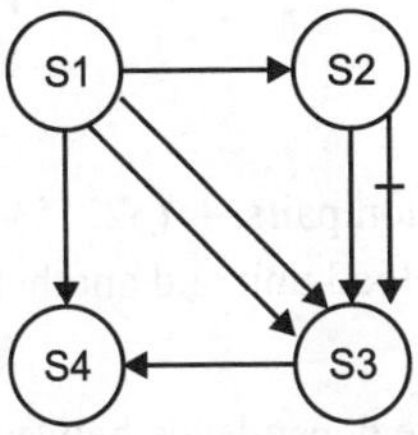

(*b*) 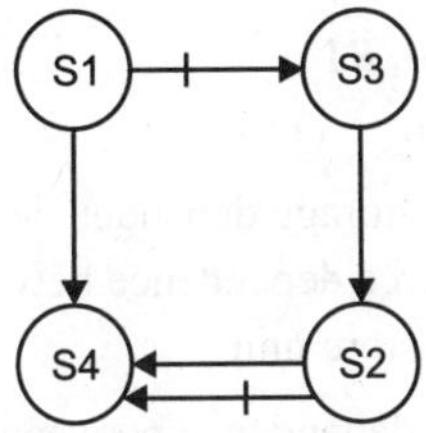

EXAMPLE 8.3: Consider the following FORTRAN code:

```
        DO 10 1 = 2, N
S1:     A (I + 1) = B (I – 1) + C (I)
S2:         B (I) = A (I) × K
S3:         C (I) = B (I) – 1
10 continue
```

Determine the data dependencies in this program?

SOLUTION: The graph is shown below. The subscript is used to indicate the iteration:

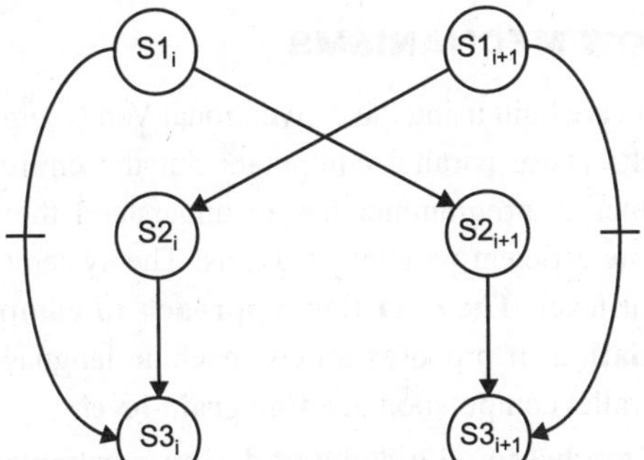

EXAMPLE 8.4: Analyze the data dependencies among the following statements in a given program:

***S*1: Load *R*1, 1024**

***S*2: Load *R*2, *M*(10)**

***S*3: Add *RI*, *R*2**

***S*4: Store *M*(1024), *R*l**

***S*5: Store *M*((*R*2)), 1024**

Where (R_i) means the context of register R_i and Memory (10) contains 64 initially.

(*a*) **Draw a dependence graph to show all the dependencies.**

(*b*) **Are there any resource dependencies if only one copy of each functional unit is available in the CPU?**

(*c*) **Repeat the above for the following program statements:**

S1: Load *RI*, *M* (100)

S2: Move *R2*, *R*l

S3: Inc *R*l

S4: Add *R2*, *R1*

S5: Store *M* (100), *R1*

SOLUTION:

(*a*) Yes, there are storage dependencies between the instruction pairs — (*S2*, *S5*) and (*S4*, *S5*). There is resource dependence between *S*1 and *S*2 on the load unit and another between S4 and *S*5 on the store unit.

(*b*) There is ALU dependence between *S*3 and *S*4 and storage dependence between *S*1 and *S*5.

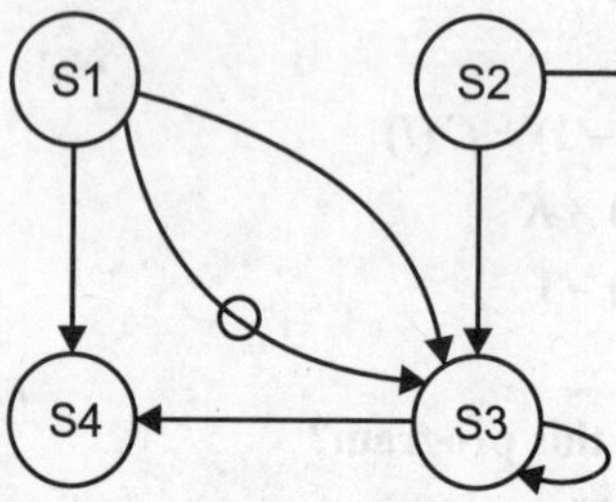

8.17 PROGRAM FLOW MECHANISMS

Many parallel computers are built using the conventional Von Neumann architecture processors (PEs) as the building block. These parallel computers put the entire burden of parallelising a procedure on the programmer. A programmer has to understand the underlying architecture of the parallel computer to write efficient parallel programs. The systems do not attack the issue of parallelism at a fundamental level. **The data flow approach to computing considers the issue of parallelism as its foundation.** It proposes a new machine language which offers a powerful formalism for describing parallel computation at a **fine grain level.**

Reduction computers are based on a demand driven mechanism. It initiates an operation based on the demand for its results by other computations. We discuss each of these now.

8.18 CONTROL FLOW, DATA FLOW AND REDUCTION COMPUTERS

We have three categories of computers:

(*a*) Control Flow Computers (or Von Neumann Computers).

(*b*) Data Flow Computers.

(*c*) Reduction Computers.

I. Control Flow or Von Neumann's Conventional Computers

These computers use a program counter (PC) to sequence the execution of instructions in a program. These machines are also called as control-driven machines because the program flow is explicitly controlled by programmers. These computers use shared-memory to store program instructions as well as data. Instructions operate on variables in shared memory. Because the memory is shared so execution of one instruction may produce side effects on other instructions too. This is not preferable as it prohibits parallelism. These systems are uniprocessor system and are sequential machines i.e., execution of instructions take place from left to right and top to bottom. However, note that these control flow machines can be made parallel by using parallel language constructs or parallel computers.

For example: 8085 CPU, 8086 CPU, Pentium-IV work on control flow mechanism.

II. Data Flow Computers/Data-driven Computers/Eager Machine

These machines are eager for data to be present. If it is present then the instruction is executed. These computers are thus known as **data driven computers or eager machines.** In a data driven program, **the instructions are not ordered. There is no shared memory.** Thus, data is stored inside instructions. The results or data tokens are passed directly between the instructions. Actually, a copy of data is passed to instructions. If an instruction has consumed these data token then they (tokens) are not available for reuse by other instructions. In these computers there is-

- No shared memory.
- No Program Counter (PC)
- No Control Sequencer.

Since there is **no memory sharing** so there are **no side effects seen** here. What these computers require is that they should be able **to detect data's presence,** to **match the data** tokens with the **needy instructions** and to enable the **chain reaction of asynchronous instruction executions.** We shall be discussing about these a bit later. **Please note however, that a pure data flow computer exploits fine grain parallelism at the instruction level.**

What is a data flow program graph?

A **machine language program** of a data flow computer is represented by a **data flow program** graph. This graph is made up of operators connected by **arcs.** Arcs carry tokens which have **values.** An operator with **two input** arcs and one output arc is shown below in Fig. 8.32.

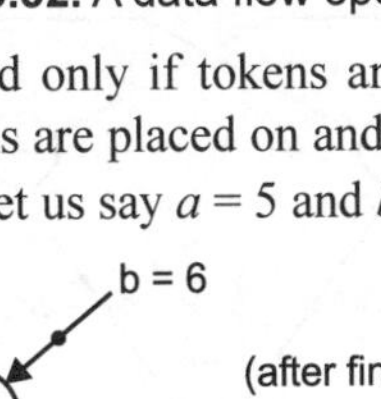

Fig 8.32. A data flow operator

The operator of Fig. 8.32 is enabled only if tokens are present in both its input arcs and no token is present in its output arc. Tokens are placed on and removed from the arcs according to the firing rules. To explain the firing rule, let us say $a = 5$ and $b = 6$ in above Fig. 8.32. Then, we have:

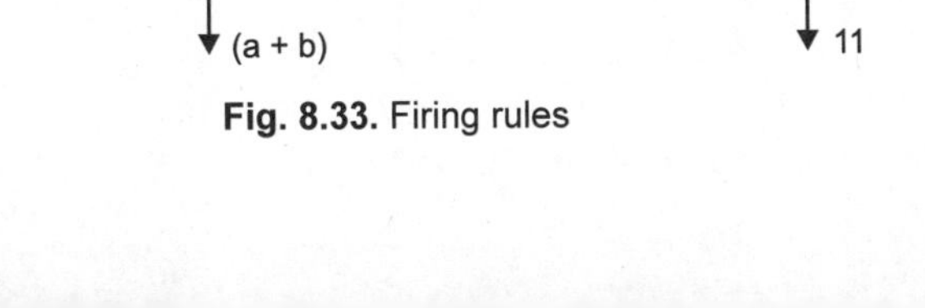

Fig. 8.33. Firing rules

Please note that here, an operator fires, i.e., the tokens in the two input arcs are removed, the operation (+) is applied on the values carried by the tokens and a token with the result value is placed on the output arc. This is what exactly happens in this example.

We are in a position to solve a problem now.

EXAMPLE 8.1: Draw a data flow graph to compute the expression given below: $(x + y) * (x - y)$? What happens when $x = 4$ and $y = 32$ appears on the input arc?

[GGSIPU, B. TECH. (CSE)-7TH SEM., 1ST MIHORS, 2012]

SOLUTION: Here, x and y are two operands and there are 3 operators (+, -, *). We draw now:

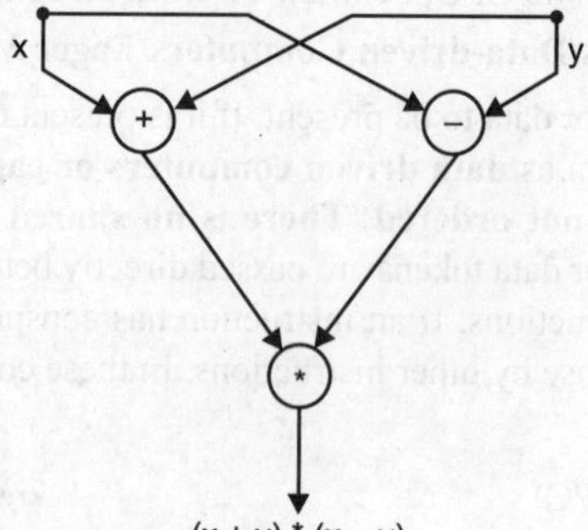

Fig. 8.34. A data flow operator

Now, say $x = 4$ and $y = 32$ appears on the input arc, then we draw:

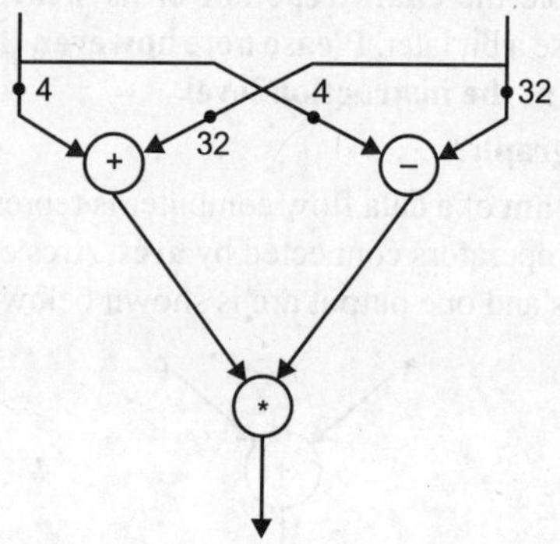

Then, in the next stage we get:

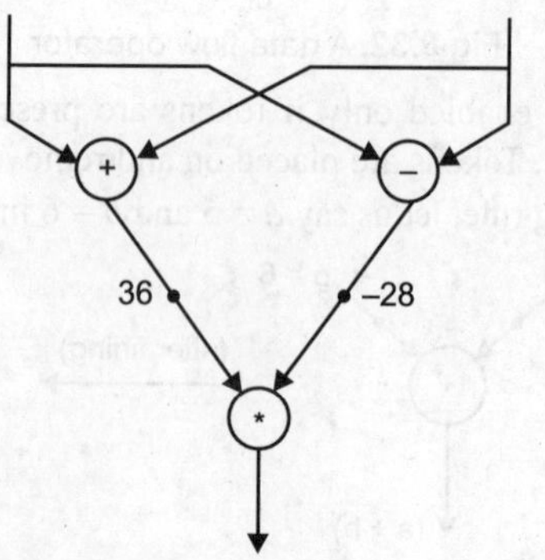

And, finally we get:

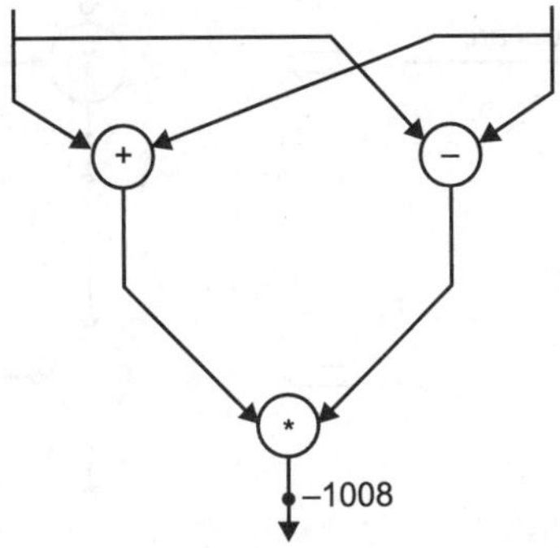

So, we find that the operators may be connected as shown above to form a data flow program graph. If the tokens with values for x and y are placed in the input arc, both operators + and - can fire simultaneously and place the result token on the respective output arcs. As soon as both the output tokens are generated, the * operator fires giving the result (as -1008 in our example).

Other operators used in Data flow graph:

1. **Fork:** A fork looks like this:

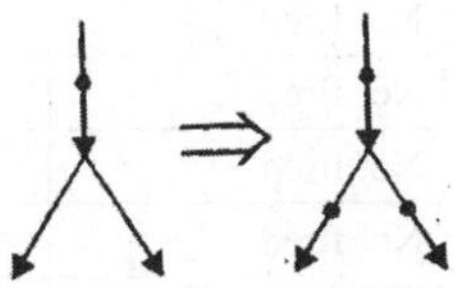

Fig. 8.35. Fork operation

In this notation, as soon as -a token arrives on the input arc it is copied in each of its output arcs; as shown in Fig. 8.35.

2. **Function:** Fig. 8.36 depicts a function.

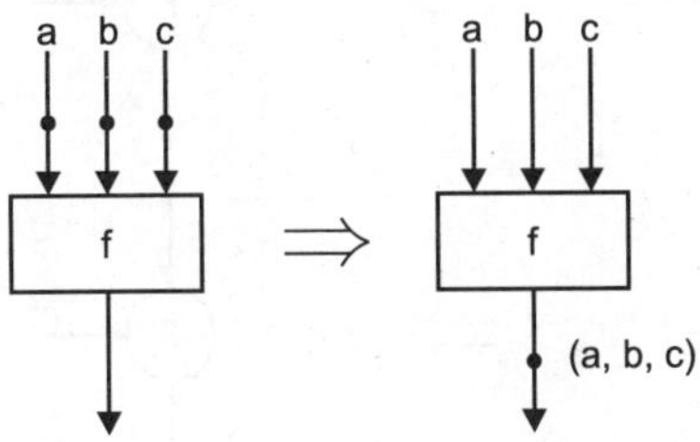

Fig. 8.36. Function operation

Herein, after the tokens arrive on all the input arcs, result token is placed on the output arc.

3. **True gate**: A true gate is shown in Fig. 8.36

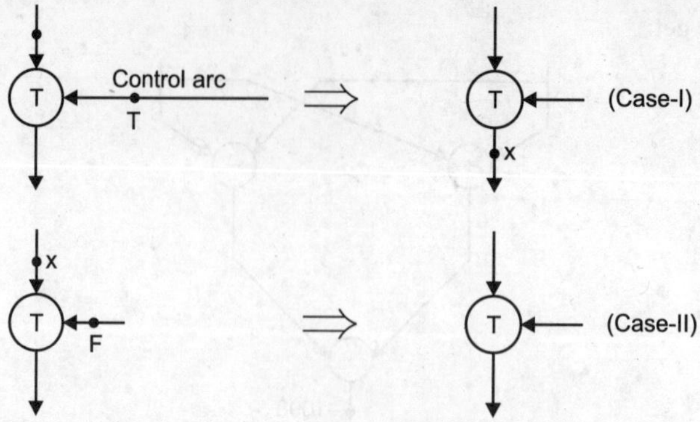

Fig. 8.37. True Gate

Case I: When a 'true' token (*T*) arrives on the control arc of this graph and a token x arrives on the input arc, the gate fires and '*x*' is transmitted to the output arc.

Case II: When a 'false' token (*F*) arrives on the control arc and '*x*' arrives on the input arc, then the gate fires with no token on the output arc. Both x' and F tokens on the input arc are destroyed.

Thus, we can draw a true gate operation table as follows:

Input arc	Control arc	Status of the operator	Output arc	Remarks
Nil	Nil	Not fired	Nil	Waiting for inputs
Nil	*T*	Not fired	Nil	Waiting for input
Nil	*F*	Not fired	Nil	Waiting for input
x	NIL	Not fired	Nil	Waiting for control
x	*T*	Fired	*x*	*x* and *T* consumed
x	*F*	Fired	Nil	*x* and *F* consumed

4. False gate. A false gate is shown in Fig. 8.38.

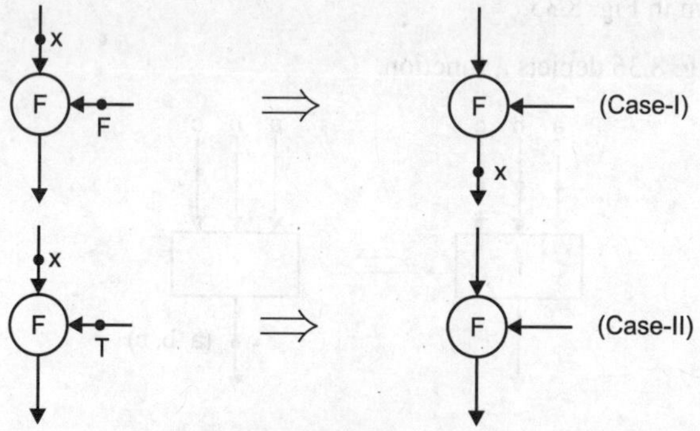

Fig. 8.38. False gate

A false gate shown above in Fig. 8.38, works in a similar fashion. It fires when an input token and a control token both arrive.

Case I. If the control token is *F* then the input token is transmitted to the output.

Case II. If the control token is *T* then both input and control tokens are destroyed and no output token appears.

5. **Merge.** A merge operator is shown below in Fig. 8.39

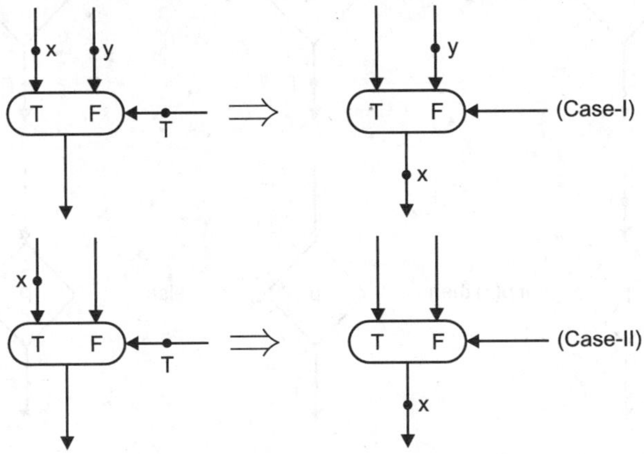

Fig. 8.39. Merge operator

It is seen in Fig. 8.39 that depending on whether the token on the control arc is *T* or *F*, the input token from the appropriate arc is placed on the output arc. The token on the input arc which is not selected is not destroyed. The firing rules of the merge-operator are listed below:

Input T arc	Input F arc	Control arc	Status of operation	Output arc	Remarks
Nil	Nil	Nil	Not fired	Nil	Both x and *y* are not destroyed
Nil	Nil	*T*	Not fired	Nil	
Nil	Nil	*F*	Not fired	Nil	
Nil	*y*	*T*	Not fired	Nil	
Nil	*y*	*F*	fired	*y*	
Nil	*y*	Nil	Not fired	Nil	
x	Nil	*T*	fired	*x*	
x	Nil	*F*	Not fired	Nil	
x	*y*	*T*	fired	*x*	
x	*y*	*F*	fired	*y*	
x	Nil	Nil	Not fired	Nil	
x	*y*	Nil	Not fired	Nil	

6. **Predicate.** A predicate operator is shown below in Fig. 8.40. The values of the token in the two input arcs are compared by the predicate operator.

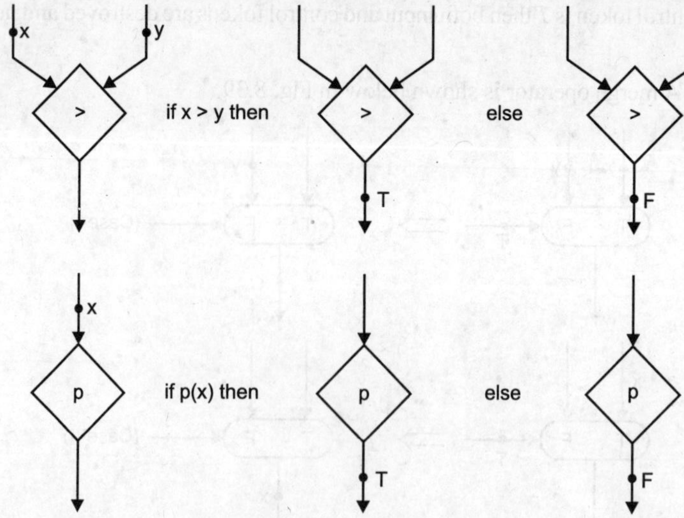

Fig. 8.40. Predicate operator

A *T*(true) or *F*(false) token is placed on the output arc based on whether the predicate succeeds or not.

7. **Switch.** A switch is not a new operator. It is a combination of *T* and *F* gates as shown below in Fig. 8.41.

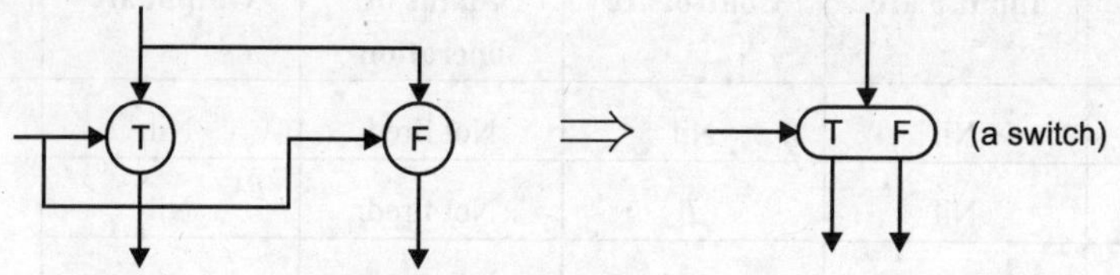

Fig. 8.41. Switch operator

The notation in concise is shown as a switch. How it works?

Case I:

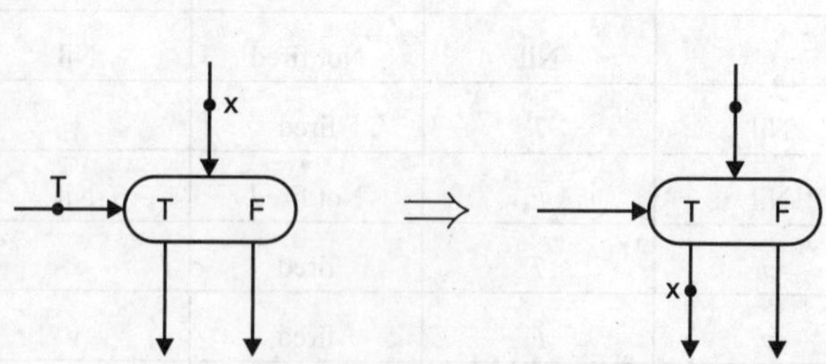

When *x* appears on the input arc and the control arc receives *T* then *x* appears on the *T* branch of the switch as an output.

Case II:

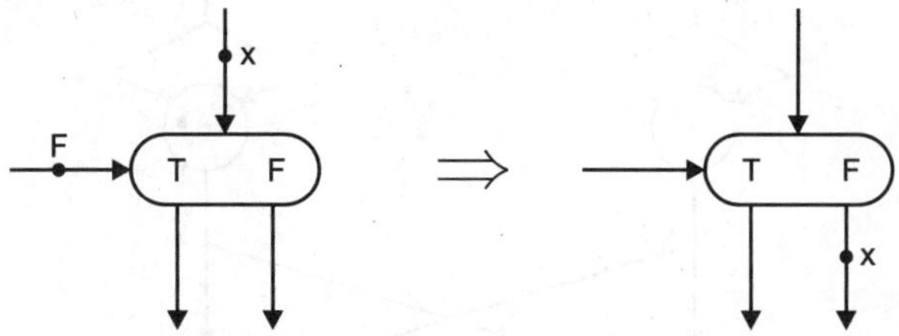

Similarly, when x appears on the input arc and F appears on the control arc then x appears on an output arc.

Note here that switch is not a new operator. It is actually a combination of T and F gates.

We are now in a position to solve some problems now.

EXAMPLE 8.1: Consider the following statements:

if x>y then (x - y)
else (x*y)

endif

Draw its data flow graph?

SOLUTION: Herein, we have used predicates merge and switch operators to implement the given statement.

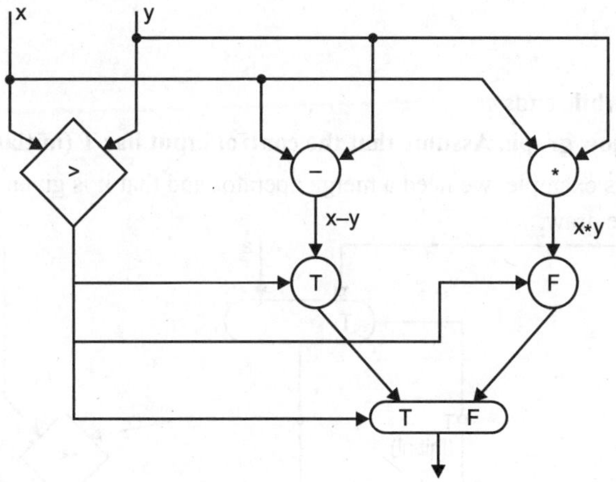

EXAMPLE 8.2: Draw a data flow graph to compute the following expression:
$(a^2 + b^2) / (a^2 - b^2)$?

SOLUTION: Say,

$$x = a * a$$
$$y = b * b$$

Then
$$z = \frac{x+y}{x-y} = \frac{a^2+b^2}{a^2-b^2}$$

So, we draw its data flow graph now:

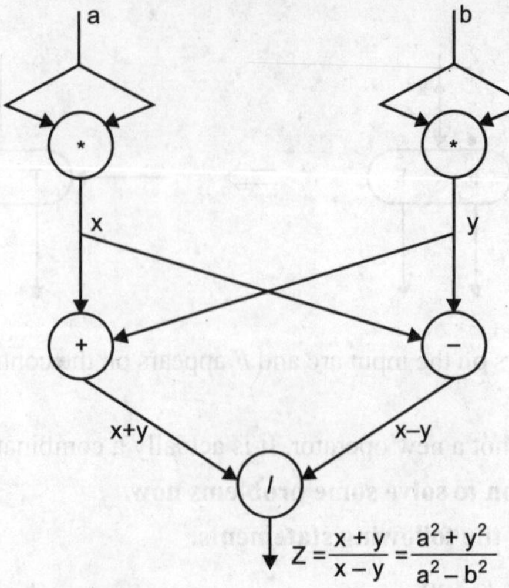

Note that the first two instructions can be carried out in parallel. That is why, we have drawn such a data flow graph.

EXAMPLE 8.3: Consider the following while loop:

x=a
while(*x*<*y*)
{
***x* = 2 **x*;**
} //while ends

Draw its data flow graph. Assume that the control input has T (initially).

SOLUTION: In this example, we need a merge operator and that it is given that the control input has *T* initially. So, we draw:

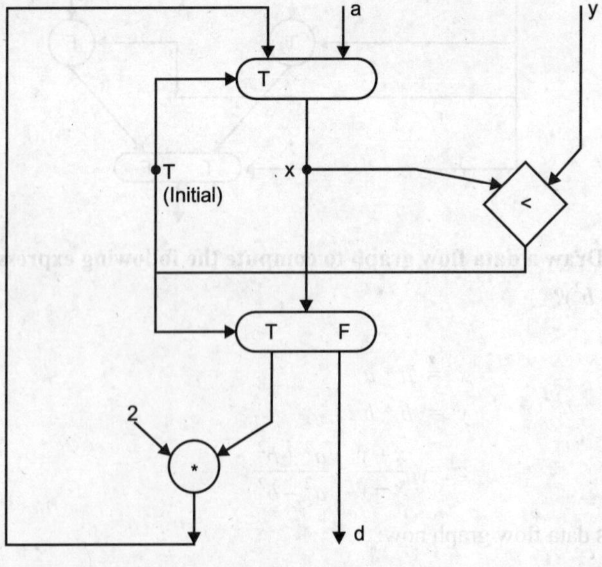

EXAMPLE 8.4: It is desired to store the sum of all array elements, a[i] for i ← 1 to n.

That is,

$$Sum = \sum_{i=1}^{n} a(i)$$

Draw its data flow graph. Also explain your results.

SOLUTION:

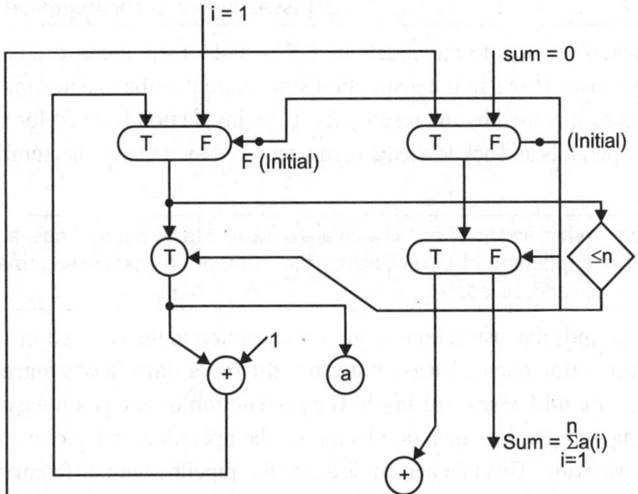

In this flow graph, an initial token, *F* is supplied to the two merge gates. The initial values of *i* and **sum** enter the loop via the *F* input of the merge gates. If the predicate evaluates to *T* then *i* and sum are routed to the loop body. The values circulate in the loop till the predicate evaluates to *F*. When this happens the result comes out of the loop.

Please note that the possibility of parallel execution will be exploited by the way in which the hardware is designed to execute the data flow graph.

What is data flow computer architecture?

A data flow computers computing element (CE) is shown below in Fig. 8.42.

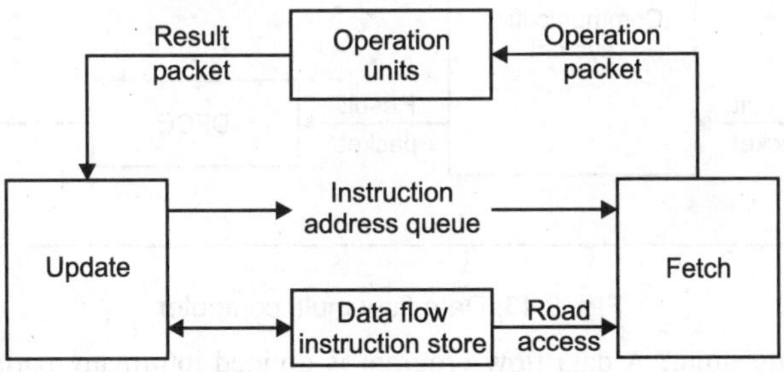

Fig. 8.42. A data flow computers computing element (CE)

How it works? The instruction store in this computer stores the machine instructions corresponding to the data flow graph. When an instruction is ready for execution, its address is sent to the instruction address queue. The fetch unit (as shown) fetches the address of the first instruction waiting in this queue. Using this address it retrieves a data flow instruction from the instruction store.

The operation code, the operands and the addresses where the results are to be sent are formed into an operation packet and then sent to the operation execution units. There can be multiple units also that can work together. The results so obtained after execution are formed into a result packet.

> **NOTE:** Result packet = result + address where the results should go
> +
> addresses where acknowledgements should go.

The result packets are sent to the update unit. This unit enters these results in the appropriate operand slots in the instructions in the instruction store Note that the update Unit will also forward acknowledgements as specified by the result packet. An instruction is ready for its execution when the count of input operands and acknowledgements received by it match the number specified in the instruction.

> **NOTE:** When the program is first invoked, all arcs are assumed to be empty. Thus, acknowledgements are needed. This is implemented by initialising the number of acknowledgements to equal the number of destination addresses.

The update unit finds the instructions ready for execution in the instruction store and puts their addresses in the instruction queue. **Please note that during a data flow program execution, the number of instruction addresses waiting in the instruction queue is a measure of parallelism present in the program.** Besides this, the fetch unit, the operation unit and the update unit can all be simultaneously working. This mechanism is a circular pipeline with different packets flowing in different parts. The degree of concurrency is limited by the number of operation units in the ring and the degree of pipelining in fetch and update units. However, the level of concurrency is limited by the parallelism within the program and the capacity of the data paths connecting the units in the ring.

A Data flow multi computing System

Many data flow computing elements (DFCE or CE) can be used to built a data flow multi computing system. It is shown below in Fig. 8.43. Each DFCE is connected to a communication system.

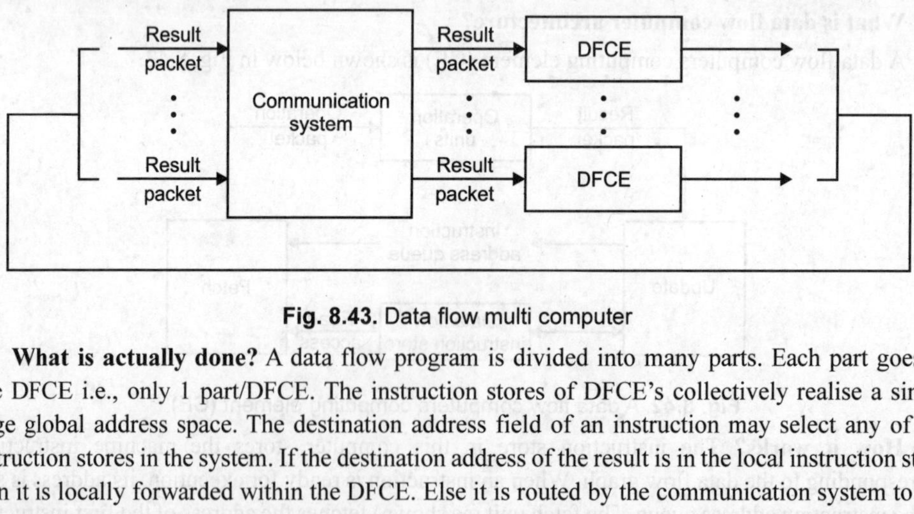

Fig. 8.43. Data flow multi computer

What is actually done? A data flow program is divided into many parts. Each part goes to one DFCE i.e., only 1 part/DFCE. The instruction stores of DFCE's collectively realise a single large global address space. The destination address field of an instruction may select any of the instruction stores in the system. If the destination address of the result is in the local instruction store then it is locally forwarded within the DFCE. Else it is routed by the communication system to the DFCE whose instruction store has that address. **Such a computer is called as a static data flow**

computer. As given by Dennis, this computer allows only one token in an arc at a time. Also, no new tokens can be accepted by an operator until the result is consumed by the receiving operators and acknowledgements to this effect are received by the operator. If this is not ensured then the results could be incorrect.

There is another type of data flow multi Computer. It is known as **a tagged token data flow computer or dynamic computer.** This model was given by Arvind and Gurd. In this model, more than one token is allowed in an arc. This will exploit more parallelism. Each token on an arc is given a tag which maintains the logical order in which tokens appear on an arc. The i-th token to flow along an arc carries a tag, i. An operator fires when all its input arcs have tokens whose tags are identical. No acknowledgement is required as each token carries its own unique tag. A token has this form

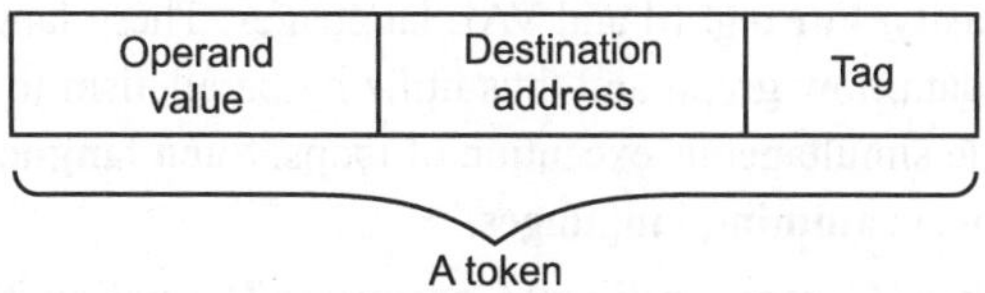

Fig. 8.44. Token format

Please note that the tagged data flow model allows concurrent computation of many iterations of a loop. This is so because the iteration number appears as a tag. Each iteration of a loop creates a new result which has an independent existence. A tagged token DFC is shown below in Fig. 8.45.

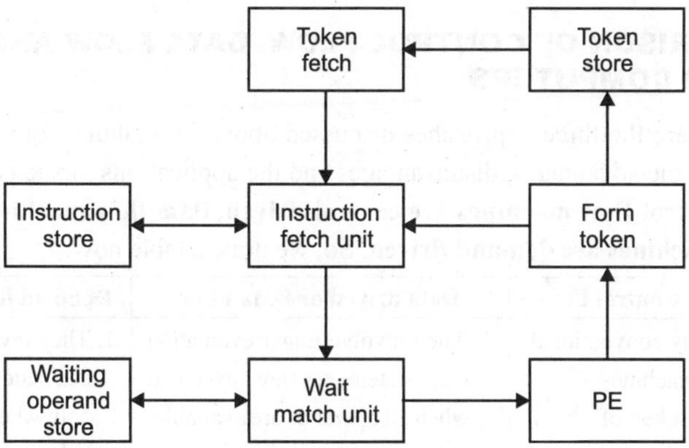

Fig. 8.45. Tagged token DFC

This model works without acknowledgement part in the instruction. When a token arrives for an instruction which requires a single input operand, the instruction can be executed immediately. When the first token containing one of the operands arrives for an instruction requiring 2 input operands, it must wait until its correct partner arrives. So, a waiting operand store is provided. This shows working of a single DFCE. We have **many DFCEs connected together using a communication medium. A large data flow program is partitioned** and stored in individual instruction memories of the DFCEs. **There is a global addressing of instructions as well as data.**

The statements like x $\leftarrow x * 10$ are not meaningful here. There is no sense in updating a variable with a new value if it is a DFC. This creates a problem when operations on some parts of arrays are to be performed by many DFCEs, in which case, arrays have to be duplicated. For this reason, .a synchronization mechanism called as **I—structure is provided within each PE. Herein, arrays are centrally stored.** Only one write operation is permitted in the structure. It can be read and written independently. It is a tagged memory unit (2-bit tag) for over lapped usage of a data structure by both producer and consumer processes. **Note that the I-structure provides the hardware aid to assist multiple computers to independently read/write into a common store without causing read/write races.**

Please note that a data flow graph is the machine language of a DFC. A HLL is needed for this machine which will use the implicit parallelism in the algorithm. The programmer is thus free to not to use statements like fork, join, send and receive. It should be independent of the machine specifications such as number of PEs, memory hierarchy etc.

Some languages which have been designed with clean rules for syntax and semantics allow a user to write programs easily. **For e.g.** Id and VAL languages. These languages have compilers to translate a program to a data flow graph and thus utilizing parallelism to its maximum. It **unfolds** loops and enables multiple simultaneous execution of loops. **Such languages are known as single assignment functional programming languages.**

III. Demand — Driven Computers/Lazy Computers/Reduction Machines

In these machines, if there is a demand for the result then only the computation is triggered. They use top down approach as compared to the bottom-up approach as used in previously described machines. It is also known as a lazy machine because the operations are executed only when their results are required by another instruction. In these machines, only required instructions are executed. There is a high degree of parallelism.

8.19 COMPARISON OF CONTROL FLOW, DATA FLOW AND DEMAND DRIVEN COMPUTERS

We now compare the three approaches discussed above in a tabular form. This also gives us an idea of what are the advantages, disadvantages and the applications of such computers. **We also know that the control-flow machines are control-driven, data flow machines are data driven and Reduction machines are demand driven.** So, we draw a table now:

Control driven or Control Flow	Data driven or Data Flow	Demand driven or Reduction
1. These are basically conventional Von Neumann's machines computations i.e. token of control indicates when a statement should be executed.	1. They involve Eager evaluation i.e., statements are executed when all operands are available.	1. They involve lazy evaluation i.e., statements are executed only when their result- is required for another computation.
2. Programmer has full control an advantage.	2. It provides very high potential for parallelism - an advantage.	2. Only required instructions are executed - an advantage.
3. Complex data and control structure are easily implemented.	3. High through put is seen here.	3. High degree of parallelism.
4. Less efficient machines.	4. Time lost waiting for unneeded arguments.	4. No sharing of objects.
5. Programming is not easy.	5. High control overhead.	5. Time is needed to propagate demand tokens.

8.20 ADVANCED PROCESSOR TECHNOLOGY

Powerful General purpose microprocessors may be divided into two groups i.e.,

(*i*) Pure complex instruction set computer (CISC) processors.

(*ii*) Pure reduced instruction set computer (RISC) processors.

Examples of CISC processors are the 8086, 80186, 80286 and 80386 belonging to INTEL family and 68000 and 68040 from MOTOROLA family.

Please note that 80386 is the last pure CISC model of the Intel family because 80486 has the facility of RISC technology partially.

The CISC microprocessors have:

- **Complex** machine instructions.
- **Micro-encoding** of machine instructions.
- Best addressing capability.
- Smaller number of useful registers.

Reduced Instruction Set Computer (RISC) has faster clock rates, ranging from 20 to 120 MHz.

Examples of RISC processors are the Intel i860, SPARC, IBM RS/6000 etc. are some of the RISC processors.

Pipelining has been used in RISC machines. RISC processors have been succeeded by super scalar processors that execute multiple instructions in one clock cycle. Very Large Instruction word (VL1W) processors are those in which one instruction word encodes more than one operation. **As per the Moore's Law —"The number of transistors which can be integrated in a chip has been doubling every 18 months"**. To enhance the speed of PEs we now make use of multithreading, VLIW and vector processors. What we actually observe is that as technology evolves rapidly, the clock rates of PEs also slowly move from lower to higher speeds. We shall also study about the super pipelined processors. These computers use multiphase clocks with clock rate ranging from 100 to 500 MHz. Vector computers (to be discussed) use this approach. We should also understand that a scalar processor is different from a vector processor. This is shown in Fig. 8.46 below. Also shown in Fig. 8.46 is the working of a vector processor. What we observe from Fig. 8.46 and Fig. 8.47 is that in case of a scalar processor — one-result / many clock cycles is produced while in case of vector processors one result/clock is produced.

Scalar vs vector processing

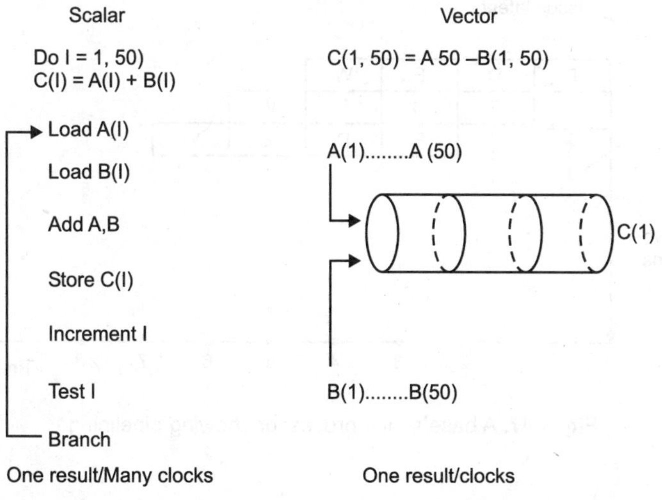

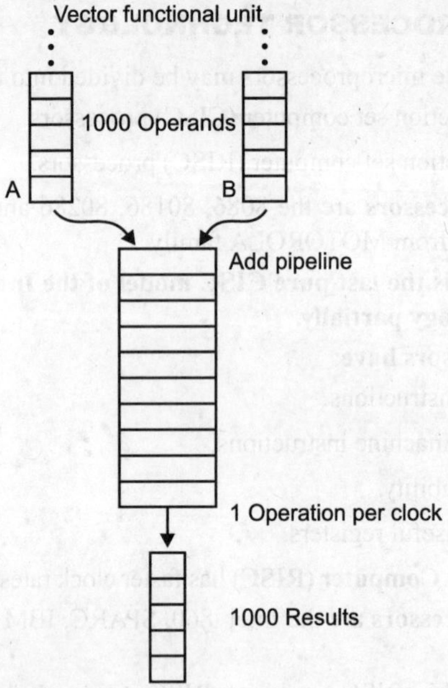

Fig. 8.46. and 8.47 scalar v/s vector processor

Please note that a base scalar processor is defined as a system in which one instruction is issued per cycle. There is one cycle latency (delay) for a simple operation and one cycle latency (delay) between the instruction issues.

As we already know that the execution of any instruction requires four phases:

Fetch (F) → Decode (D) → Execute (E) → Write-back (W) (results)

Further assuming that we have an instruction pipeline (like an assembly line production) which receives successive instructions from its input side and it executes them in an overlapped fashion. Then we have three different cases.

Case 1: Execution in a base scalar processor

Herein, if *I* draw a graph showing its execution of instruction then we get the following:

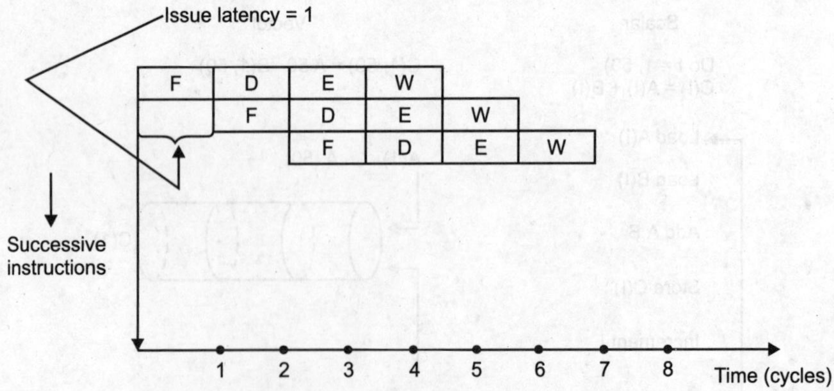

Fig. 8.47. A base scalar processor showing pipelining.

So, here in Fig. 8.47 we find that the pipeline utilization can be improved if successive instructions can execute at the rate of one per cycle.

Case 2: Pipeline underutilization

Can't we have an issue—latency of more than one? Yes, why not. Say, the issue latency is 2 now. So, we draw Fig. 8.48.

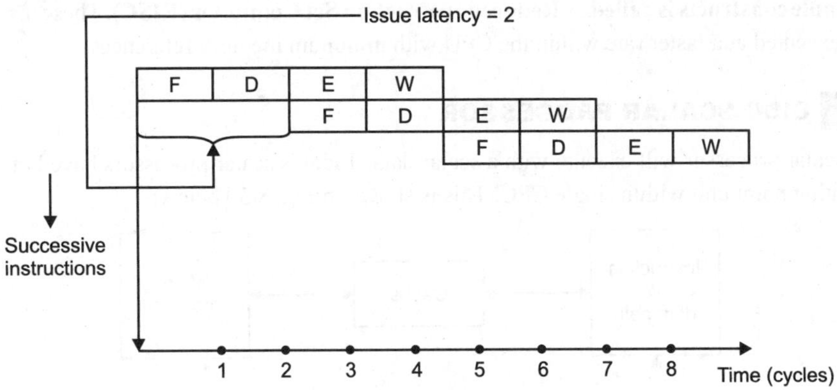

Fig. 8.48. Pipeline underutilization with 2 issue latency.

It is observed from figure 8.48 that if the issue-latency between two instructions is increased (from 1 to 2) then the pipeline can be underutilized.

Case 3: Poor pipeline utilization

It is also possible to combine two pipeline stages into one stage. So, we draw another Fig. 8.49 now.

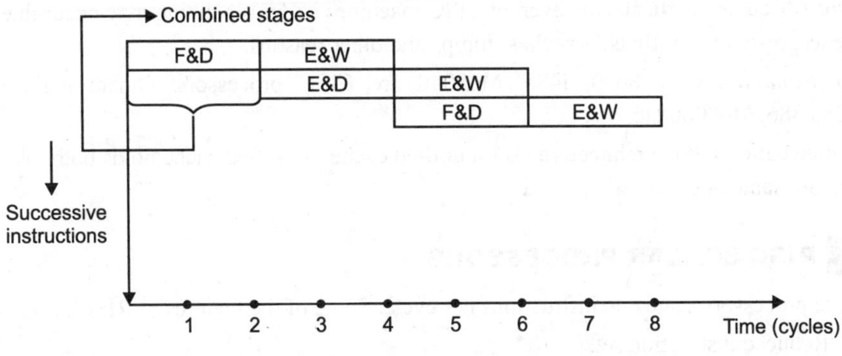

Fig. 8.49. Poor pipeline utilization.

Herein, 2 phases i.e., Fetch (*F*) and Decode (*D*) have been merged. Similarly, Execute (*E*) and write—back results (*W*) phases have been merged. But this also results in poor pipeline utilization.

Please note here that the effective CPI for case I is 1 (ideal pipeline). **Whereas for case II, it is 2 and in case III, it is ½ (half) only**. What we observe here is that the pipeline utilization is falling down only and not increasing.

8.21 INSTRUCTION—SET ARCHITECTURES

One of the important aspects of Computer architedure is the design of the instruction set for a processor. It is the instruction set chosen for a particular computer that determines the way in which machine language program are constructed. **A computer with a large number of instructions is called as a Complex Instruction Set Computer (CISC). A computer that uses a few instructions with simple constructs is called as Reduced Instruction Set Computer (RISC).** These instructions can be executed at a faster rate within the CPU with minimum memory references

8.22 CISC SCALAR PROCESSOR

A scalar processor will execute with a scalar data. Today's scalar processors have both integer and floating point unit within single CPU. This is shown in Fig. 8.50 below:

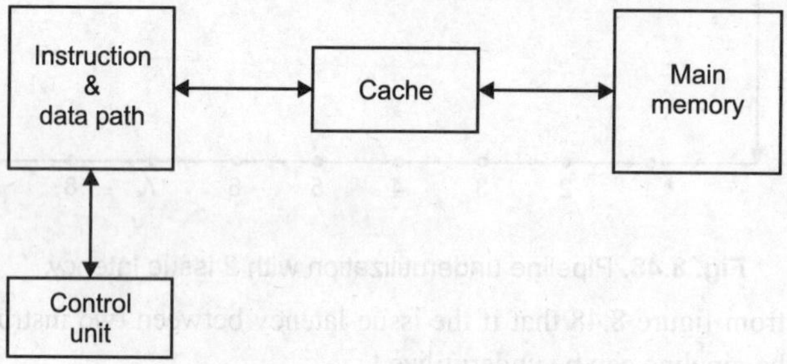

Fig 8.50. A CISC architecture.

We can use a single chip or many chips to construct a CISC scalar processor. **Please note that ideally, a CISC scalar processor should have a performance equal to that of a base scalar processor** (discussed earlier). However, in CISC machines under pipelining may occur due to data dependence, resource conflicts, branches, Jumps and other reasons.

For example: VAX 8600, i486, M68040 are CISC processors. Others include 8086, 80186/286/386, M68000 etc.

By convention-CISC architecture uses a unified cache. A unified cache holds both instructions and data. So, same bus is used.

8.23 RISC SCALAR PROCESSORS

These processors issue one instructions per cycle. Some of the features of RISC are-

(*a*) Reduced instruction set.

(*b*) Simpler instructions.

(*c*) Hardwired control unit.

(*d*) Few addressing modes.

(*e*) Instruction pipelining.

Types of Processors

For example : Intel i860, M8810a, AMD 29000 are some RISC processors. A RISC architecture is shown in Fig. 8.51

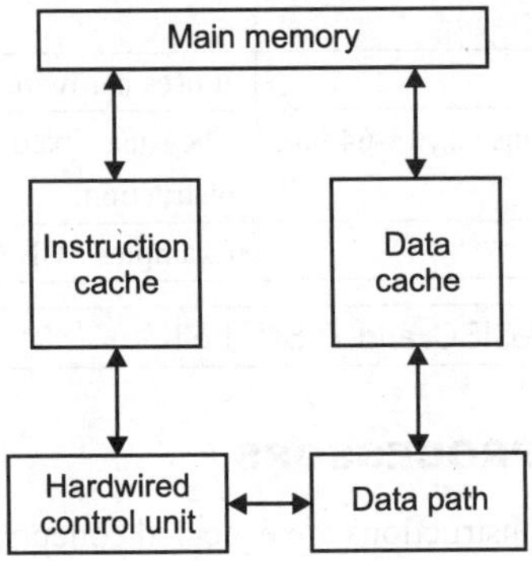

Fig. 8.51. A RISC architecture.

In RISC machines, we have separate instruction (*I*) and data (*D*) caches. Say, we want to multiply 2 numbers being stored in a 2D-memory

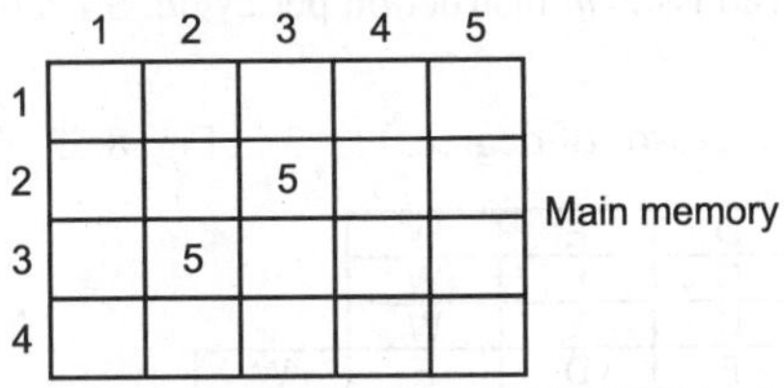

At memory location (2,3) = 5 is stored.

At memory location (3,2) = 5 is stored.

Then, CISC machine will multiply them in one instruction as follows:

MULT 2 : 3, 3 : 2

Whereas RISC machine will, use many instructions as follows

Load *A*, 2 : 3	; Get First number
Load *B*, 3: 2	; Get Second number
Prod *A*, *B*	; Multiply them i.e., $A \leftarrow A * B$
Store 2 : 3, *A*	; Move results from A to
	; mem. Loc. 2 : 3

In CISC approach, very little RAM is required to store instruction. The emphasis is on building complex instructions directly into the hardware. But in RISC approach, more RAM is required.

8.24 COMPARISON OF CISC AND RISC IN TABULAR FORM

CISC	RISC
1. These computers use large set of instructions	These computers use small set of instructions
2. They support 12-24 addressing modes	They support only 3-5 addressing mode.
3. They use 8-24 general purpose registers (GPRS).	They use 32-192 GPRs.
4. They mostly have a unified cache.	They use separate (split) data and instruction cache.
5. Clock rates are between 33-50 MHz.	Clock rates are between 50—150 MHz.
6. CPI is between 2 and 15.	Average CPI is less than 1.5.

CISC	RISC
It uses micro coded control logic.	It uses hardwired control logic.
They use variable format instructions i.e., 16-64 bits per instruction.	They use fixed instruction format i.e., 32 bits per instruction.
Examples : 8086, 186, 286, 386	Examples SUN SPARC, i860 etc.

NOTE: Pentium has features of CISC and RISC, both.

8.25 SUPERSCALAR PROCESSORS

A processor in which many instructions are executed concurrently is known as a " super scalar processor. These processors exploit more instruction level parallelism (ILP) in user programs. The instruction issue degree (m) is limited by this 1formula

$$2 < m < 5$$

These processors can use pipelining with three instructions per cycle also. In general, a super scalar processor of degree m can issue m instruction per cycle. So, a base scalar processor (RISC or CISC) has $m = 1$.

We show a super scalar processor of degree, $m = 3$ in Fig. 8.52.

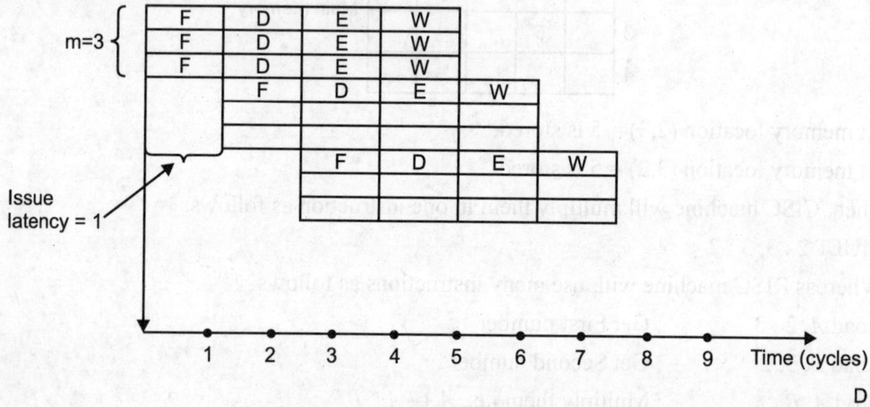

Fig. 8.52 A Super scalar with degree (m) = 3.

That is, three instructions are executed per cycle. **In general, if we want to fully utilize a super scalar processor of degree m then m instructions must be executed in parallel.** In some clock cycles this may not be true. In that case, some of the pipelines may be stalling in a wait state. In a super scalar processor, the issue latency is 1 as in case of a base scalar processor. **Please note that super scalars require a high degree of ILP in programs so it depends more on an optimizing compiler to exploit parallelism.** A super scalar machine can issue a fixed—point, floating point, load and branch, **all in one cycle also.** So, here $m = 4$; $(2 < m < 5)$. Here, the parallelism achieved will be the same as in a vector processor.

8.26 VLIW ARCHITECTURES

VL1W stands for Very Long Instruction Word. It is a technique that combines multiple standard instructions into one long instruction word. VLIW processors rely on the complier to exploit ILP for determining the instructions which may be executed in parallel. The long instruction word known as "Multi OP" is composed of multiple arithmetic, logic and control operations. VL1W processor executes these operations within a multi OP concurrently and thereby achieves TLP. VLIW processor's instruction format is shown in Fig. 8.53 below:

OP1	OP2	OP3	OP4

Fig. 8.53. VLIW Instruction (Multi OP).

Each operation in a VLIW instruction is equivalent to one instruction in a Super scalar or purely sequential processor. The number of operations in a VLIW instruction is equal to the number of execution units in the processor. Each operation specifies the instructions that will be executed on the corresponding execution unit in the cycle during which the instruction is issued. The hardware need not have to examine the instruction stream for detecting ILP. The compiler is responsible for ensuring that all the operations specified in an instruction can be executed simultaneously. Due to this the VL1W processor has very simple instruction issue logic as compared to that on a super scalar processor. In each cycle, the instruction logic fetches a VLIW instruction from the memory and issues it to the corresponding execution units.

Next, we will discuss the architecture of VLIW processor.

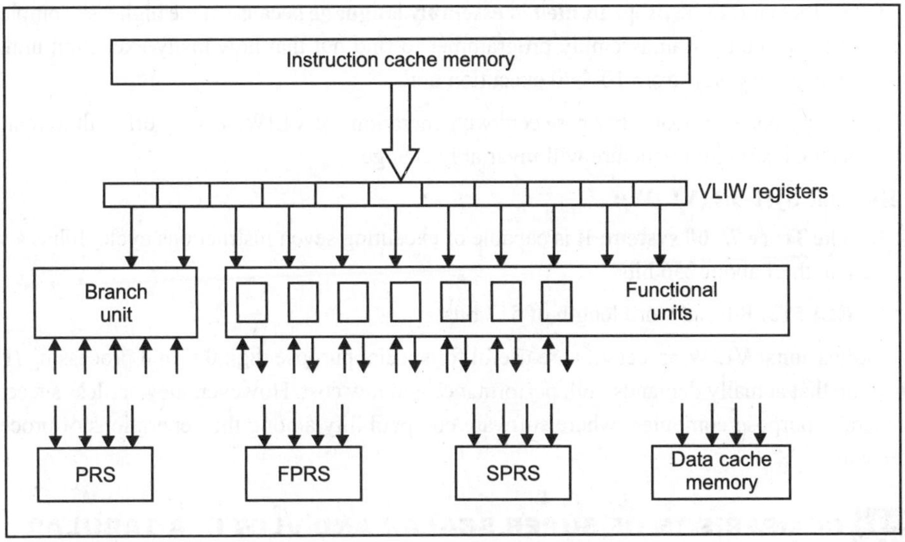

Fig. 8.54. VLIW Processor Architecture.

VLIW architectures are suitable for exploiting ILP in programs. These processors contain multiple functional units. A very long instruction word (VL1W) is fetched from the parallel execution. These capabilities are exploited by the compilers. The compilers generate code by grouping independent primitive instructions together which are executable in parallel. The processors have relatively simple control logic because they do not perform any dynamic scheduling or reordering of operations as in c se of super scalar processors.

Advantages of VLIW

The following are the advantages of VLIW processors:

1. The instruction issue logic is very simple.

2. Clock cycles required for implementing the instructions are shorter than super scalar processor.
3. The compiler has complete control for detecting ILP.
4. VLIW can fit more execution units on a given chip space because of simple instruction issue logic.

Disadvantages of VLIW

The following are the disadvantages of VLIW processors:

1. It is virtually impossible to maintain the **compatibility between generations of VLIW processor family because** VLIW programs execute correctly when executed on a processor with **same number of execution units and the same instruction latencies** as the processor for which they were compiled.
2. If a compiler cannot find enough parallel operations, it has to insert explicit NOP operations into the corresponding operation slots. This rsults in **higher memory requirement** as compared to the equivalent program for super scalar processors.
3. VLIWs **cannot be programmed in assembly language** because of the high task complexity. It is difficult for an assembly programmer to find out that how many execution units are free or busy, say, from 10—20 execution units.
4. Binary code compatibility between two generations of VLIWs is very difficult to maintain as the instruction structure will invariably change.

Example Systems (VLIW):

1. **The Trace 7/200 system:** It is capable of executing seven instructions cycle. It has a word length of about 256 bits.
2. **ELI 512:** It has a word length of 512 bits.

Applications: VLIW processors are useful for special purpose digital signal processing (DSP) application that actually demands high performance and low cost. However, they are less successful as General—purpose computers where software compatibility among the generations of processor is mandatory.

8.27 COMPARISON OF SUPER SCALAR AND VLIW IN A TABULAR FORM

A Comparison of super scalar and VLIW is given in table below:

Super-scalar	VLIW
1. The code size is small.	1. The code size is larger.
2. Complex hardware for decoding and issuing instructions.	2. Simple hardware for decoding and issuing instructions.
3. They are compatible across generations.	3. They are not compatible across generations.
4. No change in hardware is required.	4. Requires more registers but simplified hardware for register ports.
5. They are scheduled dynamically by the processor.	5. They are scheduled statically by the compiler.

8.28 VECTOR AND SYMBOLIC PROCESSORS

Vector Processor: A Vector instruction involves a large array of operands. A vector processor is a coprocessor specially designed to perform vector computations. They are used in a multi-pipelined supercomputer. We have two types of vector operations—

(*a*) Register—based vector instructions.

(*b*) Memory—based vector instructions.

Register-vector instructions appear in most register-to-register vector processors like Cray supercomputers.

Let			
	V_i	–	Vector register
	N	–	length of V_i
	S_i	–	Scalar register
	$M[1: n]$	–	memory array
	0	–	Vector operator (small circle)

Then, Vector operations can be:

V_1 o V_2	$\rightarrow$	V_3 (binary vector)
S_1 o V_1	$\rightarrow$	V_2 (Scaling)
V_1 o V_2	$\rightarrow$	S_1 (binary reduction)
$M(1: n)$	$\rightarrow$	V_1 [Vector load]
$V1$	$\rightarrow$	$M(1: n)$ (vector store)
o V_1	$\rightarrow$	V_2 (unary vector)
o V_1	$\rightarrow$	S_1 (unary reduction)

Please note here that the vector length should be equal in all operands used in a vector instruction. Also note that the reduction is an operation of one or two vectors yielding a scalar result.

On the other hand, **memory-based** vector operations are performed in memory-to- memory vector processors like in Cyber 205.

For example:

$M_1 (1 : n)$ o $M_2 (1 : n) \rightarrow M(1 : n)$

$S1$ o $M1 (1: n) \rightarrow M2 (1 : n)$

o $M1 (1 : n) \rightarrow M2 (1 : n)$

$M1 (1 : n)$ o $M2(1 : n) \rightarrow M(p)$

Here, $M1$ (1: n) and $M2$ (1 : n) are two vectors of length n.

$M(p)$ — a scalar stored in memory location p.

Please note that the vector length is not restricted by the register length. The vector pipes can be attached to any scalar processor- Super scalar, super pipelined or both. An optimizing compiler is required to convert the sequential code to vectorized form for its vector pipelining.

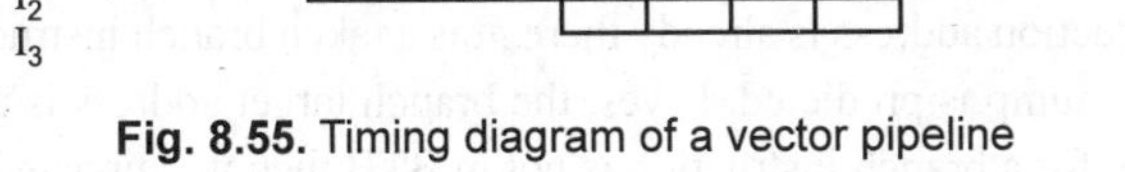

Fig. 8.55. Timing diagram of a vector pipeline

Let us now study about **symbolic processors.**

Symbolic Processing has been used in many areas like theorem proving, pattern recognition, expert systems and so on. Herein, we have a modern and non—algorithmic approach of problem solving. Symbolic processors include prolog processors Lisp processors or symbolic manipulators. It depends on various features like how knowledge is represented? What common operations are to be performed? What are the properties of algorithms? And so on. In symbolic processing, we deal with logic programs, lists, objects, scripts, net, frames and neural networks. No floating-point operations are done here.

For example: Symbolics 3600 Lisp processor.

8.29 CASE STUDY ON PENTIUM PROCESSOR (CISC)

Pentium is a CISC processor with a 2 instruction **super scalàr pipeline organization.** Pentium uses a 5 stage pipeline. It has these stages:

First Stage : Prefetch Stage

Pentium instructions are variable length and are stored in a prefetch buffer. There is a 256-bit path from instruction cache to the prefetch buffer.

Second Stage: Decode - 1 Stage

The processor decodes the instruction and finds the opcode, checks which instructions can be paired for simultaneous execution.

Third stage: Decode - 2 Stage

The addresses for memory reference are found in this stage.

Fourth Stage: Execute stage

In this stage, data cache fetch or ALU or floating point unit operation may be done. **Please note that two operations can be carried out.**

Fifth Stage: Write-back stage

In this stage, registers and flags are updated based on the results of execution.

Pentium has 2 ALUs called as U and V. Two instructions can be executed simultaneously. But there are some restrictions to ensure that no potential conflicts exist. **Two successive instructions, I_1 and I_2 can be dispatched in parallel to U and V units provided the following conditions are satisfied:**

1. Both I_1 and I_2 are simple instructions. **An instruction is called simple if it can be carried out in one clock cycle.**
2. I_1 and I_2 are not flow dependent or output dependent. **That is, the destination register of I_1 is not the source or destination of I_2 and vice versa.**
3. Only I_1 may contain an instruction prefix. An **instruction prefix** is 0-4 bytes long and has information like address size, operand size etc.
4. Neither I_1 nor I_2 contains both a displacement and an immediate operand.

Pentium employs a branch target buffer (BTB). A BTB caches information about recently encountered branch instructions. When an instruction in the instruction stream is fetched, the BTB is checked. If the instruction address is already there, it is a taken branch instruction. The history bits are checked to see if a jump is predicted. If yes, the branch target address is used to fetch the next instruction. If an entry for a branch instruction is not in BTB then it is updated.

8.30 CASE STUDY ON SPARC (RISC)

SPARC (Scalable Processor Architecture) is a RISC microprocessor architecture designed in 1985 by Sun Microsystems. SPARC is scalable across a wide range of semiconductor technologies, chip implementations and system configurations. SPARC is flexible. It is a flexible integration of cache, memory management and floating point units. So, processors are produced at a price that is suitable for systems ranging from leap-tops to super computers.

Solaris runs on SPARC—based systems.

SPARC architecture includes **register window.** SPARC has ***32 GPRS, 8 global registers and 24 registers are in a register window.*** A window consists of three groups of 8 registers— **the out, local and in registers.** They are as follows:

Register Group	Register Address	Use
1. Global	*r*[0] — *r*[7]	Contains values that vary little between executions.
2. Out	*r*[8] — *r*[15]	Contain outgoing parameters.
3. Local	*r*[16] — *r*[23]	Contain scratch registers.
4. IN	*r*[24] — *r*[31]	Contains incoming parameters.

SPARC can have 2 to 32 windows. Most implementations have 7 to 8 windows. **At any given time, only one window is visible that is determined by the current window pointer (CWP).** This is a five-bit value that can be decremented or incremented by **SAVE and RESTORE instructions** respectively. These instructions are generally executed on **the procedure call and return** respectively. **The register windows overlap partially. So the out register becomes the in registers of the called procedure. Thus, the memory traffic is reduced when going up and down the procedure call. Since this is a frequent operation, so performance is improved.**

The overlapping is shown below in Fig. 8.56.

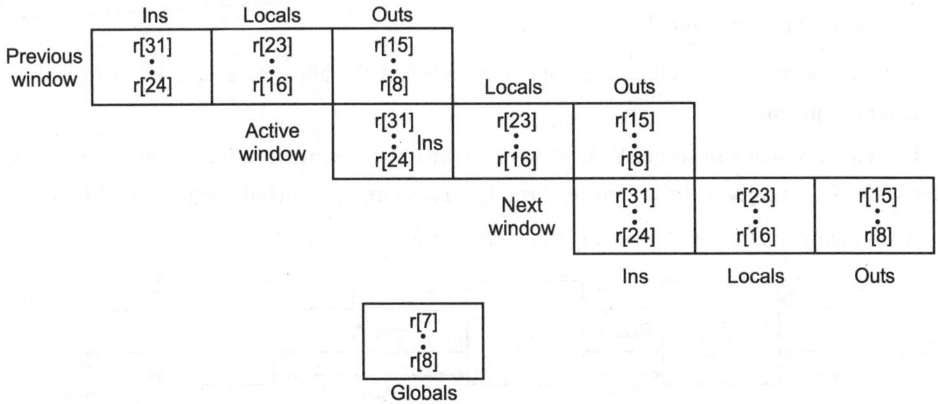

Fig. 8.56. Three overlapping register windows and global registers.

When a function is called, the in register may contain arguments that can be used. The **local registers** can be used for anything while the function executes. The out registers are used to pass arguments to functions that it calls.

Register windows are also used to save the processor contexts when traps or interrupts occur. The SPARC OS always ensure that there is a register window not being used below the current one. If a trap occurs then the current workspace pointer (CWP) is decremented and the new window saves the processor context.

8.31 PIPELINE – PRINCIPLES AND IMPLEMENTATION

Pipelining means realizing temporal parallelism in an economical way. In this technique, the problem is divided into a series of tasks that have to be completed one after the other. Each task is executed by a separate process or processor.

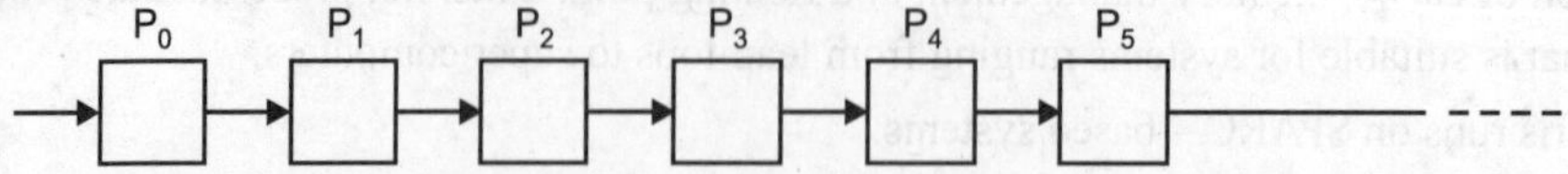

The problem is divided into separate functions that must be performed in succession. Pipelining is very much similar to assembly line in an industry. It means an overlapped parallelism.

A linear pipeline processor is a cascade of processing stages which are linearly connected to perform a fixed function over a stream of data flowing from one end to the other.

Linear pipeline is of two types:

(*a*) Asynchronous pipelines.

(*b*) Synchronous pipelines.

Pipelining involves some conditions. These conditions are:

1. The input task can be divided into sequence of subtasks.
2. Each subtask can be executed by a specialized hardware that operates concurrently with other pipeline stages.
3. There is a constant stream of tasks into the pipe and there is overlapped execution at the subtask level.

8.31.1 Linear pipeline processor

I. Asynchronous Model

In an asynchronous pipeline, the data flow between the adjacent stages is controlled by a **handshaking protocol.**

Principle: When the stage, S_i, is ready to transmit, it sends a ready signal to stage S_{i+1}. After stage S_{i+1}, receives the incoming data, it returns an acknowledgement signal to S_i.

An asynchronous pipeline model is shown in Fig. 8.57 below:

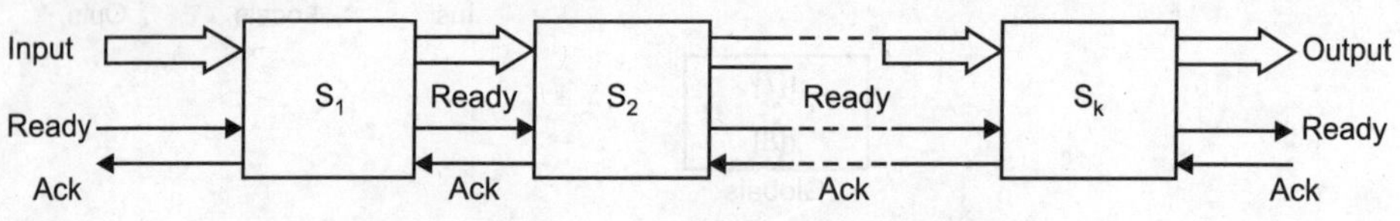

Fig. 8.57. Asynchronous pipeline model

Applications of Asynchronous pipelines: Asynchronous pipelines are useful in designing the communication channels in the message — passing multicomputers where pipeline worm whole routing is practised.

Please note that these pipelines may have a variable throughput rate. Different amounts of delay may be experienced in different stages.

II. Synchronous Model

A synchronous pipeline is shown in Fig. 8.58.

Basic structure of linear—pipelining is as follows

L : Latch (ICs)

CLK : Clock pulse

S_i : the ith stage

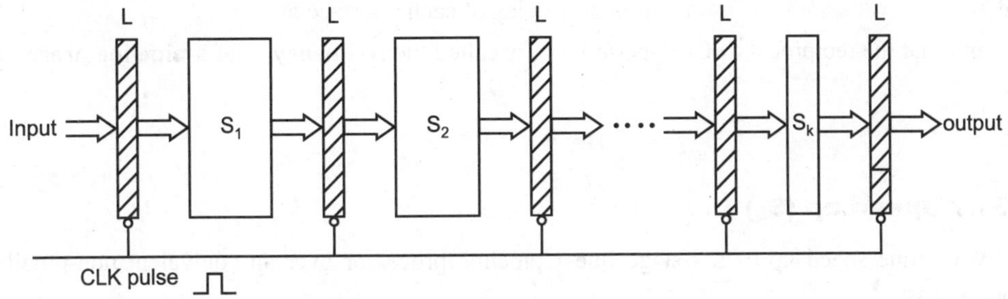

Fig. 8.58. Synchronous pipeline

Working: The pipeline consists of a cascade of processing stages. The stages are pure combinational circuits performing arithmetic or logic operations over the data stream flowing through the pipe. The stages are separated by high-speed interface latches. The latches are fast-registers for holding the intermediate results between the stages. Information-flows between adjacent stages are under the control of common CLK applied to all the latches simultaneously.

SpaceTime diagram: One can draw a space time diagram (Fig. 8.59) to show over-lapped operations in a linear pipeline processor, having 4-stages only. We can extend it to n-stages).

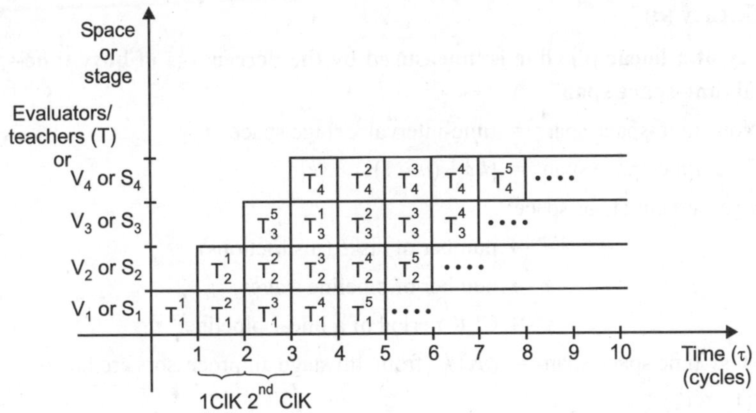

Fig. 8.59. Space-time diagram

Where, $T_j^i \rightarrow$ is j^{th} – subtask

In i^{th} – task.

Explanation: Once the pipe is filled up, it will output one result / clock period, independent of the number of stages in the pipe.

Ideally, a linear pipeline with k- stages can process n-tasks in $t_k = k + (n - 1)$ clock periods.

Where $T_1 = nk$ when pipelining is not done.

The following are the **terms** associated with linear pipeline structure of parallel computer.

III. Clock period (τ): it is defined by the formula given below:

$$\tau = \max (\tau_j)^k_{i=1} + \tau_i \; i \leftarrow 1 \text{ to } k$$

$$\tau = \tau_m + \tau_l$$

Where $\tau_i \rightarrow$ is time delay for stage – i

and $\tau_l \rightarrow$ is time delay of each interface latch.

and that the reciprocal of CLK-period, (τ), is called the **frequency, f, of a pipeline processor** i.e.,

$$f = \frac{1}{\tau} \text{Hz.}$$

8.31.2 Speed up (S_k)

We define speed up of a k-stage linear pipeline processor over an equivalent non-pipeline processor as:

$$S_k = \frac{T_1}{T_k} = \frac{n.k}{k+(n-1)} = \frac{\text{Non-pipelined speed up}}{\text{Pipelined speed up}}$$

∴ maximum speed up is, $S_k \rightarrow k$

Where $n >> k$

i.e. minimum speed up that a linear pipeline can provide is k, where k, where k is the number of stages in the pipe. This maximum speed up is never fully achievable because of **"data – dependencies"** between instructions, interrupts, program branches etc. Many pipeline cycles may be wasted on a waiting state caused by out of sequence instruction executions.

IV. Efficiency (*n*)

Efficiency of a linear pipeline is "measured by the percentage of busy time-space spans over the total time-space span".

Now, time-space span = time-interval x stage space

& Total time-space span = $[k\tau + (n-1)\tau] \times [k]$ ...(1)

i.e., k-stages are our stage-space

Where $n \rightarrow$ number of tasks (instructions)

$k \rightarrow$ number of pipeline stages

$\tau \rightarrow$ CLK period of a linear pipeline.

& Busy time space span = $(n\tau)\, k$ [from 4th stage all processors are busy] ...(2)

∴ from (1) & (2):

$$\boxed{\eta = \frac{nk\tau}{(k\tau+(n-1)\tau)k}}$$

$$\therefore \quad \eta = \frac{n}{\dfrac{(k\tau+(n-1)\tau)k}{k\tau}} = \frac{n}{(k^2\tau+nk\tau-k\tau)/k\tau}$$

or

$$\eta = \frac{n}{k+(n-1)}$$

Note that $\eta \to 1$ as $n \to \infty$ $\left[\because \frac{n}{k+(n-1)} = \frac{1}{\frac{k}{n}+\left(1-\frac{1}{n}\right)} = \frac{1}{\frac{k}{\infty}+\left(1-\frac{1}{\infty}\right)} = \frac{1}{O+1} = \frac{1}{1} = 1\right]$

i.e., larger the number of tasks (n) flowing through pipeline, the better is its efficiency.

Also we realize that $\eta = \frac{S_k}{k}$ or $\eta = \frac{S_k}{k} \times 100\%$

i.e., efficiency of a linear pipeline is also defined as the ratio of its actual speed-up to the ideal speed-up k. Since, it is a ratio of two speed ups so it doesn't have any units. However, it is expressed in %.

V. Throughput (w)

The number of results (tasks) that can be completed by a pipeline per unit time is called its throughput. This rate reflects the computing power of a pipeline. i.e.,

$$w = \frac{n}{k\tau + (n-1)\tau} = \frac{\eta}{\tau}$$

Where n equals the total number of tasks being processed during an observation period of $k\tau + (n-1)\tau$.

When $\eta \to 1$, w = throughput = $\frac{1}{\tau} = f$ (Hz).

This means that the maximum throughput of a linear pipeline is equal to its frequency, which corresponds to **one output result per clock period.**

8.32 NON-LINEAR PIPELINE PROCESSOR

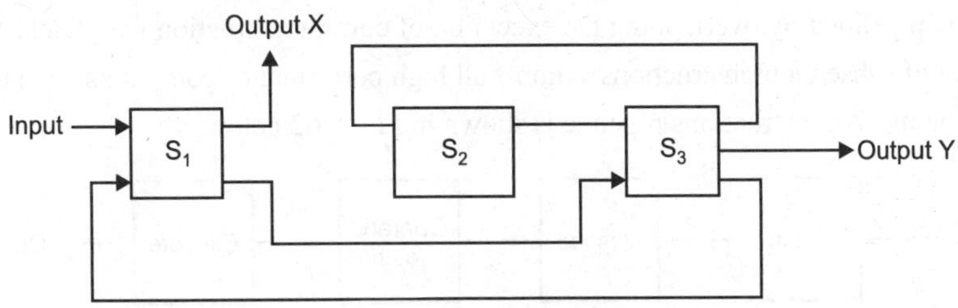

Fig. 8.60. Non-linear pipeline.

When a pipeline allows **feed-forward and feedback connections** in additions to the streamline connections then it is called as a **non-linear pipeline.**

A dynamic pipeline is sometimes called as a non-linear pipeline because of feed forward and feedback connection. It can be reconfigured to perform different functions at different times. **Please note that the linear pipelines discussed earlier are static pipelines because they perform fixed functions.** A two function non-linear pipeline is shown in Fig. 8.61.

This non-linear pipeline can perform two functions X and Y.

In practice, many of the arithmetic pipeline processes allow non-linear connections to implement **recursion and multiple functions.** If feedback and feed-forward connections are not used properly then the inherent advantage of pipelining may be lost. On the other hand, if non-linear data flow is properly sequenced then the pipeline efficiency will enhance.

8.33 CLASSIFICATION OF PIPELINE PROCESSORS

8.34.1 Based on levels of processing-Handler's classification (1977)

Handler has proposed the classification scheme according to the levels of processing as follows.

1. **Arithmetic pipelining**

In this method, the ALUs of a computer are segmented in various data formats for pipeline operations. This is shown in Fig. 8.61.

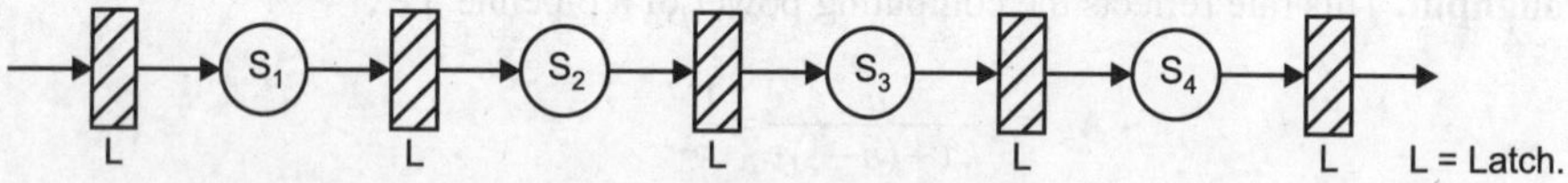

Fig. 8.61. An arithmetic pipeline.

For example : 4 – stage pipes in Star 100,

4 – Stage pipes in TI-ASC,

14 – Stage pipes in Cray - 1,

26 – Stage pipe in Cyber - 305.

2. **Instruction Pipelining**

This type of pipelining is also known as instruction look ahead. In this the execution of stream of instructions is pipelined by overlapping the execution of current instruction with fetch, decode and operand fetch of subsequent instructions. Almost all high performance computers have instructions execution pipeline. An instructions pipeline is shown in Fig. 8.62 below.

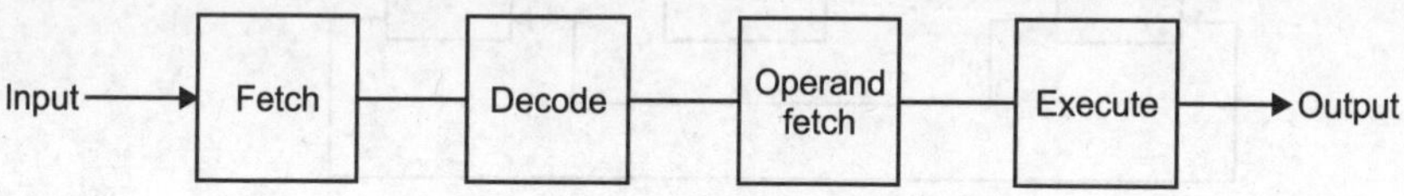

Fig. 8.62. Instruction Pipeline

3. **Processor Pipelining**

In this pipeline, same data stream is processed by the cascade of processors. Each processor performs a specific task. The data stream passes the first processor with results stored in a memory block which is also accessible by the second processor. The second processor processes this result and passes it to third and so on. This pipeline of multiple processor is not much popular. It is shown in Fig. 8.63 below.

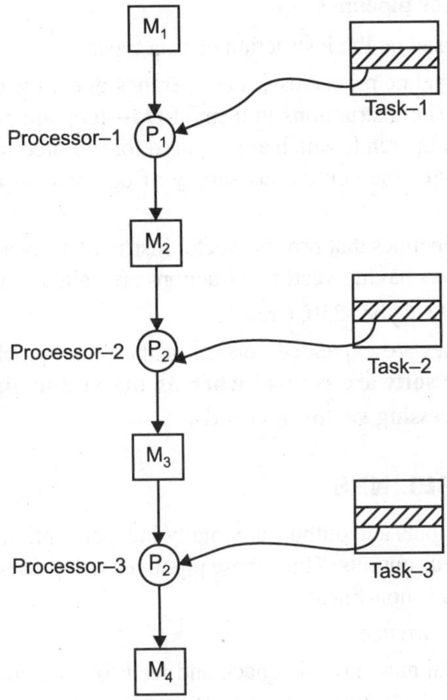

Fig. 8.63. Instruction Pipelining

8.34.2 Based on Pipeline Configuration

Ramamoorthy and Li's classification (1977)

1. **Unifunction versus Multifunction pipelines**

Unifunction Pipeline: A pipeline with fixed and dedicated function is called as unifunctional pipeline.

For example : Floating-point adder.

Please note that Cray-1 has 12 unifunctional pipeline units for various scalar, vector, fixed point and floating-point operations.

Multifunction Pipeline : A pipeline that performs different functions either at different times or at the same time, by inter connecting different subsets of stages in the pipeline is called as a multifunction pipeline.

For example : TI—ASC has 4 multifunction pipeline processors.

2. **Static versus Dynamic pipelines**

Static Pipeline: It is a pipeline that assumes only one functional configuration at a time. It can be either unifunctional of multifunctional. The function performed by' static pipeline should not change frequently. The frequent change in the function will lead to degradation of performance of static pipeline.

Dynamic Pipeline: Herein, several functional configurations can exist simultaneously. Dynamic pipeline must be multifunctional and uni-functional pipeline must be static. The control in the dynamic pipe 'is complex as compared to the control in the static pipeline. **Please note here that the unifunctional or multifunctional static pipelines are more popular in most of the existing computers.**

3. Scalar versus vector pipelines

This classification is based on the instruction or data types.

Scalar pipeline: If a pipeline processes scalar operands under the control of Do-loop then it is called as a scalar pipeline. The instructions in a small Do—loop are normally prefetched into the instruction buffer. The scalar operands which are required for repeated scalar instructions are moved into a data cache. This ensures the continuous supply of operands to the pipeline. For example : IBM—360

Vector Pipeline: The pipelines that process vector instructions over vector operands are known as vector pipelines. Computers having vector instructions are called as vector-processors.

For example: STAR-100, Cyber-250, Cray-1.

Actually, vector pipelines are expanded version of the scalar pipelines. **Please note that the scalar pipelines are under software control whereas the vector pipeline uses firmware and hardware controls for processing vector operands.**

8.34 GENERAL PIPELINES

In linear pipelines, the inputs and outputs are totally independent. In some cases, it is not so and inputs may depend on previous outputs. Thus, these pipelines will possess feedback or feed forward connections and flow of data is non-linear.

For example: Linear recurrence.

Thus, pipelines in general may have feedback and feed forward connections in addition to the cascade connections. A general pipeline is shown in Fig. 8.64 below.

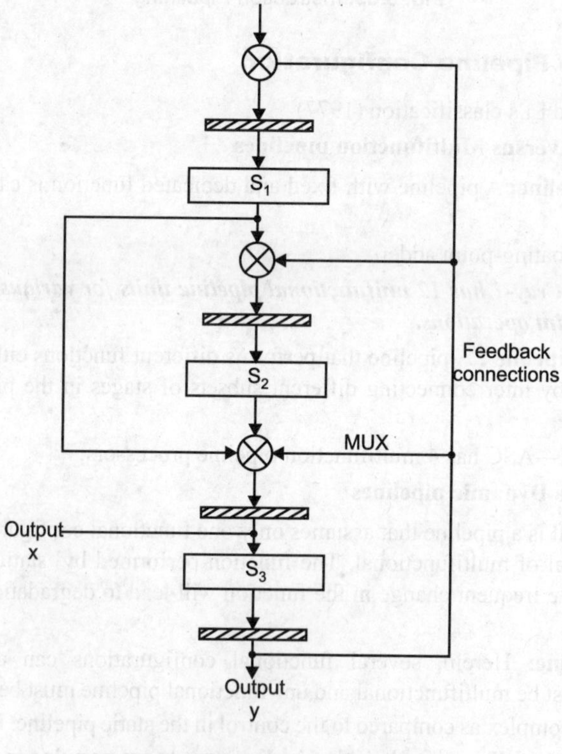

Fig. 8.64. A General Pipeline

As shown in Fig. 8.64, it is a two function pipeline with function-*X* and function-*y*. There are three stages *S*1, *S*2 and *S*3. The crossed circles are multiplexers. They are used for selecting among multiple connection paths in evaluating different functions.

Reservation Tables

Reservation table is a 2*D* chart. It is also known as a Gantt chart. **The utilization pattern of successive stages in the pipeline is specified by a reservation table.** It was introduced by Davidson in 1971. It shows the utilizations or reservation of successive stages in a pipeline for evaluation of a specific function, in successive pipeline cycles. It is very much similar to the space-time diagram. A reservation table for a linear pipeline is shown in Fig. 8.65 below.

→ Time (Clock cycles)

Stages ↓

	1	2	3	4
S_1	X			
S_2		X		
S_3			X	
S_4				X

Fig. 8.65. Reservation Table

It shows that stage-1 (S_1) is being used at time = 1 units, stage-2 (S_2) is busy at time = 2 units and so on. A reservation table consists of rows corresponding to pipeline stages and columns to clock time units. The evaluation time for a function is equal to the total number of clock units in the reservation table. The table represents the flow of data through the pipeline for one complete evaluation of a given function. One symbol like '*X*' is sufficient to mark a busy stage in a unifunction pipeline but multiple symbols are used to mark different functions like *X* and *Y*. For example,

	t_0	t_1	t_2	t_3	t_4	t_5	t_6
S_1	Y				Y		
S_2			Y			Y	
S_3		Y		Y			Y

Fig. 8.66. For function X

	t_0	t_1	t_2	t_3	t_4	t_5	t_6
S_1	Y				Y		
S_2			Y			Y	
S_3		Y		Y			Y

Fig. 8.67. For Function Y

Please note that the evaluation time of different functions may be different. Like in above Fig. 8.66, the evaluation time for *X* is 8 clock units and for Fig. 8.67, the evaluation time for *Y* is 7 clock units.

Also note that when any square of the reservation table is marked, it indicates that the corresponding stage is used at that time. If (i, j)th square is marked then it means that state, S_i, is used *j*-time units after the initiation of the function evaluation.

In a static, unifunction pipeline, one reservation table is sufficient to describe the data flow pattern. On the other hand, **in multifunctional pipeline** different reservation tables are used for different functions. **Please note that a given reservation table need not correspond to one particular hardware pipeline only. It may be used by several hardware pipelines with different interconnection structures.**

These reservation tables describe many interesting features of the pipeline utilization. Some of the features are as follows

1. **Multiple marks in a Row:** It indicates a repeated usage of a given stage if the marks are in distinct columns. It indicates a prolonged usage of a stage if the marks are in adjacent columns.
2. **Multiple marks in a column:** It indicates that multiple stages are simultaneously used.
3. **Continuous marks in a row/column:** If the marks are continuous, they may represent a slower stage needing more time slots.
4. **Number of columns in a table:** The number of columns in the table stands for the total compute time required by the computation represented by the table.
5. A general pipeline may have multiple paths, parallel usages of multiple stages and non-linear flow of data.

8.34.1 Latency Analysis Terminologies

We need to understand some terminologies used during latency analysis. They are discussed below.

1. **Collision:** The number of time units (or clock cycles) between two initiations of a pipeline is the **latency** between them. **Latency values must be positive integers only.** A latency of k means that two initiations are separated by k clock cycles. Any attempt by two or more initiations to use the same pipeline stage at the same time will cause a **collision.**
2. **Forbidden Latencies:** A collision implies resource conflicts between two initiations in the pipeline. Therefore, all collisions must be avoided in scheduling a sequence of pipeline initiations. Some latencies will cause collisions and some will not. **Latencies that cause collisions are called as forbidden latencies. Please note that in order to detect a forbidden latency, one needs to check the distance between any two checkmarks in the same row of the reservation table.**

For example : In the reservation table given below, the latencies are as follows

	1	2	3	4	5	6	7	8
S_1	X					X		X
Stage S_2		X		X				
S_3			X		X		X	

The distance between the first mark and the second mark in row S_1 above is 5 i.e., its forbidden latency is 5.

Now, consider another 3 stage pipeline:

	1	2	3	4	5	6	7	8
S_1	X					X		X
Stages S_2		X		X				
S_3			X		X		X	

Fig. 8.68 Collision with scheduling latency of 2.

We observe from this Fig. 8.68 that the initiations X_1 and X_2 collide in stage-2 at time = 4. At time = 7, these initiations collide in stage 3. Similarly, other collisions are shown in times 5, 6, 8, ... etc.

3. **Latency sequence: It is defined as a sequence of permissible non forbidden latencies between successive task initiations.**

   For example: In Fig. 8.64, we observe that 2, 4, 5, 7 are forbidden latencies. So, 1, 3, 6, and 8 are some non-forbidden latencies.

4. **Latency cycle: It is defined as a latency sequence which repeats the same subsequence or cycle indefinitely.**

   For example: Consider the following reservation table in Fig. 8.69.

Cycle repeats (from 10 to 18)

	1	2	3	4	5	6	7	8	9	10	11	12	13	14	15	16	17	18	19	20	
S_1	X_1	X_2				X_1	X_2	X_1	X_2	X_3	X_4				X_3	X_4	X_3	X_4	X_5	X_6	
S_2		X_1	X_2	X_1	X_2						X_3	X_4	X_3	X_4						X_5	....
S_3			X_1	X_2	X_1		X_1	X_2				X_3	X_4	X_3		X_3					

Fig. 8.69. Shows latency cycle (1, 8) = 1, 8, 1, 8, 1, 8 with an average latency of 4.5.

Here in, the latency cycle (1, 8) represents the infinite latency sequence 1, 8, 1, 8, 1, 8......... This implies that the successive initiations of new tasks are separated by one cycle and eight cycles alternately.

5. **Average Latency The average latency of a latency cycle is obtained by dividing the sum of all latencies by the number of latencies along the cycle.**

   For example: The latency cycle (1,8) has an average latency of (1÷8)12= 4.5

6. **Constant Cycle: A Constant cycle is a latency cycle which contains only one latency value. For example:**

	1	2	3	4	5	6	7	8	9	10	11	12	13	14	15	16	17	18	19	20	
S_1	X_1					X_1	X_2	X_1				X_2	X_3	X_2				X_3	X_4	X_3	
S_2		X_1		X_1				X_2		X_2				X_3		X_3				X_4	....
S_3			X_1		X_1		X_1		X_2		X_2		X_3		X_3	X_3		X_3		X_3	

Here, Latency cycle (6) = 6, 6, 6, 6

So, (6) is a **constant cycle.** The average latency of constant cycle is simply the latency itself.

8.35.2 Collision-free scheduling-steps to follow

Davidson provides an elegant method for identifying collision—free issue latencies and determining the possible issue sequences that are collision free. These sequences are called as **state transitions**. Davidson method involves **four steps:-**

Step 1: Compile a list of the issue latencies that will cause collisions for each row (stage) of the reservation table.

For example: Consider the following reservation table shown in Fig. 8.70.

Stage ↓	1	2	3	4	5	6	7	8	9	0
1	X								X	
2		X	X					X		
3				X						
4					X	X				
5							X	X		

Fig. 8.70. A Reservation Table

Note here that row-i will have a collision with issue latency of 8. That, is we need to check the distances between any two checkmarks in the same row of the reservation table.

∴ Row–1: 8

Row–2: 1, 5, 6

Row–3: 0

Row–4: 1

Row–5: 1

Step 2: Form the for bidden list for the reservation table that is the set union of all the non—null row forbidden issue latencies:

Forbidden list, $F = 1, 5, 6, 8$

The forbidden list tells us that new issues can be made without collisions at latencies of 2, 3, 4, 7, 9^+ (or at t3, t4, t5, t8, $t10^+$). **Note that the '+' means any latency greater than the one indicated.**

Step 3: A collision vector for the initial state is constructed from the forbidden list. This vector reads from right to left (by latency) using '1' for collision and '0' otherwise. Please note that the last non-forbidden latency of 9 can be ignored in the collision vector.

For example: In Fig. 8.71, the collision vector, V. that is formed is as follows

	0	7	6	5	4	3	2	1
Collision vector, V =	[1,	0,	1,	1,	0,	0,	0,	1]

That, is since 1 is a forbidden state in list, F, so we put a '1' as '1' shows a collision. As 2 is not a forbidden state (from step—2) so we put a '0' under it in the above collision vector. V. This goes on. We ignore the last non-forbidden latency of 9 in this collision vector, V.

Step 4: A state transition diagram is constructed from the collision vector.

The initial state collision vector is V = [10110001]. The transitions are 2, 3, 4, 7 and 9^+. To find the collision vector of the next state, the collision vector of the present state is shifted right for each transition. The shifted collision vector is ORed with the initial state collision vector to form a new state.

For example: Consider the following reservation table shown in Fig. 8.66.

Now, V = [10110001]

Right shifting V by 1-bit we get:

V' = [1011000]

Again, right shifting V by 1-bit we get:

V'' = [101100].

We have right shifted 2 times because one of the out-transitions is 2. So, now we OR this result (V'') by the original collision vector V and we get

$$\begin{array}{r} 10110001 \\ +\ 101100 \\ \hline =\ 10111101\ 1 \\ \hline \end{array}$$

So, we can now draw this in our state transition diagram. We repeat this process for 3, 4, 7 and 9 transitions also. When the out-transition is 3 we get V'' as [10110111]. When out—transition is 4, we get:

V'' = [10111011]

Similarly when transition is 7, we get :

V'' = V = [10110001]

Also, for out-transition of 9, we get:

V'' = V = [10110001]

So, we draw a state transition diagram (STD) now:

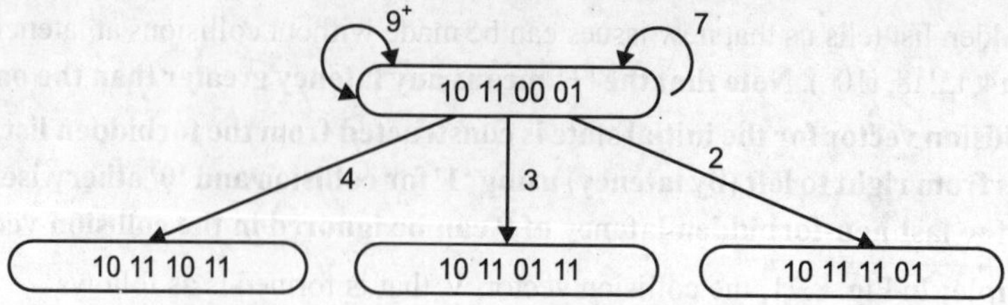

10110001	10110001	10110001
4→ 1011	3→10110	2→101100
10111011	10110111	10111101

Fig. 8.71. An initial state diagram.

Observe here that there are **three new states and two returns to the initial state. The latency used for the new state is shown by a number on the arrow connecting the states. Please note that the latency of 7 returns to the original state.** Any latency equal to or greater than 9 will also return to the original state - an effect that is indicated by 9^+. **Please note that the process of shifting continues by taking the collision vector of each new state, shifting and ORing with the initial state collision vector.** So, now we get a complete state transition diagram shown in Fig. 8.72 below:

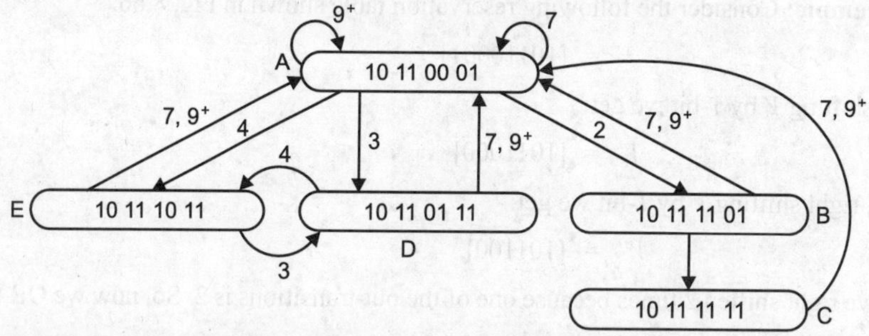

Fig. 8.72. Complete STD- Showing states - A, B, C, D and E

We can identify various issue cycles from Fig. 8.68 above. They are shown in table below:

Cycle	Path	Issue Latencies	Average Latency	Acceptance Ratio
1.	A, A, A, A	7,7	7	0.14
2.	A, D, A, D,	3, 7,3, 7	5	0.2
3.	A, D, E, D, E	3, 4, 3, 4	3.5	0.28
4.	A, D, E, A, D, E	3, 4, 7, 3, 4, 7	4.66	0.21
5.	A, E, D, E, D	4, 3, 4, 3	3.5	0.28
6.	A, E, A, E	4, 7, 4, 7	5.5	0.18
7.	A, B, A, B	2, 7, 2, 7	4.5	0.22
8.	A, B, C, A, B, C	2, 2, 7, 2, 2, 7	3.66	0.27

Please note that all cycles start with an issue into an empty pipeline-state A. We also find that in the 4th column, the minimum of average latency is 3.5.

So, we say that the minimum average latency (MAL) for the cycles 3 and 5 is 3.5. Cycles that permit issues at a constant latency can have a minimum, constant latency (MCL). ***For***

example, the only MCLs for this pipeline are 7 and of course 9^+. **The MCL is the smallest integer that is not a factor of any of the forbidden latencies.** Like, in our example, the smallest latency that is not a factor of (1, 5, 6, 8) is 7. A latency of 2 will collide with 6 and 8, a latency of 3 will collide with 6 and so on. Constant latencies are, however, of interest because then the control is easier to implement.

Now, we need to find the greedy cycles on the state diagram. **Greedy cycles are defined as those simple cycles in which each latency is the minimal latency (outgoing arc) from a state in the cycle. Please note that simple cycle is the one in which each state appears only once.**

To determine greedy cycles we follow a procedure:-

1. Start from each node of the state diagram.
2. Select arc with smallest latency label until a closed simple cycle is formed.
3. The latencies on the above correspond to the greedy cycle.

The average latency of any greedy cycle is less than or equal to the number of is in the collision vector. It is lower than those of simple cycles. Also, the average latency of greedy ccle is always greater than or equal to MAL. At least one of the greedy cycles will lead to MAL. Thus, the collision free scheduling of pipeline is nothing but finding greedy cycles from the set of simple cycles. The greedy cycles yielding MAL is the final choice to get the maximum throughput. So, Overall summary is as shown below:

From Reservation table given

↓

Issue latencies are found out

↓ then

Forbidden list/latencies are formed

↓

Collision Vector is formed

↓

State diagram is drawn Greedy cycles are found

↓

↓ MAL is calculated

We are in a position to solve some problems now.

8.34.3 Problems based on Reservation tables

EXAMPLE 8.1: Consider the following reservation table:

	t_1	t_2	t_3	t_4	t_5	t_6	t_7	t_8
S_1	X						X	
S_2			X					X
S_3		X		X				
S_4			X		X			

(*a*) Determine latencies in the forbidden list, *F* and the collision vector, *C*.

(*b*) Draw the state transition diagram.

(*c*) List all simple cycles and greedy cycles.

(*d*) Determine MAL.

(*e*) If clock period, *T* = 20ns, determine the maximum throughput of the pipeline.

[Pune Univ., B.Tech. 2nd sem; May 2004]

SOLUTION: (*a*) Forbidden latencies = {5, 4, 2}

∴ Permissible latencies = {1, 3, 6}

$$\therefore \text{ Collision Vecctor, } \quad V = \overset{6\,5\,4\,3\,2\,1}{[0\,1\,1\,0\,1\,0]}$$

Where 1 – Collision

0 – No collision

(*b*) The state transition diagram is:

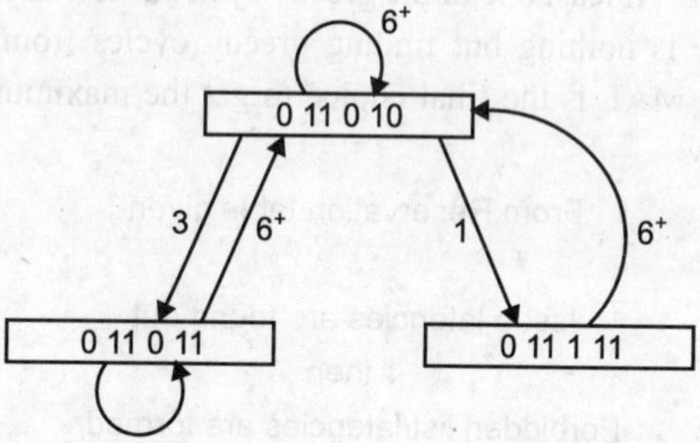

Initial collision vector (ICV) = 011010 & Permissible latencies are [1, 3, 6]

$$\begin{aligned} \therefore \quad \text{ICV} &= 0\,1\,1\,0\,1\,0 \\ 1 &\rightarrow \underline{1\,1\,0\,1}\,(+) \qquad \text{(Right shift by 1)} \\ & \underline{0\,1\,1\,1\,1\,1} \end{aligned}$$

Similarly,

$$\begin{aligned} \text{ICV} &= 0\,1\,1\,0\,1\,0 \\ 3 &\rightarrow \underline{0\,0\,0\,0\,1\,1}\,(+) \qquad \text{(Right shift by 3)} \\ & \underline{0\,1\,1\,0\,1\,1} \end{aligned}$$

Also,

$$\begin{aligned} \text{ICV} &= 0\,1\,1\,0\,1\,0 \\ 6 &\rightarrow \underline{0\,0\,0\,0\,0\,0}\,(+) \qquad \text{(Right shift by 6)} \\ & \underline{0\,1\,1\,0\,1\,0} \end{aligned}$$

So, a state transition diagram is drawn above.

(*c*) **List of Latency Cycles is** : (6), (3, 6) (1, 6), (3), (3,3,6), (3,6,6) and (6,1,6).

List of Simple Cycles is: (6), (3), (3, 6) and (1, 6).

List of Greedy Cycles is: (3), (1, 6).

(*d*) MAL = 3

(e) Throughput, $W = \frac{\eta}{t} \times \frac{1}{\text{MAL}}$

Assuming efficiency, $\eta = 1$

and $t = 20$ ns

$$w = \frac{n}{k\tau + (n-1)\tau} = \frac{\eta}{\tau}$$

$$= 1/(20 * 10^{-9}) * 1/3 = 16.67 \text{ MIPS}$$

EXAMPLE 8.2: Consider the following reservation table (RT):

	1	2	3	4	5	6	7
S_1	X		X				X
S_2				X		X	
S_3			X		X		

Calculate the following:

(*a*) Find all forbidden latencies.

(*b*) Draw a state transition diagram.

(*c*) Find all simple and greedy cycles.

(*d*) Find optimal constant latency cycle and minimal average latency.

(*e*) If pipeline clock period is 20 ns. Find the throughput of the pipeline.

SOLUTION:

(*a*) ROW 1: 2, 4, 6

ROW 2: 2

ROW 3: 3

∴ Set *F* (of forbidden latencies) = [2, 4, 6]

	1	2	3	4	5	6	7
S_1	X		X				X
S_2				X		X	
S_3			X		X		

(*b*) Permissible latencies are $\{1, 3, 5, 7^+\}$

Now, collision vector,

$$V = \{\overset{6}{1}\,\overset{5}{0}\,\overset{4}{1}\,\overset{3}{0}\,\overset{2}{1}\,\overset{1}{0}\}$$

ICV = 1 0 1 0 1 0

$1 \rightarrow \underline{1\ 0\ 1\ 0\ 1}$ [Right shifting by 1]

$\underline{1\ 1\ 1\ 1\ 1\ 1}$

Similarly for states 3, 5, 7 and 7^+ we can find the next states. Continuing in the same fashion we get the following STD:

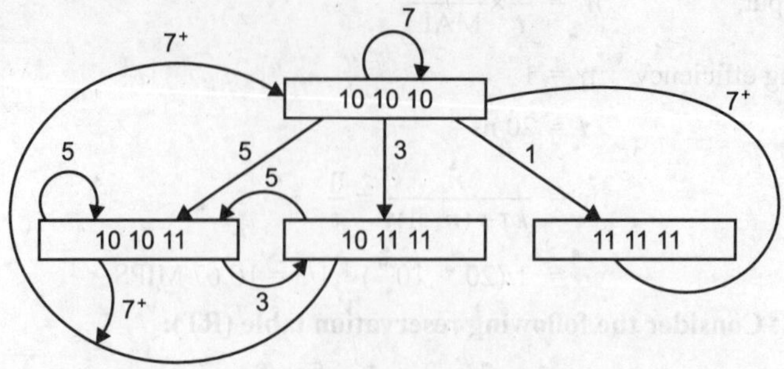

(*c*) Now, we find out the simple greedy cycles and the average latencies:-

Simple Cycles	Average Latency
5	5
7	7
(1,7) – Greedy	4*
(3,7)	5
(5,7)	6
(5,3)-Greedy	4*
3,5,7	5

(*d*) ∴ Minimum average latency (MAL) = 4.

(*e*) ∴ Maximum throughput = $\dfrac{1}{MAL \times \tau}$

Where τ – Clock Period

Now, MAL = 4

∴ and τ = 20 ns (given)

$$\therefore \text{ Maximum throughput } = \frac{1}{4\times20\times10^{-9}} = \frac{10^6}{80\times10^{-13}}$$

$$= \frac{10^6}{0.008} = 12.5 \text{ MIPS} = 12.5 \text{ MIPS}$$

EXAMPLE 8.3: Consider the execution of a program of 15000 instructions by linear pipeline processor. The clock rate of pipeline is 25 MHz. Pipeline has five stages and one instruction is issued per clock cycle. Neglect penalties due to branch instructions and out of sequence execution:

(*a*) Calculate the speed up program execution by pipeline as compared with that by nonpipelined processor.

(*b*) What are the efficiency and throughput of the pipeline processor?

SOLUTION: Given:

f = 25 MHz

Number of instructions = n = 15000

Number of pipeline stages $= k = 5$

(*a*) Speed up $= \dfrac{nk}{k+(n-1)} = \dfrac{(15000)5}{5+(15000-1)} = 4.99$

(*b*) Efficiency, $\eta = \dfrac{n}{k-(n-1)} = \dfrac{15000}{5+14999} = 0.99$

& Throughput, $W = \dfrac{nf}{k+(n-1)} = \dfrac{15000\times 25\times 10^{-6}}{5+14999} = 24.99$ MIPS

EXAMPLE 8.4: A processor (P_1) is non-pipelined and has a clock rate of 25 MHz. It has average CPI = 4. Another processor (P_2) has clock rate of 20MHz. P_2 is designed with five stages. P_2 is improved successor of P_1

(*a*) If a program of 100 instructions is to be executed on both processors, what is the speed up of P_2 compared to that of P_2?

(*b*) Find MIPS rate of P_1 as well as P_2 during execution of the program?

SOLUTION:

(*a*) CPI = 4

$f_1 = 25$ MHz $\qquad f_2 = 20$ MHz

$n = 100, \qquad k = 5$

$\therefore$ Speed-up $\quad S = \dfrac{T_1}{T_2}$

But $\quad T_1 = \dfrac{n\times CPI}{f_1} = \dfrac{100\times 4}{25\times 10^6} = 16\mu$ sec

$$T_2 = [k + (n-1)]\tau_2$$

$$= \frac{[5+99].1}{20\times 10^6} = \frac{104}{20\times 10^6} = 5.2\mu \text{ sec.}$$

$$S = \frac{T_1}{T_2} = \frac{16}{5.2} = \mathbf{3.08}$$

(*b*) Throughput, W = number of instructions executed / second

For pipelined processor, P_2

$$W_{P_2} = \frac{n\tau}{\frac{k+(n-1)}{10^6}} = \frac{100\times 20\times 10^6}{(5+99)\times 10^6} = \frac{200}{104} = \mathbf{19.23\ MIPS}$$

For Non-pipelined processor, P_1,

$$W_{P_1} = \frac{1}{4\tau} = \frac{f}{4} = \frac{1}{4}\times 25\times 10^6 = 6.25\times 10^6 \text{ instruction sec.}$$

$$= \mathbf{6.25\ MIPS}$$

EXAMPLE 8.5: Determine MAL and through put of the following instruction pipelining shown in the reservation table

	t_1	t_2	t_3	t_4	t_5	t_6	t_7
S_1	x				x		

S_2		x					x
S_3		x			X		x
S_4		x					x
S_5	x						x

[UPTU, B. TECH.(CSE/IT)-8TH SEM., 2005-08]

SOLUTION: Forbidden list, $F = \{2,4,5,6\}$

Collision vector and state diagrams are shown next:

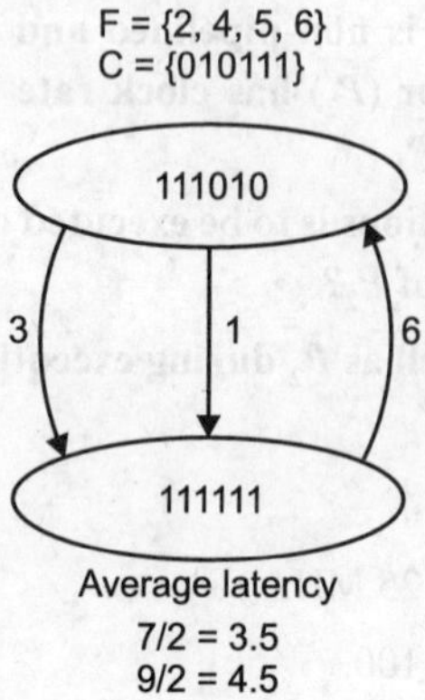

Simple cycles: 1,6 and 3,6.

$$\text{MAL} = 3.5$$

$$\text{Throughput} = 1/3.5 * 100\% = 33.3\%$$

8.34.4 Arithmetic Pipeline Design

Pipelining techniques can be applied to speed-up numerical computations.

I. Computer Arithmetic Principles

In our computers, arithmetic is performed with finite precision due to the use of fixed- size memory words or registers. This fixed-point or integer arithmetic offers a fixed range of numbers that can be operated upon. Floating-point arithmetic operates over much increased dynamic range of numbers. In modern computers, fixed-point and floating-point arithmetic operations are performed by separate hardware. Advanced RISC microprocessors usually have the hardware for both operations on the same processor chip. **Please note that the finite precision means that the numbers exceeding the limit must be truncated or rounded to provide a precision within the number of significant bits allowed.** In case of floating point numbers, exceeding the exponent range means error conditions called as overflow or underflow.

1. Fixed Point Operations

There are three notations followed for fixed-point operations:

(*a*) Signed magnitude.

(*b*) One's complement.

(*c*) Two's complement.

Out of these, twos complement notation is more popular in most of the computers because of its unique representation of all numbers including zero.

Add, subtract, multiply and divide are the four basic arithmetic operations.

2. Floating-point Operations

There are four basic arithmetic operations for a pair of floating point numbers.

Say, $x = (m_x, e_x)$

and $y = (m_y, e_y)$ are two floating point numbers.

Where m_x and m_y are their mantissa and e_x and e_y are exponents.

For simplicity and clarity, say $e_x \le e_y$ and base $r = 2$. Then the four basic operations on x and y will be: $x + y$, x-y, $x*y$ and x/y.

From these equations, it is clear that we can divide these operations into two groups— one for the exponent operations and the other for mantissa operations. These two groups of operation demand double hardware for floating point unit as compared to that required in a fixed point unit.

3. Elementary Functions

Elementary functions include trigonometric, exponential, logarithmic and other transcendental functions. Truncated polynomials or power series can be used to evaluate the elementary functions such as sin x, in x, e^x, cosh x, $\tan^{-1} y$, $\sqrt{x}$, x^3 etc. **Please note that the computer arithmetic can be implemented by hardwired random logic circuitry as well as by table lookup using ROM or RAM in the memory.** Table look ups can be used to see the values of frequently used constants. Hashing will provide a faster access to these tables.

8.34.5 Arithmetic Pipeline Stages

Depending on the arithmetic operation (like add, subtract, multiply, divide squaring, square roots, logarithm etc.) which is to be implemented, different pipeline stages in an arithmetic unit require different hardware logic. **Basically, we need some hardware for add and shift operations only since all operations involve these two operations only. Arithmetic and logical shifts can be easily implemented with shift registers.** High speed addition requires the use of carry-propagation adder (CPA) which **adds two numbers and produces an arithmetic sum or it requires a carry-save adder (CSA) to add three input numbers and produce one sum output and a carry output.** Let us now tabulate the differences between CSA and CPA.

CPA	CSA
1. It adds two numbers and produces its sum.	1. It adds three numbers and produces one sum output and a carry output.
2. When CPA is used to built a cascade of full adder then the carry-out (C_{out}) of the lower stage is connected to the carry—in (C_{in}) of a higher stage.	2. When CSA is used to built a cascade of full adder then the carryout terminals of all stages are taken as the output lines for a carry-vector, C.

8.34.6 Different pipeline designs

CPAs and CSAs can be used to design a multiply pipeline and a divide pipeline. We discuss these one by one now.

Multiply Pipeline Design

Let us now study, how to use a number of CSAs for multiple-number addition. The same will serve the purpose of pipeline multiplication. We shall consider an example of multiplication of two 6-bit numbers. This is shown below in Fig. 8.73.

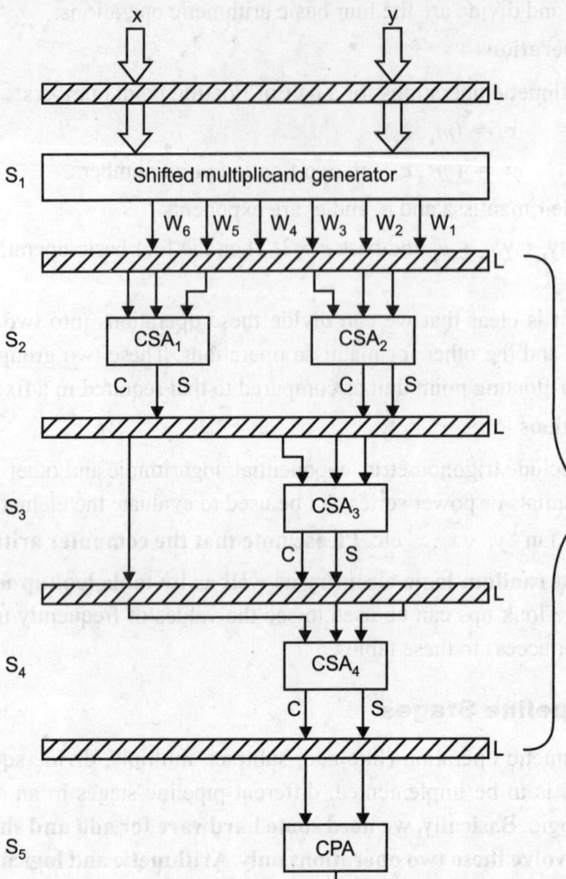

Fig. 8.73. A pipelined 6-bit multiplier

As is clear from the Fig. 8.73 that this 6-bit, 2 number multiplier pipeline has **five stages:-**

Stage 1: In this stage, we generate all 6 × 6 = 36 immediate product terms i.e., these terms form the six rows of the shifted multiplicands, W_i where $i = 1, 2, ... 6$.

These 6 numbers are passed to stage-2.

Stage 2: The six numbers are then added by forming two groups each groups having three numbers to get two sum vectors and two carry vectors. Two CSAs are ued for this addition.

Stage 3: The four, results generated by stage-2 are added in this stage by using another CSA. Thus, three of the above results are added and the fourth (Sum Vector) is forwarded to stage-4. This CSA also generates two results. In all, three results are fed to stage-4.

Stage 4: This stage consists of a CSA that adds all the three vectors received and generates one sum vector and one carry vector. They are passed to stage-5.

Stage 5: It adds the sum vector and carry vector received from stage 4, using a CPA and the result is one number which is the final output, the Product $P = X \times Y$.

Please note that there are totally four CSAs that are interconnected to form a three- level CSA tree. This CSA tree merges six numbers into two : The sum vector, S and the carry vector, C. The final stage is a CPA that adds sum vector, S and a carry vector, C to produce the product, P. The above CSA tree that adds only multiple single bit numbers is known as a bit-slice Wallace tree.

However, the cost of the hardware of this multiplier is quite high. So, **some trade-off is required between cost and evaluation time.** So, we have an **alternative approach also and it is called as an iterative CSA tree for a pipelined multiplier**. In this case, a CSA tree pipeline of Fig. 8.73 is modified to have a feedback so that it allows the multiple pass usage of CSAs. Such an iterative multiplier is shown in Fig. 8.74.

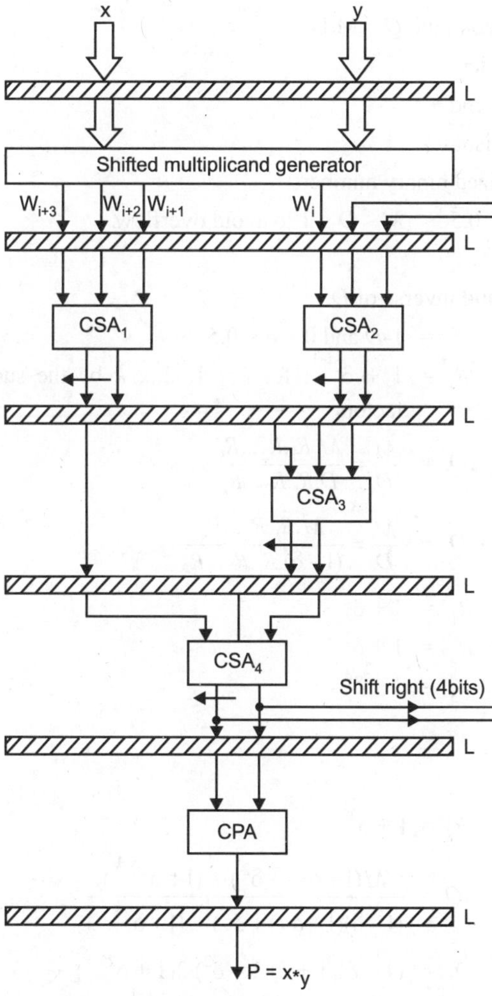

Fig. 8.74. Iterative CSA tree for Pipelined Multiplication

In this approach, two input ports of CSA tree are connected with the feedback carry vector and sum vector. CPA is needed to be expanded to handle increased operand width. This pipeline can be used to merge four additional multiplicands per iteration. For instance, to multiply two 32-bit numbers, only eight iterations will be required with this CSA tree with feedback.

Now, one pass 32-input CSA tree pipeline requires the use of 30 CSAs in eight pipeline stages. **On the other hand, the iterative CSA tree requires 4 CSAs totally. Thus, there is saving of cost of 26 additional CSA (i.e., 30 - 4 = 26 CSAs). Thus, the iterative approach saves the hardware cost significantly as compared to single pass approach.** Even though the hardware cost reduces yet the evaluation time increases.

2. Division pipeline design

Many models of high performance computers e.g., IBM 360/370, CDC-6600/7600, share the same hardware. This is possible because of application of convergence division method.

Convergence Division Method

Assume that we want to compute $Q = M/D$

Where Q is quotient

M is dividend

D is divisor.

We will consider normalized binary numbers.

$\therefore \quad 0.5 \leq M < D < 1$ to avoid overflow.

Now,

i.e., multiplication of M and inverse of D.

Let $\delta = 1-D$ and $0 < \delta < 0.5$ ...(1)

and $R_i = 1 + \delta^{2^{i-1}}$; for $i = 1, 2, \ldots k$ be the successive converging factors. ...(2)

$$\therefore \quad Q = \frac{M}{D} = \frac{M.R_1.R_2...R_k}{D.R_1.R_2...R_k}$$

$$Q = \frac{M}{D} = \frac{M.R_1.R_2...R_k}{(1-\delta).R_1.R_2...R_k} \quad \text{(from (1)}$$

$$R_1 = 1 + \delta$$

$$R_2 = 1 + \delta^2$$

$$R_3 = 1 + \delta^4$$

$$\vdots$$

$$R_k = 1 + \delta^{2^{k-1}}$$

$$Q = \frac{M(1+\delta)(1+\delta^2)\cdots(1+\delta^{2^{k-1}})}{(1-\delta)(1+\delta)(1+\delta^2)\cdots(1+\delta^{2^{k-1}})}$$

Let

$$D_i = (1-\delta)(1+\delta)(1-\delta^2)...(1+\delta^{2^{k-2}})$$

$$= (1-\delta^2)(1+\delta^2)\ldots(1+\delta^{2^{k-1}})$$

$$= (1-\delta^4)(1+\delta^4)\ldots(1+\delta^{2^{k-1}})$$

$$\therefore \quad D_i = (1-\delta^{2^i})$$

$$\text{As} \quad 0 < \delta < 0.5, \delta^{2i} \rightarrow 0 \text{ as } i \rightarrow \infty$$

$$D_i = 1$$

$$Q = M.R_1 R_2.....R_k \qquad ...(3)$$

Thus, division can be carried out by repeated multiplication as given by equation-3. **Please note here that the smaller is the fraction 6, the faster convergence is possible.** In IBM 360 machine, same hardware is shared for floating point multiply and divide operation. For speeding up multiplication operations multiplier recoding techniques are used. After recoding, SIX multiplicand multiples are obtained. A pipelined multiply/ divide unit of IBM 360 machine is shown in Fig. 8.75 below:

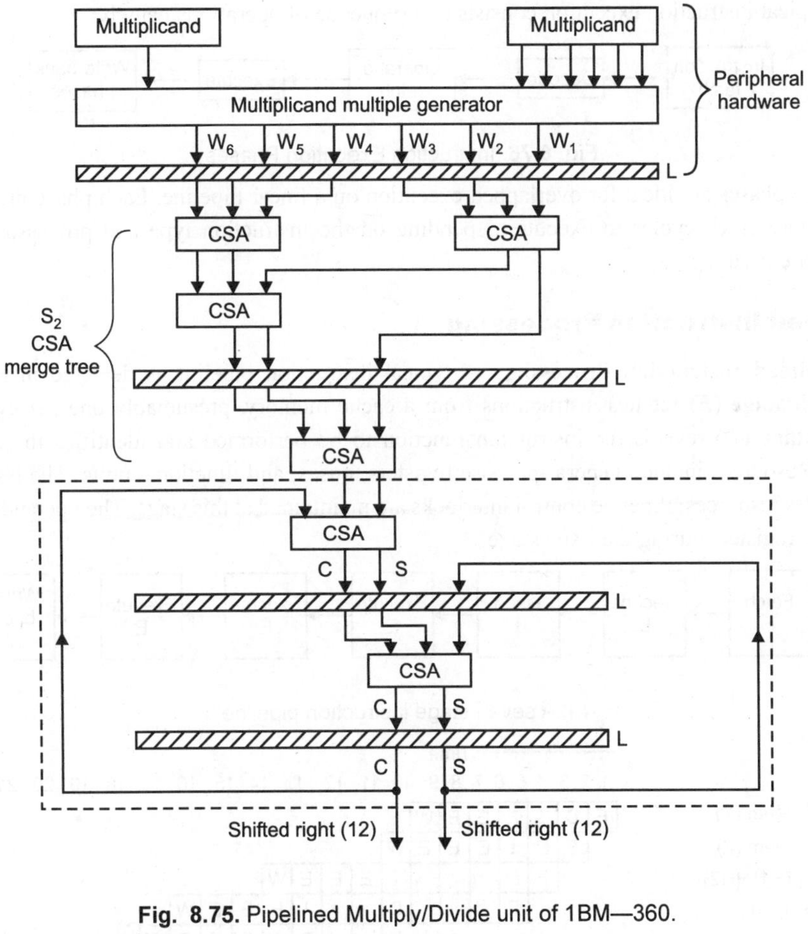

Fig. 8.75. Pipelined Multiply/Divide unit of 1BM—360.

As shown in Fig. 8.75, there are two parts of multiply/divide unit:

Part I: The iterative hardware for multiple multiplicand addition as shown inside the dashed-line box.

Part II: The peripheral hardware for input reservation, prenormalization, multiplier recoding, exponent arithmetic, carry propagation and output storage.

A convergence division method is used for division. Therefore, above iterative-multiply unit can also perform division without additional facilities. Herein, there are 4 areas where parallelism has been found:

(*a*) Parallel operations of ADD unit and multiply/divide unit within floating point unit.

(*b*) Pipelining in ADD and Multiply/Divide unit.

(*c*) Parallel execution within the iterative multiply hardware.

(*d*) Parallel operations of fixed point unit and floating-point unit.

Instruction Pipeling Design

A stream of instructions can be executed by a pipeline in an overlapped manner.

1. Phases of instruction execution

A typical instruction execution consists of a sequence of operations namely:

Fig. 8.76. Instruction Execution Phases

These phases are ideal for overlapped execution on a linear pipeline. Each phase may require one or more clock cycles to execute, depending on the instruction type and processor/memory architecture used.

Pipelined Instruction Processing

Pipelined Instruction Processing: A typical instruction pipeline is depicted in Fig. 8.77. **The fetch stage (*F*)** fetches instructions from a cache memory, presumably one per cycle. **The decode stage (*D*)** reveals the instruction function to be performed and identifies the resources needed. Resources include general-purpose registers, buses, and functional units. The **issue stage (*I*)** reserves resources. Pipeline control interlocks are maintained at this stage. The operands are also read from registers during the issue stage.

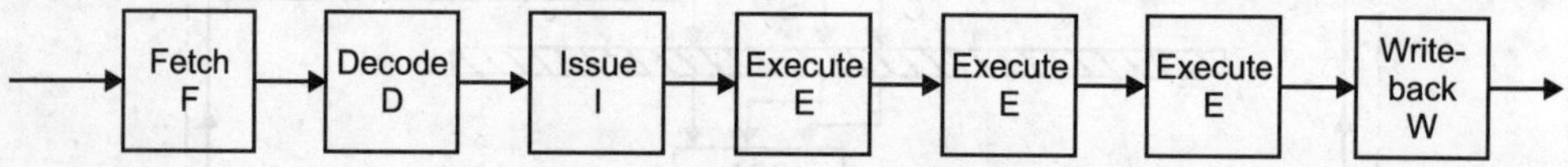

(*a*) A seven stage instruction pipeline

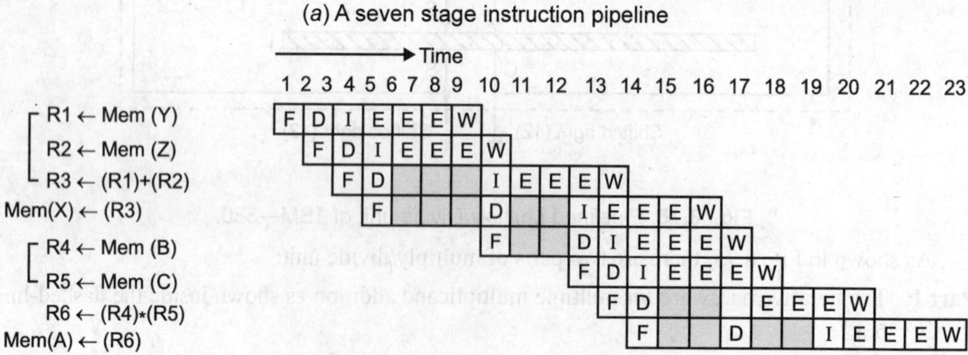

(*b*) In-order instruction issuing

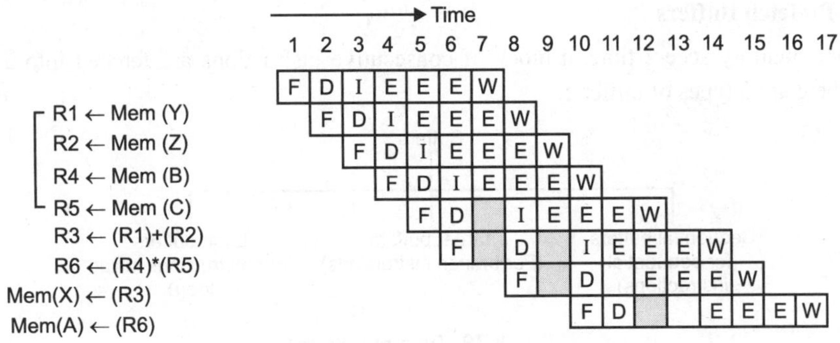

(*c*) Reordered instruction issuing

Fig. 8.77. Pipelined execution of $X = Y + Z$ and $A = B \times C$.

The instructions are executed in one or several **execute stages (*E*).** Three execute stages are shown in Fig. 8.77 (a). The last **writeback stage (*W*)** is used to write results into the registers. Memory load or store operations are treated as part of execution. Figure 8.73 shows the flow of machine instructions through a typical pipeline. These eight instructions are for pipelined execution of the high-level language statements $X = Y + Z$ and $A = B \times C$. Assume **load and store** instructions take four execution clock cycles, while floating- point **add and multiply** operations take three cycles.

Figure 8.77(b) illustrates the issue of instructions following the original program order. **The shaded boxes correspond to idle cycles when instruction issues are blocked due to resources latency or conflicts or due to data dependences. The first two load instructions issue on consecutive cycles. The add is dependent on both loads and must wait three cycles before the data (*Y* and *Z*) and loaded in.**

Similarly, the store of the sum to memory location X must wait three cycles for the **add** to finish due to a flow dependence. There are similar blockages during the calculation of A. The total time required is 17 clock cycles. This time is measured beginning at cycle 4 when the first instruction starts execution until cycle 20 the last instruction starts execution. This timing measure eliminates the unduly effects of the pipeline **'startup" or "draining" delays.**

Figure 8.77(c) shows an improved timing after the instruction issuing order is changed to eliminate unnecessary delays due to dependence. **The idea is to issue all four load operations in the beginning.** Both **add and multiply** instructions are blocked fewer cycles due to this data perfecting. The reordering should not change the end results. The time required is being reduced to 11 cycles, measured from cycle 4 to cycle 14.

8.34.8 Mechanisms for Instruction Pipelining

There are different mechanisms to smoothen the pipeline flow and to remove bottlenecks and unnecessary memory-access operations.

1. Prefetch Buffers

In one memory-access time, a block of consecutive instructions are fetched into a prefetch buffer. There are 3 types of buffers:

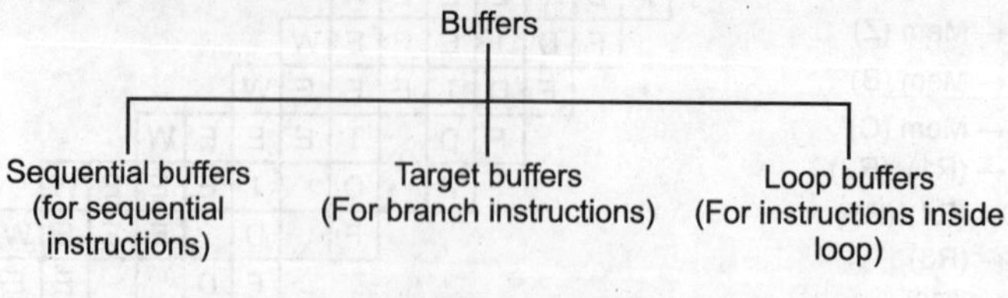

Fig. 8.78. Type of buffers.

Please note here that each buffer has its own role as shown in Fig. 8.78. Also note that both sequential and target buffers operate in a FIFO order. These buffers become part of the pipeline as additional stages. A conditional branch instruction causes **both sequential and target buffers to fill with instructions.** These two buffers work alternately to prevent a collision between the instructions flowing into and out of the pipeline.

A third type of buffer called as a loop buffer is maintained by the fetch stage of the pipeline. All these three buffers are shown in Fig. 8.79.

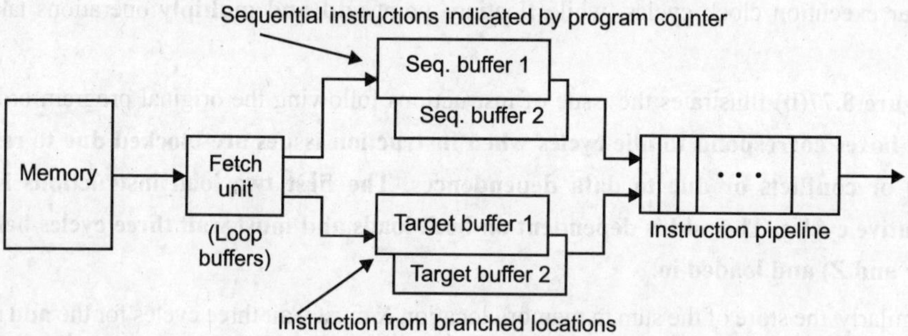

Fig. 8.79. Three Prefetch Buffers.

The *loop buffer* operates in two steps

1. It contains instructions sequentially ahead of the current instruction. This saves the instruction fetch time from memory.
2. It recognizes when the target of a branch falls within the loop boundary

The advantage of this scheme is that unnecessary memory accesses can be avoided.

For Example: CDC—6600 and Cray—1 use loop buffers.

2. Multiple functional units

Multiple Functional Units: Sometimes a certain pipeline stage becomes the bottleneck. This stage corresponds to the row with the maximum number of checkmarks in the reservation table. This bottleneck problem can be alleviated by using multiple copies of the same stage simultaneously. This leads to the use of multiple execution units in a pipelined processor design (Fig. 8.80.)

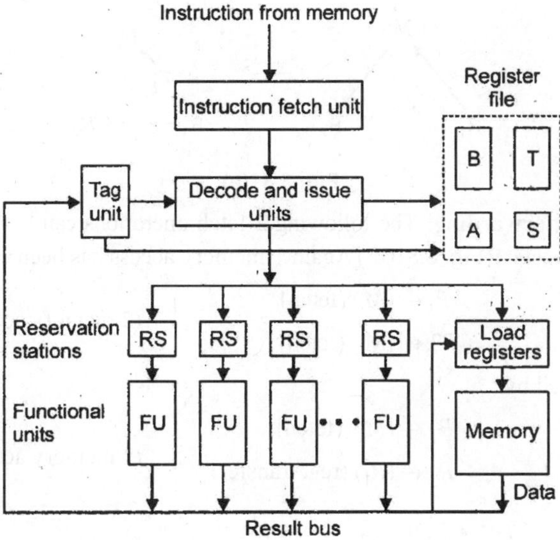

Fig. 8.80. Pipeline processor with many functional units.

Sohi (1990) used model architecture for a pipelined scalar processor containing multiple functional units (Fig. 8.80) In order to resolve data or resources dependences among the successive instructions entering the pipeline, **the Reservation Stations (RS)** are used with each functional unit. Operands can wait in the RS until its data dependencies have been resolved. Each RS is uniquely identified by a tag, which is monitored by a tag unit.

The tag unit keeps checking the tags from all currently used registers or RSs. This register tagging technique allows the hardware to resolve conflicts between source and destination registers assigned for multiple instructions. Besides resolving conflicts, the RSs also serve as buffers to interface the pipelined functional units with the decode and issue units. The multiple functional units are supposed to operate in parallel, once the dependences are resolved. This will alleviate the bottleneck in the execution stages of the instruction pipeline.

3. Internal data forwarding and Register tagging

There are 2-techniques that are used for instruction pipelining. They are discussed below.

1. **Internal forwarding: It refers to a "short-circuit" technique for replacing unnecessary memory accesses by register to register transfers** in a sequence of arithmetic-store operations. (∴ Register access is faster than memory access).

   It is also of 3 types:

   (*a*) **Store-fetch forwarding:** The following sequence of the 2—operations store then- fetch can be replaced by 2—parallel operations, one store and one register transfer:

$$\left.\begin{array}{l} M_i \leftarrow (R_i) \text{ (store)} \\ M_2 \leftarrow (M_i) \text{ (fetch)} \end{array}\right\} \quad \text{(2- Memory accesses)}$$

being replaced by

$$\left.\begin{array}{l} M_i \leftarrow (R_1) \text{ (store)} \\ R_2 \leftarrow (R_2) \text{ (Fetch)} \end{array}\right\} \quad \text{1 Memory access only now.}$$

e.g.

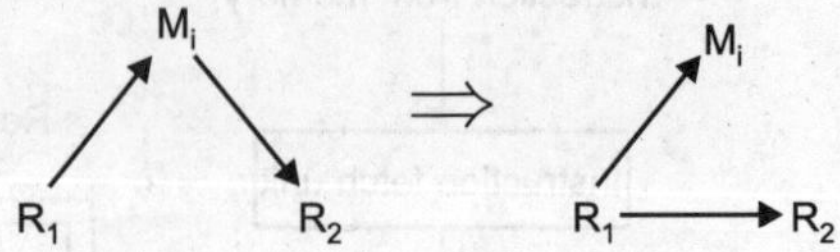

Fig. 8.81(a).

(b) Fetch-fetch forwarding: The following 2-fetch operations can be replaced by 1-fetch & 1-register transfer. (Fig. 8.81(b)) Again 1-memory access has been eliminated:

$$\left.\begin{array}{l} R_i \leftarrow (M_i) \text{ (fetch)} \\ R2 \leftarrow (\mathrm{M_i}) \text{ (fetch)} \end{array}\right\} \text{(2 memory accesses)}$$

being replaced by:

$$\left.\begin{array}{l} R_1 \leftarrow (M_1) \text{ (fetch)} \\ R_2 \leftarrow (R_1) \text{ (reg. transfer)} \end{array}\right\} \text{(1 memory access)}$$

e.g.,

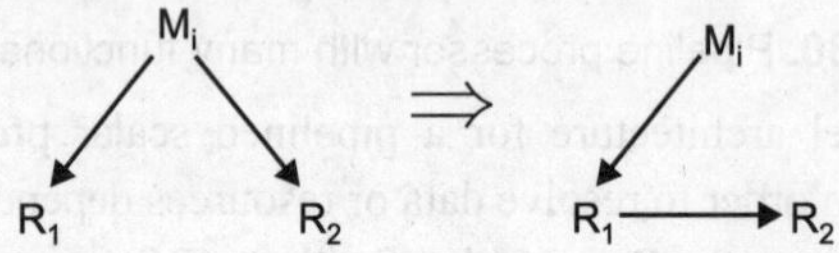

(c) Store-store overwriting: Following 2-memory updates (stores) of the same word can be combined into one, since the second store overwrites the first:

$$M_i \leftarrow (R_1) \text{ (store)} \qquad \text{(2- Memory accesses)}$$

$$M_i \leftarrow (R_1) \text{ (reg. transfer)}$$

being replaced by

$$M_i \leftarrow (R_2) \text{ (store)} \qquad \text{(1 memory access only)}$$

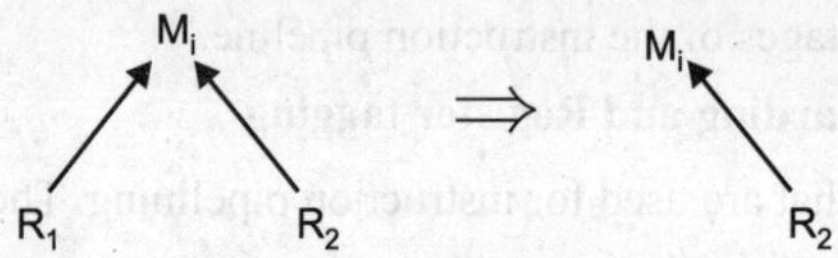

Fig. 8.81(c).

II. Register tagging: "Refers to the use of tagged registers, buffers & reservation stations for exploiting concurrent activities among multiple arithmetic units."

Application: This technique may be used in almost any computer that has multiple functional pipelines & accumulators.

We are in a position to solve the problem now.

EXAMPLE 8.1: The inner loop of a certain program is completed to perform the following operations in a sequence:

1. $\boldsymbol{R_0 \leftarrow (M_1)}$ **(fetch)**
2. $\boldsymbol{R_0 \leftarrow (R_0) + (M_2)}$ **(add)**

3. $R \leftarrow (R_0) \times (M_3)$ **(mul)**
4. $M_4 \leftarrow R_0$ **(store)**

Apply your internal-forwarding technique to simplify of sequence of such executions, so that minimum numbers of memory references are done? Explain.

SOLUTION: Now, we first draw original data flow—sequence for the given problem:

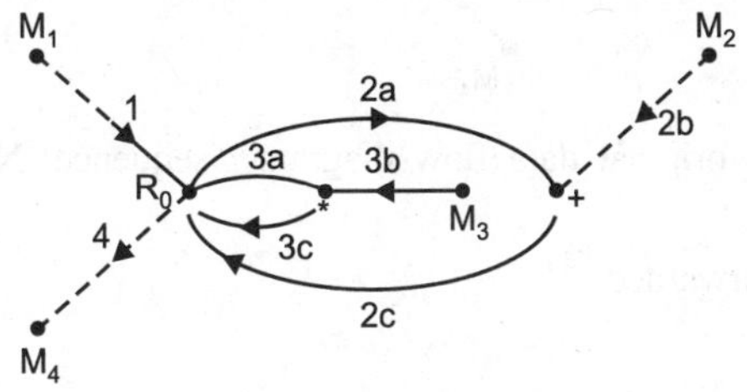

i.e., 1st instruction, is $R_o \leftarrow (M_1)$

Where '1' represents instruction 1 above. Similarly, 2nd instruction is:

$$R_0 \leftarrow (R_0) + (M_2)$$

$$R_0 \leftarrow (R_0) + (M_2)$$

i.e., Contents of R_0, are added to contents of M_2 and result in again brought to R_0, so we can draw:

i.e., add (R_0) to (M_2) by using + or "adder unit" & then bring that result to R_0 (2c step). i.e., our 2nd instruction need 3-substeps

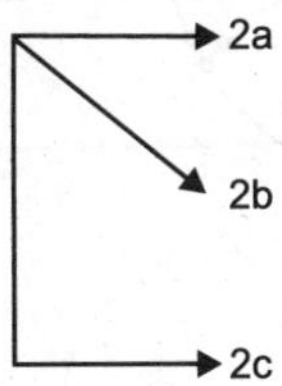

Similarly, for 3rd instruction

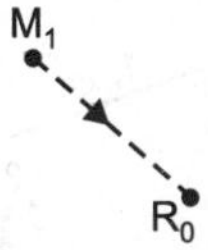

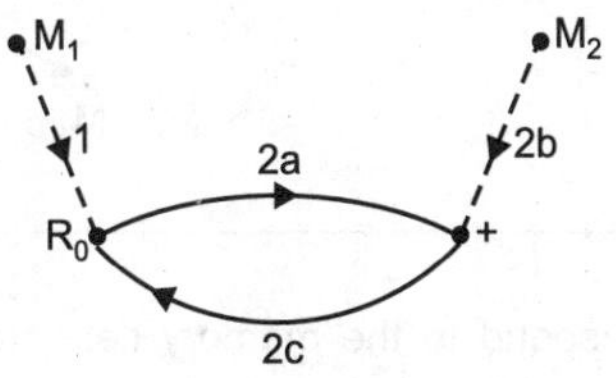

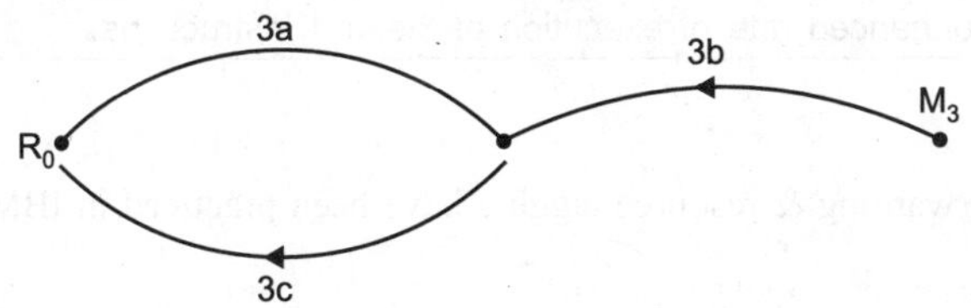

Similarly, for 4th instruction

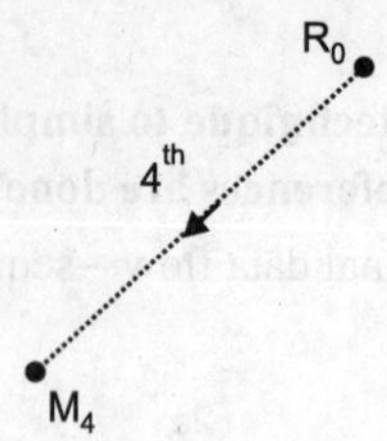

So, we get the above original data flow diagram / sequence. Now we apply our internal forwarding technique:

1. Step (1) and (2) forwarded:

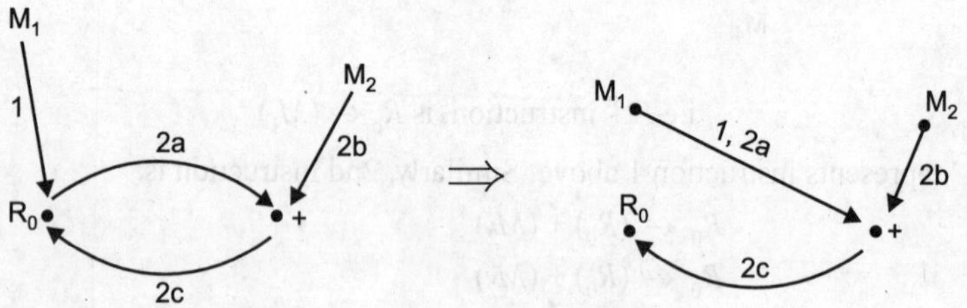

2. Step (2) and (3) forwarded:

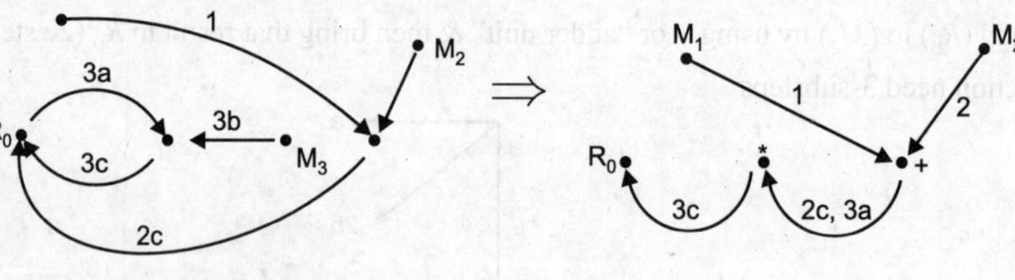

3. Step (2) and (4) forwarded:

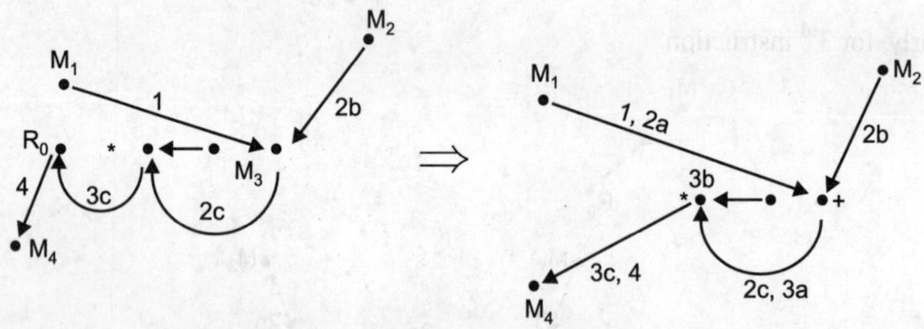

NOTE:

1. Nodes in the graph correspond to the memory cells, registers, an adder, or a multiplier.
2. Memory accesses are shown by thick arrows and register transfers by thin arrows.
3. We have, thus, enhanced rate of execution of these 4 instructions.

Application

Both internal-forwarding & resource tagging have been practiced in IBM model 91 floating-point execution unit.

8.34.9 Pipeline Hazards

1. Pipeline hazards are caused by **"resource—usage conflicts"** among various instructions in the pipeline. Such hazards are triggered by interinstruction dependencies.
2. When successive instructions **overlap** their fetch, decode and execution through a pipeline-processor, **inter instruction dependencies** may arise to prevent the sequential data flow in the pipeline.

For example, an instruction may depend on the results of a previous instruction. Until the completion of the previous instruction, the present instruction cannot be initiated into the pipeline. In other instances, two (2) stages of a pipeline may need to update the same memory location. Hazards of this sort, if not properly detected and resolved, could result in an **"interlock-situation"**, in the pipeline or produce unreliable results by overwriting.

1. Data Hazards

There are 3-classes of data dependent hazards, according to various data update patterns:

(a) **Write-After- Read (WAR) hazards:** It may occur when J-attempts to modify some data object that is read by *I*. i.e.,

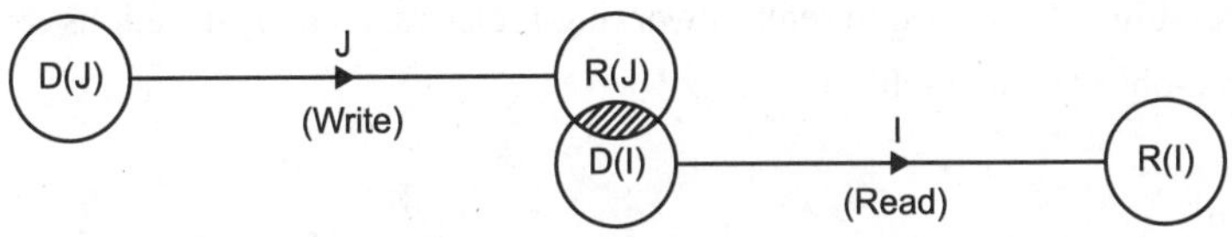

[it is modified by *J*, so *J* writes]

∴ The necessary conditions for this hazard are

$$D(I) \cap R(J) \neq \phi \text{ for WAR} \quad \text{...(la)}$$

↑

null

(b) **Read-After-Write (RAW) hazards:** A RAW hazard between the two (2) instructions *I* & *J* may occur when J attempts to read some data object that has been **modified by *I*** i.e.,

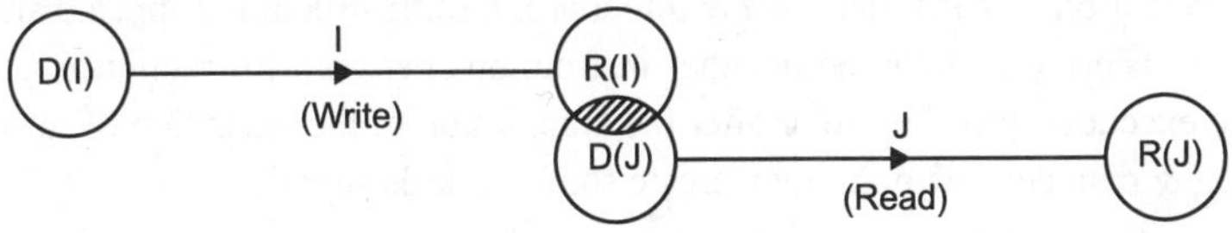

[modified by *I*, so *I* writes]

∴ The necessary condition for this hazard is:

$$R(I) \cap D(J) \neq \phi \text{ for RAW}$$

(null) . . . (1b)

(c) **Write-after-write (WAW) hazards :** A WAW hazard may occur if both *I* and *J* attempt to modify the same data object. i.e.,

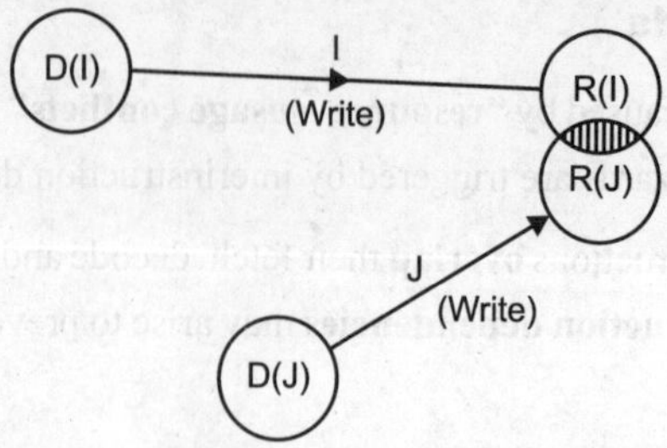

[both I & J modify, so, both write]

∴ The necessary condition for this hazard is:

> **NOTE:** RAR is not there because when we do read-after read nothing is changed, so RAR is no problem.

$$R(I) \cap R(j) \neq \phi \text{ for WAR} \qquad \ldots(\text{lc})$$

↑

null

∴ Improper timing & data dependencies may create some hazardous situations.

2. Control Hazard

"Resource-objects" are used to refer to working-registers, memory-locations & special flags.

∴ (resource-object) = data-object

↑

content of

∴ Each instruction can be considered as a mapping from set of data objects to a set of other data objects.

Domain, *D*(*I*), of an instruction I is defined as the set of 'resource-objects' whose contents may affect the execution of I (i.e., operands only).

Range, *R*(*I*), of an instruction, I is the set of resource objects whose data objects may be modified by execution of instruction I (i.e., results of execution of instruction)

Obviously, the operands to be used in an instruction execution are retrieved (read) from its domain and the results will be stored (written) in its range.

Consider, execution of 2 instructions *I* & *J* in a program. Instruction *J* appears after instruction *I* in the program. There may be none or other instructions between instruction *I* & *J*. Instruction *J* may enter the execution pipe before or after the completion of the execution of instruction *I*. The improper timing & data dependencies may create some hazards situations.

How to do Hazard detection?

1. It can be done in the **instruction fetch stage of a pipeline** by comparing the domain and range of the incoming instruction with those of the instruction being processed. When any one of the condition of equations, *Ia*, *Ib*, & *Ic* is detected, warning signal can be generated to prevent the hazard from taking place.
2. Another approach is to allow the incoming instruction through the pipeline and **distribute the detection to all potential pipeline stages.** It offers better flexibility **at the expense of increased hardware control.**

3. Hazard Resolution

How to resolve such hazards?

1. Once a hazard is detected, the system should resolve the interlock situation. Consider the instruction sequence $\{... I, I+1, ... J, J+1, ...\}$ in which a hazard has been detected between the current instruction. J and a previous instruction

A straight forward approach is to stop the pipe & to suspend the execution instruction *J*, *J* + 1, *J* + 2 ... , until the instruction. *I* has passed the point resource conflict.

In order to avoid RAW-type of hazards, IBM engineers developed a **short-circuiting approach, also called as data-forwarding,** which forwards multiple copies of the data as many waiting instruction as may wish to read it.

> NOTE: Another type of hazards is due to the job-scheduling problem.

Once a task is initiated in a static pipeline, its, flow pattern is fixed. An 'initiation' refers to the start of a single function evaluation when 2 or more initiations attempt to use the same stage at the same time, **a collision results. Thus, the job sequencing problem is "To properly schedule queued tasks awaiting initiation in order to avoid collisions and to achieve high throughput."**

4. **Problems based on pipeline Hazards**

EXAMPLE 8.1: Consider the following instructions ($I_1 - I_5$) and identify various hazards:

I_1 : $R_1 \leftarrow (M(R_4))$; **Load**

I_2 : $R_2 \leftarrow R_1 + R_2$; **Add**

I_3 : $M[R] \leftarrow R_2$; **Store**

I_4 : $R_2 \leftarrow R_6$ **and** R_3; **AND (logical)**

I_5 : $R_6 \leftarrow R_6 + 1$; **increment?**

SOLUTION: The instruction <I_1, I_2, I_3> pose a RAW hazard.

<I_2, I_4> pose WAW hazard and <I_4, I_5> pose a WAR hazard

EXAMPLE 8.2: Identify various hazards in the following instruction stream:

I_1 : $R_2 \leftarrow R_2 + R_3$

I_2 : **if zero** (R_2) **then goto** L_3**?**

SOLUTION: <I_1, I_2, I_3> show RAW Hazard.

Data dependency hazards are problematic. They may prevent simultaneous processing of two instructions in the pipeline. As a result, they disrupt and reduce throughput.

EXAMPLE 8.3: Identify the hazards in the following instruction stream:

I_1 : $R_2 \leftarrow R_2 + R_3$

I_2 : **if** $R_2 = 0$ **then goto** $L3$

I_3 : $M[500] \leftarrow R_2$

I_4 : $L3 : M[600] \leftarrow M[500] + R_5$**?**

SOLUTION: <I_1, I_2, I_3> show RAW hazard. <I_2, I_3> show control hazard

Here, I_3 is the constituent of control dependency hazard.

EXAMPLE 8.4: Identify all of the RAW, WAR, WAW and control hazards in the following instruction sequence:

DIV ***r*2, *r*5, *r*8**

SUB ***r*9, *r*2, *r*7**

ASH ***r*5, *r*14, *r*6**

MUL ***r*11, *r*9, *r*5**

BEQ ***r*10, 0, *r*12**

OR ***r*8, *r*15, *r*2 ?** **[Pune Univ., B. Tech. 2nd sem., Dec. 2003)**

SOLUTION: Let us denote all these instructions by statement numbers — SI to *S*6 as follows :

*S*1	:	$r2 \leftarrow r5/r8$
*S*2	:	$r9 \leftarrow r2/r7$
*S*3	:	$r5 \leftarrow r14 << r6$
*S*4	:	$r11 \leftarrow r9 \times r5$
*S*5	:	$r10 \leftarrow r12$
*S*6	:	$r8 \leftarrow r15$ OR $r2$.

(*i*) Now, flow dependencies in the program are:

(*a*) $S1 \rightarrow S2$

(*b*) $S3 \rightarrow S4$

(*c*) $S1 \rightarrow S6$

(*d*) $S2 \rightarrow S4$

∴ The program has 4 RAW hazards.

(*ii*) No antidependencies in the program.

∴ No WAR hazards.

(*iii*) No output dependencies in the program.

∴ No WAW hazards.

8.34.10 Dynamic Instruction Scheduling

There are three approaches used here. They are as follows:

(*a*) Static Scheduling Approach.

(*b*) Register Scoreboarding Approach.

(*c*) Tomasulo's Approach.

1. Static Scheduling

In this approach hazard detection is conducted to a fixed point in the pipeline usually at the instruction decode stage. But its main disadvantage is that all dependencies or collisions cannot be resolved in advance and hence potential hazards have to be treated actual hazards.

2. Register Scoreboarding

A separate register that has one bit to identify each register of the register file is called a **scoreboard**. This bit is set if the corresponding register is in use. A computer with registers will have a 32-bit score board to indicate the busy/free status of registers. When an instruction uses a set of registers, the bits corresponding to those registers are set to 1 in the scoreboard. They are reset to 0 as soon as the instruction using that register completes execution. Thus, the hardware will examine the scoreboard to see if the registers specified in the instruction are free before executing it.

3. Tomasulo's Approach

Let us assume that there is a usage counter, C_i, associated with each distinct store, S_i. The store includes local registers and main memory. If the memory is interleaved then each distinct memory module constitutes a distinct store. C_i may take values in the range $\{1, 0, -1, -2, ... -n_i\}$ where n_i is the maximum number of concurrently executable instructions having S_i as a source.

- If $C_i = 1$, it indicates that some instructions with store, S_i, as a destination is being processed by the pipeline at that time. i.e., S_i, is being used as a source as well as a destination by more than one instruction.
- If $C_i = 0$, it implies that the store is neither a source nor a destination for any instruction.
- If $C_i = -m$, for some $m <= n_i$ it indicates that m instructions in the pipeline are using S_i, as a source.

Let us also assume that there is a binary busy flag, B_n, associated with each distinct functional unit, FU_n. At any given time, B_n can be 1 or 0.

If $B_n = 1$, if indicates that FU_n is being used by a pipeline stage.

If $B_n = 0$, it indicates that FU_n is not busy.

It is assumed that the hazard detection is carried out in the DECODE stage of the pipeline. If the hazard is absent, DECODE stage completes decoding and pass the result to EADDR stage. If, however, hazard is detected, the DECODE stage will not issue the instruction to the next stage.

DECODE will hold the instruction in a latch until the hazard condition disappears. Let SOURCE (I_k) DEST (I_k) and UNIT (I_k) represent operand source, result destination set and functional set units set of an instruction, I_k.

There are three (3) independent procedures involved in Tomasulo's algorithm:

Procedure I: DECODE stage will issue I_k when the following conditions are satisfied:

$$C_i = 0 \text{ for all } S_i \in \text{DEST } (I_k)$$
$$C_j \leq 0 \text{ for all } S_i \in \text{SOURCE } (I_k)$$
$$B_n = 0 \text{ for all } FU_n \in \text{UNIT } (I_k)$$

These conditions confirm that:

- None of the destination stores of the instructions are being used either as a source or as a destination by any other preceding instruction in the pipeline.
- Each of the source stores of the instruction is only being used as a source for other preceding instructions in the pipeline.
- Each of the functional units required to process the instruction is free.

Procedure II: DECODE stage will change usage counters and busy flags, after issuing instruction, I_k to the next stage, as follows:

$$\text{new } C_i = 1 \text{ for all } S_i \in \text{DEST } (I_k)$$
$$\text{new } C_j = C_j - 1 \text{ for all } S \in \text{SOURCE } (I_k)$$
$$\text{new } B_n = 1 \text{ for all } FU_n, \in \text{UNIT } (I_k)$$

Procedure III: After complete processing of the instruction, usage counters and busy flags will be updated as follows:

$$\text{new } C_i = 0 \text{ for all } S, \in \text{DEST } (I_k)$$
$$\text{new } C_j = C_j + 1 \text{ for } C, \in \text{SOURCE } (I_k)$$
$$\text{new } B_n = 1 \text{ for all } FU_n \in \text{UNIT } (I_k)$$

Action to be taken after hazard detection: Once the hazard is found, it must be resolved. There are two approaches commonly followed for resolution of hazards. They are as follows:

1. Stop the pipeline initiation at the point of hazard unit the instruction has passed the point of resource conflict. Thus, if a hazard is detected between the current instruction J and a previous instruction I, pipeline is stopped and execution of instructions $J, J+1, J+2$ ... is suspended
2. Second approach is to suspend only instruction J and allow instructions $J \div 1, I+2$ ... to flow down the pipe.

First approach is simple to implement. But it will degrade the performance by losing the advantage of pipelining.

The **second approach** is more sophisticated and hence attractive, but more complex.

Resolution of Collision/Structural Hazard

When a hazard is detected between an instruction I_j and some earlier instruction, issue of I_j to the next stage is delayed until the hazard condition vanishes. As a result, I_j will remain in one of the buffers of DECODE stage. DECODE stage will continuously test the values of C_i and B_n until condition in (1) are satisfied. If it is decided to always have an in order execution of instruction stream then delaying issue of means the instruction I_{j+1}, I_{j+2} ... following I_j will also be delayed irrespective of any hazard conditions with those instructions. These succeeding instruction are delayed only because of delay of I_j. This problem can be resolved to some extent by introduction of virtual functional units. Till now, we have associated real functional Units $FU_n \in UNITS(I_j)$. Now we associate a set of virtual functional units ($VFUN_1$, $VFUN_2$ ... $VFUN_q$) with each such FU_n. The number of this virtual function unit, q, can be made as large as required. **The main aim behind this idea is to avoid delayed issue of I_j because of unavailability of functional unit.** Instead, I_j will be passed to next stage by assuming the availability of virtual functional unit capable of processing it, provided there are no data dependency hazards. Thus, only Condition that will stop I_j issue to next stage is a data dependency hazard. Of course, the assumption of virtual functional unit will not help in completing the instruction I_j. It will always need the availability of a real functional unit. But this will remove the hurdle in issue of succeeding instructions provided no data-dependency hazards are detected. Virtual functional units can save the time required to test $B_n = 0$. It is avoided altogether. A simple realization of q virtual functional units is by associating a queue of q latches with a FU_n. Assigning an instruction I_j to a virtual functional unit then means passing I_j to the queue. The instruction will be actually processed by real function unit FU_n by servicing the contents of the queue on first come first serve basis. The concept is shown in Fig. 8.82.

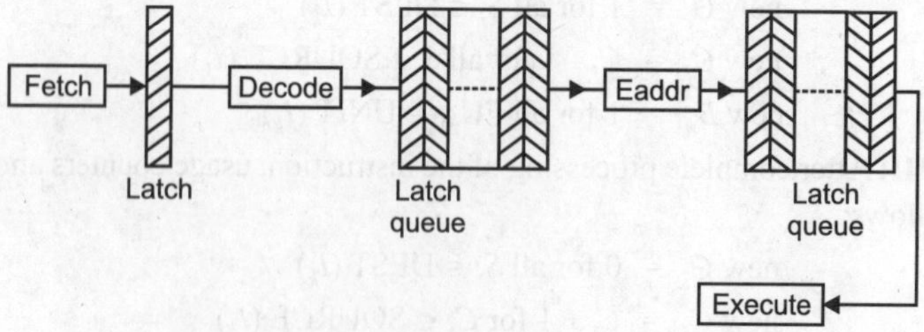

Fig. 8.82. Realization of Virtual Functional Units by Latch Queue

Forwarding: Resolution of Data Dependencies

Assumption of virtual function units will avoid the delay of instructions issue due to collisions or structural hazards. Hence, the only reason remains that will stop an instruction to be issued to next Stage is data dependency hazard. This delay of issue to instruction due to RAW type data dependency hazards can be further reduced by a technique known **as forwarding.** This technique is also introduced by Tomasulo in 1967. This is similar to internal forwarding technique. **It can be called as data forwarding.** In this technique each distinct store S_i is associated with a tag T_i. This tag T_i, is an indicator of functional unit FU_n, that is used by some instruction in the pipeline and the output of that FU_n is to be written into S_i. A tag T_i, is attached to store S_i, whenever S_i, is being used as a destination of an instruction and the instruction has been passed to DECODE stage. If for some S_i, $\in$ SOURCE (I_k) (where I_k is the instruction stream processed by pipeline), there is a tag I_k attached to S_i, then a potential RAW hazard is posed. The store S_i has to receive the value, that is produced by a functional unit FU_n and I_k tag indicates this FU_n. In this situation, I_k is conditionally issued to the next stage (EADDR) along with the tag T_i. When FU_n processes I_k and generates a value to be written to S_i, the pipeline control checks all the stores and latches for the presence of tag indicating FU_n. As S_i, is the store where such match will be found, the FU_n will write the result to S_i will be removed. When such a match is found with a latch hqlding an instruction, then the output of FU is forwarded to the conditionally issued instruction I_k or the tag associated with I_k may be reset. This indicates that the hazard is eliminated. It is possible that I_k may have to wait for several forwarded values before is its RAW hazards are fully resolved (depending on particular type of I_k). Only after the elimination of hazards I_k is processed by the next stage.

Finally note that the forwarding scheme discussed above will avoid the delaying of instructions issued by DECODE stage due to RAW hazards. However, the issued instruction cannot be completed, till the data dependencies have been resolved.

Effect of branching on pipeline performance is described below by a linear instructions. pipeline consisting of 5-segments.

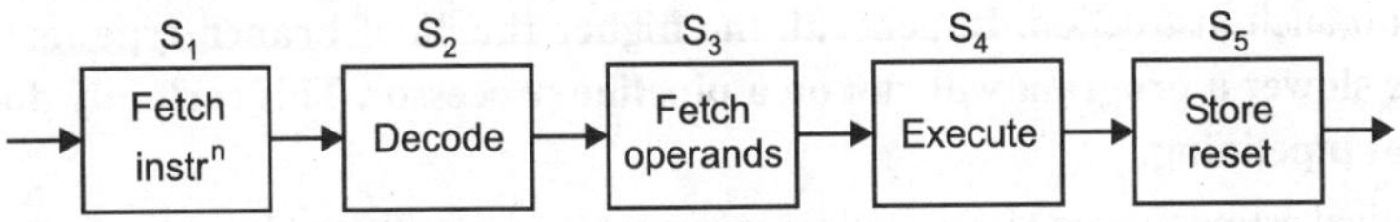

Case I: Now, consider the space-time diagram; **When no branch instructions are there:**

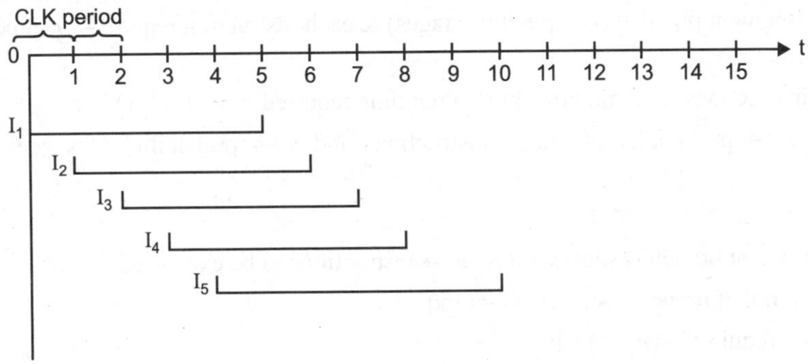

Fig. 8.83(b).

i.e., to execute I_1, 5-clock periods are required, similarly, for I_2, I_3, I_4, I_5 ... I_n. These instructions are executed by our instruction pipeline in an **"overlapped fashion"**, if branch-type of instructions do not appear. Under such circumstances, once the pipeline is filled up with sequential instructions is (non-branch type), the pipeline completes the execution 'of one instruction per a fixed latency (usually, 1 or 2 *clk* periods). (shown in Fig. 8.83 (b))

Case II: When Branching Occurs: The space time diagram is as follows

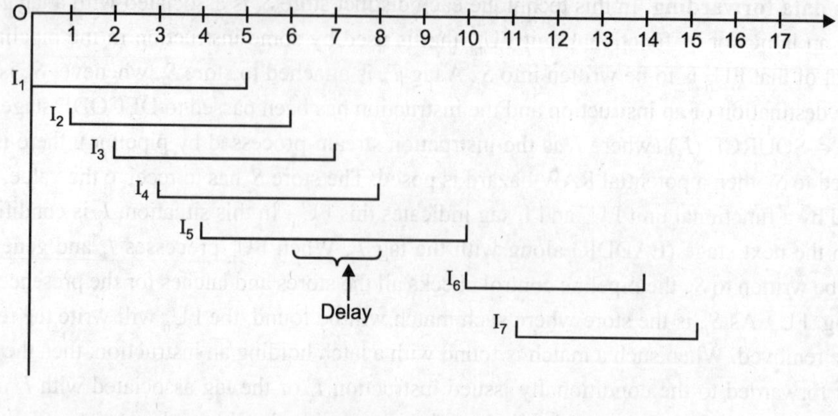

Fig. 8.83(c). Instruction I_5 is a branch instruction.

Whereas, a "branch instruction" entering the instruction pipeline may be halfway down the pipe (such as a "successful" conditional branch instruction) before a branch decision is made. This will cause the PC to be loaded with the new address to which the program should be directed, making all prefetched instructions useless. The next instruction cannot be initiated until the completion of the current branch instruction cycle. This causes extra time delays in order to drain the pipeline. The **"Overlapped-action" is suspended** and the pipeline must be drained at end of the branch cycle. The continous flow of instruction into the pipeline is thus temporarily interrupted because of presence of a branch instruction. **In general, the higher the % of branch-type instruction in a program, the slower a program will run on a pipeline processor. This certainly does not merit the concept of pipelining.**

An analytical estimation or Mathematical representation of effect of branching on an n-segment instruction pipeline in given below:

Let $n \rightarrow$ segment pipeline (i.e., pipeline stages) & each instruction require $\rightarrow$ *n*-pipeline cycles or *n-clk* periods.

If $m \rightarrow$ instructions (with no branching) then time required $= n + (m - 1)$... ...(1)

Now, if $p \rightarrow$ probability of branch-instructions and $q \rightarrow$ probability of successful branch instructions

or

Probability that branch is successful & $m \rightarrow$ instructions to be executed.

Then total no. of branch-instructions = mpq

$\therefore$ Extra time required $= (n - 1)$ Clk cycles ...(2)

(due to branching)

From (1) & (2) we get:

$\therefore$ Total no. of cycles (no branch) (branched)

required to execute $= (n + (m - 1)) +$ mpq $(n - 1)$

m-instructions.

(in branched case)

$\therefore$ Total instruction cycles =

$((n + (m - 1) + mpq(n - 1))/n$

Special Cases

1. As m becomes large, 'performance' of our instruction pipeline is measured by average no. of instructions executed per instruction cycle

$$performance = \frac{\lim_{m \to \infty}\left(\frac{m}{((n+(m-1))+mpq(n-))}\right)}{n}$$

$$= \frac{n}{1+pq(n-1)}$$

2. When $p = 0$, (i.e., no branch instructions, encountered) then performance reduces to n-instructions per n pipeline clocks, which is ideal i.e.,

$$\text{Performance} = \frac{n}{1+0} \qquad [p = \text{probability of branch instructions} = 0]$$

$$= n$$

For e.g., if $n = 5$

$p = 20\% = 0.20$

$q = 60\% = 0.60$

Then performance $= 5/(1 + (0.20)(0.60(4))$

$$= \frac{5}{1+0.12(4)}$$

$$= \frac{5}{1.48}$$

$= 3.378$ instructions / instruction cycle.

This is less than the ideal execution rate of 5 instructions/5 pipeline cycles. In other words, **an average of 35.2% cycles may be wasted because of branching.**

8.34.11 Advanced pipelining

Loops are the most fundamental source of parallelism for instruction level pipeline processors (ILP). Here, the regularity of the control structure is used to speed up the computation. **Please note that loop scheduling is a focal point of instruction schedulers** which have been developed for highly parallel ILP processors, such as VLIWS. **Also note that it is a standard feature of the emerging global schedulers.**

Loop scheduling is normally done in two ways:

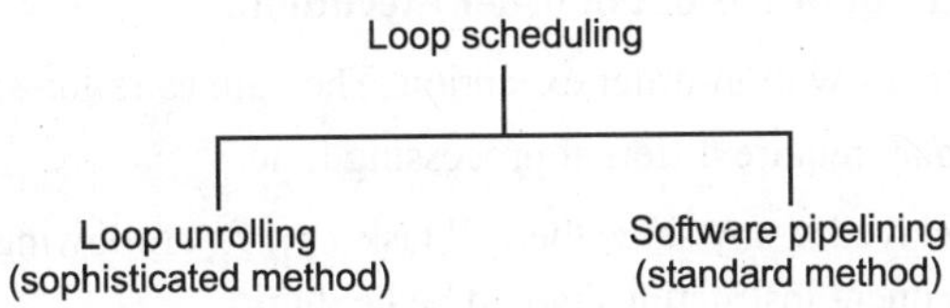

We shall be discussing these two techniques one by one now.

1. Loop Scheduling-Unrolling

Loop unrolling means repeating the loop body a number of times and thus the need of inter-iteration code, such as decrementing loop count, testing for loop ends and branching back conditionally between the iteration is eliminated. This reduces the execution time. Loop unrolling can be implemented quite easily when the number of iterations is already fixed at the compile time. This normally happens with 'do' and 'for' loops. Let us consider an example now

```
For j= 1 to 4
do
{
        B (j) = 2 × A (j)
}
```

The above loop is replaced by the following code, by the optimizing compiler:

$B(1) = 2 * A(1)$

$B(2) = 2 * A(2)$

$B(3) = 2 * A(3)$

$B(4) = 2 * A(4)$

Thus, loop unrolling reduces the execution time at the cost of code length. After loop unrolling, a larger basic block is obtained which can be scheduled to execute the instructions in an overlapped manner to improve the performance of the pipeline.

The resulting speed depends on the size of the loop. **Please note that when the loop size is large, the relative gain is less whereas if the loop size is small, the gain is more significant.**

2. Out of order Execution

Let us consider a *k*—stage pipeline. This pipeline can be imagined as a system that accepts unprocessed task in some order and generates the same set of tasks but processed in some order. There are two possibilities related to order of one processed tasks

1. **The task may merge out in the same order that they enter. This is known as in-order execution.** This is shown in Fig. 8.84 below:

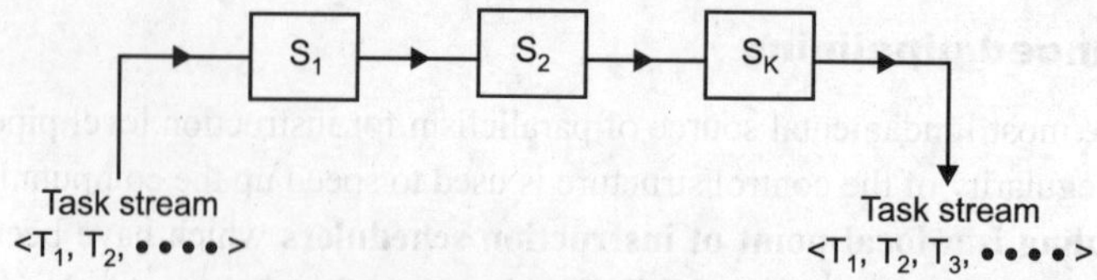

Fig. 8.84. In-order execution

2. **The task may merge-out in different order.** The necessity of preserving initiation order is relaxed. **This is known as out of order execution.**

There are some problems with in-order execution. They are as follows:

1. Different tasks may require different processing time.
2. If a task, T_i, is delayed at any stage then all task T_{i+1}, T_{i+2} following T_i will also be delayed. That is, all subsequent instructions would be held up.

Thus, second approach is more efficient. In this out-of-order execution, the necessity of preserving initiation order is relaxed. **If any task, T_i is delayed at a given stage and it is possible that T_{i+1} can proceed down the pipeline, then it is allowed. This technique is also known as forwarding.** It may lead to a situation where the output task stream order is some permutation of the initiation order. A k-stage pipeline that performs out-of-order execution is shown in Fig. 8.85.

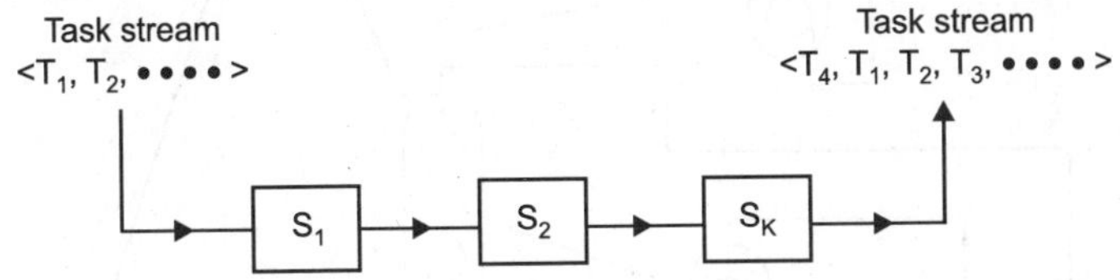

Fig. 8.85. Out-of-order execution (k-stage pipeline)

The out-of-order technique, may increase the over lapping in processing of the instructions and also the throughput. But it needs additional machinery both logical and physical. The machinery should ensure that the throughput is increased and the intended function of the original task stream is preserved.

3. Instruction Scheduling

It is usually advantageous to reorder instructions on pipelined super-computers. Reordering of instructions will lead to minimization of delays due to instruction stalls (wait) because of the dependencies. In case an instruction, '*I*' and (*I* + 1) are dependent, i.e., (*I* + 1) cannot be completed until the result of '*I*' is available then it is desirable to place other independent instructions between *I* and (*I* + 1) so that '*I*' can be complete before (*I* + 1) is attempted. **This process of arranging sequences of straight line code so that stall will be eliminated or reduced is known as Instruction Scheduling.** Usually, instruction scheduling is performed on the basic blocks. Basic blocks are the straight line code of which only the first instruction can be the target of branch instruction and only the last instruction can be a branch instruction.

4. Trace Scheduling

A technique that was initially developed for horizontally micro-coded machine. Then it is a reimplementation for VLIW (Very Large Instruction Word) machines as an instruction scheduling technique. VLIW machines demand more parallelism than is typically available within a basic block. Hence, additional instructions are found in the branches to execute. Trace scheduling is based on the point that branch decisions can be predicted at the compilation time with some reliability. Branch decisions can be taken based on software heuristics or tin using profiles of the previous program execution.

Trace scheduling involves a concept of a trace. Trace is possible execution path within a loop. A trace may include conditional branches and joint points. This is shown below in Fig. 8.80.

A trace scheduler identifies the traces in a program initially and then selects the most likely trace and schedules it as an entity. Then, the next likely trace is selected and the process is repeated till the whole program is scheduled. Inner loops of programs are unrolled so that maximum parallelism can be exposed for trace scheduling. A trace can have multiple entry and exit points. Sometimes it becomes necessary to insert a compensation code to preserve correctness.

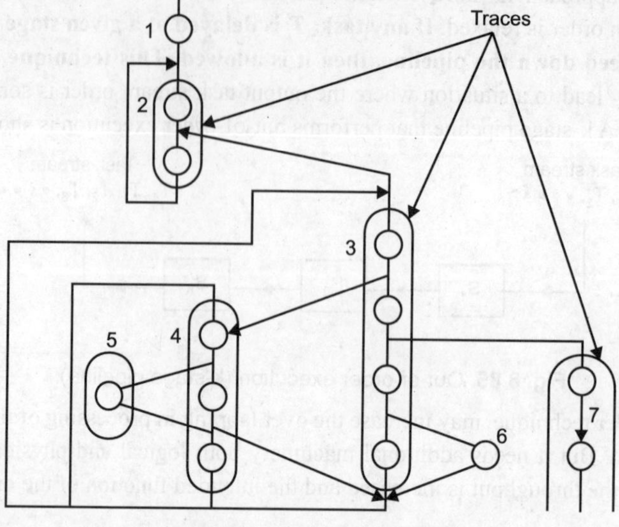

Fig. 8.86. Flow graph and traces

For example : Consider a piece of code given below:

$x = y$

if a = 1 go to L1

$z = 10$

.
.
.

$L1$: ....

Now, if an assignment statement is moved from its position to a position after the conditional branch, then it becomes necessary to insert a compensation code. It becomes necessary to repeat the assignment statement at the target of the conditional branch, so that it is always executed regardless of the value of 'a' as shown below.

if a = 1 go to $L1$

$x = y$

$z = 10$

.
.
.

$L1$: $x = y$

Drawbacks of Trace Scheduling

1. The compilation time is more.
2. The generated block size is more.

Trace scheduling was developed as a strategy for analysing VLIW architecture and it is proved to be very effective in generating highly parallel code for wide-word machines.

For processors with a large number of issues per cycle, in which conditional or predicted execution is not appropriate or not supported, trace scheduling is very useful.

In such processors, simply loop unrolling may not be possible and may not be even sufficient to uncover enough ILP so that the processor may be kept busy.

There are two steps in trace scheduling:

Step 1: **Trace Selection:** In this step, a likely sequence of basic block is found, whose operations will be put together into a smaller number of instructions i.e., **traces. Long traces are generated by loop unrolling.** Using static branch prediction, other conditional branches are also selected. **As a result, traces are produced as a straight line sequence formed by joining many such basic blocks.**

Step 2: **Trace Compaction: This process makes the trace compact by squeezing the trace into small number of wide instructions.** This is nothing else but code scheduling. The process of trace compaction also attempts to move operations as early as possible. It packs the operation into a few wide instructions.

Advantage of Trace Scheduling: It simplified the decision related to global code motion.

5. **Software Pipelining**

Software pipelining is the process of pipelining the successive iterations of a loop in the source code. The term is analogous to hardware pipelining. The operations of single iteration are divided into 'k' stages and a single iteration performs stage-1 from iteration-i, stage-2 from iteration (i-1) and so on. The concept is shown with an example now. Consider the following loop:

```
for     i = 1 to 5
        do
        {
        A(I) = A(I) * 2 + C
        }
```

This is an example of DO-all loop. All iterations are independent in this loop. **Let us assume that cycle time of memory access is one and that of arithmetic operation is two. If there is no pipelining, then each iteration will take six cycles to execute. That is,**

Cycle	Instruction	Comments
1.	Read	Fetch $A[I]$
2.	MUL	Multiply by 2
3.		
4.	ADD	Add to C
5.		
6.	Write	Store $A[A]$

Thus, N iterations will need 6N cycles. Now, in our code, $N = 5$ (for loop runs 5—times)

$\therefore$ Cycles required $= 6N = 6 \times 5 = 30$.

Please note that we are neglecting the loop control overhead.

Now, say, **we want to execute the same code with software pipelining.** Let the processor (PE) be a two-issue PE. Now, how many cycles are needed?

Cycle	Iteration				
	1	2	3	4	5
1	Read				
2	MUL				
3		Read			
4		MUL			
5	Add		Read		
6			MUL		
7		Add			
8	Write			MUL	
9			Add		
10		Write			MUL
11				Add	
12			Write		
13					Add
14				Write	
15				NOP	
16					Write

∴ The software pipelined code requires only 16 cycles to execute.

$$\therefore \text{Speed up} = \frac{30}{10} = 1.8$$

It is also possible to parallelize recurrence with software pipelining. The main feature of software pipelining is it minimizes the interval at which iterations are initiated.

Thus, the advantages of software pipelining are:

1. It reduces initiation latency and thus maximizes throughput.
2. It produces small and compact code.

Practical pipelines are not always simple because of various reasons. Some of the reasons are - Real pipelines are non-linear, different stages of a pipeline need different time periods, feedback and feed-forward connections exist and so on. A flow pattern of static pipeline is always fixed once a task is initiated. When the same stage is demanded by two or more inputs, there is a collision. So, proper job scheduling is to be done. For this some assumptions (like execution time for all pipeline stages are multiple of some basic block) are made. In case of multifunction and dynamic pipelines, path followed through the pipeline may change dramatically with each input. So, the task of defining optimal schedules becomes very difficult. This chapter solves all such problems.

MULTIPLE CHOICE QUESTIONS [MCQs]

Q. 1. It is possible to achieve parallelism

(*a*) With and within the CPU (*b*) With many CPUs only

(*c*) Without CPUs (*d*) All of the above.

Q. 2. A CPU is also called as a

(*a*) PE (*b*) Parallel computer

(*c*) ALU (*d*) None of the above.

Q. 3. 100 MFLOPs corresponds to:

(*a*) i/ 100 million floating point operations/second.

(*b*) 1/1010 million floating point operations/second.

(*c*) 100 million floating point operations/second.

(*d*) None of the above.

Q. 4. Second Generation computers belong to:

(*a*) 1945—54 (*b*) 1955—64

(*c*) 1965—74 (*d*) None of the above.

(*e*) 1010 (*d*) None of these.

Q. 5. Third generation computers uses:

(*a*) Multiprogramming and time-sharing.

(*b*) Multiprogramming

(*c*) Multithreading

(*d*) All of the above.

Q. 6. With each new generation, the circuiting size becomes:

(*a*) Bigger (*b*) Smaller

(*c*) Smaller and advanced (*d*) None of the above.

Q. 7. Which of the following computers belong to 5th generation:

(*a*) Cray—XMP (b) Intel Paragon

(*c*) VPP 500 (*d*) Both *b* and *c*.

Q. 8. ENIAC stands for:

(*a*) Electronic Numerical Integrator and Calculator.

(*b*) Electronic Number Integration and Calculation.

(*c*) Enhanced Number Integrator and Calculator.

(*d*) None of the above.

Q. 9. RTL stands for:

(*a*) Register Transfer Language (*b*) Remote Transfer Language

(*c*) RISC Transfer Language (*d*) None of the above.

Q. 10. Tera flops means:

(*a*) 10^{14} (*b*) 10^{10}

(*c*) 10^{12} (*d*) None of these

Q. 11. Parallelism is equal to

(*a*) Hardware parallelism + Software parallelism.

(*b*) Hardware parallelism only.

(*c*) Software parallelism only.

(*d*) None of the above.

Q. 12. The first mechanical adder/substractor was built in Franceby:

(*a*) Charles Bubbage (*b*) Blaise Pascal

(*c*) Luse (*d*) Howard Aiken.

Q. 13. CDC—6600 has how many functional units:

(*a*) 5 (*b*) 10 (*c*) 15 (*d*) 20

Q. 14. Instruction execution involves five phases which are:

(*a*) Fetch, decode, operand, fetch, Execution, results.

(*b*) Operand fetch, fetch, decode, Execution, results.

(*c*) Fetch, execute, decode, operand fetch, results.

(*d*) None of the above.

Q. 15. CPU means:

(*a*) ALU – CU (*b*) ALU + CPU

(*c*) ALU + CU (*d*) None of the above.

Q. 16. A COMA model comprises of:

(*a*) Multiprocessor + Cache memory (*b*) Multiprocessor + Main memory

(*c*) Microprocessor + Cache memory (*d*) None of the above.

Q. 17. NORMA means:

(*a*) Message passing multicomputers. (*b*) Mainframes

(*c*) Vector supercomputer (*d*) None of the above.

Q. 18. Array Processors are put under which of these categories:

(*a*) SISD (*b*) SIMD (*c*) MISD (*d*) MIMD

Q. 19. According to Fengs, average parallelism degree, *P* is given by the formula:

(*a*) $P_a = P/T$ (b) $P_a = \sum_{i=1}^{T} \frac{P_i}{T}$

(*c*) $P_a = P/Ti(1 \leftarrow 1 \text{ to } T)$ (*d*) None of the above

Q. 20. LAN like Ethernet is a:

(*a*) Loosely coupled (*b*) Pipelining

(*c*) Not coupled (*d*) None of the above.

Q. 21. The process of allowing instructions to execute out of order when resources are sufficient is called as

(*a*) Scaffolding (*b*) Pipelining

(*c*) Score boarding (*d*) None of the above

Q. 22. The speed-up, $S(n)$, is given by:

(*a*) $S(n) = T(1) * T(n)$ (*b*) $S(n) = T(n)/T(1)$

(*c*) $S(n) = T(1)/(n)$ (*d*) None of the above.

Q. 23. The number of machine instructions to be executed in the program is called as the:

(*a*) Cycle (*b*) Time Period

(*c*) Instruction Count (*d*) None of the above

Q. 24. The equation for Amadahl's law is:

(*a*) $\underset{n \to \infty}{S(n)} = \frac{1}{f}$ (*b*) $\underset{n \to \infty}{S(n)} = f$

(*c*) $\underset{n \to \infty}{S(n)} = \frac{1}{T}$ (*d*) None of the above

Q. 25. In temporal parallelism, temporal refers to

(*a*) Time (*b*) Space

(*c*) PEs Count (*d*) None of these

Q. 26. Performance (*P*) and execution time (*T*) of CPU are related by:

(*a*) $P \propto T$ (*b*) $P \propto \frac{1}{T}$ (*c*) $P = T$ (*d*) $P + T$

Q. 27. David Kuck of University of Illinios adopted:

(*a*) Implicit Parallelism (*b*) explicit Parallelism

(*c*) Both *a* and *b* (*d*) None of the above

Q. 28. Conditions of parallelism were given by:

(*a*) Charles Babbage (*b*) Bernstein

(*c*) Albrecht (*d*) None of the above.

Q. 29. According to Bernstein, two process, P_i and P_j can execute in parallel if and only if:

(*a*) $P_i \| P_j$ (*b*) $Pi / P_j = 1$

(*c*) $P_i * P_j = 1$ (*d*) None of the above.

Q. 30. For two statements, *S*1 and *S*2, if an execution path exists from *S*1 to *S*2 then they are said to be:

(*a*) Antidependent (*b*) Flow dependence

(*c*) Output dependence (*d*) None of the above.

Q. 31. A program segment chosen for parallel processing is known as:

(*a*) Grain (*b*) Cluster

(*c*) Work station (*d*) None of the above.

Q. 32. A compiler that automatically detects the parallelisms is known as:

(*a*) Optimizing compiler (*b*) Run-time compiler

(*c*) Interpreter (*d*) None of the above.

Q. 33. A loop level parallelism has a grain size of:

(*a*) 20 (*b*) 200 (*c*) 500 (*d*) None of the above.

Q. 34. Demand driven computers are also known as:

(*a*) Control flow computer (*b*) DFC

(*c*) Reduction computers (*d*) None of the above.

Q. 35. Pentium-IV works on:

(*a*) Control flow mechanism (*b*) Data flow mechanism

(*c*) Demand driven mechanism (*d*) All of the above

Q. 36. Static data flow computer (SDFC) was given by:

(*a*) Dennis (*b*) Bernstein

(*c*) Albrecht (*d*) None of the above.

Q. 37. Pipelining uses:

(*a*) data parallelism (*b*) temporal parallelism

(*c*) spatial parallelism (*d*) none of the above

Q. 38. The clock period (*t*) is given by:

(*a*) $\tau = \tau_m + \tau_l$ (*b*) $\tau = \tau_m \times \times_l$

(*c*) $\tau = \tau_m - \tau_l$ (*d*) None of the above

Q. 39. Scalar pipelines are under:

(*a*) Software control (*b*) Hardware control

(*c*) Firmware control (*d*) None of the above.

Q. 40. The utilization pattern of successive stages in the pipeline is

(*a*) Space-time diagram (*b*) Reservation table

(*c*) Both (*a*) and (*b*) (*d*) None of the above.

Q. 41. Latency values must:

(*a*) Negative (*b*) Positive

(*c*) Either (*a*) or (*b*) (*d*) None of the above

Q. 42. Forbidden latency means:

(*a*) Distance between any two checkmarks in the same row of the reservation table.

(*b*) Distance between any two checkmarks in the same column of the reservation table.

(*c*) Distance between all the checkmarks.

(*d*) None of the above

Q. 43. The average latency of a constant cycle is :

(*a*) Constant (*b*) Latency itself

(*c*) Not Known (*d*) None of the above

Q. 44. CPA stands for:

(*a*) Carry power adder (*b*) carry storage adder

(*c*) Carry simple adder (*d*) None of the above

Q. 45. CSA stands for:

(*a*) Carry save adder (*b*) Carry storage adder

(*c*) Carry simple adder (*d*) None of the above.

Q. 46. A separate register that has one bit to identify each register of the register file is called as a

(*a*) Black board (*b*) White board

(*c*) Score board (*d*) None of the above

Q. 47. Loop scheduling includes:

(*a*) Loop unrolling (*b*) Software Pipelining

(*c*) Both (*a*) and (*b*) (*d*) None of the above

Q. 48. In out-of-order execution, the task are:

(*a*) in different order (*b*) in same order

(*c*) no order (*d*) None of the above.

Q. 49. A possible execution path within a loop is known as:

(*a*) Control path (*b*) Flow path

(*c*) Trace (*d*) None of the above.

Q. 50. During loop scheduling, when the loop size is large, the relative gain is:

(*a*) Large (*b*) Less

(*c*) No change (*d*) None of the above.

Q. 51. Real pipelines are:

(*a*) Linear (*b*) Non Linear

(*c*) Exponential (*d*) None of the above

Q. 52. CISC stands for:

(*a*) Compound Instruction Symbolic Computer.

(*b*) Complex Instruction Set Computer.

(*c*) Common Idea Set Computer.

(*d*) None of the above.

Q. 53. CISC microprocessors have:

(*a*) Complex machine instruction. (*b*) Best addressing capability.

(*c*) Both (*a*) and (1). (*d*) None of the above.

Q. 54. A system in which one instruction is issued per cycle:

(*a*) Base Scalar processor. (*b*) Super scalar.

(*c*) Vector. (*d*) None of the above.

Q. 55. For an ideal pipeline, effective CPI is:

(*a*) 1 (*b*) 2 (*c*) 3 (*d*) 4

Q. 56. RISC stand for:

(*a*) Remote Instruction Set Computer.

(*b*) Reduced Instruction Set Computer.

(*c*) Ram Instruction Set Computer.

(*d*) None of the above.

Q. 57. 8086/186/286/386 are examples of:

(*a*) Vectors (*b*) RISC

(*c*) CISC (*d*) None of the above

Q. 58. RISC has:

(*a*) Unified cache (*b*) *I* and *D* cache

(*c*) *L*1 cache (*d*) None of the above.

Q. 59. CISC has:

(*a*) 8-24 GPRs (*b*) 32-192 GPRs
(*c*) 10-12 GPRs (*d*) 50-100 GPRs

Q. 60. For Super scalar processor

(*a*) $1 < m < 10$ (*b*) $5 < m < 15$
(*c*) $2 < m < 5$ (*d*) $10 < m < 100$

Q. 61. Pentium employs a:

(*a*) BTB (*b*) PSP (*c*) ASP (*d*) DSP

Q. 62. A pure CISC processor is:

(*a*) 186 (*b*) 286 (*c*) 386 (*d*) 486

Q. 63. More RAM is required in:

(*a*) CISC (*b*) RISC
(*c*) Vectors (*d*) None of the above

ANSWERS

1. (*a*)	**2.** (*a*)	**3.** (*c*)	**4.** (*b*)	**5.** (*a*)	**6.** (*c*)	**7.** (*d*)	**8.** (*a*)
9. (*a*)	**10.** (*c*)	**11.** (*a*)	**12.** (*b*)	**13.** (*b*)	**14.** (*a*)	**15.** (*c*)	**16.** (*a*)
17. (*a*)	**18.** (*b*)	**19.** (*b*)	**20.** (*a*)	**21.** (*c*)	**22.** (*c*)	**23.** (*c*)	**24.** (*a*)
25. (*a*)	**26.** (*b*)	**27.** (*a*)	**28.** (*b*)	**29.** (*a*)	**30.** (*b*)	**31.** (*a*)	**32.** (*a*)
33. (*c*)	**34.** (*c*)	**35.** (*a*)	**36.** (*a*)	**37.** (*b*)	**38.** (*a*)	**39.** (*a*)	**40.** (*c*)
41. (*b*)	**42.** (*a*)	**43.** (*b*)	**44.** (*c*)	**45.** (*a*)	**46.** (*c*)	**47.** (*c*)	**48.** (*a*)
49. (*c*)	**50.** (*b*)	**51.** (*b*)	**52.** (*b*)	**53.** (*c*)	**54.** (*a*)	**55.** (*a*)	**56.** (*b*)
57. (*c*)	**58.** (*b*)	**59.** (*a*)	**60.** (*c*)	**61.** (*a*)	**62.** (*c*)	**63.** (*b*)	

CONCEPTUAL SHORT QUESTIONS WITH ANSWERS

Q. 1. Define the following terms:

(*a*) Processor design space.

(*b*) Latency.

(*c*) Instruction issue rate.

(*d*) Simple latency.

(*e*) Resource conflicts.

(*f*) Processor versus coprocessor.

(*g*) GPRs.

(*h*) Addressing modes.

(*i*) Unified versus split caches.

(*j*) Hardwired versus micro coded control.

Ans. The definitions are given below:

(*a*) Processor design space: It is defined as a coordinated space with the x and y axis. x-axis represents clock-rate and y-axis represents CPI. Each coordinate i.e., point in the space. (x , y) represents a design choice of a processor whose performance is determined by the values of the coordinates.

(*b*) Latency: It is defined as the time required between issuing two consecutive instructions.

(*c*) Instruction issue rate: It is defined as the number of instructions issued per cycle.

(*d*) Simple Latency: The number of cycles required for the execution of a simple instruction such as add, move etc is known as simple latency.

(*e*) Resource conflicts: When two or more instructions attempt to use the same functional unit at the same time then it is known as resource conflict.

(*f*) Processor versus coprocessor: A coprocessor is one that is usually attached to a processor. Coprocessor performs special functions at a fast speed.

For example: Math coprocessor, graphical coprocessors etc.

(*g*) General Purpose Registers (GPRs): Those registers that are for general use of the programmer and are not designated for special usage like the special— purpose registers—base registers or index registers.

(*h*) Addressing modes: It specifies how the effective address of an operand is generated so that its actual value can be fetched from the correct memory locations.

(*i*) Unified versus split caches: In a unified cache, both data and instructions are kept in the same cache. In a split caches, both data and instructions are held in the separate caches.

(*j*) Hardwired versus micro coded control: In hardwired control, the control signals for each instruction are generated by proper circuitry such as delay elements.

In micro coded control, each instruction is implemented by a set of microinstructions, which are stored in the control memory. The decoding of microinstructions generates appropriate signals to control the execution of an instruction.

Q. 2. Answer the following questions on designing scalar RISC or super scalar RISC processors:

(*a*) Why do most RISC integer units use 32 bit GPR? Explain the concept of register windows implemented in the SPARC architecture?

(*b*) What are the design trade-offs between a large register file and a large D- cache?

(*c*) Explain the relationship between the integer unit and the floating point unit in must RISC processors with scalar or super scalar organization?

[GGSIPU, M. Tech—6th sem., May 2003]

Ans. (*a*) A windowing system divides the register file on a machine into groups which are assigned to different processors. There is usually overlap among the register sets to provide a fast communications mechanism among cooperating procedures for parameter passing. The use of a large number of GPRs allows less frequent memory accesses and thus speeds up program execution. **Please note here that access to memory is slower than GPRs.**

(*b*) A large register file and a large data .cache both serve the purpose of reducing memory traffic. From implementation point of view, the same chip area can be used for either a large register file or a large data cache. From the programming point of view, registers can be manipulated by program code but cache is transparent to the user. In fact, data cache is transparent to the user. In fact, data cache is primarily involved in load/

store operations. The addressing of a cache involves address translation and is more complicated than that of a register file. **Reservation stations and recorder buffers are used in super scalar machines** to facilitate instruction look ahead and internal data forwarding which are needed to schedule multiple instructions through multiple pipelines simultaneously.

(*c*) In most RiSC processors, the integer unit executes load, store, integer, bit and control transfer functions. It also fetches instructions for the floating-point unit in some systems. The floating-point unit performs various arithmetic operations on floating-point numbers. The two units can operate concurrently.

Q. 3. Based on your understanding of advanced processor, answer the following questions on RISC, CISC, super scalar and VLIW architecture:

(*a*) Compare the instruction set architecture in RISC and CISC processors in terms of instructions format, addressing nodes and CPI.

(*b*) Give advantages & disadvantages of using common/separate caches.

(*c*) Distinguish between scalar RISC and super scalar RISC in terms of instruction issue, pipeline architecture and processor performance.

(*d*) Explain the difference between super scalar and VLIW architecture in terms of hardware and software requirement. [GGSIPU—M. Tech. 6th sem., May 20031]

Ans. (*a*) We compare CISC and RISC in tabular form below:

Feature	CISC	RISC
1. Instruction format	16-64 bits per instruction	Fixed (32-bit) format.
2. Addressing modes	12-24	Limited to 3-5
3. CPI	2—15, on the average 5	<1.5, very close to 1.

(*b*) Advantages of Separate Caches:

1. It **doubles the bandwidth** because two complementary requests are serviced at the same time.
2. It **simplifies the logic design** as the arbitrations between instruction and data accesses to cache is simplified or eliminated.
3. The **access time is reduced** because both data and instructions can be placed close to the functional units which will access them.

For example: Instruction cache can be placed close to the instruction fetch and decode units. Disadvantages of separate caches:

1. It complicates the problem of consistency because data and instruction may coexist in the same cache block. This is true if self—modifying code is allowed or when data and Instructions are intermixed and stored in the same cache block. To avoid this we require a compiler support to ensure, that instruction and data are stored, in different cache blocks.
2. It may lead to inefficient use of cache memory because the working set size of a program varies with time and the fraction devoted to data and instruction also varies. **Therefore, the sum of data cache size and instruction cache size is usually larger than the size of a unified cache.** So, the utilization of the instruction cache and/or data cache is likely to be lower.

NOTE: For separate caches three things are a must-

1. Dedicated data paths are required for both the data and instruction caches.
2. Separate MMUs and TLBs are also needed to shorten the time of address translation.
3. A higher memory bandwidth should be used for separate caches to support the increased demand. In practice, there is a trade off between the degree of support provided and the resulting hardware complexity.

(*c*) **Instruction issue:** The scalar RISC processor issues one per cycle whereas the super scalar RISC can usually issue more than one per cycle.

Pipeline architecture: In an m-issue super scalar processor, up to m pipelines may be active in any base cycle. A scalar processor is equivalent to a super scalar processor with $m = 1$.

Processor Performance: An m-issue super scalar can have a performance m times that of a scalar processor, provided both are driven by the same clock rate, no dependence relation or resource conflicts exist among instructions.

(*d*)

Super-scalar	VLIW
1. Super scalar requires more sophisticated hardware support such as larger recorder registers and reservation tables for efficient use of resources of the system.	2. Both the hardware and software support at run time is usually simplified. For example: the decoding logic can be simple.
2. Support for software is desired to reserve data dependencies and to improve the efficiency.	The VLIW instructions are compacted by the compiler. It explicitly packs together instructions which can be executed in concurrency based on heuristics or runtime statistics.
3. The code size is small	The code size is larger
4. They are compatible across generations	They are not compatible across generations.
5. They are scheduled dynamically by the processor.	They are scheduled statistically by the compiler.

Q. 4. What causes a processor pipeline to be under—pipelined ?

Ans. There are 2 -reasons for pipelines to get underutilized

(*a*) The instruction latency is longer than one base cycle.

(*b*) The combined cycle time is greater than the base cycle.

Q. 5. What are the factors that limit the degree of super scalar design?

Ans. The dependence among instructions or resource conflicts among instructions can prevent simultaneous execution of instructions.

Q. 6. What are the differences between scalar and vector instructions?

Ans. Scalar instructions operate on a number or a pair of numbers at a time. Vector instructions perform identical operations on vectors of length usually much larger than scalars.

Q. 7. What will be the speed up gain of the vector pipeline over the scalar pipeline?

Ans. Say, the pipeline has *k*-stages and the length of vector is *N*. First output is generated in the kth cycle. Later on, an additional output is generated in each cycle.

Last result comes out of the pipeline in

$(N + K - 1)$ cycles.

Using a base scalar machine, it takes NK cycles.

$\therefore$ Speed-up $= NK/(N + K - 1)$.

Q. 8. Say, parallel issue is added to vector pipeline execution. Now a parallel issue is also added to a super scalar pipeline of the same degree. What is the speed improvement?

Ans. If an *m*-issue vector processing is used then each vector is of length = N/m.

$$\therefore \quad \text{Execution time} = \left(\frac{N}{m} + k - 1\right) \text{ cycles.}$$

If only parallel issue is used, the execution time = (N/m)k.

$$\therefore \quad \text{Speed improvement} = \frac{\frac{N}{m} + k - 1}{\left(\frac{N}{m}\right)k}$$

$$= \frac{Nk}{N + m(k-1)}$$

Q. 9. What are processors and coprocessors?

Ans. The central (heart) of a computer is known as a CPU or a processor. This CPU is actually a scalar processor, which may consist of multiple functional units like integer arithmetic, ALU etc.

To perform certain other complex numerical calculations, coprocessors are also used in conjunction with processors. **This pairing is must as coprocessors cannot be used alone. For example,** digital signal processor (DSP) or a LISP processor executes AI programs, floating—point accelerator, vector processors, Math coprocessor etc. **Please note that coprocessors cannot handle I/O operations.** So, coprocessors are also known as **attached processors (APs) or slave processors. Also note that the processor and coprocessor operate with a host—back--end relationship. An AP may be more powerful than its host.**

For example:

1. Intel 8087 coprocessor is used along with the Intel 8086/8088 processor.
2. Intel 80287 coprocessor is used with Intel 80286 processor.

Q. 10. Define the following terms:

(*a*) Instruction pipeline cycle.

(*b*) Issue latency.

(*c*) Issue rate.

(*d*) Simple operation latency.

(*e*) Resource conflicts.

Ans. (*a*) The clock period of the instruction pipeline.

(*b*) The time required, in cycles, between the issuing of two adjacent instructions.

(*c*) The number of instructions issued per cycle.

(*d*) Simple instruction like adds, loads, stores, branches, moves etc have lesser delays in execution than the complex instructions like divides, cache misses etc. These latencies are measured in number of cycles.

(*e*) A situation where two or more instructions demand use of the same functional unit at the same time.

Q. 11. Consider a shared bus parallel computer 'built using 32 bit RISC processors running at 150 MHz with CPI-1. Assume that 15% of the instructions are loads and 10% arc stores. Assume 0.95 hit ratio to cache for read and write through caches. The bandwidth of the bus is 2GB/sec.

(*a*) How many processors can the bus support without getting saturated?

(*b*) If caches are not there, how many processors can the bus support assuming the main memory is as fast as the cache. [UPTU, B. Tech (CSE) 8th Sem., 2007-08]

Ans. (*i*) RISC processor processes 32 bits in $\frac{1}{150\times10^6}$ secs [$\because$ 150 MHz = 150 x 10^6 Hz]

In 1 sec, RISC processor requires $32 \times 150 \times 10^6$ bits

$$\therefore \text{ No. of processor } = \frac{2\times10^9}{32\times150\times10^6} \quad [1\text{GB} = 1 * 10^9 \text{ bits}]$$

$$= 4.2 \cong 4.$$

(*ii*) In order to get the bus support, the processors without being saturated, the cache which has additional overhead makes the processor wait for additional memory cycles. So the number of processors goes on increasing.

Q. 12. What are the different types of parallelism?

Ans. Parallelism is of two types:

(*a*) Hardware parallelism: It is built into the machines architecture.

(*b*) Software parallelism: It is exploited by the concurrent execution of machine language instructions in a program as coded by a programmer.

Q. 13. Distinguish between Temporal and Data Parallel processing?

Ans. The following table summarizes the differences between the two:

Temporal Parallelism	Data Parallelism
1. In this parallelism, the job is divided into a set of independent tasks and tasks are assigned for processing.	1. Full jobs are assigned for processing.
2. Tasks should take equal time.	2. Jobs may take different times.
3. Pipeline stages should be synchronized.	3. No need to synchronize beginning of jobs.
4. Bubbles in jobs may lead to idling of PEs.	4. Bubbles in jobs do not cause idling of processors.
5. PEs are specialized to perform tasks.	5. PEs are general purpose.

Q. 14. Give some examples of India's supercomputers.

Ans. Some examples of India's Supercomputers are:

1. **PARAM 10000 (by CDAC ; in 1998).** It uses Sun Solaris OS for parallel programming. The peak speed is 10GFLOPS

2. **PACE + by DRDO; in 1997.** It was ANUPAM programming Environment with FORTRAN and C languages.

3. **ANUPAM Model—2 (by BARC; in 1997).** It uses DEC Alpha processors with DEC UNIX environment.

Q. 15. How is bit serial memory accessing different from bit parallel accessing?

Ans. The first electronic digital computers used a bit serial MM. Each bit of a word was read individually from memory. **For example:** EDSAC, Pilot ACE, EDVAC and UNIVAC systems (all of them had bit serial memories).

Bit-parallel arithmetic became possible once bit-parallel memory was available.

For example: IBM-701 machine used bit parallel arithmetic.

Q. 16. What do you mean by Inter leaved memory? Distinguish between low-order and high-order inter leaving.

Ans. An interleaved memory is a memory unit divided into a number of modules or banks that can be accessed simultaneously. Each memory bank has its own addressing. circuitry. Instruction and data addresses are interleaved to take advantage of the parallel fetch capability. It can be done in two ways.

(*a*) **Low-order interleaving:** This method uses low-order bits of an address to determine the memory bank containing the address. For example

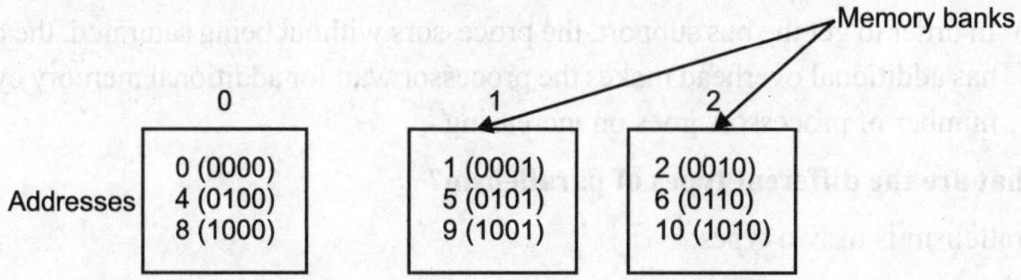

Fig 8.87(a). Low-order interleaving lets the low-order address determine the memory bank

(*b*) **High-order interleaving:** This method uses the high-order bits of an address to determine the memory bank.

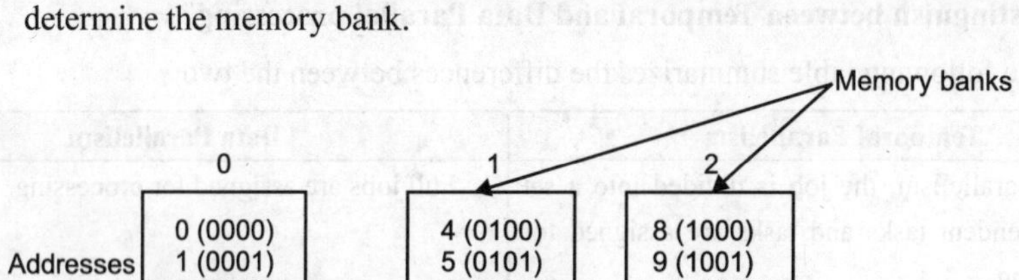

Fig 8.87(b). High-order interleaving lets the high-order address determine the memory bank.

NOTE:

1. During computer designing, it is very important to match the speed of the various components.
2. IBM STRETCH computer was the first computer to have an interleaved memory.
3. The advantage of having two memory banks was that the maximum data transfer rate to and from the memory was increased by a factor of 2 (2-times)

Q. 17. A program is run on a 40MHZ CPU with the instruction mix and corresponding clock cycle count as given in the table below. Determine

(*a*) Effective CPI.

(*b*) Execution time.

(*c*) MIPS rate for the program. **[UPTU, B. Tech. (CSE) 8th Sem.; 2003-04]**

The table is shown below:

Instruction Type	Clock Cycle Count	Instruction Count
1. Integer arithmetic	1	45000
2. Floating point	2	32000
3. Data transfer	2	15000
4. Control Transfer	2	8000

Ans. As we know that:

$$CPI = \frac{Total\ Clock\ cycles\ requires\ for\ given\ I_C}{Frequency\ of\ Clock}$$

Corresponding to the values in the table given above, we find that:

1. ***Clock cycles required for Integer Arithmetic instructions are:***

$$= 45,000 * 1 = 45,000$$

2. ***Clock cycles required for floating-point instructions are:***

$$= 32,000 * 2 = 64,000$$

3. ***Clock cycles for Data transfer instructions are:***

$$= 15,000 * 2 = 30,000$$

4. ***Clock cycles for control transfer instruction are:***

$$= 8,000 * 2 = 16,000$$

So, the Total clock cycles = 1,55,000

Also, total number of instructions

$$(I_c) = (45,000 + 32,000 + 15,000 + 8,000)$$

$$= 1,00,000$$

$$I_c = 1,00,000$$

(*a*) **Effective CPI** $= \frac{155000}{100000}$

$$= 1.55 \text{ cycles / instruction}$$

(*b*) Execution time for the program

$$= \frac{\text{Total clock cycle}}{\text{Clock period}}$$

$$= \frac{155000}{40 \times 10^6}$$

$$= 3.87 \text{ msec.}$$

(*c*)
$$\text{MIPS} = \frac{\text{Clock rate}}{\text{CPI} \times 10^6}$$
$$= \frac{40\times10^6}{1.55\times10^6}$$
$$= 25.8 \text{ MIPS}$$

Q. 17. Calculate the average CPI when the following conditions are given:

Instruction Types	Cycles	Relative Frequency
I	2	30%
II	3	25%
III	5	40%
IV	10	5%

Ans. As already explained, in this chapter that

CPI = No. of cycles / instruction= cycles * Relative Frequency

$CPI_I = 2 \text{ x } 0.30 = 0.60$ [From table above]

$CPI_{II} = 3 \text{ x } 0.25 = 0.75$

$CPI_{III} = 5 \text{ x } 0.40 = 2.0$

$CPI_{IV} = 10 \text{ x } 0.05 = 0.5$

$$\therefore \text{Average} \quad CPI = \frac{CPI_I + CPI_{II} + CPI_{III} + CPI_{IV}}{4}$$
$$= \frac{(0.60+0.75+2.0+0.50)}{4}$$
$$= \frac{3.85}{4}$$
$$= \mathbf{0.9625}$$

Q. 18. Suppose that the same program is executed on two different machines-A and B. Compilers and data set on both the machines are identical. Given that:

Machine-A:	**Average CPI**	**=**	**3.5**
	Cycle time	**=**	**1.0 ns**
Machine-B:	**Average CPI**	**=**	**1.2**
	Cycle Time	**=**	**0.5 ns**

Which out of these two machines is slower?

Ans.

Machine-A: CPI * Cycle Time

= 3.5*1.0

Machine-B: CPI * Cycle Time

= 1.2 × 0.5

= 0.6

∴ Machine-B is faster as it as a lower CPI.

Q. 19. How are performance and execution time related to each other?

Ans. $\text{Performance} \propto = \dfrac{1}{\text{Execution time of CPU}}$

So, a computer that executes a program in half the time taken by another machine has twice the performance **Please note that the performance and execution time vary in opposite directions. Also note that doubling processor performance does not mean replacing an *x*GHz CPU with a 2*x* GHz CPU.**

Q. 20. Distinguish between Implicit and Explicit Parallelism?

Ans. Let us tabulate the differences between the two in a tabular form:-

Implicit Parallelism	Expilcit Parallelism
1. To achieve implicit parallelism, the source code is written in sequential languages like C, FORTRAN 77, LISP or PASCAL.	1. To achieve explicit parallelism, the source code is written in the concurrent dialects of C, FORTRAN, LISP or PASCAL.
2. We need a parallelizing compiler.	2. Here, we need a concurrency preserving compiler.
3. A parallel object code is generated.	3. A concurrent object code is generated.
4. This approach has been used in the programming of shared-memory multicomputer development.	4. This approach has been used in multiprocessors.
5. The compiler must be able to detect parallelism,	5. The compiler need not detect parallelism as it is explicitly specified in the user programs.
Examples: (*a*) David Kuck of University of Illinois adopted implicit-parallelism approach. (*b*) Ken Kennedy of Rice University used this approach	***Examples:*** (*a*) Charles Seitz of California Institute of Technology used this approach in multi computers development. (*b*) William Daily of MIT also used this approach.

Q. 21. Given the following data:

Instruction Type	CPI	Instruction mix
1. Arithematic and logic	**1**	**60%**
2. Load/store with cache hit	**2**	**18%**
3. Branch	**4**	**12%**
4. Memory reference with cache miss	**8**	**10%**

(*a*) Calculate the average CPI when the program is executed on a uniprocessor.

(*b*) Also calculate the corresponding MIPS rate?

Ans. **(*a*) Average**

$$\text{CPI} = 1 \times 0.6 + 2 \times 0.18 + 4 \times 0.12 + 8 \times 0.1$$
$$= 2.24 \text{ cycles/instruction}$$

(*b*)

$$\text{MIPS rate} = \frac{40}{2.24} = 17.86 \text{ MIPS}$$

Q. 22. Suggest a possible circuitry which helps us in finding the next state of the pipeline using collision vector, C as the input. The output is either '0' meaning safe or '1' meaning collision?

Ans. We need an n-bit right shift register where n is the maximum forbidden latency. The circuitry is shown below:

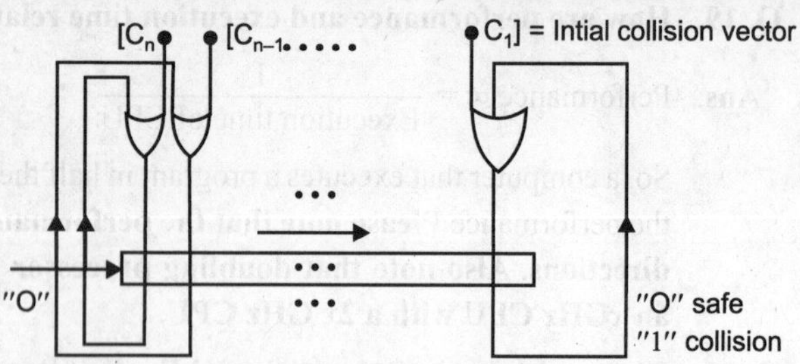

Herein, the initial collision vector (C) is initially loaded into the register. The register is then shifted to the right. Each 1-bit shift corresponds to an increase in the latency by 1. When a '0' bit emerges from the right end after P shifts, it means P is a permissible latency. Likewise, a 1-bit being shifted out means a collision thus the corresponding latency should be forbidden. Logical 0 enters from the left end of the shift register. The next step after P shift is thus obtained by bitwise-ORing the initial collision vector with the shifted register contents. **For example:** From the initial state, $C_x = (1\ 0\ 1\ 1\ 0\ 1\ 0)$, the next state of $(1\ 1\ 1\ 1\ 1\ 1\ 1)$ is reached after 3 shifts or 6 shifts.

Q. 23. How will you design a pipeline floating point adder?
[UPTU, B. Tech (CSE) 8th Sem.; 2003-04]

Ans. Let us consider the design of a pipeline floating point adder. The inputs to the pipeline are two floating point numbers in normalized form:

$A = a \times 2^p$

$B = b \times 2^q$

Where a, b are two fractions and p, q are their exponents. Aim is to compute sum,

$$C = A + B$$
$$= c \times 2^r$$
$$= d \times 2^s$$

Where $r = \max(p, q)$ and $0.5 \le d \le 1$.

This pipeline has four stages – S_1, S_2, S_3, S_4 and d is normalized (mantissa) fraction.

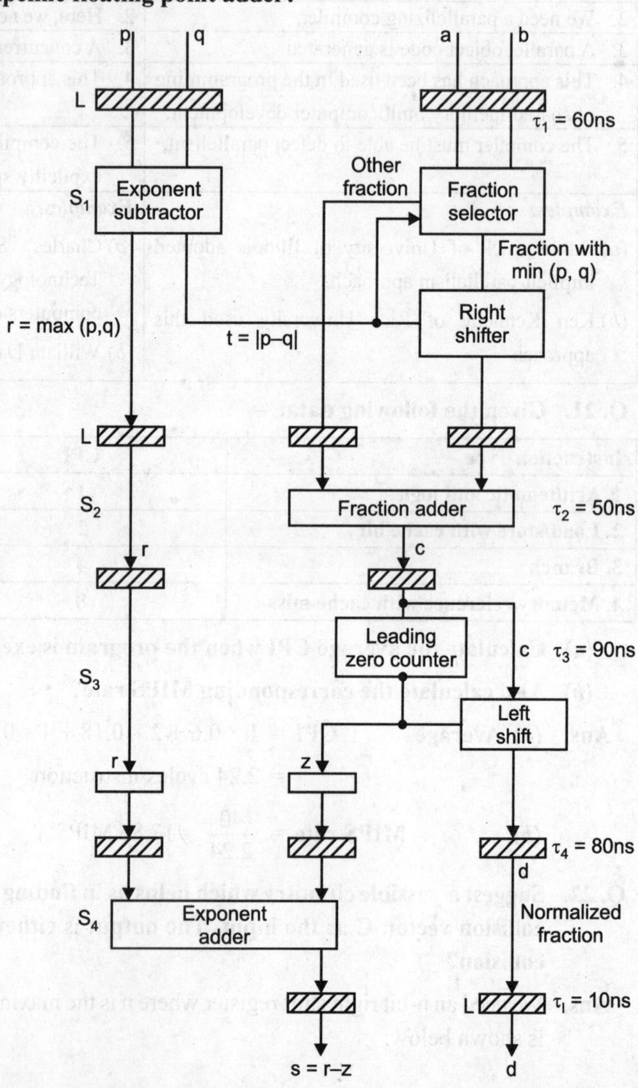

Operation performed by S_1: Comparing p and q. Compare the two exponents, p and q. Get the larger exponent, $r = \max(p, q)$ and determine the difference, $t = |p-q|$.

Operation performed by S_2: Right shifting of fraction i.e., shift right the fraction associated with lower exponent by *t*-bits to equalize the two exponent.

Operation performed by S_3: Adding two fractions—Add the preshifted fraction with the other fraction and produce the intermediate sum fraction, *C*.

Operation performed by S_4: Normalize the result-count the number of leading zeros, say *u*, in fraction *C* and shift left *C* by *u*-bits. The output is normalized fraction, sum, $d = c \times 2^r$. The exponent *S* is also modified as (*r-u*) to produce the output exponent.

All these stages can be implemented with combinational logic circuits.

Also shown in the figure:

$$\tau_1 \text{ (delay at } S_1) = 60 \text{ ns}$$

$$\tau_2 \text{ (delay at } S_2) = 50 \text{ ns}$$

$$\tau_3 \text{ (delay at } S_3) = 90 \text{ ns}$$

$$\tau_4 \text{ (delay at } S_4) = 80 \text{ ns}$$

and τ_1 (latch delay) = 10 ns

∴ The period of clock driving this pipeline will be equal to:

$$\tau = \tau_i\,(\max) + \tau_l$$

$$\tau = (90 + 10) \text{ ns}$$

$$\tau = 100 \text{ ns}$$

$$f = \frac{1}{\tau} = \frac{1}{100 \text{ ns}} = 10 \text{ MHz.}$$

Therefore, the time taken by the pipeline to complete a task will be $T = 100$ ns and time taken by non-pipelined processor to complete a task will be:

$$T_S = \tau_1 + \tau_2 + \tau_3 + \tau_2 + \tau_1$$

$$= 60{+}50{+}90{+}80{+}10{\div}10$$

$$T_s = 300 \text{ ns}$$

∴ Speed-up with pipeline adder $= S = \dfrac{T_s}{T_p}$

$$= \frac{300}{100} = 3$$

Please note that in order to achieve an ideal speed up equal to the number of stages i.e., 4, all stages should possess a uniform delay of 75 ns.

∴ Maximum speed-up $= \dfrac{300}{75}$ 4 (Ideal)

Q. 24. Write a short note on Multifunction Arithmetic pipelines.

Ans. The pipelines like floating point adder, fixed point multiplication or division etc were unifunction pipelines as they carry out one predefined operation. However, a multi-function pipeline is designed to carry out a set of **multiple operations. The basic idea is to reduce the cost of arithmetic unit by the hardware sharing.** It is implemented by connecting required number of basic functional modules. These basic modules are commonly required in several different operations. For example, normalization operation is common for all floating point operations. Figure below shows a multi-function pipeline in TI-ASC computer.

The pipeline of TI-ASC computer consists of eight stages. The figure shows all the interconnections of routes among eight stages. This pipeline can perform following functions:

(*a*) Fixed point arithematic.

(*b*) Floating point arithematic.

(*c*) Many logical shifting operations over scalar and vector operands.

The clock period is 60 ns. Different connecting paths are used based on different arithmetic and logic instructions.

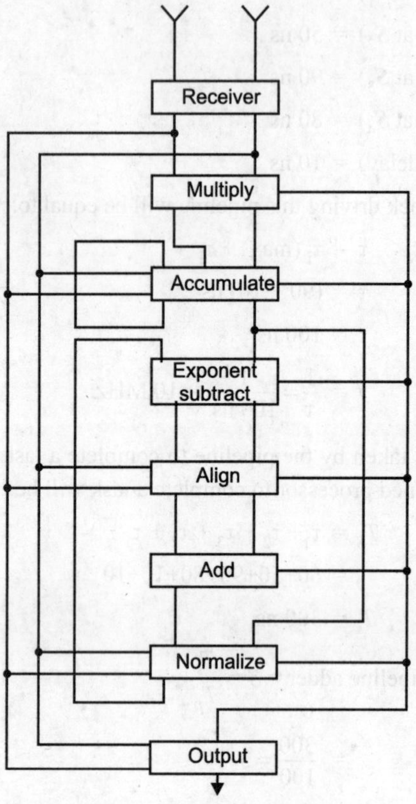

Fig. 8.88. Multifunction pipeline in TI-ASC system.

Q. 25. Explain the performance of pipelines with stalls.

Ans. A stall (wait) causes the pipeline performance to degrade from the ideal performance. Now, the speed-up from pipelining is given by a formula:

$$\text{Speed-up from pipelining} = \frac{\text{Average instruction time pipelined}}{\text{Average instruction time unpipelined}}$$

$$= \frac{\text{CPI unpipelined} \times \text{Clock period unpipelined}}{\text{CPI pipelined} \times \text{Clock period pipelined}}$$

The ideal CPI on pipelined machine is always 1.

$\therefore$ Pipelined CPI = Ideal CPI + Pipelined stall clock cycles/instruction

= 1 + Pipeline stall clock cycles/instruction.

Neglecting the cycle time overhead of pipelining and assuming the stages are perfectly balanced, the cycle time of two machines are equal and

$$\text{Speed-up} = \frac{\text{CPI unpipelined}}{1 + \text{pipeline stall cycles per instruction}}$$

If all instructions take the same number of cycles, which must also equal to the number of pipeline stages (i.e., the depth of pipeline) then unpipelined CPI is equal to the depth of the pipeline.

$$\boxed{\text{Speed-up} = \frac{\text{CPI unpipelined}}{1 + \text{Pipeline stall cycles per instruciton}}}$$

From the above equation **it is clear that if there are no stalls (waits) then the speed up is equal to the pipeline depth i.e., the number of pipeline states.**

Q. 26. Consider the following *C* statements:

$$\boldsymbol{a = x + y;}$$
$$\boldsymbol{b = x + z;}$$

Do they satisfy Bernstein conditions? Furthermore, if $a = x + y$; and $b = a + b$, then will they satisfy the same?

Ans. Consider the first two statements:

$$a = x + y;$$
$$b = x + z;$$

Now,

$$I_1 = (x, y)$$
$$I_2 = (x, z)$$
$$O_1 = (a)$$
$$Q_2 = (b)$$

$$\therefore \quad \left.\begin{array}{l} I_1 \cap O_2 = \phi \\ I_2 \cap O_1 = \phi \\ I_1 \cap O_2 = \phi \end{array}\right\}$$

are satisfied. Hence, these two statements can be executed in parallel.

Now, say

$$a = x + y;$$
$$b = a + b;$$
$$\therefore \quad I_2 \cap O_1 \neq \phi$$

$\therefore$ These two statements cannot be executed concurrently.

Q. 27. What is a communication latency?

Ans. In general, n tasks communicating with each other require $n(n — 1)/2$ communication links among them. So, the complexity grows quadratically. This puts an upper bound (limit) on the number of PEs that can be used in a computer.

Q. 28. What is the difference between the machine instruction of a conventional Von Neumann's machine to that of a data flow computer (DFC)?

Ans. The machine instruction format of a Von Neumann computer is as follows:

Operation to perform	Address in main memory of operands	address in the main memory of the result	Address of the next instruction to be carried out (PC)
Operation to perform	Slot for operand from left arc	Slot of operand from right arc	Address of the machine instruction and address of slots in which the result is to be stored.

We see that the operands in data flow machines are directly forwarded to the instructions which need them rather than being stored in memory as is done in Von Neumann computers. There is no program counter (PC) to give the address of the next instruction to be executed as in Von-Neumann computer. A data flow instruction is activated as soon as all its input operand slots are filled and can fire if the input operand slots of the instruction (s) to which the result is to be sent are empty. The operand slots of the receiving instruction will be free if it has used up whatever operands came to it earlier. Thus, as soon as a receiving instruction consumes its input operands, it sends an acknowledgement to all the sending instructions. An enabled instruction fires after it receives acknowledgements from all of the result destination addresses.

Q. 29. Consider the following sequential code in FORTRAN language:

S1 : $A = B + C$

S2 : $C = B*D$

S3 : $S = O$

S4 : **DO** $I = A$, **100**

$S = S + X(I)$

END DO

S5 : **IF (S. GT . 1000) C = C * 2**

Will this satisfy Bernstein's conditions for parallelism? Restructure the program in order to **maximize parallelism?**

Ans. Firstly, we form the input and output sets for the instructions given:

$$I_2 = \{B, C\} \qquad O_1 = \{A\}$$
$$I_2 = \{B, D\} \qquad O_2 = \{C\}$$
$$I_3 = \phi \qquad O_3 = \{S\}$$
$$I_4 = \{S, A, X(I)\} \qquad O_4 = (S)$$
$$I_5 = \{S, C\} \qquad O_5 = \{S\}$$

Using Bernstein's conditions, we find that:

(*a*) $\quad I_1 \cap O_3 = \phi \qquad I_2 \cap O_1 = \phi$

and $\quad O_1 \cap O_3 = \phi$

*S*1 and *s*3 can be executed concurrently.

(*b*) $\quad I_2 \cap O_3 = \phi \qquad I_3 \cap O_2 = \phi$

and $\quad O_2 \cap O_3 = \phi$

$\Rightarrow$ *S*2 and *S*3 can be executed concurrently.

(*c*) $I_2 \cap O_4 = \phi$ $I_4 \cap O_2 = \phi$

and $O_2 \cap O_4 = \phi$

⇒ *S*2 and *S*4 can be executed concurrently.

(*d*) $I_1 \cap O_5 = \{C\}$

⇒ *S*1 and *S*5 can not be executed concurrently.

(*e*) $I_1 \cap O_2 = \{C\}$

⇒ *S*1 and *S*5 can not be executed concurrently.

(*f*) $I_4 \cap O_1 = \{A\}$

⇒ *S*1 and *S*4 can not be executed concurrently.

(*g*) $I_5 \cap O_2 = O_5 \cap O_2 = \{C\}$

⇒ *S*2 and *S*5 can not be executed concurrently.

(*h*) $I_4 \cap O_3 = O_4 \cap O_3 = \{S\}$

⇒ *S*3 and *S*4 can not be executed concurrently.

(*i*) $I_5 \cap O_5 = \{S\}$

⇒ *S*3 and *S*5 can not be executed concurrently.

(*j*) $I_5 \cap I_4 = I_5 \cap O_4 = \{S\}$

⇒ *S*4 and *S*5 can not be executed concurrently.

We can reconstruct the program to draw the flow graph as shown below:

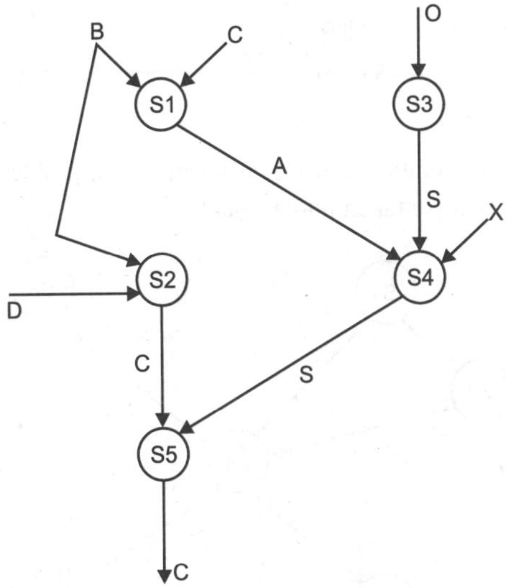

Q. 30. Consider the execution of the following code segment consisting of 7 statements. Use Bernstein's conditions to detect the maximum parallelism embedded in this code. Justify the portions that can be executed in parallel and the remaining portions that must be executed sequentially. Rewrite the code using parallel constructs such as co-begin and co-end. No variable substitution is allowed.

[GGSIPU, B. TECH(CSE)-7TH SEM. 1ST TERM. 2012].

S1: $A = B + C$

S2: $C = D + E$

S3: $F = G + E$

S4: $C = A + F$

S5: $M = G + C$

S6: $A = L + C$

S7: $A = E + A$

Ans. The input and output sets for the instructions are as follows:

$I_1 = [B, C]$ $O_1 = [A]$

$I_2 = [D, E]$ $O_2 = [C]$

$I_3 = [G, E]$ $O_3 = [F]$

$I_4 = [A, F]$ $O_4 = [C]$

$I_5 = [G, C]$ $O_5 = [M]$

$I_6 = [L, C]$ $O_6 = [A]$

$I_7 = [E, A]$ $O_7 = [A]$

Using Bernstein's conditions we find that

$S1 \parallel S3$ $S3 \parallel S5$

$S1 \parallel S5$ $S3 \parallel S6$

$S2 \parallel S3$ $S3 \parallel S7$

$S2 \parallel S7$ $S5 \parallel S6$

$S5 \parallel S7$

However, Bernstein's conditions are not sufficient for this problem. The precedence relations as shown below have to be taken into account:

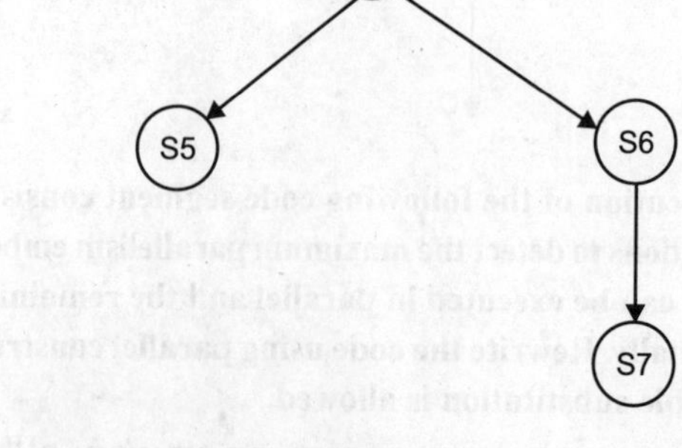

It is clear that $S1$, $S2$ and $S3$ must be executed before $S4$. Moreover, $S5$, $S6$ and $S7$ must be executed after $S4$. This consideration prohibits parallel execution among the two groups of statements. Thus, the statements that can be, executed in parallel are: $S1 \parallel S3$, $S2 \parallel S3$, $S5 \parallel S6$ and $S5 \parallel S7$.

The parallel code is given below:

```
Co begin
            S1, S3
Coend
            S2
            S4
Co begin
            S5, S6
Coend
            S7
```

Q. 32. Define the following terms:

(*a*) Computational granularity **(*b*) Communication latency**

(*c*) Flow dependence **(*d*) Anti dependence**

(*e*) Output dependence **(*f*) I/O dependence**

(*g*) Control dependence **(*h*) Resource dependence**

(*i*) Bernstein conditions **(*j*) Degree of parallelism**

Ans. (*a*) The amount of computation involved in a software process.

(*b*) The time measure of the communication overhead incurred between machine subsystems.

(*c*) A statements $S2$ is flow-dependent on statement SI if an execution path exists from Si to $S2$ and atleast one output of Si feeds in as input to $S2$.

(*d*) A statement $S2$ is antidependent on statement Si if $S2$ follows Si in program order and the output of $S2$ overlaps the input to SI.

(*e*) Two statements are output dependent if they produce the same variable.

(*f*) I/O dependence occurs when the same file or I/O device is requested by two statements.

(*g*) This refers to the situation where the order of execution of statements cannot be determined before run-time.

(*h*) Resource dependence is concerning the conflicts in using shared resources such as integer units, floating-point units, registers and memory areas among the parallel events.

(*i*) Bernstein's condition states that two processes can execute in parallel if their input sets I_1, I_2 and the output sets O_1, O_2 satisfy the following conditions

$$I_1 \cap O_2 = \phi$$

$$I_2 \cap O_1 = \phi$$

$$O_1 \cap O_2 = \phi$$

(*j*) For each time period, the number of processors used to execute a parallel program is defined as the 4-egree of parallelism.

Q. 33. (*a*) Compare control flow, data flow and reduction computers in terms of the program flow mechanism used.

(*b*) What are the differences between string reduction and graph reduction machines?

Ans. (*a*) A control flow computer use Program Counter (PC) to sequence the execution of instructions in a program. In a data flow computer, the execution of an instruction is driven by data availability. In a reduction computer, the computation is triggered by the demand for an operation's result.

(*b*) In string reduction, each demander gets a separate copy of the expression for its own evaluation. In graph reduction, each demander is given a pointer to the result of the reduction.

Q. 34. Consider the following code:

input d,e,f

$C_O = 0$

For i from 1 to 8 do

begin

$a_i := d_i + e_i$

$b_i := a_i * f_i$

$c_i := b_i + C_{i-1}$

end

output *a, b, c*

Find out how many cycles are required to run this code on:

(*a*) Sequential (uniprocessor) machine.

(*b*) Data flow computer (DFC) ?

Ans. (*a*) On a sequential machine:

when i = 1, in above code then

$$a_1 = d_1 + e_1$$
$$b_1 = a_1 * f_1$$
$$c_1 = b_1 + c_0$$

and so on; till i = 8.

On a sequential machine the execution is as follows:

1	4	6	7	10	12		43	46	48
a_1	b_1	c_1	a_2	b_2	c_2	...	a_8	b_8	c_8

∴ 24 instructions are there as 3 * 8 = 24

Each add, multiply and divide takes 1, 2 and 3 cycles respectively (say).

∴ Sequential machine takes 48 cycles to execute these 24 instructions.

(*b*) On a DFC (data flow computer)

On a data driven computer, the scenario is different. That is

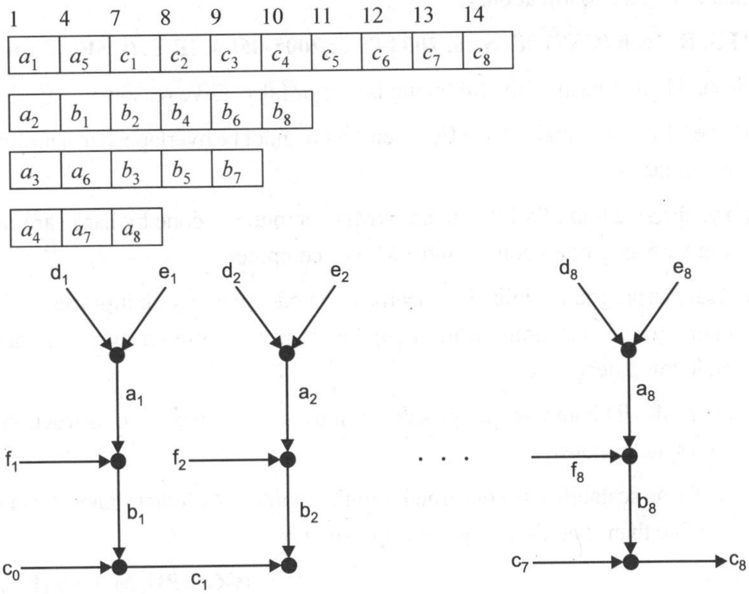

i.e., if a_1 and a_5 are available then all c_1 to c_8 results are available. So, a DFC will take only 14 cycles.

Q. 35. Write a note on — Role of compilers in parallel computing?

Ans. We list the roles of compilers:

1. Compilers are used to exploit hardware features to improve performance.
2. CDC STACKLIE, Cray CFT, Rice PFC and Yale Bulldog are some of its examples.
3. The general guideline is to increase the flexibility in hardware parallelism and to exploit software parallelism.
4. Hardware and software design trade offs exist in terms of cost, complexity, expandabilit compatibility and performance.
5. Multi processors compilation is much move involved than for uniprocessors.
6. Granularity and communication latency play important roles in code optimizations

EXERCISE QUESTIONS

Q. 1. Write short notes on

(*a*) Application Areas Supercomputers.

(*b*) Techniques used in B.W. matching of a uniprocessor?

[B.E. (CSE); Pune Univ., 2001, 2002, 2005,

Q. 2. "Finer the grain size, the higher the potential for parallelism, but higher the commun and scheduling overhead." Justify this statement. **[B.E. (CSE); Pune Univ**

Q. 3. What are the fundamental issues in parallel processing?

[B.E. (CSE) ; Pune Uni

Q. 4. Explain Feng's classification.

[UPTU, B. Tech (CSE) 8th Sem. 2004-05 & 2005-06] & [B.E. (CSE); Pune Univ. 2006]

Q. 5. Indicate whether each of the following is true or false. Give reasons:

(*a*) The CPU computations and I/O operations cannot be overlapped in a multiprogrammed computer.

(*b*) Synchronization of all PEs in an S1MD computer is done by hardware rather than by software as is often done in most MIMI) computers.

(*c*) As for as programmability is concerned, shared—memory multiprocessors offer simpler inter processor communication support than that offered by a message— passing multicomputer.

(*d*) In an MIMD computer, all processors must execute the same instruction at the same time synchronously.

(*e*) As far as scalability is concerned, multicomputers with distributed memory are more scalable than shared-memory multiprocessors.

[GGSIPU, M.Tech (IT), Dec. 2003]

Hint:

(*a*) False. The fundamental idea of multiprogramming is to overlap the computations of some programs with the I/O operations of other programs.

(*b*) True. In an SIMD machine, all processors execute the same instruction at the same time. Hence, it is easy to implement synchronization in hardware. In an MIMD machine, different processors may execute different instructions at the same time. Hence, it is difficult to support synchromsation in hardware.

(*c*) True. Inter processor communication is facffitated by sharing variables on a multiprocessor and by passing messages among nodes of a multicomputer. The multicomputer approach is usually more difficult to program since the programmer must pay attention to the actual distribution of data among the processors.

(*d*) False. In general, an MIMD machine executes different instruction streams on different processors.

(*e*) True. The contention among processors to access the shared memory may create hot spots, making multiprocessors less scalable than multicomputers.

Q. 6. Give five performance factors and explain four system attributes?

[GGSIPU, B.Tech. 7th sem (CSE), Dec. 2004—07]

Q. 7. Explain the architectural operations of SIMD and MIMI) computers. distinguish between multiprocessors and multicomputers based on their structures, resource sharing and IPC.

[GGSIPU, B.Tech. sem. CSE, Dec. 2007]

Q. 8. With the help of block diagrams, explain Flynn's classification of computer architectures.

[GGSIPU, M.Tech (IT) 1st Sem; Dec. 2004 & UPTU, B. Tech (CS) 7th Sem.; 2005-06 & 2008-09]

Q. 9. (*a*) Define the following terms:

(*i*) Parallel processing (*ii*) Speed-up

(*iii*) Scalability (*iv*) Parallel computer

(*v*) Pipelining. **[KUD, B.E (CSE) 8th sem.; 1997]**

(*b*) What is a supercomputer? Explain the need for supercomputers.

[UPTU, B. Tech (CSE) 8th Sem.; 2005-06 & KUD, B.E. (CSE) 8th sem; 1997]

Q. 10. (*a*) Why do you need high speed computing? List the points and explain in brief.

(*b*) List and explain the interesting features of parallel computers.

[KUD, B.E. (CSE) 8th sem., 1997]

Q. 11. How does a multiprocessor machine differ from a multicomputer machine? Give two examples of each. **[DTU-ME (CS); 2006]**

Q. 12. (*a*) Which is the best classification for parallel system — Flynn's or Handler's. Discuss their limitations, if any. **[DTU-ME (CS); 2006]**

(*b*) How does a multiprocessor machine differ from a multicomputer machine.

(*c*) What are the limitations of speed-up 7 Can we have superlinear speed-up? Justify your answer. **[DTU-ME (CS); 2006]**

Q. 13. (*a*) What are the different methods increasing the speed of computers.

(*b*) Compare temporal and Data parallel processing methods. **[DTU- ME (CS); 2002]**

Q. 14. Describe a place of the following computer system in the Flynn's classification scheme:

1. Illiac-IV
2. nCUBE
3. Cray T90 series
4. CM-5
5. PARAM 10000 **[DTU- ME (CS); 2003]**

Hint:

1. SIMD
2. MIMD
3. SISD
4. SIMD
5. MIMD

Q. 15. Suppose a multiprocessor is built out of individual processors capable of sustaining 50 MFLOPS. What is the largest fraction of a program's execution time that could be devoted to sequential operations if the parallel computer is to exceed the performance of a supercomputer capable of sustaining IGFLOPS. **[DTU-ME (CS); 2002]**

Q. 16. Explain how the degree of parallelism (DOP) and number of processors effect the performance of a parallel computing system. Give Amdahl's law and find the expression for fixed load speed-up. **[UPTU, B. Tech (CSE) 8th Sem.; 2005-06]**

Q. 17. (*a*) State Amdahl's law and prove it.

(*b*) Describe with block diagram, shared memory architecture. Enumerate its features.

Q. 18. Explain how instruction set, compiler technology, CPU implementation and control and memory hierarchy affect the CUP performance and justify the efforts in terms of program length, clock rate and effective CPI. **[UPTU, B.Tech (CSE) 8th Sem.; 2007-08]**

Q. 19. (*a*) Define parallel computing. What are the fundamental used in parallel processing? Discuss various applications of parallel computing?

(*b*) Explain how DOP and number of processors affect the performance of a parallel computing system. Discuss various speedup performance laws.

[UPTU, B. Tech (CSE) 8th Sem.; 2008-09]

Q. 20. Use Bernstein's conditions to detect the parallelism embedded in this code:

$P1 : C = D*E$

$P2 : M G + C$

$P3 : A = B + C$

$P4 : C = L + M$

$P5 : F = G + E$

Also draw a dependence graph showing both data dependence and resource dependence.

[GGSIPU, B.Tech.(CSE); 7th sem., Dec. 2007]

Q. 21. Answer the following questions related to data flow computers:

(*a*) Distinction between static and dynamic data flow computers.

(*b*) Draw a data flow graph showing the computations of the roots of quadratic equation:

$$A_i x^2 + B_i x + c_i = 0 \ (i = 1, 2, \ldots N)$$

[GGSIPU, M-Tech. (IT) ; 7th sem. ,May 2003]

Q. 22. What is non-Von Neumann architecture computer? Compare Von Neumann architecture vis-a-vis data flow architecture computer. Which architecture is more suitable for parallel algorithm and why? **[GGSIPU, M.Tech (IT)- 6th sem., May 2003]**

Q. 23. Explain Bernstein's conditions for parallelism.

[GGSIPU, M.Tech (IT)- 1st sem., Dec. 2004]

Q. 24. (*a*) Discuss the concept of grain packing and scheduling with the help of an example. (l) Compare control flow and data flow computers.

[GGSIPU, M.Tech (IT),7th sem., Dec. 2004]

Q. 25. List the special features of data flow computers and differentiate between static and dynamic data flow computers.

[UPTU, B. Tech. (CSE) 8th Sem.; 2006-07 & KUD, BE (CSE) 8th sem., 1996]

Q. 26. List the different operators used in data flow graphs along with their usage. Draw data flow graphs to compute factorial of a positive integer, *N*. **[KUD, BE (CSE), 8th sem., 1996]**

Q. 27. (*a*) Describe the following:

(*i*) Data driven computation.

(*ii*) Event driven computation.

(*iii*) Static data flow graph.

(*iv*) Dynamic data flow graph.

(*b*) Draw data flow graphs to represent the following computations:

(*i*) if(($a = = b$)&($c < d$)) than $c = c - a$ else $c = c + a$

(*ii*) for (i =0; i< 10; i++)

{

cout << i;

{ **[KUD, BE (CSE), 8th sem., 1997]**

Q. 28. Write short notes on:

1. Classification of parallel computers based on

(*a*) Mode of Accessing Memory. (*b*) Grain Size. **[DTU, M.E. (CSE), 2003]**

Q. 29. Analyze the data dependencies for the following program. Draw a dependency graph to show all dependencies:

Load $R1$, M(100)

Move $R2$, $R1$

Inc $R1$

Add $R2$, $R1$

Store M(100), $R1$? **[Pune University; B.E. (CSE), Dec. 2001]**

Q. 30. Consider the following loopnest:

```
DO I = 1, N
DO J = 2, N
A (I,J)  = B (1 - J) + C (1,J)
C (1, J) = D (I, J) / 2
E (I, J) = A (I, J-1)**2 + E (1,J-1)
END DO
END DO
```

[UPTU, B. Tech. (CSE) 8th Sem.; 2003-04]

Q. 31. Distinguish between Medium grain and fine grain multicomputer in their architecture **[UPTU, B. Tech. (CSE), 8th Sem.; 2007-08]**

Q. 32. (*a*) Compare CISC and RISC architectures.

(*b*) With the help of pipeline diagrams, explain super scalar and VL1W processors.

[UPTU, B. Tech. (CSE) -8th Sem.,2005-06 & GGSIPU—M.Tech. 1st sem., Dec. 2004].

Q. 33. Compare RISC architecture with CISC architecture. **[KUD—B.E. (CSE)-7th sem., 1996]**

Q. 34. Discuss the salient features and important applications of RISC and CISC architectures.

[KUD, BE (CSE); 8th sem., 1997]

Q. 35. Explain major attributes of RISC machines. **[KUD, BE (CSE) -8th sem., 1996]**

Q. 36. What are the features of scalable processor architecture? Explain register window and its parameter passing between procedures of SPARC architecture.

[Pune Univ., B.E. (CSE) 2nd sem., May 2004 & Dec. 2005]

Q. 37. Explain SPARC architecture & VL1W processors.

[Pune Univ., B.E. (CSE)- 2nd sem., May 2004 & Dec. 2005]

Q. 38. Draw and explain SPARC architecture. **[Pune Univ., B.E. (CSE)- 2nd sem., Dec. 2004]**

Q. 39. Discuss the CISC and RISC architectures with the help of their functional block diagrams. Also indicate their advantages and drawbacks.

[UPTU, B. Tech (CSE)-7th Sem., 2003-04]

CHAPTER

9 COMPUTER ARITHMETIC

9.0 INTRODUCTION

Basically, number systems are of two types –

(*a*) Non-positional.

(*b*) Positional.

Non-Positional Number System was used long back by humans to count on fingers. But fingers are only 10, so they used stones, pebbles or sticks to count further this method of counting uses an additional approach or the non-positional number system. Even Roman numerals like I for 1, II for 2 and so on is an example of non-positional number system.

Positional Number Systems use a few symbols called **digits.** These symbols represent different values depending on the position they occupy in the number. The value of each digit in such a number is determined by three things –

(*a*) The digit itself.

(*b*) The position of the digit in the number.

(*c*) The base of the number system.

For eg. The number system used in our daily life is called as a decimal number system.

NOTE: **Base** is defined as the total number of digits available in the number system. We define the base or radix of a number system as the number of digits it uses to represent numbers in the system. **For eg.** Decimal number system uses 10 digits, from 0 to 9, so its base or radix is 10.

9.1 NUMBER SYSTEMS

Positional number systems are also of four types

(*a*) Binary number system (base 2)

(*b*) Octal number system (base 8)

(*c*) Decimal number system (base 1z0)

(*d*) Hexadecimal number system (base 16)

The overall chart is –

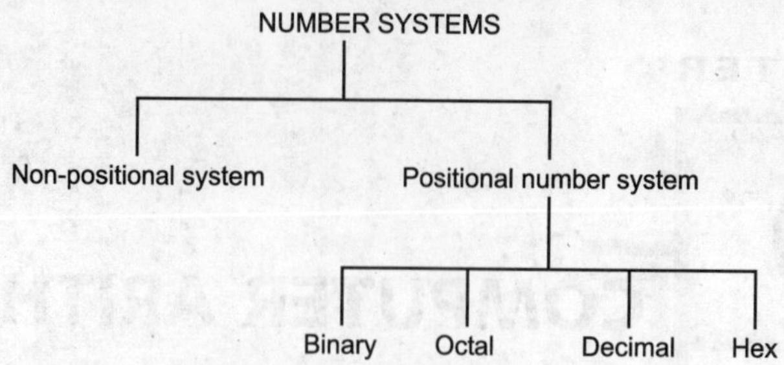

Fig. 9.1. Types of Number Systems

Let us compare these four number systems in a tabular form –

Table 9.1: Number Systems

Number system	Data unit	Digits used	Usage
Decimal (10)	Digit	0 to 9	Commonly used daily.
Binary (2)	Bit	0 and 1	Used internally by computer.
Octal (8)	Nibble	0 to 7	Used earlier by mini computers for easy communication of object programs and data.
Hexadecimal (16)	Byte	0 to 9 and A to F	Currently in use.

There are three rules for representation of any number system. They are as follows –

Rule 1: Total number of digits available i.e., base or radix of these numbers.

Rule 2: First digit is always zero.

Rule 3: Last digit = Base – 1.

For binary number system,

Base = 2

1st digit = 0

So, Last digit = (Base – 1) = (2–1) = 1

Hence, Final digits = 0,1

Similarly, for decimal number system,

Base = 10

1st digit = 0

Last digit = (Base – 1)

= (10–1)

= 9

Final digits = 0,1,2,3,4,5,6,7,8,9

For octal number system,

Base = 8

1st digit = 0

Last digit = (Base – 1)

= (8 – 1) = 7

Final digit = 0,1,2,3,4,5,6,7

For hexadecimal number system,

Base = 16

1st digit = 0

Last digit = (Base – 1)

= (16 – 1) = 15

Final digits = 0,1,2,3,4,5,6,7,8,9,A,B,C,D,E,F

Where A = 10

B = 11

C = 12

D = 13

E = 14

F = 15

The following table – 2 summarizes all numbers (from 0 to 20) in a tabular form –

Table 9.2: Numbers in Decimal, Binary, Octal and Hexadecimal

Decimal	Binary	Octal	Hexadecimal
0	0	0	0
1	1	1	1
2	10	2	2
3	11	3	3
4	100	4	4
5	101	5	5
6	110	6	6
7	111	7	7
8	1000	10	8
9	1001	11	9
10	1010	12	A
11	1011	13	B
12	1100	14	C
13	1101	15	D
14	1110	16	E
15	1111	17	F
16	10000	20	10
17	10001	21	11
18	10010	22	12
19	10011	23	13
20	10100	24	14

Note: As with all numbering systems most significant digits are at left, least significant digits are at right.

9.2 DECIMAL AND BINARY NUMBERS

As we know that in a decimal number system, ten digits are available. These are 0 to 9. The base of the decimal number system is 10. This number system is also called as **the base 10 number system. Please understand that in such a system the weight of each bit of a decimal number system depends on its relative position.** That is,

The value of 1st of number from right side = 1st bit $* 10^0$

The value of 2nd bit of number from right side = 2nd bit $* 10^1$

The value of 3rd bit of number from right side = 3rd bit $* 10^2$

• • • •

• • • •

• • • •

• • • •

∴ The value of *n*th bit of number from right side = n^{th} bit $* 10^{n-1}$

= n^{th} bit $*$ (base)$^{n-1}$

In any number system, there are certain symbols used called as **digit or base or radix** of that system. The value is determined by two things-

(*a*) Face value.

(*b*) Place value.

Also understand that the face value is fixed for any symbol or digit by raising base to increasing order of numbers 0,1,2,3 .... from right to left. When we multiply the face value by its place value and add all such digits then we get add all such digits then we get the exact value of that particular number.

> **NOTE:** When we use more than one number system at a time, we use base as a subscript to distinguish both number systems.

In binary number system, we have only two symbols or digits i.e., 0 and 1. **The binary digits are called as bits. The base of binary system is 2. Each position in a binary number represents a power of the base 2.** So, in this system the right most position is the units (2^0) position, 2's (2^1) position and so on.

For eg. Decimal equivalent of the binary number $(1010)_2$ is –

[1 0 1 0]

$2^3\ 2^2\ 2^1\ 2^0$

or $1 \times 2^3 + 0 \times 2^2 + 1 \times 2^1 + 0 \times 2^0$

$= 8 + 0 + 2 + 0$

$= 10$

$\therefore (1010)_2 \equiv (10)_{10}$

Please note that the weight of each bit of a binary number depends on its relative position. Also note that –

The value of 1st bit of number from right side $= 1^{st}$ bit $\times 2^0$

The value of 2nd bit of number from right side $= 2^{nd}$ bit $\times 2^1$

• • • • • • • •

• • • • • • • •

• • • • • • • •

• • • • • • • •

The value of nth bit of number from right side $= n^{th}$ bit* 2^{n-1}

9.3 OCTAL AND HEX NUMBERS

In octal number system, the base is 8. So, here we have only symbols (digits) i.e., 0,1,2,3,4,5,6,7. Here, each position in an octal number represents a power of the base (8).

For eg. $(456)_8$ is written in decimal as follows –

(4 5 6)

8^2 8^1 8^0

or $4 \times 8^2 + 5 \times 8^1 + 6 \times 8^0$

$= 256 + 40 + 6$

$= 302$

Hence, $(456)_8 = (302)_{10}$

Please note here that the weight of each bit of an octal number depends on its relative system. Also note that

The value of 1st bit of number from right side $= 1^{st}$ bit $\times 8^0$

The value of 2nd bit of number from right side $= 2^{nd}$ bit $\times 8^1$

• • • • •

• • • • •

• • • • •

• • • • •

The value of nth bit of number from right side $= n^{th}$ bit $* 8^{n-1}$

$= n^{th}$ bit $*$ $(\text{base})^{n-1}$

We are in a position to solve some problems now.

EXAMPLE 9.1: Convert the following decimal numbers to binary form. Also give the set of rules you follow for such a conversion. Numbers are 50, 0.3125 and 42.4.

SOLUTION: Let us see the rules of converting any decimal numbers to its binary form, first of all-

Rule 1: Write down the decimal number.

Rule 2: This decimal number is divided by new base i.e., 2 ; until the integer position is '0'.

Rule 3: Read the remainder from upward direction indicated by arrow mark.

For eg.

2	50	
2	25	0 ↑
2	12	1
2	6	0
2	3	0
2	1	1
	0	1

i.e., $(50)_{10} = (110010)_2$

But please note the second number given in question. It is 0.3125. It is a decimal fractional number.

Rules to convert decimals with fraction into a binary form –

Rule 1: Write down the decimal fractional number.

Rule 2: Multiply this number by 2 and carry binary number.

Rule 3: If decimal fraction becomes same or approximate nearly then stop process.

Rule 4: Required binary numbers are in downward arrow direction.

So, decimal fractions can be converted to binary by repeated multiplication by 2 until the fractional product is zero or same. The carry generated by each multiplication forms the binary number.

For eg. $(0.3125)_{10} = (?)_2$

Number given is $= 0.3125$

$$\begin{aligned}
& & & \underline{\text{carries}} \\
\therefore \quad 0.3125 \times 2 &= 0.6250 & & - 0 \\
0.6250 \times 2 &= 1.250 & & - 1 \\
0.250 \times 2 &= 0.500 & & - 0 \\
0.5 \times 2 &= 1.0 & & - 1
\end{aligned}$$

(carries read in downward arrow direction ↓)

$$\therefore \quad (0.3125)_{10} = (.0101)_2$$

What about $(42.4)_{10}$?

$$(42)_{10} = (101010)_2$$

$$(0.4)_2 = (0.011)_2$$

$$(42.4)_{10} = (101010.011)_2$$

EXAMPLE 9.2: Convert the following binary numbers to its decimal form $(10111)_2$ and $(101101.10101)_2$. Also write down the rules you follow for the same. What about the binary fractional numbers?

SOLUTION: The rules for binary to decimal conversions are as follows –

Rule 1: Write down the given binary number.

Rule 2: Write the weight of digits from right to left starting from 0 to upward.

Rule 3: Multiply binary digits with the corresponding weight and add it.

For eg. Given:

$(10111)_2 = (?)_{10}$

[1 0 1 1 1]

$2^4\ 2^3\ 2^2\ 2^1\ 2^0$

$$= 1 \times 2^4 + 0 \times 2^3 + 1 \times 2^2 + 1 \times 2^1 + 1 \times 2^0$$
$$= 16 + 0 + 4 + 2 + 1$$
$$= 23$$

Therefore, $(10111)_2 = (23)_{10}$

But what about binary-fractional numbers?

In this case we **do not** follow the rule 2 above. Instead the weights of digits start from left to right i.e., weight starting 1 and upward. A collection of digits makes a number which in general has two parts – **integer and fractional**, separated by a radix point (.) i.e.,

$$(N)_b = d_{n-1}\, d_{n-2}\, \ldots\, d_1 \ldots d_1 d_0\ .\ d_{-1}\, d_{-2} \ldots d_{-f} \ldots d_{-m}$$

Integer part   Radix   Fractional part

where

N = a number

B = radix of the number system (or base).

n = number of digits in integer portion.

m = number of digits in fractional portion.

d_{n-1} = MSD (Most Significant Digit)

d_{-m} = LSD (Least Significant Digit)

For eg. $(101101.10101)_2$ = (?)10

Given: $(101101.10101)_2$

$= [1 \times 2^5 + 0 \times 2^4 + 1 \times 2^3 + 1 \times 2^2 + 0 \times 2^1 + 1 \times 2^0 + 1 \times 2^{-1} + 0 \times 2^{-2} + 1 \times 2^{-3} + 0 \times 2^{-4} + 1 \times 2^{-5}]$

$= [32 + 0 + 8 + 4 + 0 + 1 + 1/2 + 0 + 1/8 + 0 + 1/32]$

$= [32 + 8 + 4 + 1 + 0.5 + 0.125 + 0.03125]$

$= (45.65625)_{10}$

What about $(0.1011)_2$?

Now, .1011 is –

2^{-1} 2^{-2} 2^{-3} 2^{-4}

[1 0 1 1]

$$= [1 \times 2^{-1} + 0 \times 2^{-2} + 1 \times 2^{-3} + 1 \times 2^{-4}]$$
$$= (1/2 + 0 + 1/8 + 1/16)$$
$$= (0.5 + 0 + 0.125 + 0.0825)$$
$$= (0.6875)_{10}$$
$$= (0.1011)_2 = (0.6875)_{10}$$

EXAMPLE 9.3: How will you convert binary number to its octal form Convert the following
(*a*) $(10001111)_2$ (*b*) $(11101.00101101)_2$.

SOLUTION: The following rules are followed:

Rule 1: Write down the binary number.

Rule 2: Partition the binary number into a group of three digits each. Start from right to left.

Rule 3: Write decimal equivalent of each group.

Rule 4: Combine these decimal equivalents (digits) to get the required octal number.

For eg. $(10001111)_2$

Given: 010 001 111 (rule 1)

2 1 7 (rule 2 and 3)

(2 1 7) (rule 4)

So, $(10001111)_2 = (217)_8$

Now consider another given number –

011 101 . 001 011 010 (rule 1)

3 5 . 1 3 2 (rule 2 and 3)

$(35.132)_8$ (rule 4)

Hence, $(11101001011010)_2 = (35.132)_8$

EXAMPLE 9.4: How will you convert octal number to binary number. Write down the rules you follow and apply them to the following numbers

(*a*) $(217)_8$ (*b*) $(56.57)_8$

SOLUTION: The rules followed are as follows –

Rule 1: Write down the octal numbers.

Rule 2: Convert all octal number to three bits binary equivalents.

Rule 3: Combine all binary numbers to get required number.

For eg. $(217)_8$

(2 1 7)

↑ ↑ ↑

010 001 111

Hence, $(217)_8 = (10001111)_2$

Now, consider $(56.57)_8$

i.e., (5 6 . 5 7)

(101 110 . 101 111)

$(101110.101111)_2$

$$(56.57)_8 = (101110.101111)_2$$

EXAMPLE 9.5: Convert the following binary numbers to their hex equivalents.-

(a) $(1110110)_2$ **(b) $(11011.01101101)_2$**

What rules you followed?

SOLUTION: The rules followed are as under:

Rule 1: Write down the binary number.

Rule 2: Partition these binary numbers into group of four digits each starting from right to left.

Rule 3: Write the decimal equivalent of each group.

Rule 4: Combine these decimal equivalents (or digits) to get the required HEX number.

For eg. $(1110110)_2 = (?)_{16}$

Given: 0111 0110 (using rule 1 and 2)

rf = 7 6 (using rule 3 and 4)

Hence $(1110110)_2 = (76)_{16}$

Consider second number now.

(11011 . 0110 1101)

We add 3 zero to left

0001 1011 . 0110 1101

1 11(B) . 6 13(D)

So, $(1B.6D)_{16}$

EXAMPLE 9.6: Convert the following HEX numbers into binary form and other as indicated:

(a) $(1DD)_{16}$ **(b) $(5BC.6B)_{16}$** **(c) $(5D)_{16} = (?)_8$**

(d) $(135)_{10} = (?)_{16}$ **(e) $(0.513)_{10} = (?)_8$**

SOLUTION: To convert HEX numbers to their binary form, we follow the following steps:

Rule 1: Write down the HEX numbers.

Rule 2: Each HEX number is converted to its equivalent four binary.

Rule 3: We combine these binary numbers to get the required binary number.

For eg.

(a) $(1DD)_{16} = (?)_2$

Now, [1 D D]

0001 1101 1101

So, $(1DD)_2 = (111011101)_2$

(b) $(5BC.6B)_{16} = (?)_2$

Now, 5 = 0101

B = 11 = 1011

C = 12 = 1100

6 = 0110

$$B = 11 \quad = \quad 1011$$

$$(5BC.6B)_{16} = (10110111100.0110100)_2$$

(*c*) $(5D)_{16} = (?)_8$

We firstly convert given HEX number to its binary form and then to its octal form *i.e.*

HEX number $\xrightarrow[\text{to}]{}$ Binary number $\xrightarrow[\text{to}]{}$ Octal number

i.e., $(5D)_{16} \rightarrow (?)_2 \rightarrow (?)_8$

Now, HEX to binary is

$$5 = 101$$

$$D(13) = 1101$$

So, $(5D)_{16} = (1011101)_2$

Now, we convert

$$(1011101)_2 = (?)_8$$

i.e., 001 011 101 (add zeros to left)

↓ ↓ ↓

1 3 5

So, $(5D)_{16} = (135)_8$

Please note the following points here–

1. Any number in one number system can be represented in any other number system. **They are inter-convertible.**
2. **Although computers operate on HEX values** yet the input and output are in decimals only because the users can understand decimal numbers easily.
3. Using HEX numbers is better as it requires **lesser memory.** So, the processor also becomes very fast. We need lesser memory as the long binary string is now compressed to a smaller HEX number (as we form groups of 4 bits).
4. We observe that–

Octal number	HEX number
↓ converted to	↓ converted to
Binary number	Binary number
↓ converted to	↓ converted to
HEX number	Octal number

This shows that one base is converted into another base.

Next we consider part – *d*

(*d*) $(135)_8 = (?)_{16}$

Now, $(135)_8$ is

[1 3 5]

↓ ↓ ↓

(001) (011) (101)

$\therefore \qquad (135)_8 = (1011101)_2$

and $\qquad (1011101)_2 = (?)_{16}$

i.e., 0101 $\qquad$ 1101

$\downarrow \qquad \downarrow$

5 $\qquad$ 13(*D*)

So, $\qquad (135)_8 = (5D)_{16}$

The rule followed is as given in point number 4.

(*e*) $(135)_{10} = (?)_8$

8	135	
8	16	–7
8	2	–0
	0	–2

So, the result is $(207)_8$

(*f*) $(0.513)_{10} = (?)_8$

		carries
.513 × 8	= 4.104	– 4
.104 × 8	= 0.832	– 0
.832 × 8	= 6.656	– 6
.656 × 8	= 5.248	– 5
.248 × 8	= 1.94	– 1
.984 × 8	= 17.875	– 7
	⋮	
	⋮	

Hence, $\qquad (0.513)_{10} = (0.406517..........)_8$

9.4 BINARY ARITHMETIC

There are four basic arithmetic operations on binary numbers. Binary arithmetic uses only 0 and 1. Hence, it is simpler. The following are the basic operations–

9.4.1. Binary Addition

The rules of binary addition are as follows–

Augend (*X*)	Addend (*Y*)	Sum	Carry	Result
0	0	0	0	0
0	1	1	0	1
1	0	1	0	1
1	1	0	1	10

That is,

$$0 + 0 = 0$$
$$0 + 1 = 1$$
$$1 + 0 = 1$$
$$1 + 1 = \underline{1}0$$
$$1 + 1 + 1 = \underline{1}1$$

Note: It is read as one zero but its meaning is two.
Please note that the carry in first three rows is zero i.e., carry = 0 but in the fourth row carry = 1. Similar to a decimal addition, it is added to the next higher binary position. Also note that the carry = 1 is generated only when two bits to be added are 1.

An aid to memory: If the number of 1s to be added in a column is even then the sum bit is 0 and if the number of 1s to be added in a column is odd then the sum bit is 1. Every pair of 1s in a column produces and carry (1) to be added to the next higher bit column.

We are in a position to some problems now.

Q. 1. Add the following binary numbers –

(*a*) 0101 and 1111 **(*b*) 1111 and 10.**

Ans. (*a*)

```
  0101    (5₁₀)
  1111    (15₁₀)
 ------
 10100    (20₁₀)
```

So, Carry = 1

(*b*)

```
  1 0 1 1    (11₁₀)
  1 0 0 1    (9₁₀)
 ---------
1 0 1 0 0    (20₁₀)
```

Again carry = 1.

Q. 2. Add the following binary numbers –

1101.101 + 111.011.

Ans. Given: 1101.101 + 111.011.

```
(1) (1) (1) (1)   (1) (1)
 1   1   0   1 . 1  0  1
     1   1   1 . 0  1  1
--------------------------
1  0   1   0 1 . 0  0  0   (carry = 1)
```

9.4.2. Binary Subtraction

The rules of binary subtraction are as follows –

Minuend (*X*)	Subtrahend (*Y*)	Difference	Borrow
0	0	0	0
0	1	1	1
1	0	1	0
1	1	0	0

That is,

$$\begin{aligned} 0-0 &= 0 \\ 1-0 &= 1 \\ 1-1 &= 0 \\ 0-1 &= 1 \quad \text{(borrow = 1 from next column)} \\ 10-1 &= 1 \end{aligned}$$

In 2nd row, borrow = 1. This is to be subtracted from the next higher bit as it is done in decimal subtraction. **We are in a position to solve some problems now.**

Q. 1. Subtract $(0110)_2$ from $(1011)_2$

	C_1	C_3	C_2	C_1	(Minuend)
Ans.	1	0	1	1	(Minuend)
	−0	1	1	0	(subtrahend)
	0	1	0	1	

Note that in column 1 and 2, borrow = 0 and in column 3, it is 1.

In C_1, firstly subtract 0 from 1 and from this result obtained, subtract the borrow bit.

Q. 2. Subtract $(111.111)_2$ from $(1010.01)_2$

Ans. [C7	C6	C5	C4		C3	C2	C1]
1	0	1	0	.	0	1	0
−	1	1	1	.	1	1	1
0	0	1	0	.	0	1	1

In C_1, a 1 cannot be subtracted from zero (0). So, borrow a 1 from C_2, making C_2 column 0. The 1 borrowed from C_2 column becomes 10 in C_1 column. So, in C_1 we do (10 − 1) = 1.

In C_2, 1 cannot be subtracted from a 0. So, a borrow of 1 is taken from C_3 column, but it is also a 0. So, we borrow a 1 from the C_4 column. It is also a 0, so borrow a 1 from C_5, making C_5 column 0. Proceeding this way we find that –

$$\begin{aligned} \text{In } C_2,\ 10-1 &= 1 \\ \text{In } C_3,\ 1-1 &= 0 \\ \text{In } C_4,\ 1-1 &= 0 \\ \text{In } C_5,\ 10-1 &= 1 \\ \text{In } C_6,\ 1-1 &= 0 \\ \text{In } C_7,\ 0-0 &= 0 \end{aligned}$$

So, Answer = $(0010.011)_2$

9.4.3. Binary Multiplication

There are two methods of binary multiplication –

(*a*) The paper and pencil method.

(*b*) The computer method.

The complete set of rules for binary multiplication is as follows –

(*a*) $0 \times 0 = 0$

(*b*) $0 \times 1 = 0$

(*c*) $1 \times 0 = 0$

(*d*) $1 \times 1 = 1$

Both the above mentioned methods follow these rules. The paper method is just like multiplication of decimal numbers on paper. In this method –

1 Multiply the multiplicand with each bit of the multiplier and add the partial products.

2 The partial product is same as the multiplicand if the multiplier bit is a 1 and is zero if the multiplier bit is a 0.

3 Numbers are in signed magnitude form.

For eg.

```
        1 0 0 1 (multiplicand)
        1 1 0 1 (multiplier)
        -------
        1 0 0 1
      0 0 0 0 ×
    1 0 0 1 × ×
  1 0 0 1 × × ×
  -------------
  1 1 1 0 1 0 1
```

We are in a position to solve an example now.

Q. 1. Multiply $(1011.101)_2$ by $(101.01)_2$

Ans.

```
            1 0 1 1 . 1 0 1   (3dp)
                1 0 1 . 0 1   (2dp)
            ---------------
            1 0 1 1 1 0 1
          0 0 0 0 0 0 0 ×
        1 0 1 1 1 0 1 × ×
      0 0 0 0 0 0 0 × × ×
    1 0 1 1 1 0 1 × × × ×
  -------------------------
      1 1 1 1 0 1.0 0 0 0 1  (5dp)
```

Multiplicand has 3 decimal places (3dp) whereas multiplier has 2 dp. So, total is 5dp. So, we add decimal dot at 5 decimal places from right to left.

Hence, Answer = $(111101.00001)_2$ using paper and pencil method.

Please note that a computer can add only two numbers at a time with a carry. So, the paper and pencil method cannot be used by the digital computer. Also, as the system (PC) has only a fixed number of bit positions available. A *n*-bit number when multiplied by another *n*-bit number yields a 2*n*-bit number. So, now we need (*a*) A *n*-bit multiplicand register.

(*b*) A 2*n*-bit multiplier or result register.

The multiplier is placed in the left *n*-bits of the multiplier/ quotient (*MQ*) register and the right *n*-bits are set to 0. So, *MQ* is used here as a **dual register** that holds the multiplier and the partial and then final results. The multiplicand is placed in the M register. Then the *MQ* register is shifted one bit to the left. **If a 1 is shifted out, M is added to the *MQ* register. If a 0 is shifted out, a 0 is added to the *MQ* register.** We repeat this process *n*-times i.e., the number of bits in the multiplier. The final result is in *MQ* register.

> **NOTE:** The accumulator and the *MQ* registers are physically joined so that their contents can be shifted together either left or right.

Binary multiplication can be performed by shifting the binary number towards left. **Please remember that a left shift by a single bit is equivalent to multiplication by 2. Also note that on similar lines, a left shift by two bits is equivalent to multiplication by 4. In general, the multiplication factor is determined by 2^n where *n* is the number of bit shifts.**

9.4.4. Binary Division

Binary division uses the following rules –

(*a*) 0/1 = 0 (*b*) 1/1 = 1

(*c*) Division by zero is meaningless.

Binary division follows the following steps –

1. Start from the left of the dividend.
2. Perform a series of subtractions in which the divisor is subtracted from the dividend.
3. If subtraction is possible, put a 1 in the quotient and subtract the divisor from the corresponding digits of dividend.
4. If subtraction is not possible (i.e., divisor is greater than remainder), record a 0 in the quotient.
5. Bring down the next digit to add to the remainder digits.

We are in a position to solve an example now.

For eg. Divide $(1011)_2$ by $(11)_2$.

```
        11    | 0 1 0 1 1 |  0 0 1 1   (Divisor = 11, dividend = 01011, quo = 0011)
              | 1 1       |
             ------------
borrow  -->  1 1 0
restore -->    1 1
             ------------
               0 1 0
                 1 1
             ------------
borrow  -->      1 1 1
restore -->        1 1
             ------------
                   1 0 1
                     1 1
             ------------
No borrow -->        1 0 1
                       1 1
             ------------
No borrow -->          1 0    ----------- Remainder
```

Please note the following points here:

1. Preserve divisor as it is to be successively subtracted from the dividend.
2. Use dividend bits starting from MSB.
3. Once a bit is used to develop a quotient it is not needed again.
4. The bit to its right is appended to the remainder for developing the next quotient bit.
5. As each quotient bit is developed, the corresponding MSB of the dividend may be discarded.

Even binary division can be done by 2 methods –

(*a*) Paper and pencil method (as discussed above).

(*b*) Computer method.

Let us discuss method–II now. **The computer method of division involves successive subtraction.** Say, if we divide an eight bit dividend by a four bit divisor then the quotient will be in the right half of the *MQ* register and the remainder in the left half. Firstly, dividend is placed in the *MQ* register and the divisor in the *D* register. Then, the divisor subtracted from the dividend. **Please understand here that-**

(*a*) The result is considered **negative** if a borrow is required.

(*b*) The result is considered **positive** is no borrow is required.

(*c*) **If this result is positive,** the quotient will be greater than four bits, hence an error occurs. We cannot complete the division with those registers.

(*d*) **If the result is negative,** then the quotient will be four or less bits. Now, it is smaller to be contained in the right half of the *MQ* register.

(*e*) *MQ* register is then shifted left by 1 bit.

(*f*) The bit shifted out (0 or 1) is NOT lost, actually.

(*g*) It is stored in *CF* (carry flag) and is used for the subtraction following the left shift.

(*h*) If the result of subtraction is positive, a 1 is added to the LSB of *MQ* register (where quotient is formed).

(*i*) If it is negative, the divisor is added to the *MQ* and *MQ* is shifted left one bit. This puts a 0 in this bit of the quotient.

(*j*) The process is continued till *MQ* register has been shifted left four bits i.e., number of bits in *D*-register.

(*k*) The remainder is in the left half of the *MQ* register and the quotient in the right half.

We need three registers for division and multiplication (discussed earlier) both. The three registers used here are –

(*a*) An *N*-bit register to store the divisor.

(*b*) An (N + 1) bit accumulator in which the dividend is originally stored and from which the divisor is subtracted in each step, and

(*c*) An *N*-bit quotient register.

Please note that the accumulator and the *MQ* register may be again physically joined so that their contents can be shifted together.

We are in a position to solve an example now.

Q. 1. Divide (*a*) 1010 by 10 (using paper method).

(*b*) 1011 by 11 (using computer method).

Ans. 1010 by 10

```
10 |1010 |101
     10
   × 10
      10
      ××
```

So, Answer = 101

(*b*)

Initial state		
ACC	MQ	MD
0 0 0 0 0	1 0 1 1	0 0 1 1
COUNT = 1		
	ACC	
Shift-Left	0 0 0 0 1	
ACC; = ACC – MD	1 1 1 0 1	MQ
ACC [1] = 1	1 1 1 1 0	0 1 1 0
Set MQ [N] = 0	0 0 0 1 1	0 1 1 0
Restore	0 0 0 0 1	0 1 1 0

COUNT = 2	ACC	MQ
		1 1 0 0
Shift-Left	0 0 0 1 0	
ACC: = ACC – MD	1 1 1 0 1	
ACC [1] = 1	1 1 1 1 1	
Set MQ [N] = 0	0 0 0 1 1	1 1 0 0
Restore	0 0 0 1 0	1 1 0 0

COUNT = 3		MQ
	ACC	
Shift-Left	0 0 1 0 1	1 0 0 0
ACC: = ACC – MD	1 1 1 0 1	
ACC [1] = 0	0 0 0 1 0	
Set MQ [N] = 1	0 0 1 0 1	1 0 0 1

COUNT = 4		
	ACC	MQ
Shift-Left	0 0 1 0 1	0 0 1 0
ACC; ACC – MD	1 1 1 0 1	
ACC [1] = 0	0 0 0 1 0	
Set MQ [N] = 1	0 0 0 1 0	0 0 1 1
	Remainder	Quotient

9.5 SIGNED AND UNSIGNED BINARY NUMBERS

Both positive and negative numbers are handled by digital systems. In the decimal number system,

(*a*) '+' indicates positive numbers eg +80, +95 etc.

(*b*) '–' indicates negative numbers eg. –80, –95 etc.

But in a binary system, we cannot use + ve and – ve signs as above. Instead we use MSB of these numbers.

(*a*) MSB = 1 ; shows negative numbers.

(*b*) MSB = 0; shows positive numbers.

∴ +13 = 01101 (+ve no.)

and –13 = 11101 (–ve no.)

Such numbers having MSB and 0 or 1, sign bit are called as signed binary numbers and their representation is known as signed-magnitude representation.

Digital systems also handle binary numbers which are assumed to be positive and thus do not have the MSB's sign bit. Such numbers are known as **unsigned numbers.**

For eg. $(11101)_2$ is –13 (signed binary)

And 29 (unsigned binary)

Please note that the negative numbers are a particular problem with binary numbers. So, there are 3 types of common numbering systems used –

Type	Meaning	Range
Unsigned	Binary numbers can have only +ve values.	0 to 255
Signed	MSB of binary number is used to indicate +ve or –ve no.	–127 to +127
2s complement	–ve nos. are represented by complementing the binary number and then adding 1 to it	–128 to +127

In digital computers, complements are used for simplifying logical manipulations and for subtractions there are 2 methods for each *r*-base system –

(*a*) *r*'*s* complement.

b) (*r* – 1)'*s* complement.

The value of *r* is referred to two types as the 2*s* complement and 1*s* complement for binary numbers and 10*s* and 9*s* complement for decimal numbers.

The 2*s* (or 1*s*) complement system for representing signed numbers is as follows –

1. If the number is +ve, the magnitude represented in its true binary form and a sign bit 0 is placed in front of the MSB.
2. If the number is –ve, the magnitude is represented in its 2*s* (or 1*s*) complement form and a sign bit 1 is placed in front of the MSB.

In general, to represent the numbers in sign 2*s* complement form, determine the 2*s* or 1*s* complement of the magnitude of the number and then attach the sign bit. Also note that the

2*s* complement operation on a signed number will change a positive number to a negative number and vice versa.

It implies that the conversion of complement to binary is the same as the process to convert true binary to complement.

Let us take some decimal numbers and convert them to

(*a*) Signed 2*s* complement form.

(*b*) Signed 1*s* complement form.

(*c*) Signed magnitude form.

Decimal	2*s* complement form (signed)	1*s* complement form (signed)	Sign magnitude form
+2	0010	0010	0010
+1	0001	0001	0001
+0	0000	0000	0000
–0	–	1111	1000
–1	1111	1110	1001
–2	1110	1101	1010

How to find 1*s* and 2*s* complement?

1*s* complement – "Replace each 1 by 0 and 0 by 1 in a binary number".

2*s* complement – "Find 1***s*** complement of the binary number and add 1 to it".

In above table, the +ve numbers in all three representations have a 0 in the leftmost position. Signed 2*s* complement representation has only one representation for 0, which is always positive. **Also note that all negative numbers have a 1 in the left most bit position.** Also observe that whenever a signed number has a 1 in the sign bit and all 0*s* for the magnitude bit then the decimal equivalent is -2^n where *n* is the number of bits in the magnitude. For eg. In above table, 1000 is –8.

Both binary number and its 1*s* complement are complementary to each other. If one of these numbers is +ve then the other number will be negative with the same magnitude and vice versa. For eg. $(0101)_2$ represents $(+5)_{10}$ whereas $(1010)_2$ represents $(-5)_{10}$ in 1*s* representation. For an *n*-bit number, the maximum +ve no. which can be represented in 1*s* complement representation is $-(2^{n-1}-1)$.

But 2*s* complement numbers have the following properties –

1. 2*s* complement of 0 is 0.
2. MSB is a sign bit, (1 = –ve no. and 0 = + ve no.)
3. A –ve no. is converted to its +ve no. by finding its 2*s* complements.
4. 2*s* complement of a number is the number itself.
5. For an *n*-bit number, the maximum +ve no. which can be represented in 2*s* complement form is (2^{n-1}) and the maximum –ve number is -2^{n-1}.
6. If the LSB of the number is 1, its 2*s* complement is obtained by changing each 0 to 1 and 1 to 0 except LSB.
7. If the LSB of the number is 0, its 2*s* complement is obtained by scanning the number from the LSB to MSB bit by bit and retaining the bits as they are up to and including the occurrence of the first 1 and complement all other bits.

Advantages of 2*s* complements form

Both addition and subtraction can be performed using 2*s* complement representation for signed numbers. Even subtraction is done by addition in this representation. *i.e.*,

$$A - B = A + 2s \text{ complement of } B$$
$$= A + (1s \text{ complement of } B + 1)$$

We consider 4 cases now.

Case I: When both numbers are positive.

```
Eg.    +5 = 0101   (in 2s form)
       +2 = 0010   (in 2s form)
       +7   0111
```

Reasons—

```
∵ +5 = 0101          and
Its 1s = 1010            +2 = 0010
           + 1       Its 1s = 1101
          1011                  +1
                              1110
```

Case II: When both numbers are negative.

```
Eg.    –5 = 1011
       –2 = 1110
       –7  11001
```

Carry generated above from MSB is discarded.

Case III: When one number is positive and its magnitude is larger than the negative number

```
Eg.    +5 = 0101
       –2 = 1110
       +3  10011
```

Carry generated from MSB is discarded.

Case IV: When one number is positive and its magnitude is smaller than the negative number

```
Eg     -5 = 1011
       +2 = 0010
       –3   1101
```

From these 4 cases, we observe that the add and subtract operations can be carried out by an adder circuit if the numbers are represented in their 2*s* complements form. So, no separate circuit is needed to perform subtractions.

Advantages of 1*s* complement form

1*s* complement of a number is obtained by simply complementing each bit of the number or by subtracting each bit of the number from 1. Actually, this complement value represents the negative of the original number. It is easier to implement this logic in hardware by simply inputting all bits through inverters.

Problem with 1*s* complement form

Problem occurs when we wish to represent zero. Both 00000000 and its 1*s* complement 11111111 represent zero. The $(00000000)_2$ is called as **positive zero** and the $(11111111)_2$ is called as a **negative zero.**

Now, let us discuss about 9*s* and 10*s* complement forms.

9*s* complement of a decimal number

Each digit of a decimal number is subtracted from 9. For eg.

9s complement of 80 is = 99

$$\begin{array}{r} 99 \\ -80 \\ \hline 19 \end{array}$$

i.e., 19

Similarly, 9*s* complement of 1234 is =

$$\begin{array}{r} 9999 \\ -1234 \\ \hline 8765 \end{array}$$

i.e., $(1234)_{10}$ = (8765) in 9*s* complement.

Please note that the given a number *N* in base *r* having *n*-digits, the (*r* – 1)'s complement of *N* is defined as $(r^n - 1) - N$, for decimal number, *r* = 10 and *r* – 1 = 9.

Hence, 9*s* complement of *N* is $(10^n - 1) - N$.

Now, 10^n represents a number that consists of a single 1 followed by *n* 0'*s*. $10^n - 1$ is a number represented by *n* 9'*s*.

For eg. If $n = 4$

i.e., $10^4 = 10{,}000$

And $10^4 - 1 = 9999$

It follows that the 9*s* complement of a decimal number is obtained by subtracting each digit from 9.

Also note that for binary numbers,

$r = 2$

And $r - 1 = 1$

So, 1*s* complement of *N* is $(2^n - 1) - N$.

Again, 2^n is represented by a binary number that consists of a 1 followed by *n* 0'*s*. $2^n - 1$ is a binary represented by *n* 1*s*.

However, when we subtract binary digits from 1, we can have

either $1 - 0 = 1$

or $1 - 1 = 0$

This causes the bit to change from 0 to 1 or from 1 to 0. Therefore, the 1*s* complement of a binary number is formed by changing 1*s* to 0*s* and vice versa.

10*s* complement of a decimal number

We just say that –

10*s* complement of a decimal number = 9*s* complement the number + 1

For eg. 10*s* complement of 80 is =

$$\begin{array}{r} 99 \\ -80 \\ \hline 19 \\ +1 \\ \hline 20 \end{array}$$

$$(80)_{10} = 20 \text{ (10s complement)}$$

The 10*s* complement of a decimal number represents its negative valve.

So, the *r's* complement of an *n*-digit number *N* in base *r* is defined as $r^n - N$ for *N* not equal to 0 and 0 for $N = 0$. On comparison with the $(r - 1)$'*s* complement we find that the *r's* complement is obtained by adding 1 to the $(r - 1)$'s complement.

As $$r^n - N = [(r^n - 1) - N] + 1$$

So, 10*s* complement of 1234 =

```
 9999
-1234
 8765 (9s)
   +1
 8766 (10s)
```

As 10^n is a number represented by a 1 followed by *n* 0's.

$10^n - N$, which is 10*s* complement of *N*, can be formed by leaving all least significant 0's unchanged, subtracting the first non-zero least significant digit from 10 and subtracting all higher significant digits from 9.

In a similar way, 2*s* complement can also be obtained by leaving all least significant 0*s* and the first 1 unchanged and replacing 1*s* with 0*s* and 0*s* with 1*s* in all other higher significant digits.

What if the numbers have radix point?

The method is – **If a number (*N*) has a radix point then that point should be removed temporarily in order to form its *r's* (or *r* – 1's) complement. Then the radix point is restored to the complemented number in the same relative position. Also note here that the complement of the complement restores the number to its original value.**

That is, *r's* complement of $N = r^n - N$

$$\text{It's complement} = r^n - (r^n - N)$$
$$= N$$
$$= \text{the original number.}$$

How to do subtraction with complements?

The subtraction of two *n*-digit unsigned numbers $(M - N)$ in base *r* is done as follows –

1. Add the minuend, *M* to the *r's* complement of the subtrahend, *N*. This performs –
$$M + (r^n - N) = M - N + r^n$$
2. If $M >= N$, the sum will produce an end carry, r^n, which is discarded. Left is the result $(M - N)$.
3. If $M < N$, the sum does not produce an end carry and is equal to $r^n - (N - M)$, which is the *r's* complement of $(N - M)$. To obtain the answer in a similar form, we take the *r's* complement of the sum and place a negative sign in front.

9.5.1. Octal Arithmetic

For this, we convert octal numbers to binary and then use the rules of binary arithmetic only. **Please note that octal subtraction can be performed using 1*s* complement or 2*s* complement method.**

We are in a position to solve some examples now.

Q. 1. Find the decimal equivalents of the following binary signed numbers -

(*a*) 10110 **(*b*) 001000?**

Ans. (*a*) 10110

Sign bit MSB is 1. It means that the number is –ve.

It's magnitude = 0110

= $(12)_{10}$

Hence, $(10110)_2 = (-12)_{10}$

(*b*) 001000

Sign bit (MSB) is 0. It means that the number is positive.

It's magnitude = 01000 = 8

Hence, $(001000)_2 = +8$

Q. 2. Represent the following in 1*s* complement form–

(*a*) +8 and –8 **(*b*) +15 and –15 ?**

Ans. (*a*) $(+8)_{10} = (01000)_2$

$(-8)_{10} = (10111)_2$

(*b*) $(+15)_{10} = (01111)_2$

$(-15)_{10} = (10000)_2$

Q. 3. Represent $(-17)_{10}$ in the following forms–

(*a*) Sign magnitude

(*b*) One's complement

(*c*) Two's complement form.

Ans. The minimum number of bits required to represent $(+17)_{10}$ in signed number format is six.

$(+17)_{10} = (010001)_2$

Hence, $(-17)_{10}$ is represented as –

(*a*) $(110001)_2$ for part – *a*

(*b*) $(101110)_2$ for part – *b*.

(*c*) $(101111)_2$ for part – *c*.

Q. 4. Perform as indicated using 1s complement logic-

(*a*) 25 – 14 **(*b*) –25 + 14**

(*c*) –25 – 14 **(*d*) +25 + 14**

(*e*) +25 + (–25) ?

Ans. (*a*) (25 – 14) = ?

Now, 25 = 00011001

–14 = 11110001 (1*s* complement form)

+11 100001010

+ 1 (bring down carry and add)

Result = 00001011

So, MSB is a 0. Hence, result is +ve i.e., $(+11)_{10}$.

(*b*) +14 = 00001110

−25 = 11100110 (1*s* form)

11110100 (No carry)

As MSB = 1

No. is −ve and 1*s* complement of result is (11110100) = 00001011

= $(-11)_{10}$

(*c*) −25 = 11100110 (1*s* form)

−14 = 11110001 (1*s* form)

−39 111010111

+1

11011000

As MSB = 1, so the result is −ve

It's 1s complement = ?

i.e. (11011000) = 00100111 = $(-39)_{10}$

(*d*) +25 = 00011001 (1*s* form)

+14 = 00001110 (1*s* form)

+39 = 00100111

As MSB = 0 and carry is not there, so the result is +ve and is $(00100111)_2 = (+39)_{10}$

(*e*) +25 = 00011001

−25 = 11100110 (1*s* form)

11111111

As MSB = 1 and carry is not there, so the result is 1*s* complement of $(11111111)_2$ = 00000000 (i.e., 0)

NOTE: Rule followed is - "In 1*s* complement subtraction, we add the 1*s* complement of the subtrahend to the minuend. If there is a carry then bring the carry around and add it to the LSB. If the MSB (sign bit) is a 0, then the result is +ve and is our final result. Else if the MSB is a 1, and carry is there or no carry is there then the result is −ve and we take its 1*s* complement to get the magnitude in binary".

Q. 5. Perform as indicated using 2*s* complement logic-

(*a*) −75 to + 26 (addition)

(*b*) 14 from 46 (subtraction).

Ans. (*a*) Now +75 = $(01001011)_2$ and (−75) = $(10110101)_2$ (in 2*s* form)

So, +26 = 00011010

−75 = +10110101 (2*s* form of −75)

–49 11001111

As MSB = 1 and no carry is generated. So the result is –ve.

So, 2*s* complement of result = 2*s* complement of (11001111) = $(00110001)_2$ = 49

Hence the final result = –49.

(*c*) As +14 = 00001110

–14 = 11110010 (2*s* form)

So, +46 = 00101110

–14 = 11110010 (2*s* form)

+32 100100000

So, carry = 1; ignore it.

MSB = 0, so the result is +ve.

Hence, result = 00100000 = +32

Q. 6. Given two binary numbers–

A **= 1010100**

and ***B*** **= 1000011. Perform the following–**

(*a*) ***A–B***

(b) ***B–A*** **using both 1*s* and 2*s* complement forms?**

Ans. Case 1: Using 1*s* complement arithmetic

(*a*) *A* = 1010100

1*s* of *B* = 0111100

So, 1010100

+ 0111100

10010000

+1 (carry is added to LSB)

0010001

So, *A–B* = $(0010001)_2$

(*b*) *B–A* = ?

As *B* = 1000011

And 1*s* of *A* = 0101011

So, 1000011

+ 0101011

1101110

Hence, no end-around carry is generated.

Therefore, (*B–A*) = –(1*s* complement of 1101110)

= –0010001

Case 2: Using 2*s* complement arithmetic

(*a*) *A* – *B* **(*b*) *B* – *A***

Ans. (*a*) $A = 1010100$

$B = 1000011$

So, 2*s* complement of B = (1*s* of B + 1)

So, 1*s* of B = 0111100

$$\begin{array}{r} 0111100 \\ +1 \\ \hline 0111101 \end{array}$$

So, A = 1010100

$$\begin{array}{r} 1010100 \\ +0111101 \\ \hline 10010001 \end{array} = \text{SUM}$$

As $A > B$, SO WE DISCARD END CARRY.

Hence, $A - B = (0010001)_2$

(*c*) $B = 1000011$

$A = 1010100$

So, 2*s* of A = (1*s* of A + 1)

And 1*s* of A = 0101011

$$\begin{array}{r} 0101011 \\ +1 \\ \hline 010110 \end{array}$$

So, $B - A = B$ + 2*s* of A

$$\begin{array}{r} = 1000011 \\ +0101100 \\ \hline 1101111 \end{array}$$

As $A < B$ and there is no end carry.

So, $(B - A)$ = – (2*s* complement of Result)

= – 0010001

9.6 POSITIVE NUMBERS MULTIPLICATION ALGORITHM

Multiplication of two binary numbers may be–

(*a*) Unsigned (i.e. positive) multiplication.

(*b*) Signed (i.e. negative) multiplication.

In this section, we discuss unsigned (*i.e.*, positive) multiplication. In next section, we discuss about signed binary multiplication.

Unsigned (or positive) multiplication circuitry is shown in Fig. 9.2.

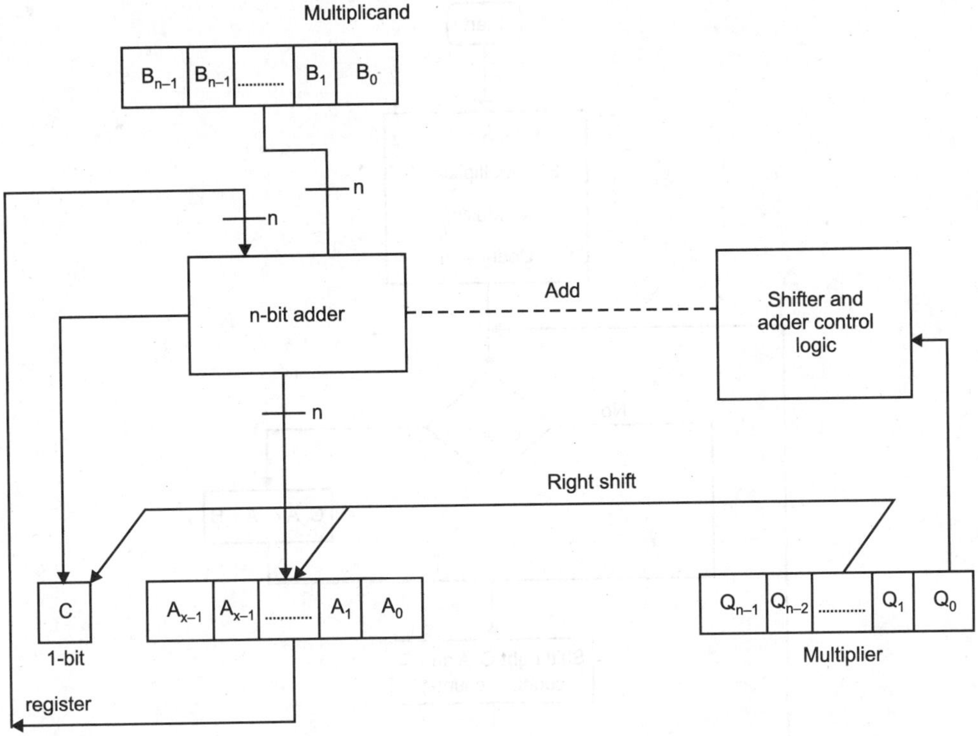

Fig. 9.2. Hardware circuitry for positive (unsigned) binary multiplication

In Fig. 9.2, we have used 2 notations–

(*a*) —/—→

This shows *n*-bit bus.

(*b*) ------------→ dotted lines showing control signals.

Working: The working steps are very simple and are as follows –

Step 1: Bit 0 of multiplier operand (*i.e.*, Q_0 bit of *Q*-register in Fig. 9.2) is checked.

Step 2: **If bit Q_0** (*i.e.*, bit 0) **is one(1)** then we add multiplicand and partial product and all bits of *C*, *A* and *Q* register are shifted to the right one bit, so that the *C*-bit goes into A_{n-1}, A_0 goes into Q_{n-1} and Q_0 is lost.

Step 3: If bit Q_0 (i.e. bit 0) is zero then no addition is performed. Only shift operation is performed.

Step 4: Repeat steps (1) through 3, *n*-times to get the desired result in *A* and *Q* registers. Let us draw its flowchart now. It is shown in Fig. 9.3

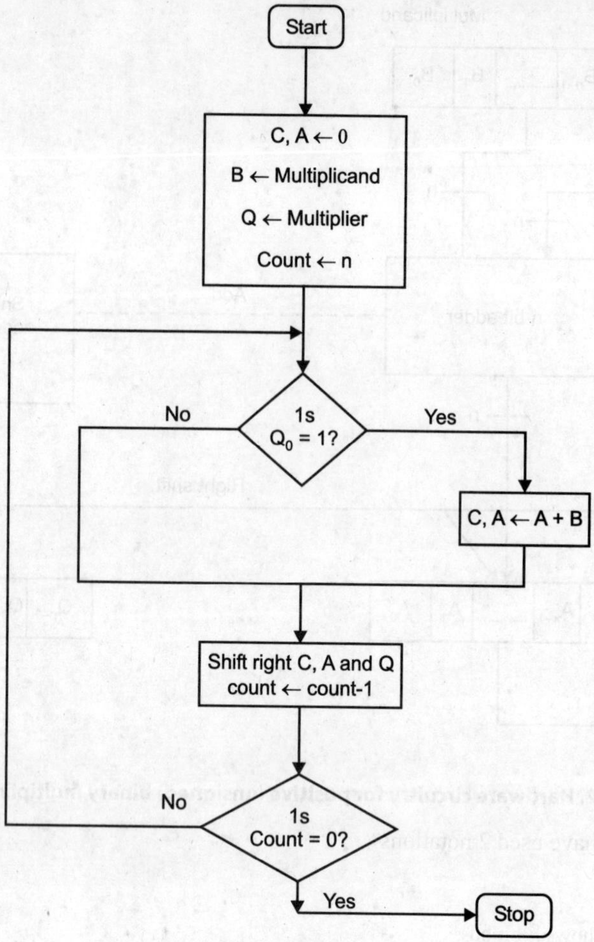

Fig. 9.3

Let us consider an example to stimulate this flowchart now.

Say, Multiplicand (B-reg) = 1101

And Multiplier (Q-reg) = 1011

∴

C	A	Q	
0	0000	1011	
0	1101	1011	Add, Shift } 1st cycle
1	0011	1101	Add, Shift } 2nd cycle
0	1001	1110	
0	1001	1110	

0	0100	1111	Add Shift	3rd cycle
1	0001	1111		
0	1000	1111	Add Shift	4th cycle

Final resultant product

9.7 2s COMPLEMENT SIGNED MULTIPLICATION

We have seen in the previous sections that the multiplication of two numbers in signed magnitude form is easy. But if the numbers are in 2*s* complement form then the earlier method cannot be used. The number may be converted to signed magnitude form firstly. Then the product may be reconverted into 2*s* complement form. This is time consuming. However, Booth designed an algorithm for **signed number multiplication which is popularly known as Booth's algorithm.** It works well for both negative and positive multiplier. It treats both positive and negative multipliers uniformly.

As per this algorithm, we can reduce the number of operations required for multiplication by representing multiplier as a difference between two numbers. **This algorithm handles both positive and negative 2*s* complement operands without any need of result correction.** When the multiplier has a stream of 1*s*, the number of additions required is minimized. This speeds up multiplication process. **Please understand that this speeds up the multiplication process as the time reduction depends on the bit pattern in the multiplier.**

Actually, Booth's algorithm involves **recoding of the multiplier,** firstly. In recoding format, each bit in the multiplier can take any of the three values : 0, 1 and –1.

For example, the multiplier

001110	(14)	can be represented as -	
010000	(16)	=	2^4
000010	(2)	=	2^1
001110	(14)		

Also understand that the product can be computed by adding 2^4 times the multiplicand to the 2*s* complement of 2^1 times the multiplicand, as shown above. In standard multiplication algorithm, three additions are required but in above algorithm, one addition and one subtraction can give the result.

How to recode the multiplier now?

The rule is : "–1 times the shifted multiplicand is selected when moving from 0 to 1 , +1 times the shifted multiplicand is selected when moving from 1 to 0 and 0 times the shifted multiplicand is selected for none of the above case, as the multiplier is scanned from right to left".

But please remember the following points:

1. We assume an implied 0 to the right of the multiplier LSB.
2. When we add a negative multiplicand, we must extend the sign bit value of the multiplicand to the left as far as the product will extend.
3. Booth's algorithm generates 2*n*, bit product.

We are in a position to solve some problems now.

EXAMPLE 9.1: Convert the following numbers into Booth's recoded format:

(*a*) 101100 **(*b*) 011001** **(*c*) 11011**

(*d*) 001100 **(*e*) 101100**

SOLUTION:

Implied zero

(*a*) 1 0 1 1 0 0 0 (Multiplier)

←

Using the rule given above, we recode it as follows:

–1 +1 0 – 1 0 0 (move from right to left and use rule stated above)

Implied zero

(*b*) 0 1 1 0 0 1 0 (Multiplier

←

+1 0 –1 0 +1 –1 (Move from right to left and use rule stated above)

Implied zero

(*c*) 1 1 0 1 1 0 (Multiplier)

←

0 –1 1 0 –1 (Using rules)

Implied zero

(*d*) 0 0 1 1 0 0 0 (Multiplier)

←

0 +1 0 –1 0 0 (Using rules)

Implied zero

(*e*) 1 0 1 1 0 0 0 (Multiplier)

←

–1 +1 0 –1 0 0 (Using rules)

EXAMPLE 9.2: Perform the following multiplications using Booth's method -

(*a*) 010011 and 001100

(*b*) 01110 and 11011

(*c*) 110011 and 101100?

Ans.

(*a*) 010011 (Multiplicand)

001100 (Multiplier)

Firstly we recode the multiplier–

i.e. 0 0 1 1 0 0 recoded as

0 0 1 1 0 0 0 Implied Zero

←

0 +1 0 –1 0 0

Now, we multiply

						0	1	0	0	1	1	
					×	0	+1	0	–1	0	0	
0	0	0	0	0	0	0	0	0	0	0	0	
0	0	0	0	0	0	0	0	0	0	0	×	2*s* complement of multiplicand
1	1	1	1	1	0	1	1	0	1	×	×	
0	0	0	0	0	0	0	0	0	×	×	×	
0	0	0	1	0	0	1	1	×	×	×	×	
0	0	0	0	0	0	0	×	×	×	×	×	
0	0	0	0	1	1	1	0	0	1	0	0	

Please note in this example, whenever the multiplicand is multiplied by –1, its 2*s* complement is taken as a partial result. Also remember that the same algorithm can be used for negative multiplier also.

(*b*) 0 1 1 1 0 (+14) Multiplicand

1 1 0 1 1 (–5) Multiplier

Firstly, we recode the multiplier –

1 1 0 1 1 0 ← Implied Zero

←

0 –1 1 0 –1 (Recoded multiplier)

Now, we multiply –

					0	1	1	1	0	
				×	0	–1	+1	0	–1	
1	1	1	1	1	1	0	0	1	0	2*s* complement of multiplicand
0	0	0	0	0	0	0	0	0	×	
0	0	0	0	1	1	1	0	×	×	
1	1	1	0	0	1	0	×	×	×	
0	0	0	0	0	0	×	×	×	×	
1	1	1	0	1	1	1	0	1	0	(≡ –70)

We can use this method even if our both multiplicand and multiplier are negative.

(*c*) 1 0 1 1 0 0 (Multiplier given)

–1 +1 0 –1 0 0 (Recoded Multiplier)

∴ We perform multiplication now

						1	1	0	0	1	1	(Multiplicand)
					×	−1	+1	0	−1	0	0	Recoded multiplier)
0	0	0	0	0	0	0	0	0	0	0	0	
0	0	0	0	0	0	0	0	0	0	0	×	
0	0	0	0	0	0	1	1	0	1	×	×	2s complement of multiplicand
0	0	0	0	0	0	0	0	0	×	×	×	
1	1	1	1	0	0	1	1	×	×	×	×	
0	0	0	1	1	0	1	×	×	×	×	×	
0	0	0	1	0	0	0	0	0	1	0	0	(≡ 260)

$$\text{Multiplicand} = (110011)_2 = (-13)$$
$$\text{\& Multiplier} = (101100)_2 = (-20)$$

And $(-13 \times -20) = 260$ which is easily obtained above using Booth's method.

9.7.1. Hardware Implementation

The Booth's algorithm can be implemented as shown in the Fig. 9.4. The circuit is similar to circuit for positive number multiplication. It consists of n-bit adder, shift, add subtract control logic and four registers, A, B, Q and Q_{-1}. As shown in Fig. 9.4 multiplier and multiplicand are loaded into register Q and register B respectively, and register A and Q_{-1} are initially set to 0.

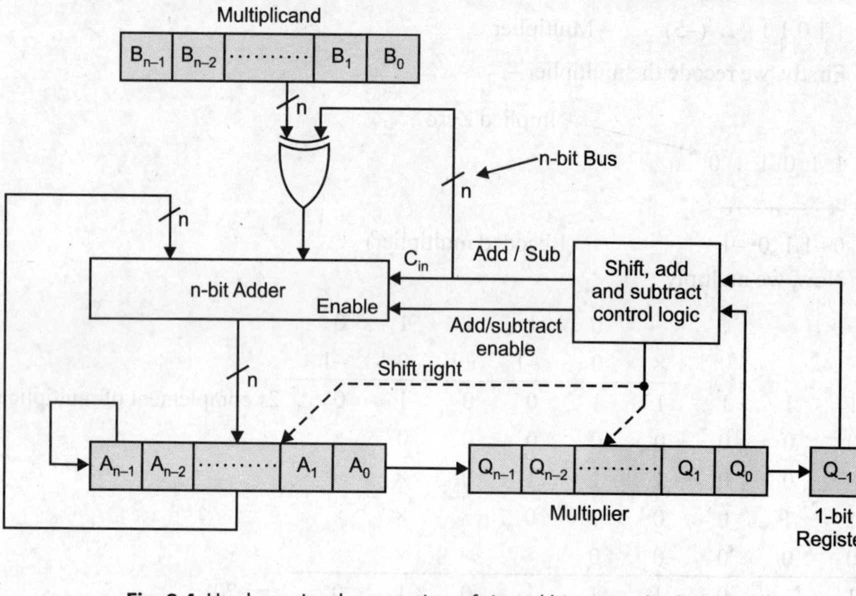

Fig. 9.4. Hardware implementation of signed binary multiplication

(Initial settings: $A \leftarrow 0$ and $Q_{-1} = 0$)

The n-bit adder performs addition of two inputs. One input is A register and other input is multiplicand.

(*a*) In case of addition, Add' / Sub line is 0, therefore $C_{in} = 0$ and multiplicand is directly applied as a second input to the n-bit adder.

(*b*) In case of subtraction, Add'/ Sub line is 1, therefore $C_{in} = 1$ and multiplicand is complemented and then applied to the *n*-bit adder. As a result, the 2's complement of multiplicand is added in the *A* register.

The shift, add and subtract control logic scans bits Q_0 and Q_{-1} one at a time and generates the control signals as shown in the table. If the two bits are same (1 –1 or 0 –0), then all of the bits of the *A*, *Q* and Q_{-1} registers are shifted to right 1 bit without addition or subtraction (Add / Subtract Enable = 0). If the two bits differ, then the multiplicand (*B* register) is added to or subtracted from the *A* register depending on the status of bits. If bits are $Q_0 = 0$ and $Q_{-1} = 1$ then multiplicand is added and if bits are $Q_0 = 1$ and $Q_{-1} = 0$ then multiplicand is subtracted. After addition or subtraction right shift occurs such that the leftmost bit of $A(A_{n-1})$ is not only shifted into A_{n-2} but also remains in A_{n-1}. **This is required to preserve the sign of the number in *A* and *Q*. It is known as an arithmetic shift, since it preserves the sign bit.**

Table 9.3: Truth table for shift, add and subtract control logic

Q_0	Q_{-1}	Add'/sub	Add/Subtract Enable	Shift
0	0	*X*	0	1
0	1	0	1	1
1	0	1	1	1
1	1	*X*	0	1

The sequence of events in Booth's algorithm can be explained with the help of flow chart shown in Fig. 9.5

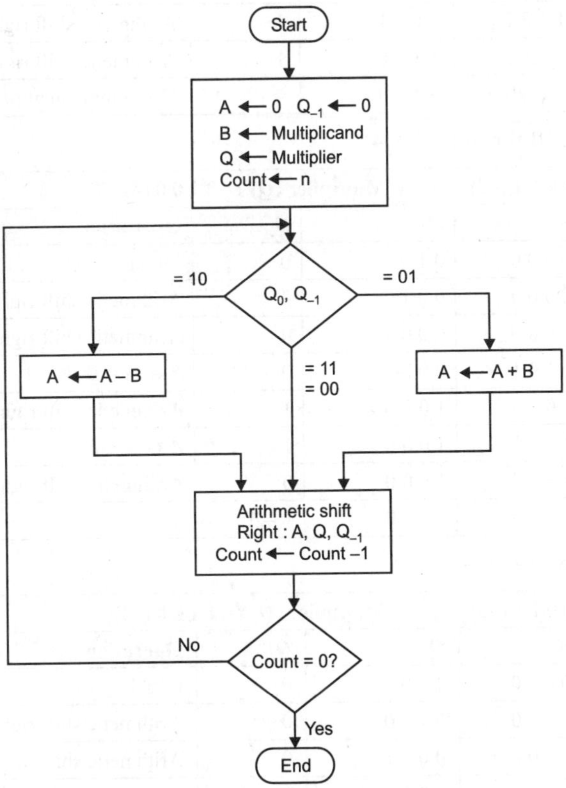

Fig. 9.5. Booth's algorithm for signed multiplication

Let us see the multiplication of 4 bit numbers, 5 and 4 with all possible combinations

Case 1: Both Positive (5 × 4)

Multiplicand (B) ← 0 1 0 1 (5)		**Multiplier (Q) ← 0 1 0 0 (4)**		
Steps	***A***	***Q***	Q_{-1}	**Operation**
	0000	0100	0	Initial
Step 1:	0000	0010	0	Arithmetic Shift Right
Step 2:	0000	0001	0	Arithmetic Shift Right
Step 3:	1011	0001	0	$A \leftarrow A - B$
	1101	1000	1	Arithmetic Shift Right
Step 4:	0010	1000	1	$A \leftarrow A + B$
	0001	0100	0	Arithmetic Shift Right
Result	0001	0100	= +20	

Case 2: Negative Multiplier (5 × –4)

Multiplicand (B) ← 0 1 0 1 (5)		**Multiplier (Q) ← 1 1 0 0 (–4)**		
Steps	***A***	***Q***	Q_{-1}	**Operation**
	0 0 0 0	1 1 0 0	0	Initial
Step 1:	0 0 0 0	0 1 1 0	0	Arithmetic shift right
Step 2:	0 0 0 0	0 0 1 1	0	Arithmetic shift right
Step 3:	1 0 1 1	0 0 1 1	0	$A \leftarrow A - B$
	1 1 0 1	1 0 0 1	1	Arithmetic shift right
Step 4:	1 1 1 0	1 1 0 0	1	Arithmetic shift right
Result	1 1 1 0	1 1 0 0	= –20	(2's complement of 20)

Case 3: Negative Multiplicand (–5 × 4)

Multiplicand (B) ← 1 0 1 1 (–5)		**Multiplier (Q) ← 0 1 0 0 (4)**		
Steps	***A***	***Q***	Q_{-1}	**Operation**
	0 0 0 0	0 1 0 0	0	Initial
Step 1	0 0 0 0	0 0 1 0	0	Arithmetic shift right
Step 2:	0 0 0 0	0 0 0 1	0	Arithmetic shift right
Step 3:	0 1 0 1	0 0 0 1	0	$A \leftarrow A - B$
	0 0 1 0	1 0 0 0	1	Arithmetic shift right
Step 4:	1 1 0 1	1 0 0 0	1	$A \leftarrow A + B$
	1 1 1 0	1 1 0 0	0	Arithmetic shift right
Result	1 1 1 0	1 1 0 0	= –20	

Case 4: Both Negative (–5 × –4)

Multiplicand (B) ← 1 0 1 1 (–5)		**Multiplier (Q) ← 1 1 0 0 (–4)**		
Steps	***A***	***Q***	Q_{-1}	**Operation**
	0 0 0 0	1 1 0 0	0	Initial
Step 1	0 0 0 0	0 1 1 0	0	Arithmetic shift right
Step 2:	0 0 0 0	0 0 1 1	0	Arithmetic shift right
Step 3:	0 1 0 1	0 0 1 1	0	$A \leftarrow A - B$

Multiplicand (B) ← 1 0 1 1 (–5)		Multiplier (Q) ← 1 1 0 0 (–4)		
Steps	A	Q	Q_{-1}	**Operation**
	0 0 1 0	1 0 0 1	1	Arithmetic shift right
Step 4:	0 0 0 1	0 1 0 0	1	Arithmetic shift right
Result	0 0 0 1	0 1 0 0	= +20	

9.7.2. Modified Booth's Algorithm

To speed up the multiplication process in the Booth's algorithm a technique called **bit pair recoding** is used. **It is also called Modified Booth's algorithm.** It halves the maximum number of summands. In this technique, the Booth-recorded multiplier bits are grouped in pairs. Then each pair is represented by its equivalent single bit multiplier reducing total number of multiplier bits to half.

For example, pair (+1 –1) is equivalent to the pair (0 + 1). This means that instead of adding –1 times multiplicand at shifted position *i* to +1 times the multiplicand at position *i* + 1, the same result is obtained by adding +1 times multiplicand at position *i*.

Similarly, (+1 0) is equivalent to (0 + 2), (–1 + 1) is equivalent to (0 – 1) and so on. **Please note that by replacing pairs with their equivalents we can get bit pair recorded multiplier. Also note that instead of deriving bit pair recorded multiplier from Booth recorded multiplier, we can directly derive it from original multiplier.** The following table shows how bit pair recording of multiplier can be directly derived:-

Multiplier bit pair		Multiplier bit on right	Bit pair recorded multiplier bit at position *i*
$i+1$	i	$i-1$	
0	0	0	0
0	0	1	+1
0	1	0	+1
0	1	1	+2
1	0	0	-2
1	0	1	-1
1	1	0	-1
1	1	1	0

We are in a position to solve some examples now.

EXAMPLE 9.1: Find the bit pair code for multiplier – $(11010)_2$

SOLUTION: Using table given above, we can derive the bit pair code as follows:

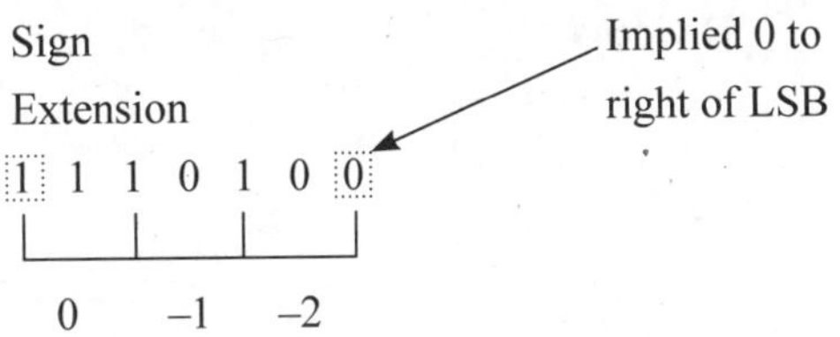

EXAMPLE 9.2: You are given two signed 2s complement numbers. Multiply them using bit pair recoding

X = **110101** **(Multiplicand)**

& Y = **011011** **(Multiplier)**

SOLUTION: Given:

X = 110101 (–11) (Multiplicand)

Y = 011011 (+27) (Multiplier)

We need to find the bit pair code for multiplier, Y, firstly –

```
Sign                          Implied 0 to
Extension                     right of LSB
0  1  1  0  1  1  0
+2    –1    –1
```

∴ We multiply X and Y now:

```
            1 1 0 1 0 1
            +2  –1  –1
     000000001011   <------- 2s complement of multiplicand
     0000001011XX   <------- 2s complement of multiplicand
     11101010XXXX   <------- multiplicand * (+2)
     111011010111 (= –297)
```

9.8 DIVISION ALGORITHMS

Let us see how 2 binary numbers are divided-

Rule: "The bits of the dividend are examined from left to right until the set of bits examined represents a number greater or equal to the divisor. Till this condition occurs, 0*s* are placed in the quotient from left to right. When the condition is satisfied, a 1 is placed in the quotient and the divisor is subtracted from the partial dividend. This result is known as the partial remainder. Then the division process follows repetition of steps. In each repetition cycle, additional bits from the dividend are brought down to the partial remainder until the result is greater than or equal to the divisor and the divisor is subtracted from the result to produce a new partial remainder. This process continues till all bits of the dividend are brought down and the result is still less than the divisor".

Let us take an example to understand this:

```
     1100 | 10101001 | 1110  <------ Quotient
            1100
Divisor     10010              Dividend
             1100
            01100
             1100
            00001  (Remainder)
```

Please note the following points here

1. Division is more complex than multiplication.

2. The division process is same, the difference is that the binary division's quotient bits are 0 and 1.

For e.g.
```
12 | 169 | 14
     12
     ---
      49
      48
      ---
       1   (same as above)
```

9.8.1. Restoring Division

Figure. 9.6 shows the hardware for implementation of division process described in the previous section. It consists of $(n + 1)$ bit binary adder, shift, add and subtract control logic and registers *A*, *B* and *Q*. As shown in the Fig. 9.6, divisor and dividend are loaded into register *B* and register *Q*, respectively. Register *A* is initially set to Zero. The division operation is then carried out. After the division is complete the *n*-bit quotient is in register *Q* and the remainder is in register *A*.

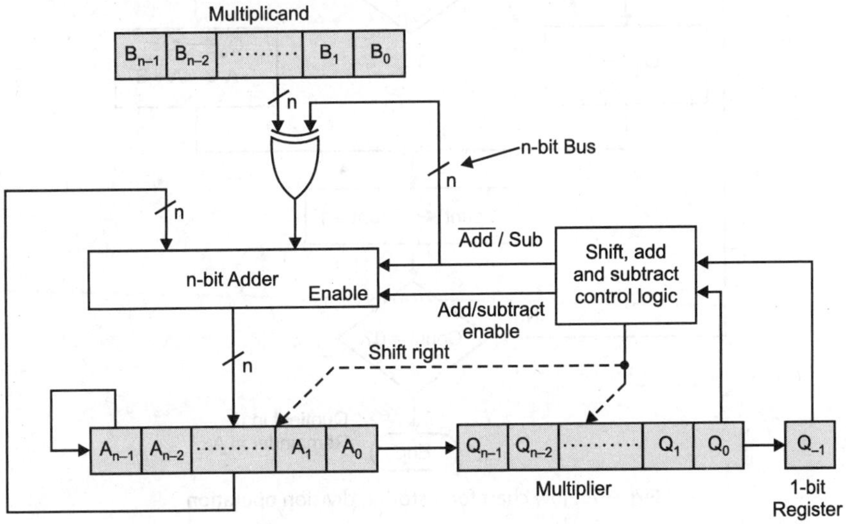

Fig. 9.6. Hardware to implement binary division

Division Operation Steps are as follows:

Step 1: Shift *A* and *Q* left one binary position.

Step 2: Subtract divisor from *A* and place answer back in *A* ($A \leftarrow A - B$).

Step 3: If the sign bit of *A* is 1, Set Q_0 to 0 and add divisor back to *A* (that is restore *A*); Otherwise, set Q_0 to 1.

Step 4: Repeat steps 1, 2 and 3 *n*-times.

Flow chart for division operation is as shown in Fig. 9.7

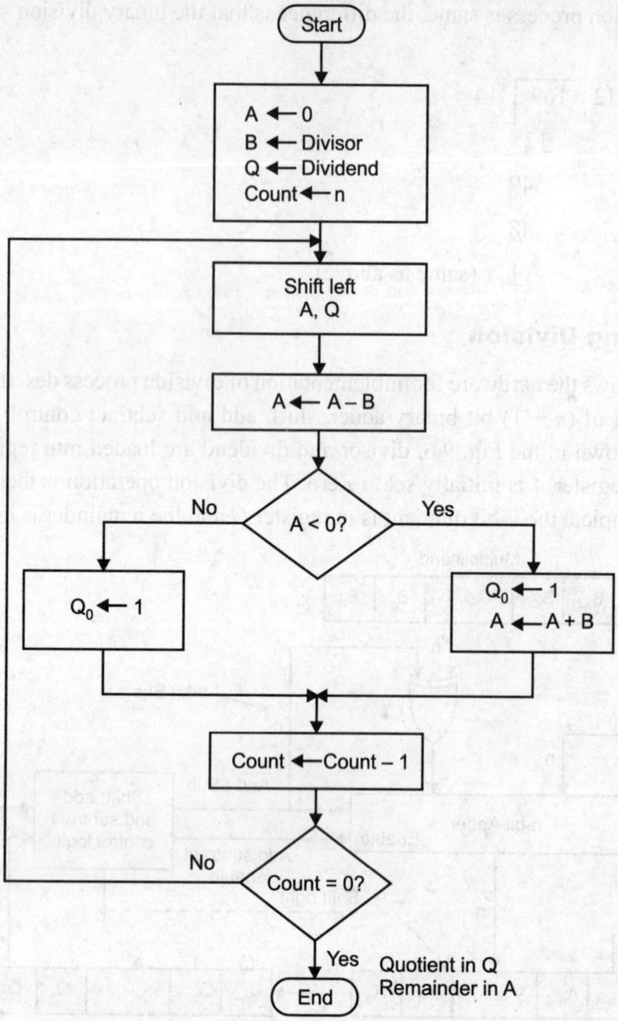

Fig. 9.7. Flow chart for restoring division operation

Let us solve an example now.

Say, we have a 4-bit dividend and a 2 bit divisor.

$$\text{Dividend} = 1\,0\,1\,0$$

$$\text{Divisor} = 0\,0\,1\,1$$

We follow the steps (1) through (4) given above and divide.

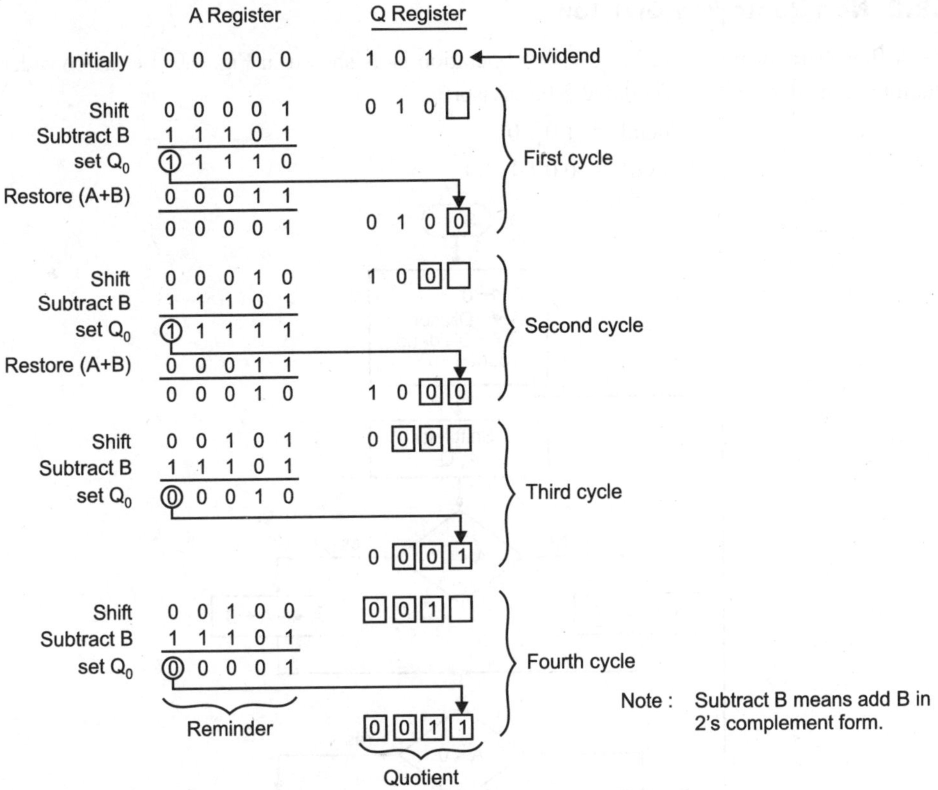

Fig. 9.8. A restoring division example

The division algorithm just discussed needs restoring register A after each unsuccessful subtraction. (Subtraction is said to be unsuccessful if the result is negative). **Therefore it is referred to as restoring division algorithm. This algorithm is improved, giving non restoring division algorithm.** Consider the sequence of operations that takes place after the subtraction operation in the restoring algorithm.

If A is positive	If A is negative
Shift left and subtract divisor → $2A - B$	Restore → $A + B$ Shift left and subtract divisor → $2(A + B) - B = 2A + B$

Observe the above operations, we can thus write following steps for non restoring algorithm:-

Step 1: If the sign of A is 0, shift A and Q left one bit position and subtract divisor from A; otherwise, shift A and Q left and add divisor to A.

If the sign of A is 0, set Q_0 to 1; otherwise, set Q_0 to 0.

Step 2: Repeat steps 1 and 2 for n times.

Step 3: If the sign of A is 1, add divisor to A.

Step 4: Step 3 is required to leave the proper positive remainder in A at the end of n cycles.

9.8.2. Non Restoring Division

A flowchart for non restoring division operation is as shown in Fig. 9.9. Let us consider an example. Consider 4-bit dividend and 2-bit divisor:

Dividend = 1 0 1 0

Divisor = 0 0 1 1

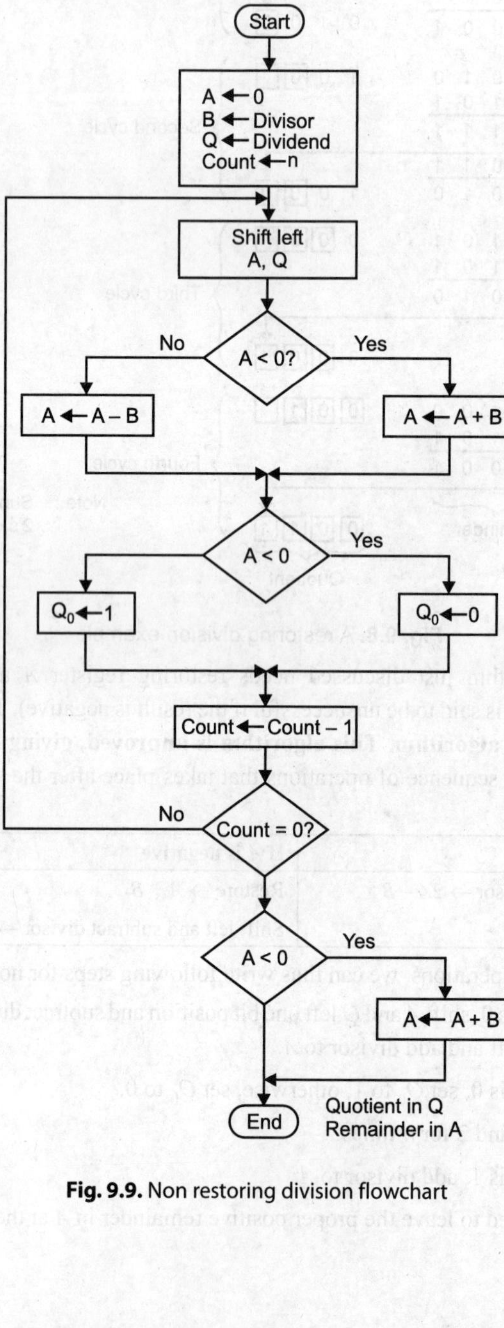

Fig. 9.9. Non restoring division flowchart

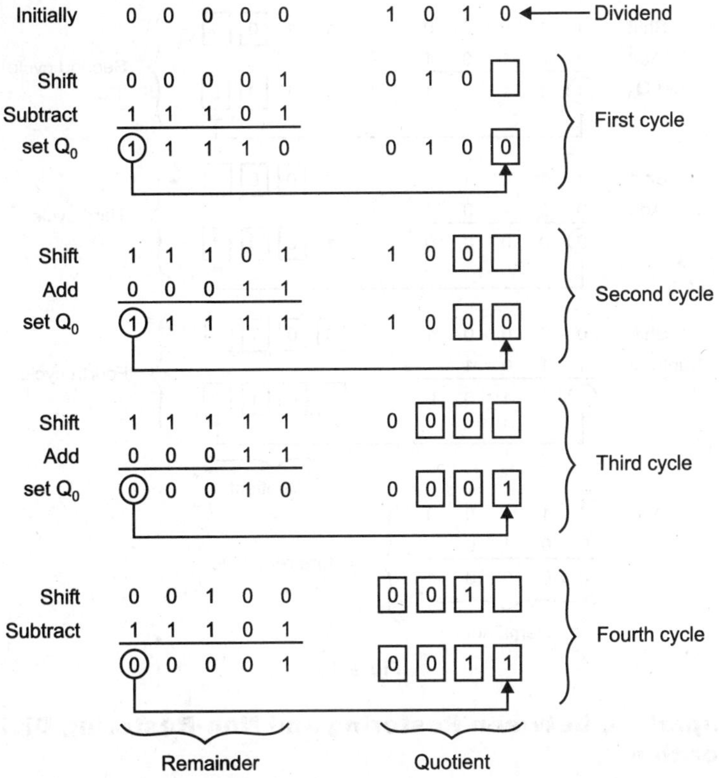

Fig. 9.10. A non restoring division example

In the above example, after 4 cycles, register A is positive and hence step 3 is not required. Let us see another example where we need step 3. Consider 4-bit dividend and 3 bit divisor:

$$\text{Dividend} = 1\,0\,1\,1$$
$$\text{Divisor} = 0\,1\,0\,1$$

Figure 9.10 shows steps involved in the non-restoring binary division.

The hardware shown in Fig. 9.11 can also be used to perform non restoring algorithm. There is no simple algorithm for signed division. In signed division, the operands are pre-processed to transform them into positive values. Then using one of the algorithms just discussed quotients and remainders are calculated. The quotients and remainders are then transformed to the correct signed values.

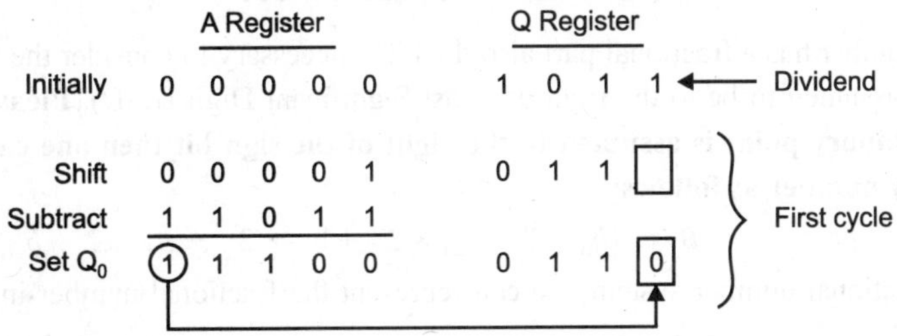

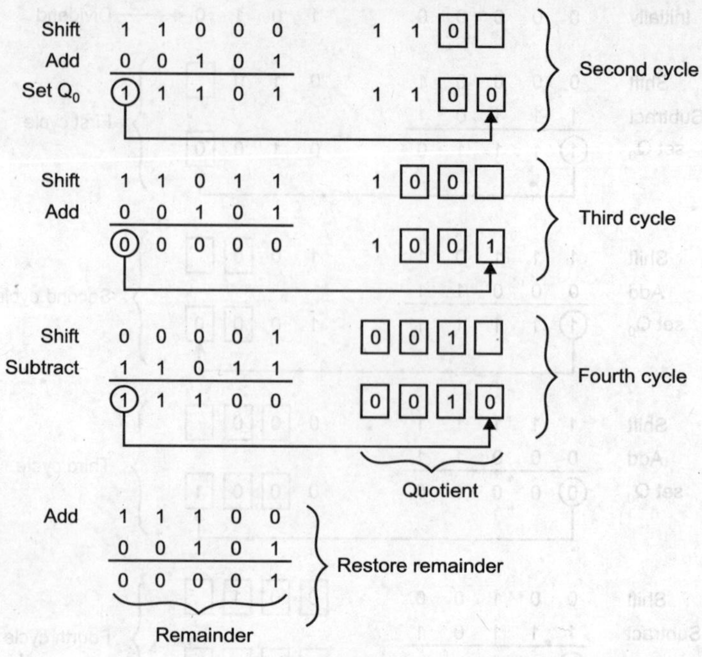

Fig. 9.11

9.8.3. Comparison between Restoring and Non-Restoring Division Algorithm

Let us tabulate the differences.

Restoring Division	Non-Restoring Division
1. This division process involves the restoring of register *A* if the result of subtraction is negative	1. There is no need of restoring of register *A*.
2. In each cycle, the content of register *A* is first shifted left and then divisor is subtracted from it.	2. In each cycle, the content of register *A* is first shifted left and then divisor is added or subtracted with the content of register *A* depending on the sign of *A*.
3. There is no need of restoring the remainder.	3. It needs restoring of remainder if it is negative.
4. It is a slower algorithm.	4. It is a faster algorithm.

9.9 FLOATING POINT IEEE REPRESENTATION

If a binary number has a fractional part also then it is necessary to consider the **decimal point** which is always assumed to be to the right of Least Significant Digit (LSD). **Please understand here that if the binary point is assumed to the right of the sign bit then one can represent a fractional binary number as follows:**

$$B = [b_0 \times 2^0 + b_{-1} \times 2^{-1} + b_{-2} \times 2^{-2} + \ldots\ldots + b_{-(n-1)} \times 2^{-(n-1)}]$$

In such a fractional number system, we can represent the fractional number in the following range:

$$2^{-(n-1)} \leq F \leq 1 - 2^{-(n-1)}$$

$\therefore$ For $n = 32$, range (value) is

$$2^{-31} \leq F \leq 1 - 2^{-31}$$

$$\leq F \leq (1 - 2.3283 \times 10^{-10})$$

Also understand that this range is NOT sufficient to represent fractional numbers. Our system must be able to store very large integers and very small fractions, both. The operation should be such that the position of the binary point is variable as is automatically adjusted as the computations proceed. **Thus, now the binary point is said to float and the numbers are called as floating point numbers.** So, the position of a binary point in floating point number is **variable** and thus the numbers must be represented in a specific representation i.e. **floating point representation.**

For eg. $(111101.1000110)_2$ can be represented in the floating point format as follows:

1. Right shift binary point to the right of the first bit.
2. Multiply the number of correct scaling factor (to get the same value).
3. The number is thus said to be in its normalized form.

Applying steps 1 through 3 we get:

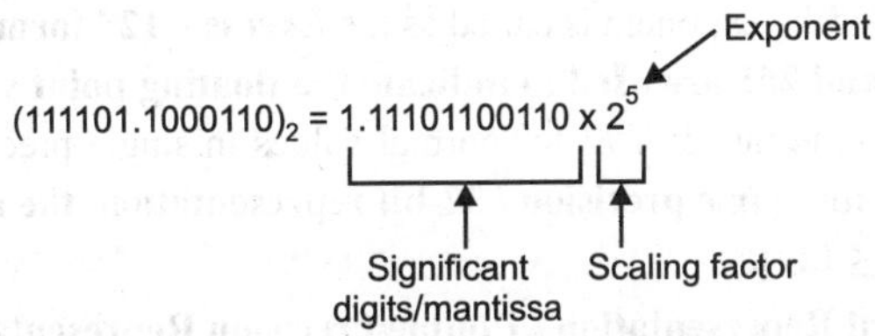

This is its normalized form. **Please note that the base in the scaling factor is fixed as 2.** So it need not appear explicitly in the machine representation of a floating point number. Hence, three fields – **sign field, significant digits and exponent** represent a floating point number. **The string of the significant digits is known as the mantissa.**

For eg. In above example,

Sign = 0

Mantissa = 11101100110

Exponent = 5

Also note that in floating point numbers, bias value is added to the true exponent which solves the problem of representation of negative exponent. Hence the magnitude of two numbers can be compared by doing arithmetic on the exponent first.

However, IEEE has developed standards for representing floating point numbers in 32 bits and 64 bits format, (IEEE 754 standard). Let us discuss these representation standards now.

(*a*) 32 Bit Standard Representation / Single Precision Representation

It is so named as it occupies a single 32-bit word. Fig. 9.10 shows this schema –

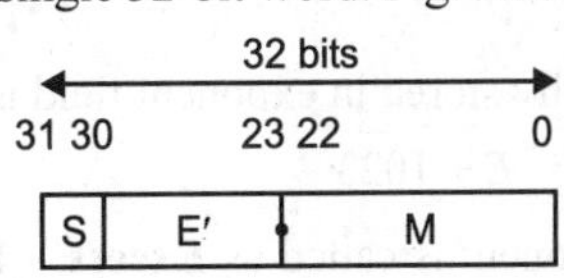

Where S = Sign bit (0 for + and 1 for –)

E' = 8-bit signed exponent in excess – 127 representation.

M = 23 bit mantissa fraction.

And value represented = $\pm 1.M \times 2^{E' - 127}$

Fig. 9.12. 32- bit / single precision representation

From Fig. 9.12, we observe that the 32 bits are divided into three fields–

(*a*) Sign (1-bit).

(*b*) Exponent (8-bits).

(*c*) Mantissa (23-bits)

That is, the sign bit is given in the first bit, followed by a representation for the exponent (to the base 2) of the scale factor. **Also note from Fig. 9.10 that instead of the signed exponent (*E*).** The value actually stored in the exponent field is –

$$E' = E + \text{bias}$$

where bias = 127 in this representation schema.

$$E' = E + 127$$

This representation of the exponent is called as the **Excess – 127 format. Please note that the end values of *E'* i.e., 0 and 255 are used to indicate the floating point values of exact zero and infinity respectively.** So the range of E' for normal values in single precision is $0<E'<255$. **Also note that it means that for single precision / 32-bit representation, the actual exponent is *E*, in the range of ($-126 \le E \le 127$).**

(*b*) 64-bit Standard Representation / Double Precision Representation

It is so named as it occupies two 32-bit words (2 * 32 = 64 bits). These 64 bits are divided as shown in Fig. 9.13

64 bits

63	62 – 52	51 – 0
S	E'	M

where S = Sign bit (0 for + and 1 for –)

E' = 11-bit excess – 1023 exponent.

M = 52-bit Mantissa fraction.

And value represented = $\pm 1.M \times 2^{E' - 1023}$

Fig. 9.13. 64 bit / Double Precision Representation

From Fig. 9.11 we observe that the 64-bits are divided into three fields–

(*a*) Sign (1-bit).

(*b*) Exponent (1-bit).

(*c*) Mantissa (52-bits).

In this method, the value actually stored in exponent field is –

$$E' = E + 1023$$

This representation of the exponent is called as **Excess – 1023 format. Please note that the end values of *E'* i.e., 0 and 2047 are used to indicate the floating point exact values of exact zero and infinity respectively.** So, the range of E' for normal values in double precision is

$0 < E' < 2047$. **Also note that it means that for double precision format of ($-1022 \leq E \leq 1023$).**

The extreme values of biased exponent E' are used to represent **special values.** Two cases arise:

Case-I: When $E' = 0$ and $M = 0$

When $E' = 0$ and the mantissa fraction (M) = 0, the value, exact 0 is represented. The biased exponent with all 1*s* is reversed to represent infinity where infinity is the result of dividing a normal number by zero. The **sign bit** is still part of these representations, so there are ± 0 and $\pm \infty$ representations.

Case II: When $E' = 0$ and $M \neq 0$

When $E' = 0$ and mantissa fraction (M) $\neq 0$ then denormal numbers are represented. We define **denormal is such a result that causes an underflow and has leading 0*s* in the mantissa even after the exponent is adjusted to its smallest possible values. E' with all 1*s* and $M \neq 0$ is reserved to represent Not – A Number (NaN). A NaN is the result of performing an invalid operation such as 0/0 or $\sqrt{-1}$.**

As per IEEE standards, the processor sets exception flags if **underflow, overflow, divide by zero, inexact or invalid conditions occur during the program execution. Underflow occurs** when a number requires an exponent less than – 126 (in single precision) or less than – 1022 (in double precision). Similarly, **overflow occurs** if the number requires exponent greater than + 127 (in single precision) or greater than + 1023 (in double precision).

Divide by zero occurs when any number is divided by zero. **Inexact condition occurs** when final result needs rounding off, so as to represent it in normal formats. **Invalid condition / Exception occurs** if operations such as 0/0 or $\sqrt{1}$ are encountered. **Please note that when exceptions occur, the results are set to special values. Also note that now inbuilt or user defined functions are needed to handle exceptions.**

We are in a position to solve some problems now.

EXAMPLE 9.1: Represent the following:

(*a*) $(1259.125)_{10}$

(*b*) $(-307.1875)_{10}$

(*c*) $(0.0625)_{10}$

in single precision (32-bits) and double precision (64-bits) formats.

SOLUTION:

(*a*) Given : $(1259.125)_{10}$

Firstly, we convert this decimal number into its binary form

Integer part is:

```
16 ) 1259 ( 78                      16 ) 78 ( 4
     112                                 64
     ----                                ---
      139                                14    (≡ E)
      128                                ---
     ----
      011       (≡ B)
     ----
```

$\therefore$ We get 4EBH (= 100 1110 1011)$_2$

Fractional Part is:

$$0.125 \times 2 = 0.25 \text{ ------------ } 0$$
$$0.25 \times 2 = 0.5 \text{ --------------- } 0$$
$$0.5 \times 2 = 1.0 \text{ --------------- } 1$$
$$0$$

$\therefore \quad (0.125) = (0.001)_2$

$\therefore \quad (1259.125)_{10} = (100\ 1110\ 1011 + 0.001)$
$= 10011101011.001$

Next, we normalize this result

$$10011101011.001 = 1.0011101011001 \times 2^{10}$$

Now, its single precision representation is –

For this number,

$$S = 0$$
$$E = 10$$
$\&$ $\quad M = 0011101011001$

$\therefore$ Bias for single precision format is 127.

$\therefore \quad E' = E + 127$
$= 10 + 127$
$= (137)_{10}$
$= (10001001)_2$

$\therefore$ Number in single precision format is

0	10001001	0011101011001.......0
Sign(s)	Exponent (E)	Mantissa (M) (23-bits)

Now, let us see its double precision representation–

For a given number here,

$$S = 0$$
$$E = 10$$
$\&$ $\quad M = 0011101011001$

$\therefore$ Bias for double precision format is 1023

$\therefore \quad E' = E + 1023 \quad = 10 + 1023$
$= (1033)_{10}$
$= (10000001001)_2$

So, the number in double precision format is–

0	10001001	0011101011001.......0
Sign(s)	Exponent (E)	Mantissa (M) (52-bits)

(*b*) **Given: $(-307.1875)_{10}$**

Firstly, we convert this decimal number in binary format–

Integer part is

$$16 \overline{)\,307\,} (19 \quad\quad 16 \overline{)\,19\,} (1$$

```
16 ) 307 ( 19          16 ) 19 ( 1
     16                     16
     ---                    --
     147                     3
     144                    --
     ---
       3        (≡ 3)
     ---
```

133H = 1 0011 0011 → 1 3 3

Fractional part is–

$$0.1875 \times 2 = 0.3750\text{-------} \quad 0$$
$$0.3750 \times 2 = 0.750\text{--------} \quad 0$$
$$0.750 \times 2 = 1.5\text{------------} \quad 1$$
$$0.5 \times 2 = 1.0\text{----------------} \quad 1$$
$$0$$
$$= 0.0011$$

$\therefore$ Binary Number $= -100110011 + .0011$

$= -100110011.0011$

Now, we normalize this number as follows

$$-100110011.0011 = -1.001100110011 \times 2^8$$

$\therefore$ **Number in single precision form is as follows–**

For given number,

$$S = 1$$
$$E = 8$$

And $M = 0011\ 0011\ 0011$

Now, bias for single precision format is 127

$\therefore$ $E' = E + 127 = 8 + 127 = 135_{10}$

$= (10000111)_2$

$\therefore$ Number in single precision format is

0	10000111	00110011001100……0
Sign(s)	Exponent(E)	Mantissa(M) (23-bits)

Now, let us see it's **double precision representation–**

For a given number here,

$$S = 1$$
$$E = 8$$

& $M = 0011\ 0011\ 0011$

Now, bias for double precision format is 1023

$\therefore$ $E' = E + 1023 = 8 + 1023 = (1031)_{10}$

$= (10000000111)_2$

∴ Number in Double precision format is–

0	100 0000 0111	0011001100110......0
Sign(s)	Exponent(E)	Mantissa(M) (52-bits)

(*c*) Given: $(0.0625)_{10}$

Firstly, we convert this decimal number into its binary form

Integer part: 0

Fractional part:

$$0.0625 \times 2 = 0.125 \text{---------------- } 0$$
$$0.125 \times 2 = 0.250 \text{---------------- } 0$$
$$0.250 \times 2 = 0.5 \text{---------------- } 0$$
$$0.5 \times 2 = 1.0 \text{---------------- } 1$$
$$0$$
$$= 0.0001$$

∴ Binary number = 0.0001

Now, we normalize this number–

$$0.001 = 1.0 \times 2^{-4}$$

∴ Number in single precision form is–

For given number, we see that

$$S = 0$$
$$E = -4$$
& $$M = 0001$$

Bias for single precision format is 127

∴ $$E' = E + 127 = -4 + 127 = (123)_{10}$$
$$= (01111011)_2$$

∴ Number in single precision format is–

0	0111 1011	00010000000000......0
Sign(s)	Exponent(E)	Mantissa(M) (23-bits)

Now, let us see its **double precision representation–**

For a given number,

$$S = 0$$
$$E = -4$$
& $$M = 0001$$

Bias for double precision format is 102.3

∴ $$E' = E + 1023$$
$$= -4 + 1023 = 1019$$
$$= (011111111011)_2$$

∴ Number in double precision format is =

0	011 1111 1011	0001000000000……0
Sign(s)	Exponent(E)	Mantissa(M) (52-bits)

9.9.1. Floating Point Additions and Subtractions (Arithmetic)

Consider two floating point numbers-

$$A = m_1.r^{el}$$

& $$B = M_2r^{e2} \text{ (where } e1 >= e2)$$

To add (or subtract) A and B, we follow the following rules –

Step 1: Select the number with a **smaller exponent** and shift its mantissa right, a number of steps equal to the difference in exponents $|e2 - e1|$.

For eg. Say, $A = 1.754 \times 10^2$

& $B = 6.8 \times 10^4$

Then, as per rule –1, A is selected and is converted to 0.0175×10^4.

Step 2: Set the exponent of result **equal to** the larger exponent.

Step 3: Perform **addition / subtraction** on the mantissas and determine the sign of the result.

Step 4: If required, **normalize** the result.

We are in a position to solve some problems now.

EXAMPLE 9.1: Perform as indicated

(*a*) $A + B$ **(*b*) $A - B$**

If A **= 44900000 H**

& B **= 42A00000H**

SOLUTION: (*a*) $A + B$

We follow the steps as explained above –

Step 1: Represent the number in single-precision format –

A = 0 1000 1001 001 0000 …0

B = 0 1000 0101 010 0000 …0

Exponent for A = 1000 1001 = 137

∴ Actual exponent = 137 – 127 (bias)

= 10

Exponent for B = 1000 0101 = 133

∴ Actual exponent = 133 – 127 (bias) = 6

> = Number B has small exponent with difference 4.

> = We shift right mantissa by 4-bits.

Step 2: Shift Mantissa

Shifted mantissa of B = 00000100 …0

Step 3: Add Mantissas

Mantissa of A = 00100000 ….0

$$
\begin{aligned}
\text{Mantissa of } B &= \underline{00000100 \quad \ldots.0} \\
\text{Mantissa of Result} &= \underline{00100100 \quad \ldots.0}
\end{aligned}
$$

Both the numbers are +ve, so the sign of the result is positive.

$$
\begin{aligned}
\text{Hence the result} &= 010001001\ 00100100\ldots..0 \\
&= \mathbf{44920000H}
\end{aligned}
$$

(b) ***A* – *B***

During subtraction process, two mantissas are subtracted instead of addition and the sign of greater mantissa is assigned to the result. So, we follow the steps:

Step 1: Represent numbers in single precision format-

$$
\begin{aligned}
A &= 0\ 10001001\ 0010000\ldots.0 \\
B &= 0\ 10000101\ 0100000\ldots.0 \\
\text{Exponent for } A &= 10001001 = 137 \\
\therefore \quad \text{Actual exponent} &= 137 - 127 \text{ (bias)} = 10 \\
\text{Exponent for } B &= 10000101 = 133 \\
\therefore \quad \text{Actual Exponent} &= 133 + 127 \text{ (bias)} = 6
\end{aligned}
$$

Number B has smaller exponent with a difference of 4.

We shift right its mantissa by 4 bits.

Step 2: Shift Mantissa

$$\text{Shifted mantissa of } B = 0000\ 0100 \quad \ldots 0$$

Step 3: Subtract Mantissa

$$
\begin{aligned}
\text{Mantissa of } A &= 00100000 \quad \ldots 0 \\
\text{Mantissa of } B &= \underline{00000100 \quad \ldots 0} \\
\text{Mantissa of Result} &= \underline{00011100 \quad \ldots 0}
\end{aligned}
$$

Mantissa of A is greater than mantissa of B.

$$
\begin{aligned}
\therefore \quad \text{Sign of result} &= \text{sign of } A. \\
\therefore \quad \text{Result} &= 01000100100011100\ldots 0 \\
&= \mathbf{448E0000H} \quad \textbf{(Answer)}
\end{aligned}
$$

9.9.2. Drawbacks of FP Arithmetic

The following are some of the shortcomings of FP Arithmetic

1. **Mantissa Overflow**

   The addition of two mantissas of the same sign may result in a carryout of the MSB. In such a case, we right shift the mantissa and increment the exponent.

2. **Mantissa Underflow**

   In the process of aligning mantissas, digits may flow off the right end of the mantissa. In such a scenario, truncation methods (like chopping, rounding off) are used.

3. **Exponent Overflow**

   It occurs when a positive exponent exceeds the maximum possible exponent value. In some systems, this may be designated as +∞ or –∞.

4. **Exponent Underflow**

   It occurs when a negative exponent exceeds the maximum possible exponent value. In such scenario, the number is designated as zero.

9.9.3. Flow charts for FP Additions and Subtractions

Let us write their algorithms first.

Declare Registers

$AM[0:M-1]$	; for Mantissa of A.
$BM[0:M-1]$	; for Mantissa of B.
$AE[0:E-1]$	; for exponent of A.
$BE[0:E-1]$	; for exponent of B.
$E[0:E-1]$	; for temporary storage of exponent.

Step 1: Read the numbers

$AM \leftarrow$ Mantissa of A

$BM \leftarrow$ Mantissa of B

$AE \leftarrow$ Exponent of A

$BE \leftarrow$ Exponent of B

Step 2: Compare the two exponents

$E = AE - BE$

Step 3: Equalize

If $E < 0$ then

Right shift AM;

$E = E + 1$ and go to step 3;

If $E > 0$ then

Right shift BM

$E = E - 1$ goto step – 3;

Step 4: Add Mantissas

$AM = AM + BM$

& $E =$ Max (AE, BE)

Step 5: Check exponent overflow

If overflow occurs during mantissa addition

If $E = E_{max}$ then report 'overflow'

else

Right shift AM

$E = E + 1$ goto stop.

Step 6: Adjust for zero result.

If $AM = 0$ then $E = 0$; goto stop.

Step 7: Normalize the Result

If AM normalized then goto stop.

Step 8: Check exponent underflow

If $E > E_{min}$ then

Left shift AM;

$E = E - 1$, goto step 7

Step 9: Stop.

Figure 9.14 shows the corresponding flowcharts

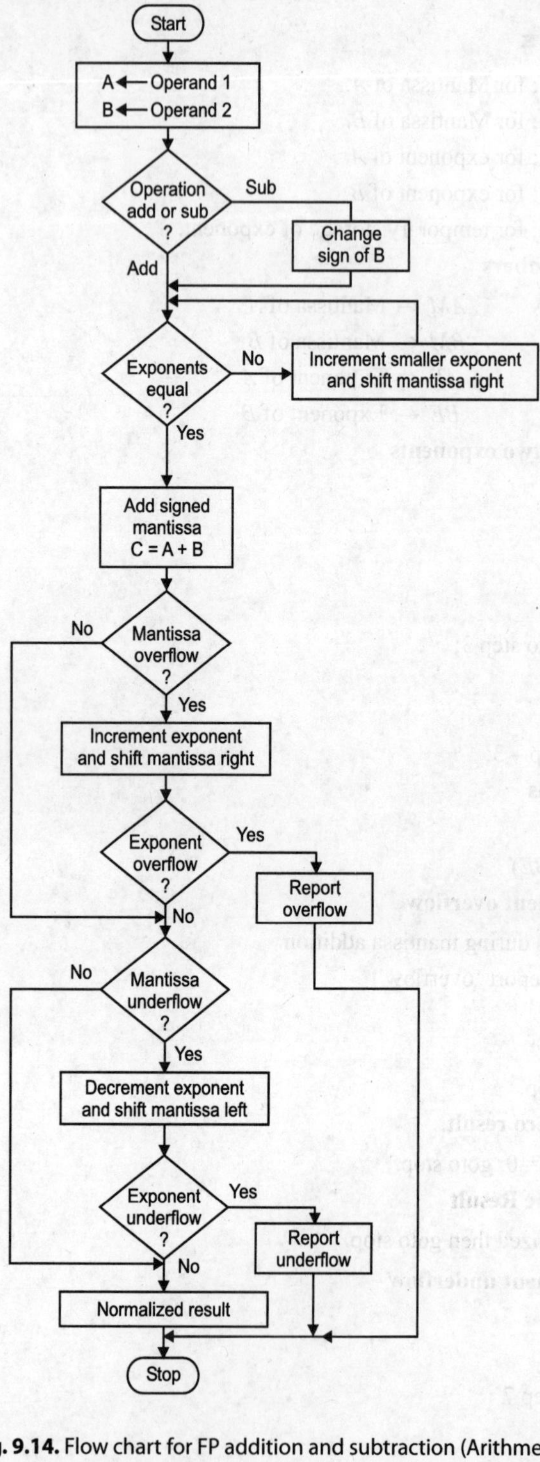

Fig. 9.14. Flow chart for FP addition and subtraction (Arithmetic)

9.9.4. IMPLEMENTATION OF FP OPERATIONS

The hardware required for doing FP operations (addition and subtraction) are shown in Fig. 9.15

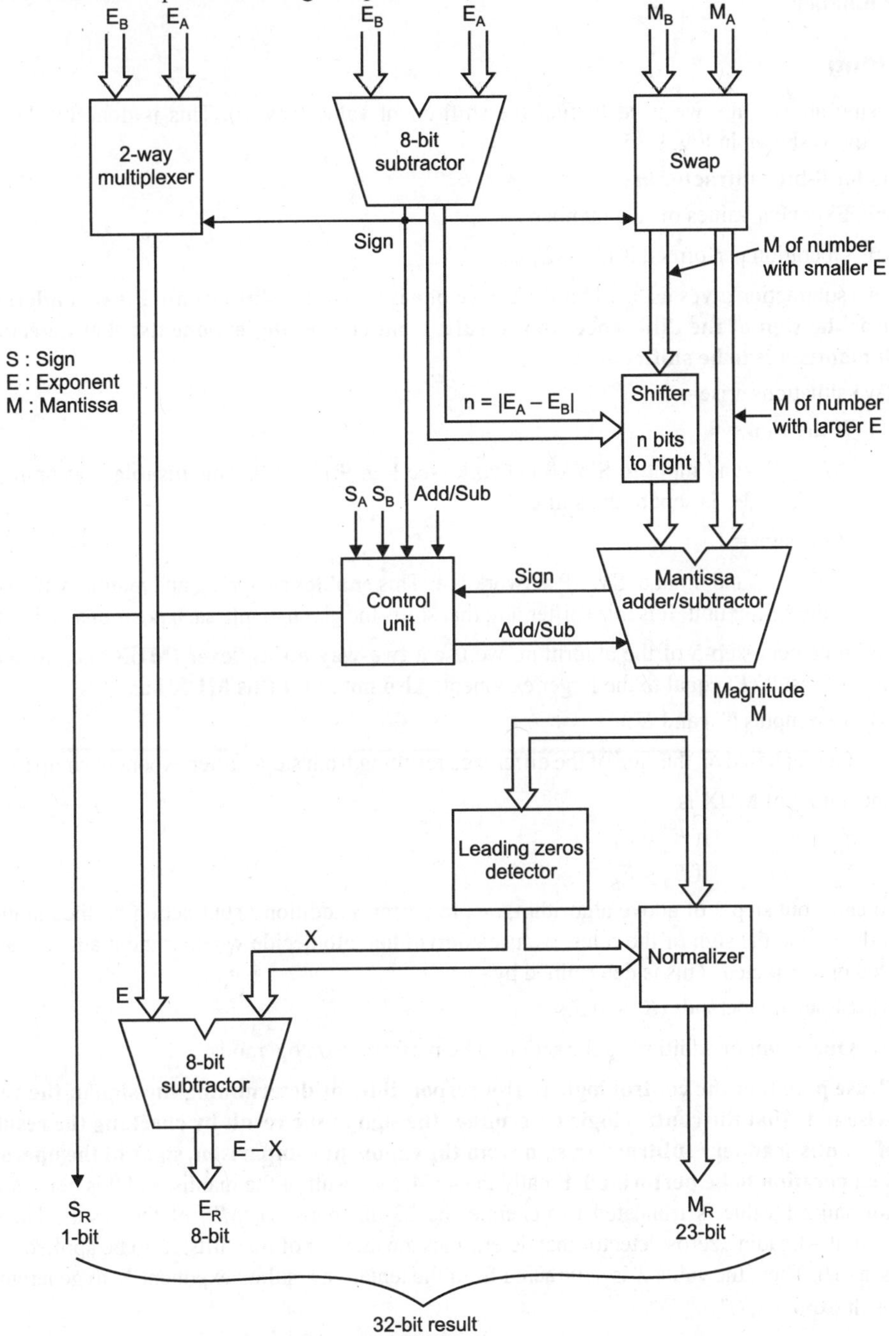

Fig. 9.15. Hardware for FP operations

Figure 9.15, shows the hardware needed to add / subtract two floating point, 32-bit operands (using single precision format : 1-bit for sign, 8-bits for signed exponent and 23 bits for mantissa). We follow the rules of addition and subtraction of *FP* numbers–

"Compare the exponents of numbers to find out the smaller exponent number and then to find out how far to shift the mantissa of that number so that its exponent matches with the other number".

Working

Using above rule, we need to find the shift-count value (say, *n*). This is done by the 8-bit subtractor as shown in Fig. 9.15.

Inputs for 8-bit subtractor are–

(*a*) Exponent values of two numbers,

(*b*) Operation performed is $(E_A - E_B)$.

This subtraction gives us '*n*'. This difference of *n* is sent to the **shifter unit. Please understand that it is the sign of the difference (that results from comparing exponents) that determines which mantissa is to be shifted.**

Two situations arise–

(*a*) If the sign = 0

$\therefore E_A \geq E_B$ and input to SWAP network (see Fig. 9.15) is 0. This **disables** swapping and mantissa, M_B is sent to the shifter.

(*b*) If the sign = 1

$\therefore E_A - E_B$ and input to SWAP network is 1. This **enables** swapping and mantissa M_A is sent to the shifter unit. It is this shifter unit that shifts the given mantissa, *n* positions to the right.

To implement step-5 of the algorithm, we use a **two-way multiplexer (MUX)** *i.e.*, to set the exponent of result (*E*) equal to the larger exponent. **Also note that this MUX has –**

(*a*) Two inputs (E_A and E_B).

(*b*) Output based on the sign of the difference resulting from step-1 after exponent comparisons.

The output of MUX is –

$E = E_A$ if $E_A \geq E_B$

Or $E = E_B$ if $E_A \leq E_B$

To carry out step 3 of above algorithm, *i.e.*, to perform addition / subtraction on the mantissas and to determine the sign of the rules, we use **control logic** to decide whether the mantissas are to be added or subtracted. This is determined by –

(*a*) **Signs** of Operands (S_A and S_B).

(*b*) **Operation** of addition / subtraction to be performed on operands.

Please note that the control logic is also responsible for determining the sign of the result (S_R). Also note that the control logic determines the sign of the result by checking the resulted sign of mantissa adder / subtract or, sign from the exponent comparison, signs of the operands and the operation to be performed. Finally in step 4, the result of the mantissa (*M*) is normalized. The normalized value is truncated to generate the 23-bit mantissa, *MR*, of the result. There is another unit – Leading zeros detector that determines the number of bit shifts, *X*, to be applied to the mantissa (*M*). Then, the value *X* is subtracted from the tentative resulted exponent *E*, to generate the true result exponent (E_R).

9.9.5. FP Multiplication and FP Division Algorithms

Rules for multiplication of FP numbers

Step 1: Add the exponents and subtract bias.

Note: Bias is 127 for single precision number
Bias is 1023 for double precision numbers

Step 2: Multiply the mantissas and determine the sign of the result.

Step 3: Normalize the result.

Tip: No need of alignment of mantissas for FP multiplications and divisions.

It's flow chart is shown in Fig. 9.16

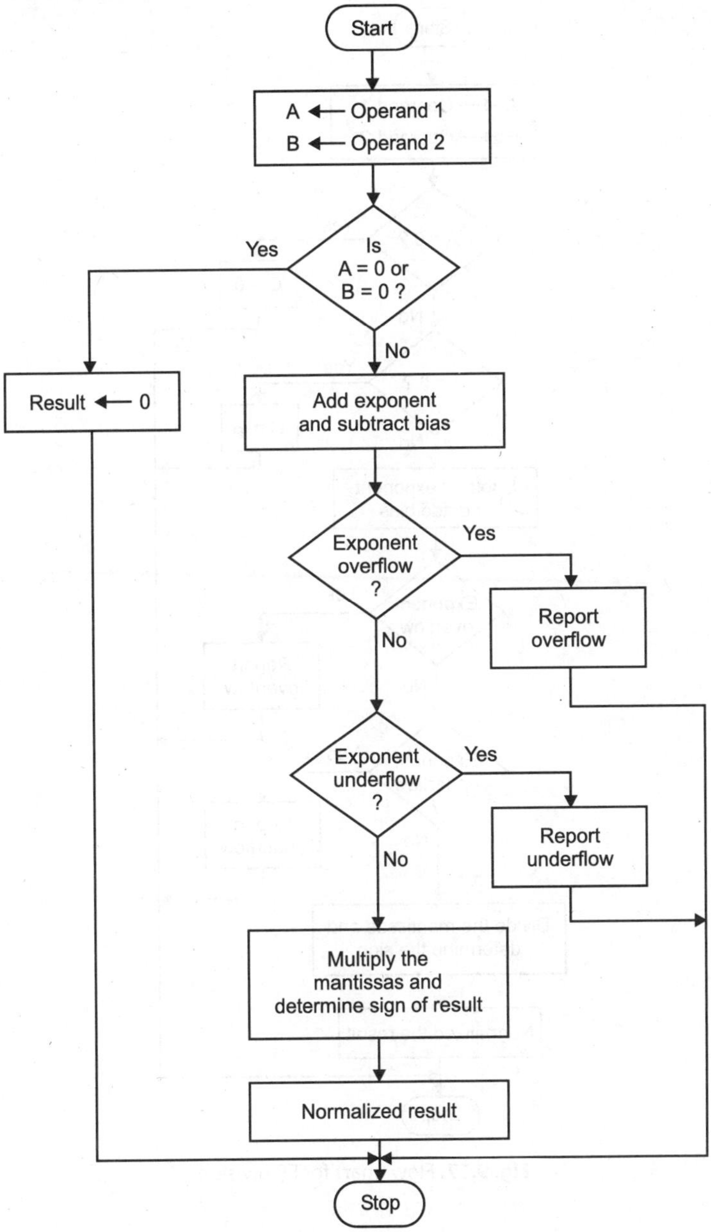

Fig. 9.16. Flow chart for FP multiplication

Next, let us see the rules for division of FP numbers

Step 1: Subtract the exponents and add the bias.

> **Note:** Bias is 127 for single precision numbers. Bias is 1023 for double precision numbers.

Step 2: Divide the mantissas and find out the sign of the result.

Step 3: Normalize the result.

Its flowchart is shown in Fig. 9.17

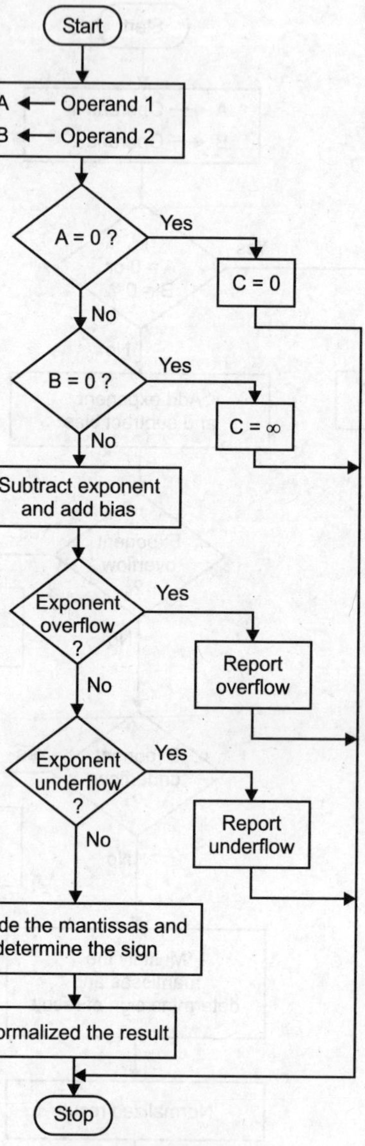

Fig. 9.17. Flow Chart for FP division

SUMMARY

In this chapter we have dealt with different types of number systems, binary arithmetic for both signed and unsigned numbers. We have also studied about positive and negative numbers multiplication, division addition and abstraction algorithms and flowcharts. Without booth's algorithm, studying computer system architecture is incomplete. The major challenge is to store floating point numbers, add, subtract, multiply and divide them. Several numericals have been solved for the same.

MULTIPLE CHOICE QUESTIONS [MCQs]

Q. 1. Roman numerals like I, II, III and so on are the examples of

(*a*) Binary number system. (*b*) Non positional number system.
(*c*) Positional number system. (*d*) None of the above.

Q. 2. Octal number system means

(*a*) Base 2 (*b*) Base 8 (*c*) Base 10 (*d*) Base 16

Q. 3. The binary digits are called as

(*a*) Bits (*b*) Dits (*c*) Hits (*d*) None of the above

Q. 4. Computers operate on

(*a*) HEX values (*b*) Decimal values
(*c*) Octal values (*d*) None of the above

Q. 5. HEX numbers are better because they need

(*a*) Lesser memory. (*b*) Lesser time. (*c*) Lesser speed. (*d*) None of the above.

Q. 6. $(A–B)$ is computed as

(*a*) A + 1s complement of B. (*b*) A + 10s complement of B.
(*c*) A + 2s complement of B. (*d*) A + 9s complement of B.

Q. 7. In 1s complement form, the number $(00000000)_2$ is called as

(*a*) Positive zero. (*b*) Negative zero.
(*c*) Zero only. (*d*) None of the above.

Q. 8. 10s complement of a decimal number is

(*a*) 9s complement of number +1 (*b*) 9s complement of the number –1
(*c*) 2s complement of the number +1 (*d*) None of the above.

Q. 9. An algorithm that treats both positive and negative multipliers uniformly is known as

(*a*) Shift algorithm (*b*) Booth's algorithm
(*c*) Neumann's algorithm (*d*) None of the above

Q. 10. Which one of the following is a faster algorithm

(*a*) Restoring division. (*b*) Non restoring division.
(*c*) FP division. (*d*) None of the above.

Q. 11. The binary system has a radix of

(*a*) 0 (*b*) 1 (*c*) 2 (*d*) 8

Q. 12. ASCII and EBCDIC differ in

(*a*) Their efficiency in strong data. (*b*) Random and sequential access method.
(*c*) Number of bytes used for character storage.
(*d*) Their collecting sequences.

Q. 13. 1s complement of 1010 is

(*a*) 0000 (*b*) 1010 (*c*) 0101 (*d*) 1111

Q. 14. Half of a byte is called as a

(*a*) Nibble (*b*) Bit

(*c*) Word (*d*) None of the above table

Q. 15. In binary arithmetic, 0 × 0 is

(*a*) Not allowed (*b*) 0 (*c*) 0.0 (*d*) 1

ANSWERS

1. (*b*)	**2.** (*b*)	**3.** (*a*)	**4.** (*a*)	**5.** (*a*)	**6.** (*c*)	**7.** (*a*)	**8.** (*a*)
9. (*b*)	**10.** (*b*)	**11.** (*c*)	**12.** (*d*)	**13.** (*c*)	**14.** (*a*)	**15.** (*a*)	

CONCEPTUAL SHORT QUESTIONS WITH ANSWERS

Q. 1. The complementer shown in figure below is not needed if instead of performing $A + \overline{B} + 1$ we perform $B + \overline{A}$. Derive an algorithm in flowchart form for addition and subtraction of fixed point binary numbers in signed magnitude representation with the magnitudes subtracted by the two micro operations $A \leftarrow \overline{A}$ and $EA \leftarrow A + B$.

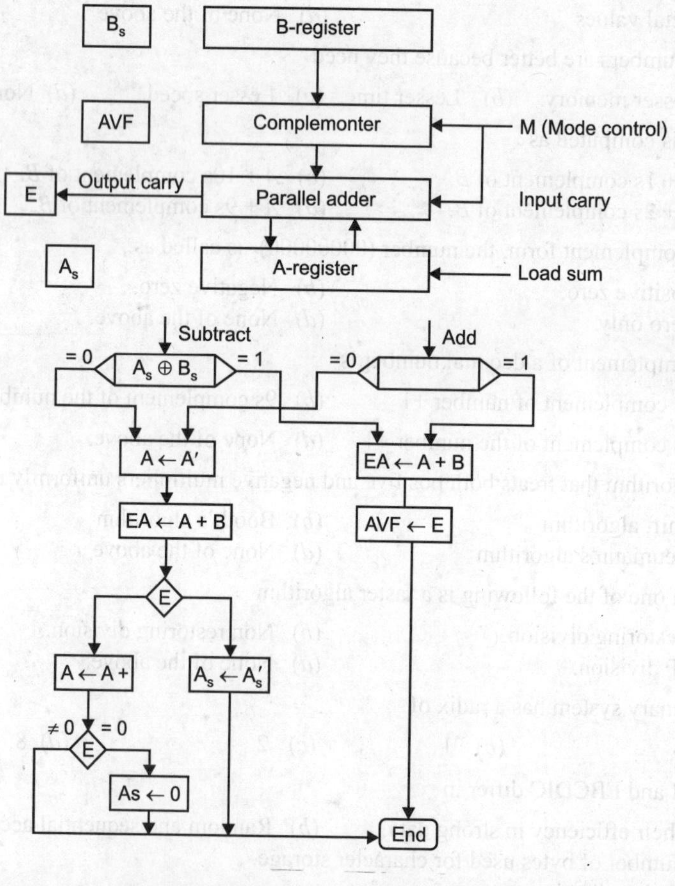

This figure shows hardware for signed magnitude addition and subtraction.

Q. 2. Perform the arithmetic operations below with binary numbers and with negative numbers in signed 2s complement form. Use 7-bits to accommodate each number together with its sign. In each case, determine if there is an overflow by checking the carries into and out of the sign bit position:

(*a*) (+35) + (+40) **(*b*) (–35) + (–40).**

Ans.

(*a*) +35 = 0100011

+40 = 0101000

+75 = 1001011

Here, $F = 0$ and $E = 1$

$\therefore$ $F \oplus E = 1$; overflow occurs.

(*b*) +35 = 1011101

–40 = 1011000

–70 = 0110101

Here, $F = 1$ and $E = 0$

$\therefore$ $F \oplus E = 1$; overflow occurs.

Q. 3. Prove that the multiplication of two *n*-digit numbers in base *r* gives a product no more than 2*n* digits in length. Show that this statement implies that no overflow can occur in the multiplication operation.

Ans. Maximum value of numbers = $r^n - 1$

It is necessary to show that the maximum product is less than or equal to $r^{2n} - 1$

$$\therefore \quad \text{Maximum product} = (r^n - 1)(r^n - 1)$$
$$= r^{2n} - 2r^n + 1$$
$$\leq r^{2n} - 1$$

This gives, $2 \leq 2r^n$

or $1 \leq r^n$

This is always true as $r \geq 2$.

Q. 4. Formulate a hardware procedure for detecting an overflow by comparing the sign of the sum with the signs of the augend and addend. The numbers are in signed 2s complement form.

Ans. *S*1: Transfer augend sign into T_s

*S*2: Add:

$$AC \leftarrow AC + BR$$

A_s will have the sign of the SUM.

The circuit is shown in figure –

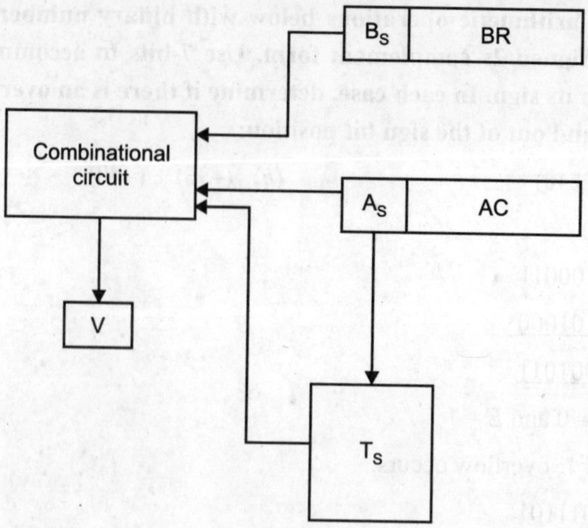

∴ It's Boolean function, F is

$$F = T_s' B_s' A + T_s B_s A_s'$$

Q. 5. Show that adding B after the operation $A + B + 1$ restores the original value of A. What should be done with the end carry?

Ans 5. $A + B + 1$ performs: $A + 2^n - B$

$$= 2^n + A - B$$

Adding B: $(2^K + A - B) + B$

$$= 2^n + A$$

Remove end carry, 2^n to obtain A.

Q. 6. (*a*) Perform the operation (–9) + (+16) = –15 with binary numbers in signed is complement representation using only five bits to represent each number (including the sign). Show that the over flow detection procedure of checking the inequality of the last two carries fails in this case.

(*b*) Suggest a modified procedure for detecting and over flow when signed 1s complement numbers are used.

Ans. (*a*) $-9 = 10110$

$\underline{-6 = 11001}$

$\underline{-15 = 01111}$

Note: Add end around carry, F as needed in signed 1s complement addition.

∴ 01111

$\underline{+1}$

10000 = – 15

∴ $F = 1, E = 0$

$E \oplus F = 1$; however, there should be no overflow since result is – 15.

(*b*) The procedure $V \leftarrow E \oplus F$ is valid for 1s complement numbers provided we check the result.

$\underline{Q}$ $\underline{1111...11}$ When $V = 1$

A_s A

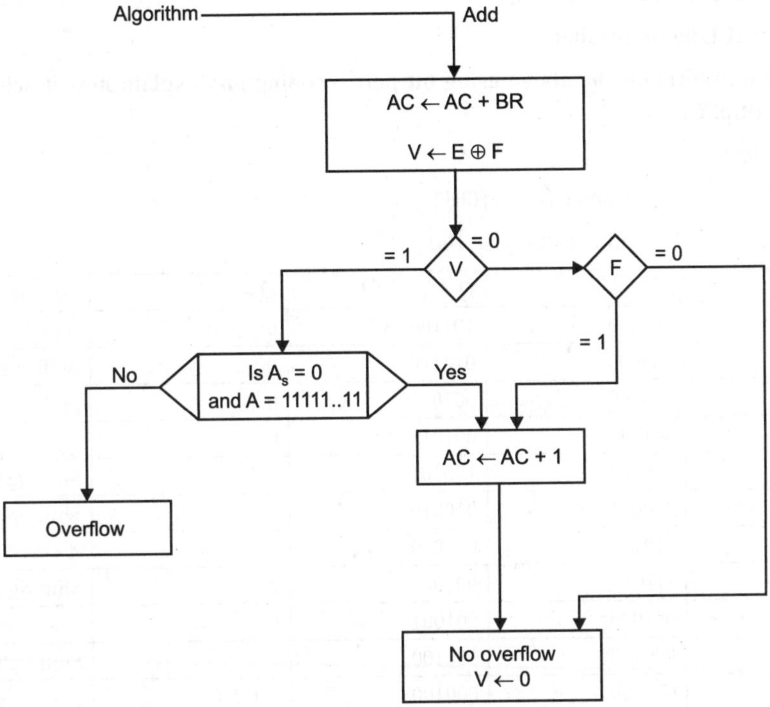

Q. 6. Why should the sign of the remainder after a division be the same as the sign of the dividend? **[GGSIPU, B.Tech (CSE)- 5th Sem., Dec. 2011]**

Ans. In general $\frac{A}{B} = Q + \frac{R}{B}$

Where A is dividend

Q is quotient

R is remainder

Four possible signs for A and B:

1. $\frac{+52}{+5} = +10 + \frac{+2}{+5} = +10.4$

2. $\frac{-52}{+5} = -10 + \frac{-2}{+5} = -10.4$

3. $\frac{+52}{-5} = -10 + \frac{+2}{-5} = -10.4$

4. $\frac{-52}{-5} = +10 + \frac{-2}{-5} = +10.4$

Note: The Sign of remainder must be same as the sign of dividend.

Q. 7. Explain Booth's algorithm to multiply the following pairs of signed as complement numbers

A = 110011 (multiplicand)

B = 101100 (multiplier)

Also implement the above using bit pair recoding and explain how it achieve faster multiplication.

Ans. Given:

Multiplicand (B) ← 110011 (–13)

Multiplier (Q) ← 101100 (–20)

Steps	A	Q	$Q-1$	Operation
	000000	101100	0	Initial
1	000000	010110	0	Shift right
2	000000	001011	0	Shift right
3	001101	001011	0	$A \leftarrow A \leftarrow B$
	000110	100101	1	Shift right
4	000011	010010	1	Shift right
5	110110	010010	1	$A \leftarrow A + B$
	111011	001001	0	Shift right
6	001000	001001	0	$A \leftarrow A - B$
	000100	000100	1	Shift right
Result	000100	000100	= + 260	

Using Bit – Pair Recoding

Bit pair recoding for multiplier is (–1 –1 0)

∴ We multiply now–

1 1 0 0 1 1

× –1 –1 0

0 0 0 0 0 0 0 0 0 0 0

0 0 0 0 0 1 1 0 1 × × ← 2s complement of multiplicand

0 0 0 1 1 0 1 × × × × ← 2s complement of multiplicand

0 0 1 0 0 0 0 0 1 0 0 = (+260)

Please note the following points here

1. Booth's algorithm may need the summation at each step.
2. The number of steps required in Booth's algorithm are equal to the length of the multiplier in bits.
3. The bit – pair recoding halves the maximum number of summations. So, it is a faster method.

Q. 8. Perform (1100 ÷ 11) using

(a) Restoring Division Algorithm.

(b) Non-Restoring Division Algorithm.

Ans. (a) By Restoring Division Algorithm

$Q \leftarrow$ Dividend (1100), $B \leftarrow$ Divisor (11)

	A-Register	Q-Resister	
Initially	00000	1 1 0 0	(Dividend)
Shift	00001	1 0 0 □	1st Cycle
Subtract B	11101		1st Cycle
	(1)1110		1st Cycle
Restore (A + B)	00011		1st Cycle
	00001	1 0 0 0	1st Cycle
Shift	00011		2nd Cycle
Subtract B	11101	0 0 0 0	2nd Cycle
	(0)0000		2nd Cycle
		0 0 0 1	2nd Cycle
Shift	00000	0 0 1 □	3rd Cycle
Subtract B	11101		3rd Cycle
	11101		3rd Cycle
	(1)1101		3rd Cycle
		0 0 1 0	3rd Cycle
Restore (A + B)	00000	0 1 0 □	4th Cycle
Shift	00000		4th Cycle
Subtract B	11101		4th Cycle
	(1)1101		4th Cycle
Restore (A + B)	00000 (Remainder)	0 1 0 0 (Quotient)	4th Cycle

(b) Non-Restoring Division

	A-Register	Q-Register	
Initially	0 0 0 0 0	1 1 0 0	(Dividend)
Shift	0 0 0 0 1	1 0 0 □	1st Cycle
Subtract B	1 1 1 0 1	1 0 0 0	1st Cycle
	(1)1 1 1 0		1st Cycle

Shift	1 1 1 0 1	0 0 0 □	2nd Cycle
Add	0 0 0 1 1	0 0 0 1	
	(0)0 0 0 0		
Shift	0 0 0 0 0	0 0 1 □	3rd Cycle
Subtract *B*	1 1 1 0 1		
	(1)1 1 0 1	0 0 1 0	
Shift	1 1 0 1 0	0 1 0 □	4th Cycle
Add	0 0 0 1 1		
	(1)1 1 0 1	0 1 0 0	
		Quotient	
	1 1 1 0 1		
Add	0 0 0 1 1		
Divisor	0 0 0 0 0	(Restoring Remainder)	

Q. 9. Multiply + 15 and – 6 using Booth' algorithm.

Ans. Given:

Multiplicand (B) ← 01111 (+15)

Multiplier (Q) ← 1010 (–6)

We draw a table first -

Steps	*A*	*Q*	*Q – 1*	*Operation*
	00000	1010	0	Initial
1	00000	0101	0	Right shift
2	10001	0101	0	A ← A – B
	11000	1010	1	Right shift
3	00111	1010	1	A ← A + B
	00011	1101	0	Right shift
4	10100	1101	0	A ← A – B
	11010	0110	1	Right shift
Result	11010	0110	= – 90	2s complement of 90

Q. 10. Discus the three methods of truncation. Compare them. [PTU, MCA 3rd Sem., 2009]

Ans. There are 3 methods of truncation as follows :-

(*a*) **Chopping**

As we have studied that the mantissas of initial operands and final results are limited to 24 bits, which includes the implicit leading 1. But if extra bits are added in the intermediate steps of calculations then we get the maximum accuracy in the final result. **These extra bits used in the intermediate calculations are called as the guard bits. This means that the operands are used with guard bits for calculations and then**

final result of calculation is truncated to create 24 bit number that approximates the longer final result. This process of removing the guard bits without making any changes in the retained bits is known as chopping.

For eg :

Before chopping number: $0.\,b_{-1}\,b_{-2}\,b_{-3}\,b_{-4}\,b_{-5}\,b_{-6}$

After chopping number: $0.\,b_{-1}\,b_{-2}\,b_{-3}$

That is if we want to truncate a fraction from 6 to 3-bits then we remove 3 LSBs (from right). Here in this example, the error in 3-bit result ranges from 0 to 0.000111. The value .000111 is almost equal to .001. **In general, the error in chopping process ranges from 0 to almost 1 in the best significant position of the retained bits.** Herein the least significant position of the retained bit is b_{-3}. **Please understand that in this method, the error range is not symmetrical about 0, so the result of chopping is a biased approximation.**

(*b*) **Von Neumann's Rounding**

In this method of rounding, two rules are followed –

Rule – 1: If the bits to be removed are all 0s, they are simply removed with no changes to the retained bits.

Rule – 2: If any of the bits to be removed are 1, then the LSB of the retained bits is set to 1.

For example,

If (say) original number is –

$0.\,b_{-1}\,b_{-2}\,b_{-3}\,b_{-4}\,b_{-5}\,b_{-6}$

With $b_{-4}\,b_{-5}\,b_{-6} = 000$

Then, using **rule – 1** above, we get the following truncated number –

$0.\,b_{-1}\,b_{-2}\,b_{-3}$

Another example, following **rule – 2** is given now-

Say, original number is-

$0.\,b_{-1}\,b_{-2}\,b_{-3}\,b_{-4}\,b_{-5}\,b_{-6}$

With $b_{-4}\,b_{-5}\,b_{-6} \neq 000$

Then, using **rule – 2** above, we get the following truncated number –

$0.\,b_{-1}\,b_{-2}\,1$

In this method, error ranges between –1 and +1 in the LSB position of the retained bits. **Please note that in this method, the range of error is larger than it is in chopping method. Also however, note that the error range is symmetrical about 0. That is why the result of this type of Von Neumann's rounding method is an unbiased approximation.**

> **NOTE:** Unbiased approximations are better if many operands and operations are involved in generating a result because +ve errors tend to offset – ve errors as computation proceeds.

For eg: Say, if the original number is ------ 0.010010

Its truncated form is 0.011 **(Positive Error).**

But if the number is 0.011010. Its truncated form is 0.011 **(Negative Error).**

(*c*) **Rounding Method**

In this difficult method, a 1 is added to the LSB position of the bits to be retained if there is a 1 in the MSB position of the bits being removed.

For eg: If (say) original number is

$0.b_{-1}\, b_{-2}\, b_{-3}\, b_{-4}\, b_{-5}\, b_{-6}$ with $b_{-4} = 0$

Then, using this method, we get the following truncated number -

$0.\, b_{-1}\, b_{-2}\, b_{-3}$

Another example

Say, if original number is-

$0.\, b_{-1}\, b_{-2}\, b_{-3}\, b_{-4}\, b_{-5}\, b_{-6}$ with $b_{-4} = 1$

Then, its truncated number is-

$0.\, b_{-1}\, b_{-2}\, b_{-3} + 0.0001$

In this method, the **error range** is (approx.) – ½ to + ½ in the LS position of the retained bits and is symmetrical about 0. **Hence, the result of rounding is a unbiased approximation.**

For eg: If original number is 0.011011

Then, after truncation we get 0.011 **(Negative Error)**

But if original number is 0.011100 then its

truncated form is = 0.100 **(Positive Error).**

Please understand that this method of rounding is most difficult as it requires and addition operation and a possible renormalization.

> **Note:** IEEE floating point representation uses this method by default.

Rounding method can be implemented using only 3-guard bits:

(*a*) **First two of these are two MSBs** of the section of the mantissa to be removed.

(*b*) **Third bit is** the logical OR of all bits beyond these first two bits in the full representation of the mantissa. **This bit is called as a sticky bit.** It must be initialized to 0. If a 1 is shifted out through this position, the bit becomes 1 and retains that value.

EXERCISE QUESTIONS

Q. 1. Convert the decimal number – 2.675 in IEEE 754 format and -35 in all possible signed binary representations, if number of bits used for representation is eight.

[GGSIPU, B.Tech. (CSE) – 5th sem. Dec. 2004]

Q. 2. Write short notes on – Booth's algorithm for multiplication.

[GGSIPU, B.Tech (CSE) – 5th sem. Dec. 2006]

Q. 3. (*a*) Discuss the basic of Booth's algorithm. Draw the flowchart of booth's algorithm for multiplication of signed as complement numbers.

(*b*) Suggest a procedure for detecting are overflow when signed is complement numbers are used. **[GGSIPU, B.Tech (CSE) – 5th sem. Dec. 2008]**

Q. 4. (*a*) Explain booth algorithm in detail.

(*b*) Explain floating point number representation.

[GGSIPU, B.Tech (CSE)- 5th sem., Dec 2009]

Q. 5. (*a*) With the help of a flowchart discuss the hardware divide algorithm. Explain how the divide overflow conditions are handled?

(*b*) Draw the diagram showing hardware for signed magnitude addition and subtraction.

[GGSIPU, B.Tech (CSE) – 5th sem. Dec 2010 & 2011]

Q. 6. Design an array multiplier that multiplies two 4 bits numbers. Use AND gates and binary adders. **[GGSIPU, B.Tech (CSE) – 5th sem. Dec 2011]**

Q. 7. (*a*) A 36-bit FP binary number has 8-bit plus sign for the exponent and 26-bit plus sign for the mantissa. The mantissa is a normalized fraction. Numbers in the mantissa and exponents are in signed magnitude representation. What are the largest and smallest positive quantities that can be represented, excluding zero?

(*b*) Perform the arithmetic operations (+42) + (–13) and (–42) – (–13) in binary using signed 2s complements representation for negative number.

[MDU, BE (CSE) – 4th Sem. 2000 and 2001]

Q. 8. (*a*) Explain algorithm for FP addition Draw its flow chart.

(*b*) Draw flowchart of fixed – point multiplication.

[MDU, BE (CSE) – 4th Sem. 2000 & 2004]

Q. 9. Explain the algorithm for multiplying two 4-bit unsigned numbers by taking a suitable example. **[PTU, B. Tech (CSE) – 3rd sem. 2009]**

APPENDIX–A SYLLABUS AND LECTURE PLANS

Syllabus (Computer Organization) — UPTECH SYLLABUS

Unit 1: [Chapter – 1]

Register transfer language, Bus and memory transfers, Bus architecture, Bus arbitration, Arithmetic, logic, shift microoperation, Arithmetic logic shift unit, Design of fast adders, Arithmetic algorithms (addition, subtraction, Booth multiplication), IEEE standard for floating point numbers.

Unit 2: [Chapter – 2]

Control Design

Hardwired and micro programmed (Control Unit) : Fundamental concepts (Register Transfers, Performing an arithmetic or logical operations, Fetching a word from memory, Storing a word in memory), Execution of a complete instruction, Multiple-Bus organization, Hardwired control, Micro programmed control (Microinstruction, Microprogram sequencing, Wide-Branch addressing, Microinstruction with next-address field, Prefetching microinstruction).

Unit 3: [Chapter – 3]

Processor Design

Processor organization: General register organization, Stack organization, Addressing mode, Instruction format, Data transfer and manipulations. Program control, Reduced instruction set computer.

Unit 4: [Chapter – 4]

Input/Output Organization

I/O Interface, Modes of transfer, Interrupts and interrupt handling, Direct memory access, Input-Output processor, Serial communication.

Unit 5: [Chapter – 5]

Memory Organization

Memory hierarchy, Main Memory (RAM and ROM Chips), Organization of 2D and (2*2)D, Auxiliary memory, Cache memory, Virtual memory, Memory management hardware.

MDU Syllabus

Computer System Architecture and Organisation

(Strictly As Per New Syllabus M.D. University, Rohtak)

UNIT-1 : Basic Principles

Boolean Algebra and Logic Gates, Combinational Logic Blocks (Adders, Multiplexers, Encoders, Decoder), Sequential Logic Blocks (Latches, Flip-Flops, Registers, Counters).

UNIT-2 : General System Architecture

Store Program Control Concept, Flynn's Classification of Computers (SISD, MISD, MIMD); Multilevel Viewpoint of a Machine; Digital Logic, Micro Architecture, ISA, Operating Systems, High Level Language; Structured Organization; CPU, Caches, Main Memory, Secondary Memory Units and I/O; Performance Metrics; MIPS, MFLOPS.

UNIT-3 : Instruction Set Architecture

Instruction Set Based Classification of Processors (RISC, CISC, and Their Comparison); Addressing Modes: Register, Immediate, Direct, Indirect, Indexed; Operations in the Instruction Set: Arithmetic and Logical, Data Transfer, Control Flow; Instruction Set Formats (Fixed, Variable, Hybrid); Language of the Machine: 8086; Simulation Using MSAM.

UNIT-4 : Basic Non Pipelined Cpu Architecture

CPU Architecture Types (Accumulator, Register, Stack, Memory/Register) Detailed Data Path of a Typical Register Based CPU, Fetch-Decode-Execute Cycle (Typically 3 to 5 Stage); Microinstruction Sequencing, Implementation of Control Unit, Enhancing Performance With Pipelining.

UNIT-5: Memory Hierarchy and I/O Techniques

The Need for a Memory Hierarchy (Locality of Reference Principle), Memory Hierarchy in Practice: Cache, Main Memory and Secondary Memory; Memory Parameters: Access/Cycle Time, Cost Pei Bit; Main Memory (Semiconductor RAM and ROM Organization, Memory Expansion, Static and Dynamic Memory Types); Cache Memory (Associative and Direct Mapped Cache Organizations.)

UNIT-6 : Introduction to Parallelism

Goals of Parallelism (Exploitation of Concurrency, Troughput Enhancement); Amdahl's law; Instruction Level Parallelism (Pipelining, Super Scaling—Basic Features); Processor Level Parallelism (Multiprocessor Systems Overview).

UNIT-7: Computer Organization [80 × 86]

Instruction Codes, Computer Register, Computer Instructions, Timing and Control, Instruction Cycle, Type of Instructions, Memory Reference, Register Reference, I/O reference, Basics of Logic Design, Accumulator Logic, Control Memory, Address Sequencing, Micro-Instruction Formats, Micro-Program Sequencer, Stack Organization, Instruction Formats, Types of Interrupts; Memory Hierarchy.

Computer Organisation (TCS-401)

New Syllabus UP. Technical University

UNIT-1

Register Transfer Language, Bus and Memory Transfers, Bus Architecture, Bus Arbitration, Arithmetic Logic, Shift Micro operation, Arithmetic Logic Shift Unit, Design of Fast address, Arithmetic Algorithms (addition, subtraction, Booth Multiplication), IEEE standard for Floating-point numbers.

UNIT-2

Control Design Hardwired & Micro Programmed (Control Unit): Fundamental Concepts (Register Transfers, Performing of arithmetic or logical operations, Fetching a word from memory, storing a word in memory), Execution of a complete instruction, Multiple-Bus organization, Hardwired Control, Micro programmed control (Microinstruction, Micro program sequencing, Wide-Branch addressing, Microinstruction with Next-address, Field, Prefetching Microinstruction).

UNIT-3

Processor Design Processor Organization: General register organization, Stack organization, Addressing Mode, Instruction format, Data transfer & manipulations, Program Control, Reduced Instruction Set Computer.

UNIT-4

Input-Output Organization I/O Interface, Modes of transfer, Interrupts & Interrupt handling, Direct Memory access, Input-Output processor, Serial Communication.

UNIT-5

Memory Organization Memory Hierarchy, Main Memory (RAM and ROM Chips), organization of 2D and 21/2 D, Auxiliary memory, Cache memory, Virtual Memory, Memory Management Hardware.

GGSIPU SYLLABUS

Code No.: BCA 203	**I**	**T**	**C**
Paper: Computer Architecture	**3**	**1**	**4**

Instrucuons to Paper Setters:

1. Question No. 1 should be computer and cover the entire syllabus. This question should have objective or short answer type questions. It should be of 25 marks.

2. Apart from question No. 1 rest of the paper shall consist of four units as per syllabus every unit should have two questions. However student may be asked to attempt only 1 question from each unit. Each question should be 12.5 marks.

UNIT-I

Register Transfer and Microoperations: transfer language. Resister transfer bus and memory transfers, arithmetic microoperations, logic micro-operations, shift microoperation arithmetic logic shift unit

Basic Computer organizations and design instruction codes computer resisters computer Instructions timing and control, **[No. Of Hrs: 11]**

UN IT-II

Basic Computer organizations and design instruction cycle memory-reference instructions register reference instructions input instructions design of accumulator logic unit

Central processing unit: Introduction general register organization stack organization instruction formats address modes, **[No. Of Hrs: 11]**

UNIT-III

Computer arithmetic: Introduction multiplication algorithms division algorithms for fixed point-members.

Input output organization: peripheral devices input output interfaces. Asynchronous data transfer modes of transfer priority interrupt direct memory access (DMA) **[No. Of Hrs: 11]**

UNIT-IV

Memory organization: memory hierarchy, main memory, auxiliary memory, associative memory, cache memory, virtual memory, Memory Management Hardware **[No. Of Hrs: 11]**

	L	T	C
Code No.: **MCA 106**			
Paper: Computer System Architecture	3	1	4

Instructions To Paper Setters:

1 Question No. I should be compulsory and cover the entire syllabus. This question should have objective or short answer type questions. It should be of 20 marks.

2. Apart from Question No. I, rest of the paper shall consist of four units as per the syllabus. Every unit should have two questions. However, student may be asked to attempt only I question from each unit. Each question should be 10 marks.

UNIT-I

Introduction and overview: Review of digital components, Evolution of computers.

Register Transfer and Microoperation: Register transfer language, register transfer, bus and memory transfer, arithmetic microoperations, logic microoperations, shift microoperations.

Basic Computer Organization and Design: Instruction codes, computer registers, computer instructions, timing & control, instruction cycle, memory reference instructions, input-output and interrupts, design of basic computer, design of accumulator logic. **[No. of Hrs: 14]**

UNIT- II

Microprogrammed Control Unit: Control memory, address sequencing.

Central Processing Unit: Introduction, general register organization, stack organization, instruction formats, addressing modes. Pipeline and vector processing Parallel Processing, pipelining, arithmetic pipeline, RISC **[No. of Hrs: 12]**

UNIT-III

Computer Arithmetic: Introduction, addition and subtraction, multiplication algorithms, division algorithms, floating point arithmetic operation, decimal arithmetic unit, decimal arithmetic operations.

Input-Output Organization: Peripheral devices, input-output interface, asynchronous data transfer, modes of data transfer, priority interrupt, direct memory access, input-output processor. **[No. of Hrs: 12]**

UNIT-IV

Memor organization: Memory hierarchy. main memory. auxiliary memory. Associative memory, cache memory, virtual memory, memory management hardware. Multiprocessors: Characteristics of multiprocessor. Interconnection Structure, Interprocessor Communication & Synchronization. **[No. of IIrs: 12]**

Delhi University, Deptt. of Computer Science-MCA Programme

MCA 1O4 COMPUTER SYSTEMS ARCHITECTURE and LAB.

Basic Building Blocks: Boolean logic and Boolean algebra, tristate logic; flip-flops, counters, shift registers, adders, substractor, encoders, decoders, multiplexers, demultiplexers

Register Transfer and Micro Operations: Bus and memory transfers, arithmetic, logic shift micro operations; basic computer organization: common bus system, instruction formats, instruction cycle, interrupt cycle, input/output configuration, CPU organization, register organization, stack organization, micro programmed control unit RISC architecture; microprocessor architecture. Memory Unit: Primary memory, secondary memory, associative memory, sequential access, direct access storage devices.

Input-Output Architecture: Input/Output devices; data transfer schemes - programmed I/O and DMA transfer; data transfer schemes for microprocessors.

Lecture Plans (MDU & GGSIPU)

FOR FACULTY AND STUDENTS-STUDY GUIDE PLAN

M.D. University Syllabus For CSE and ECE

B.Tech – course code: CSE-210-E: semester-IV

Computer Architecture and Organization

Lec/Tut	Course Plan
	UNIT-I: BASIC PRINCIPLES
L1	Boolean Algebra And Logic Gates
L2	Combinational Logic Blocks

Lec/Tut	Course Plan
	Adders, Multiplexers
	Encoders And Decoders
L3	Sequential Logic Blocks
	Latches, Flip Flops, Counters And Registers
T1	Problems On K-Map Simplification
	UNIT-II: GENERAL SYSTEM ARCHITECTURE
L4	Stored Program Control Concept Flynn's Classification of Computers: SISD, MISD, SIMD and MIMD Architectures
L5	Multilevel View Point of a Machine Digital Logic-Macro and Micro Architecture And ISA
L6	Operating Systems and High Level Language
L7	Structured Organization Performance Metrics (MIPS, MFLOPS)
T2	Problems On MIPS and MFLOPS
L8 L9	CPU-Central Processing Unit Cache, Main Memory and Secondary Memory Units I/O Devices
	UNIT-III: INSTRUCTION SET ARCHITECTURE
L10	Instruction Set Based Classification of Processors Three, Two, One, Zero Address Instructions RISC and CISC Address Instructions and RISC Vs. CISC
L11	Addressing Modes
T3	Numerical On Addressing Modes And Address Instructions
L12	Operations in The Instruction Set Arithmetic and Logical Instructions Data Transfer And Control Flow
L13 L14	Instruction Set Format : Fixed, Variable And Hybrid 8086 CPU and Simulation Using MASM
	UNIT-IV: BASIC NON-PIPELINED ARCHITECTURE
L 1 5	CPU Architecture Types Accumulator, Register, Stack, Memory/Register Detailed Data Path of a Register Based CPU
T4	Summary And Numerical On Stacks
L16	Microinstruction Sequencing Implementation of Control Unit
L17	Fetch, Decode and Execute Cycle Control Unit- Enhancing Performance With Pipelining
	UNIT-V: MEMORY HIERARCHY AND I/O TECHNIQUES
L18	Need For Memory Hierarchy Locality of Reference Principle
L19	Main Memory Semiconductor RAM and ROM Organization Memory Expansion
T5	Summary and Problems on Main Memory Expansion
L20 L21	Static and Dynamic Memory Types-Associative Memory Cache Memory-Associative And Direct Mapped Cache Organizations-Cache Coherence Problem
	UNIT-VI: INTRODUCTION TO PARALLELISM
L22	Goals of Parallelism Segmentation of Processor in Functional Units-Amdahl's Law
T6	Problems On Cache Memory
L23	Pipelining Concept
L24	Instruction Level Parallelism Piepline Hazards
L25	Processor Level Parallelism

Lec/Tut	Course Plan
L26	Vector Processors- Super Scaling
L27	Memory Interleaving- Array Processors
T7	Problems On Amdahl's Law And Pipelining
	UNIT-VII: COMPUTER ORGANISATION-8086
L28	Instruction Codes type of Instructions (Register Reference, Memory Reference and I/O Reference)
L29	Computer Registers- Computer Instructions Basics of Logic Design
L30	Instruction Cycle Flowchart For Determining the Type of Instruction
L31	Timing and Control Circuit
T8	Numerical on Register Transfer and Revision on Instructions.
L32	Control Memory - Mapping Logic Microprogram Example
L33	Microinstructions- Microinstruction Formats Micro Program Sequencer
T9	Summary and Numerical on Stacks
L34	Direct Memory Access-DMA
L35	Types of Interrupts-Software, Internal And External Interrupts-Flowchart For Interrupt Cycle
T10	Revision of Previous Exam Papers of MDU
L36	Virtual Memory And Memory Management

GGSIPU, Delhi

Lecture plan for computer architecture 3rd sem.

Subject code: EICS-305 **Credits: 4**

S.No	Contents	No. Of Lectures	Tutorials
	1st Term		
1.	Introduction to computer architecture (difference between computer architecture. Computer hardware & computer organization)	1	
2.	Understanding Register Transfer Language (RTL)	1	
3.	Common bus & memory transfer (hardware implementation)	2	
4.	Arithmetic micro operation: binary adder binary adder subtractor arithmetic circuit (hardware implementation)	2	
5.	Logical shift micro operation (hardware implementation)	1	
6.	Instruction code: stored program organization indirect addresses	2	
7.	Computer resisters, instruction timing & control	2	
8.	Basic computer design	2	
9.	Accumulator design	1	
10.	Control memory	1	
11.	Address sequencing: conditional branching mapping of instruction.	1	
12.	CPU- Introduction and organization stack organization	1	

S.No	Contents	No. Of Lectures	Tutorials
	1st Term		
13.	Instruction format: 3,2,1,0 address instructions.	2	
14.	Addressing modes explanation and numerical example solving.	2	
	2nd Term		
15.	Parallel processing	3	
16.	Pipe lining arithmetic pipelining	2	
17.	RISC pipelining		
18.	Vector processing: vector operations, matrix multiplication supercomputers.	1	
19.	Array processing: SIMD processor	1	
20.	Computer arithmetic		
(a)	Introduction	1	
(b)	Addition and subtraction	1	
(c)	Multiplication and division	2	
(d)	Floating point operation	1	
(e)	Decimal architecture	1	
21.	Peripheral devices	1	
22.	I/O interface	1	
23.	Modes of data transfer	2	
24.	I/O processor	1	
	3rd Term		
25.	Memory hierarchy main memory auxiliary memory RAM, ROM, chips magnetic disk magnetic tapes	1	
26.	Associative hardware organization cache memory difference mappings	1	
27.	Virtual memory	1	
28.	Characteristics of multiprocessor interconnection structure	1	
29.	Inter process communication & synchronization	1	

APPENDIX–B
EXPERIMENTS IN CSA LAB.

List of Experiments

Experiment No. 1: To study AND gate & verify its truth table.

Experiment No. 2: To study OR gate & verify its truth table.

Experiment No. 3: To study NAND gate & verify its truth table.

Experiment No. 4: To study NOR gate & verify its truth table.

Experiment No. 5: To study NOT gate & verify its truth table.

Experiment No. 6: To study shift register & verify its truth table.

Experiment No. 7: To study 7490 counter & verify its truth table.

Experiment No. 8: To study Tristate buffer & verify its truth table.

Experiment No. 9: To study DAC & verify its truth table.

Experiment No. 10: To study ADC & verify its truth table.

Experiment No.1

AIM: To study the 2 input AND gate and verify its truth table.

Theory: AND gate is a gate with two or more inputs. The gate has high output only when all the inputs are high.

Symbol:

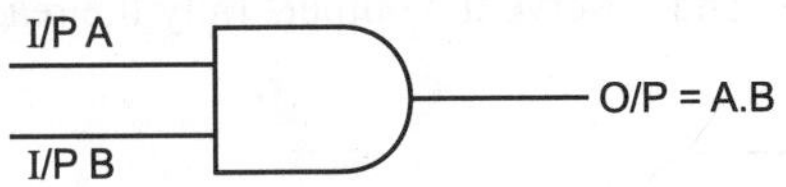

2 Input AND gate

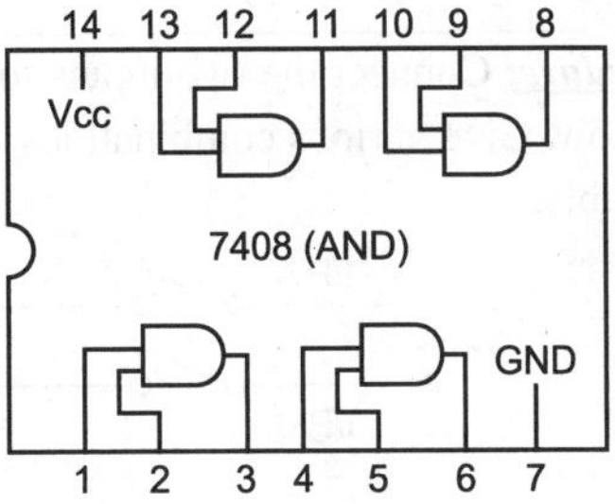

Truth table:

Truth table for two input gate:

Input A	Input B	Output Y=A.B
0	0	0
0	1	0
1	0	0
1	1	1

Procedure: Connect the two inputs to the logic switch and the output to the LED indicator as shown below. Give various combinations to inputs and observe the output. Tally the readings with the truth table.

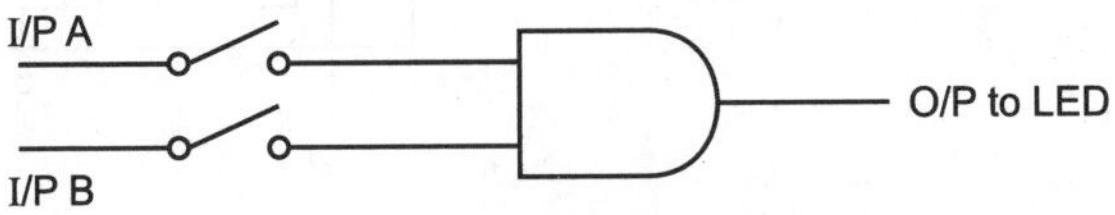

Experiment No. 2

AIM: To study the 2 input OR gate and verify its truth table.

Theory: OR gate is a gate with two or more inputs and one output. The gate has high output if any, or all the inputs are high.

Symbol:

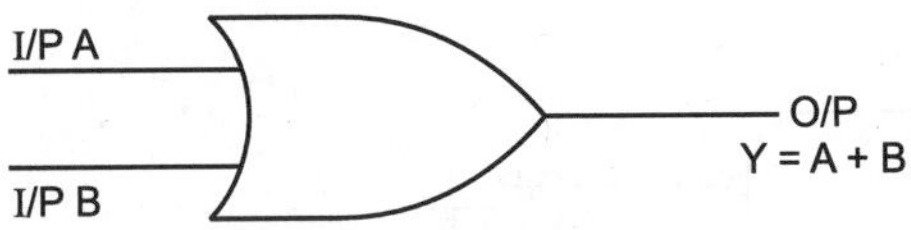

2 Input or gate

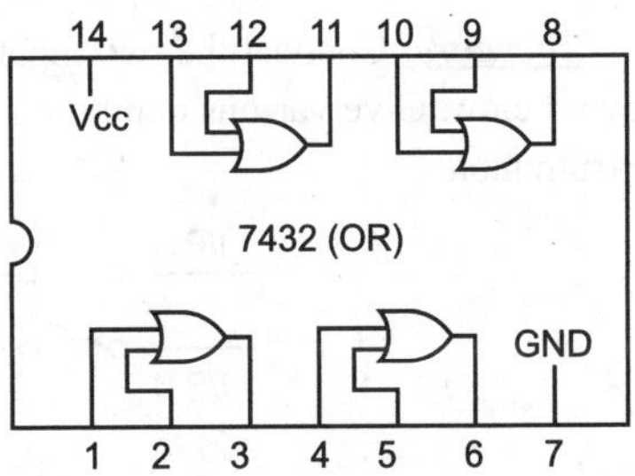

Truth Table:

Truth table for two input OR gate:

Input A	Input B	Output Y=A+B
0	0	0
0	1	1
1	0	1
1	1	1

Procedure: Connect the two inputs to the logic switch and the output to the LED indicator as shown below. Give various combinations to inputs and observe the output. Tally the readings with the truth table.

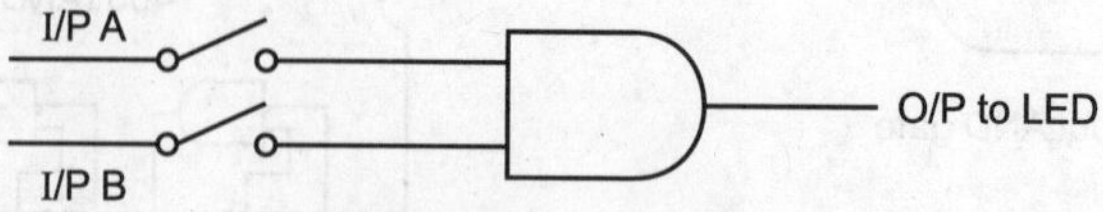

Experiment No. 3

AIM: To study the 2 input NAND gate and verify its truth table.

Theory: NAND gate is a gate with two or more inputs. It represents a NAND gate followed by an inverter.

Symbol:

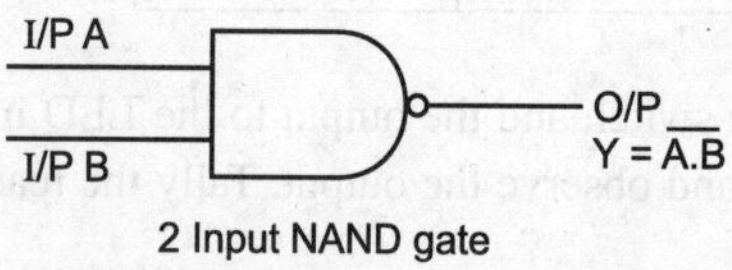

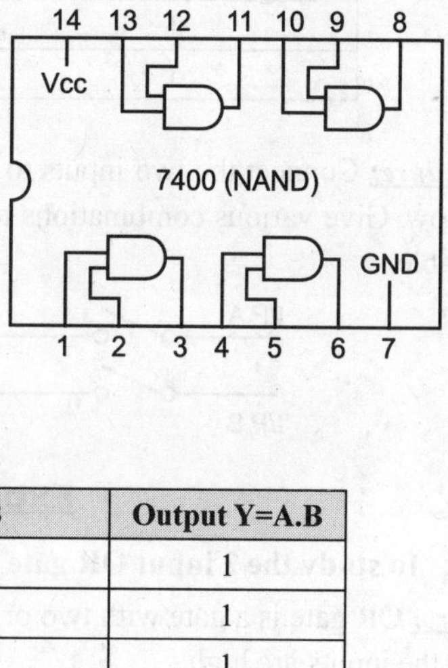

Truth table:

Truth table for two input or gate:

Input A	Input B	Output Y=A.B
0	0	1
0	1	1
1	0	1
1	1	0

Procedure: Connect the two inputs to the logic switch, and the output to the LED indicator as shown below. Give various combinations to inputs and observe the output. Tally the readings with the truth table.

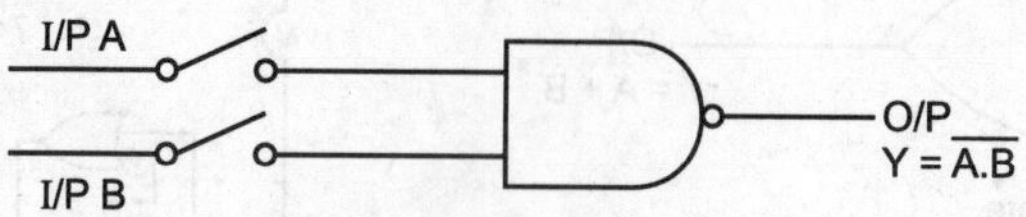

Experiment No. 4

AIM: To study the 2 input NOR gate and verify its truth table.

Theory: NOR gate is a gate with two or more than two inputs. NOR gate is equivalent to an OR gate following by an inverter. Only one of the inputs must be high to get low outputs if both the inputs are low, the output is high. NOR gate is a universal gate as any logic circuit can be built with NOR gates only.

Symbol:

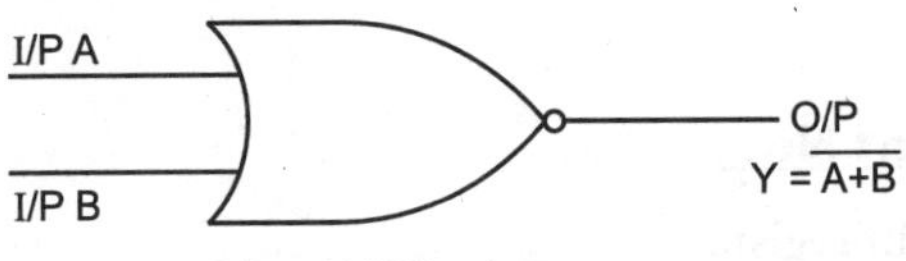

2 Input NOR gate

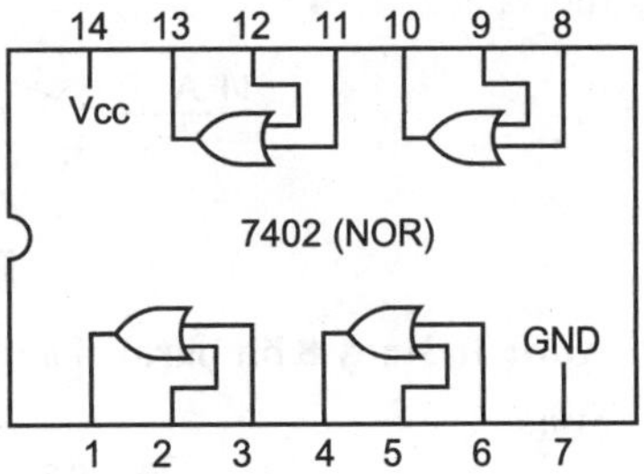

Truth Table:

Truth table for two input NOR gate:

Input A	Input B	Output Y=A+B
0	0	1
0	1	0
1	0	0
1	1	0

Procedure: Connect the two inputs to the logic switch and the output to the LED indicator as shown below. Give various combinations to inputs and observe the output. Tally the readings with the truth table.

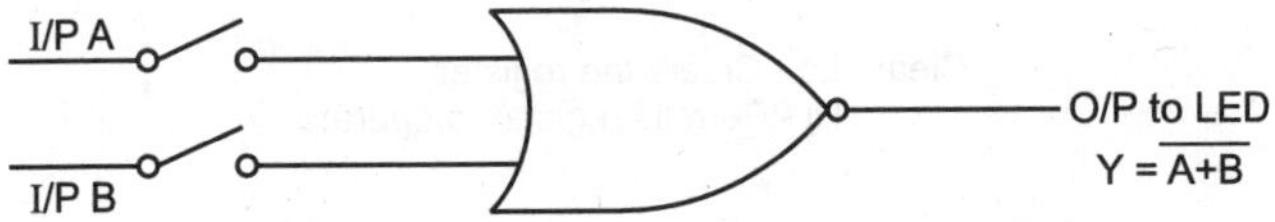

Experiment No. 5

AIM: To study the NOT gate and verify its truth table.

Theory: OR gate is a gate with two or more inputs and one output. The gate has high output if any, or all the inputs are high.

Symbol:

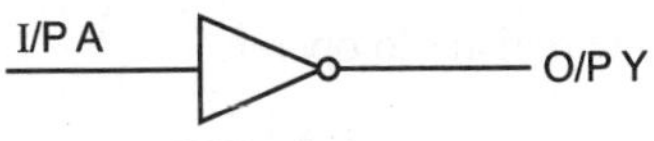

NOT gate

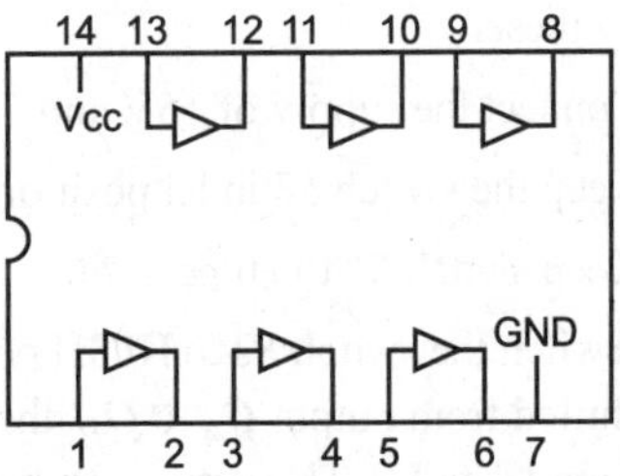

Truth Table :

Truth table for two input or gate:

Input A	Output Y=A
0	1
1	0

Procedure: Connect the two inputs to the logic switch and the output to the LED indicator as shown below. Give various combinations to inputs and observe the output. Tally the readings with the truth table.

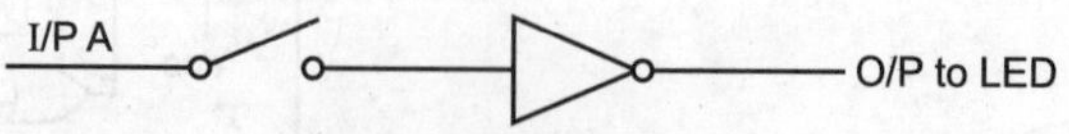

Experiment No. 6

AIM: To study 8 bit parallel out serial in shift register.

Symbol:

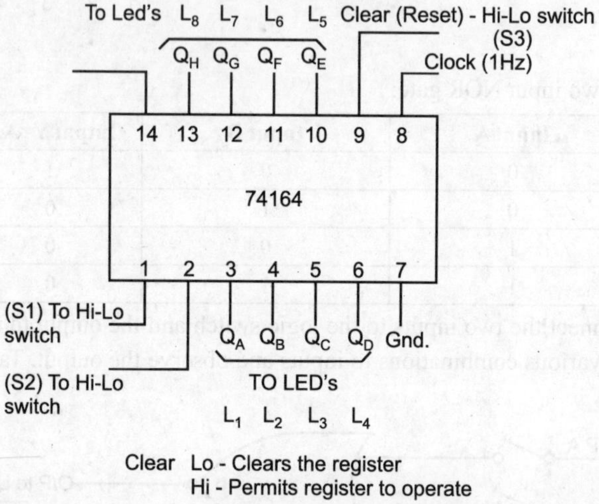

Procedure:

1. Pin nos. 1 &2 are two serial inputs. *QA* to Q_H are 8 bit parallel outputs. Pin no. 9 is the Clear line. Clock is to be connected to pin no. 8.
2. Connect the two inputs pin Nos. 1 & 2 to two Hi- Lo switches *S*1 & *S*2.
3. Connect the Clear line Pin no. 9 to a Hi- Lo switch *S*3.
4. Connect pin no. 8 to Clock output, 1 Hz. At this point, clock of 1Hz is available.
5. Connect the O/P's Q_A to Q_H to eight LED's *LI* to 1.8. You will be able to monitor the 0/P5 by these.
6. Connect the supply of +5V and Ground to pin numbers 14 & 7 respectively.
7. Keep the switch *S*3 in Hi position, this permits the register to operate.
8. Keep switch *S*1 to Hi position.
9. Switch the switch *S*2 to HIGH position. As the clock of 1 Hz arrives at pin 8, the logic 1 is shifted from output Q_A to Q_H the clock progresses. This can be seen by the lamp glowing from L1 to L8. The output can be said to be shifting from output Q_A to Q_H.

10. If the position of switch $S1$ is now kept at Low, logic 0 is shifted from output Q_A to Q_H. This can be observed by lamps going off from $L1$ to $L8$.
11. It is necessary to keep one out of the two switches $S1$ & $S2$ in the HIGH position to enable to shift the input given to the other I/P. If the input to be shifted is to be given to $S1$, then $S2$ should be in the HIGH position, and, if the input to be shifted is to be applied to $S2$, then $S1$ should be kept in the HIGH position. The input is inhibited if the other switch is kept in the LOW position.

This explains and demonstrates the working of the Shift Register.

Experiment No.7

AIM: Study of 7490 counter.

THEORY:

The circuit used for counting the pulses in known as a counter. When the pulses to be counted are applied to a counter it goes from, state to state and the output of the flip-flops in the counter is decoded to read the count. The counters are composed of flip-flops. A circuit with n-flip-flops can count from 0 to $2n$.

It is a divide-by-two and divide-by-five decade counter or mod 10 counter. It consists of four master slave flip flops internally connected to provide a mod -2 counter and a mod-5 counters. The mod - 2 and mod - 5 counters can be used independently or in combinations.

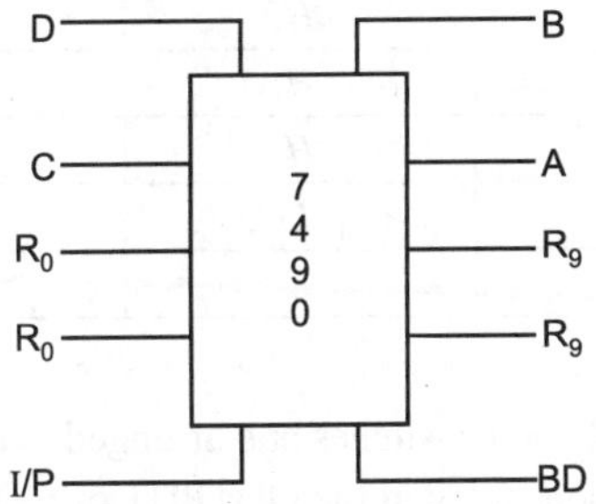

$A\ B\ C\ D$ = **Outputs.**

$R_0\ R_0\ R_9\ R_9$ = **Reset inputs.**

Input = **Clock to A flip flop.**

BD = **Clock to B flip flop.**

To use IC 7490 maximum count length (i.e. as mod 10 counter), the 'BD' input is connected to the Q_A output The input count pulses are applied to input A and the outputs are as described in the function table. There are four reset inputs namely R_0, R_0, R_9, R_9.

1. When both the R_9's are high and any one of 'R_9' is low the output **displays zero.**
2. When both the R_9's are high and R_0's are don't care, the output **displays nine.**
3. To use the rounter in counting mode, make one R_0 Rand R_9, low and others are don't care.

RESET INPUTS					OUTPUTS			
R_0 (1)	R_0 (2)	R_9 (1)	R_9 (2)		D	C	B	A
H	H	L	X		L	L	L	L
H	H	X	L		L	L	L	L

RESET INPUTS				OUTPUTS			
X	*X*	*H*	*H*	*H*	*L*	*L*	*H*
X	*L*	*X*	*L*	COUNT			
L	*X*	*X*	*L*	COUNT			
L	*X*	*L*	*X*	COUNT			
X	*L*	*L*	*X*	COUNT			

NOTE:

1. Output A is connected to input B for BCD count.
2. Output D is connected to input A for bi-quinary count and BD is given clock.

BCD Count Sequence:

COUNT	OUTPUTS			
	D	***C***	***B***	***A***
0	*L*	*L*	*L*	*L*
1	*L*	*L*	*L*	*H*
2	*L*	*L*	*H*	*L*
3	*L*	*L*	*H*	*H*
4	*L*	*H*	*L*	*L*
5	*L*	*H*	*L*	*H*
6	*L*	*H*	*H*	*L*
7	*L*	*H*	*H*	*H*
8	*H*	*L*	*L*	*L*
9	*H*	*L*	*L*	*H*

PROCEDURE :

Reset inputs are connected to logic switches and arranged in counting mode as shown in Reset function in table. INPUT (A) is connected at the OUTPUT of **COARSE CLOCK.** All outputs are connected (*A*, *B*, *C*, *D*) to either LED's to see counting in BCD code or to the 7-segment display to see counting in the decimal numbers. Output *A* is connected to input BD for BCD count.

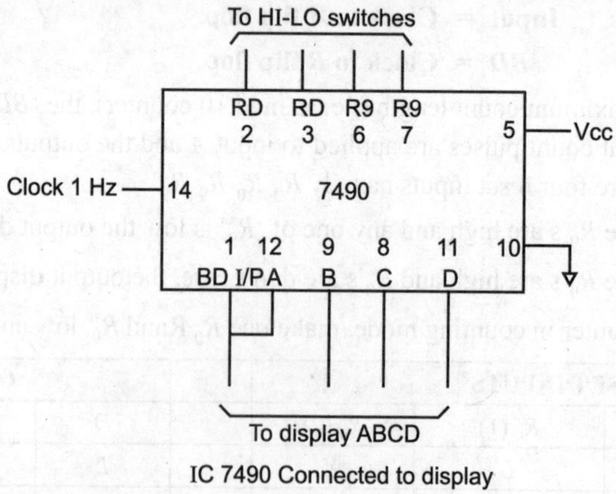

IC 7490 Connected to display

Experiment No.8

AIM: **To study three state buffer and verify its truth table.**

THEORY:

The three state buffer has three states of outputs. The DISABLE plays a very important role in selecting the output state. The three states of the output are:

1. High State
2. Low State
3. High impedance state (i.e. output is not connected in the circuit, it floats.)

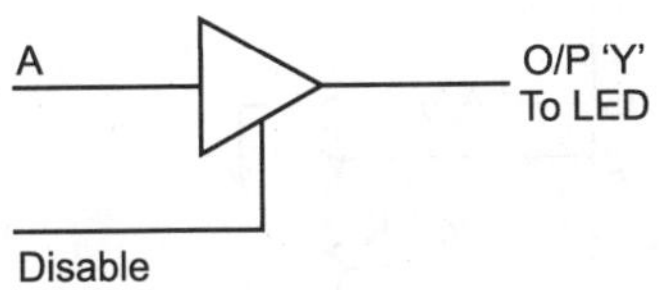

Tristate Buffer

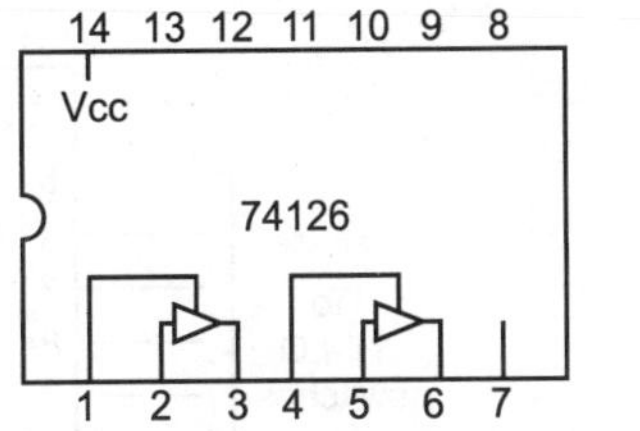

If pin 1 = Logic 1 then pin2 = pin 3
If pin 1 = Logic 0, then pin3 is open.

When DISABLE is HIGH:

The three state buffer acts as a non - inverting buffer. So that INPUT A = OUTPUT Y. Whatever may be the input (logic 0 or 1) ,the same appears at the output. If input is low then output is also low. If input is high then output is also high.

When DISABLE is low:

When DISABLE is low, irrespective of the state of input, the output floats i.e. (the output is not connected in the circuit).

TRUTH TABLE:

DISABLE	INPUT A	OUTPUT Y
Low	0	*
	1	*
High	0	0
	1	1

* stands for tristate, i.e high impedance state.

PROCEDURE:

The DISALBLE and input of three state buffer are connected to logic switches and output to the LED indication as shown in the figure below:

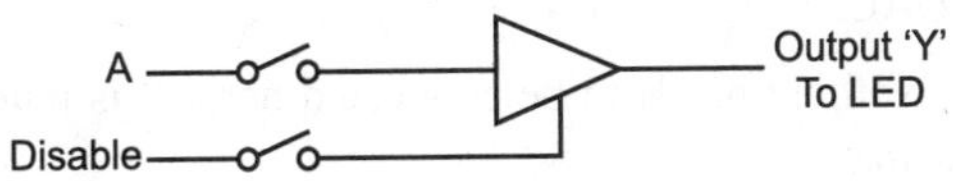

CIRCUIT DIAGRAM

Give all combinations of logic signals at inputs, and observe the output. Tally the result with the Truth Table.

Experiment No : 9

AIM: To convert digital signals into an analog signal using DAC 0808/0800.

CAUTION: Observe the Digital Trainer supplied to you. It may have DAC 0808 or DAC 0800 fitted into it. These two chips are similar, but not identical. Both are 8 bit D to A converters. Follow the procedure for the type fitted in your trainer. Procedure for both is given below:

PROCEDURE FOR DAC 0808:

It is a 16 Pin chip. Rig the circuit as shown below:

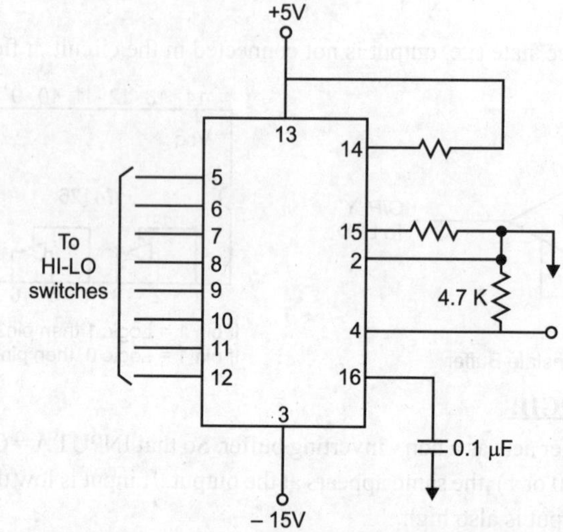

1. Connect socket marked GND to GND bus. This applies ground to the DAC, pin no.2.
2. Connect socket marked -V to socket marked -15V. This applies -15V the -V pin of DAC, pin no. 3.
3. Connect sockets marked A_1 to A_8 to HI-LO switch output sockets numbered 1 to 8 respectively, pin nos. 5, 6, 7, 8, 9, 10, 11, 12. A_1 represents the most significant bit (MSB). A_8 represents the least significant bit (LSB). Now by setting the switches 1 to 8, you can feed desired digital binary number from 00000000 to 11111111.
4. Connect external digital multimeter with red lead to pin no. 4, and black lead to socket marked GND.

> **NOTE:** The DVM black lead should be connected to the GND socket located near the DAC IC and NOT anywhere on the GNU bus. This will avoid voltage drops across the ground bus and improve the accuracy of result.

5. **COMP** : Pin no. 16. Nothing needs to be connected here as it is a very sensitive point. It has been internally grounded through a 0.01uF ceramic disc capacitor to reduce parasitic responses in the DAC.
6. V_R- : Pin no. 15. Nothing needs to be connected here. It is internally returned to ground through 4.7K resistor.
7. V_R+ : Pin no. 14. Nothing needs to be connected here. It is internally returned to +5V through a 2.5K resistance, yielding a reference input current of 2mA.
8. V_{cc} : Pin no. 13. Connect socket marked V_{cc} to +5V bus. This provides operating positive voltage to the DAC.

Experiment:

Set toggle switches 1 to 8 to various combinations, and observe DVM readings. Obtain the table below, showing DAC operation:

0808 DAC

A_1	A_2	A_3	A_4	A_5	A_6	A_7	A_8	**ANALOG O/P**
1	1	1	1	1	1	1	1	–4.94v
1	0	0	0	0	0	0	0	–2.48v
0	1	0	0	0	0	0	0	–1.244v
0	0	1	0	0	0	0	0	–620mv
0	0	0	1	0	0	0	0	–310mv
0	0	0	0	1	0	0	0	–155mv
0	0	0	0	0	1	0	0	–77mv
0	0	0	0	0	0	1	0	–38mv
0	0	0	0	0	0	0	1	–19mv
0	0	0	0	0	0	0	0	0mV

Experiment No: 10

AIM: To convert an analog signal into digital using ADC 808/809.

Theory:

ADC 808 as well as ADC 809 are similar 8 bit analog to digital converters. Whereas one can refer to data books on the subject for details, the operating procedure is explained as below:

Procedure:

This multiplexer cum ADC is a 28 pin IC. Implement the connections as shown below:

Pin no. **Connect to**

11 .... +5V

13 .... GND

12 .... Reference Voltage (+5V)

Address lines

23 ....*C*.... HI-LO Sw.(S3)

24 ....*B*.... HI-LO Sw.(S2) (address of input lines)

25 ....*A*.... HI-LO Sw.(S1)

Input lines

26 ---------------- I/P line 0

27 ---------------- I/P line 1

28 ---------------- I/P line 2

1 ---------------- I/P line 3

2 ---------------- I/P line 4

3 ---------------- I/P line 5

4 ---------------- I/P line 6

5 ---------------- I/P line 7

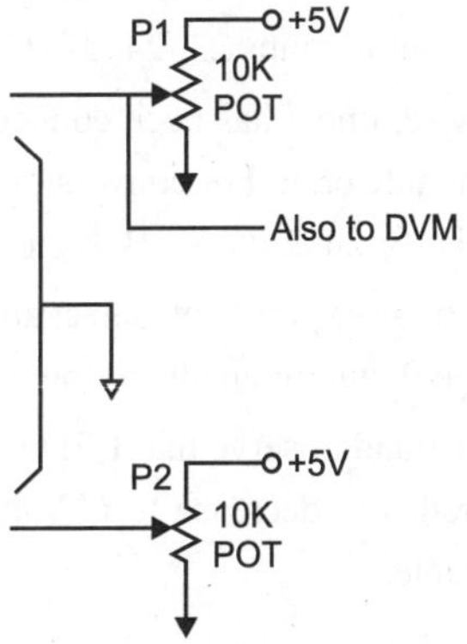

Pin no.		Connect to
16	....	Reference –ve
10	....	Clock 100KHz
9	....	O/P enable – Hi-Lo switch (S4)
7	....	End of conversion – to 10Hz clock
6	....	start – to clock 10Hz
21	....	2^{-1} – to LED1
20	....	2^{-2} – to LED2
19	....	2^{-3} – LED3
18	....	2^{-4} – to LED4
8	....	2^{-5} – to LED5
15	....	2^{-6} – to LED6
14	....	2^{-7} – to LED7
17	....	2^{-8} – to LED8

The address lines C,B,A on pins 23,24,25 respectively select the input lines from INPUT 0 to INPUT line 7 (Pin 26,27, 28, 1,2,3,4 & 5) for conversion of the analog INPUT applied there to (input lines) to digital code as given below:

C	*B*	*A*	I/P line selected for *A* to *D* conversion
0	0	0	I/P line 0, pin 26
0	0	1	I/P line 1, pin 27
0	1	0	I/P line 2, pin 28
0	1	1	I/P line 3, pin 1
1	0	0	I/P line 4, Pin 2
1	0	1	I/P line 5, pin 3
1	1	0	I/P line 6, pin 4
1	1	1	I/P line 7, pin 5

In the present case we have connected line 0 to a pot *P*1 wherefrom we feed an analog voltage variable from 0 to 5 V. This analog voltage will be converted to digital signal provided line 0 is selected by setting pins 23, 24, 25 (C,B,A) to 0, 0 and 0 (all zeroes).

Likewise, line 7 has been connected to Pot *P*2 and by adjusting *P*2 analog voltage of 0 to 5 V can be available on it. For conversion of voltage at line 7 to digital code, line *7* has to be selected by setting pills 23, 24 & 25 (C, B, A) to 1, 1, 1(all ones).

To start the experiment, select any one line, say line 0, by setting pins 23, 24 & 25 to all zeroes. Also set pin 9, output enable to logic High.

Vary P1 and observe that LED's *L*1 to L8 change in status. Start from *P*1, set to maximum, i.e. 5V and gradually decrease to *U* Volts. Observe the corresponding status of LED's and verify the enclosed table.

The experiment can be repeated for line 7 by selecting line 7 instead of line 0.

Analog Input	DB7	DB6	DB5	DB4	DB3	DB2	DB1	DB0
0-5mv	0	0	0	0	0	0	0	0
8mv-25mv	0	0	0	0	0	0	0	1
27mv-45mv	0	0	0	0	0	0	1	0
65mV-84mV	0	0	0	0	0	1	0	0
142mV-158mB	0	0	0	0	1	0	0	0
298mV-314mV	0	0	0	1	0	0	0	0
610mV-625mV	0	0	1	0	0	0	0	0
1.23V	0	1	0	0	0	0	0	0
2.47V	1	0	0	0	0	0	0	0
3.73V	1	1	0	0	0	0	0	0
4.36V	1	1	1	0	0	0	0	0
4.65V	1	1	1	1	0	0	0	0
4.83V	1	1	1	1	1	0	0	0
4.90V	1	1	1	1	1	1	0	0
4.94v	1	1	1	1	1	1	1	0
4.97v	1	1	1	1	1	1	1	1

APPENDIX–C
GLOSSARY

A

A/D converter (Analog to Digital Converter) A device that can convert continuous analog signals from instruments that monitor condition like movement, temperature, sound, etc., into discrete digital numbers or binary code for the computer.

AJUX Apple's version of UNIX for the Macintosh.

A20 PC address line that points to memory beyond one legabyte. For compatibility with 808618088s, this line is gated in 286s and up. It is controlled by circuitry on the motherboard. When disabled, it keeps the machine operating in Real Mode (under 1MB), and when enabled, it helps the CPU address memory beyond 1MB (Protected Mode).

A: The usual designation for the first floppy disk drive in a PC.

abacus An ancient mechanical calculator. It consists of movable beads threaded on a grid of wires. Though first developed in ancient Mediterranean cultures, it is still used in several far-eastern Asian countries.

ABC (Atanasoff-Berry Computer) First electronic digital computer, completed in 1942 by Professor John Atanasoff and his graduate student Clifford Berry of Iowa State University, which embodied the basic concepts of future computers . input, memory and arithmetic unit.

abend (ABnormal END) Also called a crash or bomb. This occurs when the computer is presented with instructions or data it cannot recognIze or when a program is atteilipting to reach beyond its protective boundary. This can happen as the result of erroneous software logic or hardware failure.

abort To exit a function or application midway and without saving any data that has been changed. It is also, in DOS commands, the-option for cancelling a command -that cannot be implemented (eg. trying a DIR of A:withodt a floppy in it). The key combination –CTRL+BREAK or ESC also abort commands.

abscissa The x axis of a graph or chart. Contrast with ordinate.

absolute In programming, a mathematical function that always returns a positive number. For example, ABS(25-100) yields 75, not -75.

absolute address Explicit identification of a peripheral device, of a location within the peripheral device or of a specific location in memory. For example, all these are absolute addresses:

disk drive no. 1, sector no. 12 and byte no. 65,536 are absolute addresses. During low level programming, the computer must be given absolute addresses to reference its memory and peripherals. See base address, relative address.

absolute coding Program coding that uses machine instructions and absolute address. Such programs can be directly executed by a computer without prior translation to a different form. Contrast with symbolic coding.

absolute vector In computer graphics, a vector with end points designated in absolute coordinates. Contrast with relative vector.

absolute zero Theoretical temperature at which molecular activity ceases (-273.15° C, -459.67 F).

AC (Alternating Current) The form of electricity from power plant to home/office. Its direction is reversed 50 or 60 times per second. Contrast with DC.

accelerator Key combination that is used to activate a task. See accelerator board.

accelerator board An add-in board that replaces the existing CPU with a higher performance CPU. These boards are usually specific to a task and take over the functions of the main CPU in performing these tasks.

access To store data on and retrieve data from a disk or other peripheral device. See access arm, access method.

access arm Mechanical arm of the disk drive that moves the read/write head across the surface of a disk. It is directed by instructions in the operating system to move the read/write head to the specific track on the disk. The rotation of the disk positions the read/write head over the required sector of the track.

access code Characters and/or numbers that identifies a user to the computer system. It allOws only authorised users with access the computer.

access control The process of using access codes whereby use of a computer is restricted to authorized users.

access light The light on the front of a system unit that signals when the computer is reading from or writing to a disk. This is sometimes on the disk drive itself.

access mechanism Them mechanical device in the disk storage Unit that positions the read/write heads on the proper tracks.

access method The software routine that is part of the operating system or network control program which handles the storing! retrieving; in a network control programme, it looks after the transmitting/receiving of data. It is also responsible for detecting errors in these processes either caused by hardware or network malfunction and correcting it if possible.

Tapes use the Sequential Access Method for storing data. This places the next block of data after the previous one. Disks normally use Indexed Access Methods. The index is a table of contents for each file or each record within the file. Random Access Methods are common disk access methods when the read/write head does not have to travel sequentially to reach the specific location on the storage device (disk). The index allows it to jump to any position without going through the intervening positions. Quite naturally, the random access method is considerably faster than the sequential access method.

Communications access methods, such as IBM's TCAM and VTAM, transfer data between a host computer and remote terminals. LAN access methods, such as DSMA/CD (Ethernet) and token passing (Token Ring), transfer data to and from connected computers on the network.

access monitoring A method of access control in which the system user is given only a certain number of attempts to provide the correct password.

accessory card An additional circuit card that can be mounted inside a personal computer and connected to the system bus.

access time (1) Memory access time is how long it takes for a character in memory to be transferred to or from the CPU. In a personal computer, fast RAM chips have an access time of 80 nanoseconds or even less. Though this is a common speed measurement, disk performance is also influenced by other factors like channel speed (transfer rate), interleaving, caching, file fragmentation, etc. (2) Disk access time is an average of the time it takes to position the read/write head over the requested track. Fast personal computer hard disks have access time of 18 milliseconds or less.

account number The number assigned, in a database, to an employee, customer, vendor or product for identification.

accounting machine Early office machine used to compute and prepare invoices and payroll, etc., using magnetic strip ledger cards or punched cards.

accumulator Hardware register used to hold the results or partial results of arithmetic and logical operations.

accuracy The degree of exactness of an approximation or measurement. While accuracy normally denotes absolute quality of computed results; precision usually refers to the amount of detail used in representing those results.

ACK (Acknowledgment code) Communications code sent from a receiving station to a transmitting station to indicate that it is ready to accept data. It is also used to acknowledge the error-free receipt of transmitted data. Contrast with NAK.

acoustical sound enclosure A device that fits over a printer or other machine to dampen noise. It is more noticeable when absent.

acoustic coupler Device that connects a terminal or computer to the handset of a telephone. It contains a shaped foam bed that the handset is placed in, and it may also contain the modem.

action The activity resulting from a given condition.

action entry One of the four sections of a decision table. Specifies what actions should be taken.

action-oriented management report An exception report used to alert management to abnormal situations that require special attention.

action statement A statement that tells the computer to perform some action.

active cell In an electronic spreadsheet, the cell that is highlighted by the cursor, Information may be entered, altered, or deleted by the user when the cell is active. Also called current cell.

active file A file currently being used.

active matrix LCD Advanced LCD technology that improves contrast by adding a transistor to each monochrome or red, green and blue dot. The transistor allows more current to illuminate the pixel. This means that the display is brighter and more readable. Contrast with passive matrix LCD.

active window In a window environment, the window in which the user is currently working.

activity One of the subunits of work that comprise a task.

actuator Mechanism that moves an object; for example, the device that moves the head assembly on a disk drive or an arm of a robot.

Ada High-level programming language designed for embedded applications and process control but is also used for logistics applications. ADA is a Pascal-based language that is very comprehensive.

ADA was named after Augusta Ada Byron (1815-1852), Countess of Lovelace and daughter of Lord Byron. She was a mathematician and colleague of Charles Babbage, who was developing his Analytical Engine. Some of her programming notes for the machine have survived, giving her the distinction of being the first documented programmer in the world.

adapter Device that allows one system to connect to and work with another. Display adapters and network adapters are really controllers, not adapters. See host adapter, expansion bus.

adapter boards Printed circuit boards that connect a system board to peripheral I/O devices or add specialized functions to the system.

adaptive system (1) A system displaying the ability to learn, change its state, or otherwise react to a stimulus. (2) Any system capable of adapting itself to changes in its environment.

ADB (Apple Desktop Bus) Macintosh communications port for keyboards, mice, trackballs, graphics tablets and other input devices.

ADC See A/D converter.

add-in, add-on Refers to hardware modules, such as printed circuit boards, that are designed to be plugged into a socket within the computer.

address (1) Number of a particular memory or peripheral storage location. Each byte of memory and each disk sector has its own unique address. Programs are compiled into machine language, which references actual addresses in the computer. (2) As a verb, to manage or work with. For example, "The computer can address 2MB of memory."

address bus Internal channel from the processor to memory across which the addresses of data (but not the data itseft) are transmitted. The number of lines (wires) in the address bus determines the amount of memory that can be directly addressed as each line carries one bit of the address. For example, the 8088 processor has 20 address lines and can address 1,048,576 bytes. The 68020 has 32 address lines and can address four gigabytes. Various swapping and switching techniqnes can be added to the hardware that allow a computer to use more memory than is directly addressable by its address bus. See EMS.

addressing (1) Locating a required piece of data by specific techniques. (2) A data communications control method whereby the host computer specifies the particular terminal for which it has data.

address mode Method by which an instruction references memory. An indexed address is modified by the contents of an index register before execution. An indirect address points to another address. Ultimately, in order to do any actual processing, the instruction must derive real, or absolute addresses, where the required data is located.

address register High-speed circuit that holds the addresses of data to be processed or of the next instruction to be executed.

address space Total amount of memory that can be used by a program. The address space may refer to a physical memory limit or to a virtual memory limit, which includes memory and disk. For example, the 386 can address 4GB of memory and 64TB of virtual memory.

add time The time required for a computer to perform an addition, exclusive of the time required to obtain the quantities from storage and put the sum back into storage.

address translation Transforming one address into another. For example, assemblers and compilers translate symbolic addresses into machine addresses. Virtual memory systems translate a virtual address into a real address.

addressable cursor Screen cursor that can be programmed to move to any row or column on the screen.

administrative data processing The field of data processing concerned with the management or direction of an organization.

Adobe fonts See PostScript.

Adobe Illustrator See Illustrator.

Adobe Photoshop See photoshop.

Adobe Type Manager PostScript font utility for the Macintosh and Windows from Adobe Systems. It scales Type 1 fonts into screen fonts and prints them on non-PostScript dot matrix and HP laser printers. Rather than downloading the font to the printer, it sends a bitmap of the entire page of text to the printer.

ATM technology is built into OS/2 and NeXTstep, and was originally developed to provide WYSIWYG screen fonts for the Mac. See PostScript.

advanced BASIC A generic term used to describe versions of the BASIC programming language that include features and operations not found in standard BASIC.

AFE (Apple File Exchange) Macintosh utility that converts data files between Mac and PC formats. It also includes a file translator between IBM's DCA format and MacWrite; however, MacLink Plus Translators can be used for additional capability.

AFP (AppleTalk Filing Protocol) Client/server protocol used in AppleTalk communications networks. In order for non-Apple networks to access data in an AppleShare server, their protocols must translate into the AFT language.

aftermarket The market for peripherals and software created by the sale of a large number of a specific brand of computer.

agent Software routine that waits in the background and performs an action when a specified event occurs. For example, agents could transmit a summary file on the first day of the month or monitor incoming data and alert the user when a certain transaction has arrived. See workflow automation.

AI (Artificial Intelligence) Devices and applications that exhibit human 'intelligence' and behaviour including robots, expert systems, voice recognition, natural and foreign language processing. It also implies the ability to learn or adapt through experience.

In the future, everything we now know and think about a computer will change. By the turn of the century, you should be able to converse with the average computer. Future systems will ask you what help you need and automatically call in the appropriate applications to aid you in solving your problem.

In the 1990s, the Al buzzword will used extensively to refer to any and all advancements. However, the acid test of Al was defined in the 1940s by the English scientist, Alan Turing, who said, A machine has artificial intelligence when there is no discernible difference between the conversation generated by the machine and that of an intelligent person." This test is called the 'Turing Test'.

Note: The term 'intelligence' refers to processing capability; therefore, every computer is intelligent. But, artificial intelligence implies human-like intelligence. An ironic twist in terminology.

aiming symbols A movable screen cursor on a display screen.

aircraft simulator A computer-controlled device that is used to train pilots. All of the instruments of a modern jet cockpit are there to make the simulation as close to reality as possible. The simulator includes a large screen, like a windshield, on which a mind- boggling array of graphics are generated. These sophisticated simulators are extremely realistic and are considered as good as training on an actual aircraft.

ALC (Assembly Language Coding) Generic term for IBM mainframe assembly languages.

Aldus PageMaker See Pagemaker.

Aldus Persuasion Desktop presentation program for the Macintosh from Aldus Corp. It can create output for overheads, handouts, speaker notes and film recorders. It is noted for its sophisticated transition features, such as fades, gravel, swipes and wipes.

alert box A screen display, usually in a small window, which asks a question or warns the user of impending disaster if his next move is the wrong move. The user answers by clicking a mouse button on a choice or giving a key command.

alert messages Messages that inform the user that the operation being performed is improper or impossible.

algebra A form of mathematics in which letters representing numerical values can be operated upon according to basic rules of arithmetic.

algebaric expression One or more characters or symbols associated with algebra; for example, $A + B = C$ or A/B.

algebra of logic A system of logical relations expressed as algebraic formulas first introduced by George Boole. See Boolean Algebra.

ALGOL (ALGOrithmic Language) High-level compiler language that was developed as an international language for the expression of algorithms between people and between people and machines.

algoritlun Set of ordered steps for solving a problem, such as a mathematical formula or the instructions in a program.

alias (1) Alternate name used in databases for identification, such as for naming a field or a file. (2) Phoney signal created under certain conditions when digitizing voice.

allasing In computer graphics, the stair-stepped or jagged appearance of diagonal lines, the poorer the resolution, the greater the degree of 'jaggies'. See anti-aliasing.

aligning edge That edge of a form that serves to correctly position a document to be scanned by an OCR device. Also called reference edge.

alignment Adjustment of tolerances within the mechanism of a device so it will operate properly.

allocate To reserve a resource such as memory or disk for instructions or data. Sometimes done by a programmer, or sometimes automatically by a program. See memory allocation.

all points addressable A graphics mode in which each pixel on the display screen can be accessed independently a program.

alphabetic stung A string in which the characters are letters or pertain to an agreed alphabet set.

aiphageometric See alphamosaic.

aiphamosaic Very-low-resolution display technique that uses elementary graphics characters (the upper part of the ASCII) as part of its character set.

alphanumeric Use of alphabetic letters mixed with numbers and special characters as in name, address, city and state. The text you are reading is alphanumeric.

alphanumeric sort The process in which a computer system puts a list into alphabetical or numerical order, or both.

alpha test The preliminary testing stage of software development or system development

AltaIr 8800 Microcomputer kit introduced in 1974 from Micro Instrumentation and Telemetry Systems. It used an 8080 microprocessor. In 1975, it was packaged with Microsoft's MBASIC. An estimated 10,000 Altairs were sold, making it the first commercially successful microcomputer.

Alto Xerox personal computer that pioneered the mouse! icon environment. It was the progenitor of Apple's Lisa and Macintosh. Designed in 1973 with 128K RAM, a 608x808 pixel screen and a 2.5MB removable hard disk, it connected directly to an Ethernet network. By 1979, about 1,000 Altos were in use.

ALU (Arithmetic Logic Unit) High-speed circuit in the CPU that does the actual calculating and comparing. Numbers are transferred from memory into the ALU for calculation, the results of which are sent back into memory. Alphanumeric data is sent from memory into the ALU for comparing. The results of the comparison are tested by GOTOs. For example, IF ITEMA EQUALS ITEMB GOTO UPDATE ROUTINE.

AM (Amplitude Modulation) Transmission technique that blends the data signal into a carrier by varying (modulating) the amplitude of the carrier. See modulate.

AM386 386-compatible chip running at 40MHz from Advanced Micro Devices. The AM386SXL is a 386SL-compatible chip.

ambient Surrounding. For example, ambient temperature, humidity and other conditions are atmospheric conditions that exist at the moment.

Amdahl Corporation A computer ma nufacturer founded in 1970 by Gene Amdahl. Its purpose was to build IBM-compatible mainframes with better performance. Its first mainframe was the 470/V6 computer, released in 1975.

American National Standards Institute (ANSI) An organization that acts as a national clearinghouse and coordinator for voluntary standards in the United States. It was founded in 1918 and is supported by more than a thousand professional societies, trade organizations, and companies.

American Standard Code for Information Interchange See ASCII.

Anuigat[th] Brand name for a family of microcomputers manufactured by Commodore Business Machines. Due to its excellent graphics, it is used extensively in the area of computer graphics and animation. The Amiga personal computers are based on the Motorola 68000 family of microprocessors.

The Amiga 500 is geared for home use and includes built-in speech synthesis, four-voice stereo sound and color graphics (4,096 cols.). The Amiga 2000 is designed for office applications, including CAD and desktop publishing. It has optional PC compatibility and NTSC video processing. The high-speed Amiga 3000(68030) provides enhanced graphics and the Workbench interface.

AMI BIOS Popular PC-compatible ROM BIOS from American Megatrends, Inc., Norcross, GA.

Ami Pro Windows word processing program from Lotus that includes desktop publishing features. It allows for the creation of presentation-quality charts and graphs. Ami was one of the first full-featured word processors for Windows and was originally developed by Samna Corp.

amp (AMPere) Unit of electrical current in a circuit. Volts measure the force or pressure behind the current. Watts are a total measurement of power derived from multiplying amps times volts. It is the base SI unit of electric current. A current of 1 ampere means that 6.25 X 1018 electrons are flowing by a point each second. 1 ampere equals 1 coulomb per second.

amplifier An electronic circuit that increases the voltage, current, or power of an input signal, or that isolates one part of a system from another.

amplitude Strength or volume of a signal, usually measured in decibels.

amplitude modulation See AM.

analog Analog devices monitor conditions, such as movement, temperature and sound, and convert them into analogous electronic or mechanical patterns. For example, an analog watch represents the planet's rotation with the rotating hands on the watch face. Telephones tuft voice vibrations into electrical vibrations of the same shape. Analog implies continuous operation in contrast with digital, which is broken up into numbers.

Traditionally, audio and video recording has been analog. Sound, which is continuously varying air vibrations, is converted into analogous electrical vibrations. Video cameras scan their viewing area a line at a time and convert the infinitely varying intensities of light into analogous electrical signals.

The ability to capture the subtle nature of the real world is the single advantage of analog techniques. However, once captured, modem electronic equipment, no matter how advanced, cannot copy analog signals perfectly. Third and fourth generation copies of audio and video recordings show marked deterioration.

By converting analog signals into digital, the original audio or video data can be preserved indefinitely and copied over and over again without deterioration. Once continuously varying analog signals are measured and converted into digital form, they can be stored and transmitted without loss of integrity due to the inherent accuracy of digital methods.

The key to conversion is the amount of digital data that is created from the analog signal. The shorter the time interval between samples and the more data recorded from that sample, the more the digital encoding reflects the original signal.

analog channel In communications, a channel that carries voice or video in analog form as a varying range of electrical frequencies. Contrast with digital channel.

analog computer Device that processes infinitely varying signals, such as voltage or frequencies. A thermometer is a simple analog computer. As the temperature varies, the mercury moves correspondingly. Although special-purpose, complex analog computers are built, almost all computers are digital. Digital methods provide more programming flexibility.

analog data The physical representation of information such that the representation bears an exact relationship to the original information. Electrical signals on a telephone channel are analog data representations of the original voice data.

analog model A model that relates physical similarity to the actual situation.

analog monitor Video monitor that accepts analog signals from the computer after the digital signals have been converted to analog by the video display board). It may accept only a narrow range of display resolutions; for example, only VGA or VGA and Super VGA, or it may accept a wide range of signals including TV. See multisync monitor, ROB monitor. Contrast with digital monitor.

analog representation A representation that does not have discrete values but Is continuously variable.

analog sIgnal A signal that varies continuously in wave form, such as the human voice.

analog transmission The transmission of data as continuous wave patterns.

analysis See systems analysis & design. analyst See systems analyst.

analytical graphics Traditional line graphs, pie charts, and bar charts used to illustrate and analyze data. A type of presentation graphics built into a spreadsheet, database, or word processing program.

Analytical Engine Programmable calculator designed by the British scientist, Charles Babbage in mid- 1830's. Although it was never completed due to lack of funds and constant redesign, it was a significant advance and embodied the principles of the stored program computer. Babbage's colleague, Augusta Ada Byron, daughter of the poet Lord Byron, explained the machine's concepts to the public. See Ada.

AND, OR & NOT Fundamental operations of Boo lean logic. AND is true if both inputs are true, OR is true if either input is true, and NOT is an inverter; the output is always the opposite. See Boolean search, chip, gate.

		AND			OR		NOT
Input		Output	Inputs		Outputs	Inputs	Outputs
0	0	0	0	0	0	0	1
0	1	0	0	1	1	1	0
1	0	0	1	0	1		
1	1	1	1	1	1		

AND gate (1) A binary circuit with two or more inputs and a single output, in which the output is logic 1 only when all inputs are logic 1, and the output is logic 0 if any one of the inputs is logic 0. (2) In a computer, a gate circuit with more than one input terminal. No output signal will be produced unless a pulse is applied to all inputs simultaneously.

angstrom Unit of measurement equal to approximately 1/250 millionth of an inch (.1 nanometre). It is used to measure the elements in a chip.

animated graphics Moving diagrams or cartoons, often found in computer-based courseware. Animated graphics take up far less disk space than video images.

animation The process of making an object appear to move by rapidly displaying a series of pictures of it, each one in a slightly different position; a techniques used for producing computer-generated movies.

anisotropic Refers to properties, such as transmission speed, that vary depending on the direction of measurement. Contrast with isotropic.

anode In electronics, positively charged receiver of elections that flow from the negatively charged cathode.

anomaly Abnormality or deviation. It is a favourite word among computer people when complex systems produce output that is inexplicable.

annotation symbol A symbol used to add message or notes to a flowchart, attached to other flowcharting symbols by dashed lines.

ANSI-COBOL A version of COBOL standardized in 1974 by the American National Standards Institute.

ANSI See American National Standards Institute.

ANSI character set ANSI-standard character set that defines 256 characters. The first 128 are ASCII, and the second 128 contain math and foreign language symbols (different than PC extended ASCII).

ANSI terminal Display terminal that follOws commands in the ANSI standard terminal language. It uses 'escape sequences' to control the cursor, clear the screen and set colors. Communications programs often support the ANSI terminal.

ANSI.SYS See DOS ANSI.SYS.

answer mode The ability of a modem to accept an incoming call from another modem.

answer/originate In telecommunications, the alternatives of receiving (answering) or sending (originating) a phone call.

anthropomorphism A figure of speech used to describe inanimate objects or computers and devices controlled by computers, as though they were persons. The tradition of addressing a ship as 'she' is an example.

anti-aliasing In computer graphics, a category of techniques that is used to smooth the jagged appearance of diagonal lines. For example, the pixels that surround the edges of the line are filled in with varying shades of grey or color in order to blend the sharp edge into the background. See dithering.

antistatlc mat A floor mat placed in front of a device, such as a disk unit, that is sensitive to static, to prevent shocks that could cause loss of data during human handling of the unit.

antivirus programme Program that detects and removes a virus. See also vaccine.

APA See All Points Addressable.

aperture card Punched card that holds a frame of microfilm.

API (Application Program Interface) Language and message format used by a program to activate and interact with functions in another program or in the hardware. See interface.

APL (A Programming Language) High-level, interactive scientific language noted for its brevity and matrix generation capabilities. Developed by Kenneth Iverson in the mid 1960s, it runs on micros to mainframes and is often used to develop mathematical models. It is primarily an interpreted language, but compilers are available.

APL uses unique character symbols and requires special software or ROM chips to enable the computer to display and print them. APL is popular in Europe.

Apollo (Apollo Systems Div. of HP) Formerly Apollo Computer, this manufacturer of high-performance workstations became a division of HP in early 1989. Founded in 1980, it pioneered the concept of networked workstations.

app See application.

app code (APPlication code) Instructions in a program that actually process data.

append To add data to the end of an existing structure. For example, the dBASE APPEND command starts the data entry mode and allows users to add records to the end of the file. Also refers to adding a text block at the end of a tile in word processing applications. In DOS, a text file can be attached (appended) to the end of another text file.

Apple (Apple Computer, Inc.) One of the first and certainly the most influential of the microcomputer manufacturers. Founded in 1976 by Steven P. Jobs and Stephen G. Wozniak, using the family garage as a base and $100 in capital, Apple made computers that became wildly successful. Today, Apple is the largest independent manufacturer of non-IBM-compatible personal computers.

Apple was formed on April Fool's Day in 1976. Soon after, it introduced the Apple I. In 1977, it introduced the Apple Ii, a fully-assembled computer with 4K RAM for $1,298. The 11+ was introduced with 48K in 1979. The Apple H's open architecture encouraged third-party vendors to build plug-in hardware to enhance its capability. This, plus its superior sound and color graphics, caused Apple us to become the most widely used computer in the home and classroom. They were also used in business primarily for the innovative VisiCalc software that was launched on it. Indeed it is often commented that VisiCaic launched Apple rather than the other way round! VisiCalc was the forerunner of spreadsheet programmes.

In 1983, Apple introduced the Lisa, the fore-runner of the Macintosh. Lisa was aimed at the corporate market, but was soon dropped in favour of the Mac. As a graphics-based machine, the Mac was successful as a low-cost desktop publishing system. Although it was praised by many for its ease of use, its slow speed, small screen and closed architecture was not exciting for most corporate buyers.

Since the advent of the Mac II in 1987, that has changed dramatically. Macs offer full-size screens, open architecture and color. Numerous entry-level and high-speed models have been added and are widely accepted.

In 1991, Apple surprised the industry by announcing an alliance with IBM to fully integrate Macs into IBM enterprise networks, to develop the PowerPC with Motorola, to develop Power Open, an industry standard UNIX that runs AIX and Mac applications on the PowerPC, and to form Taligent o develop and license an object-oriented operating system for the PowerPC and Kaleida to develop and license multimedia software, tools and scripting languages for a diverse variety of computers and consumer electronic gear.

Apple II Personal computer family from Apple that helped pioneer the microcomputer revolution. It has been widely used in schools and home. It uses the 8- bit 6502 microprocessor running at 1MHz, an 8-bit bus and runs under Apple's DOS or ProDOS operating system with AppleSoft BASIC, built into ROM, always available to the user. With a Z80 microprocessor board plugged into it, Apple us can run CP/M programs, such as dBASE II. The Apple lie, IIGS, and a lie card for the Macintosh LC are currently manufactured.

APPLE II AND 11+ Introduced in April 1977, the Apple II came with 4Kof memory and was designed to hook up to a TV and cassette tape recorder. The floppy disk arrived by mid 1978. In June 1979, the Apple 11+ was introduced with 48K of RAM and an improved auto-start ROM for easier startup and screen editing. Screen resolution is 280x192 with six colors.

APPLE lie AND lic In 1983, the Apple lie was the 'e"nhanced model. It included four cursor keys instead of two, and memory was increased to 128K. In 1984, the lie portable was launched with a sleek design, but limited expandabitity. Apple makes an Apple lie board that plugs into the Macintosh LC, turning it into an Apple II.

APPLE IIGS Introduced in 1986, the IEGS is a major upgrade. It uses the 16-bit 65C816 CPU that runs at 2.8MHz and features enhanced graphics and sound (GS). Screen resolution is 320x200 with 256 colors. It has 15 separate and simultaneous sounds and has built-in AppleTalk connectivity. The OS will accept most Apple II plug-in boards, but requires software written for the GS in order to activate its enhanced capabilities.

APPLE III An enhanced Apple II intended for business use (1980). It was not 100% compatible with the II and never caught on.

Apple key Original name of the Command key.

Apple Macintosh See macintosh.

Apple menu Menu at the top left side of a Macintosh screen that is always available to provide access to desk accessories.

AppleShare Software for PCs from Apple that allows a PC workstation to reside in an AppleTalk network. It requires a LocalTalk PC Card from Apple for AT- bus workstations, or a LocalTalk Card from DayStar Communications for Micro Channel Pcs.

AppleSoft BASIC Apple's version of BASIC that comes with Apple II models. It is installed in firmware (ROM) and is always available.

applet Small application, such as a utility program.

AppleTalk OSI-based LAN from Apple introduced in 1985. It supports Apple's proprietary Local Talk access method as well as Ethernet and Token Ring. The AppleTalk protocol and Local Talk access method are built into all Macs, IIGS's and LaserWriters. With products from Apple and others, AppleTalk can run in Pcs, VAXs and UNIX workstations.

AppleWorks Integrated software package (1983) for Apple IIs from Claris Corp which combines word processing, file management, spreadsheet, business graphics and communications.

application (1) Specific use of the computer, such as payroll, inventory and billing. (2) Same as application program and software package.

application developer Individual that develops a business application and usually performs the duties of a systems analyst and application programmer.

application development system Programming language and associated utility programs that allow for the creation, development and running of application programs. A DBMS, including query languages and report writers, may be included.

application generator Software that generates application programs from descriptions of the problem rather than by traditional programming. It is one or more levels higher than a high-level programming language, but still requires that the user enter mathematical, or algorithmic, expressions in order to describe complex functions.

application notes instructions and recommendations from the vendor provided in addition to the normal reference manuals.

application-oriented language A problem-oriented programming language whose statements contain or resemble the terminology of the computer user.

application package Software package that is created for a specific purpose or industry.

application processor Computer that processes data in contrast with one that performs control functions, such as a front end processor or database machine.

application program Any data entry, update, query or report program that processes data for the user. Contrast with system program.

application program library Application programs used by an organization.

application programmer Individual who writes application programs in a user organization. Most programmers are application programmers. Contrast with systems programmer.

applications programming Preparation of programs for application to specific problems to find solutions.

applications programs Programs normally written by programmers within an organization that enable the computer to perform specific useful tasks.

application-specific Integrated circuit An integrated circuit designed to fill the specific requirement of an application.

applied mathematics Mathematics put to practical use as in mechanics, physics, or computer science.

approximation A number that is not exact, but has been rounded off to a prescribed decimal place; e.g., 3.14 and 3. 14159 are both approximations of pi. There are statistical rules which govern this rounding off.

APT (Automatic Programmed Pool) A programming system used in numerical control applications for the programmed control of machine functions. APT allows a user to define points, lines, circles, planes, and conical and geometric surfaces.

Arago dBASE IV-compatible DBMS and compiler from WordTech Systems, with enhanced report writing, screen generation and business graphics. Arago dBXL is the interactive DBMS. Arago Quicksilver is the compiler.

arbitration Set of rules for allocating machine resources, such as memory or peripheral devices, to more than one user or program.

ARC, ARC+Plus (1) PC compression programs from System Enhancement Associates

ARC was one of the first compression utilities to achieve popularity in the early 1980s. ARC+Plus provides enhanced features and increased speed. (2) ARC extension previously used by PKWARE Inc. in its PKARC program. (3) (Advanced RISC Computing) Open system specification based on the MIPS R3000 and R4000 processors. It includes the EISA and Digital's TURBOchannel bus.

arcade games Computer video games popularized by coin-operated machines, characterized by high-resolution color graphics, high-speed animation, and sound. Players often use joysticks to control a screen object, and the computer scores point based on the game's rules.

architecture See computer architecture, network architecture, software architecture.

archival Pertaining to long-term storage of data.

archive (1) To copy data onto a different disk or tape for backup. Archived files are often compressed to maximize storage media. (2) To save data onto the disk.

archive attribute An attribute state which can be set to classify files. This state can be checked by certain copy and backup programs.

Arcnet A computer networking scheme.

area search Examination of a large group of documents to select those that pertain to one group, such as a specific category or class.

argument In programming, a value that is passed between programs, subroutines or functions. Arguments are independent items, or variables, that contain data or codes. When an argument is used to customize a program for a user, it is typically called a parameter.

arithmetic (1) The branch of mathematics concerned with the study of the positive real numbers and zero. (2) Pertaining to such operations as addition, subtraction, multiplication, and division, or to the section of the computer hardware that performs these Operations.

arithmetic coding Statistical data compression method that converts strings of data into single floating point numbers between 0 and 1.

arithmetic expression (1) In mathematics, one or more characters or symbols associated with arithmetic, such as 1+2=3 or 8÷6. (2) In programming, a non-text expression.

arithmetic logic unit See ALU.

arithmetic operations Various manipulations of numerical quantities, including the fundamental operations of addition, subtraction, multiplication, and division, as well as aggregation, exponentiation, and extraction of roots.

arithmetic operators Symbols for arithmetic functions: + for 'add',- for 'subtract', * for 'multiply', / for 'divide'. See precedence.

arithmetic overflow Result from an arithmetic calculation that exceeds the space designated to hold it.

arithmetic shift To multiply or divide a quantity by a power of the number base. For example, if binary 1101, representing decimal 13, is arithmetically shifted twice to the left, the result is 110100, representing 52, which is also obtained by multiplying 12 by 2 twice; however, if decimal 13 is shifted to the left twice, the result will be the same as multiplying by 10 twice, or 1,300.

arithmetic underflow Result from an arithmetic calculation that is too small to be expressed properly. For example, in floating point, a negative exponent can be generated that is too large (too small a number) to be stored in its allotted space.

arithmetic unit Same as arithmetic-logic unit.

arrangement The order of index terms or items of data in a system.

array Ordered arrangement of data elements. A vector is a one dimensional array, a matrix is a two-dimensional array. Most programming languages have the ability to store and manipulate arrays in one or more dimensions. Multi-dimensional arrays are used extensively in scientific simulation and mathematical processing; however, an array can be as simple as a pricing table held in memory for instant access by an order entry program. See subscript.

array element One item in an array.

array processor Computer, or extension to its arithmetic unit, that is capable of performing simultaneous computations on elements of an array of data in some number of dimensions. Common uses include analysis of fluid dynamics and rotation of 3-D objects, as well as data retrieval, in which elements in a database are scanned simultaneously. See vector processor, math coprocessor.

arrival rate The number of characters or messages arriving over a data communications medium per unit of time.

ART A PFS First Publisher graphics format used for clip art.

artificial Intelligence See Al.

artificial language Language that has been predefined before it is ever used. Contrast with natural language.

Artline An illustrative graphics program for use with IBM-compatible microcomputers. Features include multilayer editing an autotrace facility, scalable fonts, 3-D shading effects, a blending function to change one image into another, and access to a large supply of clip art images.

Arts & Letters tin Graphics Editor An illustrative graphics program that runs on Windows and OS/2. A special effect function allows text, clip art and freeform graphics to be warped, bent, stretched, and twisted by specifying the shape into which the object is to fit. A Graduated Fill function allows colourful blends and the 3-D illusion of depth by a variety of linear and radial fill for text and graphic artwork. The program has several thousand files of clip art and an autotrace feature.

artwork Visual and graphic elements on a page, such as line drawings, halftones, or solids.

AS (Application System) IBM mainframe fourth-generation language that runs under MVS. It was originally designed for non-computer people and includes commands for planning, budgeting and graphics. However, a programmer can also produce complex applications. It also provides computer conferencing.

AS/400 (Application System/400) IBM minicomputer series introduced in 1988 that supersedes and advances the System/36 and System/38. System/36 programs run in the AS/400 in System/36 mode after they have been recompiled. System/38 programs run intact in System/38 mode. After recompilation, SystemJ38 programs will run in native AS/400 mode, which takes advantage of all system resources.

The AS/400 serves in a variety of networking configurations: as a host or intermediate node to other AS/400s and Systeml3x machines, as a remote system to mainframe-controlled networks and as a network server to PCs. The AS/400 offered the widest range of connectivity in an IBM introduction.

ascender The part of lowercase b, d, f, h, k, I, and t, that extends above the body of the letters.

ascending order An order that ranges from smallest to largest or first to last. Alphabets and counting numbers are in naturally ascending order. Contrast with descending order.

ASCII (American Standard Code for Information Interchange) Pronounced 'ass-key." A binary code for data that is used in communications, most minicomputers and all personal computers.

ASCII is a 7-bit code providing 128 possible character combinations, the first 32 of which are used for printing and transmission control. Since the common storage unit is an 8-bit byte (256 combinations) and ASCII uses only 128, the extra bit is used to hold a parity bit or special symbols. For example, the PC uses the additional values for foreign language and graphics symbols. In the Macintosh, the additional values can be user-defined to enhance a font. See ASCII chart, hex chart.

ASCII chart

Standard ASCII Extended ASCII

ASCII tile Data or text file that contains characters coded in ASCII. Text files, word processing documents, batch files and source language programs are usually ASCII files. Only the first 128 characters (0- 127) within the 256 combinations in a byte conform to the ASCII standard. The rest are used differently depending on the computer and the software

Files created by database and most word processing programs are usually not ASCII files since they contain binary numbers and additional codes. The ASCII file can be used as a common denominator between incompatible formats. For example, if program A cannot convert its data to the format of program B, but both programs can handle ASCII files, conversion is often possible using built-in import and export functions. Dates, floating point and binary numbers may still cause conversion problems, however.

ASCII protocol Simplest form of transmitting ASCII data and implies little or no error checking. Each character can be transmitted with a parity bit in order to provide some degree of error checking, but important data, such as numbers, and source and machine language programs, should be transmitted with a more sophisticated protocol.

ASCII sort Sequential order of ASCII data. In ASCII code, lower case characters follow upper case. True ASCII order would put the words DATA, data and SYSTEM into the following sequence: DATA SYSTEM data

Ashton-Tate Software company founded in 1980 by Hal Lashlee and George Tate to market DBASE II. Borland acquired it in 1991.

ASIC (Application Specific Integrated Circuit) Custom chip designed for a specific application. It is designed by integrating standard cells from a library. ASIC design is faster than designing a chip from scratch, and design changes can be made more easily.

askSam Text management system for PCs from askSam Systems, Perry FL. It holds unstructured text as well as standard data fields. The product is noted for its flexible text retrieval and hypertext capabilities.

ASM File extension for assembly language source programs.

aspect ratio Ratio of width to height of an object.

assemble The automatic process by which a computer converts a symbolic source-langauge program into a machine langauge, usually on an instruction-by-instruction basis.

assembler Software that translates assembly langiage into machine language. Contrast with compiler, which is used to translate a high-level language, such as COBOL or C, into assembly language first and then into machine language.

assembly language Programming language that is one step away from machine language. Each assembly language statement is translated into one machine instruction by the assembler. Programmers must be well versed in the computer's architecture since assembly language is hardware dependent; there is a different assembly language for each CPU series.

Assembly language allows the most efficient of hardware and is consequently the fastest language. In the past, control programs (operating systems, database managers, etc.). were written in assembly language to maximize the machine's performance. Part of the lightening speed of 1-2-3 is because it was written in assembly language. Today, C is often used instead. Like assembly language, C can manipulate the bits at the machine level, but it is also more portable to different computer platforms. There are C compilers for most computers.

Although erroneously used synonymously, assembly language and machine language are not the same. Assembly language is turned into machine language.

assembly listing Printing output produced by an assembler. Lists the original assembly-language program, the machine-language version of the program, storage assignments, error messages, and other information useful to the programmer.

assertions A concept referring to the storage of procedures as a part of an object-oriented database. An assertion is a property of the object with which it is associated, typically some condition that the object must satisfy. Assertions are like methods, but are not encapsulated along with the local data on which they operate.

assignment statement In programming, a compiler directive that assigns a value into a variable. For example, COUNTER = 0 creates a variable named counter' and fills it with zeros. The VARIABLE NAME = VALUE syntax is common among programming languages.

associative storage Storage accessed by comparing the antent of the data stored in it rather than by addressing predetermined locations.

ASSP (Application Specific Standard Part) ASIC chip originally designed for one customer and then released to the general public.

asterisk (1) A symbol (*) used in many programming languages to represent a multiplication operator. (2) Symbol used as a 'Wildcard' in DOS commands.

asymmetric modem Full-duplex modem that transmits data in one direction at one speed and simultaneously in the other direction at another speed. For example, data flows at high-speed in one direction while acknowledgement is returned at low-speed in the other. Contrast with ping pong.

asymmetric multiprocessing Multiprocessing design in which each CPU is dedicated to a specific function. Contrast with symmetric multiprocessing.

asymmetric system (1)System in which major components or properties are different. (2) In video compression, a system that requires more equipment to compress the data than to decompress it.

asynchronous (1) Unsynchronized events, for example, the time interval between event A and B is not the same as B and C. (2) Able to initiate a transmission eithered. (3) In SNA, refers to independent events rather than concurrent events. For example, if one m sends mail to a party who is not available, the ability to forward the mail at a later time is consided asynchronous. (4) Starting the next I/O operation before the current one is completed. (5) In SCSI, the acknowledgment of each byte of data transferred. (6) Contrast with synchronous.

asynchronous computer A computer in which each operation starts as a result of a signal generated by the completion of the previous operation or by the availability of the equipment required for the next operation.

asynchronous Input Input data having no time-dependable pattern or cycle when related to the computer system.

asynchronous protocol Communications protocol that controls an asynchronous transmission, for example, ASCII, TTY, Kermit and Xmodem. Contrast with synchronous protocol.

asynchronous transmission Transmission of data in which each character is a self-contained unit with its own start and stop bits. Intervals between characters may be uneven. It is the common method of transmission between a computer and a modem, although the modem may switch to synchronous transmission to communicate with the other modem. Also called start/stop transmission. Contrast with synchronous transmission.

AT (Advanced Technology) IBM's first 286-based PC, introduced in 1984. It was the most advanced machine in the PC line and featured a new keyboard, 1.2MB floppy and 16-bit data bus. AT-class machines run approximately three to four times faster than XTs (8088-based PCs). See PC.

AT bus 16-bit data bus used in the AT. Also called ISA bus. See PC bus. Contrast with Micro Channel.

AT class PC that uses the Intel 286 CPU and the AT bus.

AT command set Series of machine instructions used to activate features on an intelligent modem. Developed by Hayes Microcomputer Products, and formally called the Hayes Standard AT Command Set, it is used entirely or partially by most every modem manufacturer. AT is a mnemonic code for ATtention, which is the prefix that initiates each command to the modem. See Hayes Smartmodem.

AT interface Refers to the 16-bit PC bus or to the devices that connect to it via expansion card and slot or an IDE connector. See XT interface, PC bus.

AT keyboard 84-key keyboard provided with the PC AT. It corrected the non-standard placement of the PC's return and left shift keys. See PC keyboard, Enhanced keyboard.

AT&T (American Telephone & Telegraph Company) Largest long distance communications carrier in the U.S. It has gone through a major change from the world's largest monopoly to a competitive enterprise. Its ventures into the PC market have been modest, but in 1991, it acquired NCR, a seasoned computer company.

Atari (Atari Computer) Manufacturer of personal computers. Originally founded in 1972 by Nolan Bushnell and famous for its "Pong" video games. In 1976, it was sold to Time Warner, and in 1984, it was sold to Jack Tramiel and investors. Within six months, the 520ST was introduced, the first personal computer designed for MID! (music) applications. Its product line, aimed at providing quality computing at affordable prices, includes the 104OSTE and

MEGA STE personal computers, T1'030 workstation and Portfolio palmtop computer. Atari also continues to be a major competitor in video games.

Atari ST A personal computer series from Atari Corporation.

ATM Abbreviation for automated teller machine. See Automated Teller Machine.

atom In list processing languages, a single element in a list.

atomic Indivisible. An atomic operation, or atomicity, implies an operation that must be performed as a whole, that is, entirely or not at all. For example, if machine failure prevents a transaction to be processed to completion, the system will be rolled back to the start of the transaction. See two-phase commit.

atomic operation An operation that cannot be divided into smaller operations.

attach To connect a peripheral to a computer to increase its capacity.

attached processor Additional CPU connected to the primary CPU in a multiprocessing environment. It operates as an extension of the primary CPU and shares the system software and peripheral devices.

attenuation Loss of signal power in a transmission.

atto A prefix meaning one-quintillionth, or a billionth of a billionth, as in 10^{-18} Abbreviated as a.

attribute (1) In relational database management, a field within a record. (2) For printers and display screens, a characteristic that changes a font, for example, from normal to boldface or underlined, or from normal to reverse video. (3) See file attribute.

audio. Range of frequencies within human hearing (approx. 20Hz at the low to a high of 20,000Hz). Traditional audio devices are analog, because they handle the sound waves in an analogous form. Radios maintain the audio signal as rippling waves from antenna to speaker. Sound waves are "carved" into plastic phonograph records, and audio tape records sound as magnetic waves. Audio is processed in a computer by converting the analog signal into a digital code using various techniques, such as PCM.

audio board Personal computer expansion board that generates sound and provides amplification for small external speakers. Frequently called sound board. See MPC.

audio device Any computer device that accepts and/or produces sound.

audio output Computer output generated through voice synthesizers that create audible signals resembling a human voice.

audio response See voice response.

audio-response device A device that converts data in internal storage to vocalized sounds understandable to humans. Also called voice output unit or voice synthesizers.

audiotex Voice response application that allows users to enter and retrieve information over the telephone. In response to a voice menu, users press the keys or answer questions to select their way down a tree of choices. It is used for obtaining the latest financial quotes as well as for ordering products. It is also built into interactive systems that allows databases to be changed. See VIS.

audiovisual Audio and/or video capability.

audit Examination of systems, programming and datacenter procedures in order to determine the efficiency of computer operations.

audit software Specialized programs that perform a variety of audit functions, such as sampling databases and generating confirmation letters to customers. It can highlight exceptions to categories of data and alert the examiner to possible error.

audit trail Record of transactions in an information system that provides verification of the activity of the system.

authentication A process for verifying the correctness of a piece of data.

authenticity The integrity of a message.

author (1) A person who designs instructional material for computer-assisted instruction system. (2) A person who creates a hypertext document.

authoring system standard A computer system capable of executing authoring program. Software that allows for the development of tutorials and CBT programs.

authorization A system control feature that requires specific approval before processing can take place.

authorization code Identification number or password that is used to gain access to a local or remote computer system.

authorized program A computer program capable of altering the fundamental operation or status of a computer system.

Authorware Macintosh authoring program from Authorware. Courseware developed on the Mac can be converted to the PC.

auto (AUTOmatic) Refers to a wide variety of devices that perform unattended operation.

auto answer Modem feature that accepts a telephone call and establishes the connection. See auto dial.

auto attendant Voice store and forward system that replaces the human operator and directs callers to the appropriate extensions or voice mailboxes.

auto bypass Ability to bypass a terminal or other device in a network if it fails, allowing the remaining devices to continue functioning.

auto resume Feature that lets you stop working on the computer and take up where you left off at a later date without having to reload applications. Memory contents are stored on disk or kept active by battery d/or AC power. This feature is found most often on laptops and notebook PCs.

AutoCAD Full-featured CAD program from AutoDesk Inc., that runs on PCs, VAXs, Macs and UNIX workstations. Originally developed for CP/M machines, it was one of the first major CAD programs for personal computers and became an industry standard. Many software packages import and export graphics fil in DXF, AutoCAD's external file format.

autochart A type of documentor used for the automatic production and maintenance of charts, principally flowcharts.

autocoder IBM assembly language for 1960s-vintage 1400 and 7000 series computers.

auto-dia A modem capable of connecting to the telephone system and dialling a number. The modem and communications software perform the proper communications procedures so that computers may exchange data.

AUTODIN (Automatic Digital Network) The data-handling portion of the military communications system.

auto-disconnect Automatic disconnecting by one modern when it receives a disconnect message or when the other party hangs up.

AUTOEXEC.BAT (AUTOmatic EXECute BATch) DOS batch file that executes automatically when the computer is started. The OS/2 counterpart is STARTUP.-CMD. See DOS AUTOEXEC. BAT.

autoflow Wrapping text around a graphic image or from one page to the next.

autofont A self-training OCR system that automatically adjusts to the type designs of different typefaces in order to read a wide range of documents quickly and accurately.

auto Indexing A system of indexing that superimposes additional information at any of several given addresses.

AutoLISP AutoCAD language used to create customized menus and routines.

auto-load A key on some computer keyboards that activates the computer. Essentially boots the operating system into internal storage and starts execution of the system.

automata A theory related to be study of the principles of operation, behavioral characteristics, and application of automatic devices. It is an open-ended computer science discipline that concerns an abstract device called an "automaton," which performs a specific computational or recognition function. Networks of automata are designed to mimic human behaviour.

automated data processing A largely self-regulating process in which information is handed with a minimum of human effort and intervention.

automated flowchart A flowchart drawn by a computer- controlled printer or plotter.

automated office The result of the merger of computers, office electronic devices, and telecommunications technology in an office environment.

automated teller machine (ATM) A banking terminal that provides customer with 24-hour deposit-and- withdrawal service; a special-purpose device connected to the bank's computer system. To use the automatic teller, the customer inserts a plastic identification card, enters a special password code, and communicates with the system by using a numeric keypad and visual display.

automatic feature negotiation Ability of a modem to determine and adjust to the speed, error control and data compression method of the modem at the other end of the line.

automatic Pertaining to a process or device that, under specified conditions, functions without intervention by a human operator.

automatic carriage A control mechanism for a printer that can automatically control the feeding, spacing, skipping and ejecting of paper or preprinted forms.

automatic check An equipment check built in specifically for checking purposes.

automatic coding Machine-assisted preparation of machine-language routines.

automatic controller A device or instrument capable of measuring and regulating by receiving a signal from a sensing device, comparing this data with a desired valUe, and issuing signals for corrective action.

automatic error correction A technique for detecting and correcting errors that occur in data transmission or within the system itself.

automatic hyphenation A feature that hyphenates words automatically, often found in word processor and page layout programs.

automatic loader A hardware loader program, usually implemented in a special ROM, that allows loading of an auxiliary storage unit (a hard disk or floppy disk).

automatic pagination A feature that automatically breaks text into pages; often found in word processing and page layout programs.

automatic programming (1) The process of using a computer to perform some stages of the work involved in preparing a program. (2) The production of a machine-language computer program under the guidance of a symbolic representation of the program.

automatic reformatting In word processing, automatic adjustment of text to accommodate changes.

automatic shutdown The ability of some systems software to stop a network or a computer system as a whole in an orderly fashion.

automation Replacement of manual operations by computerized methods. Office automation refers to integrating clerical tasks such as typing, filing and appointment scheduling. Factory automation refers to computer-driven assembly lines.

automaton A machine designed to simulate the operations of living things. See Robot.

automonitor (1) computer's record of its functions. (2) A computer program that records the operating functions of a computer.

autopolling Contraction of automatic polling, a process whereby terminals in a computer network are scanned periodically to determine whether they are ready to send information; a combination of hardware and software that polls the terminals in a computer network.

auto-redial A modem feature for redialling a number until contact is established.

auto-repeat A feature of keyboards that allows a key to repeat automatically when held down. Also called typmatic.

auto-restart The capability of a computer to perform automatically the initialization functions necessary to resume operation following an equipment or power failure.

autosave Saving data to the disk at periodic intervals without user intervention.

autoscore In word processing, an instruction that causes text to be underlined.

autosizing Ability of a monitor to maintain the same rectangular image size when changing from one resolution to another.

autostart routine Instructions built into the computer and activated when it is turned on. The routine performs diagnostic tests, such as checking the computer's memory, and then loads the operating system and passes control to it.

autotrace Routine that locates outlines of raster graphics images and converts them into vector graphics.

AUX (AUXiliary) DOS name for the first connected serial port. See DOS device names. See A/UX.

auxiliary equipment Equipment not under direct control of the central processing unit.

auxiliary memory High-speed memory bank used in mainframes and supercomputers. It is not directly addressable by the CPU, rather it functions like a disk. Data is transferred from auxiliary memory to main memory over a high-bandwidth channel. See auxiliary storage.

auxiliary operation An operation performed by equipment not under control of the central processing unit.

auxiliary storage External storage devices, such as disk and tape.

availability The ratio of the time that a hardware device is known or believed to be operating correctly to the total hours of scheduled operation.

avaable time Time that a computer is available for use but is not being used.

Avant Grade A modem sans serif typeface design owned by the International Typeface Corporation (ITC) and included as a built-in font with many postscript laser printers.

AVC (Audio Visual Connection) Multimedia software from IBM that works in conjunction with IBM's Audio Capture and Video Capture boards for the PS! 2. It allows users to integrate sound and pictures into applications and includes an authoring language.

avionics Electronic instrumentation and control equipment used in airplanes and space vehicles.

Award BIOS Widely-used PC-compatible ROM BIOS from Award Software, Inc. By 1991, over 20 million Award BIOS's have been installed.

awk (Aho Weinberger Kernighan) UNIX programming Wility developed in 1977 by Mo, Weinberger and Kernighan. Due to its unique pattern-matching syntax, it is often used in data retrieval and data transformation. DOS versions are also available.

axws (Plural of axis) In a two-dimensional coordinate system, lines used as references for vertical (Y) and horizontal (X) measurement. See cartesian coordiante system.

azimuth Trajectory of an angle measured in degrees going clockwise from a base point. A disk azimuth algnment test checks for the correct positioning of the read/write head to the track.

Abstract data type: In SQL3, a user-defined structure having methods, data items, and identifiers. A version of an OOP object; persistence is provided by binding the ADT to a column of a relation.

Action/object menu: A system of menus in which the top menu refers to actions and the lowest menus refer to the objects on which those actions are taken.

ActiveX: An architecture of program elements developed and promulgated by Microsoft. ActiveX provides a means by which independent programs can interface with one another dynamically. ActiveX controls are program segments that conform to the ActiveX interface. See IUnknown and Query Interface.

ADT: See Abstract data type.

After-image: A record of a database entity (normally a row or a page) after a change. It is used in recovery to perform rollforward.

Al: Artificial intelligence. A group of related disciplines providing capabilities that in the past were attributed only to humans. Vision, robotics, and expert systems are branches of artificial intelligence. Sometimes a vague term, artificial intelligence is used in marketing literature to mean new and exciting.

Anomaly: An undesirable consequence of a data modification used primarily in discussions of normalization. With an insertion anomaly, facts about two or more different themes must be added to a single row of a relation. With a deletion anomaly, facts about two or more themes are lost when a single row is deleted.

API: See Application program interface.

Application: A business computer system that processes a portion of a database to meet a user's information needs. It consists of menus, forms, reports, queries, and application programs.

Application design: The process of creating the structure of programs and data to meet the application's requirements. Also the structure of the users' interface.

Application metadata: Data dictionary data concerning the structure and contents of application menus, forms, and reports.

Application plan: In DB2, a set of access paths for each SQL statement in an application program. It includes information about database tables' structures, available indexes, and data storage structures.

Application program: A custom-developed program for processing a database. It can be written in a standard procedural language such as COBOL, C, or BASIC or in a language unique to the DBMS.

Application program interface (API): A set of program procedures or functions that can be called to invoke a set of services. The API includes the names of the procedures and functions and a description of the name, purpose, and data type of parameters to be provided. For example, a DBMS product could provide a library of functions to call for database services. The names of procedures and their parameters constitute the API for that library.

Application view: That portion of a database processed by a particular application program.

Archetype/version object: A structure of two objects that represents multiple versions of a standardized item. For example, a SOFT-PRODUCT (the archetype) and PRODUCT-RELEASE (the version of the archetype). The identifier of the version always includes the archetype object.

Association object: An object that represents the combination of at least two other objects and that contains data about that combination. It is often used in contracting and assignment applications.

Atomic: A set of actions that is completed as a unit. Either all actions are completed or none is.

Atomic transaction: A group of logically related database operations that is performed as a unit. Either all of the operations are performed, or none of them is.

Attribute: (1) A column of a relation; also called a column, field, or data-item. (2) A property in an entity or semantic object. (3) A data or relationship property in an OOP object. (4) In the ODMG-93 model, an implementation of an object property in an OOP implementation such as C++ or Smailtalk.

Authorization rules: A set of processing permissions that describes which users or user groups can take particular actions against particular portions of the database.

B

B-spline In computer graphics, a curve that is genered using a mathematical formula which assures continuity with other b-splines.

B-tree (Batanced-tree) Technique for organizing inxes. In order to keep access time to all data to a imum, it stores the data keys in a balanced hierathv that continually realigns itself as items are inled and deleted. Thus, all nodes in the hierarchy wys have a similar number of keys.

B+tree is a version of B-tree that maintains a aachv of indexes while also linking the data Seentially. It provides both fast direct access and sequential access to data.

Abbreviation for binary or bit; for example, bps for bits per second and ilOib for the binary number 1101.

B: Abbreviation for byte or baud. Used for bytes when referring to storage, or baud rate when referring to communications, for example, KB means 1 kilobyte (1,024 bytes).

B: Designation for the second floppy disk in a PC. It was sometimes used for the hard disk in earlier non-IBM PCs.

babble The cross-talk from a large number of channels in a system.

back-end CASE CASE tools that generate program code. Contrast with front-end CASE.

back end processor Same as database machine.

back up To make a copy of important data or (lies onto a different storage medium for safety. This is an essential part of computer use.

backbone In communications, the part of a network that handles the major traffic. It may interconnect multiple locations, and smaller networks may be attached to it.

backfilling Assigning EMS memory to conventional memory in 8086/88 and 286 PCs. Original motherboard chips are disabled and the EMS chips are assigned the low memory addresses. Backfilling lets multitasking programs, such as DESQview, run more programs simultaneously in expanded memory.

background (1) Non-interactive processing in the computer. See foreground/background. (2) Base, or default screen or backdrop, color on screen.

background Ink Highly reflective ink in optical character recognition that is used to print the parts of the form that are not to be detected or recognized by the scanner.

background noise Extraneous and unwanted signals that creep into a line, channel or circuit.

background processing The execution of lower-priority computer programs during periods when system resources are not required to process high-priority programs.

background program A program that can be executed whenever the facilities of a multiprogramming computer system are not required by other programs of higher priority. Contrast with foreground program.

backing storage Same as auxiliary storage.

backlash In a mechanical operation, the 'play" between interacting arts, such as two gears, which develops due to use and as a result of tolerance.

backlit LCD screen that has its own light source from the back of the screen, making the background brighter and characters appear sharper.

back panel The back of a computer case, with a number of sockets for connecting peripheral devices to the computer.

backplane (1) Reverse side of a panel or board that contains interconnecting wires. (2) Printed circuit board, or device, containing slots, or sockets, for plugging in boards or cables.

backsolver See solver.

backspace (1) The keyboard operation to move the screen cursor one column to the left, deleting the character that was displayed in that position. A backspace to the printer moves the print head one column to the left. (3) The key marked with an arrow pointing to the left (not the cursor movement key). (2) To move to the previous block on a magnetic tape.

backspace tape The process of returning a magnetic tape to the beginning of the preceding record.

backtracking The operation of scanning a list in reverse. backup Additional resources or duplicate copies of data on different storage media for emergency purposes.

backup & recovery Combination of manual and machine procedures that can restore lost data in the event of hardware or software failure. Routine backup of databases and system logs that keep track of the computer's operations are part of a backup & recovery program. See checkpoint/restart.

backup copy Disk, tape or other machine readable copy of a data or program file. Making backup copies is a tedious. but essential discipline that most computer users learn the hard way - after irreplaceable work is lost.

backup disk Disk that is used to hold duplicate copies of important files. High-density floppy disks and removable disks cartridges are used for backup disks.

backup power Additional power source that can be used in the event of power failure. See UPS.

backup programmer A programmer who is an assistant to the chief programmer.

backup tape See tape backup.

Backus-Naur form Also known as Backus normal form, it was the first metalanguage to define programming languages, developed by John Backus and Pejer Naur in 1959.

backward chaining In Al, a form of reverse reasoning that starts with the conclusion and works backward. The goal is broken into many subgoals, or sub- subgoals, which can be solved more easily. Known as top-down approach. Contrast with forward chaining.

backward compatible Same as downward compatible.

backward read A feature avaitable on some magnetic tape systems whereby magnetic tape units can transfer data to computer storage while moving in reverse.

badge reader A terminal equipped to read credit cards or specially coded badges.

bad sector Segment of disk storage that cannot be read or written due to a physical problem (eg. scratch) in the disk. Bad sectors on hard disks are marked by I the operating system and bypassed. If data is recorded in a sector that becomes bad, special software, and sometimes special hardware, must be used to recover it, but bad sectors themselves cannot be physically repaired.

BAK file (BAcKup file) DOS and OS/2 file extension for backup files.

BAL (1) (Basic Assembly Language) Assembly language for the IBM 370/3000/4000 mainframe series. (2) (Branch And Link) Instruction used to transfer control to another part of the program.

ballistic gain Trackball or mouse feature that changes cursor travel relative to hand speed. The faster the ball is moved, the farther the cursor is moved.

ball printer A printer that has the printing elements on the face of a ball-like replacement element. Type fonts can easily be changed by changing the typeball.

balloon help On-screen help displayed in a cartoon-style dialogue box that appears when the pointer (cursor) is placed over the object in question. Most effectively used in the Mac.

band (1) Range of frequencies used for transmitting a signal. A band can be identified by the difference between its lower and upper limits as well as by its actual lower and upper limits, for example, a 10MHz band in the 100 to 110MHz range." (2) Contiguous group of tracks that are treated as a unit. (3) Printing element in a band printer.

band pass filter Electronic device that prohibits all but a specific range of frequencies to pass through it.

band printer Line printer that uses a metal band, or loop, of type characters as its printing mechanism. The band spins horizontally around a set of hammers. When the desired character is in front of the selected print position, the corresponding hammer hits the paper into the ribbon and onto the character in the band.

bandwidth Transmission capacity of a computer channel, communications line or bus. It is expressed in cycles per second (Hertz), the bandwidth being the difference between the lowest and highest frequencies transmitted. The frequency is equal to or greater than the bits per second. Bandwidth is also often stated in bits or bytes per second. See video bandwidth.

bank Arrangement of identical hardware components. Eg. Memory chips.

bank switching Engaging and disengaging electronic circuits. Bank switching is used when the desigrr of a system prohibits all circuits from being addressed or activated at the same time requiring that one unit be turned on while the others are turned off.

bar chart Graphical representation of information in the form of bars. Also called bar graph. See business graphics.

bar code Code used for recognition by a scanner. Traditional one-dimensional bar codes use the bar's width as the code, but encode just an ID or account number. Two-dimensional systems, such as PDF 417 from Symbol Technology, can hold 1,800 characters in an area the size of a postage stamp.

bar code reader A photoelectric scanner that reds bar codes by means of reflected light.

bare beard A printed circuit board with no electronic components on if.

bar printer An impact printing device that uses several type bars positioned side by side across the line.

barrel distortion Screen distortion in which the sides bow out. Contrast with pincushioning.

barrel printer Same as drum printer.

base (1) Starting point or reference point. (2) Component in a bipolar transistor that activates the switch. Same as gate in a MOS transistor. (3) Multiplier in a numbering system. In a decimal system, each digit position is worth 10x the position to its right. In binary, each digit position is worth 2x the position to its right.

base address Location in memory where the beginning of a program is stored. The relative address from the instruction in the program is added to the base ad. dress to derive the absolute address. See base/displacement.

base alignment Alignment of a variety of font sizes on a baseline.

baseband transmission A method of using low-frequency transmission of signals across coaxial cables for short-distance, local area network transmission.

base class In object-oriented programming, the most generalized class in a class structure. Most applications have many such base classes. Some language define a primitive base class, which serves as the ultimate superclass of all classes.

base 8 See octal.

base/displacement Technique for running programs from any location in memory. The addresses in the machine language program are displacement addresses (relative to the beginning of the program). As the program is running, the hardware adds the displacement address to the base address (where the beginning of the program is currently stored) and derives the absolute address.

base font Default font used for printing if none other is specified.

baseband In baseband, the full bandwidth of the channel is used, and simultaneous transmission of multiple sets of data is accomplished by interleaving pulses using TDM (time division multiplexing). Contrast with broadband transmission, which transmits data, voice and video simultaneously by modulating each signal onto a different frequency, using FDM (frequency division multiplexing).

baseline Horizontal line to which the bottoms of lowercase characters (without descenders) are aligned. See typeface.

baseline document The reference document for changes to a data processing system.

base 16 See hexadecimal. - base 10 See decimal.

base 2 See binary.

BASIC (Beginners All purpose Symbolic Instruction Code) Programming language developed by John Kemeny and Thomas Kurtz in the mid 1960s at Dartmouth College. Originally developed as an interactive, mainframe timesharing language, it has become widely used on all sizes of computers including pocket computers.

BASIC is available in both compiler and interpreter form, the latter being more popular for the casual user and first-time programmer. As an interpreter, the language is conversational and can be debugged a line at a time since it runs one line at a time.

BASIC is considered one of the easiest programming languages to learn. Simple programs can be quickly written on the fly. However, BASIC is not a structured language, such as Pascal, dBASE or C, and it's easy to end up with spaghetti code that's difficult to decipher later.

BASICA A version of the BASIC programming language developed by Microsoft Corporation for the IBM PC family of computers.

basIc Input-output system (BIOS) A set of programs encoded in readonly memory (ROM) in IBM-compatible microcomputers. These programs facilitate the transfer of data and control instructions between the computer and peripherals.

BASIC in ROM BASIC interpreter stored in a read only memory chip that is available to the user at all times

basic linkage The linkage used repeatedly in one routine, program, or system that follows the same set of rules each time.

BAT file (BATch file) A file of consisting of a set of DOS or OS/2 commands, which are executed one after the other. The file has a .BAT extension and is created with a text editor or word processor in ASCII. See DOS batch file, DOS AUTOEXEC.BAT.

batch Group, or collection, of items. batch file See BAT file.

batch job Same as batch program.

batch operation Some action performed on a group of items at one time.

batch processing Processing a group of transactions at one time. Transactions are collected and processed against the master files (master files updated) at the end of the day or some other time period. Contrast with transaction processing.

batch program Non-interactive (non-conversational) program such as a report listing or sort.

batch session Transmitting or updating an entire tile. Implies a non-interactive or non-interruptible opera- lion from beginning to end. Contrast with interactive session.

batch stream Collection of batch processing programs that are scheduled to run in the computer.

batch system See batch processing.

batch total Sum of a particular field in a collection of items that is used as a control total to ensure that all data has been entered into the computer. For example, using account number as a batch total, all account numbers would be summed manually before entry into the computer. After entry, the total is checked with the computer's sum of the numbers. If it does not match, source documents are manually checked against the computer's listing.

baud (1) Signalling rate of a line. It is the switching speed, or number of transitions (voltage or frequency changes) that are made per second. Only at low speeds are bauds equal to bits per second; for example, 300 baud is equal to 300 bps. However, one baud can be made to represent more than one bit per second. For example, the V.22bis modem generates 1200 bps at 600 baud. (2) Commonly (and erroneously) used to specify bits per second for modem speed; for example, 1200 baud means 1200 bps. See previous paragraph.

baudot code Pronounced "baw-doh." One of the first standards for international telegraphy developed in the late 19th century by Emile Baudot. It uses five bits to make up a character.

baud rate The speed at which telecommunicated data is transmitted, measured in bits per second. Common baud rates are 300, 1,200, and 2,400. Technically, since baud is itself a rate, the reference is redundant.

bay The cabinet or rack in which electronic equipment is installed; also called equipment bay.

BBS (Bulletin Board System) Computer system used as an information source and message switching system for a particular interest group. Users dial into the BBS, review and leave messages for other users as well as communicate to other users on the system at the same time. BBSs are used to distribute shareware and may provide access (doors) to other application programs.

BCD Abbreviation for binary coded decimal.

BDOS error See read error, write error.

beacon In a network, a special message sent by a node indicating a serious network problem.

beaconing Signalling error conditions in a LAN.

bead (1) Small programming subroutine. A sequence of beads that are strung together is called a thread. (2) Insulator surrounding the inner wire of a coaxial cable.

beam penetration CRT A vector display system that produces color by varying the strength of an electron beam directed at a screen coated with (typically) both red and green phosphor layers.

bebuggIng The intentional seeding of a program with known mistakes to measure the rates of debugging by student programmers.

beep An audible sound produced by a computer's speaker. Also a command in some programming lan-i guages that causes the computer's speaker to emit a sound.

behaviour In object-oriented programming, how an object acts and reacts, in terms of its state changes and message passing.

bell character Control code used to sound an audible bell or tone in order to alert the user (ASCII 7, EBCDIC 2F).

Bell Laboratories The research and development centre of the AT&T Company and one of the most renowned scientific laboratories in the world. Many computer hardware developments, software concepts, and programs were generated at Bell Laboratories.

bell 103 The standard for 300-baud modems.

bells and whistles An informal description of the spe. cial or extra features of a computer system, including graphics, color displays, sound, and many peripherals.

bell 212A The standard for 1,200-baud modems.

belt-bed plotter A pen plotter that uses a wide continuous belt for holding the paper.

benchmark Tests used in the measurement of computer equipment performance under typical conditions of use for the purpose of comparing execution speed, throughput, and so forth, while running an actual set of applications. Unless the end user environment can be duplicated closely, the benchmark may be inaccurate. It may be more effective to find a user organizatibn with a similar processing environment and sim-. ply monitor the operation. See Linpack, Dhrystones, Whetstones, Khornerstones, SPECmark.

benchmark problem A problem designed to evaluate and compare the performance of digital computers.

Bernoulli Box Removable disk system from Iomega Corp., that connects to personal computers through a SCSI interface. The name comes from the 18th century Swiss scientist, Daniel Bernoulli, whose principle of fluid dynamics is demonstrated in the disk mechanism. When the floppy disk is spun at high speed, it bends up and maintains a thin band of air between it and the read/write head. Unlike a hard disk in which the read/write head flies over a rigid disk, the floppy disk in the Bernoulli Box flies up to a rigid read/write head. Upon power failure, a hard disk has to retract the head to prevent a recording failure or head crash, whereas the Bernoulli Box Happy automatically bends down. This prevents the risk of the head crashing on the disk surface. Introduced in 1983, the first Bernoulli Box was a 10MB, 8" floppy disk cartridge.

Beta First home VCR format. Developed by Sony, it records video on 1/2" tape cassettes.

beta test Test of hardware or software that is performed by users under normal operating conditions. See alpha test.

betaware Software in beta test that has been provided to a large number of users prior to the formal release.

Bezier Atype of curve generated by an algorithm. Named after French mathematician Pierre Bezier, it is used to display nonuniform curves bases upon a fitting algorithm. Bezier curves need only a few points to define a large number of shapes, hence their usefulness over other mathematical methods for approximating a given shape. Within drawing programs, they are typically reshaped by moving the handles that appear off the curve.

BFT (Binary File Transmission) Standard for transmitting data between fax boards in less time than conventional modems. It does not allow transfer between fax boards and data modems.

bias The amount by which the average of a set of values departs from a reference value.

bibliography (1) An annotated catalog o documents. (2) An enumerative list of books. (3) A list of documents pertaining to a given subject or author. (4) The process of compiling catalogues or lists.

bidirectional When data flow may go in either direction on a wire. Transceivers at each end both receive and transmit. Common bidirectional buses are tristate or open collector transistor-transistor logic.

bidirectional printer Printer that prints alternate lines from right to left.

BIFF (Binary Interchange File Format) Spreadsheet file format that holds data and charts, introduced with Excel Version 2.2.

blform In typography, a typeface that combines tower-case and smallcap characters to form the lowercase alphabet.

bifurcate To divide into two.

bifurcation A condition whereby two, and only two, outcomes can occur, such as on or off,- 1 or true of false.

Big Blue Slang for IBM coined derived from the blue covers on most of its earlier mainframes.

billion One thousand times one million. See giga, nanosecond.

bin (BINary) Popular directory name for storing executable programs, device drivers, etc. (binary files).

binaries Executable programs in machine language.

binary Meaning two. The fundamental principle behind digital computers. All input to the computer is converted into binary numbers made up of the two digits O and 1 (bits). For example, when you press the "A" key on your personal computer, the keyboard generates and transmits the number 01000001 to the computer's memory as a series of pulses. The 1 bits are transmitted as high voltage; the 0 bits are transmitted as low voltage. The is and Os are stored as a series of charged and uncharged memory cells in the computer.

On magnetic disk and tape, the bits are stored as positively and negatively charged spots. Display screens and printers convert the binary numbers into visual characters.

The electronic circuits that process these binary numbers are themselves binary in concept. They are made up of on/off switches (transistors) that are electrically opened and closed. The current (lowing through one switch turns on (or off) another switch, and so on. These switches open and close in nano-seconds and picoseconds (billionths and trillionths of a second).

A computer's capability to do work is based on its storage capacity (memory and disk) and internal transmission speed. Greater storage capacities are achieved by making the memory cell or magnetic spot smaller. Faster transmission rates are achieved by shortening the time it takes to open and dose the switch and developing circuit paths that can handle the increased speeds. In order to improve the performance of a computer, we simply continue to refine the binary concept.

binary arithmetic (1) A mathematical numeration system equivalent to the decimal arithmetic system but involving only two digits: 1 and 0 (2) An expression recognizing that all arithmetic calculations are done with two values at a time.

binary code Coding system made up of binay digits. See BCD, data code, numbers.

binary coded character One element of a notaticn system representing alphanumeric character - such as decimal digits, alphabetic letters, and special symbols-by a predetermined configuration of consecutive binary digits.

binary coded decimal (BCD) A computer coding system in which each decimal digit is represented by a group of four binary l's and 0's.

binary coded decimal number Any number, usually consisting of successive groups of figures, in which each group of four figures is a binary number that represent, but does not necessarily equal arithmetically, a particular figure in an associated decimal number; for example, the decimal number 264 is represented as the binary coded number 0010 01100100.

binary compatible Refers to any data, hardware or software structure (data file, machine code, instruction set, etc.) in binary form that is totally identical to another.

binary device (1) A device that can register two conditions, such as an electrical switch that can be on or off. (2) In computer science, equipment that records data in binary form or that reads the data so coded.

binary digit Either the character 0 or 1. Abbreviated as bit.

binary field Field that contains binary numbers. It may refer to the storage of binary numbers for calculation purposes, or to a field that is capable of holding any information, including data, text, graphics images, voice and video. See BLOB.

binary file (1) Program in machine language ready to execute in the CPU/operating system it was created for. Binary files cannot be transmitted by protocols that handle only ASCII text. (2) File that contains binary numbers. Proprietary data formats often use binary numbers and must be treated like machine language for transmission.

binary format (1) Numbers stored in pure binary form in contrast with BCD form. (2) Information stored in a binary coded form, such as data, text, images, voice and video. See binary file, binary field, BLOB. (3) File transfer mode that transmits any type of file without loss of data.

binary notation Use of binary numbers' to represent values.

binary numbers Numbers stored in pure binary form. Within one byte (8 bits), the values 0 to 255 can be held. Two contiguous bytes (16 bits) can hold values from 0 to 65,535. See numbers, binary values.

binary point The radix point in a mixed binary numeral, separating the fractional part from the integer part. In the binary numeral 110.011, the binary point is between the two 0's.

binary search Technique for quickly locating an item in a sequential list. The desired key is compared to the data in the middle of the list. The half that contains the data is then compared in the middle, and so on, either until the key is located or a small enough group is isolated to be sequentially searched.

binary synchronous See bisync.

binary system A numeral system with a base or radix of 2. The numeral 111 in the binary system represents the quantity 1, x 2, plus 1 x that is, 7 in the decimal system.

binary-to-decimal conversion The process of converting a numeral written in base 2 to the equivalent numeral written in base 10.

binary-to-hexadecimal conversion The process of converting a numeral written in base 2 to the equivalent numeral written in base 16.

binary-to-octal conversion The process of converting numeral written in base 2 to the equivalent numeral written in base 8.

binary tree Data structure in which each node contains one parent and no more than two children.

binary values The following table shows the maximum number of numeric combinations in a binary structure with all bits set to zero equivalent to one combination. For example, in one bit, which can be. 0 or 1, there are two possible values.

Bits	Total values	
1	2	
2	4	
3	8	
4	16	
5	32	
6	64	
7	128	
8	256	
9	512	
10	1,024	1K
11	2,048	2K
12	4,096	4K
13	8,192	8K
14	16,384	16K
15	32,768	32K
16	65,536	64K

bind (1) To assign a machine address to a logical or symbolic reference or address. (2) To assign a type or value to a variable or parameter. See binding time. (3) To link modules together. See linkage editor.

binding In object-oriented programming, the process of weaving a program together to resolve all the connections among its components. Static, or early, binding resolves these connections before the program is run. Dynamic, or late, binding occurs while the pro. gram is running.

binding time (1) In program compilation, the point in time when symbolic references to data are converted into physical machine addresses.. (2) In programming languages, when a variable is assigned its type (integer, string, etc.). Traditional compilers and assemblers provide early binding and assign types at compilation. Object-oriented languages provide late binding and assign types at runtime when the van- able receives a value from the keyboard or other source.

biochip An organic device that assembles itself and requires no electricity to operate. If biochip research proves to be successful, one billion times as much data as that now stored on a silicon chip will be able to be stored on a biochip.

biocomputer A computer that will have its central processor and memory stored on biochips.

biomechanics Study of the anatomical principles of movement. Biomechanical applications on the computer employ stick modelling to analyze the movement of athletes as well as racing horses.

biometrics The science of measuring individual body characteristics; used in some security systems and forensic research.

bionic Machine that is patterned after human or natural physiological principles; for example, robots. It also refers to artificial devices implanted into humans replacing or extending normal human functions.

BIOS (Basic I/O System) Detailed instructions that activate peripheral devices. See ROM BIOS.

bipolar Category of high-speed microelectronic circuit design, which was used to create the first transistor and the first integrated circuit. The most common variety of bipolar chip is TTL (transistor transistor logic). Bipolar and MOS are the two major categories of chip design.

bipolar read-only memory See brom.

bipolar transmission Digital transmission technique that alternates between positive and negative signals. The is and Os are determined by varying amplitudes at both polarities while non-data is zero amplitude.

BIPS (Billion instructions Per Second) See MIPS.

biqulnary code A seven-bit weighted code used primarily to represent decimal numbers.

birefringence Using a crystal to split light into two frequencies that travel at different speeds and at right angles to each other. It is used to filter out a color in an LCD display.

bis Second version. It means twice in Old Latin, or encore in French.

bistable device A device with only two stable states, such as on and off.

bi-state A situation in which a computer component take on either of two possible conditions.

bisync (Binary SYNChronous) Major category of synchronous communications protocols used in mainframe networks. Bisync communications require that both sending and receiving devices are synchronized before transmission of data is started. Contrast with asynchronous transmission.

blsynchronous See bisync.

bit (Binary digiT) Single digit in a binary number (0 or 1). Within the computer, a bit is physically a memory cell (made up of transistors or one transistor and a capacitor), a magnetic spot on disk or tape or a pulse of high or low voltage travelling through a circuit. Conceptually, a bit is like a light bulb; either on or off.

Groups of bits make up storage units in the computer, called characters, bytes, or words, which are manipulated as a group. The most common is the byte, which is made up of eight bits and is equivalent to one alphanumeric character.

bit cell Boundary in which a single bit is recorded on a tape or disk.

bit control The means of transmitting serial data in which each bit has a significant meaning and a single character is surrounded with start and stop bits.

bit density Number of bits that can be stored within a given physical area.

bit flipping The process of inverting bits - changing 1's to 0's and vice versa. For example, in a graphics prpgram, to invert a black-and-white bit-mapped image (to change black to white and vice versa), the program could simply flip the bits that make up the bit map.

bit Image A collection of bits stored in a computer's memory, arranged into a rectangular matrix. The computer's display screen is a bit image that is visible to the user.

bit level device A device, such as a disk drive, that inputs and outputs data bits or data blocks. Contrast with pulse level device.

bit manipulation Processing individual bits within a byte. Bit-level manipulation is very low-level programming, often done in graphics and systems programming.

bitmap (1) In computer graphics, an area in memory that represents the video image. For monochrome screens, one bit in the bitmap represents one pixel on screen. For gray scale or color, several bits in the bitmap represent one pixel or group of pixels on screen. (2) Binary representation in which each bit or set of bits corresponds to some object (image, font, etc.) or condition.

bitmap file formats See art, cut, gif, iff, img, macpaint, neo, pcx, tga, tiff. Contrast with object file graphic formats.

bit-mapped font A set of characters in a particular size and style, in which each character is described in a unique pattern of dots. Bit-mapped screen or printer fonts represent characters with a matrix of dots. To display or print-mapped fonts, the computer or printer must keep a full representation of each character in memory. Contrast with scalable font.

bit-mapped graphics A method of generating screen images by creating a one-for-one correspondence between bits in memory and pixels on the screen. In color graphics, three or more bits are required in the bit map to represent the red, green and blue value of an individual pixel. Bitmapped graphics are created by paint programs and some scanners.

bit parallel Transmission of several bits at the same time, each bit travelling over a different wire in the cable.

bit pattern Specific layout of binary digits.

bit plane Segment of memory used to control an object, such as a color, cursor or sprite. Bit planes may be reserved parts of a common memory or independent memory banks each designed for one purpose.

bit rate Transmission speed of binary coded data. Same as data rate.

bit serial Transmission of one bit after the other on a single line or wire.

bit slice processor Logic chip that is used as an elementary building block for the computer designer.

bit specifications (1) Size of the computer's internal word, or registers, which is the amount of data the CPU can compute at the same time. (2) Size of the computer's data bus, which is the pathway over which data is transferred between memory and the CPU and between memory and the peripheral devices. (3) Size of the address bus, which determines how much memory the processor can address directly. Each bit doubles the number. (4) Number of colors that can be displayed at onetime. Unless some of the memory is used for cursor or sprite movement, an 8-bit graphics adapter generates 256 colors; 16-bit, 64K colors; 24-bit, 16.8 million colors. See alpha channel.

bit stream Transmission of binary signals.

bit stuffing Adding bits to a transmitted message in order to round out a fixed frame or to break up a pattern of data bits that could be misconstrued for control codes.

black box Custom-made electronic device, such as a protocol converter or encryption system. Yesterday's black boxes often become today's off-the-shelf products.

blank (1) Part of a medium in which no characters are recorded. (2) In electronic spreadsheets, a command that will erase the contents of a cell or range of cells. (3) An empty space with dimension of one character of data.

blank character Space character that takes up one byte in the computer just like a letter or digit. When you press the space bar in an ASCII computer, a character with the numeric value of 32 is created.

blanking On a display screen, not displaying a character although it is present; leaving a space.

blank squash Removal of blanks between items of data. For example, in the expression CITY + "," + STATE, the data is concatenated with a blank squash resulting in AUSTIN, TX rather than AUSTIN TX.

bleed In a printed document, any element that runs off the edge of the page. Also when colors spill over their boundaries.

blind search A time-consuming type of search that uses can orderly scheme, but no prescience, to exhaust all possibilities.

blinking A graphics aid that causes a predefined graphic entry to blink on the CRT to attract the designer' attention.

blip Mark, line or spot on a medium, such as microfilm, that is optically sensed and used for timing or counting purposes.

BLOB (Binary Large OBject) Coined by Borland, a database field that holds any digitized information.

block (1) Group of disk or tape records that is stored and transferred as a single unit. (2) Group of bits or characters that is transmitted as a unit. (3) In word processing, a group of text characters marked for moving, copying, saving or other operation.

block device Peripheral device that transfers a group of bytes (block, sector, etc.) of data at a time such as a disk. Contrast with character device.

block diagram Chart that contains squares and rectangles connected with arrows to depict hardware and software interconnections. For program flow charts, information system flow charts, circuit diagrams and communications networks, more elaborate graphical representations are usually used.

block graphics Graphics images created by using block graphics characters, ASCII characters. Because these characters are handled the same way as ordinary characters, the computer can display block graphics considerably faster than bitmapped graphics. Their transport-ability is also substantially more.

block header A brief record of data that described a block of memory and its contents.

blockIng The process of grouping a specified number of logical records into one contigubus unit of storage called a block, usually to increase the efficiency of computer input and output operations. In word processing, the process of setting apart a text portion as a block.

blocking factor The number of logical records per physical record on a magnetic tape or disk.

blocking object In object-oriented programming, a passive object whose semantics are guaranteed in the presence of multiple threads of control.

block length The measure of the size of a block, usually specified in units such as records, words, characters, or bytes.

block move Ability to mark a contiguous segment of text or data and move it.

block sorting A sorting technique used to break down a file into related groups.

blocks world An artificially created environment of blocks used in the study of robotics and natural language.

block transfer The relocation of an entire block of data from one area of storage to another.

blow To write code or data into a PROM chip by blowing the fuses of the 0 bits. The 1 bits are left alone.

blow up Same as crash, bomb or abend.

blue ribbon problem A computer program that executes properly on the first try and does not require any debugging.

BMP (Bit MaP) Windows graphics format that may be device dependent or independent. Device independent BMP files (1MB) are coded for translation to a wide variety of displays and printers.

BNC Commonly used connector for coaxial cable. The plug looks like a cylinder with two short pins on the outer edge on opposite sides. After the plug is inserted, the socket is turned, causing the pins to tighten the plug within it.

BNF Abbreviation for backus normal form. board See printed circuit board, BBS.

board computer A computer in which all electronic components are laid out on a single circuit board.

board exchange warranty A warranty that provides a customer with a new replacement board when the original needs repair.

board level Electronic components that are mounted on a printed circuit board instead of in a cabinet or finished housing.

BOF (Beginning Of File) Status of a file when it is first opened or when an instruction or command has reset the file pointer.

boilerplate Common phrase or expression used over and over. Boilerplate is stored on disk and copied into the document as needed.

boilerplate document A document created by combining selected paragraphs from a set of standard paragraphs which only a small amount of original information.

boldface Characters that are heavier and darker on printed output and brighter than normal on a display screen.

boldface attribute Code that turns normal characters into boldface characters on a printer or display screen.

boldface font Set of type characters that are darker and heavier than normal type. In a boldface font, all characters have been designed as bold characters.

bold printing The ability to make certain letters darker than the surrounding text. Some printers produce bold characters by over-striking or shadow printing.

bomb Same as abend and crash.

bookkeeping See housekeeping.

Bookman Aserif typeface frequently used for body type. Bookman, a design owned by the International Typeface corporation (ITC), is included as a built-in font with many PostScript laser printers.

Booleon algebra A branch of symbolic logic similar in form to algebra but dealing with logical relationship instead of numerical relationships. Boolean algebra has now become an important subject in logic design of electronic computers. It was developed by English mathematician and logician George Boole (1815- 1864).

Boolean data Yes/no or true/false data.

Boolean expression Statement using Boolean operators that expresses a condition which is either true or false.

Boolean logic The 'mathematics of logic," developed by the English mathematician George Boole in the mid 19th century. Its rules and operations govern logical functions (true/false) rather than numbers. As add, subtract, multiply and divide are the primary operations of arithmetic, AND, OR and NOT are the primary operations of Boolean logic.

Boolean operator One of the Boolean logic operators such as AND, OR and NOT.

Boolean search Search for specific data. It implies that any condition can be searched for using the Boolean operators AND, OR and NOT.

boot Causing the computer to start executing instructions. Personal computers contain built-in instructions in a ROM chip that are automatically executed on startup. These instructions help the computer figure out components (peripherals), search for the operating system, load it and pass control to it. Starting up a large computer may require more button pushing and keyboard input. The te1m comes from boot strap," since bootstraps help you get your boots on, booting the computer helps it get its first instructions. See cold boot, warm boot.

boot drive Disk drive that contains the operating system.

boot failure Inability to locate and/or read the operating system from the designated disk.

boot ROM Memory chip that allows a workstation to be booted from the server or other remote station.

boot sector The area on disk that contains instructions and/or data that cause the computer to locate and load the operating system. It is usually the first sector of a disk partition. Any physical damage to this sector means that the disk is unusable.

bootstrapping Starting up a computer system. "Cold boot" refers to complete restarting after switching the power on, while 'swarm boot" means partial restarting under operating system control. Warm boot is done by pressing Ctrl-Alt-Del keys simultaneously.

boot virus Virus written into the boot sectors of a floppy disk. If the floppy is booted, it infects the system. For example, the Michel-angelo virus, which destroys data on March 6th, Michelangelo's birthday, infects a computer if it is booted with the infected disk.

bootable disk Disk that contains the operating system (i.e., the two hidden tiles and COMMAND. COM) and typically refers to a floppy disk. If a hard disk personal computer does not find a bootable floppy disk in the primary floppy drive (A:) at startup, it boots from the hard disk.

bootstrap See boot.

border (1) In on-screen windows, the edge surrounding the user's workspace. Window borders provide a visible frame around a document or graphic. (2) In printing, a decorative line or pattern along one or more edges of an illustration or a page.

bore The diameter of a hole, such as on a floppy disk of magnetic tape reel.

Borland (Borland Int'l) Leading PC software company founded in 1983 by Philippe Kahn. Its Turbo Pascal moved Pascal out of the academia into a commercial product, and its Turbo C has become an industry standard. Borland C++ and Turbo Pascal for Windows are committed to Windows and object-oriented programming.

Borland C++ ANSI C and C++ compiler from Borland for DOS and Windows applications. It is Turbo C- compatible and its debugger also supports Windows programs written in Microsoft C.

borrow An arithmetically negative carry that occurs in direct subs-traction by raising the low-order digit of the minuend by one unit of the next higher-order digit.

BOT Acronym for Beginning Of Tape mark that shows where to start recording on a magnetic taps.

bottleneck See limiting operation.

bottom-up technique An implementation technique wherein the bottom level modules are written and tested, after which the next-lowest level of modules are written and tested. This process continues until all of the modules have been completed. Contrast with top-down development.

bound Pertaining to whatever limits system performance. Processor bound or I/O bound indicates which component of a system determines the speed of the system.

boundary fill The process of filling a region with color by switching to a new value (color) all pixels that are bounded by pixels having the boundary value.

box drawing characters Set of charcters from extended ASCII which are used for drawing boxes.

bpl (Bits Per Inch) Used to measure the number of bits stored in a linear inch of a track on a recording surface, such as on a disk or tape.

bps (Bits Per Second) Used to measure the speed of data transfer in a communications system.

brain-damaged A term describing a program that performs in an ill- behaved or destructive manner.

branch (1) Same as GOTO. (2) Connection between two blocks in a flowchart or two nodes in a network.

branch Instruction An instruction to a computer that enables it to choose between alternative program paths, depending upon the conditions determined by the computer during the execution of the program.

branchpoint The place in a program where a branch is selected.

breadboard Thin plastic board full of holes used to hold components (transistors, chips, etc.) that are wired together. It is used to develop electronic prototypes or one-of-a-kind systems.

break To temporarily or permanently stop executing, printing or transmitting.

break key Key that is pressed to stop the execution of the current program or transmission, usually the ESC key.

breakpoint A specified point in a program at which the program may be interrupted by manual intervention or by a control routine. Generally used as an aid in testing and debugging programs.

bridge (1) To purposefully or inadvertently cross from one circuit, channel or element over to another. (2) Device that connects two networks of the same type together. Contrast with gateway. See router, brouter.

bridgeware Hardware or software that converts data or translates programs from one format into another.

briefcase computer A portable computer that will fit' inside a briefcase.

brightness Light level on a display screen. Contrast with contrast.

broadband Technique for transmitting large amounts of data, voice and video over long distances. Using high frequency transmission over coaxial cable or optical fibres and the same technique as in cable TV, several streams of data can be transmitted simultaneously. Contrast with baseband.

broadcast To disseminate information to several recipients simultaneously.

Brooklyn Bridge PC file transfer program from Fifth Generation Systems, that transfers data between laptops and desktop computers.

BROM Acronym for Bipolar Read-Only Memory, a read-only memory with no write function that uses bipolar semiconductor devices.

brownout A period of low-voltage electrical power caused by unusually heavy demand. Brownouts can cause computers to operate erratically or to crash. It is different from blackouts which are total loss of electricity.

browse (1) To view and possibly edit a file on screen like text in a word processing document. Browse commands let the user scroll through the data horizontally by field and vertically by row or screenful. (2) To view and edit the class hierarchy of the objects in an object-oriented programming language.

browser A tool supplied with the programming language that lets the programmer view the hierarchy and edit code in object-oriented languages.

browsing Looking at files or computer listings in search of something interesting, often without authorization to do so.

brush In computer paint programs, a tool used to produce brushstrokes of varying width, and in some cases with calligraphic or shadowing effects.

brute-force technique Any mathematical technique that depends on the raw power of a computer to arrive at an inelegant solution to a mathematical problem. Most computer users try to avoid brute-force tech-, niques unless they have no practical alternative.

BSC Abbreviation for Binary Synchronous Communication, a procedure used for data transmission.

BTAM Abbreviation for Basic Telecommunications Access Method, an access, method that permits read/ write communications with remote devices.

Btrleve Database management system from Novell that accompanies its NetWare operating systems.

bubble Bit in bubble memory or a symbol in a bubble chart.

bubble chart Chart that uses bubble-like symbols often used to depict data flow diagrams.

Bubble Jet Canon's ink jet printer technology. Considerably cheaper than laser printers.

bubble memory It is conceptually a stationary disk with spinning bits. The unit, only a couple of square inches in size, contains a thin film magnetic recording layer. Globular-shaped bubbles (bits) are electromagnetically generated in circular strings inside this layer. In order to read or write the bubbles, they are rotated past the equivalent of a read/write head. It is about as fast as a slow hard disk and holds its content without power.

bubble sort Multiple-pass sorting technique that starts by sequencing the first two items, then the second with the third, then the third with the fourth and so on until the end of the set has been reached. The process is repeated until all items are in the correct sequence.

bucket Another term for a variable. It is just a place to store something.

buffer Reserved segment of memory used to hold data while it is being processed. In a program, buffers are created to hold some amount of data from each of the files that will be read or written. A buffer may also be a small memory bank used for special purposes.

buffered computer A computer that provides for simultaneous input/output and process operations.

buffer flush Transfer of data from memory to disk.

buffering The delaying and temporary storing of data in a data communications-path.

buffer pool Area of memory reserved for buffers.

bug Persistent error in software or hardware. If the bug is in software, it can be corrected by changing the program. If the bug is in hardware, new circuits have to be designed. The term was coined in the 1.940s when a moth was found squashed between the points of an electromechanical relay in the Mark I. This is the origin of the term 'debugging'. Contrast with glitch.

bug compatible Hardware device that contains the same design flaws as the original.

building block principles A system design that, like building blocks, permits addition of other equipment units to form a larger system. See modularity.

built-in check See Automatic Check.

built-in font A printer font encoded permanently in the printer's read-only memory (ROM).

bulk eraser A device used to erase information from a storage medium such as floppy disk or type.

bulk storage Storage media that is used for its high capacity rather than high-speed execution. May refer to auxiliary menlory, tape or disk.

bullet Anpen or closed circle used to set off items in a list.

bulletin board service See BBS.

bump mapping In computer graphics, a technique for simulating rough textures by creating irregularities in shading.

bundled/unbundled Complete package of hardware and software for a single price. Unbundled systems have separate prices for each component.

bundled software The software included with a computer system as part of the system's total price. Contrast with unbundled.

bunny suit Protective clothing worn in a clean room that keeps human bacteria from infecting the chip- making process.

burn To ruin circuity by subjecting it to excessive current or heat.

burn In To test an electronic system by running it for a specified length of time. Although an electronic component can fail at any time, weak components will generally fail within the first few hours of running. The longer the burn in period, the better the test.

burning The process of programming a read-only memory.

burst (1) in computer operations, to separate continuous-form paper into discrete sheets. (2) In data transmission, a sequence of signals counted as one unit.

burst mode Alternate method of high-speed transmission in a communications or computer channel. Burst mode implies that due to certain conditions, the system can send a burst of data at higher speed for a shorter period of time.

bus Common channel (pathway) between hardware devices either internally between components in a computer, or externally between stations in a communications network. When you plug in a board into one of the expansion slots in your personal computer, you are plugging into the bus.

When bus architecture is used in a computer, the processor(s), memory banks and peripheral control units are all interconnected through the bus. The bus is divided into two channels, one to select where data is located (address bus), and the other to transfer the data (data bus).

When bus architecture is used in a network, all terminals and computers are connected to a common channel that is made of twisted wire pairs, coaxial cable or optical fibres. Ethernet is the most common LAN architecture that uses a bus topology.

bus bridge Device that connects two busses together.

bus card Expansion board (card) that plugs into the computer's expansion bus.

bus extender (1) Board that pushes a printed circuit board out of the way of surrounding boards for testing purposes. It plugs into an expansion slot which, in turn, plugs into the bus extender. (2) Device that extends the length of a communications channel. (3) Device that increases the number of expansion slats. It is either an expansion board containing multiple expansion slots, or an expansion board that cables to a separate housing that contains the slots and its own power supply.

bus mouse Mouse that plugs into an expansion board rather than into a serial port. Thus, it takes up an expansion slot whereas- a serial mouse takes up a serial port.

business data processing Data processing for business purposes such as payroll, scheduling, and accounting.

business graphics Numeric data represented in graphic form. While line graphs, bar charts and pie charts are the common forms of business graphics, there are many additional graphic representations available. By transforming numerical data into graphic form, patterns of business activity can be viewed, conclusions drawn and trends noticed more quickly.

business machine Any' office machine, such as a typewriter or calculator, that is used in clerical and accounting functions, The term has traditionally excluded computers and terminals.

business-oriented programming language A language designed for handling large data files in business applications. See COBOL.

business programming The branch of computer programming in which business problems are coded for computer solution. This usually involves relatively few calculations but extensive tiles with a large number of data inputs and outputs.

business software: Programs specifically designed for business applications. Examples include electronic spreadsheets, database management systems, business graphics packages, payroll programs, and accounting programs.

bus network A system in which all stations, or computer devices, communicate by using a common distribution channel, or bus.

bus system A network of paths inside the computer that facilitate data flow. Important buses in a computer are identified as data bus, control bus, and address bus.

button Physical button on a device (eg. mouse), or a simulated button on screen (icon) that is "pushed" by moving the cursor onto it and clicking a mouse button.

bypass In communications to avoid the local telephone company by using satellites and microwave systems.

bypass capacitor - A capacitor used to reduce electrical noise from the power supply.

byte Common unit of computer storage (micro to mainframe). It is made up of eight, binary digits (bits). A bytç holds the equivalent of a single character, such as the letter A, a dollar sign or decimal point. For numbers, a byte can hold a single decimal digit (0 to 9), two numeric digits (packed' decimal) or a number from 0 to 255 (binary numbers).

Byte Specifications The primary specifications of hardware are rated in bytes; for example, a 80-megabyte (also written as 80M or 80MB) disk holds 80 million characters of instructions and data. A one-megabyte (1M or 1MB) memory allows one million characters of instructions and data to be stored internally for processing.

With database files and word processing documents, the file size is slightly larger than the number of data characters stored in it, since word processing files contain embedded codes for layout settings (margins, tabs, boldface); and database files contain codes that describe the structure of the records. Unlike data and text, a 100,000-byte graphics file is not indicative of the size of the image contained in it. There are many graphics standards, and the higher the image quality, the more bytes are needed to represent it. A low-resolution graphics file can take as little as 8,000 bytes, while high-resolution files can take 100,000 or more bytes per picture.

byte addressable Computer that can address each byte of memory independently of the others. Contrast with word addressable.

byte-oriented protocol Communications protocol that uses control codes made up of full bytes. The bisynchronous protocols used by IBM and other vendors are examples. Contrast with bit-oriented protocol.

bytes per Inch (BPI) The number of bytes that can be contained on one inch of magnetic tape. A common measure of recording density.

Band: The section of a report definition that contains the format of a report section. There normally are bands for the report heading and footing, page heading and footing, and the detail line of the report. There are also bands for group or break points within the report.

Banded report writer: A report writer in which the sections of the reports are defined by bands. (See Band.)

Base table: In relational implementations, the table from which relational views are defined.

Before-image: A record of a database entity (normally a row or a page) before a change. It is used in recovery to perform rollback.

Bill of materials: A recursive data structure in which a part (or, in general, any element) can be both an assembly of other parts and a component of other assemblies.

Binary relationship: A relationship between exactly two entities or tables.

Bind: A verb meaning to connect a program variable or a GUI control to a column of a table or query.

Bottom-up database design: The design of a database that works from the detailed and specific to the general. Although this sort of design takes little time, it may result in a database that is too narrow in scope.

Boyce—Codd normal form: A relation in third normal form in which every determinant is a candidate key.

Branch: A subelement of a tree that may consist of one or many nodes.

Buffer : An area of memory used to hold data. For a road, data is read from a storage device into a buffer; for a write date is written from the buffer to storage.

Built-in function: In SQL, any of the functions COUNT, SUM, AVG, MAX or MIN.

C

C High-level programming language developed at Bell Labs that is able to manipulate the computer at a low level. After late 1980s, C has become the language of choice for developing commercial software. C has very high transportability and can run in a wide variety of micros, minis and mainframes.

C is programmed as a series of functions that call each other for processing. Even the body of the program is a function named "main." Functions are very flexible, allowing programmers to choose from the standard library that comes with the compiler, to use third party functions from other C suppliers, or to develop their own.

Compared to other high-level programming languages, though C appears complicated, its intricate appearance is due to its extreme flexibility.

C++: Object-oriented version of C created by Bjarne Stroustrup that is becoming very popular. C++ combines traditional C programming with object-oriented capability.

C: Designation for the primary hard disk in a PC.

cable Flexible metal or glass wire or group of wires. All cables used in electronics are insulated with a material such as plastic or rubber.

cable connector The male/female plug used for connecting cables between a computer and peripherals.

cable matcher Same as gender changer.

cabletext Videotex service that uses coaxial cable. See videotex.

cache Pronounced cash." A disk cache is a reserved section of normal memory or additional memory on the disk controller board. When the disk is read, a large block of data is copied into the cache. If subsequent requests for data can be satisfied from the cache, slower disk access is not required. If the cache is used for writing, data is queued up in memory and written to the disk in larger blocks.

caching Retaining data in cache memory for rapid access.

caching controller Disk controller with a built-in cache. See cache.

CAD (Computer-Aided Design) Using computers to design products. CAD systems are high-speed and high resolution workstations or personal computers. CAD software is available for general design or specialized uses, such as architectural, electrical and mechanical design. CAD software may also be highly specialized for creating products such as printed circuits and integrated circuits, Except in a few cases, CAD systems rely extensively on graphics. See graphics, CADD, CAE.

CAD/CAM (Computer-Aided Design/Computer-Aided Manufacturing) Integration of computer-aided design with computer-controlled manufacturing. The products designed in the CAD system are input directly into the CAM system. For example, after a machine part is designed in CAD, its electronic image is transferred to a numerical control programming language, which generates the instructions to control the machine that makes the part.

CADAM Full-featured IBM mainframe CAD application, which includes 3-D capability, solid modelling and numerical control. Originally developed by Lockheed for internal use, it was distributed by IBM after the late 1970s.

CADD (Computer-Aided Design and Drafting) CAD systems with additional features for drafting, such as dimensioning and text entry.

CAE (1) (Computer-Aided Engineering) Software that analyzes designs which have been created in the computer or that have been created elsewhere and entered into the computer. Different kinds of engineering analyses can then be performed, such as structural analysis and electronic circuit analysis. (2) (Common Application Environment) Software development platform that is specified by X/Open.

CAI (1) (Computer-Assisted Instruction) Same as CBT.

CAL (Computer-Assisted Learning) Same as CBT.

calculated field Numeric or date field that is derived from the calculation of other fields. Data is not entered into a calculated field by the user.

calculatIng Reconstructing or creating new data by compressing certain numeric facts.

calculatIons Any mathematical process performed on data.

calculator Machine that provides only arithmetic capabilities. It accepts keypad input and displays results on a readout and/or paper tape. Unlike a computer, it cannot handle alphabetic data.

calculator mode The operating mode on some interactive computer systems that allows the terminal (or keyboard/display, in the case of microcomputers) to be used as a desk calculator. The user types an expression, the computer then evaluates it and returns the answer immediately.

calibration The process of determining by measurement or by comparison with a standard the correct value of each scale reading on a meter or the correct value of each setting of a control knob.

call (1) In programming, a statement that references an independent subroutine or program. The call is turned into a branch instruction by the assembler, compiler or interpreter. The routine that is called is responsible for returning to the calling program after it has finished processing. (2) In communications, the action taken by the transmitting station to establish a connection with the receiving station in a dial-up network.

callback PPD A port protection device that screens incoming calls.

call by reference In programming, call to a subroutine that passes addresses of the parameters used in the subroutine.

call by value In programming, a call to a subroutine that passes the actual data of the parameters used in the subroutine.

call instruction An instruction that, after diverting execution to a new sequence of instructions, permits return to the program's original sequences.

called routine In programming, a program subroutine that performs a specific task and is accessed by a call or branch instruction in the program.

calligraphic graphics A method of forming an image from scan lines oriented in arbitrary directions and drawn in an arbitrary order. Though expensive electronics are required, spatial antialiasing is not. Typical of this style of graphics are the "wire-frame" models that were considered synonymous with computer graphics in the early days.

calling program In programming, a program that initiates a call to another program.

calling sequence The specified set of instructions and data necessary to call a given subroutine.

CAM (1) (Computer-Aided Manufacturing) Automated manufacturing systems and techniques, including numerical control, process control, robotics and materials requirements planning (MRP). See CAD/CAM. (2) (Content Addressable Memory) Same as associative storage.

cancel A keyboard operation that deletes the line currently being typed.

candidates Any of the alternative plans offered in the preliminary design phase of a project.

canned program Software package that provides a fixed solution to a problem. These programs prepared by computer manufacturers or software developers are provided to a user in read-to-use-form that are general enough to be used by many business and individuals. Contrast with custom software.

canned routine Program subroutine that performs a specific processing task.

Canon engine The internal mechanism of a Canon office photocopier, used in many Laser Printers.

canonical synthesis Process of designing a model of a database without redundant data items. A canonical model, or schema, is independent of the hardware and software that will process the data.

Canvas[tm] A drawing and painting program for the Apple Macintosh computer. With 24-bit color, unlimited layers, Bezier curves, precision tools, bit-mapped editing at high resolutions, and full-color separation, it combines color capabilities and powerful object- editing options with a friendly interface and ease of use.

CAP Acronym for computer-aided publishing.

capacitance The measure of the ability to store electric charge, the basic unit of measurement being a farad.

capacitor Electronic component that holds a charge. It comes in varying sizes for use in power supplies to the tiny cells in dynamic RAM chips.

capacitor storage A storage device that utilizes the capacitance properties of materials to store data.

capacity The number of items of data that a storage device is capable of containing. Frequently defined in terms of computer words, bytes, or characters.

cap height The height of a capital letter from the baseline.

caps Capital letters or upper case. All caps means that all letters are capitalized, initial caps (also called 'proper case') refers to the capitalization of the first letter of each significant word.

capstan On magnetic tape drives, a motorized cylinder that traps the tape against a free-wheeling roller and moves it at a regulated speed.

capture (of data) The recording of data on a form or its entry into a computer.

CAR (Computer-Assisted Retrieval) Systems that use the computer to keep track of components, text documents or records stored on paper or on microform. The computer is used to derive the location of a requested item, which must be manually retrieved from a shelf, bin, or microform.

carbon ribbon A ribbon used with printers to produce extremely sharp characters with excellent definition.

card See printed circuit board, magnetic stripe, punched card, HyperCard.

card cage Cabinet or metal frame that holds printed circuit cards.

card code The combinations of punched holes that represent characters in a punched card.

card column Vertical column that is used to represent a single character of data by its pattern of punched holes. The common IBM card contains 80 card columns.

card field The fixed number of consecutive punched card columns assigned to a unit of information.

card hopper A device that holds punched cards and makes them available for the feeding mechanism of card handling equipment.

card Image Representation of punched cards in which each hole in the card is represented by a bit on tape or disk.

cardinality In object-oriented programming, the number of instances that a class may have, the number of instances that participate in a using class relationship.

cardinal number A number that indicates how may items there are in a set. For example, if "word 21 has 10 letters," 21 is ordinal; 10 is cardinal. See ordinal number.

card punch (1) Early peripheral device that pudches holes into cards at 100 to 300 cards per minute. (2) Same as keypunch machine.

card reader (1) Peripheral device that reads magnetic stripes on the back of a credit card. (2) Early peripheral device that reads punched cards at 500 to 2,000 cards/minute. The code is detected by light patterns created by the holes in the card.

card row One of the horizontal lines of punching position on a punched card.

caret Up-arrow (") symbol used to represent a decimal point or the control key. For example, 'Y means CtrlY. It is the shift-6 key on the keyboard.

carpal tunnel syndrome Compression of the main nerve to the hand due to scarring or swelling of the surrounding soft tissue in the wrist (area formed by car- pal bones on top and muscle tendons below). Caused by trauma, arthritis and improper positioning of the wrist, it can result in severe damage to the hands. Once a malady of carpenters and mechanics, it is now an ailment of computer and data entry personnel. See RSI, Wrist Pro.

carriage Printer or typewriter mechanism that holds the platen and controls paper feeding and movement.

carriage return (CR) In a character printer, the operation that causes the next character to be printed at the left margin. Usually along with a line feed (LF) which means left margin of the next line. See return key.

carrier Alternating current that vibrates at a fixed frequency, used to establish a boundary, or envelope, in which a signal is transmitted. Carriers are used to transmit several signals simultaneously through a wire or cable. For example, several voice, data and! or video signals can travel over the same line as long as each one resides within its own carrier vibrating at a different frequency.

carrier based Transmission system. that generates a fixed frequency (carrier) to contain the data being transmitted.

carrier frequency Unique frequency used to "carry" data within its boundaries. It is measured in cycles per second, or Hertz. See FDM.

carry The process of bringing forward. The special condition that occurs when the sum of two digits in a single column is equal to or greater than the number base. The carry digit is the digit to be added to the next higher column.

Cartesian coordinate system The system named for French mathematician Rene Descartes (1596-1650) whereby, in a flat plane, a point can be located by its distances from two intersecting straight lines, called the axes, the distance from one axis being measured along a parallel to the other axis. The number associated with the point are called the coordinates of the point.

cartridge font A series of typefaces contained in ROM clips mounted within a plastic module called a cartridge. The cartridge is placed in a compatible laser printed to allow it to use the typefaces.

CAS (Communications Application Specification) Intel communications protocol, introduced in 1980, for a combination fax and modem board that allows personal computer users to exchange data more easily with fax machines.

cascade connection Two or more similar component devices arranged in tandem, with the output of one connected to the input of the next.

cascade control An automatic control system in which the control units are linked chain fashion, each feeding into, as well as regulating, the next stage.

cascade sort An external tape sort that sorts by merging strings from all but one tape onto the remaining tape. Subsequent passes merge fewer tapes until one tape contains all items.

CASE (Computer Aided Software Engineering or Computer Aided Systems Engineering) Software that is used in any and all phases of developing an information system, including analysis, design and programming. CASE tools provide automated methods for designing and documenting traditional structured programming techniques. The ultimate goal of CASE is to provide a language for describing the overall system that is sufficient to generate all the necessary programs.

case sensitive Distinguishing lower case from upper case. In a case sensitive language, 'a' is treated differently than 'A'.

case statement In programming, a variation of the if- then-else statement that is used when several ifs are required in a row. Used in C and in dBase programming.

cashless society A computerized system in which purchase transactions would be settled instantaneously by transferring credits from the buyer's bank account to the seller's account.

cashmemory See cache.

cassette Self-contained, removable storage module that contains a supply reel of magnetic tape and a takeup reel.

cassette recorder A device designed to use cassettes to record and store digital data and, at a later time, reload this data into the computer's internal storage. It was used with early microcomputer systems.

casting In programming, the conversion of one data type into another.

cat (conCATenate) UNIX command that displays the contents of a file.

catalog Directory of disk files or files used in an application. Also any map, list or directory of storage space used by the computer.

catena A connected series.

cathode In electronics, a device that emits electrons, which flow from the negatively charged cathode to the positively charged anode.

cathode ray tube See CRT.

CATV (Community Antenna TV) Original name for cable TV which used a single antenna at the highest location in the community.

CAU (Controlled Access lJnit) Intelligent hub from IBM for Token Ring networks. Failed nodes are identified by the hub and reported via IBM's LAN Network Manager software.

CAV (Constant Angular Velocity) Disk technique that spins the disk at a constant speed. The number of bits in each track is the same, but their 'density varies because the inner tracks have smaller circumferences than the outer tracks and are- more densely packed. Contrast with CLV.

CB simulator See teleconferencing (3).

CHASIC A compiled basic programming language. A CBASIC program is translated into object code before it is executed. Program execution time is much faster than the more popular interpreter BASIC.

CBR (Computer-Based Reference) Reference materials accessible by computer in order to help people do their jobs quicker.

CBT (Computer-Based Training) Using the computer for training and instruction. CBT programs are called courseware and provide interactive training sessions for all disciplines. It uses graphics extensively, as well as CD ROM and videodisc. CBT courseware is developed with authoring languages, such as Adroit, PILOT and Demo II, which allow for the creation of interactive sessions.

CBX (Computerized Branch eXchange) Same as PBX. CCA (1) (Common Cryptographic Architecture) IBM encryption software for MVS and DOS applications. (2) (Compatible Communications Architecture) Network Equipment Technology protocol for transmitting asynchronous data over X.25 networks.

CCD (Charge Coupled Device) Electronic memory made of a special type of MOS transistor that can store patterns of charges in a sequential fashion. CCDs are used in TV and scanning devices since they can be charged by light as well as by electricity.

CCFL (Cold Cathode Fluorescent Lamp) Same as CCFT.

CCFI (Cold Cathode Fluorescent Tube) Type of light source for a backlit screen. It weighs more and uses more power than other backlights.

CD (Compact Disc) Audio disc that contains up to 72 minutes of stereo sound. A 4.75" diameter CD is like a miniature phonograph record, except only one side is recorded. It is a direct access device; individual selections can be played Eck in any sequence. Unlike phonograph records which contain "carved sound waves", CDs are recorded in digital form as a series of microscopic pits (binary code) covered with a clear, protective plastic layer. Instead of a needle vibrating in the groove, a laser shines onto the pits and the reflections are decoded and converted into digital code by sampling the sound waves and converting each sample into a 16-bit number. It requires about 1.5 million bits of storage for each second of stereo hi-fl sound. Digital sound is so clear because the numbers are turned into sound electronically. There's no tape hiss or needle pops and clicks. In addition, the CD can handle a wider range of volume (dynamic range), providing more realism.

Other forms of CDs (CD ROM, CD ROM XA, CD-I and DVI) all stem from the audio CD. Introduced in the U.S. in 1983, sales of CDs and CD players exceeded sales of LPs and turntables in 1986.

CD audio Same as CD and DAD.

CD caddy Plastic container that holds a CD ROM disc. The caddy is inserted into the disc drive.

CD-I (Compact Disc-Interactive) Compact disc format that holds data, audio, still video and animated graphics. It provides up to 144 minutes of CD-quality stereo, up to 9.5 hours of AM-radio-quality stereo or up to 19 hours of monophonic audio. Developed by Phillips and Sony, CD-I is designed for home and business use with CD-I players connected to TVs and personal computers. CD-I includes an operating system standard as well as proprietary hardware methods for compressing the data further in order to display video images. CD-I discs require a CD-I player and will not play on a CD ROM player. See CD, CD ROM, DVI.

CD ROM (Compact Disc Read Only Memory) Compact disc format used to hold text, graphics and hi-fl stereo sound. Though basically similar to a music CD, it uses a different track format for data. So, a music CD player cannot play CD ROMs, but CD ROM players can usually play music CDs and have headphone and amplifier jacks, A CD ROM player connects to a controller card, which is plugged into one of the computer's expansion slots.

CD ROMs hold in excess of 600MB of data, which is equivalent to about 250,000 pages of text or 20,000 medium-resolution images. See CD ROM XA, CD-I, DVI.

CD ROM Extensions Software required to use a CD ROM player on a PC running DOS. It usually comes with the player and includes a driver specialized for the player and Microsoft's MSCDEX.EXE RAM resident program.

CD ROM XA (CD ROM eXtended Architecture) CD ROM enhancement introduced in 1988 by Phillips, Sony and Microsoft that lets text and pictures be narrated by allowing concurrent audio and video. It also functions as a bridge between CD ROM and CD-I, since CD ROM

XA discs can be played on a CD-I player. CD ROM XA uses a staqdard CD ROM player, but requires a CD ROM XA controller card in the computer. See CD-I, DVI.

CD+Graphics CD format that adds video. You can listen to the opera and read the text on screen.

CDA (Compound Document Architecture) Compound document format from Digital that creates hot links between documents.

CDC See Control Data.

cdev (Control Panel DEVice) Customizable settings in the Macintosh Control Panel that pertain to a particular program or device. Cdevs for the mouse, keyboard and startup disk, among others, come with the Mac. Others are provided wih software packages and utilities.

CDIP (Sidebrazed Ceramic DIP) High-quality ceramic DIP that typically uses gold-plated leads attached by brazing.

CD player A device that reads the information stored on a compact disc.

CDR A Coreldraw object file format.

CDTV (commodore Dynamic Total Vision) CD system from Commodore that combines audio, graphics and text. Introduced in 1991, it is an inter-active multimedia system for the home. The player connects to a TV and also plays music CDs, including CD+Graphics and CD+MIDI.

Ceefax Teletext service of the British Broadcasting Corporation.

CEG (Continuous Edge Graphics) VGA RAMDAC chip from Edsun Labs that adds anti-aliasing on the fly. It can also calculate intermediate shades, thus providing thousands of colors on an 8-bit board that could normally generate only 256 colors.

cell (1) Elementary unit of storage for data (bit) or power (battery). 2) In a spreadsheet, the intersection of a row and column.

cell address In a spreadsheet, the column and row coordinates of a cell.

cell animation An animation technique in which a background painting is held stationary while animated images are moved over the painting producing the illusion of movement. Animation programs that perform cell animation are available.

cell contents The label, value, formula, or function contained in a spread sheet cell.

centering The word processing and page layout program feature that places a line of text midway between the left and right margins - in the center of a horizontal line.

centering cone Short plastic or metal cone that is used to align a 5.25" floppy disk to the drive spindle. It is inserted into the diskette's centre hole when .the drive door is closed.

centralized data processing The concept by which a company has all its computing equipment located at the same site and field-office operations have no effective data processing capability. Contrast with distributed computing.

centralized network configuration The structure of a computer network whose dominating feature is a central computer that, one way or another, is involved in everything that happens in the system.

central processing unit See CPU. central processor Same as CPU.

centralized processing Processing performed in one or more computers in a single, centralized location. It implies that all terminals throughout the organization are connected to the computers in the datacenter. Contrast with distributed processing and decentralized processing.

Centronlcs Interface Standard 36-pin parallel interface for connecting printers and other devices to a computer. It defines the plug, socket and signals used and transfers data asynchronously up to 200 Kbytes/ sec.

The male connector contains a plug approximately 1.5" wide and 1/8" thick that has 18 contacts each on the top and bottom. The female socket contains one opening with matching contacts on the inside top and bottom.

This de facto standard was developed by Centronics Corp., maker of the first commercially successful dot matrix printers. The printer, was introduced in 1970, and the company was bought by Genicom Corp. in 1987. See printer cable.

CEO (Comprehensive Electronic Office) Office software from Data General introduced in 1981. It includes word processing, e-mail, spreadsheets, business graphics and desktop accessories.

CERDIP (CERamic DIP) Type of DIP that uses two ceramic layers epoxied together.

certificatIon (1) The acceptance of software by an authorized agent, usually after the software has been validated by the agent, or after its validity has been demonstrated to the agent. (2) A system of attesting that a person has achieved a certain professional status, usually by passing a standardized and rigorous examination.

CG Abbreviation for computer graphics, any graphic element created with the aid of a computer.

CGA (Color/Graphics Adapter) IBM video display standard that provides low-resolution text and graphics. It was the first graphics standard for the IBM PC and has been superseded by EGA and VGA. CGA requires a digital RGB Color Display monitor. See PC display modes.

CGI (Computer Graphics Interface) Device independent graphics language for display screens, printers and plotters that stemmed from GKS.

CGM (Computer Graphics Metafile) Standard format for interchanging graphics images. CGM stores images primarily in vector graphics, but also provides a raster format. Earlier GDM and VDM formats have been merged into the CGM standard.

chad Piece of paper that is punched out on a punched card, paper tape or on the borders of continuous forms.

chain (1) The linking of records by means of pointers in such a way that all like records are connected, the last record pointing to the first. (2) A set of operations that are to be performed sequentially.

chained files Data files where data blocks are chained together by using pointers.

chained list A list in which each item points to the next items and the order of retrieval need not have any relation to the storage order.

chain field The field in record that defines the location and storage device of other data items logically related to he original record but not physically attached.

chaining (1) The process of linking a series of records, programs or operations together. (2) The method of allowing the execution of programs larger than the main memory of a computer by loading and executing modules of the same program sequentially.

chaining search A technique used for retrieving data from a file by using address in the records that link each record to the next in the chain.

chain printer Line printer that uses character typefaces linked together in a chain as its printing mechanism. The chain spins horizontally around a set of hammers. When the desired character is in front of the selected print position, the corresponding hammer hits the paper into the ribbon and onto the character in the chain.

chamfer A bevelled edge between two intersecting lines. change agent The role of the systems analyst in overcoming resistance to changing within an organization.

change file Transaction file used to update a master file.

channel (1) High-speed metal or optical fibre pathway between the computer and the control units of the peripheral devices. Channels imply independent transmission paths in which multiple channels can transfer data concurrently with each other and with other processing. In a personal computer, the bus serves as a common, shared channel. (2) In communications, any pathway between two computers or between a terminal and a computer. It may refer to the physical medium, such as coaxial cable, or to a specific carrier frequency (subchannel) within a larger channel or wireless medium.

channel adapter A device that enables data communications between channels on different hardware devices.

channel capacity In Data Communications, an expression of the maximum number of bits per second that can be accommodated by the channel. This maximum number is determined by the bandwidth modulation scheme and certain types of noise. The channel capacity is most often measured in bauds, or bits per second.

channel program Set of instructions executed by a high- speed peripheral channel. The program instruction that initiates the I/O operation indicates where the channel program resides. The channel executes the channel program independently, allowing other operations to take place concurrently in the computer.

character Single alphabetic letter, numeric digit, or special symbol such as a decimal point or comma. A character is equivalent to a byte.

character based Same as text based.

character cell Matrix of dots used to form a single character on a display screen or printer. For example, an '8x16 character cell is made up of 16 horizontal rows each containing eight dots. The combination of dots determines the character being formed.

character checking The checking of each character by examining all characters as a group or field.

character code A code designating a unique numerical representation for a set of characters. Same as data code.

character data Alphanumeric data or text. Contrast with numeric data.

character device Peripheral device that transfers data one byte at a time at a time, such as a parallel or serial port. Contrast with block device.

character field Data field that holds alphanumeric characters. Contrast with numeric field.

character generator (1) Circuitry that converts data characters into dot patterns for a display screen. (2) Device that creates text characters that are superimposed onto video frames.

character graphics Set of special symbols that are strung together like letters of the alphabet to create graphics. For example, the following character graphics are used to print forms, charts and simple graphics. They form part of the ASCII characters. See Box drawing characters.

character mode Same as text mode.

characters per Inch The method of expressing the output from dot matrix and daisy wheel printers as determined by type size and style. Abbreviated CPI.

characters per second A unit for measuring output of low-speed serial printers. Abbreviated CPS.

character pitch Measurement of the number of characters per inch.

character printer Printer that prints one character at a time, such as a daisy wheel or dot matrix printer. See printer.

character recognition Ability of a machine to recognize printed text. See OCR, MICR.

character set: (1) Group of unique symbols and codes. For example, the ASCII character set contains 128 characters numbered 0 to 127. The English character set is 26 symbols (A-Z). (2) See symbol set.

character string Group of alphanumeric characters. Contrast with numeric data.

character terminal Display screen without graphics capability.

characteristic In logarithms and floating point, the number that indicates where the decimal point is placed.

charge coupled device See CCD.

CHARGECARD Hardware memory manager for 286 PCs from ALL Computers Inc., that turns extended memory into EMS and uses unused high memory (640-1024K) for drivers and TSRs. The 286 chip is removed and plugged into the CHARGECARD, which is plugged back into the socket.

Charles Babbage Institute An organization for the study of the information revolution from a historical perspective.

chart The visual representation of quantitative information, such as a bar graph, in which the information is made visual by heavy horizontal or vertical lines, or a circle graph or pie chart. See flowchart, structure chart.

chassis The metal frame upon which the wiring, sockets, and other parts of an electronic assembly are mounted.

chat mode Communications option that lets users type messages back and forth to each other. Each keystroke is transmitted as it is pressed.

check bits Bits used for error checking purposes. The bits hold a number which has been calculated from a segment of data that has been transmitted or stored. See parity checking, checksum, CRC.

check box Method of showing the current status of a selectable option by displaying an X or checkmark symbol in a small box next to it when selected.

check digit Digit used to ensure that account numbers are correctly entered into the computer. Using a formula, the check digit is calculated from the original account number and is added to and maintained as part of the number at all times, usually the last digit of the number.

check problem A testing problem designed to determining whether a computer or a computer program is operating correctly.

check sum See checksum. checkout See debug.

checkpoint/restart Method of recovering from a system failure. A checkpoint is a copy of the computer's memory that is periodically saved on disk along with the current register settings (last instruction executed, etc.). In the event of any failure, the last checkpoint serves as a recovery point.

When the problem has been fixed, the restart program copies the last checkpoint into memory, resets all the hardware registers and starts the computer from that point. Any transactions in memory after the last checkpoint was taken until the failure occurred will be lost.

checksum Value used to ensure data is transmitted with out error. It is created by adding the binary value of each alphanumeric character in a block of data and sending it with the data. At the receiving end, a new checksum is computed and matched against the trans-mitted checksum. A non-match indicates an error.

Just as a check digit tests the accuracy of a single number, a checksum tests a block of data. Checksums detect single bit errors and some multiple bit errors, but are not as effective as the CRC method.

chicklet keyboard Keyboard with small, square keys not suitable for touch typing.

child In database management, the data that independent on its parent. See parent-child.

child program Secondary or subprogram called for and loaded into memory by the main program. See parent program.

chip Integrated circuit. Chips are squares or rectangles that measure approximately from 1/46th to 5/8th of an inch on a side. They are about 11.30th of an inch thick, although only the top 1/1000th of an inch holds the actual circuits. Chips contain from a few dozen to several million electronic components (transistors, resistors, etc.). The terms chip, integrated circuit and microelectronic are synonymous.

The base material of a chip is usually silicon. Silicon is found in quartz rocks and is purified in a molten state. It is then chemically combinei(doped) with other materials to alter its electrical properties. The result is a silicon crystal ingot from three to five inches in diameter. Wafers, about 1/30th of an inch thick, are cut from this "crystal salami." Circuit building starts out by adhering a layer of silicon dioxide insulation on the wafer's surface. The insulation is coated with film and exposed to light through the first photomask, hardening the film and insulation below it. The unhardened areas are etched away exposing the silicon base below. By shooting a gas under heat and pressure into the exposed silicon (diffusion), a sublayer with different electrical proper-ties is created beneath the surface.

Through multiple stages of masking, etching, and diffusion, the sublayers on the chip are created. The final stage lays the top metal layer (usually aluminum), which interconnects the transistors to each other and to the outside world.

Each chip is tested on the wafer, and bad chips are marked for elimination. The chips are sliced out of the wafer, and the good ones are placed into spiderlike packages (DIPs, SIMMs, SIPs, etc.). The chip is connected to the package with tiny wires, then sealed and tested as a complete unit. Depending on the design complexity, more chips can fail than succeed this tedious process.

Chip making is extremely precise. Operations are performed in a "dean room," since air particles can mix with the microscopic mixtures being created and easily render a chip worthless.

The story of chips begins in late 1947 with the invention of the transistor by John Bardeen, Walter Brattain and William Shockley. The transistor would eventually replace all the bulky, hot, glass vacuum tubes. The original transistors were soldered individually onto a circuit board to connect to other individual transistors, resistors and diodes. Since hundreds of transistors were made on one round silicon wafer and cut apart only to be reconnected again, the idea of building them in the required pattern to begin with was obvious. In the late 1950s, Jack Kilby and Robert Noyce created the integrated circuit, a set of interconnected transistors and resistors on a single chip. Since then, the number of transistors that have been put onto a single chip has increased exponentially, from a handful in the early 1960s to millions by the late 1980s. Today, a million transistors take up no more space than the first transistor.

A byproduct of miniaturization is speed. The shorter the distance a pulse travels, the faster it gets there. The smaller the components making up the transistor, the faster the transistor switches. Switch times of transistors are measured in billionths and trillionths of a second. In fact, a Josephson junction transistor has been able to switch in 50 quadrillionths of a second. In time, instead of adding more circuits across the surface, the circuits will be built in over lapping layers. Within the next 10 to 15 years, it is conceivable that the electronics in today's multi-million-dollar supercomputer can be built within a cube one inch square!

Logic Chip is a single chip that can perform some or all of the functions of a processor. Memory Chips or Random Access Memory (RAM) chips contain from a couple of hundred thousand to several million storage cells (bits). They are the computer's working storage and require constant power to keep their bits charged. Special Purpose Chips are used in low-cost consumer items (watches, calculators, etc.) as well as higher-cost products (video games, automobile control, etc.) may be designed from scratch to obtain economical and effective performance.

chip card See smart card, memory card.

chip carrier (1) Package that a chip is mounted in. (2) chip package with connectors on all sides. See leaded chip carrier, leadless chip carrier.

chip family A group of related chips, each of which (except the first) evolved from an earlier chip in the family; for example, the Intel Corporation's family of 80 x 86 microprocessors: 80286, 80386, 80486.

chip set Group of chips designed to work together to perform a function.

Chkdsk See DOS Chkdsk.

Chooser Macintosh desk accessory that allows the user to select a printer, file server or network device, such as a network modem.

chop To discard unneeded data.

chroma Color attributes such as saturation, shade, and hue.

chromaticity The dominant wavelength and purity of a color as objectively measured; corresponds to hue and saturation of the color without regard to brightness.

chrominance Those portions of a composite video signal controlling color.

CICS (Customer Information Control System) TP monitor from IBM that provides transaction processing for IBM mainframes. It controls the interaction between applications and users and lets programmers develop screen displays without detailed knowledge of the terminals used. It also provides terminal routing, password security, transaction logging for error recovery and activity journals for performance analysis.

CIF (Common Intermediate Format) Video format that transmits 36.45 Mbits/sec at 30 frames/sec.

CIM (1) (Computer-Integrated Manufacturing) Integrating office/accounting functions with automated factory systems. Point of sale, billing, machine tool scheduling and supply ordering are part of CIM. (2) CompuServe Information Manager.

CIO (Chief Information Officer) Executive officer in charge of all information processing in an organization.

cipher A secret method of representing information to ensure computer security.

ciphertext Data that has been coded (enciphered, encrypted, encoded) for security purposes.

circuit (1) Set of electronic components that perform a particular function in an electronic system. (2) Same as communications channel.

circuit analyzer (1) Device that tests the validity of an electronic circuit. (2) In communications, same as data line monitor.

circuit board Same as printed circuit board.

circuit breaker Protective device that opens a circuit upon sensing a current overload. Unlike a fuse, it can be reset.

circuit capacity The number of channels in a circuit that can be dealt with simultaneously.

circuit card Same as printed circuit board.

circuit switching Temporary connection of two or more communications channels. Users have full use of the circuit until the connection is tenninated. Contrast with message switching, which stores messages and forwards them later, and contrast with packet switching, which break up a message into packets and routes each packet through the most expedient path at that moment.

circuitry A complex of circuits describing the interconnection within or between systems.

circular list A linked list, usually of data elements, in which the last element points to the first one.

circular shift A shifting operation whereby bits or characters shifted off one end of a register enter the register on the opposite end.

CIS CompuServe Information Service.

CISC (Complex Instruction Set Computer) Pronounced "sisk." Traditional computer architecture that uses microcode to execute very comprehensive instructions. Instructions may be variable in length and use all addressing modes, requiring complex circuitry to decode them. Contrast with RISC.

Cl/1 (Connectivity Language/i) Database language from Apple that lets a Macintosh access an SQL-based database in another computer.

cladding Plastic or glass sheath that is fused to and surrounds the core of an optical fibre. It keeps the light waves inside the core and adds strength to it. The cladding is covered with a protective outer jacket.

clamping ring The part of a 5.25" floppy disk drive that presses the disk onto the spindle. It is usually part of the centering cone.

Clarion PC application development programs from Clarion Software Corp. The main product is Professional Developer, which includes a Pascal-like programming language, DBMS and prototyping generator. Personal Developer is for non-programmers.

Claris CAD Full-featured 2-D CAD program for the Macintosh from Claris Corp. that is noted for its ease of use. It provides an easy-to-learn path into CAD, while offering most features found in CAD programs.

class In object-oriented programming, a user-defined data type that defines a collection of objects that share the same characteristics. A class member (object) is an "instance" of the class. Concrete classes are designed to be 'instantiated." Abstract classes are designed to pass on characteristics through inheritance.

Class A, B See FCC Class.

class category In object-oriented programming, a collection of classes, some of which are visible to other class categories and other of which are hidden.

class diagram In object-oriented programming, part of the notation of object-oriented design, used to show the existence of classes and their relationships in the logical design of a system. A class diagram may represent all or part of the lass structure of a system.

class library Object-oriented programming classes supplied by third parties; for example, a GUI library.

class structure In object-oriented programming, the "kind or hierarchy of a system; a graph whose vertices represent classes and whose arcs represent relationships among these classes. The class structure of a system is represented by a set of class diagrams.

class variable In object-oriented programming, a place- holder for part of the state of a class. Collectively, the class variables of a class constitute its structure. A class variable is shared by all instances of the same class.

Classic See Macintosh.

classify To categorize or place data with similar characteristics into the same category.

CLCC (Ceramic LCC) See LCC.

clean room Room in which the air is highly filtered in order to keep out dust and impurities.

clear (1) The keyboard function that remove the contents from the display screen. (2) Same as zap.

clearing Replacing the information in a register, storage location, or storage unit with zeros or blanks.

clear memory To reset all RAM and hardware registers to a zero or blank condition. Rebooting the computer may or may not clear memory, but turning the computer off and on again guarantees that memory is cleared.

click To seject an object by pressing the mouse button when the cursor is pointing to the required menu option or icon.

click art Clip art on a diskette or CD-ROM; a floppy or CD-ROM of professionally drawn pictures that are ready to copy and use in computer-produced documents.

client (1) In object-Oriented programming, an object that uses the resources of another, either by operating upon it or by referencing its state. (2) An individual or organization contracting for systems analysis.

client application (1) Application running in a network workstation. (2) See OLE.

client/server (1) Architecture in which the client is the requesting machine (PC or workstation) and the server is the supplying machine (LAN file server, mini or mainframe). The client provides the user interface and performs some or most of the application processing. The server maintains the databases and processes requests from the client to extract data from or update the database. The server also controls the application's integrity and security. (2) Request/supply relationship between programs. Applications can be designed, whether running within the same computer or in multiple computers, in which one program (the client) requests data from another program (the server). For example, in X Window, the server is software that manages the display screen, and the client is the application that asks the server to display something.

dient/server protocol Communications protocol that provides a structure for requests between a workstation (client) and a server in a network. It refers to layer 7 in the OSI model.

dip art Set of canned images used to illustrate word processing and desktop publishing documents.

clipboard Reserved memory temporarily used to hold data that has been copied from one application in order to be inserted into another.

clipping Removing portions of n image that are outside the boundaries of the edge of a window or display screen. Certain graphics programs also support clipping as a means of masking everything but a certain object so that painting tools, for example, can be applied to the object alone.

clipping path A curve or polygon that is used to mask an area in a document. Only what is inside the clipping path appears when the document is printed.

Clipper Application development system from Computer Associates. Originally a dBASE compiler, it has become a complete stand-alone development environment with many unique features. Clipper was developed by Nantucket Corp., which was acquired by CA in 1992.

clipping Cutting off outer edges or boundaries of a word, signal or image. See scissoring.

clipping level Disk's ability to maintain its magnetic properties and hold its content. A high-quality level range is 65-70%; low quality is below 55%.

clobber To write new data over the top of good data in a file or otherwise damage a file so that it becomes useless; to wipe out a file. This is usually an irreversible process.

clock Internal timing device. The different varieties of clocks are: CPU Clock which uses a quartz crystal to generate a uniform electrical frequency from which digital pulses are created and used. See clock speed.

Realtime Clock or Time-of- day clock that keeps track of hours, minutes and seconds and makes this data available to the programs. Timesharing Clock A timer set to interrupt the CPU at regular intervals in order to provide equal time to all the users of the computer. Communications Clock In a synchronous communications device, the clock maintains the uniform transmission of data between the sending and receiving terminals and computers.

clock/calendar Internal time clock and month/year calendar that is kept active with a battery. Its output allows software to remind users of appointments, to determine the age of a transaction and to activate tasks at specified times.

clock pulse Signal used to synchronize the operations of an electronic system. Clock pulses are continuous, precisely spaced changes in voltage. See clock speed.

clock rate The time rate at which pulses are emitted from a clock.

clock track The track on which a pattern of signals has been recorded to provide a time reference.

clock speed Internal heartbeat of a computer. The clock circuit uses fixed vibrations generated from a quartz crystal to deliver a steady stream of pulses to the CPU.

A faster clock will speed up internal processing provided the computer's circuits can handle the increased speed. For example, the same processor run- fling at 20MHz is twice as fast internally as one run- fling at 10MHz.

clocking The technique used to synchronize a sending and receiving data communications device, permits synchronous transmission at high speeds.

clockwise Moving from left to right.

clone Identical copy of another device. A clone functions like the original, but does not necessarily look identical. It implies 100% compatibility.

closed architecture System whose technical specifications are not made public. Contrast with open architecture.

closed file A file that cannot be accessed for reading or writing. Contrast with open file.

closed loop A loop that is completely circular. closed routine See closed subroutine.

closed shop Environment in which only data processing staff is allowed access to the computer. Contrast 'with open shop.

closed subroutine A subroutine stored at one place and linked to one or more calling routines. Contrast with open subroutine.

closed system System that does not accept interconnection to foreign terminals or devices. Contrast with open system.

cluster Some number of disk sectors (typically 2 to 16) treated as a single unit. The entire disk is divided into clusters, each one a minimum increment of storage. Thus a 30-byte file may use up 2,048 bytes on disk if the disk cluster is four 512-byte sectors. See lost cluster, cluster controller.

cluster controller Control unit that manages several peripheral devices, such as terminals or disk drives.

clustered devices A group of terminals connected to a common controller.

clustering (1) In object-oriented programming, the storing of objects contiguously on a disk for efficient accessing. (2) Grouping things with similar characteristics.

CLUT (Color Look Up Table) Hardware or software table that contains color mixing information (intensity of red, green and blue) for each color in a palette or series of palettes.

CLV (Constant Linear Velocity) Disk technique that spins a disk at different speeds. By varying the speed depending on which track is being accessed, the physical density of bits in each track can be the same, thus allowing the outer tracks to hold more data than the inner tracks. CLV mechanisms are used in CD ROM players in order to store larger amounts of data. Contrast with CAV. See ZBR.

CMI (Computer-Managed Instruction) Using computers to organize and manage an instructional program for students. It helps create test materials, tracks the results and monitors student progress.

CMIP (Common Management Information Protocol) Pronounced "C-miss." OSI protocol that defines the format for network monitoring and control information.

CMIS (Common Management Information Services) Pronounced "C-miss." OSI standard that defines the functions for network monitoring and control.

CML Abbreviation for current mode logic.

CMOS (Complementary MOS) Pronounced "C moss." Type of integrated circuit widely used for processors and memories. It uses PMOS and NMOS transistors in a complementary fashion that results in less power to operate.

CMOS RAM (1) Memory made of CMOS chips. Due to their low power requirement, they are increasingly being used for main memory in portable computers. (2) Small, battery-backed memory bank in a personal computer that is used to hold time, date and system information such as drive types.

CMY Abbreviation for cyan, magenta, yellow, a color mixing system used to print colors.

CMYK (Cyan Magenta Yellow black Color model used for printing. In theory, cyan, magenta and yellow (CMY) can print all colors, but inks are not pure and black comes out muddy. Black ink is required for quality printing. See colors, RGB.

co-resident Program or module that resides in memory along with other programs.

coaxial cable High-capacity cable used in communications and video, commonly called co-ax. It contains an insulated solid or stranded wire that is surrounded by a solid or braided metallic shield, which is wrapped in an external cover. There are several types of coaxial cable, each designed with a different width and impedance for a particular purpose (TV, baseband, broadband), Coax provides a much higher bandwidth than twisted wire pair.

COBOL (Common Business Oriented Language) High-level business programming language that has been the primary business application language on mainframes and minis. It is a compiled language and was one of the first high-level languages developed. Formally adopted in 1960, it stemmed from a language called Flowmatic in the mid 1950s. Although COBOL requires more writing than other languages, it is more readable as a result.

code (1) Set of machine symbols that represents data or instructions. See data code, machine language. (2) Any representation of one set of data for another. For example, a parts code is an abbreviated name of a product, product type or category. A discount code is a percentage. (3) To write a program. See source code, line of code. (4) To encode for security purposes. See encryption.

code conversion A process for changing the bit groupings for characters in one code into the corresponding character bit groupings for a second code.

code generator See application generator, macro recorder.

code page In DOS 3.3 and higher, a table that sets up the keyboard and display characters for various foreign languages.

code set A complete set of representation defined by a code, for example, all of the two-letter post office identifications for the 50 states constitute a code set.

codec (COder-DECoder) Electronic circuit that converts voice or video into digital code (and vice versa) using techniques such as pulse code modulation and delta modulation. A codec is an A/D and D/A converter.

coded decimal number A number consisting of suessive characters or a group of characters that usually represents a specific figure in an associated decimal number.

coder (1) Junior, or trainee, programmer who writes simple programs or writes the code for a larger program that has been designed by someone else. (2) Person who assigns special codes to data.

Code View Microsoft debugger for programs written with Microsoft C and CodeView-compatible compilers. Like other modern debuggers, it links source and object program letting the programmer step through the source code as the program is executed.

coding (1) Writing a list of instructions that will cause a computer to perform specified operations. (2) An ordered list or lists of the successive instructions that will cause a computer to perform a particular process.

coding form A form on which the instructions for programming a computer are written. Each programming language has its own coding form.

coercion In programming-language expressions, an automatic conversion from one data type to another.

COFF (Common Object File Format) UNIX System V macnine language format.

COGO (Coordinate Geometry) Programming language used for solving civil engineering problems.

coherence An assumption used in raster scan display technology that attributes the same value of an individual pixel to its adjacent pixel.

cohesion A measure of the inner strength of a program module.

cold boot Starting the computer by turning power on. Turning power off and then back on again clears memory and many internal settings. Some program failures will lock up the computer and require a cold boot to use the computer again. In other cases, only a warm boot is required. See warm boot, boot.

cold fault A computer fault that is apparent as soon as the machine is switched on.

cold start Same as cold boot.

collate To merge two or more sequenced data sets to produce a resulting data set that reflects the sequencing of the original sets.

collating sequence Sequence, or order, of the character set built into a computer. See ASCII chart.

collating sort A sort that uses a technique of continuous merging of data until one sequence is developed.

collator (1) Punched card machine that merges two decks of cards into one or more stacks. (2) Utility program that merges records from two or more files into one file.

collection The, process of gathering data from various sources and assembling it at one location.

collector Output side of a bipolar transistor. Same as drain in a MOS transistor.

collision (1) The result of keys colliding at the same address when two keyboard operators are ordered simultaneously. Programming in the computer's operating system defines which operations will be performed. (2) The problem that occurs when two records have the same disk address.

collision detection (1) In computer graphics, particularly in arcade-type games, the determination of when objects have collided. Several programming techniques may be used to detect a collision. (2) A task performed in a multiple-access network to prevent two computers from transmitting at the same time.

color The hue perceived for different wavelengths in the portion of the electromagnetic spectrum to which the human eye responds. It is possible to create almost all visible colors using two systems of primary colors. Transmitted colors use red, green, and blue (ROB), and reflected colors use cyan, magenta, and yellow (CMY). Color displays use RGB and color printers use CMY.

color bits Number of bits associated with each pixel that represent its color. For 16 colors, four bits are used; for 256 colors, eight bits.

color burst signal The signal present in composite video output that provides color information. Sometimes turning off the color burst signal improves the quality of pictures on black-and-white monitors.

color cycling In computer graphics, a technique that simulates animation by continuously changing colors rather than moving the objects. Also called color lookup table animation.

color graphics Ability to display graphic images in colors.

color keying Technique for, superimposing a video image onto another. For example, to float a car on the ocean, the car image is placed onto a blue background. The car and ocean images are scanned together. The ocean is made to appear in the resulting image wherever background (blue) exists in the car image.

color model Any method for representing color in graphics arts and desktop publishing. In the graphic arts and printing areas, colors are often specified with the Pantone system. In computer graphics, colors can be described using any of several different color systems; RGB (red, green, blue), CMY (cyan, magenta, yellow), and HSB (hue, saturation, brightness).

color monitor A computer display designed to work with a video card or adapter to produce text or graphics images in color. A color monitor has a screen coated internally with three phosphors one each for red, green, and blue. To light the phosphor and produce a sport of color, such a monitor also usually contains three electron guns -again, one for each of the three colors. See monitor.

color printer Printer that prints in color using dot matrix, electro photographic, Cycolor, electrostatic, ink jet or thermal-transfer techniques. See printer.

color resolution The number of different colors or gray- scale values, a system can produce or work with. A value is usually given in bits.

color saturation The amount of a hue contained in a color, the more saturation, the more intense the color.

color separation Separating a picture by colors in order to make negatives and plates for color printing. Full color requires four separations, cyan, magenta, yellow and black (CMYK).

ColorRIX A draw/paint program for IBM-compatible microcomputers. In addition to the usual draw/paint tools, the program includes several scalable bitmapped fonts, a printing/screen capture feature, a presentation slide show, an application/language independent screen loader, and sophisticated animation effects.

ColorStudio^{tm} An Apple Macintosh 24-bit true color imaging program for graphics art professionals. It allows for merging high-resolution color photos, video captures, pixel artwork, and PostScript type. Features include powerful paint and retouching tools, a full- density gray scale mask, and six pressure tools: airbrush, charcoal, paintbrush, pencil, waterdrop, and finger tip.

column (1) The vertical numbers of one line of an array. (2) One of the vertical lines of punching positions on a punched card. (3) The position of information in a computer word. (4) The horizontal division of an electronic spreadsheet. Together with rows, columns serve to form the spreadsheet matrix. Contrast with row.

column move Relocating a rectangular block of characters within a text document or a column in a spreadsheet.

COM (Computer Output Microfilm) Creating microfilm or microfiche from computer output. A COM machine receives print-image output from the computer and creates a film image of each page. Additional graphics (lines, logos, etc.) may be added.

COM file (1) (COMmand file) Executable DOS or OS! 2 program that takes up less than 64K and fits within one memory segment. It is an exact replica of how it looks in memory. It has the extension COM. See EXE file. (2) VMS file containing commands to be executed.

COM port Serial communications port on a PC. See COM1.

COM1 Logical name assigned to the first serial port in DOS and OS/2. COM ports are usually connected to a modem or mouse and sometimes to a printer. Contrast with LPT1.

combination logic A circuit arrangement in which the output state is determined by the present state of the input; a digital system not utilizing memory elements.

combinatorial explosion A condition that occurs in problem solving when the possibilities to be examined become too numerous for the computer. It can occur even with very large computers.

combinatorics The study of methods of counting how many objects there are of some type, or how many ways there are to do combinations and permutations.

COMDEX (Computer Dealers Exposition) Trade show intended for PC manufacturers, developers, dealers and distributors held in the spring (usually in Atlanta) and fall (Las Vegas). Sponsored by The Interface Group, Inc., Fall Comdex draws the largest attendance of all computer shows.

comma delimited Record layout that separates data fields with a comma and usually surrounds character data with quotes.

command (1) Order given to the computer by the user. See command-driven, menu-driven. (2) Programming language directive. Contrast with function.

command-driven Program that accepts commands as typed-in phrases. It is usually harder to learn, but my offer more flexibility than a menu-driven program. Once learned, command-driven programs may be faster to use, because the user can state a request suazinctly. Contrast with menu-driven.

command interpreter Same as command processor.

Command key On Apple keyboards, a key with the outline of an Apple, a propeller, or both. It is pressed along with another key to command the computer.

command language Special-purpose language that accepts a limited number of commands, such as a query language, job control language (JCL) or command processor. Contrast with programming language, which is a general purpose language.

command line In a command-driven system, the area on screen that accepts typed-in commands.

command mode Operating mode that causes the computer to accept commands for execution.

command processor System program that accepts a limited number of user commands and converts them into the machine commands required by the operating system.

command queuing Ability to store multiple commands and execute them one at a time.

command set Same as instruction set.

command shell Same as command processor.

command tree A hierarchical diagram that shows all the choices from a main command menu and the associated submenus.

COMMAND.COM Command processor for DOS and OS/2 in Real Mode. See DOS COMMAND. COM.

comment Descriptive statement in a source language program that is used for documentation and will not be implemented.

comment out To disable lines of code in a program by surrounding them with comment-start and comment- stop characters.

commercial software Software that is designed and developed for sale to the general public.

Commodore (Commodore Business Machines, Inc.) In 1977, Commodore introduced the PET computer and launched the personal computer industry along with Apple and Radio Shack In , 1982 it introduced the Commodore 64(64K RAM) and later the / Commodore 128. These were very popular home computers, and over 10 million units have been sold. The MC, which includes an icon-based operating system is still on the market. In 1985, the successful Amiga series was introduced, which features advanced capabilities at affordable prices. Also offered are a complete line of IBM-compatible PC.s. In 1991, it introduced the CDTV system, an interactive multimedia CD for home use.

common language A computer programming language sensible to two or more computers with different machine languages. BASIC, COBOL, FORTRAN, and PASCAL are common languages.

Common storage The section of memory for each user tat holds data or parameters that are accessible to all programs.

communicating word processors A network of word processor used to transmit electronic mail.

communications Electronic transfer of information from one location to another. Data communications refers to digital transmission, and telecommunications refers to all forms of transmission, including analog voice and video. Protocol is the way communications systems "talk to" each other. Protocols work in a hierarchy starting at the top with the user's program and ending at the bottom with the plugs, sockets and electrical signals. To learn about this hierarchy, see OSI.

Personal computer communications takes on several forms: (1) Data can be transferred between two distant personal computers by using modems, a telephone line and a communications program in each computer. (2) Data can be transferred between two local computers by cabling them together with a null modem cable and using a communications program in each computer. (3) Personal computers can act like a remote terminal to a minicomputer or mainframe. (4) Personal computers can be part of a local area network (LAN), in which databases and printers can be shared among users. If the LAN interconnects with a mini or mainframe networks, then personal computers can communicate with larger computers.

Minicomputer communications systems control as many as several hundred terminals connected to a single computer system. They support a variety of low-speed dial-up terminals and high-speed local terminals. With larger minicomputers, the communications processing is handled in separate machines, called communications controllers.

Mainframe systems can control several thousand remote terminals. They support a variety of low-speed dial-up terminals and high-speed local terminals. Large mainframes use separate machines, called communications controllers or front end processors, to handle the communications processing.

The most common form of long-distance communications has been the telephone system, which, up until a few years ago, transmitted only voice frequencies. This technique, known as analog communications, has been error prone, because the electronic frequencies get mixed together with unwanted signals (noise) that invade the line for a variety of reasons.

In a digital network, only binary code is transmitted, in which only two distinct frequencies or two distinct voltages are sent over the line. Instead of amplifiers, repeaters are used, which analyze the incoming signal and regenerate a brand new outgoing signal. Any noise that invades the line will get only as far as the next repeater and be filtered out.

communications channel Also called a circuit or line, it is a pathway over which data is transferred between remote devices. It may also refer to the entire physical medium, such as a public or private telephone line, optical fibre, coaxial cable or twisted wire pair, or, it may refer to the specific carrier frequency transmitted within the medium, such as in a microwave or satellite channel or in a broadband local area network.

communications controller Peripheral control unit that connects several communications lines to a computer and performs the actual transmitting and receiving as well as various message coding and decoding activities.

communications network (1) Communications channels that interconnect terminals and computers. (2) Communications channels, all hardware that supports the interconnections and all software that manages the transmission.

communications parameters Basic settings for modem transmission, which include bit rate (300, 1200,2400, etc.), parity (none, even, odd), number of data bits (7 or 8) and number of stop bits (typically 1). See N-8-1.

communications processor A computer that provides a path for data transfer between the computer system and the data communications network.

communications program Programs that allow computers to communicate through a modem. Some communications programs are capable of automatic telecommunications such as auto-answering, auto-dialling, and even dialling another computer at a preset time to establish communication and send and receive information. Some programs allow operation of an unattended remote computer - accessing disk files, operating peripherals, and so forth.

communications protocol Hardware or software standard for transmitting data between terminals and computers and between computers. The international OSI standard and IBM's SNA define seven layers of protocols for enterprise-wide networks; however, exchanging data between personal computers uses protocols in only the bottom two to four layers.

Protocols are complex as one protocol can be a subset of another. Regardless of complexity, the conceptis the same: protocols are the rules used to govern transmission of data between two devices without error.

communications satellite Radio relay station in orbit 22,300 miles above the equator. It travels at the same rate of speed as the earth (geosynchronous), so that it appears stationary. It contains many communications channels that receive analog and digital signals from earth stations. All signals are transmitted within a carrier frequency.

The signals are amplified and transmitted back to earth, covering either a small geographical area (spot beam) or almost a third of the earth's surface. In the latter case, private data is often encrypted.

communications server Computer in a network that manages access to external networks. It may manage a pool of modems and/or provide gateways to dissimilar networks.

communications software See Communications program.

compact disc See CD.

COMPACT II High-level numerical control programming language used to generate instructions for numerical control (machine tool) devices.

compact keyboard A keyboard with reduced-size keys or reduced spacing between keys. Essentially for use in laptops and notebook PCs.

compaction The packing of data structures to make room in storage.

compandor (COMpressor/exPANDOR) Device that improves the signal for AM radio transmission. On outgoing transmission, it raises the amplitude of weak signals and lowers the amplitude of strong signals. On incoming transmission, it restores the signal to its original form.

Compaq (Compaq Computer Corp.) PC manufacturer founded in 1982 by Rod Canion, Bill Murto and Jim Harris. The PC-compatible COMPAQ Portable which was a major product in 1983 owed its success to its rugged construction, ability to run all PC software and its semi-portability (it weighed 30 pounds!). In 1984, it introduced its DESKPRO desktop computers and achieved a computer-industry sales record in its second year. In 1986, it was the first to offer a 386-based machine. Compaq is an industry leader known for its rugged and reliable computers.

comparator A device for checking the accuracy of transcribed data by comparing it with a second transcription, nothing any variation between the two.

compare Fundamental computer capability. By comparing one set of data with another, the computer can locate, analyze, select, reorder and make decisions. After comparing, the computer can indicate whether the data were equal or which set was greater or less than the other. See computer.

comparative sort A sort by comparison of two or more keys.

comparator A device for checking the accuracy of transcribed data by comparing it with a second transcription, nothing any variation between the two.

compart Computer art.

compatibility (1) A property of some computers that allows programs written for one computer to run on another (compatible) computer, even though it is a different model. (2) The ability of different devices, such as a computer and a printer, to work together. (3) The ability of specific software to work with a specific brand and model of computer. All software is not "compatible" with all computers. See standards & compatibility.

compatibility mode Feature of a computer or operating system that allows it to run programs written for a different system. Programs often run slower in compatibility mode.

compatible (1) A term describing the degree of interworking possible between two devices or systems. If an element in a system is fully compatible with the functional and physical characteristics of that system, it can be incorporated into the system without modification. (2) A personal computer that can run software designed for the IBM PC and/or IBM P8/ 2 computers.

compatible software Programs that can be run on different computers without modification.

compilation One of two principal means of translating programs written in high-level languages into machine-language instructions that can be directly executed by the processor. Entails translating a complete program before any execution, Contrast with interpretation, in which each instruction is translated when it is to be executed. See compiler.

compile To prepare a machine-language program or a program expressed in symbolic coding from a program written in a high- level programming language, such as cobol or pascal.

compile time Time it takes to translate a program from source language into machine language. Link editing time may also be included in compile time.

compile-and-go An operating technique by which the loading and execution phases of a program compilation are performed in one continuous run. Especially useful when a program must be compiled for a onetime application.

compiler (1) Software that translates a high-level programming language (COBOL, C, etc.) into machine language. A compiler usually generates assembly language first and then translates the assembly language into machine language. (2) Software that converts a higher-level language or set of commands and text into a lower-level representation that can be executed. For example, a help compiler converts a text file embedded with user directives into a coded file that has been linked into the operating environment. A dictionary compiler converts terms and definitions into a dictionary lookup system.

compiler compiler Same as metacompiler.

compiler language High-level programming language that is translated into machine language before the program is executed. See compiler.

complement Number derived by subtracting a number from a base number. For example, the tens complement of 8 is 2. In set theory, complement refers to all the objects in one set that are not in another set.

complementary MOS (CMOS) A method of making metallic oxide semiconductor (MOS) chips that uses almost no power and works and works faster than MOS. Not very good for LSI, but used in electronic watches and clocks where power has to come from a battery.

completeness check A procedure that establishes that none of the fields is missing and that the entire record has been checked.

component One element of a larger system. A hardware component can be a device as small as a transistor or as large as a disk drive as long as it is part of a larger, system. Software components are routines or modules within a larger system.

composite symbol A symbol consisting of more than one character, such as the composite symbol *, which stands for "not equal to" in some software systems.

composite video Video-only (no audio) portion of the standard NTSC TV signal in which the red, green and blue signals and the horizontal and vertical sync signals are mixed together. It is not as crisp as RGB (red, green and blue transmitted separately). Earlier personal computers had composite video output for TV connections.

composition The selection of type sizes and styles and the positioning of type on a page.

compound document Text file that contains both text and graphics. Eventually compound documents will hold voic and video.

compound statement A single instruction that contains two or more instructions that could otherwise be used separately.

compress (1) To compact data to save space. See data compression. (2) UNIX utility for compressing data. A .Z suffix is added to the file name. The utility "uncompress" decompresses files.

compression See data compression.

compression ratio Measurement of compressed data. For example, a file compressed into 1/4th of its original size can be expressed as 4:1, 25%, 75% or 2 bits per byte.

compressor (1) Device that diminishes the range between the strongest and weakest transmission signals. See compandor. (2) Routine or program that compresses data. See data compression.

Compsurf Netware utility that performs a high-level hard disk format. NetWare servers require their own proprietary format.

CompuServe Online information service that provides conferencing, news, sports, weather, e-mail and access to a large number and variety of databases. The CompuServe Information Manager (CIM) is software for the user's personal computer that makes it easier to navigate through the system.

computability The property by which computational problems are classified.

computation The result of computing.

compute To perform mathematical operations or general computer processing. See computer.

compute bound Same as process bound.

computer General-purpose machine that processes data according to a set of instructions that are stored internally either temporarily or permanently. The computer and all the equipment attached to it are called hardware. The instructions that tell it what to do are called software. A set of instructions that perform a particular task is called a program, or software program.

The computer can selectively retrieve data into its main memory (RAM) from any peripheral device (terminal, disk, keyboard, etc.) connected to it. Instructions are copied into memory from a disk, tape or other source before any data can be processed. The processor is directed to go to the first instruction in the program and begin. It copies the instruction from memory into its control unit circuit and matches it against its built-in set of instructions. If the instruction is valid, the processor carries it out. If it is not, the computer comes to an abnormal end (abend). After processing the data internally, the computer can send a copy of the results from its memory out to any peripheral device (screen, printer, disk storage, etc.) The more memory it has, the more programs and data a computer can work with at the same time. Once the data has been stored in the computer's memory, the computer can process it by calculating, comparing and copying it. By calculating, comparing and copying, the computer accomplishes all forms of data processing.

First-generation computers, starting with the UNIVAC I in 1951, used vacuum tubes as their primary switching component. Memories were made of thin tubes of liquid mercury and magnetic drums.

Second-generation systems in the late 1950s replaced vacuum tubes with transistors and used magnetic cores for memories (IBM 1401, Honeywell 800, etc.). Size was reduced and reliability was significantly improved.

Third-generation computers, beginning in the mid 1960s, used the first integrated circuits (IBM360, CDC 6400, etc.) and the first operating systems and DBMSs. Online systems were widely developed, although most processing was still batch oriented using punched cards and magnetic tapes.

Starting in the mid 1970s, the fourth generation brought us computers made entirely of chips. It spawned the microprocessor and the personal computer. It introduced distributed processing and office automation. Query languages, report writers and spreadsheets brought the average person in contact with computers for the first time.

The fifth generation ought to become more visible by the mid 1990s with voice recognition, natural and foreign language translation, fibre optics, optical disks and technologies still in the research labs. By the 21st century, a computer should be able to converse somewhat intelligently with us.

Computers can be as small as a chip or as large as a truck. The difference is in the amount of work they can perform within the same time frame. Its power is based on many factors, including its word size and the speed of its CPU, memory and peripherals.

computer accessories The equipment that can be attached to a computer, such as mouse, disk drive, visual display device, keyboard, or printer. Also called peripherals.

computer anxiety The fear of computers.

computer architecture Design of a computer system. It sets the standard for all devices that connect to it and all the software that runs on it. It is based on the type of programs that will run (business, scientific, etc.) and the number of them that must be run concurrently. It specifies how much memory is needed and managed.

computer art A broad term that can refer either to art created on a computer or to art generated by the computer, the difference being whether the artist is human or electronic. When created by human beings, computer art is done with painting and drawing programs that offer a range of drawing tools, brushes, pencils, patterns, shapes, and colors.

computer awareness Generally, an understanding of what a computer is, how it works, and the role and impact of computers in society.

computer camp A camp, usually in session during the summer weeks, where campers learn to use microcomputers in addition to participating in more traditional activities.

computer centre Same as datacenter.

computer chess A computer program that plays the game of chess. Since 1970, the ACM North American Computer Chess Championships have served both as a catalyst for progress and as a historical record of this most exciting area of artificial intelligence research. During these 20-plus years, programs, have improved from the level of rank club players to among the best in the world. The names of some of the popular chess programs are CHESS, RIBBIT, BELLE, CRAY BLITZ, HITECH, and DEEP THOUGHT.

computer conferencing A method of sending, receiving and storing typed messages within a network of users.

computer crime The unauthorized use of computer systems, including software or data, for unlawful purposes.

computer designer Person who designs the electronic structure of a computer.

computer games Any interactive software or firmware in which the input data consists of the human player's physical actions and the output is an interactive graphics display.

computer graphics See graphics.

computer language Programming language, machine language or the language of the computer industry.

computer literacy Understanding computers and related systems. It includes a working vocabulary of computer and information system components, the fundamental principles of computer processing and a perspective for how non-technical people interact with technical people. It does not deal with how the computer works (digital circuits), but does imply knowledge of how the computer does its work (input, process, output). It requires a conceptual understanding of systems analysis & design, application programming, systems programming and datacenter operations.

computer on a chip Single chip that contains the processor, RAM, ROM, clock and I/O control unit. It is used for myriads of applications from automobiles to toys.

computer operations That part of a computer installation responsible for the day-to-day collection, production, distribution, and maintenance of data.

computer operator A person skilled in the operation of the computer and associated peripheral devices. This person performs other operational functions that are required in a computer centre, such as loading a disk drive, removing printouts from the line printers rack, and sometimes bursting and decollating.

computer power Effective performance of a computer. It can be expressed in MIPS (millions of instructions per second), clock speed (10Mhz, 16Mhz) and in word or bus size, (16-bit, 32-bit). However, as with automobile horsepower, valves and cylinders, such specifications are only guidelines. The real power of a computer system is net throughput, which is how long it takes to get the job done. A software package is "powerful" if it has a large number of features.

computer program A formal expression of the sequence of actions required for a data processing task; the programmer's specification of the task(s) to the computer in a formal notation that can be processed by the computer. Consists of a series of statements and instructions that cause a computer to perform a particular operation or task.

computer programmer The person whose job is to design, write, and test programs that cause a computer to do a specific job.

computer readable Same as machine readable.

computer science Field of computer hardware and software. It includes systems analysis & design, application and system software design and programming and datacenter operations. The emphasis is on learning a programming language or making a personal computer work with little or no study of the data and information required in a typical business.

computer security The preservation of computing resource against abuse or unauthorized use, especially the protection of data from accidental or deliberate damage, disclosure, or modification.

Computer Select CD ROM service from Computer Library that provides full-text articles and abstracts from over 140 computer-related periodicals.

computer services Data processing (timesharing, batch processing), software development and consulting services.

computer simulation The representation of a real or hypothetical system, constructed from a computer program.

computer system Complete computer made up of the CPU, memory and related electronics (main cabinet), all the peripheral devices connected to it and its operating system. Computer systems fall into ranges called microcomputers (personal computers), minicomputers and mainframes, roughly small, medium and large.

computer users group A group whose members share the knowledge they have gained and the programs they ave developed on a computer or class of computers of a certain manufacturer. Most groups hold meetings and distribute newsletters to exchange information, trade equipment, and share computer programs.

computer utility A service that provides computational ability, usually in the form of a time-shared computer system. Programs, as well as data, may be made available to the user. The user may also have her or his own programs immediately available in the central processing unit, have them on call at the computer utility, or load them by transmitting them to the computer prior to use. Certain data and programs are shared by all users of the service; other data and programs, because of their proprietary nature, have restricted access.

computer virus A program that attaches itself to other programs or data. A virus's typical purpose is to disrupt the processing of information by infecting the system. When an infected program is executed, the virus reproduces and spreads by searching for other software that is not infected, and then attaching itself to previously "clean" software.

Comspec See DOS Comspec.

CON (CONsole) DOS name for the keyboard and screen. See DOS device names, DOS Copy con.

concatenate To link structures together. Concatenating files appends one file to another. In speech synthesis, units of speech called phonemes (k, sh, ch, etc.) are concatenated to produce meaningful sounds.

concentrator Device that joins several communications channels together. It is similar to a multiplexor, excapt that it does not spread the signals back out again on the other end. The receiving computer performs that function.

conceptual view See view.

concordance An alphabetical list of words and phrases appearing in a document, with an indication of where those words and phrases appear.

concurrency In object-oriented programming, the property that distinguishes an active object from one that is not active, concurrency is one of the fundamental elements of the object model.

concurrency control In a DBMS, managing simultaneous access to a database. It prevents two users from editing the same record at the same time and is also concerned with serializing transactions for backup and recovery.

concurrent Pertaining to the occurrence of two or more events for activities within the same specified interval of time.

Concurrent DOS DOS-compatible, multiuser, multitasking operating system from Digital Research. It allows serial terminals to connect to Intel 8086 and higher machines. See Multiuser DOS.

concurrent language A language that supports the simultaneous execution of multiple objects, usually on parallel architecture hardware.

concurrent object In object-oriented programming, an active object whose semantics are guaranteed in the presence of multiple threads of control.

concurrent operation See multitasking, multiprocessing, parallel processing.

concurrent processing See multiprocessing.

concurrent program execution Two or more programs being executed at the same time.

condensed type Type narrowed in width so that more characters will fit a linear inch.

condition (1) A given set of circumstances. (2) A définite state of being.

conditional branch In programming, an instruction that directs the computer to another part of the program based on the results of a compare. In the following (simulated) assembly language example, the second line is the conditional branch.

conditional paging A word processing feature that causes printing to begin on the next page if a specified block of text will not fit completely within the remaining space on a page.

conditional replace A word processing function that ask the user whether to replace copy each time the program finds a particular item.

conditional statement In programming, a language statement, such as IF THEN ELSE or CASE, which tests a condition and branches to a subroutine based on the results of that test.

conditional transfer An instruction that may cause a departure from the sequence of instructions being followed, depending upon the result of an operation, the contents of a register, or the settings of an indicator. Contrast with unconditional transfer.

condition code A limited group of program conditions - such a carry, borrow, and overflow-pertinent to the execution of instructions.

condition entry One of the four sections of a decision table. Answer all questions in the condition stub.

conditioning Extra cost options in a private telephone line that improve performance by reducing distortion and amplifying weak signals.

condition stub One of the four sections of a decision table. Describes all factors (options) to be considered in determining a course of action.

conductor Material that can carry electrical current. Contrast with insulator.

conference tree A type of bulletin board structured around topics and user comments, with each main branch being a broad topic that the user can then elaborate on as the branch lengthens.

confidentiality The quality of protection against unauthorized access to private or secret information.

CONFIG.SYS DOS and OS/2 configuration file. It resides in the root directory and is used to load drivers and change settings at startup. See DOS CONFIG.SYS.

configuration Makeup of a system, such as a computer system or communications network. To configure a system is to choose from a variety of options in order to create a customized system.

configuration file File that contains information about a specific user, program; computer or file. See Config.sys.

configuration management System for gathering current hardware configuration information from all nodes in a LAN. See version control.

configure To assemble a selection of hardware or software into a system and to adjust each of the parts so that they all work together.

connect time Amount of time a user at a terminal is logged on to a computer system. See service bureau.

connecting cable The cable used to transfer electrical impulses between two pieces for equipment.

Connection Machine Family of parallel processing computers from Thinking Machines Corp., containing from 4,096 to 65,536 processors. They can be set up as hypercubes or other topologies, and are used in applications such as signal processing, simulation and database retrieval, and require a VAX or other computer as a front end.

connection-oriented In communications, requiring a direct connection or established session between two nodes for transmission. Contrast with connectionles.

connectionless In communications, the inclusion of source and destination addresses within each packet so that a direct connection or established session between nodes is not required. Contrast with connection-oriented.

connectivity Communications between computers.

connector (1) Any cable or wire that links two devices together. (2) In database management, a link or pointer between two data structures. (3) In flow- charting, a symbol that is used to break a sequence and resume the sequence elsewhere. It is often a small circle with a number or other identification written in it.

connector symbol A flowcharting symbol used to represent a junction in a line of flow. A small circle, possibly containing some identifier, connects broken paths in the line of flow on the same page. A pentagonal shape connects the flow on different ages of the same flowchart.

consecutive Pertaining to the occurrence of two sequential events without the intervention of any other such event.

consistency check A check to ensure that specific input data fall within a predetermined set of criteria; a control method wherein like data items are checked for consistency of value and from.

console (1) Main operator's terminal on a large computer. (2) Any display terminal.

console operator Same as computer operator.

consortium A joint venture to support a complete computer facility to be used in an emergency.

constant In programming, any data with fixed values within the program. Minimum and maximum amounts, dates, prices, headlines and error messages are examples of constants.

constant ratio code Code that always contains the same ratio of Os to is.

constraint Any condition that limits the solutions to a problem.

constructor In object-oriented programming, an operation that creates an object and/or initializes its state.

consultant Independent specialist. Consultants can act as advisors, or they can perform detailed systems analysis & design functions. They can help users formulate information requirements and produce a generalized or detailed set of specifications from which hardware or software vendors can respond. Consultants are often used as project advisors throughout the entire system development cycle.

contact Metal strip in a switch or socket that touches a corresponding metal strip in order to make a connection that allows current to pass. Contacts may be made of precious metals to avoid corrosion.

container cl In object-Oriented programming, a class whose instances are collections of other objects.

contention Condition that arises when two devices attempt to use a single resource at the same time. See CSMA/CD.

contention resolution Process of resolving which device gains access to a resource when both are in contention.

contents directory A series of queues that indicate the routines in a given region of internal storage.

context sensitive help Help screens that provide specific information about the condition or mode the program is in at the time help is sought.

context switching (1) In a multitasking environment, to turn control over to another program under direction of the operating system. A program's context is its current state. (2) To stop working in an application and go work in another under direction of the user.

contextual search To search for records or documents based upon the text contained in them as opposed to searching on key field or by file name.

contiguous Adjacent or touching. Contrast with fragmentation.

contiguous data structure See sequential data structure.

contiguous graphics iagrams with certain characters that touch each other.

contingency plan plan for recovery of a computer information system following emergencies or disasters.

continuity check Test of a line, channel or circuit to determine if the pathway exists from beginning to end and can transmit signals.

continuous carrier In communications, a carrier frequency that is transmitted even when data is not being sent over the line.

continuous forms Paper forms that are manufactured as a series of sheets joined together with perforated edges. The forms are moved by sprockets that interlock with the holes on the left and right sides of the sheets. After printing, forms are separated manually or by a bursting machine.

continuous processing The input of transactions into a system in the order they occur and as soon after they occur as possible.

continuous tone Any photograph or- artwork that is not yet screened for printing.

continuous-tone image A color or black-and-white image formed of combinations of separate areas made up of different color tones or gray tones.

contouring (1) In computer graphics, the creation of the outline of a body, mass, or figure. For example, in a CAD model, the representation of the surface of an object its bumps and crannies. (2) In image processing, the loss of detail that occurs in a shaded image when too few gradations of gray are used to reproduce a graphic such as a photograph.

contrast Difference between the lightest and darkest areas on a display screen. Contrast with brightness.

contrast enhancement The improvement of light-to- dark distinctions. A real digitizing process typically involves some kind of nonlinear detector that destroys the light-to-dark relationships of the object scanned. Correct contrast can be reintroduced if the characteristics of the detector are known. Contrast can even be heightened if desired.

control The function of performing required operations when certain specific conditions occur or when interpreting and acting ,upon instructions. See control section, control unit.

control ball Same as track bail.

control block Segment of disk or memory that contains a group of codes used for identification and control purposes.

control break (1) Change of category used to trigger a subtotal. (2) See Ctrl-Break.

control bus In a computer, the path linking the CPU'S control register to memory.

control character See control code.

control circuits The electrical circuits within a computer that interpret the program instructions and cause the appropriate operations to be performed.

control clerk The person who has responsibility for performing duties associated with the control over data processing operations.

control code One or more characters used to control a device, such as a display screen or printer. Control codes often begin with an escape character (ASCII 27); however, this is only one example. There is an endless number of codes used to control electronic devices. The first 32 characters of the ASCII character set are used for controlling communications devices and printers (See ASCII chart).

control field Same as key field.

control key Abbreviated "ctrl" or "ctl," Key that is pressed with a letter or digit key to command the computer; for example, holding down control and pressing U, turns on underline mode in many word processors. The caret (shift-6) symbol also represents the control key: "Y means control-Y.

control logic The order in which processing functions will be carried out by a computer.

Control Panel Routine that changes the computer's environment settings, such as keyboard and mouse sensitivity, sounds, colors and communications and printer access. It is a desk accessory in the Macintosh and a utility program in Windows.

control program Software that controls the operation of and has highest priority in a computer. Operating systems, network operating systems and network control programs are examples. Contrast with application program.

controls The order in which processing functions will be carried out by a computer.

control section That part of the central processing unit responsible for directing the operation of the computer in accordance with the instructions in the program.

control sequence The normal order of selection of instructions by a computer wherein it follows one instruction order at a time.

control signal A computer-generated signal-for automatic control of machines and processes.

control statement: An operation that terminates the sequential execution of instructions by transferring control to a statement elsewhere in the program.

control station The network station that supervises control procedures such as addressing, poling, selecting and recovery. Also responsible for establishing order on the line in the event of contention or any other abnormal situation.

control structures The facilities of a programming language that specify a departure from the normal Se-quential execution of statements. control total Same as hash total.

control unit (1) Within the processor, the circuitry That locates, analyzes and executes each instruction in the program. (2) Within the computer, a control unit, or controller, is hardware that controls peripheral activities such as a disk or display screen. Upon signals from the CPU, it performs the physical data transfers between memory and the peripheral device.

control variable In programming, a variable that keeps track of the number of iterations of a process. Its value is incremented or decremented with each iteration, and it is compared to a constant or other variable to test the end of the process or loop.

control words A series of reserved character sequences that ave a special meaning to the program that reads them.

controlled variable A variable that takes on a specific set of values in an iterative structure in a programming language.

controller See control unit (2).

convention Standard and accepted procedures in computer program development and the abbreviations, symbols, and their meanings as developed for particular programs and systems any programming style rule providing consistency among different programs.

conventional memory In a PC, the first megabyte of memory. The term may also refer only to the first 640K The top 384K of the first megabyte is called "high DOS memory" or "upper memory area." See UMA, extended memory.

conventional programming Using a procedural language.

convergence Intersection of red, green and blue electron beams on one CRT pixel. Poor convergence decreases resolution and muddles white pixels.

conversational Interactive dialogue between the user and the computer.

conversational interaction Interaction with a computer that takes the form of a dialogue between the user and the machine.

conversational language A programming language that uses a near - English character set that facilitates communication between the user and the computer. BASIC is a conversational language.

conversational mode A mode of operation that implies a dialogue between a computer and its user in which the computer program examines the input supplied by the user and formulates questions or comments that are directed back to the user.

conversational system See interactive system.

conversion (1) data conversion - Changing data from one file or database format to another. (2) media conversion - Changing storage media such as from tape to disk. (3) program conversion - Changing the programming source language from one dialect to another, or changing application programs to link to a new operating system or DBMS. (4) computer system conversion - Changing the computer model and peripheral devices. (5) information system conversion - Requires data conversion and either program conversion or the installation of newly purchased or created application programs.

conversion table A table comparing numerals in two different numeral systems.

convert (1) To change data from radix to radix. (2) To move data from one type of storage to another, such as from cd-rom to floppy disk.

converter (1) Device that changes one set of codes, modes, sequences or frequencies to a different set. See A/D converter. (2) Device that changes current from 60Hz to 50Hz, and vice versa.

cookbook A step-by-step book or manual that describes a program, a system, or some other topic.

cooling fan A small fan that keeps the circuit boards and ICs cool.

cooperative processing Sharing a job among two or more computers such as a mainframe and a personal computer. It implies splitting the workload for the most efficiency.

coordinate (1) An ordered set of absolute or relative that values that specify a location in a Cartesian a> ordinate system. (2) In an electronic spreadsheet, the intersection of two numbers and/or letters that uniquely identify the column and row of a cell. (3) Any two number used to position the cursor, or pointer, on the screen.

coordinate indexing (1) A system of indexing individual documents by descriptors of equal rank so that a library can be searched for a combination of one or more descriptors. (2) An indexing technique whereby the interrelationship of terms is shown by coupling individual words.

coordinate paper The continuous-feed graph paper used for graphs or diagrams produced on a digital plotter.

coprocessor Secondary processor used to speed up operations by handling some of the workload of the main CPU. See math coprocessor.

copy To make a duplicate of the original. In digital electronics, all copies are identical. See DOS Copy.

copy buster Program that bypasses the copy protection scheme in a software program and allows normal, unprotected copies to be made.

copyflt To get text to fit within the available area.

copy holder A device used to hold papers so the user can easily read them when typing on a keyboard. Its purpose is to reduce back, shoulder, neck, and eye strain.

copy program (1) A program designed to duplicate one or more files to another disk. (2) A program that circumvents the copy-protection device on a computer program so that the software can be copied to another disk.

copy protection Resistance to unauthorized copying of software.

In the early days of floppy-based personal computers, many copy protection methods were used. However, with each scheme introduced, a copy buster program was developed to get around it. When hard disks became the norm, copy protection was abolished. In order to manage a hard disk, files must be easily copied. This is a constant dilemma for software vendors. Every user has the manufacturing facilities to produce a perfect copy of the original!

copyright The recognized ownership of creative work; protection against unauthorized use of the work.

copyrighted software Software that costs money and must not be copied without permission from the software developer.

copyright notice A notification of copyright that is part ala program and is often printed on the display screen at the start of the program. It reminds the user that the program has a copyright, and than making copies for any purpose other than for backup is illegal.

Corel Draw^{tm} Popular windows-based illustration program for 286 and higher PCs from Corel Systems Corp. Introduced in early 1989, it includes over 100 fonts and is known for its sped and ease of use. It generates its own CDR vector graphics files, but can import other graphics formats. Has an advanced autotracing feature that quickly and easily builds a vector-based image from an entire bit-mapped black/ white/gray scale, or color clip art, paint program, or scanned image file.

core storage Non-volatile memory that holds magnetic charges in ferrite cores about 1/16th" diameter. The direction of the flux determines the 0 or 1. Developed in the late 1940s by Jay W. Forrester and Dr. An Wang, it was used extensively in the 1950s and 1960s. Since it holds its content without power, it is still used in specialized applications in the military and in space vehicles.

Core System First proposed standard for computer graphics, developed by the Graphics Standards Planning Committee of SIGGRAPH and used in the late 1970s and early 1980s. Its objectives were portability of programs between computers and the separation of modelling graphics from viewing graphics. Almost all features of the Core System were incorporated into the ANSI-endorsed GKS standard.

corrective maintenance The activity of detecting, isolating, and correcting failures after they occur.

corrupted file Data or program file that has been altered in some manner causing the bits to be rearranged, thus rendering it unreadable.

corruption Altering of data or programs due to hardware or software failure.

cost analysis A technique used to determine the overall costs of a given system and to compare them to cost factors estimated for a new design.

cost/benefits analysis Study that projects the costs and benefits of a new information system. Costs include people and machine resources for development as well as running the system. Tangible benefits are derived by estimating the cost savings of both human and machine resources to run the new system versus the old one. Intangible benefits, such as improved customer service and employee relations, may ultimately provide the largest payback, but are harder to quantify.

cost-effectiveness The effectiveness of a system or an operation in terms of the relationship of the benefits received to the resources expended to attain them. A system in which the received benefits exceed the associated costs is considered to be cost-effective.

costing A method of assigning costs to a project, job, or function. cottage key people: People who work at home and transmit work to the company by telecommunications, diskettes, or other means.

count The successive increase or decrease of a cumulative total of the number of times an event occurs.

counter (1) In programming, a variable that is used tokeep track of anything that must be counted. The programming language determines the number of counters (variables) that are available to a programmer. (2) In electronics, a circuit that counts pulses and generates an output at a specified time.

counting loop A program loop used to perform some action a fixed number of times.

coupling The interaction between systems or between properties of a system.

Courier Monospaced typeface originating from the typewriter.

courseware Educational software. See CBT

covert channel Transfer of information that violates a computer's built-in security systems. A covert storage channel refers to depositing information in a memory or storage location that can be accessed by different security clearances. A covert timing channel is the manipulation of a system resource in such a way that it can be detected by another process.

CP/M (Control Program for Microprocessors) Single user operating system for the 8080 and Z80 microprocessors from Digital Research. Created by Gary Kildall, CP/M had its heyday in the early 1980s. CP/M was an unsophisticated program that didn't instill confidence in users, yet it was a major contributor to the personal computer revolution. Although IBM asked Kildall to provide the operating system for its new personal computer, he would not agree to certain demands. IBM then went to Microsoft, which purchased an operating system from another company and turned it into DOS. Ironically, DOS was modeled after CPIM.

CPF (Control Program Facility) IBM System!38 operating system that includes an integrated relational DBMS.

CPGA (Ceramic PGA) See PGA.

cpi (1) (Characters Per Inch) Measures the density of characters per inch on tape or paper. A printer's CPI button switches character pitch. (2) (Counts Per Inch) Measures the resolution of a mouse/trackball as flywheel notches per inch (horizontal and vertical fly-wheels rotate as the ball is moved). Notches are converted to cursor movement.

cps (Characters Per Second) Measures the speed of a serial printer or the speed of a data transfer between hardware devices or over a communications channel. CPS is equivalent to bytes per second.

CPU (Central Processing Unit) Computing part of the computer. Also called the processor, it is made up of the control unit and ALU. A personal computer CPU is contained on a single microprocessor. A minicomputer CPU is contained on one or several printed circuit boards. A mainframe CPU is contained on many printed circuit boards. The CPU, clock and main memory make up a computer. A complete computer system requires the addition of control units, input, output and storage devices and an operating system. The terms CPU and processor imply the use of main memory as in the sentence "data is sent to the CPU and then processed," since the data must be stored in memory in order to be processed.

CPU bound Same as process bound.

CPU time Amount of time it takes for the CPU to execute a set of instructions and explicitly excludes the waiting time for input and output to occur. It is always less than the total duration of time for a data processing job to be completed from start to finish.

CR (Carriage Return) Return (Enter) key on a keyboard or the actual code that is generated when the key is pressed (decimal 13, hex OD).

CR/LF (Carriage Return/Line Feed) End of line characters used in standard PC text files (ASCII 13 10). In the Mac, only the CR is used; in UNIX, the LF.

cracker A programmer who gains access to a system without authorization. See Hacker.

CRAM (Card Random Access Memory) Mass storage device developed by NCR in the 1960s that used magnetic cards. In order to read or write data, a card was pulled out of the cartridge and wrapped around a rotating drum.

crash Unplanned program termination due to a hardware or software failure. See abend, head crash.

Cray (Cray Research, Inc., Eagan, MN) Supercomputer manufacturer founded in 1972 by Seymour Cray, a leading designer of large-scale computers at Control Data. In 1976, it shipped its first computer, the CRAY- 1, a 75MHz, 64-bit machine with a peak speed of 160 megaflops, making it the world's fastest vector processor. In 1982, Cray introduced the X-MP family with models calculating near 500 mflops with as much as 512MB memory and 4GB disk cache. In 1985, the four-processor.CRAY-2 system had liquid- cooled circuits, 2GB memory and was 12 times faster than the CRAY-i. In 1988, the $20 million, eight- processor, 165MHz Y-MP was introduced which calculates well into the gigaflop range. In May 1989, Cray left Cray Research and founded Cray Computer Corp.

CRC (Cyclical Redundancy Checking) Error checking technique used to ensure the accuracy of transmitting digital code over a communications channel. The transmitted messages are divided into predetermined lengths which, used as dividends, are divided by a fixed divisor. The remainder of the calculation is appended onto and sent with the message. At the receiving end, the computer recalculates the remainder. If it does not match the transmitted remainder, an error is detected.

create To make a new file on a disk as opposed to modifying an existing file.

creative designer In desktop publishing, the individual who lays out and designs a page.

Cricket Presents Desktop presentation program for the Macintosh from Computer Associates. It provides the ability to create output for overheads, handouts, speaker notes and film recorders.

Cricket Stylist A popular object-oriented drawing program for the Apple Macintosh computer. Using Cricket Stylist one can create drawings using the familiar line, rectangle, and oval tools.

crippleware Demonstration software with built-in limitations; for example, a database package that lets only 50 records be entered.

criteria range Conditions for selecting records.

critical path That path through a network that defines the shortest possible time in which the entire project can be completed.

critical path method (CPM) A management technique for control of large-scale, long-term projects involving the analysis and determination of each critical step necessary for project completion.

CROM Acronym for control rom, an integral part of most CPU chips Storage for the micro instructions that the CPU assembles into a sequence to form the complex macro instructions, such as Multiply or Branch-On-Negative Accumulator, available to the computer user.

crop marks Printed lines on paper used to cut the form into its intended size.

cross assembler Assembler that generates machine language for a foreign computer. It is used to develop programs for computers on a chip or microprocessors used in specialized applications, which are either too small or are incapable of handling the development software.

cross-check To check the computing by two different methods.

cross compiler Compiler that generates machine language for a foreign computer. See cross assembler.

cross-compiling/assembling A technique whereby one uses a minicomputer, mainframe, or time-sharing service to write and debug programs for subsequent use on microcomputers.

cross-footing check: The process of cross-adding, or subtracting, then zeroing-out in results.

cross hairs On an input device, two intersecting lines - one horizontal and one vertical - whose intersection marks the active cursor position of a graphics system.

cross tabulate To analyze and summarize data. For example, cross tabulation is used to summarize the details in a database file into totals in a spreadsheet.

crossfoot Numerical error checking technique that compares the sum of the columns with the sum of the rows.

crosshatch Criss-crossed pattern used to fill in sections of a drawing to distinguish them from each other.

cross-reference dictionary A printed listing that identifies all references of an assembled program to a specific label. In many systems, this listing is provided immediately after a source program has been assembled.

crossover cable Same as null modem cable.

crosstaLk (1) In communications, an interference from an adjacent channel. (2) Crosstalk. Family of PC communications programs from DCA'Crosstalk Communications.

crowbar A circuit that protects a computer system from dangerously high voltage surges.

CRT (Cathode Ray Tube) Vacuum tube used as a display screen in a video terminal or TV. The term often refers to the entire terminal.

CRT plot A computer-generated drawing or graph projected onto the screen of a cathode ray tube.

CRT terminal (1) A visual display unit (VDU). (2) A display device with keyboard as used by an operator to communicate with a computer. As the operator types a message or text on the keyboard, the characters are displayed on the screen.

crunch (1) To process data. See number crunching. (2) To compress data for reduced storage or transmission. See data compression.

cryoelectronic storage A storage device consisting of materials that become superconductors at extremely low temperatures.

cryogenics Using materials that operate at very cold temperatures. See superconductor.

cryosar A new-terminal semiconductor switching device that operates at very low temperatures.

cryptanalysis The operation of converting encrypted messages to the corresponding plaintext without initial knowledge of the key employed in the encryption, i.e, decrypting without knowledge of the key used to encrypt.

cryptographic techniques Methods of concealing data by representing each character or group of character by others.

cryptography Conversion of data into a secret code for security purposes. Same as encryption.

crystal Solid material containing a uniform arrangement of molecules. See quartz crystal.

crystailin Solid state of a crystal. Contrast with nematic.

CSJC (Customer Specific Integrated Circuit) Pronounced "C-sick." Custom-developed chips from Motorola.

CSMA/CD (Carrier Sense Multiple Access/Collision Detection) Baseband communications access method that uses a collision-detection technique. When a device wants to gain access to the network, it checks to see if the network is free. If it is not, it waits a random amount of time before retrying. If the network is free and two devices attempt access at exactly the same time, they both back off to avoid a collision and each wait a random amount of time before retrying.

CSV(Comma Separated Value) Same as comma delimited.

CT Abbreviation for computed tomography. See computerized axial tomography.

CU See control key.

Ctrl See control key.

Ctrl-Alt-Del In a PC, holding down the CTRL and ALT keys and pressing the DEL key reboots the system. See Boot.

Ctrl-Break In a PC, holding down the CTRL key and pressing the BREAK key cancels the running program or batch file. Same as Ctrl-C. See DOS Break.

Ctrl-C In a PC, holding down the CTRL key and pressing the C key cancels the running program or batch file. Same as Ctrl-Break. See DOS Break.

Ctrl-S In a PC, holding down the CTRL key and pressing the S key pauses a programme or scrolling of text and continues when another key is pressed.

CTS (1) (Clear To Send) RS-232 signal sent from the receiving station to the transmitting station that indicates it is ready to accept data. Contrast with RI'S. (2) See carpal tunnel syndrome.

CUA (Common User Access) SAA specifications for user interfaces, which includes OS/2 PM and character-based formats of 3270 terminals. It is intended to provide a consistent look and feel across platforms and between applications.

cue See Call.

CUT (Character-based User Interface) User interface that uses the character, or text, mode of the computer and typically refers to typing in commands. Contrast with GUI.

current (1) Present activities or the latest version or model. (2) Flow of electrons within a wire or circuit, measured in amps. (3) (Current) Windows PIM from IBM that includes a calendar, address book, phone dialler, outliner, word processor and Gantt charts for keeping track of projects.

current awareness system A process whereby a user is notified periodically by a centra file or library when selected items of information have been acquired.

current cell The cell currently available for use on a spreadsheet.

current directory Disk directory the system is presently working in. Unless otherwise specified, commands that deal with disk files imply the current directory.

current drive The disk drive currently being used by thecomputer system.

current location counter A counter kept by an assembler to determine the address that has been assigned to either an instruction or a constant being assembled.

current loop Transmission system that detects the presence or absence of current as is and Os rather than voltage levels.

current mode logic (CML) A logic circuit that employs the characteristics of a differential amplifier circuit in its design.

current page box In desktop publishing programs, an area that displays the current page being worked on.

cursive scanning A scanning technique used with video display terminals in which the electrons being sent toward the screen are deflected to form the outlines of the picture, one line at a time in the same way an artist might draw the same image.

cursor (1) Movable symbol on screen that is the contact point between the user and the data. In text systems, the cursor is a blinking rectangle or underline. On graphic systems, it is also called a pointer, and it can take any shape (arrow, square, paintbrush, etc.) and changes as it is moved into different parts of the screen. (2) Pen-like or puck-like device used with a graphics tablet. As the tablet cursor is moved across the tablet, the screen cursor moves correspondingly. See mouse.

cursor control The ability to move a video display prompt character to any position on the screen.

cursor keys Keys that move the cursor on screen, which include the up, down, left and right arrow, home, end, PgUp and PgDn keys. In addition to cursor keys, a mouse or tablet cursor also moves the cursor.

cursor tracking Positioning a cursor on a display screen by moving a stylus on a graphics tablet connected to the computer.

curve fitting A mathematical technique for finding a formula that best represents a collection of data points. Usually the formula is used to plot the best- fit line through the points.

custodian The person or organization responsible for physical maintenance and safeguarding of data stored on disk packs, tape reels, diskettes, removable hard disks, and so forth. See librarian.

customer engineer (CE) A person who repairs or does preventive maintenance on a computer or on its input/output devices and other off-line equipment. Also called field engineer.

custom IC An integrated circuit (1C) manufactured to a customer's design and specification.

customize To alter a piece of general-purpose software or hardware to enhance its performance, usually to fit a specific user's need.

customized form letters Personalized form letters produced by word processing systems and special form- letter programs.

custom software Programs prepared specifically for a business or organization and tailored to the business's needs.

customized software Software designed for an individual customer, in contrast with software packages available off-the-shelf for a particular industry, such as insurance or banking.

cut To remove text or graphics from a document. Compare paste.

CUT A bitmap format used by Dr. halo and a few other graphics programs.

cut & paste To move a block of text from one part of a document to another or from one file to another.

CUT mode (Control Unit Terminal mode) Mode that allows a 3270 terminal to have a single session with the mainframe. Micro to mainframe software emulates this mode to communicate with the mainframe. Contrast with DFT mode.

cut form A data-entry form, such as a utility bill, used by OCR devices.

cut-sheet feeder A device that feeds sheets of paper to the printer, one at a time. Usually a friction-feed device.

cutter path A line described by the motion of a cutting Rool controlled by a computer-aided manufacturing system.

cyan The shade of blue frequently used on vdts for color graphics.

CYBER Trade name for Control Data computers that includes models from high-speed workstations to supercomputers.

cybernetics Comparative study of human and machine processes in order to understand their similarities and differences. It often refers to machines that imitate human behaviour. See Al, robot.

cyberphobla The fear of computers.

cyberpunk Relating to futuristic delinquency: hackers breaking into computer banks, survival based on high- tech wits. Stems from science fiction novels such as Neuromancer and Shockwave Rider.

cyberspace Term coined by William Gibson in his novel "Neuromancer," to refer to a futuristic computer network that people use by plugging their brains into it! See virtual reality.

cycle (1) Single event that is repeated. For example, in a carrier frequency, one cycle is one complete wave. (2) Set of events that is repeated. For example, in a polling system, all of the attached terminals are tested in one cycle. See machine cycle, memory cycle.

cycle stealing CPU design technique that periodically "grabs" machine cycles from the main processor usually by some peripheral control unit, such as a DMA (direct memory access) device. In this way, processing and peripheral operations can be performed concurrently or with some degree of overlap.

cycle time Time interval between the start of one cycle and the start of the next cycle.

cycles per second Number of times an event or set of events is repeated in a second. See Hertz.

cyclic redundancy check (CRC) An error-detection scheme often used tin disk devices. When data are stored, a CRC value is computed once again. If the two values are equal, the data is assumed to be error free.

cyclic shift A shift in which the digits dropped off at one end of a word are returned at the other in a circular fashion. If a register holds eight digits, 23456789, the result of the cyclic shift two columns to the left would be to change the contents of the register to 45678923.

Cycolor Printing process from Mead Imaging that prints full tonal images like photographs.

cylinder Aggregate of all tracks that reside in the same location on every disk surface. On multiple-platter disks, the cylinder is the sum total of every track with the same track number on every surface. On a floppy disk, a cylinder comprises the top and corresponding bottom track. When storing data, the operating system fills an entire cylinder before moving to the next one. The access arm remains stationary until all the tracks in the cylinder have been read or written.

cylinder method The method or concept that data on all tracks above and below the one currently being used are available by merely switching read/write heads. Allows access to large amounts of information with no extra movement of the access device.

cylinder skew Offset distance from the start of the last track of the previous cylinder so that the head has time to seek from cylinder to cylinder and be at the start of the first track of the new cylinder. See head skew.

cypher A form of cryptography in which the plaintext is made unintelligible to anyone who intercepts it by a transformation of the information itself, based on some key.

Callback: An OOP design practice by which an object passes its identity to another object with the expectation that the called object will notify the calling object when some event occurs. Often the event is the destruction of the called object, but used for other purposes as well.

Candidate key: An attribute or group of attributes that identifies a unique row in a relation. One of the candidate keys is chosen to be the primary key.

Cardinality: In a binary relationship, the maximum or minimum number of elements allowed on each side of fhe relationship. The maximum cardinality can be 1:1, 1:N, N:1, or N:M. The minimum cardinality can be optional—optional, optional—mandatory, mandatory—optional, or mandatory—mandatory.

Cartesian product: A relational operation on two relations, A and B, producing a third relation, C, with C containing the concatenation of every row in A with every row in B.

CCP: Communications control program. A program that controls and administers transactions requests and responses in a teleprocessing system. The CCP routes transactions to the correct application programs and returns responses to the correct user terminal.

CGI: See Common gateway interface.

Check box: In a GUI environment, an element of the user interface in which a user can select one or more items from a list, Items are selected by clicking on them.

Checkpoint: The point of synchronization between a database and a transaction log. All buffers are force- written to external storage. This is the standard definition of checkpoint, but this term is sometimes used in other ways by DBMS vendors.

Child: A row, record, or node on the many side of a one-to-many relationship.

Child and twin pointer scheme: In DL/I, a technique used to represent segment relationships of a data base record in storage.

Child pointer: In the child and twin pointer scheme, the address of a child node.

Client computer: A microcomputer on a local area network with client—server architecture. In a database application, the client computer processes database application programs. Requests for actions on the database are sent to the database computer.

Client—server database architecture: The structure of a networked computing system in which one computer (usually a microcomputer) performs services on behalf of other computers (usually a microcomputer). For a database system, the server computer, which is called a database server, processes the DBMS, and client computers process the application programs. All database activities are carried out by the database server.

Client—server system: A system of two or more computers in which at least one computer provides services for one or more other computers. The services can be database services, communication services, printer services, or some other function.

COBOL: Common Business Oriented Language. The most widely used third-generation language for business applications.

CODASYL: Conference on Data Systems ‘anguages. A nonprofit committee of vendor, user, and academic personnel who established and now maintain the conventions for COBOL. The DBTG, or DataBase task group, developed a network model that was popular in the 1970s and early 1980s but is now being phased out.

Column: A logical group of bytes in a row of a relation or a table. The meaning of a column is the same for every row of the relation.

Command: A statement input to a database application by which users specify the activity to be performed. Contrast this with Menu.

Commit: A command issued to the DBMS to make database modifications permanent. Once the command has been processed, the changes are written to the database and to a log in such a way that they will survive system crashes and other failures. A commit is usually used at the end of an atomic transaction. Contrast this with Rollback.

Common gateway interface: A standard for defining forms and sending and receiving form data in HTML documents.

Communications control program: See CCP.

Complex network: A collection of entities, objects, or relations and their relationships, of which at least one of the relationships is complex (many to many).

Composite group: A group of attributes in a semantic object that is multivalued and contains no other object attributes.

Composite key: A key with more than one attribute.

Composite object: An object with at least one multi- valued attribute or attribute group. It is called a composite object because the key of the relation that represents the multivalued attribute or group is a composite key.

Compound object: An object that contains at least one other object.

Computed value: A column of a table that is computed from other column values. Values are not stored but are computed when they are to be displayed.

Concurrency: A condition in which two or more transactions are processed against the database at the same time. In a single CPU system, the changes are interleaved; in a multi-CPU system, the transactions may be processed simultaneously, and the changes on the database server are interleaved.

Concurrency transparency: In a distributed database system, the condition in which application programs do not know and do not need to know whether data is being concurrently processed. The DDBMS organizes update activities so that the results produced when concurrent processing is underway are consistent with the results that would occur if there were no concurrent processing.

Concurrent processing: In teleprocessing applications, the sharing of the CPU among several transactions. The CPU is allocated to each transaction in a round robin or in some other fashion for a certain period of time. Operations are performed so quickly that they appear to users to be simultaneous. In local area networks and other distributed applications, concurrent processing is used to refer to the (possibly simultaneous) processing of applications on multiple computers.

Concurrent update problem: An error condition in which one user's data changes are overwritten by another user's data changes. Same as Lost update problem.

Conflict: Two operations conflict if they operate on the same data item and at least one of the operations is a write.

Consistency: Two or more concurrent transactions are consistent if the result of their processing is the same as it would have been if they had been processed in some serial order.

Consistent schedule: An ordered list of transaction operations against a database in which the result of the processing is consistent.

Constraint: A rule concerning the allowed values of attributes whose truth can be evaluated. A constraint usually does not include dynamic rules such as "SalesPersonPay can never decrease" or "Salary now must be greater than Salary last quarter."

CPU: Central processing unit. The portion of the computer hardware that processes arithmetic and logic instructions. The term CPU usually includes main memory as well.

Currency indicator: In the CODASYL DBTG model, a variable that identifies the most recently accessed record or set. There are currency indicators for run- unit, record type, and set.

Cursor: An indicator of the current position or focus. (1) On a computer screen, a blinking box or underscore that indicates the position into which the next entry will be made. (2) In a file or embedded SQL SELECT, the identity of the next record or row to be processed.

D

D/A converter (Digital to Analog Converter) Device that converts digital pulses into analog signals. See A/D converter.

D-RAM See dynamic RAM.

DAD (1) (Database Action Diagram) Documentation that describes the processing performed on data in a database. (2) (Digital Audio Disc) Same as CD.

daisy chain Arrangement of devices connected in series, one connected to the next. Transmitted signals go to the first device and from the first to the second and so on.

daisy wheel Print mechanism that uses a plastic or metal hub with spokes like a bicycle wheel. At the end of each spoke is the carved image of a type character. When the required character spins around to the print hammer, the image is banged into a ribbon and onto paper. The mechanism is then moved to the next location. Daisy wheel printers produce typewriter-like output quality at the rate of 10 - 75 cps. They have been superseded by dot matrix and laser printers.

DAL (Data Access Language) Database interface from Apple that allows the Mac to access DAL-supported databases on Macs or non-Apple computers.

damping Technique for stabilizing an electronic or mechanical device by eliminating unwanted or excessive oscillations.

dark bulb A type of cathode ray tube, almost black in appearance when turned off, that gives good contrast to video displays.

darkness Intensity, especially low intensity or limited brightness.

Darlington circuit Amplification circuit that uses two transistors coupled together.

DASD (Direct Access Storage Device) Pronounced "dazdee." Peripheral device that is directly addressable, such as a disk or drum.

DAT (1) (Digital Audio Tape) CD-quality, digital recording technology for magnetic tape. A 4mm, helical-scan DAT drive holds 1.3GB (up to 2GB with extended-length tapes when adapted for data storage use). See tape backup. (2) (Dynamic Address Translator) Hardware circuit that converts a virtual memory address into a real address.

data (1) Technically, raw facts and figures which are processed into information. However, in common usage, both data and information are used synonymously.

The amount of data kept in the computer versus the amount of information is a tradeoff. Data can be processed into different forms of information, but it takes time to sort and sum transactions. Data is "processed". Software is "run". (2) Any form of information whether on paper or in electronic form. In electronic form, data refers to data fields, records, files and databases, word processing documents, graphic images and digitally-encoded voice and video. (3) Data items in data files and databases in contrast with text, graphics, voice and video files.

data abstraction In object-oriented programming, creating user-defined data types that contain their own data and processing.

data acquisitiomn (1) Automatic collection of data from sensors and readers in a factory, laboratory, medical or scientific environment. (2) Gathering of source data for data entry into the computer.

data administration Database administration is the technical design and management of the database. Analysis, classification and maintenance of an organization's data and data relationships. It includes the development of data models and data dictionaries, which, combined with transaction volume, are the raw materials for database design. Data administration functions provide the overall management of data as an organizational resource.

data administrator Person who coordinates activities within the data administration department. Contrast with database administrator.

data aggregate Any collection of data items within a record that is given a name and referred to as a whole, such as an array.

data bank Any electronic depository of data. data base See Database.

data bus Internal pathway across which data is transferred to and from the processor. The expansion slots in personal computers are connected to the data bus.

data byte An eight-bit binary number representing one character of data the computer will use in an arithmetic or logical operation, or store in memory.

data carrier (1) Any medium such as a disk or tape that can hold machine readable data. (2) Carrier frequency into which data is modulated for transmission in a network.

data cartridge Removable storage module containing magnetic tape.

data catalog An organized listing by full name of all data elements used by an organization.

data centre The department that houses the computer systems, related equipment, and data tiles.

data chaining The process of linking data items together. Each data item contains the location of the next.

data channel The communications link between two devices or points.

data code (1) Digital coding system for data in a computer. See ASCII and EBCDIC. (2) Coding system used to abbreviate data, for example, codes for regions, classes, products and status.

data collection Acquiring source documents for the data entry department It comes under the jurisdiction of the data control or data entry department. See data acquisition.

data command A command that consists of a period followed by letters. Used in some older types of word processing programs for embedded commands.

data communications Same as communications.

data communications equipment The equipment associated with the transmission of data from one device to another. Examples are modems. remote terminals, and communications processors.

data communications system A system consisting of computers, terminals, and communications links.

data compatibility The ability of two or more computers to read from and write to each other's data disks or use each other's data files, even if they cannot run the same programs.

data compression Encoding data to take up less storage space. For example, short names in fixed length fields waste a lot of space. A simple method called run length encoding converts the spaces into a code that indicates how many blanks follow. There are two major methods used for data compression: statistical and dictionary, and two widely-used examples of each: Huffman coding and LZW (Lempel-Ziv-Welch).

Text files can be compressed the most. Dense, machine language files can be compressed about a third. While some graphics files leave little room for compaction, others compress well.

data concentration (1) The collection of data at an intermediate point from several low- and medium-speed lines for retransmission across high speed lines. (2) The addition of one item at the end of others to produce one longer data item.

data control department Function responsible for collecting data for input into a computer's batch processing operations as well as the dissemination of the finished reports.

data conversion The process of changing the form of data representation.

DATA/DAT (DATA/Digital Audio Tape) DAT format for data backup that can be divided into as many as 254 partitions allowing for updating in place. See tape backup.

data declaration Same as data definition (1).

data definition (1) In a source language program, the definitions of data structures (variables, arrays, fields, records, etc.). (2) Description of the record layout in a file system or DBMS.

data definition language (DDE) The language used by a database administrator to create, store, and manage data in a database environment. Also called data description language.

data description language (DDE) The language that specifies the manner in which data are to be stored and managed in a database environment by a database management system. Also called data definition language.

data dictionary Database about data and databases. it holds the name, type, range of values, source, and authorization for access for each data element in the organization's files and databases. It also indicates which application programs use that data so that when a change in a data structure is contemplated, a list of affected programs can be generated.

data diddling The technique whereby data is modified before it goes into a computer file where it is less accessible.

data directory An ordered collection of data element names and/or identifiers and their attributes that provides the location of the elements.

data directory/dictionary An ordered collection of data elements that combines the features of a data catalog data dictionary, and data directory. Describes and locates each data element.

data division The part of a COBOL program that defines the data files and record layouts.

data editing A procedure to check for irregularities in input data. Typical checks are a range check, reasonableness check, and checks to determine whether data is properly alphabetic or numeric, as required.

data element Fundamental data structure in a data processing system. Any unit of data defined for processing is a data element. A data element is defined by size (length) and type (alphanumeric, numeric only, true/false, date, etc.). A specific set of values or range of values may also be part of the definition. Technically, a data element is a logical definition of data, whereas a field is the physical unit of storage in a record. Data element, data item, field and variable all describe the same unit of data and are used interchangeably.

data encryption See encryption and DES.

data encryption standard The standardized public key by- which senders and receivers can scramble and unscramble their message.

data entry Entering data into the computer, which includes keyboard entry, optical scanning and voice recognition.

data entry device The equipment used to prepare data so the computer can accept it.

data entry operator Person who enters data into the computer, via keyboard or other reading or scanning device.

data entry program Application program that accepts data from the keyboard or other input device and stores it in the computer. It may be part of an application that also provides updating, querying and reporting. The data entry program establishes the data in the database and should test for all possible input errors. See validity checking, table lookup, check digit and intelligent database.

data export The capacity to transport (write) information from one database in a form that can be used (read) by another program, such as a word processor for form letters and reports, a spreadsheet, or a different database. Opposite of data import.

data field (1) One column or consecutive columns on a coding form or punched card used to record a particular piece of data. (2) Part of a data record.

data field masking Using special characters to offset or divide data fields. for data fields, the slash or hyphen characters are often used to divide the month, day, and year. O9t23,i. For telephone numbers, the parentheses and hyphen characters may be desired: (999) 999.9999. This feature greatly simplifies data entry and ensures standardization. Some programs routinely mask such fields as dates and telephone number.

data file Collection of data records. Contrast with word processing file and graphics file.

data file processing The updating of data files by adding, changing, or deleting records to reflect the effects of current data.

data flow (1) In computers, the path of data from source document to data entry to processing to final reports. Data changes format and sequence (within a file) as it moves from program to program. (2) In communications, the path taken by a message from origination to destination and includes all nodes through which the data travels.

dataflow analysis The study of the movement of data among processing activities.

data flow diagram Description of data and the manual and machine processing performed on the data.

data fork The part of a Macintosh file that contains data. For example, in a HyperCard stack, text, graphics and HyperTalk scripts reside in the data fork, while fonts, sounds, control information and external functions reside in the resource fork.

data format Same as file format.

Data General Corporation (DGC) A computer manufacturer founded in 1968 by Edson de Castro. In 1969, the company introduced the Nova, an advanced minicomputer. During its early years, the company was successful in marketing its minicomputers in university, scientific, and OEM markets. Over the years .DGC has developed a variety of minicomputer systems.

data glove See DataGlove.

data Import The ability to use (read) information developed with another program, particularly important in the use of integrated software where several programs will use the information gathered or produced by one program.

data Independence Fundamental DBMS technique that separates data from the processing and allows the database to be structurally changed with minimal disruption to existing programs. Programs access data in the DBMS by field and are concerned with only the data fields they use, not the format of the complete record. Thus, when the record layout is updated (fields added, deleted or changed in size), the only programs that must be changed are those that use those new fields.

data integrity Process of preventing accidental erasure or adulteration in a database.

data interchange format (DIF) The standard among software developers that allows data from one program to be accessible to another program.

data item See data element.

data leakage The illegal removal of data from a computer facility.

data library Section of the datacenter that houses offline disks and tapes. Data library personnel are responsible for custody and control of disks, tapes, and procedures manuals by cataloguing and monitoring the use of these data resources.

data line Individual circuit, or line, that carries data within a computer or communications channel.

data line monitor In communications, a test instrument that analyzes the signals and timing of a communications line. It either visually displays the patterns or stores the activity for further analysis.

data link In communications, the physical interconnection between two points (OS! layers 1 and 2). It may also refer to the modems, protocols and all required hardware and software to perform the transmission.

data link escape Communications control character which indicates that the following character is not data, but a control code.

data link protocol In communications, the transmission of a unit of data from one node to another (OS! layer 2). It is responsible for ensuring that the bits received are the same as the bits sent. The major categories of data link protocols are: (a) Asynchronous Transmission: Originating from mechanical teletype machines, asynchronous transmission treats each character as a unit with start and stop bits appended to it. It is the common form of transmission between the serial port of a personal computer or terminal and a modem. ASCII, or teletype, protocols provide little or no error checking and are only acceptable for text messages. Xmodem, Ymodem and Kermit are typical error checking protocols. (b) Synchronous Transmission: Developed for mainframe networks using higher speeds than teletype terminals, synchronous transmission sends contiguous blocks of data, with both sending and receiving stations synchronized to each other. Synchronous protocols include error checking. Examples are IBM's SDLC, Digital's DDCMP, and the international HDLC. (c) Local Area Networks: Developed for medium to high transmission speeds between stations, LANs typically use collision detection (CSMA/CD) or token passing methods for transmitting data between nodes. Examples are IBM's Token Ring, Datapoint's ARCNET, Xerox's Ethernet and AT&T's Starlan.

data logging The recording of data about events that occur in time sequence.

data management Refers to several levels of managing data. From bottom to top, they are: (1) The part of the operating system that manages the physical storage and retrieval of data on a disk or other device. See access method. (2) Software that allows for the creation, storage, retrieval and manipulation of files interactively at a terminal or personal computer. See file manager and DBMS. (3) Function that manages data as an organizational resource. See data administration. (4) Management of all data and information within an organization. It includes data administration, the standards for defining data and the way in which people perceive and use it in their day-to-day tasks.

data management system See DBMS.

data manipulation See Data Processing.

data manipulation language Language that requests data from a DBMS. It is coded within the application program such as COBOL or C.

data medium The material in or on which a specific physical variable may represent data, such as magnetic disk or cd-rom.

data model Description of the principles of organization of a database.

data modelling Identification of the design principles for a data model.

data module Sealed, removable storage module containing magnetic disks and their associated access arms and read/write heads.

data movement time The time taken to transfer data to or from a disk once the read/write head is properly positioned on a disk track.

data name Name assigned to an item of data, such as a field or variable.

data network Communications network that transmits data. See communications.

data origination The translation of information from its original form into machine-sensible form.

data pocket A means of transmitting serial data in an efficient package that includes an error-checking sequence.

data point A numeric value for charting purposes. In a single line chart, time may be plotted across the X axis and another value against the Y-axis, the intersection being a data point.

data preparation The process of organizing information and storing it in a form that can be input to the computer.

data preparation device A device that permits data capture in which the source data is collected and transformed into a medium or form capable of being read into a computer.

Datapro A research/publishing company that provides in-depth information about computer hardware and software products.

data processing Capturing, storing, updating and retrieving data and information. It may refer to the entire computer industry, to only datacenter operations, or to only data processing activities, in contrast with word processing and office functions.

data processing center A computer center equipped with devices capable of receiving information, processing it according to human made instructions, and producing the computed results. Same as information processing center.

data processing curriculum A course of study, normally offered by a business school or college, that prepares students for entry-level jobs as applications programmers or system analysts.

data processing cycle The combined functions of input, processing, and output.

data processing management Management of the data processing function, its people, and its equipment. This activity follows the well-recognized principles of planning, control, and operation.

data processing manager The person who runs the data processing center, usually including the operation of the computer. The biggest part of the manager's job is concerned with developing new systems and keeping them running.

data processing system The network of data processing hardware, software, people, and procedures capable of accepting information, processing it according to a plan, and producing the desired results.

data processing technology The science of information handling.

data processor (1) Person who works in data processing. (2) Computer that is processing data.

data projector Video machine that projects output from a computer onto a remote screen. It is bulkier than a flat LCD panel, but is faster for displaying high-speed animation.

Data Propagator IBM query language that maintains consistency between DB2 and IMS/ESA DB databases. When data is changed in the IMS database, it is automatically changed in the DB2 database.

data protection Any measure to safeguard data from undesired occurrences that intentionally or unintentionally lead to destruction, modification, or disclosure of data.

data rate (1) Data transfer speed within the computer or between a peripheral and computer. (2) Data transmission speed in a network.

data record A collection of data fields, pertaining to a particular subject. Part of a data file.

data reduction The process of transforming raw data into useful, condensed, or simplified intelligence. Adjusting, scaling, smoothing, compacting, editing, and ordering operations are often used.

data scope A special display device that monitors a data communications channel and displays the content of the information being transmitted over it.

data resource management Same as data administration.

data security The protection of data from accidental or malicious destruction, disclosure, or modification.

data set (1) Data file or collection of interrelated data. (2) AT&T name for modem.

data sharing The ability of computer processes or a computer users at several nodes to access data at a single node.

data signal Physical data as it travels over a line or channel (pulses or vibrations of electricity or light).

data sink Device or part of the computer that receives data.

data source Device or part of the computer in which data is originated.

data storage techniques Methods used by a program to store data files.

data stream Continuous flow of data from one place to another.

data striping See disk striping.

data structure Physical layout of data. Data fields, memo fields, fixed length fields, variable length fields, records, word processing documents, spreadsheet, data files, database files and indexes are all examples of data structures.

data switch Switch box that routes one line to another. For example, it is used to connect multiple printers to one computer or multiple computers to one printer. It can be done either manually or through an automatic switch.

data system Same as information system. data tablet Same as digitizer tablet.

data terminal The point in a computer system or data communications network at which data can be entered or retrieved.

data transfer Movement of data within the computer system. Typically, data is said to be transferred within the computer, but it is "transmitted" over a communications network. A transfer is actually a copy function since the data is not automatically erased at the source.

data transfer operations The operations that move data, whether externally through data communications or within main computer storage, by copying from one location to another.

data transfer rate Same as data rate.

data transmission Sending data over a communications network.

data transparency Ability to easily access and work with data no matter where it is located or what application created it.

data type Category of data. Typical data types are numeric, alphanumeric (character), dates and logical (true/false). Programming languages allow for the creation of different data types.

When data is assigned a type, it cannot be treated like another type. For example, character data cannot be calculated, and digits within numeric data cannot be isolated. Date types can only contain valid dates.

data validation The measures taken to ensure that data fields conform to desired specifications. Fields may be checked for inappropriate characters or for deviation from specified lengths or value. See edit.

data value Any string of symbols that serves as the representative of some item of information.

data word An ordered set of characters, usually of a present number, that is stored and transferred by the computer's circuits as a fundamental unit of information.

data word size The specific length of data word that a particular computer is designed to handle.

datacenter Department that houses the computer systems and related equipment. The data library is part of the datacenter, and the data entry and systems programming departments may also come under its jurisdiction. A control section is usually provided that accepts work from and releases output to the different user departments.

datacom (DATA COMmunications) See communications.

DataBase Relational DBMS for PCs from DataEase Inc. It provides a menu-driven interface for developing applications without programming and is noted for its ease of use.

DataGlove Glove used to report the position of a user's hand and fingers to a computer from VPL Research, Inc. See virtual reality.

datagram TCP/IP message unit that contains internet source and destination addresses and data.

date math Calculations made upon dates. For example, January 30 + 5 yields February 4.

datum Singular form of data, for example, one datum. It is rarely used, and data, its plural form, is commonly used for both singular and plural.

daughter board Small printed circuit board that is attached to or plugs into removable printed circuit board. Contrast with mother board.

dazdee See DASD.

DB See database and decibel.

DB-9, DB-15, DB-25, DB-37, DB-50) Plugs and sockets with 9, 15, 25,37 and 50 pins respectively, used to hook up communications and computer devices. The DB refers to the physical structure of the connector, not the purpose of each line. DB-9 and DB25 connectors are commonly used for RS-232 interfaces. The DB-25 is also used on the computer end of the parallel printer cable for PCs (the printer end isa Centronics 36-pin connector). A high-density DB15 connector is used for the VGA port on a PC, which has 15 pins in the same shell as the DB-9 connector.

DB/DC (DataBase/Data Communications) Refers to software that performs database and data communications functions.

DB2 (DataBase 2) Relational DBMS from IBM that runs on large mainframes. It is a full-featured DBMS that has become IBM's major database product. It uses the SQL language interface.

DBASE Relational DBMS for Pcs from Borland. It was j the first comprehensive DBMS for personal computers. Originally named Vulcan, DBASE was created by Wayne Ratliff to manage a company football pool.

Renamed DBASE II when Hal Lashlee and George Tate formed Ashton-Tate to market it (Ashton Tate was acquired by Borland in 1991), dBASE became a huge success within a couple of years. It is the most widely used PC database system, and its file formats have become de facto standards.

dBASE provides a Pascal-like, interpreted programming language and fourth-generation commands for interactive used BASE II: Introduced in 1981, it was the original command-driven dBASE for CP/M machines and later for PCs. dI3ASE II data formats and programs must be converted to run under dBASE III. dBASE III & III PLUS: Introduced in 1984, dBASE III was a major upgrade of dBASE II for PCs only. It handles larger databases, has more programming commands and includes a memo field and menus. In 1986, dBASE III PLUS introduced redesigned menus and added new features including the ability to store queries and relational views. dBASE IV: Introduced in 1988, it is a major upgrade of dBASE III PLUS with redesigned menus and report and forms generation screens. It adds a QBE method for asking questions as well as an SQL language interface. Many new programming commands and features are added, including arrays and windows.

Versions of dBASE IV are also available for UNIX on 386s, Sun workstations and VAXs under VMS, and a runtime version is available for the Macintosh.

dBASE complier Software that converts dBASE source language into machine language. The resulting programs execute on their own like COBOL or C programs and do not run under dBASE. See Clipper, Force and Quicksilver.

dBASE Mac Macintosh DBMS from Ashton-Tate that never caught on because it was incompatible with dBASE.

DBF file dBASE data file extension.

DBMS (DataBase Management System) Software that controls the organization, storage, retrieval, security and integrity of data in a database. It accepts requests from the application and instructs the operating system to transfer the appropriate data.

DBMSs let information systems be changed more easily as the organization's requirements change. New categories of data can be added to the database without disruption to the existing system.

MAJOR FEATURES OFA DBMS: 1. Data Security: The DBMS can prevent unauthorized users from viewing or updating the database. Using passwords, users are allowed access to the entire database or subsets of it.

2. Data Integrity: The DBMS can ensure that no more than one user can update the same record at the same time. It can keep duplicate records out of the database.

3. Interactive Query: Most DBMSs provide query languages and report writers that let users interactively interrogate the database and analyze its data. This important feature gives users access to all management information as needed. Complex business systems can be developed in dBASE and Paradox, etc., but not without programming. This is not the same as creating lists of data for your own record keeping.

4. Interactive Data Entry and Updating: Many DBMSs provide a way to interactively enter and edit data, allowing you to manage your own files and databases.

DATABASE DESIGN: A business information system is made up of subjects (customers, employees, vendors, etc.) and activities (orders, payments, purchases, etc.). Database design is the process of organizing this data into related record types. The DBMS that is chosen is the one that can support the organization's data structure while efficiently processing the transaction volume.

Organizations may use one kind of DBMS for daily transaction processing and then move the detail to another DBMS better suited for random inquiries and analysis.Overall systems design decisions are performed by data administrators and systems analysts. Detailed database design is performed by database administrators.

HIERARCHICAL, NETWORK AND RELATIONAL DATABASES: Information systems are made up of related files: customers and orders, vendors and purchases, etc. A key DBMS feature is its ability to manage these relationships.

Hierarchical databases link records like an organization chart. A record type can be owned by only one owner. In network databases, a record type can have multiple owners. Relational databases do not link records together physically, but the design of the records must provide a common field, such as account number, to allow for matching. Often, the fields used for matching are indexed in order to speed up the process.

INTELLIGENT DATABASES Though all DBMSs provide some data validation, most validation is left up to the application programs. Intelligent databases provide more validation; for example, table lookups can reject bad spelling or coding of items. Common algorithms can also be used such as one that computes sales tax for an order based on zip code.

When validation is left up to each application program, one program could allow an item to be entered while another program rejects it. Data integrity is better served when data validation is done in only one place.

FUTURE DATABASES The world of information is made up of data, text, pictures and voice. Many DBMSs manage text as well as data, but very few manage both with equal proficiency. Throughout the 1990s, DBMSs will begin to integrate all forms of information. Eventually, it will be common for a database to handle data, text, graphics, voice and video with the same ease as today's systems handle data. When this happens, the office of the future will have finally arrived!

DBS (Direct Broadcast Satellite) One-way broadcast service direct from a satellite to a user's dish (antenna). They are used to deliver private information and TV services.

dBXL dBASE III PLUS-compatible DBMS from WordTech Systems, that features a menu-driven option for interactive use. See Arago dBXL.

DC (1) (Direct Current) Electrical current that travels in one direction and used within the computer's electronic circuits. Contrast with AC. (2) (Data Communications) See DB/DC.

DCA (1) (Document Content Architecture) IBM file formats for text documents. DCA/RFT (Revisable- Form Text) is the primary format and can be edited. DCA/FFT (Final-Form Text) has been formatted for a particular output device and cannot be changed. For example, page numbers, headers and footers are placed on every page. (2) (Distributed Communications Architecture) Network architecture from Unisys. (3) (Digital Communications Associates, Inc.) Communications products manufacturer-. See IRMAboard.

DD See double density disk.

DDBMS (Distributed Database Management System) See distributed database.

DDE (Dynamic Data Exchange) Message protocol in Windows that allows application programs to request and exchange data automatically. A program in one window can query a program in another window using the DDE protocol.

DDL (1) (Data Description Language) Language used to define data and their relationships to other data. It is used to create files, databases and data dictionaries. (2) (Document Description Language) Printer control language from Imagen that runs on the HP LaserJet series. (3) (Direct Data Link) Ability of a supplier to directly interrogate a customer's inventory database in order to manage scheduling and shipping more efficiently.

DDM (Distributed Data Management) Software in an IBM SNA environment that allows users to access data in remote data files within the network. DDM works with IBM's LU 6.2 session to provide peer-to- peer communications and file sharing.

DDP (Distributed Data Processing) See distributed processing.

DDS (Digital Data Storage) DAT format for data backup. It is sequential recording method; data must be appended at the end of previous data. See tape backup.

de facto standard A programming language, product, design, or program that has become so widely used and imitated that it has little competition but whose status has not officially been declared by a recognized standard-establishing organizations.

dead halt A half situation in which the system cannot return to the point at which it halted.

dead letter box In message switching systems, a file capturing undeliverable messages.

deadlock See deadly embrace.

deadly embrace Stalemate that occurs when two elements- in a process are each waiting for the other to respond. For example, in a network, if one user is working on file A and needs file B to continue, but another user is working on file B and needs file A to continue, each one waits for the other. Both are temporarily locked out.

deallocate To release a computer resource that is currently assigned to a program or user, such as memory or a peripheral device.

deblock To separate records from a block.

debounce To prevent spurious closures of a key or switch from being recognized. One method is to introduce time delays that give the switch contacts time to settle down.

debug To correct a problem in hardware or software. Debugging software is finding the errors in the program logic. Debugging hardware is finding the errors in circuit design. See bug.

debugger Software that helps a programmer debug a program. It lets you stop the program at a specified statement, step through it one statement at a time as well as capture and view system data and program variables. Modern debuggers link source and object code so that the programmer can step through the source program while instructions are being executed.

debugging aids The computer routines - such as a tracing routine, snapshot dump, and post-mortem dump- that are helpful in debugging programs.

DEC (Digital Equipment Corp.) Digital trade name for products (DECmate, DECnet, DECsystem, etc.). Many people refer to the company as DEC.

decatenate To separate into two or more paths. Contrast w-ith concatenate.

decay Reduction of strength of a signal or charge.

deceleration time The time required to stop a magnetic tape after reading or recording the last piece of data from a record on that tape.

decentralized computer system System in which the computer and somestorage devices are in one location, but the devices that access the computer are elsewhere.

decentralized processing Computer systems in different locations. Although data may be transmitted between the computers periodically, it implies limited daily communications. Contrast with distributed processing and centralized processing.

decibel (dB) Unit that measures loudness or strength of a signal. Humans perceive loudness from a whisper of 10 dB up to about 140 dB. A noisy factory generates 90 dB and loud thunder is 110 dB. 120 dB is painful. A decibel is a relative measurement that is derived from an initial reference level and a final observed level.

decimal Meaning 10. Universal numbering system that uses 10 digits. Computers use binary numbers because it is easier to design electronic systems that can maintain two states rather than 10, See Binary.

decimal code A formal of notation by which each decimal digit is expressed separately in some other number system.

decimal digit A numeral in the decimal numeral system. The radix of the decimal system is 10, and the following symbols are used: 0, 1, 2, 3, 4, 5, 6, 7, 8,and 9.

decimal point The radix point in a mixed decimal numeral, separating the fractional part from the integer part. In the decimal number 741.12, the decimal point is between the two ones.

decimal systems A base-l0 positional, numeration system.

decimal-to-binary conversion The process of converting a numeral written in base 10 to the equivalent numeral written in base 2.

decimal-to-hexadecimal conversion The process of converting a numeral written in base 10 to the equivalent numeral written in base 16.

decimal-to-octal conversion The process of converting a numeral written in base 10 to the equivalent numeral in base 8.

decision A computer operation of determining whether a certain relationship exists between data storage or registers and of taking alternative courses of action. Determination of future action.

decision box Diamond-shaped symbol that is used to document a decision point in a flowchart. The decision is written in the decision box, and the results of the decision branch off from the points in the box.

decision Instruction In programming, an instruction that compares one set of data with another and branches to a different part of the program depending on the results.

decision making Making choices. The proper balance of human and machine decision making is an important part of a system's design.

From a programming point of view, decision making is performed two ways: algorithmic, a precise set of rules and conditions that never change, or heuristic, a set of rules that may change over time (self-modify) as conditions occur. Heuristic techniques are employed in Al systems.

decision structure Same as selection structure.

decision support system See DSS and EIS.

decision symbol A diamond-shaped flowcharting symbol used to indicate a choice or-a branching in the formation processing path.

decision table List of decisions and their criteria. Designed as a matrix, it lists criteria (inputs) and the results (outputs) of all possible combinations of the criteria. It can be peace into a program to direct its processing. By changing the decision table, the program is changed accordingly.

decision theory Abroad spectrum of concepts and techniques that have been developed both to describe and to rationalize the process of making a choice among several possible alternatives.

decision tree Graphical representation of all alternatives in a decision making process.

deck (1) The part of a magnetic tape unit that holds and moves the tape reels. (2) Set of punched cards. (3) See DEC.

declaration In programming, an instruction or statement that defines data (fields, variables, arrays, etc.) and resources, but does not create executable code.

declaration statement The part of a computer program that defines the nature of other elements of the program or reserves part of the hardware for special use.

declarative language A programming language that frees the programmer from specifying the exact procedure the computer needs to follow to accomplish a task. Instead, the user informs the program what he or she wants to accomplish.

DECmate Family of computer systems from Digital specialized for word processing. Introduced in 1981, DECmates use the PDP-8 architecture.

DECmcc (DEC Management Control Center) Digital's network management software for DECnet and TCP/ IP. DECmcc Management Stations for VMS and ULTRIX support X Window and provide color-coded alarms.

DECnet Digital's communications network, which supports Ethernet-style LANs and baseband and broadband WANs over private and public lines. It interconnects PDPs, VAXs, PCs, Macs and workstations. In DECnet philosophy, a node must be an intelligent machine and not simply a terminal as in other systems. See DNA.

DECnet/DOS allows DOS machines to function as end nodes in DECnet networks, and DECnet/OSI is the implementation of DECnet Phase V that supports OSI and provides compatibility with DECnet Phase IV and TCP/IP.

decode To translate or determine the meaning of a coded information Reverse of encode.

decoder Hardware device or software program that converts a coded signal back into its original form.

decollate To arrange copies of continuous forms in sets and remove the carbon paper from them.

decollators Device that separates multiple-part paper forms while removing the carbon paper.

decompiler Program that converts machine language back into a high-level source language. The resulting code may be very difficult to comprehend as variables and routines are named generically: A0001, A0002, etc.

decompress To restore compressed data back to its original size.

decrement To subtract a number from another number. Decrementing a counter means to subtract 1 or some other number from its current value.

decryption The process of taking an encrypted message and reconstructing from it the original meaningful message, or plaintext. Opposite of encryption.

DECstation Computers from Digital - RISC-based single-user workstations from Digital; PC series from Digital introduced in 1989. Small computer system from Digital used primarily for word processing.

DECsystem (1) Series of RISC-based, 32-bit computers from Digital that run under ULTRIX. Introduced in 1989, the 5400 model is a Q-bus system; the 5800 model uses the XMl bus. (2) Series of mainframes from Digital that were introduced from 1974 through 1980 and were the successor to the 36-bit PDP-10 computers.

DECtalk Voice synthesizing system from Digital that accepts serial ASCII text and converts it into audible speech. It is used in Touch-tone telephone response systems as well as for voice-output for visually handicapped users.

DECwindows Digital's windowing architecture, based on X Window, Version 11. It is compatible with X Window while adding a variety of enhancements.

dedicated Pertaining to programs, machines, or procedures that are designed or reserved for special use.

dedicated channel Computer channel or communications line that is used for one purpose.

dedicated chip A chip that performs one task only, such as a memory chip.

dedicated computer A computer whose use is reserved for a particular task. Compare special-purpose computer.

dedicated device A device designed to perform only certain functions that cannot be programmed to perform other functions.

dedicated lines Telephone lines leased for exclusive use by a group or individual for telecommunications. Users pay a set for leased lines rather than the per- call or per-minute charges for switched lines.

dedicated service Service that is not shared by other users or organizations.

dedicated system A computer-based device with one primary function, such as word processing. Usually easier to use for its intended task than for any other. General-purpose systems are usually more flexible.

default Standard setting or action taken by hardware or software if the user has not specified otherwise. For example, defaults in word processing programs define the margins, tabs and page length, all of which can be changed by the user.

default directory Same as current directory.

default drive Disk drive used if no other drive is specified in the command.

default font Typeface and size of the character used for printing if none other is specified.

default settings The settings automatically used by a program unless the user specifies otherwise.

deferred address An Indirect address.

deferred entry Entry into a subroutine that occurs as a result of a deferred exit from the program that passed control to it.

deferred exit The passing of control to a subroutine at a time determined by an asynchronous event rather than at a predictable time.

defragment See defragmentation.

defragmentation A process in which all the files on a hard disk are rewritten so that all parts of each file are written to contiguous sectors.

degausser Device that removes unwanted magnetism from a monitor or the read/write head in a disk or tape drive.

degradation A device used to erase information from magnetically recorded media such as a floppy disk or magnetic tape.

degradation A condition in which a system continues to operate but at a reduced level of service. Unavailability of proper equipment maintenance and computer programs not maintained to accommodate current needs are the two most common causes.

deinstall To remove a program or hardware device from active service.

dejagging A computer graphics technique for drawing smooth lines, characters, and polygons.

de jure standard Standards that exist in the marketplace due to their adoption by standard-approving bodies, such as the American National Standards Institute (ANSI) and so.

DEL key (DELete key) Keyboard key used to delete the character under the screen cursor or some other block of data. It is often used in combination with the shift, control and alt keys to delete various text Segments.

delay circuit An electronic circuit that deliberately delays the delivery of a signal for a present interval.

delay line Communications or electronic circuit that has a built-in delay.

delay line storage A storage device that consists of a delay line and a means for regenerating and reinserting information into that line Used in early computers.

delete To remove an item of data from a file or to remove a file from the disk. See undelete.

deletion record A new record that will replace or remove an existing record of a master file.

delimit To fix the limits of something, such as to establish maximum and minimum limits of a specific variable.

delimiter Character or combination of characters used to separate one item or set of data from another. For example, in comma delimited records, a comma is used to separate each field of data.

delivery The final step in the program development cycle where the program or system is given to be users for execution against actual data.

Dell Computer Corporation A manufacturer of IBM-compatible microcomputers that was founded in 1984 by Michael Dell in Austin, Texas, Dell provides a complete line of microcomputers from laptops to high-end machines.

delta modulation Technique that is used to sample voice waves and convert them into digital code. See PCM.

Deluxe Paint[tm] A popular paint program for Commodore Amiga and IBM-compatible microcomputers.

demagnetization The process of erasing information stored on magnetic disks or tape. See degausser.

demand paging Copying a program page from disk into memory when required by the program.

demand processing Same as transaction processing.

demand report A report produced only upon request and used in strategic decision-making to provide responses to unanticipated queries.

demo A demonstration program designed to emulate some of the functions of an application program for advertising and marketing purposes.

Demo II Demonstration, authoring and prototyping program for PCs from Intersolv.

democratic team A software development team structure in which team members share responsibility.

demodulate To filter out the data signal from the carrier. See modulate.

demodulation In data communications, the process or retrieving an original signal from a modulated carrier wave; used in data sets to make communications signals compatible with computer terminal signals. Counterpart to modulation.

demodulator A device that receives signals transmitted over a communications link and converts them into electrical pulses, or bits, that can serve as inputs to a data processing machine. Contrast with modulator.

demount To remove a magnetic storage medium from a device that reads or writes on it, such as to remove a disk pack from the disk drive.

demoware Demonstration software that shows some or all of the features of a commercial product. See crippleware.

demultiplex To reconvert a transmission that contains several intermixed signals back into its original separate signals.

demultiplexor A circuit that applies the logic state of a single input to one of several outputs. Contrast with multiplexor.

dense binary code A code in which all possible states of the binary pattern are used.

dense binary code A code in which all possible states of the binary pattern are used.

dense list See sequential list.

density See packing density and bit density.

departmental computing Processing a department's data with its own computer system. See distributed processing.

dependency A relationship where the execution of one job has to be completed before another can begin.

dependent segment In database management, data that depends on data in a higher level for its full meaning.

dependent variable The output of a model, so called because it depends on the inputs.

depth queuing A technique, such as shading, used to enhance the three-dimensional appearance of a two- dimensional object.

dequeue Pronounced "d-q." To remove items from a queue in order to process or transmit them.

DES (Data Encryption Standard) NIST-standard encryption technique that scrambles data into an unbreakable code for transmission over a public network. It uses a binary number as the key for encryption that offers more than 72 quadrillion combinations. The number, which can be randomly chosen for each transmission, is used as a pattern to convert the bits at both ends of the transmission.

descenders The parts of the lower case characters g, j, p. q and y that fall below the line.

descending order An order that ranges from highest to lowest in numeric value or alphabetically. Contrast with ascending order.

descending sort Arranging data from high to low sequence (from Z to A, from 9 to 0).

descriptor (1) Word or phrase that identifies a document in an indexed information retrieval system. (2) Category name used to identify data.

deserlalize To convert a serial stream of bits into parallel streams of bits.

design aids Computer programs or hardware elements intended to assist in Implementing a computer system. See debugging aids and programming aids.

design automation The use of computers in the design and production of circuit package, new computers, and other electronic equipment.

design costs The costs associated with systems design, programming, training, conversion, testing, and documentation.

design cycle (1) In a hardware system, the complete cycle of development of equipment, which includes breadboarding, prototyping, testing, and production. (2) IN a software system, the complete plan for producing an operational system, which includes problem description, algorithm development, flowcharting, coding, program debugging, and documentation. See program development cycle.

design engineer A person involved in the design of a hardware product, such as a disk unit or microprocessor chip.

Designer Popular Windows drawing program from Micrografx. It is a full-featured design program for illustrations and CAD (64 layers). It creates its own proprietary DRW file format and also supports PIC files that are compatible with other Micrografx products.

desk accessory In the Macintosh, a program that is always available from the Apple menu no matter what application is running. With System 7, all applications can be turned into desk accessories.

design heuristics The guidelines that can be followed when dividing a larger problem or program into smaller, more manageable modules.

design language A programming language whose statements and syntax facilitate its use in design work.

design phase The process of developing an information system based upon previously established system requirements.

design specifications Results of an analysis of information needs of a specific system within the organization. Included are specifications for input, processing, and output.

design walkthrough A overview of a system design by users, programmers, and consultants.

desk accessory (DA) In a graphical user interface, helpful utilities (e.g., calculator, notepad, thesaurus, paint program, or word processor) that you can open when you are in the middle of any program. Desk accessories are accessed by selecting them from a special pull-down menu. They are conveniences that can be activated wfrn needed and then either put away or moved to a small part of the display screen.

desk checking Manually testing the logic of a program.

DeskPaint/DeskDraw^{tm} An Apple Macintosh paint/draw application in desk accessory from. The application features a full set of paint and draw tools that allow creation or editing of black-and-white, gray scale, and color images, and work with macpaint, pict, and tiff file formats.

DESKPRO Compaq trade name for its PCs.

desktop (1) On-screen representation of a desktop. See Macintosh user interface and Windows. (2) Buzzword that is attached to almost any application traditionally performed on more expensive machines that are now on a personal computer, such as desktop publishing and desktop presentations.

desktop accessory Software that simulates an object normally found on an office desktop, such as a calculator, notepad and appointment calendar. It is typically RAM resident. See TSR.

desktop application See desktop accessory.

desktop computer Same as personal computer or microcomputer.

desktop mapping Using a desktop computer to perform digital mapping functions.

desktop media Integration of desktop presentations, desktop publishing and multimedia (coined by Apple).

desktop organizer See desktop accessory.

desktop presentations Creation of presentation materials on a personal computer, which includes charts, graphs and other graphics-oriented information. It implies a wide variety of special effects for both text and graphics that will produce output for use as handouts, overheads and slides as well as sequences that can be viewed on screen. Advanced systems generate animation and control multimedia devices.

desktop publishing Abbreviated "DTP" Using a personal computer to produce high-quality printed output for commercial printing. It requires a desktop publishing program, high-speed personal computer, full- or two-page display monitor and a laser printer.

The key feature of desktop publishing is its ability to merge and manage text with graphics and display it on screen WYSIWYG style. The program can flow text around graphic objects in a variety of ways.

Text and graphics may be created in the DTP program, but very few of them have full-featured word processing and graphics capability. Usually, the creation of the work is done in word processing, CAD, drawing and paint programs and then copied into the publishing system. DTP programs accept common file formats directly.

DTP programs provide the ultimate in page layout capabilities, including a multitude of different type fonts, magazine style columns, rules and borders and page numbering in a variety of styles.

desktop publishing template An already prepared page layout stored on disk.

desktop video The creation and editing of video images on a computer.

DESQview Popular multitasking, windows environment for DOS from Quarterdeck Office Systems. It runs multiple DOS text and graphics programs in resizable windows. Calendar, notepad, calculator and communications utilities are also available. DESQview 386 for 386s and up includes the widely-used QEMM386 expanded memory manager and utilizes the virtual machine capability of the 386.

DESQview/X is a version of DESQview that runs DOS, Windows and X Window applications locally or remotely on other DESQvIew/X PCs or X workstations.

destination A device or address that receives the data during a data transfer operation.

destructive memory Memory that loses its content when it is read, requiring that the circuitry regenerate the bits after the read operation.

destructive operation A process of reading or writing data that erases the data that is read or that was stored previously in the receiving storage location.

destructive read The process of destroying the information in a location by reading the contents.

destructor In object-oriented programming, an operation that frees the state of an object and/or destroys the object itself.

detachable keyboard A keyboard not built into the same case as the video display or desk unit. Connects to the system with a cable and allows greater flexibility in positioning of the keyboard display.

detail A small section of a larger file or graphics picture.

detail diagram A diagram used in hipo to describe the specific function performed or data items used in a module.

detail file Same as transaction file.

detail printing An operation in which a line of printing occurs for each record read into the computer.

detail report A printed report in which each line usually corresponds to one input record that has been read.

detection The passive monitoring of an event for the purpose of discovering a problem.

developer A person who designs, writes, and tests software. Also called a programmer.

developer's toolkit Set of software routines used in programming to link an application program to a particular operating environment (graphical user interface, operating system, DBMS, etc.).

development cycle See system development cycle.

development system (1) Programming language and related components. It includes the compiler, text editor, debugger, function library and any other supporting programs that enable a programmer to write a program. (2) Computer and related software for developing applications.

development time The time used for debugging new programs of hardware.

development tool Any hardware or software that assists in the creation of electronic machines or software programs. See developer's toolkit.

device Electronic or electromechanical machine or component from a transistor to a disk drive. Device always refers to hardware.

device adapter Same as interface adapter. device address See address.

device cluster A group of terminals or other devices that share a communications controller.

deviccode An eight-bit code for a specific input or output device.

device control character Communications code that activates a function on a terminal. See ASCII chart (17-20).

device dependent Refers to programs that address specific hardware features and work with only one type of peripheral device. Contrast with device independent. See machine dependent.

device driver See driver.

device Independent Refers to programs that work with a variety of peripheral devices

The hardware-specific instructions are in some other program (operating system, DBMS, etc.). Contrast with device dependent. See machine independent.

device level (1) In circuit design, refers to working with individual transistors rather than complete circuits. (2) Refers to communicating directly with the hardware at a machine language level

device media control language The language used by the database administrator to-create the physical description of a database on a disk storage device.

device name Name assigned to a hardware device that represents its physical address. For example, LPT1 is a DOS device name for the parallel port.

device number A number assigned to a particular peripheral device, used to identify it in the computer.

DFX A common object format for CAD files from several CAD programs.

DGS Paint A professional PC-based program for painting, composition, image retouching, and image processing.

Dhrystones Benchmark program that tests a general mix of instructions. The results in Dhrystones per second are the number of times the program can be executed in one second. See Whetstones.

Diablo emulation Printer that accepts the same commands as the Diablo printer.

diacritical Small mark added to a letter that changes its pronunciation, such as the French cedilla (c).

diagnosis The process of isolating malfunctions in computing equipment and of detecting mistakes in programs and systems. See debug.

diagnostic board Expansion board with built-in diagnostic tests that reports results via its own readout. Some boards for PCs have their own POST system and can test a malfunctioning computer that does not boot.

diagnostic routine A routine designed to locate a malfunction in the central processing unit or a peripheral device.

diagnostic tracks Spare tracks on a disk used by the drive or controller for testing purposes.

diagnostics (1) Software routines that test hardware components (memory, keyboard, disks, etc.). In personal computers, they are often stored in ROM and activated upon startup. (2) Error messages in a programmer's source code that refer to statements or syntax that the compiler or assembler cannot understand.

diagram The schematic representation of a sequence of operations or routines. See flowchart.

dialect A particular version of a computer language. Usually a minor modification of sone base language like BASIC or Pascal, but because of vast differences in modifications it may be significantly different from other dialects of the same language.

dialog A question-and-answer session between a computer system and a human.

dial-up line Two-wire line as found in the dial-up network. Contrast with leased line.

dial-up network Switched telephone network regulated by government and administered by common carriers.

dialog box Small, on-screen window that is displayed in response to some request. It provides the options currently available to the user.

diazo film Film used to make microfilm or microfiche copies. It is exposed to the original film under ultraviolet light and is developed into identical copies. Copy color is typically blue, blue-black or purple.

DIB (Device Independent Bit map) See BMP. dichotomizing search See binary search.

dictionary program A spelling-check program, often used with word processing systems.

diddle To tamper with data.

die Formal term for the square of silicon containing an integrated circuit. The popular term is chip.

dielectric Insulator (glass, rubber, plastic, etc.). Dielectric materials can be made to hold an electrostatic charge, but current cannot flow through them.

DIF (1) (Data Interchange Format) Standard file format for spreadsheet and other data structured in row and column form. Originally developed for VisiCalc, DIF is now under Lotus' program that lets users build custom programs for online access to data. (3) (Document Interchange Format) File standard developed by the U.S. Navy in 1982. (4) (Dual In-line Flatpack) Type of urface mount DIP with pins extending horizontally outwatd.

difference The amount by which one quantity or number is greater or less than another.

Difference Engine Early calculator designed by Charles Babbage (18205) and subsidized by the British government. It used rods and wheels, which was tried before by other designers. Never completed, Babbage turned his attention to the Analytical Engine.

Differential Analyzer Analog computational evice built to solve differential equations by Vannevar Bush (MIT, 1930s). Less than a dozen were built, but they were effective in calculating ballistics tables in World War II. The machine took up an entire room and was programmed by changing camshaft-like gears with screwdriver and wrench.

differential configuration Use of wire pairs for each electrical signal for high immunity to noise and crosstalk. Contrast with single-ended configuration.

diffusion Semiconductor manufacturing process that infuses tiny quantities of impurities into a base material, such as silicon, to change its electrical characteristics.

digit Single character in a numbering system. In decimal, digits are 0 through 9. In binary, digits are 0 and 1.

digital (1) Traditionally, the use of numbers and comes from digit, or finger. Today, digital is synonymous with computer. (2) Digital. See Digital Equipment.

digital camera Video camera that records its images in digital form. Unlike traditional analog cameras that convert light intensities into infinitely variable signals, digital cameras convert light intensities into discrete numbers.

It breaks down the picture image into a fixed number of pixels (dots), tests each pixel for light intensity and converts the intensity into a number. In a color digital camera, three numbers are created, representing the amount of red, green and blue in each pixel.

digital channel Communications path that handles only digital signals. All voice and video signals have to be converted from analog to digital in order to be carried over a digital channel. Contrast with analog channel.

digital circuit Electronic circuit that accepts and processes binary data (on/oft) according to the rules of Boolean logic.

digital communications The transmission of information by coding it into discrete on/off electronic signals.

digital computer Computer that accepts and processes data that has been converted into binary numbers. All common computers are digital. Contrast with analog computer.

digital control The use of digital technology to maintain conditions in operating systems as close as possible to desired values despite changes in the operating environment.

Digital Darkrm Macintosh graphics editing program from Silicon Beach Software, Inc., for enhancing black & white photographs. Version 2.0 supports color overlays for colorizing gray scale images.

digital data Data in digital form. All data in the computer is in digital form.

Digital Equipment (Digital Equipment Corp.) Major computer manufacturer, commonly known as DEC or Digital. Founded in 1957 by Kenneth Olson, who still heads the company, it pioneered the minicomputer industry with its PDP series.

Its early success came from the scientific, process control and academic communities; however, after the VAX was announced in 1977, Digital gained a strong foothold in commercial data processing. The VAX evolved into a complete line from desktop to mainframe, using the same VMS operating system in all models and causing Digital to achieve substantial growth in the 1980s.

Over the years, Digital has been widely recognized for its high-quality systems. Its strategy for the 1990s and beyond is its powerful, RISC-based Alpha architecture introduced in 1992, which will evolve into a complete family of systems.

digital mapping Digitizing geographic information for a geographic information system (GIS).

digital monitor Video monitor that accepts a digital signal from the computer and converts it into analog signals to illuminate the screen. Common examples are MDA, CGA and BOA monitors. Contrast with analog monitor.

digital PADX See digital PBX.

Digital Paper Non-erasable storage material from ICI Electronics used for tape and disk archival storage. It uses a polyester film coated with a reflective layer on top of which is adhered a dye polymer layer that is sensitive to infrared light. A laser burns pits into the film as close as half a micron apart. Capacities are about one Gbyte on a 5.25" disk and 600 GBytes on a 2,400 foot tape reel.

digital PBX (digital Private Branch Exchange) Modern PBX that uses digital methods for switching in contrast to older PBXs that use analog methods.

digital plotter An output device that uses an ink pen (or pens) to draw graphs, line drawings, and other illustrations.

digital radio Microwave transmission of digital data via line of sight transmitters.

digital recording See magnetic tape & disk.

Digital Research (Digital Research, Inc., Monterey, CA) Software company founded in 1976 by Gary Kildall that spearheaded the microcomputer revolution with its CP/M operating system. DRI's products include the GEM windows environment, FlexOS realtime operating system and DR DOS, a DOS-compatible operating system with advanced features.

In 199-1, it was acquired by Novell, Inc., Provo, UT, makers of the widely-used NetWare operating systems.

digital signal Two electrical states that communicate a code in binary data (l's and 0's) the computer can understand. Each 1 or 0 is a bit, while eight bits equal a byte, a one character. The digital signal is converted by a modem into an analog signal (modulated) that may be transmitted over phone lines. Incoming analog signals detected by the modem are converted into digital signals (demodulated) the computer can understand.

digital signal processing Category of techniques that analyze signals from a wide range of sources, such as voice, weather satellites, earthquake monitors and nuclear tests. It converts the signals into digital data and analyzes it using various algorithms.

Once a signal has been reduced to numbers, its components can be isolated and analyzed more readily than in analog form. It is used in such fields as biomedicine, sonar, radar, seismology, speech and data communications.

digital signature Coded message that can be verified by the receiver as being sent by an authentic sender. See RSA and DSS (2).

digital speech Recorded speech broken into tiny units of sound. Each tiny unit has characteristics - such as pitch, loudness, and timbre - that can be represented by numbers, which become the digital code for speech.

digital-to-analog converter (D-A converter) Mechanical or electronic devices used to convert discrete digital numbers to continuous analog signals. Opposite of analog-to-digital converter.

digital tracer A special hinged arm that can be used to trace over drawings and graphs and that sends the information to the computer.

digital transmission The transmission of data as discrete impulses.

digitize To convert an image or signal into digital code for the computer. It includes scanning an image, tracing a picture on a graphics tablet or converting camera images into the computer. 3-D objects can also be digitized using specialised equipment. Sound, temperature and movement are also said to be digitized when they are converted into digital code.

digitize To register a visual image or real object in a format that can be processed by the computer. digitized data are read into the system with graphics input devices. Digitizing includes scanning an image, tracing a picture on a graphics tablet, and converting camera images into the computer.

digitized type Type stored in computer-readable form as a collection of dots or line elements.

digitizer A graphics input device that converts images into digital data that the computer can accept.

digitizer A graphics input device that converts images into digital data that the computer can accept.

digitizing The process of converting graphic representations, such as pictures and drawings, into digital data that can be processed by a computer system.

digitizing camera A camera coupled with a processor used for highly detailed images such as pictures or three-dimension 7? digital data.

digitizer tablet Graphics drawing tablet used for sketching new images or tracing old ones, selecting from menus or simply for moving the cursor around on the screen, all of which can be provided within a single program.

The user makes contact with the tablet with a pen-like or puck-like device called a cursor (mistakenly called a mouse), which is connected to the tablet by a wire. For sketching, the user draws with the tablet cursor and the screen cursor "draws" a corresponding image. When tracing an image on the tablet, a series of x-y coordinates (vector graphics) are created, either as a continuous stream of coordinates, or as end points.

Menu selection is accomplished by a tablet overlay or by a screen display. The tablet cursor selects an item by making contact with it on the overlay, or by controlling the screen cursor. See mouse.

digit place In positional notation, the site where a digit is located in a word representing a numeral. The decimal system has the units place, the tens place, and so on.

dimension One axis in an array. In programming, a dimension statement defines the array and sets up the number of elements within the dimensions.

dimensioning In CAD programs, the management and display of the measurements of an object. There are various dimensioning, or drafting, standards which determine such things as tolerances, sizes of arrowheads and orientation onthe paper.

dimmed command A command in a pull-down menu that is grayed. A dimmed command means that choice is not currently available to the user, perhaps because another function needs to be accomplished before that selection can be made.

dimmed icon A grayed-black icon, which indicates tat the object it represents, such as a disk, folder, or document on a disk, has either been opened or been ejected from the disk drive.

DIN Acronym for. Deutsche Industrie; Norm, the German industry standard.

DIN connector (Deutsches Institut für Normung - German Standards Institute) Plug and socket used to connect .a variety of devices; for example, the PC keyboard uses a five-pin DIN. DIN plugs look like an open metal can about a half inch in diameter with pins inside in a circular pattern.

dingbats Group of typesetting and desktop publishing symbols from International Typeface Corp. that include arrows, pointing hands, stars and circled numbers. They are formally called ITC Zapf Dingbats.

diode Electronic component that acts primarily as a one- way valve. As a discrete component or built into a chip, it is used in a variety of functions. It is a key element in changing AC into DC. They are used as temperature and light sensors and light emitters (LED5). In communications, they filter out analog and digital signals from carriers and modulate signals onto carriers. In digital logic, they are used as one-way valves and as switches similar to transistors.

diode transistor logic See dtl.

DIP (Dual In-line Package) Common rectangular chip housing with leads (pins) on both long sides. Tiny wires bond the chip to metal leads that wind their way down into spider-like feet that are inserted into a socket or are soldered onto the board.

DIP switch (Dual In-line Package switch) Set of tiny toggle switches built into a DIP, which is mounted directly on a circuit board. The tip of a pen or pencil is required to flip the switch on or off.

Dir (DIRectory) CP/M, DOS and OS/2 command that lists the file names on the disk. See DOS Dir.

direct access Ability to go directly to a specific storage location without having to go through what's in front of it. Memories (RAMs, ROMs, PROMs, etc.) and disks are the major direct access devices.

direct access method Technique for finding data on a disk by deriving its storage address from an identifying key in the record, such as account number. Using a formula, the account number is converted into a sector address.

direct access processing The same as direct processing and random processing. Contrast with sequential processing.

direct access storage device (DASD) A basic type of storage medium that allows information to be accessed by positioning the medium or accessing mechanism directly to the information required, thus permitting direct addressing of data locations.

direct address An address that specifies the storage location of an operand. Contrast with indirect address.

direct-connect modem Modem that connects to a telephone line without the use of an acoustic coupler.

direct conversion The method of converting from one system to another by ceasing to operate the old systern when the new one is implemented.

direct current The flow of electrons in one direction such as supplied by a battery.

direct data entry The entry of data directly into the computer through machine-readable source documents or though the use of on-line terminals.

direct distance dialling See ddd.

direct file organization The organization of records so each is individually accessible.

direct file processing Processing that allows the user to access a record directly by using a record key.

direct memory access (DMA) A method by which data can be transferred between peripheral devices and internal memory without intervention of the central processing unit.

directory Simulated file drawer on disk. Programs and data for each application are typically kept in a separate directory (spreadsheet, word processing, etc.). Directories create the illusion of compartments, but are actually indexes to the files which may be scattered all over the disk.

direct processing A technique of handling data in random order, without preliminary sorting, and utilizing files on direct access storage devices.

directory management Maintenance and control of directories on a hard disk. Usually refers to menuing software that is easier to use than entering commands.

directory tree Graphic representation of a hierarchical directory. See DOS Tree.

dirty power Non-uniform AC power (voltage fluctuations, noise and spikes), which comes from the electric utility or from electronic equipment in the office.

disable To turn off a function. Disabled means turned off, not broken. Contrast with enable.

disassembler A program that takes machine-language code and generates the assembler-language code from which the machine langauge was produced. See assembly language.

disc Alternate spelling for disk. Compact discs and videodiscs are spelled with the "c." Most computer disks are spelled with a

disclaimer A clause associated with many software products that states the vendor is not responsible for any business losses incurred due to the use of the product.

discrete Component or device that is separate and distinct and treated as a singular unit.

discrete component Elementary electronic device constructed as a single unit. Before integrated circuits (chips), all transistors, resistors and diodes were discrete. They are widely used in high-power applications and are still used on circuit boards intermingled with the chips.

discrete cosine transform Algorithm that converts data (pixels, waveforms, etc.) into sets of frequencies. The first frequencies in-the set are the most meaningful; the latter, the least. For compression, latter frequencies are stripped away based on allowable resolution loss.

discretionary hyphen User-designated place in a word for hyphenation. If the word goes over the margin, it will split in that location.

dish Saucer-shaped antenna that receives, or transmits and receives, signals from a satellite.

disk Direct access storage device See magnetic disk.

disk array Two or more disk drives combined in a single unit for increased capacity, speed and/or fault tolerant operation. See RAID.

disk access time The time required to locate a specific track on a disk. Also called seek time. Part of total access time.

disk buffer The area of a computer's memory set aside to hold information not yet written to disk.

disk based (1) Computer system that uses disks as its storage medium. (2) Application that retrieves data from the disk as required. Contrast with memory based.

disk cache See cache.

disk cartridge Removable disk module that contains a single hard disk platter or a floppy disk.

disk controller Circuit that transmits and retrieves signals to the disk drive. In a personal computer, it is an expansion board that plugs into an expansion slot in the bus. See hard disk specs.

disk controller card A peripheral circuit card that connects disk drives to a computer and controls their operation.

disk copying The process of transferring the entire contents of one disk to another.

disk crash See head crash.

disk directory A catalog. This is the computer's own record of where each file or program is stored on the disk. The directory usually takes up a few tracks at the beginning of a disk.

disk doctor A program that enables the user to investigate directly what is stored on a disk. The use of a disk doctor may be the only way of recovering valuable data following a disk crash.

disk drive Peripheral storage device that holds, spins, reads and writes magnetic or optical disks. It may be a receptacle for disk cartridges or disk packs, or it may contain non-removable disk platters like most personal computer hard disks.

disk dump Printout of disk contents without report formatting.

disk duplicator Device that -formats and makes identical copies of floppy disks for software distribution. Simple units contain two floppy disks and require manual loading, elaborate units have automatic loading and may also attach the labels.

disk emulator Solid state replication of a disk drive. Used frequently for nodes and terminals.

disk envelope A removable protective paper sleeve used when handling or storing a 5.25-inch diskette. Must be removed before inserting the diskette in a disk drive.

diskette A single magnetic disk on which data is recorded as magnetic spots. Available in both 3.5-inch and 5.25-inch formats. See magnetic disk.

diskette tray A container used to protect and store diskettes.

disk file A file that resides on a magnetic disk. An organized collection of data stored on a disk.

disk file Set of instructions or data that is recorded, catalogued and treated as a single unit on a disk. Source language programs, machine language programs, spreadsheet, data files, text documents, graphics files and batch files are examples.

disk format (1) Storage layout of a disk as determined by its physical medium and as initialized by a format program. For example,-a 5.25" 360KB floppy versus a 3.5" 1.44MB floppy. See also low-level format, high-level format and DOS format. (2) Format of a particular database, word processing or graphics file on disk.

disk jacket A permanent protective covering for a disk, usually made of plastic. The disk is never removed from the jacket, even when inserted in a disk drive.

disk library A special room that houses a file or disk packs under secure, environmentally controlled conditions, or a storage facility that houses a file of diskettes. –

disk management (1) Maintenance and control of a hard disk. Refers to a variety of utilities that provide format, copy, diagnostic, directory management and defragmenting functions. (2) Organization structure used for storing data on a disk. See access method and DOS FAT.

disk memory Same as disk storage. Memory is no longer used in reference to disks.

disk mirroring Recording of redundant data for fault tolerant operation. Data is written on two partitions of the same disk, on two separate disks within the same system or on two separate computer systems.

disk operating system See DOS.

disk pack Removable hard disk module used in mini and mainframe systems. It is made up of several hard disk platters mounted on a central spindle and is housed in a dust-free plastic container when offline.

disk partition The logical portion of a disk that provides an organization allowing smaller blocks of data to be handled more conveniently.

disk sector A sector corresponding to a block of a data storage area between two successive radials on the disk. The cutting of a disk into sectors is analogous to the way a pie would be sliced.

disk unit See magnetic disk unit.

disk striping Spreading data over multiple disk drives. Data is interleaved by bytes or by sectors across the drives.

disk unit Same as disk drive.

Diskcopy DOS and OS/2 utility used to copy entire floppy disks track by track. See DOS Diskcopy.

diskette Same as floppy disk.

diskless workstation Computer in a network that has no disk storage. All programs and data are retrieved from the network server.

DISOSS (DIStributed Office Support System) IBM mainframe centralized document distribution and filing application that runs under MVS. It allows fore- mail and the exchange of documents between a variety of IBM office devices, including word processors and PCs.

dispatcher Same as scheduler.

dispersed Intelligence Same as distributed intelligence. displacement Same as offset. See base/ displacement. display (1) To show text and graphics on a video or flat panel screen. (2) Screen or monitor.

display adapter Same as video display board.

display attribute See attribute.

display background The part of displayed graphic data that is not part of the image being processed and is not subject to change by the user. Used to highlight the image part of the display, called the display foreground.

display board Same as video display board. display card Same as video display board.

display composition In desktop publishing, lines of type that are in bold, ornamental, or contrasting typefaces; used to attract attention.

display console An input/output device consisting of a :‘ display screen and an input keyboard.

display cycle In computer graphics, the series of operations required to display an image.

display device See display screen and video display board.

display surface The medium upon which a visual representation of graphic-data is made, such as a visual display screen, printer paper, plotter paper, or film.

display terminal Terminal with a display screen. Same as terminal, video display unit, video display terminal, CRT, monitor and console.

display tolerance The measure of accuracy with which graphic data can be output.

display type Technology of the display, such as cathode ray tube (CR1). light-emitting diode (LED), and liquid crystal display (LCD).

display unit A device that provides a visual representation of data.

DisplayWrlte Full-featured IBM word processjng program for PCs that stems from the typewriter-oriented DisplayWriter word processing system first introduced in 1980.

disassembler Software that converts machine language back into assembly language. The resulting code is difficult to maintain as variables and routines are named generically (A001, A002, etc.).

distortion Any undesired change in the waveform of an electric signal passing through a circuit, including the transmission medium. In the design of any electronic circuit, one important problem is to modify the input signal in the required way without producing distortion beyond an acceptable degree.

distributed computing See distributed processing and parallel computing.

distributed data processing See distributed processing.

distributed database Database physically stored in two or more computer systems. Although geographically dispersed, a distributed database system manages and controls the entire database as a single collection of data. If redundant data is stored in separate databases due to performance requirements, updates to one set of data will automatically update the additional sets in a timely-and controlled manner.

distributed design An information structure that identifies the existence of independent operating units but recognizes the benefits of central coordination and control.

distributed file system Software that keeps track of files stored across multiple networks. Files are identified by name rather than location.

distributed function Distribution of processing functions throughout the organization.

distributed Information processing system A set of interacting computer systems of databases situated in different locations.

distributed intelligence Placing processing capability in terminals and other peripheral devices. Intelligent terminals handle screen layouts, data entry validation and other pre-processing steps. Intelligence placed into disk drives and other peripherals relieves the central computer from routine tasks.

distributed logic See distributed intelligence.

distributed network A network configuration in which all node pairs are connected either directly or by redundant paths through intermediate nodes.

distributed processing System of computers connected together by a communications network. The term is loosely used to refer to any computers with communications between them. However, in true distributed processing, each computer system is chosen to handie its local workload, and the network has been designed to support the system as a whole. Contrast with centralized processing and decentralized processing.

distributive sort A sort performed by separating the list into parts and then rearranging the parts in order.

disturbance Any irregular phenomenon that interferes with the interchange of intelligence during transmission of a signal. See noise.

dithering In computer graphics, the creation of additional colors and shades from an existing palette. In monochrome displays, shades of grays are created by varying the density and patterns of the dots. In color displays, colors and patterns are created by mixing and varying the dots of existing colors.

Dithering is used to create a wide variety of patterns for use as backgrounds, fills and shading, as well as for creating halftones for printing. It is also used in anti-aliasing.

divide overflow Program error in which a number is accidentally divided by zero or by a number that creates a result too large for the computer to handle.

division check A multiplication check in which a zero- balancing result is compared against the original dividend.

DL/1 (Data Language 1) Database language in IMS.

DLC (1) (Data Link Control) See data link and OSI. (2) (Data Link Control) Protocol used in IBM's Token Ring networks. (3) (Digital Loop Carrier) See loop carrier.

DEL See dynamic link library.

DMA (Direct Memory Access) Specialized circuitry or a dedicated microprocessor that transfers data from memory to memory without using the CPU. Although DMA may periodically steal cycles from the CPU, data is transferred much faster than using the CPU for every byte of transfer.

DME (Distributed Management Environment) See OSF. DML Abbreviation for Data Manipulation Language. DMPL (Digital Microprocessor Plotter Language) Vector graphics file format from Houston Instruments that was developed for plotters. Most plotters support the DMPL or HPGL standards.

DNA (Digital Network Architecture) Introduced in 1978, DNA defines Digital's protocols, formats and control of message exchange over a network. DECnet is the implementation of this architecture.

DNS (Domain Naming System) E-mail addressing system used in networks such as Internet and Bitnet.

DOA Abbreviation for dead on arrival. Used to describe a product that does not work when received from the manufacturer or supplier.

do loop High-level programming language structure that repeats instructions based on the results of a comparison. In a DO WHILE loop, the instructions within the loop are performed if the comparison is true. In a DO UNTIL loop, the instructions are bypassed if the comparison is true.

docking station Base station for a laptop that includes a power supply and expansion slots as well as monitor and keyboard connectors.

docs Short for "documents" or "documentation."

document (1) Any paper form that has been filled in. (2) Word processing text file. (3) In the Macintosh, any text, data or graphics file that is created in the computer.

document handling Procedure for transporting and handling paper documents for data entry into scanning machines.

document mark In micrographics, a small optical blip on each frame on a roll of microfilm that is used to automatically count the frames.

document processing Processing text documents, such 'as in word processing, but also includes indexing methods for text retrieval based on document content.

documentation Narrative and graphical description of a system.

documentation aids Aids that help automate the documentation process, such as programs description write-ups, flowcharts, hipo, program runs, and pseudocode.

documentor A program designed to use data processing methods in the production and maintenance of program flowcharts, text material, and other types of tabular or graphic information.

document reader Any OCR or OMR equipment that reads a limited amount of information.

document retrieval The process of acquiring data from storage devices and, possibly, manipulating the data and subsequently preparing a report.

docuterm Word or phrase in a text document that is used to identify the contents of the document.

domain (1) In database management, all possible values contained in a particular field for every record in the file. (2) In communications, all the resources that are under control of a single computer system. (3) In magnetic storage devices, a group of molecules that makes up one bit. (4) In a hierarchy, a named group that has control over the groups under it, which may be domains themselves.

domain expert A human expert who contributes to the development of an expert system.

domain knowledge Knowledge of the application en- vironment.

dominant carrier Telecommunications services provider that has control over a large segment of a particular market.

dongle Same as hardware key.

door (1) In a BBS, a portal, or interface that lets an online user run an application stored in the BBS computer. (2) See drive door.

dopant Element diffused into pure silicon in order to alter its electrical characteristics.

dope vector A vector wherein an atom of a linked list describe the contents of the other atoms in the list.

doping Altering the electrical conductivity of a semiconductor material, such as silicon, by chemically combining it with foreign elements. It results in an excess of electrons (n-type) or a lack of electrons (p-type) in the silicon.

DOS (1) (Disk Operating System) Pronounced "dahss." Generic term for operating system. (2) (Disk Operating System) Single-user operating system for the PC, PS/i and PS/2 series from IBM. DOS is also called PC-DOS to distinguish it from MS-DOS, the version for non-IBM PCs. DOS and MS- DOS are developed by Microsoft, are almost identical, and both are referred to as DOS. IBM has participated in DOS development in varying degrees. See 'Operating Environment" in the PC definition.

DOS / Slashes are used to identify switches, or parameters, in a DOS command. They precede letters or numbers and their meaning is pertinent only to the command they are used with. See DOS backslash (\).

DOS % Percent signs are used in DOS batch files to define user input.

DOS. The single dot in a DOS command refers to all files in the current directory. For example, del . is the same as del *•*, which deletes all files.

DOS The double dots refer to the directory one level above the current directory. The command cd.. switches you to the higher directory. Double clicking on a [..] in a file menu does the same thing.

DOS 5.0 Major DOS upgrade introduced in June 1991 that includes a greatly enhanced DOS shell with task swapping, a utility for restoring deleted files and formatted disks, a full-screen text editor and online help. It uses less memory by loading drivers and part of itself into high memory, and it supports 2GB hard disks and 2.88MB floppies. DOS 5.0 includes Microsoft's QBasic language, which supersedes OW- BASIC in the MS-DOS version and accompanies BASICA in the IBM version. Following are new features in DOS 5.0: Doskey, Editor, EMM386.EXE, Loadhigh, Mirror, online help, Setver, Task Swapper, Undelete, Unformat, upgrading to 5.0

DOS Abort, Retry See DOS error messages.

DOS ANSI.SYS Driver used for screen control (cursor movement, screen clearing) and as a keyboard macro processor to assign commands to a function key or reassign awkwardly placed keys. Some applications require ANSI.SYS. See DOS CONFIG.SYS.

DOS Append External command that lets programs open data files as if they were in the current directory. It is used only with older programs that cannot access different directories.

DOS Assign External command used to reassign drives when programs work only with specific drives. The following example allows an install program that requires the floppy to be in drive A: to run from drive B:.

DOS Attrib External command that changes file at-tributes, which are settings in every DOS file. Settings are Read Only status, Archive, and System and Hidden.

DOS AUTOEXEC.BAT Special DOS batch file that is automatically executed whenever the computer is started or restarted. It must be stored in the root directory. Any DOS commands in AUTOEXEC.BAT will be executed like a normal DOS batch file.

DOS backslash (\) Backslashes are used to represent the root directory when it precedes the first directory of file name in a path. Used elsewhere in the path, it is a symbol that separates file and directory names. It is distinct from the slash (/).

DOS Backup/Restore External commands that let you back up your hard disk onto as many floppies as required. You can backup only those files which have been altered files from within subdirectories, add files, create a log, etc. Backup has the advantage of filling up disks completely. However, files backed up have to 'Restored' using another command.

DOS batch file File of DOS commands for "batch" processing. Each line of a batch file is a separate DOS command and is executed by DOS until the end of the file is reached. Batch files are text files and have a rudimentary 'language' or commands.

Batch Commands

cls Clear the screen

rem Remarks (program documentation) echo off Turn off display.

@echo off Turn off display (3.3 and up).

echo on Turn on display.

echo Display message; for example, echo Hello!!

call Call other batch file.

pause Stop (wait for keystroke).

Advanced Batch Commands

if not exist filename goto :line

if not stringlstring2 goto :line

if not errorlevel 0 goto :line

for %%vamame in (files) do command

%0 - Batch file name.

- %9 - Input variables.

%varname% - Variable used with Set.

DOS box DOS compatibility mode. The "box" is an OS! 2 or Windows window that is running a standard DOS application.

DOS Break Ctrl-C and Qtrl-Break are key commands that stop the current operation; however, certain functions such as disk I/O cannot normally be halted. Break is also a CONFIG.SYS setting that tests the keyboard more frequently for Ctrl-C and Ctrl-Break. Note that applications can be programmed to ignore Qrl-C and Ctrl-Break regardless of the Break setting.

DOS buffers See DOS CONFIG.SYS.

DOS cache See DOS SMARTDRV.SYS.

DOS Chdir Internal command that changes the current directory. CD is the abbreviated form. See DOS directories.

DOS Chkdsk External command that checks disk status, memory status, files and flags unidentifiable files. Improperly closed files (turning the computer off before saving) generates lost clusters, which are files that have lost their file name.

DOS CIs Internal command that clears the screen.

DOS combining files To combine text files, use the Copy command. For example, to combine the files FIRST and SECOND, creating a new file named THIRD, type:

copy first+second third

To append SECOND to the end of FIRST, type:

copy first+second

DOS command history See DOS Doskey.

DOS COMMAND.COM Command interpreter that displays the DOS prompt and accepts and executes your typed-in commands. If a command interpreter other than COMMAND.COM is used, it is specified with the Shell command (see DOS Shell).

DOS loads COMMAND.COM from the disk at startup. Part of COMMAND.COM is always resident in memory. The rest of it, or transient part, may be overwritten when a program is executed. When the program is done, the transient portion will have to be reloaded into memory. See DOS Sys.

DOS Comp External command that compares two files for identical content and reports up to 10 mismatches. See also DOS FC.

DOS comparing files See DOS FC and DOS Comp.

DOS Comspec DOS environment variable that holds the• path to COMMAND.COM. See DOS COMMAND.COM and DOS Set.

DOS CONFIG.SYS Configuration file that DOS looks for in the root directory upon startup. It is used to load drivers and change system settings. Adding a new type of peripheral to the computer usually requires installing the driver program to make it operate.

Commands	Purpose
DEVICE	Names a driver to be loaded.
FILES	Files open at one time (8-255). Default is 8, but this is often set to 20-40. Some apps open a lot of files.
BUFFERS	528-byte areas of RAM reserved for input and output (1-99). Default is usually 15, but this is often set to 20 or 30. The more buffers, the faster the I/O Ix switch in 4.x puts buffers in EMS.
LKSTDRIVE	Last drive letter (see DOS Subst). Look up DOS 5.0 Devicehigh for storing drivers in high memory in DOS 5.0.

Drivers	Purpose
ansi.sys	Screen and keyboard control.
display.sys	Supports code-page switching.
driver.sys	Identifies third & fourth floppy drives.
mouse.sys	Code-page support for printers.
printer.sys	Extended memory (XMS) manager
himem.sys	386 EMS manager.
emm386.exe	Quarterdeck's 386 EMS manager. RAM disk (extended or EMS memory).
ramdrive.sys	Disk cache (extended or EMS memory).

DOS Copy Internal command for making duplicate disk files. The command can be used to copy to/from floppies, floppies to hard disk, hard disk to floppy, directory to directory, copy and rename simultaneously, verify while copying, combine one text file to another and create a third, append the contents of one text file to another, etc. See related commands XCOPY, DISKCOPY, REPLACE and BACKUP.

DOS Copy con Internal command for creating a quick batch file. Copy Con works a line at a time. You can't go back and change lines, but you can Use backspace to delete characters on the same line.

DOS Ctty Internal command that redirects the keyboard and screen to the serial port.

DOS Date See DOS Time/Date.

DOS Debug External command that performs a variety of machine language functions. Debug is used to edit memory, executable files, input/output ports, assemble small programs and perform hex arithmetic.

DOS Del Internal command that removes a file from the disk. Tough deleted files can be undeleted with DOS 5.0, this has to be done before any other write activity.

DOS device names DOS reserved names for common input and output devices. They are: AUX, PRN, COM1-COM4, LPT1-LPT4, CON, NUL. These words cannot be used as filenames. See DOS redirection, DOS Sort and DOS Dir.

DOS device See DOS CONFIG.SYS.

DOS Dir Internal command for displaying the names of files within a single directory. It can be used alongwith a variety of switches to make listing more specific (specific files, only directories, print list, wide display, pause after every screenful, list files alphabetically, list in lowercase, etc.) A Dir list contains the following information: Drive name; Drive serial no.; Current directory name; a"." th represent the entire cunent directory and shows the creation date; a ".." to represent that the directory is attached to a higher level; and Name, extension, size, creation date/time of each file selected.

DOS directories Simulated file drawers on a disk. DOS directories are hierarchical in structure. The starting point is the root directory. A subdirectory is a directory that is subordinate to (below, or attached to) another directory. Since all directories are below the root directory, all directories are technically subdirectories. The two terms become intertwined. Directories are the same as files, with a name up to eight characters and an optional extension: of up to three. See DOS filenames. Directories are made with the MD command and removed with the RD command.

DOS disk cache See DOS SMARTDRV.SYS.

DOS Diskcomp External command that compares two floppy disks track by track and reports the side and tradc number if it finds a mismatch.

On one-drive compares, you'll be prompted to insert the source and target diskettes a few times.

DOS Diskcopy External command that makes an exact copy of a floppy disk. Disk types MUST BE THESAME. On one-drive copies, you will be prompted to insert the source and target diskettes a few times.

DOS Dos CONFIG.SYS setting in DOS 5.0 that allows part of DOS to be loaded into the HMA area (1024- 1088K). In order to do this, HIMEM.SYS or some other XMS driver must precede the Dos command in CONFIG.SYS. See DOS Loadhigh and DOS HIMEM.SYS.

DOS Doskey External command in DOS 5.0 that provides command history and macros (typed-in commands stored for later use). The command buffer (reserved space) is 512 bytes long unless otherwise specified.

Use Up and Down Arrow to move through command history, and press Page Up and Page Down for the oldest and most recent command. Doskey uses these additional key commands:

Key	**Function**
F7	Display command history
Alt-F7	Clear command history
Alt-FlO	Clear macros
F9	Recall command by number
Qrl <——>	Cursor previous/next word
Home/End	Cursor beginning/end line
Esc	Clear line

Ins Insert mode for this line

Fl, F3 and F6 work as usual. See DOS key commands.

DOS Dozen Twelve DOS commands that let you do almost everything.

The DOS Dozen

Format	Initialize a floppy
dir	List file names
del	Remve a file
rename	Change names
type	Display a text file
Xcopy	Copy file and directories
Copy	Copy file
md	Make directory
cd	Go to a directory
rd	Remove directory
chkdsk	Test for corrupted files
cls	Clear screen

DOS drive Identification DOS drives are identified with a letter and colon.

A:	First floppy
B:	Second floppy
C:	Main hard drive
D:	Second hard drive, second partition within the main hard disk or some other device such as a CD ROM drive.

Drive letters E: through Z: also used.

DOS DRIVERSYS Driver used to add newer devices (typically floppy disks) to older PCs that did not originally support them. It's also used to assign a second drive letter to a single drive to allow you to copy to and from the same drive, It will assign the highest drive letter to the new drive.

DOS Drlvparm CONFIG.SYS command that redefines the current settings for a device and maintains the same drive letter.

DOS Editor DOS 5.0 full-screen text editor for creating ASCII text files (batch files). DOS Editor is easy to use and help is online. Use the Arrow keys to move around. Press Alt-F for the File menu and select Exit when you are done.

DOS Edlin Text editor that comes with every version of DOS. It allows only one line to be edited at a time. In DOS 5.0, use the full-screen editor (see DOS Editor). Edlin can be used for small files.

DOS EMM386.EXE Memory manager for 386s and up that comes with DOS 5.0 and Windows 3.0. It converts extended memory into EMS memory and also allows programs to be stored in the UMA (area between 640K and 1M). It is activated with a statement in the CONFIG.SYS file. The HIMEM.SYS driver must also be activated before EMM386.EXE.

DOS environment Reserved area in DOS for holding values used by DOS and other applications. The values stored in this area are called "environment variables" and are created with the Set command (see DOS Set).

DOS Erase See DOS del.

DOS error messages There are dozens of error messages in DOS; however, the most common are cxplained below:

Not ready (error) reading drive I Abort, Retry, Ignore? (Fail?)

...means the drive door is left open, or the floppy disk is not in the drive. Either put the appropriate floppy disk in the drive or close the drive door (turn lever) and press R.

Not ready (error) writing device PRN

Abort, Retry, Ignore? (Fail?)

...means the printer is turned off or unavailable. Press A to cancel, or turn the printer oi and press R. You might also check the cable connection to the printer. General failure (error) reading drive X

Abort, Retry, Ignore? (Fail?)

...usually means that an unformatted floppy is being used. Press A to Abort, format the floppy and try again. You'll also get this if you try to read a high density disk in a low density drive. High density disks require high density drives.

Non-System disk or disk error

Replace and press any key when ready

.....usually means there's a non-bootable floppy in drive A. The computer looks for DOS on a floppy before it looks for DOS on the hard disk. If an ordinary floppy is in drive A at startup, it causes this error. Remove the disk and press any key.

Write protect error

....means that the floppy disk has been protected and data cannot be recorded on it. Either unprotect it or use another disk. See file protection.

Data error reading drive X

.....means that an area of the disk is unreadable. Press R to retry. Most likely, you'll have to press A to stop (abort). If the data or program is critical and there's no backup, use a utility program to try to reconstruct the damaged area.

Invalid Parameter

.....means DOS doesn't understand the command line. It indicates that a switch is used incorrectly. If you're typing path names, be sure to use a backslash (\), not a forward slash (,). The forward slash is used to enter parameters (see DOS switch).

Packed file is corrupt

See DOS Loadfix.

DOS Exit Internal command that returns control from DOS to the previous level. Many applications can "shell out" to DOS, letting you run DOS commands and then return to the application. Simply type exit to return.

DOS extender Software that is combined with a DOS application to allow it to run in extended memory (beyond 1MB). Some DOS extenders work with 286s and up, others require a 386. To gain access to extended memory, it runs the application in Protected Mode. When the application requests DOS services, the DOS extender either handles them itself or, with functions such as disk accesses, resets the machine to Real Mode, lets DOS service the request and then switches back into Protected Mode.

DOS extensions Names used to identify DOS file types. See extension and DOS file names.

DOS external commands Separate utility programs that come with DOS, such as Format, Diskcopy, XCopy, Tree, Backup and Restore, but is not resident within DOS, such as Copy and Dir. Contrast with DOS internal commands.

DOS Fastopen External command starting in DOS 3.3 that reopens hard disk files quickly. If a drive is specified with Fastopen, the locations of the files opened are stored in memory. When opened again within the same session, their exact location is known. Fastopen is put in the AUTOEXEC.BAT file with the number of files you want to hold in memory.

DOS FAT (DOS File Allocation Table) The part of the DOS and 0S12 file system that keeps track of where data is stored on disk. When the disk is high-level formatted, the FAT is recorded twice and contains a table with an entry for each disk cluster.

The directory list, which contains file ID (name, extension, date of last update...) points to the FAT entry where the file starts. If a file is larger than one cluster, that entry points to another entry and so on. If a cluster becomes damaged, its FAt' entry is marked and not used again.

DOS FC External command that compares two files for content. .EXE, .COM, .SYS, .OBJ, .LIB and .BIN files are compared byte for byte, otherwise, comparison is line by line.

DOS FCB (DOS File Control Block) Method of handling files in DOS 1.0. Applications still exist that remain compatible with 1.0 and use this method. See DOS Share.

DOS Fdlsk External command used to partition a hard disk after low-level formatting and before high-level formatting. To run Fdisk, boot the computer with a floppy in drive A that contains DOS as well as the Fdisk program. See DOS Format.

DOS file (1) Any computer file created under DOS. (2) ASCII text file. See DOS batch file.

DOS file names On a disk, every independent collection of instructions or data is a "file." Programs, databases, word processing documents, spreadsheet and graphics images are examples of files. All filesmust have a file name, and most files have an extension. Extensions are attached to the name with a period (no spaces in between).

The name can be from one to eight characters in length. The extension, if used, can be from one to three characters long.

All runnable programs in DOS have either a BAT, COM or EXE extension.

Valid characters in names and extensions are: A-Z, a-z, 0-9 ! @ # $ % & ( )" - { } ~

DOS files See DOS CONFIG.SYS.

DOS filters & pipes Filters are external commands that change data in some manner. The filters are:

FIND - Searches for text

SORT - Rearranges data in alpha order

MORE - Displays data a screenful at a time

Pipes let you direct the output of one command as input to another. The pipe symbol is a vertical bar (shift backslash key). Pipes are used with filters as follows. See DOS Find, DOS Sort and DOS Dir.

DOS Find External command used to search for a particular string of text in a text file. Find is case sensitive. See DOS filters & pipes.

DOS Format File structure used by DOS to keep track of data on a disk. All disks must be formatted (initialized) before use. This process creates the sectors on the disk (low-level format) that are later filled with data and also generates the tables that DOS uses (high-level format) to keep track of the data.

Hard disks are regularly formatted at the factory, but floppies are usually not. The Format external command creates both low- and high-level format on floppies, but only a high-level format on hard disks.

A hard disk format requires:

1. Low-level format

2. Create partitions (Fdisk)

3. High-level format (Format)

The low-level format is performed by a utility program that comes from the disk manufacturer or other software provider. It is also often contained in the BIOS of the disk controller card.

Fdisk is an external command that creates partitions, or "logical drives" on the hard disk. See DOS Fdisk.

The final step is to run Format for each logical drive (C:, D:, etc.). This step prepares the root directory, FAT tables and records startup data in the boot sector.

DOS hidden file DOS file with a status that prevents it from being altered, erased or normally recognized. DOS system files are all hidden files. See DOS Attrib.

DOS high memory Area between 640K and 1024K reserved for system use. Also may refer to the area between 1024K and 1088K (HMA). See PC memory map.

DOS HIMEM.SYS Extended memory (XMS) driver included with DOS 5.0 and Windows 3.0. HIMEM.SYS must be activated in CONFIG.SYS in order to load DOS into the HMA, to use extended memory for RAM disks and disk caches and to use EMM386.EXE to turn extended memory into EMS memory. See DOS Dos and DOS EMM386.EXE.

DOS history See DOS Doskey.

DOS Installing from drive B See DOS Assign.

DOS Internal command Command capability within DOS (COMMAND.COM) at all times, such as Dir, Copy, Del, Ren, Type and CIs. Contrast with DOS external command.

DOS Join External command that assigns a drive to a directory.

DOS key commands The following keyboard keys can be used:

Ctrl-Alt-Del	Reset Computer
Qrl-C or	
Ctrl-Break	Cancel operation

Ctrl-S	Stop scrolling
Ctrl-P	Print what's displayed (on/off)
Shift-PrtSc	Print current screen
Fl or —>	Redisplay last DOS entry a character at a time
F3	Redisplay last DOS entry
F6 Enter or	
Ctrl-Z (end-of-file character)	
Alt-Digit	Enter ASCII character by value (use numeric keypad)

DOS Label External command that names a disk (volume label). The name can be up to 11 characters long, and it can contain spaces.

DOS Lastdrlve Used in the CONFIG.SYS file, it specifies the maximum number of drives that can be accessed.

DOS Loadflx External command in DOS 5.0 that loads a program beyond the first 64K of RAM, solving aproblem with some earlier programs. With DOS 5.0, part of DOS can be loaded into high memory, thus freeing up more lower memory. Some programs cannot run in this lower RAM and generate a "Packed file corrupt" error. "Packed" refers to an older method for compressing EXE files, and this method had a bug in it that prevents it from running in lower RAM.

DOS Loadhlgh Internal command in DOS 5.0 that loads a program into the UMA (upper memory area: 640K- 1M) in 386s and up. It requires that the HIMEM.SYS and EMM386.EXE memory managers be loaded and the dosumb command be present.

If you have programs that need expanded memory (EMS), the following three lines in CONFIG.SYS are required to use Loadhigh. The RAM parameter informs EMM386 to manage both the UMA and expanded memory. See DOS Dos and DOS Mem.

DOS Mem External command starting with DOS 4.0 that displays the amount of memory currently used and free.

DOS memory manager Software that manages extended memory and expanded memory (EMS) in a DOS PC. By analyzing the PC's current configuration and using a variety of techniques, including relocating BIOS routines to extended and EMS memory, it allows TSRs and drivers to be moved out of the lower 640K and into the upper memory area (UMA). In 386s and up, it turns extended memory into EMS memory and may be able to automatically allocate both kinds of memory on demand. See memory allocation, EMS, XMS, VCPI and DPMI.

DOS Mirror External command in DOS 5.0 that tracks deletions and records disk information for the Undelete and Unformat commands. If you run Mirror routinely, for example, in your AUTOEXEC.BAT file, you will be able to undelete large numbers of files and uformat your disks. Mirror takes up 6.4K of RAM and creates a PCTRACKR.DEL file in the root directory of each drive monitored. It can also be used to save partition information so that if the disk partition data becomes corrupted, the Unformat command can use PARThSAV. FIL to restore it.

DOS Mkdir Internal command that makes a new directory. MD is the abbreviated form. See DOS directories.

DOS Mode External command that allows changes to a variety of settings. Eg. set the serial port for communications, set the serial port for the printer, redirect the printer port, change keyboard speed, to change to 40-column or 80 column modes and other display modes supported by your display card.

DOS online help As of DOS 5.0, online help is available from the DOS prompt. It èan be accessed by typing:

help <command> or <command> /?

DOS Path Internal command that sets up a search path to one or more directories. If DOS can't find a program in the current directory, it looks in the other directories mentioned in the path. See DOS AUTOEXEC.BAT.

DOS pipes See DOS filters & pipes.

DOS Print External command that prints text files or pre- formatted word processing files in the background allowing you to continue work on something else. Files can be placed in a queue and wildcards can also be used. For printing text from the screen, Type command, Shift-Print and Ctrl-P can also be used.

DOS Prompt Message DOS displays when ready to accept user input. The default prompt (C>, D>...) displays the current drive and doesn't say which directory you're in. Since this can be changed, PCs are usually configured with the following line in the AUTOEXEC.BAT file: prompt pg.

Prompt

Code	Display
$p	Current drive/directory
$g	">"
$1	"<"
$b	"I"
$$	"$"
$n	Default drive
$t	Time
$d	Date
$v	DOS version
$-	Go to next line

DOS RAM disks RAM disks simulate a diskdrive in memory and provide fast retrieval of programs and data. If operations are disk intensive, they can be speeded up considerably by using RAM disks; for example, copying files within a RAM disk is almost instantaneous. RAM disk contents are lost if the power fails or the computer is turned off. RAM disks take on the next available drive letter. RAM disks are activated by adding a line in CONFIG.SYS.

DOS RAMD1UVE.SYS See DOS RAM disks.

DOS redfrectlon Redirecting keyboard input and scren output (see DOS Mode to redirect the printer port). Normally, DOS gets input from the keyboard and displays output on screen. However, you can redirect input from the keyboard to another file and redirect output from the screen to the printer or a disk file. The symbols are:

< Redirect input

> Redirect output to a new file

>> Redirect output to an existing file

Redirection can be used with the Pipe command, which funnels output of one command into another. See DOS Sort.

DOS Rename Internal command that changes the name of one file at a time.

DOS Replace External command (DOS 3.3 and up) that copies files that have been updated. The /u checks time and date and copies only files from the source directory that are newer than the files in the target directory.

DOS Rnidir Internal command that removes a directory. RD is the abbreviated form. Directories must be empty first, and the command must be entered from the previous level. See DOS directories.

DOS root First directory on a disk.

DOS Set Internal command that sets environment variables, which are stored values used by DOS and certain applications.

DOS Selver External command in DOS 5.0 that updates a version table containing names of programs and the DOS version number they need to run under. Programs may test version numbers and function differently as a result (all DOS's are not the same), but some programs did not plan on 5 as a future number. This command fools them into getting the version number they need.

DOS Share External command that provides file sharing and file locking in a network environment.

DOS shell Shells provide the user interface in DOS, or the way you interact with the system. cOMMAND.COM is the program that provides the command-driven user interface described in this tutorial. Other shells can be substituted for COMMAND.COM, by adding the Shell command in the Config.sys file; for example:

shellxyzmenu.com

DOS 5.0 comes with a completely revised interface, and the DOSSHELL.COM file loads it. Run it by typing:

dosshell /t text (character) mode

dosshell /g graphics mode

dosshell /bw black & white (laptops)

DOS SMARTDRV.SYS Disk cache software included with DOS 4.0 and up. The driver is loaded from CONFIG.SYS, and its default setting uses 256K of extended memory. In order to use extended or expanded (EMS) memory for your disk cache, you must load the extended memory or EMS driver from CONFIG.SYS before loading SMARTDRV.SYS. See DOS HIMEM.SYS, DOS EMM386.EXE and cache.

DOS Sort External command that sorts a text file or Dir list into alphabetical order. Lines in the text files must be uniform and columns (fields) must line up. You can sort Dir lists by file characteristics. Use the /+ switch to begin the sort on other than column one of the line:

dir sort /+10 by extension

dir sort /+14 by file size

dir sort 1+23 by month

dir sort /+29 by year

This list can be written to another file, printed out or appended to an already existing file.

DOS Subst External command that creates a virtual drive and provides a shortcut for referencing long path names. See DOS Lastdrive.

DOS switch Code that modifies a command. DOS switches use a forward slash (not backslash) followed by som letter, digit or code.

DOS Sys External command that transfers hidden DOS system files. DOS is made up of IBMBIO. COM and IBMDOS.COM or IO.SYS and MSDOS.SYS hidden system files along with COMMAND.COM.

DOS Sys files DOS extension used with driver programs. See DOS CONFIG.SYS.

DOS system file DOS file that contains the fundamental part of DOS (the kernel). See DOS Sys.

DOS Task Swapper As of DOS 5.0, you can run multiple applications and switch between them. This is done through DOSSHELL. But this is not the same as multi-tasking where several programs can RUN simultaneously. Neither can you cut-and-paste between programs.

DOS text file Text file that does not contain any proprietary coding schemes. Batch files and source language programs are examples. They may contain only ASCII characters and have a CRILF (carriage return/line feed) code at the end of each line. Text files are read by text editors as well as word processors with "ASCII" or "text" input options.

DOS Time/Date Internal commands that set the system time and date and update the internal battery-powered clock. Versions previous to 3.3 do not set the internal clock.

DOS Tree External command that displays a list of the subdirectories in the current directory.

DOS Type Internal command that displays the contents of text files. Output can be redirected to a printer also.

DOS Undelete Prior to DOS 5.0, bringing a file back that has just been deleted requires an undelete utility such as found in the Norton Utilities or PC Tools. DOS 5.0 provides its own undelete utility. To recover a deleted file, you must not write anything else on the disk before using the undelete program.

DOS Unformat External command in DOS 5.0 that restores a formatted disk to its previous contents. It works best when used in conjunction with the Mirror command (see DOS Mirror).

DOS upper memory See UMA and UMB.

DOS/V Japanese version of DOS that supports two-byte- long characters for handling the Kanji character set. It can switch between English and Japanese and is geared for 286s and up with VGA graphics.

DOS VDISK.SYS See DOS RAM disks.

DOS Ver Internal command that displays the DOS version.

DOS Verify Internal command that tests each write operation by reading it back.

DOS versions Like most software, DOS improves with age:

Version	Major new features

1.0 1981	8-sector 160KB floppy (SS)
1.05	Bug fix
1.1 1982	8-sector 320KB floppy (DS)
2.0 1983	1OM hard disk, 9-sector 360KB floppy, directories, more batch commands
2.1 1983	PCjr cartridge support and bug fixes
3.0 1984	20MB hard disk, 1.2MB floppy, VDISK, PATH, new commands
3.1 1985	Network support, bug fixes
3.2 1986	720KB floppy, new commands
3.3 1987	1.44MB floppy, FDISK, XCOPY
4.0 1988	Menu and mouse support (DOS shell), improved commands, EMS support, 512MB hard disks
4.01 1988	Bug fix
5.0 1991	Major upgrade: new DOS shell, ability to use high memory, task swapping, online help, new text editor, 2GB harddisks, 2.88MB floppies, enhanced commands
6.0 1993	New features like AntiVirus, MemMaker, Interlink, Power, Smartdrive, Deframenter etc.
6.22 1994	Bugs fixed

DOS Vol Internal command that displays the name of the current drive (volume).

DOS/VSE See VSE.

DOS wild cards Wild cards are symbols that let you reference groups of related files. As in card games, wild cards take on any value. DOS wild cards are the '*" and"?." The asterisk takes the value of any number of characters. The question mark matches any single character. The dot is a shortcut for also.

DOS Xcopy External command starting with DOS 3.2 that copies files and subdirectories. Unlike the COPY command, it can copy files in subdirectories also, making the appropriate subdirectories as it copies, it can also be used as a backup command (along with the ATI'RIB command) to copy only files with their attribute set or those which have ben modified after a particular date. It does not however, copy hidden and system files with DOS 5.0.

**DOS ** See DOS backslash. Dosshell See DOS shell.

dot (1) Tiny round, rectangular or square spot that is one element in a matrix, which is used to display or print a graphics or text image. See dot matrix. (2) A period; for example, file dot extn is the same as file.extn.

dot addressable Ability to program each individual dot on a video display, dot matrix printer or laser printer.

dot chart Same as scatter diagram.

dot gain Increase in size of each dot of ink when printed due to temperature, ink and paper type.

dot matrix Pattern of dots that form character and graphic images on video screens and printers. Display screens use a matrix (rows and columns) of dots just like TVs. Serial printers use one or two columns of dot hammers that are moved across the paper. Laser printers "paint" dots of light a line at a time onto a light-sensitWe photugtaphic dtum. The mote dots per square inch, the higher the resolution of the characters and graphics.

dot matrix printer Printer that forms images out of dots. The common desktop dot matrix printer uses one or two columns of dot hammers that are moved serially across the paper. The more dot hammers used, the higher the resolution of the printed image. 24-pin dot matrix printers produce almost typewriter-like output.

dot pitch Distance between a one pixel and another monitor (typically from .28 to .51mm; large presentation monitors may go up to 1.0mm). The smaller the dot pitch, the crisper the image. A .28 dot pitch means dots are 28/lOOths of a millimeter apart. A dot pitch of .31 or less provides a sharp image, especially on text.

dots per Inch (1) A linear measure of the number of dots a printer can print in an inch. For example, a 300 dpi printer can print up to 300 dots for each horizontal or vertical inch on the paper. (2) A measure of screen resolution that counts the dots that the device can produce per linear inch.

double buffering Programming technique that uses two buffers to speed up a computer that can overlap I/O with processing. For example, data in one buffer is being processed while the next set of data is read into the second buffer.

double click To press the mouse button twice in rapid succession.

double density Having twice the storage capacity of a normal (single-density) disk or tape. In IBM-compatible microcomputers, a double-density 5.25-inch disk has a capacity of 360K bytes, while a double- density 3.5-inch disk has a capacity of 720K bytes.

double density disk Floppy disk with twice the capacity of the prior format. It originally meant high den-sity; now it means low density. The 5.25" 360KB and 3.5" 720KB floppies are examples.

double dots See DOS..

double precision Using two computerwords instead of one to hold a number used for calculations, thus allowing twice as large a number for more arithmetic precision. Contrast with single precision.

double quote Another name for the quote mark (").

double scan CGA Hardware circuit that improves CGA resolution.

double sided disk Floppy disk that is recorded on both of its sides. This means all disks now but previously there were single sided disks.

double strike Printing a character twice in order to darken the image.

doublestriking See overstriking. double twist Same as supertwist.

double word An entry of storage that is two words in length.

doubly linked list A list in which each atom contains one pointer that relates to the successor atom.

do until One of the variations of the primitive loop construct of structured programming.

do while A variation of the primitive loop construct of structured programming.

Dow Jones Information Service A computer database containing current information on stock prices and other financial news. It can be accessed by subscribers with microcomputers and modems.

down Refers to a computer that fails to operate due to hardware or software failure. A communications line is down when it is unable to transfer data.

down-line processor A processor at or near the terminal point in a data communications network that facilitates the transmission of data.

downlink Communications channel from a satellite to an earth station. Contrast with uplink.

download To transmit a file from one computer to another. When conducting the session, download means receive, upload means transmit. It also implies sending a block of data rather than interacting in a conversational mode.

downloadable font Same as soft font.

downsizing Converting mainframe and mini-based systems to personal computer LANs.

downtime Time during which a computer is not functioning due to hardware or system software failure.

downward compatible Also called backward compatible. Refers to smaller or earlier models of a computer system that can run the same software as larger or newer models. Contrast with upward compatible.

DP See data processing and dot pitch.

dpi (Dots Per Inch) Measurement of printer resolution. A 300 dpi printer means 90,000 dots are printable in one square inch (300x300).

DPMI (DOS Protected Mode Interface) DOS extender specification for 286s and up that allows DOS extended programs to cooperatively run under Windows 3.x. Developed by Microsoft, it keeps a DOS-extended application from crashing the computer and usurping Windows' control.

DPSK (Differential Phase Shift Keying) Common form of phase modulation used in modems. It does not require complex demodulation circuitry and is not susceptible to random phase changes in the transmitted waveform. Contrast with FSK.

DR DOS DOS-compatible operating system from Digital Research that is noted for its advanced features and ease of use. Version 5.0 includes a smart install program, built-in help, password protection, disk cache, serial port file transfer, the ability to store itself and drivers in high memory and an optional graphical interface. Version 6.0 includes automatic file compression that doubles hard disk capacity.

Draflx 2-D and 3-D CAD packages for PCs and Atari STs from Foresight Resources Corp. It features professional functions and a unique user interface that provides constant on-screen information during drawing.

draft mode Highest-speed, lowest-quality printing mode.

draft quality A measure of quality for printed output. Usually refers to the result of top-speed printing and therefore not the most precisely defined or fully filed- in characters. Considered acceptable for working copies but not final work. Contrast with letter quality.

drag To move an object on screen in which its complete movement is visible from starting location to destination. The movement may be activated with a stylus, mouse or keyboard keys.

drag & drop Ability to execute a function graphically without typing in a command. For example, in the Macintosh, selecting a floppy disk icon and dragging it onto the trashcan icon causes the floppy to be ejected.

drain Output (receiving) side of the bridge in a field effect transistor. When the gate is charged, current flows from the source to the drain. Same as collector in a bipolar transistor.

DRAM See dynamic RAM.

DRAW (Direct Read After Write) Reading data immediately after it has been written to check for recording errors.

drawing The process of creating a graphic image with an object- oriented drawing program.

drawing program Graphics software that allows the user to design and illustrate products and objects. All elements of the graphic object can be isolated and manipulated individually.

Drawing programs and CAD programs are similar; however, drawing programs usually provide a large number of special effects for fancy illustrations, while CAD programs provide precise dimensioning and positioning of each graphic element in order that the objects can be transferred to other systems for engineering analysis and manufacturing. Contrast with paint program.

DrawPerfect A drawing program for IBM-compatible microcomputers. This charting, drawing, and presentation program provides 256 colors. It creates 2-D bar, pie, and graph charts.

DRDBMS (Distributed Relational DBMS) Relational DBMS that manages distributed databases. See distributed database.

Dr. Halo A print program for IBM-compatible microcomputers.

DRI See Digital Research.

dribbleware Software that is publicly displayed and previewed well in advance of its actual release. Dribbleware is one stage beyond vaporware.

drift Change in frequency or time synchronization of a signal that occurs slowly.

drill-and-practice program Teaching software that reinforces old lessons.

drill down To move from summary information to the detailed data that created it.

drive (1) Electromechanical device that spins disks and tapes at a specified speed. Also refers to the entire peripheral unit such as disk drive or tape drive. (2) To provide power and signals to a device. For example, "this control unit can drive up to 15 terminals."

drive bay Slot for a disk drive in a computer cabinet.

drive door Panel, gate or lever used to lock a disk in a disk drive. In a 5.25" floppy drive, the drive dooi is the lever that is turned down over the slot after inserting the disk.

drive number The naming convention for disk drives. For example, the drives in a two-drive Apple Macintosh system are 0 and 1; in a two-drive IBM- compatible microcomputer system, the drives are A and B.

driver (1) Also.called a device driver, a program routine that links a peripheral device or internal function to the operating system. It contains the precise machine language necessary to activate all device functions and includes detailed knowledge of its characteristics, such as sectors per track or the number af pixels of screen resolution.

Basic drivers come with the operating system, and drivers are added when new peripheral devices are installed. For example, if you add a mouse or CD ROM player to your personal computer, you have to install the appropriate driver so that the operating system knows how to handle it.

In the DOS world, applications provide their own screen and printer drivers in order to provide complete control over the display and printing of a document.

Memory managers, RAM disks and disk caches are also activated by drivers. See DOS CONFIG.SYS for list of DOS drivers. (2) Device that provides signals or electrical current to activate a transmission line or display screen. See line driver.

DRO Abbreviation for destructive read out.

drop (1) In a network, the remote terminal location. (2) The distance between top and bottom of a sheet of computer stationery, measured in millimeters or inches.

drop cap In typography, a large first letter that drops below the first line.

drop dead halt A halt from which there is no recovery. drop-down menu See pull-down menu.

drop In Extraneous bit on a magnetic medium that was not intentionally written, due to a surface defect or recording malfunction.

drop out (1) On magnetic media, a bit that has lost its strength due to a surface defect or recording malfunction. (2) In data transmission, a momentary loss of signal that is due to system malfunction or excessive noise.

drop shadow A shadow placed behind an image, slightly off-set horizontally and vertically, that creates the illusion that the topmost image has been lifted off the surface of the page.

drouple (Data gROUPIE) Person who likes to spend time in the company of programmers and data processing professionals.

drum See magnetic drum.

drum plotter Graphics plotter that wraps the paper around a drum. The drum turns to produce one direction of the plot, the pen moves to provide the other.

drum printer Line printer that uses formed character images around a cylindrical drum as its printing mechanism. There is a band of characters for each print position. When the desired character for the selected print position has rotated around to the hammer line, the hammer hits the paper from behind and pushes it into the ribbon and onto the character.

dry plasma etching Method for inscribing a pattern on a wafer by shooting hot ions through a mask to evaporate the silicon dioxide insulation layer. Dry plasma etching replaces the wet processing method that uses film and acid for developing the pattern.

dry run A program-checking technique of examining the logic and coding of a program from an algorithm and written instructions and recording the results of each step of the operation before running the program on the computer.

drystone See Dhrystone.

DS/DD (Double Sided/Double Density) Refers to floppy disks, such as the 5.25 360KB PC format and 3.5' 720KB PC and 800KB Mac formats.

DS/HD (Double Sided/High Density) Refers to floppy disks, such as the 5.25" 1.2MB PC format and 3.5" 1.44MB PC and Mac formats.

DSA (1) (Directory Systems Agent) X.500 routine that looks up the location of a message recipient. It accepts requests from the Directory User Agent counterpart in the workstation. (2) (Digital Storage Architecture) Disk controller standard from Digital. (3) (Digital Signal Analyzer) Tektronix oscilloscope that samples high-frequency signals.

DSL Abbreviation for dynamic simulation language. DSP See digital signal processing.

DSR (Data Set Ready) RS-232 signal sent from the modem to the or terminal indicating that it is able to aaxØ Coiitrast with DTR.

DSS (Decision Support System) In formation and planning system that provides the ability to interrogate computers on an ad hoc basis, analyze information and predict the impact of decisions before they are made.

DBMSs let you select data and derive information for reporting and analysis. Spreadsheet and modelling programs provide both analysis and 'what if?" planning. However, any single application that supports decision making is not a DSS. A DSS is a cohesive and integrated set of programs that share data and information. A DSS might also retrieve industry data from external sources that can be compared and used for historical and statistical purposes.

An integrated DSS directly impacts management's decision-making process and can be a very cost- beneficial computer application. See EIS.

DSTN (Double SuperTwisted Nematic) LCD display that uses an extra display layer (compensating layer) between the main display and the rear polarizer, resulting in mi almost-pure black and white display with little color tinge.

DSU/CSU (Data Service Unit/Channel Service Unit) Communications device that connects an inhouse line to an external digital circuit (Ti, DDS...). The DSU converts data into the required format, while the CSU terminates the line, provides signal regeneration and remote testing.

DTE (Data Terminating Equipment) Communications device that is the source or destination of signals on a network. It is typically a terminal or computer. Contrast with DCE.

DTL Abbreviation for diode transistor logic, microelectronic logic based on connections between semiconductor diodes and the transistor.

DTP See desktop publishing.

DTR (Data Terminal Ready) RS-232 signal sent from the computer or terminal to the modem indicating that it is able to accept data. Contrast with DSR.

DTS (1) (Digital Termination Service) Microwave- based, line-of-sight communications provided directly to the end user. (2) (DeskTop Server) Motorola 68000-based network server from Banyan.

dual boot Computer that can be started with either one of two different operating systems.

dual channel controller A controller that enables reading from and writing to a device to occur simultaneously.

dual density (1) Pertaining to tapes or disks on which data is densely recorded. (2) A floppy disk with double-sided recording capability.

dual disk drive A floppy disk system that contains two disk drives, providing an increased storage capacity.

dual In-line package See DIP.

dual intensity The ability of a terminal or printer to produce characters in regular as well as highlighted or bold formats.

dual processors (1) Two central processing units within a computer system that can function simultaneously. (2) computers that use two microprocessor. Dual processor provide faster and more efficient processing. The main objective is to relieve the main processor of the task of memory management, graphics displays, and, sometimes, advanced mathematical functions.

dual-sided disk drives Disk drivers that use two read! write head to store and retrieve data on both the top;and bottom sides of a disk.

dual Y-axls graph In presentation graphics, a graph that uses two Y-axes with comparing two data series with different measurement scales. Useful when comparing two different data series that must be measured with two different values axes.

dumb terminal Display terminal without processing capability. It is entirely dependent on the main computer for processing. Contrast with smart terminal and intelligent terminal.

dummy Pertaining to an artificial argument, instruction, address, or record of data inserted solely to fulfil prescribed conditions.

dummy argument Variables, used as function arguments, that do not have any values.

dummy instruction (1) An artificial instruction or address inserted in a list to serve a purpose other than its execution as an instruction. (2) An instruction in a routine that, in itself, does not perform any functions. Often used to provide a point at which to terminate a program loop.

dummy module A selection of a module with entry and exit, but no actual processing. Particularly useful in top-clown testing when subordinate subfunctions are not ready for integration.

dump To print the contents of memory, disk.or tape without any report formatting. See memory dump.

dumping Copying all or part of the contents of a storage unit, usually from the computer's internal storage, into an auxiliary storage unit or onto a p1inter.

duplex channel See full-duplex.

duplexed system Two systems that are functionally identical. They both may perform the same functions, or one may be standby, ready to take over if the other fails.

duplexing The use of duplicate computers, peripheral equipment, or circuity so that, in the event of a component failure, an alternate component can enable the system to continue.

duplex printing Printing a document on both sides of the sheet, so that the verso (left) and recto (right) pages face each other after the document is bound.

duplicate To copy so that the result remains in the same physical form as the source, such as to make a new diskette with the same information and in the same format as an original diskette. Contrast with copy.

duplicate keys Identical key data in a file. Primary keys, such as account number cannot be duplicated, since no two customers or employees should be assigned the same number. Secondary keys, such as date, product and city, may be duplicated in the file or database.

duplication check A check requiring that the results of two independent performances of the same operation be identical. May be made concurrently on duplicate equipment or at different times on the same equipment.

duration The amount of working time it takes to compete a task.

dust cover A plastic cover used to protect microcomputers, disk units, terminals, printers, and so on from one of their worst enemies.

DVI (Digital Video Interactive) Intel compression technique for data, audio and full-motion video. On a CD ROM, it provides up to 72 minutes of full-screen video, 2½ hours ofhalf-screen video, 40,000 medium- resolution or 7,000 high-resolution images. It compresses full-motion video at ratios greater than 100 to 1 and still images at 10 to 1. Split screen capabilities allow still and moving images side by side. DVI uses standard storage devices, but requires a DVI controller board in the personal computer. See CD, CD ROM, CD-I.

Dvorak keyboard Keyboard layout designed in the 1930s by August Dvorak, Univ. of Washington, and his brother-in-law, William Dealey. 70% of words are typed on the home row compared to 32% withqwerty, and, more words are typed using both hands. In eight hours, fingers of a qwerty typist travel 16 miles, but only one for the Dvorak typist.

	Qwerty
52%	QWERTYUIOP
32%	ASDFGHJKL;'
16%	ZXCVBNM,./
Dvorak	
22%	',.PYFGCRL?
70%	AOEUIDHTNS
8%	;QJ KXBMWVZ

DVST (Direct View Storage Tube) Early graphics screen that maintained an image without refreshing. The entire screen had to be redrawn for any change.

DX See 386 and 486.

DX2 See 486.

DXF AutoCAD 2-D graphics file format. Many CAD systems import and export the DXF format for graphics interchange.

dyadic Pertaining to an operation that uses two operands.

dyadic operation Any operation on two operands.

dyadic Two Refers to two components being used.

dye diffusion See thermal dye diffusion.

dye polymer recording Optical recording technique that uses dyed plastic layers as the recording medium. A single dye polymer layer is used in some WORM devices. Erasable optical disks use two dyed plastic layers, a top retention layer and a bottom expansion layer. A bit is written by shining a laser through the retention layer onto the expansion layer, which heats the area and forms a bump that expands into the retention layer. The retention layer bumps are the actual bits read by the unit. To erase a bit, another laser (different wavelength) strikes the retention layer and the bump subsides.

dynamic Refers to operations performed while the program is running. The expression, "buffers are dynamically created," means that space was created when actually needed, not reserved beforehand.

dynamic address translation In a virtual memory system, the ability to determine what the real address is at the time of execution.

dynamic binding Linking a routine or object at runtime based on the conditions at that moment. See polymorphism.

dynamic compression Ability to compress and decom pressdata in realtime; for example, as it's being written to or read from the disk.

dynamic dump A dump taken during the execution of a program. See snapshot dump.

dynamic link Connection established at runtime from one program to another.

dynamic link library Program routines that are available to applications at runtime.

dynamic network services Realtime networking capabilities, such as adaptive routing, automatically reconfiguring the network when a node is added or deleted and the ability to locate any user on the network.

dynamic RAM Most common type of computer memory, also called D-RAM ("dee-RAM") and DRAM. It usually uses one transistor and a capacitor to represent a bit. The capacitors must be energized hundreds of times per second in order to maintain the charges. Unlike firmware chips (ROMs, PROMs, etc.) both major varieties of RAM (dynamic and static) lose their content when the power is turned off. Contrast with static RAM.

dynamic range Range of signals from the weakest to the strongest.

dynamic relocation The movement of part or all of an active (currently operating) program from one region of storage to another. All necessary address references are adjusted to enable proper execution of the program to continue in its new location.

dynamic scheduling Job scheduling determined by the computer on a moment-to-moment basis, depending upon the circumstances.

Dynamic Simulation Language (DSL) A high-level programming language, suited primarily for simulation of engineering and scientific problems of a continuous nature. Because DSL facilitates the solution of ordinary different equations that frequently are functions of time, it is particularly useful for transient analysis of dynamic systems.

dynamic storage Any memory device that must constantly be recharged or refreshed at frequent intervals to avoid loss of data, very volatile storage.

dynamic storage allocation Automatic storage allocation.

dynamic SQL SQL statements interpreted by the SQL database at runtime. Dynatpic SQL may be generated by programs or entered interactively by the user. Contrast with embedded SQL.

dynlink See dynamic link.

Data access language: See Data sublanguage.

Data admidistration: The enterprisewide function that concerns the effective use and control of the organization's data assets. It can be a person but more often is a group. Specific functions include setting data standards and data policies and providing a forum for conflict resolution. Also see Database administrator.

Data base: In DL/I, a collection of data base records.

Database: A self-describing collection of integrated records.

Database administration: The function that concerns the effective use and control of a particular database and its related applications.

Database administrator: The person or group responsible for establishing policies and procedures to control and protect a database. He (she or it) workswithin guidelines set by data adminisi trol the database structure, manage d. and maintain DBMS programs.

Database data: The portion of a database that data of interest and use to the applia users.

Data base description: In DL/I, a data structiL describes the structure of a data base record.

Database machine: A special-purpose CPU designed specifically for processing a database. It is sometlines called a backend machine because it resides between the operating system and the data. The database machine has not been commercially successful, however, and is seldom used today.

Database manager (DBM): A program that processes some portion of a distributed database.

Database node: A computer that processes a database manager and its related database(s).

Data base record: In DL/I, a hierarchical arrangement of data segments. See Logical data base record and Physical data base record.

Data base request module: In DB2, a data structure that describes the SQL statements that need to be executed.

Database save: A copy of database files that can be used to restore the database to some previous, consistent state.

Database server: On a local area network with client—server database architecture, the microcomputer that runs the DBMS and processes actions against the database on behalf of its client computers.

Data definition language (DDL): A language used to describe the structure of a database.

Data dictionary: A user-accessible catalog of both database and application metadata. An active data dictionary is a dictionary whose contents are automatically updated by the DBMS whenever changes are made in the database or application structure. A passive data dictionary is one whose contents must be updated manually when changes are made.

Data dictionary and database administration subsystem: A collection of programs in the DBMS used to access the data dictionary and to perform database administration functions such as maintaining passwords and performing backup and recovery.

Dataflow diagram: A graphical display by system developers that illustrates business processes and the data interfaces. It also shows the flow of the system ftom the perspective of the data.

Data integrity: The state of a database in which all constraints are fulfilled. Usually refers to intertable constraints in which the value of a foreign key is required to be present in the table having that foreign key as its primary key.

Data-item: (1) A logical group of bytes in a record, usually used with file processing. (2) In the context of the relational model, a synonym for attribute.

Data Language I: See DL/I.

Data manipulation language (DML): A language used to describe the processing of a database.

Data mart: A facility similar to a data warehouse but for a restricted domain. Often the data are restricted to particular types, or to particular business functions, or to particular business units.

Data model: (1) A model of the users' data requirements expressed in terms of either the entity-relationship model or the semantic-object model. It is sometimes called a users' data model. (2) A language for describing the structure and processing of a database. See Hierarchical data model, Network data model, and Relational data model.

Data owner: Same as Data proponent.

Data proponent: In data administration, a department or other organizational unit in charge of managing a particular data item.

Data replication: A term that indicates whether any portion (or all) of a database resides on more than one computer. If so, the data are said to be replicated.

Data source: In the ODBC standard, a database together with its associated DBMS, operating system, and network platform.

Data structure diagram: A graphical display of tables (files) and their relationships. The tables are shown in rectangles, and the relationships are shown by lines. A many relationship is shown with a fork on the end of the line; an optional relationship is depicted by an oval; and a mandatory relationship is shown with hash marks.

Data sublanguage: A language for defining and processing a database intended to be embedded in programs written in another language—in most cases, a procedural language such as COBOL, C, or BASIC. A data sublanguage is an incomplete programming language, as it contains only constructs for data access.

Data warehouse: A store of enterprise data that is designed to facilitate management decision making. A data warehouse includes not only data, but also metadata, tools, procedures, training, personnel, and other resources that make access to the data easier and more relevant to decision makers.

DBA: See Database administrator.

DBM: Database manager. In a DDBMS, software that processes some portion of a distributed database in accordance with action requests received from distributed transactions managers (DTM5).

DBMS: Database management system. A set of programs used to define, administer, and process the database and its applications.

DBMS engine: A DBMS subsystem that processes logical I/O requests from other DBMS subsystems and submits physical I/O requests to the operating system.

DBTG: (1) A subcommittee of CODASYL that developed the DBTG network data model. (2) A network data model that models data as records and record relationships as sets. Only simple networks can be directly represented. Although the DBTG network data model is fading in popularity, it still is in use on mainframe computers.

DB2: Database 2. A relational DBMS developed and licensed by IBM for use on mainframe computers.

DDBMS: Distributed database management system. (1) The collection of DTM5 and DBMs on all computers that processes a distributed database (see Chapter 16). (2) A commercial DBMS product that has been modified to allow processing a distributed database.

DDL: Data definition language. The portion of a data model used to define the structure of the database, views, and subschemas.

Deadlock: A condition that can occur during concurrent processing in which each of two'(or more) transactions is waiting to access data that the other transaction has locked. It is also called a deadly embrace.

Deadlock detection: The process of determining whether two or more transactions are in a state of deadlock.

Deadlock prevention: A way of managing transactions so that a deadlock cannot occur.

Deadly embrace: See Deadlock.

Definition tools subsystem: The portion of the DBMS program used to define and change the database structure.

Degree: For relationships in the entity-relationship model, the number of entities participating in the relationship. In almost all cases, such relationships are of degree 2.

Deletion anomaly: In a relation, the situation in which the removal of one row of a table deletes facts about two or more themes.

Determinant: One or more attributes that functionally determine another attribute or attributes. In the functional dependency (A, B) — C, the attributes (A, B) are the determinant.

Difference: A relational algebra operation performed on two union-compatible relations, A and B, that produces a third relation, C. Each row in C is present in A but not in B.

Distributed database: A database stored on two or more computers. Distributed data can be partitioned or not partitioned, replicated or not replicated.

Distributed database application: A business computer system in which the execution of transactions and the retrieval and updating of data occur across two or more independent and usually geographically distributed computers.

Distributed database management system (DDBMS): In a distributed database, the collection of distributed transaction and database managers on all computers.

Distributed database processing: Database processing in which transactions are executed and data is retrieved and updated across two or more independent and usually geographically separated computers.

Distributed database system: A distributed system in which a database or portions of a database are distributed across two or more computers.

Distributed system: A system in which the application programs of a database are processed on two or more computers.

Distributed two-phase locking: Two-phase locking in a distributed environment, in which locks areobtained and released across all nodes on the netwo& See Two-pJia locking.

DL/L: Data Language I. A data model developed by IBM in 11w 1960s to define and process hierarchical on DL/I. Although IMS is still in widespread use on mainframes, such database are being replaced by relational databases.

DML : Data manipulation language. The portion of a data model used to describe the processing of a database.

Domain : (1) The set of all possible values an attribute can have (2) A description of the format (data type, length) and the semantics (meaning) of an attribute.

Domain/key normal form (DK/NF): A relation in which all constraints are logical consequences of domains and keys.

Download: Copying database data from one computer to another, usually from a mainframe or mini to a microcomputer or LAN.

Drill down: User-directed disaggregation of data; used to break higher-level totals into components.

Driver: In ODBC, a program that serves as an interface between the ODBC driver manager and a particular DBMS product. Runs on the client machines in a client-server architecture.

Driver manager: In ODBC, a program that serves as an interface between an application program and an ODBC driver. It determines the driver required, loads it into memory, and coordinates activity between the application and the driver. On Windows systems, it is provided by Microsoft.

DSD: See Data structure diagram.

DSS: Decision support system. An interactive, computer-based facility for assisting decision making, especially for semistructured and unstructured problems. Such a system often includes a database and a query/update facility for processing ad hoc requests.

DTM: Distributed transaction manager. In a DDBMS, software that receives processing requests from users or application programs and translates them into DBM requests for actions. A DTM can send requests to DBMs on nodes different from its own.

E

E See exponent.

e-beam See electron beam.

e-disk (Emulated-disk) Same as RAM disk. e-mail See electronic mail.

E-tlme See execution time.

early binding Assigning types in the compilation phase. See binding time.

EAROM (Electrically Alterable ROM) Same as EEPROM.

earth station Transmitting/receiving station for satellite communications. It uses a dish-shaped antenna for microwave transmission.

EasyCAD 2 Full-featured PC CAD program from Evolution Computing, that is known for its ease of use. EasyCAD users can migrate to FastCAD, which looks almost identical on screen, but provides multiple windows and is designed for high-speed operations.

Easy Color Paint An Apple Macintosh graphics program designed for non-professionals. The user simply picks a color and pattern, chooses a tool, and starts painting.

eavesdropping Passive wiretapping, the interception of messages, usually without detection.

EBCDIC (Extended Binary Coded Decimal Interchange Code) Pronounced "eb-suh-dick." IBM character code originating with System/360, used in its mainframes and most of its midrange computers. It is an 8-bit code (256 combinations) that stores one alphanumeric character or two decimal digits within a byte. EBCDIC and ASCII are the two codes most widely used to represent data.

ECAD Acronym for electronic computer-aided design. ECF (Enhanced Connectivity Facilities) IBM software that allows DOS PCs to query and download data from mainframes as well as issue mainframe commands. It also allows printer output to be directed from the PC to the mainframe.

echo (1) Same as echoplex. (2) DOS and OS/2 screen command that displays messages and turns off/on screen responses. See DOS batch file.

echo cancellation High-speed modem technique that isolates and filters out unwanted signals caused by echoes from the main transmitted signal. This permits full-duplex modems to send and receive on the same frequency.

echo check In communications, an error checking method that retransmits the data back to the sending device for comparison with the original.

echo suppressor Communications technique that turns off reverse transmission in a telephone line, thus effectively making the circuit one way. It is used to reduce the annoying elects of echoes in telephone connections, especially in satellite circuits.

ECLIPSE Series of 32-bit minicumputers from Data General. The development of the initial 32-bit ECLIPSE MV/Family supermini, the MV,OOO, was the subject of Tracy Kid&rs bestsellingbook, "Soul of a New Machine."

ECOM Acronym for elec1ronic'..u,.iIri-4xiented mail, a process of sending and reciv ages in digital form over telecommuna iInies.

ED (1) (Extra High Density) Res ZRSM floppy disks. (1) (EDitor) Early UNIX eahix.

edge connector Row of etched lines on the edge of a printed circuit board that is inserted into an expansion slot. [[PIX FROM MINASI, P.78]]

EDI (Electronic Data Interchange) Electronic communication of transactions between organizations, such as order, confirmations and invoices. Independent service organizations provide EDI services that enableusers to interconnect with another organization's network regardless of type of equipment used.

edit To make a change to existing data. See update edit checking Same as validity checking.

edit instruction Computer instruction that fom field for display or printing. Using an edit m. inserts decimal points, commas and dollar signs the data.

edit key Key combination or function key that chai the program into edit mode when pressed.

edit line The "status report" line displayed on the scre when certain word processing programs are in i Tells the user the present location of the cursor, the amount of memory left, and (in some word processing programs) the name of the file in use. In spreadsheet, it will also show the contents or formula of the cell at the cursor location, and one or two more iten of information (depending on which spreadsheet being used).

edit mask Pattern of characters that represent formatting codes through which data is filtered for display or printing. See picture.

edit mode Operational state in a program that allows existing data to be changed.

edit program (1) Data entry program that validates user input and stores the newly created records in the file. (2) Program that allows users to change data that already exists in a file. See update.

edit routine Routine in a program that tests for valid data. See validity checking.

editable PostScript File of PostScript commands that can be edited by a word processor or other program. This allows PostScript documents to be changed without requiring the use of the application that originally created it.

editor See text editor and linkage editor.

Edlin Archaic text editor used in DOS. The OS/2 counterpart is SSE. See DOS Edlin.

EDP (Electronic Data Processing) First name used for the computer field.

education Teaching concepts and perspectives. Computer education includes computer systems and information systems. Contrast with training.

edutainment Entertaining educational material. Another related buzz word is infotainment.

EE See Extended Edition.

EEMS See EMS.

EEPROM (Electrically Erasable Programmable Read Only Memory) Memory chip that holds its content without power. It can be erased, either within the computer or externally and usually requires more voltage for erasure than the common +5 volts used in logic circuits. It functions like non-volatile RAM, but writing to EEPROM is much slower than writing to RAM. EEPROMs are used in devices that must keep data up-to-date without power.

eesa See EISA and ESA/370.

EFT (Electronic Funds Transfer) Computerised trans fer f money from one account to another.

EGA (Enhanced Graphics Adapter) IBM video display standard that provides medium-resolution (as compared to VGA) text and graphics. It supports previous display modes and requires a digital RGB Enhanced Color Display or equivalent monitor. EGA has been superseded by VGA. See PCdizplay modes.

egoless programming The concept of arranging the programming tasks so that credit for success or blame for failure must be shared by the team rather than just one person. Uses structured walkthroughs and other techniques.

EIA Interface The standard interface between peripherals and microcomputers, and modems and terminals. Another name for RS-232C interface.

EIS (Executive Information System). Information system that consolidates and summarizes ongoing transactions within the organization. It constantly provides management with all the information it requires from internal as well as external sources. See decision support system.

EISA (Extended ISA) Pronounced "e-sah." PC bus standard that extends the AT bus (ISA bus) to 32 bits and provides bus mastering. It was announced in 1988 as a 32-bit alternative to the Micro Channel that would preserve investment in existing boards. PC and AT cards (ISA cards) can plug into an EISA slot.

EL See electroluminescent.

elastic banding In computer graphics, the movement of a line drawn from a specific point on the screen to another point. The second point can be moved around the screen by using a mouse, and the line length will expand or contract as if the line were made of elastic material. Elastic banding is much used in computer aided design programs. Also called rubber banding.

electricity Flow of electrons in a circuit. The speed of electricity is the speed of light, though in a wire it is slowed due to the resistance in the material. Its pressure, or force, is measured in volts and its flow, or current, is measured in amperes. The amount of work it produces is measured in watts (amps X volts).

electrode Device that emits or controls the flow of electricity.

electroluminescent Flat panel display that provides a sharp, clear image and wide viewing angle. It contains a powdered or thin film phosphor layer sandwiched between an x-axis and a y-axis panel. When an x-y coordinate is charged, the phosphor in that vicinity emits visible light. Phosphors are typically amber, but green is also used.

electromagnet Magnet that is energized by electricity. A coil of wire is wrapped around an iron core. When current [lows in the wire, the core generates an energy called magnetic flux.

electromagnetic radiation Energy that exists in all things, including humans, which incorporates cosmic rays, gamma rays, x-rays, ultraviolet light, visible light, infrared light and radar.

electromagnetic spectrum Range of electromagnetic radiation.

electromechanical Use of electricity to run moving parts. Disk drives, printers and motors are examples. Electromechanical systems have to be designed for the eventual deterioration of moving parts.

electromotIve force Pressure in an electric circuit measured in volts.

electron Elementary particle that circles the nucleus of an atom. Electrons are considered to be negatively charged.

electron beam Stream of electrons, or electricity, that is directed towards a receiving object.

electron beam deflection system A narrow stream of electrons moving in the same direction under the influence of an electric or magnetic field. See gun and yoke.

electron gun Device which creates a fine beam of electrons that is focused on a phosphor screen in a CRT.

electron tube Same as vacuum tube.

electronic Use of electricity in intelligence-bearing devices, such as radios, TV5, instruments, computers and telecommunications. Electricity used as raw power for heat, light and motors is considered electrical, not electronic. Although coined earlier, "Electronics" magazine (1930) popularized the term. The term was derived from the electron (vacuum) tube.

electronic bulletin board Acomputer system that maintains a list of messages so people can call up (with their computer systems) and either post a message or read the message already there.

electronic circuit Integrated series of electronic components. It is a pathway through which electricity is directed in a prescribed pattern to accomplish a task. Electronic circuits used in digital computers deal with discrete binary digits (on/off pulses). Electronic circuits used in analog devices, such as radio and TV, deal with electrical vibrations (frequencies). See digital circuit.

electronic cottage The concept of permitting workers to remain at home to perform work, using computer terminals connected to a central office.

electronic magazine A magazine published in a floppy disk, video disk, CD ROM or videotape format. A type of electronic publishing.

electronic mail Transmission of messages over a network. E-mail systems are implemented in mainframe, mini and personal computer LANs. Users can send mail to a single recipient or broadcast it to multiple users on the system. Sophisticated systems prompt recipients for a reply if they have not responded within a certain time frame. With multitasking workstations, mail can be delivered and announced while the user is working in an application. Otherwise, mail is sent to a simulated postal box in the network server or host computer, which must be interrogated.

Though the fax machine has become the most universal form of electronic mail today, showing the power of a single, common standard, it, however, is not considered true e-mail since the text cannot be edited at the other end without scanning it and using text recognition software. See X.400, X.500 and EDI.

electronic marketplace The buying and selling of information through information services and video- text services. Examples of services that can be subscribed to include the Source, Compuserve, and Prodigy.

Electronic Message Service See EMS (2).

electronic messaging Same as electronic mail.

electronic printer Printer that uses electronics to control the printing mechanism, such as a laser printer and certain line printers.

electronic publishing Providing information in electronic form to readers or subscribers of the service. See information utility and videotex.

electronic switch On/off switch activated by electrical current.

electronic typewriter See memory typewriter and word processing.

electrophotographic Copy machine and laser printer printing technique. A negative image made of dots of light is painted onto a photosensitive drum or belt that has been electrically charged. The light comes from a laser, LEDs or liquid crystals that shutter a light source. Wherever light is applied, the drum becomes uncharged. A toner (dry ink) is applied and it adheres to the charged areas of the drum. After the drum transfers the toner to the paper, pressure and heat fuse the toner and paper permanently.

eiectrosensitive printer Dot matrix printer that bums away dots on the outer silver coating of a special black paper.

electrostatic Stationary electrical charges in which no current flows. Commonly called just static.

electrostatic plotter Plotter that uses a special paper that is charged as it passes by a line of electrodes. Toner is then applied to the charged paper. Models print in black and white or color, and some handle paper up to six feet wide.

electrostatic printer Same as electrostatic plotter.

elegant program Program that is simple in design, uses the least amount of memory and runs fast.

ELF (Extremely Low Frequency) See low radiation.

elite A size of typeface that fits twelve characters into each inch of type. Contrast with pica.

em In typography, a unit of measure equal to the width of the capital letter M in a particular font.

E-mail Electronic mail, a communications service for computer users wherein textual messages are sent to a central computer system, or electronic "mailbox," and later retrieved by the addresses. E-mail usually refers to private messages; bulletin board usually refers to public messages.

embedded command (1) Command inserted within text or other codes. (2) In word processing, proprietary codes inserted into the text that commands the printer to change fonts, print underline, boldface, etc. They may be partially or totally invisible on screen, but usually can be revealed when necessary. When a document is printed, the text is copied to a temporary file, and the embedded commands are converted into printer commands for a specific printer. When printing is finished, the temporary file is erased. See print to disk.

embedded SQL SQL statements written into a high- level language source program, such as C or Pascal. In a separate compiling phase, the SQL may be optimized and converted into special function calls. Contrast with dynamic SQL.

embedded system Specialized computer used to control a device. Used extensively in automobiles, appliances, avionics and space vehicles, it implies software that integrates operating system and application functions.

EMI (ElectroMagnetic Interference) Electromagnetic waves that emanate from an electrical device. It often refers to both low-frequency waves from electromechanical devices and high-frequency waves (RFI) from chips and other electronic devices.

emitter Supply of current in a bipolar transistor. Same as source in a MOS transistor.

emitter-coupled logic See ECL.

EMM (Expanded Memory Manager) Software that manages expanded memory (EMS). In 8086/88s and 286s, expanded memory boards must also be used. In 386s and up, the EMM converts extended memory into EMS.

EMM3S6 See DOS EMM3S6.EXE.

EMS (1) (Expanded Memory Specification) Technique for increasing memory in DOS PCs. EMS Version 4.0 allows DOS to work with up to 32MB of extra memory by bank switching 16K segments of EMS memory, known as the "page frame," into conventional memory. In order to use EMS, the application is either written to use it directly, or the application is run within a windows environment that uses it, such as DESQview. In XTs (8088/86s) and ATs (286s), EMS is installed by plugging in an EMS memory board and adding an EMS driver. In 386s and up, EMS is created by expanded memory manager (EMM) software that turns extended memory into EMS. Expanded memory (EMS) and extended memory are not the same. EMS can be installed in XT-class machines and up, whereas extended memory requires at least a 286. With 286s now the low-end CPU, extended memory is increasingly being used with DOS extended applications and Windows 3.0. See EMS emulator.

EMS emulator Before the 386, it referred to a driver for 8086/88s and 286s that simulated EMS memory in extended memory or disk. It is slower than an EMS board that provides high-speed bank switching, because the emulator copies data within memory or between memory and disk. Since the 386, it refers to a memory manager (EMM) that runs in 386s and up and creates EMS out of extended memory. Technically, the 386 is really not emulating anything. The 386 can map any memory to any other memory, thus it is merely mapping memory according to the EMS specification.

EMS memory manager See EMM and EMS emulator. emulation mode Operational state of a computer when it is running a foreign program under emulation.

emulator Device that is built to work like another. A computer can be designed to emulate another model and execute software that was written to run in the other machine. The emulator can be hardware, software or both.

en In typography, a unit of measure equal to one half the width of an em. An en is typically the width of one numeric digit.

enable To turn on. Contrast with disable.

Encapsulated PostScript PostScript file format that contains PostScript code for the document as well as optional preview images in TIFF, Windows Metafile or Macintosh PIG!' formats. The PostScript code drives a PostScript printer directly, and the preview formats allow the image to be manipulated on screen. DOS and OS/2 files use an EPS extension.

encapsulation (1) In object-oriented programming, making the data and processing private within an object, which allows it to be modified without causing problems elsewhere in the program. (2) In communications, inserting the frame header and data from a higher level protocol into the data frame of a lower level protocol.

encipher To encode data for security purposes. See encryption.

encode (1) To assign a code to represent data, such as a parts code. (2) Same as encipher or encrypt.

encryption Encoding data for security purposes by converting the standard data code into a proprietary code. The encrypted data must be decoded in order to be used. It is used to transmit documents over a network or to encode text so that it cannot be easily changed in a word processor or read by an unauthorized person. See DES.

end key Keyboard key commonly used to move the cursor to the end of line , but also by some programs to the bottom of the screen or file or to the next word.

end points In vector graphics, the two ends of a line (vector). In 2-D graphics, each end point is typically two numbers representing coordinates on x and y axes. In 3-D, each end point is made up of three numbers representing coordinates on x, y and z axes.

end user A person who busy and uses computer software or who has contact with computers.

end user computing Using personal computers.

endless loop Series of instructions that are constantly repeated. It can be caused by an error in the program or it can be intentional.

endnote See footnote.

end-of-block (EOB) The termination of a block.

end-of-file (EOF) The termination or point of completion of quantity of data. End-of-file marks are used to indicate this point on magnetic files. See end-of-tape marker.

end-of-job (EOJ) A condition that alerts the program that a job is done and starts another action.

end-of-message (EOM) The termination of a message. end-of-page halt A feature that stops the printer at the end of each completed page of output, usually to allow another sheet to be inserted.

end-of-tape marker A marker on a magnetic tape used to indicate the end of the permissible recording area.

end-of-text (EOT) A transmission control character used to indicate to receiving hardware that the previous character was the last character of message text.

end-of-transmission A control character used to indicate that a transmission has been completed.

engine (1) Specialized processor, such as a graphics processor. (2) Software that performs a routine function; for example, a database engine or graphics engine. (3) Slang for processor.

engineering cylinder See diagnostic tracks. Enhanced keyboard IBM 101-key keyboard that superseded the PC and AT keyboards. It has a separate cursor key cluster located between the original numeric/cursor keypad and the letter keys and also has two extra function keys - Fli and F12.

enhancement Any improvement made to a software package or hardware device.

ENIAC (Electronic Numerical Integrator And Calculator) First operational electronic digital computer developed for the U.S. Army by John Eckert and John Mauchly at the Univ. of Pennsylvania.

Completed in 1946, it was decimal-based, used 18,000 vacuum tubes, took up 1,800 square feet and performed 5,000 additions/second.

enquiry character In communications, a control character that requests a response from the receiving station.

enter key See return key.

enterprise data Centralized data that is shared by many users throughout the organization.

entity In a database, anything about which information can be stored for example, a person, concept, physical object or event. Typically refers to a record structure.

entity relationship model In a database, a data model that describes attributes of entities and the relationships among them.

entity type In a database, a particular kind of file; for example, a customer or product file.

entropy In data compression, a measure of the amount of non-redundant, non-compressible information in an object.

entry Input of an item or set of items at a terminal. See data entry.

entry point In programming, the starting point of the instructions in a subroutine.

enumerate To count or list one by one. An enumerated data type defines a list of all possible values for a variable, and no other value can then be placed into it.

envelope (1) Range of frequencies for a particular operation. (2) Group of bits or items that is packaged and treated as a single unit.

environment Computer configuration that includes the CPU model and system software (operating system, data communications and database systems). It may also include the programming language used. It sets the standards for the applications that run in it. The term often refers only to the operating system; for example, 'This program is running in a DOS environment."

environment variable See DOS Set. EOB Abbreviation for end-of-block.

EOB (End Of File) File status when its end has been reached or when an instruction or command resets the file pointer to the end.

EOF Abbreviation for end-of-job.

EOL Abbreviation for End Of Line

EOLN Abbreviation for end-of-line, a flag indicating the end of a line of data. Sometimes abbreviated EOL.

EOM (End Of Message)

EOT (End Of Transmission)

EP Abbreviation for electronic presentation, a process where a user creates a presentation using a desktop computer system. The diskette (containing the presentation) is then inserted into an EP player, which can produce an animated video presentation.

epitaxial layer In chip making, a semiconductor layer that is created on top of the silicon base rather than below it. See molecular beam epitaxy.

epoch date Starting point from which time is measured as the number of days, minutes, etc., from that time. EPROM (Erasable Programmable ROM) Reusable

PROM chip that holds its content until erased under ultraviolet light. See PROM programmer.

EPROM programmer A special machine used to program EPROM chips. Compare from programmer.

EPS See Encapsulated PostScript.

Epson A well-established make of dot-matrix printers that can print graphics as well as text.

Epson emulation Compatible with Epson dot matrix printers. The command set in the Epson MX, RX and FX printers has become an industry standard.

EPSS (Electronic Performance Support System) Computer system that provides quick, comprehensive assistance and information usually without any prior training. It may incorporate all forms of multimedia delivery as well as Al techniques such as expert systems and natural language recognition.

EQ (EQual to) See relational operator.

equalization Techniques used to reduce distortion and compensate for signal loss (attenuation) over long distances.

equation Arithmetic expression that equates one set of conditions to another; for example, A = B + C. In a programming language, assignment statements take the form of an equation. The above example would assign the sum of B and C to the variable A.

erase See delete.

erase head In a magnetic tape drive, the device that erases the tape before a new block of data is recorded.

ergonomics Science of people-machine relationships. An ergonomically-designed product implies that the device blends smoothly with a person's body or actions.

Erlang Unit of traffic use that specifies the total capacity or average use of a telephone system. One Erlang is equivalent to the continuous usage of a telephone line. Traffic in Erlangs is the sum of the holding times of all lines divided by the period of measurement.

error checking (1) Testing for accurate transmission of data over a communications network or internally within the computer system. See parity checking and CRC. (2) Same as validity checking.

error control Same as error checking.

error detection & correction See error checking & validity checking.

error-free channel Interface (wire, cable, etc.) between devices that is not subject to external interference.

error handling Routines in a program that respond to errors. The measurement of quality in error handling is based on how the system informs the user of such conditions and what alternatives it provides for dealing with them.

error rate Measurement of the effectiveness of a communications channel. It is the ratio of the number of erroneous units of data to the total number of units of data transmitted.

ES See expert system.

ES/3090, ES/9000 High-end IBM mainframe systems. ESA/390 (Enterprise System Architecture/390) Extensions to ESA/370 for System!390 series. It includes MVS/ESA, VM/ESA and VSE/ESA operating systems.

Esc See escape character and escape key.

escape character Control character often used in conjunction with other codes. In ASCII, escape is decimal 27, hex 1B; in EBCDIC, it is hex 27.

escape key Keyboard key commonly used to exit a mode or routine, or cancel some function.

escape sequence Machine command that starts with escape character.

ESD (1) (ElectroStatic Discharge) Sparks (electrons) that jump from an electrically-charged object to an approaching conductive object. (2) (Electronic Software Distribution) Installing software by transmitting it to the destination machines over a network.

ESDI (Enhanced Small Device Interface) Hard disk interface that transfers data in the one to three MByte! sec range. ESDI has always been known as the high- quality, high-speed interface for small computers. IDE drives now incorporate similar technology and are beginning to rival ESDI performance. See hard disk specs.

ESF (1) (Extended SuperFrame) Enhanced Ti format that allows a line to be monitored during normal operation. It provides room for CRC bits and other diagnostic commands. (2) (External Source Format) Specification language for defining an application in IBM's (DSP/AD application generator.

ESP (1) (E-tech Speçdy Protocol) Proprietary protocol of E-Tech Research used in its modems. (2) (Electronic Still Photography) Digitizing and transmitting images over a telephone line. (3) (Emulex SCSI Processor) Proprietary chip used in Emulex's SCSI disk controller.

ESS (1) (Electronic Switching System) Large-scale computer used to switch telephone conversations in a central office. (2) (Executive Support System) See EIS. (3) (Electronic SpreadSheet) See spreadsheet.

Ethernet IEEE 802.3 LAN standard originally developed by Xerox, Digital and Intel that transmits at ioMbps and can connect up to 1,024 nodes in total. Standard Etbernet (also called thick Ethernet) uses a bus topology with a maximum cable segment length of i,640 ft. without the use of a repeater. Attachment is made to the cable by clamping a transceiver onto it. Thin Ethernet (also called ThinNet and CheaperNet) is a bus topology with a maximum cable length of 607 feet. Nodes are daisy chained together with T-type BNC connectors as the transceivers are contained within the network adapter cards. Twisted pair Ethernet allows installed telephone wire to be used (if the right type) and Fiber Optic Ethernet is impervious to external radiation. Both use a star topology, which is considered easier to debug as networks expand.

EtherTalk Macintosh software from Apple that accompanies its Ethernet Interface NB Card and enables the MAC to adapt to Ethernet networks.

ETX Abbreviation for end-of-text.

Eurocard Family of European-designed printed circuit boards that uses a 96-pin plug rather than edge connectors.

even parity See parity checking.

event driven Application that responds to input from the user or other application at unregulated times. It's driven by choices that the user makes (select menu, press button, etc.). Contrast with procedure oriented.

EVGA (Extended VGA) See VGA.

Excel Full-featured spreadsheet for PCs and the Macintosh from Microsoft. It can link many spreadsheet for consolidation and provides a wide variety of business graphics and charts for creating presentation materials.

exception report Listing of abnormal items or items that fall outside of a specified range.

exclusive NOR See NOR.

exclusive OR See OR.

EXE file (EXEcutable file) Runnable program in DOS, OS/2 and VMS. In DOS, if a program fits within 64K, it may be a COM file.

executable Program in machine language that is ready to run in a particular computer environment.

execute To follow instructions in a program. Same as run.

execution time Time in which a single instruction is executed. It makes up the last half of the instruction cycle.

executive Same as operating system.

exit (1) To get out of the current mode or quit the program. (2) In programming, to get out of the loop, routine or function that the computer is currently in. (3) Also to get out of a DOS shell of an application.

expanded memory See EMS and expanded storage.

expanded memory emulator Memory manager for 386s and up that converts extended memory into EMS memory. See EMM.

expanded memory/manager See EMS and EMM.

expanded storage Auxiliary memory in IBM mainframes. Data is usually transferred in 4K chunks from expanded storage to central storage (main memory).

expansion board (1) Printed circuit board that plugs into an expansion slot (2) See bus extender.

expansIon bus (1) The computer's bus comprised of a series of receptacles or slots into which expansion boards (video display, disk controller, etc.) are plugged. (2) Sometimes refers to bus extender.

expansIon card Same as expansion board.

expansion slot Receptacle inside a computer or other electronic system accepts printed circuit boards. The number of slots determines scope for future expansion. In personal computers, expansion slots are connected to the bus.

ExperLogo Macintosh version of Logo from ExperTelligence. It contains more functions similar to LISP than most versions of Logo.

expert system Al application that uses a knowledge base of human expertise for problem solving. Its success is based on the quality of the data and rules obtained from the human expert. It derives its answers by run- fling the knowledge base through an inference engine, which is software that interacts with the user and processes the results from the rules and data in the knowledge base. Examples of uses are medical diagnosis, equipment repair, investment analysis, financial, estate and insurance plannin.g, vehicle routing, contract bidding, production control and training. See EPSS.

explreware Software with a built-in expiration date, either by date or number of uses.

explode (1) To break down an assembly into its component pieces. Contrast with implode. (2) To decompress data back to its original form.

exponent Number written above the line and to the right of a number that indicates the power of a number, or how many zeros there are in it. For example 10 to the 3rd power indicates three zeros. On a screen or printout, the number is expressed as 467E3. See floating point.

exponential growth Extremely fast growth. On a chart, the line curves up rather than being straight. Contrast with linear.

exponential smthing Widely-used technique in forecasting trends, seasonality and level change. Works well with data that has a lot of randomness.

export To convert a data file in the current program into a foreign format for some other program. Contrast with import.

expression In programming, a statement that describes data and processing.

extended application DOS application that runs in extended memory under the control of a DOS extender.

extended ASCII Second half of the ASCII character set (125 through 255). The symbols are defined by IBM for the PC and by other vendors for proprietary uses. It is non-standard ASCII.

Extended Binary Coded Decimal Intercange Code See EBCDIC.

extended maintenance On-call service that is ordered for periods in addition to the primary period of maintenance.

extended memory In Intel 286s and up, standard memory above one megabyte used for RAM disks, disk caches and applications using DOS extenders. Windows also uses extended memory. Contrast with expanded memory (EMS), which is specialized memory above one megabyte. Memory boards can usually be setup as a mix of the two. See EMS, XMS and DOS extender.

extensible Capable of being expanded or customized. For example, with extensible programming languages, programmers can add new control structures, statements or data types.

extension DOS and OS/2 file category added to the end of the file name with a dot. An extension can have up to three letters or digits. Executable files use .EXE, .COM and .BAT extensions. All programs and most data files use extensions. However, many word processing files do not, and users can set up their own filing system by making up their own. There are some common extensions used by certain programs by convention. Eg. .WK1 is used by Lotus 1-2-3, .BAS as source program for BASIC, .TXT for text files, .TMP for temporary files, .BAT for batch files, .PCX for PC Paintbrush picture files, etc.

external command (1) In DOS and OS/2, a function performed by a separate utility program that accompanies the operating system and is not part of (in DOS) the COMMAND.COM. (2) A user-developed HyperCard command. See XCMD.

external interrupt Interrupt caused by an external source such as the computer operator, external sensor or monitoring device, or another computer.

external modem Self-contained modem that can be connected to the serial port of any computer. It gets its power from a wall outlet. Contrast with internal modem.

external reference In programming, a call to a program or function that resides in a separate, independent library.

external sort Sort program that uses disk or tape as temporary workspace. Contrast with internal sort.

external storage Storage outside of the CPU, such as disk and tape.

Encapsulated data: Properties or attributes contained in a program or object not visible or accessible to other programs or objects.

Encapsulated structure: A portion of an object that is not visible to other objects.

Entity: (1) Something of importance to a user that needs to be represented in a database. (2) In an entity-relationship model, entities are restricted to things that can be represented by a single table. Also see Existence-dependent entity, Strong entity, and Weak entity.

Entity class: A set of entities of the same type, for example, EMPLOYEE and DEPARTMENT.

Entity instance: A particular occurrence of an entity, for example, Employee 100 and the Accounting Department.

Entity-relationship diagram: A graphic used to represent entities and their relationships. Entitiesare normally shown in squares or rectangl, and wlationships are shown in diamonds. The cardinally of the relationship is shown inside the diamond..

Entity-relationship model: The constructs and conventions used to create a model of the users' data (see Data model). The things in the users' world are represented by entities, and the associations among those things are represented by relationships. The results are usually documented in an entity-relationship diagram.

Entry-point relation: Used with regard to the relations representing an object. The entry-point relation is the relation whose key is the same as the key of the object it represents. The entry-point relation is normally the first relation processed. Also, the name of the entry-point relation is normally the same as the name of the object.

Enumerated list: A list of allowed values for a domain, attribute, or column.

Equijoin: The process of joining relation A containing attribute Al with B containing attribute Bl to form relation C, so that for each row in C, Al = Bl. Both Al and Bl are represented in C.

E-R diagram: See Entity-relationship oiagram.

Exclusive lock: A lock on a data resource that no other transaction can either read or update.

Existence-dependent entity: Same as a weak entity. An entity that cannot appear in the database unless an instance of one or more other entities also appears in the database. A subclass of existence-dependent entities is ID-dependent entities.

Explicit lock: A lock requested by a command from an application program.

Export: A function of the DBMS, to write a file of data in bulk. The file is intended to be read by another DBMS or program.

Extent (of object): In the ODMG model, the union of all object instances. Attributes can be declared to be unique across an object's extent.

Extract: A portion of an operational database downloaded to a local area network or microcomputer for local processing. Extracts are created to reduce communications cost and time when querying and creating reports from data created by transaction processing.

F

F connector Coaxial cable connector used to connect antennas, TVs and VCRs.

F keys See function keys.

Fabrication The processing of manufacturing materials to desired specifications. See Computer-Aided Manufacturing.

face (1) In computer graphica or geometry, one side of a solid object. such as a cube. A cube has six faces. (2) In printing and typography, a shortened form of typeface,

facing pages The two pages of a bound, document that face each other when the document is open. The even- numbered page (verso) is on the left, and the odd- numbered page (redo) is on the right.

facsimile See fax.

factorial Number of sequences that can edst with a set of items, derived by multiplying the number of items by the next lowest number until 1 is reached. For example, three items have six sequences (3x2x16): 123, 132, 231, 213, 312 and 321.

fail safe Same as fault tolerant.

fail soft Ability to fail with minimum destruction. For example, a disk drive can be built to automatically park the heads when power fails. Although this does not correct the problem, it minimizes destruction.

failure predictIon A technique that attempts to determine the failure schedule of specific parts of equipment so they may be discarded and replaced before failure occurs.

fan-fold paper Same as continuous forms.

far pointer In an Intel 80x86 segmented address, a memory address that includes both segment and offset. Contrast with near pointer.

Farad Unit of electrical charge that is used to measure the storage capacity of a capacitor. In microelectronice, measurements are usually in microfarads or picofarads.

Fast Asynchronous communications protocol used to quickly transmit files over high-quality lines. Error checking is done after the entire file has been transmitted.

Fast Fourier Transform Class of algorithms used in digital signal processing that break down complex signals into elementary components.

FastCAD Full-featured PC CA]) program from Evolution Computing, known for its well-designed user interface. It requires a math coprocessor. Users with less sophisticated requirements can start out with FastCAD's baby brother, Ea5yCAD.

FAT See DOS FAT.

fatal error Error condition that halts processing due to read errors, program bugs or anomalies.

FatBits MacPaint option in the "Goodies" menu that lets a user edit an image a pixel at a time.

father file See grandfather, father, son.

fault tolerant Continuous operation in case of failure. A fault tolerant system can be created using two or more computers that duplicate all processing, or having one system stand by if the other fails. It can also be built with redundant processors, control units and peripherals architecturally integrated from the ground up. Fault tolerant operation requires backup power in the event of power failure. It may also imply du. plication of systems in disparate locations in the event of natural catastrophe or vandalism.

fax (FAcSimile) Originally called telecopying, it is the communication of a printed page between remote locations. Fax machines scan a paper form and transmit a coded image over the telephone system. The receiving machine prints a copy (facsimile) of the original. A fax machine is made up of a scanner, printer and fax modem

fax board Fax transmission on an expansion board. It uses software that generates fax signals directly from disk files or the screen and transmits a sharper image than a fax machine, which gets its image by scanning. Incoming faxes are printed on the computer's printer.

fax/modem Combination fax board and data modem available as an external unit or expansion board. It includes a fax switch that routes the call to the fax or the data modem.

fax switch Device that tests a phone line for a fax signal and routes the call to the fax machine. When a fax machine dials a number and the line answers, it emits a tone to identify itself. Some devices handle voice, fax and data modem switching and may require keying in an extension number to switch to the modem.

FCB See DOS FCB.

FCC Class FCC certification of radiation limits on digital devices. Class A certification is for business use. Class B for residential use is more stringent in order to avoid interference with TV and other home reception.

FCFS First come, first served also FIFO or first in, first out.

FD (Floppy Disk) For example, FD/HD refers to a floppy disk/hard disk device.

FDDIm (Fiber Distributed Data Interface) ANSI standard token passing LAN that uses optical fiber cabling and transmits at 100 Mbits/sec up to 62 miles. FDDI specifications deal with OSI layers 1 and 2. It provides an optional "dual counter-rotating ring" topology that contains primary and secondary rings with data flowing in opposite directions. If the line breaks, the secondary ring is used to bypass the fault. Stations can be configured as Single Attached Stations (SAS) connected to concentrators, or as Dual Attached Stations (DAS), connected to both rings. Groups of stations are typically wired to concentrators connected in a hierarchical tree to the main ring. Large networks may be configured as a "dual ring of trees," in which the dual ring provides the backbone to which multiple hierarchies of concentrators are attached. FDDI provides a quantum leap in speed over Ethernet, Token Ring and other LANs and allows high-resolution graphics and digital video to be quickly transmitted. See CDDI.

FDISK See DOS Fdisk.

FDM (Frequency Division Multiplexing) Method used to transmit multiple signals over a single channel. Each signal (data, voice, etc.) modulates a carrier with a different frequency and all signals travel Simultaneously over the channel. Contrast with TDM. See baseband.

FDX See full-duplex.

FEA (Finite Element Analysis) Mathematical technique for analyzing stress, which breaks down a physical structure into substructures, called finite elements. The finite elements and their interrelationships are converted into equation form and solved mathematically.

feasibility study Analysis of a problem to determine if it can be solved effectively. The operational (will it work?), economical (costs and benefits) and technical (can it be built?) aspects are part of the study. The results of a feasibility study provide data for a go/no-go decision to start the project.

feathering Adding an even amount of space between each line on a page or column to force vertical justification.

feature negotiation See automatic feature negotiation. feedback (1) A means of automatic control in which the actual state of a process is measured and used to obtain a quantity that modifies the input to initiate the activity of the control system. (2) In data processing, infprmation arising from a particular stage of processing could provide a feedback to affect the processing of subsequent data; for example, the fact that an area of storage was nearly full might either delay the acceptance of more data or divert it to some other storage area. (3) Any process whereby output from a sequential task server to modify subsequent tasks.

female connector Receptacle into which the male counterpart of the connector is plugged.

femto A prefix indicating one-quadrillionth, or a millionth of a billionth, 10.

FEP See front end processor.

ferric oxide (Fe203) Oxidation of iron used in the coating of magnetic disks and tapes.

ferromagnetic Capability of a material, such as iron and nickel, to be highly magnetized.

FET (Field Effect Transistor) Type of transistor used in MOS integrated circuits.

fetch To locate next instruction in memory for execution by the CPU.

Fiber Channel Future ANSI standard under development for a high- speed computer channel incorporating IPI, SCSI and HiPPI command sets. Speeds range from 12.5 to 100 MBytes/sec using coax and optical fiber.

fiber optic Communications systems that use optical fibers for transmission. See optical fiber.

Fibonaccl numbers Series of whole numbers in which each number is the sum of the two preceding ones: 1, 1, 2, 3, 5, 8, 13, etc. It is used to speed up binary searches by dividing the search into the two lower numbers.

fiche Same as microfiche.

FidoNet E-mail protocol that originated from the Fido BBS created by Tom Jennings in 1984. Over 10,000 FidoNet nodes are in use.

field Physical unit of data that is one or more bytes in size. A collection of fields make up a record. A field also defines a unit of data on a source document, screen or report. The field is the common denominator between the user and the computer. When you interactively query and update your database, you reference your data by field name. Technically, a field is the physical unit of storage, whereas a data element or data item refers to the data itself. For example, it is correct to say, 'These data elements are stored in this field." The terms field, data element, data item and variable refer to the same unit of data and are often used interchangeably.

field engineer Person who is responsible for hardware installation, maintenance and repair. Formal training is in electronics, although many people have learned on the job.

field name Assigned name for a field (NAME, ADDRESS, CITY, STATE, etc.) that will be the same in every record. It is the field's identifier, not the data entered into it,

fields of view In computer graphics, the limits of what a simulated camera can see, usually expressed as a horizontal angle centred at the camera. For simplicity of computation, computer graphicists assume that what a camera sees lies within a pyramid – rather than a cone - with the apex at the camera.

field separator Character that is used to mark the separation of fields in a record. See comma delimited.

field service See field engineer.

field squeeze In a mail merge, a function that eliminates extra blank spaces in a data field so that it prints correctly within the text of the letter. See line squeeze.

field template See picture.

FIF (Fractal Image Format) Graphics file format from Iterated Systems that stores fractal images with compression ratios as high as 2,500:1.

FIFO (First In-First Out) Storage method that retrieves the item stored for the longest time. Contrast with LIFO.

fifth-generation computer Computer designed for Al applications. Appearing in the mid 1990s, these systems will represent the next technology leap.

file In computer operations, any collection of data that is treated as a single unit on a peripheral device, such as a collection of related records in data management, a single text document in word processing, an image in computer graphics, or the source program and machine language program in programming.

ifie and record locking Techniques for managing data in a multiple user environment. File locking prevents users from gaining access to a data, text or image file. Record locking prohibits access to a single record within a data file.

ifie attribute File access classification that allows for more secure and safe handling of a file. Typical attributes are read/write, read only, archive and hidden.

ifie compression See data compression. file conversion See conversion.

file extension See extension.

file format Structure of a file. There are proprietary formats for database, word processing and graphics files. See record layout.

file layout Same as record layout.

file maintenance (1) Periodic updating of master files. (2) Periodic reorganization of the disk drives. Data that has been continuously updated becomes physically fragmented over the disk space and requires regrouping. An optimizing program is run (daily, weekly, etc.) that rewrites all files contiguously or 'defragments' files.

ifie manager (1) Software that manages data files. Often erroneously called database managers, file managers provide the ability to create, enter, change, query and produce reports on one file at a time. They have no relational capability and usually don't include a programming language. (2) Software used to manage files on a disk. It provides functions to delete, copy, move, rename and view files as well as create and manage directories.

file name Name assigned by the user or programmer that is used to identifr a file. See under DOS for details of valid file names.

file protection Preventing accidental erasing of data. Physical file protection is provided on the storage medium by turning a switch, moving a lever or covering a notch. On 112" tape, a plastic ring in the center of the reel is removed (no ring-no write). 3.5" On the back of the 3.5" disk, slide the square, plastic window (bottom right) downward uncovering a hole through the disk. On a 5.25" disk, cover the side notch with a stick-on label. In these cases, writing is prohibited even if the software directs the computer to do so. Logical file protection is provided by the operating system, which can designate a single file as read only. This method allows both regular (read/write) and read only files to be stored on the same disk volume. Files can also be designated as hidden files, which makes them invisible to most software programs.

file recovery program Software that recovers disk files that have been accidentally deleted or damaged.

file server High-speed computer in a LAN that stores the programs and data files shared by users on the network. Also called a network server, it acts like a remote disk drive. See database server.

file sharing protocol Communications protocol that provides a structure for file requests (open, read, write, close, etc.) between stations in a network. If file sharing is strictly between workstation and server, it is also called a client/server protocol. It refers to layer 7 of the OS! model.

file spec (file SPECification) Reference to the location of a file on a disk, which includes disk drive, directory name and file name.

file system (1) Method for cataloguing files in a computer system. See hierarchical file system. (2) Data processing application that manages individual files. Files are related by customized programming. Contrast with relational database.

file transferprotocol Communications protocol that can transmit files without loss of data. It implies that it can handle binary data as well as ASCII data.

file viewer Software that displays the contents of a file as it would be normally displayed by the-application that created it. It is usually capable of displaying a variety of common formats.

FlleMaker II Macintosh file manager from Claris. It is a popular program for general data management and provides a variety of statistical functions, fast search capabilities and extensive reporting features.

FlleMan (1) Public-domain MUMPS software that provides a stand-alone, interactive DBMS as well as a set of utilities for the MUMPS programmer. (2) Slang for Windows' file manager.

filespec See file spec.

fill (1) In a paint program, to change the color of a bordered area. (2) In a spreadsheet, to enter common or repetitive values into a group of cells.

fill pattern (1) Color, shade or pattern used to fill an area of an image. (2) Signals transmitted by a LAN station when not receiving or transmitting data in order to maintain synchronization.

film recorder Device that makes a 35mm slide picture from a graphics file, which has been created in a CAD, paint or business graphics package. It generates very high resolution, typically 2,000 to 4,000 lines. FiJm recorders can be connected to personal computers by plugging in a controller board cabled to the recorder.

filter (1) Process that changes data, such as a sort routine that changes the sequence of items or a conversion routine (import or export filter) that changes one data, text or graphics format into another. (2) Pattern or mask through which only selected data is passed.

financlal plannlng language Language used to create data models and command a financial planning system.

financial planning system Software that helps the user evaluate alternatives. It allows for the creation of a data model, which is a series of data elements in equation form; for example, gross profit gross sales- cost of goods sold. Different values can be plugged into the elements, and the impact of various options can be assessed (what if?). It is a step above spreadsheet by providing additional analysis tools; however, some of these capabilities are being added to spreadsheet. Examples are sensitivity analysis assigns a range of values to a data element, which causes that data to be highlighted if it ever exceeds that range; and goal seeking provides automatic calculation.

Finder The part of the Macintosh operating system that manages the desktop. It keeps track of icons, controls the Clipboard and Scrapbook and allows files to be copied. Finder manages one application at a time. Multifinder manages multiple applications on screen.

fingerprint reader Scanner used to identify a person's fingerprint for security purposes. After a sample is taken, access to a computer or other system is granted if the fingerprint matches the stored sample. A PIN may also be used with the fingerprint sample.

firmware Category of memory chips that hold their content without electrical power and include ROM, PROM, EPROM and EEPROM technologies. Firmware becomes 'hard software' when holding program code.

first-generation computer Computer that used vacuum tubes as switching elements; for example, the UNIVAC I.

fixed disk Non-removable hard disk such as is found in most personal computers.

fixed-frequency monitor Monitor that accepts one type of video signal, such as VGA only. Contrast with multiscan monitor.

fixed head disk Direct access storage device, such as a disk or drum, that has a reacVwrite head for each track. Since there is no access arm movement, access times are significantly improved.

fixed length field Constant field size; for example, a 25-byte name field takes up 25 bytes in each record. It is easier to program and read, but wastes disk space and restricts file design. Contrast with variable length field.

fixed length record Data record that contains fixed length fields.

fixed point Method for storing and calculating numbers in which the decimal point is always in the same location. Contras.l with floating point.

Fkey (Function key) Macintosh command sequence using command, shift and option key combinations. For example, Fkey 1 (command-shift 1) ejects the internal floppy.

flag (1) In communications, a code in the transmitted message which indicates that the following characters are a control code and not data. (2) In programming, a status indicator that may be built into hard-ware or programmed in software. Flags are usttally no more than a bit or a byte that store a YES or NO.

flame Slang for communicating emotionally and/or excessively via electronic mail.

flashing The blinking on and off a characters on a display screen; used to call attention to something on the screen.

flash memory Memory chip that holds its content without power, but must be erased in bulk. Originally coined by Toshiba, the term comes from its ability to be erased "in a flash." Derived from BEPROMs, flash memory chips are less expensive and provide higher bit densities. As future designs provide for less-than-whole-chip erasure, and ultimately, byte by byte erasure, flash memory may provide an alternative to today's RAM.

fiat address space Memory addressing in which each byte is referenced by a different sequential number starting with 0. Contrast with segmented address space.

flatbed scanner A scanner with a glass surface upon which material to be scanned is placed. Because the original never moves during the scanning process, flatbeds produce more precise results than sheetfed scanners. The scanner can transform a full-page graphic or page of text into a digitized file.

flat file Data file that does not physically interconnect with or point to other files. Any relationship between two flat files is logical, for example, matching account numbers. The term usually refers to file managers that have no relational capability, but in the past, it has referred to the type of file used by a relational database (no predefined pointers).

flat panel display Thin display screen that uses any of a number of technologies, such as LCD, electroluminscent or plasma. Used today in laptops to reduce size and weight, they will eventually supersede CRTs.

flat shading In computer graphics, a technique for computing a one-tone shaded surface to simulate simple lighting.

flatbed plotter Graphics plotter that draws on sheets of paper that have been placed in a bed.

flexible disk Same as floppy disk and diskette. mcker Fluctuating image on a video screen.

flight computer A computer resident in a spacecraft, an airplane, or a missile.

flight simulator (1) The computer-controlled simulator bsed by airline companies to train pilots on new aircraft. Some simulators are so realistic that they are acceptable to the FAA for use in renewal of pilot licenses. (2) On personal computers, software that provides entertainment and practice in instrument reading and navigation.

Lip-flop Electronic circuit that alternates between two states. When current is applied, it changes to its opposite state. Made of several transistors, it is used in the design of static memories and hardware registers.

flippy board PC expansion board that connects to both AT and Micro Channel buses. AT connectors are on one side of the board, MCA on the other.

flippy-floppy Single-sided 5.25" floppy converted to double-sided use by punching a second notch into the disk so that it can be flipped over and inserted upside down. This is not recommen4ed as the disk's rotation is alternated.

float In programming, a name used to declare a floating point number.

floating point Method for storing and calculating numbers in which the decimal points don't line up as in fixed point numbers. The significant digits are stored as a unit called the mantissa, and the location of the radix point (decimal point in base 10) is stored in a separate unit called the exponent. Floating point methods are used for calculating a large range of numbers quickly. Floating point operations can be implemented in hardware (math coprocessor), or they can be done in software. They can also be performed in a separate floating point processor that is connected to the main processor via a channel.

floating point processor Arithmetic unit designed to perform floating point operations. It may be a coprocessor chip in a personal computer, a CPU designed with built-in floating point capabilities or a separate machine, often called an array processor, which is connected to the main computer.

floppy disk Removable storage medium. Also called a diskette, the medium is a single round disk of flexible, tape-like material housed in a square envelope or cartridge. The disk drive grabs the disk at its center and spins it inside its envelope.Like tape, floppy disks can be recorded and erased over and over. Older floppies were recorded on only one side (single sided); however, most are recorded on both sides (double sided).

The original floppy, developed by IBM, is housed in an 8' square envelope that holds from 100 to 500KB. Shugart introduced the now-common minifloppy which resides in a 5.25" square envelope and holds from 100KB to about 1.2MB. Sony developed the 3.5" microfloppy, which is now the most popular, due to its compact and rigid case. Micro- floppies hold from 400KB to 4MB and more.

A floppy disk, fresh out of the box, is blank. The disk drive it is used in determines its storage capacity. Most floppies are soft sectored disks, which requires that they be run first through a format program to record the sector identification on them. All floppies are vulnerable to extremes in temperature and magnetic influences; however, the older (5.25" and 8") floppies are more susceptible to physical damage than the 3.5" disks.

FLOPS (FLoaiing point Operations Per Second) Unit of measurement of floating point calculations. For example, 100 megallops is 100 million floating point operations per second.

Floptlcal Floppy disk from Insite Peripherals that records data magnetically, but uses grooves in the disk to optically align the head over the tracks. They have very high storage capacities, normally above 20Mb.

flow chart Graphical representation of the sequence of operations in an information system or program. Information system flow charts show how data flows from source documents through the computer to final distribution to users. Program flow charts show the sequence of instructions in a single program or subroutine. Different symbols are used to represent each type of processing in the flow chart.

flow control (1) In communications, the management of data transmission. It ensures that the receiving station can process the data before the next block is sent. (2) In programming, the if-the, and ioop statements that make up the program's logic.

flush To empty the contents of a memory buffer onto disk.

flush center In typography, refers to centering text uniflrmly between the left and right margins.

flush left In typography, the alignment of all text uniformly to the left margin.

flush right In typography, the alignment of all text uniformly to the right margin while the left margin is set ragged.

flux Energy field generated by a magnet.

FM (1) (Frequency Modulation) Transmission technique that blends the data signal into a carrier by varying (modulating) the frequency of the carrier. See modulate. (2) (Frequency Modulation) Earlier magnetic disk encoding method that places clock bits onto the medium along with the data bits. It has been superseded by MFM and RLL.

Fn key (FuNction key) Keyboard key that works like a shift key to activate the second function on a dual- purpose key, typically found on laptops to reduce keyboard size. It is different than the function keys Fl, F2, etc.

FOCUS DBMS from Information Builders, that runs on PCs, mainframes and minis. It allows relational, hierarchical and network data structures and can access a variety of databases. It includes a fourth-generation language and a variety of decision support facilities.

FOIRL (Fiber Optic Inter Repeater Link) IEEE standard for fiber optic Ethernet.

folder In the Macintosh, a simulated file folder that holds documents (files), applications and other folders. A folder is like a DOS directory. Folders can be placed within other folders.

folio In typography, a printed page number. For example, folio 3 could be the 27th physical page in a book.

Folio VIEWS Text management software for PCs from Folio Corp. that provides storage, retrieval and hypertext capability for text databases: It can import text from over 40 file formats.

font Set of type characters of a particular design and size. The characteristics include typeface (Courier, Roman, etc), orientation (portrait or landscape, symbol set, spacing, pitch, point size, style (upright or italic) and strokç weight.

In daisy wheel printers, fonts are changed by changing the daisy wheel. In dot matrix printers, fonts are built in and can be selected by software or a control panel switch. In laser printers, some fonts are built in and others can be plugged in with a cartridge or downloaded from a computer. Fonts can be bitmapped or scalable.

Bitmapped Fonts: In a laser printer, characters are printed as patterns of dots, or bitmaps, and these bitmaps can be derived from several sources. Laser printers have some number of built in fonts in a limited number of point sizes that are always available. Additional fonts are available as plug-in cartridges that contain from a couple to a dozen or rnore.di'fferent typefaces. Fonts can also be purchased like software ("soft fonts"), copied into and stored in the computer and downloaded into the printer before printing. A font- generation system can also be used, such as Bitstream's Fontware, which comes with a set of font outlines that can be scaled into any point size (within a range) that you want. Like any bitmapped set of images, all the different point sizes take up room on the hard disk.

Scalable on the Fly: Scalable fonts, such as Adobe's Post&ript, are outline fonts that are generated into the bitmaps when needed either by the printer itself, or by a controller board in the computer. They take a bit longer to print, because the fonts are created with every print session, but there is no wasted hard disk space for fonts that are used only occasionally. Like bitmapped fonts, scalable outline fonts come built-in,, as plug-in cartridges or as soft fonts that are downloaded into the printer for scaling.

font cartridge Set of bitmapped or outline fonts for one or more typefaces contained in a module that plugs into a printer slot. The fonts are stored in a ROM chip within the cartridge. Contrast with soft font and internal font.

font compiler Same as font generator.

font editor Software that allows fonts to be designed and modified.

font family Set of fonts of the same typeface in assorted sizes, including the italics and bold variations for each size. See font.

font generator Software that converts an outline font into a bitmap (dot pattern required for a particular font size). Font generation is not linear, simply expanding a letter to atly size. As fonts get bigger, their characteristics must change in order to make them attractive. See font scaler.

font metric Typographic information (width, height, kerning) for each character in a font.

font rasterizer See font scaler.

font scaler Software that converts outline fonts into bitmaps. The term is used synonymously with font generator, but usually refers to re-generating the fonts on the fly each time they are required. See scalable font.

bat style (1) Same as typeface. (2) In the HP LaserJet, refers to upright or italicized text.

it utility Software that provides functions for managing fonts, including the ability to download, install, design and modify fonts.

font weight Thickness of characters (light, medium or bold).

Fontware Font generation system for PCs from Bitstream Inc., that includes a library of outline fonts and a font generator. Typeface packages include normal, italic, bold and bold italic weights.

footer In a document or report, common text that appears at the bottom of every page. It usually contains the page number.

footnote Text that appears at the bottom of a page, which adds explanation. It is often used to give çredit to the source of information. When accumulated and printed at the end of a document, they are called endnotes.

footprint Amount of geographic space covered by an object. A computer footprint is the desk or floor surface it occupies. A satellite's footprint is the earth area covered by its downlink.

for statement High-level programming langUage structure that repeats a series of instructions a specified number of times. It creates a loop that includes its own control information.

Force dBASE compiler from Sophco that combines C and dBASE structures. It is noted for generating very small executable programs.

forced page break A page break inserted by the user.

foreground/background Priority assigned to programs running in a multitasking environment. Foreground programs have highest priority, and background programs have lowest. In a personal computer, the foreground program is the one the user is currently working with, and the background program might be a print spooler or communications program.

Formt & Trees Data analysis program for PCs from (lannel Computing, that integrates data from a variety of applications.

form (1) Paper form used for printing. (2) Screen display designed for a particular application.

form factor Physical size of a device.

form feed Advancing a printer form to the top of the next page. It is done by pressing the printer's form feed (FF) button or by sending the form feed code (ASCII 12) to the printer from the computer.

form view Screen display showing one item or record arranged like a preprinted form. Contrast with table view.

format (1) Physical structure of an item. (2) A screen format is the layout of fields cm the screen. (3) A report format is the layout of the printed page including print columns, page headers and footers. See layout setting. (4) A record format is the layout of fields within the record. (5) A file or database format is the layout of fields and records within a data file, layout codes within a word processing document or display lists (vector) or bitmaps (raster) within a graphics file. It also includes the structure of header data, or identification data, that is typically affixed to the beginning of the file. (6) See disk format, low- level format and DOS Format.

format program Software that initializes a blank disk by recording sector identification on every storage sector that the disk can hold.

formula (1) Arithmetic expression that solves a problem. For example, (fahrenheit32)*5/9 is the formula for converting fahrenheit to centigrade. (2) In spreadsheet, an algorithm that identifies how the data in a specific number of cells is to be calculated. For.example, +A3+B8 means that the contents of cell A3 are to be added to the contents of cell B8 and the results are to be placed where the formula is located.

FORTH (FOuRTH-generation language) High-level programming language created by Charles Moore in the late 1960s as a way of providing direct control of the computer. Its syntax resembles LISP, it uses reverse polish notation for calculations, and it is noted for its extensibility. It is both compiler and interpreter. The source program is compiled first and then executed by its operating system/interpreter. It is used in process control applications that must quickly process data acquired from instruments and sensors. It is also used in arcade game programming as well as robotics and other Al applications.

FORTRAN (FORmula TRANslator) First high-level programming language and compiler, developed in 1954 by IBM. It was originally designed to express mathematical formulas, and although it is used occasionally for business applications, it is still the most widely used language for scientific, engineering and mathematical problems. FORTRAN IV is an ANSI standard, but FORTRAN V has various proprietary versions.

forward clialning In Al, a form of reasoning that starts with what is known and works toward a solution. Known as bottom-up approach. Contrast with backward chaining.

forward compatible Same as upward compatible.

forward error correction Communications technique that can correct bad data on the receiving end. Before transmission, the data is processed through an algorithm that adds extra bits for error correction. If the transmitted message is received in error, the correction bits are used to repair it.

fourth-generation computer Computer made up almost entirely of chips with limited amounts of discrete components. We are currently in the fourth generation.

fourth-generation language Computer language that is more advanced than traditional high-level programming languages. For example, in dBASE, the command LIST displays all the records in a data file. In second- and third- generation languages, instructions would have to be written to read each record, test for end of file, place each item of data on screen and go back and repeat the operation until there are no more records to process.

First-generation languages are machine languages; second-generation are machine dependent assembly languages; third-generation are high-level programming languages, such as FORTRAN, COBOL, BASIC, Pascal, and C. Although many languages, such as dBASE, are called fourth-generation languages, they are actually a mix of third and fourth. The dBASE LIST command is a fourth- generation command, but applications programmed in dBASE are third-generation.

Query language and report writers are also fourth-generation languages. Any computer language with English-lilEe commands that doesn't require traditional input-process-output logic falls into this category.

FoxBASE+ dBASE III PLUS-compatible DBMS for the Macintosh from Microsoft. Originally developed by Fox Software for the PC, FoxBASE gained a reputation for its high speed and compatibility.

FoxPro dBASE IV-compatible DBMS from Microsoft for PCs. An enhanced version of FoxBASE, FoxPro includes windowing, SQL and QBE interfac'es and "Rushmore" tedmology for fast queries on large databases.

fps Frames Per Second. See frame.

FPU (Floating Point Unit) Computer circuit that handles floating point operations.

fractals In computer graphics, the use of fractional mathematics to describe an image. It allow images of natural objects, such as trees, clouds and rivers, to be highly compressed for computer storage and transmission. Instead of turning an image into bitmaps (raster graphics) or lines (vector graphics), fractals turns an image into a set of data and an algorithm for expanding it back to the original. Fractals come from the science of "chaos," which, contrary to its name, reveals orderly patterns in the apparently chaotic universe.

fragmentation Uneven distribution of data on disk. As a file is updated, new data is stored in available free space, which may not be contiguous to the current data. Reading fragmented files requires extra head movement, slowing down the operation. A disk maintenance, or optimizer, program is used to reorder the files contigu9usly.

FRAM (1) (Ferroelectronic RAM) Non-volatile semiconductor memory that retains its content without power for up to 10 years. (2) (Ferromagnetic RAM) Non-volatile memory that records microscopic bits on a magnetic surface.

frame (1) In computer graphics, one screenful of data or its equivalent storage space. (2) In communications, a group of bits that make up an elementary block of data for transmission by certain protocols. (3) In Al, a data structure that holds a general description of an object. The description is derived from basic concepts and experience.

frame buffer In computer graphics, a separate memory component that holds a graphic image.

frame grabber In computer graphics, a device that converts video images into the computer manipulatable images. The frame grabber accepts standard TV signals and digitizes the current video frame into a computer graphics image.

frame relay High-speed packet switching protocol that provides faster transmission than X.25. It is suited for data and image transfer rather than voice.

FrameMaker Desktop publishing program from Frame Technology Corp., that runs on UNIX platforms, the Macintosh and Windows. Suited for structured documents, it is noted for its fully-integrated word processing and graphics capabilities. Optional viewers let documents run on machines without FrameMaker, providing a way to distribute hypertext-based help systems.

framework (1) In object-oriented programming, a genéralized subsystem design for building applications. It consists of abstract classes and their object collaboration as well as concrete classes. While objectoriented programming supports software reuse, frameworks support design reuse. (2) (FrameWork) Integrated software package for PCs from AshtonTate that included, a programming language. One of the first integrated packages.

framing bit Same as start bit and stop bit.

free-form database Database system that allows entry of text without regard to length or order. Although it accepts data as does a word processor, it differs by providing better methods for searching, retrieving and organizing the data.

free-form language Language in which statements can reside anywhere on a line or even cross over lines. It does not imply less syntax structure, just more freedom in placing statements. For example, any number of blank spaces are allowed between symbols. Most high-level programming languages are free- form.

FreeHand Full-featured Macintosh drawing program from Aldus Corp., that combines a wide range of drawing tools with special effects.

freeware Software distributed without charge. Ownership is retained by the developer who has control over its redistribution, including the ability to change the next release of the freeware to payware. See shareware and public domain software.

frequency Number of oscillations (vibrations) that are in an alternating current within one second. See carrier.

frequency division multiplexing See FDM. frequency modulation See FM.

frequency shift See FSK.

friction feed Mechanism that allows cut paper forms to be used in a printer. The paper is passedbetween the platen and a roller that presses tightly against it. Contrast with tractor feed.

frobnlcate Slang for manipulating and adjusting dials and buttons for fun.

front-end CASE CASE tools that aid in systems analysis and design. Contrast with back-end CASE.

front end processor Computer that handles the communications processing in a mainframe environment. It connects to the communications channels on one end and the mainframe on the other. It transmits and receives messages, assembles and disassembles packets and detects and corrects errors. It is sometimes synonymous with a communications controller, although the latter is usually not as flexible. In a LAN, the network adapters perform the functions of the front end processor.

fry To ruin circuitry by subjecting it to excessive heat or current.

fs Abbreviation for femtosecond.

FSK (Frequency Shift Keying) Simple modulation technique that merges binary data into a carrier. It creates only two changes in frequency: one for 0, another for 1.

FSR (Free System Resource) In Windows, the amount of unused memory in a 64K block (128K for Version 3.1) reserved for managing current applications- Every open window takes some space in this area.

FTAM (File Transfer Access and Management) Communications protocol for the transfer of files between systems of different vendors.

FTP (File Transfer Protocol) TCP/IP protocol that is used to log onto the network, list directories and copy files. It can also translate between ASCII and EBCDIC. See TFTP.

full-duplex Transmitting and receiving simultaneously. In pure digital networks, this is achieved with two pairs of wires. In analog networks or in digital networks using carriers, it is achieved by dividing the bandwidth of the line into two frequencies, one for sending, one for receiving.

full-featured Hardware or software that provides capabilities and functions comparable to the most advanced models or programs in the same category.

full page display A monitor that allows viewing an entire page at actual size. Makes for greater flexibility and ease in desktop publishing or word processing application.

full path Path name that includes the drive, starting, or root, directory, all subdirectories and ending with the file or object name. See also file specs.

full project life cycle Project from inception to completion.

full-screen Programming capability that allows data to be displayed in any row or column on screen. Contrast with teletype mode.

full-screen editing The ability to move the cursor over the entire screen to alter text.

fully populated Refers to a printed circuit board which contains the maximum number of chips that can be plugged into it.

function In programming, a routine that does a particular task. When the program passes control to a function, it performs the task and returns control to the instruction following the calling instruction. It may perform a stand-alone task, such as printing a message, or it may accept values (arguments) from the calling instruction, process them and pass the results back. Programming languages generally provide a set of standard functions and allow programmers to detine their own. C is built entirely around functions. Contrast with command, which is a fundamental instruction within the language. Though in programming, the term is specific, outside of programming, it is used to describe any operation such as the "data entry function."

function keys Set of keyboard keys used to command the computer (labelled Fl, F2, etc.). The commands associated with these keys are defined by the program. Function keys are also used with the control, alt and shift keys, allowing 40 functions to be performed with 10 keys. Software packages that make extensive use of these keys come with plastic templates that fit around them for visual identification. PC and AT keyboards have 10 function keys in a cluster on the left (Fi-FlO). On the Enhanced keyboard, all function keys were relocated across the top of the keyboard (F1-F12).

function library Collection of program routines. See function.

functional decomposition Breaking down a process into non-redundant operations.

functional specification Blueprint for the design of an information system. It provides documentation for the database, human and machine procedures, and all the input, processing and output detail for each data entry, query, update and report program in the system.

fuse (1) Protective device that is designed to melt, or blow, when a specified amount of current is passed through it. PROM chips are created as a series of fuses that are selectively blown in order to create the binary patterns in the chip. (2) To bond together.

fusible link Circuit line in a PROM chip or similar device that is designed to be blown apart. See PROM programmer.

fuzzy computer Specially-designed computer that employs fuzzy logic. Using such architectural components as analog circuits and parallel processing, fuzzy computers are designed for artificial intelligence applications.

fuzzy logic Mathematical technique for dealing with imprecise data and problems that have many solutions rather than one. It can deal with values between 0 and 1 and is more analogous to human logic than digital logic. Results can be mostly true and mostly false rather than true and false.

fuzzy search Inexact search for data that finds answers that come close to the desired data. It can get results when the exact spelling is not known or help users obtain information that is loosely related to a topic.

Failure transparency: In a distributed database system, the condition in which application programs are isolated from failure.

Field: (1) A logical group of bytes in a record; used with file processing. (2) In the context of a relational model, a synonym for attribute.

File-processing system: An information system in which data is stored in separate files. There is no integrated data dictionary. The format of the files is usually stored in application programs.

File server: In a local area network, a microcomputer containing a file that it processes on behalf of other microcomputers on the network. The term file server is normally used for the resource-sharing architecture. See Client computer, Client—server database architecture, Database server, and Resource-sharing architecture.

Firewall: A computer that serves as a security gateway between an intranet and the Internet. Firewalls monitor the source and destination of network traffic and filter it.

First normal form: Any table that fits the definition of a relation.

Flat file: A file that has only a single value in each field. The meaning of the columns is the same in every row.

Force-write: A write of database data in which the DBMS waits for acknowledgment from the operating system that the after-image of the write has been successfully written to the log.

Foreign key: An attribute that is a key of one or more relations other than the one in which it appears.

Form: (1) A display on a computer screen used to present, enter, and modify data, A form is also called a data entry form or panel. (2) A paper document used in a business system to record data, usually concerning a transaction. Forms are analyzed in the process of building a data model.

Forms generator: A portion of the application development subsystem used to create a data entry form without having to write any application program code.

Formula domain: A domain whose values are computed by an expression containing arguments that are themselves domains.

Fourth normal form: A relation in third Boyce—Codd normal form in which every multivalued dependency is a functional dependency.

Fragment: A row in a table (or record in a file) in which a required parent or child is not present. For example, a row in a LINE-ITEM table for which no ORDER row exists.

FTP: File transfer protocol. A standard Internet service for copying files to or from a remote server.

Fully concatenated key: In DL/I, a composite of the sequence fields of a segment and the sequence fields of all its parents. The root occupies the leftmost position in the concatenated key, and the segment occupies the rightmost position.

Functional dependency: A relationship between attributes in which one attribute or group of attributes determines the value of another. The expressions X — Y, "X determines Y," and "Y is functionally dependent on X" mean that given a value of X, we can determine the value of Y.

G

G See giga.

G-byte See gigabyte.

gain Amount of increase that an amplifier provides on the output side of the circuit. -

gallium arsenide Alloy of gallium and arsenic compound (GaAs) that is used as the base material for chips. It is several times faster than silicon.

games theory The branch of mathematics concerned with probability, among other things; the mathematical process of selecting an optimum strategy in the face of an opponent who also has a strategy. The term was first used by John von Neumann in 1928 to describe the strategy of winning at poker.

gamma correction In computer graphics, using a formula to provide a range of intensities that appear uniform to the human eye.

gang punch To punch an identical set of holes into a deck of punched cards.

Gantt chart Form of floating bar chart usually used in project management to show resources or tasks over time.

gap (1) Space between blocks of data on magnetic tape. (2) Space in a read/write head over which magnetic flux (energy) flows causing the underlying magnetic tape or disk surface to become magnetized in the corresponding direction.

gapless Magnetic tape that is recorded in a continuous stream without interbiock gaps.

garbage (1) A term often used to describe incorrect answers from a computer program, usually resulting from inaccuracies in data entry or a mistake in a computer program but sometimes from equipment malfunction. (2) Unwanted and meaningless data carried in storage. (3) Incorrect input to a computer.

garbage collection Routine that searches memory for program segments or data that are no longer active in order to reclaim that space.

garbage In, garbage ou see GIGO.

garbage In, gospel out See GOGI.

gas discharge display See plasma display.

gas plasma See plasma display.

gate (1) One of the AND, OR and NOT Boolean logic gates that ties transistors together. See Boolean logic and gate array. (2) The line that triggers the switch in a MOS transistor.

gate array Chip type that contains unconnected logic elements. The finished, customized chip is obtained by adhering the top metal layer of pathways between the elements. This final masking stage is. less costly than designing the chip from scratch.

It usually contains only two-input NAND gates, which can be used singularly or connected with other NAND gates to provide all the Boolean operations required for digital logic.

gateway Computer that interconnects and performs the protocol conversion between two different types of networks. For example, a gateway between a personal computer LAN and a mainframe network, Contrast with bridge.

gather write To output data from two or more noncontiguous memory locations with one write operation. See scatter read.

gauss Unit of measurement of magnetic energy.

Gaussian distribution Random distribution of events that is often graphed as a bell-shaped curve. It is used to represent a normal or statistically probable outcome.

Gaussian noise In communications, a random interference generated by the movement of electricity in the line. Also called white noise.

GB, Gb See gigabyte and gigabit. Gblt See gigabit.

Gblts/sec (G1gaBITS per SECond) Billion bits per second.

GBps, Gbps (GigaBytes Per Second, GigaBits Per Second) Billion bytes per second. Billion bits per second.

GByte See gigabyte.

Gbytes/sec (GigaBYTES per SECond) Billion bytes per second.

GCR (1) (Group Code Recording) Encoding method used in tape drives and certain low-density floppy disks. (2) (Gray Component Replacement) Method for reducing amount of printing ink used. It substitutes black for the amount of gray contained in a color, thus black ink is used instead of the three CMY inks. See UCR and dot gain.

GDDM (Graphical Data Display Manager) Software that generates graphics images in the IBM mainframe environment. It contains routines to generate graphics on terminals, printers and plotters as well as accepting input from scanners. Programmers use it for creating graphics, but users can employ its Interactive Chart Utility (ICU) to create business graphics without programming.

GDI (Graphics Device Interface) Windows graphics language used to provide output to the screen, printer or other device. Applications create images on screen by calling GDI functions.

GDM See CGM.

GE (Greater than or Equal to) See relational operator.

GEM (Graphics Environment Manager) Graphical user interface for PCs from Digital Research. Ventura Publisher comes with a runtime version of GEM.

gender changer Coupler that reverses the gender of one of the connectors in order that two male connectors or two female connectors can be joined together.

general-purpose computer Refers to computers that follow instructions, thus virtually all computers from micro to mainframe are general purpose. Even computers in toys, games and single-function devices follow instructions in their built-in program. In contrast, computational devices can be designed from scratch for special purposes (see ASIC).

general-purpose controller Peripheral control unit that can service more than one type of peripheral device; for example, a printer and a communications line.

general-purpose language Programming language used to solve a wide variety of problems. All common programming languages (FORTRAN, COBOL, BASIC, C, Pascal, etc.) are examples. Contrast with special- purpose language.

generalized program Software that serves a changing environment. By allowing variable data to be introduced, the program can solve the same problem for different users or situations.

bgenerator (1) Software that creates software. See application.generator and macro generator. (2) Device that creates electrical power or synchronization signals.

Generic CADD Full-featured PC CADD package from Generic Software, that offers levels for beginner, intermediate and advanced users.

GEnie (General Electric Network for Information Exchange) Online information service from GE Information Services that provides business information, news and access to special interest groups.

Genifer dBASE application generator from Bytel Corp., that creates dBASE source code.

genlock (generator lock) Circuitry that synchronizes video signals for mixing. In personal computers, a genlock display adapter converts screen output into an NTSC video signal, which it synchronizes with an external video source.

bgeostationary Same as geosynchronous.

geosynchronous Earth aligned. Refers to communications satellites that are placed 22,300 miles above the equator and travel at the same speed as the earth's rotation, thus appearing to be stationary from earth's point of view.

GeoWorks Ensemble Popular graphical operating environment for DOS from GeoWorks, that includes word processing, drawing, communications, card file and calendar applications. It provides complete DOS file management and simulates file folders like the Macintosh. Users can launch all applications from within Ensemble. GeoWorks Pro also includes the Quattro Pro spreadsheet.

germanium (Ge) Material used in making the first transistors

Although still used in very limited applications, germanium was replaced by silicon years ago.

gesture recognition Ability to interpret simple handwritten symbols such as check marks and slashes.

get In programming, a request for the next record in an input file. Contrast with put.

Gilops See gigaflops.

ghost (1) Faint second image that appears close to the primary image on a display or printout. On a display, it is caused by phosphor. In transmission, it is a resuit of secondary signals that arrive ahead of or later than the primary signal. On a printout, it is caused by bouncing print elements as the paper passes by. (2) To display a menu option in a dimmed, fuzzy typeface, indicating it i.s not selectable at this time.

GHz (GigaHertZ) One billion cycles per second.

GIF (Graphics -Interchange Format) Popular raster graphics file format develooed by CompuServe that handles 8-bit color (256 colors) and uses the LZW method to achieve compression ratios of approximately 1.5:1 to 2:1.

glga Billion. Abbreviated "0." It often refers to the precise value 1,073,741,824 since computer specifications are usually binary numbers. See binary values and space/time.

gigabit One billion bits. Also Gb, Gbit and G-bit. See giga and space/time.

gigabyte One billion bytes. Also GB, Gbyte and G-byte. See giga and space/time.

gigaflops (GIGA FLoating point OPerations per Second) One billion floating point operations per second.

GIGO "Garbage in, garbage out" or Invalid input causes invalid output. Variation is "Garbage in, gospel out" or putting too much faith in computer output!

GIS (1) (Geographic Information System) Digital mapping system used for exploration, demographics, dispatching and tracking. (2) (Generalized Information System) Early IBM mainframe query and data manipulation language.

GKS (Graphical Kernel System) Device-independent graphics language for 2-D, 3-D and raster graphics images. It allows graphics applications to be developed on one system and easily moved to another with minimal or no change. It was the first true standard for graphics applications programmers and has been adopted by both ANSI and ISO.

glare filter Fine mesh screen that is placed over a CRT screen to reduce glare from overhead and ambient light.

glitch Temporary or random hardware malfunction. It is possible that a bug (permanent error) in a program may cause the hardware to appear as if it had a glitch in it and vice versa. At times it can be extremely difficult to determine whether a problem lies within the hardware or the software.

global Pertaining to an entire file, database, volume, program or system.

global search and replace In word processing, the ability to find string anywhere it appears in a document and to substitute another string for it.

global variable In programming, a variable that is used by all modules in a program.

glue chip Support chip that adds functionality to a microprocessor, for example, an I/O processor or extra memory.

goal seeking Ability to calculate a formula backward to obtain a desired input. For example, given the goal gross margin 50% as well as the range of possible inputs, goal seeking attempts to obtain the optimum input.

gooey See GUI.

GOTO (1) In a high-level programming language, a statement that directs the computer to go to some other part of the program. Low-level language equivalents are branch and jump. (2) In dBASE, a command that directs the user to a specific record in the file. (3) In word processing, a command that directs the user to a specific page number.

GOTO-less programming Writing a program without using GOTO instructions, an important rule in structured programming. A GOTO instruction points to a different part of the program without a guarantee of returning. Instead of using GOTOs, structures called subroutines or functions are used, which automatically return to the next instruction after the calling instruction when completed.

Gouraud shading In computer graphics, a technique developed by Henri Gouraud that computes a shaded surface based on the color and illumination at the corners of polygonal facets.

GPF (General Protection Fault) Application program abend in Windows Version 3.1. See UAE.

GPI (Graphical Programming Interface) Graphics language in OS/2 Presentation Manager. It is a derivative of the GDDM mainframe interface and includes Bezier curves.

GPSS (General Purpose Simulation System) Programming language for discrete event simulation, which is used to build models of operations such as manufacturing environments, communications systems and traffic patterns.

grabber (1) A device for capturing data, e.g., a video digitizer. (2) A computer program that takes a "snapshot" of the currently displayed screen image by transferring a portion of view of memory to a file on disk. (3) The fixture on the end of a test equipment lead wire with a spring actuated hook and claw designed to connect the measuring instrument to a pin of an integrated circuit, socket, transistor, and so foi lb.

grabber hand Pointer in the shape of a hand that is moved by a mouse to "grab" and relocate objects on screen.

graceful degradation A system that,-after a failure of one of its components, can continue to perform at some reduced level of performance.

graceful exit Ability to get out of a problem situation in a program without having to turn the computer off

grade Transmission capacity of a line. It refers to a range or class of frequencies that it can handle; for example, telegraph grade, voice grade and broadband.

gradient Color spread from light to dark to shade an object or give it a sense of depth. It is also used to create a colorful background.

grammar checker Software that checks the grammar of a sentence. It can check for and highlight incomplete sentences, awkward phrases, incorrect punctuation, wordiness and poor grammar.

Grammatik Popular grammar checking program for DOS, Windows, Macintosh and UNIX from Refer- ence Software. Now bundled along with WordPerfect 6.0.

grandfather, father, son Method for storing previous generations of master file data that are continuously updated. The son is the current file, the father is a copy of the file from the previous cycle, and the grandfather is a copy of the file from the cycle before that one.

grandfather file The oldest backup file copy. See father file.

graph Pictorial representation of information. See business graphics.

graphic character Printable symbol that includes digits and letters

graphical Interface See GUI.

graphics With regard to the computer, the creation and management of pictures. Pictures can be entered into the computer using input devices such as graphics tablets, mice or light pens, and existing pictures on paper can be also scanned using scanners or cameras, frames of video recordings can also be captured.

Once stored, pictures can be manipulated and copied in many ways. Colors can be changed, objects can be increased and decreased in size, slanted,

squeezed and squashed, text added and the image can be printed out or otherwise stored.

A graphics computer system requires a graphics display screen, a graphics input device (tablet, mouse, scanner, camera, etc.), a graphics output device (dot matrix printer, laser printer, plotter, etc.) and a graphics software package; for example, a CAD, draw or paint program.

The higher the resolution of the graphics output device, the better the printed image will look. The higher the resolution of the display screen, the more realistic the images will appear on it.

Vector Graphics and Raster Graphics: Two methods are used for storing and maintaining pictures in a computer. The first method, called vector graphics (also known as object-oriented graphics), maintains the image as a series of points, lines, arcs and other geometric shapes. The second method, called raster graphics, resembles television, where the picture image is made up of dots.

Vector graphics is the method employed by CAD (computer-aided design) and drawing packages. As you draw, each line of the image is stored as a vector (two end points on an x-y matrix). For example, a square becomes four vectors, one for each side. A circle is turned into dozens or hundreds of tiny straight lines, the number of which is determined by the resolution of the drawing. The entire image is commonly stored in the computer as a list of vectors, called a display list. Older CAD systems used vector display screens that 'drew" the image directly from the vectors. Today, most screens are raster graphics displays (made up of dots), and the vectors are 'rasterized" into the required dot patterns by hardware or software.

Raster Graphics for Imaging and Painting Raster graphics is the TV-like method that uses dots to display an image on screen. Raster graphics images are created by scanners and cameras and are also generated by paint packages. A picture frame is divided into hundreds of horizontal rows, with each row containing hundreds of dots, called pixels. Raster graphics images take up more space on disk than their vector graphics counterpart, since storage for each pixel is required even if it's part of the background. A small object in vector graphics format will take up only a few vectors in the display list file.

When you scan an image or paint an object into the computer, the image is created in a reserved area of memory called a bitmap, with some number of bits corresponding to each dot (pixel). The simplest monochrome bitmap uses one bit (on/off) for each dot. Gray scale bitmaps (monochrome shades) hold a number for each dot large enough to hold all the gray levels. Color bitmaps require three times as much storage in order to hold the intensity of red, green and blue.

The image in the bitmap is continuously transmitted to the video screen, dot for dot, a line at a time, over and over again. Any changes made to the bitmap are instantly reflected on the screen. Animation is accomplished by continuously copying new sequences from other areas in memory into the bitmap, one after the other.

Desktop laser printers and graphics plotters connected to personal computers have higher resolutions than the standard graphics screens that are used to display the images. That means the jagged lines on a display screen can print more uniformly on a laser printer.

graphics accelerator High-performance video display board for graphical user interfaces that has line drawing and pixel block move functions (bitblt) built into hardware. See graphics engine.

graphics adapter Same as video display board

graphics based Display of text and pictures as graphics images; typically bitmapped images. Contrast with text based.

graphics card Same as video display board.

graphics engine Specialized hardware that performs graphics processing independently of the main CPU. It can perform any of a variety of functions, such as generating graphic geometry (display list processing), converting vectors to rasters (rasterization), compression, matrix multiplication (for fast rotation) as well as providing faster data transfer from memory to the display. Graphics engines are programmed in a graphics language.

graphics file File that contains only graphics data. Contrast with text file and binary file.

bgraphics Interface See graphics language and GUI. graphics language Set of instructions that let a programmer express a graphics image in a high-level language. The language is translated into graphics images by software or specialized hardware. See graphics engine.

graphics mode Screen display mode that displays graphics. Contrast with text mode and character mode.

graphics port (1) Socket on the computer for connecting a graphics monitor. (2) Macintosh graphics structure that defines all the characteristics of a graphics window (also called GratPort).

graphics primitive Elementary graphics building block, such as a point, line or arc. In a solid modelling system, a cylinder, cube and sphere are examples of primitives.

graphics processor Same as graphics engine. graphics tablet See digitizer tablet.

graphics terminal (1) I/O device that displays pictures in raster graphics, vector graphics format or both. Images are received via communications or entered with a mouse or light pen. The keyboard may have specialized function keys, wheels or dials. (2) Terminal or personal computer that displays graphics.

graPHIGS See GDDM.

gray scale In computer graphics, a series of shades from white to black. The more gray scale, the more realistically an image can be recorded and displayed, especially a scanned photo. Scanners differentiate typically from 16 to 256 levels of gray scale, but the amount that can be entered into the computer depends on display system, memory and disk space. Although compression techniques help reduce the size of graphics files, high-resolution gray scale requires huge amounts of storage.

Gray scale is widely used in laptop displays. While good for graphics, colors used in many text applications translate into shades that are difficult to differentiate. Many applications provide an optional monochrome display mode for laptop use that changes colors to black and white for sharpest contrast.

greek To display text in a representative form in which the actual letters are not discernible. For example, when previewing a finished document in desktop publishing, if the display screen is not large enough to handle the resolution, the text is greeked.

grep (Global Regular Expression and Print) UNIX pattern matching utility that searches for a string of text and outputs any line that contains the pattern.

ground Electrically conductive body, such as the earth, which maintains a zero potential (not positively or negatively charged) for connecting to an electrical circuit.

ground current Current found in a ground line. May be caused by imbalanced electrical sources; for example, the ground line in a communications channel between two computers deriving power separately.

ground fault Temporary current in the ground line, caused by a failing electrical component or interference from an external electrical source such as a thunderstorm.

ground loop Unwanted ground current flowing back and forth between two devices that are grounded at two or more points.

ground noise injection Intentional insertion of unwanted noise by a power supply into the ground line.

groupware Software that is designed for use in a network and serve a group of users that work on a related project.

GSOS (OS Operating System) Graphical operating system for the Apple IIGS that also accepts ProDOS applications.

GT (Greater Than) See relational operator.

guard band Frequency that insulates one signal from another. In an analog telephone line, the low band is 0-300; the high band is 3300-4000FIz.

GUI (Graphical User Interface) Graphics-based user interface that incorporates icons, pull-down menus and a mouse. Macintosh, Windows, Presentation Manager (OS/2), Motif and Open Look are examples. See Star. Contrast with CUI.

GUI accelerator See graphics accelerator. gulp Some number of bytes!

gutter In typography, the space between two columns.

GW-BASIC (Gee Whiz-BASIC) BASIC interpreter that accompanied MS-DOS in versions prior to 5.0. See QBasic.

Generalization hierarchy: A set of objects or entities of the same logical type that are arranged in a hierarchy of logical subtypes. For example, EMPLOYEE has the subtypes ENGINEER and ACCOUNTANT, and ENGINEER has the subtypes ELECTRICAL ENGiNEER and MECHANICAL ENGINEER. Subtypes inherit characteristics of their supertypes.

Generalization object: An object that coxitains subtype objects. The generalization object ad its subtypes all have the same key. Subtype objfrts inherit attributes from the generalization objec1. A generalization object is also called a supertype hbject.

Granularity: The size of database resource that can be locked. Locking the entire database is large granularity; locking a column of a particular row is small granularity.

Graphical user interface: An interface having windows, graphical symbols, pop-down menus, and other structures that are often manipulated with a mouse pointer. Popular graphical user interface products are Windows from Microsoft and the Macintosh System Software from Apple.

Group identifier: An attribute that identifies a unique instance of a group within a semantic object or another group.

Growing phase: The first stage in two-phase locking in which locks are acquired but not released.

GUI: See Graphical user interface.

H

h (Hexadecimal) Symbol that refers to a hex number. For example, 09h has a numeric value'of 9, whereas OAh has a value of 10. See hex chart.

hacker Person who writes programs in assembly language or in system-level languages, such as C. Although it may refer to any programmer, it implies very tedious “hacking away” at the bits and bytes. It sometimes refers to a person who breaks a code and gains illegal entrance into a system.(1) A skilled computer enthusiast who works alone and is obsessed with learning about prqgramming and exploring the capabilities of computer systems. (2) A person who gains access to a computer system or network without authorization.

half-adder Elementary electronic circuit in the ALU that adds one bit to another, deriving a result bit and a carry bit.

half-duplex Transmission of data in both directions, but only one direction at a time. Thro-way radio was the first to use half-duplex, for example, while one party spoke, the other party listened. Contrast with full- duplex.

half height drive 5.25” disk drive that takes up half the vertical spade of first-generation drives, It is 1 5/8” high by 5.75” wide.

halftone In printing, the simulation of a continuous-tone image (shaded drawing, photograph) with groups of dots. MI printing processes, except for Cycolor, print dots. The smaller the dots and the wider they are spaced apart, the lighter the image. The denser the dots, the darker the image. Looking at a newspaper or magazine photograph through a magnifying glass shows how different dot densities simulate continuous shades. See dithering.

hammer In a printer, the mechanism that pushes the typeface onto the ribbon and paper or pushes the paper into the ribbon and typeface.

Hamming code Communications error correction method that intersperses three check bits at the end of each four data bits. At the receiving station, the check bits are used to detect and correct one-bit errors automatically.

hand-held scanner A optical scanner that is operated by manually running a scanning head an image. Small rollers on the bottom of the scanning head serve to guide the hand movement.

handle (1) In computer graphics, a tiny square attached to a graphic image used for moving or reshaping the image. The handle is selected by moving the cursor onto it and pressing a key or mouse button. (2) Temporary name or number assigned to a file, font or other object. For example, an operating system may assign a sequential number to each file that it opens as a way of identifying and keeping track of it.

handler Software routine that performs a particular task. For example, upon detection of an error, an error handler is called upon to recover from the error condition.

handset The part of the telephone that contains the speaker and the microphone.

handshaking Signals transmitted back and forth over a communications network that establish a valid connection between two stations.

hands-on Pertaining to the process of physically using a computer system.

handwriting recognition Scanning handwritten material with a computer, controlled visual scanning device to determine information content or to verify a signature.

hanging indent A paragraphing style with a full-measure first line and indented succeeding lines (called turnover lines).

hanging paragraph In typography, a paragraph of text in which the first line starts at the left margin, but the second and subsequent lines are indented.

hard boot Same as cold boot.

hard coded Software that performs a fixed number of tasks or works with only a fixed number of devices. For example, a program could be written to work with only two types of printers and not allow any Other types to be introduced. Hard coded solutions to problems are usually the fastest, but do not allow for future flexibility.

hard copy Printed output. Contrast with soft copy.

hard disk Metal disk covered with a magnetic recording material. It comes in removable and fixed varieties that hold from five to several hundreds megabytes. Contrast with floppy disk.

Hard Disk Measurements: Capacity is measured in bytes, and speed is measured in bytes per second (transfer rate) and in milliseconds (access time). Fast personal computer hard disk access times range from 12 to 28ms in larger computers as fast as ims.

bard error (1) Permanent, unrecoverable error such as a disk read error. Contrast with soft error. (2) Group of errors that requires user intervention and includes disk read errors, disk not ready (no disk in drive) and printer not ready (out of paper).

hard hyphen Hyphen that always prints. Contrast with soft hyphen.

hard return Code entered into a text document by pressing the return (enter) key. DOS and OS/2 text files use a CRLF (carriage return/line feed) pair, but this is not standard (WordPerfect uses only an LF). The Macintosh uses a CR and UNIX uses an LF. Itmay be represented by a visible symbol on screen, or it may remain invisible until revealed in an expanded screen mode. Contrast with soft return.

hard sectored Sector identification technique that uses a physicaL mark. For example, hard sectored floppy disks have a hole in the disk that marks the beginning of each sector. Contrast with soft sectored.

hard space Special space character that acts like a letter or digit, used in word processors to prevent multiple-word proper names from breaking between lines.

Hardcard Family of PC hard disks from Plus Development Corp., that houses the disk and controller on an expansion board. It is noted for its high reliability and allows for the inclusion of hard disks when all drive bays are filled.

hardware Machinery and equipment (CPU, disks, tapes, modem, cables, etc.). In operation, a computer is both hardware and software. One is useless without the other. The hardware design specifies the commands it can follow, and the instructions tell it what to do. See instruction set. The more memory and disk storage a computer has, the more work it can do. The faster the memory and disks transmit data and instructions to the CPU, the faster the work gets done.

hardware failure Malfunction within the electronic circuits or electromechanical components (disks, tapes) of a computer system. Contrast with software failure.

hardware Interrupt Interrupt caused by some action of a hardware device, such as the depression of a key or mouse movement. See interrupt.

hardware key Copy protection device supplied with software that plugs into a computer port. The software interrogates the key's serial number during execution to verify its presence. The hardware key acts as a pass-through, but tests for a special code that reads the serial number.

hardware monitor Device connected to the circuits of a computer in order to analyze its performance.

hardware virtual memory Virtual memory management built into a chip. Although virtual memory can be performed by software only, it is far more efficient to do it in hardware. See DAT and PMMU.

bardwlred (1) Electronic circuitry that is designed to perform a specific task. See hard coded. (2) Devices that are closely or tightly coupled. For example, a hardwired terminal is directly connected to a computer without going through a switched network.

harmonic distortion In communications, frequencies that are generated as multiples of the original frequency due to irregularities in the transmission line.

Harvard Graphics Popular PC business graphics program from Software Publishing Corp. It was one of the first business graphics packages and provides the ability to create columnar and free form text charts.

hash total Method for ensuring the accuracy of processed data. It is a total of several fields of data in a file, including fields not normally used in calculations, such as account number. At various stages in the pro. cessing, the hash total is recalculated and compared with the original. If any data has been lost or changed, a mismatch signals an error.

Hayes compatible Refers to modems controlled by the Hayes command language. See AT command set.

Hayes Smartmodem Family of intelligent modems for personal computers from Hayes Microcomputer Products. Hayes developed the intelligent modem for first- generation personal computers in 1978, and its command language (Hayes Standard AT Command Set) for modem control has become an industry- standard. An intelligent modem has a command state and an online state. In the command state, it accepts instructions. In the online state, it dials, answers, transmits and receives.

Once connected, it performs the handshaking with the remote modem, which is similar to the opening exchange of a telephone call. Once the handshake is completed, you are online with the other computer, and data can be transmitted back and forth.

An important part of the Hayes standard is the escape sequence, which tells the modem to switch from online to the command state.

HD (1) (High Density) Refers to 1.2MB 5.25" floppy disks and 1.44MB 3.5" floppy disks, See high density. (2) (Hard Disk) For example, FD/HD refers to a floppy disk/hard disk device such as a controller.

HDA (Head Disk Assembly) Mechanical components of a disk drive (minus the electronics), which includes the actuators, access arms, read/write heads and plat ters.

HDD (Hard Disk Drive) See hard disk.

HDTV (High Definition TV) TV with double the resolution of the current 525-line NTSC standard. The problem is deciding on a standard for transmitting both signals at the same time.

HDX See half-duplex.

head See read/write head.

head crash Physical destruction of a hard disk. Misalignment or contamination with dust can cause the read/write head to collide with the disk's recording surface. Not only is the data is destroyed, both the disk platter and head have to be replaced.

head-per-track disk Disk drive that has a read/write head positioned over each track, thus eliminating the access arm movement from track to track.

head skew Offset distance from the start of the previous track so that the head has time to switch from top of platter to bottom of platter and be at the start of the new track. See cylinder skew.

header (1) In data processing, the first record in a file that identifies the file. The name of the file, date of last update and various other status data are stored in the header. (2) In a document or report, common text that is printed at th top of every page. (3) In communications, the first part of the message that contains controlling data, such as originating and destination stations, message type and priority level. (4) Any caption or description used as a headline.

header label Record used for file identification that is recorded at the beginning of the file.

heap In programming, the free memory currently available to load and run programs.

heat sink Material or device that absorbs heat.

helical scan Diagonal tracking used on videotape and digital audio tape (DAT), which increases storage capacity over parallel methods.

help On-screen instruction regarding the use of a program. On PCs, pressing Fl is the de facto standard for getting help. With graphics-based interfaces (Mac, Windows, etc.), clicking a"?" or HELP button gets help. See context sensitive help.

help complier Software that translates text and compiler instructions into an online help system.

Hercules Graphics Video display standard for PCs from Hercules Computer Technology, that provides monochrome graphics and text with a resolution of 720x348 pixels. IBM's first PC monochrome display did not provide graphics, and Hercules introduced its display adapter to fill the void in 1982. It quickly became a de facto standard incorporated into all monochrome display boards.

hermaphroditic A term referring to connectors in which each piece has protruding and receptacle parts, rather than one piece configured as male and one as female.

Hertz Frequency of electrical vibrations (cycles) per second. Abbreviated "Hz," one Hz is equal to one cycle per second. In 1883, Heinrich Hertz detected electromagnetic waves.

heterogeneous environment Equipment from a variety of manufacturers.

heuristic Method of problem solving using exploration and trial and error methods. Heuristic program design provides a framework for solving the problem in contrast with a fixed set of rules (algorithmic) that cannot vary.

heuristic learnIng A discovery method of learning from experience. A way that computers can learn their mistakes by eliminating unsuccessful or unproductive options from their operations. See artificial intelligence and machine learning.

Hewlett-Packard See HP.

hex (HEXadecimal) Hexadecimal means 16. Base 16 numbering system used as a shorthand for representing binary numbers.

hexadecimal See hex.

HFS (Hierarchical File System) Macintosh file system that allows files to be placed into folders, and fold.ers to be placed within other folders.

hi-res Same as high resolution.

hidden codes The hidden text formatting codes embedded in a document by an on-screen formatting program.

hidden file File classification that prevents a file from being accessed. it is usually an operating system file; however, utility programs let users hide files to prevent unauthorized access.

hidden lines (1) When displaying a three-dimensional object, any line that would normally be obscured from the viewer's sight by the mass of the object itself, visible as a rest of the projection. (2) Lines that have been drawn on the screen in background color and will not become visible until the colors are switched. (3) Lines of a diagram that are invisible.

hidden line removal The process of deleting line segments from a drawing when they would be obscured were the object displayed as a solid three-dimensional figure. Many types of computer graphics software and hardware can removesuch hidden lines automatically.

hierarchIcal Structure made up of different levels like a company organization chart. The higher levels have control or precedence over the lower levels. Hierarchical structures are a one to many relationship; each item having one or more items below it. In communications, a hierarchical network refers to a single computer that has control over all the nodes connected to it.

hierarchical communications Network controlled by a host computer that is responsible for managing all connections. Contrast with peer-to-peer communications.

hierarchical file system File organization method that stores data in a top-to-bottom organization structure. All access to the data starts at the top and proceeds throughout the levels of the hierarchy.

In DOS and OS/2, the root directory is the starting point. Files can be storejin the root directory, or directories can be created off the root that hold files and subdirectories.

In the Macintosh, the disk window is the starting point. Files can be stored in the disk window, or folders can be created that can hold files and additional folders.

high color (1) Ability to generate 32,768 colors (15 bits) or 65,536 colors (16-bit). See true color. (2) Ability to generate a large number of colors.

high definition TV See HDTV.

high density Refers to increased storage capacity of bits and/or tracks per square inch, primarily in disks. See HD.

high DOS memory Same as UMA.

high-level format Information (indexes, tables, etc.) recorded on a disk that is required by a specific operating system. See low-level format.

high-level language Machine-independent programming language, such as FORTRAN, COBOL, BASIC, Pascal and C. It lets the programmer concentrate on the logic of the problem to be solved rather than the intricacies of the machine architecture such as is reqwred with low- level assembly languages.

high memory (1) Uppermost end of memory. (2) In PCs, the area between 640K and 1M, or the 64K HMA area between 1024 and 1088K

high resolution High-quality image on a display screen or printed form. The more dots used per square inch, the higher the quality. To display tot'dly realistic images including the shades of human skin requires about 1,000 × 1,000 pixels on a 12" diagonal screen.

High Sierra First CD ROM standard named for an area near Lake Tahoe where it was.conceived in 1985. Later evolved into the 150 9660 standard.

high tech Refers to the latest advancements in computers and electronics as well as to the social and political environment and consequences created by such machines.

highlight To identify an area on screen in order to select, move, delete or change it in some manner. Highlighted area shows un on the monitor in reverse video.

highlight bar Line in an on-screen menu that is displayed in reverse video or in a different color to signal the current selection/cursor position.

HLJaak Graphics file conversion and screen capture program for PCs from Inset Systems Inc. It supports a wide variety of raster and vector graphics formats as well as fax boards. It also handles conversion between PC and Mac formats.

HIMEM.SYS XMS driver in DOS 5.0 and Windows 3.0 that allows programs to cooperatively allocate extended memory in 286s and up. See XMS and DOS HIMEM,SYS.

hints Special additions to PostScript fonts that instruct the imaging device to alter space and other font features based on type size, especially for small font sizes.

HIPO (Hierarchy plus Input-Process-Output) Pronounced "hy-po." IBM flow-charting technique that provides a graphical method for designing and documenting programs.

histogram Chart displaying horizontal or vertical bars. The length of the bars are in proportion to the values of the data items they represent.

history User input within the current session. A history feature keeps track of user commands and/ or retrieved items so that they can be quickly reused or reviewed.

hit The successful comparison of two items of data. Compare match.

HMA (High Memory Area) In PCs, the first 64K of extended memory from 1024K to 1088K, which can be accessed by DOS in Real Mode. It is managed by the HIMEM.SYS driver.

HMOS (High-density MOS) NMOS chip that packs a higher number of electronic components per surface area than the original NMOS designs.

hog Program that uses an excessive amount of computer resources, such as memory or disk, or takes a long time to execute.

Hollerith machine First automatic data processing system. It was used to count the 1890 U.S. census. Developed by Herman Hollerith, a statistician who had worked for the Census Bureau, the system used a hand punch to record the data in dollar-bill-sized punched cards and a tabulating machine to count them. It was estimated that, with manual methods, the 1890 census would have taken ten years, but with Hot lerith 's machines, it took two years and saved five million dollars.

Hollerith later formed the Tabulating Machine Company and sold his machines throughput the world for a variety of accounting functions. In 1911, his company was merged into the company that was later to become IBM.

hologram A three-dimensional "photograph" created by holography

holographic store Storage in the form of a hologram. holography A method of storing data by making a multidimensional photograph on a storage medium.

home brew Products that are developed at home by hobbyists.

home button Icon that represents the beginning of a file or a set of operations.

home computer Low-priced personal computer such as the Apple II, Commodore 64 and 128, Tandy Color Computer and Atari ST.

home key Keyboard key used to move the cursor to the top of the screen or file or to the previous word or beginning of line. See home button.

home row The row of keys on the keyboard where users rest their fingers between keystrokes.

Honeywell See Bull HN.

hook In programming, instructions that provide logical breakpoints fus future expansion. Hooks may be changed to call some outside routine or function or may be places where additional processing is added.

hooked vector Trapped interrupt in a PC. The pointer for a particular interrupt in the interrupt vector table has been modified to jump.to a new routine to service that interrupt.

hookemware Free software that contains a limited number of features designed to entice the user into purchasing the more comprehensive version.

hopper Tray, or chute, that accepts input to a mechani-' cal device, such as a disk duplicator.

horizontal resolution Number of elements, or dots, on a horizontal line (columns in a matrix). Contrast with vertical resolution.

horizontal scan frequency Number of lines illuminated on a video screen in one second. For example, a resolution of 400 lines refreshed 60 times per second requires a scan rate of 24KHz plus some overhead (time to bring the beam back to the beginning of the next line). Same as horizontal synchronization frequency in TV. Contrast with vertical scan frequency.

horizontal sync See horizontal scan frequency.

host Main computer in a distributed processing environment. It typically refers to a large timesharing computer or a central computer that controls a network.

host adapter Device that connects a peripheral unit to a computer (com,puter may be any size). It contains less electronics than a controller. For example, an IDE disk drive has a built-in controller and connects to a non-IDE-ready motherboard via an IDE host adapter (often erroneously called an IDEcontroller).

host based Communications system that is controlled by a large, central computer system.

host mode Communications mode that allows a computer to answer an incoming telephone call and receive data without human assistance.

hot link Predefined connection between programs so that when information in one database or file is changed, related information in other databases and files are also updated.

hot spot Exact pixel location on screen that is affected when the mouse is clicked, such as the end point of an arrow pointer, tip of a finger pointer.

hotkey Key or key combination that causes some function to occur in the computer, no matter what else is currently running. It is commonly used to activate a memory resident (ThR) program.

housekeeping Set of instructions that are executed at the beginning of a program. It sets all counters and flags to their starting values and generally readies the program for execution.

HP (Hewlett-Packard Company, Palo Alto, CA) Major manufacturer of computers and electronics. It was founded in 1939 by William Hewlett and David Packard in a garage. Its first product, an audio oscillator for measuring sound, was the beginning of a line of electronics that made HP an international supplier of electronic test and measurement instruments.

HP entered the computer field in 1966. In 1972, HP branched into business computing with the 3000 series, a multiuser system that became well known for its extremely high reliability, especially for that time. Also in 1972, HP introduced the first scientific handheld calculator, the HP-35, obsoleting the slide rule and ushering in a new age of pocket-sized calculators. In 1982, the first HP 9000 workstation was introduced. HP's first personal computer was the Touchscreen 150, an MS-DOS personal computer that gained only modest acceptance. In 1985, it introduced the Vectra, a 286-based machine that was the first of a complete line of IBM-compatible PCs.

In 1984, HP revolutionized the printer market with its desktop LaserJet printer, which has set the standard for the industry. In 1986, it introduced a new internal design for its 3000 and 9000 families that will carry the company into the 1990s. The new HP Precision Architecture provides a significant increase in performance. In 1989, HP acquired Apollo Computer, which combined with its own line, made HP the market leader in workstations.

HP sells over 10,000 different products in the electronics and computer field, and it has gained a worldwide reputation for its rugged and reliable engineering.

HP 1000 Family of realtime computers from HP introduced in 1966.

HP 3000 Family of business-oriented computers from HP introduced in 1972.

HP 9000 Family of high-performance UNIX workstations and business servers from HP. Introduced in 1982.

HP Precision Architecture Proprietary RISC architectore from HP introduced in 1986 that is incorporated into new models of its 3000 and 9000 computer families.

HP-UX HP's version of UNIX that runs on its 9000 family. It is based on SVID and incorporates features from BSD UNIX along with several HP innovations.

HPC See High-Performance Computing.

RPFS (High Performance File System) File system, introduced with OS/2 Version 1.2, that handles larger disks (2TB volumes; 2GB files), long file names (256 bytes) and can launch the program by referencing the data as in the Macintosh. It coexists with the existing FAT system.

HPGL (Hewlett-Packard Graphics Language) Vector graphics file format from HP that was developed as a standard plotter language. Most plotters support the HPGL and DMPL standards.

HSB (Hue Saturation Brightness) See HSV. HSL (Hue Saturation Lightness) See HLS.

HST (1) Asymmetrical modem protocol from U.S. Robotics that includes error control and compression and transmits from 4800 to 14400 bps in one direction and from 300 to 400 bps in the other. (2) (Hubble Space Telescope) Launched in April 1990, it views star material some 10 to 12 billion light years from earth.

BSV (Hue Saturation Value) Color model that uses a cylindrical coordinate system structured as an inverted hexcone (six-sided pyramid). Hue is measured by the angle around the vertical axis with red at 00, yellow 600, green 120°, cyan 180°, blue 240° and magenta 300°. Saturation is amount of color from 0 to 1 or 0 to 100%. Value is from black to white (0-1 or 0-100%). Pure green would be 11120, Si and Vi.

hub Central switching device for communications lines in a star topology. It may add nothing to the transmission (passive hub) or may contain electronics that regenerate.signals to boost strength as well monitor activity (active hub, intelligent hub). Hubs may be added to bus topologies; for example, a hub can turn an Ethernet network into a star topology to improve trouble shooting.

hub ring Flat ring pressed around the hole in a 5.25' floppy disk for rigidity. The drive's clamping ring presses the hub ring onto the spindle.

hue In computer graphics, a particular shade or tint of a given color.

Huffman coding Statistical compression method that converts characters into variable length bit strings. Most frequently occurring characters are converted to shortest bit strings; least frequent, the longest. Compression takes two passes. The first pass analyzes a block of data and creates a tree model based on its contents. The second pass compresses the data via the model. See LZW.

hybrid circuit See hybrid microcircuit.

hybrid computer Digital computer that processes and log signals which have been converted into digital form. It is used in process control and robotics.

hybrid microcircuit Electronic circuit composed of different types of integrated circuits and discrete components, mounted on a ceramic base. Used in military and communications applications, it is especially suitable for building customized analog circuits (AID, D/A converters, amplifiers, modulators, etc.).

hybrid network In communications, a network made up of equipment from multiple vendors.

Hydra (1) (Hybrid Document Reproduction Apparatus) A printer, photocopier, scanner and fax built into one machine. (2) Device that converts analog signals to ISDN Basic Rate Interface (BRI). (3) Utility from the Austin Mac Developer's Assn. that tests Macintosh graphics card performance.

Hyperaccess PC communications program from Hilgraeve, that provides data compression, has its own script language and supports a variety of terminals and protocols.

HyperCard Application development system from Apple that runs on the Macintosh and Apple IIGS and provides an array of advanced and integrated features. As a database system, it lets users build files in the form of a stack of cards that can hold data, text and graphics. As a control system, it is used as a main menu to launch applications. It can control multimedia devices, such as CD ROM and videodisc, and supports the building of educational applications.

A HyperCard card is designed with fixed fields, scrolling fields and graphics. It is also designed with button icons that, when clicked, activate processes. For example, a button can be set up to run a script in the HyperTalk programming language, or it can link the user to another associated card.

hypercube Parallel processing architecture made up of binary multiples of computers (4, 8, 16, etc.). The computers are interconnected so that data travel is kept to a minimum. For example, in two eight-node cubes, dach node in one cube would be connected to the counterpart node in the other.

hypermedia Use of data, text, graphics, video and voice as elements in a hypertext system. All the various forms of information are linked together so that a user can easily move from one to another.

HyperPAD Application development system for- PCs from Brightbill-Roberts & Company. It is a HyperCard-like program that works in text mode and includes the PADtalk scripting language.

HyperScript Advanced macro (scripting) 1angage that - is provided with the WINGZ spreadsheet. — HyperTalk Programming language used in HyperCard. hypertext Linking related information. For example, by selecting a word in a sentence, information about that word is retrieved if it exists, or the next occurrence of the word is found. The concept was coined by Ted Nelson as a method for making the computer respond to the way humans think and require information.

hyperware Hypertext products.

hyphen ladder Hyphens on two or more consecutive lines, which causes distraction to the reader.

hyphenation Breaking words that extend beyond the right margin. Software hyphenates words by matching them against a hyphenation dictionary or by using a built-in set of rules, or both. See discretionary hyphen.

hyphenation dictionary Word file with predefined by - phen locations.

hyphenation zone Distance from the right margin within which a word may be hyphenated.

hysteresis Lag between making a change, such as increasing or decreasing power, and the response or effect of that change.

Hz (HertZ) See Hertz.

HAS-A relationship: A relationship between two entities or objects that are of different logical types, for example, EMPLOYEE HAS-A(n) AUTO. Contrast this with an IS-A relationship.

Hierarchical data model: A data model that represents all relationships using hierarchies or trees. Network structures must be decomposed into trees before they can be represented by a hierarchical data model. DL/I is the only surviving hierarchical data model.

Hierarchy: See Tree.

Horizontal partition: A subset of a table consisting of complete rows of the table. For example, in a table with ten rows, the first five rows.

Host variable: A variable in an application program into which a DBMS places a value from the database.

HTML: See Hypertext markup language.

HTrP: See Hypertext transfer protocol.

Hybrid object: An object containing a multivalued group that contains at least one object attribute.

Hypertext markup language: A standardized system of tagging text for formatting, locating images and other nontext files, and placing links or references to other documents.

Hypertext transfer protocol: A standardized means for using TCP/IP for communicating HTML documents over networks.

I

I-beam pointer In a graphical user interface, a special pointer shaped like a capital "I" that indicates the insertion point of text editing.

I-CASE (Integrated CASE) CASE systems that generate applications code directly from design specifications. Features include support for rapid prototyping, modelling the data and processing and drawing logic diagrams.

I/E time See instruction cycle.

I/O (Input/Output) Transferring data between the CPU and a peripheral device. Every transfer is an output from one device and an input into another.

I/O area Reserved segment of memory used to accept data from an input device or to accumulate data for transfer to an output device. It may be located within the application program, operating system or DBMS. Same as buffer.

I/O bound Refers to an excessive amount of time getting data in and out of the computer in relation to the time it takes for processing it. Faster I/O channels and disk drives will improve the performance of an I/O bound computer.

I/O card (1) I/O controller or expansion board. (2) PC Card used to connect a modem, fax, LAN or other 1/ 0 device.

I/O channel High-speed pathway between the cu and a peripheral device. See channel.

I/O Interface Channel, or pathway, between the CPU and a peripheral device. See port and expansion slot.

I/O processor Hardware or software dedicated to handling only I/O operations. See front end processor.

I/O statement Programming instruction that requests lb.

I-time See instruction time.

1486 See 486.

1860 See 860.

IBM (International Business Machines corp., Armonk, NY) World's largest computer company. It started in New York in 1911 when the Computing-Tabulating- Recording Co. (CTR) was created by a merger of The Tabulating Machine Co. (Hollerith's punched card company in Washington), and several other companies. CTR started out with 1,200 employees and a capital value of $17.5 million.

In 1914, Thomas J. Watson, Sr., became general manager. During the next 10 years, he dispensed with its non-tabulating business and turned it into an international enterprise renamed IBM in 1924. Watson was responsible for instilling a strict professional demeanour in his employees that set IBMers apart from the rest of the crowd.

IBM achieved spectacular success by manufacturing tabulating machines and the punched cards fed into them. From the 1920s through the 1960s, it developed a huge customer base that was ideal for conversion to computers.

IBM launched its computer business in 1953 with the 701 and introduced the 650 a year later. By the end of the 1950s, the 650 was the most widely used computer in the world with 1,800 systems installed. The 1401, announced in 1959, was its second computer winner, and by the mid 1960s, an estimated 18,000 were in use.

In 1964, it announced System/360, the first family of compatible computers ever developed. The 360s were enormously successful and set a standard that evolved into IBM mainframes to this day.

In 1981, IBM introduced the PC into a chaotic personal computer field, and it became a success almost overnight. IBM set the standard, but the industry took on a life of its own. Although IBM is still the largest single supplier, the majority of PC sales come from the PC industry at large, from companies such as Compaq and Dell to clone shops by the thousands.

The 1990s are going to be the most challenging era for this industry giant. With technology advancing in an never-ending spiral, with PC networks springing up daily, and with downsizing on the lips of every budget-conscious IS manager, IBM will use every ounce of its marketing genius to keep growing.

In 1991, IBM thoroughly surprised the industry by forming an alliance with Apple to more closely integrate Macintoshes into IBM enterprise networks and to jointly develop a complete new line of future desktop systems (see Apple for details).

IBM-compatible PC Personal computer that is compatible with the IBM PC and PS/2 standards.

IBM mainframes Large-scale computers from IBM, The series stems from the System/360 architecture introduced in 1964.

IBM minicomputers Midrange computers from IBM. This series begins with the System/3 introduced in 1969.

IBM PC Personal computers from IBM. May refer to the first IBM personal computer model (the "PC") introduced in 1981, or generically to the entire PC, PS/i and PS/2 line.

IC See integrated circuit and information center.

IC card See PC card and memory card.

Icon Small, pictorial, on-screen representation of an object (file, program, disk, etc.) used in graphical interfaces to represent a function.

Iconic Interface User interface that uses icons.

IDA (Intelligent Drive Array) High-performance hard disk interface from Compaq that controls a disk array via the EISA bus.

IDE (1) (Integrated Drive Electronics) Hard disk and built-in controller (also called AT and XT interface). IDE-ready motherboards have a 40-pin socket that connects directly to an IDE drive eliminating the use of an expansion slot. In non-IDE-ready machines, the drive connects to an IDE host adapter that plugs into a slot. See hard disk specs. (2) (Integrated Development Environment) Set of programs run from a single

user interface. For example, programming languages often include a text editor, compiler and debugger, which are all activated and function from a common menu.

IDE controller (1) Controller built into an IDE drive. (2) Often (erroneously) refers to an IDE host adapter that connects an IDE drive to a non-IDE-ready motherboard.

IE See information engineering.

IEEE See institute of electrical and electronics engineers.

IEEE 802 A set of standards developed by the IEEE to define methods of access and control on local area networks.

IEEE 488 The interface standard mainly used to connect laboratory instruments and other scientific equipment to computers. A type of parallel interface.

IEEE 696/5-100 The identification of a standard, developed by the Institute of Electrical and Electronic Engineers. Ensures the compatibility of all computing products designed to this standard.

if-then-else High-level programming language statement that compares two or more sets of data and tests the results. If the results are true, the THEN instructions are taken; if not, the ELSE instructions are taken. In certain structured programming languages, the THEN is implied. All statements between the IF and the ELSE are carried out if the condition is true. All instructions between the ELSE and the ENDIF are carried out if the condition is not true.

IFS (Installable File System) OS/2 feature that supports multiple tile systems. Different systems can be installed (UNIX, CD ROM, etc.) just like drivers are installed for new peripherals.

IGES (Initial Graphics Exchange Specification) ANSI graphics file format that is system independent and also intended for human interpretation. It evolved out of the US Air Force's Integrated Computer Automated Manufacturing (ICAM) program in 1979.

Illustration program Same as drawing program.

Illustrator 88 Mcintosh drawing program from Adobe Systems, Inc., that enhanced the original Illustrator program in 1988. It provides sophisticated tracing and text manipulation capabilities, as well as colors and color separations.

IM See information management.

Image (1) A picture (graphic). (2) See system image.

Image enhancement Improving graphics images either manually using a paint program or by using software routines that change contrast, smooth lines or filter out unwanted data. See anti-aliasing.

Image-oriented backup Any backup system that creates a mirror image of the disk, without regard to the files themselves. With such a system, the entire disk must be restored from the backup medium to allow access to the files.

Image processing (1) Analysis of a picture using techniques that can identify shades, colors and relationships. It is used to solve identification problems, such as in forensic medicine or in creating weather maps from satellite pictures and deals with images in raster graphics format that have been scanned in or captured with digital cameras. (2) Image improvement, such as refining a picture in a paint program that has been scanned or entered from a video source. (3) Same as imaging.

hnagesetter Typesetting machine that handles text and graphics. See phototypesetter.

Imaging Recording pictures into machine format: microfilm, videotape or computer. It refers to raster graphics formats generated by scanning or photographing pictures in contrast to vector graphics generated in CAD and drawing programs.

Imaging model Set of rules for representing images. hnmedlate access Same as direct access.

Immediate address Absolute value within a machine instruction used as data by the instruction.

Impact printer Printer that uses a printing mechanism that bangs the character image into the ribbon and onto the paper. Line printers, dot matrix printers and daisy wheel printers are examples. See printer.

Impedance Resistance to the flow of alternating current in a circuit.

Implementation (1) Computer system implementation is the installation of new hardware and system software. (2) Information system implementation is the installation of new databases and application programs and the adoption of new manual procedures.

implode To link component pieces to a major assembly. It may also refer to compressing data using a particular technique. Contrast with explode.

Import To convert a file in a foreign format to the format of the program being used.

Incident light In computer graphics, light that strikes an object. The color of the object is based on how the light is absorbed or reflected by the object.

increment To add a number to another number. Incrementing a counter means adding 1 to its current value.

incremental backup Backing up only files that have been changed since the last backup, rather than backing up everything.

incremental spacing See microspacing.

IND$FILE IBM mainframe program that transfers flies between the mainframe and a PC functioning as a 3270 terminal.

indent To align text some number of spaces to the right of the left margin. See hanging paragraph.

Indentation The white space found at the beginning of a line of text; often denotes the beginning of a paragraph.

index (1) In data management, the most common method for keeping track of data on a disk. Indexes are directory listings maintained by the OS, DBMS or the application. An index of files contains an entry for each file name and the location of the file. (2) In programming, a method for keeping track of data in a table. See indexed addressing.

Index hole Small hole punched into a hard sectored floppy disk that serves to mark the start of the see-tors on each track. V

index mark Physical hole or notch, or a recorded code or mark, that is used to identitr a starting point for each track on a disk.

Index register High-speed circuit used to hold the current, relative position of an item in a table (array). At execution time, its stored value is added to the instructions that reference it.

Indexed addressing Technique for referencing memory that automatically increments the address with the value stored in an index register. See subscript (2).

indexed sequential See ISAM.

Indexing (1) Creating indexes based on key data fields or key words. (2) Creating timing signals based on detecting a mark, slot or hole in a moving medium.

indirect addressing Address mode that points to another pointer rather than the actual data. This mode is prohibited in RISC architecture.

Inductance Opposition to the changing flow of current in a circuit, measured in Henrys.

Induction Process of generating an electric current in a circuit from the magnetic influence of an adjacent circuit as in a transformer or capacitor.

inference engine Processing program in an expert system. It derives a conclusion from the facts and rules contained in the knowledge base using various artificial intelligence techniques.

Infix notation Common way arithmetic operators are used to reference numeric values. For example, A+B/ C is infix notation. Contrast with Polish notation and reverse Polish notation.

Infopreneur Person who is in business to gather and disseminate electronic information.

information Summarization of data. Technically, data are raw facts and figures that are processed into information, such as summaries and totals. But since V information can also be raw data for the next job or person, the two terms cannot be precisely defined. Both terms are used synonymously and interchangeably;

As office automation and data processing merge, it may be more helpful to view information the way data is defined and used, namely: data, text, spreadsheet, pictures, voice and video. Data are discretely defined fields. Text is a collection of words. Spreadsheet are data in matrix (row and column) form. Pictures are lists of vectors or frames of bits. Voice is a eontjnuous stream cf sound waves. Video is a sequence of frames.

Future databases will routinely integrte all these forms of information.

Information center Division within the IS department that supports end-user computing. Responsible for training users in applications and solving related personal computer problems.

information engineering Integrated set of methodologies and products used to guide and develop information processing within an organization.

information explosion The exponential increase in the growth ahd diversification of all forms of information.

information hiding Keeping details of a routine private. Programmers only know what input is required and what outputs are expected. See encapsulation and data abstraction. V

information industry (1) Information publishing. Organizations that provide information via online services or through distribution by diskette or CD ROM. (2) All computer, communications and electronksrelated organizations, including hardware, software and services.

information management (1) Discipline that analyzes information as an organizational resource. It covers the definitions, uses, value and distribution of all data and information within an organization whether processed by computer or not. It evaluates the kinds of data/information an organization requires in order to function and progress effectively. Information is complex because business transactions are complex. It must be analyzed and understood before effective computer solutions can be developed. See data administration. (2) Same as information processing.

Information processing Same as data processing.

Information resource management See Information Systems and information management.

information science See information management.

Information service Any information retrieval, publishing, timesharing or BBS facility.

Information Services See Information Systems.

information system Business application of the computer. It is made up of the database which stores the data, application programs which generate information, manual and machine procedures and also encompasses the computer systems that do the processing.

Information Systems Formal title for a data processing, MIS, or IS department. Other titles are Data Processing, Information Processing, Information Services, Management Information Systems, Management Information Services and Information Technology.

Information utility (1) Service bureau that maintains up-to-date databases for public access. (2) Central source of information for an organization or group.

INFORMIX Family ofDBMSs from Informix Software, that includes an SQL-based relational DBMS, fourth- generation language and toolkits for embedding SQL in application programs.

infoware Information sold electronically.

InfoWindow Trade name for IBM display screens.

infrared Invisible band of radiation at the low-frequency end of the tight spectrum. Contrast with ultraviolet.

INGRES (INteractive Graphica and REtrieval System) Relational DBMS from Ingres Corp., that runs on VAXs and UNIX workstations. It includes a 4GL, QBE and lets users create and manage a database as a series of forms. Its Knowledge Management extension allows rules to be programmed into the database.

Inheritance In object-oriented programming, the ability of one class of objects to inherit properties from a higher class.

inhouse Operation that takes place on the user's premises.

INITN (INITiate) Macintosh routine that is run when the computer is started or restarted. It is used to load and activate drivers and system routines. Many INITs are memory resident and may conflict with each other like TSRs in the PC environment.

Initial program load See IPL.

initialization string Same as setup string.

Initialize To start anew, which typically involves clearing all or some part of memory or disk.

Ink jet Printer mechanism that sprays ink onto paper and produces high-quality printing like that of a laser printer. The continuous stream method produces droplets that are aimed onto the paper by electric field detlectors. The drop-on-demand method uses a set of independently controlled injection chambers. Solid ink liquefies quickly when heated and dries instantly when it reaches the paper.

INMARSAT (INternational MARitime SATellite) International organization involved in providing satellite communications to and from ships and offshore rigs.

inoculate To store characteristica of an executable program in order to detect a possible unknown virus if the file is changed.

input (1) Data that is ready for entry into the computer. (2) To enter data into the computer.

input area Reserved segment of memory that is used to accept data from a peripheral device. Same as buffer.

input device Peripheral device that generates input for the computer such as a keyboard, scanner, mouse or digitizer tablet.

input/output See I/O.

Input program Same as data entry program.

Input queue Reserved segment of disk or memory that holds messages that have been received or job control statements describing work to be done.

input stream Collection of job control statements entered in the computer that describe the work to be done.

inquiry program Same as query program.

Ins key (INSert key) A keyboard key that is used to switch between insert and overwrite mode or to insert an object at the current cursor location.

Insert mode Data entry mode that causes new data typed on the keyboard to be inserted at the current cursor location on screen. Contrast with overwrite mode.

Install program Software that prepares a software package to run in the computer. It makes subdirectories on the hard disk, copies the files from the distribution diskettes to the hard disk and decompresses them, if required. It may ask the user to identify the peripheral devices attached to the computer in order to link in the appropriate drivers. It may also request a serial number and name to customize the startup screen.

Installation spec Documentation from an equipment manufacturer that describes how a product should be properly installed within a physical environment.

instance In object-oriented programming, a member of a class; for example, "Lassie" is an instance of the class "dog." When an instance is created, the initial values of its instance variables are assigned.

Instance variable In object-oriented programming, the data in an object.

Instant print Ability to use the computer as a typewriter. Each keystroke is transferred to the printer.

instantiate In object-oriented programming, to create an object of a specific class. See instance.

instruction (1) A statement in a programming language. (2) A machine instruction.

Instruction cycle Time in which a single instruction is fetched from memory, decoded and executed. The first half of the cycle transfers the instruction from memory to the instruction register and decodes it. The second half executes the instruction.

instruction mix Blend of instruction types in a program. Often refers to writing generalized benchmarks, which requires that the amount of I/O versus processing versus math instructions, etc., reflects the type of application the benchmark is written for.

instruction register High-speed circuit that holds an instruction for decoding and execution.

instruction repertoire Same as instruction set.

instruction set Entire group of machine language instructions that a computer can follow. It is designed into the CPU and is one of the major components of its architecture. A set may contain from a handful (RISC) to several hundred instructions (CISC). Machine instructions are generally from one to four bytes long.

Instruction time Time in which an instruction is fetched from memory and stored in the instruction register. It is the first half of the instruction cycle.

insulator Material that does not conduct electricity. Contrast with conductor.

mt See interrupt and integer.

integer Whole number. In programming, the integer function would yield 123 from 123.898.

Integer BASIC Apple version of BASIC for the Apple II that handles only fixed point numbers (non-floating point). Due to its speed, many games are written in it.

integrated Collection of distinct elements or components that have been built into one unit.

integrated CASE See I-CASE.

integrated circuit Formal name for chip.

Integrated injection logic Type of bipolar transistor design known for its fast switching speeds.

integrated software package Software that combines several applications in one program, typically database management, word processing, spreadsheet, business graphics and communications. It may even provide the capacity to cut-and-paste across applications. However, no single package can provide all the capabilities of stand-alone applications. Framework, AppleWorks and Microsoft Works are examples.

Integrator In electronics, a device that combines an input with a variable, such as time, and provides an analog output; for example, a watt-hour meter.

integrity See data integrity.

Intel (Intel Corp., Santa Clara, CA) Leading manufacturer of semiconductor devices founded in 1968 by Bob Noyce and Gorden Moore in Mountain View, CA. A year later it introduced its first product, a 64- bit bipolar static RAM chip. By 1971, its very successful memory chips began to replace magnetic core storage.

Intel is best known for its 80x86 microprocessor family, but it also developed the first microprocessor in 1971. In response to a calculator chip order from Japanese manufacturer Busicom, Intel engineer Marcian E. "Ted" Hoff decided it would make more sense to design a general-purpose machine. The resulting 4004 chip was the world's first microprocessor. Intel startedwith 12 people and first year revenues of $2672. In 1990, it had 24j100 employees and revenues of four billion.

Intellect Natural language query program from Al Corp., that runs on IBM mainframes and other computers. It can answer many English language questions; for example, "Tell me the number of employees in the personnel department."

Intellifont Scalable typefaces from Agfa CompuGraphic, several of which are built into the LaserJet III family. HP Intellifont for Windows is a font scaler that creates matching screen fonts for Windows from Intellifont and compatible typefaces.

intellIgence Processing capability. Every computer is intelligent!

intelligent cable Same as smart cable.

Intelligent controller Peripheral control unit that uses a built-in microprocessor for controlling its operation.

intelligent database Database that contains knowledge about the content of its data. A set of validation criteria are stored with each field of data, such as the minimum and maximum values that can be entered or a list of all possible entries. See DBMS (Intelligent Databases).

Intelligent form Data entry application that provides help screens and low levels of Al in aiding the user to enter the correct data.

intelligent hub Network hub that performs a variety of functions such as regenerating signals, monitoring transmission for network management, allowing connections to a variety of cable types and routing. Contrast with passive hub. See hub.

intelligent modem Modem that responds to commands and can accept new instructions during online transmission. It was originally developed by Hayes.

intelligent terminal Terminal, with built-in processing capability, but no local disk or tape storage. It may use a general-purpose CPU or may have specialized circuitry as part of a distributed intelligence system. Contrast with dumb terminal.

INTELSAT (Int'l. TELecommunications SATellite) International organization involved in launching and operating cdmmercial satellites. It was created in 1964 with only 1.1 countries participating. Today, over 100 nations have ownership.

Inter To cross over boundaries; for example, internetwork means from one network to another. Contrast with intra.

Interactive Back-and-forth dialog between the user and a computer.

interactive cable TV Service in which viewers take part in TV programs by reacting to issues. It implies full TV viewing, in contrast with videotex or teletext. In time, all of these services may be provided over cable TV channels. A decod r and keyboard are required.

Interactive session Back-and-forth dialogue between user and computer. Contrast with batch session.

interactive video Use of videodisc or CD ROM controlled by computer for an interactive education or entertainment program. See videodisc and CD ROM.

InterBase Relational DBMS from Borland that runs on UNIX workstations and VAXes, designed to handle online complex processing (OLCP). It can be a peer- to- peer or client/server system and uses SQL plus its own data manipulation language.

Interblock gap Same as interrecord gap.

interface Connection and interaction between hardware, software and the user. Hardware interfaces are the plugs, sockets and wires that carry electrical signals in a prescribed order. Software interfaces are the languages, codes and messages programs use to communicate with each other. User interfaces are the keyboards, mice, commands and menus used for communication between you and the computer.

Hardware "communicates to" other hardware. All this is interfacing. The software "communicates to" the hardware and other software. Users "communicates to" the software. All this is interfacing.

Interface adapter In communications, a device that connects the computer or terminal to a network.

interframe coding In video compression, coding only the differences between frames. See intraframe coding.

interlaced Illuminating a CRT by displaying odd lines and then even lines (every other line first; then filling in the gaps). TV signals are interlaced (60 half frames/sec) as well as lower-cost high-resolution computer display systems. Interlacing uses half the signal information as non-interlacing and is less expensive to create. TV's constant animation pro' Ides acceptable viewing, but flicker can be annoying on interlaced computer screens. Contrast with non-interlaced.

Interleaf Full-featured desktop publishing software for 386 and higher PCs from IBM. Includes text and graphics editing, free-hand drawing, supports PostScript and provides connectivity to shared AS! 400 folders.

Interleave See sector interleave and memory interleaving.

Interleck Device that prohibits an action from taking place.

Intermediate language Same as pseudo language.

intermediate node routing Routing a message to nonadjacent nodes; for example, if three computers are connected in series A—B-—C, data transmitted from A to C can be routed through B.

intermittent error Error that occurs sporadically, not consistently. It is very difficult to diagnose and repair.

internal font Set of characters for a particular typeface that is built into a printer. Contrast with font cartridge and soft font.

internal interrupt Interrupt that is caused by processing, for example, a request for input or output or an arithmetic overflow error. Contrast with external interrupt.

internal modem Modem that plugs into a particular computer's expansion slot from which it derives its power. Contrast with external modem.

Internal sort Sorting accomplished entirely in memory without using disks or tapes for temporary files.

internal storage Same as memory.

Internet Large network made up of a number of smaller networks.

Internet address Format for addressing a message to an Internet user.

InterNet Router Macintosh software from Apple that internetworks different access methods (LocalTalk, EtherTalk, TokenTalk, etc.) and can reside in any network station. Each Router can connect up to eight networks with a maximum of 1,024 networks and 16 million nodes.

internetwork To go between one network and another.

Interoperable Ability for a system to function properly with another system.

Interpolate To estimate values that lie between known values.

Interpress Page description language from Xerox used on the 2700 and 9700 page printers (medium to large. scale laser printers). Ventura Publisher provides output in Interpress.

Interpret To run a program one line at a time. Each line of source language is translated into machine language and then executed.

Interpreter High-level programming language translator that translate and runs the program at the same time. It translates one program statement into machine language, executes it,,then proceeds to the next statement. Though interpreted programs run slower than their compiler counterparts; because the coinpiler translates the entire program before it is run, it is more convenient to write an interpreted program, since a single lIne of code can be tested interactively. Interpreted programs must always be run with the interpreter. For example, in order to run a BASIC or dBASE program, the BASIC or dBASE interpreter must be in the computer.

If a language can be both interpreted and compiled, a program may be developed with the interpreter and later compiled for production.

Interpretive language Programming language that requires an interpreter to run it.

Interprocess communication See IPC.

Interrecord gap Space generated between blocks of data on tape, created by the starting and stopping of the reel.

interrogate (1) To search, sum or count records in a file. (2) To test the condition or status of a terminal or computer system.

interrupt Signal that gets the attention of the CPU and is usually generated when I!O is required. For example, hardware interrupts are generated when a key is pressed or when the mouse is moved. Software interrupts are generated by a program requiring disk input or output.

An internal timer may continually interrupt the computer several times per second to keep the time of day current or tbr timesharing purposes. When an interrupt occurs, control is transferred to the operating system, which determines the action to be taken. Interrupts are prioritized; the higher the priority, the faster the interrupt will be serviced.

Interrupt-driven Computer or communications network that uses interrupts.

Interrupt mask Internal switch setting that controls whether an.interrupt can be processed or not. The mask is a bit that is turned on and off by the program.

Interrupt priorities Sequence of importance assigned to interrupts. If two interrupts occur simultaneously, the interrupt with the highes.t priority is serviced first. In some systems, a higher-priority interrupt can gain control of the computer while it's processing a lower-priority interrupt.

interrupt vector In the PC, one of 256 pointers that reside in the first 1KB of memory. Each vector points to a routine in the ROM BIOS or elsewhere in memory, which handles the interrupt.

intersect In relational database, to match two files and produce a third file with records that are common in both. For example, intersecting an American file and a programmer file would yield American programmers.

intra Within a boundary; for example, intraoffice refers to operations that take place within the office. Contrast with inter.

Inti-aframe coding Compressing redundant areas within a video frame. See interframe coding.

inverse video Same as reverse video.

inverted file In data management, a file that is indexed on many of the attributes of the data itself. It's faster to search the indexes than every record. Inverted file indexes use lots of disk space; searching is fast, updating is slower.

inverted list Same as inverted file.

inverter (1) Logic gate that converts the input to the opposite state for output. If the input is true, the output is false, and vice versa. An inverter performs the Boolean logic NOT operation. (2) Circuit that converts DC current into AC current. Contrast with rectifier.

Invoke To activate a program, routine, function or process.

ion deposition Printing technology used in high-speed page printers. It is similar to laser printing, except instead of using light to create a charged image on a drum, it uses a printhead that deposits ions. After toner is attracted to the ions on the drum, the paper is pressed directly against the drum fusing toner to paper. Quality approaches that of a laser printer, however, since the ink has not been embedded as deeply, and the paper can smear more easily.

IPC (InterProcess Communication) Exchange of data between one program and another either within the same computer or over a network. It implies a protocol that guarantees a response to a request. Although IPCs are performed automatically by the programs, an analogous function is performed interactively when user cut and paste data from one file to another using the diphoand.

JPDS (lntdiigenLPrer Data Stream) IBM format for sending full pag of text and graphics from a mainframe or mini to a heer printer.

IPI (Intelligent Peripheral Interface) High-speed hard disk interface used withininis and mainframes thai transfers data in the 10 to .25 MBytes/sec range. WI- 2 and IPI-3 refer to differences in the command set that they execute. See hard disk specs.

IPL: Initial Program Load Same as boot.

Ips (Inches Per Second) Measures the speed of tape passing by a read/write hea4 or.paper passing through a pen plotter.

IRMAboard Micro to mainframe board for PCs from DCA, Inc. It emulates an IBM 3278 (mono) or 3279 (color) mainframe terminal. IRMA is not an acronym.

IRMALAN Family of gateway products from DCA, Inc., that allow PC users connected to NetBIOS-compatible LANs to access an SNA host. It includes gateways for IEEE 802.2, SDLC and DFT environments.

iron oxide Material used to coat the surfaces of magnetic tapes and lower-capacity disks.

IRQ (Interrupt ReQuest) Hardware interrupt on a PC. Eight lines (0-7 on 8086/88s) and 16 lines (0-15 on 286s and up) accept interrupts from input devices, such as a scanner and network adapter. Two devices may not use .the same line, and it is often necessary to change the IRQ line on a new peripheral by setting switches on its expansion board.

ISA (Industry Standard Architecture) Pronounced '9- suh." Refers to the original PC bus architecture, specifically the 16-bit Al' bus. Contrast with EISA and Micro Channel.

ISAM (Indexed Sequential Access Method) Common disk access method that stores data sequentially, while maintaining an index of key fields to all the records in the file for direct access. The sequential order would be the one most commonly used for batch processing and printing (account number, name, etc.).

ISDN (Integrated Services Digital Network) International telecommunications standard for transmitting voice, video and data over a digital communications line. It uses out of band signalling, which provides a separate channel for control information. ISDN services come in two forms: Basic Rate Interface (BRI) and Primary Rate Interface (PRI). ISDN's 64Kbps transmission rate provides a big boost for PCs communicating via modem, even at 9,600 bps, but it doesn't provide an alternative for interconnecting LANs transmitting in the 10+ megabit per second range. However, Broadband ISDN (BISDN) should materialize around 1993, which utilizes broadband transmission and fiber optic cables to jump transmission speed to 150 megabits per second.

ISO (Int'l. Standards Organization) Organization that sets international standards, founded in 1946 and headquartered in Geneva. It deals with all fields except electrical and electronics, which is governed by the older Int'l. Electrotechnical Commission (IEC), also in Geneva. With regard to information processing, ISO and IEC created JTC1, the Joint Technical Committee for information technology. It carries out its work through more than 160 technical committees and 2,300 subcommittees and working groups and is made up of standards organizations from more than 75 countries, some of them serving as secretariats for these technical bodies. —ANSI is the U.S. member body.

Isochronous Time dependent. Realtime voice, video and telemetry are examples of isochronous data.

Isometric view In computer graphics, a picture of a 3-D object that shows all three dimensions in equal proportions. Isometric views do not show true perspective.

isotropic Refers to properties, such as transmission speed, that are the same regardless of the direction that is measured. Contrast with anisotropic.

IT (Information Technology) Same as Information Systems.

item One unit or member of a group. See data item.

Iteration One repetition of a sequence of instructions or events. For example, in a program loop, one iteration is once through the instructions in the loop.

iterative operation Operation that requires successive executions of instructions or processes.

IV See interactive video.

IVD (Interactive VideoDisc) See interactive video.

Iverson notation Set of symbols developed by Kenneth Iverson for writing statements in APL.

IVR (Interactive Voice Response) See voice response.

ID-dependent entity: An entity that cannot logically exist without the existence of another entity. An APPOINTMENT, for example, cannot exist without a CLIENT to make the appointment. The ID-dependent entity always contains the key of the entity on which it depends. Such entities are a subset of a weak entity. See also Strong entity and Weak entity.

Immutable object: In the ODMG standard, an object whose attributes cannot be changed.

Implementation: In OOP, a set of objects that instantiates a particular OOP interface.

Implicit lock: A lock that is automatically placed by the DBMS.

Implied object: An object that exists in the user's mind when he or she requests a report "sorted by x" or "grouped by x." For example, when the user requests all ORDERs sorted by OrderDate, the implied object is the set of all ORDER objects.

Import: A function of the DBMS, to read an entire file of data in bulk.

IMS: Information management system. A transaction- processing system developed and licensed by IBM. It includes IMS/DC, a communications control program, and IMS/DB, a DBMS that implements the DL/I data model.

Inconsistent read problem: An anomaly that occurs in concurrent processing, in which transactions execute a series of reads inconsistent with one another. It can be prevented by two-phase locking and other strategies.

Index: Overhead data used to improve access and sorting performance. Indexes can be constructed for a single column or for groups of columns. They are especially useful for columns used for control breaks in reports and for columns used to specify conditions in joins.

Index space: An area of disk storage in which DB2 stores an index.

Information-bearing set: In the CODASYL DBTG data model, a set in which the relationship between records is not represented in the data values. The relationship, though not visible in the data, is recorded in overhead data created and processed by the DBMS. Contrast this with Non-information- bearing set.

Inheritance: A characteristic of objected-oriented systems in which objects that are subtypes of other objects obtain attributes (data or methods) from their supertypes.

Insertion anomaly: In a relation, the condition that exists when, to add a complete row to a table, one must add facts about two or more logically different themes.

Insertion status: In the CODASYL DBTG model, a rule that determines how records are to be placed into sets. Records can be placed automatically by the DBMS or manually by the application program.

Interface: (1) The means by which two or more programs call each other; the definition of the procedural calls between two or more programs. (2) In OOP, the design of a set of objects that includes the objects' names, methods, and attributes.

Internet: A worldwide, public network of computers that communicate using TCP/IP.

Internet mail service: A standard service of the Internet that provides personal electronic mail.

Internet newsgroup: A standard service of the Internet that provides for public electronic mail.

Interrelation constraint: A restriction that requires the value of an attribute in a row of one relation to match the value of an attribute found in another relation. For example, CustNumber in ORDER must equal CustNumber in CUSTOMER.

Intersection: A relational algebra operation performed on two union-compatible relations, A and B, forming a third relation, C, so that C contains only rows that appear in both A and B.

Intersection relation: A relation used to represent a many-to-many relationship. It contains the keys of the relations in the relationship. When used to represent many-to-many compound objects, it has no nonkey data. When used to represent entities haying a many-to-many relationship, it may have non- key data if the relationship contains data.

Intranet: (1) A private local or wide area network that uses TCP/IP, HTML, and related browser technology on client computers and web server technology on serves. (2) Less commonly, any private LAN or WAN that involves clients and servers

Intrarelation constraint: A restriction on data values in a relation. For example, in PART (Part , name, Units), the rule is that if Part starts with a then Units must equal Pounds.

I/O: Input/output. The process in the operating system that reads and writes data from and to peripheral storage devices.

IS-A relationship: A relationship between two entities or objects of the same logical type. In reference to ENGINEER IS-A(n) EMPLOYEE, both of these entities are employees and are of the same logical type. Contrast this with a HAS-A relationship.

IUnknown: An ActiveX interface in which one ActiveX program can call another, unknown ActiveX program. Once a connection has been established, the first program can use the Query Interface to determine what objects, methods, and properties the second program supports.

J

J-lead See SOJ.

jack Receptacle into which a plug is inserted.

jacket Plastic housing that contains a floppy disk. The 5.25" disk is built into a flexible jacket; the 3.25' disk uses a rigid jacket.

Jacquard loom Automated loom that transformed the 19th century textile industry and became the inspiration for future calculating and tabulating machines. Developed by the French silk-weaver, Joseph-Marie Jacquard (1752-1834), it used punched cards to control its operation. Although punched cards were used in earlier looms and music boxes, Jacquard's loom was a vast improvement and allowed complex patterns to be created swiftly.

jaggles Stairstepped appearance of diagonal lines on a low- resolution graphics screen.

Javelin Pius PC spreadsheet from Information Resources, Inc. Instead of row and column numbers, it uses names to identify cells and consolidate data.

JCL (Job Control Language) IBM term that has become generic for command languages that direct the operating system to run application programs. It specifies information such as priority, program size and run- fling sequence, as well as the files and databases used.

JES (Job Entry Subsystem) Software that provides batch communications for IBM's MVS operating system. It accepts data from remote batch terminals, executes them on a priority basis and transmits the results back to the terminals. The JES counterpart in VM is called RSCS.

jiff See GIF.

jitter Flickering transmission signal or display image.

job Unit of work running in the computer. Ajob may be a single program or a group of programs that work together.

job class Descriptive category of a job that is based on the computer resources it requires when running.

job control language See JCL.

job management language Same as JCL.

job processing Handling and processing jobs in the computer.

job queue Lineup of programs ready to be executed.

job stream Series of related programs that are run in a prescribed order. The output of one program is the input to the next program and so on.

join (1) In relational database management, to match one file against another based on some condition creating a third file with data from the matching files. For example, a customer file can be joined with an order file creating a file of records for all customers who purchased a particular product. (2) See DOS Join.

Josephson junction Ultrá-fast switching technology that uses superconductor materials, originally conceived by Brian Josephson. Circuits are immersed in liquid helium to obtain near-absolute zero degrees required for operation. A Josephson junction has been observed to switch in as little as 50 femtoseconds.

journal same as log.

joy stick Pointing device used to move an object on screen in any direction. It employs a vertical rod mounted on a base that contains one or two buttons. It is used extensively in video games and in some CAD systems.

JPEG (Joint Photographic Experts Group) ISO/CCITT standard for compressing images using discrete cosine transform. It provides compression at variable ratios, providing 20 to 30:1 without noticeable loss. Ratios of 50:1 to 100:1 may be used if the loss in image can be tolerated.

JPEG is implemented in hardware as well as software; for example, a PC with a 1992-vintage JPEG board can compress a full-color 25MB image into 1MB in one second. C-Cube Microsystems introduced the first JPEG chip. See MPEG.

Julian date Representation of month and day by a consecutive number starting with Jan. 1. For example, Feb. 1 is Julian 32. Dates are converted into Julian dates for calculation.

Jump Same as GOTO.

jumper Metal bridge used to close a circuit. It can be a short length of wire or a plastic-coveredinetal block that is pushed onto two pins on a circuit board. It is often used in place of DIP switches.

Junction Point at which two elements make contact. In a transistor, a junction is the point where an N-type material makes contact with a P-type material.

Justification In typography, the alignment of text evenly between left and right margins. Contrast with ragged right.

Justify (1) To shift the contents of a field or register to the right or left. (2) To align text evenly between left and right margins.

Java: An object programming language that has better memory management and bounds checking than C++. Used primarily for Internet applications, but also can be used as a general-purpose programming language. Java compliers generate Java byte code that is interpreted on client computers.

Join: A relational algebra operation on two relations, A and B, that produces a third relation, C. A row of A is concatenated with a row of B to form a new row in C if the rows in A and B meet restrictions concerning their values. For example, Al is an attribute in A, and Bi is an attribute in B. The join of A with B in which Al <Bl will result in a relation, C, having the concatenation of rows in A and B in which the value of Al is less than the value of Bi. See Equijoin and Natural join.

K

K See kilo.

K-byte See kilobyte.

K&R C (Kemighan and Ritçhie C) Version of C defined by Brian Krnighan and Dennis Ritchie that preceded the ANSI standard.

KB, Kb See kilobyte and kilobit.

Kbit See kilobit.

Kbits/sec (KiloBITS per SECond) Thousand bits per second.

KBps, Kbps (KiloBytes Per Second, KiloBits Per Second) Thousand bytes per second. Thousand bits per second.

Kbyte See kilobyte.

Kbytes/sec (KiloBYThS per SECond) Thousand bytes per second.

Kermit Asynchronous file transfer protocol developed at Columbia Univ., noted for its accuracy over noisy lines. Several extensions exist, including SuperKermit, a full-duplex, sliding window version. Kermit is popular on minis and mainframes and can also handle byte-oriented transfers over 7-bit ASCII systems.

kernel Fundamental part of a program, such as an operating system, that resides in memory at all times.

kerning In typography, the spacing of letter combinations, such as WA, MW and TA, where each character overlaps into some of the space of the other for improved appearance.

key (1) Keyboard button. (2) Data item that identifies a record. As an identifier, each key value must be unique in each record. See sort key. (3) Numeric code used by an algorithm to create a code for encrypting data for security purposes.

key bounce A characteristic of some poorly designed keyboards where a character registers twice for each time the user presses the key.

key cap Replaceable, top part of a keyboard key. To identify commonly-used codes, it can be replaced with a aistom key cap.

key dick -Audible feedback provided when a key is pressed. It may be adjustable by the user.

key aimmand Key combination (Alt-G, Qrl-B, Commaad-M, etc.) used as a command to the computer.

key-driven Any device that is activated by pressing keys.

key entry Data entry using a keyboard.

key field See key (2).

key In To enter data by typing on a keyboard.

key rollover See n-key rollover.

key-to-disk machine Stand-alone data entry machine that stores data on magnetic disk for computer entry.

key-to-tape machine Stand-alone data entry machine that stores data on magnetic tape for computer entry.

key word (1) Word used in a text search. (2) Word in a text document that is used in an index to best describe the contents of the document. (3) Reserved word in a programming or command language.

key-word-In-context See KWIC.

keyboard Set of input keys. On terminals and personal computers, it includes the standard typewriter keys, several specialized keys and features outlined below. See PC keyboard, AF keyboard and Enhanced keyboard. Enter(Retum) Key: In text applications, it ends a paragraph or short line. In data applications, it signals the end of the input for that field or line.

Cursor Keys: The four arrow keys move the cursor on screen. They are used in conjunction with shift, alt and control to move the cursor in bigger jumps; for example, CONTROL UP ARROW might scroll the screen. Some earlier keyboards didn't have cursor keys, in which case, control or alt was used with some letter key. Control, Alt, Command and Option Keys: Used like a shift key, these keys are held dçwn while another key is pressed to command the cod*uter in a variety of ways. Escape Key: Commonly used to exit or cancel the current mode such as exiting from a menu. Also used to clear an area or repeat a function such as redrawing the screen. Numeric Lock: Locks a combination number/cursor keypad into numeric mode only. Home and End Keys: Commonly used to move the cursor to the extreme left or right side of the current line. Often used in conjunction with shift, control and alt; for example, CONTROL HOME and CONTROL END usually move the cursor to the beginning and end of file. Page Up and Page Down Keys: Used to move the cursor up and down a page, screen or frame. Often used in combination with shift, control and alt.

Function Keys: Used to call up a menu or per- form a function, they are located in a cluster on the left side or in a row across the top of the keyboard (labelled Fl, P2, etc.). Often used with the shift, control and alt keys providing 40 separate functions with Fl through FlO.

Backspace Key: Used to delete the character to the left of the cursor (erase typos) and may be used with the shift, control and alt keys to erase segments of text. The extra-wide, typewriter-style key is preferred.

Delete Key: Used to erase the character at the current cursor location. Used in conjunction with the shift, control and alt keys, it is used to erase any segment of text, such as a word, sentence or paragraph.

Insert Key: Usually a toggle switch to go back and forth between insert and overwrite mode. Also used to "paste" a segment of text or graphics into the document at the current cursor location.

Repeating Keys: Most computer keys repeat when held down, a phenomenon first-time computer users must get used to. This is also referred to as its typmatic feature.

Audible Feedback: Keyboards may cause a click or beep to be heard from the computer when keys are pressed. This is done to acknowledge that the character has been entered. It should be adjustable for personal preference.

keyboard buffer Memory bank or reserved memory area that stores keystrokes until the program can accept them. It lets fast typists continue typing while the program catches up. The keyboard will beep if its buffer is full.

keyboard controller Circuit that monitors keystrokes and generates the required data bits when pressed.

keyboard enhancer Same as macro processor.

keyboard Interrupt Signal that gets the attention of the CPU each time a key is pressed. See interrupt.

keyboard macro processor See macro processor.

keyboard processor (1) Circuit in the keyboard that converts keystrokes into the appropriate character codes. (2) See keyboard enhancer. (3) See keyboard controller and keyboard enhancer.

keyboard template Plastic card that fits over the function keys to identify each key's purpose in a particular software program.

keyframe In computer graphics animation, a frame that indicates the beginning or end of an object in motion.

keypad Small keyboard or supplementary keyboard keys; for example, the keys on a calculator or the number/cursor cluster on a computer keyboard.

keypunch To punch holes in a punched card. It is sometimes used to refer to typing on a computer keyboard.

keypunch department Same as data entry department.

keypunch machine Punched-card data entry machine. A deck of blank cards is placed into a hopper, and, upon operator command, the machine feeds one card to a punch station. As characters are typed, a series of dies at the punch station punch the appropriate holes in the selected card column.

Khornerstones Benchmark program that tests CPU, If O and floating point performance.

KHz (KiloHertZ) One thousand cycles per second.

kill (1) To terminate a process before it reaches it natural conclusion. (2) A method of erasing information. (3) To stop; frequently, to abort. (4) To delete a file.

kilo Thousand. Abbreviated "K" It often refers to the precise value 1,024 since computer specifications are usually binary numbers.

kllobit One thousand bits. Also KB, Kb, Kbit and K- bit. See kilo and space/time.

kilobyte One thousand bytes. Also KB, Kbyte and K- byte. See kilo and space/time.

kiudge Also spelled "kluge" and pronounced "klooj." A crude, inelegant system, component or program. It may refer to a makeshift, temporary solution to a problem as well as to any product that is poorly designed or that becomes unwieldy over time.

knowledge acquisition Process of acquiring knowledge from a human expert for an expert system, which must be carefully organized into IF-THEN rules or some other form of knowledge representation.

knowledge base Database of rules about a subject used in Al applications. See expert system.

knowledge based system Al application that uses a database of knowledge about a subject. See expert system.

knowledge domain Specific area of expertise of an expert system.

knowledge engineer Person who translates the knowledge of an expert into the knowledge base of an expert system.

knowledge representation Method used to code knowledge in an expert system, typically a series of IFTHEN rules (IF this condition occurs, ThEN take this action).

KSR terminal (Keyboard Send Receive terminal) Same as teleprinter. Contrast with RO terminal.

KWIC Acronym for key-word-in-context, a method of indexing information by preselected words or phrases that takes into consideration the content in which the words are used.

Key: (1) A group of one or more attributes identifying a unique row in a relation. Since relations may not have duplicate rows, every relation must have at least one key, which is the composite of all of the attributes in the relation. A key is sometimes called a logical key. (2) With some relational DBMS products, an index on a column used to improve access and sorting speed. It is sometimes called a physical key.

L

label (1) In data management, a made-up name that is assigned to a file, field or other data structure. (2) In spreadsheet, descriptive text that is entered into a cell. (3) In programming, a made-up name used to identify a variable or a subroutine. (4) In computer operations, a self-sticking form attached to the outside of a disk or tape in order to identify it. (5) In magnetic tape files, a record used for identification at the beginning or end of the file.

label prefix In a spreadsheet, a character typed at the beginning of a cell entry. For example, in 1-2-3, a single quote identifies a descriptive label that is to be left-aligned in the cell; double quote for right- aligned.

LAN (Local Area Network) Communications network that serves users within a confined geographical area. It is made up of servers, workstations, a network operating system and a communications link.

Servers are high-speed machines that hold programs and data shared by all network users. A workstation is a user's machine, which can also function as standalone personal computer. Diskless workstations or floppy-only workstations retrieve all software and data from the server. A printer can be attached to the workstation or it can be attached to a server and be shared by network users.

Small LANs can allow each workstation to function. as a server, allowing all users access to data on all machines. These peer-to-peer networks are often simpler to install and manage, but a dedicated server will always be able to handle transactions faster. Multiple servers are used in high-transaction-volume networks.

Bridgcs are used to connect like networks together and gateways connect one type of network to another, allowing a personal computer network to interconnect with a mini or mainframe network, for example.

The controlling software in a LAN is the network operating system, such as NetWare, Lantastic and Appletalk, which resides in the server. A component part of the software resides in each workstation and allows the application to read and write data from the server as if it were on the local machine.

The physical transfer of data is performed by the access method, such as Ethernet or Toiren Ring, which come in the form of network adapters (NICs) that plug into each computer. The actual link, or communications path, is the cable (twisted pair, coax, optical fiber, etc.) that plugs into each network adapter and connects workstations and servers together. See MAN and WAN.

LAN Manager LAN operating system from Microsoft that runs as an application under OS/2 in a server and supports both DOS, OS/2 and UNIX workstations. It uses the Microsoft File Sharing protocol (SMB) for file sharing, the NetBIOS protocol for its transport mechanism and uses Named Pipes for interprocess communication (IPC).

LAN Network Manager IBM Token Ring network management software used by the network administrator to monitor and control the network. LAN Station Manager is the workstation counterpart that collects data for LAN Network Manager.

LAN Requester LAN Server software that resides in the workstation.

LAN Server IBM's version of LAN Manager. Although these two versions have drifted apart, they may eventually be merged.

LAN station (1) Workstation in a local area network. (2) See LAN Network Manager.

Landmark rating Widely-used PC performance test from Landmark Research Int'l, that measures CPU, video and coprocessor speed. CPU speed is rated as the clock speed required in an AT-class machine that would provide equivalent performance.

landscape Printing orientation that prints data across the wider side of the form. Contrast with portrait.

landscape monitor Monitor that is used to display 2 facing text pages. It is wider than it is high.

language Set of symbols and rules used to convey information. See machine language, programming language, graphics language, page description language, fourth-generation language, standards & compatibility and user interface.

language processor Language translation software. Programming languages, command languages, query languages, natural languages and foreign languages are all translated by software.

LanguageAccess SAA-compliant query language from IBM that translates a user's English-language request into SQL language for QMF. QMF retrieves the data.

LANtastlc Popular peer-to-peer LAN operating system for PCs from Artisoft, that is noted for its ease of use. Its supports Ethernet, ARCNET and Token King adapters as well as its own twisted- pair adapter at two Mbits/sec. Artisoft also makes Ethernet adapters. Included are e-mail and chat functions. Voice mail and conversation are optional.

LapLink PC file transfer program from Travelling Software, that transfers data between laptops and desktop computers. LapLink Mac transfers files between PCs and Macs.

laptop computer Portable computer that has a flat screen and usually weighs less than a dozen pounds. It uses AC power and/or bat teries. Most have connectors for an external monitor transforming them into desktop computers. Some important features of the laptop are its ability to conz nect an external CRT and a full sized keyboard. Most laptops have built-in mouse port or a track ball and also a model. Most also have an auto-resume feature that lets you return to the computer and pickup where you left off without having to reload your applications. Most laptops use VGA gray scale, and colors translate to a shade of gray. They have low powered CPUs like the Intel's 386SL or AMD's Ajn386-SXL that prolong battery life. They use a nickel hydride battery. See notebook computer and pocket computer.

laser (Light Amplification from the Stimulated Emission of Radiation) Device that generates a very uniform light that can be precisely focused. It is used in a wide variety of applications, such as communications, printing and disk storage. It is used to transmit light pulses over optical fibers which, unlike electrical wires, are not affected by nearby electrical interferences. In 1957, the laser was conceived by Gordon Gould, a graduate student in physics at Columbia Univ.

laser printer Printer that uses the electrophotographic method and "paints" the dots of light onto a photographic drum or belt. The toner is applied to the drum or belt and then transferred onto the paper.

In 1975, IBM introduced the first laser printer, called the 3800, designed for high-speed printing. In 1978, Siemens introduced the ND 2 and Xerox introduced the 9700. In 1984, HP introduced the LaserJet, the first desktop laser printer, which revolutionized personal computer printing and propelled desktop publishing. The desktop laser printer cormpetes directly with the dot matrix printer.

Although high-resolution color laser printers are also available, less expensive deskto versions should become Widely used throughout the 1990s.

inset-disc See videodisc.

LaserJet Family of desktop laser printers from HP. Introduced in 1984, the first LaserJet revolutionized the desktop laser printer market. LaserJets print up to 300 dpi, although third-party enhancements increase resolution to 800 dpi and more. The III series adds Resolution Enhancement Technology, which uses smaller dots to smooth out the jaggies. PCL is the printer command language.

LaserJets accept bitmapped fonts from plug-in cartridges or from the computer (soft fonts). Adobe PostScript cartridges are available for the IID, lip and Iii series, and third-parties provide PostScript for the Ii. With the Ill series (PCL Version 5), scalable fonts have been added, some built in, others via cartridges. The Series II is upgradable to PCL 5.

LaserWriter Family series of 300 dpi desktop laser printers from Apple introduced in 1985. All models handle bitmapped fonts, and, except for the SC models, include Postscript, built-in AppleTalk connections, as well as RS-232 ports for connecting PCs via Diablo emulation.

LAT (Local Area Ttansport) Communications protocol from Digital for controlling terminal traffic in a DECnet envroiunent.

latch Electronic ciratit that maintains one of two states. See flip-flop.

late binding Linking routines at runtime.

latency Time between initiating a request for data and the beginning of the actual data transfer. On a rotating medium, such as a disk, latency is the time it takes for the selected sector to come around and be positioned under the read/write head. Channel latency is the time it takes for a computer channel to become unoccupied in order to transfer data.

latent Image Invisible image typically of electrical charges. For example, in a copy machine,a latent image of the page to be copied is created on a plate or drum as an electrical charge.

launch To cause a program to load and run.

layer (1) In computer graphics, one of several on-screen "drawing boards" for creatinielements within a pic ture. Layers can be manipulated independently, and the sum of all layers make up the total image. (2) In communications, a protocol that interacts with other protocols to provide all the necessary transmission services. See OSI.

layout setting Value used to format a printed page. Margins, tabs, indents, headers, footers and column widths are examples.

LC (Low cost Color) See Macintosh. LCC See leaded chip carrier.

LCD (Liquid Crystal Display) Display technology commonly used in digital watches and laptops. Because it uses less power, LCD replaced LED (light emitting diode

Power is used only to move molecules rather than to energize a light-emitting substance. Liquid crystals are rod-shaped molecules that flow like liquid and are used to direct light between two polarizing filters. In their normal state, the crystals direct the light through the polarizers, allowing a natural light gray background color to show. When energized, they redirect the light to be absorbed in one of the polarizers, causing the dark appearance of crossed polarizers to show.

LCD panel Data projector that accepts computer output and displays it on a see-through liquid crystal screen which can be placed on top of an overhead projector.

LCD printer Electrophotographic printer that uses a S single light source directed by liquid crystal shutters.

LE (Less than or Equal to) See relational operator.

leaded chip carrier Square chip housing with pin connectors on all four sides (provides more I/O paths than a DIP). Contrast with leadless chip carrier.

leader (1) Length of unrecorded tape used to thread the tape onto the tape drive. (2) Dot or dash used to draw the eye across the printed page, such as in a table of contents.

leading In typography, the vertical spacing between lines of type (between baselines). The name comes from the early days of typesetting when the space was achieved with thin bars of lead.

leading edge (1) Edge of a punched card or document that enters the reading station first. (2) In digital electronies, a pulse as it changes from a 0 to a 1. (3) In programming, a loop that tests a condition before the loop is entered.

leading zeros Zeros used to fill a field that do not increase the numerical value of the data. For example, all the zeros in 0001234 are leading zeros.

leadless chip carrier Square chip.housing with flat contact connectors on all four sides (provides more I/O paths than a DIP). Contrast with leaded chip carriet.

leaf In database management, the last node of a tree.

leapfrog test Storage diagnostic routine that replicates itself throughout the storage medium.

leased line Private communications channel leased from a common carrier. It can be ordered in pairs, providing a four-wire channel for full-duplex transmission (dial-up system provides only two-wire lines). To improve line quality, it can also be conditioned.

leased line modem High-speed modem used in private lines. It may have built-in lower speeds for alternate use in dial-up lines.

least significant digit Rightmost digit in a number.

LED (Light Emitting Diode) Display technology that uses a semiconductor diode that emits light when charged. It usually gives off a red glow, although other colors can be generated. It is used in readouts and on/off lights in myriads of electronic appliances. It was the first digital watch display, but was superseded by LCD, which uses less pover.

LED printer Electrophotographic printer that uses a matrix of LEDs as its light source rather than a laser.

left Justify Same as flush left.

Lempel Ziv Data compression algorithm that uses an adaptive compression technique.

letter quality Print quality of an electric typewriter. Laser printers, ink jet printers and daisy wheel printers provide letter quality printing. 24-pin dot matrix printers provide near letter quality (NLQ), but the characters ar not as dark and crisp.

lexicographic sort Arranging items in alphabetic order like a dictionary. Numbers are located by their alphabetic spelling.

LF See line feed.

LHARC Popular freeware compression program developed by Haruyasu Yoshizaki that uses a variant of the LZW (LZ77) dictionary method followed by a Huffman coding stage. It runs on PCs, UNIX and other platforms as its source code is also free.

librarian Person who works in the data library.

library (1) Collection of prcgrams or data files. (2) Collection of functions (subroutines) that are linked into the main program when it is compiled. (3) See data library.

library automation The application of computers and other technology to library operations and services.

library routine Subroutine that is part of a macro or function library.

LIFO (Last In First Out) Queuing method in which the next item to be retrieved is the item most recently placed in the queue. Contrast with FIFO.

ligature Two or more typeface characters that are designed as a single unit (physically touch). Fi, ffi, ae and oe are common ligatures.

light bar Same as highlight bar.

light guide Transmission channel that contains a number of optical fibers packaged together.

light pen Light-sensitive stylus wired to a video terminal used to draw pictures or select menu options. The user brings the pen to the desired point on screen and presses the pen button to make contact.

Screen pixels are constantly being refreshed. When the user presses the button, allowing the pen to sense light, the pixel being illuminated at that instant identifies the screen location.

light source In computer graphies, used to simulate the visual effect of a light on a 3-D object. Some programs can compute multiple light sources.

lightwave Light in the infrared, visible and ultraviolet ranges, which falls between x-rays and microwaves. Wavelengths are between 10 nanometers and one millimeter.

lightwave system Device that transmits light pulses over optical fibers at extremely high speeds (Gbits/sec range). Many intercity telephone trunks have been converted to lightwave systems.

LIM EMS See EMS.

limited distance modem Same as short-haul modem. limuiator See EMS emulator.

Linda Set of parallel processing functions added to languages, such as C and C++, that allows data to be created and transferred between processes.

line (1) In text-based systems, a row of characters. (2) In graphics-based systems, a row of pixels. (3) Any communications channel.

line adapter In communications, a device similar to a modem, that converts a digital signal into a form suitable for transmission over a communications line and vice versa. It provides parallel/serial and serial/par allel conversion, modulation and demodulation.

line analyzer Device that monitors the transmission of a communications line.

line concentration See concentrator.

line conditioning See conditioning.

line dot matrix printer Line printer that uses the dot matrix method. See printer.

line drawing Graphic image outlined by solid lines. The mass of the drawing is imagined by the viewer. See wire frame.

line driver In communications, a device that is used to extend the transmission distance between terminals and computers that are connected via private lines. It is used for digital transmission and is required at each end of the line.

line editor Simple editing program that allows text to be created and changed one line at a time.

line feed (1) Character code that advances the screen cursor or printer to the next line. The line feed is used as an end of line code in UNIX. In DOS and OS/2 text files, the return/line feed pair (ASCII 13 10) is the standard end of line code. (2) Printer button that advances paper one line.

line frequency Number of times each second that a wave or some repeatable set of signals is transmitted over a line. See horizontal scan frequency.

line level In communications, the signal strength within a transmission channel, measured iii decibels or nepers.

line load (1) In communications, the percentage of time a communications channel is used. (2) In electronics, the amount of current that is carried in a circuit.

line number (1) Specific line of programming language source code. (2) On display screens, a specific row of text or row of dots. (3) In communications, a specific communicati9ns channel.

line of code Statement in a source program. In assembly language, it usually generates one machine instruction, but in a high-level language, it may generate a series of instructions. 20 lines of code in COBOL might require 200 lines of code in assembly language.

line of sight Unobstructed view from transmitter to receiver.

line printer Printer that prints one line at a time. Line printers are usually connected to mainframes and minicomputers. See printer.

line segment In vector graphics, same as vector. line speed See data rate.

line squeeze In a mail merge, the vertical adjustment of the body of text when a blank line is encountered in the name nd address.

linear Sequential or having a graph that is a straight line.

linear address space See flat address space.

linear programming Mathematical technique used to obtain an optimum solution in resource allocation problems, such as production planning.

linear video Continuous playback of videotape or videodisc. Contrast with interactive video.

link (1) In communications, a line, channel or circuit over which data is transmitted. (2) In data management, a pointer embedded within a record that refers to data or the location of data in another record. (3) In programming, a call to another program or subroutine.

link edit To use a linkage editor to prepare a program for running.

linkage editor Utility program that links a compiled or assembled program to a particular environment. It formally unites references between program modules and libraries of subroutines. Its output is a load module, a program ready to run in the computer.

linked list In data management, a group of items, each of which points to the next item. It allows for the organization of a sequential set of data in nonczntiguous storage locations.

Inker See linkage editor.

Unpack Package of FORTRAN programs for numerical linear algebra that is commonly used to create benchmark programs for testing a computer's floating point performance.

LIPS (Logical Inferences Per Second) Unit of measurement of the thinking speed of an Al application. Humans do about 2 LIPS. In the computer, one UPS equals from 100 to 1,000 instructions.

liquid crystal shutters Method of directing light onto the drum in an electrophotographic printer. A matrix of liquid crystal dots function as shutters that are opened and closed.

Lisa First personal computer to include integrated software and use a graphical interface. Introduced in 1983 by Apple, it was ahead of its time, but never caught on due to its price and slow speed.

LISP (LISt Processing) High-level programming language used in non-numeric programming. Developed in 1960 by John McCarthy, it is very different in syntax and structure than languages like BASIC and COBOL. For example, in LISP there is no syntactic difference between data and instructions. LISP is used extensively in Al applications, as well as in compiler creation, and is available in both interpreter and compiler versions. It automatically handles more program activities than conventional languages, such as dynamic memory management, and lets the programmer concentrate on manipulating the objects. The language itself can be modified and expanded. Many varieties of LISP have been developed, including versions that perform calculations efficiently.

list (1) Arranged set of data, often in row and column format. (2) In fourth-generation languages, a co'mmand that displays or prints a group of selected records.

list processing Processing non-numeric data.

list processing language Programming language used for processing non-numeric data, such as LISP, Prolog and Logo. It provides special commands that work with lists of data, such as names, words and objects. Although these functions can be performed in a traditional programrhing language, list processing languages make it easier. Recutsion is also provided, which lets a subroutine call itself over again, thus allowing objects in a list to be repetitively analyzed.

listing Any printed output generated from the computer.

literal In programming, an unchanging item written into the program, sucn as a message displayed on screen. It is translated into machine language without conversion.

little endlan See big endian. liveware People.

LLCC See leadless chip carrier.

lo-res or lo-rez. See low resolution.

load (1) To copy a program fróm some source, such as a disk or tape, into memory for execution. (2) To fill up a disk with data or programs. (3) To insert a disk or tape into a drive. (4) In programming, to store data in a register. (5) In performance measurement, the current use of a system as a percentage of total capacity. (6) In electronics, the flow of current through a circuit.

load high To load programs into high memory. See DOS 1.oadhigh.

load module Program in machine language form ready to run in the computer. It is the output of a link editor.

load sharing Sharing the workload in two or more computers.

loader Program routine that copies a program into memory for execution.

loader routine Same as loader. local area network See LAN.

local bus Channel that runs at CPU speed. To increase screen performance on PCs, a local bus is used between the CPU and video adapter.

local bypass Interconnection between two facilities without the use of the local telephone company.

local loop Communications line between a customer and the telephone company's central office. See loop carrier.

local memory Memory used by a single CPU or allocated to a single program or function.

local storage Disk storage used by a single CPU.

local variable In programming, a variable used only within the routine or function it is defined in.

LocalTalk LAN access method from Apple that uses twisted pair wires and transmits at 230,400 bps. It runs under AppleTalk and uses a daisy chain topology that can connect up to 32 devices within a distance of 1,000 feet. Third party products allow it to hook up with bus, passive star and active star topologies. Apple's LocalTalk PC Card lets a PC gain access to an AppleTalk network.

lock (1) To permit exclusive use of a computer resource. (2) To protect a disk or tape file tiom being changed or erased.

locked-up keyboard A situation in which the computer does not respond to key presses.

locking a disk Ensuring that the contents of a disk are preserved from being written over by other data from a computer. a disk is locked when it has been write protected.

lockout (1) The suppression of an interrupt. (2) A programming technique used in a multiprocessing environment to prevent access to critical data by both CPU at the same time.

lock-up A situation in which no further action may occur.

log Record of computer activity used for statistical purposes as well as backup and recovery.

logic Sequence of operations performed by hardware or software. Hardware logic is made up of circuits that perform an operations. Software logic (program logic) is the sequence of instructions in a program. Logic is not the same as logical. See logical vs physical and logical expression.

logic analyzer (1) Device that monitors computer peeformance by timing various segments of the running programs. The total running time and the time spent in selected program modules is displayed in order to isolate the the least efficient code. (2) Device used to test and diagnose an electronic system, which includes an oscilloscope for displaying various digital states.

logic array Same as gate array or PLA.

logic bomb Program routine that destroys data; for example, it may reformat the hard disk or insert random bits into data files. It may be brought into a personal computer by downloading a corrupt public-domain program. Once executed, it does its damage right away, whereas a virus keeps on destroying.

logic chip Processoi or controller chip. Contrast with memory chip.

logic circuit Circuit that performs some processing or controlling function. Contrast with memory.

logic controller See PLC.

logic diagram Flow chart of hardware circuits.

logic error Program bug due to an wrong sequence o hons.

logic gate Collection of transistors and electronic coinponents that make up a Boolean logical operation, such as AND, NAND, OR and NOR. Transistors make up logic gates. Logic gates make up circuits. Circuits make up electronic systems.

logic operation Operation that analyzes one or more inputs and generates a particular output based on a set of rules. See AND, OR and NOT and Boolean logic.

logic seeking The ability of a printer that works bidirectionally to seek out the shortest printing path.

logic-seeking printer Printer that analyzes line content and skips over blank spaces at high speeds.

logical (1) Reasonable solution to a problem. (2) Higher level view of an object; for example, the user's view versus the computer's view. See logical vs physical.

logical data group Data derived from several sources. Same as view.

logical drive Allocated part of a physical drive that is designated aiid managed as an independent unit.

logical expression Expression that results in true or false. Same as Boolean expression.

logical field Data field tiat contains a yes/no, true/false condition.

logical lock Prevention of user access to data that is provided by marking the file or record through the use of software. Contrast with physical lock.

logical operator One of the Boolean logical operators (AND, OR and NOD.

logical record Reference to a data record that is independent of its physical location. It may be physically stored in two or more locations.

logical vs physical High-level versus low-level. Logical implies a higher view than the physical. When you command your program to change the output from the video screen to the printer, that's a logical request. The program will perform the physical change of address from, say, device number 02 to device number 04.

login Same as logon.

Logo High-level programming language noted for its ease of use and graphics capabilities. It is a recursive language that contains many list processing functions that are in LISP, although Logo's syntax is more understandable for novices. Logo's graphics language is also called turtle graphics, which allows complex graphics images to be created with a minimum of coding. The turtle is a triangular-shaped cursor, which 1s moved on screen with commands that activate the WrtIe as if you were driving it. Stemming from a National Science Foundation project, Logo was created by Seymour Papert in the mid 196fu along with colleagues at MIT and members of Bolt Beranek & Newman. Originally developed on large computers, it has been adapted to most personal computers.

logoff To quit, or sign off, a computer system.

logon To gain access, or sign in, to a computer system. If restricted, it requires users to identify themselves by entering an ID number and/or password. Service bureaus base their charges for the time between logon and logoff.

logout Same as logoff.

long In programming, an integer variable. In C, a long is four bytes and can be signed (-2G to +2G) or unsigned (4G). Contrast with short.

long card In PCs, a full-length controller board that plugs into an expansion slot. Contrast with short card.

long-haul In communications, modems or communications devices that are capable of transmitting over long distances.

long lines In communications, circuits that are capable of handling transmissions over long distances.

longItudInal redundancy check See LRC.

look-alike (1) A program that imitates another program so closely that users of the original program can use the look-alike program without learning any new opcrating instructions. (2) Any product that copies another. Often when a vendor produces a successful j product, its competitors offer look-alike products.

lookup Data search performed within a predefined table of values (array, matrix, etc.) or within a data file.

loop In programming, a repetition within a program. Whenever a process must be repeated, a loop is set up to handle it. A program has a main loop and a series of minor loops, which are nested within the main loop. Learning how to set up loops is what programming technique is all about. Loops are accomplished by various programming structures that have a beginning, body and end. The beginning generally tests the condition that keeps the ioop going. The body comprises the repeating statements, and the end is a GOTO that points back to the beginning.

loop carrier In telephone communications, a system that concuntrates a number of analog or digital lines from a remote termination station into the central office. It normally converts analog voice into digital at the remote station; however, it can be adapted to provide ISDN service to a customer.

loopback plug Diagnostic connector that directs the sending line back into the reêeiving line for test purposes.

loosely coupled Refers to stand-alone computers connected via a network. Loosely coupled computers process on their own and exchange data on demand. Contrast with tightly coupled.

lossless compression Compression techniques that decompress data 100% back to original. Contrast with lossy compression.

lossy compression Compression techniques that do not decompress data 100% back to original, Images and audio samples may be able to afford small losses of resolution in order to increase compression. Contrast with lossless compression.

lost cluster Disk records that have lost their identification with a file name. This can happen if a file is not closed properly, which can sometimes occur if the computer is turned off without formally quitting an application. See DOS Chkdsk.

Lotus (Lotus Development Corp., Cambridge, MA) Software company founded in 1981 by Mitch Kapor. It achieved outstanding success by introducing the first spreadsheet for the IBM PC (see Lotus 1-2-3). Over the years, it has developed a variety of applications and has been a major force in setting industry standards. In 1990, it- acquired Samna Corp., makers of the popular, Windows-based Arni word processors.

Lotus 1-2-3 Spreadsheet for PCs and a variety of computers from Lotus. Introduced in 1982, it was the first, new and innovative spreadsheet for the PC. It was the first to include graphics, file management and limited word processing along with traditional spreadsheet capabilities. Its ability to instantly convert numeric data into a graph was a dazzling feature for its time. The program's user interface was also easy to learn and use (see Lotus menu).

Versions 2.0 and subsequent 2.01 introduced in 1986,. have sold over four million copies. In 1989, Lotus introduced Version 2.2 and 3.0. Version 2.2 needs 320K of memory and adds features such as macro recording, an undo and a dynamic link from one spreadsheet to another.

Version 3.0 uses extended memory and runs on 286 and higher CPUs with at least 1MB RAM. It provides 3-D and dynamic linking capabilities as well as more sophisticated graphing. It also provides OS/2 compatibility and can access database files directly. Lotus Add-In Toolkit Pascal-like programming language from Lotus that allows automated processes to be created and executed in Lotus 1-2-3 Version 3.0. It includes an editor, compiler and debugger and allows makers of add-in products to convert them to Version 3.0.

Lotus menu Menu introduced with Lotus 1-2-3 that became a de facto standard. It is a row of words, each of which is an option that can be selected by highlighting it and pressing Enter or by pressing the first letter of the word. When the word is highlighted, an explanation line is displayed above or below it. Contrast with pull-down menu.

low frequency Electromagnetic wave that vibrates in the range from 30 to 300,000 Hertz.

low-level format Sector identification recorded on a disk. Disks have two levels of formatting. The low- level format initiates the disk and creates the physical layout of the sectors required by the disk's controller. The high-level format lays out the indexes and tables used by the operating system to keep track of the data it writes into the sectors.

low-level language Programming language that is very close to machine language. All assembly languages are low-level languages. Contrast with high-level language.

low radiation Refers to video terminals that emit less VLF (Very Low Frequency) and ELF (Extremely Low Frequency) radiation. This level of radiation cannot be shielded by office partitions. It must be cancelled out from the CRT. Health studies on this are not conclusive and are very controversial.

low resolution Low-grade display or printing quality due to a lower number of dots or lines per inch.

lower CASE See back-end CASE.

lpi (Lines Per Inch) The number of lines printed in a vertical inch.

lpm (Lines Per Minute) Number of lines a printer can print or a scanner can scan in a minute.

LPT1 Logical name assigned to parallel port #1 in DOS and OS/2 (usually connected to a printer). A second parallel device is assigned LPT2. Contrast with COM1.

LQ See letter quality.

LRC (Longitudinal Redundancy Check) Error checking method that generates a parity bit from a specified string of bits on a longitudinal track. In a row and column format, such as on magnetic tape, LRC is often used with VRC, which creates a parity bit for each character.

LSI (Large Scale Integration) Between 3,000 and 100,000 transistors on a chip. See SSI, MSI, VLSI and ULSI.

LT (Less Than) See relational operator.

lumen Unit of measurement of the flow (rate of emission) of light. A wax candle generates 13 lumens; a 100 watt bulb generates 1,200. See candela.

Lumena PC paint program from Time Arts, that provides sophisticated, special effects. It accepts and generates NTSC video output and requires a video graphics board.

luminance In computer graphics, the amount of brightness, measured in lumens, that is given off by a pixel or area.on a screen.

LZW (Lempel-Ziv-Welch) Widely-used dictionary compression method that stems from two techniques introduced by Jacob Ziv and Abraham Lempel in 1977 and 1978. LZ77 scans a fixed length block of data and creates pointers back to data when it repeats. LZ78 scans the data and creates a dictionary of repeating phrases. Pointers are created to those phrases.

LAN: Local area network. A group of microcomputers connected to one another by means of communications lines in close proximity, usually less than a mile. See Client—server database architecture and Resource-sharing architecture.

LDBR: See Logical data base record.

List box: In a GUI environment, an element of the user interface in which a list of choices is presented in a rectangle. The user moves the cursor to shade the item to be selected from the list.

Location transparency: In a distributed database system, the condition in which application programs do not know and do not need to know where data are located. The DDBMS finds data, wherever they are located, without the involvement of the application program.

Lock: The process of allocating a database resource to a particular transaction in a concurrent-processing system. The size of the resource locked is known as the lock granularity. With an exclusive lock, no other transaction may read or write the resource. With a shared lock, other transactions may read the resource, but no other transaction may write it.

Lock granularity: The size of a locked data element. The lock of a column value of a particular row is a small granularity lock, and the lock of an entire table is a large granularity lock.

Log: A file containing a record of database changes. The log contains before-images and after-images.

Logical data base (LDB): In DL/I, the collection of all the logical data base records in the data base.

Logical data base record (LDBR): In DL/I, a hierarchy of segments as perceived by an application program. Such a structure may or may not exist physically; it may be taken from other structures using pointers and other overhead data.

Logical key: One or more columns that uniquely determine the row of a table or a record of a file. A synonym for a key. Contrast this with a physical key, which is a synonym for an index.

Logical unit of work: A group of logically related database operations that is performed as a unit. Either all of the operations are performed, or none of them is. A logical unit of work is the same as an atomic transaction. It is a term used with the DBMSDB2.

Look up: The process of obtaining related data by using the value of a foreign key, for example, when processing a row of ORDER (OrderNumber, Ord-Date, CustNumber, ...), using the value of CustNumber to obtain the related value of CustName from CUSTOMER (CustNumber, CustName, ...).

Lost update problem: Same as Concurrent update problem.

LUW: See Logical unit of work.

M

M See mega.

M-byte See megabyte.

Mac A nickname for the Apple Macintosh computer.

MAC driver (Media Access Control driver) Network adapter driver that implements the Microsoft NDIS standard.

MacDraw Pro Macintosh drawing program from Claris Corp. that is an enhanced version of the original MacDraw from Apple and includes full on-screen slide presentation capability. It is used for illustrations and elementary CAD work. MacDraw files are a subset of the Claris CAD file format.

Mach UNIX-like operating system developed at Carnegie- Mellon Univ.

machine Any electronic or electromechanical unit of equipment. A machine is always hardware; however, "engine" refers to hardware or software.

machine address Same as absolute address. machine code Same as machine language.

machine cycle Shortest interval in which an elementary operation can take place within the processor. It is made up of some number of clock cycles.

machine dependent Refers to software that accesses specific hardware features and runs in only one kind of computer. Contrast with machine independent. See device dependent.

machine Independent Refers to software that runs in a variety of computers. Contrast with machine dependent. See device independent.

machine Instruction Instruction that the computer understands directly. It is made up of the op code (operation code) and one or more operands. The op code specifies the type of instruction, such as INPUT or COMPARE. The operands specify the references to data or peripheral devices. For example, the programming statement if a b is converted into a COMPARE op code and operands that state the memory locations that hold A and B.

There are machine instructions to INPUT and OUTPUT, top data by CALCULATING, COMPARING and COPYING it, and to go to some other part of the program with a GOTO instruction.

In addition, there are machine instructions that test and control peripherals. For example, an instruction can check the printer to see if there is paper in it, or an instruction can cause the access arm to seek (go to) a specific track on a disk.

machine Intelilgence See artificial intelligence.

machine language Native langauge of the computer. In order for a program to run, it must be in the machine language of the computer that is executing it. Although programmers may modify machine language in order to fix a running program, they do not create it. It is created by programs called assemblers, compilers and interpreters, which convert programming language into machine language. Machine language tells the computer what to do and where to do it. A programmer deals with data logically, "add this, subtract that," but the computer must be told precisely where this and that are located. Machine languages differ substantially. What may take one instruction in a mainframe, can take 15 instructions in a

microcomputer. See assembly language.

machine learning (1) A heuristic process whereby a device improves its performance based on past actions. (2) A field of artificial intelligence that attempts to build programs that learn from experience.

machine readable Data in a form that can be read by the computer, which includes disks, tapes and punched cards.

machine-readable Informallon Information recorded on any medium in such a way that it can be sensed or read by a machine. Also called machine-sensible.

Macintosh Series of 32-bit floppy-based computer with 128K of memory personal computers from Apple introduced in 1984. It uses the Motorola 68000 processor family and a proprietary operating system that simulates a user's desktop on screen. This standard graphical user interface, combined with its built-in QuickDraw graphics language, has provided a measure of consistency and uniformity that is unmatched. Its "high-rise" cabinet and built-in 9" monochrome screen was unique. Although clothed in traditional computer cabinetry, starting with the Mac II models, its original design is still retained in the Classic models. The Macintosh family is the largest non-IBM compatible personal computer series in use. Since the advent of the Mac II models in 1987, Macintoshes are increasingly being used in corporations. Apple's 1990 introduction of its lower-cost Classic, LC and Ilsi models have proved very popular, and the 1991 introduction of its high-end Quadra line and notebook portables added to its popularity. See Macintosh user interface. Macintosh user Interface Method of operating a Macintosh, originally developed by Xerox and introduced on the

Xerox Star in 1981. It uses a graphics screen that places familiar objects on a two-dimensional desktop. Programs, files, folders and disks are represented by small pictures (icons) on screen. An object is selected by moving a mouse over the real desktop, which correspondingly moves a pointer on the screen desktop. When the pointer touches an icon, the object is selected by clicking the mouse button. A hierarchical file system is provided that lets a user "drag" a document icon into and out of a folder icon, Folders (subdirectories in DOS) can also contain other folders. For people that are not computer enthusiasts, managing files is a delight. The Macintosh always displays a row of menu titles at the top of the screen and options are pulled down from it. The option within the menu is selected by pointing to it and releasing the button. Unlike the PC world, which, before Windows, left the design of the user interface up to the software developer, Macintosh developers always conform to the Mac interface. As a result, users feel more comfortable with any new program. Although this interface provides consistency, it does not guarantee a well- designed application. Not only must the menus be clear, but mouse movement must be kept to a minimum. The Macintosh style has been adapted to many non-Apple products. Windows, Presentation Manager, GEM, NewWave, Motif and others incorporate some of the features popularized on the Macintosh.

MacIRMA Micro to mainframe communications board for the Macintosh from DCA, Inc., Alpharetta, GA. It a 3270 terminal.

MacPaint II Full-featured Macintosh paint program from Claris that was originally developed by Apple and bundled with every Mac up until the Mac Plus. MacPaint's PICT file format is used for printing the screen.

macro (1) Series of menu selections, keystrokes and/or commands that have been recorded and assigned a name or key combination. When the name is called or the key is pressed, the macro is executed from beginning to end. It is used to shorten long menu sequences into one keystroke as well as to create miniature programs within an application. Macro languages often include programming controls (IF THEN, GOTO, WHILE, etc.) that automate sequences like any programming language. See macro recorder, batch file and shell script. (2) In assembly language, a prewritten subroutine that is called for throughout the program. At assembly time, the macro calls are substituted with the actual subroutine or instructions that branch to it. The highlevel language equivalent is a function. (3) In dBASE programming, a variable which references another variable that actually contains the data. At runtime, the macro variable is substituted with the data variable.

macro assembler Assembler program that lets the programer aeate and use macros.

macro call Same as macro instruction.

macro generator See macro recorder.

macro Instrudion Instruction that defines a macro. In assembly language, MACRO and ENDM are cxamples that define the beginning and end of a macro.

macro language - (1) Commands used by a macro processor. (2) Assembly language that uses macros.

macro processor (1) Software that creates and executes macros from the keyboard. (2) The part of an assembler that substitutes the macro subroutines for the macro calls.

macro recorder Program routine that converts menu selections and keystrokes into a macro. A user turns on the recorder, performs the process which is to be recorded, turns the recorder off and assigns a key command to the macro. When the key command is pressed, the selections are executed.

MacWrite II Full-featured Macintosh word processing program from Claris Corp., that was originally packaged with every Mac 12 and 512.

mag Abbreviation for 'magnetic."

magazette A magazine tecorded on a diskette.

Magellan Disk management utility for PCs from Lotus that searches for file names and contents. It popularized the file viewer, which lets you look into various data files as if you were using the applications that created them.

magnetic card (1) See magnetic stripe. (2) Magnetic tape strips used in early data storage devices and word processors. See CRAM, RACE and Data Cell.

magnetic coerclvlty Amount of energy required to alter the state of a magnet. The higher a magnetic disk's coercivity index, the more data it can store.

magnetic disk Primary computer storage device that uses magnetic- coated disk platters. Like tape, it can be re-recorded over and over.

The disk surface is divided into concentric tracks (circles within circles). The thinner the tracks, the more storage. The data bits are recorded as tiny spots on the tracks. The tinier the spot, the more bits per inch and the greater the storage. Most disks hold the same number of bits on each track, even though the outer tracks are physically longer than the inner ones. Some disks pack the bits as tightly as possible within each track. The circular tracks are further divided into sectors, which hold the least amount of data that can be read or written at one time. In order to update [the disk, a sçctor is read into the computer, changed r and written back to disk. A sector can contain sevr era! records, or one record can span seyeral sectors. The operating system figures out how to.fit data into these fixed spaces. Hard disks on personal computers hold from 20MB to over 1GB of data. Minicomputer and mainframe hard disks hold even more. Fixed hard disks are permanently seMedaiid cannot be removed from the drive, whereas removable hard disks are encased in modules called disk packs or disk cartridges and can be moved from one computer to another. Hard disks provide fast retrieval because they rotate at 3,600 rpm and higher and spin constantly (laptops stop the spinning to preserve battery). Hard disks are made of one or more aluminum platters of the same size, from about two to 15" in diameter, each side coated with a ferromagnetic material. See hard disk specs.

Floppy disks are a removable medium that hold about 250KB to 3MB of data. They are slower than hard disks, since the disk does not spin until a data transfer is requested, and then it only reaches a rotation speed of 300 rpm. It has a single plastic platter with magnetic coating on both sides and is encased in eithera stiff but bendable, plastic envelope (5.25") or in a plastic shell (3.5").

magnetic drum Early high-speed, dilect access atorage device that- used a magnetic-coated cylinder with tracks around its circumference. Each track had its own read/write head.

magnetic field Invisible energy emitted by a magnet. Same as flux.

magnetic ink Magnetically detectable ink used to print the MICR characters that encode account numbers on bank checks.

magnetic oxide See ferric oxide.

magnetic recording Technique used to record digital data - on disks and tapes. Writing (recording) is accomplished by passing the recording surface on or near a read/write head that discharges an electric impulse onto the surface. Although various electromagnetic signalling techniques are used, the concept is simple. A tiny spot with either a positive or negative polarity (0 or 1 bit) is deposited on the disk or tape surface. When tapes are recorded, an erase head clears the surface first, since blocks of data are not fixed in size as they are with disks. Reading is accomplished by passing the surface by the read/write head and sensing the polarity of the bit or the changes of polarity. Bubble memory is a form of magnetic recording, however, unlike tapes and disks, the surface is not moved.

magnetic stripe Small length of magnetic tape adhered to ledger cards, badges and credit cards. It is read by specialized readers that may be incorporated into accounting machines and terminals. Due to heavy wear, the data on the stripe is in a low-density format that may be duplicated several times.

magnetic tape Sequential storage medium used for data collection, backup and historical purposes. Like videotape, computer tape is made of flexible plastic with one side coated with a ferromagnetic material. Tapes come in reels, cartridges and cassettes of many sizes and shapes. As with any tape, locating a specific item requires reading everything before it. There is no way to fast forward. Data bits are usually recorded on parallel recording tracks that run the length of the tape. For example, 9-track tape holds one byte of data across the tape's width (8 bits plus parity). Data is recorded in blocks of contiguous bytes, separated by a space called an interrecord or interblock gap. Tape is often used to exchange data between minis and mainframes, since 1/2" open-reel tape provides a common standard. Storage capacity is measured in bits per inch (bpi). Since tape is laid out in parallel tracks, bpi is equivalent to bytes per inch. Common 1/2" recording densities are 1650 and 6250 bpi; early densities were 200,556 and 800 bpi. Tape drive speed is measured in inches per second (ips), thus, transfer rate is computed as: ips X bpi.

magneto-optic High-density, erasable recording method. Data is recorded magnetically like disks and tapes, but the bits are much smaller, because a laser is used to pinpoint the bit. The laser heats the bit to about 3000 Celsius, at which temperature the bit is realigned when subjected to a magnetic field. In order to record new bits on the surface, existing bits have to be prealigned in one direction first. See optical disk.

magstripe The small stripe of magnetic material found on the back of most major credit cards and computerized transit fare cards. Contains information such as account number and card holder's name, or points of entry and exit and amount of paid fare remaining.

mail box Computer storage assigned to a user for electronically transmitted mail.

mail merge Printing customized form letters. A common feature of a word processor, it uses a letter and a name and address list. In a common letter form, the names and addresses are inserted for each letter. See field squeeze and line squeeze.

main line See main ioop.

main loop Primary logic in a program. It contains the instructions that are repeated after each event or transaction has been processed. See loop.

main memory Same as memory. main storage Same as memory.

mainframe Large computer. In the mid 1960s, all computers were called mainframes, since the term referred to the main cabinet that held the CPU. Today, it refers to a large computer system. There are small, medium and large-scale mainframes, handling from a handful to several thousand online terminals. Large- scale mainframes can have hundreds of megabytes of main memory and hundreds of gigabytes of disk storage. Medium and large-scale mainframes use smaller computers as front end processors that connect directly to the communications networks.

maintenance (1) Hardware maintenance is the testing and cleaning of equipment. (2) Information system maintenance is the routine updating of master files, such as adding and deleting employees and customers and changng credit limits and product prices. (3) Software or program maintenance is the updating of application programs in order to meet changing information requirements. (4) Disk or file maintenance is the periodic reorganizing of online disk files that have undergone fragmentation due to continuous updating.

maintenance credits Monetary credits issued to a customer by the vendor for qualified periods during which the vendor's products are not functioning properly.

maintenance programme An individual who works with programs that have already been implemented into an information system, making changes as needed from time to time. See software maintenance.

maintenance servic Service provided to keep a product in good operating condition.

major key Primary key used to identit' a record, such as account number or name.

make To compile a multi-module program. The make utility recompiles only those modules that have been updated since the last compilation.

male connector Plug that is designed to fit into a particular ocket.

Maltron keyboard Keyboard that uses independent left- and right-hand modules shaped to conform to the natural, position of the hands, designed to prevent strain (RSI).

MAN (Metropolitan. Area Network) Communications network that covers a geographic area such as a city or suburb. See LAN and WAN.

management graphics Cbarts, graphs, and other visual representations of the operational or strategic aspects of a business, intended to aid management in assimilating and presenting business data.

management science Study of statisticaL methods, such as linear programming and simulation, in order to analyze and solve organizational problems. Same as operations research.

management support See DSS and EIS.

management system Leadership and control within an organization. It is made up of people interacting with other people and machines that, together, set the goals and objectives, outline the strategies and tactics, and develop the plans, schedules and necessary controls to run an organization.

Manchester Code Self-clocking data encoding method that divides the time required to define the bit into two cycles. The first cycle is the data value (0 or 1) and the second cylce provides the timing by shifting to the opposite state.

mantissa Numeric value in a floating point number. See floating point.

manual Input Data entered manually by the computer user to modify, continue, or resume processing of a computer program.

map (1) Set of data that has a corresponding relationship to another set of data. (2) List of data or objects as they are currently stored in memory or disk. (3) To transfer a set of objects from one place to another. For example, program modules on disk are mapped into memory. A graphic image in memory is mapped onto the video screen. An address is mapped to another address. (4) To relate one set of objects with another.

MAPI (Mail API) Microsoft e-mail and messaging interface. See OMI and VIM.

mapping See map and digital mapping.

marginal test System test that introduces values far thove and far below the expected values.

mark (1) Small blip printed on or notched into various storage media used for timing or counting-purposes. (2) To identify a block of text in order to per6rm some task on it such as deletion, copying and moving. Also called highlight. (3) To identify an item for future reference. (4) In digital electronics, a 1 bit. Contrast with space. (5) On magnetic disk, a re- corded character used to identify the beginning of a track. (6) In optical recognition and mark sensing, a pencil line in a preprinted box. (7) On magnetic tape, a tape mark is a special character that is recorded after the last character of data.

Mark I Electromechanical calculator designed by professor Howard Aiken, built by IBM and installed at Harvard in 1944. It strung 78 adding machines together to perform three calculations per second. It was 51 feet long, was made of 765,000 parts, weighed five tons and used punched cards and typewriters for I/O. The experience helped IBM develop its own computers a few years later.

mark sensing Detecting pencil lines in predefined boxes on paper forms or punched cards. The form is designed with boundaries for each pencil stroke that represents a yes, no, single digit or letter, providing all possible answers to each question. A mark sense reader detects the presence or absence of the marks and converts them into the appropriate digital code, or in the case of punched cards, punches holes in the card for punched card entry into the computer.

marquee A rectangular area surrounded by dotted lines, used to select objects or portions of an image in a drawing/painting program.

maser Acronym for Microwave Amplification by the Stimulated Emission of Radiation, a device capable of ampl1i1ling or generating radio frequency radiation.

mask (1) Pattern used to transfer a design onto an object. See photomask. (2) Pattern of bits used to accept or reject bit patterns in another set of data.

mask bit 1 bit in a mask used to control the corresponding bit found in data.

maskable interrupts Hardware interrupts that can be enabled and disabled by software.

masked State of being disabled or cut off

MASM (Macrn Assembler) Assembly language that allows macros to be defined and used.

mass storage High-capacity, external storage such as disk or tape.

massage To ocass data.

massively perallel Parallel processing architecture that mm hundreda or thousands of processors.

master Primary, controlling. See master-slave communications and master file.

master card Master record in punched card format.

master clock Clock that provides the primary source of internal timing for a procesor or stand-alone control unit.

master console Main terminal used by the computer operator or systems programmer to command the computer.

master control program See operating system.

master tile Collection of records pertaining to one of the main subjects of an information system. Master files contain descriptive data as well as summary information. Contrast with transaction file.

master record Set of data for an individual subject, such as a customer, employee or vendor. See master file.

master-slave communications Communications in which one side, called the master, initiates and controls the session. The other side (slave) responds to the master's commands.

math coprocessor Mathematical circuit that performs high-speed floating point operations. It increases the performance of CAD applications, but the programs must activate its use. See array processor and vector processor.

mathematical expression Group of characters or symbols representing a quantity or an operation. See arithmetic expression.

mathematical function Rule for creating a set of new values from an existing set; for example, the function f(x) 2x creates a set of even numbers (if x is a whole number).

matrix Array of elements in row and column form. See x-y matrix.

matrix printer See dot matrix and printer.

MAU (Multi-station Access Unit) Central hub in a token ring local area network.

maximize In a graphical environment, to enlarge a window to full size. Contrast with minimize.

MB, Mb See megabyte and megabit.

Mbit See megabit.

Mbits/sec (MegaBITS per SECond) Million bits per second.

MBps, Mbps (MegaBytes Per Second, MegaBits Per Second) Million bytes per second: Million bits per second.

Mbyte See megabyte.

Mbytes/sec (MegaBYTES per SECond) Million bytes per second.

MCA See Micro Channel.

MCB (Memory Control Block) identifier (16-bytes) that DOS places in front of each block of memory it allocates.

MCGA (Multi Color Graphics Array) IBM video display standard built- into low-end PS/2 models. It is not well supported by software vendors. See PC display modes.

MCI (Media Control Interface) IBM/Microsoft programming interface for controlling multimedia dei-vices. See RIFF.

MDA (Monochrome Display Adapter) First IBM PC monochrome video display standard for text-only. Due to its lack of graphics, MDA cards were often replaced with Hercules cards, which provided both text• and graphics. See PC display modes.

mechanical mouse Mouse that uses a rubber ball that rolls against wheels inside the unit. Contrast with optical mouse.

mechanization The use of machines to simplify or replace work previously accomplished by human workers. Compare automation.

media Material that stores or transmits data, for example, floppy disks, magnetic tape, coaxial cable and twisted wire pair.

media access method Access method used in a local area network, such as Token Ring, Ethernet and ARCNET.

media compatibility The ability, of two or more different style units to use the same type of disks as blank disks, whether or not each can read data recorded by the other.

media conversion Converting data from one storage medium to another, such as from disk to tape or from one type of disk pack to another.

media failure Condition of not being able to read from or write to a storage device, such as a disk or tape, due to a defect in the recording surface.

media interchangeability 'The extent to which disks' recorded on one machine can play back on anothr with the same type of drive. .

media specialist The person responsible for catalogipg and maintaining storage media such as CD-ROMS, diskettes, disk packs, magzetic tapes, and other related materials.

medium frequency Electromagnetic wave that oscillates in therange from 300,000 to 3,000,000 Hz. Sec electromagnetic spectrum.

meg Same as mega.

mega (1) MillIon: Abbieiated "M." It often refers to the precise value 1,048,576 since computer specifications are usually binary numbers. See binary values and space/time. (2) (MEGA) Personal computer series from Atari that uses a Motorola 68000 CPU and includes the GEM interface, ROM-based TOS operating system, MIDI interface and a three-voice sound chip. Current model is the MEGA STE

Mega VGA 1024x768, 256 color Super VGA mode that requires one megabyte of video RAM.

megabit One million bits. Also Mb, Mbit and M-bit. See mega and space/time.

megabyte One million bytes. Also MB, Mbyte and Mbyte. See mega and space/time.

megaflops (mega FLoating point OPerations per Second) One million floating point operations 'per second.

megahertz One million cycles per second. See' MHz. megapel dIsplay In computer graphics, a display system that handles a million or more pixels. A resolution of 1,000 lines by 1,000 dots requires a million pixels for the full screen image.

membrane keyboard Dust and dirtproof keyboard constructed of two thin plastic sheets (membranes) that contain flexible printed circuits made of electrically conductive ink. The top membrane is the printed keyboard and a spacer sheet with holes is in the middle. When a user presses a simulated key, the top membrane is.pushed through the spacer hole and makes contact withtbebdttom membrane, completing the circuit.

memo field Data field that holds a variable amount of text. The tekt may be stored in a companion file, but it is treated as if it were part of the data record.

memory (1) The computer's workspace (physically, a collection of RAM chips). It is an important resource, 'since it determines the size and number of programs that be run at the same time, as well as the amount of data thatcanbe processed instantly. The program's instructions are copied into memory from a disk oE tape and are then extracted from memory for analysis

The instant this memory is updated by software, the screen is displaying the new data.

memory protection Technique that prohibits one program from accidentally clobbering another active program. A protective boundary is created around the program, and instructions within the program are prohibited from referencing data outside of that boundary.

memory resident Program that remains in memory at all times. See TSR.

memory sniffing Coined by Data General, a diagnostic routine that tests memory during normal processing. The processor uses cycle stealing techniques that allow it to test memory during unused machine cycles. A memory bank can be "sniffed" every few minutes.

memory typewriter Typewriter that holds a few pages of text ic its memory and provides limited word processing functions. With a display screen of only one or two lines, editing is tedious.

menu List of available options on screen. Selection is accomplished by highlighting the option with a mouse or cursor keys and clicking the mouse or pressing Enter. See Lotus menu and pull-down menu.

menu bar Row of on-screen menu options.

menu-driven Using menus to command the computer. Contrast with command-driven.

menuing software Software that provides a menu for launching applications and running operating system commands.

merge See mail merge and concatenate.

merge purge To merge two or more lists together and eliminate unwanted items. For example, a new name and address list can be added to an old list while deleting duplicate names or names that meet certain criteria.

mesh network Net-like communications network in which there are at least two pathways to each node. Since the term network means net-like as well as communications network, the term mesh is used to avoid saying network communications network.

message (1) In communications, a set of data that is transmitted over a communications line. Just as a program becomes a job when it's running in the computer, data becomes a message when it's transmitted over a network. (2) In object-oriented programming, communicating between objects, similar to a function call in traditional programming.

message handling (1) In communications, a system of electronic mail that handles text (memos, letters) in document form. (2) In communications, the lower level protocols that transfer data over a network, which assemble and disassemble the data into the appropriate codes for transmission.

message queue Storage space in memory or on disk that holds incoming transmissions until the computer can process them.

message switch Computer used to switch data from one point to another. Computers have always been ideal message switches due to their input/output and compare capabilities. When a computer acts as a message switch, it inputs the message, compares its destination with a set of stored destinations and then outputs it to a selected communications channel.

metafile File that can define and store more than one type of information. For example, a Windows Metafile (WMF) can hold pictures in vector graph- los and raster graphics formats as well as text.

metalanguage Language used to describe another language.

meter Basic unit of the metric system (39.37 inches). A yard is about 9/lOths of a meter (0.9144 meter).

method In object-oriented programming, an algorithm that governs an object's behaviour and performance. When a message is sent to an object, a method is implemented and data may or may not be returned.

methodology Specific way of performing an operation that implies precise deliverables at the end of each stage.

metropolitan area netowrk (MAN A computer network that serves customers in the same city or region and can be accessed by mobile (cellular) telephone.

Mflops See megaflops.

MFM (Modified Frequency Modulation) Magnetic disk encoding method used on floppy disks and most hard disks under 40MB. It has twice the capacity of the earlier. FM method, transfers data at 625 Kbytes per second and uses the ST506 interface. See hard disk specs.

MGA (Monochrome Graphics Adapter) Display adapter that employs Hercules Graphics, combining graphics and text on a monochrome monitor.

MGP (Monochrome Graphics Printer port) Display adapter that employs Hercules Graphics and a parallel printer port on the same expansion board.

MHz (MegaHertZ) One million cycles per second. Often references a computer's clock rate, which is a raw measure of its internal speed. For example, a 12MHz 286 computer processes data internally (calculates, compares, etc.) twice as fast as a 6MHz 286. However, disk speed and caching play a major role in the computer's actual performance.

mickey Unit of mouse movement typically set at 1/200th of an inch.

MICR (Magnetic Ink Character Recognition) Machine recognition of magnetically-charged characters typically found on bank checks and deposit slips. MICR readers detect the characters and convert them into digital data.

micro (1) Microcomputer or personal computer. (2) One millionth. See space/time. (3) Microscopic or tiny.

Micro Channel Also known as MCA (Micro Channel Architecture), it is an IBM 32-bit bus used in most PS/2s, the RS/6000 series and certain USi9370 models. MCA boards can be designed for bus mastering and also contain built-in identification that eliminates manual settings often required with ISA boards. MCA transfers data at 20 MBytes/sec and has modes for increasing speeds to 40 and 80MB. Future enhancements may take it to 64 bits and 160MB. MCA boards are not interchangeable with ISA and EISA boards.

microjustification In some word processing programs, the ability to add small slivers of blank space between words had between letters within words. The result is easier to read than ordinary justified copy, where the computer merely adjusts space between words. See microspacing.

micro manager Person who manages personal computer operations within an organization and is responsible for the analysis, selection, installation, training and maintenance of personal computer hardware and software. See information center.

micro to mainframe Interconnection of personal computers to mainframes. See 3270 emulator.

microchip Same as chip.

microcircuit Miniaturized, electronic circuit, such as is found on an integrated circuit. See chip.

microcode Permanent memory that holds the elementary circuit operations a computer must perform for each instruction in its instruction set. It acts as a translation layer between the instruction and the electronic level of the computer and enables the computer architect to more easily add new types of machine in strucions without having to design electronic circuits. See microprogramming.

microcomputer Same as personal computer.

microelectronics Miniaturization of electronic circuits. See chip.

microfiche Pronounced 'micrq-feesh." A 4x6" sheet of film that holds several hundred miniaturized document pages. See micrographics.

microfilm Continuous film strip that holds several thousand miniaturized document pages. See micrographics.

microfloppy disk Floppy disk encased in a 3.5" wide, rigid plastic shell. Developed by Sony, it has become the medium of choice as it holds more data, is tougher and is easier to handle than its 5.25" counterpart.

microform In micrographics, a medium that contains microminiaturized images such as microfiche and microfilm.

micrographics Production, handling and use of microfilm and microfiche. Images are created by cameras that accept output directly from the computer. The documents are magnified for human viewing by readers, some of which can automatically locate a page using indexing techniques. Microfiche and microfilm have always been an economical alternative for high-volume data and picture storage. However, optical disks are competing with film-based systems and may ultimately become the preferred storage medium.

microimage In micrographics, any photographic image of information that is too small to be read without magnification.

microinstruction Microcode instruction. It is the most elementary computer operation that can take place; for example, moving a bit from one register to another. It takes several microinstructions to carry out one machine instruction.

microjacket In micrographics, two sheets of transparent plastic that are bonded together to create channels into which strips of microfilm are inserted and stored.

micromaiaframe Personal computer with mainframe or near mainframe speed.

micromini Personal computer with minicomputer or near minicomputer speed.

microminiature chip An LSI or VLSI chip used for computer storage (memory chip) or control (microprocessor chip).

microminiaturization A term implying very small size, one step smaller than miniaturization.

micron One millionth of a meter. Approx. 1/25,000 of an inch. The tiny elements that make up a transistor on a chip are measured in microns. Measurements below the micron level are made in Angstroms, in which 10,000 Angstroms equals one micron.

microprocessor CPU on a single chip. In order to function as a computer, it requires a power supply, clock and memory. First-generation microprocessors were Intel's 8080, Zilog's Z80, Motorola's 6800 and Rockwell's 6502. The first microprocessor was created by Intel.

microprogram Same as microcode.

microprogrammable computer Any computer whose instruction set is not fixed but can be tailored to individual needs by the programming of roms or other memory devices. Consequently, whether the computer is a mainframe, microcomputer, or microcomputer, theoretically it can be microprogrammed.

microprogramming Programming microcode.

micropublishing In micrographics, the issuing of new or reformatted information on microfilm for sale or distribution.

microsecond One millionth of a second. See space/time. Microsoft (Microsoft Corp., Redmond, WA) Leading software company founded in 1975 by Paul Allen and Bill Gates, two college students who wrote the first BASIC interpreter for the Intel 8080 microprocessor. This accompanied the Altair 8800 kit. By the end of 1976, more than 10,000 Altairs were sold with MBASIC. Versions were licensed to Radio Shack, Apple and many other vendors. Later, a version called GW-BASIC (Gee Whiz BASIC) was developed for 16-bit personal computers. Although Microsoft became a leader in microcomputer programming languages, its outstanding success is due to supplying IBM with DOS and the compatible companies with MS-DOS. Extending into graphical interfaces with Windows is also proving highly successful, ever since Version 3.0 was introduced in 1990.

Microsoft is also a major force in the applications market with pioducts such as Excel, Microsoft Word and Word for Windows. However, Microsoft's position as the supplier of the major operating system to the world's largest computer base gives it considerable influence over this industry.

Microsoft C C compiler from Microsoft used to create a wide viety of commercial products. Windows programmrng aiso requires the Microsoft Window Software Development Kit. Microsoft C and Borland's Turbo C are the most widely used C languages for PC application development.

Microsoft Word Full-featured word processing program for PCs and the Macintosh from Microsoft. The DOS version provides both graphics-based and text-based interfaces for working with a document. Microsoft Word for Windows, often called Word for Windows (WinWord), is a separate and distinct product with sophisticated capabilities designed for the Windows interface.

MIcrosoft Works Integtated software package for PCs and the Macintosh from Microsoft. It provides file management with relational-like capabilities, word processing, spreadsheet, business graphics and communications capabilities in one package.

microspacing Positioning characters for printing by making very small horizontal and vertical movements. Many dot matrix printers and all laser printers have this ability.

microwave Electromagnetic wave that vibrates at 1GHz and above. Microwaves are the transmission frequencies used in communications satellites as well as in line-of-sight systems on earth.

MIDI (Musical instrument Digital Interface) Standard protocol for the interchange of musical information between musical instruments, synthesizers and computers. It defines the codes for a musical event, which includes the start of a note, its pitch, length, volume and musical attributes, such as vibrato. It also defines codes for various button, dial and pedal adjustments used on synthesizers. A computer with a MIDI interface can be used to record a musical session, but instead of recording the analog sound waves, the computer stores the music as keystroke and control codes. The recording can be then be edited in an entirely unique manner; for example, the rhythm can be changed by editing the timing codes in the MIDI messages. In addition, the computer can easily transpose a performance from B major into D major. The original objective of MID! was to allow the keyboard of one synthesizer to play notes generated by another. However, since Version 1.0 in 1983, the standard has synthesized more than just music; it has brought the world of electronic control of music to virtually everybody and has benefitted musicians and teachers alike. MIDI devices have a connector (port) built into the musical instruments and synthesizers. It is standard on Atari STs and can be adapted to other personal computers. The Macintosh is also popular among MID! enthusiasts.

midlcomputer Computer with performance and capacity between a minicomputer and a mainframe.

midrange computer Same as minicomputer, but excludes single-user minicomputer workstations.

milestone An essential activity or step in a project that helps measure its progress.

milk disk A disk used to gather data from a small computer with a view to processing the data in a large computer later.

mill Very old term for processor (number crunching!).

millimeter One thousandth of a meter, or lj25th of an inch.

million One thousand times one thousand. See mega and microsecond.

millisecond One thousandth of a second. See space/time. minI See minicomputer.

mini-supercomputer Computer that is 25% to 100% as fast as a supercomputer, but costs less. Note: A mini- supercomputer is not the same as a supermini.

minicomputer Medium-scale computer that functions as a single workstation, or as a multiuser system with up to several hundred terminals. In 1959, Digital launched the minicomputer industry with its PDP-1. Soon after, Data General and HP introduced minis, and eventually Wang, Tandem, Datapoint and Prime joined them. IBM has introduced several minicomputer series (see IBM minicomputers). Today, the term "midrange" is becoming popular for medium- sized computer. High-end microcomputers and low- end mainframes overlap in minicomputer price and performance.

minifloppy Floppy disk encased in a 5.25" wide, stiff plastic jacket. Introduced by Shugart in 1978, it superseded IBM's 8" floppy and has been used extensively ever since.

minimize In graphical environments, to reduce a window to an icon.

MINIX Version of UNIX for the PC, Mac, Amiga and Atari ST developed by Andrew Tannenbaum and published by Prentice-Hall. It comes with complete source code.

minor key Secondary key used to identify a record. For example, if transactions are sorted by account number and date, account number is the major key and date is the minor key.

minor sort key A data field that provides a secondary source of distinctions by which to sort records. Used only when duplications occur in the major sort key.

MIPS (Million Instructions Pea' Second) Execution speed of a computer. For example, .5 MIPS is 500,000 instructions per second. High-speed personal computer and workstation CPUs perform in the 20-50 MIPS range. MIPS rates are not uniform. Some are best-case mixes while others are averages. In addition, it takes more instructions in one machine to do the same thing as another (RISC vs CISC, mainframe vs micro). However, MIPS rate is just one factor in overall performance. Bus and channel speed and bandwidth, memory speed, memory management techniques and system software also determine total throughput.

mirroring See disk mirroring.

MIS (1) (Management Information System) Information system that integrates data from all the departments it serves and provides operations and management with the information they require. It was 'the" buzzword of the mid to late 1970s, when online systems were implemented in all large organizations. See DSS. (2) (Management Information Services) See Information Systems.

mission critical Vital to the operation of an organization.

mixed object Same as compound document. MME See Multimedia Extensions.

MMU (Memory Management Unit) Virtual memory circuit that translates logical addresses into physical addresses.

mnemonic Pronounced "nuh-monic." Means memory aid. A name assigned to a machine function. For example, in DOS, COM1 is the mnemonic assigned to serial port #1. Programming languages are almost entirely mnemonics.

MNP (Microcom Networking Protocol) Family of communications protocols from Microcom, that have become de facto standards for error correction (classes 2 though 4) and data compression (class 5).

MO See magneto-opt4c.

mod See modulo.

modal Mode oriented. A modal operation switches from one mode to another. Contrast with non-modal.

mode Operational state that a system has been switched to. It implies at least two possible conditions. There are countless modes for hardware and software. See Real Mode, Protected Mode, burst mode, insert mode, supervisor state and program state.

model (1) Style or type of hardware device. (2) Mathematical representation of a device or process used for analysis and planning. See data model, data administration, financial planning system and scientific applications.

model-based expert system Expert system based on fundamental knowledge of the design and function of an object. Such systems are used to diagnose equipment problems, for example. Contrast with rule-based expert system.

modelling Simulating a condition or activity by performing a set of equations on a set of data. See data modelling, data administration, financial planning system and scientific applications.

modem (MOdulator-DEModulator) Device that adapts a terminal or computer to a telephone line. It converts the computer's digital pulses into audio frequencies and converts them back into pulses at the receiving side. An internal modem is fitted inside the system in a free expansion slot, while an external modem requires a free serial port. A communications program provides the user interface and the software protocols (Xmodem, Kermit, etc.). The modem handles the dialling and answering of the call and controls transmission speed, which ranges from 300 to 14,400 bps and higher. The common dial-up modem speed is 2,400 bps with 9,600 becoming popular. At 2,400 bps, it takes about seven seconds to fill up a text-based screen of

2,000 characters, but most interactive sessions display less than a full screen. The character rate is 10% of the bit rate; thus, 2,400 bps is equivalent to 240 cps. Features to look for in a modem re high speed, error checking and data compression. Newinodems have automatic feature negotiation, which adjusts to the other modem's speed and hardware protocols.

modem eliminator Device that allows two close computers to be connected without modems. For personal computers, it is the same as a null modem cable with appropriate software. In synchronous systems, it provides active intelligence for synchronization.

modify structure Database command that changes file's structure. Field lengths and field names can changed, and fields can be added or deleted. It ma convert the old data file into the new structure. with out data loss, unless fields have been truncated or deleted.

Modula-2 (MODUlar LAnguage-2) Enhanced versio of Pascal introduced in 1979 by Swiss professor Nicklaus Wirth, creator of Pascal. It supports separate compilation of modules.

modular programming Breaking down the design of a program into individual components (modules) that• can be programmed and tested independently. It is a requirement for effective development and maintenance of large programs and projects,

modulate To vary a carrier wave. Modulation blends a data signal (text, voice, etc.) into a carrier for transmission over a network. Major methods are AM (amplitude modulation) -, modulate the height of the carrier wave, FM (frequency modulation) - modulate the frequency of the wave, and PM (phase modulation) - modulate the polarity of the wave. Contrast with demodulate. See carrier.

module Self-contained hardware or software component that interacts with a larger system. Hardware modules are often made to plug into a main system. Program modules are designed to handle a specific task within a larger program.

module Mathematical operation (modulus arithmetic) in which the result is the remainder of the division. For example, 20 MOD 3 results in 2 (20/3 6 with a remainder of 2.

moire Pronounced "mor-ray." An objectionable pattern that results from families of curves being superimposed on one another. For example, many halftones are made up of curved patterns that can cause moire patterns when scanned into the computer.

molecular beam epitaxy Technique that "grows" atomic-sized layers on a chip rather than creating layers by diffusion.

monadic One Single item or operation that deals with one item or operand.

monitor (1) High-resolution display screen for output from a computer, camera, VCR or other video generator. A monitor's clarity is based on video bandwidth, dot pitch, refresh rate and convergence. See analog monitor, digital monitor and interlaced. (2) Software that provides utility and control functions such as setting communications parameters. It typically resides in a ROM chip and contains startup and diagnostic routines. (3) Software that monitors the progress of activities within a computer system. (4) Device that gathers performance statistics of a running system via direct attachment to the CPU's circuit boards.

monochrome Display of one foreground color and one background color, for example, black on white, white on black and green on black.

monolithic integrated circuit Common form of chip design, in which the base material (substrate) contains the pathways as well as the active elements that take part in its operation.

monophonic Sound reproduction using a single channel. Contrast with stereophonic.

monospadng Uniform horizontal spacing, such as 10 characters per inch. Contrast with proportional spacing.

Monte Cnrlo method Technique that provides approximatc solutions to problems expressed mathematically. Using random numbers and trial and error, it repeatedly calculates the equations to arrive at a solution.

MORE II Macintosh desktop presentation program and outline processor from Symantec Corp., and includes writing, spell checking, presentation- quality text and graphics and 35mm slide output.

murray See moire.

Morse code Data code represented by dots and dashes, developed by Samuel Morse in the mid-l9th century. A dot can be a voltage, carrier wave or light beam of one duration, while a dash is a longer duration. It was used to send telegraph messages before the telephone.

MOS (Metal Oxide Semiconductor) Pronounced "moss." One of two major categories of chip design (the other is bipolar). It derives its name from its use of metal, oxide and semiconductor layers. There are several varieties of MOS technologies, including PMOS, NMOS and CMOS.

MOSFET (Metal Oxide Semiconductor Field Effect Transistor) Common type of transistor fabricated as a discrete component or into MOS integrated circuits.

most significant digit Leftmost, non-zero digit in a number. It is the digit with the greatest value in the number.

motherboard Main printed circuit board in an electronic device, which contains sockets that accept additional boards. In a.personal computer, the motherboard contains the bus, CPU and coprocessor sockets, memory sockets, keyboard controller and supporting chips. Chips that control the video display, serial and parallel ports, mouse and disk drives may or may not be present on the motherboard. If not, they are independent controllers that are plugged into an expansion slot on the motherboard.

Motif Graphical user interface endorsed by the Open Software Foundation. See OSF.

motion path In computer graphics, the path to be followed by an animated object.

Motorola (Motorola, Inc., Schaumburg, IL) Leading manufacturer of semiconductor devices founded in Chicago in 1928 by Paul V. Galvin as the Galvin Manufacturing Corp. Its first product allowed radios to operate from household current instead of batteries. In the 1930s, the company commercialized car radios under the Motorola brand and in 1947, changed the company name. By the 1960s, it was a leader in communications and consumer electronics and had built its first semiconductor facility. It eventually moved from the consumer side, selling its color TV business in the mid-1970s. Although Motorola is known in computers for its 68000 microprocessor family, it isalso involved in radio and data communications systems and automotive and industrial producis, among others.

mouse Puck-like object used as a pointing and drawing device. As it is rolled actoss the desktop, the screen cursor (pointer) moves correspondingly. With a mouse, movement is relative; the screen cursor moves from its existing location. The mouse could be moved across your arm, and the screen cursor would move as well. See mechanical mouse, optical mouse, serial mouse, bus mouse and mickey.

mouse pad Fabric-covered rubber pad roughly 9" square that provides a smooth surface for rolling a mouse.

mouse pointer The on-screen icon or cursor, the movement of which is controlled by the mouse.

mouse port Socket in the computer into which a mouse is plugged.

MOV (1) (Metal Oxide Varister) Electronic component that diverts excessive voltage to ground. (2) Assembly language instruction that moves (copies) data from one location to another.

move (1) In programming, to copy data from one place in memory to another. At the end of the move, source and destination data are identical. (2) In word processing and graphics, to relocate text and images to another part of the document or drawing.

MPC (Multimedia PC) Microsoft minimum requirements for a multimedia PC: 10Mhz 286 CPU, VGA display 2MB RAM, 30MB hard disk Two-button mouse CD ROM with CD ROM extensions 2.2 Audio board with 8-bit Linear PCM sampling, music synthesizer and analog mixing capabilities Serial, parallel, MIDI and joystick ports DOS 3.1, Windows 3.0 with multimedia extensions

MPEG (Moving Pictures Experts Group) ISO/CCIIT standard for compressing full-motion video. See JPEG.

MPR II Swedish government standard for maximum video terminal radiation. The earlier MPR I is less stringent. See TCO.

MPU (MicroProcessor Unit) Same as microprocessor. ms (1) (MilliSecond) See space/time. (2) (MS) See Microsoft.

MS-DOS (MicroSoft-Disk Operating System) Single user operating system for PCs from Microsoft. It is almost identical to IBM's DOS version, and both versions are called DOS generically. See PC (Operating Environment).

MS-Net (MicroSoft Network) Microsoft's version of PC- Network introduced in 1985.

MS-Windows (MicroSoft Windows) See Windows.

MSI (Medium Scale Integration) Between 100 and 3,000 transistors on a chip. See SSI, LSI, VLSI and ULSI.

MTBF (Mean Time Between Failure) Average time a component works without failure. It is the number of failures divided by the hours under observation.

MTS (Modular TV System) Stereo channel added to the NTSC standard, which includes the SAP audio channel for special use.

MVER (Mean Time To Repair) Average time it takes to repair a failed component.

mu Name of the Greek letter u, the symbol used to denote the prefix micro, For example, us means microsecond.

MULTIBUS Advanced bus architecture from Intel used in industrial, military and aerospace applications. It includes message passing, auto configuration and software interrupts. MULTIBUS I is 16-bits; MULTIBUS II is 32-bits.

multicomputer Same as parallel computer.

multifrequency monitor Monitor that adjusts to all frequencies within a range (multiscan) or to a set of specific frequencies, such as VGA and Super VGA.

Multlilne Cable, channel or bus that contains tw or more transmission paths (wires or optical fibers).

multimasterlng See bus mastering.

MultlMate PC word processing program from AshtonTate that was originally noted for its similarity to the Wang word processors of the 1970s. Version 4.0 (1989) introduced a number of advanced features.

multimedia Disseminating information in more than one form. Includes the use of text, audio, graphics, animated graphics and full-motion video. See MPC.

Multimedia Extensions Windows routines that support audio recording and playback, animation playback, joysticks, MIDI, the MCI interface for CD ROM, videodiscs, videotapes, etc., and the RIFF file format. See MPC.

multiplexing Transmitting multiple signals over a single communications line or computer channel. The two common multiplexing techniques are FDM, which separates signals by modulating the data onto different carrier frequencies, and TDM, which separates signals by interleaving bits one after the other.

multiplexor In communications, a device that merges several low-speed transmissions into one high-speed transmission and vice versa.

multiplexor channel Computer channel that transfers data between the CPU and several low-speed peripherals (terminals, printers, etc.) simultaneously. It may have an optional burst mode that allows a high-speed transfer to only one peripheral at a time.

multiplier-accumulator General-purpose floating point processor that multiplies and accumulates the results of the multiplication. Newer versions also perform division and square roots.

multipoint line In communications, a single line that interconnects three or more devices.

multiported memory Memory that provides more than one access path to its contents. It allows the same bank of memory to be read and written simultaneously.

multiprocessing Simultaneous processing with two or more processors in one computer, or two or more computers processing together. When two or more computers are used, they are tied together with a high- speed channel and share the general workload between them. If one fails, the other takes over. It is also accomplished in special-purpose computers, such as array processors, which provide concurrent processing on sets of data. Although computers are built with various overlapping features, such as executing instructions while inputting and outputting data, multiprocessing refers specifically to concurrent instruction executions. See bus mastering and fault tolerant.

multiprogramming Same as multitasking.

multiscan monitor Monitor that adjusts to all frequencies within a range. See multifrequency monitor.

MultiSync monitor Family of multiscan monitors from NEC. NEC popularized the multiscan monitor.

multitasking Running two or more programs in one computer at the same time. It is controlled by the operating system. The number of programs that can be effectively multitasked depends on the amount of memory available, CPU speed, hard disk capacity and speed, as well as the efficiency of the operating system. Multitasking is accomplished due to the differences in I/O and processing speed. While one program is waiting for input, instructions in another program are executed. In interactive programs, the delay between keystrokes is used to execute instructions in other programs. In batch processing systems, the milliseconds of delay transferring data to and from a disk are used to execute instructions in other programs.

multithreading Multitasking within a single program. It is used to process multiple transactions or messages concurrently. It is also required for creating synchronized audio and video applications. Multithreading functions are often written in reentrant code.

multiuser Computer shared by two or more users.

multiuser DOS (1) DOS-compatible operating system that allows multiple dumb terminals to run from a single PC. (2) (Multiuser DOS) Multiuser DOS operating system from Digital Research that allows up to 10 terminals and/or PCs to hookup to a 386SX CPU or higher machine. Supersedes Concurrent DOS.

multivarlate

Use of multiple variables in a forecasting model.

MUMPS Advanced, high-level programming language and integrated database used for business applications. It has extensive string handling making it suitable for databases with vast amounts of free text. MUMPS has unique features including the ability to store both data and program statements in its database. In addition, formulas written in a program can be stored and used by other programs.

MUX (MUltipleXor) See multiplexor.

MVGA (Monochrome VGA) Non-color VGA (gray scale).

Mask: A format used when presenting data in a form or report.

Materialization: (1) The physical appearance of data in a form or report. (2) The appearance of a view of a semantic object in a form or report.

Maximum cardinality: (1) The maximum number of values that an attribute may have within a semantic object. (2) In a relationship between tables, the maximum number of rows to which a row of one table may relate in the other table.

Me: In OOP, a special pointer to the current object instance. For example, Me.Name refers to the Name attribute of the current object.

Member: In the CODASYL DBTG model, a record type that is on the many side of a one-to-many or set relationship.

Menu: A list of options presented to the user of a database (or other) application. The user selects the next action or activity from a list. Actions are restricted to those in the list. Contrast this with Command.

Metadata: Data concerning the structure of data in a database stored in the data dictionary. Metadata are used to describe tables, columns, constraints, indexes, and so forth. Compare this with Application metadata.

Method: A program attached to an object-oriented programming (OOP) object. A method can be inherited by lower-level OOP objects.

Method: In OOP, a program attribute of an object.

MIME: See Multipurpose Internet mail code.

Minimum cardinality: (1) The minimum mimber of values that an attribute may have within a semantic object. (2) In a relationship between tables, the number of rows to which a row of one table may relate in the other table.

Mixed partition: A combination of a horizontal and a vertical partition. For example, in a table with five columns and five rows, the first three columns of the first three rows.

Modeless processing: In a database application, the characteristic of inferring the mode of the user's processing from the user's actions, for example, on entering a key field, if the value exists in the database, inferring that an update is to occur; if the value does not exist in the database, inferring that an insert is to occur.

Modem: Modulator-demodulator. A device used to convert digital signals to analog signals and the reverse. It is most often used to communicate over telephone lines.

Modification anomaly: The situation existing when the storing of one row in a table records two separate facts or when the deletion of one row of a table eliminates two separate facts.

Multiple-tier driver: In ODBC, a two-part driver, usually for a client-server database system. One part of the driver resides on the client and interfaces with the application; the second part resides on the server and interfaces with the DBMS.

Multipurpose Internet Mail Code: A standardizetl list of symbols that indicate the type of a file embedded in an HTML document. Each MIME type code is associated with a program that processes files of that type. MIME types are defined for images, sounds, movies, etc. The code can be extended by adding new codes (and affiliated programs) to MIME code lists on clients and servers.

Multivalued attribute: The attribute of a semantic object that has a maximum cardinality greater than one.

Multivalued dependency: A condition in a relation with three or more attributes in which independent attributes appear to have relationships they do not have. Formally, in a relation R (A, B, C), having key (A, B, C) where A is matched with multiple values of B (or of C or both), B does not determine C, and C does not determine B. An example is the relation EMPLOYEE (EmpNumber, Emp-skill, Dependentname), where an employee can have multiple values of Emp-skill and Dependent-name. Emp-skill and Dependent-name do not have any relationship, but they do appear to in the relation.

Mutable object: In the ODMG standard, an object whose attributes may be changed.

N

n-dimensional Some number of dimensions.

naive user A person who wants to do something with a computer but does not have the experience needed to program the computer.

N-key rollover Keyboard circuit design for fast typing. To test this, press four adjacent keys in sequence without removing any finger from any of the keys. If all four letters appear on screen, it has this feature.

NAK (Negative AcKnowledgement) Communications code used to indicate that a message was not received, or that a terminal does not wish to transmit. Contrast with ACK

name service Software that converts a name into a physical address. Names can be user names, computers, printers, services or files. It provides logical to physical conversion.

Named Pipes IPC facility in LAN Manager that allows data to be exchanged from one application to another either over a network or running within the same computer. The use of the term pipes for interprocess communication was coined in UNIX.

NAND (Not AND) Boolean logic operation that is true if any single input is false. Two-input NAND gates are often used as the sole logic element on gate array chips, because all Boolean operations can be created from NAND gates.

nanoacre One-billionth of an acre, used figuratively to describe the area of an integrated circuit.

nanocomputer A computer capable of processing data in billionths of a second.

nanometer One billionth of a meter.

nanosecond One billionth of a second. Used to measure the speed of logic and memory chips, a nanosecond can be visualized by converting it to distance. In one nanosecond, electricity travels about six inches in a wire. Even at 186,000 miles per second, eketricity is never fast enough for the hardware designer who worries over a few inches of circuit path. The slightest delay is miltiplied millions of times, since millions of pulses are sent through a wire in a single second. See space/time.

narrowband In communications, a voice grade transmission of 2,400 bps or less, or a sub-voice grade transmission from 50 to 150 bps.

NASA Acronym for National Aeronautics and Space Administration.

National Computer Graphics Assoication (NCGA) A nonprofit organization dedicated to developing, promoting, and improving computer graphics applications in business, government, science, and the arts.

native language Same as machine language. See native mode.

native mode (1) Normal running mode of a computer, executing programs from its built-in instruction set. Contrast with emulation mode. (2) Highest-performance state of a computer, such as the 386 running in Protected Mode.

NATURAL Fourth-generation language from Software AG, that runs on a variety of computers from micro to mainframe.

natural language Languages of human communication. English, Spanish, French, German, Japanese, Russian, etc.

NAU (1) (Network Access Unit) Interface card that adapts a computer to a local area network. (2) (Network Addressable Unit) SNA component that cáo be referenced by name and address.

NB card (NuBus card) See NuBus.

NC See numerical control.

NCR (Network Control Block) Packet structure used by the NetBIOS transport protocol.

NCR paper (No Carbon Required paper) Multiple-part paper form that does not use carbon paper. The ink is adhered to the reverse side of the previous sheet.

NDIS (Network Driver Interface Specification) Microsoft specification for writing hardware-indepen-' dent drivers at the data link (media access method) layer.

NE (Not Equal to) See relational operator.

near pointer In an Intel 80x86 segmented address, a memory address within a single segment (the offset). Contrast with far pointer.

NEAT chipset (New Enhanced AT chipset) Set of chips used to build an AT-dass machine from Chips and Technologies, Inc. EMS capability is included. The CPU, BIOS and NEAT chipset are the primary logic chips on a 286-based PC.

negative logic Use of high voltage for a 0 bit and low voltage for a 1 bit. Contrast with positive logic.

nematic Stage between a crystal and a liquid that has a threadlike nature; for example, a liquid crystal.

nemonic See mnemonic.

neper Unit of measurement based on Napierian logarithms that represents the ratio between two values, such as current or voltage.

nerd Person typically thought of as dull socially. Nerds often like technical work and are generally introspective. Contrast with hacker, a technical person that may or may not be a nerd.

nesting In programming, the positioning of a loop within a loop. The number of loops that can be nested may be limited by the programming language. See loop.

NetBIOS Commonly used transport protocol for PC local area networks introduced with IBM's PC Network and implemented in Microsoft's MS-Net and LAN Manager. Application programs use NetBIOS for client/server or peer-to-peer communications. There are two NetBIOS modes for communicating. The Datagram is the fastest method, but does not guarantee delivery of a message. It is a self- contained packet with sender and receiver name, usually limited to 512 bytes. If the recipient device is not listening for messages, the datagram is lost. The Session mode establishes a connection until broken. It guarantees delivery of messages up to 64K bytes long. NetBIOS-compliant protocols refer to layers 3, 4 and 5 on the OSI model.

NETROOM DOS memory manager from Helix Software Co., noted for squeezing large network drivers into high DOS memory. Its DISCOVER utility reports on the system's current configuration.

NetView IBM SNA network management software that provides centralized monitoring and control for SNA, non-SNA and non-IBM devices. NetView/PC interconnects NetView with Token Ring LANs, Roim CBXs and non-IBM modems, while maintaining control in the host.

NetWare Family of network operating systems from Novell, Inc., that runs on 286 PCs and up and supports DOS, 0812 and Mac workstations. It works with a variety of LAN access methods, including Token Ring, Ethernet, ARCNET and Starlan. ELS NetWare (Entry Level System) provide support for four and eight workstations respectively and allow the same machine to act as workstation and server (peer-to- peer network). The most widely used NetWare is Advanced NetWare 286 (Netware 2.x), which runs in a dedicated file server and supports up to 100 users. It is the sole control program in the server. SFT NetWare (System Fault Tolerant) provides automatic recovery from network malfunctions. NetWare 386 (Netware 3.x) runs on 386 and 486 servers and provides increased performance. Versions are available from 10 to 4,000 nodes. NetWare for VMS provides NetWare connectivity to VAX networks, and Portable NetWare provides NetWare source code for conversion to other platforms. NetWare Lite is designed for small peer- to-peer PC networks with upward migration to Novell's larger systems. The starter kit connects two PCs.

network (1) Affangement of objects that are interconnected. See LAN and network database. (2) In communications, the transmission channels and supporting hardware and software.

network adapter Printed circuit board that plugs into a workstation or server and controls the exchange of data over a network. It performs the electronic functions of the access method (data link protocol), such as Ethernet, Token Ring and LocalTalk. The transmission medium (twisted pair, coax or fiber optic cable) physically interconnects all the adapters in the network.

network administrator Person who manages a communications network and is responsible for its efficient operation. Tasks include installing new applications and monitoring network activity.

network architecture (1) Design of a communications system, which includes the hardware, software, access methods and protocols used. It also defines the method of control: whether computers can act independently or are controlled by other computers monitoring the network. It determines future flexibility and connectability to foreign networks: (2) Access method in a LAN, such as Ethernet, Token Ring and LocalTalk.

network card See network adapter.

network control program See NCP.

network database (1) Database that runs in a network. It implies that the DBMS was designed with a client/server architecture. (2) Database that holds addresses of other users in the network. (3) Database organization method that allows for data relationships in a net-like form. A single data element can point to multiple data elements and can itself be pointed to by other data elements. Contrast with relational database.

network management Monitoring an active network in order to diagnose prQblems and gather statistics for administration and fine tuning.

network operating system Control program that resides in a file server in a LAN. It handles the requests for data from the workstations in the network.

network server See file server.

neural network Modeling technique based on the observed behavior of biological neurons and used to mimic the performance of a system. It consits of a set of elements that start out connected in a random pattern, and, based upon operational feedback, are molded into the pattern required to generate the required results. It is used in applications such as robotics, diagnosing, forecasting, image processing and pattern recognition.

New Century Schoolbook An easily read typeface developed for textbooks and magazines.

newilne End of line code. See CRILF.

NewWave PC operating environment from HP that runs between DOS and Windows. It integrates data and activates tasks within the system. Its object-management facility allows data from different applications to be merged to create a compound document. Hot links automatically update the document if data in one of the source files is updated. It allows for the creation of agents (automatic procedures) that can be activated based on time or events. Programs must be modified to run under NewWave.

NeXT Computer Family of UNIX-compatible workstations from NeXT, Inc., that use the 68040 CPU and includes 1120x832 gray-scale or color graphics, Display PostScript, 2.88MB floppy and a digital signal processing chip for CD-quality sound, image processing, data compression and voice recognition. Also included is NeXTstep, several applications and JPEG software for compressing still color or black- and- white images. The first workstation was introduced in 1988. NeXT was founded in 1985 by Steven Jobs, co-founder and former chairman of Apple.

NeXTstep Graphical user interface and object-oriented development environment from NeXT, Inc. It allows for the creation of graphics- based, windows applications under UNIX using Objective C. IBM has licensed NeXTstep for its UNIX-based (AIX) workstations.

NFS (Network File System) Distributed file system from Sun that allows data to be shared with many users in a network regardless of processor type, operating system, network architecture or protocol.

nibble Half a byte (four bits).

nibble mode memory Type of dynamic RAM that outputs four consecutive bits (nibble) at one time.

NIC (Network Interface Card) Same as network adapter. NiCad (Nickel CADmium) Material used for making

rechargeable batteries. NiCad batteries have a memory. If recharged before completely drained, the next charge lasts only as long as the previous charge. For maximum storage capacity, a complete draining is periodically required. See nickel hydride.

nickel hydride Material used for making rechargeable batteries that provides more power per pound than NiCad batteries and does not exhibit the memory effect.

NLQ (Near Letter Quality) Print quality that is almost as sharp as an electric typewriter. The slowest speed of a dot matrix printer often provides NLQ.

NMI (NonMaskable Interrupt) High-priority interrupt that cannot be disabled by another interrupt. It is used to report malfunctions such as parity, bus and math coprocessor errors.

NMOS (N-Channel MOS) Pronounced "N moss." Type of microelectronic circuit used for logic and memory chips. NMOS transistors are faster than their PMOS counterpart and more of them can be put on a single chip. It is also used in CMOS design.

no-op Instruction that does nothing, used to hold the place for a future machine instruction.

no wait state memory Memory fast enough to meet the demands of the CPU. Idle wait states do not have to be introduced.

node (1) In communications, a junction or connection point in a network (a terminal or a computer). (2) In database management, an item of data that can be accessed by two or more routes. (3) In computer graphics, an endpoint of a graphical element.

noise Extraneous signal that invades an electrical transmission. It can come from strong electrical or magnetic signals in nearby lines, from poorly fitting electrical cofttacts, and from power line spikes.

non-blocking Ability of a signal to reach its destination without interference or delay.

non-breaking space See hard space.

non-document mode Word processing mode used for creating source language programs, batch files and common text files for transfer to other programs. It creates a file containing only text without proprietary format codes. Text processors, such as Norton Editor, XyWrite, and all text editors automatically generate ASCII text files and do not require this option.

non-Impact printer Printer that prints without banging a ribbon onto paper, such as a thermal or ink jet printer. See printer.

non-Interlaced Illuminating a CRT by displaying lines sequentially from top to bottom. A monitor, by itself, is not inherently interlaced or non-interlaced. Amonitor said to be non-interlaced has the ability to handle the horizontal scan frequency from the video controller generating a non-interlaced signal at a particular resolution. See interlaced.

non-modal Not mode oriented. A non-modal operation moves from one situation to another without apparent mode switching.

non-numeric programming Programming that deals with objects, such as words, board game pieces and people, rather than numbers. Same as list processing.

non-preemptive multitasking Environment in which an application is able to give up control of the CPU to another application at specific points in its running; for example, when it is ready to accept user input. One program can dominate a machine with this method. Contrast with preemptive multitasking.

nonprint Pertaining to an impulse that inhibits line printing under machine control.

non-prucedural language Computer language that does not require traditional programming logic to be stated. For example, a- command, such as LIST, might display all the records in a file on screen, separating fields with a 4lank space. In a procedural language, such as COBOL, all the logic for inputting each record, testing for end of tile and formatting the screen has to be explicitly programmed. Query languages, report writers, interactive database programs, spreadsheets and application generators provide non-procedural languages for user operation.

non-return-to-zero See NRZ.

non-volatile memory Memory that holds its content without power. Firmware .chips (ROMs, PROMs, EPROMs, etc.) are examples. Disks and tapes may be called non-volatile memory, but they are usually considered storage devices.

nonlinear System in which the output is not a uniform relationship to the input.

NonStop Family of fault tolerant computer systems from Tandem.

NOR (Not OR) Boolean logical operation that is true if all inputs are false, and false if any input is true. An exclusive NOR is true if both inputs are the same.

normal wear Deterioration due to natural forces that act upon a product under average, everyday use.

normalization In relational database management, a process which breaks down data into recerd groups for efficient processing. There are six stages. By the third stage (third normal form), data is identified only by the key field in the record. For example, ordering information is identified by order number, customer information, by customer number.

Norton SI (Norton System Information) Norton utility that measures computer performance. It provides a computing index (CI) for CPU speed, a disk index (DI) for disk speed and a performance index (P1) that blends CI and DI. The IBM XT is used as a reference of 1.0.

Norton Utilities Disk management utility programs for the PC and Macintosh from Symantec Corp. Includes programs to search and edit files, undelete files and restore damaged files among others. Originally from Peter Norton Computing, these programs were among the first to popularize disk utilities for the PC. They are a bundle of utilities which are fast, oriented to a specific task and have few, if any, frills.

NOS (Network Operating System) Software that controls the transmission in a network.

NOT Boolean logic operation that reverses the input. If a 0 is input, a 1 is output, and vice versa. See AND, OR & NOT.

Nota Bene PC word processing system from Dragonfly Software, that uses the XyWrite engine and adds revised menus, keyboard layout and advanced handling of foreign characters and laser printers. It includes a text handling system that retrieves correspondence from pages of unstructured. notes. It is consideed efficient for academic writing.

notation How a system of numbers, phrases, words or quantities is written or expressed. Positional notation is the location and value of digits in a numbering system, such as the decimal or binary system.

notebook computer Portable computer that typically weighs less than six pounds (heavier than a pocket computer, lighter than a laptop).

Nova Minicomputer series from Data General. When introduced in 1969, it was the first 16-bit mini to use four CPU accumulators. Novas and its RDOS operating system were used extensively in the OEM marketplace.

NovaNET Satellite-based network for educational services created by the Education Research Lab of the Univ. of Illinois. It includes over 10,000 hours of lesson material from third grade to post graduate work in over a hundred subject areas.

Novell network LAN controlled by one of Novell's NetWare operating systems. See NetWare.

nroff (Nontypesetting RunOFF) UNIX utility that formats documents for terminals and dot matrix printers. Using a text editor, trot! codes are embedded into the text and the nroff command converts the document into the required output. Complex troff codes are ignored. See troff.

NRZ (Non-Return-To-Zero) Signalling method used in magnetic recording and communications that does not - automatically return to a neutral state after each bit is transmitted.

ns (NanoSecond) See nanosecond.

NT See Windows NT.

NTSC (National TV Standards Committee) U.S. TV standard administered by the FCC that is currently 525 lines transmitted at 60 half frames/sec (interlaced). It is a composite of red, green and blue signals for color and includes an FM frequency for audio and an MTS signal for stereo.

Nulius 32-bit bus architecture originally developed at MIT and defined as a Eurocard (9U). Rights to the bus were purchased by Western Digital and TI. Apple licenses it from TI and has changed its electrical and physical specs for the Mac.

NUI (1) (Notebook User Interface) Term coined by Go Corp. for its PenPoint pen-based interface. (2) (NetWare Users International) NetWare operating systems user group. (3) (Network User Identifier) Code used to gain access into local European packed- switched networks.

NUL See null.

null First character in ASCII and EBCDIC. In hex, it prints as 00; in decimal, it prints as a blank. It is naturally found in binary numbers when a byte contains no 1 bits. It is also used to pad fields and act as a delimiter; for example, in C, it specifies the end of a character string.

null modem cable RS-232-C cable used to connect two personal computers in close proximity. It connects to both serial ports and crosses the sending wire on one end to the receiving wire on the other.

null pointer In programming, a reference to zero. May be the response of an unsuccessful search function.

null string In programming, a character string that contains no data.

Num Lock (NUMeric Lock) Key used to switch acornbination number/cursor keypad into number key mode.

number crunching Refers to computers running mathematical, scientific or CAD applications, which perform large amounts of calculations.

numeric data Refers to quantities and money amounts used in calculations. Contrast with string or character data.

numeric field Data field that holds only numbers to be calculated. Contrast with character field.

numeric keypad Four-row keyboard on the right end of the computer keyboard.

numerical control Category of automated machine tools, such as drills and lathes, that operate from instructions in a program. Numerical control (NC) machines are used in manufacturing tasks, such as milling, turning, punching and drilling. First-generation machines were hardwired to perform specific tasks or programmed in a very low- level machine language. Today, they are controlled by their own microcomputers and programmed in high-level languages, such as APT and COMPACT II, which automatically generate the tool path (physical motions required to perform the operation). The term was coined in the 195(when the instructions to the tool were numeric codes. Just like the computer industry, symbolic languages were soon developed, but the original term remained.

NZ (Non Zero) Value greater or less than 0.

Natural join: A join of a relation A having attribute Al with relation B having attribute Bl where Al equals Bl. The joined relation, C, contains either column Al or Bl but not both. Contrast this with Equi join.

Natural language interface: An interface to an application program or DBMS by which users can enter requests in the form of standard English or another human language.

Network: (1) A group of interconnected computers. (2) an intranet. (3) the Internet.

Network database application: A database application in which the clients use an HTML-based browser and the server includes both an Internet- style server and a database. The application could reside on either the Internet or an intranet.

Network data model: A data model supporting at least simple network relationships. The CODASYL DBTG, which supports simple network relationships but not complex relationships, is the most important network data model.

N.M.: An abbreviation for a many-to-many relationship between the rows of two tables.

Node: (1) An entity in a tree. (2) A computer in a distributed-processing system.

Non-information-bearing set: In the CODAYSL DBTG model, a set in which the child record type contains the key of the parent record type. The set ownership is implied by the value of the key in the child record instances.

Nonobject attribute: An attribute of a semantic object that is not an object.

Normal form: A rule or set of rules governing the allowed structure of relations. The rules apply to attributes, functional dependencies, multivalued dependencies, domains, and constraints. The most important normal forms are 1NF, 2NF, 3NF, BoyceCodd NF, 4NF, SNF, and domain/key normal form.

Normalization: The process of evaluating a relation to determine whether it is in a specified normal form and, if necessary, of converting it to relations in that specified normal form.

Nothing: In 001', a null object reference. Used to set an object pointer to null, or to test an object pointer to determine if it is null.

Null value: A value that is either unknown or not applicable. A null value is not the same as a zero or blank, although in most commercial DBMS products, null values are represented by zeros or blanks.

O

obey The process whereby a computer carries out an operation as specified by one or move of the instructions forming the program currently being executed.

object (1) In object-oriented programming, a self- contained module of data and its associated processing. (2) In a compound document, an independent block of data, text or graphics that was created by a separate application.

object code Same as machine language.

object computer Same as target computer.

object language (1) Language defined by a metalanguage. (2) Same as target language. (3) Object-oriented programming language.

object module Output of an assembler or compiler, which must be linked with other modules before it can be executed.

object-oriented analysis Examination of a problem by modeling it as a group of interrelatered objects. An object is defined by its class, data elements and behavior.

object-oriented database Database that holds abstract data types (objects). It can store objects directly from an object-oriented programming language. Because any type of data can be stored (the rules for processing the data are part of an object), the object database promises fully integrated databases that will hold data, text, pictures and voice; essentially an endless variety of ever-changing formats.

object-oriented DBMS DBMS that manages an object- oriented database. It is capable of handling complex queries about objects that would be difficult in relational database programs.

object-oriented design Transforming an object-oriented model into the specifications required to create the system. Moving from object-oriented analysis to object- oriented design is accomplished by expanding the model into more and more detail.

object-oriented graphics Same as vector graphics.

object-oriented Interface Graphical interface that uses icons and a mouse, such as the Macintosh, Windows and GEM environments.

object-oriented programming Abbreviated "OOP," a programming technology that is more flexible than standard programming. Important features are: 1. encapsulation; 2. inheritance; and, 3. polymorphism.

Encapsulation is the creation of self-sufficient modules that contain the data and the processing (data structure and functions that manipulate that data). These user-defined, or abstract, data types are called classes. One instance of a class is called an object.

Classes are created in hierarchies, and inheritance allows the knowledge in one class to be passed down the hierarchy. New objects can be created by inheriting characteristics from existing classes. Object-oriented programming allows procedures about objects to be created whose exact type is not known until runtime.

Xerox's Smalltalk was the first OOP language and was used to create the graphical user interface whose derivations are so popular today. C++ is becoming the mainstay OOP language, because it combines traditional C programming with object- oriented features.

object-oriented technology Paradigm that views the world as objects rather than procedures. Object-oriented analysis (OOA), object-oriented design (OOD) and object-oriented programming (OOP) employ the concepts of encapsulation, classification and inheritance. See object-oriented programming.

object program Machine language program ready to run in a particular operating environment. It has been assembled, or compiled, and link edited.

Objective-C Object-oriented C programming language from The Stepstone Corp. that runs on PCs and popular workstations. It was the first commercial object- oriented extension of the C language.

ObjectVision Application development system from Borland for creating Windows applications. Uses visual techniques for user interface design as well as for programming logic. It also provides links to spreadsheets and databases.

Object Windows Class library of Windows objects from Borland that helps developers create Windows applications. It is an open standard available from Borland and the Object Management Group.

occam Parallel processing language designed to handle concurrent operations.

OCE (Open Collaboration Environment) Extension to System 7 from Apple that provides e-mail and document sharing across multiple platforms in an enterprise.

OCR (Optical Character Recognition) Machine recognition of printed characters. OCR systems can recognize many different OCR fonts, as well as typewriter and computer-printed characters. Advanced OCR systems can even recognize hand printing.

octal Numbering system that uses eight digits. It is used as a shorthand method for representing binary numbers that use six-bit characters. Each three bits (half a character) is converted into a single octal digit. Okta is Greek for 8.

odd parity See parity checking.

ODI (Open Data link Interface) Novell driver specification that allows multiple transport protocols to be run on one network adapter. For example, a PC can connect to a NetWare network running SPX/IPX and a UNIX network running TCP/IP.

OEM (Original Equipment Manufacturer) Manufacturer that sells equipment to a reseller. The term is also used to refer to the reseller, as well. OEM customers often purchase hardware from a manufacturer and resell it under their own brand name. They may combine units from several vendors as well as add software. The terms OEM and VAR are often used synonymously.

off-hook State of a telephone line that allows dialing and transmission but prohibits incoming calls from being answered. The term stems from the days when a telephone handset was lifted off of a hook. Contrast with on-hook.

off-the-shelf Refers to products that are packaged and available for sale.

office automation Integration of office information functions, including word processing, data processing, graphics, desktop publishing and e-mail. The backbone of office automation is a LAN, which allows users to traismit data, mail and even voice to any other user in the organization. All office functions, including dictation, typing, filing, copying, fax, Telex, microfilm and records management, telephone and telephone switchboard operations, are candidates for integration.

Office Vision Integrated office automation applications from IBM that run in all IBM computer families. It was the first major implementation of SAA and in-corporates the Presentation Manager. Introduced in 1989, it includes e-mail, scheduling, document creation and distribution as well as decision support and graphics capabilities among all users.

offline Not connected to or not installed in the computer. If a terminal, printer or other device is physically connected to the computer, but is not turned on or in ready mode, it is still considered offline, Contrast with online.

offline storage Storage not on the computer or not immediately available to the computer. Eg. disks and tapes that are kept in a data library.

offload To remove work from one computer and do it on another. See cooperative processing.

offset (1) Distance from a starting point, either the start of a file or the start of a memory address. Its value is added to a base value to derive the actual value. An offset into a file is simply the character location within that file, usually starting with 0; thus "offset 240" is actually the 241st byte of the file. See relative address. (2) In word processing, the amount of space a document is printed from the left margin. This is usually more than the right margin leaving space for binding.

ohm Unit of measurement for electrical resistance. One Ghm is the resistance in a circuit when one volt maintains a current of one amp.

OLE (Object Linking and Embedding) Windows compound document protocol. The "client" application creates the document; the "server" application creates an object within the document. When a user double clicks on an embedded object in a client app, the server app is loaded and the appropriate data file is retrieved.

OLTP (OnLine Transaction Processing) See transaction processi1g and OLCP.

OMI (Open Messaging Interface) E-mail protocol developed by Lotus, now included in VIM.

omnidirectional In all directions. For example, an omnidirectional antenna can pick up signals from all directions.

OmniPage Character recognition software for PCs and the Macintosh from Caere Corp. It was the first personal computer software that could distinguish text from graphics and convert a wide variety of fonts into text.

on-hook State of a telephone line that can receive an incoming call. Contrast with off-hook.

on the fly As and when needed, often without any user interaction. Implies little or no degradation in performance to accomplish the task. See realtime and realtime compression.

one-chip computer See computer on a chip.

one-for-one (1) A phrase often associated with an assembler in which one source-language statement is converted to one machine-language instruction. (2) The most commonly used type of correspondence.

one-pass compiler A language processor that passes through a source language program one time and produces an object module.

onion diagram Graphical representation of a system that is made up of concentric circles. The innermost circle is the core, and all outer layers are dependent on the core.

online (1) Peripheral device (terminal, printer, etc.) that is ready to operate. A printer can be attached and tumd on, yet still not online, if the ONLINE or SEL light is out. Pressing the ONLINE button will usually turn it back online. (2) An online computer system refers to a system with terminals, but does not imply how the system operates. An interactive system is an online system that implies data entry and updating. A transaction processing system is an online system that updates the necessary files as the work comes in, such as in an order processing system. A realtime system is an online system that provides an immediate response to a question.

online help On-screen instruction that is immediately available from within 'he program.

on-screen pasteup A layout on a computer monitor.

on-the-fly encryption The encryption of data just before it is written to the disk and decrypted after it ahs been read from the disk. Software for on-the-fly encryption can be simple to use, as it is often transparent to the user.

OOObject oriented.

OOA See object-oriented analysis.

OOD See object-oriented design.

00DB See object-oriented database.

OODBMS See object-oriented DBMS.

OOP See object-oriented programming.

OOPL (OOP Language) See object-oriented programming.

OOPS (Object Oriented Programming System) See object-oriented programming.

op amp (Operational Amplifier) Device that amplifies analog signals. It uses two inputs; one for power and one for data. It is used in myriads of applications from communications to stereo.

op code See operation code.

open To identify a disk or tape file for reading and writing. The open procedure 9ocks on" to an existing file or creates a new one.

open architecture System in which the specifications are made public in order to encourage third-party vendors to develop add-on products.

Open Desktop See SCO Open Desktop.

open shop Computing environment that allows users to program and run their own programs. Contrast with closed shop.

open system Vendor-independent system that is designed to interconnect with a variety of products. It implies that standards are determined &o!n a consensus of interested parties rather than one or two vendors. Contrast with closed system. See OS!, OSF and X/Open.

operand The part of a machine instruction that references data or a peripheral device. In the instruction, ADD A to B, A and B are the operands (nouns), and ADD is the operation code (verb).

operating system Master control program that runs the computer. It is the first program loaded when the computer is turned on, and its main part, called the kernel, resides in memory at all times. It is an important component of the computer system, because it sets the standards for the application programs that run in it. All programs must work through the operating system. It performs the following functions:

Job Management: In small computers, it responds to commands from the user and loads tin requested application program into memory for execution. In large computers, the operating system carries out its job control instructions (JCL), which describe the programs that must be run for an entire shift.

Task Management: In single tasking computers, the operating system has virtually no task management to do, but in multitasking computers, it is responsible for the concurrent operation of one or more programs (jobs). Advanced operating systems have the ability to prioritize programs so that one job gets done before the other. Multitasking is accomplished by executing instructions for one function while data is coming into or going out of the computer for another. In small computers, the operating system can monitor idle time when a user is interactively working with a program to execute another program in the background.

Data Management: A major operating system function is to keep track of data on disk; hence the term DOS, or disk operating system. The application program does not know where the data is actually stored or how to get it. That knowledge is contained in the operating system's access method, or device driver, routines. When a program is ready to accept data, it signals the operating system with a message. The operating system finds the data and delivers it to the program. Conversely, when the piogram is ready to output, the operating system transfers the data from the program onto the available space on disk.

Device Management: In theory, the operating system is supposed to manage all devices, not just disk drives. It is supposed to handle the input and output to the display screen as well as the printer. This is done to ensure that new developments can be easily incorporated. However, software developers often bypass the operating system, to make the application run faster or for other reasons.

operation code The part of a machine instruction that tells the computer what to do, such as input, add or branch. The operation code is the verb; the operands are the nouns.

operations See datacenter.

operations research See management science.

operator Person who operates the computer and performs such activities as commanding the operating system, mounting disks and tapes and placing paper in the printer.

optical computer A type of computer, still largely experimental, that uses laser beams instead of wires to process information and works far faster than traditionally wired computers.

optical disk Direct access disk written and read by light. CDs, CD ROMs and videodiscs are optical disks that are recorded at the time of manufacture and cannot be erased. WORM disks are recorded in the user's environment, but cannot be erased once they are recorded. Erasable optical disks function like magnetic disks and can be rewritten over and over. Throughout the 1990s, erasable optical disks may become a viable alternative to magnetic disks. Optical disks have greater storage capacity per square inch than their magnetic counterparts, and optical technology will eventually replace magnetic media.

optical fiber Thin glass wire designed for light transmission, capable of transmitting billions of bits per second. Unlike electrical pulses, light pulses are not affected by random radiation in the environment. When the telephone companies eventually replace the copper wire from their central stations into everyone's home with optical fiber, all varieties of information services will be interactively available to the consumer.

optical mark recognition (OMR) Information processing technology that converts data into another medium for computer input by the presence of a mark in a given position, each position having a value known to the computer that may or may not be understandable to humans.

optical mouse Mouse that uses light to get its bearings. It is rolled over a small desktop pad that contains a reflective grid. The mouse emits a light and senses its reflection as it is moved. Contrast with mechanical mouse.

optical reader Input device that recognizes typewritten or printed characters and bar codes and converts them into their corresponding digital codes.

optical recognition See OCR. optical scanner See scanner.

optimizing compiler A compiler tht atempt to correct inefficiences in a program's logic to improve execution times, main storage requirements, and so forth.

opthnizer Hardware or software that improves performance. See disk management.

option key A modifier key on some keyboards; a special controi key. When held down, it gives a different interpretation to the characters next typed.

optoelectronics Merging light and electronics technologies, such as in optical fiber communications systems.

OR Boolean logic operation that is true if any of the inputs is true. An exclusive OR is true if only one of the inputs is true, but not both.

ORACLE Reiational DBMS from Oracle Corp., that runs on a wide variety of computers from micro to mainframe. It was the first DBMS to incorporate the SQL language. Database applications can be created on a PC and easily mcwed k dware platforms.

ordinal number Number th Lf-'. the sequence of an item, for example, id #34. Contrast with cardinal number.

organization chart A diagram showig the organization of a business (how respousilhlies are divided whith the business). Pictorial representation of the organizational hierarchy, showing the foimal relationships among employees.

orientation In typography, the direction of print across a page. See portrait.

orphan See widow & orphan.

OS See operating system.

OS/2 Singie user, multitasking PC operating system for 286s and up. The 16-bit versions have been developed jointly by Microsoft and IBM. The 32-bit versions are developed independently. It is an advanced operating system that is not confined to DOS's infamous 1MB limit. Although new commands have been added, many OS/2 commands are the same as in DOS. The 16-bit versions can address 16MB of RAM and 1GB of virtual memory. OS/2 requires 4MB of RAM (except for Version 1.3), but is often found running in computers with 8MB and more. OS/2's Presentation Manager (OS/2 PM), which is also part of IBM's SAA, provides a user interface similar to Windows 3.x. IBM has a proprietary Extended Edition that includes communications and database management. Windows NT, by Microsoft, was originally OS! 2 Version 3.0, this 32-bit version, scheduled for 1992/ 93, was renamed Windows NT. OS/2 compatibility was dropped, then later reannounced. See Windows NT.

oscillate To swing back and forth between the minimum and maximum values. An oscillation is one cycle, typically one complete wave in an alternating frequency.

oscillator Electronic circuit used to generate high-frequency pulses. See clock.

oscilloscope Test instrument that displays eledzonicsignals (waves and pulses) on a screen. It creates its own time base against which signals can be measured, and display frames can be frozen for visual inspection.

OSI (Open System Interconnection) ISO standard for worldwide communications that defines a framework for implementing protocols in seven iays. Control is passed from one layer to the next, starting at the application layer in one station, proceeding to the bottom layer, over the channel to the next station and back up the hierarchy. Similar functionality exists in all communications networks; however, existing nonOSI systems often incorporate two or three layers of functionality into one. Most vendors have agreed to support OSI in one form or another. See OSI model.

OTPROM (One Time PROM) PROM chip that can be programmed only once.

out of band See signaling out of band.

outdent Same as hanging indent and hanging paragraph. outline font Type of font made from basic outlines of each character. The outlines are scaled into actual characters (bitmaps) before printing. See scalable font.

outline processor Software that allows the user to type in thoughts and organize them into an outline form.

output (1) Any computer-generated information displayed on screen, printed on paper or in machine readable form, such as disk and tape. (2) To transfer or transmit from the computer to a peripheral device or communications line.

output area Reserved segment of memory used to lay out data or text in order to be transferred to an output device such as a disk or tape. Same as buffer.

output bound Excessive slowness due to output functions, typically slow-speed communications lines or printers. See print buffer.

output device Any peripheral that receives output from the computer, such as a video screen, printer, card punch or COM unit. Although disk and tape drives receive output from the computer, they are considered storage devices.

outsourcing Contracting with outside consultants, software houses or service bureaus to perform systems analysis, programming and datacenter operations. See facilities management.

OverDrive Intel's 486 upgrade CPUs. See. 486.

overflow error Error that occurs when calculated data cannot fit within the designated field. The result field is usually left blank or is filled with some symbol to flag the error condition.

overhead (1) Amount of processing time used by system software, such as the operating system, TP monitor or database manager. (2) In communications, the additional codes transmitted for control and error checking purposes.

overlay (1) Preprinted, precut form that is placed over a screen, key or tablet for indentification purposes. See keyboard template. (2) Program segment called into memory when required. When a program is larger than the memory capacity of the machine, the parts of the program that are not in constant use can be set up as overlays. When called in, instructions and data from the previous overlay are lost. In a virtual memory computer, overlays are swapped in and out automatically without loss.

overlay card Controller that digitizes NTSC signals from a video source for display in the computer.

overloading In programming, the ability to use the same name for more than one variable or procedure, requiring the compiler to differentiate them based on context.

overprint The process of printing more than once at the same position in order to emphasize or improve the type. For example, to print an element of one color over one of another color.

overscan Area outside of the normal rectangular viewing area on a display screen. Contrast with underscan.

overstrike (1) To type over an existing character. (2) Character with a line through it.

overwrite (1) Data entry mode that writes over existing characters on screen when new characters are typed in. Contrast with insert mode. (2) To record new data on topof existing data such as when a disk record or file is updated.

Object attribute: An attribute of a semantic object that represents a link to an object.

Object class: In object-oriented programming, a set of objects with a common structure.

Object class library: In object-oriented programming, a collection of object dasses, usually a collection that serves a particular purpose.

Object constructor: In object-oriented programming, a function that creates an object.

Object destructor: In object-oriented programming, a function that destroys an object.

Object diagram: A portrait-oriented rectangle that represents the structure of a semantic object.

Object identifier: An attribute that is used to specify an object instance. Object identifiers can be unique, meaning that they identify one (and only one) instance, or nonunique, meaning that they 'identify exactly one object instance.

Object instance: The occurrence of a particular semantic object, for example, the SALESPERSON semantic object having LastName equal to Jones.

Object-Oriented Programming: A style of computer programming in which programs are developed as sets of objects that have data members and methods. Objects interface with one another by calling each other's methods.

Object persistence: In object-oriented programming, the characteristic that an object can be saved to nonvolatile memory, such as a disk. Persistent objects exist between executions of a program.

Object view: The portion of a semantic object that is visible to a particular application. A view consists of the name of the semantic object plus a list of the attributes visible in that view.

1:N: An abbreviation for a one-to-many relationship between the rows of two tables.

ODMG-93: A report issued by the Object Data Management Group, which is a consortium of object database vendors and other interested industry experts. The report applies the ideas of another group, the Object Management Group, to the problem of object databases. The first ODMG report was produced in 1993 and is accordingly referred to as ODMG-93.

OOP: See Object-oriented programming.

Open Database Connectivity Standard (ODUC): A standard interface by which application programs can access and process SQL databases in a DBMS-independent manner. ODBC was developed by a committee of industry experts from the X/Open and SQL Access Group committees and was incorporated as a part of Windows by Microsoft.

Option button: In a GUI environment, an element of the user interface in which the user can select an item ftom a list. Clicking on one button de-selects the button currently pressed (if any). It operates like the radio buttons on a car radio and in fact is the same as a radio button (see Radio button) but was introduced under a different name to avoid litigation among vendors.

Orphan: Any row (record) that is missing its parent in a mandatory one-to-many relationship.

Overhead data: Metadata created by the DBMS to improve performance, for example, indexes and linked lists.

Owner: (1) In the CODASYL DBTG model, a record type that is on the one side of a one-to-many or set relationship. (2) In data administration, the department or other organizational unit in charge of the management of a particular data item. An owner can also be called a data proponent.

P

p-code See pseudo language and UCSD p-System. p-System See UCSD p-System.

PABX (Private Automatic Branch eXchange) Same as PBX.

pack (1) To compress data in order to save space. Unpack refers to decompressing data. See data compression. (2) Instruction that converts a decimal number into a packed decimal format. Unpack converts a packed decimal number into decimal. (3) In database programs, a command that removes records that have been marked for deletion.

package See software package.

packaged software See software package.

packed decimal Storage mode that places two decimal digits into one byte, each digit occupying four bits. The sign occupies four bits in the least significant byte.

packet switching Technique for handling high-volume traffic in a network by breaking apart messages into fixed length packets that are transmitted to their destination through the most expedient route. All packets in a single message may not travel the same route (dynamic routing). The destination computer reassembles the packets into their proper sequence. This method is used to efficiently handle messages of different lengths and priorities in large networks.

packetized voice Transmission of realtime voice in a packet switching network.

packing density Number of bits or tracks per inch of recording surface. It also refers to the number of memory bits or other electronic components on a chip.

pad (1) To fill a data structure with padding characters. (2) (PAD) (Packet Assembler Dissassembler) Communications device that formats outgoing data into packets of the required length for transmission in a packet switching network. It also strips the data out of incoming packets.

padding Characters used to fiH up the unused portion of a data structure, such as a field or communications message. A field might be padded with blanks, zeros or nulls.

paddle Input device that controls the cursor on screen in a back-and-forth motion. It has a dial and one or more buttons and is typicaLly used in video games to hit balls and steer objects. See joy stick.

page (1) In virtual memory systems, a segment of the program that is transferred into memory. (2) In videotex systems, a transmitted frame. (3) In word processing, a printed page.

page break In printing, a code that marks the end of a page. A hard page break is inserted by the user, and the page will always break at that location, eg. at the end of a chapter. A soft page break is created by a word processing or report program based on current settings. Soft page breaks change as data is added or when the page length is changed.

page composition The addition of type to a layout.

page composition program A program for designing and producing professional-looking documents; also called desktop publishing program.

page description language High-level language for defining printer output. If an application generates output in a page description language, the output can be printed on any printer that supports it. Much of the character and graphics shaping is done within the printer rather than in the user's computer.

page fault Virtual memory interrupt that reads the required page from disk when the next instruction or item of data is not in memory.

page frame See EMS.

page header Common text that is printed at the top of every page. It generally includes the page number and headings above each column.

page layout program In desktop publishing, an application program that assembles text and graphics from a variety of files with which one can determine the precise placement, scaling, sizing, and cropping of material in accordance with the page design represented on screen. Popular page layout programs include PAGEMAKER, QUARK XPRESS and VENTURA PUBLISHER.

page makeup Setting up (formatting) a printed page, which includes the layout of headers, footers, columns, page numbers, graphics, rules and borders.

page mode memory Common dynamic RAM chip design. Memory bits are accessed by row and column coordinates. Without page mode, each bit is accessed by pulsing the row and column select lines. With page mode, the row (page) is selected only once for all bits (columns) within the row, resulting in faster access.

page preview A mode found on many page layout and word processing programs that shows a full page view of how a page will look when printed out, including added elements such as headers, footers, and margins.

page printer Type of printer that prints a page at a time. See laser printer and ion deposition.

page recognition Software that recognizes the content of a printed page which has been scanned into the computer. It uses optical character recognition to convert the printed words into computer text, but it implies that the text can be automatically differentiated from other elements on the page, such m pictures and captions.

PageMaker Full-featured desktop publishing program for the PC and Macintosh from Aldus Corp. Originally introduced for the Mac in 1985, it set the standard for desktop publishing. In fact, Paul Brainerd, president of Aldus, coined the term desktop publishing. The PC version was introduced in 1987.

page skip A control character that causes a printer to skip the rest of the current page and move to the top of the next page.

pagination (1) Page numbering. (2) Laying out printed pages, which includes the setting up and printing of columns, rules and borders. Although pagination is used synonymously with page makeup, the term often refers to the printing of long manuscripts rather than ads and brochures.

paging In virtual memory, the transfer of program segments (pages) into and out of memory.

paint (1) In computer graphics, to literally "paint" the screen using a tablet stylus or mouse to simulate a paintbrush. (2) To create a screen form by typing anywhere on screen. To "paint" the screen with text.

paint program Graphics program that allows the user to simulate painting on screen with the use of a graphics tablet or mouse, Paint programs create raster graphics images.

PAL (1) (Paradox Application Language) Paradox's programming language. (2) (Programmable Array Logic) Programmable logic chip (PLD) technology from Advanced Micro Devices. (3) (Phase Alternating Line) European TV standard that uses 625 lines of resolution (100 more than NTSC).

palatino A serif typeface included as a built-in font with many POSTSCRIPT laser printers.

palette (1) In computer graphics, the total range of colors that can be used for display, although typically only a subset of them can be used at one time. May also refer to the collection of painting tools available to the user. (2) Set of functions or modes.

palmtop Computer small enough to hold in one hand and operate with the other. Palmtops may have specialized keyboards or keypads for data entry applications or have small qwerty keyboards.

pan (1) In computer graphics, to move (while viewing) to a different part of an image without changing magnification. (2) To move (while viewing) horizontally across a text record.

pane The term for each of the windows that result from splitting a single window.

paper tape (1) Slow, low-capacity, sequential storage medium used in the first half of the 20th century to hold data as patterns of punched holes. (2) Paper roll printed by a calculator or cash register.

paperless office Long predicted, the paperless office is still a myth. Although paper usage has been reduced in some organizations, it has actually increased in most others. Furthermore, a paper document is still considered the pr000f ofa transaction. In time, laptop computers with immense storage and high-resolution screens will serve to replace paper when travelling. Optical fiber networks will make it easy to send data, pictures, voice and video quickly. As color laser printers become commonplace, it will be easy to reproduce any document, no matter how complex.

paradigm: Pronounced "para-dime A model, example or pattern.

Paradise Popular video display boards from the Paradise subsidiary of Western Digital Corp.

Paradox Network-ready relational DBMS for PCs from Borland that is known for its ease of use and query by example method for asking questions. Its PAL programming language is unique. Many PAL statements are interactive Paradox commands, so that a Paradox user can adjust to programming more easily. The Paradox engine (database part of Paradox) is available separately. It can be accessed by C programs, allowing C applications to manage Paradox databases.

paragraph In DOS programming, a 16 byte block. Memory addresses are generated as "segment:of[et," where the segment is expressed in paragraphs. To compute an address, the segment register is shifted left four bits (multiplying it by 16).

paragraph assembly A process in which a document is assembled on a word processor from paragraph stored on disks.

parallel computing Solving a single problem with multiple computers or computers made up of multiple processors. See array processor and hypercube.

parallel Interface Multiline channel that transfers one or more bytes simultaneously. For example, personal computers often connect printers via a Centronics 36- wire parallel interface, which transfers one byte at a time over eight wires, the remaining wires used for control signals. Large computer parallel interfaces transfer more than one byte at a time. Contrast with serial interface. See Centronics.

parallel port I/O attachment used to hook up a printer or other parallel interface device. On a PC, it is a 25- pin female DB-25 connector. See printer cable.

parallel processIng (1) Architecture within a single computer that can perform more than one operation at the same time. See pipeline processing and vector processor. (2) Multiprocessing architecture made up of multiple processors or multiple computers. See hypercube and multiprocessing.

parallel transmission Transmitting data one or more bytes at a time. Contrast with serial transmission.

parallelizing To generate instructions for a parallel processing computer.

parameter (1) Any value that customizes or adds specific information to a commandor program. Parameters include such information as file names, coordinates, ranges of values and specific codes. They are often entered along with the program name when the program is loaded. See DOS switch. (2) In programming, a value passed to a subroutine or function for processing.

parameter-driven Software that requires external values. It solves a problem that is partially or entirely described by the values (parameters) that are entered.

parametric Pertaining to the technique by which a line, curve, or surface is defined by equations based on some independent variable. Used often in COMPUTER-AIDED DESIGN systems.

parent-child In database management, a relationship between two files. The parent file contains required data about a subject, such as employees and customers. The child is the offspring; for example, the child of a institutional file may be the employee file.

parent program Main or primary program, or first program loaded into memory. See child program.

parity bit Extra bit attached to the byte, character or word used to detect errors in transmission.

parity checking Error detection technique that checks for the accurate transmission of digital data either within the computer system or over a network. Parity checking uses an extra bit (ninth bit) that holds a o or 1 depending on the data content of the byte. In order to detect a transmission error, the parity bit is tested each time a byte is transmitted.

parity drive Separate disk drive that holds parity bits in a disk array. See RAID.

parity error Error condition that occurs when the parity bit of a character is found to be incorrect.

park To retract the read/write head on a hard disk to its home location before the unit is physically moved in order to prevent damage which is caused if the head touches the hard disk. Most modern drives park themselves when the power is turned off.

parse To analyze a sentence or language statement. Parsing breaks down words into functional units that can be converted into machine language.

parser Routine that performs parsing operations on a computer or natural language.

partition Reserved part of disk or memory that is set aside for some purpose.

parts programmer A programmer who translates the physical explanation for machining a part into a series of mathematical steps and then codes computer instructions for those steps. See APT and NUMERICAL CONTROL.

Pascal High-level programming language (interpreted and compiled) developed by Swiss professor Niklaus Wirth in the early 1970s and named after the French mathematician, Blaise Pascal. It is noted for its structured programming, which caused it to achieve popularity initially in academic circles. Pascal has had strong influence on subsequent languages, such as Ada, dBASE and PAL. See Turbo Pascal:

Pascaline Calculating machine developed in 1642 by French mathematician Blaise Pascal. It could only add and subtract, but it gained attention because 50 units were placed in prominent locations throughout Europe.

passive hub Network hub that contains no active electronics and adds nothing to the signals being transmitted. Contrast with intelligent hub. See hub.

passive matrix LCD Common LCD technology that illuminates a pixel by sending current down the appropriate row and column. Contrast with active matrix LCD.

passive star Network topology that joins wires from several nodes without providing any additional processing. Contrast with active star.

password Word or code used to serve as a security measure against unauthorized access to data. However, since the computer can only verify the legitimacy of the paword, not the legitimacy of the user, any unauthorized user with a valid password is considered a valid user by the computer. See NCSC.

paste See cut & paste.

patch Temporary or quick fix to a program. Too many patches in a program make it difficult to maintain. It may also refer to changing the actual machine code when it is inconvenient to recompile the source program.

path (1) In communications, the route between any two nodes. Same as line, channel, link or circuit. (2) In database management, the route from one set of data to another, for example, from customers to orders. (3) In programming, a set route taken by the program to process a set of data. (4) The-complete route to a file on a disk including drive, directory, subdirectory. See DOS Path.

PAX (1) (Private Automatic Exchange) Inhouse intercom system. (2) (Parallel Architecture Extended) Parallel processing environment standard based on Intel's i860 RISC chip, UNIX System V and Alliant Computer's parallel and 3-D graphics technologies. PAX-1 Software from VXM Technologies, Boston, MA, that allows a network of computers to function as a single parallel processing system. It runs in an Ethernet network with the TCP/IP protocol and supports personal computers, minis and mainframes.

payware Software distributed for money. Contrast with freeware.

PBX (Private Branch eXchange) Inhouse telephone switching system that interconnects telephone extensions to each other, as well as to the outside telephone network. It may include functions such as least cost routing for outside calls, call forwarding, conference calling and call accounting.

PC (1) (Personal Computer) Machines that conform to the PC standard, originally developed by IBM and subsequently governed by Intel, Microsoft and major PC vendors collectively. The PC is the world's largest computer base. (2) (Personal Computer) Any personal computer. (3) Sometimes refers to first-generation IBM models PC, 2CT and AT in contrast with second-generation PS/2s. (4) See printed circuit board. See Personal computer for details of (2).

PC-8 Symbol set that contains the extended ASCII characters of the IBM PC.

c board See printed circuit board.

PC bus Bus architecture used in first-generation IBM PCs. It refers to the original 8-bit bus and the 16-bit extension introduced with the AT. 8-bit boards fit in 8-bit and 16-bit slots, but 16-bit boards fit only in a 16-bit slot. Also called ISA bus. Contrast with EISA and Micro Channel.

PC card (1) Memory card, I/O card or memory and I/O card. (2) Expansion board for a PC.

PC-compatible Personal computer compatible with the IBM PC and PSI2 standards.

PC-DOS DOS operating system supplied by IBM for its personal computers in contrast with MS-DOS for the compatibles. Both versions are almost identical, and both are simply called DOS.

PC keyboard Keyboard introduced with the IBM PC that provides a dual-function keypad for numeric entry and cursor movement. It was severely criticized for its non-standard shift key placement, which was corrected with the AT keyboard. Regardless of key placement, users often praise the feel of IBM keyboards. See Keyboard.

PC LAN (1) Network of IBM or IBM-compatible PCs. (2) Network of any variety of personal computers.

PC memory card See memory card.

PC memory map The following chart shows how conventional memory (first megabyte of RAM) is used in a PC:

Address		
11000:0000	1088K	Extended
		High Memory Area
		(HMA) Memory
10000:0000	1024K	PC ROM BIOS PS/2
F000:0000	960K	ROM BIOS & VGA ROM
E000:0000	896K	Available
Top 384K	for drivers and of the	
D000:0000	832K	EMS page frame first megabyte
C800:0000	800K	EGA, VGA ROM BIOS of RAM is
C000:0000	768K	called the
		Free Upper
BCOO:0000	752K	Memory Area
	CGA	(UMA),
	Graphics	Hercules comprised
	CGA, EGA, Graphics of Upper	
VGA Text Memory		
B800:0000	736K	Blocks
	Free	(UMB5)
B400:0000	720K	MDA RAM
B000:0000	704K	EGA, VGA Graphics
		RAM
A000:0000	640K	Lower 640K
		is used by User DOS and Programs user programs.
		DOS and COMMAND.COM Interrupt vectors
		OK

PC-MOS/386 Multiuser PC operating system from The Software Link. It runs most standard DOS applications as well as applications written for the 386's Protected Mode.

PC network (1) Network of IBM and/or IBM-compatible PCs. (2) Network of any variety of personal computers. (3) (PC Network) First PC LAN from IBM introduced in 1984. It uses the CSMAJCD access method and introduced the NetBIOS interface. Token Ring Network support was later added. Microsoft's version is called MS-Net.

PC Paintbrush PC paint program from ZSoft Corp., that is widely used and has set an industry standard graphics format. Its PCX raster graphics format is generated and accepted by many graphics, word processing and desktop publishing programs.

PC Tools Deluxe Comprehensive package of PC utilities from Central Point Software, that includes a DOS shell as well as file management, communications, disk caching, backup and data compression utilities.

PCB See printed circuit board.

PCJr (PCjunior) IBM's first home computer introduced in 1983. Its original keyboard was unsuitable for typing, but adequate keyboards were later added. It was discontinued in 1985.

PCL (Printer Control Language) Command language for the HP LaserJet printers. It has become a de facto standard used in many printers and typesetters. PCL Level 5, introduced with the LaserJet III in 1990, also supports Compugraphic's Intellifont scalable fonts.

PCM (1) (Pulse Code Modulation) Technique for digitizing speech by sampling the sound waves and converting each sample into a binary number. It uses waveform coding that samples a 4KHz bandwidth 8,000 times a second. Each sample is an 8 bit number, resulting in 64K bits of data per second. See ADPCM. (2) (Plug Compatible Manufacturer) Organization that makes a computer or electronic device that is compatible with an existing machine.

PCX Widely-used raster graphics file format developed by Zsoft Corp., that handles monochrome, 2-bit, 4- bit, 8-bit and 24-bit color and achieves compression ratios of approximately 1.1:1 to 1.5:1.

PD software See public domain software.

PDIP (Plastic DIP) Common type of DIP made of plastic.

PDL See page description language.

peek/poke Instructions that view and alter a byte of memory by referencing a specific memory address. Peek displays the contents; poke changes it. These are commands in BASIC.

peer In communications, a functional unit that is on the same protocol layer as another.

peer-to-peer communications Communications in which both sides have equal responsibility for initiating the session. Contrast with master-slave communications.

peer-to-peer network Local area network that allows all users access to data on all workstations. Dedicated file servers are not required, but may be used.

pel Same as pixel.

pen-based computing Using a stylus to enter hand writing and marks into a computer. See gesture recognition.

pen plotter See plotter.

PenPoint Operating system from Go Corp., that provides a stylus (pen) interface for hand- written input. It uses a DOS-compatible file system, but does not run DOS applications. The direction, speed and order of the user's pen strokes is analyzed for recognition. See NUI.

PEPPER board Family of graphics display boards for PCs from Number Nine Computer Corp., that provide extremely high-resolution images required in CAD and high-end graphics applications.

perfory Detachable perforated strips on the two sides of fanfold computer paper.

perfs Perforations in paper to facilitate removing pin- feed edges and tearing continuous paperinto seperate pages.

peripheral Any hardware device connected to a computer, such as a monitor, keyboard, printer, plotter, disk or tape drive, graphics tablet, scanner, joy stick, paddle and mouse.

peripheral controller See control unit (2).

permanent font (1) A soft font that is kept in the printer's memory until the printer is turned off. (2) Same as internal font.

permanent memory Same as non-volatile memory.

permutation One possible combination of items out ofa larger set of items. For example, with the set of numbers 1, 2 and 3, there are six possible permutations: 12, 21, 13, 31, 23 and 32.

perpendicular recording See vertical recording. persistence In a CRT, the time a phosphor dot remains illuminated after being energized. Long-persistence phosphors reduce flicker, but generate ghost-like images that linger on screen for a fraction of a second.

persIstent link See hot link.

personal computer Personal computers are used as stand-alone machines or as workstations and file servers in a local area network. They are predominantly used as single-user systems under DOS. , IBM's first personal computers used acronyms and names: XT, AT, Convertible, etc. The PS/2 series use numbers: Model 30, 55, 80, etc. (see IBM PC). Compatibles often use the CPU designation in the name, such as "386 Turbo."

THE HISTORY OF PERSONAL COMPUTERS: The personal computer industry began in 1977, when Apple, Radio Shack and Commodore introduced the first off-the-shelf computers as consumer products. These used an 8-bit microprocessor with a maximum of 64K of memory and floppy disks for storage. In 1981, IBM introduced the PC, an Intel 8088-based machine, slightly faster than the genre, but with 10 times the memory. It was floppy-based, and its DOS operating system from Microsoft was also available for the clone makers (MS-DOS). The 8088 was cleverly chosen so that CP/M software vendors could convert to it easily. dBASE II was introduced in 1981 bringing mainframe database functions to the personal computer level and launching an entire industry of compatible products and addons. Lotus 1-2-3 was introduced in 1982, and its refined interfaceand combined graphics helped spur sales of the new standard. he IBM PC was successfully cloned by Compaq and unsuccessfully by others. However, by the time IBM announced the AF in 1984, vendors were effectively cloning the personal computer and, as a group, eventually grabbed the majority of the personal computer market. Apple introduced the Macintosh in 1984. The graphics- based desktop environment caught on, especially in desktop publishing, and the graphical interface, or "gooey," (GUI) worked its way to the personal computer world with Microsoft Windows, and, eventually Ventura Publisher with its GEM interface. n 1986, the Compaq 386 ushered in the first Intel 386- based machine. In 1987, IBM introduced the PS/2, its next generation of personal computers, which added improved graphics, 3.5" floppy disks and an incompatible bus to help fend off the cloners. OS/2, jointly developed by IBM and Microsoft, was also introduced to handle the new machines, but it has been slow to catch on. In the same year, more powerful Macintoshes were introduced, including the Mac SE and Mac II, which opened new doors for Apple. In 1989, the personal computer makers introduced 486-based computers, and Apple gave us faster Maca, which it has continued to do each year since. In 1990, Microsoft's introduced Windows 3.0, which is rapidly catching on as the graphical environment for personal computers. Software publishers are rapidly developing Windows versions of their products. Important features of the personal computer are as follows:

CPU: The XT CLASS - 8086, 8088, launched in 1981 used the 16-bit 8088 chip. Today, XT-class machines are rarely sold new, but survive in the second-hand market. They are used for many data processing functions, but are considered too slow for intensive graphics or Windows applications. The 286, first used in the IBM AT in 1984, is a 16-bit machine that is more responsive than the XT and was the first personal computer to directly address more than one megabyte of memory. AT-class machines are fast enough for many applications, but are sluggish under Windows and are not geared for future 32-bit applications. The 386, first used by Compaq in 1986, is a 32-bit machine that runs faster than the 286 and can address an unbelievable four gigabytes of memory. 386s will also run future 32-bit applications and operating systems. The 386SX is slower than the 386, but retains the same advanced features. The 386SL is designed for battery conservation in laptops. With initial models introduced in late 1989, the 486, or 486DX, is about twice as fast as the 386 and has a built-in math coprocessor. The 486SX runs at slower speeds than the 486DX and makes the coprocessor an optional item. For more details on CPUs, see specs below and look up 286, 386, etc.

OPERATING ENVIRONMENT: Almost all personal computers use Microsoft's DOS operating system, which was developed for the 8088 chip, thus all DOS applications are written to address only one megabyte of RAM. The personal computer was also designed so that the first 640K of the one megabyte is used for applications, while the next 384K (upper memory area, UMA) is used by the operating system to control peripheral devices (see PC memory map). Since some of the 640K is also used by DOS, only about 570K to 600K is actually available to user programs. As users became comfortable with personal computers, they wanted more than one application open and active at the same time. In order to get around DOS' single task nature and the personal computer's 640K limit, a variety of add-ons, techniques and remedies have been created to solve this dilemma. Among these techniques are the TSRs, expanded memory, task switchers and multitaskers, memory managers, extended memory and windows, DOS 5.0 added a task switching capability that runs multiple DOS applications and swaps inactive ones to disk, etc. Innovations in operating systems are DR DOS with advanced features like on-the-fly compression, Windows NT, etc.

INPUT AND OUTPUT: There are three ways of getting data into and out of the personal computer. The first is via the keyboard, which plugs into a keyboard connector always built onto the motherboard. The second is via the data bus, or expansion bus, into which are s1ctted expansion boards which control circuits for disk drives, the video display, CD ROM reader and network adapter for example. The third way is through serial and parallel ports which are input/output pathways built into the motherboard or contained on a separate expansion board. The serial ports are typically used for modems, mice, scanners and digitizer tablets, and the parallel port is generally used for the printer. Both serial and parallel ports are used for data transfer between computers.

VIDEO DISPLAY: Since 1981, IBM has introduced several display standards, implemented by plugging a graphics adater into an expansion slot and connecting the appropriate monitor to it. Each new standard incorporates the previous ones for compatibility; however, vendors have to modit their programs to handle the higher resolution graphics each time. personal computers operate in two software- selectable modes: text mode (character mode) and graphics moçle. The former is faster but the latter can also be speeded up by use of specialized "accelerator" chips.

PRINTERS: There are hundreds of printer models that work with personal computers from dot matrix to ink jet to laser printers and most of them plug into the personal computer's parallel port. Printing text files directly from DOS works with all printers, but in order to select fonts, boldface, underline and other print attributes, the application must support the printer.

KEYBOARDS: The original personal computer keyboard used an awkward return and left shift key placement. Finally corrected on the AT keyboard, the backspace key was made harder to reach. Then came the Enhanced keyboard with a host of relocated keys, making it impossible to assign function keys intelligently.

FLOPPY DISKS: The most common floppy is the 360KB, 5.25' disk introducedsoon after the first IBM PC. Later, the AT model introduced the 1.2 megabyte floppy. The 1.2MB drives can read and write the 360KB disks, but earlier models of the drive cannot be used to format 360KB disks. IBM introduced the 720KB, 3.5" microfloppy on its Convertible laptop, then doubled the capacity to 1.44MB with the PS/2 line. Due to their greater capacity and convenience, the 3.5" floppies have been retrofitted to many machines and have become the medium of choice. HARD DISKS: Non-removable, hard disks for personal computers are available with storage capacities from 20MB to 1.5GB and above. If a hard disk is added that is not compatible with the existing disk controller, a new controller board must be plugged in. However, one disk's internal standard does not conflict with another, since all programs and data must be copied onto it. Removable disk cartridges that hold 40 to 80 and more megabytes are also becoming popular. As the storage capacity grows, so does performance. Disk access times run from 15 milliseconds (fast) to 100 ms (slow). The larger ESDI and SCSI drives also transfer data faster. Hard disks, 100 megabytes and over, are generally very fast and are the type required for use as a network server. See hard disk specs.

THE FUTURE: The personal computer industry developed with little planning. All of a sudden, it was there, and machines were bought to solve individual problems, such as automating a budget, typing a letter or searching a file. However, in large organizations, the real data exists in the mainframe, and it doesn't serve the organization to have an employee retype the mainframe reports into the micro in order to analyze and manipulate it. Personal computers can serve as invaluable tools for the user when they are designed into the fabric of the organization. Fast personal computers are changing the marketplace. Not only do they begin to compete with minicomputer workstations, but, during the 1990s, networks of these machines will be installed for applications that were previously relegated to minis and mainframes. These high-powered desktop computers will encourage the development of more artificial intelligence applications that are the backbone of the next computing generation. By the turn of the century, voice recognising computers will not be unusual. As stand-alone machines, personal computers place creative capacity into the hands of an individual that would have cost nourmous sums of money a few years ago. Its use is slowly but surely shifting the balance of power from the large company to the small, from the elite to the masses, from the wealthy to individuals of modest means. The personal computer has truly revolutionized the computer industry and the world.

personal computing The use of a personal computer by individuals for applications such as entertainment, home management, education word processing, and family business.

personal workstation Same as personal computer or workstation.

PERT chart A diagram representing the interdependencies of work elements against time, typically shown graphically as circles and connecting line.

PET computer (Personal Electronic Transaction computer) CP/M and floppy disk-based personal computer introduced in 1977 by Commodore. It was one of the three first personal computers.

PFS First Choice: Integrated software package for PCs from Spinnaker Software Corp., that provides word processing, database, spreadsheet, graphics and communications capabilities.

PFS Write: See Professional Write.

PGA (1) (Pin Grid Array) Chip housing with high density of pins (200 pins can fit in 1.5' square). Used for large amounts of I/O, its underside looks like a "bed of nails." (2) (Programmable Gate Array) Type of gate array that is programmed by the customer. (3) (Professional Graphics Adapter) Early high-res PC display standard (640x480, 256 cols.) with 3-D processor that had minimal support.

PgUp/PgDn keys Page Up and Page Down keys are typically used to move text up and down one screenful, but they can be programmed to do anything.

phase change recording Optical recording technique that uses a laser to create a bit by altering the crystalline structure of a metallic surface. The bit either reflects or absorbs light when read.

phase encoding See PE

phase locked Technique for maintaining synchronization in an electronic circuit. The circuit receives its timing from input signals, but also provides a feedback circuit for synchronization.

phase modulation Transmission technique that blends a data signal intoa carrier by varying (modulating) the phase of the carrier. See modulate.

Phoenix BIOS PC-compatible ROM BIOS from Phoenix Technolgies, Ltd. Phoenix was the first company to successfully mass produce the ROM BIOS for the PC.

phone connector (1) Plug and socket fo a two or three- wire coaxial cable used to plug microphones and headphones into amplifiers. The plug is a single, nail- like ¼" thick prong about 1¼" in length. See phono connector. (2) Plug and socket for a telephone line, typically the RJ-11 modular connector.

phone hawk Slang for a person who calls up a computer via modem and either copies or destroys data.

phoneme Speech utterance, such as "k,""ch," and "sh," that is used in synthetic speech systems to. compose words for audio output.

phosphor Rare earth material used to coat the inside face of a CRT. When struck by an electron beam, the phosphor emits a visible light for a few milliseconds. In color displays, red, green and blue phosphor dots are grouped as a cluster.

photocomposition Laying out a printed page using electrophotographic machines, such as phctotypesetters and laser printers. See page makeup and pagination.

photolithography Lithographic technique used to transfer the design of the circuit paths and electronic elements on a chip onto a wafer's surface. A photomask is created with the design for each layer of the chip. The wafer is coated with a light-sensitive film and is exposed to light shining through the photomask. The light reaching the wafer hardens the film, and when the wafer is exposed to an acid bath (wet processing) or hot ions (dry processing), the unhardened areas are etched away.

photomask Opaque image on a transluscent plate that is used as a light filter to transfer an image from one device to another. See chip.

photomicrography Photographing microscopic images. photon Elementary particle of light. It is much smaller than its electron counterpart and can thus allow even greater miniaturization within photonic circuits.

photonics Science of building machine circuits that use light instead of electricity.

photooptic memory Storage device that uses a laser beam to record data onto a photosensitive film.

photorealistic Image synthesis In computer graphics, a format for describing a picture that depicts the realism of the actual image. It includes such attributes as surface texture, light sources, motion blur and reflectivity.

photoreslst Light-sensitive film used in photolithography that temporarily holds the pattern to be etched away.

photosensor Light-sensitive device that is used in optical scanning machinery.

phototypesetter Device that creates professional-quality text. Input to the phototypesetter comes from the keyboard, over a communications channel or via disk or tape. The output is a paper-like or transparent film that is processed into a camera-ready master for printing. The phototypesetter has been used to print books, magazines and all commercially printed materials, and was originally the only machine that could handle multiple fonts and text composition capabilities, such as kerning. Today, though desktop laser printers are being used to typeset text, a majority of them cannot produce the ultra-fine lines of the high-resolution (1200 to 2400 dpi) phototypesetters.

physical Refers to devices at the electronic, or machine, level. Contrast with logical. See logical vs physical.

physical address Actual, machine address of an item or device.

physical format See record layout and low-level format.

physical link (1) Electronic connection between two devices. (2) In data management, a pointer in an index or record that refers to the physical location of data in another file.

physical lock Prevention of user access to data provided by a locking on/off switch or file protection mechanism such as on a floppy disk. Contrast with logical lock.

PlC (1) (PiCture) File extension used for graphics formats. Lotus PlC is a vector format for 1-2-3 charts and graphs. (2) (Programmable Interrupt Controller) Intel 8259 chip that controls interrupts in PCs.

pica (1) In word processing, a monospaced font that prints 10 characters per inch. (2) In typography, about 1/6th of an inch (0.166") or 12 points

picosecond One trillionth of a second. Pronounced "peeco- second."

PlCT (PICTure) Macintosh graphics file format that stores images in the QuickDraw vector format. When PlC!' files are converted to the PC, they use the .PCI' file extension.

picture element See pixel.

pie chart Graphical representation of informatiot in which each unit of data is represented as a pie-shaped piece of a circle. See ousiness graphics.

piezoelectric Generation of electricity from a crystal subjected to pressure. Certain crystal oscillators and microphones are piezoelectric devices.

HF file (Program Information File) Windows data file used to hold requirements of non-Windows applications. Windows supplies PIFs for many applications, but new PIFs can be created with the PIF Editor if a non-Windows application has special requirements or does not work properly. It includes such data as conventional and extended memory required, graphics mode and optional parameters. An application can be launched by clicking on its PIF file.

piggyback board Small printed circuit board that plugs into another circuit board (rather than onto the motherboard) in order to enhance its capabilities.

PIL (Publishing Interchange Language) Standard for document interchange that defines the placement of text and graphics objects on the page. It does not address the content of the objects.

PILOT (Programmed Inquiry Learning Or Teaching) High-level programming language used to generate question-and-answer courseware. A version that incorporates turtle graphics runs on Atari personal computers.

PIM (Personal Information Manager) Combination word processor, database and desktop accessory program that organizes a variety of information. It allows the user to tie together more loosely structured information than traditional programs. PIMs vary widely, but all of them attempt to provide methods for managing information the way people think about their jobs and functions.

pin (1) One of the male leads on a multiline plug, such as an RS-232 connector. Each pin is connected with its female counterpart to close a circuit. It is also one of the footlike leads on a chip that plugs into a socket on the circuit board. (2) PIN (Personal Identification Number) Personal password number chosen by the user for identification purposes.

pin feed Method for moving paper that contains a set of pins on a platen or tractor. The pins engage the paper through perforated holes in its sides.

pinch roller Small, freely-turning wheel in a tape drive that pushes the tape against a motor-driven wheel in order to move it.

pincushioning Screen distortion in which the sides bow in. Contrast with barrel distortion.

ping pong (1) Half-duplex communications method in which data is transmitted in one direction and acknowledgement is returned at the same speed in the other. The line is alternately switched from transmit to receive in each direction. Contrast with asymmetric modem. (2) To go in one direction and then in the other.

ping-pong buffer See double buffering.

pinouts Description and purpose of each pin in a multiline connector.

pipe Shared space that accepts the output of one program for input into another. In DOS and OS/2, the pipe command is a vertical line (I). The statement, dir sort directs the output of the directory list to the sort utility. See DOS filters & pipes and DOS redirection.

pipeline processing Category of techniques that provide simultaneous, or parallel, processing within the computer.

piracy Illegal copying of software for personal or commercial use.

pitch Number of printed characters per inch. With proportionally spaced characters, the pitch is variable and must bc measured as an average. See dot pitch.

pixel (FIX ELement) Smallest element on a video display screen. A screen is broken up into thousands of tiny dots, and a pixel is one or more dots that are treated as a unit. A pixel can be one dot on a monochrome screen, three dots (red, green and blue) on color screens, or clusters of these dots. For monochrome screens, the pixel, normally dark, is energized to different light intensities, creating a range from dark to light. For color, each red, green and blue dot is energized to different intensities, creating a range of colors perceived as the mixture of these dots. The number of bits assigned to each pixel in its associated digital memory determines the number of shades and colors that can be represented. The most economical system is monochrome in which one bit is used per pixel (on or oft). In the most elaborate color displays, which use up to four full bytes for each of the red, green and blue dots, each pixel can display billions of different shades. Considering that a high-resolution screen may use a million pixels, many megabytes of memory would have to be reserved to hold such an image.

pixel graphics Same as raster graphics.

PK software Popular PC shareware compression programs from PKWARE Inc., (PKstands for Phil Katz). PKZIP compresses files into a ZIP file and PKUNZIP decompresses them. PKSFX compresses files into a self-extracting EXE file that decompresses when loaded and doesn't require the PKUNZIP program. ZIP2EXE creates the self-extracting file from an existing ZIP file. PKLITE compresses only EXE and COM program files.

PLA (Programmable Logic Array) Programmable logic chip (PLD) technology from Philips/Signetics.

plaintext Normal text that has not been encrypted and is readable by text editors and word processors. Contrast with ciphertext.

planar Technique developed by Fairchild Instruments that creates transistor sublayers by forcing chemicals under pressure into exposed areas. Planar superseded the mesa process and was a major step toward creating the chip.

planar area In computer graphics, an object that has boundaries, such as a square or polygon.

planning system See spreadsheet and financial planning system.

plasma display Also called gas discharge, a flat-screen technology that contains an inert ionized gas sandwiched between x- and y-axis panels. A pixel is selected by charging one x- and one y-wire, causing the gas in that vicinity to glow a bright orange.

platen Long, thin cylinder (normally black) in a typewriter or printer that guides the paper through it and serves as a backstop for the printing mechanism to bang into.

platform Hardware architecture of a particular model or computer family. It is the standard to which software developers write their programs. The term may also include the operating system. See environment.

PLATO (Programmed Logic for Automatic Teaching Operations) Developed by Donald Bitzer and originally marketed by CDC, it was the first CBT system to combine graphics and touch-sensitive screens for interactive training.

platter One of the disks in a disk pack or hard disk drive. Each platter provides a top and bottom recording surface. See magnetic disk.

PLC (Programmable Logic Controller) Computer used in process control applications. PLC microprocessors are typically RISC-based and are designed for high- speed, realtime and rugged industrial environments.

PLCC (Plastic LCC) Widely-used type of leaded chip carrier. See LCC.

PLD (Programmable Logic Device) Logic chip that is programmed at the customer's site. The PLD is not a storage chip like a PROM or EPROM, although fuse- blowing techniques are used. It contains different configurations of AND, OR and NOR gates that are "blown" together. Contrast with gate array, which requires a manufacturing process to complete the programming.

plot To create an image by drawing a series of lines. In programming, a plot statement creates a single vector (line) or a complete circle or box that is made up of several vectors.

plotter Graphics printer that draws images with ink pens. It requires data in vector graphics format, which makes up an image as a series of point-to-point lines. See flatbed plotter and drum plotter.

Plotter In a Cartridge HPGL emulation in a cartridge for laser printers from Pacific Data Products, San Diego, CA.

plug compatible Hardware that is designed to perform exactly like another vendor's product. A plug compatible CPU runs the same software as the machine it's compatible with. A plug compatible peripheral works the same as the device it's replacing.

plugboard Socket board with used to program early tabulating machines and computers. A wire is inserted into one output and one input socket, closing a circuit and activating a function. Complicated programs looked like "mounds of spaghetti."

plugs & sockets Physical connectors used to Jink together all variety of electronic devices. See DB-9, RS-232-C, and Centronics.

PM See preventive maintenance, Presentation Manager and phase modulation.

pocket computer Hand-held, calculator-sized computer that runs on batteries. It can also be plugged into a personal computer for data transfer.

point (1) To move the cursor onto a line or image on screen by rolling a mouse across the desk or by pressing the arrow keys. (2) In typography, a unit equal to 1/72nd of an inch, used to measure the vertical height of a printed character.

point and shoot To select a menu option or activate a function by moving the cursor onto a line or object and pressing the return key or mouse button.

point of sale Capturing data at the time and place of sale. Point of sale systems use personal computers or specialized terminals that are combined with cash registers, optical scanners for reading product tags, and/or magnetic stripe readers for reading credit cards. Point of sale systems may be online to a central computer for credit checking and inventory updating, or they may be stand-alone machines that store the daily transactions until they can be delivered or transmitted to the main computer for processing.

pointer (1) In database management, an address embedded within the data that specifies the location of data in another record or file. (2) In programming, a variable that is used as a reference to the current item in a table (array) or to some other object, such as the current row or column on screen. (3) On-screen symbol used to identify menu selections or the current screen location. It is moved by a mouse or other pointing device.

pointing device Input device, such as a mouse or graphics tablet, used to move the cursor on screen or to draw an image.

Poisson distribution Statistical method developed by the 18th century French mathematician S. D. Poisson, which is used for predicting the probable distribution of a series of events. For example, when the average transaction volume in a communications systern can be estimated, Poisson distribution is used to determine the probable minimum and maximum number of transactions that can occur within a given time period.

poke See peek/poke.

polarity (1) Direction of charged particles, which may determine the binary status of a bit. (2) In micro- graphics, the change in the light to dark relationship of an image when copies are made. Positive polarity is dark characters on a light background; negative polarity is light characters on a dark background.

polarized One-way direction of a signal or the molecules within a material pointing in one direction.

Polish notation Method for expressing a sequence of calculations developed by the Polish logician Jan Lukasiewicz in 1929. For example, A(B+C) would be expressed as * A + B C. In reverse Polish notation, it would be A B C + .

polling Communications technique that determines when a terminal is ready to send data. The computer continually interrogates its connected terminals in a round robin sequence. If a terminal has data to send, it sends back an acknowledgement and the transmission begins. Contrast with interrupt- driven, in which the terminal generates a signal when it has data to send.

polling cycle One round in which each and every term inal connected to the computer or controller has been polled once.

polygon In computer graphics, a multi-sided object that can be filled with color or moved around as a single entity.

polyhedron Six- or more-sided object. A group of connected polygons.

polyline In computer graphics, a single entity that is made up of a series of connected lines.

polymorphic tweenlng Animation technique that, based on starting and ending shapes, creates the necessary 9n-between" frames to change one object into another.

polymorphism Meaning many shapes. In object-oriented programming, the ability of a generalized request (message) to produce different results based on the object that it is sent to.

Polyvlslon Flat panel display from Alpine Polyvision Inc. that uses a piastic film of metal ions sandwiched between horizontal and vertical electrodes. Where current intersects, the metal ions turn black.

pop See push/pop.

pop-down menu See pull-down menu.

populate To plug in chips or components into a printed circuit board. A fully populated board is one that contains all the devices it can hold.

popup (1) Type of menu called for and displayed on top of the existing text or image. When the item is selected, the menu disappears and the screen is restored. (2) Same as TSR.

port (1) Pathway into and out of the computer. The serial and parallel ports on a personal computer are external sockets for plugging in communications lines, modems and printers; however, the computer has several internal sockets (expansion slots) that accept control units for such devices as disk drives and video displays. (2) To convert software to run in a different computer environment.

port address Physical identification of an I/O port.

port expander Device that connects several lines to one port in the computer. A line is given access to the port either by a hardware switch or through software selection.

portability See portable.

portable Refers to software that can be easily moved from one type of machine to another. It implies a product that has a version for several hardware platforms or has built-in capabilities for switching between them. However, a program that can be easily converted from one machine type to another is also considered portable.

portable computer Personal computer that can be easily transported. Compared to desktop models, it has limited expansion slots and disk capacity. The first portable was the Osborne I, a CP/M machine that was soon followed by many others, such as the Kaypro and Otrona's Attache. In late 1982, Compaq introduced the first MSDOS portable. See laptop computer, notebook computer and pocket computer.

Portable NetWare OEM version (C source code) of Novell's NetWare operating system that can be compiled for a specific vendor's machine.

porting See port.

portrait Orientation in which the data is printed across the narrow side of the form.

positive logic Use of low voltage for a 0 bit and high voltage for a 1 bit. Contrast with negative logic.

POST (Power On Self Test) Series of built-in diagnostics that are performed when the computer is first started. Proprietary codes are generated (POST codes) that indicate test results. See diagnostic board.

postflx notation See reverse Polish notation.

postprocessor Software that provides some final processing to data, such as formatting it for display or printing.

PostScript Page description language from Adobe Systems, Inc., used in a wide variety of printers, imagesetters and display systems. PostScript commands do not drive the printer directly. They are language statements (ASCII text) that are translated into the printer'machine language by a PostScript interpreter built into the printer. Fonts are scaled to size by ,the interpreter, thus eliminating the need to store a variety of font sizes on disk. PostScript fonts come in Type 1 and Type 3 formats, and Adobe makes only Type 1. Type 1 fonts are widely used and are made by other companies as Adobe later made the format public. Type 1 fonts are encrypted and compressed and also allow for hints, which improve the appearance of text, especially at desktop laser printer resolutions. Type 1 fonts use a simpler, more efficient command language than Type 3. With Adobe 1'pe Manager, Type 1 fonts can also be used on nonPostScript printers. Typz 3 fonts do not use encryption or hints, but can use the entire PostScript language to create complex designs that include fills and patterns. Type 3 fonts can also be bitmaps. In order to speed up printing small fonts on PostScript printers, Windows 3.1 creates Type 3 bitmaps from its TrueType outlines. Originally developed as a device-independent imaging language, PostScript is used extensively on Macs and PCs. It has also migrated to workstations, minis and mainframes.

pot See potentiometer.

potentiometer Device that controls the amount of current that flows through a circuit, such as a volume switch on a radio.

power See computer power.

power down To turn off the computer in an orderly manner by making sure all applications have been closed normally and then shutting the power.

power supply Electrical system that converts AC current from the wall outlet into the DC currents required by the computer circuitry.

power up To turn the computer on in an orderly manner.

power user Person who is very proficient with personal computers. It implies knowledge of a variety of software packages.

PowerPC Proposed RISC chip from Motorola for IBM/ Apple's joint venture.

PowerPoint Macintosh desktop presentation program from Microsoft. It was the first desktop presentation program for the Mac and provides the ability to create output for overheads, handouts, speaker notes and film recorder. Color palettes for Genigraphics slides accompany the product.

PPGA (Plastic PGA) See PGA.

pph (Pages Per Hour) Measurement of printing speed.

ppm (Pages Per Minute) Measures the speed of a page printer, such as a laser printer.

PQFP (Plastic Quad FlatPack) Surface mount chip housing with flat leads on all four sides.

PRAM (Parameter RAM) Pronounced "P RAM." A battery-backed part of the Macintosh's memory that holds Control Panel settings and the specifications for the hidden desktop file. If the command and option keys are held down at startup, the desktop specifications are cleared and a dialog to rebuild the desktop is initiated.

precedence Order in which an expression is processed.

precision Number of digits used to express the fractional part of a number. The more digits, the more precision. See single precision and double precision.

predicate In programming, a statement that evaluates an expression and provides a true or false answer based on the condition of the data.

preemptive multitasking Multitasking that shares processing time with all running programs. For example, background programs can be given recurrent CPU time no matter how heavy the foreground load. Contrast with non-preemtive multitasking.

prefix notation See Polish notation.

prepress In typography and printing, the preparation of camera-ready materials up to the actual printing stage, which includes typesetting and page makeup.

preprocessor Software that performs some preliminary processing on the input before it is processed by the main program.

presentation graphics Business graphics, such as bar charts and graphs, that are used as presentation material in meetings and lectures. It implies the ability to create stylized graphics such as 3-D charts.

Presentation Manager Windows environment and graphical user interface that is built into OS/2. Similar to Windows for DOS, it allows users to keep applications open as multiple windows on screen and to command the computer with icons and a mouse.

pressure-sensitive keyboard A keyboard constructed of two thin plastic sheets coated with a circuit made of electrically conductive ink. An economical, flat keyboard used in several older, low-priced microcomputer.

pressure-sensitive pen The stylus used with a DIGITIZER. Contains a pressure transducer that detects and transmits writing pressure as Z-axis data.

preventive maintenance Routine checking of hardware that-is performed by a field engineer on a regularly scheduled basis. See remedial maintenance.

prhnary index The index that controls the current processing order of a file. See secondary index.

primary storage The computer's internal memory (RAM). Contrast with secondary storage.

primer An elementary instruction manual.

prImitive (1) In computer graphics, a graphics element that is used as a building block for creating images, such as a point, line, arc, cone or sphere. (2) In programming, a fundamental instruction, statement or operation. (3) in microprogramming, a microinstruction, or elementary machine operation.

print buffer See printer buffer.

print column Column of data on a printed report that may be subtotalled or totalled. Print columns are the heart of a report writer's description.

print engine See printer engine.

print head Mechanism that deposits ink onto paper in a character printer.

print image Text or graphics document that has been prepared for the printer. Format codes for the required printer have been embedded in the document at the appropriate places. With text files, headers, footers and page numbers have been created and inserted in every page.

print image format See print image.

print queue Disk space that holds output designated for the printer until the printer can receive it.

print screen Ability to print the current on-screen image. See screen dump.

print server Computer in a network that controls one or more printers. It stores the print-image output from all users of the system and feeds it to the printer one job at a time. This function may be part of the network operating system or an add-on utility.

print spooler Software that allows printing to take place in the background while other tasks are being performed in the foreground.

print to disk: To redirect output to the disk that is normally sent to a printer. The file that is created contains the text and all the required layout, or format, codes embedded within it. The file can be printed at a later date or at a remote location by transmitting it to the printer without requiring the word processor or desktop publishing program that created it. Actually all print jobs first create a disk file which is retreived by the printer. The print to disk process eliminates the last stage of actually printing the file.

print zone In BASIC programming, a fixed length area on an output device within which data are aligned in columns.

printed circuit board Fiat board that holds chips and other electronic components. The board is "printed" with electrically conductive pathways between the components. The main printed circuit board in a system, such as the motherboard, is called a board, while the smaller ones that plug into the slots in the main board are called boards or cards.

printer Device that converts computer output into printed images. The following is an overview of printer types. Serial printers print a character at a time and use dot matrix and character printer technologies. Serial printers are referred to as character printers regardless of the printing technology employed. Line printers print a line at a time and, due to their higher speeds, are the standard impact printers found in the datacenter. They use drum, chain, train, band, dot matrix and dot band technologies. Page printers, also called laser printers, print a page at time and generally use the copy machine electrophotographic technique. High-speed page printers are widely used in large datacenters, and desktop laser printers are now commonplace for personal computers. Color printers use impact dot matrix with multiple color ribbons, electrophotographic with multiple color toners, electrostatic plotters with multiple color toners and ink jet with multiple color inks.

Impact printers can use dot matrix, band, chain, train or drum printing techniques. Character printers are similar to Selectric typewriters, printing one character at a time by using a daisy wheel or similar mechanism. In a serial dot matrix printer, a vertical set of printing wires moves serially across the paper, formulating characters by impacting a ribbon and transferring dots of ink onto the paper. The clarity of the character is determined by how close the dots print together.

Non-impact printers use electrophotographic techniques where a drum is charged with a high voltage and an image source paints a negative light copy of the image to be printed onto the drum. Where the light falls onto the drum, the drum is discharged. A toner (ink) is allowed to adhere to the charged portion of the drum. The drum then fuses the image onto the paper by pressure and heat. See electrophotographic. They can a!so use electrosensitive techniques where dot are charged onto specially coated silver- colored paper, usually in a serial fashion. The charge removes the aluminum coating, leaving a black image. Other non-impact techniques are electrotatic, ink jet, ionographic, magnetographic and thermal techniques.

printer buffer Memory device that accepts printer output from one or more computers and transmits it to the printer. It lets the computërdisposeóf its printer output at full speed without waiting for each page to print. Printer buffers with automatic switching are connected to two or more computers and accept their output on a first-come, first-served basis.

printer cable Wire that connects a printer to a computer. On a PC, the cable has a 25-pin DB-25 male connector for the computer and a 36-pin Centronics male connector for the printer.

printer driver Software routine that converts an application program's printing request into the language the printer understands.

printer engine Unit within the printer that does the actual printing.

printer ifie (1) Document in print image format ready to be printed. See print to disk. (2) Same as printer driver.

printer font Font used for printing. Printer and screen resolutions are not the same, thus fonts generated for the printer will not display accurately on screen. Contrast with screen font.

printout (PRINTer OUTput) Same as hard copy.

PRN (PRiNter) DOS name for the first connected parallel port. See DOS device names.

problem-oriented language Computer language designed to handle a particular class of problem. For example, COBOL was designed for business, FORTRAN for scientific and GPSS for simulation.

problem solving The solving of a program by a computer. It need not be described by an exact mathematical equation, but it does need a certain set of rules that the computer can follow. If a solution to a problem depends upon intuition or guessing, or if a problem is badly defined, the computer cannot be used to solve it. A computer cannot perform tasks properly unless problems are specified correctly in every detail. The instructions must also list in complete detail each step of the solution.

procedural language Programming Janguage that requires programming discipline, such as COBOL, FORTRAN, BASIC, C,. Pascal and dBASE. Programmers writing in such languages mustdevelop a proper order of actions in.order to solve the. problem, based on a knowledge of data prbcessingand,prgramming. Contrast with non-procedural 1anguage'

procedure (1) Manual procedures are human tasks. (2) Machine procedures are lists of routines or programs to be executed, such as described by the job control language (JCL) in a mini or mainframe, or the batch processing language in a personal computer. (3) In programming, another term for a subroutine or function.

procedure oriented Application that forces the user to follow a predefined path from step A to step B. Data entry programs are typical examples. Contrast with event driven.

process To manipulate data in the computer. The computer is said to be processing no matter what action is taken upon the data. It may be updated or simply displayed on screen.

process bound Excessive amount of processing causing an imbalance between I/O and processing. Process-bound applications may slow down other users in a multiuser system. A personal computer is process bound when it is recalculating a spreadsheet, for example.

process control Automated control of a process, such as a manufacturing process or assembly line. It is used extensively in industrial operations, such as oil refining, chemical processing and electrical generation. It uses analog devices to monitor real-world signals and digital computers to do the analysis and controlling. It makes extensive use of analog/digital, digital/analog conversion.

processing Manipulating data within the computer. The term is used to define a variety of computer functions and methods. See centralized processing, distributed processing, batch processing, transaction processing, multiprocessing and computer.

processor (1) Same as CPU. (2) May refer to software. See language processor and word processor.

processor unit Same as computer.

Procomm Popular PC shareware communications program from Datastorm Technologies, that supports a wide number of protocols and terminals. Procomm Plus is the commercial version with more features.

ProDOS (PROfessional Disk Operating System) Operating system for the Apple II family that superseded Apple's DOS 3.3. It provides a hierarchical file system with file names up to 15 characters in length.

production database Central database containing an organization's master files and daily transaction files.

production system Computer system used to process an organization's daily work. Contrast with a system used only for development and testing or for ad hoc inquiries and analysis.

Professional Write Word processing program for DOS and Windows from Software Publishing Corp. It is easy to use and meets the needs of many who write uncomplicated letters and memos. Originally called PFS:Write, it was one of the earliest PC word processors.

program Collection of instructions that tell the computer what to do. A program is also called software; hence, program, software and instructions are synonymous. A program is written in a programming language and is converted into the computer's machine language by software called assemblers, compilers and interpreters.

program generator See application generator.

program logic Sequence of instructions in a program. There are many logical solutions to a problem. But the solution that runs the fastest is usually the most desired. Program logic is written using three classes of instructions: sequential processing, selection and iteration. 1: Sequential processing is the series of steps that do the actual data processing. Input, output, calculate and move (copy) instructions are used in sequential processing. 2. Selection is the decision making within the program and is performed by comparing two sets of data and branching to a different part of the program based on the results. In assembly languages, the compare and branch instructions are used. In high-level languages, IF THEN ELSE and CASE statements are used. 3. Iteration is the repetition of a series of steps and is accomplished with DO LOOPS and FOR LOOPS in high-level languages and GOTOs in assembly languages. See loop.

program maintenance Updating programs to reflect changes in the organization's business or to adapt to new operating environments. -

Program Manager Control center for Windows 3.x operation. It provides the means to launch applications and manage the desktop.

program state Operating mode of the computer that executes instructions in the application program. Contrast with supervisor state.

program statement Phrase in a high-level programming language. One program statement may result in several machine instructions when the program is compiled.

program step Elementary instruction, such as a machine language instruction or an assembly language instruction. Contrast with program statement.

programmable Capable of following instructions. What sets the computer apart from all other electronic devices is its programmability.

programmable calculator Limited-function computer capable of working with only numbers and not alphanumeric data.

programmatic interface Same as API.

programmer Person who designs the logic for and writes the lines of codes of a computer program. See application programmer and systems programmer.

programmer analyst Person who analyzes and designs information systems and designs and writes the application programs for the system. A programmer analyst is both systems analyst and applications programmer.

Programmer's Switch Physical buttons included with the Macintosh ((key on the LC) that include a System Reset button and a Debugging button that will invoke MacsBug if present or switch to the built in monitor in ROM.

programming Creating a computer program. The steps are:

1. Developing the program logic to solve the particular problem.
2. Writing the program logic in a specific programming language (coding the program).
3. Assembling/compiling the program- to turn it into machine language.

4. Testing and debugging the program.
5. Preparing the necessary documentation.

programming language

Language used to write instructions for the computer. It lets the programmer express data processing in a symbolic manner without regard to machine- specific details.. The statements that are written by the programmer are called source language or code, and they are translated into the computer's machine language by programs called assemblers, compilers and interpreters. Like human languages, each programming language has its own grammar and syntax. There are many dialects of the same language, and each dialect requires its own translating system. Each language is particularly suited to a particular type of situation or problem. FORTRAN and APL are used in scientific areas, and C is used extensively for commercial software. LISP and Prolog are used in Al applications and FORTH is used in process control. Standards have been set by ANSI for many programming languages, and ANSI-standard languages are dialect free. However, it can take years for new features to be included in ANSI standards, and new dialects inevitably spring up as a result.

Programming languages fall into two major categories: low-level assembly languages and high-level languages. Assembly languages are available for every CPU family, and each assembly instruction is translated into one machine instruction by the assembler program. With high-level languages, a programming statement may be translated into one or several machine instructions by the compiler. Today's popular high-level languages for business are BASIC, COBOL, dBASE and Pascal.

progressive scan Same as non-interlaced.

project manager Software used to monitor the time and materials on a project. All tasks to complete the project are entered into the database, and the program computes the critical path, the series of tasks with the least amount of slack time. Any change in the critical path slows down the entire project.

Prokey Keyboard macro processor for PCs from RoseSoft, that allows users to eliminate repetitive typing by setting up an occurrence of text or a series of commands as a macro.

Prolog (PROgramming in LOGic) Programming language used for developing Al applications (natural language translation, expert systems, abstract problem solving, etc.). Developed in France in 1973, it is used throughout Europe and Japan and is gaining popularity in the U.S. Similar to LISP, it deals with symbolic representations of objects.

PROM (Programmable Read Only Memory) Permanent memory chip that is programmed, or tilled, by the customer rather than by the chip manufacturer. Contrast with ROM, which is programmed at the time of manufacture. See PROM programmer.

PROM blower Same as PROM programmer.

PROM programmer Device that writes instructions and data into PROM and/or EPROM chips. The bits in a new PROM are all is (continuous lines). The PROM programmer only creates fu, by blowing" the middle out of the is. The bits in EPROMs, which are not permanently altered, can be erased under ultraviolet light and reprogrammed.

prompt Software message that requests action by the user. Command-driven systems issue a cryptic symbol when ready to accept a command; for example, in dBASE it is simply a dot (.), in UNIX, a $, and in DOS, the venerable C:\>.

proof (1) A trial copy of a page or publication used to check accuracy. (2) Short for proofread, meaning to check for mistakes.

proofing program Same as dictionary program or Spelling checker.

proofreader's marks In desktop publishing, a standard set of notations for indicating errors or corrections on a proof.

propagation Transmission (spreading) from one place to another.

propagation delay Time it takes to transmit a signal from one place to another.

proportional spacing Character spacing based on the width of each character. For example, an I takes up less space than an M. In monospacing (fixed), the I and M each take up the same space. See keming.

proprietary software Software owned by an organization or individual. Contrast with public domain softwares

Protected Mode In Intel 286s and up, an operational state that allows the computer to address all of memory. It also prevents one program from entering into the memory boundary of another, thus enabling multiple programs to run in a guarded environment. See Real Mode, Virtual 8086 Mode and memory protection.

protocol Rules governing transmitting and receiving of data. See communications protocol and OSI.

protocol stack Hierarchy of protocols used in a communications network. See OSI.

protocol suite Same as protocol stack.

prototyplng Creating a demo of a new system. It has become essential for clarifying information requirements. The design of a system (functional specs) must be finalized before the system can be built. Using fourth-generation languages, systems analysts and users can develop the new system together. Databases can be created and manipulated while the user monitors the progress. Once users see tangible output on screen or on paper, they can figure out what's missing or what the next question might be if this were a production system. If prototyping is carefully done, the end result can be a working system.

Prt Sc: See print screen.

PS/1 IBM home computer series introduced in 1990 that features an integrated monitor and easy-to-open case. Original models use the 286 CPU and PC bus. See PC.

P5/2 IBM personal computer series introduced in 1987 that supersedes the original PC line. It features the 3.5" microfloppy disk, VGA graphics and Micro Channel bus. The 3.5" disks and VGA are now commonly used in all PCs and the Micro Channel is offered by some PC-compatible vendors. Smaller PSI 2 models use the original PC bus. See Personal Computer.

PS/2 bus Same as Micro Channel.

pseudo compiler Compiler that generates a pseudo language, or intermediate language, which must be further compiled or interpreted for execution.

pseudo-duplexing Communications technique that simulates full-duplex transmission in a half-duplex line by turning the line around very quickly.

pseudo language Intermediate language generated from source language, but not yet executable. It has to be interpreted or compiled into machine language for execution. Since a large amount of the translation has already been done in the pseudo language, creating pseudo language compilers for new CPU architéctures is easier than creating source language compilers.

PSN 1) (Packet-Switched Network) Communications network that uses packet switching technology. (2) See Personal Server Network.

public domain software Software in which ownership has been relinquished to the public at large. See freeware and shareware.

public file File made available to all other users connected to the system or network.

Publish and Subscribe Macintosh System 7 capability that provides hot links between files. All or part of a file can be published into an "edition file," which is imported into a subscriber file. When any of the published files are updated, the subscriber file is also updated.

puck Puck-like tablet cursor used on a digitizer tablet.

pull-down menu Also called a pop-down menu, a screen menu that is displayed from the top of the screen downward when its title is selected. The menu remains displayed while the mouse button is depressed. To select a menu option, the highlight bar is moved (with the mouse or the keyboard cursor keys) to the appropriate line and the mouse button is let go. The drop-down menu is a variation that keeps the menu open after its title is selected. To select a menu option, the highlight bar is moved to the ine and the mouse button is clicked. Key commands may also activate drop-down menus.

punched card Early storage medium made of thin cardboard stock that holds data as patterns of punched holes. Each of the 80 or 96 columns holds one character. The holes are punched by a keypunch machine or card punch peripheral and are fed into the computer by a card reader.

push/pop: Instructions that store and retrieve an item on a stack. Push enters an item on the stack, and pop rettieves an item, moving the rest of the items in the stack up one level. See stack.

push/pull tractor Printer tractor that can be switched from pushing paper onto the platen to pulling it from the platen. Single-sheet continuous forms can be pushed, but most multipart forms and labels must be pulled to prevent jamming.

put In programming, a request to store the current record in an output file. Contrast with get.

PVGA (Paradise VGA) VGA display board or VGA chips from Paradise Division of Western Digital.

Page: A unit of disk storage. In DB2, a 4K block of contiguous disk space used to hold the database, data dictionary, and overhead data.

Paired attribute: In a semantic object, object attributes are paired. If object A has an object attribute of object B, then object B will have an object attribute of object A; that is, the object attributes are paired with each other.

Parent: A row, record, or node on the one side of a one-to-many relationship.

Partition: (1) A portion of a distributed database. (2) The portion of a network that is separated from the rest of the network during a network failure.

Partitioned table space: In DB2, a table space that holds data for exactly one table.

Pathologically Eclectic Rubbish Lister: The programming language PERL, also known as Practical Extraction and Report Language.

PDBR: See Physical data base record.

PERL: The Practical Extraction and Report Language. An interpreted programming language developed by Larry Wall and originally for UNIX. PERL interpreters are now available for Windows and Macintosh. Often used for server programs on the Internet and on intranets.

Persistent object: An OOP object that has been written to persistent storage.

Pervasive key: In a database application, a key that performs the same function throughout the application. The meaning of the key always remains the same.

Physical data base record (PDBR): In DL/I, a hierarchy of segments stored in data base files.

Physical key: A column that has an index or other data structure created for it. A synonym for an index. Such structures are created to improve searching and sorting on the column values.

Pointer: An address to an instance of a data structure. The address of a record often is in a directly addressed file.

Polymorphism: In OOP, the situation in which one name can be used to invoke different functions. Polymorphism in which the functions are dlistinguished by having different parameter sequences is called parametric polymorphism. For it, names are resolved by the compiler at compile time. Polymorphism in which the functions are distinguished by object inheritance is called inheritance polymorphism. Such names are resolved at run time by determining the type of object being invoked.

Pop-down list box: In a GUI environment, the list box that appears when the user selects an icon that represents that box.

Precompiler: A program that translates the database access commands of a particular DBMS product. Such commands are embedded in an application program normally written in a third-generation language. The commands are translated into data structures and calls to DBMS-processing routines in the syntax of the third-generation language.

Primary key: A candidate key selected to be the key of a relation.

Processing-interface subsystem: The portion of the DBMS routines that executes commands for processing the database. It accepts input from interactive query programs and from application programs written in standard languages or in DBMS-specific languages.

Processing rights and responsibilities: Organizational policies regarding which groups can take which actions on specified data-items or other collections of data.

Product: A relational operation on two relations, A and B, producing a third relation, C, with C containing the concatenation of every row in A with every row in B. It is the same as a Cartesian product.

Program/data independence: The condition existing when the structure of the data is not defined in application programs. Rather, it is defined in the database, and then the application programs obtain it from the DBMS. In this way, changes can be made in the data structures that may not necessarily be made in the application programs.

Projection: A relational algebra operation performed on a relation, A, that results in a relation, B, where B has a (possibly improper) subset of the attributes of A. Projection is used to form a new relation that reorders the attributes in the original relation or to form a new relation that has only some of the attributes from the original relation.

Property: Same as an Attribute.

Proponent: See Data proponent.

Prototype: A quickly developed demonstration of an application or portion of an application.

Q

Q&A Integrated PC file manager and word processor from Symantec Corp., that includes mail merge capability as well as a programming language for customizing data entry forms and reports. Its Intelligent Assistant feature provides a query language that can learn new words from the user.

QBasic BASIC interpreter from Microsoft that comes with DOS 5.0 (both PC-DOS and MS-DOS). It supersedes Microsoft's GW-BASIC.

QBE (Query By Example) Method for describing a query originally developed by IBM for mainframes. A replica of an empty record is displayed and the search conditions are typed in under their respective columns.

QEMM-386 (Quarterdeck EMM-386) Popular DOS memory manager for 386s and up from Quarterdeck Office Systems. Its Stealth feature in Version 6.0 remaps ROM BIOS routines into EMS to free up high DOS memory. It is also part of DESQview 386. QEMM-50/60 is a version for PS/2 Models 50 and 60 (286s).

quadblt Group of four bits used in QAM modulation.

quadrillion One thousand times one billion. See femtosecond.

quantize To break into discrete values for sampling purposes.

QuarkXpress Desktop publishing program for the Macintosh and Windows from Quark. Originally developed for the Mac, it is noted for its precise typographic control and advanced text and graphics manipulation.

quartz crystal Slice of quartz ground to a prescribed thickness that vibrates at a steady frequency when stimulated by electricity. The tiny crystal, about 1/ 20th by 1/5th of an inch, creates the computer's heartbeat.

Quattro Pro PC spreadsheet from Borland that provides advanced graphics and presentation capabilities. It has an optional interface that is keystroke, macro and file compatible with Lotus 1-2-3. Version 2.0 adds goal seeking, 3-D graphing and the ability to create multi-ayered slide shows.

query To interrogate a database (count, sum and list selected records). Contrast with report, which is usually a more elaborate printout with headings and page numbers. The report may also be a selective list of items; hence, the two terms may refer to programs that produce the same results.

query by example See QBE.

query language Generalized language that allows a user to select records from a database. It uses a command language, menu-driven method or a query by example (QBE) format for expressing the matching condition. Query languages are usually included in DBMSs, and stand-alone packages are available for interrogating files in non-DBMS applications. See query program.

query program Software that counts, sums and retrieves selected records from a database. It may be part of a large application and be limited to one or two kinds of retrieval, such as pulling up a customer account on screen, or it may refer to a query language that allows any condition to be searched and selected.

queue Pronounced "Q." Temporary holding place for data in memory or on disk. See message queue and print queue.

queuing theory A form of probability theory useful in studying delays or lineups at servicing points;

a research technique concerned with the correct sequential orders of moving units. May include sequence assignments for bits of informations or whole messages.

QuickBASIC Popular BASIC compiler from Microsoft that adds advanced features to the BASIC language.

QuickC C compiler from Microsoft that is compatible with its larger C compiler and is used by the beginner or occasional programmer. QuickC for Windows is a version that works entirely within Windows environment for developing Windows applications. It includes the QuickWin library.

QuIckdraw Graphics display system built into the Macintosh. It accepts commands from the application and draws the corresponding objects on the screen. It provides a consistent interface that software developers can work with.

QulckPascal Pascal compiler from Microsoft that is compatible with Turbo Pascal and provides object oriented capabilities.

Quicksilver dBASE III PLUS compiler from WordTech Systems, Inc., that adds scrolling text windows to the dBASE language. The Quicksilver/UNIX version translates dBASE source code into the UNIX environment, and Oracle Quicksilver allows dBASE commands to manage an Oracle database.

QuickTime Multimedia extensions to Macintosh's System 7 that add sound and video capabilities.

QuickWin Library of C and FORTRAN routines from Microsoft that allows quick porting of DOS applications to the Windows environment. Character-based apps run in resizable windows.

quit To exit the current program. It's a good habit to quit a program before turning the computer off. Some programs don't close all files properly until quit is activated.

qwerty keyboard Standard English language typewriter keyboard. Q, w, e, r, t and y are the first letters starting at the top left, alphabetic row. It was originally designed to slow down the typist to prevent the keys from jamming. See Dvorak keyboard.

QBE: Query by example. A style of query interface, first developed by IBM but now used by other vendors, that allows users to express queries by providing examples of the results they seek.

Query Interface: An interface in ActiveX (and Microsoft COM) that can be used to determine the objects, methods, and properties supported by an ActiveX program.

Query/update language: A language that can be employed by end users to query the database and to make changes in the database data.

R

R3000, R4000 Families of 32-bit and 64-bit RISC processors from MIPS. MIPS licenses the design to other companies.

RBASE Relational DBMS for PCs from Microrim, that provides interactive data processing, a complete programming language and an application generator. It was the first DBMS to compete with dBASE II in the early 1980s.

rack Frame or cabinet into which components are mounted.

rack mounted Components that are built to fit in a metal frame. Electronic devices, such as testing equipment and tape drives, and industrial computers, are often rack mounted units.

RAD (Rapid Application Development) Approach to systems development that incorporates a variety of automated design tools (CASE). Developed by James Martin, it focuses on human management and user involvement as much as on technology.

radio Transmission of electromagnetic energy (radiation) over the air or throtigh a hollow tube called a waveguide. Although radio is often thought of as only AM or FM, all airborne transmission is radio, including satellite and line-of-sight microwave.

radio buttons Series of on-screen buttons that allow only one selection. If a button is currently selected, it will de-select when another button is selected.

radio frequency See RF.

radix Base value in a numbering system. For example, in the decimal numbering system, the radix is 10.

radix point Location in a number that separates the integral part from the fractional part. For example, in the decimal system, it is the decimal point.

ragged right In typography, non-uniform text at the right margin, such as manual typewriter text.

RAID (Redundant Arrays of Inexpensive Disks) Cluster of disks in which data is copied onto multiple drives. It provides faster throughput, fault tolerance (mirroring) and error correction.

RAM (Random Access Memory) Computer's primary workspace. Although true of most memory chips (ROMs, PROMs, etc.), "random" means that the contents of each byte can be directly accessed without regard to the bytes before or after it. RAM chips require power to maintain their content. See dynamic RAM, static RAM and memory.

RAM cache See cache.

RAM card (1) Printed circuit board containing memory chips that is plugged into a socket within the computer. (2) Credit-card-sized module that contains memory chips and battery for palmtops. See memory card.

RAM chip (Random Access Memory chip) Memory chip See dynamic RAM, static RAM, RAM and memory.

RAM cram Insufficient memory to run applications, especially in DOS PCs with its 1MB memory limit.

RAM disk Disk drive temporarily simulated in memory. I/O that normally goes to the magnetic disk is diverted to the RAM disk. Processing is speeded up, because there's no mechanical disk action, only memory transfers. However, if the power fails, all the updated data in the RAM disk will be lost. Same as E-disk and virtual disk.

RAM refresh Recharging dynamic RAM chips many times per second in order to keep the bit patterns valid.

RAM resIdent Refers to programs that remain in memory in order to interact with other programs or to be instantly popped up when required by the user. See TSR.

RAMDAC (Random Access Memory Digital to Analog Converter) The VGA controller chip that maintains the color palette and converts data from memory into analog signals for the monitor.

Ramdrive See DOS RAM disks.

random access Same as direct access.

random noise Same as Gaussian noise.

random number generator Program routine that produces a random number. Random numbers are created easily in a computer, since there are many random events that take place; for example, the duration between keystrokes. Only a few milliseconds' difference is enough to seed a random number generation routine with a different number each time. Once seeded, an algorithm computes different numbers throughout the session.

range (1) In data entry validation, a group of values from a minimum to a maximum. (2) In spreadsheets, a series of cells that are worked on as a group. It may refer to a row, column or rectangular block defined by one corner and its diagonally opposite corner.

raster display Display terminal that generates dots line by line on the screen. TVs and almost all computer screens use the raster method. Contrast with vector display.

raster fill The process used by a graphics camera to fill in the spaces between the raster lines of a video screen to give a screen picture a more finished appearance.

raster graphics In computer graphics, a technique for representing a picture image as a matrix of dots. It is the digital counterpart of the analog method used in TV See graphics. Contrast with vector graphics.

raster Image processor See RIP.

raster scan Displaying or recording a video image line by line.

rasterization of vectors Conversion of graphic objects made up of vectors, or line segments, into dots for output to raster graphics screens, dot matrix and laser printers. Unless vector graphics terminals and plotters are used, all object-oriented graphics must be converted to raster images for display and printing. See font scaler.

rat's nest The feature on printed circuit design systems that allows users to view all the computer-determined interconnections between components. This makes it easier to determine whether further component placement improvement is necessary to optimize signal routing.

raw data Data that has not been processed.

ray tracing In computer graphics, the creation of reflections, refractions and shadows on a graphics image. It follows a series of rays from a specific light source and computes each pixel in the image to determine the effect of the light. It is a very processintensive oneration.

RBASE See R:BASE.

RCA connector Same as phono connector.

RDBMS (Relational DataBase Management System). See relational database.

read To input into the computer from a peripheral device (disk, tape, etc.). Like reading a book or playing an audio tape, reading does not destroy what is read. A read is both an input and an output (I/O), since data is being output from the peripheral device and input into the computer. Memory is also said to be read when it is accessed to transfer data out to a peripheral device or to somewhere else in memory. Every peripheral or internal transfer of data is a read from somewhere and a write to somewhere else.

read error Failure to read the data on a storage or memory device. Although it is not a routine phenomenon, magnetic and optical recording surfaces can become contaminated with dust or dirt or be physically damaged, and cells in memory chips can malfunction.

read only (1) Refers to storage media that permanently hold their content; for example, ROM and CD ROM. (2) File which can be read, but not updated or erased. This is done by changing the file attribute.

read-only attribute File attribute that, when turned on, indicates that a file can only be read, but not updated or erased.

read/write (1) Refers to a device that can both input and output or transmit and receive. (2) Refers to a file that can be updated and erased.

read/write channel Same as I/O channel.

read/write head Device that reads (senses) and writes (records) data on a magnetic disk or tape. For writing, the surface of the disk or tape is moved past the read/write head. By discharging electrical impulses at the appropriate times, bits are recorded as tiny, magnetized spots of positive or negative polarity. For reading, the surface is moved past the read/write head, and the bits that are present induce an electrical current across the gap.

read/write memory Same as RAM.

reader Machine that captures data for the computer, such as an optical character reader, magnetic card reader and punched card reader. A microfiche or microfilm reader is a self-contained machine that reads film and displays its contents.

readme file Text file copied onto software distribution disks that contains last-minute updates or errata that have not been printed in the documentation manual.

readout (1) Small display device that typically shows only a few digits or a couple of lines of data. (2) Any display screen or panel.

real address Same as absolute address.

Real Mode Operational state in Intel 286s and up in which the computer functions as an 8086/8088. It is limited to one megabyte of memory. See Protected Mode and Virtual 86 Mode.

real storage Real physical memory in a virtual memory system.

realtime (1) Immediate response. The term may refer to fast transaction processing systems in business; however, it is always used to refer to process control applications. (2) Any electronic operation that is performed in the same timeframe as its real-world counterpart. Realtime video transmission produces a live broadcast.

realtime clock Electronic circuit that maintains the time of day. It may also provide timing signals for timesharing operations.

realtime compression Quickly compressing and decompressing data. PC products such as Stacker, SuperStor and DBLSpace (Dos 6.0) let you allocate some amount of hard disk space to create a compressed drive. Any data written on that drive by any program is compressed and decompressed when read back. See JPEG.

realtime conferencing See teleconferencing (3).

realtime image In computer graphics, a graphics image that can be animated on screen in the same time frame as in real life.

realtime Information system Computer system that responds to transactions by immediately updating the appropriate master files and/or generating a response in a time frame fast enough to keep an operation moving at its required speed. See transaction processing.

realtime operating system Master control program that can provide immediate response to input signals and transactions.

realtime system Computer system that responds to input signals fast enough to keep an operation moving at its required speed.

reasonableness check A technique whereby tests are made on processed data to indicate whether a gross data exists. Programming instructions would check if the data lies within preset upper and lower limits and initiate some action if the data are not reasonable. See DATA EDITING.

reasonable test Type of test that determines if a value falls within a range considered normal or logical. It can be made on electronic signals to detect extraneous noise as well as on data to determine possible input errors.

reboot To reload the operating system and restart the computer. See boot.

receiver Device that accepts signals. Contrast with transmitter.

record (1) Group of related fields that store data about a subject (master record) or activity (transaction record). A collection of records make up a file. Master records contain permanent data, such as account number, and variable data, such as balance due. Transaction records contain only permanent data, such as quantity and product code. (2) In a data organization method, a block of data that is read and written at one time, which has no relationship to records in a data processing system.

record format Same as record layout.

record layout Format of a data record, which includes the name, type and size of each field in the record.

record locking See file and record locking.

record mark Symbol used to identify the end of a record. record number Sequential number assigned to each physical record in a file. Record numbers change when the file is sorted or records are added and deleted.

records management Creation, retention and scheduled destruction of an organization's paper and film documents. Computer- generated reports and documents fall into the records management domain, but traditional data processing files do not.

rectifier Electrical circuit that converts AC into DC current with the use of diodes that act as one-way valves. Contrast with inverter.

recto The right hand (odd-numbered) page in a two sided printing of a book or document.

recursion In programming, the ability of a subroutine or program module to call itself. It is helpful for writing routines that solve problems by repeatedly processing the output of the same process.

redirection Diverting data from its normal destination to another; for example, to a disk file instead of the printer, or to a server's disk instead of the local disk. See DOS redirection and redirector.

redirector In a LAN, software that routes worbtation requests for data to the server.

redundancy check In communications, a method for detecting transmission errors by appending a calculated number onto the end of each segment of data. See CRC.

reentrant code Programming routine that can be used by multiple programs simultaneously. It is used in operating systems and other system software as well as in multithreading, where concurrent events are taking place. It is written so that none of its code is modifiable (no values are changed) and it does not keep track of anything. The calling programs keep track of their own progress (variables, flags, etc.), thus one copy of the reentrant routine can be shared by an any number of users or processes.

referential Integrity In relational database management, a built-in safeguard that ensures every foreign key matches a primary key.

reflection mapping In computer graphics, a technique for simulating reflections on an object.

reflective spot Metallic foil placed on each end of a magnetic tape. Light is shined onto the tape and re[lected back to a photosensor, signalling the end of tape.

reformat (1) To change the record layout of a file or database. (2) To initialize a disk over again.

refraction Bending of light, heat or sound as it passes through different materials.

refresh To continously charge a device that cannot hold its content. For example, CRTs must be constantly refreshed, because the color phosphors hold their glow for only a few milliseconds. Dynamic memory chips (DRAMs) require constant refreshing to maintain their charged bit patterns.

refresh rate (1) Number of times per second that a device is re- energized, such as a CRTor dynamic RAM chip. (2) In computer graphics, the time it takes to redraw or redisplay an image on screen.

regenerator (1) In communications, the same as a repeater. (2) In electronics, a circuit that repeatedly supplies current to a memory or display device that continuously loses its charges or content.

register Small, high-speed circuit that holds addresses and values of internal operations. For example, registers keep track of the address of the instruction being executed and the data being processed. When an assembly language program is debugged, register contents are displayed to determine the computer's status at the time of failure. In microcomputer assembly language programming, registers are referenced for routine functions, such as calculating and moving data within memory. Assembly languages in larger computers are often at a higher level.

register level compatibility Hardware component that is 100% compatible with another device. It implies that the same type, size and names of registers are used.

related files Two or more data files that can be matched on some common condition, such as account number or name.

relational algebra (1) Branch of mathematics that deals with: relations for example, AND, OR, NOT, IS and CONTAINS. (2) In relational database, a collection of rules for dealing with tables; for example, JOIN, UNION and INTERSECr.

relational calculus Rules for combining and manipulating relations; for example Dc Morgan's law, "the complement of a union is equal to the union of the complements."

relational database Database organization method that links files together as required. In non-relational systems (hierarchical), records in one file point to the locations of records in another. These links are set up ahead of time in order to provide fast daily processing. However, in a relational database, relationships between files are created by comparing data. A relational system can take any two or more files and genërate a new file from the records that meet the matching criteria. Routine queries often involve more than one data file. In practice, a pure relational query can be very slow. In order to speed up the process, indexes are built and maintained on the key fields used for matching. Sometimes, indexes are created whenever the data is requested. Although relational database became a popular buzzword in the mid 1980s, the term was coined in 1970 by Edgar Codd, whose objective was to easily accomodate a user's ad hoc request for selected data.

relational operator A symbol that specifies a comparison between two values.

Relational	*Operator*	*Symbol*
EQ	Equal to	=
GT	Greater than	>
GE	Greater than or equal to	>=
NE	Not equal to	<> or# or!
LE	Less than or equal to	<=
LT	Less than	<

relational spreadsheet See spreadsheet.

relative address Address that is relative to the first location of the program rather than a fixed location of memory. It is added to the base address in order to derive the absolute address, the actual location of the data. See relocatable code and base/displacement.

relative vector In computer graphics, a vector with end points designated in relative coordinates. Contrast with absolute vector.

relay Electrical switch used to allow a small current to control a larger one. The small current energizes the relay, which then closes a gate, allowing the large current to flow through.

relocatable code Machine architecture that allows programs to reside anywhere in memory. It is accomplished with a relative addressing scheme in which the hardware increments the addresses of the ma chine instructions at runtime. The increment is the starting location where the program was loaded.

REM (REMarks) Programming language statement used to document the program and contains no executable code. Can be used in Batch files or in BASIC source code.

remedial maintenance Repair service that is required due to a malfunction of the product. Contrast with preventive maintenance.

remote access software See remote control software. remote batch See RJE.

remote communications (1) Communicating via long distances. (2) See remote control software.

remote control software Software that allows a user at one computer to interact with a computer in a different location as if the remote computer were the local machine. One part of the program resides in the local machine and another resides in the remote. Commonly used by technical personnel to help users with support problems, it is also used to perform a function on a remote machine that the remote user cannot do.

remote job entry See RJE.

removable disk Disk unit that is inserted into its respective disk drive for reading and writing and removed when not required. Floppy disks and disk cartridges are removable disk media.

render To draw a real-world object as it actually appears.

rendering In computer graphics, creating a 3-D image that incorporates the simulation of lighting effects, such as shadows and reflection.

repagination A process in which a page layout or word processing program adjusts a multipage document as it is revised to ensure uniform page length and appearance.

repeater In communications, a device that amplifies or regenerates the data signal in order to extend the distance of the transmission. It is used in LANs.

repeating decimal number A nonterminating decimal number, such as .3333333... or 31282828....

repertofre A complete set of instructions that belongs to a specific computer or family of computers. Also called INSTRUCI'ION SET.

report Printed or microfilmed collection of facts and figures with page numbers and page headings. In a DBMS or file manager, the report option is typically used to prepare any kind of printed output, including mailing labels. See query.

report tile File that describes how a report is printed. report format Layout of a report showing page and column headers, page numbers and totals.

report generator Same as report writer.

report writer Software that prints a report based on a description of the layout. As a stand-alone program or part of a DBMS, it retrieves selected records from a file and may sort them into a new sequence before printing. A report is designed by entering text for the page header, identifying the print columns (data fields) and indicating which columns are totalled or subtotalled. Once created, it is stored in a report file for future use. Developed in the early 1970s, report writers, or report generators as they were originally called, were the precursor to today's query languages and were the first programs to generate computer output without having to be programmed.

reprographics Duplicating printed materials using various kinds of printing presses and high-speed copiers.

reserved word Verb or noun in a programming or command language that describes some action or object. Reserved words cannot be used for user-defined variables and may or may not be used as field names.

reset button Computer button or key that reboots the computer. All current activities are stopped cold, and any data in meliory is lost. On a printer, the reset button clears the printer's memory and readies it to accept new data from the computer.

resident module The part of a program that must remain in memory at all times. Instructions and data that stay in memory can be accessed instantly.

resident program Program that remains in memory at all times. See TSR.

resistor Electronic component that resists the flow of current in an electronic circuit.

resolution Degree of sharpness of a displayed or printed character or image. On screen, resolution is expressed as a matrix of dots. A 640x480 resolution means 640 dots across each of 480 lines. The same resolution looks sharper on a small screen than a large one. For printers, resolution is expressed as the number of dots per linear inch. A 300 dpi resolution means 90,000 dots per square inch (300x300).

resource fork Resource part of a Macintosh file. For example, in a text document, it contains format codes with offsets into the text in the data fork. In a program, it contains executable code, menus, windows, dialog boxes, buttons, fonts and icons.

response time Time it takes for the computer to comply with a user's request, such as looking up a customer record.

restart To resume computer operion after a planned or unplanned termination. See boot, warm boot and checkpoint/restart.

restricted function Computer or operating system function that cannot be used by an application program.

retrieve To call up data that has been stored in a computer system. When a user queries a database, the data is retrieved into the computer first and then transmitted to the screen.

return key Also called the Enter key, the large key on the right side of the keyboard. In data entry operations, it is used to end the line of input and signal the computer to process it. In word processing, it ends the line or paragraph and inserts a return code into the document. It is not used like a typewriter return key to end lines within a paragraph. The computer wraps words to the next line automatically. See CR.

reusabillty Ability to use all or the greater part of the same programming code or system design in another application.

reverse engineer To isolate the components of a completed system. When a chip is reverse engineered, all the separate circuits that make up the chip are identified.

reverse polish notation Mathematical expression in which the numbers precede the operation. For example, 2 + 2 would be expressed as 22+, and 10 -3 * 4 would be 10 3 4 * -. See FORTH.

reverse video Display mode used to highlight characters on screen. For example, if the normal display mode is black on white, reverse video would be white on black.

revision level See version number.

RF (Radio Frequency) Range of electromagnetic frequencies above the audio range and below visible light. All broadcast transmission, from AM radio to satellites, falls into this range, which is between 30KHz and 300GHz.

RF/ID (Radio Frequency/IDentification) Identification system that uses tags that transmit a wireless message. The tags derive their power from a hand- held gun/reading unit.

RF modulation Refers to transmitting a signal through a carrier frequency. Some home computers and all VCRs provide RF modulation of a TV channel, typically Channel 3 or 4, to allow connection to the antenna inputs of a TV that does not have separate video inputs.

RD shielding Material that prohibits electromagnetic radiation from penetrating it.

RD (Radio Frequency Interference) High-frequency electromagnetic waves that eminate from electronic devices such as chips.

RGB (Red Green Blue) Method of recording and generating colors in a video system. On a TV or color monitor, colors are displayed as varying intensities of red, green and blue dots. When red, green and blue are all turned on high, white is produced. As the intensities are equally lowered, shades of gray are produced. When all dots are turned off, the base color of the screen appears. Color printing uses the CMY or CMYK (Cyan Magenta Yellow blacK) system for mixing colors. In RGB, colors are added to create white. In CMY, colors are subtracted to create white. See colors.

RGB monitor (1) Video display screen that requires separate red, green and blue signals from the computer. It generates a higher-quality image than composite signals, in which the three colors are transmilled together (standard TV). It comes in both analog and digital varieties. (2) Often refers to a monitor that accepts CGA signals (digital).

ribbon cable Thin, flat, multiconductor cable that is widely used in electronic systems; for example, to interconnect peripheral devices to the computer internally.

right justify Same as flush right.

ring One stage or level in a set of prioritized stages or levels, typically involved with security and password protection.

ring network Communications network that connects terminals and computers in a continuous loop.

RIP (Raster Image Processor) In computer graphics, the component (hardware, software or both) that prepares data for a raster output device, which is typically a printer. RIPs are designed for a specific type of input, such as vectors, PostScript as well as different raster data.

RISC (Reduced Instruction Set Computer) Computer architecture that reduces the complexity of the chip by using simpler instructions. RISC compilers have to generate software routines to perform complex instructions that were previously done in hardware by CISC computers. In RISC, the microcode layer and associated overhead is eliminated. RISC keeps instruction size constant, bans the indirect addressing mode and retains only those instructions that can be effectively overlapped and made to execute in one machine cycle or less. The RISC chip is speedier than its CISC counterpart and is designed faster and built more economically.

RISC Systein/6000 See RS/6000.

robo stick An input device used to manipulate the cursor and to create graphics.

robot Stand-alone system that can perform physical and computational activities. It is a multiple-motion device with one or more arms and joints that is capable of performing many different tasks like a human. It is used extensively in manufacturing for welding, riveting, scraping and painting. Robots, designed with Al, can respond to unstructured situations. For example, specialized robots can identify objects in a pile, select the objects in the appropriate sequence and assemble them into a unit. Robots use analog sensors for recognizing objects in the real world and digital computers for their direction. Analog to digital converters convert temperature, motion, pressure, sound and images into binary code for the robot's computer. The outputs of the computers direct the physical actions of the arms and joints by pulsing their motors.

robotIcs Art and science of the creation and use of robots.

robust Refers to a solid program that works properly under all normal and most abnormal conditions.

rollback A system that will restart the running program after a system failure. Snapshots of data and programs are stored at periodic intervals, and the system rolls back to restart at the last recorded snapshot.

ROM (Read Only Memory) Memory chip that permanently stores instructions and data. Its contents are created at the time of manufacture and cannot be altered. Used extensively to store control routines in personal computers (ROM BIOS) and in peripheral controllers, it is also used in plug-in cartridges for printers, video games and other systems. See PROM, EPROM and EEPROM.

ROM BIOS (ROM Basic Input Output System) Instructions contained in a ROM chip that activate peripheral devices in a PC. It includes routines for the keyboard, screen, disk, parallel and serial port and for internal services such as time and date. It accepts requests from the device drivers in the operating systern as well as from application programs. It also contains autostart functions that test the system on startup and prepare the computer for operation. It searches for other BIOS's on the plug-in boards and sets up pointers (interrupt vectors) in memory to access BIOS routines. It loads the operating system and passes control to it.

ROM BIOS swapping Alternating areas in the UMA (640K-1M) between ROM BIOSs and applications as needed.

ROM card Credit-card-sized module that contains permanent software or data. See memory card.

ROMable Machine language capable of being programmed into a ROM chip. Being "read only" the chip cannot be updated and ROMable programs must use RAM or disk for holding changing data.

ROM cartridge A plug in module that contains software permanently stored in ROM; a method of entering data and/or programs into a computer. The module can contain one or more printer fonts, programs, games, or other information.

ROM stimulator A general-purpose device used to replace ROMs and PROMs in a system during program checkout. Because it offers real-time in-circuit stimulation, it can be used in the engineering prototype or reproduction model to find and correct program errors, or in the production model to add new features.

round-off error The error resulting from rounding off a quantity by deleting the less significant digits and applying theappropriate rule of correction to the part retained; for example, 0.275 1 can be rounded to 0.275 with a round-off error of 0.0001, or rounded to 0.28 with a round-off error of 0.0049.

root directory In hierarchical file systems, the starting point in the hierarchy. When the computer is first started, the root directory is the current directory. Access to directories in the hierarchy requires naming the directories that are in its path. See path.

rotational delay Amount of time it takes for the disk to rotate until the required location on the disk reaches the read/write head.

router In communications, a device that examines the destination address of a message and selects the most effective route. It is used in complex networks where there are many pathways between users. See bridge, gateway and brouter.

routine Set of instructions that perform a task. Same as subroutine, module, procedure and function.

row Horizontal set of data or components. In a graph, it is called the x-axis. Contrast with column.

rpm (Revolutions Per Minute) Used to measure the speed of a disk drive. Floppy disks rotate at 300 rpm, while hard disks rotate at 2,400 to 3,600 rpm.

RPN See reverse polish notation.

RS-170 NThC standard for composite video signals.

RS-232-C EIA standard for a serial interface between computers and peripheral devices (modem, mouse, etc.). It uses a 25-pin DB-25 or 9-pin DB-9 connector. RS-232 defines the purposes, electrical characteristics and timing of the signals for each of the 25 lines.

RS-422, RS-423, RS-449 EIA standards for serial interfaces that extend distances and speeds beyond RS 232.

RS/6000 (RISC System/6000) IBM family of RISC- based workstations introduced in 1990.

RSI (Repetitive Strain Injury) Ailments of the hands, neck, back and eyes due to computer use. The remedy for RSI is frequent breaks which should include stretching or yoga postures. See carpal tunnel syndrome.

RTS (Request To Send) RS-232 signal sent from the transmitting station to the receiving station requesting permission to transmit. Contrast with CTS.

rubber banding In computer graphics, the moving of a line or object where one end stays fixed in position.

rubout key Keyboard key on a terminal that deletes the last character that was entered.

rule-based expert system Expert system based on a set of rules that a human expert would follow in diagnosing a problem. Contrast with model-based expert system.

ruler line Graphic representation of a ruler on screen that is used for laying out text and graphics.

rules (1) Set of conditions or standards which have been agreed upon. (2) In printing, horizontal and vertical lines between columns or at the top and bottom of a page in order to enhance the appearance of the page.

run (1) To execute a program. (2) Single or multiple programs scheduled for execution.

run around In desktop publishing, the flowing of text around a graphic image.

run length limited See RLL.

run on top of To run as the control program to some other program, which is subordinate to it. Contrast with run under.

run time See runtime;

run under To run within the control of a higher-level program. Contrast with run on top of.

runtirne Refers to the actual execution of a program.

runtime version Software that enables another program (or DOS) to execute files developed with the application. For example, a runtime version of a DBMS allows the programs to be run on computers that don't have the DBMS installed.

Radio button: In a GUI environment, an element of the user interface in which the user can select one item from a list. Clicking on one button de-selects the button currently pressed (if any). It operates like the radio buttons on a car radio.

Read—write conflict: The situation in which two actions operate on the same data item. One of the actions is a read, and the other is a write.

Real output: Output transmitted to the client of an information system, such as an order confirmation. When produced in error, such outputs cannot be changed by recovering the database. Instead, compensating transactions must be executed.

Record: (1) A group of fields pertaining to the same entity; used in file-processing systems. (2) In a relational model, a synonym for Row and Tuple.

Recursive relationship: A relationship among entities, objects, or rows of the same type. For example, if CUSTOMERs refer other CUSTOMERs, the relationship refers is recursive.

Referential integrity constraint: The condition in a database in which all interrelation constraints are satisfied.

Relation: Same as a table. A two-dimensional array containing single-valued entries and no duplicate rows. The meaning of the columns is the same in every row. The order of the rows and columns is immaterial.

Relational database: A database consisting of relations. Usually such a database is structured according to the principles of normalization, although in practice, relational databases contain relations with duplicate rows. Most DBMS products include a feature that removes duplicate rows when necessary and appropriate. Such a removal is not done as a matter of course because it can be time-consuming and expensive.

Relational data model: A data model in which data is stored in relations and relationships between rows are represented by data values.

Relational schema: A set of relations with interrelation constraints.

Relationship: An association between two entities, objects, or rows of relations.

Replicated data: In a distributed database, data that is stored on two or more computers.

Replication transparency: In a distributed database system, the condition in which application programs do not know and do not need to know whether data is replicated. If it is replicated, the DDBMS will ensure that all copies are updated consistently, without the involvement of the application program.

Report: An extraction of data from a database. Reports can be printed, displayed on a computer screen, or stored as a file. A report is part of a database application. Compare this with a Form.

Report band: See Band.

Resource locking: See Lock.

Resource-sharing architecture: The structure of a local area network in which one microcomputer performs file-processing services for other microcomputers. In a database application, each user computer contains a copy of the DBMS that forwards input/output requests to the file server, Only file I/O is processed by the file server; all database activities are processed by the DBMS on the user's computer.

Retention status: In the CODASYL DBTG model, a rule that states whether or not a record must exist in a set. If FIXED, a record may never be removed from its original set. If MANDATORY, a record must be a member of a set once it is placed into a set. If OPTIONAL, a record may or may not reside in a set.

Rollback: The process of recovering a database in which before-images are applied to the database to return to an earlier checkpoint or other point at which the database is logically consistent.

Rollforward: The process of recovering a database by applying after-images to a saved copy of the database to bring it to a checkpoint or other point at which the database is logically consistent.

Root: The top record, row, or node in a tree. A root has no parent.

Row: A group of columns in a table. All the columns in a row pertain to the same entity. A row is the same as a Tuple and a Record.

Row identifier: In SQL3, a unique, system-supplied identifier, a surrogate key. The row identifier can be made visible by stating WITH IDENTITY in the table definition.

Run-unit: In the CODASYL DBTG model, the execution of an application program by a user. Several run-units may use the same application program concurrently.

S

S-100 bus IEEE 696, 100-pin bus standard used extensively in first-generation personal computers (8080, Z80, 6800, etc.).

S3 chip Graphics accelerator chip (86C911) from S3, Inc., used in a variety of graphics accelerator boards.

SAA (System Application Architecture) Introduced in 1987, a set of IBM standards that provide consistent interfaces among all IBM computers from micro to mainframe. It is made up of user interfaces, programming interfaces and communications protocols.

sabermetriclan Slang for a statistician who uses computers to predict future performance of sports teams and players.

sag Momentary drop in voltage from the power source. Contrast with spike.

salami technique The theft of small amounts (slices) of assets from a large number of sources; an embezzlement technique that gets its name from taking a "slice" at a time, such as few cents from many bank accounts. Used frequently in computer crimes.

SAM (1) (Symantec AntiVirus for Macintosh) Popular Mac antivirus program from Symantec Corp. (2) See sequential access method.

Samna One of the first fufi-featured word processors for PCs (1983) from Samna Corp., now part of Lotus.

sampling (1) In statistics, the analysis of a group by determining the characteristics of a percentage of its members chosen by various scientific methods. (2) In digitizing operations, the conversion of real-world signals or movements at regular intervals into digital code.

sampling rate In digitizing operations, the frequency with which samples are taken and converted. The higher the sample rate, the closer real-world objects are represented in digital form.

sampling ratio When electronically scanning art or photographs, the number of pixels recorded fromthe original image vs. the final line screen during printing. The scanner may record at 300 dpi but the finished piece is printed at 150 dpi, a ratio 2:1. The desired ratio of desktop scans is 1.5:1 to 2:1; that is, 1.5 or 2 pixels are scanned for every halfone dot printed.

sans-serif Typeface style without serifs (the small horizontal lines added at the tops and bottoms of the vertical member of the letter). Helvetica is a common sans-serif font.

SAS (Statistical Analysis System) This integrated statistical package from SAS Institute Inc., includes data management, spreadsheets, CBT, presentation graphics, project management, operations research, scheduling, linear programming, statistical quality control, econometric and time series analysis, mathematical, engineering and statistical applications as well as full application development.

SASI (Shugart Associates Systems Interface) Peripheral interface developed by Shugart and NCR in 1981 that evolved into the ANSI SCSI standard in 1986.

satellite See communications satellite.

satellite channel Carrier frequency used for satellite transmission.

satellite computer Computer located remotely from the host computer or under the control of the host. It can function as a slave to the master computer or perform offline tasks.

satellite link Signal that travels from the earth to a communications satellite and back down again. Contrast with terrestrial link.

saturation (1) On magnetic media, occurs when the magnetizable particles are completely aligned and even a powerful writing signal will not improve the reading back. (2) In a bipolar transistor, occurs when the current on the gate (the trigger) is equal to or greater than what is necessary to close the switch. (3) In a diode, occurs when the diode is fully conducting.

save To write the contents of memory to disk or tape. Some applications save data automatically, others do not. Memory-based word processors, database programs and almost all spreadsheets require that the user saves the data before exiting the program.

scalablilty Ability to expand. Implies minimal change in current procedures in order to accomodate growth.

scalable Capable of being changed in size and configuration.

scalable font Font that is created in the required point size when needed to display or print a document. The dot patterns (bitmaps) are generated from a set of outline fonts, or base fonts, which contain a mathematical representation of the typeface. Scalable fonts eliminate storing dozens of different font sizes in the computer. Contrast with bitmapped font.

scalar Single item or value. Contrast with vector and rray, which are made up of multiple values.

scalar processor Computer that performs arithmetic computations on one number at a time. Contrast with vector processor.

scalar variable In programming, a variable that contains only one value.

scale (1) In computer graphics and printing, to resize an object, making it smaller or larger. (2) To change the representatinn of a quantity in order to bring it into prescribed limits of another range. (3) To designate the position of the decimal point in a fixed or floating point number.

scaling (1) The process of changing one bit-map density into a bit-map of another density. Scaling usually involves enlarging or contracting an image. (2)The process of changing the size of an image. Scaling by a factor of 3 multiples all dimensions of an image by 3.

scan (1) In optical technologies, to view a printed form a line at a time in order to convert images into bitmapped representations, or to convert these characters into ASCII text or some other data code. (2) In video, to move across a picture frame a line at a time, either to detect the image in an analog or digital camera, or to refresh a CRT-based video screen. (3) To sequentially search a (IIe.

scan head Optical sensing device in an scanner or fax machine that is moved across the image to be scanned.

scan line One of many horizontal lines in a graphics frame.

scan rate Number of times per second a scanning device samples its field of vision. See horizontal scan frequency.

scanner Device that reads text, images and bar codes. Text and bar code scanners recognize printed fonts and bar codes and convert them into a digital code. Graphics scanners convert a printed image into a video image (raster graphics) without recognizing the actual content of the text or pictures.

scatter diagram Graph plotted with dots or some other symbol at each data point. Also called a scatter plot or dot chart.

scatter plot Same as scatter diagram.

scatter read Capability that allows data to be input into two or more noncontiguous locations of memory with one read operation. See gather write.

scheduler The part of the operating system that initiates and terminates jobs (programs) in the computer. Also called a dispatcher, it maintains a list of jobs to be run and allocates computer resources as required.

scheduling algorithm Method used to schedule jobs for execution. Priority, length of time in the job queue and available resources are examples of criteria used.

schema Definition of an entire database. See subschema. scientific applications Applications that simulate real-world activities using mathematics. Real-world objects are turned into mathematical models and their actions are simulated by manipulating the models using mathematical formulas. For example, geographic terrain like rivers, lakes and mountains can be simulated. Virtually any objects with known characteristics can be modeled and simulated. Simulations use enormous calculations and often require supercomputer speed. As personal computers become more powerful, more laboratory experiments will be converted into computer models that can be interactively examined by students without the risk and cost of the actual experiments.

scientific computer Computer specialized for high- speed mathematic processing. See array processor and floating point processor.

scientific language Programming language designed for mathematical processing, such as ALGOL, FORTRAN and APL. Although all programming languáges allow for this kind of processing, statements in a scientific language make it easier to express these actions.

scientific notation Display of numbers in floating point form. The number (mantissa) is always equal to or greater than one and less than 10, and the base is 10. For example, 2.345E6 is equivalent to 2,345,000. The number following E (exponent) represents the power to which the base should be raised (number of zeros following the decimal point).

scissoring In computer graphics, the deleting of any parts of an image which fall outside of a window that has been sized and laid over the original image. Also called clipping.

SCL Extension used for ColoRiX rQster graphics file format (640x400 256 colors).

SCO (The Santa Cruz Operation, Inc.) System software company noted for its UNIX operating systems.

SCO Open Desktop Multiuser, virtual memory graphical operating system for 386s and up from SCO that runs UNIX, XENIX, DOS and X Window applications.

SCO UNIX System V AT&T-licensed implementation of UNIX System V/386 3.2 for 386s and up from SCO.It is a multiuser, multitasking environment that can run both XENIX and UNIX applications. It has more security, networking features and standards conformance than SCO XENIX. When used with SCO VP/iic or SCO Open Desktop, it can also run DOS applications.

SCO VP/ix System program for 386s and up from SCO that allows DOS applications to run concurrently with SCO UNIX or SCO XENIX in a virtual memory environment. Each application runs in its own secure virtual address space.

SCO XENIX System V AT&T-licensed, implementation of UNIX System V for 286 PCs and up from SCO. Developed by Microsoft, it was the original UNIX system for personal computers. Faster and smaller than SCO UNIX, it includes improved documentation and easier installation.

scope (1) CRT type of screen, such as used on an oscilloscope or common display terminal. (2) In programming, the visibility of variables within a program. (3) In dBASE, a range of records, such as the "next 50" or "current record to end of file."

scrambler Device or software program that encodes data forencryption.

scrambling Encoding data to make it indecipherable. See encryption and DES.

Scrapbook Macintosh disk file that holds frequently- used text and graphics objects, such as a company letterhead. Contrast with Clipboard, which holds data only for the current session.

scratch tape Magnetic tape that can be erased and reused.

scratchpad Special register or a reserved section of memory or disk used for temporary storage.

screen Display area of a video terminal or monitor. It is either a CRT or one of the flat panel technologies.

screen capture Transfering the current on-screen image to a text or graphics file. Most applications, especially word processors and graphics programs, have a utility called GRAB, CAP or something similar to do this.

screen dump Printing the current on-screen image. In PCs, pressing Shift-PrtSc prints the screen. If the screen contains graphics, the DOS Graphics utility must be loaded. Third party screen capture programs also dump graphic screens to the printer or to disk. In the Macintosh, pressing Command-shift-3 creates a MacPaint file of the current screen.

screen font Font used for on-screen display. For true WYSIWYCr systems, screen fonts must be matched as close as possible to the printer fonts. Contrast with printer font.

screen overlay (1) Clear, fine-iñesh screen that reduces the glare on a video screen. (2) Clear touch panel that allows the user to command the computer by touching displayed buttons on screen. (3) Temporary data window displayed on screen. The part of the screen that was overlaid is saved and restored when the screen overlay is removed.

screen saver After a specified duration without keyboard input, this utility blanks the screen or displays moving objects that can be quite entertaining, such as swimming fish or flying toasters! Pressing a key restores the original screen. This is to save the screen from being burnt in by a static image.

scrIpt (1) Typeface that looks like handwriting or calligraphy. (2) Program or macro.

scroll To continuously move forward, backward or sideways through text or images on screen or within a window. Scrolling implies continuous and smooth movement, a line, character or pixel at a time, as if the data were on a paper scroll being rolled behind the screen.

scroll arrow Icon that points up, down, left or right and is clicked in order to scroll the screen in the corresponding direction. The screen moves one line, or increment, with each mouse click.

scroll back buffer Reserved memory that holds a block of transmitted'ata, allowing the user to browse back through it.

scroll bar Horizontal or vertical bar that contains a box that looks like\a elevator in a shaft. The bar is clicked to scroll the scIn in the corresponding direction, or the box (elevator, thumb) is clicked and then dragged to the desired direction.

scrollable See scroll.

scrollable field Short line on screen that can be scrolled to allow editing or display of larger amounts of data in a small display space.

SCSI (Small Computer System Interface) Pronounced "scuzzy." An interface for up to seven peripherals (disk, tape, CD ROM, etc.). It is an 8-bit bus interface for up to eight devices, but the host adapter, which connects to the computer's bus, also counts as a device. The SCSI bus allows any two devices to communicate at one time (host to peripheral, peripheral to peripheral). SCSI (SCSI-i) provides up to five MBytes/sec data transfer and can connect multiple peripherals while taking only one expansion slot in the computer. SCSI-2 provides command queuing and a "Fast SCSI" synchronous option that provides 10MB data transfer (8-bit). With a secondary "B" cable for 16- and 32-bit data, "Wide SCSI" provides up to 40MB transfer. SCSI-3 proposes enhanced features and the, ability to handle more than eight devices. See hard disk specs.

SDF (Standard Data Format) Simple file format that uses fixed length fields. It is commonly used to transfer data between different programs.

SDI (1) (Single Document Interface) In Windows, a single window that is minimized or maximized independently. Contrast with MDI. (2) (Serial Data Interface) See serial interface. (3) (Strategic Defense Initiative) Proposed U.S. high-tech defense system.

SDK (Software Developer's Kit) See developer's toolkit.

seamless Integration Addition of a new aplication, routine or device that works smoothly with the existing system. It implies that the new feature can be activated and used without problems. Contrast with transparent, which implies that there is no discernible change after installation.

search and replace To look for an occurrence of data or text and replace it with another set of data or text.

search key In a search routine, the data entered and used to match other data in the database.

second-generation computer Computer made of discrete electronic components. In the early 1960s, the IBM 1401 and Honeywell 400 were examples.

second source Alternative supplier of an identical or compatible product. A second source manufacturer is one that holds a license to produce a copy of the original product from another manufacturer.

secondary channel In communications, a subchannel that is derived from the main channel. It is used for diagnostic or supervisory purposes, but does not carry data messages.

secondary Index Index maintained for a data file, but is not used to control the current processing order of the file. See primary index.

secondary storage External storage, such as disk and tape.

sector Smallest unit of storage read or written on a disk. Sectors are fixed in length, and the same number of sectors usually reside in one track. However, the hardware may vary the disk speed to fit more sectors into tracks located on the outer edges of the disk platter.

sector Interleave Sector numbering on a hard disk. A one to one interleave (1:1) is sequential: 0,1,2,3, etc. A 2:1 interleave staggers sectors so that the next sector is every second one: 0,4,1,5,2,6,3,7. In 1:1, after data in sector 1 is read, the disk controller must be fast enough to read sector 2, otherwise the beginning of sector 2 will pass the read/write head and must rotate around to come under the head again. If it isn't fast enough, a 2:1 or 3:1 interleave gives it time to read all sectors in a single rotation, eliminating wasted rotations. The optimum interleave depends on the disk controller and operating system. It can be changed with a low-level format program.

sector map See sector interleave.

security Protection of data against unauthorized access. Programs and data can be secured by issuing identification numbers and passwords to authorized users of a computer. However, systems programmers, or other technically competent individuals, will ultimately have access to these codes. Passwords can be checked by the operating system to prevent users from either logging onto the system in the first place, or they can be checked in software. Any application program running in the computer can also be designed to check for passwords. Data transmitted over communications networks can be secured by encryption to prevent eavesdropping. Although precautions can be taken to detect an unauthorized user, it is extremely difficult to determine if a valid user is performing unauthorized tasks. Effective security measures are a balance of technology and personnel management. See NCSC.

security kernel The part of the operating system that grants access to users of the computer system.

seed Starting value used by a random number generation routine to create random numbers.

seek (1) To move the access arm to the requested track on a disk. (2) Assembly language instruction that activates a seek operation on disk. (3) High-level programming language command used to select a record by key field.

seek time Time it takes to move the read/write head to a particular track on a disk after the instruction has been executed. The majority of a disk's access time is made up of seek time.

segment (1) Any partition, reserved area, partial component or piece of a larger structure. (2) One of the bars that make up a single character in an LED or LCD display. (3) For DOS segment addressing, see paragraph.

segmented address space Memory addressing in which each byte is referenced by a segment, or base, number and an offset that is added to it. Contrast with flat address space.

Sd (SELect) Printer switch that takes the printer alternately online and offline.

selection sort Search for specific data starting at the beginning of a file or list. It copies each matching item to a new file so that the selected items are in the same sequence as the original data.

selective calling In communications, the ability of the transmitting station to indicate which station in the network is to receive the message.

selector channel High-speed computer channel that connects a peripheral device (disk, tape, etc.) to the computer's memory.

selector pen Same as light pen.

Selectric typewriter Introduced in 1961 by IBM, the first typewriter to use a golf-ball print head that moved across the paper, rather than moving the paper carriage across the print mechanism. It rapidly became one of the world's most popular typewriters.

self-booting Refers to automatically loading the operating system upon startup.

self-checking digit See check digit.

self-clocking Recording of digital data on a magnetic medium such that the clock pulses are intrinsically part of the recorded signal. A separate timer clock is not required. Phase encoding is a commonly-used self- clocking recording technique.

self-documenting code Programming statements that can be easily understood by the author or another programmer. COBOL provides more self-documenting code than does C, for example. The other way is to write the code with adequate REMarks.

self-extracting file

One or more compressed files that have been converted into an executable program which decompresses its contents when run without requiring another utility.

semantic error In programming, writing a valid programming structure with invalid logic.

semantic gap Difference between a data or language structure and the real world.

semantic net A knowledge representation scheme that organizes human knowledge into a weblike structure consisting of nodes-objects, concepts and events— connected by links that specify the nature of the connections.

semantics Study-of the meaning of words. Contrast with syntax, which governs the structure of a language.

semaphore (1) Hardware or software flag used to indicate the status of some activity. (2) Shared space for interprocess communications (IPC) controlled by "wake up" and "sleep" commands.

The source process fills a queue and goes to sleep until the destination process uses the data and tells the source process to wake up.

semiconductor Solid state substance that can be electrically altered. Certain elements in nature, such as silicon, perform like semiconductors when chemically combined with other elements. A semiconductor is halfway between a conductor and an insulator. When charged with electricity or light, semiconductors change their state from nonconductive to conductive or vice versa. The most significant semiconductor is the transistor, which is simply an on/off switch.

semiconductor device Elementary component, such as a transistor, or a larger unit of electronic equipment comprised of chips.

semirandom access A method of locating data in storage that combines in the search for the desired item some form of direct access, usually followed by a limited sequential search.

sensor Device that measures or detects a real world condition, such as motion, temperature or light and converts the condition into an analog or digital representation.

sequel See SQL.

sequence check Testing a list of items or file of records for correct ascending or descending sequence based on the item or key fields in the records.

sequential One after the other in some consecutive order such as by name, number or physical location.

sequential access method Organizing data in a prescribed ascending or descending sequence. Searching sequential data requires reading and comparing each record, starting &om one end of the file.

serial One after the other.

serial computer Single-processor computer that executes one instruction after the other. Contrast with parallel computer.

serial Interface Data channel that transfers digital data in a serial fashion: one bit after the other. Communications lines are generally serial, thus modems are connected to the computer via a serial port. So are mice and scanners. Serial interfaces have multiple lines, but only one is used for data. Contrast with parallel interface. See RS-232-C.

serial mouse See bus mouse.

serial port I/O &innector used to attach a modem, mouse, scanner or other serial interface device to the computer. The typical serial port uses a DB-25 or DB-9 connector, which on the back of a PC is a 25- pin male or 9-pin male connector. Contrast with parallel port. See RS-232-C.

serial printer Type of printer that prints one character at a time, in contrast to a line or page at a time. In this context, serial has no relationship to a serial or parallel interface that is used to attach the printer to the computer. See printer.

serial transmission Transmitting data one bit at a time. Contrast with parallel transmission.

serialize To convert a parallel signal made up of one or more bytes into a serial signal that transmits one bit after the other.

serif Short horizontal lines added to the tops and bottoms of traditional typefaces, such as Times Roman. Contrast with sans-serif.

server Computer in a network shared by multiple users. See file server and print server.

server application (1) Application designed to run in a server. See client/server. (2) Any program that is run in the server, whether designed as a client/server application or not. (3) See OLE.

service bureau Organization that provides data processing and timesharing services. It may offer a variety of software packages and custom programming. Customers pay for storage of data on the system and processing time used. Connection Is made to a service bureau through dial-up terminals, private lines, or other networks, such as Telenet or 1'mnet.

service programs Programs that supplement the control programs of an operating system, such as language translators, utility routines, programmer aids.

service window The hours during the day or night that are covered by a maintenance agreement. Service provided outside of the "window" is not covered by the contract.

servo Electromechanical device that uses feedback to provide precise starts and stops for such functions as the motors on a tape drive or the moving of an access arm on a disk.

session (1) In communications, the active connection between a user and a computer or between two computers. (2) Time between starting up and ending an application program.

set theory Branch of mathematica or logic that is concerned with sets of objects and rules for their manipulation. UNION, INThRSECT' and COMPLEMENT are its three primary operations.

setup program Software that configures a system for a particular environment. In personal computers, it is used to inform the operating system of a major device change, such as a new disk drive or video display. See install program.

setup string Group of commands that initialize a device, such as a printer. See escape character.

seven-segment display Common display found on digital watches and readouts that looks like a series of Ss. Each digit or letter is formed by selective illumination of up to seven separately addressable bars.

sex changer See gender changer.

sh (SHell) UNIX command that invokes a different shell. It can be used like a batch file to execute a series of commands saved as a shell.

shade (1) In computer graphics, the quantity of black mixed with a pure color. (2) To give added dimension to an image by including changes in appearance caused by light and shadow.

shading symbols Block graphics characters that are a part of some computer graphics built-in character sets. They provide different dot densities, giving the appearance of different levels of shading.

shadow mask Screen full of holes that adheres to the back of a color CRT's viewing glass. The electron bemn is aimed through the holes onto the phosphor dots.

shadow RAM In a PC, a copy of the operating system's BiOS routines is placed in RAM to improve perfor shadow RAM chips are faster than ROM chips.

shared DASD Disk system accessed by two or more aiinputers within a single datacenter. Disks shared ii personal computer networks are called file set'.'era or database servers.

shared logic Using a single computer to provide processing for two or more terminals. Contrast with shared resource.

shared resource Sharing a peripheral device (disk, printer, etc.) among several users. For example, a file server and laser printer in a LAN are shared resources. Contrast with shared logic.

shareware Software distributed through BBS's and information services free of charge on a trial basis. If you use it, you pay for it, for which you receive additional documentation, support or possibly the next upgrade at no cost. See freeware and public domain software.

sheet feeder Mechanical device that feeds stacks of cut forms (letterheads, legal paper, etc.) into a printer.

shelfware Products that remain unsold on a dealer's shelf or unused by the customer.

shell Outer layer of a program that provides the user interface, or way of commanding the computer. Shells are typically add-on programs created for command- driven operating systems, such as UNIX and DOS. It provides a menu-driven or graphical icon-oriented interface to the system in order to make it easier to use. DOS 4.0 and 5.0 come with their own shell (DOSshell).

shell out To temporarily exit an application, go back to the operating system, perform a function (like format a disk) and then return to the application.

shift-click To click the mouse button while depressing the shift key on the keyboard.

shift-key The key on a computer keyboard that, when pressed, makes letters print as capitals instead of lowercase letters and allows some special characters to be printed. On many keyboards, acts as a shift lock and must be pressed again to return to lowercase.

shift register High-speed circuit that holds some number of bits lix the purpose of shifting them left or right. It is used internally within the processor for multiplication and division, serial/ parallel conversion and various timing considerations.

short In programming, an integer variable. In C, a long is two bytes and can be signed (-32K to +32K) or unsigned (64K). Contrnst with long.

short card In a PC, a plug-in printed circuit board that is half the length of a full-size board. Contrast with long card.

short-haul modem In communications, a device that transmits signals up to about a mile.

shrink wrapped software Refers to store-bought software, implying a standard platform that is widely supported.

SI See systems integration, Norton SI and Macintosh.

sideband In communications, the upper or lower half of a carrier wave. Since both sidebands are normally mirror images of each other, one of the halves can be used for a second channel to increase the data- carrying capacity of the line or for diagnostic or control purposes.

sidebar A block of text or a graphic image placed to the side of the main body of text in a document.

Sidekick PC desktop utility program from Borland. Introduced in 1984, it was the first popup (TSR) program for the PC. It includes a calculator, WordStarcompatible notepad, appointment calendar, phone dialer and ASCII table. Sidekick Plus (1988) adds more notepad commands, calendar alarms, scientific and programming calculators, limited file management and an outliner.

SIGM (Special Interest Group) Group of people that meets and shares information about a particular topic of interest. It is usally a part of a larger group or association.

sign Symbol that identifies a positive or negative number. In digital code, it is either a separate character or part of the byte. In ASCII, the sign is kept in a separate character typically transmitted in front of the number it represents (+ and - is 2B and 2D in hex).

sign on/sign off Same as log-onhlog-ofE

signal Physical form of transmitted data (pulses or frequencies of electricity or light).

signal converter Device that changes the electrical or light characteristics of a signal.

signal processing See digital signal processing.

signal to noise ratio Ratio of the amplitude (power, volume) of a data signal to the amount of noise (interference) in the line. Usually measured in decibels, it measures the clarity or quality of a transmission channel or electronic device.

signaling in/out of band In communications, signaling "in band" refers to sending control signals within the same frequency range as the data signal. Signaling "out of band" refers to sending control signals outside of the frequency range of the data signal.

signature (1) Unique number built into hardware or software for identification and copy protection. (2) (Signature) PC word processing program from XyQuest, that is the successor to XyWrite III Plus with enhanced graphics and font capabilities. Many XyWrite commands have been changed, and XyWrite documents must be converted to the Signature format. It adds an editable graphics display mode, macro recorder and the ability to import a variety of data files.

significant digits Those digits in a number that add value to the number. For example, in the number 00001234, 1234 are the significant digits.

silica Same as silicon dioxide.

silica gel Highly absorbent form of silicon dioxide often wrapped in porous bags and packed with equipment to absorb moisture during shipping and storage.

silicon (Si) Base material used in chips. It is one of the most abundant element in nature and is found in a natural state in rocks and sand. Its atomic structure and abundance make it an ideal semiconductor material. In chip making, it is mined from rocks and put through a chemical process at high temperatures to purify it. To alter its electrical properties, it is mixed (doped) with other chemicals in a molten state.

silicon compiler Software that translates the electronic design of a chip into the actual layout of the components.

silicon dioxide (Si02) Hard, glassy mineral found in such materials as iock, quartz, sand and opal. In MOS chip fabrication, it is used to create the insulation layer between the metal gates of the top layer and the silicon elements below.

silicon disk Disk drive permanently simulated in memory. Typically used in laptops for weight reduction, it requires constant power from a battery to maintain its contents.

silicon foundry Organization that makes chips for other companies that have only design, but not manufacturing facilities. It is typically a large chip maker that uses excess manufacturing capacity in this manner.

Silicon Valley Area around San Jose (south of San Francisco) noted for its large number of high-tech companies.

SIMD (Single Instruction stream Multiple Data stream) Computer architecture that performs one operation on multiple sets of data, for example, an array processor. One computer or processor is used for the control logic and the remaining processors are used/ as slaves, each executing the same instruction. Contrast with MIMD.

SIMM (Single In-line Memory Module) Narrow printed circuit board about three inches long that holds eight or nine memory chips. It plugs into a SIMM socket on the circuit board.

simplex One way transmission. Contrast with half-duplex and full-duplex.

simulation (1) Mathematical representation of the interaction of real-world objects. See scientific applications. (2) Execution of a machine language program designed to run in a foreign computer.

sine wave Uniform wave that is generated by a single frequency.

single board computer Printed circuit board that contains a complete computer, including processor, memory, I/O and clock.

single density disk First-generation floppy disk.

single precision Use of one computer word to hold a numeric value for calculation. Contrast with double precision.

single sided disk Obsolete floppy disk that stores data on only one side.

single threading Processing one transaction to completion before starting the next.

sink Device or place that accepts something See heat sink and data sink.

SIP (Single In-line Package) Type of daip module that is similar to a SIMM, but uses pins rather than edge connectors. SIs are sometimes called SIPS (Single In-Line Pin Package).

site license License to use software within a facility. It provides authorization to make copies and distribute them within a specific jursidction.

sketching A computer-graphics technique in which a ci lines is drawn or sketched along the path of the cursor.

sketch pad A working storage area displayed on the dpiay saeen that permits the operator to add and delete graphic or textual information easily before it is entered into permanent storage.

skew (1) Misalignment of a document or punched card in the feed tray or hopper that prohibits it from being scanned or read properly (2) In facsimile, the difference in rectangularity between the received and transmitted page. (3) In communications, a change of timing or phases in a transmission signal. (4) See cylinder skew and head skew.

slave Computer or peripheral device controlled by another computer. A lerminal or printer in a remote ioo th may only receive data is a slave. When two personal computers e hooked up via their serial or parallel por for file exchange, the file tramfer ixoam may me one computer the mter and the other the slave.

slave tube Display monitor connected to aixtber monitor in order to provide an acklitiona] viewing station.

SLC See 386SLC.

sleep (1) In programming, an inactive state due to an endless loop or programmed delay. A sleep statement in a programming language creates a delay for some specified amount of time. (2) Inactive status of a terminal, device or program that is awakened by sending a code to it.

slew rate (1) How fast paper moves through a printer (ips). (2) Speed of changing voltage.

slide show Computer-graphics software that displays graphics images in a timed sequence on the video display screen, similar to a slide show.

sliding window (1) Communications protocol that transmits multiple packets before acknowledgement. Both ends keep track of packets sent and acknowledged (left of window), those which have been sent and not acknowledged (in window) and those not yet sent (right of window). (2) View of memory that can be instantly shifted to another location.

slipstream To fix a bug or add enhancements to software without identifying such inclusions by creating a new version number.

slot (1) Receptacle for additional printed chcuit boards. (2) Receptacle for inserting and removing a disk or tape cartridge. (3) In communications, a narrow band of frequencies. See time slot. (4) May refer to reserved space for temporary or permanent storage of instructions, data or codes.

SMA (1) (Systems Management Architecture) IBM network management repository. (2) Type of. fiber optic connector. (3) (Spectrum Manufacturers Assn.) DBMS standard for application compatibility.

Smalltalk Operating system and object-oriented programming language that was developed by Xerox. It eliminates the distinction between programming language and operating system and also allows the programmer to customize the user interface and behavior of the system. Smalltalk was the first object- oriented programming language. It was originally used to create prototypes of simpler programming languages and the graphical interfaces that are so popular today.

smart cable Connecting cable between two devices that has a built-in microprocessor. It analyzes incoming signals and converts them from one protocol to another.

smart card Credit card with built-in microprocessor and memory used for identification or financial transactions. When inserted into a reader, it transfers data to and from a central computer. It is more secure than a magnetic stripe card and can be programmed to self-destruct if the wrong password is entered a fixed number of times. As a financial transaction card, it can store transactions and maintain a bank balance.

smart hub See intelligent hub.

smart Install program Install program that configures itself automatically based on the hardware environment.

smart terminal Video terminal with built-in display characteristics (blinking, reverse video, underlines, etc.). It may also contain a communications protocol. Sometimes refers to intelligent terminal. See intelligent terminal and dumb terminal.

Smaricom Family of communications programs forPCs and Macs from -Hayes. Versions emulate a several terminals and support a variety of protocols, including the Hayes V-series. Smartcom EZ is for the novice.

Smartdrive Disk cache program that comes with DOS 4.0 and Windows 3.0: Driver is SMARTDRVSYS.

SmartKey PC keyboard macro processor from No Brainer Software. It was one of the first macro processors that let users eliminate repetitive typing by creating a macro for an occurrence of text or a series of commands.

SMD (1) (Storage Module Device) High-performance hard disk interface used with minis and mainframes that transfers data in the 1-4 MBytes/sec range (SMD. E provides highest rate). See hard disk specs. (2) (Surface Mount Device) Surface mounted chip.

smoothed data Statistical data that has been averaged or otherwise manipulated so that the curves on its graph are smooth and free of irregularities.

smoothing circuit Electronic filtering circuit in a DC power supply that removes the ripples from AC power.

SMP See symmetric multiprocessing.

SMT (Surface Mount Technology) See surface mount.

SNA (Systems Network Architecture) IBM's primary networking strategy, introduced in 1974. SNA is made up of a variety of hardware and software products that all interact together. In SNA, nodes are end points or junctions, and data links are the pathways between them. Nodes-can be Type 5 (hosts), Type 4 (communications controllers) and Type 2 (peripheral; terminals, PCs and midrange computers). The heart of a mainframe-based SNA network is the SSCP (System Services Control Point) software that resides in the host. NCP (Network Control Program) resides in the communications controller (front end processor) and manages the routing and data link protocols. SNA is implemented in functional layers (protocol stack) with each layer passing control to the next layer.

SN4DS (SNA Distribution Services) IBM e-mail sys. tern for SNA networks. It also provides store and forward capabilities if a user's -machine is unavailable to receive a transmission.

snapshot Storing the contents of memory including all hardware registers and status indicators. It is periodically taken in order to restore the system in the event of failure and to fid out-what went wrong and when.

snapshot dump Memory dump of selected portions of memory. -

snapshot program Trace program that provides selected dumps of memory when specific instructions are executed or when certain conditions are-met.

snd (SouND resource) Macintosh resource fork that contains sound information, including compression ratios if used and sampling rate.

SNOBOL (StriNg Oriented symBOlic Language) One of the first list processing languages (Bell Labs; early 1960s). It was used for text processjpg and compiler development.

snow Flickering snow-like spots on a video screen caused by display electronics that are too slow to respond tochanging data.

socket Receptacle which receives a plug. soft boot Same as warm boot.

soft copy Refers to data displayed on a video screen. Contrast with hard copy.

soft error Recoverable error, such as a garbled message that can be retransmitted. Contrast with hard error.

soft font Set of characters for a particular typeface that is stored on the computer's hard disk and downloaded to the printer beforepnintihg. Contrast with internal font and font - -

soft hyphen Hyphen that prints if it winds up at the end of the line, but does notprint othêwise. Contrast with hard hyphen. See discretionary hyphèi

soft key Keyboard key simulated byin icon on screen.

soft patch Quick fix to machine language currently in memory that only lasts for the current session.

soft return Code inserted by the softare into a text document to mark the end- of th line. -When more matter is inserted, this return is shiftcrdingly and text reformatted. During piintiij thsoft return is converted into the end-of-line code required by the printer. Soft returns are determined by tile iiht margin and change when the margins are changed. Contrast with hard return.

soft sectored Common method of identifying'sb'ftfrs on a disk by initially recording sector information on every track with a format program. Contrast with hard sectored.

software Instructions for the computer. A series of instructions that performs a particular task is called a program or software program. The two major categories are system software and application software. System software is made up of control programs, including the operating system, communications software and database manager. Application software is any program that processes data for the user.

software architecture Design of application or system software that incorporates protocols and interfaces for interacting with other programs and for future flexibility and expandability. A self-contained, standalone program would have program logic, but not a software architecture.

Software Carousel Task switching program for PCs from SoftLogic Solutions, that allows the user to have up to a dozen applications open at the same time and switch back and forth between them.

software engineering Design, development and documentation of software.

software failure Inability of a program to continue processing due to erroneous logic. Same as crash, bomb and abend.

software house Organization that develops customized software for a customer. Contrast with software publisher, which develops and markets software packages.

software interrupt Interrupt caused by an instruction in the program. See interrupt.

software package Application program developed for sale to the general public. Although a set of programs developed and written for only one organization may be called a package, it usually refers to an off-the- shelf program.

software programmer Sanle as systems programmer. software protection See copy protection.

software publisher Organization that develops and markets software. It does market research, production and distribution of software. It may develop its own software, contract for outside development or obtain software that has already been written.

software stack Stack implemented in memory. See stack.

software tool Program that aids in the development of other software programs. It may assist the programmer in the design, coding, compiling, link editing or debugging phases.

SOIC (Small Outline 10 Small-dimension, surface mount DIP that uses guliwing-shaped pins extending outward.

Solaris 2.0 Multitasking operating system for SPARC computers and PCs from SunSoft. Backward compatible with Solaris 1.0 (SPARC-only), it is designed for distributed computing and includes the TCP/IP protocol.

solder mask Insulating pattern applied to a printed circuit board that exposes only the areas to be soldered.

solenoid Magnetic switch that closes a circuit, often used as a relay.

solid logic Same as solid state.

solid modeling Mathematical technique for representing solid objects. It is the least abstract form of CAD. Unlike wireframe and surface modeling, solid modeling systems ensure that all surfaces meet properly and that the object is geometrically correct. A solid model can also be sectioned (cut open) to reveal its internal features.

solid state Electronic component or circuit made of solid materials, such as transistors, chips and bubble memory. There is no mechanical action in a solid state device, although an enormous amount of electromagnetic action takes place within. For data storage, solid state devices are much faster and more reliable than mechanical disks and tapes, but are more expensive.

solid state disk Disk drive made of memory chips used for high-speed data access or in adverse environments. Dynamic RAM solid state disks are used in battery- powered, hand-held devices as well as in desktop units with hundreds of megabytes of storage that contain their own UPS systems.

solid state memory Any transistorized, semiconductor or thin film memory that contains no mechanical parts.

solid state relay Relay that contains no mechanical parts. All switching mechanisms are semiconductor or thin film components.

solver Mathematical mechanisms that allow spreadsheets to perform goal seeking.

sort To reorder data into a new sequence. Sorting capabilities are provided within the operating system and many application programs,such as word processing and DBMSs. In some word processing programs, sorting allows for all the text in the document or a marked block of text to be resequenced into either an ascending (normal) or descending sequence. In database programs, sorting resequences all the records in the file by one or more fields and often generates an entirely new copy of the file. The operating system can typically sort file names and text lists.

sort algorithm Formula used to reorder data into a new sequence.

sort field Same as sort key.

sort key Field or fields in a record that dictate the sequence of the file.

sorter (1) Sort program. (2) Person who manually puts data into a specific sequence. (3) Early tabulating machine that routed punched cards into separate stackers based on the content of a card column.

sound bandwidth Range of sound frequencies. The human ear can perceive approximately from 20 to 20,000Hz, but human voice is confined to within 3,000Hz.

source Source of current in a MOS transistor. Same as emitter in a bipolar transistor.

source code Program in its original form as written by the programmer. It is not executable by the computer directly. It must be converted into machine language by compilers, assemblers and interpreters. In some cases, source code can be converted into another dialect or a different language by a conversion program.

source computer Computer in which a program is being assembled or compiled. Contrast with object computer.

source data Original data that is handwritten or printed on a source document or typed into the computer system from a keyboard or terminal.

source data acquisition Same as source data capture. source data capture Capturing data electronically when a tranaction occurs; for example, at the time of sale. source directory Directory from which data is obtained. source disk Disk from which data is obtained. Contrast with target disk.

source document Paper form onto which data is written. Order forms and employment applications are examples.

source drive Disk or tape drive from which data is obtained. Contrast with target drive.

source language Language used in a source program. source program Program in its original form, as written by the programmer.

source statement Instructional phrase in a programming language (source language).

space/time The following units of measure are used to define storage and transmission capacities.

SPACE	Bitsorbytes
Kilo (K) Thousand	1,024.

Mega (M) Millio	1,048,576
Giga (G) Billion	1,073,741,824
Tera ('1) Trillion	1,099,511,627,776
Peta (P) Quadrillion	1,125,899,906,842,624
TI M E Fraction of second	
Millisecond (ms) Thousandth	1/1,000
Microsecond Os) Millionth	1/1,000,000
Nanosecond (ns) Billionth	1/1,000,000,000
Picosecond (ps) Trillionth	1/1,000,000,000,000
Femtosecond (fs) Quadrillionth	1/100,000,000,000,000

spaghettI code Program code written without a coherent structure. It implies an excessive use of GOTO instructions. Each decision point in a program (if this, do that) directs the computer to branch to some other part of the program. See structured programming.

SPARC (Scalable Performance ARChitecture) 32-bit RISC CPU developed by Sun Microsystems and licensed by SPARC Int'l.

spatial data Data represented as 2-D or 3-D images. spawn To launch another program from the current program.

spec See specification.

special character Non-alpha or non-numeric character, such as @, #, $, %, &, * and +.

special-purpose computer Computer designed from scratch to perform a specific function. Contrast with general-purpose computer.

special-purpose language Programming language designed to solve a specific problem or class of problems. For example, LISP and Prolog are designed for and used extensively in AI applications. Contrast with general-purpose language.

specification Definition of a data structure or processing routine in a program. See functional specification.

spectral color In computer graphics, the color of a single wavelength of light, starting with violet at the low end and proceeding through indigo, blue, green, yellow and orange and ending with red.

spectral rosponse Variable output of a light-sensitive device that is based on the color of the light it perceives.

spectrum Range of electromagnetic frequencies. speech recognition Same as voice recognition.

speech synthesis Generating machine voice by arranging phonemes (k, ch, sh, etc.) into words. It is used to turn text input into spoken words for the blind. Speech synthesis performs realtime conversion with. out a pre-defined vocabulary, but does not create human-sounding speech, mainly because in human speech inflection also carries meaning. Although individual spoken words can be digitized into the computer, digitized voice takes a lot of storage.

speed buffering Technique that compensates for speed differences between input and output. Data is accepted into the buffer at high speed and transferred out at low speed, or vice versa.

Speed Doubler See 486.

speed of electricity/light Approximately 186,000 miles per second.

spelling checker Word processing function that tests for correctly spelled words. It can test the spelling of a marked block, an entire document or group of documents. Advanced systems check for spelling as the user types and can correct common typos and misspellings on the fly. Spelling checkers simply compare words to a dictionary of words, and the wrong use of a correctly-spelled word cannot be detected. Spellers can also be configured for US or UK languages. See grammar checker.

spherlzation In computer graphics, turning an image into a sphere.

spike Also called a transient, a burst of extra voltage in a power line that lasts only a fraction of a second but can be fatal ftr a computer. Contrast with sag. See surge.

spindle Rotating shaft in a disk drive. In a fixed disk, the platters are attached to the spindle. In a removable disk, the spindle remains in the drive.

SpinRite II Popular non-destructive, low-level formatting program for PCs from Gibson ResearchCorp., that reformats the hard disk without erasing the data. It rewrites only the sector ID, which may have drifted over time.

SPL (Structured Programming Language) See structured programming.

spline In computer graphics, a smooth curve that runs through a series of given points. The term is often used to refer to any curve. See Bezier and B-spline.

split screen Display of two or more sets of data on screen at the same time. It implies that one set of data can be manipulated independently of the other. Split screens, or windows, are usually created by the operating system or application software, rather than the hardware.

splitting a window The act of dividing a window into two or more panes.

spooling (Simultaneous Peripheral Operations OnLine) Overlapping of low-speed operations with normal processing. Spooling is used to buffer data for the printer as well as remote batch terminals. See print spooler.

spread spectrum Radio transmission that continuously changes carrier frequency according to a unique pattern in both sending and receiving devices. It is used for security as well as to allow multiple wireless transmissions in the same space.

spreadsheet Software that simulates a paper spreadsheet, or worksheet, in which columns of numbers are summed for budgets and plans. It appears on screen as a matrix of rows and columns, the intersections of which are identified as cells.

Spreadsheet can have thousands of cells and can be scrolled horizontally and vertically in order to view them. The cells can be filled with: 1. labels; 2. numeric values; or, 3. formulas. Formulas are easy to create, since spreadsheets allow the user to point to each cell and type in the arithmetic operation that affects it. Roughly speaking, a formula is created by saying "this cell PLUS that cell TIMES that cell." Formulas are the spreadsheet's magic. After numbers are added or changed, the formulas will recalculate the data either automatically or with the press of a key. If data in the detail column changes, its column total (formula) changes, which is then copied to the summary column, and the summary total changes. This feature allows users to create a plan, plug in different assumptions and immediately see the impact on the bottom line. This 'what if?" capability makes the spreadsheet indispensable for budgets, plans and other equation-based tasks. The standard spreadsheet creates a two-dimensional matrix of rows and columns. In order to summarize data, totals from various parts of the spreadsheet can be summed to another part of the spreadsheet. A spreadsheet with dynamic linking allows data in one spreadsheet to automatically update another spreadsheet. In a 3-dimensional spreadsheet each cell in the spreadsheet has an X, Y and Z reference. A relational spreadsheet stores the data separate and apart from the formtilas. Data is stored in a central database and the formulas are stored in the spreadsheet. When the spreadsheet is called up, the data from the database is copied into it, thus ensuring that everyone's spreadsheet contains current data.

spreadsheet compiler Software that translates spreadsheets into stand-alone programs that run without the spreadsheet package that created them.

sprIte Independent graphic object controlled by its OWn bit plane (area of memory). Commonly used in video games, sprites move freely across the screen, passing by, through and colliding with each other with much less programming.

sprocket feed Same as pin feed.

SPS (Standby Power System) UPS system that switches to battery backup upon detection of power failure.

SPSS Statistical package from SPSS, Inc., that is used extensively in marketing research. It provides a large number of statistical processes, including regression analysis, correlation and analysis of variance. Originally named Statistical Package for the Social Sciences, it was written by Norman Nie, a professor at Stanford. In 1976, he formed SPSS, Inc.

SQL (Structured Query Language) Pronounced "SQL" or "see qwill," a language used to interrogate and process data in a relational database. Originally developed by IBM for its mainframes, there have been many implementations created for mini and micro database applications. SQL commands can be used to interactively work with a database or can be embedded within a programming language to interface to a database.

SQL/DS: (SQL/Data System) Full-featured relational DBMS from IBM for VSE and VM environments that has integrated query and report writing facilities.

SQL engine Program that accepts SQL commands and accesses the database to obtain the requested data. Users' requests in a query language or database language must be translated into an SQL request before the SQL engine can process it.

square wave Graphic image of a digital pulse as visualized on an oscilloscope. It appears square because it rises quickly to a particular amplitude, stays constant for the duration of the pulse and drops fast at the end of it.

SRAM See static RAM.

SSD See solid state disk.

SSE Protected Mode full-screen editor in OS/2.

SSI (Small Scale Integration) Up to 100 transistors on a chip. See MSI, IS!, VLSI and ULSI.

ST (1) Personal computer series from Atari that uses a Motorola 68000 CPU and includes the GEM interface, ROM-based TOS operating system, a MIDI interface and a three-voice sound chip. The 520ST has 512K RAM; the 1O4OST has 1MB. Display is 640x200, 16 cdlors. (2) Type of fiber optic connector.

ST506 Hard disk interface commonly used in drives 40MB and less. It transfers data at 625 KBytes/sec and uses the MFM encoding method. See ST412 and hard disk specs. The ST506 RLL (ST506 Run-Length Limited) is a hard disk interface (also called RLL interface) that increases capacity and speed by 50% over ST506 MFM drves and transfers data at 937 KBytes/sec. See hard disk specs.

stack (1) Set of hardware registers or a reserved amount of memory used for arithmetic calculations or for keeping track of internal operations. Stacks keep track of the sequence of routines that are called in a program. For example, one routine calls another, which calls another and so on. As each routine is completed, the computer must return control to the calling routine all the way back to the first routine that started the sequence. Stacks usually work on a LIFO basis; the last item, or address, placed (pushed) onto the stack is the first item removed (popped) from the stack. An "internal stack failure" is a fatal error which means that the operating system can't find the next routine to process. Restarting the computer usually corrects this, otherwise the operating system may have to be re-installed. (2) HyperCard file.

stack overflow Error condition that occurs when there is no room in the stack for a new item. A stack underflow occurs when an item is called for, but the stack is empty.

stack pointer Address that identifies the location of the most recent item placed on the stack.

stacker (1) Output bin in a document feeding or punched card machine, Contrast with hopper. (2) (Stacker) Realtime compression program from Stac Electronics, that doubles (approximately) the disk capacity of a PC and is transparent to the user. A coprocessor board is optionally available.

stackware HyperCard application that is made up of a HyperCard stack (data) and HyperTalk programming.

STAIRS (STorage And Information Retrieval System) IBM text document management system for mainframes. It allows users to search for documents based on key words or word combinations.

standard cell Finished design of an electronic function ready for chip fabrication. It can be as small as a clock circuit or as large as a microprocessor. It is used to make custom-designed chips.

standard devlation In statistics, the average amount a number varies from the average number in a series of numbers.

Standard Mode Windows operation mode. See Windows.

standards & compatibility Standards is the most important issue in the computer field. As an unregulated industry, we have wound up with thousands of data formats and languages, but very few standards that are universally used. The standards makers are always trying to set a standard, while the innovators are trying to create a new one. Even when standards are created, they are violated as soon as a new feature is added by the vendor. If a format or language is used extensively and others copy it, it becomes a de facto standard and may become as widely used as official standards from ANSI and IEEE. When de facto standards are sanctioned by these organizations, they become stable, at least, for a while. In order to truly understand this industry, it is essential to understand the categories for which standards are created.

Machine language is the fundamental standard for hardware compatibility. Vendors often have several families of computers, each with slightly different machine languages. After a program is written, it must be translated (assembled, compiled or interpreted) into the machine language that the computer understands

If this translates differently on various machines, the effects will be unpredictable. Machine language compatibility can also be achieved by simulation or emulation. A simulator is software that translates and executes a program in a foreign machine language. An emulator is hardware that executes the machine language of another computer and is used to encour age customers to buy a new series of computers.

The data code is built into the computer and determines how each character (letter, digit or special character) is represented in binary code. Fortunately, there are only two major data codes in wide use today, EBCDIC and ASCII. That means alphabetic data and numbers stored in one code can easily be converted to the other. IBM mainframes and minicomputers and other mainframes use EBCDIC. ASCII is used by all personal computers, most minicomputers and some mainframes. However, since ASCII is only a 7-bit code with 128 character combinations, and the 8th bit (which derives another 128 values) leaves scope for innovation. In the PC, it is used for foreign language characters and line drawing symbols.

The hardware interface specifies the plugs, sockets, cables and electrical signals that pass through each line between the CPU and a peripheral device or communications network. Common hardware interfaces for personal computers are the Centronics parallel interface used for printers and the RS-232-C interface, typically used for modems, graphics tablets, mice and printers. In addition, the ST506, RLL, ESDI and SCSI interfaces are used for disks and tapes, and the GPIB IEEE 488 standard is used for process control instruments.

There are many varieties of disk packs, disk cartridges, floppy disks, reel-to-reel tapes, tape cartridges and tape cassettes. Each one has its own unique shape and size and can be used only in drives designed to accommodate them. For minicomputers and mainframes, the half-inch magnetic tape reel is a common interchangeable medium. For personal computers, the 5.25' minifloppy and the 3.5" microfloppy disks are used.

An operating system is a master control program that manages the running of the computer system. In all environments, except for specialized scientific and process control applications, the operating system interacts with the application programs. The application programs must "talk" to the operating system. If application programs are moved to a different computing environment, they have to be converted to interface with a different operating system. If a new operating system is installed that is not compatible with the old one, the application programs have to be converted to the new operating system.

Every software program is written in a programming language, and there is at least one programming language for every major CPU series. Assembly languages are largely machine specific, and the machine language they generate runs on only one CPU family. The high-level programming language was created to eliminate this machine dependency. Programming languages, such as COBOL, FORTRAN and BASIC are supposed to be able to run on many different computers. Compatibility can be achieved when a programming language conforms to the ANSI (American National Standards Institute) standard for that language. If the same version of an ANSI COBOL compiler is available for two different CPUs, a program written in ANSI COBOL will run on both machines.

Word processors and DBMSs have their own proprietary formats for printing text and storing data. But most programs have an import and export capability that converts popular database formats into their proprietary format. If not, the program usually can import and export a plain EBCDIC or ASCII file, which is stripped of all proprietary codes and can be used as a common denominator between both systems.

There are many formats for storing a picture in a computer; but, unlike text and data files, graphics formats are more complex. To begin with, there are the two major categories of graphics: vector graphics (objects made up of lines) and raster graphics (TV- like dots).

Star Xerox workstation that formally introduced the graphical user interface and desktop metaphor in 1981. Although unsuccessful, it was inspiration for Xerox's subsequent computers and for Apple's Lisa and Macintosh. See Alto.

star network Communications network in which all terminals are connected to a central computer or central hub. PBXs are prime examples as well as IBM's Token Ring and AT&T's Starlan LANs.

start bit In asynchronous communications, the bit transmitted before each character.

start/stop transmission Same as asynchronous transmission.

startup routine Routine that is executed when the computer is booted or when an application is loaded. It is used to customize the environment for its associated software.

STARTUP.CMD (STARTUP.CoMmanD) OS/2 file executed immediately upon startup. It contains instructions that can initialize operating system settings and call in a specific application program. The DOS counterpart is AUTOEXEC.BAT.

stat mux (STATistical MUltipleXor) See statistical multiplexor.

state-of-the-art Most current technique or method applied to designing and developing hardware and software.

statement In a high-level programming language, a descriptive phrase that generates one or more machine language instructions in the computer. In a low-level assembly language, programmers write instructions rather than statements, since each source language instruction is translated into one machine language instruction.

static binding Same as early binding.

static column memory A type of page mode memory that requires less electronic pulsing in order to access the memory bits.

static electricity Stationary electrical charge that is the result of intentional charging or of friction in low- humidity environments.

static RAM Memory chip that requires power to hold its content.

static SQL See embedded SQL.

status line Information line displayed on screen that shows current activity.

stepper motor Motor that rotates in small, fixed increments and is used to control the movement of the access arm on a disk drive. Contrast with voice coil.

stereophonic Sound reproduction using two or more channels. Contrast with monophonic.

stick model Picture made of lines, or vectors. For example, in biomedical applications, the limbs of a person or animal are converted into lines so that the motion can be visually observed and graphically plotted and analyzed.

stop bit In asynchronous communications, a bit transmitted after each character.

storage device Hardware unit that holds data. It normally refers only to external peripheral equipment, such as disk and tape, in contrast with memory (RAM).

storage media Refers to disks, tapes and bubble memory cartridges.

store and forward In communications, the temporary storage of a message for transmission to its destination at ,a later time. Store and forward techniques allow for routing over networks that are not accessible at all times. Messages can be stored and forwarded at night in order to obtain off-peak rates.

stream (1) Contiguous group of data. (2)1/0 management in the C programming language. A stream is a channel through which data flows to/from a disk, keyboard, printer, etc.

stream-oriented ifie Type of file, such as a text document or digital voice file, that is more openly structured than a data file. Text and voice are continuous streams of characters, whereas database records are repeating structures with a fixed or reasonably uniform format.

streaming tape High-speed magnetic tape drive that is frequently used to make a backup copy of an entire hard disk.

strlkethrough A line drawn through a selected range of text. Marking text in this manner indicates that the text is to be deleted at some future time.

string (1) In programming, a contiguous set of alphanumeric characters that does not contain numbers used for calculations. Names, addresses, words and sentences are strings. Contrast with numeric data. (2) Any connected set of structures, such as a string of bits, fields or records.

string handling Abilty to manipulate alphanumeric data (names, addresses, text, etc.). Typical functions include the ability to handle arrays of strings, to left and right align and center strings and to search for an occurrence of text within a string.

Stringy Floppy Continuous loop cartridge of 1/16" tape from Exatron, available for early personal computers.

striping Interleaving or multiplexing data to increase speed. See disk striping.

stroke (1) In printing, the weight, or thickness, of a character. (2) In computer graphics, a pen' or brush stroke or to a vector in a vector graphics image.

stroke writer Same as vector display.

structured analysis Techniques developed in the late 1970s by Yourdon, DeMarco, Gane and Sarson for applying a systematic approach to systems analysis. It included the use of data flow diagrams and data modeling and fostered the use of implementation- independent graphical notation for documentation.

structured design Systematic approach to program design developed in the mid 1970s by Constantine, Yourdon, et al, that included the use of graphical notation for effective documentation and communication, design guidelines and recipes to help programmers get started.

structured programming Variety of techniques that impose a logical structure on the writing of a pro-grain. Large routines are broken down into smaller, modular routines. The use of the GOTO statement is discouraged. For documentation, certain programining statements are indented, so that beginnings and endings of loops are easily identified. Structured'languages, such as Pascal, Ada and dBASE, force the programmer to write a structured program. However, unstructured languages such as FORTRAN, COBOL and BASIC require discipline on the part of the programmer. See spaghetti code and CASE.

Stuffit Macintosh shareware program from Aladdin Systems, Aptos, CA, that compresses files onto multiple floppies.

style sheet In word processing and desktop publishing, a file that contains layout settings for a particular category of document. Style sheets include such settings as margins, tabs, headers and footers, columns and fonts.

stylus Pen-shaped instrument that is used to draw" images or point to menus. See light pen and digitizer tablet.

sub-notebook Lightweight notebook computer. As computers get lighter, the sub-notebook (if term persists) should.weigh two to three pounds, the notebook four to five.

subdirectory Disk directory that is subordinate to (below) another directory. In order to gain access to a subdirectory, the path must include all directories above it.

submarinlng Temporary visual loss of the moving cursor on a slow display screen such as found on a laptop computer. See active matrix LCD.

submenu Additional list of options within a menu selection. There can many levels of submenus.

subroutine Group of instructions that perform a specific task. A large subroutine is usually called a module or procedure; a small one, a function or macro, but all terms are used interchangeably.

subschema Pronounced "sub-skeema." In database management, a individual users partial view of the database. The schema is the entire database.

subscript (1) In word processing and mathematical notation, a digit or symbol that appears below the line. contrast with superscript. (2) In programming, a method for referencing data in a table.

substrate Base material upon which integrated circuits are built. Silicon is the most widely used substrate for chips.

substrlng Subset of an alphanumeric field or variable. A programming language substring function extracts the subset; for example, substr(prodcode,4,3) extracts characters 4, 5 and 6 out of a product code field or variable.

subtract In relational database, an operation that generates a third file from all the records in one file that are not in a second file.

Sun (Sun Microsystems) Manufacturer of network- based, high-performance workstations founded in 1982. Product lines include stand-alone and networked systems, diskless workstations and file servers that feature its SPARC microprocessor architecture. It supports an open systems model of computing throughout its product line which allows it to interact in networks of computer systems from other vendors.

super floppy (1) PC 3.5" floppy disk that holds 2.88MB and is compatible with the 1.44MB and 720KB formats. (2) Very-high-capacity floppy disk in the 20MB range. See Floptical.

Super VGA See VGA and PC display modes.

SuperCalc PC spreadsheet from Computer Associates. It was one of the first spreadsheets following in VisiCaic's footsteps in the early 1980s. Superalc5 (1988) provides 3-D capability, enhanced graphics and can link up to 256 spreadsheets.

supercomputer Fastest computer available. It is typically used for simulations in petroleum exploration and production, structural analysis, computational fluid dynamics, physics and chemistry, electronic design, nuclear energy research and meteorology. It is also used for realtime animated graphics.

superconductor Material that has little resistance to the flow of electricity. Traditional superconductors operate at -459 Fahrenheit (absolute zero). Thus far, the major use for superconductors, made of alloys of niobium, is for higi-powered magnets in medical imaging machines that use magnetic fields instead of x-rays If superconductors can work at reasonable temperatures, they will have a dramatic impact on the future. See Josephson junction.

SuperDrive Macintosh floppy disk drive that stores 1'44MB of data in its highest density format. It also reads and writes earlier Mac 400 and 800KB disks.

SuperKey PC keyboard macro processor from Borland that lets users create keyboard macros, rearrange the keyboard and encrypt data and programs.

supermini Large-scale minicomputer that overlaps in processing capability with a small-scale mainframe.

superscript Any letter, digit or symbol that appears above the line. Contrast with subscript.

superserver Network server with very large RAM and disk capacity; multiple processors and high-speed multiprocessing (Micro Channel, EISA, etc.) buses.

supertwist LCD display that improves on the earlier TN technology by twisting the crystals up to 180 degrees or more. It provides a wider viewing angle and improved contrast. It is recognized by its yellow and greenish blue color.

supervisor Same as operating system.

supervisor call Instruction in an application program that interrupts the computer and changes it to the supervisory state. The operating system then analyzes the call and directs the appropriate routine to handle it.

supervisor control program The part of the operation system that always resides in memory. Same as kernel.

supervisor state Operating mode of the computer that executes instructions in the operating system. In this mode, the computer can execute privileged instructions that are not available to the application program, such as input/output instructions. Contrast with program state, which is the operating mode for executing the application program. These terms are normally associated with large computers; however, all computers differentiate between these two sttes.

support (1) Assistance provided, by a hardware or software vendor in installing and maintaining its product. (2) Software or hardware designed towork with some other software or hardware product. For example, if a word processor 'supports the LaserJet," it is written to utilize the special features of that printer.

surface (1) In CAD, the external geometry of an object. Surfaces are generally required for NC (numerical control) modeling rather than wireframe or solids. (2) Coined by Wayne Ratliff, creator of dBASE, a language that interfaces to a database engine.

surface modeling In CAD, a mathematical technique for representing solid-appearing objects. Surface modeling is a more complex method for representing objects than wireframe modeling, but not as sophisticated as solid modeling. Although surface and solid models can appear the same on screen, they are quite different. Surface models cannot be sliced open as can solid models. In addition, in surface modeling, the object can be geometrically incorrect; whereas, in solid modeling, it must be correct.

surface mount Circuit board packaging technique in which the leads (pins) on the chips and components are soldered on top of the board, not through it. Boards can be smaller and built faster.

surge Oversupply of voltage from the power company that can last up to several seconds. See spike.

surge protector Device that protects a computer from excessive voltage (spikes and surges) in the power line. See voltage regulator and UPS.

surge suppressor Same as surge protector. SVGA (Super VGA) See VGA.

swap file Disk file used to temporarily save a program or part of a program running in memory.

swapping Replacing one segment of a program in memory with another and restoring it back to the original when required. In virtual memory systems, it is called paging.

switch (1) Mechanical or electronic device that directs the flow of electrical or optical signals. See data switch and transistor. (2) In programming, any bit or byte used to keep track of some function. It sometimes refers to a branch in a program. (3) Modifier of a command. See DOS switch.

switch-to-computer To integrate voice telephone and database access. For example, in customer service applications, using telephone services, such as automatic number identification (ANI) and automatic call distribution (ACD), an incoming call can retrieve and route the customer's file to the next available human agent.

switched line In communications, a link that was established in a switched network.

switched network (1) International dial-up telephone system. (2) Network in which a temporary connection is established from one point to another for each transmission session.

SX See 386SX and 486SX.

SYBASE System Family of SQL development tools from Sybase, Inc., that includes SQL Server, SQL Toolset (design, development and control) and Client/Services Interfaces (distributed database architecture). See SQL Server.

symbol In data compression, a unit of data (byte, floating point number, spoken word, etc.) that is treated independently.

symbol set In printing, a group of symbols that are extensions to standard characters for use in a particular country or specific application. Symbol sets provide codes for the non-standard upper half of the ASCII character set.

symbolic language (1) Programming language that uses symbols, or mnemonics, for expressing operations and operands. All modern programming languages are symbolic languages. (2) Language that manipulates symbols rather than numbers. See list processing.

symmetric multiprocessing Multiprocessing design in which any CPU can be assigned any application task. One CPU acts as a control processor, or scheduler, which boots the system, distributes work to the next available CPU and manages I/O requests. Contrast with asymmetric multiprocessing.

Symphony Integrated software package for PCs from Lotus that includes word processing, database management, speadsheet, business graphics, communications and a macro language.

sync character In synchronous communications systems, a special character transmitted to synchronize timing.

sync generator Device that supplies synchronization signals to a series of cameras to keep them all in phase.

synchronous (1) Sequence of fixed or concurrent events. See synchronous transmission. (2) Completing the current i/O operation before the next one is started. (3) In SCSI, the transfer of data without immediate acknowledgment of each byte. (4) Contrast with asynchronous.

synchronous protocol Communications protocol that controls a synchronous transmission, such as bisync, SDLC and HDLC. Contrast with asynchronous protocol.

synchronous transmission Transmission of data in which both stations are synchronized. Codes are sent from the transmitting station to the receiving station to establish the synchronization, and data is then transmitted in continuous streams. Modems that transmit at 1200 bps and higher often convert the asynchronous signals from a computer's serial port into synchronous transmission over the transmission line. Contrast with asynchronous transmission.

syntax Rules governing the structure of a language statement. It specifies how words and symbols are put together to form a phrase.

syntax error Error that occurs when a program cannot understand the command that has been entered. See parse.

sysgen (SYStem GENeration) Installation of a new or revised operating system. It includes selecting the appropriate utility programs and identifying the peripheral devices and storage capacities of the system the operating system will be controlling.

sysop (SYStem OPerator) Pronounced "siss-op." Person who runs an online communications system or bulletin, board. The sysop may also act as mediator for system conferences.

SysReq key (SYStem REQuest key) Keyboard key on a terminal keyboard that is used to get the attention of the central computer. The key exists on PC keyboards, but is rarely used by applications.

system (1) Group of related components that interact to perform a task. (2) A computer system is made up of the CPU, operating system and peripheral devices. (3) An information system is made up of the database, all the data entry, update, query and report programs and manual and machine. procedures. (4) "The system" Qften refers to the operating system.

System 2000 (1) Hierarchical, network and relational DBMS from the SAS Institute, Cary, NC, that runs on IBM, CDC and Unisys computers. It has been integrated into the SAS System. (2) See Fl'S 2000.

System/3, System/32, System/34, System/36, Syste/ 39 Minicomputer from IBM. Introduced from 1969, introducing punched cards, multitasking, etc.

System/360, System/370, System/390 Mainframe products from IBM, introducing virtual memory, ESA! 390 architecture, etc. First family of computer systems introduced in 1964. It was the first time in history that a complete line of computers was announced at one time. Although considerable enhancements have been made, much of the 360 architecture is still carried over in current-day IBM mainframes. See IBM mainframes.

System 7 (1) Major upgrade of the Macintosh operating system (1991). It includes virtual memory, increased memory addressing, hot links (Publish & Subscribe), multitasking (MultiFinder no longer optional), TrueType fonts and a variety of enhancements to the user interface. (2) (System/7) Sensor-based minicomputer from IBM introduced in 1970 and used for process control. It was superseded by the Series 1.

system development cycle Sequence of events in the development of an information system (application), which requires mutual effort on the part of user and technical staff. This cycle begins with systems analysis & design (feasibility study, general design, prototy. ping, detail design, functional specifications), programming (design, coding, testing), implementation (training, conversion, installation) and user acceptance.

system development methodology Formal documentation for the phases of the system development cycle. It defines the precise objectives for each phase and the results required from a phase before the next one can begin. It may include specialized forms for preparing the documentation describing each phase.

system disk Hard or floppy disk that contains part or all of the operating system or other control program.

system failure Hardware or software malfunction. May refer to a problem with the operating system problem.

system file Machine language file that is part of the operating system or other control program. It may also refer to a configuration file used by such programs.

system folder Operating system folder in the Macintosh that contains the System, Finder and MultiFinder, printer drivers, fonts, desk accessories, INITs and cdevs.

system image Memory view of current operating environment, including the operating system and running programs.

system level Operation that is performed by the operating system or some other control program.

system life cycle Useful life of an information system. Its length depends on the nature and volatility of the business, as well as the software development tools used to generate the databases and applications. Eventually, an information system that is patched over and over no longer is structurally sound enough to be expanded.

system management See systems management.

system memory Memory used by the operating system. system program Component of system software.

system prompt On-screen symbol that indicates the operating system is ready for a command. See DOS prompt.

system software Programs used to control the computer and run application programs. It includes operating systems, TP monitors, network control programs, network operating systems and database managers. Contrast with application program.

system test Running a complete system for testing purposes.

system time/date Running time of day in the computer, which is maintained by a battery when the computer is turned off. It is used to time stamp all newly-created files and activate time-dependent processes.

systems testing Testing of a series of programs, including input and output, are related in the way the systems analyst intended.

system testing The testing of all programs that make up the system, in the sequence in which they will be executed.

System V Release 4.0 Unified version of UNIX released in 1989. See UNIX.

System V.4 See System V Release 4.0.

SYSTEM.INI See WIN.INI.

systems General term for the department, people or work involved in systems analysis & design activities.

systems analysis & design Examination of a problem and the creation of its solution. See system development cycle and Systemantics.

systems analyst Persons responsible for the development of an information system. They design and modify systems by turning user requirements into a set of functional specifications, which are the blueprint of the system. They design the database or help design it if data administrators are available. They develop the manual and machine procedures and the detailed processing specs for each data entry, update, query and report program in the system. It is their job to develop solutions to user's problems, determine the technical and operational feasibility of their solutions, as well as estimate the costs to develop and implement them. They develop prototypes of the system along with the users, so that the final specifications are examples of screens and reports that have been carefully reviewed. Experienced analysts leave no doubt in users' minds as to what is being developed, and they insist that all responsible users review and concur every detail. Systems analysts require a balanced mix of business and technical knowledge, interviewing and analytical skills, as well as a good understanding of human behavior. See Systemantics.

systems disk Disk pack or disk drive reserved only for system software, which includes the operating system, assemblers, compilers and other utility and control programs.

systems engineer Often a vendor title for persons involved in consulting and pre-sales activities related to computers. See systems analyst, systems programmer, programmer analyst and application programmer.

systems management (1) Management of systems development, which includes systems analysis & design, application development and implementation. See system development cycle. (2) Management of computer systems, which includes controlling multiprocessing systems, network management and backup and recovery.

systems program See system program and system software.

systems programmer (1) A technical expert on some or all of the computer's system software (operating systems, networks, DBMSs, etc.). They are responsible for the efficient performance of the computer systems. They usually don't write programs, but perform a lot of technical tasks that integrate vendors' software. They also act as technical advisors to systems analysts, application programmers and operations personnel. (2) In a computer hardware or software organization, a person who designs and writes system software.

Schedule: In a distributed database system, an ordered sequence of data requests.

Schema: A complete logical view of the database.

Screen: See Form.

Second normal form: A relation in first normal form in which all nonkey attributes are dependent on all of the key.

Segment: In DL /1, a collection of fields that is a node in a data base record.

Segment search argument: An expression in a DL /1 that indicates the segment or segments to which the command is to be applied.

Selection: A relational algebra operation performed on a relation, A, producing a relation, B, with B containing only the rows in A that meet the restrictions specified in the selection.

Semantic object diagram: Same as Object diagram. Semantic object -model: The constructs and conventions used to create a model of the users' data. The things in the users' world are represented by semantic objects (sometimes called objects). Relationships are modeled in the objects, and the results are usually documented in object diagrams.

Semantic-object view: The portion of a semantic object that is visible in a form or report.

Sequence field: In DL/I, a field that is used to order logically the segments of a given type under a given parent. The order can be ascending or descending.

Serializable: A condition pertaining to two or more transactions in which the results of the processing are the same as they would have been if the transactions had been processed in some serial manner.

Set: In the CODASYL DBTG model, a structure that represents a one-to-many relationship among records. The parent record type is called the set owner, and the child record type(s) is (are) called the set member.

Set membership: In the CODASYL DBTG model, the records that belong to a particular set instance.

SGML: Standard generalized markup language.

Shared lock: A lock against a data resource in which only one transaction may update the data, but many transactions can concurrently read that data.

Shrinking phase: In two-phase locking, the stage at which locks are released but no lock is acquired.

Sibling: A record or node that has the same parent as does another record or node.

Simple network: (1) A set of three relations and two relationships in which one of the relations, R, has a many-to-one relationship with the other two relations. The rows in R have two parents, and the parents are of different types. (2) Any set of tables and relationships containing the structure defined in (1).

Simple object: An object that contains no repeating attributes and noobject attributes.

Simple table space: In DB2, a table space that contains data from more than one table.

Single-tier driver: In ODBC, a database driver that accepts SQL statements from the driver manager and processes them without invoking another program or DBMS. A single-tier driver is both an ODBC driver and a DBMS; used for file-processing systems.

Single-valued attribute: In a semantic object, an attribute having a maximum cardinality of one.

SQL: Structured query language. A language for defining the structure and processing of a relational database. It is used as a stand-alone query language, or it may be embedded in application programs. SQL is accepted as a national standard by the American National Standards Institute. It was developed by IBM.

SQL3: SQL3 is an extension to the SQL92 database standard that includes support for object-oriented database management. Developed by both the ANSI X3H2 and the ISO/IEC JTC1/5C21/ WG3 standardization committees.

Standard generalized markup language (SGML): A standard means for tagging and marking the format, structure, and content of documents. HTML is a subset of SGML.

Storage group: In DB2, a group of disk volumes on which database data is stored.

Strong entity: In an entity-relationship model, any entity whose existence in the database does not depend on the existence of any other entity. See also ID-dependent entity and Weak entity.

Subschema: A subset of a database that is processed by one or more applications. A subschema may also be called an application view; it is used primarily with the CODASYL DBTG model.

Subtable: In SQL3, a table that is a subtype of a second table, called a supertable.

Subtype: In generalization hierarchies, an entity or object that is a subspecies or subcategory of a higher-level type. For example, ENGINEER is a subtype of EMPLOYEE.

Supertable: In SQL3, a table that has one or more sub- tables defined on it.

Supertype: In generalization hierarchies, an entity or object that logically contains subtypes. For example, EMPLOYEE is a supertype of ENGINEER, ACCOUNTANT, and MANAGER.

Surrogate key: A column of unique values that is maintained by the application or the DBMS. This column is used as the primary key of the table.

Swizzling: In OOP, the process of converting a permanent object identifier into an in-memory address and the reverse.

T

T See tera.

T-byte See terabyte.

T-carrler Digital transmission service from a common carrier. Introduced by AT&T in 1983 as a voice service, its use for data transmission has grown steadily. T-carrier service requires multiplexors at both ends. Versions are Ti, T2 and T3.

tab character Control character in a document that represents movement to the next tab stop. See ASCII chart (9 and 11).

tab delimited Text file format that uses tab characters as separators between fields. Unlike comma delimited files, alphanumeric data is not surrounded by quotes.

tab key Keyboard key that moves the cursor to the next tab stop. T

tabbing Moving the cursor on a video display screen or the print head on a printer to a specified column.

table (1) In programming, a collection of adjacent fields. Also called an array, a table contains data that is either constant within the program or is called in when the program is run. See decision table. (2) In a relational database, the same as a file; a collection of records.

table lookup Searching for data in a table, commonly used in data entry validation and any operation that must match an item of data with a known set of values.

table view Screen display of several items or records in rows and columns. Contrast with form view.

tablet See digitizer tablet.

tabular form Same as table view with respect to printed output. tabulate (1) To arrange data into a columnar format. (2) To sum and print totals.

tabulate (1) To print totals. (2) To form data into a table. tabulating equipment Punched card data processing machines, including keypunches, sorters, collators, interpreters, reproducers, calculators and tabulators.

tabulator Punched card accounting machine that prints and calculates totals.

tag (1) Set of bits or characters that identifies various conditions about data in a file and is often found in the header records of such files. (2) Name (label, mnemonic) assigned to a data structure, such as a field, file, paragraph or other object. (3) Key field in a record. (4) Brass pin on a terminal block that is connected to a wire by soldering or wire wrapping.

tag sort Sorting procedure in which the key fields are sorted first to create the correct order, and then the actual data records are placed into that order.

Tandem (Tandem Computers Inc., Cupertino, CA) Manufacturer of computers founded in 1974 by James Treybig to address the transaction processing market (reservations, financial transf&s, etc.). It introduced the first commercial computer based on a fault tolerant, multiprocessor architecture,

tandem processors Two processors hooked together in a multiprocessor environment.

Tandy (Tandy Corp.) Manufacturer of PCs and electronics. In 1963, it acquired the Radio Shack chain of nine electronics stores in the Boston area. Today, Tandy has over 7,000 stores and dealer franchises. In 1977, it introduced one of the first personal computers, the TRS-80 Model I. Tandy's Model 100 and 200 lightweight portables were also an inspiration to the laptop generation. Tandy now offers a full line of IBM-compatible PCs.

tap In communications, a connection onto the main transmission medium of a local area network. See transceiver.

tape See magnetic tape & disk.

tape backup Use of magnetic tape for storing duplicate copies of hard disk files.

tape drive Physical unit that hcilds, reads and writes the magnetic tape. See magnetic tape & disk.

tape dump Printout of tape contents without any report formatting.

tape mark Control code used to indicate the end of a tape file.

tape transport Mechanical part of a tape drive.

tar UNIX utility for archiving files, often used in conjunction with "compress."

Targa Raster graphics file format (.TGA extension) developed by Truevision, that handles 16-, 24- and 32-bit color. It is also the trade name of a line of high-resolution video graphics boards.

target computer Computer into which a program is loaded and run. Contrast with source computer. See cross assembler/compiler.

target directory Directory into which data is being sent. target disk Disk onto which data is recorded. Contrast with source disk.

target drive Drive containing the disk or tape onto which data is recorded. Contrast with source drive.

task Independent running program. See multitasking.

task management The part of the operating system that controls the running of one or more programs (tasks) within the computer at the same time.

task swapping Switching between two applications by copying the current running program to disk or other high-speed storage device (auxiliary memory, EMS, etc.) and loading another program into that program space. Not to be confused with multi-tasking.

task switching Switching between active applications. See context switching.

TB, Tb See terabyte and terabit. Tbit See terabit.

Tbits/sec (TeraBITS per SECond) Trillion bits per second.

TBps, Thps (TeraBytes Per Second, TeraBits Per Second) Trillion bytes per second. Trillion bits per second.

TByte See terabyte.

Thytes/sec (TeraBYTES per SECond) Trillion bytes per second.

TCO Stringent low-radiation standards set by the Swedish Confederation of Professional Employees. See MPRH.

tear-off menu On-screen menu or palette that can be moved off of its primary position and relocated to any part of the screen.

tech writer Person who is responsible for writing documentation for a hardware or software product.

tele Operations performed remotely or by telephone. telecom See telecommunications.

telecommunications Communicating information, including data, text, pictures, voice and video. See communications.

telecommunications specialist A person responsible for the design of data communications networks.

telecommunity Society in which information can be transmitted or received freely between all members without technical incompatibilities.

telecommutlng Working at home and communicating with the office.

teleconferencing (1) Video teleconferencing. Video conference among several users provided by video cameras and monitors set up inhouse or in a public conferencing center. (3) Computer teleconferencing. Keyboard conference among several users at term inals or personal computers provided by specialized software in a host computer or BBS.

telecopying (long distance copying) Formal term for fax.

telegraph Low-speed communications device that transmits up to approximately 150 bps. Telegraph grade lines, stemming from the days of Morse code, can't transmit a voice conversation.

telemanagement Management of an organization's telephone systems.

telemarketing Selling over the telephone.

Telematlcs Convergence of telecommunications and information processing.

telemetry Transmitting data captured by instrumentation and measuring devices to a remote station where it is recorded and analyzed. For example, data from a weather satellite is telemetered to the earth.

telephone wiring See twisted pair.

telephony Science of converting sound into electrical signals, transmitting it within cables or via radio and reconverting it back into sound.

teleprinter Terminal that includes a keyboard for input and a printer for output. Teleprinters provide hard copy; display terminals provide soft copy. Contrast with video terminal.

teleprocessing (long distance processing) Early IBM term for data communications.

teleprocessing monitor See TP monitor.

telesoftware Computer programs sent by telephone line or television as part of the teletext signal.

Teletex See Telex.

teletext Broadcasting service that transmits text to a TV set that has a teletext decoder. It uses the vertical blanking interval of the TV signal (black line between frames when vertical hold is not adjusted) to transmit about a hundred frames. See videotex.

teletype interface Same as teletype mode.

teletype mode Refers to producing output a line at a time as if typed on a typewriter. It implies that data is displayed or printed serially, one line following the other.

teletypewriter Low-speed teleprinter, often abbreviated "TTY."

Telex International dial-up communications service that uses teleprinters and transmits Baudot code t 50 bps (66 words/minute).

template (1) Plastic or stiff paper form that is placed over the function keys on a keyboard to identify their use. (2) Programmatic and descriptive part of a programmable application; for example, a spreadsheet that contains only descriptions and formulas or a HyperCard stack that contains only programming and backgrounds. When the template is filled with data, it becomes a working application.

temporary font Soft font that remains in the printer's memory until the printer is reset manually or by software. Contrast with permanent font.

ter Third version.

tern Trillion Abbreviated "T." It often refers to the precise value 1,099,511,627,776 since computer specifications are usually binary numbers. See binary values and space/time.

terabit One trillion bits. Also Th, Thit and T-bit. See tera and space/time.

terabyte One trillion bytes. Also TB, Thyte and T-byte. See tera and space/time.

teraflops (tera FLoating point OPerations per Second) One trillion floating point operations per second.

terminal (1) I/O device for a computer that usually has a keyboard for input and a video screen or printer for output. (2) Input device, such as a scanner, video camera or punched card reader. (3) Output device in a network, such as a monitor, printer or card punch. (4) Connector used to attach a wire.

terminal emulation Using a personal computer to simulate a mainframe or minicomputer terminal. See virtual terminal.

terminal mode Operating mode that causes the computer to act like a terminal; ready to transmit typed- in keystrokes and ready to receive transmitted data.

terminal server Computer or controller used to connect a variety of terminals to a network or host computer.

terminal session Time in which a user is working at a terminal.

terminal strip Insulated bar that contains a set of screws to which wires are attached.

terminate and stay resident See TSR.

terminator (1) Chaiacter that ends a string of alphanumeric characters. (2) Hardware component that is connected to the last peripheral device in a series or the last node in a network.

terrestrial link Communications line that travels on, near or below ground. Contrast with satellite link.

test data Set of data created for testing new or revised programs. It should be as close to real data as possible.

test driver A program that directs the execution of another program against a collection of test data sets.

testing Running new or revised programs to determine if they process all data properly. See test data.

text Words, sentences and paragraphs. Contrast with data, which are defined units, such as name and amount due. Text may also refer to alphanumeric data, such as name and address, to distinguish it from numeric data, such as quantity and dollar amounts. A page of text takes about 2,000 to 4,000 bytes. See text field.

text based Also called character based, the display of text and limited graphics character. For example, 25 rows of 80 columns. Contrast with graphics based.

text editingm Ability to change text by adding, deleting and rearranging letters, words, sentences and paragraphs.

text editor Software used to create and edit files that contain only text. Unlike a word processor, it usually does not provide word wrap or formatting features such as underline, boldface or font changes. Editors designed for programming may provide automatic indention and multiple windows. See DOS Edlin and DOS Editor.

text field Data structure that holds alphanumeric data, such as name and address. If a text field holds large, or unlimited, amounts of text, it may be called a memo field. Contrast with numeric field.

text file File that contains only text characters. Contrast with graphics file and binary file.

text management Creation, storage and retrieval of text. It implies flexible retrieval capabilities that can search for text based on a variety of criteria. Although a word processor manages text, it usually has limited retrieval capabilities.

text mode (1) Screen display mode that displays only text and not graphics. (2) Program mode that allows text to be entered and edited.

texture mapping In computer graphics, the creation of a special surface. These textures can be produced with algorithms. It can also be done by electronically wrapping a secondary image around an object.

TFT (Thin Film Transistor) See thin film.

TFT LCD (Thin Film Transistor LCD) See active ma-, trix LCD.

theorem A statement that can be proved; the conclusion of a valid arguement.

theorem prover A program that starts with a goal and searches for implications whose conclusions will unify with the goal. A theorem prover has a database consisting of a set of axioms. Its inference mechanism makes inferences that lead to a satisfaction of the goal.

theorem proving The branch .of artificial intelligence involved in using computers to prove mathematical and logic theorems.

thermal dye diffusion Printing process similar to thermal wax transfer except that a dye is used instead of ink. The printhead heats the ribbon causing the dye to turn from a solid to a gas and condense on special paper. The more heat, the denser the image. Continuous color can be produced that approaches photographic quality.

thermal printer Non-impact printer that uses a print head of electrically heated pins and special heat-sensitive paper. The pins are pushed against the paper, and, when selectively heated, the paper darkens upon contact. Thermal printers are quiet, low-cost devices that provide a low to medium-resolution print image.

thermal wax transfer Printing process that transfers a waxlike ink onto paper. For example, in a color printer, a mylar ribbon is used that contains several hundred repeating sets of full pages of black, cyan, magenta and yellow ink. A sheet of paper is pressed against each color and passed by a line of heating elements that transfers the dots, or pixels, of ink onto the paper.

thick film Layer of magnetic, semiconductor or metallic material that is thicker than the microscopic layers of the transistors on a chip. For example, metallic thick films are silk screened onto the ceramic base of hybrid microcircuits. Contrast with thin film.

thimble printer Letter quality printer similar to a daisy wheel printer. Instead of a wheel, characters are formed facing out and around the rim of a thimble- shaped cup. For example, the NEC Spinwriters are thimble printers.

thin film Microscopically thin layer of semiconductor or magnetic material that is deposited onto a metal, ceramic or semiconductor base. For example, the layers that make up a chip and the surface coating on high-density magnetic disks are called thin films.

thin film head Read/write head for high-density disks that is made from thin layers of a conducting film deposited onto a nickel-iron core.

thin window display A one-line display used on keyboards, pocket computers, and so on. Usually on LCD or LED display.

third-generation computer Computer that uses integrated circuits, disk storage and online terminals. The third generation started roughly in 1964 with the IBM System/360.

third-generation language Traditional high-level programming language such as FORTRAN, COBOL, BASIC, Pascal and C.

third normal form See normalization.

thrashing Excessive paging in a virtual memory computer. If programs are not written to run in a virtual memory environment, the operating system may spend excessive amounts of time swapping program pages in and out of the disk.

thread One transaction or message in a multithreaded system.

threading See multithreading.

three-state logic element Electronic component that provides three possible outputs: off, low voltage and high voltage.

throughput Speed with which a computer processes data. It is a combination of internal processing speed, peripheral speeds (I/O) and the efficiency of the operating system and other system software all working together.

THz (TerallertZ) One trillion cycles per second.

TI (Texas Instruments, Inc., Dallas, TX) Leading semiconductor manufacturer founded in 1930 to provide services to the petroleum industry. During the war, it manufactured electronic equipment for the Navy, and in 1946, formally added electronica to its product line. In 1951, Texas Instruments entered the semiconductor business. TI was the first to commercialize the silicon transistor, pocket radio, integrated circuit, hand-held calculator, single- chip computer and the LISP chip. In the early 1980s, it introduced and sold a large number of its low-priced 99/4a home computers. It later introduced a high-quality MS- DOS computer, but eventually pulled out of the personal computing business. It also creates computer systems for Al applications, composite metals, electrical control products and consumer electronica, including its well-known line of calculators and educational math and reading machines.

TIFF (Tagged Image File Format) Widely-used raster graphics file format developed by Aldus and Microsoft that handles monochrome, gray scale, 8- and 24-bit color. It uses several compression methods: LZW provides ratios of about 1.5:1 to 2:1. Ratios of 10:1 to 20:1 are possible for documents with lots of white space using CCITT Group III & IV compression methods (fax). See JPEG.

tightly coupled Refers to two or more computers linked together and dependent on each other. One computer may control the other, or both computers may monitor each other. Two computers tied together for multiprocessing are tigitly coupled. Contrast with loosely coupled, such as personal computers in a LAN.

tiled Display of objects side by side; for example, tiled windows cannot be overlapped on top of each other.

time slice Fixed interval of time allotted to each user or program in a multitasking or timesharing system.

time slot Continuously repeating interval of time or a time period in which two devices are able to interconnect.

timer mterrupt Interrupt generated by an internal clock. See interrupt.

timesharing Computer environment that allows multiple users access to selected programs and databases. It mostly refers to large computers in service bureaus and implies that users can initiate the required sessions as needed.

timing clock See clock.

timing signals Electrical pulses generated in the processor or in external devices in order to synchronize computer operations. The main timing signal comes from the computer's clock, which provides a frequency that can be divided into many slower cycles. Other timing signals may come from a timesharing or realtime clock. In disk drives, timing signals for reading and writing are generated by holes or marks on one of the platters, or by the way the digital data is actually recorded.

Tiny BASIC Subset of BASIC that has been used in first generation personal computers with limited memory.

TN (Twisted Nematic) First successful LCD technology, which twists liquid crystal molecules 90 degrees between polarizers. Requires bright ambient light, uses low voltage and is still used in low-cost applications. See supertwist.

TOF (Top Of Form) In ptinters, the beginning of a physical paper form.

toggle To alternate back and forth between two states.

token passing Communications network access method that uses a continuously repeating frame (the token) that is transmitted onto the network by the controlling computer. When a terminal or computer wants to send a message, it waits for an empty token. When it finds one, it fills it with the address of the destination station and some or all of its message.

token ring network (1) Communications network that uses the token passing technology in a sequential manner. Each station in the network passes the token on to the station next to it. (2) (Token Ring Network) IBM LAN that uses a special twisted wire cable and the token passing access method transmitting at four or 16 Mbits/sec. It uses a star topology in which all computers connect to a central wiring hub, but passes tokens to each of up to 255 stations in a sequential, ring-like sequence. Token Ring conforms to the IEEE 802.5 standard.

toner Electrically charged ink used in copy machines and laser printers. It adheres to an invisible image that has been charged with the opposite polarity onto a plate or drum or onto the paper itself.

tool (1) On-screen function in an interactive program; for example, a line draw, circle -draw or paintbrush option in a graphics program. (2) Program used for software development or system maintenance. Utility programs, editors., debuggers and graphics routines are examples. A program that helps a user customize, adapt or work with a computer may also be called a tool.

tool palette Collection of on-screen functions, typically graphics related, that are grouped in a menu structure for interactive selection.

toolbox Same as toolkit.

toolkit Set of software routines that allow a program to be written for and work in a particular environment. The routines are called by the application program to perform various functions, for example, to display a menu or draw a graphic element.

top of file Beginning of a file. In a word processing file, it is the first character in the document. In a data file, it is either the first record in the file or the first record in the index.

topdown design Design technique that starts with the highest level of an concept and works its way down to the lowest level of implementation.

topdown programming Programming design and documentation technique that imposes a hierarchical structure on the design of the program. See structured programming.

topology (1) In a communications network, the pattern of interconnection between nodes; for example, a bus, ring or star configuration. (2) In a parallel processing architecture, the interconnection between processors; for example, a bus, grid, hypercube or Butterfly Switch configuration.

total bypass Bypassing local and long distance telephone lines by using satellite communications.

touch screen Touch-sensitive display screen that uses a clear panel over on the screen surface. The panel is a matrix of cells that transmit pressure information to the software.

tower (1) Floor-standing cabinet taller than it is wide. (2) Tower Series of UNIX-based single and multiprocessor computer systems from NCR that use the Motorola 68000 family of CPUs.

tpl (Tracks Per Inch) Used to measure the density of tracks recorded on a disk or drum. TPS (1) (Transactions Per Second) Number of transactions processed within one second in a transaction processing system. (2) (Transaction Processing System) Originally used as an acronym for such a system. It now refers to the measurement of the system (#1 above).

track Storage channel on disk or tape. On disks, tracks are concentric circles (hard and floppy disks) or spirals (CD5 and videodisca). On tapes, they are parallel lines. Their format is determined by the specific drive they are used in. On magnetic devices, bits are recorded as reversals of polarity in the magnetic surface. On CDs, bits are recorded as physical pits under a clear, protective layer. See sector.

trackball Input device used in video games and as a mouse alternative. It is a stationary unit that contains a movable ball rotated with the fingers or palm and, correspondingly, moves the cursor on screen.

tractorfeed Mechanism that provides high speed movement of paper forms through a printer. It contains pins on tractors that engage the paper through perforated holes in its left and right borders. Contrast with sheet feeder.

trailer (1) In data processing, the last record in a file, which usually contains the number of records in the file and hash totals. (2) In communications, a code or set of codes that make up the last part of a transmitted message.

trailer label Last record in a file, which contains iden tification data about the file.

train printer Line printer mechanism that uses type slugs that ride in a track. See chain printer.

trainIng (1) Teaching the details of a particular subject. With regard to software, training provides instruction for each command used in an application. Contrast with education. (2) In communications, the process by which two modems determine the correct protocols and transmission speeds to use. (3) In voice recognition systems, the recording of the user's voice in order to provide samples and patterns for recognizing that voice.

transaction Activity or request. Orders, purchases, changes, additions and deletions are examples of transactions that are recorded in a business information environment. Queries and other requests are also transactions to the computer, but are usual ly just acted upon and not recorded in the system. Transaction volume is a major factor in determining the size and speed of a computer system.

transaction file Collection of records that record the activity of an organization. The data in transaction files is used to update the data in master files, which contain the subjects of the organization. Transaction files also serve as audit trails and are usually transferred from active disk files to the data library after some period of time. As optical disks become more economical, transaction files will remain online in the computer so that an organization's history will be immediately available for ad hoc queries. See information system.

transaction processing Processing transactions as they are received by the system. Transaction processing systems, also called online or realtime systems, update master files as soon as they are entered at terminals or arrive over communications lines. Contrast with batch processing, which stores transactions and updates the necessary files at a later date. If you save receipts in a shoebox and add them up at the end of the year for tax purposes, that's batch processing. However, if you buy something and immediately add the amount to the running total, that's transaction processing!

transceiver Transmitter and receiver of analog or digital signals that comes in many forms; for example, a communications satellite transponder on a network adapter.

transcribe To copy data from one medium to another, for example, from one source document to another, or from a source document to the computer. It often implies a change of format or codes.

transducer Device-that converts one energy into another, for example, a read/write head converts magnetic energy into electrical energy and vice versa. In process control applications, it is used to convert pressure into an electrical reading..

transfer To send data over a computer channel or bus. "Transfer" generally applies to transmission within the computer and peripherals, and 'transmit" refers to transmission outside of the computer (over a line, network, etc.). Transfers are actually copies, since the data is in both locations at the end of the transfer. Input, output and move instructions activate data transfers in the computer.

transfer protocol See file transfer protocol.

transfer rate Also called data rate, the transmission speed of a communications or computer channel. Transfer rates are measured in bits or bytes per second.

transfer time Time it takes to transmit or move data from one place to another. It is the time interval between starting the transfer and the completion of the transfer.

transformer Electromagnetic device that changes AC voltage. It is made up of a number of steel laminations that are wrapped with two coils of wire; the primary coil on the input side and the secondary coil on the output side. The voltage change is derived from the number of windings in each coil. For example, if the input is 120 volts, the primary coil has 1,000 windings, and the secondary coil has 100 windings, the output oltage will be 12 volts. In order to create direct CUIT ent (Dq, the output of the secondary coil is passed through a rectifier.

transient Malfunction that occurs at random intervals; for example, a rapid fluctuation of voltage in a power line or a memory cell that intermittently fails.

transient area Area in memory used to hold application programs for processing. The bulk of a computer's main memory is used as a transient area.

transient state Exact point at which a device changes modes, for example, from transmit to receive or 0 to 1.

transistor Semiconductor device used to amplify a signal or open and close a circuit. In digital computers, it functions as an electronic switch. When activated, it bridges the gap between two wires and allows current to flow. The gap is a material that normally resists electricity, but can change its state to become conductive and allow current to flow from source to drain. Transistors, resistors, capacitors and diodes, make up logic gates. Logic gates make up circuits, and circuits make up electronic systep

translate (1) To change one language into another; for example, assemblers, compilers and interpreters translate source language into machine language. (2) In computer graphics, to move an image on screen without rotating it. (3) In telecommunictions, to change the frequencies of a band of signals. V

TransLISP PLUS Version of LISP for PCs from Solution Systems, Inc. It provides an interface to Microsoft C that allows a C routine to be added to the LISP library as a function.

transmission Transfer of data over a communications channel.

transmission channel Path between two nodes in a network. It may refer to the physical cable, the signal transmitted within the cable or to a subchannel within a carrier frequency. In radio and TV, it refers to the assigned carrier frequency.

transmission control unit See TCU.

transmit To send data over a communications line. See transfer.

transmitter Device that generates signals. Contrast with receiver.

transparent Refers to a change in hardware or software that, after installation, causes no noticeable change in the operation of the computer.

transponder Receiver and transmitter in a communi cations satellite. -V

transport protocol Communications protocol responsible for establishing a connection and ensuring that all data has arrived safely. It is defined in layer 4 of the OSI model.

transponder Receiver and transmitter in a communications satellite.

transport protocol Communications protocol responsible for establishing a connection and ensuring that all data has arrived safely. It is defined in layer 4 of the OSI model.

trap To test for a particular condition in a running program. A debugging trap waits for the execution of a particular instruction in order to stop the program and analyze the status of the system at that moment.

trapdoor Alternate way of gaining access to an interactive program. It implies a special entrance or exit that can be used if necessary.

trash can Macintosh icon used for deleting files, folders and applications and ejecting a floppy disk.

tree Hierarchical structure. See directory tree.

trichromatlc In computer graphics, the use of red, green and blue to create all the colors in the spectrum.

trillion One thousand times one billion. See tera and picosecond.

triple precision Use of three computer words to hold a number used for calculation, providing an enormous amount of arithmetic precision.

triple twist Supertwist variation that twists crystals to 260 degrees for improved clarity.

troff (1) (Typesetting RunOFF) UNIX utility that formats documents for typesetters and laser printers. Using a text editor, troff codes are embedded into the text and the troff command converts the document into the required output. See nroff. (2) In BASIC this command switches off the Trace On. See TRON.

Tarjan horse Program routine that invades a computer system by being secretly attached to a valid program that will be downloaded into the computer. It may be used to locate password information, or it may alter an existing program to make it easier to gain access to it. A virus is a Trojan horse that continues to infect programs over and over.

TRON (The Realtime Operating System Nucleus) Advanced realtime computer architecture and operating system under development by Japanese universities and corporations. Its ultimate goal is a common architecture and user interface from the smallest consumer appliance to the largest supercomputer. (2) In BASIC, a command which echoes the line numbers of the source code of the program being run. Used as a Debugging tool. See TROFF.

TRS (Tandy Radio Shack) First trade name used by Tandy for its personal computers. In 1977, the TRS80 was one of the three first personal computers ever introduced. TRS-DOS was the name for its operating system.

True BASIC ANSI-standard structured-programming version of BASIC for the PC, Mac and Amiga from True BASIC. Developed in 1984 by BASIC'S creators, John Kemeny and Thomas

Kurtz (who continue to take an active role in it), it includes many enhancements over their original BASIC and is pro. vided in both interpreter and compiler form.

true color (1) Ability to generate 16,777,216 colors (24- bit color). See high color. (2) Ability to generate photo-realistic color images (requires minimum of 24-bit color).

TrueImage Enhanced PostScript interpreter from Microsoft that prints PostScript Type 1 and TrueType fonts.

TrueType Scalable font technology from Apple. Each font outline contains its own algorithm for generating the bitmaps for the screen and printer. It is used in System 7, Windows 3.1 and OS/2. See TrueImage.

truncate To cut off leading or trailing digits or characters from an item of data withoi3t regard to the accuracy of the remaining characters. Truncation occurs when data is converted into a new record with smaller field lengths than the original.

trunk Communications channel between two points. It often refers to large-bandwidth telephone channels between major switching centers, capable of transmitting many simultaneous voice and data signals.

TSR (Terminate and Stay Resident) Refers to programs that remain in memory so that they can be instantly popped up over some other application by pressing the required combination of keys (hotkey). The program is displayed either as a small window on top of the existing text or image, or it takes up the full screen. When the program is exited, the previous screen contents are restored. On DOS PCs, TSRs provide quick access to a calculator, calendar or dictionary; however, memory conflicts may arise when multiple TSRs are loaded. Older ones may not always work with newer ones. The term basically refers to loading a program, terminating its action but not removing it from memory. [[PJX OF SIDEKICK??]]

TEL (Transistor Transistor Logic) Digital circuit in which the output is derived from two transistors. Although T1'L is a specific design method, it often refers generically to digital connections in contrast with analog connections. For example, a Til input on a monitor requires digital output from the display board rather than analog output.

tube See CRT and vacuum tube.

tuple In relational .database management, a record, or row. See relational database.

turbo Trade name for hardware and software that implies high speed. It often refers to faster clock rates in personal computers. Borland has popularized its use in its language products, such as Turbo C and Turbo Pascal.

Turbo C C compiler from Borland used to create a wide variety of commercial products. It is known for its exceptionally well-designed debugger.

Turbo Mouse Macintosh trackball from Kensington Microware, Ltd., San Mateo, CA. If the ball is moved slowly, the cursor moves slowly, but if moved quickly, the same spatial movement moves the cursor a greater distance on the screen. Its PC counterpart is called the"Expert Mouse.

Turbo Pascal Pascal compiler for DOS from Borland used in a wide variety of applications from accounting to complex commercial products. Turbo Pascal for Windows provides an object-oriented programming environment for Windows development. Borland is responsible for moving the Pascal language from the academic halls to the commercial world.

turnaround document Paper document or punched card prepared for re- entry into the computer system. Paper documents are printed with OCR fonts for scanning.

turnaround time (1) In batch processing, the time it takes to receive finished reports after submission of documents or files for processing. In an online environment, turnaround time is the same as response time. (2) In half-duplex transmission, the time it takes to change from transmit to receive and vice versa.

turnkey system Complete system of hardware and software delivered to the customer ready-to-run.

turnpike effect In communications, a lock up due to increased traffic conditions and bottlenecks in the system.

turtle graphics Method for creating graphic images in Logo. The turtle is an imaginary pen that is given drawing commands, such as go forward and turn right. On screen, the turtle is shaped like a triangle.

tutorial Instructional book or program that takes the user through a prescribed sequence of steps in order to learn a product. Contrast with documentation, which, although instructional, tends to group features and functions by category or by alphabetical order.

tweak To make minor adjustments in an electronic system or in a software program in order to improve performance.

twinaxial Type of cable similar to coax, but with two inner conductors instead of one.

TWIP (TWentIeth of a Point) Equal to 1/1440th of an inch.

twisted pair Abbreviated "UTP" (Unshielded Twisted Pair), a pair of thin-diameter (22 to 26 gauge) insulated wires commonly used in telephone wiring. The wires are twisted around each other to minimize interference from other twisted pairs in the cable. Twisted pairs have less bandwidth than coaxial cable or optical fiber.

type (1) In data or text entry, to press the keys on the keyboard. (2) In programming, a category of variable that is determined by the kind of data stored in it. For example, integer, floating point, string, logical, date and binary are common data types. (3) In DOS and OS/2, a command that displays the contents of a text file.

Type 1 font See PostScript.

Type 3 font See PostScript.

type ball Golf ball-sized element used in typewriters and low-speed teleprinters that contains all the print characters on its outside surface. It was introduced with IBM's Selectric typewriter.

type family See typeface family.

type font Set of print characters of a particular design (typeface), size (point size) and weight (light, medium, heavy). See font.

type scaler See font scaler.

typeahead buffer See keyboard buffer.

typeface Design of a set of printed characters, such as Courier, Helvetica and Times Roman. It consists of the ascender area which rises above the body of the letter (called x-height), the base line and the descender area. The entire area being measured in point sizes.

typeface family: Group of typefaces that include the normal, bold, italic and bold-italic variations of the same design.

typeover mode In word processing and data entry, a state in which each character typed on the keyboard overwrites or replaces the character at the current cursor location. Contrast with insert mode.

typesetter See phototypesetter and imagesetter.

Table space: In DB2, a collection of one or more VSAM data sets, or files, used to store database data on magnetic disk.

TCP/IP: Terminal Control Program! Internet Protocol.

TelNet: A standard service on the Internet that allows a user to log on to a server from a remote computer.

Third normal form: A relation in second normal form that has no transitive dependencies.

Top-down database design: The design of a database that works from the general to the specific. The resulting database can serve an organization's overall needs; the danger is that it may never be completed. See Bottom-up database design.

Transaction: (1) An atomic transaction. (2) The record of an event in the business world.

Transaction node: In a distributed database system, a computer that processes a distributed transaction manager.

Transform-oriented language: A data sublanguage such as SQL that provides commands and capabilities to transform a set of relations into a new relation.

Transient object: In OOP, an object that has not been written to permanent storage. The object will be lost when the program terminates.

Transitive dependency: In a relation having at least three attributes, R (A, B, C), the situation in which A determines B, B determines C, but B does not determine A.

Transparency: The hiding, from a system user, of the existence of some problem or characteristic.

Tree: A collection of records, entities, or other data structures in which each element has at most one parent, except for the top element, which has no parent.

Trigger: A procedure invoked when a specified condition exists in the data of a database. For example, when Quantity-on-Hand of an item reaches zerd (or some specified amount), a procedure can be triggered to order more of the item.

Tuple: Same as Row.

Twin: A record or node that has the same parent as does another record or node.

Two-phase commitment: In a distributed database system, a process of commitment among nodes in which the nodes first vote on whether they can commit a transaction. If all the nodes vote yes, the transaction is committed, If any node votes no, the transaction is aborted. A two-phase commitment is required to prevent inconsistent processing in distributed databases.

Two-phase locking. The procedure by which locks are obtained and released in two phases. During the growing phase, the locks are obtained, and during the shrinking phase, the locks are released. Once a lock is released, no other lock will be granted that transaction. Such a procedure ensures consistency in database updates in a concurrent-processing environment.

U

UAE (Uninterruptible Application Error) Application program abend in Windows Version 3.0. See GPF.

UART (Universal Asynchronous Receiver Transmitter) Electronic circuit that transmits and receives data on the serial port.

UHF (Ultra High Frequency) Range of electromagnetic frequencies from 300MHz to 3GHz.

ULSI (Ultra Large Scale Integration) More than one million transistors on a chip. See SSI, MSI, LSI and VLSI.

ultrafiche Pronounced "ultra feesh." Microfiche that holds up to 1,000 document pages per 4x6" sheet of film. Normal microfiche stores around 270 pages.

ultraviolet Invisible band of radiation at the high-frequency end of the light spectrum. It takes about 10 minutes of ultraviolet light to erase an EPROM chip.

UMA (Upper Memory Area) PC memory between 640K and 1024K See PC memory map.

UMB (Upper Memory Block) Unused blocks in the UMA (640K-1M). A UMB provider is software that can load drivers and TSRs into this area.

unary Meaning one; a single entity or operation, or an expression that requires only one operand.

unbundled Separate prices for each component in a system. Contrast with bundled.

unconditional branch In programming, a GOTO, BRANCH or JUMP instruction that passes control to a different part of the program. Contrast with conditional branch.

undelete To restore the last delete operation that has taken place. There may be more than one level of undelete, allowing several or all previous deletions tO be restored. See DOS Undelete.

underflowm (1) Error condition that occurs when the result of a computation is smaller than the smallest quantity the computer can store. (2) Error condition that occurs when an item is called from an empty stack.

underscan Area within the normal rectangular viewing are on a display screen. Contrast with overscan.

undo To restore the last editing operation that has taken place. For example, if a segment of text has been changed, performing an undo will restore the original text. Programs may have several levels of undo, including being able to reconstruct the original data for all edits performed in the current session. Contrast with undelete.

unidirectional Transfer or transmission of data in a channel in one direction only.

union In relational database, the joining of two files. See set theory.

Unisys (Unisys Corp.) Computer manufacturer formed in 1986 as a merger of Burroughs and Sperry corporations. It traces its history, through its various mergers to the ENIAC itself. Unisys has concentrated on providing integrated solutions to vertical markets, such as financial, airlines and communications. Its commercial base accounts for about 78% of revenues, and the rest is derived from defense contracts.

unit record equipment See tabulating equipment.

UNIVAC I (UNIVersal Automatic Computer) First commercially successful computer, introduced in 1951 by Remington Rand. Over 40 systems were sold. Its memory was made of mercury-filled acoustic delay lines that held 1,000 12-digit numbers. It used magnetic tapes that stored 1MB of data at a density of 128 cpi. In 1952, it predicted Eisenhower's victory over Stevenson, and UNIVAC became synonymous with computer (for a while).

UNIX Multiuser, multitasking operating system from AT&T that runs on a wide variety of computer systems from micro to mainframe. UNIX is written in C. It is C's inherent transportability that allows UNIX to run on so many different computers. UNIX is made up of the kernel, the heart of the operating system, the file system, a hierarchical directory method for organizing files on the disk and the shell, the user interface which providqs the way the user commands the system. Normal UNIX commands are very cryptic but they can be replaced with shells that are easier to use, including graphical user interfaces (GUIs). The following list shows typical UNIX commands with their DOS counterparts:

Command	**UNIX**	**DOS**
List directory	Is	dir
Copy a file	cp	copy
Delete a file	rm	del
Rename a file	my	rename
Display contents	cat	type
Print a file	lpr	print
Check disk space	df	chkdsk

UNIX was developed in 1969 by Ken Thompson and additional work was done by Dennis Ritchie, and, by 1974, UNIX had matured into a state-of-the- art operating system. UNIX became very popular in scientific and academic environments. Considerable enhancements were made to UNIX at the Univ. of California at Berkeley, and versions of UNIX include the Berkeley extensions. By the late 1970s, commercial versions of UNIX, such as IS/i and XENIX, became available. In the early 198tk, AT&T began to consolidate the many versions of UNIX into standards which evolved into System III and eventually System V. After 1984, it began to market UNIX aggressively. In November 1989, it introduced the most significant release of UNIX: System V Release 4.0. The name UNIX was coined for a single-user (un) version of MULTICS, as it was intended to be a scaled-down version of that very elaborate operating system. Ironically today, UNIX's multiuser capabilities are one of its most important features. See UNIX International, XJOpen, OSF and POSIX.

unload To remove a program from memory or take a tape or disk out of its drive.

unmark (1) In word processing, to deselect a block of text, which usually removes its highlight. (2) To deselect an item that has been tagged for a particular purpose.

unpack See pack.

unzip To decompress a file with PKUNZIP. See PKsoftware.

up Refers to a device that is working.

UPC (Universal Product Code) Standard bar code printed on retail merchandise. It contains the vendor's identification number and the product number, which is read by passing the bar code over a scanner.

update To change data in a file or database. Update and edit are often used synonymously; however edit implies changing existing data, while update also implies adding and deleting records.

uplink Communications channel from an earth station to a satellite. Contrast with downlink.

upload See download.

upper CASE See front-end CASE.

UPS (Uninterruptible Power Supply) Backup power for a computer system when the electrical power fails or drops to an unacceptable voltage level. Small UPS systems provide battery power for only a few minutes; enough to power down the computer in an orderly manner. An online UPS provides a constant source of electrical power from the battery, while the batteries are being recharged from AC power. An offline UPS, also known as a standby power system (SPS), switches to battery within a few milliseconds after detecting a power failure. A surge protector filters out surges and spikes, and a voltage regulator maintains uniform voltage during a brownout, but a UPS keeps a computer running when there is no electrical power. UPS systems typically provide surge suppression and may also provide voltage regulation.

uptime Time during which a system is working without failure. Contrast with downtime.

upward compatible Also called forward compatible. Refers to larger or newer models of a computer that can run the same software as smaller or earlier models. Contrast with downward compatible.

user Any individual who interacts with the computer at an application level. Programmers, operators and other technical personnel are not considered users when working in a professional capacity on the computer.

user area Reserved part of a disk or memory for user data.

user defined Any format, layout, structure or language that is developed by the user.

user friendly System that is easy to learn and easy to use.

user group Organization of users of a particular hardware or software product. Members share experiences and ideas to improve their understanding and use of a particular product. User groups are often responsible for influencing vendors to change or enhance their products.

user Interface Combination of menus, screen design, keyboard commands, command language and help screens, which together create the way a user interacts with a computer. Hardware, such as a mouse and touch screen, are also included. See Macintosh user interface and Lotus menu.

utility program Program that supports the operation of the computer. Utility programs, or simply "utilities," provide file management capabilities, such as sorting, copying, comparing, listing and searching, as well as diagnostic and measurement routines that check the health and performance of the computer system.

Union: A relational algebra operation performed on two union-compatible relations, say A and B, forming a third relation, say C, with C containing every row in both A and B, minus any duplicate rows.

Union compatible: The condition in which two tables have the same number of attributes and the attributes in corresponding columns arise from the same domain.

Union incompatible: The condition in which either two tables have a different number of attributes or the attributes in corresponding columns arise from different domains.

Universal resource locator: The address of a file on the Internet.

URL: Universal resource locator. Sometimes uniform resource locator, but the meaning is the same.

User view: A particular user's view of a database.

User working area (UWA): In the CODASYL DBTG model, the area of main memory that contains data values pertaining to a particular run-unit.

UVIA: See User working area.

V

V.110, V.120, V.17, V.21, V.22, V.22bls, V.23, V.25, V.25b1s,... CCITI' standards for various aspects of computer communications.

V20, V30 8088 and 8086 pin-compatible processors from NEC. Versions running at 16MHz were introduced in 1991.

VAC (Volts Alternating Current) See volt and AC.

vacuum tube Electronic device that controls the flow of electrons in a vacuum, used as a switch, amplifier or display screen. It is primarily the CRT in monitors and TVs.

validity checking Routines in a data entry program that tests the input for correct and reasonable conditions, such as numbers falling within a range and correct spelling, if possible. See check digit.

value (1) Content of a field or variable. It can refer to alphabetic as well as numeric data. For example, in the expression, state "PA", PA is a value. (2) In spreadsheets, the numeric data within the cell.

value-added network Communications network that provides services beyond normal transmission, such as automatic error detection and correction, protocol conversion and message storing and forwarding. Telenet and Tymnet are examples of value-added networks.

vaporware Software that has been advertised but not delivered.

variable In programming, a structure that holds data and is uniquely named by the programmer. It holds the data assigned to it until a new value is asiigned to it or until the program is finished. Variables are used to hold control values. In some languages, the type of data must be declared before it is assigned. A local variable is one that can be referenced only within the subprogram, function or procedure it was defined in. A global variable can be used by the entire program.

variable length field Record structure that holds fields of varying lengths.

variable length record Data record that contains one or more variable length fields.

varname (VARiable NAME) Abbreviation for specifying the name of a variable.

VAX (Virtual Address eXtension) Family of 32-bit computers from Digital introduced in 1977 with the VAX- 11/780 model. VAX machines range from desktop personal computers to large-scale mainframes. Large VAXs can be clustered together to provide a multiprocessing environment serving thousands of online users. All VAXs use the same operating system, and programs running on one VAX can run on any other. VAX systems also provide a compatibility mode for running PDP software. Due to its compatible archi tecture, the VAX family achieved outstanding success throughout the 1980s.

VAXcluster Group of VAXs coupled together in a multiprocessing environment.

VAXELN Realtime operating environment for VAXs from Digital. It runs under VMS and provides application development in Pascal and other languages. Resulting programs are downloaded into the target systems.

VBE (VGA BIOS Extensions) VESA VGA standard for interrogating the capabilities of a graphics adapter. It allows the software developer to write a universal driver for all VBE-compliant VGA cards.

VCR (Video Cassette Recorder) Videotape recording and playback machine. Although VCRs are primarily analog recording machines, adapters allow them to store digital data for computer backup.

VDE (Video Display Editor) WordStar and WordPerfect-compatible shareware word processor written by Eric Meyer.

VDI (Virtual Device Interface) ANSI standard format for creating device drivers.

Vdisk See DOS RAM disks.

VDM See CGM.

VDS (Virtual DMA Services) Programming interface that lets bus mastering devices cooperatively manage DMA channels.

VDT (Video Display Terminal) Terminal with a keyboard and display screen.

VDT radiation Electromagnetic radiation emitted from a computer display screen. Exhaustive testing so fa seems inconclusive, but vendors recommend keeps ing the face at least 18 to 20 inches from the screen.

VDU (Video Display Unit) Same as VDT.

vector (1) In computer graphics, a line designated by its end points (x-y or x-y-z coordinates). When a circle is drawn, it is made up of many small vectors. (2) In matrix algebra, a one-row or one-column matrix.

vector display Display terminal that draws vectors on the screen. Contrast with raster display.

vector graphics In computer graphics, a technique for representing a picture as points, lines and other geometric entities. See graphics. Contrast with raster graphics.

vector processor Computer with built-in instructions that perform multiple calculations on vectors (onedimensional arrays) simultaneously.

Vectra PC series from HP. Vectras are noted for their ruggedness and reliability.

Venn diagram Graphic technique for visualizing set theory concepts using overlapping circles and shading to indicate intersection, union and complement.

Ventura Publisher Desktop publishing program for PCs and the Macintosh from Ventura Software, Inc. (a Xerox company), that provides full-scale pagination for large documents. It is designed to import data created in other graphics and word processing programs. Ventura is available for DOS, Windows, OS! 2 and the Mac. The DOS version comes with a runtime version of the GEM interface.

verify In data entry operations, to compare the keystrokes of a second operator with the files created by the first operator.

version control Management of source code in a large software project. Version-control software provides a database that keeps track of the revisions made to a program by all the programmers involved in it.

version number Identification of a release of software. The difference between Version 2.2 and 2.3 can be substantial, since new releases not only add new features, but often correct annoying bugs. Version numbers, such as 3.la or 3.11, indicate a follow-up release only to fix a bug in the previous version, whereas 3.1 and 3.2 usually indicate routine enhancements in the product.

vertical redundancy checking See VRC.

vertical refresh See vertical scan frequency.

vertical resolution Number of lines (rows in a matrix). Contrast with horizontal resolution.

vertical scan frequency Number of times an entire display screen is refreshed, or redrawn, per second. Measured in Hertz, display systems range from 45 to over 100Hz. For example, VGA in the U.S. is generally 56 to 60Hz; in Europe, 70Hz and above. TV is refreshed 60 half-frames/ sec (interlaced) resulting in 30 Lull frames/sec. Contrast with horizontal scan frequency.

VESA (Video Electronics Standards Assn.) Organization of major PC graphics vendors devoted to improving graphics standards. It is involved with video controller, monitor and multimedia standards, including VGA, Super VGA and XGA. See PC display modes.

vesicular film Film used to make copies of microforms. It contains its own developer and creates a pink negative or positive copy when exposed to a negative master through ultraviolet light.

VGA (Video Graphics Array) IBM video display standard built into most PS/i and PSI2 models that provides medium-resolution text and graphics. It has become the minimum standard for all PCs. VGA supports previous CGA and EGA modes and requires an analog monitor. Its highest-resolution mode is 640x480 with 16 colors, but VESA and third parties have boosted colors and resolution. See PC display modes.

VGA HC (VGA HiColor) VGA board that provides 32K or 64K colors using Tseng Labs' ET4000 chip or equivalent.

VGA pass through Feature of a high-resolution display adapter that couples internally with a VGA display adapter and passes its signals through to the monitor.

VHD (Very High Density) Floppy disk technologies that place 20MB and more of data on a 3.5" disk. See Floptical.

VHF (Very High Frequency) Range of electromagnetic frequencies from 30MHz to 300MHz.

VHS VCR format introduced by JVC in 1976 (to compete with Sony's Beta format) that has become the standard for home and industry. SVHS (Super VHS) is a subsequent format that improves resolution.

VHSIC (Very High Speed Integrated Circuit) Pronounced "vizik." Ultra-high-speed chips employing IS! and VLSI technologies.

vi (Visual Interface) UNIX full-screen text editor that can be run from a terminal or the system console. It is a fast, programmer-oriented utility.

video Audio/visual playback and recording technology used in TV It also refers to computer screens and terminals.

video adapter Same as video display board.

video bandwidth Maximum display resolution, measured in MHz, and calculated by horizontal x vertical resolution x refreshes/sec. For example, 800x600x60 28.8MHz. TV studio recording is limited to 5MHz; TV broadcasting is limited to 3.58Mhz.

video board Same as video display board.

video camera Camera that takes continuous pictures and generates a signal for display or recording. It captures images by breaking down the image into a series of lines. Each line is scanned one at a time, and the continuously varying intensities of red, green and blue light across the line are filtered out and converted into a variable signal. Most video cameras are analog, but digital video cameras are also available. See digital camera.

video card Same as video display board.

video codec Circuit that converts NTSC video into digital code and vice versa. It incorporates a compression technique to reduce the data and may or may not provide full-motion video.

video conferencing See teleconferencing.

vIdeo controller (1) Device that controls some kind of video function. (2) Same as video display board.

video digitizer Same as frame grabber.

video display board Expansion board that plugs into a personal computer and generates the text and graphics images for the monitor's screen. Also called a display adapter, graphics adapter, graphics card, video adapter, video card or video controller, it determines the resolution and number of colors on screen. It converts the characters or graphic patterns (bitmaps) within a reserved segment of the computer's memory into signals used to refresh the display screen.

In digital systems (CGA, EGA, etc.), the display board generates digital signals for the monitor. The monitor then does the conversion from digital to analog. In analog systems (VGA, Macintosh, etc.), the display board creates the analog signals sent to the monitor. The monitor must be capable of handling the frequency range of the display board (number of lines per second). Multisync monitors accept a range of frequencies and work with several display standards. [[FULL PAGE FROM MINASI, P.509]]

video display card Same as video display board.

video display terminal/unit Same as video terminal. video editor Dedicated computer that controls two or more videotape machines for editing purposes. It keeps track of frame numbers in its own database and switches the recording machine from playback to record.

video graphics board Video display board that generates text and graphics and accepts video from a camera or VCR. Truevision's Targa board and Vision Technologies Vision board are examples. The terms video graphics board and video display board sound alike, but video display boards (display adapters) do not handle NTSC video.

video overlay card Graphics controller that allows N1SC video and computer images to be mixed.

video RAM Specially-designed memory circuits on a video display board that are used to hold the image that appears on the video screen. The pixel data or character data stored in the video RAM by the program is translated to the monitor in the required format. Often uses dual-ported RAM, which allows simultaneous reads and writes.

video teleconferencing See teleconferencing.

video terminal Data entry device that uses a keyboard for input and a display screen for output. Although the display screen resembles a TV, it usually does not accept TV/video signals.

video window Display of NTSC video (TV) in an independent window on a computer screen.

videodisc Read-onIy optical disc that holds up to two hours of video data. Videodiscs are recorded in an analog format like videotape. Though videodiscs have not made a significant dent in the market. they are used for interactive instructional training courses, however. -

videotex Interactive information technology that includes shopping, banking, news, weather and e-mail services. Experiments have been tried in the U.S., but it has yet to catch on. It is delivered over a telephone line to a subscriber's TV through a decoder box and attached keyboard. Information is broadcast to and stored in the decoder as predefined screens (frames) which can be retrieved by menu. Videotex delivers simple graphics and limited animation.

view (1) To display and look at data on screen. (2) In relational database management, a special display of data, created as needed. A view temporarily ties two or more files together so that the combined files can be displayed, printed or queried.

viewer See file viewer.

viewport (1) In the Macintosh, the entire scrollable region of data that is viewed through a window. (2) Same as window.

virtual Simulated or conceptual environment, which, as a result, may refer to virtually anything.

Virtual 8086 Mode Operational mode in Intel 386s and up that allows it to perform as multiple 8086 CPUs. Under direction of a control program, each virtual machine runs as a stand-alone 8086 running its own operating system and applications. This is not the same as the 386's virtual memory mode, which extends main memory to disk.

virtual disk Same as RAM disk.

virtual machine (1) Computer that runs multiple operating systems with each operating system running its own programs; for example, a 386 PC running multiple DOS applications in its virtual mode. (2) One operating system and its associated application programs running within a virtual machine environment. (3) Virtual memory computer.

virtual memory Technique that simulates more memory than actually exists and allows the computer to run several programs concurrently regardless of size. Virtual memory breaks up a program into segments, called pages. Instead of bringing the entire program into memory, it brings as many pages into memory as it can fit based on the current mix of programs and leaves the remaining pages on disk. When instructions are called for that are not in memory, the appropriate disk page is called in, overlaying the page in memory.

virtual monitor In the Macintosh, the ability to dynamically configure to any monitor type and to use multiple monitors of different types including, displaying the same object across two or more screens.

virtual peripheral Peripheral device simulated by the operating system. For example, the process of printing to. disk.

virtual processing Parallel processing technique that simulates a processor for applications that require a processor for each data element. It creates virtual processors for data elements above and beyond the number of processors available.

virtual processor Simulated processor in a virtual processing system.

virtual reality Artificial reality that projects the user into a three-dimensional space generated by computer. Impleiftentations include the use of a DataGlove and head-mounted stereoscopic display, which allow users to point to and manipulate illusory objects in their view. See cyberspace.

virtual storage Same as virtual memory.

virtual terminal Terminal emulation that allows access to a foreign system. Often refers to a personal computer gaining access to a mini or mainframe.

virtualize (1) To activate a program in virtual memory. (2) To create a virtual screen.

virus Software used to infect a computer. After the virus code is written, it is buried within an existing program. Once that program is executed, the virus code is activated and attaches copies of itself to other programs in the system. Infected programs copy the virus to other programs. The effect of the virus may be a simple prank.that pops up a message on screen out c4the blue or the actual destruction of programs and data. See worm.

VisiCaic First electronic spreadsheet. It was introduced in 1978 for the Apple II. Conceived by Dan Bricklin, a Harvard student, and programmed by Bob Frankston, it became a major success. It launched an industry and was almost entirely responsible for the Apple II being used in business. Thousands of Apples were bought to run the VisiCalc. VisiCalc was a command-driven program that was followed by SuperCalc, MultiPlan, Lotus 1-2-3 and a host of othera, each improving the user interface. Spreadsheets have also been implemented on minis and mainframes.

Visual BASIC Version of Microsoft QuickBASIC for developing Windows applications. User interfaces are developed by dragging objects from the Visual BASIC Toolbox onto the application form.

visualization In computer graphics, the converting of numeric data into picture form to allow humans to recognize patterns that are difficult to identify in numeric form. It is used especially in research situations, both theoretical and practical.

VLF (Very Low Frequency) See low radiation.

VLSI (1) (Very Large Scale Integration) Between 100,000 and one million transistors on a chip. See SSI, MSJ, LSI and ULSI. (2) (VLSI Technology, Inc., Tempe, AZ) Designer and manufacturer of custom chips.

VM (Virtual Machine) IBM mainframe operating system which can run multiple operating systems within the computer at the same time, each one running its own programs. CMS (Conversational Monitor System) provides VM's interactive capability.

VM/386 (Virtual Machine/386) Multitasking operating environment for 386s from IGC Corp. It uses the 386's virtual 86 mode which runs multiple copies of DOS, each running its own application.

voice channel Transmission channel or subchannel that carries human voice.

voice coil Type of motor used to move the access arm of a disk drive in very small increments. Like the voice coil of a speaker, the amount of current determines the amount of movement. Contrast with stepper motor, which works in fixed increments.

voice grade Refers to the bandwidth required to transmit human voice, which is usually about 4,000Hz.

voice mall Computerized telephone answering system that digitizes incoming voice .messages and stores them on disk. It usually provides auto attendant capability, which uses prerecorded messages to route the caller to the appropriate person, department or mail box.

voice messaging Using voice mail as an alternative to electronic mail, in which voice messages are intentionally. recorded, not because the recipient was not available.

voice processing Computerizedhandling of voice, which includes voice store and forward, voice response, voice recognition and text to speech technologies.

voice recognition Conversion of spoken words into computer text. Speech is first digitized and then matched against a dictionary of coded waveforms. The matches are then converted into text. Systems must be trained to a voice before using, by taking samples of actual words from the person who will use it. Speaker-independent systems can recognize limited vocabularies such as numeric digits and a handful of words.

voice response Generation of voice output by computer. It provides pre-recorded information either with or without selection by the caller. Interactive voice response allows interactive manipulation of a database. See audiotex.

volatile memory Memory that does not hold its contents without power. A computer's main memory, made up of dynamic RAI'vl or static RAM chips, loses its content immediately upon loss of power.

volt Unit of measurement of force, or pressure, in an electrical circuit. The common voltage of an AC power line is 120 volts of alternating current (alternating directions). Common voltages within a computer are from 5 to 12 volts of direct current (one direction only).

volt-amps Measurement of electrical usage that is computed by multiplying volts times amps. See watts.

voltage regulator Device used to maintain a level amount of voltage in the electrical line. Contrast with surge suppressor, which filters out excessive amounts of current, and contrast with UPS, which provides backup power in the event of a power failure.

volume (1) Physical storage unit, such as a hard disk, floppy disk, disk cartridge or reel of tape. (2) Logical storage unit that spans some number of physical drives.

volume label (1) Name assigned to a disk (usually optional). (2) Identifying stick-on label attached to the outside of a tape reel or disk cartridge. (3) See header label.

VPS (Vectors Per Second) Used to measure the speed of a vector or array processor.

VRAM See video RAM.

VRC (Vertical Redundancy Check) Error checking method that generates and tests a parity bit for each byte of data .that is moved or transmitted. -

VS (Virtual Storage) Same as virtual memory.

VSAM (Virtual Storage Access Method) IBM access method for storing data, widely used in IBM mainframes. It uses the B+tree method for organizing data.

VAR: Value-added reseller. A person, company, or group that develops database applications and sells them to other companies. The VAR adds value to the DBMS product by building the application.

Vertical partition: A subset of the columns of a table. For example, in a table with ten columns, the first five columns.

View: (1) The subset of a database that can be processed by an application. (2) An object view.

W

W5086 Weitek graphics accelerator chip set.

wafer (1) Base material in chip making. It is a slice, approx. 1/30" thick, from a long silicon crystal from 3 to 6" in diameter. The wafer goes through a series of photomasking, etching and implantation steps. See chip. (2) Small, continuous-loop magnetic tape cartridge that is used for the storage of data.

wait state Amount of time spent waiting for some operation to take place. It can refer to a variable length of time a program has to wait before it can be processed, or it may refer to a specific duration of time, such as a machine cycle. When memory is too slow to respond to the CPU'S request for it, wait states are introduced until the memory can catch up. -

WAN (Wide Area Network) Communications network that covers wide geographic areas, such as states and countries. See MAN and LAN.

wand Hand-held optical reader used to read typewritten fonts, printed fonts, OCR fonts and bar codes. The wand is waved over each line of characters or codes in a single pass.

Wang (Wang Laboratories, Inc., Lowell, MA) Manufacturer of computers and applications for financial, legal and professional services, manufacturing and government. Founded in 1951 by Dr. An Wang, the company initially produced specialized electronic devices. It introduced an electronic desk calculator. In the 1970s, Wang introduced its first word processing systems and computers. By 1978, it was the largest worldwide supplier of CRT-based word pro. cessors. In 1987, it introduced its integrated image system, which enable paper documents to be stored, viewed and transmitted on a computer. For the 1990s, Wang is making its products available on industry- standard hardware platforms while continuing to focus on imaging as a leading technology.

Wangnet Broadband LAN from Wang that handles data, voice and video.

warm boot Restarting the computer by performing a reset operation (pressing reset, Ctrl-Alt-Del, etc.). See cold boot and boot.

warm start Same as warm boot.

Warnler-Orr diagram Graphic charting technique used in software engineering for system analysis and design.

watt A measurement of electrical power. One watt is one ampere of current flowing at one volt. Watts are typically rated as AMPS x VOLTS; however, AMPS x VOLTS, or VOLT-AMP (V-A) ratings and watts are only equivalent when powering devices-that absorb all the energy such as electric heating coils or incandescent light bulbs. With computer power supplies, the actual watt rating is only 60 to 70% of the VOLT-AMP rating.

wave Shape of radiated energy. All radio signals, light rays, x-rays, and cosmic rays radiate an energy that looks likes rippling waves.

waveform Pattern of a particular sound wave or other electronic signal in analog form.

Weitek coprocessor High-performance math coprocessor for micro and minicomputers from Weitek Corp. Since 1981, the company has been making coprocessors for CAD and graphics workstations. In order to use a Weitek coprocessor, software must be written for it.

well behaved Refers to programs that do not deviate from a standard.

well mannered Same as well behave4.

wetware Biological system or structure that emulates a biological system.

what If? Using a spreadsheet as a planning tool. When new data is entered, results are calculated based upon the formulas. Therefore, entering hypothetical data allows one to see the results of this data.

Whetstones Benchmark program that tests floating point operations. Results are expressed in Whetstones persecond. Whetstone I tests 32-bit, and Whetstone II tests 64-bit operations. See Dhrystones.

white noise Same as Gaussian noise.

wide area network See WAN.

widow & orphan A widow is the last line of a paragraph that appears alone at the top of the next page, and an orphan is the first line of a paragraph that appears alone at the bottom of a page.

width table List of horizontal measurements for each character in a font, used by word processing and desktop publishing programs.

wild cards Symbols used to represent any value when naming files. See DOS wild cards.

wimp interface (Windows, Icons, Menus and a Pointing device) Same as GUI.

WIN.INI (WINdows INItialization) File read by Windows on startup that contains data about the current environment (desktop, fonts, sounds, etc.) and individual applications. It is often updated by an install program to provide information for the application when it runs. SYSTEM.INI, another startup file, contains data about the hardware (drivers, 386 Enhanced Mode settings, etc.).

Win32 Programming specification (API) for Windows' 32-bit mode (386 and up) fully supported In Windows NT. Many functions are also supported in Windows 3.1 (Win32s subset).

Winchester disk' Sealed disk technology developed by IBM that incorporates the access arm, read/write heads and disk platters in a sealed unit. By aligning the heads to its own disks, greater capacities and speeds are obtainable than with removable disk cartridges. It was originally designed as a dual 30MB configuration, and its 30-30 specification (same as a Winchester rifle) gave rise to its name. Although originally a self-contained, removable module, the term is now used for any fixed hard disk.

window (1) Rectangular, scrollable viewing area. May refer to a scrollable list or to a re-sizable window that contains the entire application. See GUI and windows environment. (2) Reserved area of memory. (3) Time period.

windowing software Same as windows program.

Windows Graphics-based operating environment from Microsoft that integrates with DOS. It provides a desktop environment similar to the Macintosh, in which each active application is displayed in a resizable, movable window on screen. Though applications are written specifically for it, Windows also runs DOS applications and can be used as the primary operating environment from which all programs are launched.

Windows lx, Windows 286 (2.x) and Windows/ 386 were first attempts. Windows 3.0 created an industry (1990) with its enhanced user interface and ability to manage extended memory (up to 16MB with its built-in DOS extender). Windows 3.1 (1992) is faster, supports multimedia, TrueType fonts and drag & drop commands. Compound documents (OLE) are added and Real Mode is eliminated. Windows 3.x applications are 16-bit programs that run on all 80x86 CPUs. Windows 3.1 requires a 286 and Windows NT will require a 386. Some of the 386's native (32- bit) instructions can be accessed by applications written for Windows 3.1, using Microsoft's Win32s specification.

Windows accelerator See graphics accelerator.

windows environment Any operating system, operating system extension or application program that provides nultiple windows on screen. DESQview, Windows, PM, MultiFinder and X Window are examples. But now increasingly used to refer to Windows as an operating system.

Windows Metafile Windows file format that holds vector graphics, bitmaps and text. Its vector format is becoming popular for graphics interchange. Sometimes Windows uses the Metafiie for temporary storage, but applications mostly use it for storing all types of data that will be reused in the same or in another application.

Windows NT (Windows New Technology) Advanced 32-bit operating system for 386s and up from Microsoft. It runs applications written for DOS, Windows 3.x and NT (Win32). NT does not use DOS, it is a self-contained operating system:

windows program (1) Software that adds a windows capability to an existing operating system. (2) Application program written to run under Windows.

wlreframe modeling In CAD, a technique for representing 3-D objects, in which all surfaces are visibly 'outlined in lines, including the opposite sides and all internal components that are normally hidden from view. Compared to surface and solid modeling, wireframe modeling is the least complex method for representing 3-D images.

wireless Same as radio.

wizzu wig See WYSIWYG.

WK1 Lotus 1-2-3 Version 2.0 file extension.

WKS Lotus 1-2-3, Version 1-A file extension.

WMF See Windows Metafile.

word (1) Computer's internal storage unit and refers to the amount of data it can hold in its registers and process at onetime. For example, a 16-bit computer processes two bytes in the same time it takes an 8- bit computer to prOcess one byte, providing the timing clocks are of equal speed. (2) Primary text element, identified by a word separator (blank space, comma, etc.) before and after a group of contiguous characters. (3) 'See Microsoft Word.

word addressable Computer that can address memory only on word boundaries. Contrastewith byte addressable.

Word for Windows See Microsft Word.

word processing Creation and management of text documents. It has replaced the electric typewriter in most offices, because of the ease in which documents can be edited and printed. Advanced word processors function as elementary desktop publishing systems and support graphics as well as an infinite variety of fonts.

Some of the features of a word processor are: Ability to wrap words round to the next line (word wrap); justify text in relation to the right or left margins or the centre of the page; text editing including block move/delete/copy, search and replace; layout settings (margins, indents, fonts, etc.); headers, footers, pagination; mail merge (ability to customize form letters); printing in draft, high quality, in blocks and pages and print preview; spelling checkers and thesaurus; and elementary file management. Ad—vanced features may include ability to work with more than one file at a time, to set newspaper columns, generate tables of contents and indexes, ability to incorporate graphics into text, etc. Word processors may be text-based, which increases their speed or be graphics-based which enables one to see the final output on screen. Most word ,processors incorporate their own codes into the text to handle-these features and the codes of one may not be understood by another, necessitating a utility to translate documents if need be.

word processing machine Computer that is specialized for only word processing functions.

word processor (1) Software that provides word processing functions on a computer. (2) Computer specialized for word processing functions.

word publishing: Word processing programs that provide a certain number of desktop publishing features such as merging, displaying and printing graphics with text.

word separator Character that separates a word, such as a blank space, comma, period, -,? and!.

word wrap Feature of word processing and text handling systems that carries text automatically onto the next line when one is full. In some word processing programs, word wrap can be switched off for writing programming source code.

WordBASIC Subset of Microsoft QuickBASIC with added word processing functions used to customize Microsoft Word.

WordPerfect Full-featured word processing program from WordPerfect Corp., introduced in 1980 that runs on IBM, Apple II, Macintosh, Amiga and Atari personal computers. It is the most widely used word processor. Version 5.0 introduced significant improvements that included desktop publishing features and a WYSIWYG preview mode. Version 5.i added an optional menu system. Version 6.0 adds a graphics mode and ability to develop hypertext documents.

WordStar Full-featured PC word processing program from WordStar Int'l. Introduced in 1978 for CP/M machines, it was the first program to give sophisticated word processing capabilities to personal computer users at far less cost than the dedicated word processors of the time. It is one the most widely used programs and many WordStar keyboard commands have become de facto standards.

workgroup Two or more individuals who share files and databases. LANs designed around workgroups provide electronic sharing of required data.

working directory See current directory. worksheet Same as spreadsheet.

worksheet compiler Same as spreadsheet compiler.

workstation (1) High-performance, single user microcomputer or minicomputer that has been specialized for graphics, CAD, CAE or scientific applications. (2) In a LAN, a personal computer that serves a single user in contrast with a file server that serves all users in the network. (3) Any terminal or personal computer.

worm (1) Destructive program that replicates itself throughout disk and memory, using up the computers resources and eventually putting the system down. See virus and logic bomb. (2) Program that moves throughout a network and deposits information at each node for diagnostic purposes, or causes idle computers to share some of the processing workload. (3) (WORM) (Write Once Read Many) Storage device that uses an optical medium that can be recorded only once. Updating requires destroying the existing data (all Os made is), and writing the revised data to an unused part of the disk.

wrist rest Platform used to raise the wrist to keyboard level for typin'

wrist support Product that prevents and provides a therapy for carpal tunnel syndrome by keeping the hands in a neutral wrist position.

write To record data into or onto a memory or storage device, such as disk, tape, memory and firmware. Read and write is analogous to play and record on an audio tape recorder.

write back cache Disk or memory cache that handles writing. Data written into the high-speed cache memory from the CPU is written onto disk or into real memory.during idle machine cycles.

write error Inability to record data into or onto a memory or storage device due to contamination or damage on the media. Could also be caused by malfunctioning electronic components in memory devices.

write protect Prohibits the erasing or changing of a disk file. See file protection.

write protect notch Small, square cutout on the side of a floppy disk used to prevent it from being written and erased. On 5.25" floppies, the notch must be covered for protection. To protect a 3.5" diskette, press the slide lever toward the edge of the disk uncovering a hole (upper left side viewed from the back).

WSI See wafer scale integration.

WYSIWYG (What You See Is What You Get) Pronounced "wizzy- wig." Refers to text and graphics appearing on screen the same as they would print. It is almost impossible to get 100% identical representation, because screen and printer resolutions rarely match.

Weak entity: In an entity-relationship model, an entity whose logical existence in the database depends on the existence of another entity. See also ID-dependent entity and Strong entity.

Write write conflict: The situation in which two write actions operate on the same data item.

WYSIWIG: What you see is what you get. A term used with form and report generators, in which the DBMS re-creates exactly what the developer types on the screen while developing forms and reports.

X

x (1) In programming, symbol used to identify a hexadecimal number. For example, OxOA or \xOA specify the hex number OA. (2) (X) Refers to X Window.

x-axis See x-y matrix.

x-height In typography, the height of the letter x in lower case or the main body of the letter. Point size includes the x-height, the height of the ascender and the height of the descender. See typeface.

X Protocol Message format of the X Window system.

X Terminal Terminal with a built-in X Window Server (X Window display software).

X Window Windowing environment for graphics workstations that was developed at MIT with participation from Digital and IBM. It is designed to allow graphics generated in one computer system to be displayed on another workstation in the network. X Window is designed to run under any operating system and is supported by all major workstation vendors.

x-y matrix Group of rows and columns. The x-axis is the horizontal row, and the y-axis is the vertical column. An x-y matrix is the reference framework for two-dimensional structures.

x-y monitor In graphics, the display screen of a vector display terminal. The entire vector display comprises the monitor and vector graphics controller.

x-y plotter Same as plotter.

x-y-z matrix Three-dimensional structure. The x and y axes represent the first two dimensions; the z axis, the third dimension. In a graphic image, the x and y denote width and height; the z denotes depth.

XA See CD ROM XA and 370/XA.

Xbase dBASE-like languages such as Clipper and FoxPro. Originally almost identical to dBASE, new commands and features over the years have made them only partially dBASE compatible.

Xcopy DOS and OS/2 utility that copies files and subdirectories. See DOS Xcopy.

XDOS Software from Hunter Systems, that converts Intel 80x86 executable code into Motorola 68020 code ready to run under UNIX. A PC program can thus be translated into a running program on a UNIX-based 68020 computer.

XENIX See SCO XENIX.

xerography See electrophotographic.

XGA (EXtended Graphics Array) IBM high-resolution video display standard optimized for graphical user interfaces with a built-in pixel block move (bitblt) capability. In addition to VGA, it provides 256 colors at 640x480, 64K colors at 640x480, 256 colors at 1,024x768 and 132 column text. See high color.

XLISP Microcomputer version of the LISP programming language that has been in the public domain for a number of years.

Xmodem Widely-used asynchronous file transfer protocol developed by Ward Christensen. First versions used a checksum to detect errors; however, later versions use the more effective CRC method (XmodemCRC). Programs typically include both methods and drop back to checksum if CRC is not present at the other end. Xmodem transmits 128-byte blocks.

XMS (eXtended Memory Specification) Interface that allows DOS programs to ue extended memory in 286s and up. It provides a set of functions for reserving, releasing and transferring data to and from extended memory. DOS programs that are XMS aware can allocate extended memory without conflict, including the high memory area (HMA). See HIMEM.SYS and DOS extender.

XMT In communications, an abbreviation for transmit. xon-xoff In communications, a simple asynchronous protocol that keeps the receiving device in synchronization with the sender. When the buffer in the receiving device is full, it sends an x-off signal (transmit oft) to the sending device, telling it to stop transmitting. When the receiving device is ready to accept more, it sends the sending device an x-on signal (transmit on) to start again.

XT (EXtended Technology) First IBM PC with a hard disk, introduced in 1983. See PC.

XT class PC with Intel 8086/8088 CPU and 8-bit bus. XT interface Refers to the 8-bit PC bus or to the devices that connect to it via expansion card and slot or an IDE connector. See AT interface and PC bus.

XTree PC disk management program and DOS shell from XTree Co. Introduced in 1985, it was the first program to help users manage hard disks by providing a hierarchical display of directories. XTreePro added a built-in text editor, and XTreePro Gold added application launching, split windows and file viewers.

XyWrlte III Plus Pronounced "zy-write." PC word processing program from XyQuest, used extensively by major newspapers and magazines. It is noted for its flexibility and typesetting orientation as well as its speed on slow PCs. It is command-driven, but its interface can be completely customized by the user. It provides up to nine windows for documents and includes a programmer-oriented macro language. In 1988, menus were added to assist first-time users.

Y

y-axis See x-y matrix.

Ymodem Asynchronous file transfer protocol identical to Xmodem-1K plus batch file transfer (also called Ymodem Batch). Ymodem-G transmits without acknowledgment (for error-free channels or when modems are self correcting), but transmission is cancelled upon any error.

Z

z-axis Third dimension in a graphics image. The width is the x-axis and the height is the y-axis.

Z80 8-bit microprocessor from Zilog Corp. that was the successor to the Intel 8080. The Z80 was widely used in first-generation personal computers that used the CPIM operating system.

Z8000 16-bit microprocessor from Zilog Corporation that is the successor to the Z80.

zap Command that typically deletes the data within a file but leaves the file structure intact so that new data can be entered.

ZBR (Zone Bit Recording) Technique that records more bits on a disk. The tracks on a disk become longer the farther they are from the center. However, on regular disks, the clock rate that records the bits doesn't change, which results in the outer tracks being less densely packed than the inner tracks.

zero-slot LAN Refers to transmitting between computers over a serial or parallel port, thus freeing up an expansion slot normally used by LAN cards.

zero wait state

Refers to a high-speed memory that transfers its data immediately upon being accessed without waiting one or more machine cycles to respond.

zip (1) To compress a file with PKZIP. See PKsoftware. (2) (ZIP) (Zig-Zag Inline Package) Similar to a DIP, but smaller and tilted on its side for mounting on boards with limited space.

Zmodem Asynchronous file transfer protocol that is more efficient than Xmodem. It sends file name, date and size first and responds well to changing line conditions due to its variable length blocks. It uses CRC error correction and is effective in delay-induced satellite transmission.

Zoo Freeware compression program, including source code, used in UNIX, DOS and other environments.

O

OK (Zero Kilobytes) Typically references motherboards that do not include memory as priced.

Ox In programming, the symbol for a hexadecimal number. See x.

1-2-3 See Lotus 1-2-3.

l.2M Refers to the 1.2MB high-density 5.25" floppy disk used in PCs.

l.44M Refers to the 1.44MB high-density 3.5" disk used in PCs.

16-bit See bit specifications.

24-bit See bit specifications.

286 Officially the 80286, a 16-bit multitasking microprocessor from Intel that can address 16MB of physical memory, 1GB of virtual memory and uses a 16-bit data bus. Modes of operation are Real Mode, which performs as an 8086 CPU (limited to 1MB memory), and Protected Mode, which addresses all memory. Its optional math coprocessor is the 80287. PCs using the 286 chip are known as AT-class machines.

286/12,286/16... Specification of CPU speed for a 286. The second number is the clock rate: 286/12 means 12MHz.

3.5" (1) Refers to the common 3 1/2 inch microfloppy disk used in personal computers. (2) Refers to disk drives and other devices with a 3 1/2 inch horizontal form factor.

32-bIt See bit specifications.

32-bit processing In a PC, refers to programs written for the 386's native mode. All registers, pointers and addresses use the full 32 bits. Although the 386 is a 32-bit machine, under DOS, it runs applications in Real Mode, which functions as a 16-bit 8088, the CPU in the first PC.

3270 emulator Plug-in board that converts a personal computer or workstation into an interactive IBM mainframe terminal. The first 3270 emulator in widespread use was the IRMAboard.

34010,34020 General-purpose microprocessors from TI that are optimized for graphics and conform to the TIGA interface.

360K May refer to the 360K 5.25" minifloppy disk used with PCs.

386 Known as the 386 or 386DX, a 32-bit multitasking microprocessor from Intel that provides more flexible memory management than the 286. It supports 16-bit and 32-bit data buses and can execute both 16-bit instructions (standard DOS applications) and 32-bit instructions (386-specific applications). Its 32- bit mode is only starting to be utilized. The 387DX math coprocessor is optional. See 386SX and 386SL. 386-compatible chips from Advanced Micro Devices and Chips and

386/25, 386133... Specification of CPU speed for a 386. The second number is the clock rate: 386/25 means 25MHz.

386 Enhanced Mode Windows operation mode. See Windows.

386DX See 386.

386MAX DOS memory manager for 386s and up from Qualitas, Inc., noted for its advanced capabilities.

316SL Version of the 386 designed for laptops. It runs at variable clock rates, supports a 16-bit data bus and addresses 32MB of physical memory. In combination with the 82360SL chip, which includes I/O controllers, it allows for managing power to the CPU and peripherals. Except for memory and video controller, the two chips make up almost the entire computer.

386SLC IBM version of the 386SX that includes an internal 8KB memory cache. It includes power management capabilities and runs as fast as a 386DX.

386SX Version of the 386 that runs at slower clock speeds, supports a 16-bit data bus (not 32) and addresses 16MB of physical memory (not 4GB). It is used in laptops because it uses less power and dispel Is less heat; however, the 386SL is even more suited for laptops. The 387SX is the optional math coprocessor.

3GL See third-generation language.

4004 First microprocessor. Designed by Marcian E. 'Ted" Hoff at Intel, it was a 4-bit, general-purpose CPU that was initially developed for the Japanese Busicom calculator.

486 Known as the i486 or 486DX, a high-speed version of the 386. It includes a built-in math coprocessor, an 8KB memory cache and contains 1.2 million transistors. RISC design techniques along with its memory cache and a burst mode that quickly fills the cache cause it to run twice as fast as the 386. The DX2 is a 486 with Intel's Speed Doubler technology that doubles the internal clock speed. For example, a 486/50DX2 accesses RAM and other chips on the motherboard at 25MHz but processes internally at 50MHz. 4S6DXs may be upgraded to DX2s by replacing the DX CPU with Intel's OverDrive CPU for the 486DX. See 486SX.

486/25, 486/33... Specification of CPU speed for a 486. The second number is the clock rate: 486/25 means 25MHz.

486DX See 486.

486DX2 See 486.

486SX Version of the 486 that runs at slower clock speeds than the 486DX and does not provide the math coprocessor (optional 487 chip). 486SXs can be upgraded to 486DX2s with Intel's OverDrive chip for the 486SX, which includes the coprocessor. The OverDrive chip is plugged into the coprocessor socket, which disables the 486SX CPU. See 486.

4GL See fourth-generation language.

525" (1) Refers to the common 5 1/4 inch floppy disk used in personal computers. (2) Refers to disk drives and other devices with a 5 1/4 inch horizontal form factor.

586 The latest generation CPU from Intel. 66MHZ, 64- bit processor that is four times as fast as a 33MHz 486.

64-bit See bit specifications.

6502 8-bit microprocessor from Rockwell Int'l., Corp. used in the Apple II and earlier Atari and Commodore computers.

6800 8-bit microprocessor from Motorola. The 6801 is a computer-on-a-chip version.

68000 Family of microprocessors from Motorola that are the CPUs in Macintoshes and a variety of workstations.

68000- 32-bit CPU; can address 16MB and uses a 16-bit data bus.

68020 - 32-bit CPU; can address 4GB ançl uses a 32-bit data bus.

68030 - 32-bit CPU; can address 4GB and uses a 32-bit data bus. It runs at higher clock speeds and has built-in cache memory.

68040 - Redesigned 68030 that can run up to three times as fast.

7-bit ASCII Refers to transferring ASCII text in which an 8-bit byte holds the ASCII character plus a parity

7-track Refers to older magnetic tape formats that record 6-bit characters plus a parity bit.

720K May refer to the 720K microfloppy disk used in PCs.

8-bit See bit specifications.

8-N-I (8 bits, No parity, 1 stop bit) eters for modem transmission.

802.1, 8022, etc. See IEEE 802.1.

80286 See 286.

80287 See 286.

80386 See 386.

80386DX See 386.

80386SL See 386SL.

80386SX See 386SX.

80387 See 386.

80486 See 486.

80486DX See 486.

80486SX See 486SX.

80487 See 486SX.

80586 See 586.

8080 8-bit microprocessor from Intel introduced in 1974. It was the successor to the 8008 (first commercial 8- bit microprocessor) and precursor to the 8086 family

8086 16-bit microprocessor from Intel that can address 1MB of memory and uses a 16-bit data bus. Introduced in 1978, the 8086 defines the base architecture of the 8086 family, which includes the 8086, 8088, 286,386,486 and 586. DOS applications can run in all models of the 8086 family, but software written specifically for the 286 or 386 can only run in the required machines. OS/2 applications run in 286 and higher CPUs. The math coprocessor for the 8086 is the 8087.

8088 16-bit microprocessor from Intel that addresses 1MB of memory and uses an 8-bit data bus. This slower speed version of the 8086 was chosen for the original IBM PC in order to ease software migration from existing Z80-based CP/M applications. The math coprocessor for the 8088 is the 8087.

80x86 Refers to the Intel 8086 CPU family (8086,8088, 80186,80286,386,486,586). Starting with the 386, Intel has dropped the "80" prefix in its reference manuals.

82385 Intel controller chip that manages the memory cache in 386 and 486 CPUs.

8514 IBM monitor used with its 8514/A display adapter.

8514/A IBM high-resolution display adapter that provides an interlaced display of 1024x768 pixels with up to 256 colors or 64 shades of gray. It can coexist with VGA for dual monifor capability. It includes a video coprocessor that performs 2-D graphics functions, thus relieving the CPU of graphics tasks and improving performance. The 8514/A is faster than VGA and requires about a tenth of the CPU'S time for graphics functions.

860 Known as the i860, a 64-bit RISC-based microprocessor from Intel that uses a 64-bit data bus, has built- in floating point and 3-D graphics capability and contains over one million transistors. It can be used as a stand-alone CPU or to accelerate performance in existing systems.

88000 Family of 32-bit RISC microprocessors from Motorola. Tpe 88100 is the first processor in the 88000 family. Introduced in 1988, it incorporates four built-in execution units that allow up to five operations to be performed in parallel.

9-track Refers to magnetic tape that records 8-bit bytes plus parity, or nine parallel tracks. This is the common format for 1/2' tape reels.

APPENDIX–D

End Term University
Question papers (GGSIPU, DU, MDU, UPTECH)

GGSIPU

(Please write your roll no immediately) **Roll No.................**

End- term examination

Fifth Semester (B. Tech.) – December-2004

Paper code: ETCS 305 **Subject: Computer Architecture**

Time: 3 hours **Maximum Marks: 75**

Note: Attempt all questions.

Q. 1. (*a*) A digital computer uses a memory unit with 256k words of 32 bits each. A binary instruction code is stored in one word of memory. The instruction has 4 parts:

1. an operation code.
2. an indirect bit.
3. a register code to specify on of 64 registers.
4. an address part.

Determine the size of operation code, register code and address.

Draw and label the instruction word format.

Determine the bit-size of date and address inputs of the memory.

(*b*) The 8 bit registers AR, BR, CR and DR initially have the following values: AR= 11110010, BR=11111111, CR=10111001, DR=11101010

Determine the contents of each register after execution of following sequence of microoperations.

AR-AR.BR

CR-CR.DR, BR-BR+1

AR-AR.CR

CR-AR<BR

DR-AR>BR

AR-CR+DR

Q. 2. (*a*) State the difference between arithmetic shift and logical shift. Starting from initial value of register $R = 11011101$, determine R after a logical shift left following by a circular shift right following by a arithmetic shift left.

(*b*) What is Reverse polish notation. Convert the following expressions to RPN. 5

(*i*) $W + X*[Y * Z + P * Q*(R\text{-}S)]$

(*ii*) $W = X * W + [P + (R + S)–Q]$

(*c*) Evaluate the following arithmetic expression using the stack operation by first converting it RPN

(4*5) + (7*4) — (3*6)

Q. 3. (*a*) What are addressing modes? Give two advantages of using them. How many references to a memory are needed by direct and indirect address instruction to bring the operand into a CPU register?

(*b*) An instruction is stored at location 8000 with its address field at location 8001 .The address field has the value 4000. A processor register R contains the numeral 20. Find the effective address if addressing mode is

(*i*) direct (*ii*) immediate

(*iii*) relative (*iv*) register indirect

(*c*) Compare the auxiliary memory with cache memory. What is the use of memory hierarchy. Explain the following w.r.t. cache memory.

(*i*) hit ratio (*ii*) locality of reference (*iii*) associative mapping

Q. 4. (*a*) Draw a space time diagram for 8-segment pipeline. What is speed-up ratio? What is the maximum value of speed- up ratio that is achievable?

(*b*) What are the various ways by which the computer systems may be classified. Explain Flynn's classification in detail.

(*c*) Explain the concept of pipelining by taking the example of arithmetic pipeline for floating point addition and subtraction.

Q. 5. (*a*) Differentiate between:

(*i*) RS232 and RS422

(*ii*) Multiprocessing and parallel processing

(*iii*) Hardwired control and microprogrammed control

(*iv*) One address and two address instruction

(*v*) LIFO and FIFO

(*b*) Write a note comparing and contrasting RISC and CISC processors.

Q. 6. (*a*) What do you understand by I/O bus. Why it is needed? How many signals does **ISA** bus has? Explain the following w.r.t ISA.

(*i*) REFRESH (*ii*) $SA_0 - SA_{19}$

(*b*) How EISA differs from ISA.

(*c*) Draw a block diagram showing the architecture of IBM PC. Differentiate between the following buses on IBM PC system board.

(*i*) SD, MD and XD bus (*ii*) SA, MA and XA bus

Q. 7. (*a*) What do you understand by virtual memory. Explain the method by which a virtual address of 20 bits is mapped to a physical address of 15 bits. Explain the following with respect to virtual memory.

(*i*) Page (*ii*) Page frames

(*iii*) Page replacement (*iv*) Page fault

(*b*) Convert the decimal number-2.675 in IEEE 754 format and -35 in all possible signed binary representations, if no. Of bits used for representation is eight.

Q. 8. (*a*) Write short notes on any two:

(*i*) IDE drivers for HDD (*ii*) Device drives

(*iii*) Kernel drivers (*iv*) ALU design

(*b*) Design a common bus system with multiplexers for 16 registers each of 16 bits. Give the number of multiplexers needed, their size and selection inputs.

(*c*) Give the block diagram and timing diagram to implement the following register transfer statement

XT3: $R_2 - R1$

End-Term Examination

FIFTH SEMESTER [B. TECH.] **December 2005**

Paper Code: ETS3O5 **Subject: Computer Architecture**

Time: 3 hours **Maximum Marks : 75**

Note: Attempt any five questions. All questions carry equal marks.

Q. 1. (*a*) Design a common bus system with tristate buffers that supports 8 registers of 8 hits each. Determine the number and size of decoders. (4)

(*b*) What is micro operation' Draw a 4 hit arithmetic circuit that performs the following arithmetic micro operations: add subtract. increment and decrement. (8)

(*c*) Represent the following conditional statement by two register transfer statements with control functions.

If $P = 1$ then $(R1 < - R_2)$ else if $Q = 1$ then $R_1 - R_3$

Q. 2. (*a*) Register *A* holds the 8 hit binary 11011001. Determine the *B* operand and logic micro operation to be performed in order to change the value in A to (5)

(*i*) 01101101

(*ii*) 11111101

(*b*) Draw block diagram for the hardware that implements the following statements

$x + yz$: AR <— $AR + BR$

where *AR* and *BR* are two n hit registers and *x*, *y* and *z* are control variables. Include logic gates for control function. (6)

(*c*) How is overflow detected in 4

(*i*) Arithmetic and (*ii*) Shift microoperations?

Q. 3. (*a*) Explain IBMPC bus with reference to signals available. How PCI improves the performance of IBM PC bus? (8)

(*b*) Discuss the mechanism of communication in interparallel ports. (4)

(*c*) Most 32 bit buses permit 16 hit reads and writes. Is there an)' ambiguity about where to place the data? Discuss.

Q. 4. (*a*) A certain computer has 16 bit instruction and 6 bit address. Some instructions have one address and others have two. If there are n-two address instructions, what is maximum number of one address instructions? (4)

(*b*) Which of the following pairs of reverse polish formulae are mathematically equivalent? (4)

(*i*) *AB* + *C* + and *AB C*++

(*ii*) *ABXC* + and *ABC*+*

(*c*) A two word instruction is stored in memory at an address designated by symbol *W*. The address field of the instruction (stored at *W* + 1) is designated by symbol *Y*. the operand used during the execution of the instruction is stored at an address symbolized by *Z*. An index register contains the value *X*. Shows how *Z* is calculated from the other address if addressing of the instruction is

(*i*) direct (1)

(*ii*) indirect (2)

(*iii*) relative (2)

(*iv*) indexed (2)

Q. 5. (a) What is basic difference between branch instruction, a all subroutine and program interrupt. (3)

(*b*) Compare and contrast RISC and CISC architecture. (6)

(*c*) Two computers use register window with the following, characteristics. Determine the window size and total number of registers in each computer.

Q. 6. (*a*) Explain the concept of pipelining by taking example of instruction pipelining.

(*b*) Under what circumstances instruction pipeline deviates form its normal operation. Discuss the methods to overcome this.

(*c*) A pipeline *P* is formed to provide a speedup of 6.16 where, operating at 100 M Hz and an efficiency of 88%. How many stages does P have? What are P's MIPs and CPI performance levels.

Q. 7. (*a*) **A machine** has a 32 bit byte addressable virtual address space. The page size is 8KB. How many pages of virtual address space exist? (3)

(*b*) A computer has pages of virtual address space but only has 4 page frames. Initially memory is empty. A program references the virtual pages in the order 0, 7, 2, 5, 8, 9, 2, 4. Which reference causes a page fault with LRU and FIFO? (5)

(*c*) What is micro program control unit? How is mirco instruction sequencing performed? explain with suitable diagram. (7)

Q. 8. Write short notes on any three of three of the following: – 5 × 3 = 15

(*a*) RS232

(*b*) General purpose instrumentation bus IEEE498

(*c*) Power PC architecture

(*d*) Device drivers

(*e*) Kernel drivers

End-Term Examination
December-2006
Exam Series code: 100103DEC06200053

Paper Code: ETCS-305 ***Subject: Computer Architecture***

TIme: 3 Hours **Maximum Marks :75**

Note: Attempt any five questions.

Q. l. (*a*) The content of PC in the basic computer is 3AF. The content of AC is 7EC3. The content of memory at address 3AF is 932E. The content of memory at address 32E is O9AC. The content of memory at address O9AC us 8B9F. (8)

(*i*) What is the instruction that will be fetched and executed next?

(*ii*) Show the binary operation that will be performed in the AC when the instruction is executed.

(*iii*) Give the contents of the registers PC, AC, AR, DR and JR and the values of E, I at the end of the instruction cycle.

(*b*) Describe the instruction cycle and draw its flow chart. (4)

(*c*) Can the letter I be used as a symbolic address in the assembly language program defined for the basic computer? Justify your answer. (3)

Q. 2. (*a*) Explain how cache memory may be organized using associative mapping. (6)

(*b*) (*i*) How many 128 × 8 RAM chips are needed to provide a memory capacity of 2048 bytes? (*ii*) How many lines of the address bus must be used to access 2048 bytes of memory? How many of these lines will be common to all chips? (*iii*) How many lines must be decoded for chip select? Specify the size of the decoders? (6)

(*c*) Explain why can't we have a single large main memory instead of a hierarchy of memory. (3)

Q. 3. (*a*) Explain in brief with example all the different types of addressing modes. (6)

(*b*) Explain the basic features of RISC and CISC computers. (6)

(*c*) An output program resides in the memory starting from address 2300. It is executed after the computer recognizes an interrupt when FGO becomes a 1. (While IEN =1) (3) (*i*) What instruction must be placed at address 1?

(*ii*) What must be the last two instructions of the output program?

Q. 4. (*a*) List all the micro-operations for the following cycles in the basic computer. (8)

(*i*) Fetch cycle (*ii*) Indirect cycle

(*iii*) Interrupt cycle (*iv*) ISZ execute cycle

Give suitable example.

(*b*) What is interrupt I/0? Design a parallel priority interrupt hardware system with four interrupt sources. (7)

Q. 5. Write short notes on any three of the following: (5 × 3)

(*a*) Booth's algorithm for multiplication.

(*b*) Architecture of Pentium processor and functions of different blocks.

(*c*) Direct Memory Access (DMA) transfer

(*d*) Virtual memory

Q. 6. (*a*) What is the difference between hardwired control and micro programmed control. (4)

(*b*) What do you mean by "interrupt" and "vector interrupt"? (4)

(*c*) Write a subroutine to subtract two numbers. In the calling program the BSA instruction is followed by two parameters: the subtrahend and minuend. The difference is returned to the main program in the third location following the BSA instruction. (7)

Q. 7. Differentiate between any three of the following: (5 × 3)

(*a*) Register transfer instructions and Memory transfer instructions

(*b*) Vector processing and Parallel processing

(*c*) Synchronous data transfer and Asynchronous data transfer

(*d*) Microprocessor and Multiprocessor systems

Q. 8. (*a*) Explain interprocessor communication and synchronization. Give suitable example. (8)

(*b*) What is pipelining? Explain the systems that have pipelined processing and parallel processing. (7)

End Term Examination

FIFTH SEMESTER [B.TECH.]- DECEMBER 2009

Paper Code: ETCS-305 Subject: Computer Architecture

Paper ID: 27305 ***Time : 3 Hours*** Maximum Marks :75

Note: Attempt any five questions in all. Q.No.1 is compulsory. Attempt one question from each unit.

Q. 1. (*a*) Explain register transfer language. (5)

(*b*) Explain stack organization. (5)

(*c*) Explain priority interrupt. (5)

(*d*) Discuss memory hierarchy. (5)

(*e*) Discuss characteristics of multiprocessor. (5)

UNIT-I

Q. 2. (*a*) Explain timing sequence of instruction cycle. (6.5)

(*b*) Explain architecture of Computer System. (6)

OR

Q. 3. (*a*) Design a Accumulator logic for computers system. (6.5)

(*b*) Differentiae between direct and indirect addressing. Discuss various technique for the same. (6)

UNIT-II

Q. 4. (*a*) Differentiate between RISC and CISC. (6.5)

(*b*) Explain instruction format of computer system. (6)

OR

Q. 5. (*a*) Explain pipeline processing of instruction. (6.5)

(*b*) Explain array processor. (6)

UNIT-III

Q. 6. (*a*) Explain Booth Algorithm in detail. (6)

(*b*) Explain MAR. (3)

(*c*) Explain floating point number representation. (3.5)

OR

Q. 7. (*a*) Explain Isolator and Memory mapped I/O. (4)

(*b*) Define strobe control. (4)

(*c*) Explain UART. (4.5)

UNIT-IV

Q. 8. (*a*) Explain the organization of virtual memory. (6)

(*b*) Assume system has 48-bit virtual address, 36 bit physical address, 128 MB of main memory and page size in the system is 4096 byte (4KB) pages. Find systems support to how many virtual and physical pages in the address space. (6.5)

OR

Q. 9. (*a*) Explain CAM. (6)

(*b*) Explain interconnection structure of computer system. (6.5)

End Term Examination

Paper Code: ETCS3O5 **Subject: Computer Architecture**

FIFTH SFMESTER [B.TECH] DECEMBER-2010

Time: 3 Hours **Maximum Marks: 75**

Note : Attempt five questions in all. Select one question from each unit including Q.1 which is compulsory

Q. 1. (*a*) What is a lens? How can it he implemented?

(*b*) Explain what is a microinstruction and a microprogram.

(*c*) Why is microprogram med control unit so called?

(*d*) Differentiate between a direct and indirect addressing mode with the help of suitable examples.

(*e*) What is vector processing?

(*f*) What is an interrupt? How is it serviced?

(*g*) What is an interface?

(*h*) Define the term computer architecture.

(*i*) Write down the format of a 16-bit instruction.

(*j*) What are MRI and RRI? Give examples. (2.5 x 10=25)

UNIT-I

Q. 2. (*a*) What is a decoder? Discuss 3 to 8 line decoder with the help of a circuit diagram and a truth table. (6.5)

(*b*) What is a microperation? How many types of micro operations are mostly found in digital computers: Explain with the help of at least one example for each category. (6)

Q. 3. (*a*) Explain the three basic computer instruction formats. Give examples of each type. (4.5)

(*b*) with the help of a flow chart, explain the type of an instruction is determined. (7)

(*c*) What are program interrupts? (1)

UNIT-II

Q. 4. (*a*) How many types of address sequence are required in a control memory? Explain with the help of a diagram of a control memory and its associated hardware. (7.5)

(*b*) Explain the format of a micro instruction in the control memory. (5)

Q. 5. (*a*) What are addressing modes? Explain the following with the help of suitable examples: (1 + 8)

(*i*) Implied mode | (*ii*) Immediate mode
(*iii*) Register mode | (*iv*) Register indirect mode
(v) Direct address mode | (*vi*) Indirect address mode
(*vii*) Relative address mode | (*viii*) Base Register addressing mode

(*b*) What is arithmetic pipeline? (3.5)

UNIT-III

Q. 6. (*a*) With the help of a flow chart, discuss the hardware divide algorithm. Explain how the divide overflow conditions are handled? (10)

(*b*) Draw the diagram showing hardware for signed magnitude addition and subtraction. (2.5)

Q. 7. Discuss the following:- (2.5 x 5=12.5)

(*a*) I/O bus and interface module

(*b*) I/O bus versus memory bus

(*c*) Isolated versus memory-mapped **I/O**

(*d*) Handshaking

(*e*) Interrupt-initiated I/O

UNIT-IV

Q. 8. Write short notes on the following:

(*a*) Memory hierarchy in a computer system (7.5)

(*b*) Memory address map (2.5)

(*c*) Associative memory (2.5)

Q. 9. Write short notes on the following:

(*a*) Set associative mapping in Cache Memory (4.5)

(*b*) Cross bar switch (4)

(*c*) Interprocessor synchronization (4)

End Term Examination

FIFTH SEMESTER [B.TECH] DECEMBER-2011

PAPER CODE: ETCS305 **Subject: Computer Architecture**

Time: 3 Hours **Maximum Marks :75**

Note: Q.no.1 is compulsory. Attempt one question from each unit.

Q. 1. (*a*) What is the difference between serial and parallel transfer? Explain with required example.

(*b*) Explain the hardware implementation of logic microoperation for AND, OR, XOR and complement logic gate.

(*c*) Explain the timing control signals.

(*d*) What is the difference between microprocessor and a microprogram?

(*e*) Why should the sign of the remainder after a division be the same as the sign of the dividend? **(5 × 5 = 25)**

UNIT-I

Q. 2. A digital computer has a common bus system for 16 register of 32 bits each. The bus is constructed with multiplexers. (12.5)

(*a*) How many selection inputs are there in each multiplexer?

(*b*) What size of multiplexers are needed?

(c) How many multiplexers are there in the bus?

OR

Q. 3. What is the difference between a direct and indirect address instruction? How many references to memory are needed for each type of instruction to bring an operand into a processor register? (6)

(*b*) Explain the circuit of Accumulator Logic. **(6.5)**

UNIT-II

Q. 4. (*a*) Define the following: (4)

(*i*) Microoperation (*ii*) Microinstruction

(*iii*) Microcode

(*b*) A computer has 16 registers, an ALU with 32 operations and a shifter with eight operations. All connected to a common bus system. (8.5)

(*i*) Formulate a control word for a microoperation.

(*ii*) Specify the number of pits in each fled on the control word and give a general encoding scheme.

OR

Q. 5. (*a*) convert the following arithmetic expressions from infix to reverse Polish notation: **(6)**

(*i*) $A * B + C * D + E * F$ (*ii*) $A * B + A * (B * D + C * E)$

(*iii*) $A * [B + C * CD + E]$

$F * (G + H)$

(*b*) Draw a space-time diagram for a six-segment pipeline showing the time it takes to process eight tasks. **(6.5)**

UNIT-III

Q. 6. (a) Design an array multiplier that multiplies two 4-bit numbers. Use AND gates and binary adders. (6)

(*b*) Show the hardware to be used for the addition and subtraction of two decimal numbers in signed-magnitude representation. Indicate how an overflow is detected? (6.5)

OR

Q. 7. (*a*) Explain DMA transfer in a computer system. (6)

(*b*) What is the difference between isolated I/O and memory-mapped I/O? What are the advantages and disadvantages of each? (6.5)

UNIT-IV

Q. 8. (*a*) Explain memory hierarchy in a computer system. (6)

(*b*) A computer uses RAM chips of 1024x1 capacity. (6.5)

(*i*) How many chips are needed and how should their address lines be connected to provide a memory capacity of 1024 Bytes?

(*ii*) How many chips are needed to provide a memory capacity of 16K bytes? Explain in words how the chips are to be connected to the address bus.

OR

Q. 9. (*a*) A virtual memory has a page size of 1K word. There are eight pages and four blocks. The associative memory page table contains the following entries

Page	Block
0	3
1	1
4	2
6	0

Make a list of all virtual address (in decimal) that will cause a page fault, if used by the CPU. (6)

(*b*) Explain Cache Coherence. **(6.5)**

End Term Examination

First Semester B. TECH. — DECEMBER 2008

Paper Code: ETCS 305 **Subject: Computer Architecture**

Paper ID: 27305 **(Batch: 2004-2005)**

Time: 3Hours **Maximum Marks :75**

Note: Q. NO. 1 compulsory. Internal choice is indicated. (2.5 × 10)

Q.1. (*a*) What is Register Transfer language? How is ii different from 'C' language?

(*b*) Explain Selective Complement Operation- Give an example to illustrate your answer

(*c*) Briefly explain Stored Program Organization.

(*d*) What are the advantages of microprogrammed control over hardwired control?

(*e*) Explain Polish Notation. Give one example each to illustrate Polish Notation and Reverse Polish Notation.

(*f*) Express 3*4) + (5*6) to Reverse Polish Notation.

(*g*) Explain memory-mapped I/O organization.

(*h*) Explain the term handshaking. What is its relevance?

(*i*) Differentiate between 'hit' and 'miss' with respect to cache memory.

(*j*) How is logical memory address different from physical memory address? Give an example.

UNIT-I

Q. 2. (*a*) Design a 4 bit combinational circuit decrementer using four full-adders. Operate the circuit by giving it inputs and verify them by performing manual binary operations. (7.5)

(*b*) Check for the correctness of the following statements: (5)

(*i*) $xT : AR <-AR, AR<-0$ (*ii*) $yT : R1 <-R2, R1<-R3$

Justify your answers in each case.

OR

Q. 3. (*a*) The content of PC is $3AF_h$ in the basic computer. The content of AC is $7EC3_h$. The data stored at memory location $3AF_h$ **5** $932E_h$. The content of memory at address $32E_h$ is $09AC_h$. The content of memory at address $9AC_h$ is $8B9F_h$. (7.5)

(*i*) What is the instruction that will be fetched and executed next?

(*ii*) Show the binary operation that will be performed in AC when the instruction is executed

(*b*) Differentiate between direct and indirect addressing. How many references to memory are needed for each type of instruction to bring an operand into a processor register? (5)

UNIT-II

Q, 4. (*a*) Explain the difference between hardwired control and microprogrammed control. Can the hardwired control be associated with microprogrammed control? Give example of a processor in which both kinds of controls are implemented. (7.5)

(*b*)

(*i*) micro operation (*ii*) micro code (*iii*) propagation delay

OR

Q. 5. (*a*) Convert the following arithmetic operations from infix to reverse polish notation. (7.5)

(*i*) $A * B + C * D + E * F$ (*ii*) $A * B + A * (B * D + C * E)$

(iii) $A + B * [C * D + E * (F + G)]$

(*iv*) $A * [B + C * (D + E)]/F * (G + H)$

(*b*) Identify the following instructions and justify your answers. **(5)**

(*i*) MOV X, R_1 (*ii*) MUL *X*, *R*1, *R*2

(*iii*) STORE T (*iv*) POP X

(*iv*) MOV R2, C

UNIT-III

Q. 6. (*a*) Discuss the basics of Booth's Algorithm. Draw the flowchart of Booth's Algorithm for multiplication of signed-2's complement numbers. (7.5)

(*b*) Suggest a procedure for detecting an oveflow when signed 1's complement numbers are used.

OR

Q. 7. (*a*) How many character's per second can be transmitted over a 1200 baud line in each of the following modes? (7.5)

(*i*) Synchronous serial transmission.

(*ii*) Asynchronous serial transmission with one stop bit. (Assume a character code of eight bits.)

(*b*) What is the difference between isolated I/O mode and memory-mapped I/O mode? Give advantages arid disadvantages of each. (5)

UNIT-IV

Q. 8. The cache memory is employed in computer systems to compensate for the speed differential between main memory access time and speed of processor logic". Discuss and justify the above statement. (12.5)

OR

Q. 9. Discuss the following with reference to multiprocessors: (12.5)

(*i*) Time Shared Common Bus (*ii*) Multistage Switching

FIRST TERM EXAMINATION

FIFTH SEMESTER [B.TECH] - SEPTEMBER 2011

(Regular)

Paper Code: ETCS — 305 **Subject: Computer Architecture**

Time: 1Hr 30 Min **Maximum Marks: 30**

Note: Attempt any three questions. Question No. 1 is compulsory. Each question carries 10 marks.

Q. 1. (*a*) Explain the difference between hardwired control and microprogrammed control. (2)

(*b*) Explain the overflow condition in Arithmetic Shift microoperation. (2)

(*c*) What are the two instructions needed in the basic computer in order to set the *E* flip-flop to 1?

(*d*) The following transfer statements specify a memory. Explain a memory operation in each case:

(*i*) $M[AR]$ <-- $R3$ (*ii*) $R2$ <-- $M[AR]$ (2)

(*e*) How many bits wide memory address have to be if the computer had 16 MB of memory? (Use the smallest value possible) (2)

Q. 2. (*a*) A digital computer has a common bus system for 16 registers of 32 bits each. The bus is constructed with multiplexers (6)

(*i*) How many selection inputs are there in each multiplexer?

(*ii*) What sizes of multiplexers are needed?

(*iii*) How many multiplexers are there in the bus?

(*b*) Define the following: (4)

(*i*) Microoperation (*ii*) Microinstruction

(*iii*) Microprogram (*iv*) Microcode

Q. 3. (*a*) Explain the importance of different addressing modes in computer architecture with suitable example. (5)

(*b*) What is an instruction format? Explain different types of instruction formats in detail (5)

Q. 4. (*a*) Design an arithmetic circuit with one selection variable *S* and two *n*-bit data inputs *A* and *B*. The circuit generates the following four arithmetic operations in conjunction with the input carry Cm. Draw the logic diagram for the first two stages. (5)

S	Cin = 0	Cin = 1
0	$D = A + B$ (add)	$D = A + 1$(Increment)
1	$D = A - 1$ (decrement)	$D = A + B + 1$ (Subtract)

(*b*) Explain Shift microoperation in detail. Also draw and explain 4-bit combinational circuit shifter. (5)

Second Term Examination

FIFTH SEMESTER [B.TECH] - NOVEMBER 2011

(Regular)

Paper (code: ETCS - 305 **Subject: Computer architecture**

Time: 1 Hr 30Min **Maximum Marks: 30**

Note: Attempt any three **questions. Question No. 1 is compulsory. Each question carries 10** marks.

Q. 1. (*a*) Explain Flynn's classification of computers. (2)

(*b*) What is the difference between isolated I/O and memory mapped I/O? (2)

(*c*) Why does DMA have priority over the CPU when both request a memory transfer? (2)

(*d*) Derive an algorithm for evaluating the square root of a binary fixed point number. (2)

(*e*) What is pipeline processing? (2)

Q. 2. (*a*) Explain in detail the RISC Pipeline. Why is the cache miss penalty, greater in deeply pipelined processor? (6)

(*b*) What is direct memory access (DMA)? Why are the read and write control lines in a DMA controller bidirectional? (4)

Q. 3. (*a*) Formulate a hardware procedure for detecting an overflow by computing the sign of the sum with the signs of the augend and addend. The numbers are in signed 2's complement representation (5)

(*b*) What is the basic advantage of using interrupt initiated data transfer over transfer under program control without an interrupt? (5)

Q. 4. (*a*) What is Asynchronous data transfer? Explain in detail. (5)

(*b*) Explain Vector Processing. What is the difference between Vector & Array processing (5)

B. Tech. (Sem. – 3rd)

COMFUTER ARCHITECTURE

SUBJECT CODE: CS - 201

Paper ID [A0451]

Note Please fill subject code and paper ID on OMR

Time 03 Hours Maximum Marks: 60

Instruction to Candidates:. . . –

1. Section-A is Compulsory.

2. Attempt any Four questions from Section-B.
3. Attempt any Two questions from Section-C.

SECTION-A

Q. 1. **(10 × 2 = 20)**

(*a*) Explain the significance of a layered architecture.

(*b*) Distinguish between SIMD and MIMD.

(*c*) What is Memory Hierarchy? Explain with the help of diagram.

(*d*) What do you mean by the term DMA channel?

(*e*) What is the basic function of an interrupt controller?

(*f*) Explain the importance of interleave memory.

(*g*) How can you evaluate the performance of processor architecture?

(*h*) What is the difference between memory-mapped and peripheral mapped I/P

(*i*) Explain the various types of performance metrics?

(*j*) What is the need of virtual memory?

SECTION-B **(4 × 5 = 20)**

Q. 2. Explain the algorithm for multiplying two 4-bit unsigned numbers by taking a suitable example.

Q. 3. Explain the important features of a RISC based system architecture.

Q. 4. Discuss hardware/software part partitioning with the help of a suitable flow-chart.

Q. 5. What are superscalar machines? Discuss their important features.

Q. 6. Explain the block diagram of 8251 chip.

SECTION-C **(2 × 10 = 20)**

Q. 7. What are the various issues for designing the instruction set of a processor.

Q. 8. Explain the block diagram of 8255 chip and then explain that how this chip will be used in conjunction with 8085 microprocessor to interface a DMA controller.

Q. 9. Write short notes on the following:

(*a*) Fast carry adder. (*b*) Hazards of pipelining.

MCA **(Sem.-3rd)**

COMPUTER SYSTEM ARCHITECrURE

SUBJFCT CODE: MCA- 301(N2)

Paper ID **[B0111]**

[Note: please fill subject code and paper ID on OMR]

Time : 03 Hours Maximum Marks 60

Instruction to Candidates:

1. Attempt any one question from each Sections A, B, C, and D.

2. Section-E compulsory.
3. Use of Non-programmable Scientific Calculator is allowed.

SECTION–A

(1 × 10 = 10)

Q. 1. (*a*) Explain with a logic diagram the working of a full-adder.

(*b*) Explain the action of multiplexer and demultiplexer with suitable diagrams.

Q. 2. (*a*) Explain in detail about serial in serial out shift register.

(*b*) Design a 4-bit binary adder/subtractor circuit.

SECTION–C

(1 × 10 = 10)

Q. 3. Explain in detail the different types of instructions that are supported in a typical processor.

Q. 4. What are the various types of computer registers? Describe the control logic design with sequence register and decoder.

SECTION–C

(1 × 10 = 10)

Q. 5. Explain in detail the working of a micro programmed control unit

Q. 6. (*a*) Discuss the data transfer mechanism of the PCI bus.

(*b*) Outline some specific properties of RISC systems.

SECTION–D

(1 × 10 = 10)

Q. 7. What arc the various types of ROM? Discuss the methods of programming ROMs.

Q. 8. Discuss the various mapping schemes used in cache design. Compare the schemes in terms of cost and performance.

SECTION–E

(10 × 2 = 20)

Q. 9.

(*a*) What is an XNOR gate? Draw its truth table.

(*b*) What is the difference between latch and flip flop?

(*c*) What are Demultiplexers?

(*d*) What are opcode and operand? Give examples.

(*e*) What is the function performed by timing and control unit- in a microprocessor?

(*f*) What is an instruction cycle?

(*g*) What is the purpose of guard bits used in floating point operations?

(*h*) Give the function of memory address and memory buffer registers.

(*i*) Why are interrupt mask provided in any processor?

(*j*) Give the features oft RAM cell.

EXAMINATION PAPERS

EXAMINATION PAPER-2000
MDU UNIVERSITY (ROHTAK)
COMPUTER ORGANIZATION-CSE-303-C

1. (*a*) A 36 bit floating point binary number has 8-bit plus sign for the exponent and 26 bit plus sign for the mantissa. The mantissa is a normalized fraction. Numbers in the mantissa and exponents are in signed-magnitude representation. What are the largest and smallest positive quantities that can be represented, excluding zero? (12)

(*b*) Perform the arithmetic operations (+42) + (–13) and (–42) – (–13) in binary using signed –2's complement representation for negative no. (8)

2. What is Cache Memory? Explain different mapping procedures. Also mention their advantages and disadvantages. (20)

3. (*a*) The access time of a Cache memory is 100ns and that of main memory 1000ns. It is estimated that 80% of memory requests are for read and the remaining 20% for write. The hit ratio for read accesses only is 0.9. A write-through procedure is used:

(*i*) What is the average access time of the system considering only memory read cycles? (10)

(*ii*) What is the average access time of the system for both read and write requites?

(*iii*) What is the hit ratio taking into consideration the write cycles?

(*b*) Explain the associative memory. (10)

4. Explain the DMA mode of data transfer in detail. What do you understand by the term cycle stealing ? (20)

5. (*a*) Explain the difference between Hardware control memory and Micro programmed control memory. (5)

(*b*) What do you understand by control memory? Explain different address-sequencing procedures. (15)

6. (*a*) A computer uses a memory unit with 256 k words of 32 bits each. A binary instruction code is stored in one word of memory. The instruction has four parts-an indirect bits, an operation code, a register code part to specify on of the 64 registers and an address part.

(*i*) How many bits are there in the operation code the register code part, and the address part?

(*ii*) Draw the instruction word format and indicate the number of bits in each part.

(*iii*) How many bits are there in the data and address inputs of the Memory? (15)

(*b*) Explain the following : (5)

(*i*) MAR/AR (*ii*) MBR (*iii*) PC

7. Explain different addressing modes with suitable example. (20)

8. Write short notes of the following: (5 × 4)

   (*i*) I/O processor

   (*ii*) Daisy chain priority Interrupt System

   (*iii*) Auxiliary Memory

   (*iv*) Register Transfer Language.

EXAMINATION PAPERS 411

EXAMINATION PAPER-2001

COMPUTER ORGANIZATION-CSE-303-C

1. (*a*) Explain virtual memory in detail. Also show the implementation of page table. (8)

   (*b*) The logical address spaces in the computer system consist of 128 segments. Each segment can have up to 32 pages of 4k words in each. Physical memory consists of 4 k block of 4 k words in each. Formulate the logical and physical address formats. (12)

2. (*a*) A computer uses RAM chips of 1024 x 1 capacity:

   (*i*) How many chips are needed, and how should their address lines be connected to provide a memory capacity of 1024 bytes.

   (*ii*) How many chips are needed to provide a memory capacity of 16 k bytes, Explain in words how the chips are to be connected to the address lines. (12)

   (*b*) Write note on magnetic tapes and magnetic drums. (8)

   (*c*) Explain parallel priority Interrupt system in detail considering 8 interrupt sources. (10)

   (*d*) Explain DMA process in detail. (10)

3. (*a*) Define the following: (10)

   (*i*) Vectored Interrupt (*ii*) Non-vectored Interrupt

   (*iii*) Strobe control mode (*iv*) Handshaking mode of data transfer

   (*v*) Polling process.

   (*b*) What are the three modes of data transfer to and from peripherals? Explain in details. (10)

4. (*a*) What does the 8-bit binary string 10110110 represents in the following number system?

   (*i*) Unsigned binary (*ii*) Signed binary

   (*iii*) 2's complement (*iv*) l's complement (8)

   (*b*) Explain the micro-program sequences for a control memory in detail. (12)

5. (*a*) Explain different addressing modes in detail. (10)

   (*b*) Perform the following arithmetic operations:

   (*i*) (+ 42) + (–1 3) (*ii*) (–42) – (–1 3)

   in binary using 2's complement representation. (10)

6. Show the hardware required to implement the following logic micro-operations: (20)

(i) $T_1 : F <- A$ (intersection) B (ii) $T_2 :$ G B C V D

(iii) $T_3 : E <- E$ (iv) $Xy' T_0 + T_1 + x'y\ T_2 : A <- A + B$.

7. Write short notes on the following:

(i) I/O processor (ii) Associative Memory

EXAMINATION PAPERS 415

EXAMINATION PAPER-2004

COMPUTER ORGANIZATION

1. (a) Draw a combinational circuit that accepts a 2 bit number and generates on 0/p binary which is equal to square of i/p (8)

   (b) Explain the conversion technique of J.K. Flip Flop to T-Flip Flop. (6)

   (c) What is look ahead carry? Explain its significance. (6)

2. (a) What are different arithmetic micro-operations, when implemented in a serial computer. Assume that initially carry flip flop is clear. Use shift registers, flip-flops and adders to implement the structures. (12)

   (b) What are the advantages of hard-wired control than a micro-programmed control unit? Contrast and compare the things. (8)

3. (a) Explain all types of instructions. (10)

   (b) Explain interrupt cycle through a flow chart. (10)

4. What is addressing mode? Explain any eight addressing mode using practical data. Calculate the effective addresses in each mode. (20)

5. Write a program to evaluate the following arithmetic statement using:

   (i) Three address instructions

   (ii) Two address instructions

   (iii) One-address instructions (20)

$$X = \frac{\left[A \cdot \frac{B}{C} + D\right].E}{\frac{D}{E} \cdot F + \frac{C}{A} + B} + C$$

6. (a) Explain the algorithm for floating point addition. Draw its flow chart. (10)

   (b) Draw flow chart of fixed-point multiplication. (10)

7. Define the following terms. Also explain them. (20)

   (i) Types of interrupts (ii) Micro program sequencer

   (iii) Design of accumulator logic (iv) Bus and memory transfer

8. (a) Discuss the advantages of interleaved memory. (6)

   (b) How do we read from associative memory? (6)

   (c) Explain, how data is accessed from virtual memory. Draw its construction also. (8)

EXAMINATION PAPERS 417

EXAMINATION PAPER-2006

[BE. 4th Semester (CSE) Examination] Paper—CSE-210-E

COMPUTER ARCHITECTURE AND ORGANIZATION

Time allowed: 3 hours Maximum Marks: 100

Note : Attempt Any **FIVE** questions. All questions carry equal marks.

1. (*a*) Define the term register. Design a 4-bit bidirectional shift register with parallel load. (10)

(*b*) Draw the logic diagram and truth table for full adder. (10)

2. (*a*) What do you mean by Instruction Set Architecture (ISA) ? How it affects the design of a computer system? (10)

(*b*) Briefly discuss the stored program concept. (10)

3. (*a*) What are the advantages and disadvantages of fixed and variable instruction formats? (6)

(*b*) What are the advantages offered by complex instruction set computers? (6)

(*c*) Discuss the following addressing modes briefly:

(*i*) Relative addressing modes. (8)

4. (*a*) How a computer instruction is executed? Draw the instruction cycle. (10)

(*b*) What is control unit? Discuss any two methods briefly for implementation of control unit. (10)

5. (*a*) Compare the characteristics of static and dynamic RAM. (5)

(*b*) What is the design principle for cache memory ? Discuss the following cache mapping scheme:

(*i*) Direct cache mapping. (*ii*) Associative cache mapping. (15)

6. (*a*) What are the design issues for multiprocessor computer systems? (10)

(*b*) How you can enhance the throughput of a computer system ? Give suitable example. (10)

7. (*a*) What are the various types of interrupts supported by 80 × 86 family? (10)

(*b*) Give three examples with brief description of the following:

(*i*) Register reference instruction (*ii*) Memory reference instruction

(*iii*) I/O instructions for 80 x 86 family. (10)

8. (*a*) Draw the block diagram and briefly explain the microprogram sequencer. (10)

(*b*) Briefly discuss the Flynn's classification of digital system. (10)

418 COMPUTER SYSTEM ARCHITECTURE AND ORGANISATION

EXAMINATION PAPER-2007

[B.E. 4th Semester (CSE) Examination] Paper—CSE-2i0-E

COMPUTER ARCHITECTURE AND ORGANIZATION

Time allowed: 3 hours Maximum Marks: 100

Note : Attempt Any **FIVE** questions. All questions carry equal marks.

1. (*a*) Design a combinational circuit with three inputs *x*, *y*, *z* and three outputs *A*, *B*, *C*. When the binary input is 0, 1, 2, 3 the binary output is one greater than the input when the binary point is 4, 5, 6 or 7, the binary output is one less than the input. (10)

   (*b*) What do you meant by a multiplexer? Design a 4 × 1 multiplexer using AND, OR and NOT gate. (10)

2. (*a*) Draw and explain the multilevel viewpoint of a machine. (10)

   (*b*) What are the various types of operation systems? Discuss the characteristics of each briefly. (10)

3. (*a*) What are the characteristics of RISC computers. (5)

   (*b*) Why a number of address ing modes are needed? By taking suitable examples explain the following addressing modes:

   (*i*) Direct (*ii*) Index

   (*iii*) Relative (*iv*) Immediate

   (*v*) Register (15)

4. Draw and explain the detailed data path for a register based CPU and stock based CPU. (20)

5. (*a*) Define the term "locality of reference." How this concept is used in the design of memory system? (10)

   (*b*) What do you mean by cache memory? Draw and explain the block diagram of cache memory. (10)

6. (*a*) State and explain the Amdahl's law. (10)

   (*b*) How the throughput of a system can be enhanced with parallel mechanisms? (10)

7. (*a*) What do you mean by control memory? How is it different than simple memory? (10)

   (*b*) What are the various types of instructions supported by the 8086 family. Discuss each briefly.

8. (*a*) What are the various parameters that can be used to evaluate the performance of a memory unit. (10)

   (*b*) What do you mean by structure organization? (10)

APRIL 2011 50417/SAE5C

Time : Three hours Maximum: 75 marks

SECTION A - (10 x 2 =20 marks)

Answer any TEN questions.

All questions carry equal marks.

Each answer. should not exceed 50 words.

1. Mention four components of computer system.
2. Mention the role of Cache memory.
3. What is the use of Main memory?

4. List any four external memory storage.
5. What are addressing modes? Mention any two addressing modes.
6. List the various instruction formats.
7. Mention the use of DMA.
8. List any four features of pipelined processing.
9. Define the term instruction cycle.
10. Compare CISC and RISC processors.
11. What are micro operations?
12. What are the functions of control unit?

SECTION B—(5 × 5 25 MARKS)

Answer any FIVE questions.

All questions carry equal marks.

Each answer should not exceed 200 words.

13. What are bus interconnecting system? Explain.
14. Explain the concept of memory hierarchy.
15. Compare static and dynamic RAM.
16. Mention the features of optical storage.
17. Explain the advantages of floating point representation.
18. Mention different types of instructions available in the instruction set.
19. Write short notes on microinstruction sequencing.

SECTION C—(3 × 10 = 30 MARKS)

Answer any THREE questions.

All questions carry equal marks.

Each answer should not exceed 500 words.

20. Explain the evolution of computer systems.
21. Explain the principles of cache design.
22. Explain the structure and functions of magnetic disk storage.
23. Discuss about different addressing mode with examples.
24. Explain the Hardwired implementation of control unit.

416 COMPUTER SYSTEM ARCHITECTURE AND ORGANISATION

EXAMINATION PAPER-2005

[B.E. 4th Semester (CSE) Examination] Paper—CSE-210-E

COMPUTER ARCHITECTURE AND ORGANIZATION

Time allowed: 3 hours Maximum Marks: 100

Note : Attempt Any **FIVE** questions.

1. (*a*) Prove the following:

   (*i*) A positive logic AND gate operation is equivalent to negative logic OR operation. (5)

   (*ii*) $ABC + AC + AB + ABC = AB + BC + CA.$ (5)

   (*b*) What do you mean by a register? Draw the block diagram of a 4-bit bi-directional shift register. (10)

2. (*a*) Explain the Flynn's classification of digital computer. (10)

   (*b*) What do you mean by structured organization? Briefly discuss multi level view point of a machine. (10)

3. (*a*) Differentiate between RISC and CISC computers. (10)

   (*b*) What is addressing mode ? Clearly state how effective address is calculated in the following add modes

   (*i*) Relative (*ii*) Index

   (*iii*) Implied (*iv*) Indirect (10)

4. Draw and explain the detailed data path of a typical register based CPU. (20)

5. (*a*) What is pipelining? Discuss how performance of a system can be enhanced with pipelining. (10)

   (*b*) Which is the fastest memory in the memory hierarchy ? Why memory hierarchy is needed? (10)

6. (*a*) Write and explain any five goals for parallel processor design. (10)

   (*b*) What is cache coherence problem ? How multiprocessor resolve this problem? (10)

7. For 8086 microprocessor explain: (20)

   (*i*) Types of interrupts (*ii*) Set of registers

   (*iii*) Total memory hierarchy. (20)

8. Briefly discuss the following:

   (*a*) Static and dynamic RAM and its organization.

   (*b*) Amdahl's law. (10 + 10)

412 COMPUTER SYSTEM ARCHITECTURE AND ORGANISATION

EXAMINATION PAPER-2002

COMPUTER ORGANIZATION-CSE-303-C

1. (*a*) Design an arithmetic circuit with one selection variable *S* and two *n*-bit data *i/ps* *A* and *B*. The circuit generates the following four arithmetic operations in conjunction with the input carry C_{in} Draw the logic diagram for it.

S	$C_{in} = 0$	$C_{in} = 1$
0	$D = A + B$	$D = A + 1$
1	$D = A - 1$	$D = A + B + 1$

(6)

   (*b*) A majority function is a digital circuit whose o/p is 1 if majority of the inputs are 1. The o/p is zero otherwise:

(*i*) Obtain truth table of a 3 – *i/p* majority function

(*ii*) Draw the circuit of majority function, using NAND gates only.

(*iii*) Show that a full adder circuit consists of a 3-*i/p* × OR and a 3-*i/p* majority function. (4+ 5 + 5 = 14)

2. (a) Draw block diagram of a bus system connected to 4 registers with information transferred serially from only register to any other register. Use decoder and a multi-plexer to select the source register and decoder to select the destination register. (10)

(*b*) Draw the logic diagram of a 4-bit register with clocked JK Flip flop having control imps for increment. Complement and parallel transfer micro-operations. Show how 2's complement can be implemented in this register. (10)

3. (*a*) A memory unit has a capacity of 65536 words of 25 bit each, used with a computer. The instruction code is divided into 4 parts-an indirect mode bit. Operation code, two bits that specify a processor register and an address part.

(*i*) What is maximum no. of operation that can be incorporated in the computer if an instruction is stored in one memory word ?

(*ii*) How many processor registers are there in the computer and how many bits are in each?

(*iii*) How many bits are there in MBR, MAR and PC? (4 + 4 + 4 = 12)

(*b*) Draw a flowchart for computer cycle control and explain it. (8)

4. (*a*) Compare horizontal vs vertical micro instructions. (8)

(*b*) Micro program sequencer uses a register stack 8-levels deep.

(*i*) Draw a block diagram of the sequencer

(*ii*) Formulate the sequencer of internal operations which are required to implement call and Return from subroutine microinstructions. (12)

5. (*a*) Write a program to evaluate the arithmetic statement. With suitable comments, using

(*i*) $X = (A + B * C)/(DE * F \div G * H)$

(*ii*) Three address m/c

(*iii*) Two address m/c

(*iv*) One address m/c

(*v*) Zero address m/c (12)

(*b*) How many types of interrupts are there? Explain each with the help of an example. (8)

6. (*a*) Draw the flow-chart and hardware for Booth's algorithm of multiplication of two signed 2's complement numbers and explain. (10)

(*b*) Draw and explain flow-chart and hardware for division. (10)

7. (*a*) What is cache memory? Explain the write-through and write-back method to write in cache. (8)

(*b*) What do you understand by mapping? Explain direct mapping cache organization. (7)

(*c*) How interleaved memory is useful in multiprocessor system? (5)

8. (*a*) Obtain the Boolean function for match logic of one word in an associative memory taking into consideration a tag bit that indicates whether word is active or inactive.

(*b*) What do you understand by memory address map? Explain how main memory is connected to a CPU through data and address buses. (8)

(*c*) An address space is specified by 24 bits and corresponding memory space by 16 bits.

(*i*) How many words are there in address space?

(*ii*) How many words are there in memory space?

(*iii*) If a page consists of 2k words, how many pages and blocks are there in the system? (6)

414 COMPUTER SYSTEM ARCHITECTURE AND ORGANISATION

EXAMINATION PAPER-2002

COMPUTER ORGANIZATION

1. (*a*) Explain the associative memory and show the match logic for one word of associative memory. (10)

(*b*) A computer employs RAM chips of 256 x 8 and ROM chips of 1024 × 8. The computer system needs 2k byte of RAM, 4k byte of ROM

(*i*) How many RAM and ROM chips are required?

(*ii*) Draw a memory address map for the system.

(*iii*) Show the connection of memory with CPU. (10)

2. (*a*) Write a short note on memory hierarchy. Explain the different types of auxiliary memories. (10)

(*b*) Differentiate between Virtual memory and Cache memory. (5)

(*c*) What is page replacement? Explain any page replacement algorithm. (5)

3. (*a*) Differentiate between the following

(*i*) Micro-programmed and hardwired control memory.

(*ii*) Synchronous and asynchronous serial data transfer. (10)

(*b*) Explain daisy chain priority interrupt system. (10)

4. (*a*) Make a list of all virtual (in decimal) that will cause a page fault, if used by CPU. (10)

(*b*) What is Microinstruction format? Explain different formats available. (10)

5. (*a*) Distinguish between Integer and Floating point representation of numbers with their relative advantages and disadvantages through examples. (8)

(*b*) Explain the flow chart for multiplication and division of fixed-point numbers.(12)

(*c*) Explain the following terms:

(*i*) Memory Hierarchy (*ii*) Primary and secondary memory

(*iii*) Auxiliary memory (*iv*) Type of interrupt (20)

7. Write a program to evaluate the following arithmetic statement, using three, two and one instruction

$$X = \frac{A}{B} + \frac{C + D \cdot \frac{E}{F}}{D \cdot E - \frac{F}{C \div A}} - G$$

8. (*a*) A Virtual memory has page size of 1 k words. There are 8 pages and 4 blocks. The associative memory page table contains:

Page	Block
0	3
1	1
4	2
6	0

COMPUTER TECHNOLOGY AND APPLICATION

Paper – CS . 501

(Computer Systems Organisation)

Time 3 Hours Maximum Marks 100

Write your roll no. on the top immediately on receipt of this question paper

Answer any five questions.

Assume missing data, if any.

(*a*) Show the hardware to implement the following RTL code:

(*i*) $a : X \leftarrow X - Y$

(*ii*) $K : X + Y' + 1$

(iii) $F: X <- X\ EX\text{–}OR\ Y.$

Also show the hardware to implement all three of the RTL statements in one combined system Control hardware ensures that no more than one of the control signals a, b and r is active at any time. (10)

(b) Show the code to perform the computation $X = A + (B^* C) + D$ using microprocessors that use the following instruction formats. Do not modify the values of *A B*, *C* and *D*. If necessary, use temporary location T to store intermediate results.

(*i*) three-operand instructions;

(*ii*) two-operand instructions;

(*iii*) one-operand instruction.

(*iv*) zero-operand instructions. (10)

2. Design a CPU that meets the following specifications:

– It can access 256 words of memory, each word being 8bit wide. The CPU does this by outputing an 8-bit address on its output pins *A*[7….0] and reading in the 8-bit value from memory on its inputs *D*[7….0].

– The CPU contains an 8-bit address register (AR), program counter (PC), accumulator (AC), and data register (DR), and a 3-bit instruction register (IR).

– The CPU must realize the following instruction set. Note that a is an 8-bit value stored in the location immediately following the instruction. (20)

Instruction	Instruction Code	Operation
LDI	000XXXXXa	$AC <- a$
STO	001XXXXXa	$M[a] - AC$
ADD	010XXXXXa	$AC <- AC + M[a]$
OR	01IXXXXXa	$AC <- ACVM[a]$
JUMP	100XXXXXa	$PC <- a$
JREL	101AAAAA	$PC <- PC + 000AAAAA$
SKIP	110XXXXX	$PC <- PC + 1$
RST	111XXXXX	$PC <- 0, AC <- 0$

3. (*a*) A CPU is specified by the following RTL code. Partition the microoperations into field such that the total number of bits is minimized. Each microoperation OP**2 returns to FETCH1.

FETCH1 : $AR <- PC$

FETCH2 : $DR <- M, PC <- PC + 1$

FETCH 3 : $IR, AR <- DR$

0P001 : $DR <- M$

0P002 : $AC <- AC + DR$

0P011 : $AC <- AC\ PC + 1$

0P012 : $AC <- AC + 1$

0P101 : $DR <- M, AC <- AC + 1$

0P102 : $DR <- DR + 1$

0P11 : $DR <- M$

0P112 : $PC <- PC + DR\ (5.0)$ (10)

(*b*) Write the R.TL code For the shift add multiplication. Show the trace of the R.TL code for the shift-add multiplication, UV <– $X.Y$ for $X = 8$ and $Y = 12$ (10)

4. Write the RTL code for non-restoring division algorithm. Show the hardware for the non restoring algorithm. Also show the trace of the RTL code for the non-restoring division algorithm for:

UV = 01111011

X = 1010

5. Show the layout of a cache for a CPU that can address 1M × 16 of memory: the cache holds 8K × 16 of data and has the following mapping strategies. Give the number of bits per location and the total number of locations.

(*i*) Fully associative;

(*ii*) Direct mapped;

(*iii*) Two-way set associative;

(*iv*) Four way set associative. (20)

6. (*a*) What is the difference between isolated 110 and memory-mapped I/O ? What are the advantages and disadvantages of each? (5)

(*b*) What programming steps are required to check when a source interrupts the computer while it is still being required by a previous interrupt request from the same source? (5)

(*c*) What do you mean by programmed I/O mode of data transfer ? Explain with example. (5)

(*d*) How many times does the control unit refer to memory when it fetches and executes an indirect addressing' mode instruction if the instruction is :

(*i*) a computational type requiring an operand from memory;

(*ii*) a branch type. (5)

7. (*a*) Define the following:

(*i*) Micro-operation; (*ii*) 1icro-instruction;

(*iii*) Micro-program; (*iv*) micro-code;

(*v*) Instruction. (5)

(*b*) Formulate a mapping procedure that provides eight consecutive micro-instructions for each routine, The operation coda has six bits and control memory has 2048 words. (5)

(*c*) A two word instruction is stored in memory at an address designated by the symbol W. The address field of the instruction (stored at $W + 1$) is designated by the symbol *Y*. The operand used during the execution of the instruction is stored at an address symbolized by *Z*. An index register contains the value *X*. State how *Z* is calculated from the other addresses if the addressing mode of the instruction is:

(*i*) Direct (*ii*) Indirect

(*iii*) Relative (*iv*) Indexed.

(*d*) Differentiate between hardwired control and microprogrammed control. Is it possible a hardwired control associated with a control memory? (5)

8. Write short notes any four) of the following: (5 × 4)

(*i*) Pipelining (*ii*) Synchronous data transfer;

(*iii*) Memory Hierarchy; (*iv*) Priority interrupts;

(*v*) Virtual Memory (*vi*) Instruction Set Architecture.

APPENDIX–E
BIBLIOGRAPHY

1. Rajiv Chopra, "Advanced Computer Architecture", S. Chand & Company Ltd., Second Revised Edition, Reprint 2012.
2. Rajiv Chopra, "Operating Systems", S. Chand & Company, Third Reprint Edition, 2013.
3. Rajiv Chopra, "Introduction to Microprocessors", 1st Edition Katsons, 2011.
4. V. Rajaraman, T. Radhakrishnan, "Computer Organization and Architecture", PHI, Fourth printing, July 2011.
5. B. Govindarajalu "Computer Architecture and Organization: Design Principles and Applications", Tata Mc Graw Hill, Third Reprint 2005.
6. M. Morris Mano, "Computer System Architecture", PHI, 3rd Edition 1993.
7. John D. Corpinelli, "Computer Systems Organization and Architecture", Pearson Education, First Indian Reprint 2011.
8. V.P Henring, Harry F. Jordan, "Computer System Design and Architecture", Pearson Education, 6th Indian Reprint 2002.
9. Andrew S. Tanenbaum, "Structured Computer Organization", PHI 5th Edition 2006.
10. P. Pal Chaudhari, "Computer Organization and Design", PHI 1994.
11. B. Ram, "Computer Architecture and Organization", New Age International Publishers, 2010.
12. Web sources
    (*a*) http://www.intel.com / design/pentium4/manuals/index_new.htm
    (*b*) www.PCGuide.com
13. Hamacher, Vranesic and Zaky, "Computer Organization", 5th Edition Mc Graw Hill, 2002.
14. Shiv Shankar Mishra, "Digital Electronics", Second Reprint, Satya Prakashan 2009-10.
15. www.techgig.com
16. Amit Kumar Mishra, "Computer Architecture", First Edition, Katsons 2011.
17. William Stallings, "Operating Systems Internets and Design Principle", Pearson Education, 6th Edition 2011.
18. Rajiv Chopra, "Lab. Manual of Information Technology", First Edition, NP, 2012.

END TERM EXAMINATION

FIFTH SEMESTER ***DECEMBER-2012***

Paper Code: ETCS305 Subject: Computer Architecture

Time: 3 Hours ***Maximum Marks: 75***

Note: *Attempt all questions. Internal choice is indicated.*

Ql. Answer the following:-

(*a*) Give an example for logical and shift microoperations. (2)

(*b*) Draw a space-time diagram for a six-segment pipeline showing the time it takes to process eight tasks. (2)

(*c*) How many times does the control unit refer to memory when it fetches and executes an indirect addressing modeinstruction if the instruction is. (i) a computational type requiring an operand from memory and (ii) a branch type. (2)

(*d*) Draw the flowchart of divide operation. (2)

(*e*) Compare the characteristics features of tightly coupled and loosely coupled multiprocessor systems. (3)

(*f*) The logical address space in a computer system consists of 128 segments. Each segment can have up to 32 pages of 4K words in each. Physical memory consists of 4K blocks of 4K words in each. Formulate the logical and physical address formats. (2)

(*g*) Compare isolated I/O and memory-mapped I/O. Give their respective advantage and disadvantages. (2)

Q2. (*a*) Give an example to illustrate bus and memory transfer operations. (6)

(*b*) Represent the following conditional control statement by two register transfer statements with control functions. If P = l) then (R1<–R2) else if (Q = l) then (Rl < – R3). (4)

(*c*) Give an example to illustrate arithmetic microoperations. (5)

OR

(*a*) Draw the block diagram to illustrate addressing sequencing in control memory. (5)

(*b*) Give the classification of various types of instructions used in basic computer organization. (5)

(*c*) Explain instruction cycle in detail. Give various phases of instruction cycle. (5)

Q3. (*a*) Give an example for each of the following instruction formats and explain their working mechanism:- (6)

(*i*) RISC instruction (*ii*) Three-address instruction (*iii*) Zero-address instruction.

(*b*) Discuss the role of Reverse Polish Notation in stack organization. (3)

(*c*) compare the following address modes:- (6)

(*i*) Direct address mode (*ii*) Indirect address mode (*iii*) Relative address mode.

OR

(*a*) Explain four possible hardware schemes that can be used in an instruction pipeline in order to minimize the performance degradation caused by instruction branching. (4)

(*b*) Explain vector processing in detail. Give an example for illustration. (5)

(*c*) Explain attached array processor and SIMD array processor briefly. (6)

Q4. (*a*) Explain Booth Multiplication algorithm. Draw the respective flow chart and give an illustration. (6)

(*b*) Draw the block diagram of BCD adder and explain its working. (5)

(*c*) Design an array multiplier that multiplies two 4-bit numbers. Use AND gates and binary adders. (4)

OR

(*a*) What is the basic advantage of using interrupt-initiated data transfer over normal data transfer under program control without an interrupt? (4)

(*b*) Compare strobe control method and handshaking method used in data transfer.

Give their respective advantages and disadvantages. Give an example for each. (6)

(*c*) Draw the block diagram of DMA and explain its working. (5)

Q5. (*a*) Explain LRU and FIFO page replacement algorithms. (5)

(*b*) Explain various mapping techniques used in the cache memory. Compare the fetures of write-through and write-back cache. (5)

(*c*) Explain segmented-page mapping used in memory management hardware. (5)

OR

(*a*) Explain the following interconnected structures used in computer architecture:- (6)

(*i*) Multiport memory (*ii*) Crossbar Switch (*iii*) Time shared common bus.

(*b*) Explain multistage switching networks used in multiprocessor systems. Give an example to illustrate omega multi-stage network. (3+3)

(*c*) How many switch points are there in a crossbar switch network that connects p processors to m memory modules? (3)